The 2nd North Carolina Cavalry

for
Nicholas Jefferson Harrell
Second Lieutenant, Company C, 2nd North Carolina Cavalry,

and his
son, Herman Leslie Harrell,
and his
grandson, Roland Parker Harrell,
and his
great-great-granddaughter, Lorie Lynn Harrell Carlson,
and his
great-great-great-grandson, Alec Roger Harrell Carlson

with appreciation from
his
great-grandson, Roger Herman Harrell

The 2nd North Carolina Cavalry

Roger H. Harrell

McFarland & Company, Inc., Publishers
Jefferson, North Carolina, and London

The present work is a reprint of the illustrated case bound edition of The 2nd North Carolina Cavalry, *first published in 2004 by McFarland.*

All maps are by George F. Skoch

Library of Congress Cataloguing-in-Publication Data

Harrell, Roger H. (Roger Herman), 1936–
The 2nd North Carolina Cavalry / Roger H. Harrell.
p. cm.
Includes bibliographical references and index.

ISBN 978-0-7864-6774-7
softcover : acid free paper ∞

1. Confederate States of America. Army. North Carolina Cavalry Regiment, 2nd. 2. North Carolina — History — Civil War, 1861–1865 — Regimental histories. 3. United States — History — Civil War, 1861–1865 — Regimental histories. 4. United States — History — Civil War, 1861–1865 — Campaigns.
I. Title: Second North Carolina Cavalry. II. Title.
E573.62nd.H37   2012   973.7'457 — dc22   2004002810

British Library cataloguing data are available

© 2004 Roger H. Harrell. All rights reserved

No part of this book may be reproduced or transmitted in any form or by any means, electronic or mechanical, including photocopying or recording, or by any information storage and retrieval system, without permission in writing from the publisher.

On the cover: *(top)* Captain Pinkney Tatum (courtesy Richard A. Anthony), *(bottom)* Colonel William Paul Roberts (Library of Congress) Background image © 2012 Pictures Now

Manufactured in the United States of America

*McFarland & Company, Inc., Publishers
Box 611, Jefferson, North Carolina 28640
www.mcfarlandpub.com*

Table of Contents

List of Maps   vii

Acknowledgments   viii

Preface   1

One • **Department of North Carolina and District of Pamlico**   5
    Cavalry Leadership   5
    Organization and Training Camp   6
    The Department of North Carolina   14
    The Battle of New Bern, March 14, 1862   19
    Cavalry Duty, the Enemy Present   29
    Reorganization and Changes in the Command Structure   34

Two • **The Army of Northern Virginia and the 2nd North Carolina Cavalry**   41
    The Armies in Virginia   42
    The Confederate Cavalry under James E. B. Stuart   43
    Robert E. Lee Makes a Move; the Maryland Campaign   52
    Robert E. Lee Back in Virginia   59
    Stuart's Expedition to Maryland and Pennsylvania, October 9–12   61
    The Rappahannock Line   63
    The Union Army Crosses the Potomac   66
    W. H. F. Lee's New Brigade   71
    Four Attempts to Cross the Rappahannock River   75
    The Chancellorsville Campaign, April 29–May 5, 1863   85
    Second Squadron Detached; Duty in Virginia   95

Three • **Cavalry Shield for the Gettysburg Campaign**   109
    J. E. B. Stuart's Cavalry Division   111
    The Battle at Brandy Station, June 9   115
    Middleburg and Upperville, June 17–21   128
    The Ride-around to Gettysburg   146
    Greetings at Hanover, Pennsylvania, June 30   155
    The Cavalry Joins the Battle of Gettysburg, July 2   163
    Gettysburg's East Cavalry Field, July 3   165
    Retreat from Gettysburg: Cavalry All Around, July 4–14   173

Four • **Reorganizations and Winter Campaigns**   185
    Cavalry Reorganization and Leadership Change   191

The Fight at Jack's Shop, September 22   193
The Bristoe Campaign, October 9–20   198
The Mine Run Campaign, November 26–December 2   213
Winter Camp: "Rain, Sleet and Snow make camp-life almost unbearable"   217
Kilpatrick's Expedition to Richmond, February 28–March 4, 1864   221
Shuffling the Regiment and the Brigade, Mid-April to May 3   230

Five • **Grant's Overland Campaign, May 4 to Mid-June 1864**   233
The Battle of the Wilderness, May 4–6   234
Stalemate: Grant Moves to Spotsylvania Court House, May 7–12   242
The Cavalries Move Toward Richmond, May 9   249
Stalemate: Grant Moves to the North Anna River, May 20   265
Stalemate: Grant Moves to Cold Harbor, May 27   273
Stalemate: Grant Moves Toward Petersburg, June 12   288

Six • **The Siege of Petersburg, Mid-June 1864 to April 1865**   292
Initial Efforts to Envelop Petersburg   292
Wilson and Kautz Raid on the Railroads, June 22–July 1   296
Duty Along the Weldon Railroad, July   304
Grant's Demonstrations Against Richmond   306
Grant Makes His Move for the Weldon Railroad   318
Picket Duty, an Adventure, and More Picketing   329
Grant Moves on Richmond and Across the Weldon Again   333
Grant's Last Attempts to Encircle Petersburg Before Winter Camp   337

Seven • **The Appomattox Campaign**   348
Grant's Spring Offensive Against the Army of Northern Virginia   349
First Encounters   354
"Dreadful conflict at Chamberlain's Run on the 31st of March"   355
The Battle of Five Forks, April 1, 1865   360
The Retreat Begins   367
The Battle at Namozine Church, April 3   369
Five More Days to Appomattox Court House   373
The Last Battle: Appomattox Court House, April 9   384

Appendix: Combat Losses in the 2nd North Carolina Cavalry   391

Chapter Notes   409

Bibliography   445

Index   449

List of Maps

1.1:	Early Posts Near the North Carolina Coast	12
1.2:	Around New Bern, 1862	19
2.1:	The Peninsula and Around Richmond	47
2.2:	The Rappahannock Line and Loudoun Valley	51
2.3:	Campaigning in the North, September and October 1862	55
2.4:	Fredericksburg, Above and Below	74
2.5:	Chancellorsville, Mine Run, and Wilderness Campaigns	88
2.6:	Longstreet's Suffolk Campaign	100
3.1:	Around Brandy Station, June 1863	116
3.2:	Loudoun Valley, Middleburg and Upperville	129
3.3:	Stuart's Route to Gettysburg and Back	148
3.4:	Cavalry Encounter at Hanover	156
3.5:	Gettysburg, East Cavalry Field	167
5.1:	From the Wilderness to Petersburg	251
6.1:	Siege of Petersburg and Wilson-Kautz Raid	294
6.2:	Grant's Moves South and West of Petersburg	321
7.1:	To Chamberlain's Run and Five Forks	349
7.2:	The Route to Appomattox Court House	368

Acknowledgments

I wish I were capable of thanking all the people who over the past several years have shared their materials or sent me in useful directions, but here I can mention only a few of them. They gave of their time to discuss my project and relevant aspects, both large and small, of specific battles, the North Carolina Cavalry, and particularly the 2nd North Carolina Cavalry. Among these are Robert F. O'Neill of Stafford, Virginia; Chris Calkins of the Petersburg National Battlefield; Horace Mewborn of Springfield, Virginia; Richard Golightly of Centreville, Virginia; and Joseph Nyomarkay of Redondo Beach, California.

I would also like to express my deep gratitude to the librarians, archivists, and staff members of the institutions that have preserved and made available materials without which histories would be less than they are — if they could be written at all. In particular I would like to thank the friendly and dedicated professionals at the following institutions: Virginia Historical Society, Richmond, Virginia; Museum of the Confederacy Library, Richmond, Virginia; Library of Virginia, Richmond, Virginia; National Archives and Records Service, General Services Administration, Washington, D.C.; Library of Congress, Manuscript Division, Washington, D.C.; North Carolina Division of Archives and History, Raleigh, N.C.; Rare Book, Manuscript, and Special Collections Library, Duke University, Durham, N.C.; Southern Historical Collection, University of North Carolina, Chapel Hill, N.C.; Greensboro Historical Museum Archives, Civil War Collection, Greensboro, N.C.; South Caroliniana Library, University of South Carolina, S.C.; U.S. Army Military History Institute, Carlisle, Pennsylvania; Rare Book and other departments, Huntington Library, San Marino, California;

I would also like to thank Alison Rittger of San Francisco, California, for her professional yet friendly editorial work. She made the text more understandable and easier to read.

There are many things for which I thank my wife, Margaret, but I will confine myself to her enthusiastic support throughout this project; her willingness to accompany me on many of the field trips to North Carolina and Virginia (including long, hot walks over numerous battlefields); and her endurance while carefully reading more than one draft of this history.

Preface

One of the most remarkable features of the 2nd North Carolina Cavalry's history is its evolution from an inept and ineffective aggregate of brave men into an efficient regiment that became a pillar of strength in the Army of Northern Virginia's Cavalry Corps.

To keep such troops [the 2nd North Carolina Cavalry] in the presence of the enemy would be useless [and] criminal, and I respectfully suggest that the officers and men who have on two occasions covered themselves with shame and our arms with dishonor be debarred the privilege of combating for our liberties. The officers should be reduced, never to hold commissions; the men should be dismounted and disarmed and placed at hard labor during the war....

I respectfully recommend that all but one squadron of the regiment be transferred to the rear and there be placed in a school of instruction under competent officers. Ignorance, idleness, and incapacity so strongly characterize a large number of the officers that a thorough purging is required.
— Brigadier-General Robert Ransom, Jr., District of Pamlico, N.C., April 20, 1862.

Roberts, I think my division equal, if not superior, to any division in the army, but let me tell you that I think I am growing a little partial to your regiment, because I feel more secure and my sleep is less disturbed when the gallant "Two Horse" is in my front.
— General William H. F. Lee, Division Commander, Army of Northern Virginia, 1864.

I distinctly remember that after the battle of Chamberlain's Run [March 31, 1865], I passed the regiment on the road, and its great loss both in splendid officers and gallant men made such an impression upon me that I wept like a child. Its losses had been so many that I scarcely recognized it.
— Brigadier-General William P. Roberts, Army of Northern Virginia, April 1, 1865.

How did the men of the 2nd North Carolina Cavalry raise their regiment from the one characterized by Ransom in early 1862 to the one referred to by W. H. F. Lee in 1864 and by Roberts in 1865? It surely was not an easy course. I hope this volume answers the question.

North Carolina was late to the secessionist movement for a number of reasons. One was the relatively small number of large plantation owners willing to enter an all-or-nothing fight to retain a slave-based economy. In fact, only about 3 in 10 households in the state owned one or more slaves. To be sure, early in the debate, radical secessionists wanted North Carolina to leave the Union, but they were a minority. On January 29, 1861, the state assembly asked voters to consider calling a convention to take up the issue of secession, but on February 28, 1861, a majority of voters said no. Of course, that was an expression of sentiment at the moment, not a settlement of the question at hand.

Public opinion would have to change before that handful of wealthy planters and politicians dared join the southern secessionist movement — and change it did. After the fall of Fort Sumter on April 13, reason was largely adrift in churning adrenaline, and the Radicals were delighted as popular support for war increased. Nonetheless, many North Carolinians retained their rationality. One prominent citizen, William A. Graham, put it simply: "Truly indeed, may it be said that madness rules the hour." (His son, William A. Graham, Jr., went on to become a captain in Company K of the 2nd North Carolina Cavalry.) Later in April, President Lincoln called for troops to suppress the Southern insurrection. One of the governors he called upon was Ellis of North Carolina. The answer was predictable: "You can get no troops from North Carolina." These two April events accelerated North Carolina's slide into secession.[1]

Although few had enthusiastically embraced secession in the beginning, the thoughts and sounds of war stirred many hearts. For the most part, the people of North Carolina were now full of resentment and ready to fight. They were ready to join their southern brethren, even if it meant fighting a short war.

One of many developments to follow April 1861 was the creation of the 2nd North Carolina Cavalry. The history on these pages covers the formation, near demise (on more than one occasion), and eventual maturation of this cavalry regiment. I am often asked, Why focus on the 2nd North Carolina Cavalry? It was certainly not a famous regiment, nor did it play a pivotal role in a major battle. My initial interest developed many years ago when I learned that one of my great-grandfathers fought in the 2nd North Carolina Cavalry. Beyond that, I became interested in the lives and experiences of the nearly 1,500 other men who served in the regiment. Their lives had to have been affected in the most profound ways by their experiences during the war years, and there had to have been tens of thousands of cavalrymen living through similar circumstances. Indeed, what the North Carolina cavalrymen saw and did in the war was no doubt a more universal experience than we see in the lives of more famous men about whom much has been written.

My interest became more complicated once the research was underway. It was apparent the cavalrymen in the 2nd North Carolina journeyed through the war on a path not always traveled by others—and watching them stumble and then charge their way through the war provided an unconventional view of events. It is an interesting view, one that should not be overlooked if our goal is to understand what the ordinary soldier went through. With that in mind, I have allowed the 2nd North Carolina Cavalry, as well as cavalrymen from other units, to act as the reader's guides through four years of mayhem, sometimes calculated, sometimes not.

Historians typically lead readers through the Civil War by directing attention to famous battles, leaders, or military units of great interest. A journey with the 2nd North Carolina Cavalry often takes us to these major battles and puts us in proximity to famous generals, but it also takes us on less frequently traveled by-roads and into engagements other historians seldom discuss. As we travel, we will see many small battles that were not by themselves decisive factors in determining the outcome of the war; yet they were part of the troopers' wartime experiences, and forever part of their lives and of those who came after.

It is difficult to generalize about the meaning of these wartime experiences, but we can infer the prevailing significance by close attention to the context of their actions—the context of the war and the larger battles. Thus I have not simply focused on the known accomplishments and failures of the cavalrymen, but also on the surrounding events that influenced their performance, and on what they took from each experience. This means, for instance, though they hardly fired a shot during the famous battle of Fredericksburg, they were atop a nearby hill; came under artillery fire; and most importantly saw thousands of Union men march, wave after wave, into the well-entrenched Confederate line to a certain death. Even from the periphery, it had to have been a powerful and memorable experience.

Often a cavalry engagement seems small when isolated, but takes on major significance when viewed as a shielding operation for the movement of an army going into or coming from a major battle. The 2nd North Carolina Cavalry spent much of that long war engaged in just such operations, which are too often not viewed closely enough. The war itself or each great battle was the context and the cavalrymen knew that the larger picture gave meaning to even small actions.

Among the factors making up the cavalryman's experience were the regiments standing near them at different times. Other Confederate cavalry regiments fought alongside the 2nd North Carolina, but often competed with them for resources or preferred duty. These nonviolent battles were certainly part of the cavalryman's wartime experience.

Among the many daily battles facing the 2nd North Carolina were the struggles to get equipment and arms, to feed themselves and their horses, and to survive the often harsh physical conditions, as well as to fight their enemy. Moreover, their struggles were seldom fought one at a time. More often, they overlapped to create nearly unfathomable hardships. As we follow the 2nd North Carolina through the war, we will take the time to appreciate the variety of battles they fought.

While most days did not involve fighting the enemy, most did involve watching and being watched. The days without violence gave no relief from the commonplace struggles with hunger and cold weather, as well as boredom couched in the feared lack of purpose. Considering all the battles cavalrymen confronted month after month and year after year, we can perhaps begin to sense the cumulative fatigue and weariness of those lucky enough to avoid enemy fire or illness.

Superimposed on the physical stress was the mental exhaustion that must have come with the exultation of victory one day, defeat and despair the next. Often within minutes, a victorious charge was followed by a rapid retreat in great confusion. Even those cavalrymen who entered the war for adventure must have found the rush of mounted charges with flashing sabers and clashing bodies a little less exciting when repeated month after month and year after year.

Certainly the 2nd North Carolina Cavalry had its slackers who advanced more slowly than their comrades or found reasons to be unavailable when major battles were imminent, but the cavalrymen were mostly gallant and brave, often going beyond the call of duty, and usually doing their best under the worst of circumstances. They didn't ask for much, and they didn't get much. In the end, what they had was the experience of it all.

ONE

Department of North Carolina and District of Pamlico

By June of 1861, the Union navy had established a coastal blockade. It was not completely effective but it was in place, and eventually forced closure of the main supply line for Richmond up the James River. This increased the importance of the maritime supply line through North Carolina's Hatteras Inlet. The Confederate Capital's supply line through North Carolina entered by the Albemarle and Pamlico Sounds, then on to the interior of the state. North Carolinians knew they would be the second target, and they did not want their state occupied by their enemy, nor did the Confederate leadership in Richmond want to lose vital supply lines coming through North Carolina. The state and its water inlets would have to be defended.

North Carolina began developing regiments early in 1861 with an eye at first to defending their state, then ultimately, and sometimes reluctantly, to defending the Confederacy. They did not get serious about cavalry right away, however. Though the state was full of young men who were excellent horsemen, there was no cavalry tradition. It started with the development of the 1st North Carolina Cavalry (the Ninth Regiment North Carolina State Troops). The 1st Cavalry began recruiting in May and June of 1861 and came together in July near Asheville, North Carolina. By August they were undergoing rigorous training at Camp Beauregard. The development of the 2nd North Carolina Cavalry (Spruill's Cavalry Regiment, later named the Nineteenth Regiment North Carolina State Troops) began only about one month later than the 1st Cavalry, but that resulted in an enormous difference in the resources the state had at its disposal for its second cavalry regiment — the lack of leadership, training, and equipment accounted for the difference between the 1st and 2nd Cavalries for well over a year into the war. Becoming North Carolina's second cavalry regiment was not easy.

Cavalry Leadership

Many officers in the United States military resigned their commissions and were immediately offered commissions of equal or higher rank in the Confederate States of America's rapidly forming military units. For instance, Colonel Robert Ransom, a United States Cavalryman and West Pointer, resigned his commission and returned to North Carolina to take command of and train the 1st North Carolina Cavalry.[1] By the time the state of North Carolina decided to form another cavalry unit, apparently no experienced cavalry commanders were available for such an assignment, though a number of competent civilians were eager to gain a military rank and do their part in the coming struggle.

North Carolina drew upon what resources were available and many responsible citizens with no military experience were given commissions based on their prominence and promise to raise volunteer regiments and companies. Samuel B. Spruill (an attorney and politician) was one such citizen, as were John W. Woodfin (also an attorney) and George W. Hayes (a farmer). S. B. Spruill began his military career as Colonel of his own cavalry regiment at the age of 50; Woodfin began his new career as a Major in Spruill's cavalry regiment at the age of 43; Hayes started his military career at the age of 56 as Captain of Company A in the regiment — the other nine companies in Spruill's regiment were commanded by men of similar inexperience. Lieutenant Colonel William G. Robinson was the regiment's exception; he was a military man and a West Point graduate. (These appointments were typically made by the Governor of North Carolina with the advice of the Military Board.)[2]

In May of 1861, the state convention authorized Colonel Samuel B. Spruill to raise a legion of five cavalry companies. On August 30, the state legislature ratified an act increasing the number of cavalry companies in his legion to ten. The North Carolina legislature committed to providing the men with equipment and horses. This commitment would prove difficult to keep.

In the beginning the second cavalry unit was known as "Colonel Spruill's Cavalry Regiment." The 1st Regiment North Carolina Cavalry (Ninth Regiment N. C. Troops) had already been organized, so it should have been easy enough to name Spruill's regiment the 2nd Cavalry, which they eventually did. However, it took a while because, as the state of North Carolina worked its way through the difficult task of mobilizing for war for the first time, it ended up with two numbering systems for its regiments—the State Troops regiments, and the Volunteer regiments. They sorted out the numbering system in stages. On November 14, 1861, by Special Orders no. 222, Spruill's cavalry unit was officially labeled the 10th Regiment North Carolina Volunteers, but there was already an infantry regiment with that designation. Consequently, another name change was in the offing. To shorten an even longer story, Spruill's regiment finally became the Nineteenth Regiment North Carolina Troops by Special Orders no. 230 on November 20, 1861—but the regiment was more often known as the 2nd North Carolina Cavalry.

Organization and Training Camp

The ten companies that eventually became the 2nd North Carolina Cavalry were raised in various locations across the state. Colonel Samuel B. Spruill was from Bertie County in the northeast part of the state, so it is not surprising that most of the companies were raised in the northern counties. However, one company was raised as far south as Cumberland County (Company D), and one on the western tip of the state in Cherokee County (Company A). Typically, men enlisted in their home county, but if that was not an option, they would go to an adjacent county. In any case, most recruits entered camp as part of a company raised in or near their homes.

From the beginning North Carolinians saw the county as the most immediate and important political entity in their lives, and it still was in the 1860s. It followed that military units derived from and identified with counties would be the most immediate and important sources of a man's military identity. Most men were recruited by prominent individuals from their county, and local pride along with a large dose of social pressure were often important considerations in the call to arms—as was the lure, at a more abstract level of thinking, to defend the "Old North State." The company became a natural and major connection to the folks back home. With their primary military identity initially coming from their company, the men had difficulty developing a sense of commitment to the regiment until the latter became a source of pride, and that could take time. For instance, Company A of Cherokee County was the "Cherokee Rangers" in June of 1861 and did not become Company A until August 30—even then for many it remained the Cherokee Rangers. Also the men of Company H initially called themselves the "Northampton and Bertie Dragoons," members of Company D referred to their unit as the "Cumberland Cavalry," and the men in Company K called themselves the "Orange Cavalry." In their correspondence most of the men continued to identify their units with county-specific names long after training camp had ended. Nonetheless, at some point these companies would have to become part of a larger unit, a regiment.

Most if not all of the counties made the boys who volunteered for service in defense of their homes and culture feel very special. The young men of Cumberland County who volunteered for military service in order to add a dimension of importance to their lives, or for the adventure of it all, must have felt they had made the correct decision when they marched through the streets of Fayetteville toward the river to take passage for Wilmington and then on to Kittrell's Springs for training. They were somebody; they were the Cumberland Cavalry; they would become part of Colonel Spruill's Cavalry Regiment. On that day, August 15, 1861, the *Fayetteville Observer* described the event and listed each recruit by name. In most other places there was less pageantry but recognition nonetheless. Local pride in raising a company of cavalrymen is illustrated by a notice first published on July 10, 1861 in a Beaufort County newspaper: "A Cavalry Co. — We learn that Capt. Satherthwaite has succeeded in raising his company of Cavalry [Company G], and that in a few days they will leave for the rendezvous at Kittrell's Spring...."[3]

Companies A, B, C, D, E, F, and G began forming in June 1861; companies H and I in July; and company K in September. The counties of North Carolina provided the following companies: Cherokee County, Company A; Iredell County, Company B; Gates and Hertford Counties, Company C; Cumberland County, Company D; Nash and Wilson Counties, Company E; Guilford County, F; Beaufort County, Company G; Bertie and Northampton Counties, Company H; Moore County, Company I; and Orange County, Company K.

As the companies made their way to training camp, the sense that they were doing something important certainly grew when citizens along their routes came out to acknowledge and applaud their bravery and commitment to the southern cause. For instance, when the Cumberland Cavalry (they become Company D) stopped at Goldsboro on its journey to training camp on August 18, the tired and hungry recruits were met by local citizens, even some prominent ones; and they were fed and shown a kindness exceptional in the eyes of these young men from Cumberland County. When Captain Bryan took his company of recruits from Moore County through Fayetteville on their way to training camp at Kittrell's, they were entertained at the Fayetteville Hotel from the time they arrived until 8:00 A.M. the next day when they proudly marched through town to take passage for Wilmington — the local newspaper noted the event and named every man in the newly formed company of cavalry from Moore County (they became Company I).[4]

Except for Company A, they gathered for training at Camp Clark near Kittrell's Springs in Granville County (Kittrell is now in Vance County). The recruits and officers probably thought the war was getting off to a wonderful beginning when they arrived at Kittrell's Springs. It was the location of North Carolina's first summer resort. (Construction on Kittrell Springs Hotel began in 1858 and was finished in 1860. Most of its guests came from the deep South, and the hotel housed several hundred guests at a time.)[5]

Leadership at the company level was not only responsible for recruitment activity but also for getting the recruits to Camp Clark for their training. Most of the time a respected fellow county resident was the local recruiter — in some cases this person was as important as any other factor in recruiting young men. In most cases the officers in each company were assigning themselves ranks and actively recruiting in their home counties before they knew to which regiment their companies would be assigned. Once in camp, most company officers were appointed to rank from June 18 or 21, and August 30, 1861 — with few exceptions appointments were effective before training camp started on August 31. It appears that none of the company officers had any military training.

Once at Camp Clark the companies were formed into Colonel Spruill's Cavalry Regiment. At the regimental level most of the important appointments were made effective during the first month of training camp, in September 1861. By the end of their training camp the regiment's leadership included the following: Colonel: Samuel B. Spruill, resident of Bertie County, attorney and politician. He spent little time with the regiment and resigned on March 29, 1862. Lieutenant Colonel: William G. Robinson, resident of Wake County. He was appointed lieutenant colonel to rank from September 1, 1861. He was wounded and captured on April 13, 1862, and promoted to colonel on September 9, 1863 to rank from July 23. Robinson was dropped from the regiment's rolls on May 25, 1864 when he was transferred to the Navy Department. Major: John W. Woodfin from Buncombe County, an attorney by profession. He transferred from the 1st North Carolina Cavalry when he accepted his promotion to major on September 23, 1861 at the age of 43. He resigned from the regiment due to ill health on September 6, 1862. It appears he left the 1st Cavalry about the time they were first sent to Virginia, and just about the time the 2nd Cavalry was transferred to Virginia he resigned from that unit. Adjutant: Guilford Nicholson, resident of Halifax County. He was appointed adjutant with the rank of 1st lieutenant on November 16, 1861. He was transferred to Company A as a 1st lieutenant on June 5, 1862. Quartermaster: John S. Hines, resident of Wake County. He was appointed assistant quartermaster and captain on September 25, 1861 to rank from June 18. He resigned on February 3, 1862. (He returned later to work in the Conscript Bureau in Raleigh.) Commissary: John W. Moore, resident of Hertford County. He was appointed assistant commissary of subsistence and captain on September 25, 1861 to rank from June 18. He resigned on February 3, 1862 when promoted to major in a light artillery battalion.

As noted earlier, Colonel Spruill and Major Woodfin were attorneys by profession and had no military experience. To some, that mattered. For instance, another North Carolina civilian with perhaps a bit more wisdom than Spruill and Woodfin was also offered a position in the 2nd Cavalry by the Governor — he was Bryan Grimes. Grimes was offered the rank of major in the 2nd North Carolina Cavalry, but he refused the position and took the same rank in the 4th North Carolina (infantry). His reason for doing so was more important than the rank. Grimes also had no military experience; consequently, he knew he must learn from commanders who knew what they were doing. In his own words, his consideration was, "...Colonel George B. Anderson, a graduate of West Point, was Colonel of the 4th Infantry, whilst the others were officered by inexperienced civilians like myself, and I preferred a subordinate position with an efficient officer to higher rank with officers without experience."[6]

It is not too surprising the commanders of the regiment had difficulty training and equipping their men given the minimal level of their own military experience, as well as the fact that most of the men would be in training camp for not much more than one month, and most of that time without horses and equipment.

"THOSE CAMPS ARE GRAVE YARDS"

During training camp, the attrition rate among troopers was high. A survey of the Roster of North Carolina Troops for the 2nd North Carolina Cavalry revealed some interesting reasons. The numbers tend to understate losses, but the proportions in each of the categories is probably reliable. The recorded losses from May through October 1861 were: 8 men transferred out, 16 men discharged, 13 men rejected, 25 men died of illness or disease, 2 men deserted, and 2 officers resigned.[7]

The thirteen rejected men were in the Cherokee Rangers (Company A), and the rejections came when Lieutenant Colonel Laurence Baker of the 1st North Carolina Cavalry paid the company a visit. He had authority to review the company because the Cherokee Rangers were originally assigned to Colonel Robert Ransom's 1st Cavalry in late June of 1861. Captain Rufus Barringer and L. Baker were in Asheville with six of their newly assigned companies at the time. One of Baker's jobs was to screen new recruits. He looked over the Cherokee Rangers and rejected thirteen recruits.[8]

Records for the thirteen men simply state "Rejected by Colonel Baker, August 2–3, 1861." At least three of the men were sent home because of their advanced age — but not all the older men accepted their rejection notices gracefully. For instance, Thomas J. Colvard first enlisted in Cherokee County at the age of 54, only to be rejected by Colonel Baker. Mr. Colvard waited a couple of months and then re-enlisted in Buncombe County for the same Company A, 2nd North Carolina Cavalry. The second time, he lasted until August 12, 1862 before being discharged again (just before the regiment left for Virginia). Several of Thomas Colvard's sons were also in Company A of this regiment.

The greatest loss of men in the regiment during training camp was clearly due to death from illness and disease. The number does not reflect the number of men who were disabled for extended periods of time from illness but did not die. Many of the men noted that camp conditions contributed to the problem. For instance, Thomas Branson from Guilford County wrote home to his sister: "Our tents leak and we get wet when it rains. Some four men are sick [in Company F]. One man died in the camp yesterday."[9] While disease and illness were common to most training camps, these conditions did not go unnoticed, and were not acceptable to most North Carolinians. The following commentary was published about conditions in the 2nd North Carolina Cavalry's training camp:

> We hear great complaint concerning the character of the tents furnished to portions of our troops. The encampment at Kittrell's Springs is said to be especially cursed in this particular. The cloths of the tents, we hear, is of a miserable sleazy quality, and as there are no flies to them they furnish little or no protection against rain. We hope that those having this matter in charge will institute a reform. Camps are at best subject enough to disease without any temptation being offered for its appearance. In the case of measles, to which the troops have been in great numbers subjected, protection against rain is indispensable to a cure.[10]

Later in September, a commentary in the *Raleigh Standard* (which was reprinted in many newspapers throughout the State) tried to respond to what they referred to as "...the common saying that 'those camps are grave yards.'" The editorial referred to several "Mortality Tables" to show that annually the number of young men who died of illness and disease that year was similar to the year before the war.[11] It is doubtful many of the families and friends of the young men dying in the camps were comforted by such reasoning.

TRAINING

Aside from the health problems, camp life for the cavalrymen had additional discomforts. For instance, Private Branson sent the following observations home to his sister, Emily. He described the first sound of the morning as "the horn at 5 o'clock." It called them to order for roll call. The company was then marched out into a field and paraded for about an hour. They returned to camp for breakfast. He went on to say most of the day was "spent working about" pretty much as they pleased. They were then paraded in the field again at about 5:00 P.M. for another hour. That was apparently about all the drill they received. Lights were blown out at 9 o'clock. During training camp, their other activity consisted of guard-duty on designated days for two hours, then rest for four hours. Branson went on to describe his experience at mess. "Things are fully as bad as I expected. We had fat, middling meat, sometimes boiled with peas. Coarse bread and coffee, sometimes with sugar, sometimes none…. I could do very well on meat & bread if it was cooked, but it is not. I eat a little and make out, looking forward for other times." Private Branson also suggested that meals would probably be a better experience if each mess did its own cooking rather than having a cooking crew of one man and four servants for the entire company. In addition to getting up at five in the morning, parading for two hours a day, and not liking the food much, Branson found camp life a little confining. He noted that they were not allowed to leave camp without a furlough and those were rare.[12]

As indicated, Colonel Spruill's intentions may have been in the right place but his experience was not. By contrast, the 1st North Carolina Cavalry was organized under Colonel Robert Ransom, a West Pointer with military experience — he was a stickler for discipline and drill, and once the regiment was in the field the pay-off was evident. Colonel Ransom formed one of the finest and best trained regiments in the Army of Northern Virginia.[13] Spruill did not have the capacity to provide such training for the 2nd Cavalry, so it probably did not matter much that he spent most of his short military career in Raleigh. Except for Lieutenant Colonel W. G. Robinson, the commanders of the regiment were apparently all rookies.

W. G. Robinson's responsibility was running the training camp, and he found it necessary to pay more attention to equipping the troops than to training them — on a first things first basis. Training and drilling cavalrymen without horses and sabers is at best inadequate. A great deal of the responsibility for training the troops from necessity fell to the company commanders, the captains and lieutenants, but they too had other responsibilities and no military experience.

Lieutenant Colonel Robinson apparently also used the captains in each company to help acquire horses. For instance, in late September Captain Cole of Company F was "gone up the country to buy horses; will be gone about two weeks." While the captains were on search and acquire missions, their lieutenants were usually in charge of training the men.[14]

Thus, to the extent it happened at all, a good deal of the training and drilling took place under the direct orders and eyes of the lieutenants and sergeants — many of whom were probably spirited fighters, but totally lacking in experience needed to teach and execute commands that would direct a squadron or entire regiment to move rapidly and strike — damaging the enemy more than themselves. One can say with a good deal of certainty that most of the young North Carolinians were excellent horsemen when they enlisted, but few at the time could have executed the following set of commands: "Form column by squadron." "Gallop; march." "Right oblique." "Forward; draw saber; charge." Yet two years later, on June 9, 1863, the men of the 2nd North Carolina responded to just that set of commands at full speed, in the heat of the largest cavalry battle ever fought on the North American Continent, and they moved like a precision machine. Certainly the cavalrymen in such a charge cannot ride as wild farm-boys out for an adventure. They had to know the commands, of course, but they also had to set the proper gait of their mounts at each stage of the advance and move with the column — it would not do to ride up the rear of the horse in front or lean into the one on your right. Unfortunately, the men of the 2nd North Carolina Cavalry got little such training and drill at Camp Clark. Even had the captains and lieutenants been able to learn enough about cavalry tactics during their training camp to teach the men what they would need to know, drill in such maneuvers did not take place — most men were still without horses on which to train and virtually none of them had sabers by the end of training camp. They left training camp ill-prepared to fight any war, say nothing of the one they were about to face.

Supplying Equipment and Horses

To avoid setting an unrealistically high standard, it is again useful to look at what the 1st North Carolina Cavalry achieved. They began the process of equipping their cavalrymen about one month before the 2nd Cavalry, but what a difference a month made. The 1st Cavalry not only got excellent training and drill under Colonel Robert Ransom, Lieutenant Colonel Laurence Baker, and others; they also got first call on scarce equipment cavalrymen needed: horses, guns, and pistols. The exception was sabers. For some inexplicable reason the 2nd Cavalry had more sabers than the 1st Cavalry — a situation in need of a remedy.

When the 1st Cavalry received their final polish for graduation from training camp on October 10, 1861, they already knew they were being sent to Virginia, and they were mounted and well equipped, except for sabers. The Governor and James G. Martin, adjutant general for North Carolina troops, appealed to the officers of the 2nd North Carolina Cavalry to give up their sabers to fully equip the 1st Cavalry. They reluctantly complied with the request after they received every assurance "…that the State would do everything in its power to equip the Second Cavalry as soon as possible…."[15] Actually, the 2nd Cavalry was told they too would soon be fully equipped, but it would take awhile. As indicated, the 1st Cavalry was well trained, fully equipped, and immediately sent off to battle in Virginia, but the men of the 2nd Cavalry could expect a very different experience.

Anytime the deprived are asked to make another sacrifice, some are bound to have mixed feelings, and it is not difficult to imagine that among the men of the 2nd Cavalry were feelings of anger, resentment, and inferiority. In late September 1861, around the time they had to give up their sabers, many of the "cavalrymen" were less well equipped than they were a month before, and were probably in pretty low spirits. In a letter to his sister on September 21, Thomas Branson wrote,

We do not know yet when we will go. Have been speaking of sending us down on the coast, but do not think they will for a while, as we are not yet equipped and have only about enough horses for one company. We are anxious to go soon as they will fit us out. We have not been treated right or we would have been ready long since.[16]

As their training camp neared its end in October, still more than half of the men in the 2nd Cavalry did not have horses. Virtually none of them had sabers, and the struggle to acquire the basic equipment remained a constant.

However, the need to equip the men gained momentum as pressure for their departure grew. By early October clearly the state could not furnish all the men with horses; some privates were encouraged to furnish their own mounts. This required setting a value on each privately owned horse. A board of officers was established which consisted of Captains Boothe (Company C), Randolph (Company H), and Thomas (Company E). The officers' as well as privates' horses were listed by color, height and value — typically valued at $140 each.[17] This policy resulted in about half the companies being mounted when they left training camp.

Company A, training in Asheville, was experiencing the same difficulties getting enough horses. Private William A. Curtis wrote years later, "We were to be mounted on horses furnished by the state, and those who owned horses were required to take them before a board of valuation and have them appraised and sell them to the State, and no member was allowed to take a private horse into service...." This policy was modified later in the war, but not for the better. In any case, Company A at Asheville was more successful than most of the companies camped near Kittrell Springs, and by mid–October they were fully mounted and armed mostly with double-barreled shot-guns. Only about half of the men in Company A had saddles by that time, however.[18]

By late September, several companies had been moved from Camp Clark to the town of Hertford just above the Albemarle Sound, despite not being fully equipped. In addition to horses, they needed just about every other type of equipment. For instance, on October 12, 1861, when the Ordnance Department in Raleigh sent a request for the number of bridles and saddles Robinson at Kittrell's needed for the two squadrons still with him at Camp Clark, the Department informed Robinson that they had already sent about 10,000 cartridges to Colonel S. B. Spruill at Hertford, Perquimans County. In addition to revealing the sort of basic cavalry equipment some companies still needed, the request from Raleigh also illustrates the increased difficulty of supplying the companies as a result of dividing the regiment before it was fully equipped. Spruill had taken five companies of partially equipped men with no horses to Hertford before the 12th of October. Robinson still had the 3rd Squadron (companies C and H) and the 2nd Squadron (companies B and G) with him at Kittrell's Springs.[19]

William G. Robinson intensified his efforts to outfit the squadrons still with him at Camp Clark. On October 13 he issued Battalion Order No. 1 authorizing 1st Lieutenant James M. Wynn (Company C) to proceed the next morning to the cavalry camp near Hertford in Perquimans County "...for the purpose of procuring shoes and other articles for troops in this Camp." Apparently a good deal of the supplies and equipment for the 2nd North Carolina Cavalry had been sent to Hertford which was Colonel Spruill's original destination in late September. Lieutenant Wynn was further instructed to collect and order back to Camp Clark all troops on furlough or sick leave that he might come across on his journey — the call was for members of companies under marching orders for Hyde County. On October 18, Robinson issued Special Orders No. 3 which carried the following instructions: "Sergeant Hunt [Company F] will proceed tomorrow morning to the headquarters of the regiment with such horses as Capt. Cole may have left behind and report to the commanding officer." Captain Cole's Company F had already gone to Perquimans County, North Carolina.[20] Lieutenant Colonel Robinson was under orders to move the two squadrons with him at Camp Clark by late October even though they were not fully equipped. Thus Colonel Spruill's cavalry was not graduated as a regiment and sent out to do battle, and was certainly not fully equipped when dispersed along North Carolina's coastal waterways.

Spruill Takes Five Companies to Edenton

By early October of 1861, Colonel Spruill had moved half of his companies out of training camp for their first assignment before they were mounted, fully equipped or trained. Premature and ill-advised decisions were being made at this time because the Confederate commanders were trying to decide how to defend the North Carolina coast with too few troops.[21] As indicated, the original destination for Spruill's five companies was Hertford, Perquimans County. Companies D, E, F, I, and K were all ordered to the state's northernmost water-way where the Chowan River enters the Albemarle Sound. But on their way to Hertford the companies had to stop at Edenton in Chowan County due to illness in all the companies. Soon after they settled near Edenton, they had to relocate about a mile and a half across the sound because of the swampy conditions.[22]

In mid–November the five companies were still at Camp Washington near Edenton. Their health had improved somewhat. But it was still an important issue when Lieutenant William A. Graham Jr. of the Orange Cavalry (Company K) wrote to his hometown newspaper to thank the ladies of Hillsborough and its

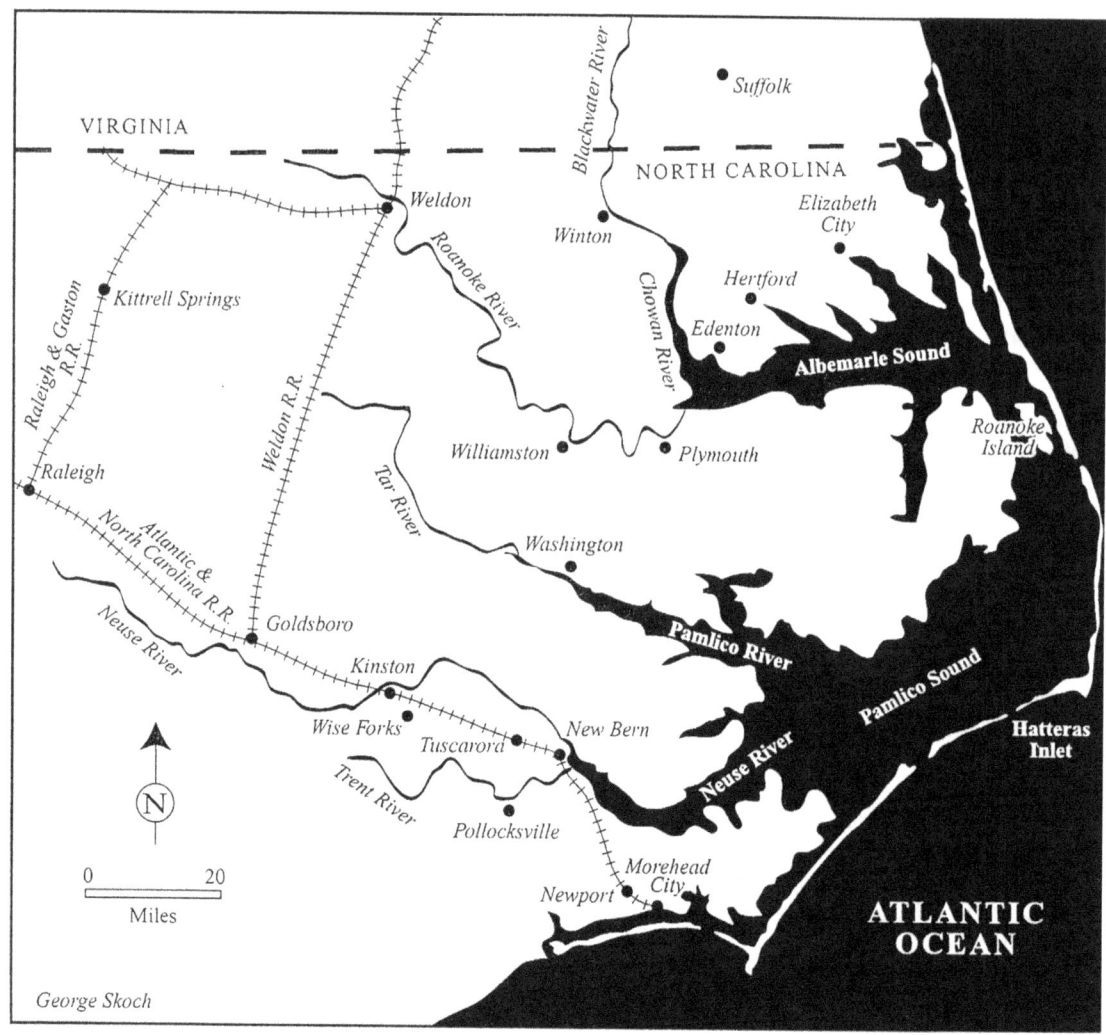

1.1: Early Posts Near the North Carolina Coast

vicinity for the uniforms they had made and sent to Camp Washington for the company. Graham went on to point out that the gift allowed them to spend the money the State had allocated for making uniforms for the comfort of the sick and needy in the company.[23]

On November 30, while still at Camp Washington, Lieutenant John P. Lockhart wrote a report on the state of the Orange Cavalry for the *Hillsborough Recorder*. He opened his report by taking note of the deaths of Sergeant W. S. Walker of his company, and R. Andrews of Captain Strange's Cumberland Cavalry (Company D). He went on to say 50 men were on the sick list at that time, but only four of them were from Captain Turner's Orange Cavalry.[24]

Around the same time, Lieutenant Lockhart's brother, Levi Y. Lockhart, also with the Orange Cavalry, wrote to their sister, Ellen, which illustrates the familiarity and closeness among the men in a company. He told his sister of their cousin, William S. Walker's, death in the camp hospital — Levi Lockhart though also sick in the camp hospital recovered. Levi wrote the following about his cousin's last days and the condition of others:

He was never well after he had the measles; we all tried to get him to take care of himself, but he would not; and he had the chance to go home, but he would not go; he would not go to the hospital until he was obliged to go, and after he went there, I never saw any person reduce so fast in all my life. He was out of his head four or five days before he died, and the day he died he could not speak a word.... We have ten men in the hospital, but none of them are very dangerous. John Nickols is sick, but nothing more than cold. Henry Neal is on the mend, but he is very weak. We expect to leave here in about eight days to go to Newbern.[25]

Levi's letter to his sister, Ellen, also illustrates how difficult it must have been to watch the young men they had grown up with in Orange County get ill and often die for reasons difficult to fathom. (Levi's and Ellen's friend, Private Jonathan M. Nichols, at the age of 25 did die in the hospital at Camp Washington, Edenton, N. C. on December 14, 1861.)

While at Camp Washington, the five companies remained without mounts during the first month or so of their stay and were threatened with the possibility of being sent to the coastal defenses as infantry, ending the short life of Colonel Spruill's Cavalry. Spruill was apparently in favor of this idea, but the officers of the companies involved successfully resisted the notion.[26] Major Woodfin was, for all purposes, in command of the five companies at Edenton during most of its stay there, and he continued the search for horses as well as equipment and arms to turn his troopers into cavalrymen. He had captains of the various companies make special efforts, such as the one described in the following item from the *Fayetteville Observer*:

100 Horses and Double-Barrel Guns Wanted for Cavalry Service. SOUND, ACTIVE HORSES and good Guns will be required, for which will be paid full CASH prices by the subscriber, at the following times and places, town: Clinton, Friday the 15th November; Fayetteville, Monday and Tuesday the 18th and 19th; Jonesboro, Moore County the 20th; Ritter's Muster Ground, Thursday the 21st; Carthage, Friday the 22nd; Pittborough, Monday the 25th; In Brooks's X Roads the 26th.
    J. L Bryan
    Capt. Moore County
    Cavalry [Company I]
    November 12, 1861.[27]

In spite of the hardships, after Spruill moved the five companies to Camp Washington in late September, life for cavalrymen who stayed healthy was better than it had been during training camp. For instance, Lieutenant John P. Lockhart ended his report, mentioned above, with a lighter note referring to information they had received of their pending departure for New Bern. Their expected move apparently raised some mixed feelings as indicated by his acknowledgment of the kindness shown the troopers by the people of Edenton, particularly the women, who frequently visited the hospital with kind words and cheer. In addition, Lockhart mentioned that healthy soldiers were also cared for — in his words:

Invitations to dine, and to tea, are often extended to the officers of the Regiment; and the young men of the camp have a happy time, and no doubt they will receive orders to leave here with many regrets; for, say what you please about it, young girls will love young soldiers, and old people had as well be reconciled to it.[28]

Marching Orders for the Other Five Companies

The four companies remaining at Camp Clark with Lieutenant Colonel Robinson did not leave training camp until early November, and they did not have a common destination. Robinson's Special Orders No. 5 on November 5 authorized 2nd Lieutenant Mills Eure of Company C to draw $800 from the Assistant Quartermaster "...for the use of the squadron now under orders for the Coast." At that time, Companies C and H were the Third Squadron and they were sent to New Bern, where the Neuse River spreads into Pamlico Sound.[29]

Companies C and H, under the command of Captain John Boothe of Company C, were accompanied by W. G. Robinson. Robinson and the Third Squadron arrived at New Bern and camped in the Fair Grounds on the Neuse River.

The Second Squadron, Companies B and G under Captain Clinton M. Andrews, was assigned to Washington, North Carolina near the confluence of several rivers with the Pamlico River — this is the major water-way entering North Carolina north of the Neuse River. Company G was raised in Washington so this duty probably had its compensations if not adventure for some of the men stationed there.

Company A had not joined the other companies of the regiment at Camp Clark, and they were apparently in no great hurry to meet the other companies. They left Asheville on October 23, marched for five days to the nearest railroad depot and departed for Raleigh in stages. They were camped near the railroad depot in Raleigh until November 12, when they began their six day march to New Bern. When they arrived, they went directly to the Fair Grounds where they met Lieutenant Colonel Robinson and the men of Companies C and H for the first time.[30]

The five companies at Edenton joined the others at New Bern in December 1861 and at that time were still not completely mounted — it would take well into February 1862 before that was accomplished.

In December of 1861, as the regiment continued to gather, it began building its first winter camp south of New Bern, across the Trent River, only about a mile from town. This was Camp Fisher and it was home until taken by the Yankees.[31] During this time the companies continued to search for equipment.

The companies in the 2nd North Carolina Cavalry were scattered along the coastal region as a response to the great concern among North Carolinian and Confederate officials for an invasion into North Carolina's interior via its many and vulnerable waterways. Officials in Raleigh did not want to lose control of their state and were concerned for the welfare and property of the people of North Carolina, while the Confederate government in Richmond wanted its supply routes and communication channels to the south to remain open. To meet these concerns, Union forces had to be kept out of the interior of North Carolina.

Recognizing this concern about an invasion of North Carolina from the sea helps explain the placement of the 2nd North Carolina cavalrymen when they left training camp. It also, to some extent, accounts for the fluctuating command structure in North Carolina that often responded to rumors of the next and most likely invasion from the sea by Union forces.

The Department of North Carolina

While the 2nd North Carolina Cavalry was still in training camp, authorities in Raleigh and Richmond were preparing for the difficult to predict yet inevitable Union invasion of North Carolina. The Confederate authorities in Richmond were not in a position to offer additional troops or equipment to North Carolina for the protection of her vulnerable coast line as tension built. Richmond did assist them, however, with organization and leadership appointments. Major Richard C. Gatlin was made a brigadier general on August 19, 1861 and put in command of the Department of North Carolina after he resigned his commission in the U.S. army — he was a West Point graduate and knew something of military matters. Gatlin set up his headquarters at Goldsboro.[32]

Colonel Daniel H. Hill was called up from the Charlotte Military Institute by the Governor of North Carolina to command Camp Ellis — there he formed and trained the First North Carolina Regiment (infantry) and sent them off to Virginia by late May of 1861. On September 29, 1861, D. H. Hill was put in command of the defenses of Albemarle and Pamlico Sounds within R. C. Gatlin's Department of North Carolina (Special Orders No. 166). Soon after Hill took command of his District, Gatlin received information from General Huger at Norfolk that a Union fleet was going to sail from New York for the South. On October 26, Gatlin received a telegram from the Secretary of War in Richmond announcing the enemy fleet had sailed. Gatlin and others believed the fleet would head for New Bern. (This was when W. G. Robinson and some of the 2nd Cavalry were sent in that direction.) This began a period of several months in which the commanders of the Department of North Carolina would be warned of the imminent arrival of Ambrose E. Burnside's fleet in the New Bern area. Obviously more rumors than facts about Burnside's arrival were circulating adding to an atmosphere of urgency that lasted until mid–March of 1862.[33]

D. H. Hill knew immediately he had too few troops to cover the coast, the sounds, and the rivers — all of which had to be defended from the land. After a partial tour of his command, Hill reported to General R. C. Gatlin on October 27. Hill described his activity in these words: "...having a line of defense thrown up to defend the approaches to New Berne, Washington, Hyde, and Roanoke. The spade has been set again everywhere I have been, even in lazy Elizabeth. I have also got the promise of a little work from Beaufort. Should it be done, the age of miracles is not yet over." Not coincidentally, most of the locations mentioned were places to which 2nd North Carolina cavalrymen were intended to be sent or in fact had been sent around October of 1861. In his report from Fort

Macon on October 27, Hill also expressed the following concern: "The Yankee force at Hatteras is said to be 8,000. I fear for Roanoke Island. That place and this [Fort Macon] are the weak points in my department."[34]

Shortly after D. H. Hill expressed his concerns about North Carolina's coastal defenses, the five companies Spruill sent to Edenton were threatened with being sent to Roanoke Island as infantry. On October 28, Gatlin responded to D. H. Hill's request for more troops in the District of Pamlico by first explaining he had none to send, then he added this paragraph:

I have urged upon the Governor to send every man he can arm to this Coast. As yet I have heard of no other troops than four companies of Cavalry under Lt. Col. Robinson, who have been ordered to Washington via Newbern, to report to you. Please let me know where you prefer having them sent. They may come by this place, perhaps to-morrow or next day. If they do, I shall direct the Col. to halt at Newbern and await your orders, unless I hear from you in regard to them.[35]

General Gatlin sent another message to D. H. Hill a few days later in which he revealed a bit of frustration, not just at the lack of troops in his department but also at not being able to keep track of the troops nominally under his command. It seems the Governor of North Carolina was as involved in troop movements within the State as was General Gatlin and others. Gatlin appeared to be ready to throw his hands into the air and tell his command to simply do whatever works — this is suggested in his comments to D. H. Hill on October 30:

In regard to Colonel Jordan's regiment, it has never reported to me; is not in Beaufort County by any other than the Governor's order. If it is in the service of the Confederate States, dispose of it as you may think best. I had hoped that the cavalry [companies from the 2nd North Carolina Cavalry] would have reached New Berne by this. I have directed my adjutant-general to write you in regard to them. Dispose of them and any other troops sent to report to you as you may think best.[36]

Gatlin's expressed hope that the 2nd Cavalry would have arrived in New Bern by October 30, reflects how little was known about troop movements in the State because, as pointed out previously, W. G. Robinson did not request travel funds for the journey from Camp Clark to New Bern until November 5.

On November 16, 1861, with his work just underway, D. H. Hill was sent to Virginia to command the North Carolina brigade in the Potomac District. Brigadier General Lawrence O'B. Branch was Hill's replacement. Ten days later, the Secretary of War in Richmond placed Roanoke Island under Branch's command in Gatlin's Department of North Carolina and removed the 3rd Regiment of Georgia Volunteers from the island. The Secretary instructed Gatlin to replace the Georgians with a North Carolina regiment. (Again this was about the same time as talk of sending the five companies from the 2nd North Carolina Cavalry without mounts to the island as infantry.) The orders from Richmond had the effect of increasing the territory Branch had to cover and reducing the number of troops available in the Department of North Carolina.[37]

On November 29, Gatlin responded to Richmond by pointing out that Brigadier General D. H. Hill had been replaced by a commander with less experience who was then asked to command a greater area. Gatlin pointed out that "General Hill, with all his activity, was never able to make a tour of his command in less than fifteen days, such is its extent coastwise." He then went on to repeat his request that the Department of North Carolina be divided into more and smaller districts with a commander in each.[38]

A month after D. H. Hill was replaced by Branch, North Carolina's governor, Henry Clark, recommended to President Jefferson Davis that Hill's former command be divided into three rather than two commands — arguing it was more than one officer could manage. With Special Orders No. 272 on December 21, 1861, the Secretary of War in Richmond ordered "...North Carolina east of the Chowan River, together with the counties of Washington and Tyrrell, is hereby constituted a military district under Brigadier-General Wise, and attached to the command of Major-General Huger commanding the Department of Norfolk." Wise was in charge of the coast from Norfolk to Roanoke Island — which included Albemarle Sound and the Chowan River. That part of North Carolina then was removed from the Department of North Carolina's command and placed in the Department of Norfolk.

Colonel Spruill and the five companies of the 2nd North Carolina Cavalry with him at Edenton were nearly affected by this division, but they had moved to join their comrades in the New Bern area just in time. Gatlin wrote Branch and opened his correspondence with this line: "The adjutant-general will foreword to you an order in relation to the movement of a portion of Spruill's regiment. By the time of its arrival it is presumed the permanent camp will have been selected." When Wise left Norfolk to survey his new command on January 3, 1862, the men from the 2nd North Carolina had gone to New Bern and thus remained in the Department of North Carolina. Below Roanoke, Branch's command still included the inland waterways off the Pamlico Sound on which most of the 2nd North Carolina Cavalry was then located. The 2nd Cavalry was almost united for the first time in the New Bern area to welcome in the new year of 1862 (companies B and G were still at Washington, North Carolina).[39]

With the new year came a heightened sense of the inevitable Union invasion of North Carolina. On January 5, Governor Clark sent the following message to Secretary of War Benjamin in Richmond:

We have reliable information that the Burnside expedition at Fort Monroe is destined for Pamlico Sound and New Berne. The batteries at New Berne are slight, and manned with inexperienced volunteers, and there are only two imperfect regiments there. We have no arms for volunteers or militia. [This comment includes the 2nd N.C. Cavalry.] Will you send us troops from Richmond or some of our own regiments from James River?....

Secretary of War Benjamin did little to hide his annoyance with Clark's message when he replied the next day in these words, "We are fully alive to the necessity of defending your coast; have much better sources of information than you can possibly have. Be assured we are vigilant, and will use our utmost means for your defense."[40]

R. C. Gatlin also expressed his concern on the issue, but the Secretary of War's assurances apparently did little to ease General Gatlin's own concerns as evidenced by his correspondence with Governor Clark on January 16, 1862 when he said, "No arms have yet arrived here for Leventhorpe's or Lee's regiments, or sabers for Spruill's [2nd Cavalry].... I am fearful that the arms to be sent from Richmond will be too late to meet the fleet [Burnside's] should it land upon our coast."[41]

Governor Clark and General Gatlin were not the only ones on edge because of rumors and inaccurate information about the inevitable Union invasion of New Bern. The rumors circulated statewide on a regular basis, prompting the *Raleigh Register* to print the following commentary on January 15:

There is something quite mysterious in the movements of this much talked about Armada. The other day it was said to be in Pamlico Sound. It appears, however, that it has never been in the Sound, and is now in Hampton Roads, and its probable destination will be up the Rappahannock River, or against the city of Norfolk.[42]

After as well as before this commentary, the newspaper had reported every rumor about the "approaching" Union fleet without skepticism.

Concern about the pending invasion also penetrated to the ranks of the 2nd North Carolina Cavalry. In a letter written by Thomas A. Branson of Company F to his sister, Marinda, on January 8, 1862, he mentioned, "We are *since* expecting an attack on New Berne soon. While I was gone home, the camp was excited twice by the intelligence that the Yankees..." were coming. In his letter, Private Branson went on to echo the Governor's concern, expressing his anxiety about the regiment's readiness for such an invasion, "We are not yet prepared for an engagement for we are not fully armed yet and not enough sabers and pistols." He estimated it would be another six months before they were able to defend themselves. However, Branson's comment contained an air of optimism about their future preparedness which was a new feeling among the troopers in the regiment. They were getting more horses and some arms which prompted Branson to mention in a January 21 letter to his sister how the regiment was by then drilling on horseback, most with guns, sabers and pistols, and how it was a "beautiful sight."[43]

While troopers like Thomas Branson were very concerned, yet a little optimistic about their readiness for the coming battle, others in the regiment were still preoccupied with battling illness and disease even in their new camps in the New Bern area.

The young men in Company K were not much better off when they got to New Bern from Camp Washington. Private James W. Bacon wrote to his friend, Ellen, while in the hospital at Camp Fisher near New Bern, on January 26, 1862.

Sad news has just come in; George James is dead. Anthony Cole I think will not get well. Seven of our Company have died, and whose time will be next, God only knows. Most of his (A. W. Cole) friends have given him out. This death of James is a great loss; he has left a wife and some poor children to mourn his loss, but I hope God will take care of them. We have lost more men than any other company....[44]

George James was 27 years old when he died of "disease." James Bacon and his friends were right. Anthony W. Cole died at the age of 22 from "pneumonia" in the camp hospital the next day — James also mentioned that Anthony was "...in great pain" the day before he died. Company K's battle with disease resulted in nine deaths from the end of training camp through April 1862. They had lost 15 men to illness and disease by the time they left for Virginia in September of 1862. This period of time was undoubtedly Company K's longest battle of the war. While the battles to become equipped and the battles with illness continued, the war between the states came closer to home.

THE BURNING OF WINTON ON FEBRUARY 20, 1862

By February of 1862 the major military activity in the Pamlico area was still in response to the anticipated invasion of New Bern by Burnside — but week after week they did not invade. Part of Burnside's delay was caused by his decision to first clear the Albemarle Sound in the northeastern part of the state. He sent a force into Albemarle Sound and up the Chowan River. These were waterways that had been removed from Branch's district and placed under the distant eye of Huger's Department of Norfolk. It was easy sailing for the Federal force. One of their targets was the town of Winton in Hertford County on the southwest side of the Chowan River and thus in Gatlin's Department of North Carolina. Winton became the first North Carolina town burned in the war by the enemy.

On February 18, 1862, eight gunboats started up the Chowan River for the small village of Winton — population, around 300. Expecting the Union to want control of Winton and to destroy nearby railroad bridges, the Confederate command had sent Lieutenant Colonel William T. Williams[45] and his First Battalion of North Carolina Volunteers with a four-gun battery to assist some local militia companies in the defense of Winton.

W. T. Williams positioned his troops well and fired on the first gunboat that approached the wharf. The gunboat circled, fired its big guns and scattered the confederate artillerymen. The gunboats went down river, out of sight for the night. The Confederate troops and villagers celebrated their apparent victory but the gunboats returned on the morning of February 20, and began to shell the town again. After getting little or no response, the Federals under the command of Colonel Rush C. Hawkins were convinced that the village was not defended so went ashore and entered the town without incident.

Rush C. Hawkins inspected the main buildings and homes in town and decided to burn them to the ground because Confederate forces probably had used them for some purpose, and as retaliation for the Confederates firing on his gun boats the day before. Hawkins ordered his 9th New York, "Zouaves" to roll barrels of tar into the Court House and the other major buildings to insure they, with all their contents, would burn completely. While Hawkins was taking care of such important military matters, he allowed his troops to loot the village, hardly missing a home.[46]

Burnside's adventures in the Albemarle Sound struck very close to home for many of the men in the 2nd Cavalry who were from counties adjacent to the sound — especially those from the counties that clustered around Hertford County (companies C and H). Most of these men had been on picket duty around New Bern for nearly 5 months, waiting for Burnside to attack in that area.

While the men of the 2nd Cavalry waited for the Union attack at New Bern, they had plenty of time in camp to read newspaper accounts of what Burnside was doing before coming to New Bern. During February that included the clearing operation which swept up the Chowan River as far as Winton. The Governor of North Carolina was able to anticipate some of the frustration felt by the troops in the 2nd Cavalry who were from the Winton area, and he heard from citizens along the sound and rivers who demanded more protection. Among his gestures toward protecting the people and their property along the waterways, he dispersed more of the 2nd North Carolina Cavalry from the New Bern area.

On February 19, 1862, the first day of the fighting at Winton, Governor Clark contacted military headquarters for the Department of North Carolina in Goldsboro and requested that "Randolph's and Boothe's companies" of the 2nd North Carolina Cavalry be sent to the area. The cavalrymen in Boothe's Company C were from Hertford and Gates Counties. Winton is the county seat of Hertford and just across the Chowan River from Gates County. The men from Randolph's Company H were from Bertie and Northampton counties—both adjacent to, and south and west of Hertford County respectively. General Gatlin then notified Branch of the request for Companies C and H on February 21 and included the comment, "I hope you can spare either the two companies named, or two others, and will send them with dispatch." Companies C and H were immediately sent to Williamston (about 10 miles southeast of Hamilton) on the Roanoke River and the Bertie and Martin county line—about 10 miles south of Windsor, the county seat for Bertie. Colonel Leventhorpe and his 34th Regiment of North Carolina troops were already stationed at Williamston. Companies C and H came under his command. Colonel Leventhorpe's duty on the lower Roanoke was to keep enemy boats from going up river at that point. When Colonel Spruill, on February 24, 1862, got the order to send the cavalry companies, his assignment was to "harass the enemy and assist the inhabitants."[47]

Companies C and H stayed in Leventhorpe's command on the Roanoke River until he and his troops were moved to Hamilton in the first half of March. When they left Williamston, Company H returned to Camp Fisher, near New Bern, and Company C was assigned to the Washington, North Carolina area—Companies B and G were still stationed near Washington at that time. Company C was recalled to the New Bern area on the evening of March 12 or early the following morning—Burnside's fleet actually appeared near New Bern on March 12, 1862.[48]

Given the placement and periodic relocation of companies from the 2nd North Carolina Cavalry, one might suspect that their commanders felt their presence could make a difference. That was not the case however. In fact, as Governor Henry T. Clark received word and read advertisements in the newspapers about efforts to raise new cavalry battalions and regiments in North Carolina for Confederate service, he let his feelings be known. On March 11, 1862, the day before Burnside's arrival at New Bern, Clark wrote the Secretary of War in Richmond, voicing his concern about what he thought was an unauthorized endeavor. He further wanted the Secretary of War to be reminded that the Confederacy had not yet met its present commitment to existing North Carolina units—specifically the 2nd North Carolina Cavalry. The Governor pointed out that:

Three months ago we tendered Colonel Spruill's regiment of cavalry (Nineteenth) to the Confederacy. They were accepted. After three months' efforts I was unable to obtain arms and equipments for them (from New Orleans to Richmond). We tried in vain to get swords or carbines. This regiment was received by you but partly armed (from necessity). They are yet without sabers, although we spared neither effort nor money. We did engage from the Eastvan & Froelich sword factory at Wilmington, and paid high prices, but three-fourths of the swords proved worthless. If more cavalry is to be received, let me ask that this regiment (Nineteenth North Carolina Volunteers), four or five months in your service without arms, be furnished before others are received. If cavalry is preferred, I can raise you two or more regiments, but I have refused all tender of cavalry companies because I could not equip them.... My own opinion about cavalry is that unless they can have six or eight months' drilling, with arms and horses, they are only valuable as scouts or vedettes, and these can be temporarily had in any section.

But to return to the Nineteenth Regiment North Carolina Volunteers [2nd Cavalry]. If you can let them have sabers they will be useful. They have been many months in your service without arms, and consequently are almost useless, though drawing pay and rations.[49]

This assessment was apparently not posted for viewing by the men of the 2nd Cavalry.

In any case, by March 11, 1862 the Governor of North Carolina regretfully had to acknowledge that the 2nd North Carolina Cavalry was "almost useless" as a fighting force—their use was still limited to scouting and picketing. He also raised the question of

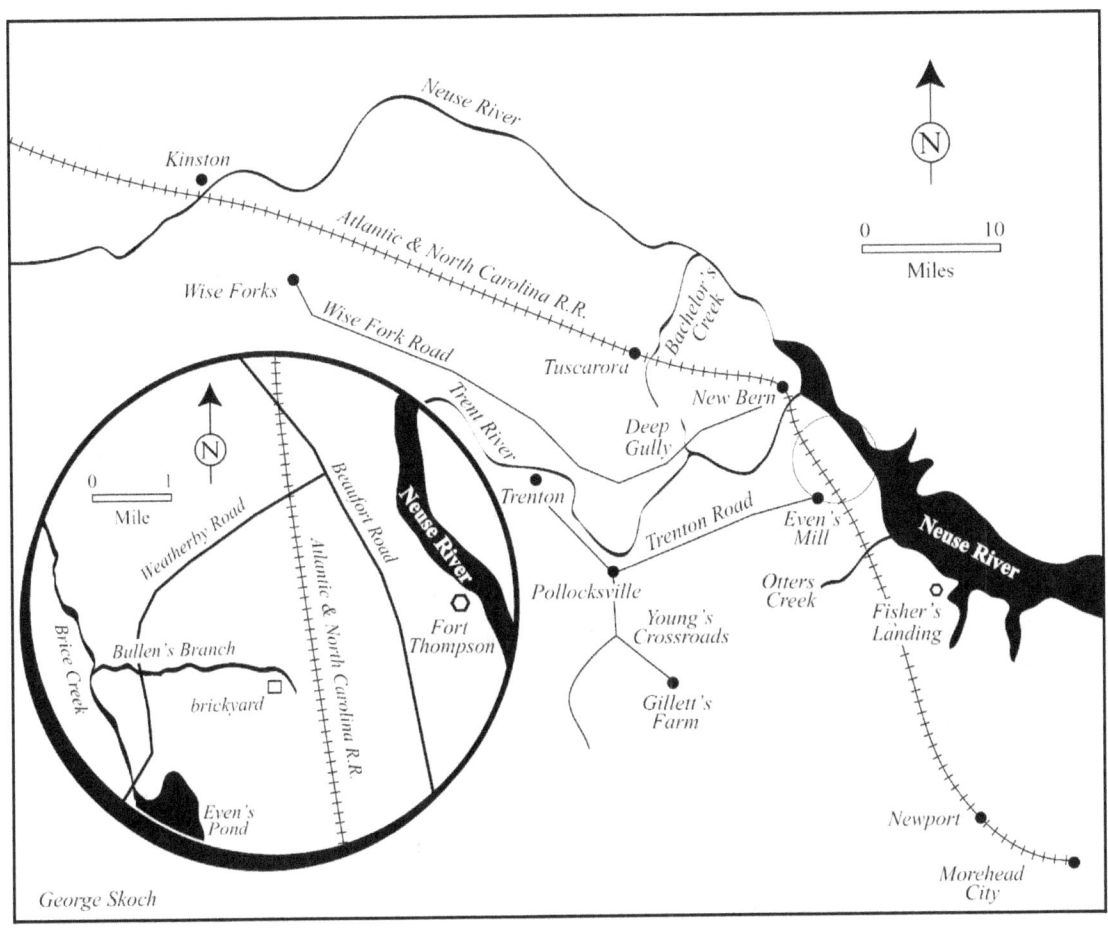

1.2: Around New Bern, 1862

the amount as well as the quality of training a trooper receives when without arms and horses. This was probably a pretty good assessment of the 2nd Cavalry's effectiveness after seven months of service, and on the eve of their first major battle.

The Battle of New Bern, March 14, 1862

During the night of March 11, 1862, Union forces gathered at Hatteras Inlet and started early the next morning for the Neuse River, then to a point just below New Bern. By evening on the 12th they had anchored off the mouth of Slocum's Creek about 16 miles from New Bern. Confederate defenses extended down the Neuse River as far as Otter Creek, just above Slocum's Creek, but the line was not adequately manned.[50]

The morning of March 13 was cold, rainy and dark, when Federal troops brought more gloom to the North Carolina coast. After shelling the wooded areas near the coast, they began to land 13 regiments and 8 pieces of artillery. The Union troops spent the day on a mud-march up the river-bank meeting with very little resistance until evening when they encountered Confederate pickets. They spent the night in the mud and cold rain, just short of the Confederate main line of defense starting at Fort Thompson and running west across their path.[51]

THE CONFEDERATE RESPONSE

Branch divided his command into two wings and placed them under Colonels Charles C. Lee of the 37th North Carolina and Reuben P. Campbell of the 7th North Carolina. He kept Colonel C. M. Avery's 33rd North Carolina and

Samuel B. Spruill's 2nd Cavalry in reserve. Campbell's command included his 7th Regiment under Lieutenant Colonel Haywood, Sinclair's 35th North Carolina, Whitehurst's independent company, Colonel H. J. B. Clark's Militia Battalion, Latham's Battery, and two sections of Brem's Battery. When Campbell listed the units in his command, he made no mention of Colonel Zebulon Baird Vance's 26th North Carolina or companies from Spruill's 2nd North Carolina Cavalry, but they were on his wing and presumably under his command. (In his Official Report, S. B. Spruill mentioned that he was under Campbell's direct command.) Colonel Vance also seems to have been under Campbell's command from the outset, up near Fisher's Landing on March 13, and Vance returned to the Fort Thompson line with Campbell and Sinclair. There is little to suggest that Campbell was aware of his responsibility for the troops on the western side of the railroad — they apparently did not communicate during the fighting and Campbell made no effort to notify the men west of the railroad when he spread the word of the general retreat. Colonel C. C. Lee was in charge of the 27th and 37th North Carolina Regiments plus some artillery.[52]

When L. O'B. Branch was certain Burnside had landed, he moved troops south to resist the Union advance. He sent Colonel James Sinclair and his 35th Regiment to Fisher's Landing just above Otter Creek (about 10 miles south of New Bern). Branch also sent Z. B. Vance's 26th North Carolina under the command of Lieutenant Colonel Henry K. Burgwyn down to occupy the Croatan breastworks. A small cavalry force under Haughton consisting of ten men from the Macon Mounted Guards was sent to Evans's Mill just north of the Croatan Line, but they were shelled by Union gunboats and pulled back early. Other regiments were strung along the coast to defend against further enemy landings. Colonel C. M. Avery's 33rd Regiment and E. G. Haywood's 7th were in reserve at the intersection of Beaufort Road and the Atlantic & North Carolina Railroad just north of Fort Thompson.[53]

Heavy shelling of the coastal defenses from Federal vessels preceded the Union march up the coast. The Confederate force sent south to meet the invaders was not of sufficient strength to offer serious resistance, so R. P. Campbell himself went forward and ordered them to pull back. Z. B. Vance arrived just in time to board the retreating rail cars with his regiment, J. Sinclair and his 33rd North Carolina, and Campbell — all boarded waiting rail cars which took them up the coast to the nearly completed breastworks stretching inland from Fort Thompson. They left the Union troops to slog their way north through the difficult mud.[54]

L. O'B. Branch collected his forces near Fort Thompson, and had plenty of time to deploy them but not enough to complete the breastworks running west from the railroad or get all of his artillery where most needed. The 27th and 37th North Carolina regiments were posted on the Confederate left, between Fort Thompson and the Old Beaufort Road. The 7th and 35th regiments were between Beaufort Road and the railroad line. The Militia battalion under Colonel H. J. B. Clark was at the railroad to the right of the 35th Regiment. The Militia was placed to secure the right flank of the front line and in front of the gap between the front line and the recessed line west of the railroad — the Militia was just east of the brickyard. The brickyard on the west side of the railroad was part of the weakest point in the line.

The Confederate line west of the railroad was held by Vance's 26th Regiment. It was set back, north of the Confederate line stretching from Fort Thompson to the railroad. Vance's command was behind Bullen's Branch and a line of fallen trees. Initially, his command included two, then three companies of dismounted men from the 2nd North Carolina Cavalry. The 33rd Regiment was in reserve about 400 yards north of the brickyard, near the railroad, but they were brought forward to secure Vance's left flank as far as the railroad and to fill the gap on the Militia's right when the action began.[55]

During the night of the 13th, L. O'B. Branch received information that led him to believe a Union force was moving north along the Weathersby Road which would allow them to easily flank the Confederate right. Colonel Vance was then instructed to extend his line westward to Weathersby Road. Vance put Lieutenant Colonel Henry K. Burgwyn in command of the troops on his far right — Burgwyn's command then included a section of T. H.

Brem's battery, Captain McRae's independent infantry company, and two dismounted companies from the 2nd North Carolina Cavalry. The cavalrymen were Captain G. W. Hayes and his Company A, and Company K under the command of Lieutenant W. A. Graham (Captain J. Turner was off rounding up more horses for his company).

Early on the morning of March 14, Branch realized his center at the brickyard was a weak point in his line and began to make adjustments. C. M. Avery's 33rd Regiment was brought forward in line with Z. B. Vance, straddling the railroad — Lieutenant Colonel R. F. Hoke was in command of five companies from the 33rd North Carolina on the west side of the railroad. Hoke was then on Vance's left, and Colonel Avery had the remainder of the 33rd on and east of the railroad, behind the Militia. The weak spot in the staggered line of defenses was still at, and east of the brickyard, however, so Branch moved some artillery into the gap. But they were not manned in time. Federal forces attacked at about 7:30 in the morning on the 14th of March.[56]

THE FIGHT FOR NEW BERN, MARCH 14, 1862

The battle began with a blast from a Confederate battery aimed at the edge of a wooded area where a small group of Yankees on horseback appeared. The Yankees had come forward to see what the enemy had for them — the mounted group included General Burnside himself. They acknowledged the Confederate greeting by pulling back into the woods and sending J. G. Foster's brigade forward along Beaufort Road. Then J. L. Reno's command was sent along the railroad. Artillery as well as musket fire broke out along the line extending from Fort Thompson to the railroad. Foster sent four regiments forward with two more close behind — he held three regiments in reserve. Nevertheless, the Confederate line in front of Foster's command held.

The 21st Massachusetts led Reno's brigade up the railroad until they heard the firing from Foster's fight on their right. Reno's first view of the enemy through the fog came when he and the 21st Massachusetts were already at the right flank of the Confederate front line. Reno's men had marched through the fog to the brickyard before they saw an unmanned battery and the Confederate Militia on their right. Reno and his forces were still unaware of Vance's line in front of them running from the railroad west to Weathersby Road. Initially, Reno had thought he was on the right flank of the entire Confederate line. Vance's 26th North Carolina was also unaware of Reno's 21st Massachusetts until they heard the invaders firing at the Militia's position. The 21st Massachusetts formed facing the railroad, facing east into the Confederate Militia's flank and opened a heavy fire. The 21st Massachusetts was followed by the remainder of Reno's command coming up the railroad tracks.[57]

When the Militia's flank was fired upon and ordered to fall back, some of the men broke ranks. The commander of the Militia sent word to Branch that the enemy was in strength on his right flank. This was about the time Branch ordered Hoke with five companies from the 33rd North Carolina to move south, from Vance's left. He also had Avery take the remainder of the 33rd Regiment down toward the brickyard to support the Militia's right and rear. Avery and Hoke could not get to the Militia in time so they pulled back in line with Vance's position. With firing at their front and flank and an order to pull back, most of the Militia broke into disorderly retreat. Their commander, H. J. B. Clark, later said that first a panic seized his men, then order was restored and a new line formed, but from there "...the panic was renewed and increased and my influence as a commander gone."[58]

With the Militia rapidly making for the rear, the right flank of Sinclair's 35th Regiment lay exposed to Reno's force. Some of the 35th North Carolina also broke for the rear, but Sinclair rallied most of them. Nonetheless, some of the 35th followed the Militia in rapid and disorderly retreat. By 10:00 A.M. the Union force on Sinclair's right flank had increased beyond his ability to hold. Sinclair's Lieutenant Colonel fell back again with some of the men from the right flank. Sinclair could see his force unable to hold the flank and sent for Colonel Campbell, who arrived and ordered the 35th North Carolina to retire. As they pulled back, the fire on their right flank continued and several more men were wounded or killed. In Sinclair's words: "This created somewhat of a panic, as the enemy were firing upon us from the railroad and brick-yard; but soon my men rallied and retired in perfect order till we reached that portion of the railroad intersected by the county road, where I formed them into line ready to advance to meet the foe if called upon."[59] Sinclair may well have restored order at the intersection, but the situation he left behind for the 7th North Carolina was anything but orderly.

When the 35th Regiment pulled back, the right flank of the 7th Regiment was completely exposed to Reno's brigade which was up in force by then. Initially, the 7th held position with bayonets and drove back the enemy at their flank. The Federal force was too overwhelming, however, and soon the 7th North Carolina was forced to begin an orderly withdrawal. All the while, Foster's Union regiments increased pressure at the front of the line east of the railroad. At that point, Branch was mainly concerned with getting his troops back across the Trent River bridges into New Bern.

Branch ordered his men who were east of the railroad and had not already retreated to pull back in an orderly fashion. Colonel Charles C. Lee communicated with the 27th and 37th Regiments, Colonel Campbell with the Militia and the 35th North Carolina, and then the 7th Regiment. Campbell apparently did not concern himself with notifying the troops on Vance's line, west of the railroad. Branch ordered the general retreat and sent couriers to Vance, Avery, and Hoke ordering their pull back, but unfortunately not one of them received the message.[60]

Earlier, just about the time the Militia panicked and broke for the rear, Vance's left flank saw the 21st Massachusetts facing eastward and opened a heavy fire of musketry and artillery into their flank. Reno was surprised but in short order turned part of the 21st Massachusetts, the 51st New York, and the 9th New Jersey toward the northwest at the flank of Vance's line — most of Avery's 33rd North Carolina was by then in place on Vance's left.[61]

Colonel S. B. Spruill had dismounted and sent Captain B. L. Cole with his Company F and Captain C. A. Thomas with his Company E, all from the 2nd North Carolina Cavalry, to Z. B. Vance's line at about the same time the 33rd Regiment was moved up. The cavalrymen moved up on foot and were soon joined by Major J. W. Woodfin who led them to the front. Captain Thomas with Company E moved to the far right and joined their comrades in Companies A and K also from the 2nd Cavalry — Companies E, A, and K were under the direct command of Lieutenant Colonel Henry K. Burgwyn of the 26th North Carolina and were holding the line from Vance's right to Weathersby Road. Apparently Captain Cole with Company F and Major Woodfin remained near the 33rd North Carolina on Vance's left. The point has been made that the men of the 2nd Cavalry had little training as cavalrymen, but it should also be noted that they had no training to fight as infantrymen — of course, none of them had battle experience.

Nonetheless, Vance's line held and brought Reno's advance in their direction to a temporary halt — the fighting was severe. The commander of the 21st Massachusetts described Vance's force in these words: "These consisted of the Thirty-third North Carolina and the Sixteenth [Twenty-sixth] North Carolina Regiments, and were the best-armed and fought the most gallantly of any of the enemy's forces. Their position was almost impregnable so long as their left flank, resting on the railroad, was defended, and they kept up an incessant fire for three hours, until their ammunition was exhausted and the remainder of the rebel forces had retreated from that position of their works lying between the river and the railroad."[62]

While Vance's line held, under the assault on their left flank, they also received increased pressure at their front which began to threaten the center of his line — the point from which he had moved troops during the night toward Weathersby Road. Hoke sent two companies from the 33rd to help strengthen the weak spot in the line, but the connection between Vance and Hoke remained very thin at best. The Union force that came at Vance's front had a hard time and were pushed back several times. However, around mid-day a strong Union force pushed its way into a large gap that had developed between Vance's left and Hoke's right, resulting in the latter fighting on three fronts.[63]

About the same time, noon, Z. B. Vance's quartermaster arrived in great haste to inform him that the left flank of his line had been turned near the railroad by a large Union force and his entire camp had already been pillaged. In addition, Vance was told the enemy had flanked the companies with Avery and were moving up the railroad beyond his line as well as west in an effort to encircle his command and take the two bridges across the Trent — he was losing his escape route. Vance could no longer see Hoke's men of the 33rd North Carolina through the dark blue haze of men and smoke — Union forces had not only pushed into the gap between Hoke and Vance, but had also overwhelmed Avery. It was at this time Vance learned that the entire Confederate force was in retreat except for his command. Without hesitation Vance executed an orderly retreat.[64]

The Disorderly Retreat

The Confederate retreat was first disorderly and then orderly. As indicated, the first to retreat were the men from Colonel H. J. B. Clark's Militia, and they were followed by some troopers from J. Sinclair's 35th North Carolina. Clark, Sinclair and Branch all tried to rally the men who were retiring in a very disorderly manner, but they had only limited success. Branch later noted, in his Official Report on the battle, that all his units behaved well except the 35th Regiment and the Militia (he also pointed out that the 7th and 33rd Regiments absorbed the main Union assault). It is not difficult to understand how men facing their first battle might panic when flanked by an overwhelming enemy. Nonetheless, they were condemned from many quarters — Sinclair brought charges against his lieutenant colonel, and the Militia was tried in the newspapers and elsewhere. The dismounted men from the 2nd North Carolina Cavalry, however, received the most severe condemnation, because as the panicked men of the Militia and the 35th Regiment retreated they came upon the riderless horses of the cavalrymen and apparently without breaking stride, mounted them and sped off across the bridge over the Trent River. Colonel S. B. Spruill, who was still in the rear of the lines, noticed the Militia was beginning to break, so he rode to the area where the horses were being held. At that time Spruill's companies A, K, F, and E were dismounted on Vance's line — Spruill described the scene as follows:

I immediately rode back where the horses of my dismounted men were held, and found many of them mounted and being mounted by the infantry. Captain Cole, most of his command [Company F], and a portion of Captain Thomas' command [Company E], succeeded in getting their horses, but Lieutenant Graham's command [Company K] was left on foot, except those that had charge of his horses; also a portion of Captain Thomas' command, which retreated in company with Colonel Vance's command. I remained a short time, expecting Lieutenant Graham and Captain Thomas to come up, so as to inform them what had become of their horses; but they not arriving..., I rode off and overtook my command at Colonel [C. C.] Lee's camp.[65]

S. B. Spruill's inventory of lost horses was fairly accurate. Most of the men in the dismounted companies on the far right of Z. B. Vance's command did not get back to retrieve their horses. The cavalrymen on the far right in company K and Captain Thomas with most of Company E retreated on foot with Vance's command. A portion of Thomas's company may have retreated with Hoke and some of the infantrymen from the 33rd North Carolina. Company A managed to move their horses nearer to the far right of the line during the night or early on the 14th, and consequently were able to escape over the county bridge on horseback, and meet with Spruill on the Kinston Road later in the day. In any event, this situation created an image problem for the cavalrymen in the 2nd North Carolina. Many observers back at the bridge and in town assumed the fleeing men on horseback were all men of the 2nd North Carolina Cavalry. In fact, they were troopers from the 35th Regiment and the Militia.

The process of laying blame for the rout began immediately after the battle and escalated for weeks. Of course, newspapers knew what should have been done; how it should have been executed; and who was at fault when plans went awry. For instance, by late March in one of its commentaries the *Raleigh Register* carried the following statement: "The Militia, it is said, did not commence retreating until ordered to do so, and the question is who gave that order? It is agreed on all hands that Sinclair's regiment and the Cavalry behaved very badly, indeed...." Early on, the media was softening the criticism of the Militia, and in this same issue, they helped focus attention on Sinclair's scapegoat by pointing out that he had arrested and brought charges of cowardice against his lieutenant colonel.[66] It took longer for them to look more closely at the behavior of the 2nd North Carolina Cavalry, and the stain on their image had more time to set, and consequently it would be more difficult to remove.

The *Raleigh Standard* also rushed to judgment and was weak in its clarification. Its first position read as follows: "At first the retreat was made in good order, but a panic occurring among the cavalry, the regiments became somewhat disorganized. The cavalry having passed over the bridge, burned it, and thus cut off the retreat of two regiments." The troops cut-off were Vance's 26th, part of the 33rd North Carolina, and company K as well as part of Company E from the 2nd Cavalry. In fact, Colonel Campbell and much of his command crossed after Spruill took the cavalrymen riding with him across the county bridge. A week after this newspaper report, the same source had a better idea of what had taken place at the county bridge and printed a partial clarification: "Col. Campbell here held the enemy at bay until every retreating soldier passed the bridge, and then if we recollect rightly, set fire to the bridge." The clarification made no mention of the 2nd North Carolina Cavalry.[67]

After about two weeks of negative treatment at the hands of the press and others, many of the men in the 2nd Cavalry had had enough — they sought to clarify matters themselves. For instance, Lieutenant John P. Lockhart of Company K said in an open letter to the press:

That the Militia and Cavalry were the first to give way I know to be a slander. So far as our company is implicated, our horses were stationed a mile to our left, near the Railroad. Militia and infantry rode them off, and that early in the action; hence the report that the cavalry first gave way. Cavalry horses were seen early in the flight, but foot soldiers rode them. But enough of that fight.... We expect to have that fight over. Tell all the seceders, who could whip twelve Yankees a year ago, to come and whip one now, and we will give them a furlough after the fight.[68]

It is not difficult to detect Lieutenant Lockhart's resentment over the continual accusations about the manner in which the cavalry retreated after he and his comrades had placed their lives on the line.

THE ORDERLY RETREAT

Most of S. B. Spruill's mounted cavalry, including those from companies E and F who had regained their horses, gathered with Major J. W. Woodfin near the intersection of the Beaufort Road and the railroad, near Colonel C. C. Lee's former camp. Near that same place, L. O'B. Branch was trying to collect his command for an orderly withdrawal across the two bridges spanning the Trent. Spruill's mounted cavalrymen also moved toward the county bridge in an orderly retreat.[69]

L. O'B. Branch planned to have his command cross the Trent at the railroad bridge going directly into southern New Bern or at the smaller county bridge where Beaufort Road crossed the river. Branch sent Colonel C. C. Lee to the railroad bridge with instructions to collect their forces in the northern part of New Bern.

C. C. Lee and most of his command made it across the railroad bridge and headed toward the northern part of town. They joined the other infantry regiments near the depot. While at the depot, they connected with Lieutenant Colonel William G. Robinson, General Branch's acting assistant general, who directed them to take the command toward Kinston. W. G. Robinson was communicating Branch's orders to all officers he came in contact with. Around sundown, Branch's command moved to Tuscarora Depot about 8 miles outside of New Bern. During the night, the infantry assembled and boarded trains for Kinston.[70]

Before crossing the Trent River himself, L. O'B. Branch sent R. P. Campbell and the 7th Regiment to the smaller county bridge farther up the river and instructed him to hold it. Branch remained at the intersection of Beaufort Road and the railroad directing traffic and hoping to delay the Union advance while others crossed the bridges. When Branch felt no more stragglers were coming north and the enemy was in sight, he followed Campbell and the other troops who had collected around C. C. Lee's former camp back toward the county bridge. Campbell was then instructed to hold the bridge until Vance and Hoke arrived and then to join Branch in town.[71] (Vance did not try for the county bridge, and the bridge was burning by the time Hoke got there, but the remounted men of the 2nd Cavalry and stragglers from Avery's command had crossed before Campbell left the bridge).

When Branch arrived in New Bern most of his forces had already left, and Federal gunboats had docked in several areas. He then orders in all directions for officers to collect their men and head for Tuscarora, the nearest railroad depot outside of town.[72]

WEST OF THE RAILROAD, VANCE'S RETREAT

The troopers under Colonels Z. B. Vance and C. M. Avery, and Lieutenant Colonels R. F. Hoke and Henry K. Burgwyn held the Confederate line west of the railroad until Branch's disorderly retreat was complete and the orderly pullback was well under way.

When Avery, who was on Vance's left at the railroad, realized he was nearly surrounded, he ordered a pullback. A gap had developed between the companies directly under his command and the other companies of the 33rd North Carolina under Hoke. Consequently, when Avery pulled back, Hoke's command continued to hold. As Avery retired north along the railroad, he came upon Foster's 25th Massachusetts which was already at his rear. Colonel C. M. Avery with about 150 of his men were captured — many of the Confederates on Avery's part of the line managed to escape into woods. Major J. W. Woodfin along with part of Company E and Company F from the 2nd North Carolina Cavalry probably also escaped at this point. Most of these cavalrymen retrieved their horses and joined S. B. Spruill back at the crossroads, crossing the Trent at the county bridge.

R. F. Hoke's command was among the last to leave the fight — they were engaged in front and on the left and right before they pulled back. When Hoke discovered Avery had been driven back, he ordered the men of the 33rd North Carolina with him to begin a pullback. Unable to cross the river, Hoke then headed west for Bryce's Creek. In his words:

> I fell back some distance and intended to unite with Colonel Avery and Major Lewis, but found the troops had continued to fall back, so kept on and intended to join my regiment at the bridge, but found it on fire, so had to cross Bryce's Creek…; continued the retreat to Trenton, in connection with Colonel Vance, who crossed the creek with me, and learning at Trenton our troops were making a stand at Kinston, made a forced march, and reached that point on Sunday morning about 10 o'clock, which made a march of 50 miles in about thirty-six hours.[73]

Vance knew the Union forces were north of his position and increasingly at his rear, so he decided to take his men west to cross the Weathersby Road and then Bryce's Creek. He took the dismounted cavalrymen from companies E and K of the 2nd North Carolina with him.

THE 2ND NORTH CAROLINA CAVALRYMEN'S EXPERIENCES

The 2nd Cavalry held positions on the line that caused them to miss most of the hand-to-hand fighting, and consequently they avoided serious combat losses— nonetheless most of them were in the thick of their first real battle and experienced it close up. But their experiences varied greatly because they had not been sent up as a regiment. Four companies dismounted and stood side-by-side with the infantry on Vance's line. The other companies were held in reserve or did not arrive in time.

As indicated earlier, on the morning of the 13th, S. B. Spruill had been ordered to take his cavalry command to the crossing of Beaufort Road and the railroad. Once there he was ordered to hold a position just east of the railroad, between the intersection and Z. B. Vance's encampment. Spruill had companies D, E, F, H, and K with him when he first moved up — Company A joined him shortly. Spruill's command was placed under Colonel R. P. Campbell. At about 2 P.M., Spruill was ordered to send his two best armed companies to Colonel Vance on the extreme right of the line. Spruill sent Captain G. W. Hayes with his Company A and Lieutenant William A. Graham with Company K — every fourth man in the companies stayed back with their comrades' horses. These two companies were armed with long-range guns: Company A had Mississippi rifles, and Company K carried Hall's carbines. Spruill and the other four companies stayed in reserve.

Later in the afternoon, enemy shelling of their position forced them to move west of the railroad, behind Vance's line. The cavalrymen had hardly settled in their new position when Spruill was ordered to send two of the four companies still with him to Lieutenant Colonel William G. Robinson for vedette duty during the night (Robinson had been detached from the 2nd Cavalry to Branch's staff as Assistant Adjutant-general). He sent Captain James W. Strange with his Company D and Captain John Randolph with Company H —

both companies under the command of Major J. W. Woodfin. The cavalrymen moved about six miles down river where they halted in the rain. By nightfall they were on picket duty at the railroad until relieved at 5:00 A.M. on March 14.

Late in the evening of March 13, Spruill requested permission from R. P. Campbell to take the troops still under his direct command and the horses of his dismounted men back to camp for feeding. He was told to use his own discretion, so between 9 and 10 o'clock Spruill took companies E and F along with the horses of Companies A and K back to their camp for feeding.[74]

After getting some rest in camp, Spruill began to mobilize his men around 4:00 A.M. on March 14, and return to the front. Before leaving he sent Captain Cole's Company F to relieve Companies D and H from their night as videttes. Spruill and Company E returned to the front with the horses of the dismounted men who were still under Vance's command.[75]

When companies D and H returned to camp from their night duty as videttes, Captains Strange and Randolph found that Spruill had left orders for them to keep their companies in camp for food and rest. He also left Company C, under the command of Lieutenant James M. Wynn, in camp for some much needed rest until ordered up. Company C had been in Washington, North Carolina with companies B and G. Lieutenant Wynn and Company C were ordered to Camp Fisher early on March 13, so they marched all day and most of the night, covering about 40 miles before reaching camp around 2:00 A.M. on March 14.[76]

When Spruill returned to the intersection of the railroad and Beaufort Road with Company E and the men tending the horses from the dismounted companies, R. P. Campbell instructed him to hold and stand ready. Their position received heavy fire from enemy vessels on the river until Spruill was ordered to dismount the remainder of his men and send them to Z. B. Vance on the Confederate line west of the railroad. He put Captain C. A. Thomas in command of the two companies available — Thomas's own Company E and Cole's Company F which had returned to Spruill from vedette duty by that time. Shortly after Thomas took his command toward the front, Major J. W. Woodfin returned, and Spruill sent him after Thomas with orders to take command of Companies E and F. At about the same time, Spruill sent a courier to Camp Fisher with instructions for Companies C, D, and H to report for duty on the front. Companies D and H had just returned to camp and begun savoring thoughts of food and rest when the order to head for the front arrived. They immediately remounted their horses and along with Company C, left camp at a gallop. As they approached the New Bern area, they began to pass retreating men and horses, wounded and bloody.[77]

As indicated above, Spruill stayed behind the line and was in a position to see the Militia and the 35th Regiment break and flee the line for the Trent River — many of them stopping to mount and ride off with horses from the dismounted men of the 2nd cavalry. Apparently the dismounted men of Company F and Captain Cole along with Major Woodfin had their horses brought near their positions once the fighting got under way because most of them were able to regain their horses — the same was true for a portion of Captain Thomas's Company E. On the other hand, many of the men of Company E and almost all of the men in Companies K lost their horses to their own infantry. Spruill and his men who had collected under Major Woodfin near Colonel C. C. Lee's camp retreated along with the rest of Branch's command.

Spruill and the mounted cavalrymen with him crossed ahead of Colonel Campbell's command, but after Colonel C. C. Lee's command. (The Militia and the 35th North Carolina had crossed the railroad bridge into town.) Spruill sent his mounted cavalry across the narrow county bridge "by file." After about half of his command was across the bridge, Spruill left Major Woodfin in charge and crossed the bridge himself. Once on the other side, Spruill met W. G. Robinson who was in the process of forming the cavalrymen as they came across. Robinson also had companies D, H, and C with him — he had intercepted them on their route from Camp Fisher to meet Spruill at the front. When Spruill left the bridge only Captain Hayes and his company A had yet to cross the river, so he sent his command ahead with Robinson on the road to Kinston.

After S. B. Spruill left the bridge, he joined his mounted men and Major J. W. Woodfin on the Kinston Road. By the time he got there, W. G. Robinson had ridden into New Bern. Spruill and Woodfin rode to the railroad depot where they met the infantry. Once there, they were instructed to rally around the depot, at which time Spruill was given the order to burn all the cotton and naval stores in New Bern. After questioning the source of such an order, Spruill "...ordered Major Woodfin to make a detail of men to do so, which he promptly did, and left my [Spruill's] command for the purpose of executing the same." Among the troopers sent into town were five men from Company D and perhaps some from Companies C and I. When the detail finished torching the naval stores they headed for Kinston, arriving there around midnight.[78]

Burning stores of cotton and other goods was certainly a new experience for the young men of the 2nd Cavalry most of whom were farmers or merchants, and knew of the work that went into producing the goods they were ordered to destroy.

Spruill and the cavalrymen with him stayed at the depot until the last of the rail cars had pulled out with troops heading for Kinston. By that time enemy shells from gunboats were falling all around them. Finally, Spruill ordered his troopers out onto the road to Kinston. Soon after they were on the road, someone in the rear of the column gave the order to "Gallop, march." The nervous troopers became even more excited, and the cavalrymen along with some infantry began to break ranks. Order was soon restored but no one could find out who had given the order. Word had been passed forward that 700 Union cavalrymen were closing on their rear. Captain Randolph of Company H rode up to Spruill and asked if they were going to make a stand. Spruill decided they would at a bridge about two miles in front of them. While Spruill's command was preparing to make a stand, Lieutenant Colonel W. G. Robinson rode up and told Spruill that he did not believe there was any enemy cavalry at their rear, and he was correct. At about this time, Captain Hayes and Company A caught up with Spruill and joined their comrades on the road to Kinston.[79]

When the day started, the dismounted cavalrymen in companies A and K were on the far right of Vance's line, beyond the swamp to Weathersby Road, with a section of Brem's battery and Captain McRae's company of infantry. Thomas's Company E joined Companies A and K on the far right just before the fighting started. The fighting began on the left of Vance's line just before 8:00 A.M. worked its way along the line until it reached the men west of the swamp around 8:30 that morning. The most severe fighting was at Vance's left, but the men in companies A, K, and E of the 2nd Cavalry nonetheless got their first real war experience. As indicated earlier, the fighting continued on this front until about 12:00 P.M. when Vance learned that Branch was in retreat and Avery on the left of his line had been overrun. Vance ordered his command to retire and sent a message to Lieutenant Colonel Burgwyn, who was in direct command of the men from the 2nd Cavalry and the other troops between the swamp and Weathersby Road, instructing him to join the retreat. According to one report, companies A, K, and E under Hayes, Graham, and Thomas "who were on foot, and placed on the right of our line, were among the last to leave, and came off the field in good order, with the right wing of the 26th regiment N. C. Troops under the command of Lieutenant Colonel H. K. Burgwyn."[80]

As indicated above, Captain Hayes's Company A managed to reach their horses and cross the county bridge to join Spruill and the rest of the mounted cavalrymen on the road to Kinston later in the day. The men of Company K and some from Company E were not so fortunate, but not for the lack of trying. Around 11:00 A.M., more than two hours into the fighting, Lieutenant Graham, commanding company K, sent private William Rhew to retrieve their horse from where they had left them the day before, well to the rear near the railroad. Around 12:00 P.M., when Lieutenant Colonel Burgwyn, in full retreat, came by Graham's position and told him to follow suit, Graham took his men to the place on Weathersby Road where Private Rhew was supposed to have brought the horses only to find they were not there. In Graham's words: "They had been ridden off before Rhew reached them, some say by the Militia; others, by men with uniforms. I don't know who rode them; but the men came off on foot with me, and we found the horses in Kinston on our arrival there on Sunday morning."[81]

Vance led his men across Weathersby Road to Bryce's Creek where they had to do battle with the creek while keeping an eye on the enemy at their rear. Colonel Vance described the experience in these words:

On arriving at the creek we found only one small boat, capable of carrying only three men, in which to pass over. The creek here is too deep to ford and about 75 yards wide. Some plunged in and swam over, and, swimming over myself, I rode down to Captain Whitford's house, on the Trent, and through the kindness of Mr. Kit Foy, a citizen, procured three more small boats, carrying one on our shoulders from the Trent, with which we hurried up to the crossing. In the mean time Lieutenant-Colonel Burgwyn with the [men] of the right wing in excellent condition, and assisted me with the greatest coolness and efficiency in getting the troops across, which after four hours of hard labor and the greatest anxiety we succeeded in doing. Lieutenant-Colonel Burgwyn saw the last man over before he entered the boat. I regret to say that three were drowned in crossing.[82]

The cavalrymen of the 2nd North Carolina had marched to the creek with Burgwyn and assisted him until all were across.[83] Once Vance had his command across the creek, he took them on the road to Trenton. At Trenton they learned that Branch was planning a stand at Kinston, so they crossed the Trent River and headed north for that place. They marched day and night with little rest until they reached Branch at Kinston around noon on March 16. Vance had the highest praise for the men who made the march with him — he spoke of their "spirit of determination and power of endurance" and described them as "Drenched with rain, blistered feet, without sleep, many sick and wounded, and almost naked, they toiled on through the day and all the weary watches of the night without murmuring...." Lieutenant Colonel Hoke of the 33rd North Carolina said they marched about 50 miles in about thirty-six hours.[84] According to one trooper, who witnessed their arrival at camp and recalled many years later, "Only the muddy, motley and weary troops of the Twenty-sixth North Carolina seemed to be in good spirits ... for Zebulon Baird [Vance] had found a keg of brandy which had restored his soldiers courage and cheered their souls."[85] Probably the dismounted cavalrymen of the 2nd North Carolina had a share as they were under Vance's direct command during the retreat.

2ND NORTH CAROLINA CAVALRY'S LOSSES DURING THEIR FIRST FIGHT

During either the fighting or the retreat, the 2nd Cavalry lost at least four men — it is difficult to know when the losses occurred. Three of the cavalrymen were from Company C, which did not make it to the front. Company C was stopped by Lieutenant Colonel W. G. Robinson en route to the battle field after the retreat was already under way. They were on hand, however, to join the others for the burning detail and covering the infantry's retreat. The detail that went into town to burn the stores and warehouses had several close encounters with their enemy which may have resulted in the losses. None of the reports mention the presence of Company I, but they may have been on picket duty nearby during the fighting and retreat.

Combat Losses in the 2nd North Carolina Cavalry During the Battle of New Bern, 1862

Trooper	Age	Co.	Fate
Tully M. Forbes		C	captured, March 14
Joseph J. Ellis		C	captured, March 14
Nicholas J. Battle	32	C	captured, March 15
Hiram Barber	30	I	captured, March 15–August

The source for this table is *North Carolina Troops 1861–1865, A Roster*, compiled by Louis H. Manarin (Raleigh, N.C., State Division of Archives and History), vol. II, Cavalry, pp. 104–177. The Roster of Troops took most of its information from the Compiled Service Records which are primarily based on Company Muster Roll cards. A major deficiency in the Service Records is lack of information in many cases resulting in an understatement of the losses. (See Appendix for more information on the men listed above, page 391)

CHANGES IN THE NORTH CAROLINA COMMAND STRUCTURE AFTER THE BATTLE

Humiliating defeats are often followed by changes in command structure, and the loss of New Bern was no exception. Changes started at the top in North Carolina when on March 15, 1862, with Special Orders No. 60, Brigadier General Richard C. Gatlin was relieved from duty on account of ill health. He was temporarily replaced by Brigadier General Joseph

R. Anderson. Major General Theophilus H. Holmes was soon afterwards appointed commander of the Department of North Carolina.[86]

By the time L. O'B. Branch wrote his report on the battle, he had already been replaced by Brigadier General Samuel G. French — however, he was scheduled to replace Branch before the battle took place. S. G. French took command of the District of Pamlico on March 17. In that post he was commander of the First Brigade which included the 7th, 26th, 27th, 35th North Carolina Regiments, Major S. H. Rogers's battalion of infantry, North Carolina Troops; Captain William Sutton's battalion of foot artillery; Captains Jones and Grisham's batteries; and Spruill's 2nd North Carolina Cavalry.[87]

Just after the defeat at New Bern, more Confederate troops were moved to the Kinston area — they included the return of Brigadier General Robert Ransom, who had done an excellent job of training the 1st North Carolina Cavalry before he took them to Virginia where they preformed well. The 1st Cavalry returned also.

As more resources became available, Holmes reorganized his force into four brigades. The First Brigade was commanded by R. Ransom, the Second by J. R. Anderson, the Third by L. O'B. Branch, and the Fourth by J. G. Walker — Samuel G. French was put in command of the District of Cape Fear. R. Ransom's First Brigade was the largest of the four with 4,295 effective troopers (4,954 present), and included the following units by April 19, 1862:[88]

Ransom's First Brigade

25th North Carolina
26th North Carolina
27th North Carolina
35th North Carolina
A Battalion, North Carolina
9th North Carolina (1st Cavalry)
19th North Carolina (2nd Cavalry)
Evans's North Carolina Troop
Grisham's Mississippi Battery
Jones's North Carolina Battery

It was probably a combination of factors such as the stern leadership in Ransom's brigade, the presence of the highly acclaimed 1st Cavalry, and the ineptitude demonstrated by Spruill, the lawyer and politician, during the battle of New Bern that prompted the latter's resignation on March 29, just a few days after Ransom took command. Matthew L. Davis was appointed colonel of the 2nd North Carolina Cavalry but he became ill while on his way to Goldsboro, North Carolina and died there on April 23, 1862. Lieutenant Colonel William G. Robinson took temporary command of the regiment while waiting for M. L. Davis.

While waiting for their new Colonel, the 2nd Cavalry was kept busy drilling and training under the watchful eye of their new brigadier general, Ransom, and his staff. They were also immediately put to work as a buffer between their infantry and the enemy in and around New Bern. The 2nd Cavalry had pulled picket duty before but never with a large enemy force at their front.

Cavalry Duty, the Enemy Present

Picket duty was a basic part of cavalry activity, but the job took on additional dimensions when the enemy was near. The cavalry was expected to provide a protective screen between their army and the enemy; and they were expected to keep the enemy's pickets and scouts at arm's length — to keep their enemy's eyes and ears at a good distance. If a sizable enemy force moved toward their army, it was the cavalry's job to slow their advance, giving their comrades time to ready their stand or withdraw. In addition, they were expected to be the eyes and ears of their army. This often meant they had to go on the offensive — perform raids on enemy positions and scouting missions behind enemy lines. Basically, the cavalry had to control the space between the two opposing armies. The full scope of a cavalryman's job would soon be learned by the men of the 2nd Cavalry, because the enemy was there in force.

For several months after the fall of New Bern, some members of the 2nd Cavalry felt their duty was the most severe service the regiment would experience. This assessment was partly due to the regiment's state of readiness to be in front of their enemy. The 2nd Cavalry did not have the training or arms to handle such a formidable enemy nor, in the days immediately following the defeat, did they have even the clothes and blankets to cope with the weather.

The first week or two were the worst. For instance, in a letter written on April 1, Lieutenant John P. Lockhart wrote the following to a hometown newspaper: "We had one severe week of picket duty, without blankets or clothes, save what we wore upon our backs from Newbern. Many things have since come for our comfort, for which we thank the 'old folks at home.' The officers of our company are now without tents—but we expect them soon." By early April clothing and blankets had begun arriving for the cavalrymen in other companies also.[89]

There is no question the men of the 2nd Cavalry faced difficulties a large part of which was the duty itself. Their assignment was to picket the roads between Kinston and New Bern. This typically meant a party of between 30 and 60 men would go about 25 miles toward New Bern and establish its picket camp within a half or quarter mile of enemy pickets. The inexperienced troopers in the 2nd Cavalry knew that General Burnside's entire force was just behind the Federal pickets, while the cavalrymen of the 2nd North Carolina knew they had no support for more than a hard days march to their rear.

Any sense of vulnerability had to be enhanced by the manner in which they were armed. With the partial exception of companies A and K, the regiment was still armed with the weapons brought from home by the men— needless to say, nothing was state of the art in arms. Lieutenant W. A. Graham of Company K spoke of going on picket around that time with 35 men, "...armed about as follows: Two Sharp's carbines, six Hall's, five Colts' (six shooters), four Mississippi rifles and twelve double-barreled shotguns, and perhaps a half dozen pairs of old one-barrel 'horse pistols.' There was not exceeding twenty cartridge boxes in the company; the others carried their ammunition (twenty rounds) in the pockets of their cloths and in their haversacks."[90] The cavalrymen also knew that Burnside had about 30,000 troops fully equipped and with modern arms. Add to their feeling of isolation their inadequate arms, the physical conditions, and one can begin to imagine the men's level of discomfort.

Each company from the 2nd Cavalry would rotate into picket duty for about 10 days at a time. While out on picket, it was not uncommon for a horse to remain saddled for up to 5 days at a time. It was also common to have rain on each of the days. These conditions often resulted in three-quarters of the horses returning from picket duty with sore backs—the men generally not in much better condition.

This was the first time most of the companies of the 2nd Cavalry were together. (One or two companies were usually detailed for duty on the Pamlico or Roanoke Rivers.) The picket duty was constant for the next six months or so. Most of the 2nd Cavalry was camped near Wyse's Fork, five miles southeast of Kinston, and most of the duty was in front of New Bern. However, two companies were posted across the river, near Trenton, to picket the river and roads leading east and south from that point. The first squadron sent to picket south of the Neuse River included companies C and D. These companies picketed along the Trent River and the road to Pollocksville.[91]

The 2nd Cavalry typically had one encounter with the enemy each week, but nothing very notable for the first month after the defeat at New Bern. From time to time, however, the nervous boredom of picketing was broken by exhausting scouts and raids into enemy territory.

An example of a scouting mission occurred on Saturday, April 5, 1862 when Lieutenant Colonel William G. Robinson (commanding the 2nd Cavalry while waiting for Spruill's permanent replacement) ordered Captain John Boothe of Company C to lead a scout from the Trenton area south into Careret County to determine their enemy's strength south of New Bern. Captain Booth was instructed to take his cavalrymen toward Morehead City—a distance of about 40 miles southeast of New Bern, depending on the route taken. In his report to W. G. Robinson, Boothe described the experience as follows:

I took my march toward Carteret County on Saturday, and reached Mr. Foscue's, on the Beaufort road, 20 miles below Trenton.

Sunday I was joined by Captain Hill and 50 of his men and proceeded toward Beaufort. At sunset I halted, and sent forward to ascertain the number and position of the enemy's advance reported to be ahead. At 1 o'clock in the night my scouts came in, not able to find anything, and I proceeded to Eli Saunders' and fed my horses and men.

Monday morning I was joined by Lieutenant Humphreys with about 30 men. By agreement with Captain Hill and Lieutenant Humphreys I divided the whole force into four platoons of about 30 men each, placing the men with the best arms in the first platoon. This platoon I placed under command of Lieutenant Eure and sent it forward as an advance down the road from Saunders' toward Newport. I followed with the other three platoons and their commanders a short distance behind the advance. After going within 5 miles of Newport the advance saw a squad of 5 of the enemy and charged them, capturing 3 and killing 2. About 200 yards in advance of the first squad there was another squad of 12, which being discovered, Lieutenant Eure rallied his platoon and charged them, killing 1 and capturing 6. Most of the enemy fired their muskets without injuring a horse or man on our side. In five minutes after the firing ceased two companies of the enemy came in sight and fired upon us and fell into the marsh. By their fire the only damage done was the killing of my horse under me. I ordered the men to retire down the hill, as there was no chance to charge them from a miry causeway. With our 9 prisoners I retraced my steps to this place last night.

I let Lieutenant Humphreys take charge of 3 prisoners, Captain Hill 3, and I send the remainder to you and through you to General Ransom.

I am very anxious that you should recall me forthwith, as my horses and men are completely exhausted and tired out.

I also send 7 muskets captured from the enemy and Captain Hill took two.

The number of the enemy at Newport and stationed at intervals from Newport to the place we encountered them is about 600 or 700 from the best information. At and about Morehead City one regiment.

P. S.—Since writing the above one of my pickets has come in from Haughton's, about 4 miles from Pollocksville, toward Wilmington, saying the enemy had fired upon him and killed or taken the two pickets that were with him, and that there was 500 or 600 of the enemy.[92]

Combat Losses in the 2nd North Carolina Cavalry Mid-March to Mid-April, 1862

Trooper	Age	Co.	Fate
Andrew N. Reid	20	B	killed, March 30
Hugh W. Collins	22	C	captured, c. April 8
James H. Kelly	22	C	captured, c. April 8
Willie H. Perry	21	E	captured, before April 16

The source used here is: *North Carolina Troops 1861–1865, A Roster*, compiled by Louis H. Manarin (Raleigh, N. C., State Division of Archives and History), vol. II, Cavalry, pp. 104–177. (See Appendix for more information on the men listed above, page 391.)

The two pickets Captain Boothe referred to in his post script as "killed or taken," were in fact taken prisoners.

During their first month of picket and scouting duty with their enemy present, the 2nd Cavalry was cautious, but still took at least four losses: one killed and three captured.

THE ATTACK AT GILLETT'S FARM, APRIL 13, 1862

Late in the night of April 13, Lieutenant Colonel William G. Robinson became a little bolder and led a force of about 200 men from the 2nd North Carolina Cavalry in a mounted attack on some Federal troops occupying a house at Gillett's farm south of Pollocksville. W. G. Robinson had most of Captain Strange's Company D (54 men), Captain Turner's Company K (45 men), Captain Bryan's Company I (45 men), Captain Thomas's Company E (25 men), and some cavalrymen from Captain Hayes's Company A (4 men), Captain Andrew's Company B (14 men), and Captain Cole's Company F (15 men) with him at the time. The entire force consisted of 1 Lieutenant Colonel, 3 captains, 8 lieutenants, and 202 men.

W. G. Robinson had a plan of attack which called for the cavalrymen from Company I to charge the house from the front, Company D from the left and Company K from the right. Not only were the attacks ill-conceived but also not coordinated, and consequently not separately effective. All the cavalrymen approached the house from the lane leading directly to the front of the house. Captain Bryan's Company I was in front of the column and had the shortest distance to his point of attack which was the front of the house—they advanced and fired until they ran out of ammunition. Captain Strange's Company D was next in line and was supposed to tear down a fence along the lane and circle around the left side of the house. Coming up the lane after Company D were some men from Company E who were under the command of a Sergeant and apparently had no specific orders. They succeeded in blocking Captain Turner's Company K, making it necessary for them to stop long enough to throw down a fence and enter the field to the right of the lane. By this time, Captain Turner had already been hurt or seriously wounded while still in the lane. Lieutenant Colonel Robinson made it around the back of the house along with Captain Strange and about 30 men from Company D only to lead a misguided charge, probably motivated by frustration, in which he was wounded in the leg, fell from his horse, and was captured. After many of the young horsemen did some charging around, probably feeling a sense of adventure in their first important mounted charge, the disorganized Confederate cavalrymen found that they were easy targets for the Union troopers in the farm house so pulled back in confusion.[93]

As indicated, the attack was poorly planned, confused, and ended in an embarrassing defeat for the 2nd Cavalry. They had a plan of attack before charging the farm house on horseback, but virtually no one followed any plan. One wonders if in the heat of battle, it occurred to Lieutenant Colonel Robinson that his troopers were sorely lacking in discipline and drill necessary to carry out the sort of attack he had led them into—training that he had by default primary responsibility for providing.

We might expect that some of the blame for such a poorly planned and executed adventure might fall upon Lieutenant Colonel Robinson who was in charge and led the attack. In addition, Robinson, more than anyone, must have known how ill-equipped and ill-trained his men were at that time. Nonetheless, the judgment of his superior and fellow West Pointer, Brigadier General Ransom, was that Robinson had been a victim of his men's ineptitude and cowardice.

Indeed, the event at Gillett's farm was as outrageous to the Confederate command in North Carolina, as it was demoralizing to the men of the 2nd Cavalry. Major General Thomas H. Holmes, commander to the Department of North Carolina, ordered Brigadier General Robert Ransom to conduct an inquiry into the incident. After his study of the matter, R. Ransom could not find anything of value in the 2nd Cavalry once Lieutenant Colonel W. G. Robinson was gone. He even personally examined the wounds of Captain J. Turner of Company K, and decided "...all his injuries were caused by the fall from his horse." R. Ransom's report of April 20, 1862, was devastating, and nearly had a terminal impact on the 2nd Cavalry. He concluded:

The officers should be reduced, never to hold commissions; the men should be dismounted and disarmed and placed at hard labor during the war.... It may, perhaps, appear severe that the few who seemed willing to do their duty should suffer with the multitude of those who failed in all that becomes the officer or soldier, but they are so inextricably mingled that human ingenuity would fail to make the just discrimination.[94]

Ransom goes on to say he would exclude one squadron of the regiment from punishment—presumably that would have included those companies not involved in the skirmish, but that is not clear in his report.

Ransom's report and actions at the time suggest he had a certain lack of understanding when it came to his volunteer troops, and an inability to notice the men lacked training and discipline rather than potential. Apparently he also had a problem with being just or fair. From a variety of sources, one historian concluded, "A gallant spirit was Ransom's but he was not altogether popular with his men. He was too much the regular, the West Pointer, in handling troops." One veteran who had served under Ransom said, "If he had understood volunteer soldiers, and realized that four-fifths of the men in the ranks were as careful of their personal honor, and as anxious for the success of the cause as he, he would have been one of the greatest generals in Lee's army...."[95]

In any case, R. Ransom was such a disciplinarian it is understandable that he was humiliated by the behavior of a detachment from a regiment in his brigade. But his lack of understanding of how to build the morale of his troops was also evident in the quote above. He recommended punishing all those in the detachment, and others in the regiment, because some of them failed in the performance of their duties—he would commit the injustice of punishing those who did their duty, just to be sure and punish those who did not. This judgment was supported by Major General Holmes when he received the report and passed it on to the Secretary of War in Richmond.

Fortunately for the 2nd North Carolina Cavalry, when the report and its recommendations got to Richmond, it was passed on to one of President Jefferson Davis's senior military advisors—General Robert E. Lee.

A letter (attached to Ransom's report in the Official Records) from General R. E. Lee to

Holmes tactfully agreed with the findings in the report, but not the recommended punishment. R. E. Lee demonstrated a level of wisdom not evident in the leadership of Ransom or Holmes, when he concluded,

While deeply mortified at the conduct of the men, as reported by General R., I cannot see how his suggestions to reduce the officers and disarm the men and condemn them to hard labor can be carried out, unless charges be properly preferred and the matter submitted for investigation to a court-martial, when it could be ascertained how far the whole companies might be disbanded and their arms given to others. But it would appear from the report of the detachments engaged that but a few men from some of the companies were present. For the bad behavior of a few it would not appear just to punish the whole. I would suggest that these men be stationed at some point, if possible, where their drill could be perfected, as it would seem that their unfortunate behavior was attributable in a great measure to lack of drill and discipline.[96]

It would seem R. E. Lee's conclusion necessarily placed a major part of the blame for the incident on the regiment's lack of training, again directing blame toward W. G. Robinson, something R. Ransom was not publicly willing to do.

The difference in leadership qualities is apparent in this event. While Ransom and Holmes were ready to discard the men as worthless soldiers, General R. E. Lee could see their failure as the result of a lack of training rather than weakness of character. More importantly, however, was R. E. Lee's tendency to place a higher value on justice for the many than on punishment of a few when he dealt with his men. This is probably one of the most important factors in R. E. Lee's ability to get more from his soldiers than was normally possible.[97]

The issue did not die easily for Ransom and others, however, partly because of the scope of the attack on the 2nd Cavalry. For instance, in an apparent effort to twist the blade in the wound, Ransom not only used a harsh tone in his report and discussions with others, but felt it necessary to revive the unjust accusations that were leveled at the cavalrymen after the Battle of New Bern. His knowledge of the cavalrymen's retreat at New Bern was based on hearsay and he apparently neglected to recall the press reports that clarified the role of the cavalrymen in the earlier battle. Ransom's unfortunate comment reads as follows: "To keep such troops in the presence of the enemy would be useless [and] criminal, and I respectfully suggest that the officers and men who *have on two occasions covered themselves with shame* [my italics] and our arms with dishonor be debarred the privilege of combating for our liberties."[98] Perhaps Ransom felt it necessary to recall an inaccurate accusation from past events to justify his harsh recommendations in the Gillett farm affair. Nonetheless, the tarnished image of the 2nd Cavalry rapidly spread beyond the commanding officers as the newspapers printed some of the information and all of the condemnation.

Always eager to accuse, the Raleigh newspapers followed Ransom's lead and also condemned the men of the 2nd Cavalry for their behavior at Gillett's farm, and they also felt it important to remind people of accusations leveled at the cavalrymen just after the Battle of New Bern. An example of what the public read follows:

...companies of the Second Regiment of Cavalry... came upon a body of about two hundred and fifty Yankees, and having surrounded them, were about to deprive them of their arms, when one of his own men cried out, 'Boys, a large party of the enemy are upon you — take care of yourselves.' This alarm created a perfect stampede on the part of all our cavalry, except Col. Robinson and about fifty of his men, who ... were captured by the enemy whom we could so easily have taken prisoners. There, by the dastardly cowardice or black hearted treachery of one of our own men, were we deprived of the opportunity of capturing a large number of Yankees.... We hope the coward or villain who gave the alarm can be identified, and that he will be speedily brought to a drum-head court-martial, and shot.[99]

Such harsh condemnation certainly must have seemed unreasonable to the men of the 2nd Cavalry, and it clearly angered some of their supporters in home counties. For instance, a commentary in the *Hillsborough Recorder* pointed out that the 2nd Cavalry had been from the beginning treated as "the stepchild of the State," and that accusations of bad behavior at New Bern were false. The *Recorder* goes on to note that the *Raleigh Register* and *Standard*, both inappropriately recalled the inaccurate information about the behavior of the cavalry at New Bern, unjustly and thoughtlessly echoing Ransom's overreaction. Furthermore, the commentary observes that "The frequency of falsehoods respecting events of the war, is sufficient to put all on their guard against disparaging rumors as to the courage of our troops. Soldiers in the field have little opportunity for defense against street jesters, railroad travelers or the statements of the press...."[100] Nonetheless, the affair at Gillett's Farm added to the tarnish still on the 2nd Cavalry's image, and probably their self-image as well.

There were certainly more wounded men from the 2nd Cavalry than listed in the following table, and according to one source, Lieutenant Colonel W. G. Robinson was not the only Confederate captured.

Combat Losses in the 2nd North Carolina Cavalry at Gillett's Farm, April 13, 1862

Trooper	Age	Co.	Fate
William G. Robinson		F&S	wounded & captured
John A. Braddy	36	D	killed
Alexander C. McDougald	33	D	wounded
Love Melvin	20	D	mortally wounded
Jesse R. E. Pittman	25	E	wounded
John M. Gaster	32	I	wounded
Josiah Turner Jr.		K	wounded
John H. Vanstory		F	wounded

The source used here is: *North Carolina Troops 1861–1865, A Roster*, compiled by Louis H. Manarin (Raleigh, N.C., State Division of Archives and History), vol. II, Cavalry, pp. 104–177. In this and subsequent tables, F&S means Field & Staff. (See Appendix for more information on the men listed above, page 391.)

With the loss of Lieutenant Colonel W. G. Robinson, the remaining leadership of the 2nd North Carolina Cavalry was even less experienced in the ways of war than before. Nonetheless, it is very probable that intense training and drill were added to the cavalrymen's already difficult duty, and that it certainly took place under the watchful eyes of their Brigadier General Ransom — for at least a couple of weeks until Ransom was recalled to Virginia by General R. E. Lee for more serious duty.

Reorganization and Changes in the Command Structure

The 2nd North Carolina Cavalry was only in Robert Ransom's brigade from mid–March through April of 1862 — five or six weeks, but there is little reason to believe Ransom paid a great deal of attention to the regiment until after the Gillett farm affair. When Ransom left North Carolina in late April, however, he probably left instructions for rigorous training for the 2nd Cavalry.

By mid–April, General Robert E. Lee was already asking T. H. Holmes of the Department of North Carolina to return R. Ransom to Fredericksburg, Virginia with his brigade. On April 27, Holmes told R. E. Lee that he would "…send Ransom's brigade to Fredericksburg as soon as I can relieve it, unless you will be satisfied with the new one to be organized out of the troops at Raleigh." The next day, Lee responded making it clear he wanted an experienced brigade, not the new recruits in training at Raleigh. Nonetheless, Holmes was reluctant to weaken his force in North Carolina and R. E. Lee had to restate his request on April 30 in the following words: "Your letters of the 27th instant and telegram of 29th are received.... It would not be well to send the new brigade to be organized at Raleigh to Fredericksburg instead of Ransom's. The new men would no doubt suffer greatly, and their efficiency be much impaired by the usual diseases of the camp." On the same day, Holmes responded to Lee informing him that with grave concern he had contacted the railroad authorities about transportation for the brigade requested and was told transportation would be available by May 1.[101]

On May 3, 1862, R. Ransom and his troops were in Virginia, but he left most of the 2nd North Carolina Cavalry behind. It is not clear if Ransom made the decision to leave them because they still needed training, or if Holmes requested they be left behind because they were by then the most experienced cavalrymen available to him. In any case, both Ransom and Holmes were apparently pleased to leave the 2nd Cavalry at Camp Johnston near Kinston. However, Ransom did take companies H and I of the 2nd Cavalry with him to Virginia for a short while.[102]

By mid–May, R. E. Lee was again informing Holmes that he must pull more of the experienced troops from North Carolina for duty in Virginia. Lee was sympathetic to Holmes's need for troops and informed him of the recent appointment of General James G. Martin and Colonel Clingman to brigadier generals, and that they were being sent to him as commanders of North Carolina brigades made up mostly of new recruits.[103] The 2nd Cavalry became part of Brigadier General Martin's new brigade — with companies H and I still detached to R. Ransom in Virginia.

On June 1, 1862, Brigadier General James G. Martin took command of his new brigade which included the 2nd North Carolina Cavalry, four regiments of infantry, three batteries of light artillery, and two independent companies of cavalry. Martin's brigade also included Captain Whitford's company of heavy artillery, and Captain Nethercutt with 20 men all acting as Partisan Rangers. His command totaled 5,329 men, but only 3,928 were reported present for duty.

The first issue Brigadier General James G. Martin raised in his report to Goldsboro on June 17 dealt with the unhealthy conditions he observed when he arrived in camp. The 1,407 men who were in his command but not present for duty were mainly "...sick in hospitals in camp, some absent sick, with a few on detached service and furloughs."[104]

All his regiments were infected, even the cavalry. In the 2nd Cavalry alone, just for the period of time surrounding his arrival, there were at least twenty non-combat losses recorded — mostly from disease. Fortunately for the men in his brigade, James G. Martin made the effort to improve their conditions. In his words,

My first attention was called to the large amount of sickness in camp and the probable cause, with the view to remedy it if possible. The ground on which the troops were camped was low, without any drainage, and a swamp on the side of each regiment.

After careful examination in every direction in the vicinity of Kinston I found it necessary to remove my camp to Falling Creek, where there is a high and dry encampment on the railroad, and to all appearances healthy, at least as much as any place in this section of the country. There is an excellent drill ground at the camp, large enough for the entire brigade.[105]

Relocating the camp about six miles out of Kinston was probably more beneficial to the infantry than the cavalry because the latter was often out on picket duty — the picket camps were not as well constructed as the infantry camps, but at least they were easily moved to cleaner and drier locations as called for. Nonetheless, the men of the 2nd Cavalry certainly appreciated the move as well as the concern.[106]

In his June 17 report, J. G. Martin also described his placement of troops. He placed one regiment of infantry back at Kinston. Captain Carraway's company of cavalry and Captain Whitford's Partisan Rangers were assigned to picket duty on the northeast side of the Neuse River, near Swift Creek. Captain Tucker's cavalry pulled picket duty on the Tar River from Greenville to just outside Washington, North Carolina. Martin placed the 2nd North Carolina Cavalry between his new camp and the enemy at New Bern. In his words, "The cavalry pickets extended to within a few miles of New Bern, nearly to Deep Gully on the Trent road, and from the railroad near Tuscarora running across to the Neuse. This duty was done by five companies of cavalry, which I intend to strengthen by three more." Captain Nethercutt and his Partisan Rangers formed part of the picket line south of the 2nd North Carolina Cavalry — from near Deep Gully, to and across the Trent River in Jones County. As before, this was a typical use of the cavalry — their job was to control the space between the armies while the latter were at rest.

The five companies of the 2nd North Carolina Cavalry on picket duty between Camp Johnston and New Bern at that time were B, C, D, G, and K. (Companies H and I were in Virginia with Ransom.) There is no information for Companies A, E, and F during the May–June reporting period which suggests they were also on detached duty.[107] In any case, companies A, E, and F were certainly the ones Martin indicated he hoped to add to the five companies already in place, so they were probably not far off.

The single most important change for the 2nd North Carolina Cavalry during this period was the appointment of Solomon Williams as its colonel on June 6, 1862 — just five days after

Martin took command of the brigade. They had been without a colonel in residence since Spruill resigned on March 29. Lieutenant Colonel Robinson had been in temporary command of the regiment until April 13 when he was captured at Gillett's farm. The process of selecting a new Colonel was apparently not simple. For instance, Colonel Junius Daniel was offered the command of the 2nd Cavalry but he declined the appointment in favor of Colonel Solomon Williams, whom Daniel considered more qualified than himself for the job.[108]

Not only did Solomon Williams develop a close relationship with the men of the 2nd Cavalry, but he recognized what they needed to become a more efficient fighting unit. With him, the cavalrymen received both training and leadership.

THE 2ND CAVALRY CONTINUES ITS DUTIES AND REPAIRING ITS IMAGE

After the nasty affair at Gillett's farm on the evening of April 13, 1862, and while the change in brigade commanders was underway, most of the 2nd Cavalry continued picket duty and involvement in skirmishes and raids against the enemy. It was exhausting and risky, as the following examples illustrate.

On April 21–22, Company B of the 2nd North Carolina Cavalry clashed with Union pickets and drove them back — seven Federals were killed and one captured. There were no losses for Company B. Then later in April, in their turn, Company B had its pickets surprised at Tuscarora Depot, and lost equipment and a horse.

A picket of 18 men from the 2nd Cavalry, Company C, under the command of Lieutenant William P. Roberts, while on duty just below Trenton around May 1, 1862, stopped for dinner at a farm house near Sawyer's Mill. They posted several pickets and sat down to their meal. In short order, one of the pickets was driven in by a company of Union cavalry. The Confederates in the farm house did not hear the commotion until the enemy was upon them and they had been cut off from their horses. The Union commander called for Roberts and his men to surrender, which was a reasonable request under the circumstance, but Lieutenant W. P. Roberts ordered his men to charge the Federal troops. Early in the charge, the Union commander was shot and fell from his horse. The fighting became general, and the men of the 2nd North Carolina Cavalry stood firm.

One Confederate observer later said around 20 Union men were on the ground by the time Lieutenant Roberts noticed Union infantry support was rapidly approaching. At which point Roberts had his men gather several sabers, pistols and other Union equipment before they made good their escape. The men from the 2nd Cavalry suffered one reported loss — Private John Taylor Cross was seriously wounded.

Such actions illustrated the determination of the 2nd Cavalry to become a fighting force at least equal to the sum of each individual's courage, and to have their public image match their self-image — and it was working. After describing the skirmish, the *Raleigh Standard* closed coverage with this commentary: "Captain Boothe's company [Company C] is winning laurels by its intrepidity. This is the second or third skirmish in which it had met with success. If all our cavalry were properly equipped and officered, we might expect every day to hear of success. Coolness, judgment and courage will do wonders."[109]

Shortly after mid–May, five companies of the 1st North Carolina Cavalry were stationed on the road to New Bern on the north side of the Trent River. They relieved several companies from the 2nd Cavalry on that section of the picket line. Fortunately, one member of the esteemed 1st Cavalry was also a valued correspondent for the *Raleigh Standard*, and he took it upon himself to investigate among the residents of the area a story about a skirmish that involved the 2nd Cavalry the week before. This cavalryman then wrote a long letter to the *Standard* which is notable for a couple of reasons. First it is another example of the *Raleigh Standard* recounting and praising the men of the 2nd Cavalry, an important factor in establishing a positive image for the unit; secondly, the news item was a letter written by a cavalry peer, a member of the highly respected 1st North Carolina Cavalry.

The skirmish described took place near Foscue's farm on the North side of the Trent River, early in the morning on May 15. The men from the 2nd Cavalry consisted of troopers primarily from Captain Hayes's Company A, but also including a number of men from companies B and K — about 40 to 50 cavalrymen in all. Videttes, mostly from Company B, had been sent up the road toward New Bern where they encountered the cavalry advance of a large enemy force (about 200 cavalry, 2000 infantry, and cannon). The Union cavalry advance gave chase to the Confederate videttes, who retreated rapidly along the road, past their reserves. The Union advance was followed by the remainder of their cavalry, and as they came down the road passing the 2nd Cavalry's reserves, the men from Company A under Lieutenant Rogers (who replaced Captain Hayes as commander of the company at the end of May) and from Company K led by Lieutenant Graham, charged the Union column. In the words of the letter writer from the 1st Cavalry:

Then commenced the ball. Our men discharged their firearms as promptly as possible — then drew their sabres, and went to work in regular style. The galling fire they had given the enemy on coming up, and their thrilling yells as they bore down on them, added decidedly to the discomfort of the blue coats, and they commenced falling back. The platoon which had pursued the videttes, hearing the fighting in their rear, wheeled, and our men found themselves attacked by this body also in their rear.... The steel of foeman rang vividly against that of his antagonist, and cries of agony (I am told by one who *heard.*) mingled with the shouts of enthusiasm and the sharp cracks of small arms. The Yankees contested well the ground for about half a mile, and until their infantry and cavalry made their appearance on the roadside.... Our men having cut through the force attacking them in their rear, on seeing their infantry, immediately withdrew out of range to await further demonstrations.[110]

After a short while, the Union forces gathered their dead and wounded, burned the local church and other buildings then withdrew back toward New Bern. The letter writing cavalryman from the 1st North Carolina was obviously taken by what he learned of the action he called "...decidedly marvelous and improbable that so small a force as ours should effectively check and whip so superior a force of cavalry they encountered...." His final praise, and undoubtedly what the men of the 2nd Cavalry wanted to hear, came with these words:

But the 2nd Cavalry that were engaged, are certainly *fighting men*. I am convinced that the regiment has been belied by the slanderous reports circulated. It had undoubtedly some of the best fighting material that the State has in the field — and if they were efficiently armed, equipped and officered, the regiment would win as high a reputation as any in the service has achieved.

One day after the success near Foscue's farm, cavalrymen from Company C of the 2nd Cavalry drew more positive attention with their actions on the opposite side of the Trent River, near Pollocksville. Lieutenant William P. Roberts with 20 men from Company C had a skirmish with the enemy on May 16, 1862. Roberts and his men repulsed a force of Union cavalry making its way toward Trenton. There were no Confederate losses in this engagement, and they took three prisoners. The Union cavalry had also advanced along other roads that day and encountered cavalrymen from Companies B and G from the 2nd North Carolina Cavalry — three Confederate losses were recorded from these two companies.[111]

In addition the 2nd Cavalry was involved in numerous small skirmishes, which received less attention. One such encounter took place

Combat Losses in the 2nd North Carolina Cavalry April 14 through July 27, 1862

Trooper	Age	Co.	Fate
H. Zimmerman	22	A	killed, April 14
Lambert P. Garrard		K	injured, April 15
William B. Whitworth		F	killed, April 17
John Taylor Cross	24	C	wounded, May
W. T. Brown		A	captured, May 5
Jesse A. Cahoon	23	G	captured, May 9
Joseph W. Tarkenton	19	G	captured, May 9
George McLelleand Jr.	19	A	captured, May 13
Beauford Rhea	25	A	killed, May 15
William H. Neal	18	K	wounded & captured, May 15
James J. McLean	37	B	captured, May 16
John F. Miller	33	B	captured, May 16
Jones S. Henderson	21	G	wounded, May
John A. Battle	27	C	captured, May 27
Thomas Bunch		K	captured, July 26
Robert S. Walker		K	captured, July 26
N. B. Dudley	23	K	captured, July 27

The source used here is: *North Carolina Troops 1861–1865, A Roster*, compiled by Louis H. Manarin (Raleigh, N. C., State Division of Archives and History), vol. II, Cavalry, pp. 104–177. (See Appendix for more information on the men listed above, page 391.)

on May 19 below Kinston in which the regiment lost nine men, killed and wounded, while the enemy losses may have been as high as 75.[112]

From the fights and skirmishes the 2nd Cavalry was engaged in from the embarrassment on April 13 until July of 1862, the regiment came away with remarkably few losses. The losses that were recorded are presented in the table following.

THE ATTACK AT BACHELOR'S CREEK, JULY 28, 1862

Naturally, all such skirmishes did not result in victory for the cavalrymen of the 2nd North Carolina, and on July 28, 1862, everyone in the regiment was reminded picket camps near enemy lines were dangerous. Nearly twenty men from Company B established their picket headquarters at French's house on Bachelor's Creek (about 13 miles from New Bern). They were attacked by infantrymen from the Massachusetts 27th, some men from the 3rd New York Artillery, and 3rd New York Cavalry — 105 troopers in all.

Early on Sunday morning the Federals moved up a railroad track, through their own picket line, then cut over to the Confederate videttes and drove them back at a great speed, not giving them time to sound an alarm for their comrades camped at the farm house they were using as a headquarters on the Neuse road. The Union troops quickly but only partially, surrounded the house, and fired a volley into it to announce their arrival.

According to a report filed by Union Captain Charles D. Sanford, Commanding Guard at Batchelor's Creek, they had the following encounter with 15 to 20 troopers:

I immediately moved forward and came on the house very suddenly, it being almost entirely concealed by trees.... I therefore ordered a charge and a fire while charging.... They fired a volley through the windows and yard, the volley being the first intimation the rebels had of our presence. They ran quickly, but only 4 escaped, 1 of them being wounded in the leg. The prisoners were brought in from the swamp and placed under guard and the house searched. Nothing was found of any value but a few sabers, the rifles and pistols being mostly worthless and condemned. Some 20 good horses were captured, only 4 escaping. The wounded of the enemy were placed in a wagon and sent under charge of the cavalry to the railroad. Everything having been cleared out of the house, it, together with most of the outbuilding, were fired, and were burning finely when we left.

We took 10 prisoners, 1 dead man being unintentionally left behind unburied, and 1 dying (Corp. Grier Black, of Mecklenburg County, North Carolina) on the return home. One with his arms shattered was immediately sent to the hospital; the remainder, by General Foster's order, being sent to the provost-marshal. The prisoners belonged to Company G, Second North Carolina Cavalry, and had been at French's some three weeks.[113]

Captain Sanford's report incorrectly described the Confederate prisoners as from Company G — they were in fact all from Company B. Union reports put the losses to the 2nd North Carolina Cavalry at: 1 killed, at least 3 wounded, and 10 soldiers captured. The numbers are close to accurate, except there were probably many more with wounds that were not reported for the records. Plus, the 2nd Cavalry did lose 20 of their valuable horses that day.[114] Experiences such as this would remind the troopers that the tedium of picket duty can escalate rapidly to the dangers of war. By most accounts, the duty in the New Bern area was one of the least popular for the troopers in the 2nd Cavalry.

Combat Losses in the 2nd North Carolina Cavalry Bachelor's Creek, July 28, 1862

Trooper	Age	Co.	Fate
Grier R. Black	22	B	killed
John J. Harden	27	B	captured
Samuel A. Knox	19	B	captured
Cornelius Medlock	26	B	captured
James H. Puckett	30	B	captured
William F. Reid	20	B	captured
William J. Reid	20	B	wounded & captured
Edwin P. Rogers	25	B	captured
Marcus J. Shook	26	B	captured
George C. White	24	B	captured

The source used here is: *North Carolina Troops 1861–1865, A Roster*, compiled by Louis H. Manarin (Raleigh, N. C., State Division of Archives and History), vol. II, Cavalry, pp. 104–177. (See Appendix for more information on the men listed above, page 392.)

The 2nd Cavalry had at least one encounter with the enemy every week during this period of time, most of which resulted in Confederate successes and helped rebuild some of the pride the men had before the defeat in the battle of New Bern and the humiliating engagement at Gillett's farm involving several of the companies of the 2nd North Carolina Cavalry.

More Changes in the Command Structure

While the men of the 2nd Cavalry were still working on their image problem and adjusting to a new colonel and brigade commander in June, more changes were put into place. Brigadier General J. G. Martin had been with his command near Kinston for only a few weeks when orders began to circulate about changes in the command and moving Martin with his brigade to Virginia.

On June 21, 1862, in Special Orders No. 140, Robert. E. Lee notified the troops that "The department of Maj. Gen. Theo. H. Holmes is hereby extended to the south bank of the James River, including Drewry's Bluff. He will establish his headquarters at Petersburg, or at such other point as he may deem more convenient."[115] By July 5, Holmes issued Special Orders No. 143 from his new headquarters in Drewry's Bluff, which continued the pull out from North Carolina.[116]

On August 8, R. E. Lee corresponded with Governor Clark in an effort to explain why General Holmes had pulled the more "Serviceable" troops from North Carolina to Virginia. The correspondence included the following:

He [Holmes] brought the brigades of Generals Martin and French because, the enemy being in and upon James River, it was thought proper to provide against any attempt he might make to penetrate North Carolina and cut the railroad from the north, which might have been among his designs. With this view General Holmes was ordered back to the south side of the river immediately after the battles, where he was joined by Generals Martin and French. The information received by General Holmes led him to believe, as I do, that the principal part of General Burnside's command had been transferred to Virginia, where I believe they now are.[117]

The correspondence goes on to remind the Governor that Holmes's command was by then in the hands of Major General D. H. Hill. R. E. Lee's explanation also made it clear that J. G. Martin had left North Carolina by the first week of August.

When J. G. Martin pulled out of the Kinston area, however, he did not take his entire brigade. In fact, when Union forces began to move out of New Bern toward Kinston, Colonel Solomon Williams of the 2nd North Carolina Cavalry was then acting brigadier general, and he moved that portion of Martin's brigade that had been left under his command down to meet the advancing enemy.[118] While day-to-day operations had not changed much for the men of the 2nd Cavalry, they were by then operating under the command structure recently based at Drewry's Bluff and Petersburg, and personnel changes continued.

By mid–August, J. G. Martin had submitted his resignation but it was not accepted, and he was instructed to report to D. H. Hill, commanding the Department of North Carolina, and to take immediate command of the troops in North Carolina.[119]

Several days later, D. H. Hill, from his Headquarters in Petersburg, issued Special Orders No. 180 dated August 18, 1862, which included the following:

Brig. Gen. J. G. Martin is assigned, in accordance with instruction from the General Commanding the Army, to the District of North Carolina, extending from the right banks of the Roanoke to the South Carolina line. Brig. Gen. J. J. Pettigrew will relieve General Martin of the charge of his brigade.[120]

Around the time J. G. Martin's brigade was being shuffled about, Martin was telling R. E. Lee the Department of North Carolina had a cavalry regiment that could be sent to Virginia. Delighted with the prospect of getting another cavalry regiment, R. E. Lee then reported to the Secretary of War on August 25 that he was told "...a regiment of cavalry (the Second North Carolina Regiment, I think) which was not required for service in that State, and, indeed, from the locality of its then station (Goldsborough District), it was difficult to forage." R. E. Lee went on to say, "I wrote to General D. H. Hill on the subject, but have not received a reply. Cavalry is very much needed in this region; the service is hard, and the enemy strong in that arm. If the regiment in question is not needed in [North] Carolina, I respectfully request it be ordered to join General Hampton's brigade."[121]

The 2nd Cavalry did not at that time end

up in Wade Hampton's brigade. However, efforts to send them in various other directions continued. For example, on September 15, G. W. Smith offered the services of the 2nd Cavalry to S. G. French for use by Colonel Daniel in his expedition into North Carolina. His correspondence reads as follows:

Colonel Daniel takes with him two of his best regiments and a fine battery. If the Second North Carolina Cavalry will be of use to you in this expedition suspend the order sending them forward until after you get back. I have directed Colonel Daniel to return with his command as soon as the expedition is over. Strike the hardest blow you can.[122]

There is no evidence at this point to suggest the 2nd Cavalry was attached to Colonel Daniel for his expedition after September 15. The Second Squadron (Companies C & K) of the 2nd Cavalry did, however, fall under Daniel's command at Drewry's Bluff about this time, after they moved up from Hamilton, North Carolina.

Their Last Duty in North Carolina

By the first of August, Confederate forces had substantially moved out of North Carolina. Holmes had moved his headquarters from Goldsboro to Drewry's Bluff above Petersburg in late June (D. H. Hill replaced Holmes there on July 17, 1862.), and Martin had also been moved to the Petersburg area — the latter leaving much of his brigade in North Carolina. Around this same time, Union forces began to probe more deeply into the interior of North Carolina — one of their major objectives to interrupt the railroad going through Goldsboro. One of their first probes was toward Kinston where the bulk of the 2nd Cavalry was still stationed. (Companies C and K, the Second Squadron, were detached to Hamilton, N. C., and Companies H and I were still with Ransom's brigade, Ewell's division, Army of Northern Virginia for the Peninsular Campaign.)[123]

While the 2nd Cavalry and others under the command of Colonel Solomon Williams were confronting the advancing enemy under very difficult circumstances, D. H. Hill, their new commander of troops in North Carolina, apparently still had concerns about some of his officers. Brigadier General T. L. Clingman, then at Goldsboro, for example, wrote the following to D. H. Hill: "I fear, as you suggest, that Colonel Williams is not in all respects fully qualified for the position he holds [acting brigadier general], but the other two colonels there [Kinston area] are much less so. In fact, Williams complains of their want of discipline, &c. The greatest difficulty, however, arises from the small force on the line."[124]

Whether or not Solomon Williams and his small command were qualified for their position did not concern their enemy; however, as Union forces began to move out of New Bern toward Kinston with land forces on the Trent and Dover roads and gunboats up the Neuse River. Colonel Solomon Williams of the 2nd North Carolina Cavalry did not have time to question his own qualifications for the job — he just did what could be done. Sol Williams moved down from the Kinston area to meet the advancing enemy.[125] This was among the last holding actions the 2nd Cavalry participated in before moving to northern Virginia.

By early October 1862, the 2nd North Carolina Cavalry under the command of Major Clinton M. Andrews had made its way to northern Virginia. Colonel Sol Williams was on leave, and Major Woodfin had resigned, thus putting the regiment in the hands of newly promoted Major C. M. Andrews.

The Second Squadron, Companies C and K, remained detached, and it took them until May of 1863 to catch up with the rest of the regiment.

Once again, undoubtedly many minor wounds did not get recorded, and many of the more serious wounds that resulted in eventual discharge or transfer to the Invalid Corps are also not reflected in the tables of "Combat Losses in The 2nd North Carolina Cavalry." The only recorded losses for the regiment, less the four detached companies, for the month of August are listed below.

Combat Losses in the 2nd North Carolina Cavalry August 1862

Trooper	Age	Co.	Fate
Alexander Autry	25	D	captured, August 6
John H. Hubbard	27	D	captured, August 6
George R. Britton	26	E	captured, August 6

The source used here is: *North Carolina Troops 1861–1865, A Roster*, compiled by Louis H. Manarin (Raleigh, N. C., State Division of Archives and History), vol. II, Cavalry, pp. 104–177. (See Appendix for more information on the men listed above, page 392.)

Two

The Army of Northern Virginia and the 2nd North Carolina Cavalry

By the time the 2nd North Carolina Cavalry moved to Virginia in September of 1862, it was still trying to become a regiment rather than a collection of squadrons to be employed where needed. As we might expect, the squadrons did not go to the battlefields of Virginia as a unit. Companies C and K remained detached and moved up from Hamilton separately in late September, settling at Drewry's Bluff by October 19. However, once most of the companies had arrived, companies H and I, which had moved to Virginia with Robert Ransom's brigade in June 1862, returned to the regiment. When Companies C and K arrived, the other eight companies, had already moved through Drewry's Bluff (Headquarters of their brigade) and on to Richmond. Indeed, they were in Richmond by October 1, and camped at Culpeper Court House by October 6. While at Culpeper Court House, they had picket and limited scouting duties. The regiment was moved to Warrenton on the 12th of the month — but the Second Squadron, companies C and K, remained detached while at Drewry's Bluff and elsewhere. They did not rejoin the regiment until May 20, 1863.[1]

The likelihood of developing a regimental identity was certainly not enhanced by the prolonged absence of their commanding officer. Colonel Solomon Williams remained on leave, then detached duty, and did not accompany his 2nd Cavalry to Virginia — he also would not join the regiment until May of 1863. The regiment was under the direct command of Major Clinton M. Andrews for its journey north. Andrews had been moved to the regiment's Field and Staff when he was promoted to major on June 6, 1862 — Major Woodfin resigned on that date.

By September 1862 the 2nd North Carolina Cavalry's commanders above the regimental level had settled around the Petersburg-Richmond area, but they and their command structure were still very much in flux. In addition, the war in Virginia was moving at a rapid pace and the need for cavalry changed from week to week. Major General Gustavus W. Smith was commanding the forces in North Carolina from Richmond — and he was still moving his troops up to the Richmond area. However, he remained reluctant to send his troops north of the James River, though he was increasingly under pressure to do so. During the year, Robert E. Lee had managed to move the fighting from the Richmond area to northern Virginia, and by October he needed cavalry there.

To better understand the military environment into which the 2nd North Carolina Cavalry entered in September 1862, it is helpful to consider what the Confederate army in Virginia had been through during the previous several months and what sort of command structure had developed during that time. Consider why Robert E. Lee was so anxious and expressed such urgency in his requests for more troops from G. W. Smith at the time. What R. E. Lee and his army had just been through and the losses they had experienced were living memories, and help explain why Lee was certainly relieved when the 2nd North Carolina Cavalry and other troops arrived from G. W. Smith's command. Also, we should briefly survey the activities and relationship between the Army of Northern Virginia and its new cavalry command under James E. B. Stuart on the eve of the arrival of the 2nd Cavalry.[2]

The Armies in Virginia

The military campaigns in Virginia during 1862 did not start well for the Confederacy, or the Union for that matter. Most notably, they were among the bloodiest of the war. And the command structures of the opposing armies were responsible for much of this turmoil; neither President Lincoln nor Davis was happy with his commander in Virginia by May of 1862.

President Davis and General Joseph Johnston

Friction existed among the top commanders of the Confederate army in and around Richmond — principally between President Davis and General Joseph Johnston. Davis did not have full confidence in Johnston's ability to do the job at hand, and Johnston knew it. Johnston did not communicate well with his superior or the commanders of troops under him. Misunderstanding and confusion characterized preparations for defending the Confederate capital.

Fighting around Richmond began on May 15, when Union gunboats attempted with no success to break through the fortification at Drewry's Bluff. In spite of successfully defending the James River, Johnston pulled his line of defense closer to Richmond on that day and again on May 17, until he was, in many areas, at the earthworks built in 1861 around the suburbs of the capital. If Johnston had a plan, he did not communicate it to his fellow commanders — all of whom needed to know where and how the stand against the attacking Union forces would take place.

On May 20, General George B. McClellan took a large Union force across the Chickahominy River, and still President Davis and others had no idea what Johnston had in mind for defending Richmond, or if defending the city were part of the plan. President Davis and his military advisor, General Robert E. Lee, rode to the Confederate front near Mechanicsville and spoke with several commanders, inquiring about the plan of operations; about their orders. No one they spoke with seemed to know what had been planned for the defense of Richmond. Davis sent requests to Johnston for information and received no hint of his plans.

G. B. McClellan was clearly in no hurry, though by May 26, he was within ten miles of Richmond, and the Federal cavalry had occupied Mechanicsville, just five miles north of the city. Johnston learned of the enemy's proximity when he received word that G. B. McClellan was to be reinforced by McDowell's men coming down from near Fredericksburg. Johnston then decided to attack the invading Union army before McDowell could reach G. B. McClellan's troops. General Gustavus W. Smith was assigned the task of hitting G. B. McClellan's right before they were joined by McDowell. G. W. Smith formulated and presented his plan to a council of war on May 28 only to be informed that J. E. B. Stuart had provided information indicating that McDowell was no longer moving toward G. B. McClellan.

President Davis's military advisor, Robert E. Lee, caused McDowell's force to be drawn back when he sent Thomas J. "Stonewall" Jackson to the Shenandoah Valley. The diversion had worked — when T. J. Jackson captured Front Royal on May 23, President Lincoln sent reinforcements to the Valley and held McDowell's force back from G. B. McClellan. As a result, G. B. McClellan hesitantly readied his troops for a siege of Richmond, and President Davis pressured Johnston to launch an attack on the Union forces in front of Richmond.

The Confederate council of war, however, did not know with certainty where McDowell was, and they debated the wisdom of attacking G. B. McClellan. It was late on the night of May 28, when the generals decided to change the plan of attack — and, of course, President Davis was not informed. General James Longstreet's idea prevailed — he proposed to attack in the vicinity of Seven Pines on the morning of May 29. Early on that day, General D. H. Hill found Federal troops, infantry, cavalry, and artillery on the move near Seven Pines. As a result, J. Johnston favored delay. On May 30, D. H. Hill reported that Federal forces had again moved closer and were west of Seven Pines. Johnston decided to attack at Seven Pines on May 31. Again, this decision was not communicated to Jefferson Davis nor to his military advisor, Robert E. Lee.

Joseph Johnston planned to overwhelm the Union force at Seven Pines before it received reinforcements. This plan required coordinating the troops in his various commands. Longstreet was to advance along the Nine Miles Road; D. H. Hill was to move first along the Williamsburg Road; Huger was to come down from the Oakwood area and follow D. H. Hill onto the Charles City Road. Through lack of communication and coordination, Longstreet ended up on the wrong road. Indeed, three of the four divisions were on or heading for the same road. They met at Gillies Creek which was full and forceful from the previous night's storm — crossing was a slow process. The prospects for destroying the Union's IV Corps were passing with the sun. After a bit, Johnston could hear the sounds of Longstreet's engagement off to the south and soon received a message from Longstreet indicating he was in heavy fighting and was gaining ground. Fighting continued until nightfall on May 31. The Confederates missed several opportunities due to conflicting orders, miscommunications, and uncertainties. Basically, Johnston had launched a poorly executed assault, one brigade at a time. His plan was not as much at fault as was his poorly worded and circulated orders during the operation.

Joseph Johnston was wounded twice during the day's battle and was replaced by Robert E. Lee. In addition, the Confederates lost over 6,000 men in the attack — the Federals lost about 5,000. R. E. Lee pulled back on June 1, and set his men to strengthening the fortifications around Richmond. The Union forces did not follow.

During the first days of R. E. Lee's command, new troops were arriving from North Carolina and other places. T. H. Holmes's brigades from North Carolina were sent up. One under John G. Walker arrived at Petersburg and was moved to Drewry's Bluff. Ransom's brigade followed. He brought with him only two companies from his 2nd North Carolina Cavalry. While integrating the newly arriving units was important, fixing the army was essential.

R. E. Lee knew that the Confederate army in Virginia had problems. These problems led General Chilton of Lee's staff to characterize the army in June of 1862 as not much more than an "armed mob.... In a word, it was magnificent material, of undisciplined individuality, and as such correspondingly unreliable and disorganized."[3] To remake the army in Virginia, R. E. Lee knew he would have to communicate well with President Davis and with his generals, as would the latter among themselves. He knew he had to build a new army in Virginia while pushing and drawing Union troops away from Richmond. President Davis had the man he needed.

PRESIDENT LINCOLN AND GENERAL GEORGE B. MCCLELLAN

In May of 1862, George B. McClellan had more than 100,000 Union troops in front of the Confederate capital. Smart money was on the imminent fall of Richmond. President Lincoln had another 35,000 troops under McDowell between Fredericksburg and Washington, ready to join G. B. McClellan's right in an assault on Richmond.

However, G. B. McClellan was too hesitant at Richmond's door during May of 1862 and Lincoln was frustrated. He did not conduct a well coordinated pursuit of R. E. Lee after the battle near Seven Pines, and President Lincoln was again frustrated. While R. E. Lee was entrenching to defend Richmond, G. B. McClellan continued to frustrate President Lincoln by communicating a series of reasons for delaying his attack — mainly because he wanted more troops. President Lincoln did not yet have his man in Virginia. Lincoln's confidence in G. B. McClellan finally reached a new low, so the general would not be getting more troops for the siege of Richmond. Lincoln was casting his eye and troops toward the Shenandoah Valley.

The Confederate Cavalry under James E. B. Stuart

Robert E. Lee saw great potential in having a well developed and independent cavalry long before the Union commanders did, and as he formed the new army of Virginia, the cavalry became an important part. He realized if the cavalry were united and free to roam as needed, it could facilitate communication with and locate units in the field — their enemy's as well as their own. R. E. Lee was acutely aware of the need for better information, and he would increasingly look to his cavalry for it.

R. E. Lee's inclination to develop his cavalry was already evident on June 10, 1862 when he sent Brigadier General J. E. B. Stuart with his cavalrymen to locate and determine the strength of G. B. McClellan's right wing. He told Stuart of his planned offensive north of the Chickahominy River, and of his need to locate the right wing of the Army of the Potomac. He needed to know how far it extended and what it was doing.

As the plan was being formulated, R. E. Lee apparently heard of or sensed Stuart's desire to make more of the information gathering mission — to perhaps ride around G. B. McClellan's army and make an expedition of it. This was evident when R. E. Lee sent written instructions to Stuart the next day; he felt compelled to include the following advice, "...but be content to accomplish all the good you can without feeling it necessary to obtain all that might be desired. I recommend that you take only such men as can stand the expedition, and that you take every means in your power to save and cherish those you take..., and remember that one of the chief objects of your expedition is to gain intelligence for the guidance of future operations...."[4] R. E. Lee clearly recognized the sense of adventure and ambition in Stuart and had elevated the mission to the status of expedition. Lee obviously also felt the need to temper the 29-year-old cavalryman's inclinations while not stifling them.

Among those Stuart selected for his first expedition were the colonel of the 1st Virginia Cavalry, Fitzhugh "Fitz" Lee, R. E. Lee's nephew; William H. F. "Rooney" Lee, colonel of the 9th Virginia Cavalry and R. E. Lee's second son; and John S. Mosby. Several other officers and 1,200 of the best men Stuart had under him were also selected.

Robert E. Lee had emphasized the need for secrecy so at the outset neither the officers nor the men knew the nature of their mission. On the morning of June 12, Stuart awakened his staff and told them he expected every man to be in his saddle in ten minutes. They struck north then east and located the Union right. Having accomplished his mission, finding no Union forces of consequence in the area he covered, he had the option of returning to camp the way he came. However, he realized Union cavalry were closing in on his rear, so his logic and sense of adventure inspired him to continue south behind G. B. McClellan's army and circle the entire Union force before heading back to Richmond.

Stuart was able to observe and communicate what R. E. Lee needed to know, and in the process, capture men, horses, and supplies before returning to Richmond on June 16. R. E. Lee was pleased and felt he had a useful and inspiring cavalry. Stuart and his cavalrymen were the talk of the town, indeed of the Confederacy. No great battle; no great victory; but pride enough for all.

With the information Stuart gathered, R. E. Lee decided he would bring Thomas J. Jackson back from the Shenandoah Valley, and have him hit the Union army on its right flank while the balance of the Confederate army near Richmond attacked G. B. McClellan's front.

The Seven Days' Battles, June 25–July 1, 1862

R. E. Lee recalled T. J. Jackson from the Valley, and on June 24, when G. B. McClellan learned of Jackson's return, he instinctively hesitated. As Jackson approached the capital, he moved ahead of his troops and on to R. E. Lee's headquarters a few miles above Richmond for a council of war. R. E. Lee held council with his four generals: Thomas J. Jackson, James Longstreet, Daniel H. Hill and Ambrose P. Hill. They discussed the plan for attacking G. B. McClellan north of the Chickahominy River. R. E. Lee had already discussed the plan at length with President Davis. The plan called for Jackson to move from Frederick's Hall (Frederickshall) to a position southeast of Ashland and communicate with L. O'B. Branch of A. P. Hill's division. Then they were to move down the east side of the River.

As the armies moved into position, Union forces clashed with Confederates near Seven Pines on June 25. It was not a major assault by either army; nonetheless, the skirmish resulted in about 1,000 casualties. It was the first day of the Seven Days' Battles.[5]

The Confederate plan called for Jackson and Branch, once they were in position, to communicate with A. P. Hill who was to cross the Chickahominy at Meadow Bridge. Robert E. Lee, Longstreet and D. H. Hill were south of A. P. Hill. D. H. Hill was to follow A. P. Hill across the river. However, from the outset communication with Jackson and Branch broke down — when the fighting was underway, R. E. Lee did not know where Jackson was.

On June 26, near Beaver Dam Creek R. E. Lee attacked even though Jackson was not in place yet. A. P. Hill went first, but he was not able to advance beyond the creek. D. H. Hill got up and Longstreet's troops pushed in behind D. H. Hill, but confusion reigned and they could do little. A. P. Hill was exposed and took the greatest abuse.

G. B. McClellan apparently got the best of it that day in the battle of Beaver Dam Creek and went on the defensive. During the night, G. B. McClellan learned that Jackson had finally arrived on his right, so he ordered troops on the right to drop back to a better defensive position near Gaines's Mill. In addition, he felt his supply lines might be threatened, so he moved his base and supplies to the south side of the Peninsula on the James River. The end of the threatened siege of Richmond was in sight. Sensing victory, G. B. McClellan occupied himself with covering his retreat, and Lincoln was again frustrated.

The next fight in the Seven Days' Battles took place around Gaines's Mill, where the Union right was well entrenched. G. B. McClellan had to fight there because he feared a withdrawal of his troops at that point would make his rear too vulnerable. On the morning of the 27th, R. E. Lee planned to dislodge the Union forces at the mill with a coordinated attack; Longstreet at the left, A. P. Hill at the center moving toward Gaines's Mill, and at the Union right D. H. Hill followed by Jackson. Once again, the attack lacked the essential ingredients of coordination and effectiveness. It was near the end of the day, when a brigade of Texans under John B. Hood broke through the Union center; but what a costly victory! More than 8,000 Confederate troopers were lost.

After the fight at Gaines's Mill the Union force was still superior in numbers and in pretty good shape. Nonetheless, G. B. McClellan felt beaten and proceeded to pull his army back to the James River on the night of the June 27, and President Lincoln was frustrated once more.

On the morning of June 28, Confederate forces again faced the enemy; this time near Cold Harbor and White Oak Swamp, but they were not certain what G. B. McClellan was up to. However, once R. E. Lee became convinced G. B. McClellan was retreating to the James River, he conceived of another great plan, this time to hit the retreating Union army in the flank while it was in motion.

R. E. Lee's preparations to attack G. B. McClellan developed slowly on June 29. Nine columns were to converge from six directions to hit G. B. McClellan in the flank. Natural and unnatural (and R. E. Lee probably thought some supernatural) forces combined to render this well-conceived Confederate plan ineffective.

At Savage's Station, three miles south of the Chickahominy on June 29, and again near Glendale (Riddell's Shop) on June 30, the Confederates were not able to coordinate their attacks and R. E. Lee was unable to destroy his enemy in retreat. Longstreet and A. P. Hill did show an ability to stay in touch with one another in the battle near Frayser's farm on June 30, however. Nonetheless, after several days of fighting, R. E. Lee had failed to destroy G. B. McClellan's retreating army. More than 10,000 Confederate soldiers had been lost in the defense of Richmond to date.

On July 1, the Union rear guard made a stand on Malvern Hill near the James River. Here, once again, the Confederate command failed to communicate and consequently was lacking in coordination. Thousands of Confederate troopers marched into un-neutralized Union artillery fire and many died. That day, more than 5,500 men were killed or wounded largely because generals had not yet learned to communicate. The heaviest losses were in D. H. Hill's (1,743) and Huger's (1,137) divisions (Ransom's brigade, with Companies H and I of the 2nd North Carolina Cavalry, was detached from Holmes's division and was with Huger's at that time).[6]

During the night, G. B. McClellan retreated again. This time to Harrison's Landing where he was under the shelter of Union gunboats on the James River. Once R. E. Lee discovered his enemy had retreated during the night, he attempted a pursuit with Stuart's cavalry in the advance, but it was slowed by a heavy storm during the day. Stuart managed to harass and follow closely the retreating Union troops but to little effect. R. E. Lee remained in the area of Malvern Hill until July 3, but the pursuit was over for the time being, with Richmond no longer threatened, there was time to reflect and regroup.

From June 25 through July 1, more than 20,000 Confederate troopers were killed, wounded or missing. The Union lost fewer than half that number. In Virginia that week, the Union retreated in the face of victory, and the Confederates pursued them in a most disorderly, ineffective, and costly fashion—but Robert E. Lee was learning the parameters of the war. He and his generals would get better at it.

Stuart's Cavalrymen During the Seven Days' Battles

The activities in this period affected Robert E. Lee's notion of how and when the cavalry could be useful, and it affected their self-image. The character of the cavalry in the Army of Virginia that grew out of these days and the months is particularly important because this cavalry would be the "home" of the 2nd North Carolina for years to come.

On June 26, Stuart covered Jackson's left during the latter's advance and performed that task routinely. In the battle at Gaines's Mill, the thick forests and underbrush immobilized the cavalry. On June 28, Stuart was sent to cut G. B. McClellan's communications at the York River Railroad, which he did with little opposition. After finishing their work on the railroad, they camped near Tunstall's Station. During the night, they could hear explosions set off by the burning Federal depot at the White House on the Pamunkey River (property owned by Robert E. Lee's middle son, cavalryman W. H. F. Lee, who was with Stuart at the time).[7]

The next morning, June 29, residents warned Stuart that usually better than 5,000 Union troops guarded the nearby base so the cavalrymen advanced slowly and carefully. When they approached the smoldering property that had been the White House, Stuart saw a Federal gunboat still at the landing—perhaps a trophy for the taking. W. H. F. Lee, commanding the 9th Virginia Cavalry, knew the environment well so helped Stuart decide from where and how they might best attack the gunboat.

Stuart sent seventy-five men forward with rifled carbines. They were spread along the bank with orders to fire on the deck of the gunboat. A number of sharpshooters from the 17th New York were sent ashore to greet the Confederate riflemen, and a heated exchange took place. Stuart finally caused the Union sharpshooters and the gunboat to pull back and leave the area by shelling them with his howitzer.[8]

Upon inspecting the ruins of the storage base, Stuart's men were struck by the amount of supplies the Union forces had to burn. They were also undoubtedly impressed with the amount of the Sutlers' stores that survived the fires. These stores provided a feast for the Confederate cavalrymen. For the remainder of the day, they feasted, packed what they could carry, and destroyed the rest.

Before they were on the road again, R. E. Lee sent a courier with a request for information and Stuart's evaluation of what he saw: G. B. McClellan's troop movements in the area and what Stuart thought G. B. McClellan was up to. Stuart replied that there was no evidence of a retreat down the Peninsula, and he was sure G. B. McClellan was moving to the James River.[9] Stuart was right and it helped R. E. Lee determine his next move. More importantly perhaps, the reply increased R. E. Lee's confidence in his cavalry commander's ability to gather information and interpret its meaning.

Stuart and his men ended their feast and destruction on the morning of June 30, and set out to fulfill the second part of their assignment: to intercept and slow G. B. McClellan's retreat if possible. With that in mind, Stuart headed for the bridges on the Chickahominy, about 13 miles away. He had already sent scouts to the bridges on the day of feasting. Stuart's column made good time on the 30th and around 11:00 A.M. they were overlooking Forge Bridge, and Colonel Fitz Lee was at Long Bridge about six miles upstream. Union troops were near Long Bridge but when Stuart's horse artillery brought its guns up, they were able to push the enemy's guns and cavalry back from the bridge. Fitz Lee and his command crossed the Chickahominy, cleared the roads for a distance and then settled in for the night.

Early the next morning, July 1, Stuart received orders written the day before to overtake and support Jackson. The orders were of little help in locating Jackson but after some fast riding and reasoning, Stuart was able to return to his men and take them back across the Chickahominy, and head South toward the sounds of battle. Beyond Forge Bridge, Stuart found a detachment of Jackson's 2nd Virginia Cavalry, Munford's regiment, and from them learned of their army's location. Stuart and his cavalrymen had covered forty-two miles that day but

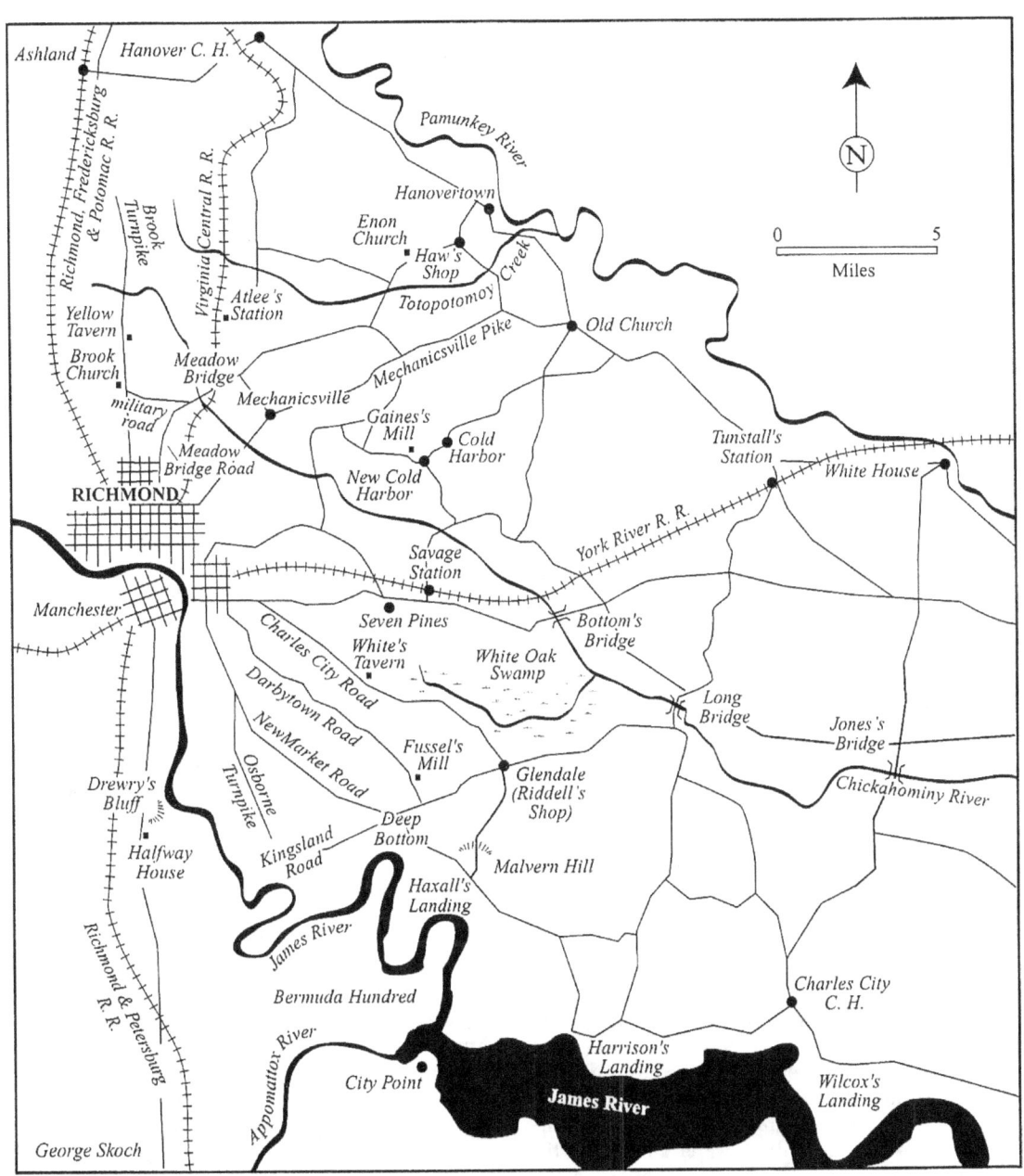

2.1: The Peninsula and Around Richmond

they were still a mile and a half east of the Confederate line. As they went down for the night, they could hear the last shots of the day coming from Malvern Hill.

On July 2, Stuart stayed in touch with R. E. Lee, while his men canvassed the area for Union stragglers, abandoned weapons, and engaged in minor skirmishes most of the day. One member of Stuart's staff described the most important event in his day—it centered on desensitizing his new horse to wartime experiences. His description is instructive because in addition to getting a better understanding of horse sense, we implicitly get a first glance at a Virginia horseman's romanticized view of the world while surrounded by the horrors of war.

Recall that the horrors included 5,590

Confederates wounded or killed near Malvern Hill on July 1, of which 1,743 were from General D. H. Hill's division. D. H. Hill's description of the day was not romanticized and included this observation, "It was not war — it was murder.... We saw men going about with lanterns, looking up and carrying off the dead and wounded." Even with the nighttime effort to clear the field; the next day there was still enough on the ground to violate horse sense and permit a romantic to rise above it. Romanticized views of war were held, from time to time, by many Confederate cavalry officers and as such were part of the character of the army soon to be experienced by the men of the 2nd North Carolina Cavalry. Let Lieutenant Colonel W. W. Blackford of General Stuart's staff describe his day — the day his new horse, Magic, arrived:[10]

The first thing I did after getting settled in camp, while still near Malvern, was to try Magic. She has been resting several days and Gilbert [Blackford's slave] led her out looking sleek and fine but with the devil in her eye.

General Stuart and staff assembled to see the start. Out she came, trotting round and round Gilbert, tossing her head and snorting at almost everything. After much coaxing I got her to allow me to come alongside, then to put my foot in the stirrup and hand on her mane, and that was all I needed her consent for. As I lit in the saddle she reared and bolted off and I gave her half a mile or so of a full run and then pulled her gently but firmly down to a moderate gait.

For miles in every direction the country was strewn with carcasses of men and horses, and her terror at sight of them was great. She would come to a halt a long way off, snort and try to wheel, but I kept her head to the object and tried to reason the matter with her by soothing with voice and hand. Putting her nose to the ground she would take a long snuff and then go a little nearer and repeat the process, and so on; after perhaps an hour the first time, she would come up close to it. Each time the fear was less, until finally the unsightly objects scarcely attracted her attention.

One hopes that Magic was soon able to rise above the horrors of war as her owner had clearly been able to do. Blackford's description provided above was preceded and followed by a discussion of what a magnificent horse he had and how "ignorant horsemen" fail to understand their animal's needs. War did indeed offer men of breeding the opportunity to demonstrate their refinement — the qualities that set them apart from ordinary troopers. The latter seldom expressed romanticized and lofty views of war.

During the night of July 2, Stuart sent Captain Pelham of his horse artillery out, with his one serviceable howitzer, to find a position from which he could harass the retreating enemy. Pelham reported back to Stuart that he had located Union forces below a long ridge known as Evelington Heights.

Stuart took the 9th Virginia Cavalry and headed for Pelham. By daylight of July 3, Stuart could see Union camps and wagon trains spread along the river, under the heights. They pushed a Federal squadron off the heights and Pelham found a good position for his single gun. Stuart instructed Pelham to begin shelling their enemy, and he set out collecting Union stragglers and questioning residents to find the true extent of the Federal forces below the heights. When he determined that most of the enemy was collected below him, he sent word to R. E. Lee. General Lee replied that Jackson and Longstreet were on the way. Thinking that infantry support was soon to arrive, Stuart continued to harass his enemy below with his one little howitzer. As Union troopers began to move up the ridge on Pelham's flank, Stuart spread his sharpshooters along the ridge. Then Federal guns began to shell Pelham's position until he was forced to fall back about half a mile. A Federal battery then moved up and continued to shell Pelham and the cavalrymen. By early afternoon, Pelham was about out of ammunition, and Stuart learned that Longstreet was still six or seven miles away. The heights could not be held, and Stuart had to fall back about two miles and go into camp for the night.

The next morning, July 4, Longstreet and Jackson were close enough to attack the enemy, but Federal forces had a commanding position on the heights so there would be no fireworks. Stuart received abundant criticism for prematurely unleashing Pelham's one Howitzer on G. B. McClellan's army, but in the end, it was just another lost opportunity to destroy G. B. McClellan in retreat.

Robert E. Lee retained his high opinion of Stuart and before the month of July was done, R. E. Lee promoted him to major general.

Stuart's new division consisted of two brigades—the first cavalry brigade under Wade Hampton from South Carolina and the second cavalry brigade under Colonel Fitz Lee from the 1st Virginia Cavalry. Stuart and his cavalry remained below Richmond for a couple of weeks and then on July 21, moved up to recruit and rest near Hanover Court House for another several weeks.

Union Forces After the Seven Days' Battles

When the Seven Days' Battles were over, President Lincoln still had about 100,000 men under General G. B. McClellan in the Army of the Potomac on the Peninsula, and about 50,000 with John Pope in the Army of Virginia. Yet, Lincoln had little confidence in G. B. McClellan's ability to defeat R. E. Lee, so did not send him the additional troops he continued to request for another attack on Richmond.

From the other side of the line, however, there was still concern that the size of the Union force around Richmond would increase. This concern increased when Major General A. E. Burnside was put in motion—R. E. Lee had to speculate on his destination; was he on the way to support McClellan or Pope? Or was Burnside's movement going to be a third possible point of Union assault?

Since late June, Pope's mission had been to shield Washington, control the Shenandoah Valley, and disrupt the lines of communications near Gordonsville between the Shenandoah Valley and the Confederate capital. Pope's mission moved from threat to reality when his cavalry began raiding the Virginia Central Railroad. Pope's activity, G. B. McClellan's hesitation at Richmond, and Burnside's movement led R. E. Lee to make the next important move.

Robert E. Lee Reacts

On July 13, R. E. Lee sent Jackson with about 12,000 men to Gordonsville to protect the rail junction from attacks by Pope. Sensing no immediate threat to Richmond from G. B. McClellan, R. E. Lee then sent another 13,000 men under A. P. Hill to Jackson.

Robert E. Lee had been troubled by the lack of coordination among his divisions during the Seven Days' Battles, so he informally grouped his divisions into corps. In effect he had moved A. P. Hill up with Jackson at Gordonsville and formed "Jackson's Command" near the Rapidan, and the infantry around Richmond came to be known as "Longstreet's Command."[11]

Jackson had lost his cavalry commander, Ashby, and without consultation had been assigned newly promoted Brigadier General Beverley H. Robertson. Robertson's new command included the 7th and 12th Virginia, the 17th Virginia Battalion, Munford's 2nd Virginia and Flournoy's 6th—they were the "Laurel Brigade." The cavalrymen collected around Jackson at Gordonsville.

Lee's movement of Jackson's command and G. B. McClellan's hesitation at Richmond helped President Lincoln decide to pull G. B. McClellan's troops from the Peninsula and send them to Pope. On August 3, McClellan was ordered to move from his position near Richmond to Aquia Creek, near Fredericksburg. Burnside was already on his way up to cover G. B. McClellan's arrival and join Pope's left on the Rappahannock line.

R. E. Lee knew movement was taking place, but he was not yet certain who was moving where. He sent Stuart and his cavalrymen toward Fredericksburg to collect information. On August 5, Stuart reported that Burnside was there with about 16,000 troops, and that he believed Union forces were preparing to move on the railroad that linked Jackson to R. E. Lee at Richmond. In fact, on that day Pope was concentrating his forces near Culpeper Court House and preparing to move down to the Rapidan River and on to Charlottesville where the Virginia Central met the Orange & Alexandria Railroad. That, of course, would take them through Gordonsville, where Jackson was concentrating his command.

Before G. B. McClellan's troops could reach Pope's Army of Virginia, Jackson moved toward Pope's divisions near Cedar Mountain—about a day's march north of Gordonsville. Pope moved his cavalry forward on the morning of August 9 and attacked Jackson.

Pope had nearly 3,000 cavalrymen in front of Robertson's Confederate cavalry force of less than 1,200, and Jackson was not confident of Robertson's ability to lead his cavalry—he was worried about the Federal cavalry hovering near his train of 1,200 wagons. In the end, Jackson assigned infantry to guard the train and urged Robertson to locate the enemy who was certainly in the area. Robertson continued to give Jackson excuses for not moving instead of providing useful information.

The battle was under way on August 9 when Union forces attacked Jackson. August 10 was spent locating and burying the dead and collecting arms from the field. By the next day, Pope had the balance of his men in place, and the Confederates had about 55,000 men in the field. The opposing armies battled to a stand-off.

In Jackson's eyes, his cavalry under Robertson had contributed nothing to the fighting on August 9. Consequently, when Stuart rode into his camp the following day, Jackson was noticeably happy to see him. Jackson asked Stuart to locate and determine the size of the enemy for him, which he soon did. Stuart told Jackson that in his view the Federal force in the area was too strong to attack. On August 11, both sides, under a flag of truce, collected the wounded and continued to bury the dead. During the night, Jackson had campfires built along the front while he took his troops back across the Rapidan. The ruse worked; Pope did not follow. Jackson and Pope both claimed success. The commanders on both sides had made mistakes, making it difficult to attribute outstanding leadership to either. Jackson had 229 killed and 1,047 wounded. Pope lost more than twice that number.

R. E. Lee was increasingly uncomfortable with the stand-off—he could not sit and wait. It was apparent that Pope's army was too large for Jackson's, and Burnside was heading for Jackson's supply lines. In addition, G. B. McClellan was moving up to the Rappahannock line. Under the circumstances, R. E. Lee decided to attack Pope, the most immediate threat to Jackson and Gordonsville, before Pope could be reinforced. To this end, R. E. Lee sent ten brigades under Longstreet's command to Jackson. Basically, once R. E. Lee was certain McClellan was on the move and Jackson was threatened, he moved the bulk of his force from the Richmond area to near Gordonsville. The fighting had moved from Richmond to Northern Virginia, and R. E. Lee's command was henceforth known as the Army of Northern Virginia. Major General Gustavus W. Smith was left in command of the reduced force around Richmond, the forces at Drewry's Bluff, and those under D. H. Hill in North Carolina.[12]

After the Cedar Mountain fighting, Jackson wanted a new commander for his cavalry— he was very dissatisfied with Robertson's performance. A couple of days after R. E. Lee arrived at Gordonsville, the command problem was resolved when on August 17 Jackson's cavalry was placed under J. E. B. Stuart—who then had three brigades under his command.

General Pope was increasingly worried about the size of R. E. Lee's force across the Rapidan, so he pulled back across the Rappahannock. Then on August 20, 1862 R. E. Lee's army with Longstreet on the right and Jackson on the left crossed the Rapidan—this was the first combined move of the new Army of Northern Virginia. Lee did not think it wise to force his way across the Rappahannock in front of Pope's army. Rather, he decided to outflank Pope by moving up the river, then going east to hit Pope's right flank. Such a move called for a reconnaissance mission by the cavalry.

Stuart's Cavalry Raid on Catlett's Station, August 20–24

In periods between great battles, the cavalry was typically involved in minor encounters such as the one on August 20 when J. E. B. Stuart, riding with Robertson's cavalry brigade, encountered Union cavalry and pushed them back across the Rappahannock. Robert E. Lee was pleased by this action, but Stuart naturally wanted to do more. He formulated a plan to get behind Pope's army and cut their supply line coming down the Orange & Alexandria Railroad. He would take his cavalrymen up the river, cross at Waterloo Bridge, head for Warrenton through Auburn Mills, and hit Catlett's Station above Warrenton Junction. The plan was approved by Lee and Stuart began to select his men for the adventure. Among those he selected to join him in commanding a force of around 1,500 cavalrymen were Fitz Lee, W. H. F. Lee, William C. Wickham, and Thomas Rosser.

They went up and crossed the Rappahannock, yet by the time they got to Warrenton, J. E. B. Stuart's party had not yet encountered Union forces. Residents said no forces had been there for days. As Stuart led his cavalrymen out of Warrenton for Auburn Mills, a violent thunder storm caused his horse artillery to fall be-

Two • The Army of Northern Virginia and the 2nd North Carolina Cavalry 51

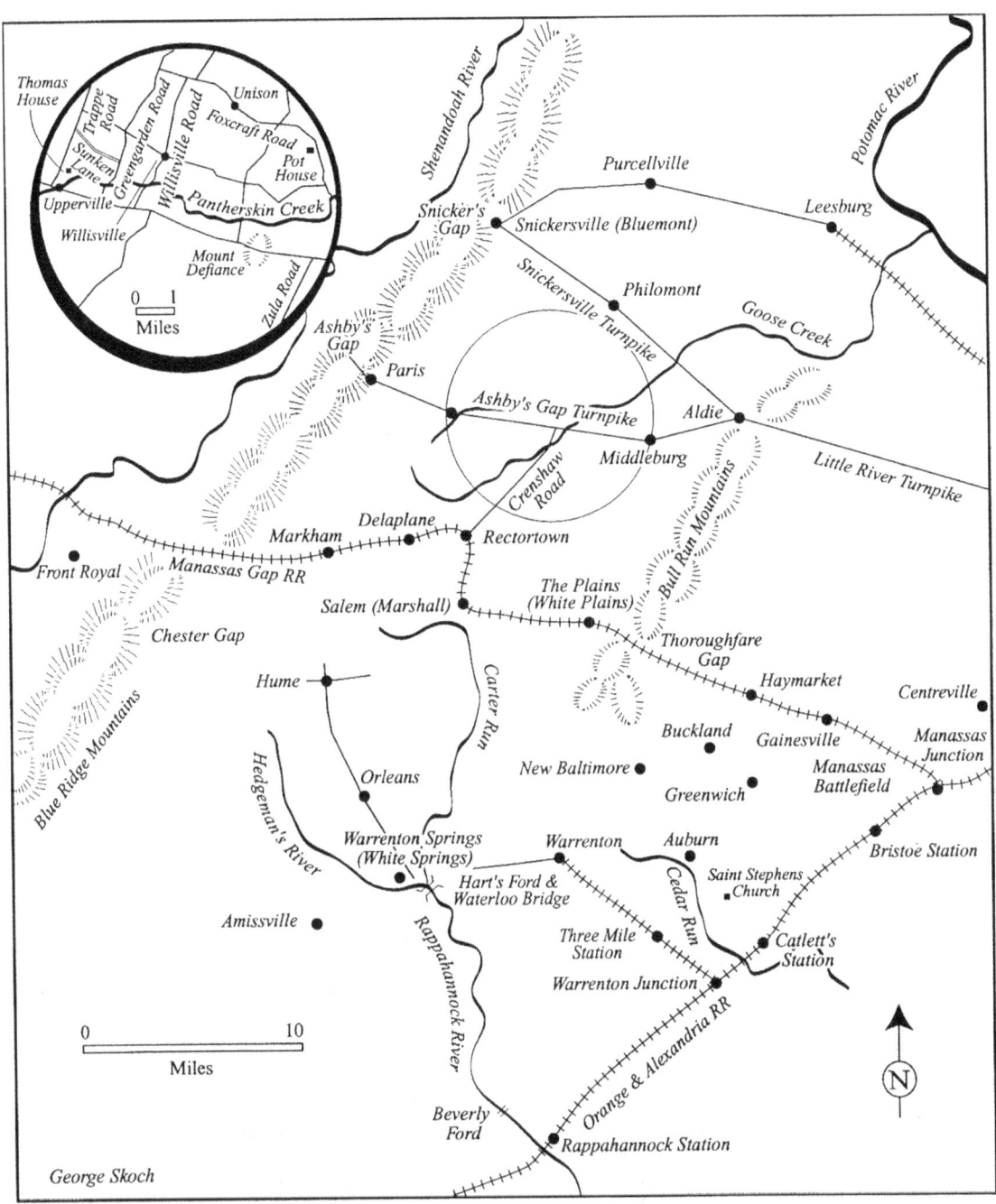

2.2: The Rappahannock Line and Loudoun Valley

hind. Rosser's command, in the lead that day, was increasingly out front. He was nonetheless able to capture some Union pickets and start leading Stuart's column through Union lines. Once behind enemy lines, Stuart had W. H. F. Lee with the 9th Virginia head for Pope's headquarters to capture what and whomever they could. The 1st and 5th Virginia Cavalries were sent to attack another camp and destroy some of the railroad. A detachment was also sent to burn the bridge over Cedar Run. Robertson covered the rear and remained on the lookout for the horse artillery and its escort, the 12th Virginia Cavalry, which had also fallen behind.

J. E. B. Stuart's cavalrymen made their attacks, captured numerous prisoners and considerable booty — some of which belonged to General Pope personally. Among the most cherished items were Pope's hat, military cloak, and a uniform frockcoat. Stuart was given the uniform coat because he had been humiliated weeks earlier when some of Pope's men surprised him during a nap and caused him to flee leaving his plumed hat and cloak for the intruders. Pope's dispatch book was also captured along with much of his correspondence from previous days. Though the Confederates could not ignite the bridge over Cedar Run in the heavy rain, they returned to R. E. Lee's side of the Rappahannock — wet yet happy.

Robert E. Lee Makes a Move; the Maryland Campaign

Watching the river's fords and their enemy on the other side was not Jackson's favorite pastime any more than it was R. E. Lee's. Stuart's return from his successful mini-campaign behind Pope's line, signaled R. E. Lee to move ahead with his larger campaign. On August 24, R. E. Lee went to Jackson's camp with a proposal that would add some spice to their duty. Jackson was given the opportunity to slip upriver, cross where possible, and get in the rear of Pope's army — the purpose was to damage the Orange & Alexandria Railroad, the main Union supply line. He was to do, on a large scale, what Stuart had shown was possible. One of R. E. Lee's main goals was to cause Pope to retreat rapidly and widen the distance between him and their expected reinforcements. Like Stuart before him, Jackson wasted no time and was soon on the march — in order were Richard S. Ewell, then A. P. Hill, then William B. Taliafferro.

Jackson's column left early on August 25, before all the men had time to fully prepare their three day's rations. The column crossed the Hedgeman's River and Carter's Run, before the two join and become the Rappahannock. Once across, Jackson's men headed for Salem and the Manassas Gap Railroad where they spent their first night. During the day, Jackson's cavalry escort, the 2nd Virginia, had scouted the front to avoid any surprises, and during the night they had guard duty.

On August 26, Jackson's men had another long march and the challenge of Thoroughfare Gap in the Bull Run Mountains as they passed eastward. If the gap was well guarded by their enemy, it could be a difficult pass. Once again, Jackson sent his cavalry escort ahead and they found the route free of all Union forces. After Jackson's column cleared the gap, they passed through Hay Market and on to Gainesville.

At Gainesville, with the bulk of his cavalry, Stuart caught up with Jackson at the head of his column. Stuart had left his camp on the Rappahannock around 2:00 A.M. August 26 and took farm roads and a gap through the Bull Run Mountains that was not suitable for a column of infantry in order to catch up with Jackson by mid-afternoon. With Stuart's cavalrymen there to cover his front and flanks, Jackson moved his column at a more comfortable pace — there was less to worry about with Stuart's cavalry there. From Gainesville they headed southeast for Bristoe Station, one of Jackson's objectives on Pope's supply line.

Thomas T. Munford's 2nd Virginia Cavalry was again in advance when they cautiously approached Bristoe Station with infantry support near their rear. The cavalrymen charged into the station and ran off a handful of Union cavalrymen and contained some infantry seeking cover in the hotel. The Confederates were disappointed to find that their arrival was during a time of day when the trains were returning from Pope's front and not carrying great quantities of supplies for the Federal army. Some residents of Bristoe, however, told Jackson and his commanders that Pope's army kept enormous supplies of rations and other goods at Manassas Junction, about seven miles up the Orange & Alexandria Railroad.

Not surprisingly, Jackson decided to go for the jackpot as soon as possible — without giving adequate rest to troops who had marched about fifty-five miles in two days. General I. R. Trimble volunteered to put his 21st North Carolina and 21st Georgia on the road to Manassas Junction immediately. To insure success, Jackson sent the cavalry along with him. Stuart's cavalry led the way and after the first encounter with enemy guards, waited for the infantry to come up. They had little difficulty taking the base, even richer in supplies than they had imagined. Though as hungry as they were exhausted, Jackson's infantrymen were hesitant to help themselves to the vast stores of food before them because Jackson had made it clear to his men in the past that all booty belonged to the Confederacy — and when the situation was under control, the officers would see to it the men were fed. However, Cavalrymen seldom operated under such constraints. Besides, everything happens faster in the cavalry so they were helping themselves to all they could eat and carry as soon as they arrived. Trimble, on the other hand, restrained his men and set them to guarding the captured supplies until Jackson arrived with the rest of his command.

Jackson had a relatively minor exchange with a Federal battery and some infantry while arriving at Manassas Junction, but they were overrun without much loss of time. By 11:00 A.M., Jackson was at the junction. Once there, he heard that Federal troops were pressing Ewell south of Bristoe. He packed all he could carry away in his wagons and turned his men loose to fill their stomachs and haversacks. Before they pulled out, the remainder of the stores were set ablaze.

Jackson was satisfied. He had completed the first part of his mission. Pope's supply line had been disrupted. His next task was to protect his men until they were reunited with Longstreet's wing of the army — after all, Jackson was still vulnerable in the rear of Pope's much larger force. Nonetheless, Jackson decided to remain in the area and wait for R. E. Lee and Longstreet.

Looking for the silver lining on the dark smoke clouds rising from Manassas Junction, General Pope knew he had Jackson isolated from the rest of R. E. Lee's army and thought he could destroy him. Pope's problem was his cavalry. It was not yet what it would become later in the war, and his cavalrymen had difficulty locating Jackson after he left Manassas Junction.

On the other hand, J. E. B. Stuart had maintained a connection between Generals Jackson and Longstreet. Jackson pulled up just west of the old Manassas battlefield and waited for Longstreet. He expected Longstreet on August 29 and felt he could wait, but Pope's men came across Jackson's camp late the next day.

Worried that Jackson was ready to withdraw, Pope decided to attack on August 29 before he had gathered all his units. He sent forward one division at a time, and they were pushed back repeatedly by a well-entrenched Confederate force. Pope finally did collect about 32,000 men in front of Jackson's 22,000, and Pope had another force of 30,000 coming up to reinforce the Union left. It was clear Jackson's troops would have a difficult time holding until reinforced. Of course, Stuart and his cavalrymen had the task of covering Jackson's flanks while waiting for Longstreet to arrive. Pope's troops proceeded to press hard at Jackson's right, but before they could overwhelm Jackson with their combined force, Longstreet arrived. Stuart had ridden out to guide the advance of Longstreet's men to Jackson's flank. Night was closing in and the scene was set for the Second Manassas.

THE SECOND BATTLE AT MANASSAS

The next day, August 30, serious fighting began in the afternoon, again at Jackson's right. Pope sent a large force to hit Jackson's right and formed a similar force for his center and left. Jackson was under great pressure when he sent word to R. E. Lee that he needed support from Longstreet's end of the line. Longstreet could see that the left flank of the Union forces attacking Jackson was vulnerable, so rather than send troops as requested, he immediately moved artillery to his left where they could and did sweep along the Union lines in front of Jackson. Pope's line was torn apart and forced to pull back. R. E. Lee then ordered a general charge, and Pope was pushed back. Nightfall ended the violence.

During the night, Pope decided to withdraw toward Washington, so R. E. Lee sent Jackson after him. It rained most of the night, and Jackson's tired troops had difficulty finding Pope's retreating flank. Stuart's cavalry was warning R. E. Lee that Pope was being heavily reinforced by G. B. McClellan's forces.

On the afternoon of September 1, Jackson's advance encountered resistance at Chantilly. Union troops were making a stand in force and Jackson pulled up to deploy his divisions. Fighting was furious in a driving rain until darkness, and the Union Forces were pulled back. Jackson sustained about 500 causalities, and the Union about twice that number.

At the end of that day and the campaign, R. E. Lee's troopers were about twenty miles from the Union capital. Most importantly for

R. E. Lee was the demonstrated ability of both Jackson and Longstreet to command large numbers of troops and to cooperate on the field of battle. In addition, R. E. Lee felt Stuart's cavalry had performed well as an independent branch of the service. The cavalry had kept Jackson's and Longstreet's commands in touch with one another, had guarded the army's flanks and their wagon trains, and had gathered important information at the right time. Robert E. Lee was pleased. His army had a greatly improved command structure by the end of his second campaign, but the cost was nearly 10,000 men lost. These losses, combined with losses during the Seven Days' Battles, meant Lee's new Army of Northern Virginia needed more troops.

Robert E. Lee continued to call for troops from General G. W. Smith's command in southern Virginia and North Carolina, even though Smith already had troops under his command on the march to the Rappahannock. The Rappahannock line had to be held whether R. E. Lee was behind it or on the move with most of his army. Smith's lines of communication with his troops on the Rappahannock, however, were long and awkward. He sensed he had lost control of his troops once they were sent to territory outside his area of command, and he apparently wanted the loss acknowledged. In a correspondence to the Secretary of War on August 31, 1862, G. W. Smith indicated that the troops under his command stationed on or above the Rappahannock in R. E. Lee's theater of the war could more effectively get their orders directly from R. E. Lee.[13]

John G. Walker had been sent by T. H. Holmes to R. E. Lee for the defense of Richmond just after the battles of Seven Pines. When G. W. Smith replaced Holmes, Walker's units with others were moved to the Rappahannock Line at Lee's request. During August, Smith sent part of the 15th Virginia Cavalry under Critcher to the Fredericksburg area and started John R. Chambliss, Jr. with the 13th Virginia Cavalry toward the Rappahannock Line — all into R. E. Lee's area of command. (The 2nd North Carolina Cavalry was destined to join Chambliss's command on the line, but not for another month.) Yet the number of troops arriving on the Rappahannock hardly kept pace with R. E. Lee's losses.

The pressure on G. W. Smith was considerable, so he continued to send troops to the Rappahannock line, though reluctantly. In early September he ordered the 2nd North Carolina Cavalry forward, but without any apparent sense of urgency. For instance, Junius Daniel was about to lead an expedition into North Carolina in mid–September and G. W. Smith offered to temporarily suspend the 2nd Cavalry's orders to move up to Richmond and let them accompany Daniels if they would be of use.[14]

Meanwhile, President Lincoln was disappointed with Pope's performance and displeased, to say the least, when G. B. McClellan had not moved in a timely manner to help Pope at the Second Manassas, so some changes were in order. Pope was sent west. Lincoln combined Pope's Army of Virginia with the Army of the Potomac and put G. B. McClellan in command. McClellan was not his first choice, but at the time his only practical choice. McClellan had only a few days to ready his army for action. R. E. Lee was taking his tired army toward the Potomac River to invade the North. President Lincoln sent McClellan after R. E. Lee with instructions to destroy the Army of Northern Virginia.

THE MARYLAND CAMPAIGN

After pushing to within 20 miles of the Union capital on September 1, Robert E. Lee did not have the resources to attack Washington, nor even to stay put. One of his options was to retire around Richmond and rebuild his army, but that was not his choice. The most acceptable course of action was to invade the North and hope the politicians in Washington would seek a peace settlement. With that in mind, R. E. Lee led his army across the Potomac on September 4, 1862.

J. E. B. Stuart and his cavalry followed R. E. Lee's army to Leesburg and crossed the Potomac on September 5. Once across, Stuart moved to Poolesville with Fitz Lee's brigade leading the way. They encountered minor resistance as they came across Union cavalry and took some prisoners. As R. E. Lee's army marched to Frederick the next day, the cavalry rode on their flank heading for Urbana.

Robert E. Lee had hoped his army could live off the lands they passed through, but this hope was not realized. He needed a supply line through the Shenandoah Valley, but a Union garrison at Harper's Ferry stood in the path. Lee expected Union troops to withdraw from Martinsburg and Harper's Ferry once he advanced on Frederick, but they did not. He then decided to dislodge them from those places. Once again R. E. Lee divided his army. He sent a large portion of his army to take Harper's Ferry and believed they could achieve their objective and return to him before G. B. McClellan arrived. General Stuart and his cavalry stayed east of Frederick to watch for and slow McClellan's approach.[15]

At Urbana, B. H. Robertson's brigade,

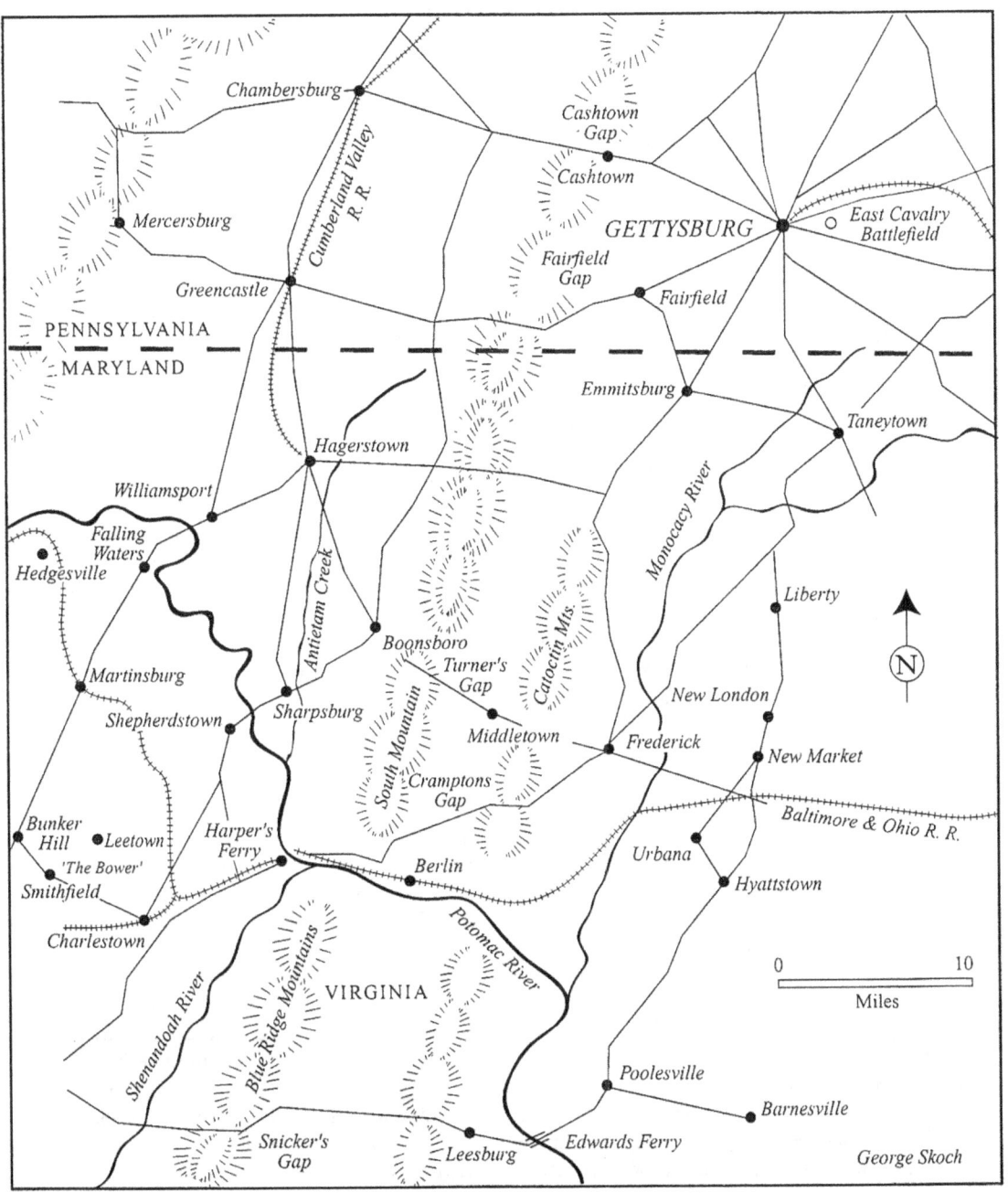

2.3: Campaigning in the North, September and October 1862

under the command of Colonel Thomas Munford, joined Stuart and the main body of the cavalry. They stayed near Urbana until September 12 covering the front of Lee's army — watching for the Army of the Potomac. This maneuver was particularly important once R. E. Lee had detached more than half his army to the Harper's Ferry area. Stuart placed Fitz Lee's cavalry brigade on his left at New Market on the Baltimore and Ohio Railroad; Wade Hampton's brigade near Hyattstown; and B. H. Robertson's brigade on his right. The latter, under T. Munford, stretched toward Poolesville.

Initially, G. B. McClellan did not know where the Army of Northern Virginia was; nor did he know that R. E. Lee had divided his army. Nonetheless, by September 8, G. B. McClellan was heading in the right direction and began to bounce off R. E. Lee's shield, Stuart's cavalry. Union forces came upon Hampton's center position first and were driven back several times. G. B. McClellan also sent a force to Poolesville, so Munford was moved there to stop the Federal advance. Munford only had the 2nd and 12th Virginia Cavalry with him at the time (the 6th Virginia had been left to collect arms and equipment from the battlefield near Centreville; the 17th Battalion had been detached for other duty before crossing the Potomac, and the 7th Virginia Cavalry had been sent to Harper's Ferry to assist Jackson). With his reduced force, Munford took and held the crossroads at Poolesville for three days.

On September 11, the Union infantry arrived in force along most of Stuart's line so he began an orderly pullback of his cavalrymen. Under pressure, Stuart pulled Fitz Lee's command back from New Market, west of the Monocacy; Robertson's brigade (Munford) back toward Jefferson; and Hampton's men were pulled back to occupy Frederick.

In front of Frederick, Hampton threw pickets out on the roads G. B. McClellan might use to approach the town. Of course, his job was to slow the advancing Union forces in an orderly manner so none of his pickets on other roads would end up behind the approaching enemy. He placed his men and artillery in front of Frederick and waited. They came in force and after a heated exchange Hampton slowly withdrew into the town. Union forces placed a gun in the suburbs supported by cavalry and infantry. The 2nd South Carolina Cavalry was called upon to secure the brigade's withdrawal from town. The 2nd South Carolina charged and scattered the enemy — taking ten prisoners and the gun. Hampton's brigade then retreated to bivouac for the night at Middletown without further incident.

In the meantime, Munford was instructed to drop back from Jefferson and hold Crampton's Gap in the South Mountain with his 2nd and 12th Virginia cavalries. Fitz Lee and his command were sent up to find the right flank of the Union army as it was advancing. The cavalry's job, even when the area was contracting, was to control the territory between the armies — Stuart was doing his job.

On the morning of the 13th, Stuart sent Hampton and his command to support Colonel Martin because Union forces were beginning to force their way through Catoctin Gap. Martin and Hampton held the crest until the arrival of two Union infantry brigades. The infantry joined the contest at about 2:00 P.M. and the Confederate forces withdrew slowly, with the 1st North Carolina Cavalry covering their rear. Stuart moved his men slowly toward Middletown giving D. H. Hill time to occupy Turner's Gap in South Mountain. In his report on the fighting at the gap in Catoctin Mountain and back toward Middletown, Stuart had special praise for the Jefferson Davis Legion and the 1st North Carolina Cavalry under Colonel L. S. Baker.[16]

Once through Turner's Gap, Stuart headed for Boonsboro and from there sent Hampton with most of his command to reinforce Munford at Crampton's Gap in the South Mountain. Stuart was at Boonsboro by nightfall, and he sent Colonel Rosser with a detachment of cavalry and horse artillery to occupy Braddock's Gap and left Hampton's Jefferson Davis Legion at Boonsboro as he headed for Crampton's Gap to join Munford and Hampton.

When Hampton was heading for Crampton's Gap along the eastern side of South Mountain, he spotted Union cavalry traveling on a parallel road. He led the Cobb Legion in a charge and dispersed the enemy cavalry — Hampton lost 13 men; the Union perhaps twice that number. Hampton's task was to control the area not simply pass through it — so, as was so often the case with the Confederate cavalry at that time, they "Attack and Die." They did not avoid. Such encounters were becoming a daily routine while in front of the enemy; a routine that intensified as G. B. McClellan's army moved closer to R. E. Lee.

The situation became critical when a Confederate officer lost his orders in a field and some of G. B. McClellan's men stumbled across the plans. From that mishap, G. B. McClellan knew the Confederate force was divided and vulnerable. In addition, R. E. Lee had underestimated McClellan's determination — McClellan had his forces in front of Lee's reduced force days before Lee had expected him. Thus, on September 13, G. B. McClellan had already located R. E. Lee and knew he had the upper hand on Lee's divided army — McClellan's response to this good fortune was to spend the rest of the day and all night preparing to move against R. E. Lee.

With his force divided, McClellan approaching, and a major battle brewing, R. E. Lee's thoughts also drifted to the rear. He was still trying to get more troops for the Rappahannock Line and above, as far as Warrenton. R. E. Lee had a special reason for wanting a force, no matter how small, at Warrenton. He had placed several thousand wounded comrades there from the Second Manassas battle. On September 13, R. E. Lee wrote to President Davis describing his loss of troops for various reasons and pointing out that he had sent wagon loads of wounded to Warrenton, a place not well protected. In General Lee's words,

Only one regiment of cavalry is in front of Warrenton, and that I fear my necessities will oblige me to withdraw. Unless General Smith can organize a force, and advance it, of sufficient strength to cover that section of country, it will be liable to raids from Washington and Alexandria by the enemy's cavalry. It is a risk we must necessarily run to use the troops elsewhere.[17]

As pointed out earlier, G. W. Smith had already started John G. Walker's infantry and John R. Chambliss's 13th Virginia Cavalry for the Rappahannock line. (In addition, General Smith would soon send the 2nd North Carolina Cavalry, but that was not yet on anyone's agenda because the 2nd North Carolina Cavalry did not arrive in Richmond until around October 1, and then they were not sent directly to Warrenton.)

Between Sharpsburg and Antietam Creek

As Robert E. Lee was requesting additional troops for the Rappahannock Line and his escape route on the other side of the Potomac, his attention was pulled back to a more immediate problem. J. E. B. Stuart learned that McClellan had R. E. Lee's invasion plan in hand and was preparing to attack R. E. Lee while his army was divided. Stuart informed R. E. Lee of this during the night of September 13, and Lee immediately began to collect his troops and block the passes through South Mountain. D. H. Hill was instructed to hold Turner's Gap, and Longstreet was called down from Hagerstown to support him.

D. H. Hill and Longstreet held G. B. McClellan's advance at Turner's Gap until nightfall on September 14. During the night R. E. Lee instructed them to fall back on Sharpsburg where the Confederate stand was to be made. The action on September 14 gave R. E. Lee an additional day to prepare and to get reinforcements from Harper's Ferry. R. E. Lee concentrated his force at Sharpsburg about a mile from the Potomac. As Longstreet's and D. H. Hill's troops marched to the Confederate line, they were escorted by Fitz Lee's cavalry command. Hopelessly outnumbered, R. E. Lee decided to stand and stop G. B. McClellan from relieving the Union garrison at Harper's Ferry. He would stand and fight at Sharpsburg (Antietam Creek).

Early on September 14, when D. H. Hill and Longstreet were holding Turner's Gap, Stuart arrived at Crampton's Gap and found that Union forces were not yet in front of Munford and Hampton. He considered the possibility that G. B. McClellan might also send troops around the Confederate right, from Frederick through Jefferson and Weverton to Harper's Ferry. To cover that possibility Stuart sent Hampton down near the Potomac. He left Munford to hold Crampton's Gap "against the enemy at all hazards." Then Stuart rode to General McLaws's camp to inform him of the situation and ask that infantry support be sent to Crampton's Gap. Shortly thereafter, Federal forces appeared at the gap. Munford and his small cavalry force held for more than three hours of intense fighting but, out of ammunition, they were in the process of falling back when Brigadier General Cobb, from McLaws's infantry, arrived. The 2nd and 12th Virginia Cavalry were singled out for their coolness and gallantry until overpowered and forced from the gap.[18]

Once Stuart learned of the struggle at Crampton's Gap, he hurried to the scene and regrouped the retreating troops from Cobb's command. He placed them across the road in Pleasant Valley, but the enemy had not pursued the retreating Confederates, so they rested for the night in that position.

Stuart's cavalry kept busy between the armies as they positioned themselves for another great battle. By early morning of September 15, Fitz Lee's command was covering the rear of Longstreet and D. H. Hill as they pulled back to Sharpsburg and formed the Confederate left. Hampton and his cavalrymen covered McLaws as he pulled out of Pleasant Valley toward Harper's Ferry. Stuart personally reported to Jackson at Harper's Ferry and described the situation, after which he was instructed to return to R. E. Lee at Sharpsburg and explain the situation at Harper's Ferry. Once Stuart arrived near Sharpsburg, R. E. Lee assigned him to the left end of the Confederate line where Fitz Lee's cavalry was already in position. Munford's small command of cavalrymen covered the right flank of the Confederate line.

While G. B. McClellan was massing his troops for the assault, and R. E. Lee was placing his troops in line at Sharpsburg, R. E. Lee received news from General G. W. Smith indicating Chambliss's cavalrymen and others were on the way to the Rappahannock line as of September 4. This news was thought important enough for R. E. Lee to respond on the pressure-filled day of September 15, 1862—the following is from his response:

Your letter of the 4th instant has just been received. I am glad to learn that you have organized a force for the Rappahannock, which I hope will be sufficient for present purposes; but I beg you will spare no effort to increase it, and, if it acquires sufficient strength, that you will advance it beyond the Rappahannock, to cover that country from the raids of the enemy's cavalry as far as possible.[19]

R. E. Lee was certainly still concerned about the wounded Confederates in Warrenton, but by September 15, he was also concerned about escape routes for his army once back across the Potomac. Chambliss did begin scouting above the Rappahannock soon after arriving in the area.

By September 16, McClellan had 60,000 men in front of R. E. Lee and 15,000 more a few miles away—Lee had fewer than 30,000 men in the field. G. B. McClellan spent most of that day considering his plan of attack for September 17. During the afternoon of September 16, however, troops on the Union right crossed the Antietam Creek to the north of the Confederate left and beyond the reach of their artillery. Stuart moved his cavalry still further in that direction and placed his artillery on a commanding hill. Skirmishing and heavy artillery exchanges took place on the left that night. Jackson sent Jubal A. Early's brigade to help Stuart, but Union forces continued to advance into the woods close enough to force Stuart to halt his artillery fire for fear of endangering his own men. Stuart then withdrew his artillery to a position in the rear where he could see the end of the Confederate line and sent J. A. Early back to Jackson. G. B. McClellan had found the Confederate left, but his carefully planned maneuver gave the Confederates another day for more reinforcements to arrive from Harper's Ferry.

In spite of all the planning, the Union attack on September 17 was not well coordinated. They hit the Confederate left first with heavy artillery fire which lasted throughout the morning, then sent a large force of infantry at Jackson. They also attacked the center throughout the day. Union forces on the Confederate right finally made it across a bridge over Antietam Creek in the afternoon. The town was burned and Confederate troopers were being beaten back along most of the line. It was a day often described as one of great slaughter.

Just as the Confederate right was about to be flanked, R. E. Lee got reinforcements from Harper's Ferry. Among those who arrived was L. O'B. Branch and his brigade. Along with other brigades, Branch led his men in a charge on the Union's flank and was killed on the field of battle. Darkness brought to the battlefield some peace that continued until the next light.

R. E. Lee stayed on the field during September 18, waiting for G. B. McClellan to follow up his success—Lee knew his army was too weak to attack so he waited, but McClellan did not come. During the day fresh Union troops were moved into the line which helped convince R. E. Lee he should withdraw his men back across the Potomac during the night. Fitz Lee's cavalry brigade covered the rear of the retreating army through the next morning when they held the enemy advance in check. During the night, Stuart took the main body of his cavalry across the river above Shepherdstown and moved up the Potomac. Then on the morning of September 19, he re-crossed the river at Williamsport and took a position that would enable him to hit the Union's right and rear should they attempt to follow R. E. Lee in force. Stuart and his men held their position under increasing pressure and skirmishing through the following day, then withdrew to the south side of the Potomac during the night.[20]

The Maryland Campaign cost the Army of Northern Virginia over 13,600 men — most of them at Sharpsburg. The Union lost about twice that number — most of them at Harper's Ferry. The losses in Stuart's cavalry did not come in the great battles as they did for the infantry. The role of the cavalry before, during, and after the great battles resulted in losses spread over many days and places — losses that too often went unnoticed. Stuart described the suffering of his cavalrymen in these terms: "...Theirs was the sleepless watch and the harassing daily *petite guerre*, in which the aggregate of casualties for the month sums up heavily. There was not a single day, from the time my command crossed the Potomac until it re-crossed, that it was not engaged with the enemy...." While R. E. Lee was certainly disappointed with the results of the campaign, he had learned a lot about his cavalry and he liked what he saw — in his words, "Its [the cavalry's] vigilance, activity, and courage were conspicuous, and to its assistance is due in a great measure, the success of some of the most important and delicate operations of the campaign."[21] Through all the battling, R. E. Lee found a good working relationship between his army and Stuart's cavalry.

Robert E. Lee moved his army in a line from Martinsburg to Winchester. Stuart's cavalrymen were between Lee's line and the Shenandoah and Potomac Rivers as the rivers approach their confluence at Harper's Ferry.

Robert E. Lee Back in Virginia

While President Lincoln and General G. B. McClellan were occupied with the Emancipation Proclamation following their victory of sorts at Antietam Creek,[22] President Davis and R. E. Lee were working to consolidate forces and rationalize lines of communications. By September 28, the link between R. E. Lee and John R. Chambliss's cavalry command was in place, and R. E. Lee's request that G. W. Smith's troops operate above the Rappahannock had been answered. President Davis sent a correspondence to R. E. Lee indicating that Chambliss had been instructed to communicate directly with him any information he obtained about enemy activity between the Rappahannock and the Potomac rivers.[23]

On October 1, 1862, R. E. Lee wrote to the Secretary of War and included the following reference to Chambliss: "Colonel Munford, with his cavalry, is at Leesburg, and reports no movement of the enemy in that quarter, and Colonel Chambliss, with the Thirteenth Virginia Cavalry, is at Warrenton Junction. I hope they will be able to check any movement toward the Rappahannock."[24] Apparently General Lee was still not certain at what point G. B. McClellan would attempt to cross the rivers.

With his usual vigilance, on the same day, R. E. Lee also wrote G. W. Smith and again included a reference to Chambliss:

Colonel Chambliss reports from Warrenton Junction that about a brigade of infantry of the enemy, with artillery and cavalry, is now at Manassas. That force is no doubt intended to watch that region, but it may also make an attempt upon Gordonsville. Have you anything to resist it, or can you make arrangements to do so?[25]

R. E. Lee was more certain of G. B. McClellan's likely targets than of his attack routes. One of R. E. Lee's concerns was the vulnerability of his supply lines at Gordonsville because he still had his Army of Northern Virginia with Stuart's cavalry above Harper's Ferry.

As R. E. Lee expressed his concern, G. W. Smith was already assigning the newly arrived 2nd North Carolina Cavalry to Chambliss's command. By October 1, 1862 Chambliss's command included: the 61st Regiment Virginia Volunteers, the 13th Regiment Virginia Cavalry, the 2nd Regiment North Carolina Cavalry, and Captain S. S. Lee's C. S. Navy, Drewry's Bluff.[26] The regiments under Chambliss were not organized into a brigade nor did they operate as a unit, but they were all heading in the same direction to form a line above the Rappahannock.

The 2nd North Carolina Cavalry would find itself temporarily under Colonel Chambliss on several occasions.

In an environment where a few units were needed in many places, the 2nd North Carolina Cavalry was not sent directly to Chambliss on the Rappahannock line (which he held above the river), rather G. W. Smith responded to R. E. Lee's more recently expressed concern about Gordonsville, and sent the small cavalry unit to Culpeper Court House to stand on the Orange & Alexandria Railroad between the enemy and Gordonsville. They were, more or less, a second line of defense should the enemy push through or around Chambliss in an effort to cut R. E. Lee's supply line.

The 2nd North Carolina Cavalry moved from Richmond soon after it arrived and was at Culpeper Court House by October 6. From that point, the 2nd North Carolina could keep an eye on Gordonsville and patrol the Rappahannock from the south side of the river.

While at Culpeper Court House, the 2nd North Carolina Cavalry was engaged in routine scouting and picketing duty — there was no major Union move on Gordonsville at that time. Nonetheless, their routine picketing was occasionally interrupted by a little exercise. For instance, while there, a detachment from the regiment, which included Company B, was patrolling the Rappahannock when it came upon and followed an enemy patrol across the river and into Fauquier County. They had surely been instructed by Chambliss to pursue the enemy well across the river if the occasion presented itself because Chambliss was still under General Lee's instructions to patrol and when possible reach beyond the Rappahannock into Fauquier County. In any case, the 2nd North Carolina Cavalry detachment followed the Union cavalrymen across the river and as far as Elk Creek in Fauquier County, before deciding they were too far from their base. They returned to camp near Culpeper Court House on October 15. Just in time, it seems, to pack up and move up to Warrenton in Fauquier County.[27]

G. W. Smith's compromise position of placing the 2nd North Carolina Cavalry between Gordonsville and the Rappahannock line did not yet address one of R. E. Lee's other concerns expressed back on September 13 for protecting the wounded Confederates still at Warrenton. The left of Chambliss's line had been pulled toward Warrenton Junction, leaving the town of Warrenton without cavalry protection.

Robert E. Lee was not the only person working to protect the wounded at Warrenton. Colonel William H. F. Payne made a considerable effort to get a unit stationed there, and he was put in command of the place and the troops there.

W. H. F. Payne was at Warrenton, his home town, on parole and recuperating from a serious wound incurred at Williamsburg — he was apparently a sight to behold, with his jaw wired shut and wearing a rubber mask made by his surgeon to hold his jaw in place. His weight was down to around 100 pounds because he could only consume fluids, but he could not remain inactive.

As indicated, after the Second Manassas R. E. Lee took his army to Sharpsburg and sent the Confederate wounded to Warrenton. From that day, the people of Warrenton and W. H. F. Payne were concerned that Union cavalry could easily enter town and capture the wounded men. This concern prompted Payne to set out for Richmond and speak to General G. W. Smith about the problem — Payne wanted a unit stationed in the town for the protection of all. Payne managed to get to Culpeper Court House in a handcar (the railroad between Manassas and Culpeper had been destroyed) and while waiting there for a train to Richmond, he observed the off-duty cavalrymen of the 2nd North Carolina — they mostly impressed him at the time with their idleness.

When Payne got to Richmond he met with General G. W. Smith and explained the situation at Warrenton. Of course, G. W. Smith had already been made aware of the problem by R. E. Lee back on September 13. G. W. Smith reportedly asked Payne what he proposed and the latter replied that he "...had seen a regiment of Confederate cavalry in Culpeper as I passed through it, apparently doing nothing; and I requested that it be ordered to join me in Warrenton. He [Smith] was very much amused at first — I suppose I must have looked more like a dead than a living man. He told me, however, to go back as fast as I could."

While Payne was gone, a regiment of Union cavalry had briefly occupied Warrenton and passed through the hospitals — they apparently captured and paroled about 1,200 of the

Confederate wounded, but the paroles were said to have been lost.

Soon after Payne's returned to Warrenton, the 2nd North Carolina Cavalry arrived from Culpeper and was placed under his command.[28] The loose organization commanded by Chambliss made it easier for Payne to take control—both Stuart and R. E. Lee made note of the fact Payne was the commander of the 2nd North Carolina Cavalry while at Warrenton. Since Payne and R. E. Lee wanted a unit at Warrenton, Payne finally got his command. The day-to-day operation of the 2nd North Carolina Cavalry was still under the command of Clinton M. Andrews. (The regiment's colonel, Solomon Williams, was still detached.)

While Payne was recruiting the 2nd North Carolina Cavalry, and the latter was moving up to Warrenton, J. E. B. Stuart was taking his cavalry on another bold adventure.

Stuart's Expedition to Maryland and Pennsylvania, October 9–12

While Chambliss's small cavalry command was performing more traditional cavalry duties, namely fighting for control of the territory between the Rappahannock and the Potomac Rivers, R. E. Lee and J. E. B. Stuart were ready to "push the envelope" one more time — to test the limit of possible roles for their new cavalry. The role for the cavalry was coming together as a bold and freewheeling arm of R. E. Lee's Army of Northern Virginia, and Lee liked what he was seeing. This new cavalry would soon be the home of the 2nd North Carolina.

Robert E. Lee and Stuart had been sitting in their camps waiting for their enemy to invade, but no word of their advance arrived. Waiting for information and action was always difficult for R. E. Lee and his commanders. Finally, after a respectable wait, R. E. Lee decided to send Stuart on a mission to discover what G. B. McClellan was doing and how his army was deployed. R. E. Lee certainly understood that any routine mission by Stuart would take on dimensions of a raid behind enemy lines, and that was clearly acceptable. In that spirit, Stuart was also instructed to destroy a bridge just outside of Chambersburg and collect horses while in Pennsylvania. Basically, R. E. Lee also gave his consent to another ride around of G. B. McClellan's army if Stuart thought it advisable.

On October 8, Stuart received his orders and prepared to leave the next morning. He selected commanders and men from Hampton's, Fitz Lee's, and Robertson's brigades. Wade Hampton led a detachment of about 600 men from his command; Colonel W. H. F. Lee[29] led a detachment of about the same number from his cousin's brigade; and Colonel W. E. "Grumble" Jones led the detachment from Robertson's brigade.

Stuart assembled his cavalrymen at Darksville and crossed the river on the morning of October 10 with Hampton's men in the lead. Colonel Matthew C. Butler of the 2nd South Carolina hit the Potomac first and successfully pushed back the Federal pickets. Stuart's column moved across, encountering only minor resistance during the early morning hours. Though minor, the encounters were noted by the enemy and McClellan knew he had been invaded by Stuart's cavalry.

According to explicit orders, no horses were to be confiscated while the troops were in Maryland. Once the Confederate cavalrymen arrived in Pennsylvania, it was a different matter. A command of 600 men were in front and another in the rear; with the center command instructed to spread out from each side of the road to collect horses from unsuspecting Pennsylvania farmers. After a long day's march, Stuart and his men reached Chambersburg on the evening of October 10. Hampton was appointed "Military Governor" by Stuart; Colonel Butler was sent to the bank to confiscate all available cash; and Grumble Jones was sent out to burn the bridge over Conococheague Creek.

Hampton was able to keep order and peace in the town during what one Yankee later termed "the day of rebel rule in Chambersburg...." One of the citizens who surrendered the town to the invaders later described the scene as follows:

General Stuart sat on his horse in the centre of the town, surrounded by his staff, and his command was coming in from the country in large squads, leading their old horses and riding the new ones they had found in the stables hereabouts. General Stuart is of medium size, has a keen eye, and wears immense sandy whiskers and moustache. His demeanor to our people was that of a humane soldier. In several instances his men commenced to take private property from stores, but they were arrested by General Stuart's provost-guard. In a single instance only, that I heard of, did they enter a store by intimidating the proprietor.[30]

Butler was not successful in getting the bank's cash because it had all been removed earlier in the day when word of the invaders arrived. Similarly, Jones was not successful in burning the bridge because it was a good Pennsylvania bridge make of steel. They did, however, find a store of Union goods, including army-blue overcoats that the threadbare Confederates greatly appreciated — what they could not wear or carry, they burned upon leaving town the next morning.

As the cavalrymen left town, they were feeling the pressure of Union forces closing in around them. Union scouts were on every road, and their cavalry was trying to determine the invader's route to intercept them before they got back across the Potomac. Stuart rode just behind his advanced guard and in front of the main body of his cavalry to set the column's direction without advance notice to even his own men. They left town heading east as if for Gettysburg, then turned south heading for Emmetsburg, then Frederick, and finally for the Potomac near Leesburg. Colonel W. H. F. Lee with the detachment from Fitz Lee's brigade was in the lead that day.

Sometime after nightfall, Stuart intercepted a Union courier from Frederick with papers showing that Colonel R. H. Rush's 6th Pennsylvania was at Frederick with a large enough force to hold the town, and Pleasonton with about 800 men was within four miles. To avoid the enemy, Stuart changed his planned route and swung east of Frederick, going instead through Woodsboro, New London, Hyattstown, and then through the Potomac to Leesburg.

Near midnight of October 11, a scouting party from the 6th Pennsylvania spotted Stuart's column and reported to Rush at Frederick and Pleasonton at Mechanicstown. It was then a race for the Potomac. By the time Stuart's advance reached the river, they had covered 65 miles in 20 hours — a pace hard to overtake. Nonetheless, by morning of October 12, in addition to Rush from Frederick and Pleasonton from Mechanicstown, George Stoneman was now closing in on Stuart's column from Poolesville.

The Union commanders did not know where Stuart would try to cross the Potomac and could not coordinate their attacks. Pleasonton was closest to being in the right place at the right time. Around 8:00 A.M. October 12, Pleasonton's advance guard found itself marching in the opposite direction on the same road as Stuart, who was riding with his advance guard at the time. It was a cold, damp morning and many of Stuart's cavalrymen were still wearing the warm blue overcoats they confiscated the day before at Chambersburg. This was undoubtedly a major cause of the Union cavalrymen's continued yet cautious advance. Stuart noticed their hesitation and held his men in order to maximize the surprise and shock of the inevitable Confederate charge. When Stuart unleashed his troopers, the Union advance guard had only enough time to fire one volley, turn and race back to the main body. The charge gave Stuart enough room to gain a commanding position near one of the river's fords. Immediately Stuart had Pelham move one of his guns forward and began firing as rapidly as possible at Pleasonton's command. Stuart then dismounted some troopers in support of Pelham. This understandably convinced Pleasonton that he was at the ford Stuart intended to use.

Meanwhile, further back on the road, Stuart's leading brigade under the command of Colonel W. H. F. Lee took a left turn on a farm road and headed directly for the river. The lead brigade was followed by Colonel W. E. Jones's command, with Hampton's command in the rear. When W. H. F. Lee reached the river, the ford he wanted to use was occupied by a large force of Union infantry. The situation seemed nearly impossible so W. H. F. Lee sent word to Stuart, who was still with the advance in front of Pleasonton, to come and assess the situation. Stuart's reply was short and to the point: He was fully occupied and the ford had to be taken "at all hazards." Colonel W. H. F. Lee knew what that meant — attack! Perhaps because he was a Harvard man rather than a graduate of West Point or the Virginia Military Institute, W. H. F. Lee wanted to try one alternative before he attacked the strong Union position at the ford. Colonel Lee sent a note to the Federal commander in which he explained that Stuart's entire force was behind him, and the Union position was hopeless — suggesting the Federal commander should surrender to avoid unnecessary bloodshed. Colonel W. H. F. Lee waited the fifteen minutes he had given them to surrender, then opened fire with his artillery and ordered his front regiments forward. The Confederates were ready to receive severe fire every second of their advance, but none came. Probably no one was more surprised than W. H. F. Lee to find that the Federal troopers had taken their leave through a dry canal bed. The Confederates continued to cross the Potomac and immediately put their guns in position on the Virginia side.[31]

After W. H. F. Lee's and W. E. Jones's commands crossed the river, Pelham gradually pulled back from Pleasonton's front. When he got to the river he held his position, firing up river, then down river, then in his front. Pelham was not going to cross until Stuart's rear guard arrived and crossed. M. C. Butler's South Carolinians and the 1st North Carolina had not yet made it to the river. Stuart sent several couriers but none could find them. Stuart arrived and was very concerned; he did not want to lose his rear guard. A member of Stuart's staff, W. W. Blackford (with his then seasoned horse, Magic), offered to go and make one last effort to find them. Stuart said "All right! And if we don't meet again good-by old fellow!" As Blackford started off Stuart called out, "Tell Butler if he can't get through, to strike back into Pennsylvania and try to get back through West Virginia. Tell him to come in at a gallop." M. C. Butler had been assigned the rear-guard position for Stuart's column since Chambersburg and was still in that position along with a detachment from the 1st North Carolina. Stuart's rear guard was delayed by their enemy, and finally when the men from the 1st North Carolina were overtaken from behind, they told Butler they had no alternative but to stand and fight, so Butler pulled back most of his regiment and a gun to make a stand. Their job, after all, was to slow the advance of the enemy while their comrades withdrew across the river. When Blackford found the rear guard, he explained that Union forces were closing in on all sides, and Stuart wanted the rear guard back at a gallop or they would surely be cut off. Butler replied he would withdraw as fast as possible, but he would not leave his gun as Blackford had suggested. In a mad dash back and through the ford, Butler and his rear guard made it to Virginia, gun, broken-down horses and all. Stuart was happy. His expedition was a success and remarkable — they had covered 80 miles in 27 hours. Perhaps most importantly was the extent to which his cavalry commands worked together under Stuart's leadership.[32] J. E. B. Stuart had fashioned a cavalry in style and purpose to suit his fancy and R. E. Lee's needs. The 2nd North Carolina Cavalry would soon be a part of this cavalry culture.

By the time Stuart returned to R. E. Lee, the 2nd North Carolina Cavalry was settled in its new camp at Warrenton, Virginia, protecting the town from Union patrols, as well as patrolling the area on the left of Chambliss's line above the Rappahannock River.

The Rappahannock Line

Colonel William H. F. Payne saw the 2nd North Carolina Cavalry's presence in Warrenton as security for the town and the wounded soldiers in its care; John R. Chambliss primarily saw their presence, to the extent he noticed them at all, as an extension of his left wing. R. E. Lee undoubtedly saw their presence as an answer to both of his concerns in that area. Indeed, once the 2nd North Carolina Cavalry settled in at Warrenton, their duties soon expanded beyond just protecting the wounded, and they became the left wing of the Rappahannock Line.

Chambliss's right was anchored by the 15th Virginia Cavalry (under Colonel Ball) as far as Fredericksburg; the center of the line was covered by the 13th Virginia Cavalry (under Colonel Chambliss) which was spread from the 15th Virginia through Warrenton Junction; and, as indicated, the left of the Rappahannock line was held by the 2nd North Carolina (temporarily under Colonel W. H. F. Payne of the 4th Virginia) and was based in Warrenton. The Union cavalry shielding Alexandria and Washington made patrols as far west as Upperville and down to Salem and Plains on a regular basis. The two cavalries were in almost daily contact during October and into November of 1862.

As indicated, while based in Warrenton, the 2nd North Carolina Cavalry's duties included scouting territory patrolled by Union cavalry. One such scout was led by Major Clinton M. Andrews on October 17. He was ordered to take 6 of the 8 companies of the 2nd North

Carolina at Warrenton, which at the time numbered 225 cavalrymen. He also took two pieces of artillery. Their assignment was to scout into enemy lines toward Centreville. After riding for eighteen hours without rest, they stopped near Centreville and camped until about 2:00 A.M. the next morning. Once back in the saddle, they set a line of march through Manassas toward Gainesville. They reached Gainesville just after daylight and learned that a Federal force had passed during the night. According to local residents, the force consisted of cavalry and artillery followed by a guarded wagon train. C. M. Andrews decided to pursue the wagon train in the direction of Haymarket. Within a half mile of Haymarket, the advance guard, Company D, came upon their enemy's videttes who did not fire, thinking the approaching horsemen were their own rear guard. Andrews sent his advance guard forward slowly while he called the 1st Squadron (Companies H and G), under Captain Randolph, to join Company D and readied them for a charge of the enemy position. After the charge and a chase for about two miles, they overtook and captured the Union party — only one man got away. The Confederates had captured 1 Lieutenant, 27 troopers, 24 mules, 32 horses, and 7 wagons loaded with sugar, coffee, pork, crackers and oats. The captured "Miserable Yankees" were required to drive the wagons back to Warrenton while the cavalrymen of the 2nd North Carolina followed.

Apparently the Union troops in advance of the wagon train were caught off guard because their pursuit of the Confederate raiding party was delayed. Andrews reported that they were back in Warrenton for about half an hour before word came that a Federal force was approaching town. He moved the two pieces of artillery that had been attached to the regiment into his line, but the enemy did not come. Andrews then had his cavalrymen in the saddle, and they set out after their enemy. The Union force had halted about three miles up the road and when the 2nd North Carolina approached, according to Andrews, "they skedaddled double quick."

C. M. Andrews ended a report to Governor Vance of North Carolina with these words, "*We have coffee, and sweetening too every day now.*" Private Samuel N. Mason of Company G, 2nd North Carolina Cavalry sent a letter home to his father describing the haul in about the same terms, but Mason added the following: "I tell you [father] you ought to of been in camp with us boys to of seen us of Siet Back and ___k [unreadable] Coffee Swetened with sugar an eat a__d [unreadable] pork and other necessaryes of life."[33]

On or about the same day, a related Union view of the scouting activity in the area was provided by Brigadier General J. Stahel in a correspondence dated October 18 to General Sigel: "This morning early I intended to march to Warrenton, to ascertain the force of the enemy there, which is variously stated as being considerable infantry and artillery; others as a brigade of cavalry, and others as only a small force of cavalry." But before Stahel got under way, he learned about the wagon train lost to the Confederate cavalry from Warrenton, the 2nd North Carolina.[34]

By October 20, G. J. Stahel had no better idea of the size and composition of the Confederate force at Warrenton than he had earlier in the month. He reported to F. Sigel that the force at Warrenton consisted of two regiments of cavalry, one battery, and about two infantry regiments — he reported the cavalry were the Nineteenth North Carolina and the Second Virginia. The "two" cavalry regiments mentioned were probably one and the same — the Nineteenth North Carolina and the 2nd North Carolina Cavalry. The 2nd Virginia Cavalry was Munford's command in Fitz Lee's brigade and they were up near Stuart at the time — near Harper's Ferry.[35]

Robert E. Lee was aware of Federal penetration into the area between the Rappahannock and Potomac Rivers approaching the Blue Ridge Mountains and was increasingly concerned about the ability of Chambliss's small force of detached units to control so vast an area. In fact, earlier, R. E. Lee was already thinking the detached regiments under Chambliss would be more effective if they were organized into a brigade with a competent brigadier general. He had someone in mind, and he began to make overtures in that direction around mid–October. Robert E. Lee sent General G. W. Smith a message on October 16, that contained the following lines,

…and what is the exact force of the cavalry on the line of the Rappahannock. The promotion of Brig. Gen. W. H. F. Lee, upon the return to duty of Brig.

Gen. Fitz Lee, will enable me to send a brigadier-general to command it, as I think it advantageous that the operations of the whole should be under one head, that it may act collectively or separately, as emergencies may require.[36]

W. H. F. Lee had been promoted to Brigadier-General on October 3 and needed a brigade. His father, R. E. Lee, was already commanding General G. W. Smith's troops under Chambliss on the Rappahannock line which in effect had distanced them from Smith's control—the time was right to incorporate them into the Army of Northern Virginia, as J. E. B. Stuart's fourth cavalry brigade.

R. E. Lee's concern about integrating Chambliss's line into his own defenses took on an air of urgency as the commanding general was increasingly convinced G. B. McClellan was about to push across the Potomac and drive the Army of Northern Virginia back across the Rappahannock. On October 22, R. E. Lee notified Longstreet that Stuart was extending his pickets toward Middleburg and would be in communication with Walker and his infantry division—and that Walker should stay alert. R. E. Lee's final instruction was for Walker to stay in touch with the temporary commander of the 2nd North Carolina Cavalry, William H. F. Payne, which suggests Payne was operating more-or-less as an independent command at Warrenton and should be communicated with directly at that point rather than through Chambliss. R. E. Lee's propensity to tighten the lines of communication among his commanders was evident, and the time was at hand.[37]

The time to incorporate Chambliss's command into a new brigade for Stuart's cavalry was right, but R. E. Lee knew it would take some time to establish a new chain of command, so he continued to communicate directly with Chambliss. For instance, on October 23, R. E. Lee responded directly to Chambliss, Commanding Forces on Rappahannock, instructing him to contact and stay in touch with Walker.[38]

R. E. Lee's message indicates that Chambliss's left, the 2nd North Carolina Cavalry at Warrenton, was instructed to extend its pickets to Walker's right wing, toward Upperville. R. E. Lee continued to reinforce his troops on the Rappahannock line, but he still did not know where McClellan would strike.[39]

The Union cavalry was also busy looking for vulnerability in the Confederate line. On October 25, 1862, Major General Franz Sigel commanding the 11th U.S. Army Corps, wrote a report at the end of which he added:

...I have further learned from refugees and other reliable sources that the enemy has a force of 2,000 cavalry, consisting of the Second North Carolina, Seventh and Twelfth Virginia, a small detachment of infantry, with some artillery, at Warrenton. The strength of the infantry force is given variously from one company to two regiments. No force but strong pickets at Warrenton Junction, Rappahannock Station, and Fredericksburg. No re-enforcements whatever have been sent lately from Winchester to Warrenton. The rebels have only been running two trains this week to Warrenton Junction and Warrenton.[40]

Sigel's information was wrong on more than one fact. His estimates of the Confederate force in the town were understandably confused because wounded representatives from just about every regiment that fought at Second Manassas were housed in Warrenton—and from time-to-time when Colonel Payne thought the town was about to be attacked, he placed some of the least seriously wounded men in town on the line of defense. More importantly perhaps, Sigel's correspondence tells us much about his focus—it was on the headquarters of the 2nd North Carolina Cavalry at Warrenton.

Increasingly it appeared R. E. Lee's concerns were justified; within a few days of Sigel's report, on October 28, another Federal report focused on the area—it included the following: "Scouts from Warrenton Junction report a force of about 600 cavalry and infantry at that place; a regiment of cavalry and about 50 infantry at Warrenton." Then another Union report from G. D. Bayard to F. Sigel contained the follow reference, "...Strong detachments of cavalry are patrolling the country from Warrenton to Middleburg, but they usually return to Warrenton."[41]

When Bayard wrote the above-mentioned report on October 31, G. B. McClellan had already started his army across the Potomac at Harper's Ferry with Union cavalry in his advance. He also had Union cavalry approaching from the east toward Middleburg and at Warrenton. J. E. B. Stuart moved to place what cavalry he could collect between the two Union cavalry forces and to slow the Union advance to the Rappahannock River. The two opposing cavalries once again stood between their armies, each pushing to control the area and monitor the enemy.

According to Colonel W. H. F. Payne, during a three week period Union cavalry made several attempts to take Warrenton and drive the 2nd North Carolina Cavalry out but were unsuccessful each time. In his words, "The Carolina regiment was a small one, but I had reinforced it by some of the convalescents, and held the town until Gen. McClellan entered it, withdrawing without losing anything."[42]

During the 2nd North Carolina Cavalry's first month in Virginia, at least 12 men were lost, 4 of the recorded losses in combat are listed below.

Combat Losses in the 2nd North Carolina Cavalry October 1862

Trooper	Age	Co.	Fate
David Panther	19	A	mortally wounded, before October 13
Henry Thornell	28	E	captured, October 17
Rufus Rentfrow	24	E	captured, October 19
Joseph Melton	31	D	captured, October 21

The source for this table is *North Carolina Troops 1861–1865, A Roster*, compiled by Louis H. Manarin (Raleigh, N.C., State Division of Archives and History), vol. II, Cavalry, pages 104–177. (See Appendix for more information on the men listed above, page 392.)

The Union Army Crosses the Potomac

When George B. McClellan finally brought his army across the Potomac, it was only a matter of time before Chambliss's 13th Virginia and 2nd North Carolina Cavalry and Stuart's cavalry were pushed back across the Rappahannock River. But time is what mattered. Once the Confederate cavalry determined the size and direction of the Union force coming across the river, it had to slow the invaders long enough for R. E. Lee's infantry to get below the Rappahannock and into position.

On October 26 and for the next several days, Federal forces crossed the Potomac, some near Leesburg, and some at Harper's Ferry—according to G. B. McClellan, the Second and some of the Fifth Corps crossed at Harper's Ferry, and the First, Fifth, and Sixth Corps were delayed a day due to heavy rains. In his report on the campaign, G. B. McClellan described his intentions as follows:

The plan of campaign I adopted during this advance was to move the army, well in hand, parallel to the Blue Ridge, taking Warrenton as the point for the main body, seizing each pass on the Blue Ridge by detachments as we approach it, and guarding them after we had passed as long as they would enable the enemy to trouble our communications with the Potomac.[43]

Given the Union army's trajectory, we might expect the 2nd North Carolina Cavalry to be in the center of the storm, and they were.

Robert E. Lee was not sure at the outset which route McClellan's army would take south—it could be east or west of the Blue Ridge Mountains. R. E. Lee divided his army to cover both possibilities. He sent Jackson to Winchester with orders to keep the passes open as he dropped down the Shenandoah Valley and to stay in communication with Longstreet on the west side of the mountains. One division from Longstreet's corps was sent to the Upperville area to watch the enemy's advance—the bulk of his command dropped below the Rappahannock toward Culpeper Court House. The job of slowing and monitoring the advancing enemy naturally fell to the cavalry.

J. E. B. Stuart was ordered to collect his cavalry in Loudoun County, located just north of Fauquier County "…with a view to watch the enemy's movements, and to delay his progress while our army was changing its position, so as to confront him on the Rappahannock." Stuart was with Fitz Lee's brigade. Hampton's brigade was still farther north near Martinsburg and was ordered to meet Stuart near Upperville by November 3. They actually met a day later and a little farther southwest, near Linden because Stuart was driven by the enemy and under constant pressure.[44]

As Stuart dropped down the east side of the Blue Ridge Mountains from Upperville, he stayed west of Warrenton; west of John R. Chambliss's Rappahannock line; with the 15th Virginia on the right near Fredericksburg; the 13th Virginia in the center; and the 2nd North Carolina on the left, headquartered in Warrenton.

Ideally, Stuart's east wing would stay in

touch with W. H. F. Payne, commanding the 2nd North Carolina at Warrenton, but the regiments under Chambliss's command were informally transferred from G. W. Smith's command to R. E. Lee and not yet into Stuart's cavalry command. R. E. Lee had been communicating directly with Chambliss, and telling others, Walker for instance, to communicate directly with Payne at Warrenton. Apparently Stuart was not in communication with the somewhat independent cavalry regiments on the Rappahannock line. Not until after the serious fighting on November 5 did Stuart know the 2nd North Carolina was holding the town of Warrenton.[45]

When the first Union troops crossed the Potomac, on October 26, Alfred Pleasonton's cavalry brigade crossed with them — he settled in at Lovettsville and waited for the army to complete its crossing. By the 31st, Pleasonton had moved his cavalry southeast to Purcellville, about 10–15 miles above Aldie, and made contact with George D. Bayard who was headquartered at Aldie.

As indicated, G. D. Bayard's cavalry had been skirmishing with Chambliss's regiments in the area between Warrenton and Aldie for weeks, and the encounters had escalated to a daily activity. In fact, on October 31, Bayard reported to Sigel that "Strong detachments of cavalry are patrolling the country from Warrenton to Middleburg, but they usually return to Warrenton."[46] He was referring to the 2nd North Carolina Cavalry headquartered in Warrenton.

On the same day, G. D. Bayard was ordered to cooperate with A. Pleasonton, and they met that morning. In the afternoon, Pleasonton, still at Purcellville, notified Bayard that G. B. McClellan wanted them to join forces for a "cavalry reconnaissance in force." to locate the enemy and determine their direction. Pleasonton then asked if he thought they should head for Snickersville or Ashby's Gap?[47] In either case, they would head west and traverse the country above the area normally patrolled by Chambliss and the 2nd North Carolina Cavalry. They were looking for Longstreet and Stuart. They found the latter.

In the meantime, early on October 31, Stuart was looking for the main Union cavalry, and he sent the 3rd Virginia Cavalry to pursue a scouting party from Bayard's command back as far as Aldie. The 4th Virginia Cavalry followed to assist the 3rd, but as daylight was nearly gone, Stuart pulled his troops back to Middleburg for the night — he knew his rear might be vulnerable to Pleasonton who was up at Purcellville. Bayard pulled back near Chantilly.[48]

The next day, November 1, Pleasonton was at Philomont, nearly halfway to Upperville with about 1000 men to cooperate with Bayard and locate R. E. Lee's army. D. H. Hill came over Ashby's Gap from the Valley with instructions to hold the Gap. Stuart pulled back to cover D. H. Hill's front.[49] Stuart's and Pleasonton's cavalrymen had sharp skirmishes at Philomont and westward four or five miles to Bloomfield. To the north of Stuart's cavalry Pleasonton was working his way over.

Bayard's men had to keep an eye on Chambliss's regiments which were in a position to hit the flack of his and Pleasonton's cavalry as they probed the area occupied by Stuart. The Company Muster Rolls show that the men of the 2nd North Carolina Cavalry were under increasing pressure by November 1. For instance, the report from Company B contained the following comment, "…we engaged enemy nearly every day, as they tried to work their way into Warrenton." A similar statement is found in the roll for Company I: we were "…engaged every day Nov. 1–8th as they tried to work their way into Warrenton."[50] At that point, however, it was unlikely the men of the 2nd North Carolina knew the size and determination of the Union force headed directly for Warrenton.

On November 2, William W. Averell was ordered to combine his cavalry with Pleasonton's. They did, and encountered Stuart near the town of Union.[51] Pleasonton's forces drove the Confederate cavalry from Union.

The next day, Pleasonton moved down to Upperville and clashed again with Stuart's troops. D. H. Hill withdrew from Ashby's Gap, back into the Valley. Stuart then divided the force he had with him in the Upperville area and sent the 3rd and 9th Virginia Cavalries to secure Ashby's Gap, and sent the 1st, 4th and 5th Virginia Cavalries south along the east side of the mountains as a rear guard for his wagons. Stuart's orders were to observe and delay G. B. McClellan's advance — which he had been doing for several days. By evening, Thomas L.

Rosser and the 4th Virginia approached Piedmont, but finding the enemy there, he went on to Markham's.[52]

On November 4, T. L. Rosser and Averell engaged one another in minor skirmishes. Pleasonton with two brigades of cavalry was ordered to push toward Chester Gap and then take the road to Culpeper Court House. Franz Sigel was instructed on November 4, "to be prepared to move on Warrenton as soon as you receive orders to do so." Bayard was instructed to take a position in front of Salem.[53]

While the Union cavalry was getting into position to continue advancing, Wade Hampton was coming east from Front Royal with his brigade and Stuart was coming down from a meeting with T. J. Jackson just west of Ashby's Gap; the two planned to meet at Markham. As Rosser had found earlier, however, the enemy was already at Markham so Hampton and Stuart met at Linden, just over four miles to the west, late at night on November 4.

Cavalry Fight at Barbee's Cross Roads

Early the next morning, Stuart, Hampton and Rosser (with Fitz Lee's command) were at Barbee's Cross Roads (near Hume, about twelve miles northwest of Warrenton).[54] Pleasonton was heading in the same direction. Stuart was determined to give battle with his enemy's cavalry at Barbee's Cross Roads—his intention was to delay their advance toward the Rappahannock. In Stuart's words events unfolded as follows:

> Dispositions were made accordingly, [Fitz] Lee's brigade being on our right and Hampton's on the left. The crest of the hill immediately north of the town was occupied by our artillery and sharpshooters, with a view to rake the enemy's column as it moved up the road; but the main position for defense was just at the crossroads, where the main body was held in reserve.
>
> Toward 9 A.M. the enemy advanced, and a fierce engagement of artillery and sharpshooters ensued, lasting for some hours. The enemy at length approached under cover of ravines and woods, and my command held the position near the cross-roads, where our artillery had complete control of the approaches. At this juncture I received information that the enemy was in Warrenton. This information, together with the delay and lack of vigor in the enemy's attack at this point, led me to believe that this was only a demonstration to divert my attention from his move on Warrenton. I accordingly gave orders to Hampton and Rosser to withdraw, the former by the Flint Hill road: the latter by the Orleans road....
>
> In withdrawing, there was a sharp conflict between the First North Carolina Cavalry, under Lieutenant-Colonel [James B.] Gordon, and the enemy on the left, that regiment suffering a good deal.[55]

Under great pressure from the advancing Union troops and apparently under the impression that Warrenton had fallen, Stuart told Hampton and Rosser to withdraw. Stuart took the road to Orleans with Rosser, and they bivouacked the night of November 5 near Orleans. While camped for the night, Stuart and his staff developed an interesting realization about the state of affairs at Warrenton. He said:

> Upon arriving at Orleans, 7 miles distant, it was ascertained that the report of the occupation of Warrenton by the enemy was a mistake. The enemy had attacked the place, but had been gallantly repulsed by a portion of the Second North Carolina Cavalry, under Lieutenant-Colonel Payne, of the Fourth Virginia Cavalry.[56]

Prior to the evening of November 5, Stuart clearly had not been in communication with Payne's command at Warrenton nor is it clear anyone else had either.

Presumably, the 2nd North Carolina Cavalry had been receiving instruction from Chambliss, who was receiving orders directly from R. E. Lee. Robert E. Lee had been pretty good about communicating with Chambliss when the latter was the Rappahannock line, but it is easy enough to imagine how communication might have broken down as the situation became more dynamic. R. E. Lee may not have found time to correspond with Chambliss about unfolding events, but even if he did think to keep Chambliss informed, there is no record that Chambliss bothered to keep W. H. F. Payne and his 2nd North Carolina at Warrenton aware of events and any plan for withdrawal. As a result, the 2nd North Carolina Cavalry may well have been the last to know Warrenton was on the brink of being surrounded on November 5 when Stuart and others were falling back to the Rappahannock.

One indication that the 2nd North Carolina was not aware of the extent to which Pleasonton was pushing Stuart to the Rappahannock can be found in the actions of the regiment on the afternoon of November 5 around

Warrenton. The cavalrymen in the 2nd North Carolina were on the attack, not preparing to withdraw. In fact, the word Stuart had received while engaged at Barbee's Cross Roads on November 5, was probably of the attack described as follows by F. Sigel: "To-day, at 2.30, our cavalry at New Baltimore was attacked by 1,500 of the enemy's cavalry and four pieces of artillery, but (they were) repulsed and pursued toward Warrenton by Colonel Percy Wyndham and four pieces of our flying artillery."[57]

New Baltimore is less than five miles from Warrenton to the northeast and was normally the area patrolled by the 2nd North Carolina Cavalry. As far as we currently know, the 2nd North Carolina was the only cavalry stationed in Warrenton, but their eight companies certainly did not amount to 1,500 men. Chambliss and his 13th Virginia Cavalry may have been in the area, but then Stuart would have referred to them as Chambliss's troops in Warrenton rather than Payne's in his comment about the activities on November 5. More than likely Sigel exaggerated the number of attackers.

In any case, on November 5, the 2nd North Carolina Cavalry was attacking the enemy, not simply holding their position until pressed back. When they were driven back to Warrenton, they successfully fought and held the town.

In all probability, Chambliss and his 13th Virginia Cavalry were not fighting alongside the 2nd North Carolina on the 5th because they apparently had moved to the west, above Warrenton, and were fighting with or just to Stuart's rear. In fact, Chambliss may have been caught between Stuart's stand and Pleasonton's advance according to a report written by Pleasonton on the evening of November 5 which includes the following:

In the houses ahead of us are a number of wounded from to-day's fight, among them 1 captain, Thirteenth Virginia Cavalry, mortally wounded. Five more wounded rebels have turned up in our lines, and several dead rebels were found by the scouting party on the road to the gap.... Stuart and Hampton last night slept in the room from which I am now writing [near Linden].[58]

These comments indicate Pleasonton was at Linden and Chambliss's 13th Virginia had been fighting near there earlier in the day. Also on November 5, Bayard had a sharp skirmish back at Salem[59] (about 6 or 7 miles northeast of Barbee's) which was most certainly with members of Chambliss's command. Clearly, Chambliss had his hands full that day above Warrenton and on the way to Linden. It is not likely then that the 13th Virginia Cavalry was part of the force that hit Colonel Wyndham at New Baltimore, just northeast of Warrenton, earlier in the day. The latter was probably attacked only by the 2nd North Carolina — they may have simply appeared to be a force numbering close to 1500 men.

Pleasonton went on to say in his report on the evening of November 5 that "If the general wishes me to keep on from here toward Flint Hill and Culpeper, Bayard ought to go toward Warrenton. Should he and I both strike that way we might make a good thing." Pleasonton's suggestion implies that no planned move on the town of Warrenton had occurred by late on November 5 — at least none Pleasonton was aware of.

Apparently during the night J. E. B. Stuart also gave some thought to the town of Warrenton, which had been held by W. H. F. Payne and the 2nd North Carolina Cavalry for nearly a month, because in his words, "On the next morning, November 6, I sent a portion of the command, under Colonel Rosser, to occupy Warrenton, and crossed the Rappahannock at Waterloo Bridge."[60] This was an interesting choice of words. He sent Rosser to occupy a town he already knew was held by the 2nd North Carolina Cavalry.

In any event, later in his report, Stuart noted that on November 6, "Rosser having reached Warrenton, found that the enemy was advancing on his rear as well as front, and was therefore compelled to leave the place. Meeting the enemy in his path, he skillfully eluded him, bringing off his little band, without loss, to the south side of the Rappahannock." Apparently Rosser did not make it into the town. Neither Rosser nor Stuart wrote of seeing Payne or the 2nd North Carolina that day. One wonders if any thought was given to how and when the 2nd North Carolina Cavalry managed to get out of Warrenton — certainly there was no mention of it. Stuart mentioned Rosser's skill in getting his command back from the Warrenton area in a correspondence to R. E. Lee, and Lee was impressed enough to write back the next day, "Your note of yesterday evening has been received. I am pleased at the adroitness with which Colonel Rosser extricated himself from Warrenton, and hope that none of his men were seriously injured."[61] There is reason to believe Payne was also "skillful and adroit" because he managed to get his men out of Warrenton and across the river without losses of any kind. Payne later wrote that he and the 2nd North Carolina Cavalry "…held the town until Gen. McClellan entered it, withdrawing without losing anything."[62]

The situation at Warrenton which Payne and his North Carolinian cavalrymen, as well as Rosser and his Virginians, skillfully and adroitly extricated themselves from had resulted from the fact that Pleasonton passed Warrenton to the west on his way to the Rappahannock, and Bayard was instructed to "…cut off what there might be in Warrenton and proceed to Rappahannock Station." He was to get between Warrenton and the river—to cut off any retreat. After the Union cavalry passed Warrenton on both sides and halted at the Rappahannock, the Union 6th Corps advanced to Warrenton.[63]

South of the Rappahannock River

Later in the day on November 6, 1862, Stuart's first day back across the Rappahannock, R. E. Lee, from his headquarters at Culpeper Court House, greeted him with the following word of caution, "I wish you to interdict, as far as possible, all communication with Amissville, as the small-pox is said to be in that region." Lee followed those words of caution with this request: "Communicate on your right with Colonel Chambliss, so that you may keep me advised of everything which takes place on the Rappahannock, and govern your movements by those of the enemy."[64]

The 2nd North Carolina was still under the command of Chambliss and had presumably joined him south of the Rappahannock sometime on November 6. That would put the 2nd North Carolina on duty at the Rappahannock to the right of Fitz Lee's brigade and to the left of Chambliss's 13th and 15th Virginia Cavalries which were still stretched to Fredericksburg.

On November 7, R. E. Lee wrote the Secretary of War and informed him of the enemy occupation of Virginia's Loudoun and Fauquier Counties, as far as the Rappahannock River. In his correspondence, Lee added the following assessment, "The enemy, apparently, is in very strong force, especially in cavalry, in which we are greatly outnumbered. Our cavalry, diminished by the casualties of battle and hard service, is now reduced by disease among the horses—sore tongue and soft hoof." Lee ended with these words, "It has been snowing all day, and I fear that our men, with insufficient clothing, blankets, and shoes, will suffer much, and our ranks be proportionally diminished."[65] It was not a happy time for R. E. Lee and his Confederates in body or spirit.

On the other side, November 7 was certainly not a happy time for George B. McClellan either—late that night, he was notified that he had been fired. A stroke of President Lincoln's pen relieved Major General McClellan from the command of the Army of the Potomac and replaced him with Major General Ambrose E. Burnside.[66]

Undoubtedly R. E. Lee and his weary troops appreciated the time spent in transition from McClellan to Burnside. By November 8, Longstreet had his corps in Culpeper County, and R. E. Lee was instructing Jackson to move south in the Shenandoah Valley and remain alert while en route to Culpeper. R. E. Lee informed him that Union forces had crossed the Rappahannock and were strong at Amissville. Jackson's advantage was that the Federal commanders knew Longstreet was in Culpeper County and they had daily contact with Stuart's cavalry but they had no idea where Jackson was.[67] Even though Union forces were at Amissville, Jackson had some comfort knowing that Hampton's cavalry brigade was near Washington, Virginia between the enemy there and the mountains with pickets extending along the Blue Ridge Mountains as far as Flint Hill. By November 10, however, Union forces had pushed into Washington, forcing Hampton to withdraw. Stuart, with Fitz Lee's brigade, pushed back the enemy each time they tried to drop below Amissville. Still on November 10, with little apparent provocation, the Union forces withdrew, and the advance begun by G. B. McClellan ended.

Stuart began scouting Union lines to determine the size and location of his enemy across the Rappahannock while Burnside was assuming command. Colonel Chambliss and his 13th Virginia and 2nd North Carolina cavalries watched the south side of the Rappahannock from the positions held by Fitz Lee's brigade on the left — Chambliss's left was between the Beverly and Kelly Fords. Their right extended to the left wing of the 15th Virginia Cavalry at Fredericksburg. It was about this time W. H. F. Payne asked for and received the command at Lynchburg — he spent the remainder of the winter there and returned to the 4th Virginia Cavalry in February of 1863. During most of this period, Major Clinton M. Andrews was again in command of the 2nd North Carolina Cavalry. Longstreet's Headquarters were just behind Chambliss's cavalrymen, near Culpeper Court House. [68]

Though placed on the right of Stuart's cavalry along the river-line, Chambliss's collection of detached regiments was still not under Stuart's command, nor were they yet officially part of R. E. Lee's Army of Northern Virginia. Nonetheless, Chambliss still received his instructions directly or indirectly, in a somewhat cumbersome manner, from Robert E. Lee himself. For instance, General Lee sent a message to Chambliss around noon on November 8; Chambliss sent a message for Lee to Longstreet around 2:00 in the afternoon of that same day; Longstreet communicated with R. E. Lee and passed on Chambliss's message that evening. R. E. Lee responded through his Aide-de-Camp to Longstreet that same evening, saying,

...he [Lee] has already directed Colonel C [Chambliss] (by letter about noon to-day) to send to the rear all surplus articles, baggage, stores, &c., and to have his command in marching condition, so that should he be compelled to retire from his present position he could do so without embarrassment. He was told to keep with him only such things as were necessary and could be moved with the command, and to make arrangements for supplying his men with provisions.... Should there be any withdrawal of the troops from this point, he should be notified....[69]

The substance of R. E. Lee's message to Chambliss not only made clear that Chambliss should be ready to pull back from the Rappahannock at a moment's notice, but also raised the issue of reorganization.

A number of organizational changes had been made during late October and some were still surfacing during the second week of November.[70] One change in particular was about to affect the 2nd North Carolina Cavalry directly. As indicated, Colonel Chambliss was instructed to move his wagons to the rear, but he and his 13th Virginia Cavalry were left in position picketing the Rappahannock, while the 2nd North Carolina Cavalry was pulled back from its position on the river and instructed to meet with the 9th Virginia Cavalry and W. H. F. Lee at Brandy Station. The 2nd North Carolina's orders to pull back are chronicled in the Company Muster Rolls: the Rolls for Company B have an entry that states they were ordered to evacuate on the 8th; for Company I, an entry says they were ordered to evacuate on November 9. The 9th Virginia Cavalry had been camped near Culpeper Court House prior to November 8 and moved to Brandy Station on the 14th of the month. A new brigade was created.

W. H. F. Lee's New Brigade

As just indicated, the 2nd North Carolina Cavalry moved to Brandy Station, as part of the larger reorganization of the cavalry on November 10, 1862. By Special Orders No. 238, Fitz Lee's brigade included the 1st, 2nd, 3rd, and 4th Virginia cavalries; Wade Hampton's brigade included the 1st and 2nd South Carolina, and 1st North Carolina cavalries along with Cobb's and Phillips's Georgia Legions; W. E. Jones's brigade included the 6th, 7th, and 12th Virginia cavalries as well as the 17th Battalion of Virginia Cavalry and White's Cavalry; and W. H. F. Lee's newly formed brigade included the 5th, 9th, 10th, and 15th Virginia cavalries, and the 2nd North Carolina Cavalry. (The 13th Virginia was soon afterward assigned to W. H. F. Lee's brigade and the 5th Virginia was returned to Fitz Lee's brigade.)[71]

The 2nd North Carolina and the 9th Virginia cavalries had a couple of days rest at Brandy Station and got used to the idea of belonging to a newly formed brigade, under a new brigadier-general, William H. F. Lee. The adjustment was easier for the 9th Virginia Cavalry because W. H. F. Lee had been their Colonel prior to his promotion. The men of the 2nd North Carolina had never been in the same command with the 9th Virginia and consequently had no prior contact with their new brigade commander. The 2nd

North Carolina Cavalry was also, for the first time, in the already celebrated cavalry division of J. E. B. Stuart and officially in Robert E. Lee's Army of Northern Virginia.[72]

W. H. F. Lee's cavalrymen probably enjoyed the rest they were afforded in their new camp at Brandy Station, though they and their horses apparently had few comforts. In fact on the same day the cavalry was officially reorganized, R. E. Lee wrote to the Secretary of War and reported that about three-fourths of Stuart's cavalry horses suffer from "sore tongue" or "foot disease." R. E. Lee went on to say that "Horses are now so scarce and dear that the dismounted men are unable to purchase them." In another report that day, R. E. Lee confided to G. W. Smith that the 9th Virginia Cavalry had only 90 effective men (mounted and fit for duty). A few days earlier, on November 7, R. E. Lee had alerted the Secretary of War to the difficulties the troops were facing with heavy snow on the ground and insufficient clothing, blankets, and shoes. It is often difficult to know the extent to which such conditions were experienced by a particular regiment, but it is even more difficult to imagine that the 2nd North Carolina Cavalry floated on an island of comfort in such a sea of misery.[73]

Robert E. Lee Watches Burnside

While W. H. F. Lee's new brigade collected at Brandy Station, R. E. Lee was increasingly concerned by the movements of Burnside's army. Stuart was reporting daily on Union troop movements. On November 12, for instance, Stuart reported that the enemy had pulled out of Amissville but saw no signs yet of their direction; on November 15, Lee was aware that the Union force was moving out of Warrenton probably marching on Fredericksburg.[74]

Also on November 15, Robert E. Lee learned of the presence of Union gunboats and transports in Aquia Creek, reinforcing his feeling that Fredericksburg was Burnside's target. R. E. Lee moved McLaws's and Ransom's divisions of Longstreet's corps in that direction along with W. H. F. Lee's cavalry brigade. On that date, R. E. Lee sent the following correspondence from his headquarters near the Culpeper Court House to his son, W. H. F. Lee:

GENERAL: I request you to order the Sixty-first Virginia Volunteers, Colonel Groner commanding, and the Norfolk Light Artillery Blues, Captain Grandy commanding, to proceed at once to Fredericksburg. They will take the route by Stevensburg, crossing the Rapidan at Raccoon Ford, till they intersect the Plank road from Orange Court-House to Fredericksburg. Should they learn that Fredericksburg is unoccupied by the enemy, they will pursue the Plank road to that city; but should they learn of its occupation, they will fall back through Spotts-sylvania Court-House, and take position on the Fredericksburg and Richmond Railroad, where it crosses the North Anna. After crossing the Rapidan, Colonel Groner must send forward his staff officers to ascertain the best roads, prepare forage for his command, &c., at points where it will be needed. He will be careful on the march to permit no straggling, depredation upon the citizens, country, &c., and be careful to pay for all articles consumed by his command, or to give proper receipts for the same.

I have the honor to be, with great respect, &c.,

R. E. Lee, General[75]

Continuing evidence suggested R. E. Lee was justified in moving troops to the Fredericksburg area. For instance, on November 17 he learned that Union troops (Sumner's corps) had moved from Catlett's Station toward Falmouth (across the river from Fredericksburg) and their cavalry arrived by afternoon. On November 18, R. E. Lee reported an enemy move on Fredericksburg had occurred on November 17. In his words, "The enemy's cavalry were prevented from crossing the Rappahannock last evening by our troops in Fredericksburg, nor have I yet heard of its occupation. There are in Fredericksburg a regiment of cavalry, one infantry, and two additional companies, and two light batteries." The cavalry regiment in Fredericksburg at that time was W. H. F. Lee's 15th Virginia under the command of Colonel William B. Ball. They were supported by four companies of Mississippi infantry and Lewis's light battery. Later, in his battle report, R. E. Lee noted that by November 17, 1862 it was known that Federal forces were positioning themselves for a move on Fredericksburg, and that he had more Confederate troops on the way to that City.[76]

In fact, Burnside had more than just his cavalry at Falmouth on November 17. He had his two advance corps there, and they would have been able to cross the river into Fredericksburg on that day if their pontoons had arrived. Burnside had managed to move his 110,000 man army and have his advance troops on the doorstep of Fredericksburg before R. E. Lee had Longstreet in front of him. Burnside's problem was while he kept R. E. Lee uncertain of where he intended to cross the Rappahannock, he apparently also keep his fellow Federals, who were supposed to have sent the pontoon bridges ahead, more than a little confused. Consequently, when Burnside arrived at his selected crossing point, he had to wait for the pontoons. He had to wait for more than a week.[77]

The delay gave R. E. Lee time to have the 2nd North Carolina Cavalry, along with most of W. H. F. Lee's brigade, at Fredericksburg, in front of Burnside — not to mention Longstreet's entire corps a couple of days later.

The movement of W. H. F. Lee's cavalry brigade was official on November 18 when Robert E. Lee, with Special Orders No. 246, sent the following instructions to his new brigadier-general, "Upon his [W. H. F. Lee] arrival he will assume command of the cavalry and other forces now there, and, if practicable, resist the occupation of Fredericksburg by the enemy and his advance into the country. He will leave the Thirteenth Virginia Cavalry, Colonel Chambliss, to picket the Rappahannock until further orders."[78] Fortunately for W. H. F. Lee and his cavalrymen, the order to "resist the occupation of Fredericksburg" by themselves was manageable because Burnside was not yet in a position to cross the river. Thus was avoided what just might have been the 2nd North Carolina Cavalry's greatest battle.

On the morning of November 19, R. E. Lee started the remainder of Longstreet's corps for Fredericksburg. About this same time, Jackson brought his corps east of the Blue Ridge Mountains and camped near Orange Court House where he waited for developments.

W. H. F. Lee's cavalry was at Fredericksburg on November 20. The next day, Burnside had most of his army in place and there was no further doubt about his intentions — he planned to take Fredericksburg, then on to Richmond. Somehow, Burnside and his Army of the Potomac remained confident even though, for several days, they faced W. H. F. Lee's three cavalry regiments supported by a handful of infantry and artillery, across the river. On November 21, the Union commander summoned the authorities at Fredericksburg to surrender the city or see it bombarded the following morning. The city was not surrendered but it was evacuated, yet the bombardment did not take place.[79]

During the week of waiting, Burnside continued to prepare for crossing the river at Fredericksburg, and Federal gunboats continued to appear at Port Royal (about 18 miles down river from Fredericksburg). By November 26, however, Longstreet's corps was well positioned on the hills behind Fredericksburg; D. H. Hill's division was stationed at Port Royal; and the rest of Jackson's corps started from Orange Court House for Fredericksburg — Jackson was soon in place to support Longstreet on the Confederate left or to support D. H. Hill on the right.[80] Burnside had lost his best chance for an easy victory at Fredericksburg.

Burnside's delay in front of Fredericksburg gave the Confederate troops a welcome period for consolidation and rest. However, it also suggested to R. E. Lee that Burnside might not cross the Rappahannock at Fredericksburg. R. E. Lee had to consider the possibility Burnside might make his crossing farther up or down river and then move on Fredericksburg. With that possibility in mind, R. E. Lee pulled W. H. F. Lee's cavalry regiments from Fredericksburg and moved them down river.

W. H. F. Lee's cavalry brigade was sent to Port Royal on the Confederate right to picket the river between Fredericksburg and Port Royal as well as below the latter. The presence of enemy gunboats in the area and infantry as well as some artillery across the river from Port Royal increasingly drew Confederate attention to that area as a likely crossing point for Burnside. According to Lieutenant Beale, of the 9th Virginia, W. H. F. Lee's brigade did not rest long in Fredericksburg before they "...were hastened on down the river road leading to Port Royal. It was made evident by the rapidity with which our march was urged that apprehensions were felt that an attempt would be made by a part at least of Burnside's troops to effect a crossing at Port Royal."[81] The cavalry brigade was spread along the river in front of D. H. Hill's division.

What the cavalrymen of W. H. F. Lee's brigade experienced while waiting for Burnside's attack was often similar for all regiments. A Lieutenant in the 9th Virginia Cavalry was

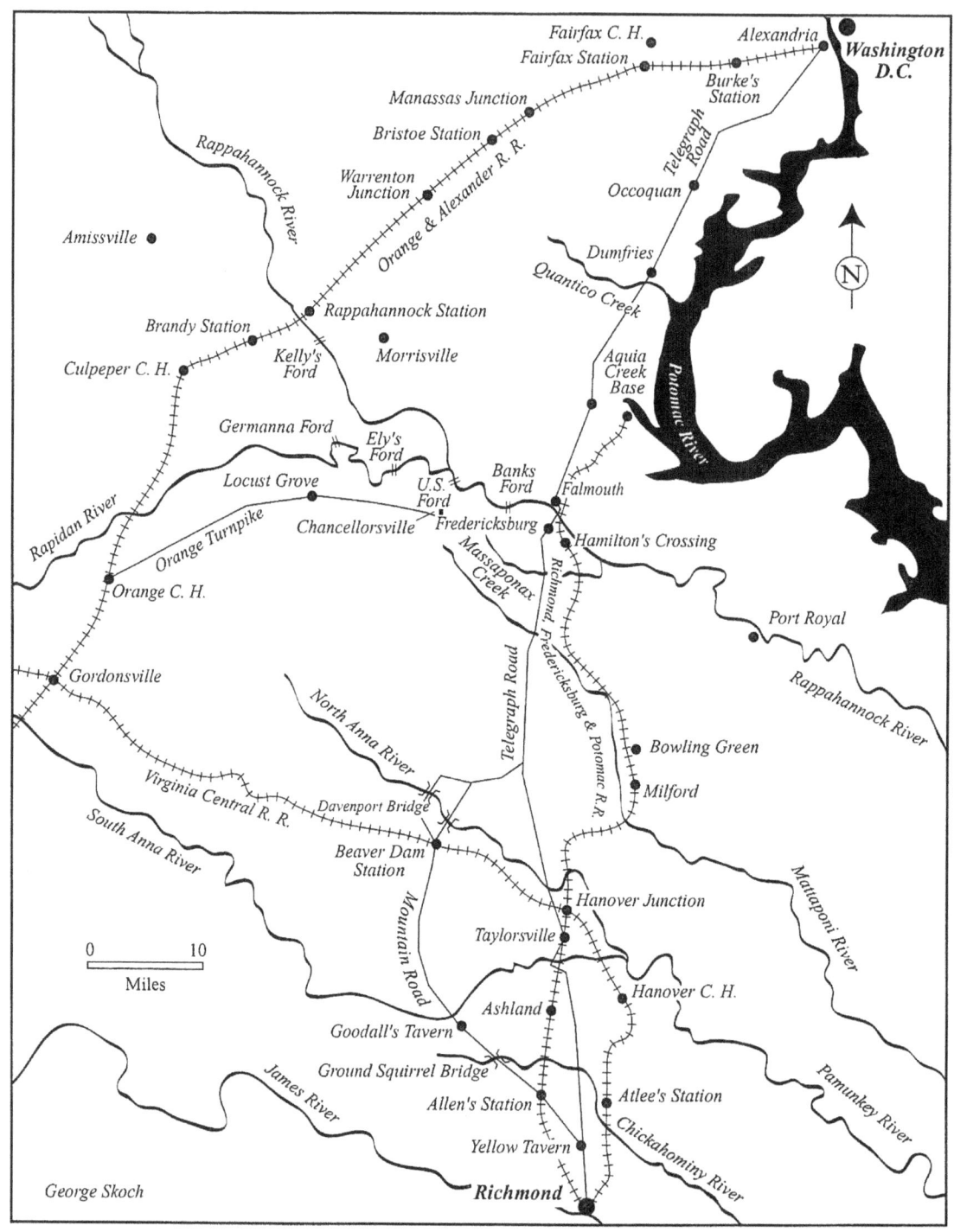

2.4: Fredericksburg, Above and Below

thoughtful enough to record some of their activities and his impressions for us. Lieutenant George Beale described their arrival at Port Royal in the following manner: "When our regiment reached the point..., I was directed to take a small detail of men to reconnoiter and establish a picket-post. Two men having been sent forward to ascertain if any of the enemy were in the place, the detail followed on to the centre of the village where we dismounted and picketed our horses, and then proceeded, as secretly as possible, to the river-bank, without discovering any hostile signs on the opposite side." However, Beale goes on to describe what followed their arrival at the river:

We perceived at once that our situation was an exposed one, there being no means of concealment or shelter.... While deliberating how to provide some means of shelter in the event of being fired on by sharpshooters, we saw a squadron of cavalry make their appearance in Port Conway, nearly opposite us, and several of them ride across the spacious grounds.... Their free and easy motions and unconcerned air so moved upon the men who were with me that they opened their carbines on them, at which they wheeled and galloped in another direction. Immediately afterwards, one or two cannon, of the presence of which we had been hitherto entirely unconscious, were placed in position..., and at the sight of these, our little squad left without standing on the order of our going. We succeeded in reaching and mounting our horses without hearing the whizzing note of bomb or ball.

As we galloped back to find a place of safety for our horses, a solid shot passed over our heads and struck a small house beside the street....[82]

Not much more excitement was experienced by most of the cavalrymen while at Port Royal. They would from time-to-time exchange rifle fire with passing gunboats or transports communicating up river with Burnside — they even had such exchanges with enemy pickets across the river. The pace was broken around December 1 when a detachment from the 9th Virginia was granted permission to raid a Union camp on the north side of the river — they captured a number of prisoners and horses and were able to free a couple of their comrades from the 15th Virginia Cavalry who had been captured by Union forces the day before.[83] The detachment from the 9th Virginia returned to camp just in time to move down river with the brigade into Essex County.

They were moved further down river a couple of days after General J. Early along with most of Jackson's corps arrived in the Fredericksburg area on December 1. Jackson's command was initially placed near Guinea Station on the Richmond Fredericksburg & Potomac Railroad, but after two or three days, J. Early was moved to support D. H. Hill near Port Royal.[84] With Port Royal covered by D. H. Hill's and Early's commands, W. H. F. Lee was permitted to move his cavalry down river and camp near Lloyd's in Essex County to secure fresh horses if possible and revitalize others.

Once down near Lloyd's, the cavalrymen were aware of the enemy's frequent patrols and foraging just across the river and they were disturbed by their presence. Nonetheless, in the words of one Lieutenant in the brigade,

...it seemed to us a happy circumstance to get into Essex, where we were able to obtain corn and provender for our horses as well as many provisions and delicacies for ourselves.

During the week of our encampment in Essex our duties were not onerous and the men longed for some diversion to break the monotony of their life. The duties of the regiment were to guard the river shore with an extended line of pickets.[85]

Private Samuel N. Mason of the 2nd North Carolina Cavalry found a diversion from the monotony of picket duty and wrote a letter home in which he described the highlight of his week as follows:

father the Yankes are on one side of the river and our army on the other The river is all that divides us we have passed a law against shooting pickets so we dont shoot each others pickets at all I tell you that soots me adzackly we stand picket within two hundred yards of each other, we talk with each other while on poast the other day a Yankey came down to the river and hollored at me he says hellow Rebbell how do you come on I toled him I come on well enough for him how did he Shine he said he was dooing along verry well if he had some tobacco chew I toled him I would gave him a chem if he would come after it he thanked me and said that he would like to have a chew says he dont you want some coffee for some tobacco So I asked the sargent commanding my post if I could go he toled me he dident recon there was any danger to go along if I wanted to so I laid down my arms and went over while at the same time he laid his down he met me half way and spolk very poitely and invited me to walk in his camp so I gave him 1 bat of tobacco and he gave me about two lbs of ground coffee and sugar enough to sweeten it with I tell you the Yankes assembled around me like a parcel of buseredes would around a lot of dead horses I chatted them about ½ hour and left I tell you I dident feel rite no way.[86]

Four Attempts to Cross the Rappahannock River

Of course, the Army of the Potomac was poised across the river for a reason — eventually they wanted to take Richmond and destroy Robert E. Lee's army in the process. They made several attempts during the winter and into the spring of 1863. General Burnside made his first attempt at Fredericksburg in December of 1862. Then President Lincoln's generals made three additional attempts farther upriver on the Rappahannock in early 1863: Burnside made his "mud march" at Lee's left on January 20, 1863; Hooker tried that again on April 13; and the third attempt from upriver was a couple of weeks later and it took them as far as Chancellorsville.

The week before the Battle of Fredericksburg, the cavalry of the Army of Northern Virginia was placed as follows: Rosser's brigade was in the Wilderness watching the left flank and the upper fords on the Rapidan River; Hampton's brigade was on Longstreet's immediate left, between Banks and U.S. fords; Fitz Lee's brigade was with Longstreet behind Fredericksburg; and W. H. F. Lee's brigade was on the Confederate right flank, below Port Royal along the river (W. E. Jones's brigade was still in the Shenandoah Valley). W. H. F. Lee's Third Cavalry Brigade at the time consisted of Colonel Solomon Williams's 2nd North Carolina, the 9th Virginia under Colonel R. L. T. Beale, the 10th Virginia under Colonel J. Lucius Davis, the 13th Virginia under Colonel J. R. Chambliss Jr., and the 15th under Colonel William B. Ball.[87]

The Battle of Fredericksburg, December 13, 1862

Early on December 11, Union engineers started placing three pontoon bridges across the Rappahannock at Fredericksburg and three others a couple of miles south of town — troops were sent across by boat to protect the bridge-builders from sharpshooters in town. Burnside's guns spent most of December 12 shelling the mostly evacuated city.

R. E. Lee moved Jackson forward between Longstreet's right and Hamilton's Crossroads. J. Early's and D. H. Hill's commands were pulled up from near Port Royal and placed on Jackson's right — they were in place on the morning of December 13 with J. Early as the second line and D. H. Hill the third.[88] Also, on December 12, Stuart moved the bulk of Fitz Lee's cavalry brigade to the right of Jackson to connect with W. H. F. Lee's cavalry brigade which had been called up from Essex County the night before.

On December 11, word had been sent to W. H. F. Lee, camped near Lloyds in Essex County, to have his men fill their haversacks and cartridge boxes and head for Fredericksburg. They reached Massaponax Run where it crossed the river road late on December 12 and bivouacked near Port Royal Road. The 2nd North Carolina Cavalry along with the 9th and 13th Virginia Cavalries had marched about forty miles and throughout the day, they heard the "ominous roar of artillery in the direction of Fredericksburg...." When the cavalrymen settled for the night, they cut and piled branches from cedar trees which lined both sides of the road and then covered the branches with their blankets making mattresses which separated them from the snow that had fallen during their day's march. At sunrise on December 13, W. H. F. Lee's troops crossed the run in a dense fog and rested in column of squadrons in a field on the extreme right of the Army of Northern Virginia. When the fog lifted, they saw in front of them and across the river on their right a "formidable array of artillery." They dismounted their sharpshooters and the rest of the brigade was ordered back behind the run at a trot. J. E. B. Stuart joined his Calvary regiments east of Hamilton's Crossing on the right flank of the Confederate line during the morning.[89]

Once the pontoon bridges were in place, Burnside's forces crossed the river with very little resistance. The three bridges in town carried Edwin V. Sumner's and Joseph Hooker's men into the center of Longstreet's well-entrenched corps. The three bridges below town, just below Deep Run, were crossed by William B. Franklin's troops in front of Longstreet's right wing and Jackson's corps.

Once across the river, Franklin's left wing had to form a right angle to his main line and extend to the river because Stuart's Confederate cavalry, Fitz Lee's and W. H. F. Lee's brigades were in line facing Franklin's flank from Hamilton's Crossroads to the river. The scene was set by early morning.

Burnside first made a feint at Longstreet on the Confederate left and sent Franklin at Jackson. The plan was for Franklin to roll up Jackson's right flank, then an all-out assault was to take place on Longstreet's front — however, this plan required more coordination than Burnside was able to manage that day. Nonetheless, as the fog lifted, Franklin's men could be seen crossing an open field into Jackson's and Stuart's waiting guns. After a bit, George G. Meade managed to penetrate the weak spot in Jackson's line before he was turned by the Confederate second line and sent back into Union lines. Franklin had failed to send support to Meade, and he did not make a second assault on Jackson's position.

On the Confederate left, the probe into Longstreet's line was in fact a series of attacks, nearly a brigade at a time, into a well entrenched enemy line. The Federal generals' slaughter of their men reached its pinnacle on Longstreet's front, and continued until darkness. The Union lost nearly 13,000 men that day, the Confederates nearly 5,000. This was a day R. E. Lee chose to resist the Southern credo of "Attack and Die." In spite of Jackson's and Stuart's desires to mount an attack before the fog lifted that morning, R. E. Lee took the day on the defensive, and most of his men were well rewarded. Jackson was not afforded the opportunity to attack, nor was Stuart.[90]

This was the second large battle the men of the 2nd North Carolina Cavalry had been a part of — the first was the Battle of New Bern some nine months earlier. What they witnessed in the previous battle, however, could not have prepared them for the carnage they saw on December 13, 1862. While the cavalrymen were subjected to enemy shelling and were deployed as sharpshooters on the Confederate right flank, they were not seriously engaged in the fighting — However, they witnessed the slaughter of thousands of men.[91] One Lieutenant in their brigade recorded these impressions:

It is quite probable the pick and flower of Burnside's army marched in this magnificent battle array....
...
During the entire march of the Federals from near the river, Major Pelham [with Stuart's command], with one or more guns of his horse artillery, first in one position and then in another, poured shot and shell into their ranks. It is intensely exciting to watch the effect of his firing, as from time to time the shells struck the enemy's lines, and, bursting, created no little confusion. Very soon, Pelham's guns were reinforced by two of Lindsey Walker's batteries, and the Federal guns opened on them with increasing vigor. The duel was fast and furious.
...
The scene of the morning as the splendid left wing of Burnside's Army march to meet the regiments of Jackson and Hill, was all changed in the afternoon. The bold front, the advancing lines, the fluttering standards, were all changed, and a motley disordered mass rushed madly for safety towards the river, with thirty or more Confederate guns pushing forward and pouring shot and shell after them.[92]

After the fighting on December 13, W. H. F. Lee's brigade settled into an uncomfortable bivouac for the night and the next day along with "a cold rain and great scarcity of provisions." On December 15, they marched toward Port Royal and camped on the hills overlooking the village. They stayed there for a day or two until J. Early's troops arrived and relieved them of picket duty in that area. Once again, the cavalry brigade moved down along the river as far as Essex County for picket duty.[93]

After the Battle of Fredericksburg, Robert E. Lee moved his army into winter quarters, but he kept an eye on Burnside's army — he knew Burnside needed a victory, so it might be an active winter. Longstreet camped opposite Fredericksburg and Jackson between there and Port Royal. They went into winter quarters but not hibernation. The eyes R. E. Lee focused on the Army of the Potomac were in Stuart's cavalry. Winter camp for the cavalry meant routinely rotating into picket duty along the Rappahannock River and occasionally participating in scouts and raids behind enemy lines.

Once W. H. F. Lee's cavalrymen were down river, they spent about a week throwing up their winter quarters, which were always more temporary than those constructed by the infantry. Then Stuart organized a post–Christmas day parade for most of them. Of course, the parade route took them behind enemy lines. Such raids were becoming a winter tradition for the cavalry, and they often brought more "gifts" for the troopers than did Christmas packages from home.

Winter Cavalry Raids

Wade Hampton's cavalrymen had already been on three raids across the Rappahannock into enemy lines that winter: the first raid was with only 158 men on November 27 in which they captured about 100 horses and 150 men; the second on December 10 employed 520 men in which they captured about 50 men from the guard at Dumfries, a wagon train, and cut telegraph lines (Hampton did not return in time to see the Battle of Fredericksburg); and after a couple of days of rest, the third raid was toward Occoquan in which the raiders swept along an eight mile stretch of the road capturing Union pickets, totaling about 150 men, and a sutlers' train with about twenty wagons (the Confederacy got the wagons; Hampton's men shared 300 pairs of good northern boots, baskets of wines, wonderful cheeses, and assorted delicacies). These raids were aimed at irritating and disrupting the enemy as well as boosting the spirits and comforts of the raiders. They were focused on the old Telegraph Road that followed the south side of the Potomac from Alexandria to near the Rappahannock. Numerous military and sutlers' wagon trains as well as the cavalry still used the road to reach the Army of the Potomac, and it was a main line of communication to Burnside. Stuart's Christmas raid focused on this same road from Occoquan to Dumfries. Stuart himself lead the fourth and final raid of 1862 — they left camp on December 26.[94]

Stuart took about 1,800 men selected from Hampton's, Fitz Lee's and W. H. F. Lee's brigades, and four guns from his horse artillery. They moved up the south side of the Rappahannock and crossed at Kelly's Ford. They passed through Morrisville and a few miles beyond before they bivouacked for the night. Some time later, Stuart stated his objective and plan for this last raid of the year:

I directed General Hampton to move round to the left in the direction of Occoquan, while General Fitz Lee aimed to strike the Telegraph road between Dumfries and Aquia, General W. H. F. Lee advancing between the two and by the road running along the right bank of the Quantico directly upon Dumfries, my object being to take possession of the Telegraph road, to capture all the trains that might be passing.[95]

Stuart was riding with W. H. F. Lee and his troopers when they arrived at Wheat's Mill, at the junction of the Telegraph Road and Quantico Creek, and encountered a small picket of twelve infantrymen. A squadron from the 9th Virginia charged the Union picket and captured the lot. The charging squadron was joined by two others and continued to the edge of town where they were driven back by two regiments of enemy infantry. W. H. F. Lee withdrew his command south of the creek, and they were then charged by a squadron of Union cavalry, which in turn, wheeled in retreat when fired upon. At that point, Stuart arrived with a battery of artillery and drove the enemy from the north side of the creek. At about the same time, Union artillery entered the scrap and an exchange took place. Stuart and W. H. F. Lee saw no opportunity or point to mounting an attack on the town — it was strongly held and most supplies had been removed. Before December 27 finished, the men from W. H. F. Lee's brigade had captured some 50 prisoners, and in the process, they had 1 private wounded and 2 noncommissioned officers and 12 privates missing. Only one man was captured from the 2nd North Carolina Cavalry.[96]

While W. H. F. Lee's men were approaching Dumfries, Fitz Lee and his command entered the Telegraph Road about two miles south of the town. At that point, their advance guard came upon a Union patrol and was able to capture two men while the remainder were able to race back to their support in Dumfries.

Fitz Lee's command joined Stuart and W. H. F. Lee's cavalrymen just out side of town. The Lees and Stuart discussed the situation and decided not to attack the town. Fitz Lee was instructed to dismount some men and position artillery to hold the enemy while the rest of his command joined their comrades on the Brentsville Road heading northwest from Dumfries. Fitz Lee's holding action continued until nightfall.[97]

In the meantime, Hampton had moved toward Occoquan and along the way encountered enemy pickets at Cole's Store. Hampton managed to capture four pickets while eleven tried to escape back to Dumfries but were captured by a detachment of W. H. F. Lee's 15th Virginia Cavalry. With the way cleared, Hampton pushed his command to Occoquan. They took the town in the face of several hundred enemy cavalry, but only captured 19 prisoners and 8 wagons. Stuart's command bivouacked near Cole's Store on the night of December 27.[98]

The next morning, Stuart moved his column toward Occoquan. At Greenwood Church, he sent a detachment from Hampton's brigade north to Bacon Race Church with instructions to cut off a detachment of enemy in Stuart's path. Just after Stuart left Greenwood Church, however, his column encountered two Union cavalry regiments drawn up in line of battle.

Fitz Lee's brigade was in front, and they were ordered to charge, which they did in the face of heavy enemy fire. The Federal force soon broke and was pursued for 5 or 6 miles back to the Occoquan River where Fitz Lee's command only hesitated before the 5th Virginia, under Rosser, charged across under enemy fire. The Union sharpshooters broke and Fitz Lee's command crossed the river and occupied the just deserted enemy camp — the Confederates collected the abandoned horses, mules, wagons, blankets and other stores. They had also taken about 100 prisoners.[99] On December 28, W. H. F. Lee's command was involved in guarding intersections of the roads crossed by Stuart's columns and in the process lost two men from Company B, 2nd North Carolina Cavalry near Dumphries and Fairfax Court House.

Stuart then moved his column toward Burke's Station on the Orange & Alexandria Railroad. The head of the column arrived there after dark, and a small party of Confederates was sent quietly to the telegraph office. It managed to occupy the office before the operators could give an alarm. This allowed Stuart, the prankster, to intercept some unimportant Union messages expressing uncertainty about where they might best intercept the Confederate cavalrymen who had penetrated Union lines — more importantly it provided Stuart the opportunity to send a few messages. Stuart sent the quartermaster-general of the U.S. Army a message in which he referred to the poor quality of the mules they had just furnished him, and how difficult that made it for him to move the wagons he had just captured.[100]

From Burke's Station, Stuart led his troopers back to the safety of the Confederate line with only minor encounters here and there as the Confederates continued to collect small trophies along the way. They proceeded through Middleburg, Warrenton, and finally Culpeper Court House by December 31. Stuart returned to his headquarters near Fredericksburg on the first of January and his commands returned to their former picket duties along the Rappahannock. According to Stuart, they had captured a large number of horses, mules, wagons, saddles, bridles, pistols, and sabers — as well as more than 200 prisoners.[101]

J. E. B. Stuart spent the months of January and February relaxing in winter quarters, but the eyes of his cavalry stayed focused on the enemy across the Rappahannock. R. E. Lee as well as others continued to believe there was a good possibility Burnside would try another major offensive that winter. Small movements by the Union cavalry increased R. E. Lee's concerns. For instance, on January 9, they carried out a reconnaissance in force against Catlett's and Rappahannock Stations. The Confederate cavalry drove the enemy back, but the operation caused the Confederate left to heighten its state of alert.[102]

Robert E. Lee was making every effort to keep his command prepared for the possibility that the enemy had not yet rested for the winter. Part of this effort included the 2nd North Carolina Cavalry and its brigade. In late January they were collected at Jackson's camp near Moss Neck to strut their stuff — a review of W. H. F. Lee's cavalry brigade was ordered. It was attended by an impatient J. E. B. Stuart who was eager to attend a wedding that day some miles away. It was almost three in the afternoon before the review ended and Stuart rushed off to party.[103] R. E. Lee's efforts to keep his cavalry focused was difficult at times but was prudent because just after the first of the year, Burnside made his next move: his first attempt to cross up-river from Fredericksburg.

BURNSIDE'S MUD MARCH, JANUARY 20, 1863

By January 19, it was apparent to many that Burnside was going to move on R. E. Lee's left flank and head for Culpeper Court House and Gordonsville.[104] On January 20, R. E. Lee wrote a note to J. E. B. Stuart, enclosing a letter for Wade Hampton. He asked Stuart to note the contents, pass it on, and "Give notice to the cavalry, and direct the two Lees to have their brigades ready to move at a moment's warning." The information R. E. Lee wanted passed along to his cavalry included the following:

From the reports of the scouts from both flanks of the enemy, he appears to be on the eve of making an advance. Sigel's corps, which is stationed at Stafford and Dumfries, I understand, has marching orders, and the impression among the men is that they will go in the direction of Warrenton. I think it probable that he will attempt to cross the Rappahannock at Kelly's Ford, or at Rappahannock Station....

I think it probable that the enemy will cross the Upper Rappahannock, with a view to turn our left flank. Make such resistance as you can to retard or defeat him, and, should he cross with a force too large for you to encounter, concentrate your troops; hang upon his flank and rear; cut up his communications; cause him embarrassment, and report all that you can discover of his movements and designs.[105]

R. E. Lee also told Stuart he had been informed "...that the enemy's pickets are all withdrawn from Westmoreland. If that is so, General W. H. F. Lee might draw up closer to Port Royal. Until the further intentions of the enemy are discovered, we will have to suspend furloughs to men and officers."

The heightened state of alert was certainly warranted. Burnside had mobilized his army for a major assault on the Confederate left, but his troops and wagons were soon immobilized on that same day when a major storm hit Virginia on January 20, 1863. The result was recorded in history as Burnside's "Mud March." The Virginia roads were so saturated not even the infantry could move in the knee-deep mud — the campaign was called off on January 22, but not for the want of trying.

Burnside apparently had little trouble placing blame for the failed campaign, and he set out for Washington to ask Lincoln to replace some of his insubordinate commanders, but he was replaced instead. General Joseph Hooker was made commander of the Army of the Potomac. Changes in the Union cavalry command were also on the agenda. On February 7, Brigadier General George Stoneman assumed command of the Army of the Potomac's cavalry.[106]

The 2nd North Carolina Cavalry Battles Winter

Even though the Army of Northern Virginia had been in winter quarters since December 20, only after January 22 could they feel confident the fighting was over for a few months. However, the cavalry's major battle with the elements was not over as another heavy storm arrived on January 27 and lasted a couple of days. The cavalrymen themselves could hardly combat the cold and hunger, but the horses suffered more.

Through early winter, Wade Hampton's brigade had been on picket duty along the river northwest of Longstreet at Fredericksburg, and W. H. F. Lee's brigade was on duty near Jackson's command at Port Royal and below. Fitz Lee's brigade was recuperating in Caroline County. The horses in Hampton's brigade suffered more than the others and the situation worsened by the day. Hampton was not pleased that his men and horses had such a prolonged stay at hard duty, and he made his feeling known to Stuart on numerous occasions — Hampton even made a point of the relatively easy duty given to the Virginia brigades — especially those in Fitz Lee's command. Stuart finally sent some members of his staff to investigate the situation on the left end of the Confederate line. Heros von Borcke, of Stuart's staff, concluded that the situation was growing worse by the day for Hampton's brigade. Major von Borcke later wrote, "It was a mournful sight to see more than half the horses of this splendid command totally unfit for duty, dead and dying animals lying about the camp in all directions. One regiment had lost thirty-one horses in less than a week." On von Borcke's recommendation, Stuart brought Fitz Lee's brigade up to relieve Hampton's troops. On February 9, Fitz Lee's brigade left their camp in Caroline County, where it had been stationed since the battle of Fredericksburg. Hampton's brigade was pulled back south of the James River to rebuild in Halifax and Campbell counties.[107]

As in January, the influence of the weather continued to be a serious problem into late February. Of course, the discomfort was not confined to the brigade on the northern end of the line. It was common to all regiments performing picket duty along the river. In a correspondence to President Davis on February 26, R. E. Lee communicated the following,

The weather for the last eight or ten days has been so unfavorable for observation that it has prevented the scouts from acquiring information.
...
The last fall of snow was fully a foot deep. The rain of last night and today will add to the discomfort of the troops and the hardship of our horses. I had hoped that the latter would have been in good condition for the spring campaign.... Now, when their labors are much increased, it is impossible to procure sufficient forage.[108]

Further south along the Rappahannock, the 2nd North Carolina Cavalry and the rest of W. H. F. Lee's brigade suffered once again from a short supply of food and exposure to the cold, as well as a shortage of forage for their horses. Often the cavalrymen were just as disturbed when they lost a comrade to the battle with the elements and camp conditions as they were when the loss was caused by their human enemy. For instance, Private Haywood Ennis of Company I died of "pneumonia" contracted in camp on March 8, and the other men of his company and from Moore County did not want it to go unnoticed. The men called a meeting, and asked Corporal Archibald B. Nicholson to chair the gathering and Sergeant John C. Baker to act as Secretary. The purpose of the meeting was to formulate "...a tribute of respect to the memory of Haywood Ennis..." They selected a committee of two sergeants and one corporal to draft resolutions to that end, and that a copy of the resolutions and report of the tribute be sent to the Ennis family and the *Fayetteville Observer* for publication.[109]

In addition to battling the conditions, the cavalrymen in W. H. F. Lee's brigade were also kept busy with routine picketing and an occasional flurry of excitement. One such instance, occurred on Friday February 20, when W. H. F. Lee's cavalrymen saw two Federal gunboats cruise past them from their position about twenty-five miles down river. When the gunboats returned on the afternoon of the next day, W. H. F. Lee had his artillery waiting, and they severely damaged the vessels—most of the men from the 2nd North Carolina and the other cavalrymen were not involved, but they certainly enjoyed the spectacle.[110]

In mid–March things began to get exciting for the cavalrymen upriver. On March 16 Fitz Lee received information of Union troop movements toward Kelly's Ford on the Rappahannock. Fitz Lee had a small band of pickets at the ford, and the Union cavalry was able to force a crossing the next morning with little difficulty. General Stuart was visiting Fitz Lee's headquarters at the time of the attack and moved to the front with the brigade where they were engaged in fierce fighting until nightfall when the Union forces withdrew the way they had come. Fitz Lee's command lost 133 cavalrymen.[111]

The Union cavalry probe on March 17 had R. E. Lee again anticipating an assault up-river from Fredericksburg. On March 20, 1863, R. E. Lee wrote Stuart of pending Federal moves and of their withdrawals from certain areas. R. E. Lee's opening paragraph concerned the 2nd North Carolina Cavalry and their brigade. He wrote,

I have written to W. H. F. Lee to be prepared to move at short notice, and to select one regiment to remain in that section [below Port Royal]. His quartermaster is ordered here [Richmond] to see Corley, and ascertain what arrangements can be made to subsist his brigade on the Rapidan. Corley is endeavoring to accumulate some forage at Gordonsville. Do not let them feed it all up. I will send Captain Johnston up to Rapidan Station to see if rifle-pits can be constructed there to protect the bridge. I think it probable that a dash may be made at it to destroy it, in connection with other movements.[112]

Around the first of April, W. H. F. Lee left the 10th Virginia Cavalry in Essex County and moved up with the 9th and 13th Virginia and 2nd North Carolina cavalries to within a mile from Orange Court House which was just a couple of miles below the bridge at Rapidan Station that R. E. Lee was so concerned about on March 20. (The 15th Virginia Cavalry was still around Fredericksburg and stayed in that area.) They arrived at Orange County Court House April 8, and after a few days in that position, W. H. F. Lee moved the 2nd North Carolina Cavalry and the other two regiments with him across the Rapidan and on toward the Botts farm near Brandy Station, just below the Rappahannock River, arriving on April 12. By that time the enemy fully occupied the north bank of the Rappahannock along their front.[113]

Once W. H. F. Lee had his brigade in motion for Orange Court House, R. E. Lee wrote the Secretary of War on April 4 and explained the movement of the brigade as follows:

General W. H. F. Lee's cavalry brigade is now moving from our extreme right to the Upper Rappahannock. It has been drawing its supplies during the winter from Essex and Middlesex Counties, and has drawn from the counties in the Northern Neck cattle and bacon sufficient for their subsistence....
My object in transferring this brigade from our right to our left, in addition to the cavalry re-enforcement it will give to our line on the Upper Rappahannock, was to enable me to throw forward Fitz Lee's brigade into Loudoun, with a view of collecting all the supplies possible.[114]

While generals thought of strategies and troop placements, privates generally had different thoughts. The men of the 2nd North Carolina

Cavalry knew they were moving closer to where the next fighting was expected. For some, knowing that coupled with returning to Culpeper County aroused mixed feelings. Just surviving the winter was an achievement for many and it was certainly in the mix of emotions. Shortly after arriving in Culpeper County, Private Milas Cavin of Company B sent a letter to his mother in which he notes how their new location feels a bit more like home; how harsh the winter has been; and the real likelihood of death. He wrote,

We again find ourselves up here in the mountainous country of Culpeper I look around and things look familiar, this seems more like home than the more sandy country nearer the coast ... we feel sad when I think of the number of our fellow soldiers who have died since we were here last fall, yet if it is the will of our heavenly father that such things be we should be *resigned to our destiny*, and by the good providence of God I have been preserved through another winter....[115]

Private Cavin appeared resigned to the realities of their war to date — winter caused more deaths among his comrades than combat. That tendency would change in the years to come but not because winters got easier.

The rest of the Army of Northern Virginia also survived the winter with great difficulty and began to position itself for the next Federal campaign.

Meanwhile, as previously indicated Joseph Hooker had taken over the Army of the Potomac and reorganized the cavalry under George Stoneman in early February.[116] They pulled together 3 divisions with over 11,000 cavalrymen by April of 1863. With this force on hand, the Army of the Potomac prepared for its second advance on the upper Rappahannock, the first under its new commander, General Hooker. The new cavalry was to play a more important role.

Responding to his own growing concern for the conduct of the war, President Lincoln paid General Hooker a visit on April 9, in the latter's camp near Falmouth, Virginia (just across the river from Fredericksburg and R. E. Lee's army). In an obvious response to President Lincoln's request for a plan of attack across the Rappahannock, Hooker wrote the President on April 11 outlining his intentions. The general planned to send George Stoneman's cavalry across first, with the goal of turning the Confederate left and destroying all their communications with Richmond — to isolate the Army of Northern Virginia. Furthermore, Hooker planned to have his cavalry slow R. E. Lee's retreat once the Union infantry started across the Rappahannock. He went on to say his cavalry would probably cross on the railroad bridge between Beverly and Kelly's Fords.[117]

At about the same time Lincoln was meeting with Hooker at Falmouth, Stuart broke his winter camp behind Fredericksburg and moved west, near Rapidan Station. On April 11, the same day Hooker submitted his plan to President Lincoln for crossing the Rappahannock and heading for Culpeper, R. E. Lee instructed Stuart to move his cavalry headquarters a little farther north, near Culpeper Court House to become his first line of defense at the Rappahannock. R. E. Lee's postscript to Stuart included the following words of caution: "From indications observed yesterday, it seems probable Hooker is contemplating some new movement. The late Washington papers seem also to indicate something."[118] W. H. F. Lee had the 2nd North Carolina Cavalry and two other regiments near Brandy Station, between Culpeper Court House and Hooker's planned crossing point on the Rappahannock before mid–April. (The 10th and 15th Virginia were not with him.)

HOOKER STARTS ACROSS THE RAPPAHANNOCK, APRIL 14, 1863

Robert E. Lee's information and instincts were correct again, President Lincoln and his generals Hooker and Stoneman put into action a plan to cross the Rappahannock and head for Richmond — this time directly into the 259 faces of the 2nd North Carolina cavalrymen and their comrades in the 9th and 13th Virginia cavalries.

Late on April 13, George Stoneman had concentrated his cavalry command at Morrisville ready to cross the Rappahannock early the next morning. Stoneman's plan called for Davis's brigade to cross the river above Beverly Ford, drop down and assist W. W. Averell's division at that ford. D. McM. Gregg's division was to follow Averell across Beverly Ford and head for Culpeper Court House. John Buford's brigade was to make an early demonstration at Kelly's Ford and then move up river to force a crossing at the railroad bridge (where the Orange & Alexandria Railroad crossed the Rappahannock) at the same time Averell was crossing his division.[119]

To slow the Union cavalry at the river, Stuart had placed three of W. H. F. Lee's small regiments—the 9th and 13th regiments of Virginia cavalry and 116 mounted men of the 2nd North Carolina Cavalry. (Fitz Lee's brigade was still on its mission across the Rappahannock toward Salem and would not return in time to help slow Stoneman's advance.) The 2nd North Carolina Cavalry regiment also had 143 men without horses in the rifle pits along the river. (These men had lost their horses in service.) The dismounted men were in the path of advancing enemy cavalry—a vulnerable situation often resulting in a high rate of losses by capture.

THE 2ND NORTH CAROLINA CAVALRY'S READINESS

A member of Stuart's staff commented on the problem of dismounted men in their ranks while the Union cavalry was getting its act together: "...they had very much improved their cavalry, while ours had deteriorated—mainly from the lack of horses. We now felt the bad effects of our system of requiring the men to furnish their own horses. The most dashing trooper was the one whose horse was most apt to be shot, and when this man was unable to remount himself he had to go to the infantry service, and was lost to the cavalry." Other alternatives included buying another horse, though by then it was already a difficult and expensive proposition; another possibility was to try for a riderless horse during or just after a battle.[120]

Many of the troopers in the 2nd North Carolina Cavalry who had lost their horses struggled for months to acquire new mounts. Private Milas Cavin, provides us with a good example of the difficulties encountered while trying to procure a horse. On more than one occasion Milas had written his younger brother, Jimmy, asking him to find a horse for him in their home county at a reasonable price. Milas had arranged to be on a horse detail on the assumption that his brother could arrange the purchase, but apparently his brother was having difficulty finding an affordable horse. If assured of an available horse, Milas would have been able to visit his family while picking up his new mount. In the process of arranging these matters, however, Milas's brother died, and Milas had to write to his father explaining that he was not able to attend the funeral services because a horse had not been found for him and if arrangements to acquire a horse were not made beforehand, then the entire time would be taken in trying to locate a mount. In his letter, he tried to explain the difficult circumstances as follows:

I know that I did not have money enough to bye a horse and did not know whether I could bye a horse with money or not from what I had earned. Our Captain also had to vouch for us that we would return to our regiment with horses within 30 days, and should we fail we would be held liable to Court Martial. believing it to be an imposition practiced upon the soldier compelling them to furnish horses for the use of the government at their own expense I did not think it right for us to allow ourselves to be imposed upon in that manner, I had made every preparation however that I could to go, and waited anxiously to hear from Jimmy.[121]

Milas went on to explain that he would wait for the next horse detail and he hoped by then his father might have one arranged for him, thus allowing Milas to visit his family for ten days or so.

Nonetheless, W. H. F. Lee's small effective force, with the 2nd North Carolina Cavalry having more men without than with horses, stood in front of Stoneman's cavalry and Hooker's army. W. H. F. Lee posted his men along the river, concentrating them at Kelly's Ford, the railroad bridge, Beverly's Ford, and Welford's Ford near the confluence of the Hazel and Rappahannock rivers. During the night of April 13, W. H. F. Lee learned of the Union forces collecting across the river, and he moved his sharpshooters from the 9th Virginia (about 150 men) to reinforce troopers from his other two regiments in rifle pits at Kelly's Ford. Up at the railroad bridge and nearby ford, W. H. F. Lee had stationed some men from the 13th Virginia and some of the dismounted men of the 2nd North Carolina—the latter under the command of Lieutenant Joseph Baker of Company D. There was also a mix of men from all three regiments in the pits at Beverly Ford. Finally, a number of the horseless men from the 2nd North Carolina were posted up river near Welford's Ford under the command of Lieutenant W. A. Luckey of Company B. The mounted men of the 2nd North Carolina, under the command of Captain J. W. Strange of Company D, were initially held back near Brandy Station as protection for two guns from Moorman's battery.[122]

By daylight on April 14, John Buford placed his Union brigade in front of Kelly's Ford for his planned demonstration. They made a dash and exchanged fire with their enemy—not much more. Further upriver, near the railroad bridge, Judson Kilpatrick of David McM. Gregg's division charged across the ford while supported by artillery. Men from the 13th Virginia Cavalry and twenty men under Lieutenant Baker from the 2nd North Carolina Cavalry held the rifle pits and a small block house near the railroad bridge. As the Union cavalry crossed at the ford, their artillery, stationed about 300 yards in front of the blockhouse, began a heavy fire, pounding the Confederate position with more than seventy rounds of fire. With their position severely threatened, the men of the 13th Virginia and 2nd North Carolina pulled back, and Kilpatrick's force crossed the Rappahannock. No sooner were they across, than W. H. F. Lee arrived at a gallop with the 9th Virginia Cavalry and joined the dismounted men of the 13th Virginia and the 2nd North Carolina in pushing Kilpatrick back across the river. This Confederate reaction was aided by Stuart's appearance on the scene with the two guns from Moorman's battery which immediately began to return the fire from the Union artillery. The mounted men of the 2nd North Carolina were also brought forward by Stuart with Moorman's guns.[123]

After the action near the railroad bridge, about 2:00 P.M., word came of Union movement up at Beverly Ford. W. H. F. Lee rushed two squadrons from the 9th Virginia, to the ford. They were followed at a near gallop by Moorman's two guns and their escort, the mounted men of the 2nd North Carolina. Skirmishing took place during the rest of the day, but no serious Union crossing was attempted at Beverly Ford. The men from the 2nd North Carolina stayed back with the guns. Around 7:00 P.M., the mounted men of the 2nd North Carolina were relieved and returned to camp. As April 14 drew to a close, the Union cavalrymen under Davis further up river near Welford's Ford had not attempted their planned crossing due to a severe rainstorm.

On the morning of April 15, Colonel G. Davis, under great pressure from Stoneman, who was under pressure from Hooker, who was in turn under great pressure from President Lincoln, took about two squadrons across the Rappahannock and overpowered the handful of dismounted men from the 2nd North Carolina Cavalry who remained unsupported during the night and morning.[124] Davis captured four men from the 2nd North Carolina Cavalry early that morning.

On more than one occasion, R. E. Lee had refused to relieve cavalrymen of picket duty with infantrymen along that and other rivers because he feared if infantrymen were charged by enemy cavalry from across the river, being on foot, they would have little or no chance to escape. In this instance, the same principle apparently was not applied to cavalrymen without horses.

In any event, after his brief clash with the men from the 2nd North Carolina Cavalry, Davis turned his men to the left and headed for Beverly's Ford. As they approached the ford, they found themselves between some dismounted cavalrymen from the 9th Virginia and their horses. The men from the 9th Virginia were forced to withdraw and lost 12 horses in the process. Before any of the men from the 9th Virginia were captured, however, W. H. F. Lee arrived from camp with the 13th Virginia Cavalry, and helped drive G. Davis and his men out of the area—many of whom tried unsuccessfully to escape across the raging river at that point. W. H. F. Lee's troopers captured fourteen men and horses; the river took several others.[125]

At 8:00 P.M. on April 15, Hooker sent the following message to President Lincoln: "Just heard from General Stoneman. His artillery has been brought to a halt by the mud, one division only having crossed the river. If practicable, he will proceed without it. All the streams are swimming." At 10:15 P.M. that evening, Lincoln replied to Hooker expressing his great displeasure with the cavalry's progress, and ending with these words of despair: "I do not know that any better can be done, but I greatly fear it is another failure already." How right he was. That night Hooker began to pull some of his troops back from the river, and by April 21 Stoneman told Hooker that he still had no opportunity to cross the Rappahannock due to the deep water at the fords. Hooker informed Lincoln of the situation late that same evening. The second attempt to take the Union army across the upper Rappahannock was defeated by the 2nd North Carolina Cavalry, their fellow cavalrymen in the 9th and 13th Virginia, and their greatest ally of all, the persistent Virginia rainstorms.[126]

The 2nd North Carolina Cavalry's recorded combat losses from the time they were pushed from Warrenton back across the Rappahannock in November 1862 until late April 1863 were as follows:

Combat Losses in the 2nd North Carolina Cavalry November, 1862–April 27, 1863

Trooper	Age	Co.	Fate
Henry Moore	46	A	wounded, December 24
Hiram L. Leister		H	captured, December 27
Joseph T. Summers	28	B	captured, December 28
Robert F. Moore	28	B	captured, December 28
Robert C. Ozment	26	F	wounded, April 1863
M. S. Coffy	21	A	wounded, April 6
John Kelly	26	A	captured, April 15
John H. Rhea	23	A	captured, April 15
Robert H. Sumrow	28	B	captured, April 15
Archibald T. Clark	23	D	captured, April 15

The source for this table is *North Carolina Troops 1861–1865, A Roster*, compiled by Louis H. Manarin (Raleigh, N.C., State Division of Archives and History), vol. II, Cavalry, pages 104–177. (See Appendix for more information on the men listed above, page 393.)

The raging Rappahannock and Hooker's need to reorganize gave W. H. F. Lee's cavalrymen almost two weeks to consider the enemy's next crossing.

The Chancellorsville Campaign, April 29–May 5, 1863

General Joseph Hooker, with his large army and consolidated cavalry under George Stoneman, still had to prove his worth as commander of the Army of the Potomac. He had clearly disappointed President Lincoln in his mid-April attempt to cross the Rappahannock River and head for Richmond through Culpeper. He would try again, as soon as possible — this time he would initially be more successful.

By late April, General Robert E. Lee had about 60,000 men along the Rappahannock to watch Hooker's army of more than twice that number. General James Longstreet with two of his divisions was still in Virginia but south of Richmond watching for enemy movements from the Norfolk area — he would not be a factor in the third Union effort to cross the upper Rappahannock.

Hooker's plan was pretty much as before, to pull the Army of Northern Virginia out of its entrenchments along the Rappahannock and fight in the open with his superior numbers. Such a move was still possible with his enlarged and now more experienced cavalry. The plan called for the major part of Hooker's force to cross the upper Rappahannock. Most of his cavalry, which numbered more than 10,000, had orders to get behind R. E. Lee's army and cut their communications with Richmond. The main Union force of more than 70,000 was also designated to cross the upper Rappahannock and defeat the Army of Northern Virginia if they stayed to fight. Another force, about 40,000 men, was designated for Fredericksburg and just below as a feint to hold R. E. Lee's attention and forces in that area.[127]

Even though R. E. Lee expected Hooker to bring his army across the Rappahannock, he was caught off guard. Hooker's feint near Fredericksburg was effective because the Confederate commander was predisposed to believe Fredericksburg was the crossing point for Hooker's main force. Consequently, R. E. Lee had Longstreet's corps south watching for a possible attack by Union forces from near Norfolk, Jackson's corps at and below Fredericksburg, and Stuart's cavalry still spread thinly across the landscape.[128]

Generals R. E. Lee and Stuart had Jones's cavalry brigade still in the Shenandoah Valley, Hampton's south of the James River, Fitz Lee's brigade was brought back from Sperryville and held at Culpeper Court House, and W. H. F. Lee's three small regiments guarding the upper

Rappahannock. While only W. H. F. Lee's cavalrymen were in the right place at the right time, they were the smallest brigade in Stuart's cavalry.[129]

At the opening of the Battle of Chancellorsville, the official organization of the Army of Northern Virginia indicates that W. H. F. Lee's brigade was relatively strong because it contained the 2nd North Carolina, as well as the 5th, 9th, 10th, 13th, and 15th Virginia cavalries.[130] Even if the above list of regiments had reflected W. H. F. Lee's strength, the brigade would have been brushed aside by Hooker's much larger force which was about to cross the river at their position — in fact, however, W. H. F. Lee did not have even this force to slow Hooker's crossing. Rosser's 5th Virginia Cavalry had originally been assigned to W. H. F. Lee's new brigade, but it never left Fitz Lee's brigade; finally it was reassigned, to stay where it was. The 15th Virginia had been on picket duty around Fredericksburg when it was assigned to the new brigade and it was still there. The 10th Virginia, on R. E. Lee's instructions, had been left on picket duty below Port Royal when W. H. F. Lee was ordered to Orange Court House and the upper Rappahannock around the first of April. This meant the Confederate force on the Rappahannock in front of two-thirds of Hooker's army was the 9th and 13th Virginia cavalries along with a portion of the 2nd North Carolina Cavalry (Companies C and K were still detached and down with Longstreet in front of Suffolk). The 2nd North Carolina Cavalry had fewer mounted men on the upper Rappahannock then any other regiment on April 28 — about 110 mounted men and 130 without serviceable mounts. Colonel W. H. F. Payne, of the 4th Virginia Cavalry, had once again been brought in to command the 2nd North Carolina Cavalry while their colonel was still detached. Fitz Lee's brigade was in reserve at Culpeper Court House and numbered around 800 men in the saddle during April.[131]

HOOKER CROSSES THE RAPPAHANNOCK RIVER

Most of Joseph Hooker's invasion force assembled above the Rappahannock on April 28 with orders to cross the river early the next morning. George Stoneman detached three regiments of cavalry and one light battery from Thomas C. Devin's brigade to lead the Union infantry through Culpeper County. They were accompanied by their division commander, Alfred Pleasonton. These cavalry units were assigned to escort the 12th Army Corps under Henry W. Slocum; the 11th Corps, temporally under Slocum for the march to the Rapidan; and the 5th Corps under the command of Meade. Slocum took the 11th and 12th Corps in the direction of Germanna Ford, while Meade headed for Ely's Ford a little further down on the Rapidan River. The 8th Pennsylvania Cavalry, under Huey, was assigned to the 5th Army Corps; the 17th Pennsylvania Cavalry, under Kellogg, was assigned to the 11th Corps; and the 6th New York Cavalry, under Duncan McVicar, accompanied the 12th Army Corps.[132]

The invasion began when Kellogg led the 17th Pennsylvania Cavalry across the river, first in small boats, then on a pontoon bridge near Kelly's Ford on April 28 to scout the area — the advance crossed around 6:00 P.M. His men covered several miles as they moved toward Culpeper Court House, and along the way they saw only a few dismounted Confederate pickets — they were probably dismounted cavalrymen from the 2nd North Carolina who were in that area. The pickets retired into the woods. The retiring Confederates pickets did their job and by 9:00 P.M. at Culpeper Court House, Stuart was notified of the crossing.[133]

Kellogg's advance force apparently cut through the middle of the dismounted 2nd North Carolina cavalrymen and in the process cut some of them off from their comrades further down river near Kelly's Ford. Although their picket line had been pierced, most of the dismounted men of the 2nd North Carolina Cavalry stayed in place. The Muster Roll for Company D of the 2nd North Carolina includes the following entry: "...most of the men remained in the rifle pits until the morning of April 29...." The same Muster Roll also includes the following statement, "On about 3 o'clock on the morning of the 29th of April all the mounted men in the regiment under Col. W. H. F. Payne (of the 4th Va. Cavalry) were ordered to Stone Mills (Stone's Mill?) at that place we charged the enemy's advance guard and drove them back, but were compelled owing to their superior numbers to fall back to Stevensburg, we lost one man and one horse."

Stone's Mill was located about two miles south of Kelly's Ford on Mountain Run, and the Union advance which was charged by the 2nd North Carolina Cavalry at that place was indeed overwhelming.[134]

At about 4:30 A.M. on April 29, the main Union force started across the Rappahannock at Kelly's Ford. The 6th New York Cavalry was in front, followed by Ruger's 3rd Infantry Brigade, and following closely, spread out on both sides of the road leading to Germanna Ford, was Slocum's 12th Corps. The 11th Corps was just behind the 12th Corps—the former was escorted by the 17th Pennsylvania Cavalry. The 6th New York Cavalry in front of Slocum's 12th Corps was under the direct command of A. Pleasonton. G. Meade led the 5th Corps across the river at a ford further down river near the entrance of Mountain Run. Meade took his command toward Ely's Ford on the Rapidan. The cavalry escort in front of Meade was under the direct command of Thomas C. Devin.[135]

As indicated, once across the river, the Union advance encountered the 2nd North Carolina Cavalry. Captain Beardsly of the 6th New York wrote in his report that after they crossed the river they "...met the rebel cavalry in considerable force at Crook's Run. A sharp skirmish ensued, when the enemy retired, leaving as prisoners 1 lieutenant and 1 private of the First North Carolina Cavalry." Beardsly mistakenly identified the 1st North Carolina Cavalry as the enemy in front of him as they crossed the Rappahannock. In fact, the "considerable force" the 6th New York Cavalry skirmished with on that morning near Crook's Run was about 110 mounted cavalrymen from the 2nd North Carolina. The mounted men of the 2nd North Carolina Cavalry had been pulled back from Kelly's Ford about 3:00 A.M. April 29.[136]

After the first encounter with the head of the Union column near Stone's Mill, the 2nd North Carolina was ordered to pull back to Stevensburg. However, at some point in the early morning the 2nd North Carolina was ordered to place itself in front of the 6th New York and slow the column advancing toward Germanna Ford on the Rapidan. Later in the morning, after the 6th New York and Ruger's brigade had passed, W. H. F. Lee acknowledged that the 2nd North Carolina Cavalry had been sent on to Germanna Ford before he placed the 13th Virginia near Kelly's Ford and took the 9th Virginia to Wallis Madden's place.[137]

While the mounted men of the 2nd North Carolina Cavalry were being pushed to the Rapidan by the main Union column, Stuart continued to place the other two regiments in W. H. F. Lee's brigade and Fitz Lee's brigade in various locations to monitor the magnitude and direction of the advancing Union column. He had W. H. F. Lee send Chambliss's 13th Virginia Cavalry and one piece of artillery to a position between Brandy Station and Kelly's Ford to support the dismounted men of the 2nd North Carolina—the latter were still on the roads leading from the ford and under instructions to harass the enemy.

The 13th Virginia Cavalry was more than likely the force encountered by Colonel Kellogg and the 17th Pennsylvania after they moved toward Culpeper around sunrise on April 29. Kellogg described the enemy force he met as "consisting of about 300 cavalry, one section of artillery, and some infantry." The 13th Virginia spent most of the morning fighting. W. H. F. Lee had the 9th Virginia on a hill nearby in support (the dismounted men of the 9th Virginia Cavalry had been in the rifle pits along with the dismounted of the 2nd North Carolina).[138] Once he sensed the magnitude of the invasion, Stuart sent for W. H. F. Lee's 10th Virginia Cavalry that had not been moved up with the other regiments on April 1.[139]

Sometime during the morning fighting, Stuart heard that the major enemy force was passing below him, near Willis Madden's place. He left the 13th Virginia Cavalry to slow the Union force, and moved with the 9th Virginia to Madden's, about half way between Stevensburg and Kelly's Ford. At the same time, he called for Fitz Lee's brigade. Around daylight, Stuart had moved Fitz Lee's brigade from Culpeper Court House to Brandy Station where they were held in reserve until instructed to drop down around Willis Madden's place. While at Madden's, word reached Colonel Wickham of the 4th Virginia (and presumably Stuart) that the enemy was crossing the Rapidan at Germanna Ford.[140]

When Stuart reached Madden's place with Fitz Lee's brigade and the 9th Virginia, he found the end of Slocum's column moving toward the Rapidan (it was about the same time the 6th New York Cavalry and Ruger's infantry

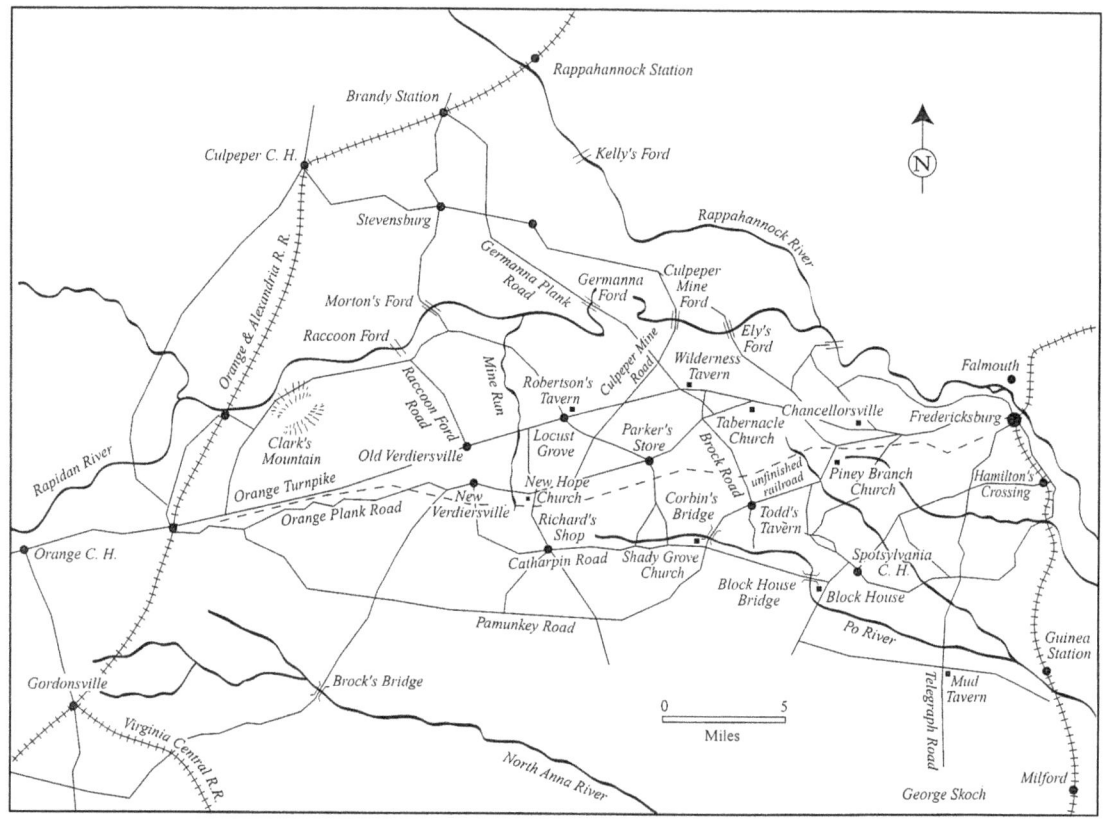

2.5: Chancellorsville, Mine Run and Wilderness Campaigns

were pushing the mounted men of the 2nd North Carolina Cavalry across the Rapidan at Germanna Ford). All Stuart could do at that point was attack the column, take prisoners and gather information about the enemy's intentions. With Fitz Lee's brigade in advance, this was accomplished. They took prisoners from the 12th, 11th, and 5th Corps—probably stragglers from the 12th Corps, the main body of which had passed beyond that point well before noon.[141]

Late on April 29, Stuart was instructed to join R. E. Lee's left below the Rapidan River. He put Fitz Lee's brigade on the road for Raccoon Ford immediately. By nightfall, W. H. F. Lee fell back to Culpeper Court House with the 9th Virginia. Chambliss's 13th Virginia was left to slow the on-coming main body of Union cavalry—Stoneman spent the night of the 29th at Madden's crossroads.[142]

Later that night the 13th Virginia Cavalry was able to cut through its near encirclement by the enemy and join their commander at Culpeper Court House. The next morning, W. H. F. Lee moved with the 9th and 13th Virginia cavalries from Culpeper Court House to Rapidan Station some twenty-five miles west of Chancellorsville. His command was to protect Gordonsville and the railroad. As it turned out, that was a monumental task because Stoneman was leading a cavalry force of over 6,000 men in that direction to sever communications between the Army of Northern Virginia and Richmond.[143]

2ND NORTH CAROLINA CAVALRY SLOWS THE UNION ADVANCE

During the day, on April 29, while W. H. F. Lee and Stuart were trying to get a handle on what was passing them near Kelly's Ford, the mounted men from the 2nd North Carolina were busy trying to slow Slocum's unstoppable column on its march for the Rapidan. The 6th New York, under McVicar, was engaged with the enemy cavalry at its front throughout the march to Germanna Ford. Naturally, in his official report, A. Pleasonton placed himself at the front of the column directing the cavalry skirmishes with the 2nd North Carolina throughout the day. According to T. H. Ruger, who commanded the lead infantry unit just behind the 6th New York Cavalry, one regiment of Confederate cavalry moved in front of them when they had traveled only 2½ miles from Kelly's Ford and skirmishing occurred between the cavalries until they were within 3 miles of Germanna Ford.[144]

This was important because later Stuart received some criticism for not placing cavalry in front of the enemy's 5th, 11th, and 12th corps as they marched to the Rapidan. Instead, his critics argued, Stuart held most of the cavalrymen with him near Kelly's Ford early in the day and then, when ordered to do so, he moved W. H. F. Lee and Fitz Lee west of the enemy columns and south toward the Rapidan to join R. E. Lee's left. The critics were wrong when they argued that no cavalry had been put in front of the advancing enemy column — the small mounted force of about 100 troopers of the 2nd North Carolina Cavalry was there.[145]

Perhaps the saddest commentary surrounding the entire issue was that the small band of brave men from the 2nd North Carolina Cavalry stood in front of and engaged an enemy column, which was propelled by the momentum of nearly 50,000 men, and no Confederate commander acknowledged their outstanding job that day.

In any case, when the advance units of the 6th New York Cavalry approached the Rapidan at several points near Germanna Ford, they encountered about 150 of their enemy who were building a bridge across the river. Many of the Confederate bridge builders were caught on the wrong side of the river, and their orderly retreat was impossible.

As noted earlier, J. E. B. Stuart had sent two couriers earlier in the day to Germanna and Ely's Fords to warn of the Union force coming their way but neither got through. The first warning the bridge builders received apparently came from the men of the 2nd North Carolina Cavalry who disengaged the approaching enemy a couple of miles before reaching the river and joined their comrades for an impossible stand at the riverside.

The dismounted bridge builders and the 2nd North Carolina Cavalry held off the 6th New York Cavalry's advance until Ruger sent the 2nd Massachusetts to the right, the 3rd Wisconsin to the left, and the 27th Indiana in behind the 6th New York Cavalry followed by artillery, all at the double-quick, toward the river. The Confederates were quickly enveloped and any attempt to retreat would have exposed them to a deadly fire from Union skirmishers already at the river's edge on their flanks. Several were killed or wounded, and over 100 prisoners were taken, while only some were able to escape through the deep waters. Only six cavalrymen from the 2nd North Carolina were among the captured in that fight. The 6th New York Cavalry had 1 killed and 4 men wounded at Germanna Ford that day.[146] The 6th New York Cavalry and Ruger's infantry crossed the Rapidan at that point.

Over on the other road to the Rapidan, Meade's column, lead by the 8th Pennsylvania Cavalry, had an easier time of it on April 29. No Confederate unit had been assigned to harass or even monitor their march. They crossed the Rapidan at Ely's Ford and drove the Confederate pickets for a couple of miles before settling in for the night on the south side of the river.[147]

Confederate Cavalry on the Rapidan River

Further upriver, after marching half the night, Stuart and Fitz Lee's brigade crossed the Rapidan near Raccoon Ford and stopped for a short rest. Fitz Lee's 3rd Virginia Cavalry, under the command of Thomas Owens, was selected to continue the march, without rest, eastward on the south side of the Rapidan to discover how far the enemy had penetrated the area south of the river, and if possible to get between the enemy and Fredericksburg. They succeeded because the Union force that crossed at Germanna Ford met resistance on the road leading down to Plank Road, and Meade's force that crossed at Ely's Ford met enough resistance on the road down to Chancellorsville to encourage them to camp for the night along the river and not push to the crossroads called Chancellorsville as the day came to an end. If they had continued to Chancellorsville, the Union troops would have been in a position to move behind R. E. Lee's army — Lee needed time to turn his left flank to meet the advance that would come along Plank Road. The meager, exhausted, and hungry Confederate cavalry on the roads leading from the river to Chancellorsville gave him the time.

A portion of W. H. F. Lee's 15th Virginia Cavalry, which had been on picket duty along the river from Fredericksburg to Ely's Ford for months, suddenly found itself in front of Meade's advance force after the latter crossed the river at Ely's Ford. Their presence gave R. E. Lee time to move infantry from near the U.S. Ford on the Rappahannock. Some of the 15th Virginia Cavalry may also have been as far up river as Germanna Ford where the 2nd North Carolina was pushed across by the 6th New York Cavalry and Ruger's infantry. On the roads coming down from the two fords, Confederate cavalrymen from the 15th Virginia and 2nd North Carolina played a role in slowing the enemy advance south of the river. In addition, some companies from W. H. F. Lee's 10th Virginia Cavalry made it to the area just in time to be pushed back from the river by the Union advance, but they like their comrades had to be pushed back, which required their enemy to deploy, skirmish and above all, spend time.[148] The 3rd Virginia from Fitz Lee's brigade arrived on the scene very late on April 29 and joined the cavalry picket lines. Both the 6th New York Cavalry and the 8th Pennsylvania Cavalry with Slocum's and Meade's columns behind them pulled their pickets in along the river, centered on Germanna and Ely's Fords respectively, and camped for the night. The 2nd North Carolina and the 15th Virginia cavalries bought R. E. Lee the time he needed.

The Confederate cavalry shield gave Major General R. H. Anderson time to move troops west on Plank Road toward Chancellorsville. At 6:45 P.M. on the 29th, R. E. Lee sent a message to Anderson instructing him to move the left wing of his division from the U.S. Ford to cover the road leading from Chancellorsville to Fredericksburg. Lee stressed the urgency of the move by pointing out that Union cavalry and infantry had crossed Germanna Ford early in the afternoon and later cavalry had crossed at Ely's Ford. He was greatly concerned that the enemy was between them and Stuart who was not yet across the Rapidan.[149]

Confederate Infantry Moves Up

Richard H. Anderson first sent the brigades of William Mahone and Carnot Posey who were on the Army of Northern Virginia's left flank. They moved up quickly from the U.S. Ford toward Chancellorsville. Anderson also ordered Wright's brigade to the front, and he met Mahone and Posey at Chancellorsville around midnight, and they could feel the presence of the Union pickets on the roads from Germanna and Ely's Fords. At that point, Anderson may not have been aware of the pickets from the 2nd North Carolina and the 15th Virginia cavalries that stood between his force and the enemy on the roads from the two fords. In any case, Anderson and his commanders did feel that the dense wilderness around them did not provide a good defensive position — it was certainly an uneasy night. Anderson had a pretty good idea of the size of the enemy forces that were resting near the two fords and knew his flank on the river side was exposed. Consequently, Anderson decided to pull his troops back early the next morning toward Fredericksburg, just out of the Wilderness, near Tabernacle Church where the old U.S. Mine Road, the Plank Road and Old Turnpike all converged. He wanted to make his stand in a place where he could entrench and face the advancing Union forces, with less concern for his right flank.[150]

By early morning April 30, Anderson's troops began their pull back, and by that time the Union cavalry was already on the attack, and they captured some of the rear guard as Anderson moved his three brigades east on Plank Road and the Old Turnpike to Tabernacle Church. They were accompanied by fog and rain.[151]

The 2nd North Carolina had been pushed down the Germanna Ford road to the Plank Road on April 29, and they became part of Anderson's unofficial rear guard for the pull back — unofficial because even though they were between Anderson's and Slocum's forces before, during, and after the pullback, they were still detached from W. H. F. Lee's brigade and under Stuart's command — and Stuart only had a general notion of where they were, and in any case he was not in a position to command them. Furthermore, we can not be certain exactly when Anderson became aware of the detached cavalry between his troops and the enemy.

Upon his withdrawal from Chancellorsville, Anderson's rear was attacked by enemy cavalry coming at them from both fords, i.e. from both the Old Turnpike and Ely's Ford road. The 2nd North Carolina Cavalry was more than likely pushed back along the Old Turnpike with its rear and northern flank exposed to the enemy coming down the Ely's Ford road. The 2nd North Carolina lost nine cavalrymen on April 30—most likely during Anderson's pullback.

As indicated, while both the 2nd North Carolina and the 3rd Virginia cavalries were detached from their brigades and under Stuart's command, he was in no position to direct them. Stuart had stayed with Fitz Lee and his brigade near Raccoon Ford until April 30. Stuart and Fitz Lee's command moved early that morning to place themselves between the enemy and Fredericksburg. They swung a little south before turning east and encountered Union cavalry at Wilderness Tavern. About that time, they got word that Union forces had already occupied Chancellorsville, Stuart then led the cavalrymen with him to Todd's Tavern and after more fighting with the enemy, on toward Spotsylvania Court House. Union cavalry had penetrated to within a mile or two of Spotsylvania Court House which resulted in another clash near that place. Stuart and the cavalrymen with him had had very little sleep or food but a full share of fighting by the morning of May 1 when they arrived on Jackson's left flank—they had finally connected with the left wing of their army as ordered April 29.[152]

In spite of the difficulties Stuart had moving below the enemy to arrive on Jackson's left, he did find time, early on April 30 to send a message to R. E. Lee informing him that two detached cavalry regiments, the 2nd North Carolina under W. H. F. Payne and the 3rd Virginia under T. H. Owen, were on Plank Road in front of the enemy, and that they had been ordered to report to the commanding general himself. At 2:30 P.M. April 30, R. E. Lee sent a message to R. H. Anderson informing him of the presence of the two detached cavalry regiments on Plank Road. R. E. Lee's message to Anderson included the following advice for the use of the two cavalry regiments: "...direct them to keep in your front, and to keep you advised of all movements of the enemy, and to delay his progress as much as possible."[153] This places the 2nd North Carolina as well as the 3rd Virginia cavalries in front of Anderson at Tabernacle Church late on April 30 covering the three roads leading eastward to the church.

By April 30, R. E. Lee was fairly certain the Union army's main attack was aiming to turn his left and get to his rear at Fredericksburg, and he notified President Davis accordingly—he ended his message to Davis with this expression of concern: "If I had Longstreet's division, would feel safe." (R. E. Lee had Anderson's and McLaws's divisions, but the bulk of Longstreet's corps was down around Suffolk.) On that same day, R. E. Lee issued Special Orders No. 121 in which he instructed Major General Lafayette McLaws to leave one brigade on the line behind Fredericksburg and then move his division as soon as possible up to support Anderson at Tabernacle Church. He also instructed Jackson to leave one division on picket behind and below Fredericksburg and move the rest of his corps to Tabernacle Church "...and make arrangements to repulse the enemy." Jackson left Early's division, and was on his way.[154] At that point, R. E. Lee and his commanders knew Hooker's main thrust was coming over the Rapidan at Germanna and Ely's Fords.

Just before sunrise on May 1, McLaws moved up to Anderson. Jackson arrived around 8:00 A.M. and put a stop to work on the trenches. He ordered the Confederate troops to get ready for an advance on the enemy—he wanted to find and fight the enemy. By 11:00 A.M. Jackson had the Confederates on the move. Anderson was on Plank Road with the 3rd Virginia Cavalry out front feeling for the enemy pickets—Jackson rode up front of Anderson with his corps in close support. McLaws and his troopers were put on the Old Turnpike heading in the same direction, toward Chancellorsville. McLaws also had cavalry in his advance, but he did not bother to identify them.[155] (The only cavalry regiment not accounted for in this action was the 2nd North Carolina and they were on or near that road.)

After marching only a short distance on the Old Turnpike, McLaws's advance came upon the enemy; then his cavalry reported that the enemy was also advancing along the Old Mine Road. McLaws sent word to Jackson who was marching on the near-parallel Plank Road, and the latter sent word to hold. In a matter of minutes, Jackson's column on Plank Road was also engaged with a heavy force of Union troops. General Stuart arrived on Plank Road and Fitz Lee's cavalry was right behind him coming from Spotsylvania Court House and their march around the enemy from Raccoon Ford over the previous two days. Jackson instructed Stuart to "Keep closed on Chancellorsville." Fighting on both roads was heavy and Hooker's men fell back a short distance, then made a stand. The process was repeated several time during the afternoon, until they came upon the Union's strong, entrenched position just before nightfall.[156]

R. E. Lee's offensive move stalled Hooker's advance — his campaign was not over by any means but it was brought to a halt and entrenched by Confederate boldness. By nightfall, the Confederate columns were within a mile or two of Chancellorsville and in sight of the Union entrenchments at that place. The 2nd North Carolina Cavalry was still attached to Anderson and they were near him down on Plank Road or still up on the pike near McLaws's command. The two cavalry regiments were moved around late in the day. The 3rd Virginia Cavalry had spent the day with Jackson and Anderson on the Plank Road but by nightfall had rejoined their brigade when Stuart and Fitz Lee arrived on the Confederate left. Fitz Lee's cavalry spent the night near Jackson — his 1st, 2nd, part of the 3rd, and 5th Virginia Cavalries on the left would accompany Jackson on his flank march the next day. Fitz Lee's 4th Virginia under the command of Wickham, and part of the 3rd Virginia under Owen guarded the Old Mine Road to the Rappahannock. At that point, the only cavalry regiment in the area detached from its brigade, was the 2nd North Carolina Cavalry. They spent the night on Anderson's and McLaws's line.[157]

R. E. Lee spent a good part of May 1 assessing Hooker's strength east and west of Chancellorsville — he decided Hooker's right was most vulnerable. How to attack it was another issue. During the night of May 1 and into the next morning, R. E. Lee conferred with Jackson on how best to take the enemy's right wing. Stuart had sent Fitz Lee to find Hooker's right, and he returned with the news that the Union right was indeed "in the air." R. E. Lee gave Jackson the go-ahead for his flank march.[158]

Early on May 2, Jackson moved his command southwest to swing around the enemy's right flank, and Anderson moved over to fill the spot vacated on the Confederate left. Fitz Lee with most of his cavalry brigade escorted Jackson on his flanking movement that day. The Confederate gamble was that Hooker would not attack early on that day. Jackson left only Anderson's and McLaws's divisions with R. E. Lee, totaling approximately 14,000 men in front of Hooker's force of about 73,000, while Jackson took his force of fewer than 30,000 around the enemy's right in the long flanking move. R. E. Lee stayed with Anderson and McLaws at the front. At that time, Hooker had the best part of five corps in the Chancellorsville area (and two more across the river below Fredericksburg). By afternoon, Fitz Lee and his cavalry had located the Union right and waited for Jackson to come up and position his troops for the attack. At about 6:00 P.M., Jackson burst upon the surprised Union troops on Hooker's right. As Jackson began his attack, R. E. Lee had his troops press the enemy along the entire front to hold Hooker's attention.[159]

Stuart did not accompany Fitz Lee's brigade on the flank march, and because the wilderness area offered few opportunities for cavalry operations, Stuart had asked permission to take the 1st Virginia Cavalry and the 16th North Carolina Infantry to hold the road leading to Ely's Ford — one of the possible escape routes should Hooker's army retreat as Jackson fully expected them to do once he reached their rear. As Stuart approached Ely's Ford, he found Averell's cavalry division there and began preparations for an attack.[160]

Late in the day, when the final push on the Union right was under way, Jackson went forward with a small party to assess the next point of attack. Upon returning through Confederate lines, he and others in his party were wounded — he was removed to the field hospital at Wilderness Tavern where his arm was amputated. The decision was made to have General J. E. B. Stuart take over Jackson's command for the remainder of the operation.[161]

About the time Stuart had the 16th North Carolina in position over on the road to Ely's Ford, he was notified that Jackson and others were down, and he was assigned Jackson's command. Stuart instructed the commander of the 16th North Carolina to fire a few rounds at the enemy camp and then return to its brigade.[162]

When Stuart reached Jackson's command around midnight, he found that the Union forces had already mounted a powerful counterattack and pushed Jackson's line hard, but the Confederates had held and their advantage was not lost. It was early morning before Stuart received orders from R. E. Lee and the command could be moved forward.[163]

The fighting was severe on May 3 around Chancellorsville, but Stuart continued to press the enemy until his right connected with Anderson's left and R. E. Lee's army was united again. Once his right was secure, Stuart massed his infantry for an all-out assault on Hooker. The entrenched Union troops held Stuart's command back twice, but they were overwhelmed by Stuart's third assault. Stuart was at the head of Jackson's command, on horseback and reportedly, as he carried the Union entrenchments, Stuart sang out in a ringing voice, "Old Joe Hooker, won't you come out of the Wilderness?" At about the same time, Anderson, with the 2nd North Carolina Cavalry on one of his flanks, took Chancellorsville.[164]

Hooker pulled out of Chancellorsville to a new position near the Rappahannock. When calling for reinforcement, late on May 2, Hooker also instructed Sedgwick to cross the Rappahannock at Fredericksburg, dispose of Early's command and close in on R. E. Lee from the rear. Sedgwick moved forcefully through Fredericksburg on the morning of May 3, and then west on Plank Road. As mentioned, Hooker had not held R. E. Lee's front, which allowed Lee to turn more of his force toward the approaching Sedgwick.

In fact, when R. E. Lee discovered that Sedgwick had crossed the river and was coming at his rear on the Plank Road, he sent McLaws's division and one of Anderson's brigades immediately to stop Sedgwick. Detachments of cavalry were placed in front of and on the flanks of McLaws's and Anderson's troops near Salem Church on Plank Road — cavalrymen from the 15th Virginia Cavalry were brought over to share the burden with the 2nd North Carolina Cavalry. The Confederate line across Plank Road was successful and on the morning of May 4, Sedgwick was in the vise rather than R. E. Lee. Sedgwick was stalled by McLaws's and Anderson's troopers about halfway between Fredericksburg and Chancellorsville. Then General Early came at him from behind, along Telegraph Road. R. E. Lee then left Stuart with Jackson's command in front of Hooker, and himself took the balance of Anderson's division to join McLaws and Early in an all-out assault on Sedgwick. Around 6:00 P.M., Anderson's and Early's commands drove Sedgwick's force back in the direction of the Rappahannock. R. E. Lee assumed Stuart with Jackson's command could hold Hooker's 90,000 men in place, because Hooker personally was already defeated. By the end of the day on May 4, Sedgwick was encircled with his back to the river and receiving Robert E. Lee's full attention. Expecting no support from Hooker, Sedgwick pulled his troops across the Rappahannock during the night. By the morning of May 5, Sedgwick was pushed back across the river and Hooker ordered his corps commanders to pull back to the U.S. Ford. With Sedgwick over the river, the Confederate commanders then turned their attention back to Hooker. General Early was left in front of Sedgwick, while McLaws and Anderson returned to Chancellorsville. R. E. Lee did not get another confrontation with Hooker, however, because by the afternoon Hooker himself was across the ford, and during the stormy night of May 5, Hooker retired his army back across the river.[165]

By May 6, Pleasonton had his and Averell's former cavalry commands back across the Rappahannock.[166] Hooker's army was again watching the Rappahannock from the northern bank. By most measures, the Army of Northern Virginia had won. Robert E. Lee outmaneuvered and flanked an army nearly twice the size of his, and was able to take control of the battle and emerge victorious. The cost, however, was high — Confederate losses were around 13,000 men and Hooker's around 17,000, but such a ratio of losses could not be sustained by the South.

THE 2ND NORTH CAROLINA CAVALRY AND W. H. F. LEE'S BRIGADE

The 2nd North Carolina Cavalry took losses on April 29 at both ends of Slocum's march from the Rappahannock to the Rapidan. They were at various times in front of or on one of R. H. Anderson's flanks during the fighting around Chancellorsville. In those positions they took losses on both April 30 and May 3. Their temporary regimental commander, W. H. F. Payne, did not write a report of their activities, and their brigade commander, W. H. F. Lee, was not in the area. The regiment was noticed briefly by R. E. Lee and J. E. B. Stuart in the beginning, but in a battle as large and dynamic as the one around Chancellorsville at that time, it is certainly understandable that the two generals lost track of a small regiment of about 100 horsemen. Early mention of the detached 2nd North Carolina Cavalry's presence came when it was assigned to R. E. Lee by Stuart, and on the same day from R. E. Lee to Anderson. Apparently all any of the commanders knew for sure was that the cavalrymen were in front of or on the flank of one of Anderson's regiments or detachments.

Losses for the 2nd North Carolina Cavalry on May 3 are consistent enough to indicate the 2nd North Carolina Cavalry was also engaged in the activities around Salem Church. They lost six cavalrymen in the fight to stop Sedgwick. Their recorded combat losses for the Chancellorsville Campaign were as follows.

Combat Losses in the 2nd North Carolina Cavalry April 29–May 7, 1863

Trooper	Age	Co.	Fate
James Eason	24	D	captured, April 29
Jacob Dale	39	A	captured, April 29
William H. Wellington	34	D	captured, April 29
Jesse Simpson	24	E	captured, April 29
James L. Drake	22	G	captured, April 29
James H. Cox	27	H	captured, April 29
Augustus Cullifer	21	H	captured, April 29
Robert W. Atkinson		E	captured, April 30
John A. P. Conoly	29	D	captured, April 30
Alexander Bedsole	21	D	captured, April 30
Richard McGlogan	47	D	captured, April 30
Warren C. Moore	43	D	captured, April 30
John W. Simms	20	D	captured, April 30
William H. Warren	22	G	captured, April 30
John W. Pritchard	32	H	captured, April 30
Ellas Williams	22	I	captured, April 30
Yancy S. Corem		F	wounded, May 2
Thomas J. Mins, Farrier	48	D	captured, May 2
James Carter	23	D	captured, May 3
William J. Davis	26	D	captured, May 3
Neill A. Johnson	24	D	captured, May 3
James F. Price	24	D	captured, May 3
Hardy Burns	25	I	captured, May 3
Rufus J. Byrum	23	I	captured, May 3

The source for this table is *North Carolina Troops 1861–1865, A Roster*, compiled by Louis H. Manarin (Raleigh, N.C., State Division of Archives and History), vol. II, Cavalry, pages 104–177. (See Appendix for more information on the men listed above, page 393.)

Once again many of the cavalrymen from the 2nd North Carolina were dismounted and in the rifle pits along the Rappahannock when Hooker's cavalry stormed across in front of their infantry early on April 29. The regiment lost at least one man in the pits. The mounted men of the 2nd North Carolina remained in front of the advancing Union column on its march to the Rapidan River during the day—they skirmished at their front during the march, slowing the invaders and fought with them at Germanna Ford on the Rapidan. They lost six men in the process, all of whom are listed as captured near Fredericksburg. The day after Hooker had his army across the Rapidan, R. E. Lee moved Anderson's division forward to stop the Union advance. The cavalrymen of the 2nd North Carolina were between them, and when Anderson decided to strengthen his position on the morning of April 30, the 2nd Cavalry covered his pullback. In the process, the 2nd North Carolina lost eight men. On May 2, R. E. Lee commanded Anderson's and McLaws's divisions in front of Hooker's army—Lee had them press hard on Hooker's line to draw attention away from Jackson's flanking move. The men of the 2nd North Carolina were on one of Anderson's flanks and lost two men in the press. On May 3, Hooker brought Sedgwick's command through Fredericksburg to attack R. E. Lee from behind. Lee turned Anderson's command to stop and hold Sedgwick until others could be turned and moved to cover the Confederate rear. The 2nd North Carolina Cavalry was still Anderson's sensor out front on that day, and 6 men were captured in the fighting.

While W. H. F. Lee's 2nd North Carolina and 15th Virginia cavalries were directly involved in the fighting around Chancellorsville, W. H. F. Lee with the 9th and 13th Virginia Cavalries were busy trying to contain George Stoneman's raids in the rear of the Army of Northern Virginia. The 9th and 13th Virginia Cavalries were the last of Stuart's command to leave the Brandy Station area after Hooker advanced across the Rappahannock. W. H. F. Lee left Culpeper Court House with his two regiments early on April 30 for Rapidan Station. His job was to keep the Army of Northern Virginia's communications open to Richmond. Stoneman left the area around Madden's Crossroads and was not far behind W. H. F. Lee's two regiments heading for the Rapidan River. His job, on the other hand, was to cut "...the enemy's communications with Richmond by the Fredericksburg route, checking his retreat over those lines" and that all else was "subservient to that object."[167]

George Stoneman crossed the Rapidan with his main force at Raccoon Ford by 10:00 A.M. on April 30. At that point, W. H. F. Lee's two regiments could not possibly monitor, let alone stop, Stoneman's dispersed activity. Stoneman continued his raiding, one step ahead of W. H. F. Lee's small cavalry force until May 5, when he began to hear rumors of Hooker's defeat and retreat back across the Rappahannock. Then Stoneman began moving back toward Raccoon Ford on the Rapidan — the second part of Stoneman's mission, to intercept the Army of Northern Virginia as they retreated to Richmond could apparently be scrapped. By daylight on May 7, Stoneman took his cavalrymen back across the Rapidan, and the head of his column reached Kelly's Ford on the Rappahannock by 9:00 that night. Pleasonton had already crossed the Rappahannock with cavalry that had been in the Battle of Chancellorsville.[168]

Though Stoneman's entire cavalry force would probably have served the Union better in and around Chancellorsville guarding the flanks of Hooker's infantry during the battle, his orders were clear and they had him elsewhere. It appears he carried out his assignment aggressively, yet he was reassigned. Pleasonton placed himself at the head of his cavalry column and led Hooker's infantry into battle. His position was high profile and hard to fault. In any case, for a number of political reasons, Pleasonton took temporary command of the cavalry on May 22; Stoneman was reassigned on June 5. (He took a desk job in Washington for several reasons, one of which was health; another was Hooker's and others' need for a scapegoat.)[169]

The fighting at Chancellorsville was followed by several weeks of rest for the Army of Northern Virginia and the inevitable reorganization. With General Jackson gone, Robert E. Lee organized the army into three corps rather than two: they were to be commanded by Longstreet, Ewell, and A. P. Hill. R. E. Lee had Longstreet on his way north from Suffolk before the Battle of Chancellorsville was over. That included bringing the Second Squadron of the 2nd North Carolina Cavalry — Longstreet joined the Army of Northern Virginia, and the cavalrymen joined the 2nd North Carolina on May 20, 1863 near Brandy Station where Stuart was collecting his cavalry.

Before we join the united squadrons of the 2nd North Carolina Cavalry, however, let us consider what the Second Squadron (Companies C and K) had experienced since leaving North Carolina in September of 1862, on detached service, ending up under James Longstreet's command.

Second Squadron Detached; Duty in Virginia

While Confederate troops pulled out of North Carolina, and the 2nd North Carolina Cavalry was busy with holding actions around Kinston, the Second Squadron of the 2nd North Carolina rotated to duty at Hamilton, North Carolina. At the time, the squadron consisted of Companies C and K and was commanded by Captain John G. Boothe of Company C. Captain Josiah Turner of Company K had been seriously injured on April 13, 1862 at Gillett's farm, so Lieutenant William A. Graham Jr. commanded Company K.

By late 1862, officials in North Carolina were increasingly concerned about minimizing losses of property. Governor Clark understood that for the time being the territory in the eastern part of the State could not be regained. Nonetheless, he continued to request sufficient troops to make raids in the Union held towns of New Bern, Plymouth, and Washington. His concerns and actions were largely responses to wealthy and prominent citizens who found their property behind enemy lines.

In those places Confederate citizens were harassed by Union soldiers and local residents sympathetic to the Union, but of greater concern to Confederate officials was the loss of property and slaves in these areas. Increasingly enslaved people had little difficulty finding their way to occupied cities, and they did in increasing numbers — from the riverside cities, they were often transported out of the area. To those who possessed slaves, that was an unsustainable loss of wealth, and they continually pressured the Governor and military commanders in the area for relief. In response, Governor Clark asked Confederate officials for enough troops to raid the population centers and regain some lost slaves and make Union sympathizers aware of the fact that the Confederacy was not defeated. There is little doubt that military officials in the state were preoccupied with these political and economic issues. For instance, on August 7, Brigadier General Clingman in a correspondence to his commander, D. H. Hill, wrote the following from Goldsboro.

Negroes are escaping rapidly, probably a million of dollars' worth weekly in all. It is estimated that one-third of the negroes in the State are east of this line of railroad, and gentlemen complain, with some reason, that that section of the State is in danger of being ruined if these things continue.

It strikes me that, if we had force sufficient to accomplish the object, negroes and other movable property of value within or near the enemy's lines should be brought away and intercourse prohibited. I think it unwise to attempt it, however, until there is an effective force....[170]

However, the Governor and military officials in North Carolina could not count on getting troops from the lines in Virginia and had to make do with what they had in the area.[171] The Second Squadron was part of the minimal force left in North Carolina for such duty.

The Second Squadron's journey from Kinston to Hamilton around August 1 was uneventful, as was their first few weeks at Camp Springreen near Hamilton. In a letter to his sister, Private Levi Lockhart wrote the following of their time: "The weather is very pleasant here at this time.... We see a fine time here; we don't have any guard duty to do hardly; we have our horses to attend to, and that is about all."[172]

The "fine time" Levi mentioned in his letter did not last long. The squadron was soon part of the effort by the Governor and military commanders in North Carolina to "secure" citizens' property in occupied areas. In spite of Clingman's reservations about taking action without adequate manpower, raids into occupied towns were made. Members of the Second Squadron participated in one such action on August 31, 1862; fourteen men from Company K, under Lieutenant John P. Lockhart, were in a skirmish near Plymouth. About a week later, they were involved in another, larger raid at Washington, North Carolina.

THE FIGHT AT WASHINGTON, NORTH CAROLINA, SEPTEMBER 6, 1862

Lieutenant Colonel Stephen D. Pool was in command of the Confederate force sent against the Federal garrison at the town of Washington. Pool collected his units just behind the Confederate picket line on the evening of September 5. He had a force of about 850 men—around 600 infantry, Adam's battery, and several companies of cavalry including the Second Squadron's companies C and K.

They moved late on September 5 and halted just outside of town early on the 6th. Seeing the enemy through the foggy daybreak, the infantry charged the Union breastworks about half a mile outside of town and drove the occupants out and across a field into town. When the infantry started its move, the cavalry on another approach to town were lined up for their charge.

Captain Tucker's Cavalry Company was first, followed by Captain John G. Boothe's companies C and K from the 2nd Cavalry. The heavy morning fog helped Confederate cavalrymen pass through the Federal pickets with very little difficulty. The cavalry units then stormed into town from several directions, yelling and firing at will. Many of the Federal troops were still asleep and were in total confusion by the time they reached the street. The Confederate cavalry continued to gallop up and down the streets, spreading confusion as their infantry moved closer.

Just after the Confederate cavalrymen had successfully charged in and occupied the main streets in town, they saw Union cavalry coming into town from another direction. Lieutenant Colonel Mix of the 3rd New York Cavalry had just led his troops out of town on the road to Plymouth when he heard the commotion in town. He turned his command and galloped back into town.

Confederate cavalrymen from Captain Tucker's company were the first to see Union cavalry entering town. The Union cavalry turned left before clashing with their enemy. The Confederates fired at them as they passed and then charged after them. One member of Tucker's company described the encounter that followed: "We pursued them at full speed, until we arrived in the main street, where we quit the chase and went to work in earnest, shooting and cutting the enemy down on every side." As this clash began, Captain Boothe and his Second Squadron arrived and entered the fighting — there were several charges and countercharges.[173]

Fierce clashes took place simultaneously in many areas of town. At one point a squad of Union cavalry countercharged the men of the Second Squadron and in the exchange, Captain Boothe was shot through his right lung.[174]

The cavalrymen of the Second Squadron, as well as the other Confederate horsemen, continued to drive the enemy back and ride through the streets keeping a reasonable distance from their enemy's big guns — they maintained all the while the sounds of men sensing victory, sounds Lieutenant Colonel Mix of the 3rd New York called "...loud, continuous cheers and demoniac yells of 'Death to the damned Yankees;' 'No prisoners;' 'No quarters,' &c." The excitement was so great that a number of the men in the Second Squadron had more difficulty controlling their horses than they had fighting the enemy. Several were thrown from their mounts but not seriously injured.[175]

When Union forces were pushed back to the cover of their gunboats, and after the fog had lifted, the gunboats began firing their big guns, and the Confederate cavalry and infantry pulled back out of range. The fighting lasted over two hours before the Confederates began to pull back.[176]

One member of Company K, Second Squadron reported in a letter to his hometown newspaper that "Contrabands [slaves in transition] in white fled with their clothes under their arms. Women and children ran about the streets, some crying, and some cursing us as d—d secessionists." The Lieutenant who made this report was clearly aware of their objectives and ended his report with this comment, "The expedition against Washington was made with no view or expectation of holding the place, but for the purpose of destroying or capturing the enemy's stores, and capturing the 'contraband' in his possession."[177]

The 2nd North Carolina Cavalry took one loss in the August 31 raid in Plymouth, and four more in the raid on Washington, North Carolina.

Combat Losses in the Second Squadron August–September, 1862

Trooper	Age	Co.	Fate
Henry T. Bowling		K	captured, August 31
William H. Brothers		C	wounded, September 6
John G. Boothe	39	C	wounded, September 6
John Gray	21	K	killed, September 6
Levi S. Walker		K	captured, September 6

The source used here is *North Carolina Troops 1861–1865, A Roster*, compiled by Louis H. Manarin (Raleigh, N.C., State Division of Archives and History), vol. II, Cavalry, pages 104–177. (See Appendix for more information on the men listed above, page 394.)

Soon after the battle at Washington, North Carolina, around October 15, the Second Squadron moved from Martin County, North Carolina into Virginia. They were still detached from their regiment when ordered by Brigadier General Martin to move toward Richmond.

DREWRY'S BLUFF, VIRGINIA

As indicated, while in Hamilton, North Carolina the squadron's captain was seriously wounded, and William A. Graham Jr. of Company K was given the command — Graham was promoted to captain on September 8 and led the squadron to Virginia. The initial plan was for the squadron to join their regiment near Richmond and then head north for R. E. Lee.

Captain Graham and his command got as far as Petersburg, however, when S. G. French ordered them to report to Brigadier General Junius Daniel at Drewry's Bluff. After arriving in the area, they camped near the Halfway House on Turnpike Road (about halfway between Petersburg and Richmond).[178]

The Second Squadron was thus placed under the direct command of J. Daniels who was commanding about 3,000 effective men (equipped and fit for duty) at Drewry's Bluff. Among his troops, Daniels had Company C, detached from the 3rd North Carolina Cavalry (the 3rd Cavalry had recently been organized, under the command of John A. Baker). Daniels placed the company from the 3rd North Carolina under Captain Graham to form a cavalry battalion with Companies C and K of the 2nd Cavalry.

Their assignment at Drewry's Bluff was to picket the James and Appomattox Rivers, while their commanders organized their expedition to Suffolk—there is a good possibility the 2nd Squadron of the 2nd North Carolina Cavalry was diverted from its rendezvous with its regiment as it passed Petersburg, because Generals Gustavus W. Smith and Samuel G. French were collecting troops for an expedition to Suffolk.

S. G. French planned to take part of Daniels's command from Drewry's Bluff along with Pettigrew's and others to check the movement of Union forces into the Suffolk area. French's effort was plagued with delays however, and perhaps a certain reluctance for the enterprise on the part of both Smith and French —consequently the expedition never materialized. Even though the Second Squadron was temporarily held in the area to participate in the expedition, they were retained for other reasons after the expedition was canceled.[179]

The proposed and canceled campaign against Suffolk was from beginning to end a response to the Union build-up in the area. Federal forces had taken Norfolk, Newport News, and moved into Suffolk on May 12, 1862. From that time on, Union commanders were fully expecting an attack on Suffolk and perhaps on Norfolk.

From late September 1862 to mid–March 1863, dozens of clashes broke out between the cavalry and artillery in the area bordered by the Nansemond and the Blackwater Rivers—an area both sides wanted to control and maintain as a buffer zone.[180] Both sides knew their opponents were building up their forces and anticipated a major attack in short order.

As indicated, however, by late September the planned Confederate campaign against Suffolk was canceled, and G. W. Smith sent the main body of the 2nd North Carolina Cavalry to Culpeper Court House to cover R. E. Lee's concern for Gordonsville. But the Second Squadron of the 2nd North Carolina remained under Daniels's command, picketing the rivers. W. A. Graham had his squadron build winter quarters at Proctor's Creek, which crosses Turnpike Road about 2 miles south of Halfway House.[181]

On the James and Appomattox Rivers, October 1862 to mid–March 1863

By October 1, the Second Squadron was settling in for the winter and spent the next several months picketing on the James and Appomattox Rivers.[182] They watched the James as far as Bermuda Hundreds—that was only about 9 miles east of their winter camp, but because the James River spends about as much time going north and south in that area as it does going east, they were picketing closer to 20 miles of riverside on the James.

Most of their picket duty was on the Appomattox River covering about 60 miles up river from Petersburg, probably as far as the Farmville area. The greater distances covered on the Appomattox meant the men were in picket camps for longer periods of time than when they pulled duty on the James.

Private William H. Strayhorn wrote his cousin from a picket outpost on January 11, 1863, and described the duty as follows, "I and five other men are stationed on the Appomattox River as pickets for the purpose of taking up stragglers from the army we are at goodee bridge near the Richmond and Danvil Railroad and I expect that we will stay here the remainder of the winter we came here on the 17th of Nove and I havnt been in the camp but once Since." Private Strayhorn made a point of the length of time they stayed away from their camp and raised the issue of watching for stragglers, a sympathetic way of stating their primary purpose on the Appomattox.[183]

By mid–October, the problem of stragglers was already catching the attention of many generals in both armies, and it was often difficult to separate the problem of stragglers from the more dangerous and unpleasant problem of catching comrades "absent without leave" and "deserters." In fact, one Lieutenant with Company C reported that men under his command were with others from Company K on the Appomattox in Amelia County as Provost Guards to arrest deserters during this period of time.[184]

Cavalrymen of the Second Squadron acting as provost marshals certainly felt an added difficulty because many deserters crossing the Appomattox were North Carolinians—many heading home to help families cope with war-imposed hardships rather than sit in winter camps. The problem persisted and by January 26, 1863, the Governor of North Carolina issued a proclamation acknowledging the seriousness of the problem.[185]

The Second Squadron had only three desertions from its own ranks during October 1862 through February 1863 which suggests the duty may have had some perks. Indeed, there was a lighter side to their duty at that time according to Private Strayhorn, who was on the Appomattox when he wrote his cousin. He provided the following view,

I am seeing a better time now than I have seen since I have been in the service we bord at Dr. Southalls a very nice man in deed and we are surrounded buy the best of friends I enjoyed finely this Christmas Miss Southall gave us one of the finest of parties on Christmas eve and I enjoyed my self finely indeed among the Ladies we don't have any thing to do but ride regular from one place to another one we go where we please and we have a fine time among the Ladies but I must say that there is a wide difference between them and the NC Ladies but in what way I will not say but will leave that for you all to decide on They are nice and entelegent but wheather it is because they are not NC Ladies is the riasen that I cant enjoy myself with them I cannot say but I mack along with them and do the best I can.[186]

Earlier in his letter, Private Strayhorn stated he thought they would remain on that duty throughout the winter. He was right. Most of the squadron was to stay put for the winter while all around them, their commanders changed. In fact, as he wrote his cousin, the Second Squadron's commander at Drewry's Bluff, Daniels, was being moved with most of his command into North Carolina to help resist Union forces there.

On December 12, as the Battle of Fredericksburg was getting under way up north, Arnold Elzey reported to G. W. Smith in Richmond and was assigned to command the defenses of Richmond which included the defenses at Drewry's Bluff (Daniels's command, including the Second Squadron of the 2nd North Carolina Cavalry).[187]

Three days after receiving his new command, Elzey received instructions from G. W. Smith that put Daniels on the road to join D. H. Hill in battles around New Bern and elsewhere in North Carolina. When the dust settled around Richmond, Elzey was in command of Richmond defenses, and under him Colonel Jack Brown was in charge of the forces at Drewry's Bluff, including the Second Squadron of the 2nd North Carolina Cavalry.[188]

Longstreet's Command and the Suffolk Campaign

On January 3, 1863, the Secretary of War, Seddon, sent a message to Robert E. Lee expressing his concern for the defenses of Richmond. The Secretary felt fewer troops were needed around Fredericksburg and more near Richmond.[189]

However, R. E. Lee was not eager to send troops from the upper Rappahannock and from Fredericksburg to the Richmond area—at least not until he was more certain Burnside had settled in for the winter. Indeed it was not until after Burnside made his abortive "Mud March" around January 20 that R. E. Lee began to relax on the northern line and give more thought to the Union build-up around Petersburg and Suffolk.

By February 17, the Secretary of War again wrote R. E. Lee explaining that he had reports that 20,000 more Union troops had arrived near Newport News and 8,000 to 10,000 more were at Suffolk. Secretary Seddon went on to say, "I am pleased to learn that with characteristic vigilance you are forwarding George E. Pickett's and John B. Hood's divisions to keep ward here." He was certainly even more pleased to learn that James Longstreet himself was coming to take command.[190]

On February 18, Pickett received the following instruction from Richmond, "...on your arrival with your division you take position on the south side of the James River in immediate vicinity of Drewry's Bluff, and there await further orders." On February 26, Longstreet took command of the Department of Virginia and North Carolina—and the Second Squadron of the 2nd North Carolina Cavalry which was still camped near Drewry's Bluff and now Pickett's division of infantry.[191] Pickett began moving some of his troops southeast toward Suffolk soon after he settled in.

Major James Dearing had recently been promoted and was in command of the artillery attached to General Pickett. In February soon

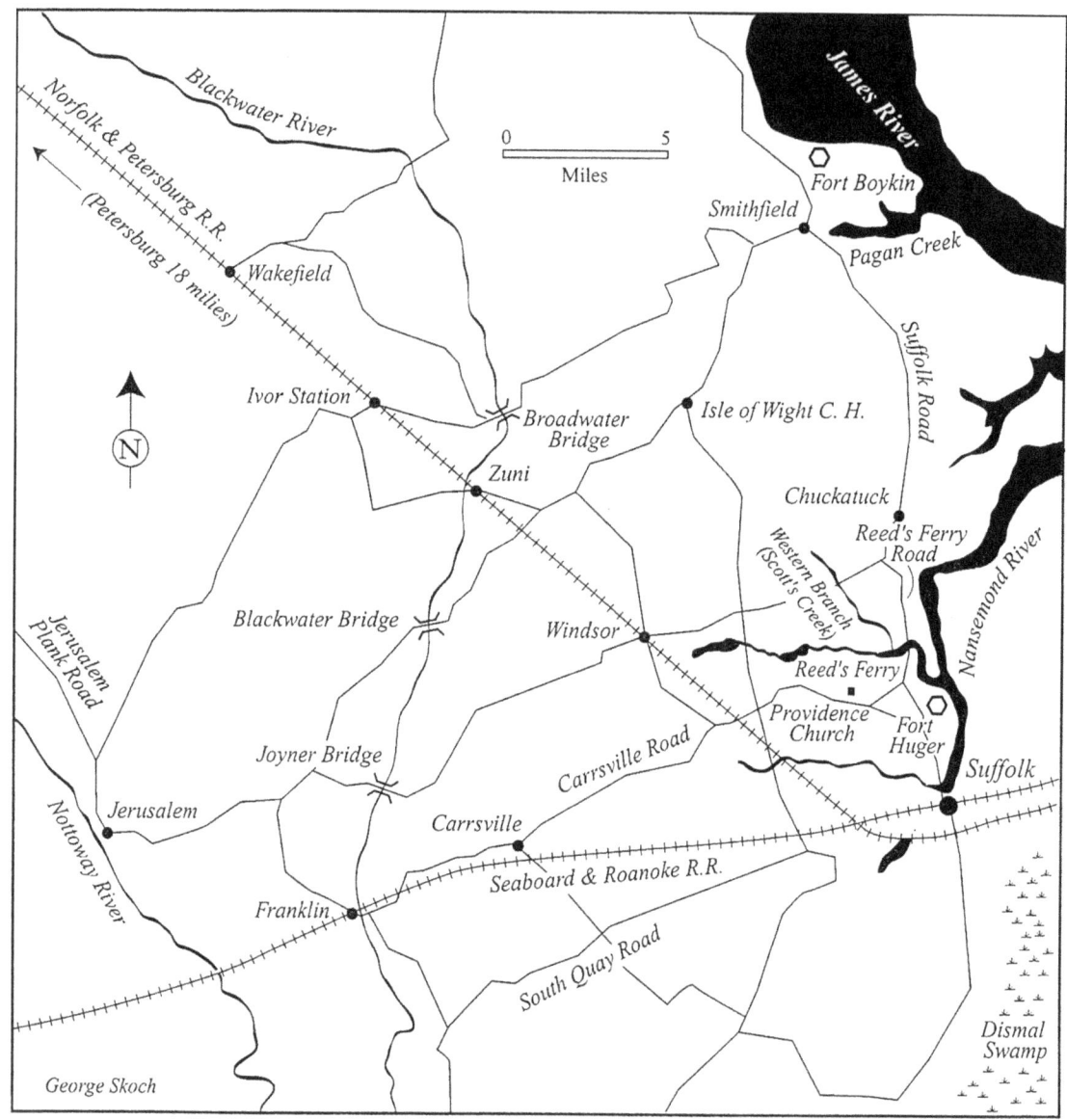

2.6: Longstreet's Suffolk Campaign

after arriving, Dearing was sent on a mission into the area between the Nansemond and Blackwater Rivers. Dearing was instructed to take a cavalry escort — he asked for twenty-five of the "best-mounted" men from the Second Squadron camped nearby.[192] He and his cavalrymen from the Second Squadron traveled to Franklin and crossed the Blackwater. They became part of Pryor's Confederate picket line from Franklin to Smithfield. Their first week in the area was relatively calm — though Confederate and Federal commanders were still sending patrols into the area between the rivers, but there was little action on the left of Pryor's line near Smithfield where the cavalrymen from the Second Squadron were posted.

Private John W. Gordon of Company C, Second Squadron, 2nd North Carolina Cavalry along with four other cavalrymen were posted about two miles from Smithfield. They were posted in open country with the nearest woods half a mile distant and not a house in sight. According to Gordon, "The weather was bitter cold, and we had neither shelter nor firewood. We had some corn meal in our haversacks, but not a thing to cook in, not even a frying pan..., having left with our wagons in Southampton every encumbrance that could be dispensed with." Nonetheless, years later, John W. Gordon recalled what he described as some of the best times of his life, while on post just outside Smithfield. Though cold and without cooking facilities, the sixteen-year-old private was apparently not old enough to know desperation — so he made the best of it. In his words:

> ...early in the afternoon of the first day at our post, I mounted my horse and went out reconnoitering. Following the road leading through the woods, I soon came to a stately mansion sitting a little off the road in a grove of oaks. My knock at the door was answered by a young lady of very attractive appearance, whom I told of our condition at the post ... encouraged by the delight the young lady manifested at the sight of a Confederate soldier, I handed her my haversack of corn meal and timidly asked if she would be kind enough to have it made into bread for us. This she cheerfully consented to do, telling me to return for it about seven o'clock in the evening.
>
> ...and you may be sure I was back at that house on time. After being introduced by the young lady to her father and sisters, of whom there were three, she being the youngest, just sweet sixteen, a few months older than myself, I was ushered into the supper room and given a seat at the table next to my fair young friend. Gee whillikens! It makes me hungry now when I think of that supper.
>
> The meal being over, I offered as an apology for hurrying away that the men at the post were hungry, and asked for my corn bread. Sweet sixteen said the bread was not ready, and invited me into the parlor to show me some oil paintings. I bashfully followed her. When a pleasant half hour had passed, and I was about to again mention that bread, she opened wide the front door and there stood my horse with a wallet thrown across her back with, at least, a half-bushel of something in each end. 'There's your corn bread,' she said, 'I hope you will enjoy it, I made it with my own hands.' The boys at the post had a royal supper and breakfast out of that wallet, but not one ounce of corn bread did they find.
>
> The next morning the whole family honored us with a visit. There was a young lady for each of us four unmarried men, and all remarkably well matched as to age. Our only married man was left to entertain the old gentleman.... They had hauled also to the post two empty hogsheads and a load of wheat straw. We laid the hogsheads down on their sides with the open ends to the fire, and with straw under us and blankets over us, we were snug as bugs in a rug.[193]

After a week of a young man's fantasy come to life, adventure, pretty young ladies enough to go around and lots of good food, the five troopers from the Second Squadron were ordered one night to be at Windsor on the Norfolk & Petersburg Railroad by the next morning — it was about twenty miles off, but young John Gordon took time to ride over to the home of his new friends and bid them farewell. He and Sweet Sixteen made promises and exchanged rings until they would meet again. Allow Private Gordon to have the closing words on this most memorable time in his life:

> As we were nearing Windsor next morning, we were overtaken by a lad in a buggy, whom we were astonished to recognize as Sweet Sixteen's young brother. He handed me a note and two large pillow cases stuffed with baked fowls, sweet potatoes, pickles, cakes, and all sorts of nice things. Immediately on my departure the night before, the sweet girl had aroused the household, and those dear people had spent the remainder of the night cooking; and this little boy, starting before daybreak, had driven hard to overtake us and present us with this additional evidence of their friendship and of their loyalty to the cause in which we were engaged.

When Private Gordon and his four comrades reported at Windsor, he wrote that they were all suffering from "cardiac wounds" received in engagements around Smithfield — but also once they arrived at Windsor, the play time was over.

Union cavalry probes near Franklin and Windsor grew more frequent as Longstreet's force in the area grew and was apparent to the Union commanders.[194]

The twenty-five cavalrymen who accompanied Dearing into the area stayed between the rivers until Longstreet was ready to make his move on Suffolk. The balance of the Second Squadron began to collect around Wakefield on the Norfolk & Petersburg Railroad.

To date, Longstreet's assignment had been simply to place his awesome presence between Richmond and the enemy — that was seldom enough for Confederate commanders, however, and his mission was revised during March of 1863.

LONGSTREET'S SUFFOLK CAMPAIGN, APRIL 11–MAY 4, 1863

Confederate commanders in Virginia spent much of March debating and then planning a move to extricate supplies from northeastern North Carolina. That area was rich in supplies badly needed by the Army of Northern Virginia — and Longstreet's troops. In fact, Longstreet's commissary, Major Raphael Moses, had been conducting conferences and inspections, and he concluded the supply situation had reached a dangerous level. More importantly, he found there were tons of "bacon and unreckoned barrels of fish" in eastern North Carolina. Some of the stores had already been gathered, purchased and were available for transport to Virginia. The supplies were so abundant and available, authorities were concerned about losing them to Union raiding parties.[195]

By March of 1863, the task at hand was to collect the supplies from various agents often in the midst of Federal forces that occupied the Norfolk area inland to Suffolk and controlled much of eastern North Carolina. At first Longstreet was reluctant and sent a message to the Secretary of War in Richmond in which he outlined his concerns. He ended his reply with a more conciliatory tone, however, "A move against Suffolk, properly aided by cavalry, might be very successful and complete, but without this aid would be but a partial success, which would hardly pay for the movement of the troops."[196] The compromise from which everyone involved got some of what they sought was to send supply trains into North Carolina to acquire what could be had, with a demonstration in front of Suffolk that might become a siege if conditions were right. This meant Longstreet had to collect the forces available to him and, of course, ask for more.

One of the first orders of business then was for General Elzey to take an inventory of his command by mid–March. In response to Elzey's request for information, Jack Brown commanding at Drewry's Bluff replied on March 15, that his command included: "Maj. B. H. Gee, commanding Fifty-ninth Georgia Infantry Regiment; Capt. W. A. Graham (since his arrival in Petersburg) commanding Second squadron, Second North Carolina Cavalry."[197] Elzey knew well that Longstreet very much wanted cavalry for his Suffolk campaign; so needless to say, Brown lost the services of the Second Squadron.

It was agreed that Elzey would send some troops from Richmond down the peninsula to hold Union troops in the Norfolk area and make it less likely they would send a force at Longstreet's left via the James River.[198] Longstreet also planned to have D. H. Hill conduct a demonstration at Washington, North Carolina.[199] Demonstrations at Washington and Yorktown were to hold enemy forces away from the Suffolk demonstration, and the Suffolk demonstration was to distract the Union forces while the supply-gathering in northeast North Carolina was underway. From the beginning the Federals were convinced that Longstreet was conducting a siege of Suffolk.

Longstreet knew he must make a convincing demonstration in front of Suffolk and, of course, take advantage of any weakness he might find there. To that end, he moved Pickett's and Hood's divisions up, and he also used French's command on the line at Suffolk — but for some reason he did not want French in charge of the operation at that point. So he transferred the young Brigadier General, Micah Jenkins, to French's division and removed Pryor of his command on the Blackwater.[200]

Longstreet collected his troops along the Norfolk & Petersburg Railroad from Wakefield to Ivor — he moved the Second Squadron of the 2nd North Carolina Cavalry into the staging area first, then Pickett's troops. Jenkins's command was already at Franklin on the Blackwater. Jenkins had most of Colonel John A. Baker's 3rd North Carolina Cavalry with him on the Blackwater line, and they worked well together — understandably he wanted J. A. Baker to lead the first thrust across the river and along Windsor road into the enemy's cavalry camp. The only other cavalry in the area were Companies C and K of the 2nd North Carolina Cavalry — the Second Squadron. Jenkins did not know them, but Longstreet did.

General Elzey had sequestered the Second Squadron and begun to collect them in a new camp halfway to Suffolk where they waiting for Longstreet. You might recall, it was on March 15, that Colonel Brown acknowledged to Elzey that he had a cavalry squadron — apparently that same evening he lost it.

On March 24, Levi Lockhart of the Second Squadron wrote his sister from near Wakefield, Virginia. According to Private Lockhart the move from their camp near Drewry's Bluff was abrupt:

I am sorry to inform you that we have left our winter quarters. We received orders on the 15th, inst., (about 6 o'clock P. M.) to report at Petersburg without delay; which we did, and got to Petersburg about 3 o'clock the next morning, where we took up camp for two days; we then received orders to report at Franklin, Virginia. After two days march through the sleet and snow, we found ourselves at Jerusalem; we then received orders to report at Wakefield Station, which is on the railroad between Petersburg and Suffolk, and about thirty miles from Jerusalem. We arrived here [Wakefield] on Sunday, last, and the next day we threw out our pickets in twenty-five miles of Suffolk.[201]

General Elzey had provided Longstreet with the cavalry he said he needed to make the Suffolk campaign a success—although Longstreet would more than likely have been happier with a larger unit. The Second Squadron at best had around 100 effective troopers at that time.[202] That number diminished day after day due to lack of nourishment and the harsh conditions. Private George W. Walker, also of the Second Squadron, wrote his cousin on March 29, from Wakefield and described their duty in that place as follows:

The duty that we have to do is not very hard though we have it, plenty of it. We had to send out 8 men on post and sill [?] and clumyer [?], and then we have to send out a scout every week. I don't think our horses will stand long, for we don't get any thing but corn to feed on. I have not seen any forage since we have been here except one load of hay, and that came in last evening.[203]

In spite of scarce provisions probably some excitement was in the air. Private Walker and the men of the Second Squadron were certainly aware that something big was in the making by the time he wrote the above letter. Because Corse's and Armistead's brigades passed through Wakefield and arrived at their collecting spot, Ivor Station, on March 25 and 28. Pickett himself arrived at Ivor on March 29. A day later, General Longstreet passed through Wakefield on his way to meet with Pickett at Ivor and stayed for several days. A couple of days later, Hood started his troops for Petersburg where they camped waiting for Longstreet to set a date for the demonstration at Suffolk.[204]

Crossing the Blackwater River and approaching Suffolk from the west was an important initial step in Longstreet's demonstration in the area — he wanted to establish a strong position rapidly east of the Blackwater in front of the enemy, which was estimated to be anywhere from 12,000 to 30,000 Federal troops at the time. Jenkins, who was then in command of the Confederate line at the Blackwater, estimated the enemy in Suffolk to be about 15,000 — but reinforcements were arriving daily.

As commander of the Blackwater line, Jenkins submitted a plan of attack and made a request for the 3rd North Carolina Cavalry, under the command of John A. Baker, to spearhead the attack. Longstreet replied with his plan of attack however. On April 6, 1863, the reply was as follows:

GENERAL: I desire that you have your command in readiness to cross the Blackwater on Friday [the 10th]. The divisions of Generals Pickett and Hood will not be able to cross before Saturday; but if the force at Suffolk is no larger than stated in your letter of the 4th you will be able to cross with the two bridges on the day before them and take up strong position between the Blackwater and Suffolk....You should have four days' rations cooked. *The squadron of Captain Graham [the Second Squadron, 2nd North Carolina Cavalry] is ordered to be at Blackwater Bridge, to cross at that point, and move on the flank via Windsor* [my italics]. The pickets [the 3rd N.C. Cavalry] that you have on the other side of the Blackwater had better be left there.... You can take them on to join you after crossing. You will require tools for entrenching. The cavalry should be provided with wires to stretch across the roads in case the enemy's cavalry should attack it, particularly for any cavalry charge.[205]

The details of Longstreet's instructions did not vary much from Jenkins's earlier suggestions—except, on March 24, Jenkins had requested Baker's 3rd Cavalry be first across the bridge and up the Windsor road to the Union cavalry camp because he had considerable confidence in Baker and his cavalry, but Longstreet wanted Graham's Second Squadron from the 2nd North Carolina Cavalry for that critical first move, on the all important left flank.

The Second Squadron's job would be to storm across the Blackwater Bridge and take the Windsor Road in the direction of the enemy cavalry camps. Then once they drove the enemy back, they were to stretch wires across the roads coming from the camps, and take positions to protect Longstreet's left flank as his army crossed the Blackwater. With his left flank protected, Longstreet planned to press the enemy and take positions in front of Suffolk. As indicated earlier, Longstreet was concerned that once the enemy had detected his presence east of the Blackwater River, they might well send troops up the James River, drop south and hit his left flank and rear. The Second Squadron was placed and remained where Longstreet felt most vulnerable. J. A. Baker's 3rd North Carolina Cavalry was primarily responsible for the right of the Confederate line. If Longstreet's worst concerns were realized and his left was attacked from the James River, the enemy would probably come through Pagan Creek at the town of Smithfield and then turn south to hit the Confederate left—the Second Squadron's left would rest at Smithfield.

In his final plan, Longstreet decided Jenkins would take his main body across at South Quay and take the center using the South Quay Road leading directly into Suffolk with a squadron of cavalry among his advanced detachment. Pickett was to take his men across at the same place behind Jenkins and then head south from South Quay Road and spread out south of Suffolk with his right wing on Dismal Swamp. Hood was slated to take his troops across at Franklin and then take his men on the Carrsville Road, through Carrsville to the intersection of the Providence Church and Reed's Ferry Roads with his squadron of cavalry covering his exposed flank on the roads to Windsor—Hood's cavalry escort was the Second Squadron from the 2nd North Carolina Cavalry. Hood's left would rest near Fort Huger just below the confluence of the Western Branch and the Nansemond River; then his line would swing down in an arch north of Suffolk.

Longstreet's campaign against Suffolk began April 11. Jenkins's troops were in place first and drove Union pickets in and past their camp until the enemy would give no more ground—they fought into the evening. Hood's men encountered the enemy near Providence Church—they hit the 1st New York Mounted Rifles (commanded by B. F. Onderdonk, part of Colonel S. P. Spear's cavalry by that time) and drove them back near Suffolk. The Second Squadron was engaged in the fight at Providence Church. Pickett's force hit and pressed the enemy south of Suffolk early on April 12.[206]

After the Confederates pushed the enemy as far as possible under the circumstance, they began to entrench themselves. As they entrenched, the cavalry pickets were sent out in all directions and continued to skirmish for several days—they pressed the Union line at all points, looking for a penetrable weakness. Graham's Second Squadron continued its assignment north of Hood—from Chuckatuck to Smithfield. (Apparently some of the 3rd North Carolina Cavalry patrolled from Western Branch to Chuckatuck occasionally.)

Longstreet's instincts were right; the greatest threats to his line came on the left from the Nansemond River where Union gunboats could come and go as they pleased with little concern for Hood's sharpshooters on the riverside. Longstreet moved more guns along the Nansemond River in an effort to gain some control of the area on his left—but he remained troubled by the gunboat activity.[207]

On more than one occasion Longstreet personally placed the Second Squadron where he felt his line was most vulnerable. Evander Law's brigade had its rifle pits on the left of Hood's line extending past French's northernmost battery, and the Second Squadron's cavalrymen were posted along and north of the rifle pits as far as Smithfield. These rifle pits and French's artillery were close enough to the river to be subjected to constant and often severe shelling as well as sharpshooter fire from Union forces both on and beyond the river. The fire was so intense that the front pits were manned by volunteers, and men did not leave or enter the batteries or rifle pits during the daylight hours.[208]

The cavalrymen of the Second Squadron who were placed along Law's line and rotated in as couriers a day at a time. The commanders in the furthermost rifle pits needed to communicate with Law's headquarters—even during the daylight hours. This was a job for horsemen.[209]

Private Gordon of Company C, discussed earlier when he was first brought to this area by Major Dearing, spent the first week of Longstreet's demonstration in and around French's battery between the river and Chuckatuck. He has left us with an example of cavalry activity on Law's line. In the young private's words:

I was a courier that day, and several times had to carry dispatches back and forth between this battery and General McLaw's [Law's] headquarters, about two miles away. I rode a fleet mare of my own raising, which I loved next best to my sweetheart. [Probably he meant "Sweet Sixteen."] We were targets for the enemy going and coming in the run we had to make across a freshly plowed field half a mile to the nearest woods. On one trip, we were nearly buried by the explosion of a shell as it struck the plowed ground in front of us, slightly wounding my mare.[210]

The first week of the demonstration was marked by both sides pressing to control the western shore of the Nansemond and James River from Suffolk to Smithfield.[211] The first important Union thrust came at Fort Huger on April 19. The guns at the fort were lost along with a number of men. That loss represented a turning point in Longstreet's campaign. For more than a week he had been aggressive and probing the Union garrison daily with little success — after this day he was compelled to be more defensive, and to orchestrate a holding action while supplies were removed from North Carolina.[212]

For those Confederate commanders who entertained the notion that the mission in front of Suffolk might find a weakness in Union defenses and be elevated to a siege of the garrison, the fall of Fort Huger was a wake-up call. The enemy garrison there was too formidable, and Longstreet's left was too vulnerable. It was clear to most Confederates by April 20, Longstreet's mission was never going to be more than a diversion at Suffolk to extract supplies from North Carolina, and with an aggressive enemy in front of them, time was of the essence. Robert E. Lee could not have agreed more with Longstreet's acknowledgment of his limited goals at Suffolk — on April 27, Longstreet received these reassuring words from his commander: "…but if the place was taken I doubt whether we could spare a garrison to hold it, and storming of his works might cost us very dear."[213]

With his revised posture in front of Suffolk, Longstreet became increasingly protective of his flanks while the supplies were drawn from North Carolina. About a week after the fall of Fort Huger, one of Longstreet's defensive actions directly involved the Second Squadron — Longstreet sent the following message to Hood: "The commanding general desires you to order Captain Graham [and his cavalrymen from the 2nd North Carolina] to burn or destroy all the wharves or landings on the Nansemond, and also those on the James, that he can reach. He should be instructed to make their destruction thorough and complete."[214]

At the time, Graham's Second Squadron was still patrolling from Chuckatuck up to and perhaps beyond Smithfield, thus on both rivers, and the squadron was apparently still getting its assignments directly from Longstreet. In any case, this assignment was clearly not that of an army on the attack.

Longstreet's new posture also had the effect of reducing the number of skirmishes. What had been daily events were much less frequent after the fall of Fort Huger, but Union probes continued to cause excitement from time to time.[215]

In a letter home Private Levi Lockhart indicated that minor skirmishing continued to take place along the entire line. Further on in his letter, he told his sister that their brother, John (Lieutenant John P. Lockhart of Company K) was sick with a sore throat and being cared for in a house near Smithfield (perhaps in the home of young Private Gordon's "Sweet Sixteen").[216]

Robert E. Lee had been urging Longstreet to send him all the cavalry he could spare but Longstreet was not eager to send what little cavalry he had on his Suffolk line to the Rappahannock just yet. He knew he would have to keep all the cavalry he had with him until he completed his pullback from the Suffolk. His withdrawal would have to be covered at the rear, and then on its flank by cavalry. Nevertheless, as late as April 27, another letter to Longstreet from R. E. Lee carried a similar and unmistakable request for a conclusion to the Suffolk expedition.[217]

Up to this point, Robert E. Lee was still trying to collect cavalry, get Longstreet and his two divisions back on the Rappahannock and be supplied by Longstreet's campaign for a spring offensive in which Lee wanted to push Hooker back to the Potomac. General Lee's needs did not change, but his sense of urgency did when on April 29 Hooker seized the initiative and pushed across the Rappahannock at Kelly's Ford and pressed W. H. F. Lee's 2nd

North Carolina Cavalry all the way to and across Germanna Ford on the Rapidan before the day ended — Hooker had five corps around Chancellorsville within a couple of days.

It was clear, Longstreet would have to wrap things up at Suffolk as soon as possible. On April 30, Longstreet received a correspondence from the Adjutant and Inspector General in Richmond, with this short but clear message: "Move without delay with your command to this place to effect a junction with General Lee." There was some delay, however, because Longstreet was not about to put his troops and the supply train at risk with a hasty and disorderly withdrawal. According to Longstreet, at one point in the urgent exchanges, he asked if he should abandon the supply trains, some of which were still in North Carolina, and return with just his troops. Later he said, "To this no answer came; and I was left to the exercise of my own judgment. As soon as the trains were safely back, we drew off, marched back to the Blackwater, and thence *en route* for Richmond and Fredericksburg."[218]

By the night of May 3, the supply trains were back, and Longstreet's plan for pulling back was in place. His instructions were specific — and included routes for Pickett's, French's (Jenkins's), and Hood's commands, and that each command should leave a picket line capable of covering their exit. Longstreet added the following:

A party of select axmen will be left with each rear guard with orders to fell such large trees in the streams and swamps as may assist in delaying pursuit on the part of the enemy. Should the enemy's cavalry attempt to annoy our rear, every effort will be made to destroy it by ambuscade or otherwise, but too much time must not be lost in endeavoring to do so. Discreet officers will be selected to relieve and conduct the picket lines. *Captain Graham's [2nd North Carolina] cavalry will report to General French at sunset to-morrow. General Pickett will give orders to the cavalry now temporarily serving with him, and General Hood to Captain Graham's cavalry* [my italics].[219]

The southernmost route, Somerton road, was to be taken by Pickett; the middle route, South Quay road, was to be used by Jenkins's (French's) troops heading west for Franklin; and the northernmost route, using Blackwater road, was to be used by Hood, before he dropped south to Franklin. It appears the Second Squadron was the only cavalry on the left with Hood's command on May 3 as they prepared to withdraw. The 3rd North Carolina Cavalry companies that had from time-to-time been on Hood's left as far as Chuckatuck were pulled early and placed to cover Pickett's withdrawal leaving just the Second Squadron to cover Hood's and their own withdrawal from as far north as Smithfield. The plan was for Hood to keep the Second Squadron at his rear until across the river, then give Graham instructions to report to General French at sunset the following day.[220]

By and large, the planned withdrawal went smoothly because Union commanders had not expected Longstreet to suddenly withdraw—consequently, Pickett and Jenkins were able to pull back in an orderly fashion.[221] It was a different story on the other end of the line. Graham's Second Squadron was suddenly forced to fend off a Union probe in force.

That morning, Federal forces launched a three-pronged attack. Their force was composed of more than 5,000 infantry, a cavalry regiment, and several batteries.[222] General Getty had his Union forces crossing the Nansemond at 9:00 A.M. on May 3.

The main Union column moved across the river and over Providence Church Road. They encountered Hood's line and were engaged in severe fighting throughout the day. At about the same time, the second column crossed the Nansemond by boats and occupied Hill's Point. They then moved up toward Western Branch to take Reed's Ferry, but Hood's troops were still in front of them and they held the Federals back. The third Union column, under the command of Major H. B. Crosby, crossed the river farther north, and moved on the road for Chuckatuck. Once Crosby's troops entered town, they were attacked by the Second Squadron of the 2nd North Carolina Cavalry.

The task of the Second Squadron was to slow the Union advance, allowing Hood to withdraw back across the Blackwater that night. The Confederate cavalrymen had a difficult job before them, and they did it well. The Union commander, Crosby, described his slow progress after crossing the River as follows:

The troops were under way for Chuckatuck at 4.30 o'clock Sunday morning, the distance being 2½ miles. My skirmishers came upon the camp of rebel pickets about half a mile from the Nansemond, their fires still burning. The rebel pickets fell back to Chuckatuck as we advanced. When within half a mile of the village we saw a company of rebel cavalry drawn up in the main street leading into the village. I ordered Lieutenant McDevitt to open fire upon them with artillery, and the rebels, after a few rounds, retired to the farther side of the village, at the junction of the Reed's Ferry and Isle of Wight roads. I advanced the skirmishers to the village and moved up the column....

I ordered Lieutenant McDevitt to put the artillery in position to command both roads until they could be reconnoitered. On discovering that the enemy intended to make no resistance at this point the column was moved ahead on the Reed's Ferry road. Captain Spittle came upon the camp on this road about half a mile beyond Chuckatuck. The enemy had but just left; their camp fires still burning.... The enemy were then reported nowhere in sight....

...passing over the same ground which our skirmishers had previously gone over. The cavalry had gone but a short distance when the enemy, who had suddenly returned, opened fire upon them, killing 1 and wounding 2 of their number. Lieutenant McDevitt opened upon them at once and shelled them toward Everett's Bridge.

The column was delayed at this point about half an hour, but there being no signs of the enemy's returning I advanced the skirmishers rapidly on the Reed's Ferry road, and again set the column in motion.

Our march was necessarily slow, owing to the thick underbrush through which the skirmishers were obliged to make their way. On approaching the West Branch we again discovered the enemy's pickets. The skirmishers ... were soon engaged. The artillery was moved up with supports and opened fire at once, commanding the opposite bank of the creek, where the enemy had two companies of sharpshooters as a support. The skirmish at this point was short and spirited, resulting in our capturing 1 lieutenant, 3 sergeants, 2 corporals, and 10 privates of the enemy. Our loss was 3 wounded, 1 of whom died some two hours afterward as we were without surgical aid.

We encamped Sunday night on the Nansemond, near the ferry, and under protection of the gunboats.[223]

After such a day, the Union force advancing on the Second Squadron, was described by its commander as, "...utterly exhausted and without food for man or horse...."[224] On several occasions the Second Squadron had appeared, then disappeared, each time requiring Crosby's forces to stop, take cover, unlimber, and position their guns to drive off the enemy cavalry standing across the road in front of them. In addition, the Federals were forced to skirmish all the way down to Reed's Ferry. The distance from Chuckatuck to Reed's Ferry was only about four and one half miles, but it took them all day to cover that distance.

When Crosby's troops reached Western Branch instead of finding that Dutton and their Union comrades had taken the ferry, they found that the Confederate cavalry that has been in front of them all day had joined with some of Hood's infantry to hold the ferry. Crosby took his men to retire for the night on the river, under the protection of Union gunboats. To Crosby's surprise, when he approached the ferry the next morning, it was his for the taking. According to the Union commander, the Confederate cavalry made their planned 11:00 P.M. withdrawal to the Blackwater.[225]

S. G. French was probably the first to notify Longstreet of the Union attack on his left that day. Longstreet, however, kept his eye on the Rappahannock and saw no necessity to alter his planned withdrawal. He told French to expect even more enemy cavalry on the day and the following night.[226]

The Second Squadron of the 2nd North Carolina Cavalry saw some difficult duty while detached to the areas around Drewry's Bluff and Suffolk but they did not suffer heavy losses. They had several men transfer and several others receive discharges for health reasons, and three men died while three others deserted during this period of time. Only two combat losses were reported during the initial push across the Blackwater River.

Combat Losses in the Second Squadron October 1862–Mid-May 1863

Trooper	Co.	Fate
James F. M. Terry	K	captured, April 9
Barzelia B. Wendley	K	captured, April 9

The source used here is: *North Carolina Troops 1861–1865, A Roster*, compiled by Louis H. Manarin (Raleigh, N.C., State Division of Archives and History), vol. II, Cavalry, pages 104–177. (See Appendix for more information on the men listed above, page 394.)

On May 4, some skirmishing took place, but Longstreet's forces did get back across the Blackwater, and the Suffolk campaign concluded.

Pickett's and Hood's divisions were instructed to move as rapidly as possible to Ivor Station and then on to Richmond, where they were met with new orders.[227] Longstreet's original plan was for Hood to have Captain Graham and his Second Squadron report to French after crossing the Blackwater River, but that part of the plan was changed. French's command was ordered to stay on the Blackwater where most of them had been before the Suffolk Campaign got underway.

The Second Squadron moved on to Ivor Station, probably on Hood's rear and flank — it is not clear whether Hood neglected to have them report to French after crossing the river or if French assigned them to the march from Franklin to Ivor Station. In any case, French kept the 3rd North Carolina Cavalry with his command on the Blackwater. Colonel Dennis Ferebee arrived with his 4th North Carolina Cavalry from D. H. Hill after their withdrawal from Washington, North Carolina and they too arrived at Ivor Station on May 5.

S. G. French may have been aware of the location of the cavalrymen, but on May 7, Longstreet's Assistant Adjutant-General sent the following correspondence to him:

Colonel Ferebee telegraphs as follows:

I have scouted through all this region to Isle of Wight Court-House, Chuckatuck, and Smithfield to this point—Ivor. I have found no enemy. Forage very scarce and my horses suffering much. *Captain Graham is here with one squadron of the Second North Carolina Cavalry and can do all the picketing necessary* [my italics].[228]

Ferebee's 4th North Carolina Cavalry and the Second Squadron of the 2nd Cavalry had been watching Hood's and Pickett's rear from Ivor Station to the James River and back down as far as Chuckatuck while those two divisions collected themselves and moved out to Petersburg. Most of Hood's division went by train and Pickett moved over to the Jerusalem Plank Road and marched toward Petersburg.

Colonel Ferebee's command and the Second Squadron performed picket and patrol duty for another day, when on May 8, they were instructed to join the Army of Northern Virginia and Stuart's cavalry. S. G. French issued the following orders: "Capt. William A. Graham, commanding squadron of Nineteenth Regiment North Carolina Troops (Second North Carolina Cavalry), will proceed with his command without delay and rejoin his regiment, Stuart's division, in the Army of Northern Virginia."[229]

The orders may have gotten to Graham by May 9 or 10. That would have given them 10 or 11 days to travel to Culpeper Court House from Ivor — about 150 miles. If they arrived at Richmond on May 11–13 they found the city preoccupied with the final departure of General Thomas J. "Stonewall" Jackson.[230] Graham and his squadron from the 2nd North Carolina Cavalry arrived at Culpeper Court House on May 20, and moved on to join W. H. F. Lee's brigade and their regiment camped near Welford's Ford, near Brandy Station. J. E. B. Stuart had been instructed to collect his cavalry around Brandy Station and ready them for a Spring campaign — Stuart had returned to his cavalry command on May 6.

Three

Cavalry Shield for the Gettysburg Campaign

When the Second Squadron of the 2nd North Carolina Cavalry arrived at Culpeper Court House, they may have been impressed by the festiveness of their apparent reception. They soon learned, however, that a great deal of the commotion was caused by J. E. B. Stuart and his staff moving their headquarters from Orange to Culpeper Court House the same day — May 20, 1863.[1] The squadron moved through Culpeper past Brandy Station and toward Hazel Run to join their regiment camped on Welford's farm.

At the time of the reunion, the 2nd North Carolina Cavalry was under the temporary command of Lieutenant Colonel W. H. F. Payne.[2] In addition, the regiment was serving in Brigadier General W. H. F. Lee's brigade.

Certainly a sense of excitement was in the air and would soon be heightened. J. E. B. Stuart in the process of collecting the largest cavalry force he had ever commanded was understandably eager to see his force in parade, so he had his staff organize an impressive review with a cast of about 5,000.[3] This was done just a couple of days after Stuart and the Second Squadron had arrived and apparently before the dust had settled — some recent arrivals were still a bit disorganized but nonetheless impressed by the spectacle.

For instance, Lieutenant John P. Lockhart of Company K, Second Squadron did not arrive with his men on May 20; he was still on sick leave, but his horse was sent along with his company. Just after the cavalry review, Lieutenant Lockhart was informed by his cousin, Robert Y. Walker, also of Company K, that his horse had "...either strayed away or [been] stolen." After very matter-of-factly conveying the news about his cousin's horse, Private Walker added the following news: "There is talk of us going on a raid over in Maryland soon. I never saw so much cavalry in all my life as there is here. We had a review the other day, and as far as I could see was cavalry."[4]

The May 22 review included the brigades of Wade Hampton, Fitzhugh Lee, and W. H. F. Lee. William E. Jones's brigade was still on its way from the Shenandoah Valley, and Beverly H. Robertson's brigade was still working its way up through southern Virginia. By all accounts the review was impressive — certainly the men of the 2nd North Carolina Cavalry had never been a part of anything so grand, and the excitement continued to escalate. Few knew, but all could sense something big was in the works.

Robert E. Lee's plan to drive Joseph Hooker back from the Rappahannock to the Potomac around the first of May had been delayed by Hooker's move across the Rapidan to Chancellorsville, but the idea had not been pushed from his mind. However, by June the plan had evolved into an ambitious campaign into Pennsylvania. He had Stuart collecting all the cavalry he could spare and placing them between Culpeper Court House and the Rappahannock, and during the first week of June R. E. Lee began moving his infantry in that direction. On June 4, R. E. Lee began moving his infantry from Fredericksburg toward Culpeper Court House. He left A. P. Hill's Corps at Fredericksburg and sent Longstreet and Ewell with their commands to Culpeper. The cavalrymen already there knew only that something grand was about to take place — so grand, another review was in order.

If Private Walker of the 2nd North Carolina Cavalry was impressed by the May 22 troop review, he must have been overwhelmed by Stuart's second act. By June 5, Robertson's and Jones's brigades had arrived, bringing Stuart's cavalry to around 10,000. These new arrivals provided Stuart with good reason to stage a second really big review. He invited Robert E. Lee and Confederate officials, including the Secretary of War — the former did not get to Culpeper in time for the review but the latter and many other prominent people did. Apparently a great many of the attendees were ladies from towns and cities as far away as Richmond. They came from near and far mostly by train and filled all the hotels and most of the homes in and around Culpeper — tents were erected to handle the over-flow. Stuart's staff was kept busy, but managed to host a ball the evening before at the Culpeper Court House. The music, dancing, and food was delightful, and many of the cavalry officers were invited.[5]

A member of Stuart's staff, W. W. Blackford, remembered "The staff was resplendent in new uniforms, and horses were in splendid condition as we rode to the field on the level plains near Brandy Station." Blackford was no doubt on his spirited mare, Magic, and he savored the moment, leaving us the following description of the pageant:

General Stuart, accompanied by his brilliant staff [including Blackford], passed down the front and back by the rear at a gallop in the usual way, the general officers and their staffs joining us as we passed, so that by the time we got back to the stand there were nearly a hundred horsemen, all officers, dashing through the field. Then the lines broke into column of squadrons and marched by at a walk, making the entire circuit; then they came by at a trot, taking the gallop a hundred yards before reaching the reviewing stand; and then the "charge" at full speed past the reviewing stand, yelling just as they do in a real charge, and brandishing their sabres over their heads. The effect was thrilling, even to us, while the ladies clasped their hands and sank into the arms, sometimes, of their escorts in a swoon, if their escorts were handy, but if not they did not. While the charging was going on, Beckman with the horse artillery was firing rapidly and this heightened the effect. It would make your hair stand on end to see them.[6]

Other members of Stuart's brilliant staff remembered the scene as Stuart approached the review site as follows: "As our approach was heralded by the flourish of trumpets, many of the ladies in the village came forth to greet us from the porches and verandahs of the houses, and showered down flowers upon our path.... Not less grateful to our soldiers' hearts were the cheers of more than 12,000 horsemen, which rose in the air as we came upon the open plain near Brandy Station...." Yet another staff-member agreed, "...the thirst for the 'pomp and circumstance' of war was fully satisfied."[7]

Unfortunately, R. E. Lee was not able to leave Fredericksburg until May 5, and did not arrive in Culpeper until late on the 7th — consequently, he missed the entire review. Nevertheless, the momentum of the preparation and the affair itself allowed Stuart to go forward with the review as well as the ball.

Also unfortunately, many of the 2nd North Carolina cavalrymen missed the review on June 5. A few days earlier, they were moved out ahead of the rest of the cavalry, presumably in advance of the campaign to the north. They had been sent about ten miles beyond the Hedgemon River, but on June 5 they were recalled. By the next day, they were once again camped near Brandy Station. The 2nd North Carolina was available for the next big cavalry review, as was Robert E. Lee.[8]

On the evening of May 7, R. E. Lee with Longstreet's and Ewell's corps arrived in and around Culpeper Court House. R. E. Lee was eager to see his cavalry and instructed Stuart to organize a review for May 8, the next morning.[9] However, this review was a more Spartan-like affair — ladies and dignitaries were not brought in by the train load. At R. E. Lee's request, there was no yelling, no extensive galloping, or firing of guns. Lee wanted to see the condition of his troops, not a spectacle.

Even though the review was to be less than a spectacle, it was not in the nature of most cavalrymen to show off without some audience to appreciate the pomp and prancing. So when Fitz Lee, who was a man of more than average humor, heard that John B. Hood had just arrived with his division, he sent the Texan an invitation to the review set for the next morning. Fitz Lee reportedly invited Hood to bring some of his friends — meaning from his staff. The next morning, Hood emerged from the woods onto the parade grounds with his entire division of infantry. Hood went over to Fitz Lee and pointed out that "You invited me, *and some of my people*, and you see I have brought them!" Fitz Lee replied, "Well, don't let them halloo, 'Here's your mule!' at the review." At which point Wade Hampton added with a laugh, "If they do we will charge you!" In any case, the cavalrymen had their audience, but paid a small price for it. As the horsemen paraded, Hood's veterans yielded to every urge to shout and deride their pampered comrades who let their horses do the walking for them. For instance, when cavalrymen lost their hats in the moment of charge, the loss was usually followed by a charge of several infantrymen who sought to capture the prize. There were probably special catcalls for the men of the Second Squadron, 2nd North Carolina Cavalry as they pranced by the infantrymen of Law's brigade who had shared the rifle-pits with them on the Suffolk line a few weeks earlier. However, the highlight for the infantrymen may have been when young Private Opie approached the point from which the cavalrymen were to charge past the reviewers, and in his words, "My horse evidently considered it a real charge and a real battle, for when our turn arrived to charge by the reviewing party, regardless of my caresses and expostulations, and although I had a heavy army bit and curb upon her, she shot out like an arrow, overtaking the squadron in front, made a rear attack upon it, and broke it in two. This episode turned this part of the review into a ridiculous farce."[10]

Overall the men of the Second Squadron were probably more impressed by the stature of Robert E. Lee — this was their first chance to see the commanding general. Passing in review for Robert E. Lee was certainly the high point of the exhausting day. The cavalrymen had been through two reviews in three days and were feeling the effects. According to one of the participants from W. H. F. Lee's brigade, "These men retired at night, hungry and weary and needing rest after the excitement and vigorous exercise through which they had passed."[11]

Weary or not, the cavalrymen were moved rapidly back to their camps, which by then resembled bivouacs. They were told to prepare for a march the following morning — this was the beginning of what came to be known as the Gettysburg Campaign. R. E. Lee planned to start Longstreet and Ewell for the Potomac. They were going to take the war to the North and take some of the burden off of the people of Virginia. Stuart's cavalry was to shield the infantry's march north.

The composition and strength of R. E. Lee's shield is worthy of note before we consider the upcoming campaigns.

J. E. B. Stuart's Cavalry Division

Generals R. E. Lee and J. E. B. Stuart had been working on ways to strengthen their cavalry in the face of the pressure they were getting from the increased size and efficiency of the Union's cavalry under George Stoneman and now Alfred Pleasonton. This issue was in their thoughts as they collected their cavalry force for the coming campaign. On May 23, just three days after Stuart moved to Culpeper Court House, R. E. Lee sent him a message in which he expressed concern over the enemy's intentions and their own readiness. At that time, he instructed Stuart to

…collect and recruit your cavalry as much as possible, and think it wise to be quiet and watchful for a little time….

Devote your attention to the organization and recuperation of your command, of which I wish a detailed report, giving the number of regiments, their strength, officers, condition, &c., and the brigades to which attached….

We could with propriety diminish the number of regiments in a brigade if they were full, but they are so small — I mean the effectives — that a brigade has hardly over two full regiments with it.[12]

In part, R. E. Lee's comment was a response to Stuart's known desire to have a couple of more brigades, so he could promote deserving officers to brigadier general — namely, Williams C. Wickham and Thomas L. Rosser. They were then commanding the 4th and 5th Virginia Cavalry Regiments — both in Fitz Lee's brigade. R. E. Lee's concern was more with the size of his effective cavalry force. The brigades lacked effective manpower, and R. E. Lee did not seem eager to reduce the size of the existing brigades.

In his message to Stuart on May 23, R. E. Lee had asked for an accounting of cavalry strength, and when he got it, his concerns were confirmed. In his report of May 25, Stuart submitted the following information (see next page).[13] Robertson and his two North Carolina regiments had arrived at Culpeper by May 25, 1863, and were included in the count. (His 3rd Cavalry remained detached on the Blackwater River.) W. E. Jones on the other hand was ordered to head for Stuart by easy marches on May 25 and his command had not yet been

Number of Effective (Healthy, Armed and Mounted) Men by Brigade in Culpeper County

	Troops	Officers
Hampton's brigade	2,032	178
Fitz Lee's brigade	1,224	108
W. H. F. Lee's brigade	1,439	90
Jones's brigade	....	....
Robertson's brigade	1,068	67
	5,736	453

counted. (A. G. Jenkins was off replacing Jones in the Valley).[14] After Jones arrived with his men, the count of effective cavalrymen near Brandy Station probably numbered close to 7,000.

While R. E. Lee's primary focus was on the number of effective men in a brigade, Stuart's attention was on the number of regiments in each and the latter seemed abundant. The regiments under Stuart's command at that time are listed below (see table).[15]

To the extent Robert E. Lee was interested in reorganizing the cavalry, he was primarily interested in creating an all North Carolina brigade by shuffling regiments—preferably with a North Carolina commander.[16] Apparently Lee's recommendation was not exactly what Stuart had in mind. Stuart was still more interested in promoting Thomas L. Rosser and Williams C. Wickham and creating two more predominantly Virginia brigades. R. E. Lee would get his all North Carolina brigade and Stuart his two new Virginia brigadier generals, but not right away. Both generals knew shuffling regiments would not increase the effective size of their force for the upcoming campaign, so nothing was done.

W. H. F. Lee's Brigade and the 2nd North Carolina Cavalry

When Stuart submitted his reports on the size and composition of his cavalry on May 25, 1863, one of the reports showed the regimental leadership in W. H. F. Lee's cavalry brigade as follows: the 2nd North Carolina, Lieutenant Colonel William H. Payne (Payne was from the 4th Virginia Cavalry, temporarily commanding the 2nd North Carolina Cavalry); the 9th Virginia, Colonel R. L. T. Beale; 10th Virginia, Colonel J. L. Davis; and the 13th Virginia, Major J. E. Gillette.[17]

Robert E. Lee's concern for the small number of effectives in the brigades is well illustrated by W. H. F. Lee's brigade and the 2nd North Carolina Cavalry. In his report, Stuart provided the following information (see table, next page). The number of effectives in the 2nd North Carolina was up considerably from the number at the Battle of Chancellorsville. At least two factors contributed to the increase: the first resulted from the return of the Second Squadron; and the second from the opportunity they had to rest and nourish their horses in lush fields—while the 2nd North Carolina

J. E. B. Stuart's Cavalry Command, June 1863

Brigadier General Wade Hampton's brigade:
   1st North Carolina
   1st South Carolina
   2nd South Carolina
   Cobb's (Georgia) Legion
   Jefferson Davis (Mississippi) Legion
   Phillips's (Georgia) Legion
Brigadier General Fitz Lee's brigade:
   1st Virginia
   2nd Virginia
   3rd Virginia
   4th Virginia
   5th Virginia
Brigadier General W. H. F. Lee's brigade:
   2nd North Carolina
   9th Virginia
   10th Virginia
   13th Virginia
   15th Virginia (detached on North Anna River)
Brigadier General W. E. Jones's brigade:
   6th Virginia
   7th Virginia
   11th Virginia
   12th Virginia
   White's Battalion
Brigadier General B. H. Robertson's brigade:
   7th Confederate
   62nd Georgia
   41st North Carolina (3rd North Carolina Cavalry—detached)
   59th North Carolina (4th North Carolina Cavalry)
   63rd North Carolina (5th North Carolina Cavalry)

Readiness of W. H. F. Lee's Men by Regiment

	Present effective mounted	Present non-effective	Absent	Percent effective of total
2nd North Carolina	213	161	247	34%
9th Virginia	616	43	308	64%
10th Virginia	286	73	361	40%
13th Virginia	414	153	170	56%
15th Virginia	....	....	....	

Readiness of North Carolina Cavalrymen by Regiment

	Present effective mounted	Present non-effective	Absent	Percent effective of total
1st North Carolina	534	156	183	61%
2nd North Carolina	213	161	247	34%
4th North Carolina	604	44	122	78%
5th North Carolina	531	129	165	64%

was camped near Culpepper they were able to send a detail with a herd of horses from each company and let them graze on a regular basis.[18]

The 10th Virginia had a small effective command by Virginia standards. The 15th Virginia Cavalry was on picket duty in central Virginia since the Battle of Chancellorsville and not counted for the upcoming fights. The 9th and 13th Virginia cavalries were the dominant forces in the brigade.

Of the 621 men on the roster of the 2nd North Carolina at that time, only 213, or about 34%, were available for combat—in good health, armed, and mounted. Within W. H. F. Lee's brigade, that was the lowest percentage, with the 10th Virginia running a close second. The low percentage of effectives was not necessarily a reflection of the training and discipline of the North Carolina men. Indeed the problem was at least twofold. First of all, many of the men in the 2nd North Carolina had considerably more difficulty getting home to acquire fresh horses than did the Virginians in their brigade. But the problem clearly goes beyond the distances between home and the battlefields, because, secondly, when we compare the 2nd Cavalry with other North Carolina regiments, they still show an unusually high rate of non-effective men. In fact, when compared to other North Carolina cavalry regiments collected near Brandy Station, the 2nd North Carolina looked even worse. For instance, the 1st North Carolina Cavalry from Wade Hampton's brigade, and the 4th and 5th North Carolina cavalries from B. H. Robertson's brigade had a much higher percentage of effective men (see following table).

The comparisons in the table highlight the relatively high number of absent men in the 2nd North Carolina. Most of the absent were on leaves, which were easier to obtain in some companies than others—many of these men did drift back into service because few of them ended up on "deserters" lists, while a good number of them sought transfers to better equipped regiments.

However, aside from the comparatively low rate of effective cavalrymen there was yet another problem—the 2nd Cavalry was the smallest regiment in total number of men within its own brigade and among the other North Carolina regiments. From the smallest to largest, the regiments contained the following numbers: 2nd North Carolina, with 621 men; 10th Virginia, 720; 13th Virginia, 737; 4th North Carolina, 770; 5th North Carolina, 825; 1st North Carolina, 873; and the 9th Virginia, 967.

These problems are difficult to account for, but certainly they were related to regimental leadership. It is commonly understood that good leadership can cause men to rise above normal endurance, strength, and courage; it is equally possible that the lack of good, consistent leadership can cause indifference, absenteeism, and low recruitment. The 2nd North Carolina's Colonel Sol. Williams had been on leave and Court Martial duty during most of their stay in Virginia; their Lieutenant Colonel, W. G. Robinson had been a captive of the Union since April of 1862 and not replaced; and several of their captains had been lost for various reasons. Up to this point the regiment had not had consistent leadership dedicated to the welfare of the regiment—there was relatively little pressure for adequate equipment and little recruiting. For example, while the regiment was under Colonel Chambliss's command, he seldom knew where it was and never seemed too concerned over it; and while under Lieutenant Colonel W. H. F. Payne's command in late 1862, the 2nd North Carolina's leader was more concerned with protecting the wounded in the town of Warrenton, getting well, and returning to active duty with his own regiment. The latter concern was still with Payne when he was reassigned to command the 2nd North Carolina Cavalry in March–May of 1863. W. H. F. Payne was a dedicated commander, but he was never happy about being detached to command the 2nd North Carolina Cavalry.

Without aggressive leadership at the brigade and regiment levels pressing for more equipment, horses, and recruits, the number of effective troops diminished over time. The reasons combined to give the 2nd North Carolina the highest absentee rate and the lowest effective rate, and the poorest recruiting effort among the regiments it was brigaded with and among other cavalry units from North Carolina.[19]

Even though the 2nd North Carolina was fully equipped for the first time after joining W. H. F. Lee's brigade, the issues of regimental leadership, acquiring horses and new recruits would not be addressed until much later in 1863. Things would get much worse before they got any better, because the 2nd North Carolina Cavalry would sustain proportionately greater combat losses than any other regiment in its brigade on the way to Gettysburg.

Leadership in the Second North Carolina Cavalry at Brandy Station

By the second week of June 1863, the 2nd North Carolina Cavalry's leadership included the following: Solomon Williams, colonel (since June 6, 1862); lieutenant colonel, vacant; Clinton M. Andrews, major; John C. Pegram, adjutant; A. Smith Jordan, assistant quartermaster; and Edward Jordon, sergeant major.[20]

Of course, as indicated above, Solomon Williams had been on Court Martial duty since the regiment left North Carolina, and he was on leave to get married around June 1. He resumed command of his regiment on June 8, 1863. During Williams's absence the 2nd Cavalry was at various times commanded by Major Clinton M. Andrews. Leaders of various companies were the men listed below.

The 2nd North Carolina Cavalry's state of readiness was not great but it was typical for them. No matter, the war would not wait for them to be ready. They were gathered in Culpeper County to help shield Robert E. Lee's next campaign north.

2nd North Carolina Cavalry: Rank by Company, May 1863

Cos.	Captain	1st Lieutenant	2nd Lieutenant
A	J. V. B. Rogers	W. B. Tidwell	Abram C. Evans
			Jacob E. Williams
B	S. J. Andrews	R. W. Allison	J. N. Turner
			William A. Luckey
C	James M. Wynn	William. P. Roberts	Abram F. Harrell
			L. R. Cowper
D	James W. Strange	Joseph S. Baker	J. A. P. Conoly
			John B. Person
E	R. W. Atkinson	K. H. Winstead	E. P. Tucke
			Eph. Robbins
F	P. A. Tatum	John G. Blassingame	N. C. Tucker
			____ Holden
G	M. L. Eure	G. P. Bryan	W. M. Owens
			J. W. Simmons
H	R. H. Reese	S. N. Buxton	F. M. Spivey
			____ Copeland
I	D. O. Bryan	Thomas H. Harrington	John C. Baker
			James A. Cole
K	W. A. Graham Jr.	John P. Lockhart	A. F. Faucette
			James R. Harris

The Battle at Brandy Station, June 9

The first fight in the Gettysburg Campaign was at Brandy Station between the cavalries. A couple of important points can be made about the Battle at Brandy Station. First, it was not planned or even expected by the Confederates; and second, though it was initiated by Hooker and Pleasonton, they had seriously misgauged what they were about to encounter as they crossed the Rappahannock River. Pleasonton surprised Stuart, yet Pleasonton was surprised by Stuart's proximity to the river.

In spite of the cavalry reviews celebrating their number and prowess, the Confederate cavalry commanders, starting with Stuart, had failed to do what they themselves considered part of their job — they had not watched the massive collection of the enemy just across the river on June 8, 1863. Aside from the attention they gave to the cavalry reviews on that day and a couple of days before, the Confederate commanders had their eyes on Pennsylvania and their plan for getting there. Stuart's men were told to be ready to march early on the morning of June 9. Much to their surprise, they had to be ready to fight rather than march on that morning in the biggest cavalry battle ever fought in America.[21]

Stuart's travel plans were put on hold because Hooker was alerted to Stuart's troop buildup around Culpeper Court House, and he wanted Pleasonton to destroy them before another Confederate cavalry campaign could get underway. On June 5, 1863, from Warrenton Junction, Brigadier General John Buford reported that Stuart was gathering the brigades of Fitz Lee, W. H. F. Lee, B. H. Robertson, A. G. Jenkins, and W. E. Jones, perhaps 20,000 cavalrymen in all — Buford's informant indicated that they might be preparing for a raid.[22]

While Buford's correspondence seriously overstated the size of Stuart's force, it clearly illustrates they were more aware of the massing of cavalry by the Confederates than the latter was of Union movements several days later. On the same day, the 5th, the War Department alerted Hooker to the following: "Prisoners and deserters brought in here state that Stuart is preparing a column of from 15,000 to 20,000 men, cavalry and artillery, for a raid. They say it will be ready in two or three days." Apparently, however, Union commanders still had no understanding of the fact that Stuart was collecting his cavalry as a part of a much bigger raid, indeed an invasion of Pennsylvania — even though they had indications that some Confederate infantry was on the move. By June 8, Union reports were a little more on the mark when Pleasonton forwarded this scouting report: "The scout ... says that the two Lees are at Culpeper. Hampton's Legion and almost 1,000 infantry at Brandy Station. Artillery at both places. Yager (the scout) says that he has reliable information that infantry are being sent to the Valley from Lee's army, and that there is a force of infantry at Culpeper."[23]

Nonetheless, Union commanders were correct to have been concerned about Stuart's cavalry build-up, given what they understood to be the composition and disposition of the enemy force at Culpeper Court House, and they took appropriate action. When Pleasonton sent the above mentioned scouting report, his orders had already been penned and they were clear. Pleasonton's instructions were as follows: "...it is recommended that you cross the Rappahannock at Beverly and Kelly's Fords, and march directly on Culpeper. For this you will divide your cavalry force as you think proper, to carry into execution the object in view, which is to disperse and destroy the rebel force assembled in the vicinity of Culpeper, and to destroy his trains and supplies of all description to the utmost of your ability."[24]

As indicated, Hooker's and Pleasonton's best information was only partially correct about the number of Confederate forces collected between Culpeper and the river, and it was considerably off the mark concerning the location of Stuart's cavalry. They still thought the main body of Confederate cavalry was concentrated near Culpeper Court House, and that the Union cavalry and infantry crossing at two different fords would be able to unite around Brandy Station and attack in force near Culpeper.

Pleasonton brought about 11,000 troopers to the Rappahannock by the morning of June 9. He had three divisions of cavalry, a reserve brigade, two infantry brigades, and four batteries of horse artillery. He sent about half his force to Beverly Ford and the rest to Kelly's Ford about six miles southeast. John Buford led the column at Beverly Ford, and David

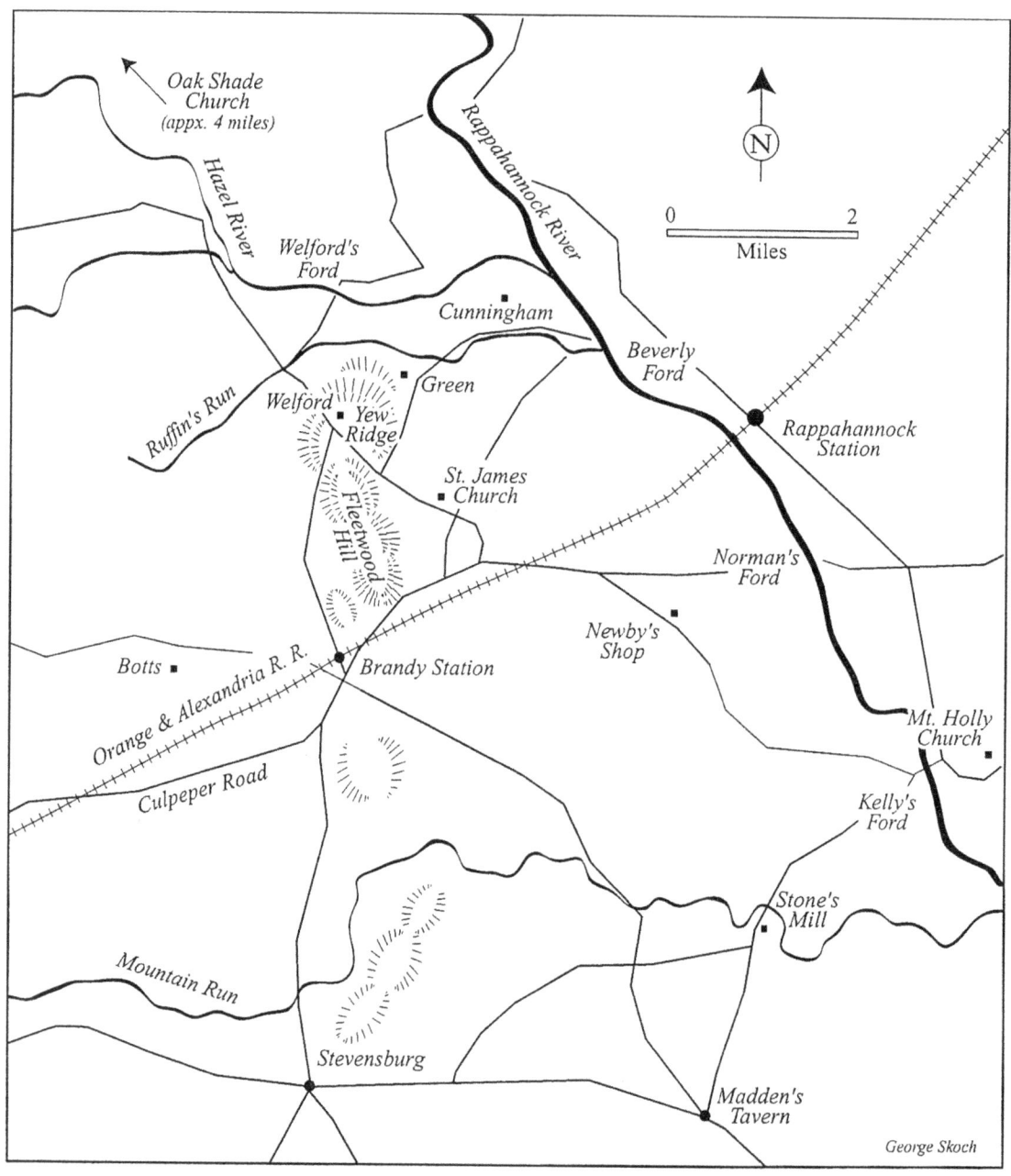

3.1: Around Brandy Station, June 1863

McM. Gregg led the others to Kelly's Ford — Pleasonton and his staff crossed with Buford on the upper ford. They planned to cross at about the same time and join forces at Brandy Station, then jointly assault Stuart near Culpeper Court House. Another column under Colonel Alfred Duffié planned to split from D. McM. Gregg's force, after crossing at Kelly's Ford and proceed to Stevensburg, then march for Culpeper Court House to join Buford and Gregg in the battle. The flaw in the plan, of course, was that Stuart and his cavalry were not at Culpeper Court House.

The Confederate cavalry was headquartered on a ridge just north of Brandy Station, known as

Fleetwood Hill. Wade Hampton's and Beverly Robertson's brigades were bivouacked from north of Brandy Station to Stevensburg, W. H. F. Lee's was just about a mile south of Welford's Ford on the Hazel River at the Welford plantation, and Brigadier General W. E. Jones's brigade bivouacked near the St. James Church about halfway up the road from Brandy Station to Beverly Ford. Fitz Lee's brigade (temporarily commanded by Colonel Thomas Munford) was located to the north about seven and a half miles, across the Hazel River up near Oak Shade Church.

Kelly's Ford, about four miles down the Rappahannock from the railroad crossing, was picketed by Robertson's troops. Jones's brigade had the responsibility of picketing the river along the Beverly Ford area. Just behind Jones's pickets, about a mile from the river, Stuart had several batteries of his horse artillery — Jones's cavalrymen were the first to know of Buford's and Pleasonton's arrival, beginning around 4:30 A.M. on June 9, 1863.

The 8th New York Cavalry stormed across Beverly Ford directly at the small Confederate picket post. The pickets fired at the oncoming Yankees, then headed back into the woods for their picket camp. Young Luther Hopkins was asleep in the picket camp when the attack began, and he was awakened in time to observe,

The pickets were hurrying up from the river in every direction, firing their pistols to give the alarm.

Our captain formed the men in the edge of the woods for the purpose of checking for a few minutes the advancing enemy, so as to give the 10,000 cavalrymen that were encamped a mile or so in the rear time to saddle and mount their horses and prepare for battle.

The enemy came pouring up from the river, and we opened fire on them, checking them for the moment. Two of our men were killed, several wounded, and two horses killed.

Two couriers had gone ahead to arouse the camp. We soon followed them along the road through the woods, the enemy hard on our heels.[25]

The Confederate pickets did their job — they made a lot of noise and immediately sent two couriers back to alert W. E. Jones of the unexpected intruders. As Jones's pickets fell back from the river, Private Luther Hopkins later recalled that his captain from the rear of the retreating men urged them to check their speed in order to slow the enemy's advance. Hopkins wrote, "I looked behind, called to the captain and told him they were right on us, and just as I spoke two bullets went hissing by my head. The captain yelled to his men to move forward, and bending low on the necks of our horses, we gave them the spur."[26]

The pickets retreated through the woods, and by the time they reached a clearing they saw some of their comrades from the 6th and 7th Virginia Cavalry racing toward them. The Virginians were heading for the sound of gunfire near the river — many of them without shirts and boots; some without saddles on their horses. Colonel Davis and the 8th New York were heading directly for the Virginians. Davis stopped to collect his men at the edge of the clearing. The Virginians continued to thunder in his direction.

At the same time, some Confederates went for their artillery batteries at the edge of the clearing. The Confederates managed to get one gun into place and begin firing at their enemy who was by then charging across the clearing to capture the guns. The guns of Stuart's horse artillery were threatened — the loss of guns would have been serious but damaged pride would have hurt more. Stuart's horse artillery had not yet lost a gun in battle. The single gun placed in the road was effective. It slowed the 8th New York Cavalry just long enough for the fastest horses from the 6th Virginia to arrive. Troopers from Jones's 6th Virginia managed to help avoid the humiliating loss, and all the guns made it to the rear.

The partially clad cavalrymen obviously did not look their best as they rode to battle, but they were at their best in their response. Remember young Private Opie whose spirited horse rode up the backs of his comrades during the theatrical charge in the cavalry review a few days earlier? Well, his mare was just as ready to follow her instincts on this day, in a charge with consequences. Thanks to his impetuous and fast mare, Opie was in a position to describe the first mounted encounter between Buford's 8th New York and Jones's 6th Virginia. His description includes the following:

Upon hearing this firing, Lieutenants ... hastily formed the men who had horses in camp, and ordered them to charge down the road.

I mounted my wild charger, for the last time, and fell into the first set of fours, when the order to charge was given, and we started down the road at a gallop. My horse did what I too well knew she would do—that is she shot out from the column like a thunderbolt and rushed down the road with the rapidity of lightning. I looked around behind me, and no one was in sight. I pulled with all my strength and vigor; I halooed, "Whoa! whoa! whoa! but to no purpose, as her mouth was fixed against her breast. I thought of killing her, but I had nothing but a sabre, as, three days before, someone had stolen my six-shooter. I expected, every moment, to rush upon the enemy.... I thought of jumping off but that would never have done.

I turned a bend in the road, and there, across my path, was a double line of cavalry. My hope was that, seeing a single horseman, they would understand the situation and not fire [Remember, John was only 18 years of age at the time, and hope for civility in the midst of war still sprang eternal];... At any rate, I saw them raise their carbines, then a line of smoke, then a crash; when, heels over head, both horse and rider tumbled through the air and fell, headlong, in a pile on the side of the road. My right leg felt as if paralyzed, but, seeing and feeling no blood, upon examination, I found that a ball had struck the toe of my boot and plowed a furrow through the sole.

I jumped up, still having my sabre in my right hand, my horse by my side dead, not having uttered a groan or made a struggle.... How I escaped remains a mystery, as I was only twenty yards distant from the enemy, and received the fire of several hundred men. After I arose to my feet, I heard the boys charging down the road. In a moment they are opposite me in the road, when another volley was fired; a man dropped dead at my feet, Lieutenant Morton.... I seized his horse and mounted him, and joined in the charge. We broke the Eighth New York....

Having by this time lost more than half of our men, we were charged by the Eighth Illinois and driven out of the woods back to our camp, where we found several regiments formed in line, ready for the coming battle.[27]

As Private Opie indicated, the charging Virginians hardly broke their pace and plunged directly into the oncoming 8th New York Cavalry. It was the first violent clash of horses and sabers on that road that morning. The Virginians pulled back and by then the 7th Virginia was charging forward and met the Union cavalries that were still advancing and by then included men from the 8th Illinois and 3rd Indiana Cavalry. The troops from the 6th and 7th Virginia pulled up in the woods, on both sides of the road, and launched charges and counter-charges until forced back by greater numbers. There were several more charges from both sides, each met with a countercharge; W. E. Jones hoped to hold Buford's forces until Stuart could send reinforcements.

The Confederate horse artillery dropped back to St. James Church and took a position near the Brandy Station road. W. E. Jones's regiments dropped back and formed on the left of the guns. About the same time, Wade Hampton arrived from the other side of Brandy Station with some of his brigade and formed to the right of the guns. J. E. B. Stuart and most of his staff came a little later. This line held Buford's regiments. Meanwhile, Union troops continued crossing the river and were pressing into the rear of regiments facing W. E. Jones's and Hampton's line.

Before leaving St. James Church for the fighting near the river, Jones had sent word to Stuart of the strong Union force coming across at Beverly Ford, but Stuart had already heard the sounds coming from the river—he knew what it meant. As he sent Hampton to support Jones, Stuart also sent instructions for B. H. Robertson to hold the road below Brandy Station coming up from Kelly's Ford; and for Colonel Matthew Butler's 2nd South Carolina from Hampton's brigade to stand in reserve and cover the road coming up from Stevensburg to Brandy Station and to keep a line of communication open to Culpeper. With Robertson and Butler covering the roads coming up from Kelly's Ford, Stuart was confident his back was covered, and with Hampton on his way to reinforce Jones's right, Stuart turned his attention to strengthening the left of the line by calling for Munford (temporally in command of Fitz Lee's brigade) to bring his men from their bivouac some eight miles from the action and cross the Hazel River—they were to join the line at that point. Stuart also sent word for W. H. F. Lee's brigade to head directly east for the enemy advance coming at them from Beverly Ford. Then Stuart and most of his staff rode hard for the action around St. James Church. Stuart left only his assistant adjutant general, H. B. McClellan, and a couple of orderlies at his headquarters on the south end of the Fleetwood ridge.

By the time Stuart arrived at St. James Church, the pressure on Jones and Hampton had eased a bit. Buford had been pressing hard on the Confederate line because his orders were to pass along the road to Brandy Station and connect with D. McM. Gregg—he was surprised to find more than a picket force between the river and Brandy and probably more than a little frustrated to find he could not force through the enemy line with his cavalry and infantry.

After much bloody fighting, Buford held his line in front of St. James Church. He then went back toward the river to collect his forces that were still crossing at Beverly Ford and to consider a sweep around the Confederate left. Buford quickly formulated and put in motion another plan—he collected a large force to head west and overpower Stuart's left. Buford moved west of the Cunningham farm and formed a line with his right near the Hazel River, dropping south opposite the Green farm. Once again, Buford was greeted by stiffer opposition than anticipated—he ran into the 9th, 10th, 13th Virginia, and the 2nd North Carolina Cavalry, all from W. H. F. Lee's brigade.

At the sound of gunfire, W. H. F. Lee's regiments were in motion. Their camp was near the Welford farm just west of Yew Ridge. It is a relatively small ridge running north and south and resting just northeast of the upper end of the Fleetwood ridge. W. H. F. Lee moved his men rapidly and formed a line east of the Yew Ridge, in front of the Green's farm house. There he dismounted men behind a stone wall on the farm facing Buford's new line.

Captain William A. Graham, of Company K, 2nd North Carolina, described the early scene as orderly and urgent. At about 6:30 A.M., the bugle sounded "Saddle up." Graham went to his regimental headquarters to find Colonel Solomon William and was told to leave only the cooks and sore-back horses in camp.[28]

About a half-hour later, Graham was notified to mount every man he had, and the call "To horse—lead out," was sounded. Graham's squadron, companies C and K, was placed at the end of Sol. William's regiment, and the 2nd North Carolina filed out after the 10th Virginia in "Column of fours." They rode about a quarter of a mile then took the road leading to Green's and then Cunningham's farms and toward the Rappahannock just above Beverly Ford. When they reached the road, they formed in platoons and immediately took the "Gallop," and held that pace for over a mile. They could hear the fighting and there was certainly a sense of urgency about them—they knew this was not the march with full provisions planned for the morning. Yet, according to Graham's estimate, still less than a third of the regiment knew the Federals had already crossed the river.

Buford's troops had passed the Cunningham farm, and set up artillery back at the farm. As soon as Graham's squadron cleared some woods and turned into the field before Cunningham's place, an artillery shell took off the top of a tree just above their heads—then they all knew the enemy was there. Indeed, they could see the enemy artillery, and they could see that part of the 10th Virginia was already engaged near Cunningham's farm.

The 2nd North Carolina Cavalry was at first placed behind a knoll to protect two guns of Breathed's horse artillery under Lieutenant Johnston that had been assigned to W. H. F. Lee. The guns were on the knoll overlooking the Confederate line being established in front of Green's farm.

From behind the knoll, Solomon Williams called up all the men in his regiment who were armed with "long range guns," and sent them to the front on foot. They were joined by dismounted men from the 9th, 10th, and 13th Virginia cavalries and commanded by John R. Chambliss of the 13th Virginia. The dismounted cavalrymen from the 2nd North Carolina and some of their comrades were ordered to move toward a stonewall behind which Buford had placed dismounted Union cavalrymen. The two lines exchanged fire for a while, the Federal cavalrymen from behind the wall—an intolerable advantage. To strengthen their position, the dismounted men of the 2nd North Carolina were ordered to charge and capture the stone wall, which they did, taking 18 prisoners and inflicting a number of causalities, and, of course, suffering some as well. By taking the wall, W. H. F. Lee's line in front of Green's farmhouse was established and strong—they communicated with W. E. Jones and formed nearly a right angle to his line.[29]

Buford's assault on W. H. F. Lee's position started in earnest around 8:30 A.M. and was severe. The fighting on the Confederate left continued throughout the morning. The Federals made numerous dismounted attacks at various places along the line, especially near the Cunningham farm — the section of the line held by W. H. F. Lee's brigade. Lieutenant Johnson's guns were still on a knoll but just behind W. H. F. Lee's line, and with open fields around them. This position threatened Buford's right flank and rear, and was the point Buford would have to break when he moved to flank Stuart's line. W. H. F. Lee's men held their end of the line under shelling from Buford's artillery most of the morning. The shelling let up from time-to-time as a number of attacks were ordered in an effort to break and drive back the left of the Confederate line. W. H. F. Lee's brigade was reinforced by the 7th Virginia from W. E. Jones's brigade which was a distance from its own brigade but connected to the 2nd North Carolina on W. H. F. Lee's right — the 7th Virginia operated with W. H. F. Lee until ordered to pull back toward Brandy Station around midday.[30]

At one point, a well-executed effort was made to break through the line where the dismounted men from the 2nd North Carolina were holding. The 2nd Cavalry had already been successful in repulsing several Union cavalry charges, before Buford called up a detachment from the Second Massachusetts and Third Wisconsin Infantry and ordered them to move forward and dislodge the Confederates behind the stone wall. The Federal infantrymen took a circuitous route around a hill for cover, crawling through fields until they came around the wall and opened fire on the very surprised dismounted sharpshooters under Colonel Chambliss's command — which included some troops from the 10th Virginia and the 2nd North Carolina. Under intense fire, Chambliss's line of sharpshooters broke and a number of his men were captured. Along with their comrades, the men of the 2nd Cavalry were surprised by the flank attack but briefly returned the enemy's fire before rapidly pulling back from the wall and regrouping.

The infantry under Buford took temporary possession of the wall and inflicted heavy losses on the dismounted men of the 2nd North Carolina Cavalry — several cavalrymen were killed or wounded and, according to Major Mudge of the of the Second Massachusetts Infantry, sixteen from the 2nd North Carolina Cavalry were taken prisoner. Lieutenant Colonel Flood of the Third Wisconsin claimed ten cavalrymen were taken prisoner in the assault.[31] The count may have been a bit off — by the end of the day, the 2nd North Carolina Cavalry had nine of its men captured by their enemy. (The difference in counts partially resulted from the ebb and flow of the line due to charges and countercharges which frequently resulted in the liberation of prisoners before they were moved to the rear.)

As indicated, there was severe fighting around the wall during the morning, but just before noon, there was a lull in the fighting as both A. Pleasonton and J. Buford realized they could not turn W. H. F. Lee's troops on the Confederate left without a massive effort and support from below by D. McM. Gregg's column. While waiting for Gregg, Buford moved troops up the line, concentrating them on his right for a massive attack on W. H. F. Lee's forces. W. H. F. Lee's cavalrymen knew Buford was massing a large force, mostly in the woods, which included the 8th Illinois, 6th Pennsylvania, 1st, 2nd, 5th, and 6th United States cavalries, as well as portions of the 2nd Massachusetts and 3rd Wisconsin infantries, and the Confederates expected a major assault at any time — but Buford had to wait for word from Pleasonton. Pleasonton awaited word from D. McM. Gregg indicating he had moved north from Kelly's Ford and was ready to link-up with his force. In fact, at 11:00 A.M. Pleasonton sent a message to Hooker explaining the lull in those terms.[32] Pleasonton and Buford would not have to wait much longer, however. There was movement south of Brandy Station, coming up from Kelly's Ford.

David McM. Gregg sent Alfred Duffié to cross the Rappahannock at the head of his column. Duffié was scheduled to cross at Kelly's Ford at the same time Buford was taking his column across at Beverly Ford at about 4:30 A.M. on the morning of June 9. Unfortunately, Duffié was misguided and did not get to the ford until around 6:00 A.M., and largely as a consequence Gregg did not complete his crossing until around 9:00 A.M..

D. McM. Gregg had been listening to the guns fire from John Buford's engagements up river and was in a hurry to get up to Brandy Station and help. When he sent his main column from Kelly's Ford up the first and most direct road to Brandy, by way of Newby's Shop, however, he was surprised to find Robinson's 4th and 5th North Carolina blocking the road and ready for battle.

D. McM. Gregg had already sent Duffié on the road from Kelly's Ford, past Stone's Mill and west to Stevensburg. From there, Duffié was instructed to take the road north to Brandy Station and the sounds of fighting. Gregg sent a force to hold Robinson's attention on the first road going northwest and took the rest of his column, behind Duffié, through Stone's Mill and up the next road, leading northwest from Willis Madden's place to Brandy Station. The road taken by Duffié to Stevensburg was not an easy course; it was blocked by Matthew C. Butler's 2nd South Carolina, supported by the 4th Virginia Cavalry.[33]

M. C. Butler and the 2nd South Carolina Cavalry made a stand across Duffié's path to Stevensburg and was more or less supported by the 4th Virginia Cavalry under Williams C. Wickham. The two Confederate regiments had difficulty communicating that day and could not manage to hold the enemy. At one point, the 4th Virginia was under severe pressure which caused it to break and run — not a common response for the 4th Virginia, "But on this day a panic possessed them." Duffié was able to push his way through Stevensburg. Butler's 2nd South Carolina dropped back along the road heading north to Brandy Station and made a stand near Mountain Run. Just after Butler reformed his line near Mountain Run, he fell in combat and passed leadership of the command to Wickham of the 4th Virginia.[34]

W. H. Payne had just returned to the 4th Virginia when Colonel Williams returned to the 2nd North Carolina the day before and had been assigned the job of communicating between Butler and Wickham. His task had to have been an incredibly difficult one in the fast moving and confused state of the Confederate "line" in front of Duffié that day.[35]

Duffié was well-positioned to continue his push through the 2nd South Carolina and the 4th Virginia when he responded to D. McM. Gregg's calls for him to back up and return to support his move on Brandy Station on another road. Before 11:00 A.M., Gregg's column approached Stuart's Headquarter on Fleetwood Hill (ridge) and was in a position to threaten Stuart's rear.

Around noon, during the lull in the fighting near St. James Church, W. E. Jones received word that Federal troops under D. McM. Gregg had made their way up from Kelly's Ford and were north of Brandy Station, approaching Fleetwood Hill — and he sent this word on to Stuart. Until then, Stuart apparently felt his rear was adequately protected by B. H. Robinson's North Carolina brigade and M. C. Butler's force he had left south of Brandy Station, so he had failed to take seriously several warnings about troops coming from Kelly's Ford. Though the force Stuart sent was not large, he felt they should have been able to hold any troops coming across the river at Kelly's Ford. In fact, however, unlike Duffié's men, Gregg's column got to Brandy Station without a serious engagement. Stuart's force below Brandy was not sufficiently effective that morning, and D. McM. Gregg sent a larger force at them than Stuart had imagined.

Stuart had left his assistant adjutant-general, H. B. McClellan, on Fleetwood Hill with no troops to defend the position. By the time McClellan could see the Federals approaching Brandy Station, he knew Stuart could not get troops there in time to hold the Station. McClellan sent word to Stuart and managed to pull a six-pounder howitzer up the hill in an attempt to slow D. McM. Gregg's attack.[36]

As soon as Stuart heard the gun firing at Fleetwood Hill, he knew the reports he had been getting were more accurate than not, and he immediately put men in motion to support H. B. McClellan on the southern end of the Fleetwood ridge. Stuart sent messengers to Hampton and W. E. Jones to bring the main bodies of their brigades immediately. According to H. B. McClellan, who wrote of these events some years later, the first to arrive were from Jones's brigade — the 12th Virginia followed closely by the 35th Battalion and 6th Virginia. Jones instructed the 7th Virginia to move toward Brandy Station and rejoin his brigade, and in the process notified W. H. F. Lee on the left of his departure. Both Jones and Hampton had to come from near St. James Church located about a mile and a half away.[37]

After stopping to respond to H. B. McClellan's single gun firing from Stuart's headquarters on Fleetwood Hill, Percy Wyndham sent three regiments around to attack the hill from the west side. These Union troops arrived at Fleetwood just as the gun had fired its last round, and the 1st New Jersey Cavalry was within fifty yards of the top. At about this time, W. E. Jones's three regiments were approaching the southern end of the ridge from the north and turned west to climb up and over the hill.

The men from W. E. Jones's brigade who had the fasted horses got to the scene first. Others were strung out behind, so the first Confederate troops were, of necessity, disorganized but just in time. The 12th Virginia charged over the crest of the hill, started down the west side and collided with the 1st New Jersey. The better organized 1st New Jersey scattered the 12th Virginia and were then hit by the 35th Virginia Cavalry Battalion. Then the 1st Pennsylvania and 1st Maryland (Federal) entered the fight and were hit by the charging 6th Virginia. At some point in the melee, Federal troops reached the top of the hill and stormed over Stuart's headquarters, capturing, among other things, much of his correspondence of the previous days.

P. Wyndham's regiments were followed by H. Judson Kilpatrick's brigade, and W. E. Jones's regiments were followed by Hampton's cavalrymen. Kilpatrick swung his regiments around to approach the hill from the southeastern end of the ridge, and as they started up the hill, they were hit in the flank by Hampton's men. Hampton arrived in near-perfect order with the Cobb Legion in front, followed by the 1st South Carolina, then the 1st North Carolina and the Jeff Davis Legion. They swept around the hill at full speed and with momentum. After a considerable battle, Hampton's troops pushed the Federals down the hill, across the railroad tracks and back toward Kelly's Ford. Jones, with those of his troops still with him, swept to the west of the hill and stopped the enemy advance there.

The fighting lasted for hours. It started with violent clashes as regiments collided with regiments, until the fighting degenerated into hand-to-hand, and saber-to-saber struggles among cavalrymen. A gunner from Chew's Battery in Stuart's Horse Artillery characterized the action with these words: "Then commenced the hand-to-hand conflict which raged desperately for awhile, then men on both sides fighting and grappling like demons, and at first it was doubtful as to who would succumb and first cry enough; but eventually the enemy began to falter and give way under the terrible strokes of the Virginian style of sabering." After the battle at Fleetwood Hill, W. W. Blackford of Stuart's staff also noted that the fight was predominately made with the saber in that field. He described the aftermath in these words: "The next morning we rode over the field and most of the dead bore wounds from the sabre, either by cut or thrust. I mean the field around Fleetwood; in other places this was not the case to so great an extent." One of the other places where weapons other than the saber were used with abandon was on the Confederate left defended by W. H. F. Lee's brigade.[38]

While the battle was raging on the southern end of Fleetwood ridge, all was not quiet on the northern front. Buford had continually reinforced his line during the morning and into the afternoon, and he was facing a thinned Confederate line. When Stuart withdrew the main bodies of Hampton's and Jones's brigades from the line holding Buford, he had W. H. F. Lee pull back and consolidate his line around the northern end of Fleetwood. About the time Stuart withdrew cavalrymen from in front of Buford, the Federal commanders were positioning their troops for a major assault on the Confederate left which gave W. H. F. Lee's brigade time to extend its line down to cover some of the gap left in the line and then pull back to Fleetwood ridge. All the while, pressure was building.

W. H. F. Lee had been watching the enemy force before him build. He knew that when he had extended his own right flank due to the withdrawal of the 7th Virginia, and a major portion of Jones's and Hampton's brigades to Fleetwood Hill, he was vulnerable. When instructions came to fall back, they certainly made sense to him — he knew it was time to fall back over Yew Ridge and form a new line with his back on the north end of the Fleetwood ridge.

W. H. F. Lee had to achieve the pullback while still impressing Pleasonton and Buford with his presence. Part of his job was to hold Buford's troops long enough for Hampton and Jones to move to and defend Fleetwood Hill.[39] The mounted and dismounted men of the 2nd North Carolina on W. H. F. Lee's right had to gather themselves for an orderly retreat over Yew Ridge along with their brigade.

Once over Yew Ridge, W. H. F. Lee formed a new line, mostly facing north with the 2nd North Carolina still on his right and turned back just enough to occupy the area between Yew Ridge and the Fleetwood ridge. Even though not yet fully reinforced, Buford had his men press hard on W. H. F. Lee's retiring cavalrymen and pursue them to their new position. During his advance, Buford was gaining confidence in his ability to achieve his goal of joining D. McM. Gregg at Brandy Station in the afternoon — he could also hear the guns over on Fleetwood Hill.

Perhaps at that point the tantalizing prospect of squeezing Stuart between Buford's line and Gregg's was an important consideration in Pleasonton's mind when at 12:30 P.M. he wrote Joseph Hooker stating, "General Gregg has joined me, and I will now attack the enemy vigorously with my whole force."[40] He meant Gregg was at Brandy and had engaged Stuart — in fact, Gregg and Pleasonton did not join forces that day south of the Rappahannock.

In any case, Pleasonton again instructed Buford to break through the Confederate left at about the same time Stuart was in the last stage of pushing Gregg's forces off Fleetwood Hill and back toward the Rappahannock. Stuart moved quickly to form a line along the eastern slope of the Fleetwood ridge with his artillery higher up — all the while, he could certainly hear the intensified fighting on the northern slope of Fleetwood between W. H. F. Lee and Buford.[41] Stuart had Jones send support to the left. Jones sent the 7th Virginia, which he had been holding in reserve between St. James Church and Fleetwood Hill, back to W. H. F. Lee — but Lieutenant Colonel Marshall and the 7th Virginia arrived just after a severe and decisive fight had ended.[42]

The afternoon fighting that had ended just as the 7th Virginia arrived had begun slowly with a series of probes, until around 4:00 P.M. when Colonel R. L. T. Beale, on W. H. F. Lee's left, was alarmed by the sight of his pickets being pushed in and rapidly pursued by Buford's troops. He described the fight as well as its aftermath as follows:

After reaching Barbour's Hill a body of the enemy's cavalry, which seemed not less than three regiments, were seen moving towards our left flank.... We did not penetrate the design of this movement at the time, but soon the few men forming the extreme left of our videttes were seen running from their posts, and Yankee troopers leaping the fence in pursuit.... The regiment, which was resting in column of fours, was ordered to charge up the hill to save the dismounted men. They came up in column, forming rapidly into line as they approached near to that of the enemy. The last squadrons [2nd North Carolina] did not halt on the alignment, but dashed upon the foe with the sabre, who broke, and were driven off in confusion. General W. H. F. Lee coming up at this moment, and seeing the enemy in retreat, commanded "Forward," and was at the same instant wounded. Fresh troops of the enemy were now seen emerging from the bottom.... and were forming a line across our rear. The rally was now sounded, and our men, breaking through this line, became involved in a hand-to-hand fight to the foot of the hill. Here we reformed and again charged, and were in turn forced down the hill by fresh troops. Just where we had reformed before we met the Second North Carolina Cavalry dashing forward, followed by the Tenth Virginia.[43]

Lieutenant George W. Beale, Colonel R. L. T. Beale's son and also a member of the 9th Virginia, added additional dimensions to the picture of the fighting that afternoon in the narrow gap between Yew Ridge and Fleetwood ridge. G. W. Beale clarified the sequence in which the participants from Buford's Reserve Brigade (commanded by C. J. Whiting) and W. H. F. Lee's brigade entered the fight that afternoon. In G. W. Beale's words:

The Pennsylvanians scarcely had been driven from the hill before the Second United States regulars dashed up on it along the line of the previous charge, attacking the Ninth Virginia on the flank, and forcing them back in a severe hand-to-hand encounter. At this juncture, the Second North Carolina Regiment, dashingly led by its young Colonel, Sol. Williams, reached the hill, and swept the regulars back, pursuing them almost to the mouth of the cannon. A charge by the Tenth Virginia Cavalry in cooperation with that of the Second North Carolina ended the combat in the saddle in this quarter of the field. The gallant Colonel of the latter regiment, Sol. Williams, had fallen, pierced in the brain with a pistol ball....[44]

The 2nd North Carolina was on W. H. F. Lee's right where it was relatively quiet when the 9th Virginia executed its charge on the 6th Pennsylvania over on the Confederate left. Eager to join the fight, Colonel Solomon Williams of the 2nd North Carolina rode over to W. H. F. Lee's position on the left and apparently pleaded for permission to have his regiment enter the fray. H. B. McClellan, of Stuart's staff, who was not in the area but had years later spoken of this fight with W. H. F. Lee, characterized Williams's request as one in which Williams "...had begged permission, inasmuch as everything was quiet on his line."[45] Under the circumstances and given the general high regard in which Colonel Williams was held by his comrades, it is unlikely Williams had to engage in extensive pleading to have his 2nd North Carolina lend a hand at the time.

Solomon Williams was granted his request and he raced off to gather his regiment and alert the 10th Virginia Cavalry as well. Which suggests W. H. F. Lee was convinced he needed not only the assistance of the 2nd North Carolina but also that of the 10th Virginia in the fighting on their left.

A view of this action from within the 2nd North Carolina was provided by Captain W. A. Graham, commanding the Second Squadron — the squadron that led the 2nd Cavalry in this charge. The picture Graham has painted adds greatly to our understanding of the roll played by Solomon Williams, and his regiment's contribution during the last charge of the day.

About 3 or 3:30 o'clock the shouts on the left told us that a brisk engagement was proceeding. Shortly afterwards Colonel Williams came at full speed towards the regiment, passing the Tenth Virginia. I suppose he gave the command, as they immediately formed by squadron and started at a gallop. As soon as he was near enough to our regiment he gave command, "Form column by squadron," and placing second squadron in front, gave the command "Gallop: march." As we rose the hill we saw the enemy driving the Ninth and Thirteenth Virginia in considerable confusion before them, in our direction. The Tenth Virginia, when it reached a position that it could fire on the enemy without firing into the Ninth and Thirteenth, halted and opened fire. Colonel Williams gave the command to his regiment "Right oblique," and as soon as we had cleared the Tenth Virginia, turning in his saddle shouted: "Forward: draw sabre: charge." The regiment raised the yell as it went by our stationary and retiring companions and the scene was immediately changed. The Federals were the fleers and the Confederates the pursuers. Our regiment drove the enemy about half a mile back upon their reserves of cavalry and infantry, who were posted on a hill, while our advance had reached an angle where two stone walls came together on an opposite hill, about two hundred yards distant. This with a volley from the reserve, checked the advance. The leading four were Colonel Williams, Sergeant Jordon, Company C; private Asbell, Company K, and this writer.

Asbell was felled from his horse with a wound through the head almost immediately. Colonel Williams gathered his horse to leap the wall shouting: "Second North Carolina, follow me." The writer called to him: "Colonel, we had better get a line, they are too strong to take this way." He replied: "That will be best: where is the flag?" and as we turned, it was not fifty yards to our rear. He rode to meet it: halted it and was shouting to the men to fall in, when he was shot through the head, and died immediately.[46]

THE END OF A LONG DAY

Once the Union forces were pushed from the field by the 2nd North Carolina, their sharpshooters and artillery in the woods stopped the pursuing Confederate cavalrymen. G. W. Beale, of the 9th Virginia, remembered the mounted men of the 2nd North Carolina and 10th Virginia drove the enemy "almost to the mouth of the cannon." Finally, Union guns drove the cavalrymen from the field and out of range. It was about this time, Buford was ordered to begin his orderly withdrawal back across the Rappahannock River. The 2nd North Carolina fell back on its line and then pursued the enemy at a distance — Chambliss was in command of the brigade at that point because W. H. F. Lee had been removed with a wound to his leg. One view of the last scene by a Confederate cavalrymen in the 9th Virginia indicated they "...followed the retreating foe without making any further attack. They moved over ground on which at intervals lay Federal dead and across a field strewn with fallen horses."[47]

Of these final encounters on W. H. F. Lee's line, the Federal commander, Pleasonton, characteristically reported he had carried the day. In his words, "Buford's cavalry had a long and desperate encounter, hand-to-hand, with the enemy, in which he drove handsomely before him very superior forces...." At another place in the same report, Pleasonton states, "...having crippled the enemy by desperate fighting so that he could not follow me, I returned with my command to the north side of the Rappahannock."[48]

Pleasonton's sketch of this last battle scene of the day was one in which he defeated Stuart's cavalry and unchallenged, casually ambled back across the river. One cannot dispute Pleasonton's characterization of the afternoon as one filled with fierce hand-to-hand fighting. However, it is a bit difficult to accept his notion that his departure for the river followed his victory over a force far greater in number than his. After all, his final cavalry charge was led by the 6th Pennsylvania Cavalry which was met and driven back by the 9th Virginia with fewer than 600 troopers (less a squadron that had been assigned to Chambliss as sharpshooters), and after the 2nd United States Cavalry had turned the 9th Virginia; the 2nd United States was in turn met and routed by the 2nd North Carolina Cavalry, which was by then fewer than 190 armed and mounted men (less the squadron of sharpshooters detached to Chambliss earlier). It should also be noted that the 6th Pennsylvania and the 2nd United States had a greater number of aggregate casualties for the day than any other Federal cavalry regiment — 146 and 66 respectively.[49]

In any case, Pleasonton knew his men were spent, and he could withdraw without being pursued by W. H. F. Lee's brigade and the 2nd North Carolina because they too were exhausted. In addition, both the 2nd North Carolina and its brigade were temporarily lacking aggressive leadership because W. H. F. Lee was down and Solomon Williams was dead.

Pleasonton's withdrawal did perhaps gain a sense of urgency when Fitz Lee's brigade, commanded by Munford, finally arrived on the Confederate left. Due to miscommunication, Munford did not get Fitz Lee's brigade south of Hazel River to join the fighting until late in the day.[50]

There were no official reports written on the 2nd North Carolina Cavalry's participation in the fighting at the north end of Fleetwood ridge. Most of what we know is based on what was in the field of vision of Colonel R. L. T. and Lieutenant G. W. Beale, both of whom saw the afternoon from within the 9th Virginia's action. Captain Graham of Company K provided useful information on the afternoon's activities but his account was very brief compared to the writings of the Beales, and Graham was not consulted for his point of view (nor apparently was anyone else from the 2nd North Carolina) by the likes of H. B. McClellan when he wrote his history of Stuart's cavalry. However, Captain Graham did mention that Captain Strange of Company D took command of the regiment when Colonel Williams fell, and at the end of the engagement, Graham knew that Strange did prepare a report on the role of the 2nd North Carolina in the fight. Graham said that Strange "...submitted it to the officers before forwarding it to headquarters." It was probably submitted to brigade headquarters, which was in some turmoil due to the wounding of Brigadier General W. H. F. Lee that same afternoon — in any case, Captain Strange's report did not survive the brigade's temporary command under Chambliss.[51]

Because the 2nd North Carolina was the last regiment to have a mounted clash with Union cavalry on June 9, and because they pushed the enemy from the field, there was a good possibility they gathered some Union equipment — such as sabers, pistols, and fully attired horses. In a fight where the enemy withdrew, the troopers who took the battlefield usually had first pick of the spoils, and that always drew the attention of the division's ordinance officer. In the case at hand, Captain John Esten Cooke, Chief of Ordnance, Cavalry Division had not received a report from the 2nd North Carolina by June 10, and he had pursued the brigade commander for an accounting of spoils taken and reported. (All equipment gathered on a battlefield legally belonged to the Confederacy, not the individuals who might be in a position to pick up, say a high quality northern pistol or saber — reality, more often than not, saw the first trooper on site fully equipped, then his friends, and then some small arms were left in the field or turned over to the ordnance officers.) Captain Cooke certainly knew as each day passed, memories would fade and gathered Union equipment would be "absorbed." On June 11, the 2nd North Carolina's brigade ordnance officer sent the following reply to the division ordnance office:

I have gotten in a report of arms captured in the recent engagement from all of my regiments excepting the Second North Carolina, which is on picket. As soon as it returns, you shall hear from it through me. There were no arms or equipments of any sort captured by any of the other regiments.[52]

Most of W. H. F. Lee's cavalrymen were on picket duty following the fight, and their regiments apparently had little difficulty reporting that no spoils were gathered by them.

There was certainly a better explanation for the delayed report from the 2nd North Carolina Cavalry. While we know the ranks of the 2nd North Carolina were depleted that afternoon, it is probably safe to conclude the men who remained were better equipped at the end of that day than the day before.

THE PRICE OF GLORY AND SPOILS

On June 9, 1863, the Confederate cavalry sustained the following losses: killed, 81; wounded, some mortally, 403; captured or missing, 382; for a total of 866 men.[53] Many of the losses were taken on the Confederate left. Lieutenant George Beale saw the activities from within W. H. F. Lee's brigade and he concluded the following about the greatest cavalry battle ever fought on American soil:

An examination of the lists of casualties on both sides shows that on no part of the field was the contest more bloody than where W. H. F. Lee and Jones repelled the last assaults of Buford's line. The men killed and wounded under Wyndham and Kilpatrick during the successive charges of their regiments on Fleetwood hill were considerably less than those sustained by the reserve brigade and Eighth Illinois.[54]

The recorded losses taken by the 2nd North Carolina are presented in the following table.

Companies C and K of William A. Graham's Second Squadron suffered more losses than other companies because they led the countercharge against the 2nd United States Cavalry in the last mounted encounter of the day. The regiment lost at least 29 men that day, or about 15 percent of its effective force. In his sketch of the regiment for the Honor Roll, Captain W. A. Graham indicated they had 35 killed and wounded. It is possible he knew of men wounded less severely than others, and of whom no mention appeared on their Muster Roll cards.[55]

The loss of Colonel Solomon Williams would impact the regiment throughout the Gettysburg campaign and perhaps beyond — as would the temporary loss of their brigadier general, W. H. F. Lee. The 2nd North Carolina started the day with the best leadership it had had to date. It ended the day with neither and continued the campaign with temporary leadership at both levels.

MORE TEMPORARY LEADERSHIP

John R. Chambliss of the 13th Virginia took command of the brigade soon after W. H. F.

Combat Losses in the 2nd North Carolina Cavalry Brandy Station, June 9, 1863

Trooper	Age	Co.	Fate
Solomon Williams		F/S	killed
John O. Brow	25	A	killed
William E. Foster	26	A	captured
Joseph Tucker	29	A	captured
S. Jay Andrews	21	B	wounded
Joseph T. Summers*	29	B	wounded
Edward M. Jordan		C	wounded
John F. Haslett		C	wounded
David E. Riddick		C	captured
George Roundtree	21	C	mortally wounded
John G. Overby*		C	wounded
John W. Gordon	17	C	wounded & captured
Lucian Baggott	25	D	wounded
William Giles	28	D	captured
John W. King	30	D	captured
Daniel W. Jones		F	wounded
Pinkney A. Tatum		F	wounded
James Jarvis	23	G	wounded
Jones S. Henderson	22	G	wounded
Thomas Raleigh	27	G	captured
James H. Bunch	24	H	killed
James A. Buxton	20	H	wounded
John G. Blassingame		I	mortally wounded
William M. Dalrymple	26	I	captured
Alexander L. Maness	20	I	captured
Henderson Asbell		K	captured
James Asbell		K	wounded
Henry J. Blalock	20	K	killed
John W. Carden	24	K	wounded
Charles R. Wilson		K	wounded

The source used here is *North Carolina Troops 1861–1865, A Roster*, compiled by Louis H. Manarin (Raleigh, N.C., State Division of Archives and History), vol. II, Cavalry, pp. 104–177, unless otherwise noted. (See Appendix for more information on the men listed above, page 394.)
*Sergeants John G. Overby and Joseph Sommers were taken to a hospital in Gordonsville and their presence there was reported in "The Rappahannock Cavalry Fight," *Fayetteville Observer*, June 22, 1863, page 2, col. 2.

Lee was carried from the field and the fight was over.[56]

This was the second time the 2nd North Carolina came under Chambliss's temporary command and nothing positive was ever mentioned about their first experience back in

October and November of 1862. Apparently Chambliss did not court the favor of his North Carolinians when he sent them to Fox's Springs for picket duty. After fighting all day and taking numerous losses, most of the men in the 2nd North Carolina marched all night to reach their new position and took their picket positions at sunrise on June 10, some 20 miles from camp. The regiment was brought back to camp near Brandy Station on June 14 to prepare for the march north. The brigade remained under Chambliss's temporary leadership throughout the Gettysburg campaign and beyond. During the campaign, the relationship between the regiment and Chambliss deteriorated further. By the end of the campaign, negative feelings ran high and for many remained for years. For instance, Captain W. A. Graham recalled and bothered to put in writing his lingering resentment of the treatment received by the men of the 2nd North Carolina. Graham put his views in these words: "I do not suppose there is a member of the Nineteenth (Second Cavalry) North Carolina that has a single pleasant recollection of his treatment of it [the regiment] during his [Chambliss's] command." Graham goes on to mention the undisputed fact that Chambliss was a brave leader who finally fell in battle fighting to his end. In fact, in Graham's view, the commanders only fault was partiality "...of treatment to the regiments under his command in the Gettysburg campaign."[57]

Temporary command was also in order at the regimental level due to the loss of Colonel Solomon Williams. Captain James W. Strange of Company D took command of the regiment on the field when Williams fell — the former was the senior officer on the field. The loss of Williams was apparently felt more by some than others. All J. E. B. Stuart had to say of Williams was that he was as "...fearless as he was efficient...." Colonel Williams clearly meant more to the men of the 2nd North Carolina Cavalry, and who felt his loss at more than one level and they, on many occasions, expressed that sense of loss.[58]

Many of the men in the 2nd North Carolina felt close to their commander and fellow North Carolinian; for instance, at a later date, October 1, 1863, Captain Graham of Company K, wrote these words about his late colonel, "On the field his bravery, dash and yet coolness was the admiration of all who beheld him. In Camps his gentle, kind, affectionate, women like manners won the hearts of his entire command both officers and men. Truly may it be said of him, none knew him but to love him, none named him but to praise him." Years later another trooper wrote, "...Perhaps no officer in the Army of Northern Virginia was more dearly beloved by his command or had more devoted friends throughout the army, than this noble young North Carolinian, who fell at Brandy Station at the head of the Brigade he commanded, in its third charge against the enemy...."[59]

His character was known even to the enemy's commander of cavalry, Alfred Pleasonton, as evident in a report on the day's activities in which he bothered to make the following comment: "Colonel Williams, of North Carolina, a great favorite, was killed."[60]

Colonel Williams's temporary replacement was readily available. He would again be Lieutenant Colonel Payne of the 4th Virginia Cavalry — he was not happy about leaving his own regiment, which he had only returned to a day or two before, and he clearly had a tough act to follow in the hearts and minds of 2nd North Carolina cavalrymen.

W. H. F. Payne apparently had had some problems with individuals in the 2nd North Carolina regiment. For instance, shortly before Colonel Williams returned from leave, and while Payne was in temporary command of the regiment, Payne had a run-in with Captain Pinkney A. Tatum of Company F, which resulted in Tatum being placed under arrest where he remained on June 9. Nonetheless, when Colonel Williams stormed back to his men that afternoon and called his regiment to arms, Captain Tatum took to horse and led the men of his company in the charge against the 2nd United States Cavalry. He led in the charge even though still stripped of all weapons and his spurs. Captain Tatum was wounded in the fight, and his Colonel Williams was killed. By night fall, after just one day of service to Colonel Williams, Captain Tatum again found himself and his company under the temporary command of the man who had placed him under arrest in the first place, Lieutenant Colonel W. H. F. Payne. Needless to say, some of the cavalrymen were no happier to see Payne return than he was to be back among them.[61]

In spite of such difficulties with temporary leadership at both the brigade and regiment levels, the cavalrymen of the 2nd North Carolina knew they had a job to do, and they inspired each other to move forward. Captain Graham observed, "As the command 'break ranks' was given, the band at Head Quarters struck up the 'Old North State.' Such cheering, jumping, etc., I have seldom witnessed. The mind of each went back over the hills and valleys to the home in the old State he loved and for which he would willingly die."[62]

Middleburg and Upperville, June 17–21

The Battle of Brandy Station caused Robert E. Lee to lose a day before he launched his campaign into Pennsylvania. The morning after, June 10, 1863, Ewell's command set out from near Culpeper Court House for Winchester through the Shenandoah Valley. On June 15, Longstreet left Culpeper and moved up the east side of the Blue Ridge Mountains to occupy Ashby's and Snicker's gaps. J. E. B. Stuart left soon after Longstreet with three cavalry brigades — Fitz Lee's (commanded by Thomas Munford), W. H. F. Lee's (commanded by John R. Chambliss), and Beverly H. Robertson's. The cavalry's job was to act as a shield between R. E. Lee's infantry and the Union cavalry which was east of the Bull Run Mountains but patrolling the area between that range and the Blue Ridge. R. E. Lee wanted to be into Pennsylvania before Hooker knew where the Confederate infantry was headed and how much of it was on the march. William E. Jones's and Wade Hampton's cavalry brigades stayed on the Rappahannock until A. P. Hill's corps was ready to move north.[63]

Stuart's job was to keep Pleasonton's Union cavalrymen out of Fauquier and Loudoun County as long as possible. Another cavalry clash was inevitable because Pleasonton had clear orders to penetrate the area with his cavalry and locate the Army of Northern Virginia.

Stuart spent his first night on the road at Salem, near Robertson's and W. H. F. Lee's brigades. The 2nd North Carolina was as far back as Warrenton, some ten miles south, where they spent the night. (The stopover was probably agreeable to their temporary commander, W. H. F. Payne, who made his home in Warrenton.) Stuart had sent three regiments from Fitz Lee's brigade to Piedmont (Delaplain), and two on to Upperville.

The next morning, June 17, Stuart sent his three brigades in as many directions but all toward the Bull Run Mountains — he decided to set his shield as far east as possible in order to have more space to withdraw into as he delayed Pleasonton on his inevitable march westward to find the Confederate army. Stuart's first priority was to send troops to slow the Union advance at Aldie and Thoroughfare Gap.

On the morning of June 17, Munford took Fitz Lee's brigade (the 1st, 2nd, 3rd, 4th, and 5th Virginia cavalries) from near Piedmont and Upperville through Middleburg to Aldie. Their instructions were "...if possible, to hold the gap in Bull Run Mountain as a screen to Longstreet's movements."[64] The Little River Turnpike came from Fairfax, through Aldie and then forked. The southern route became Ashby's Gap Turnpike as it went west through Middleburg, Upperville, and then through the Ashby's Gap in the Blue Ridge Mountains and into the Shenandoah Valley. The upper route went from Aldie, northwest through Philomont, Snickersville and Snicker's Gap — it was called the Snickersville Turnpike. Munford's job was to block those two routes. Aldie had to be a point of passage for Pleasonton's Union cavalry on its way to view the Valley.

The next most likely pass Pleasonton would use to send his troops through the Bull Run Mountains was called Thoroughfare Gap — it was cut to allow the Manassas Gap Railroad through the range. It was a narrow gorge in many places just wide enough for the railroad track and a wagon path. Colonel Chambliss and W. H. F. Lee's brigade were sent to that gap.

Chambliss entered Fauquier County on June 16 at the head of his command which included the 9th, 10th and 13th Virginia, and the 2nd North Carolina Cavalry (the 15th Virginia was left to picket the Rappahannock). The 9th Virginia was commanded by its Colonel, R. L. T. Beale; the 10th Virginia by its Colonel, J. L. Davis; the 13th Virginia was commanded by Major Gillatte (their Colonel Chambliss was commanding the brigade); and the 2nd North

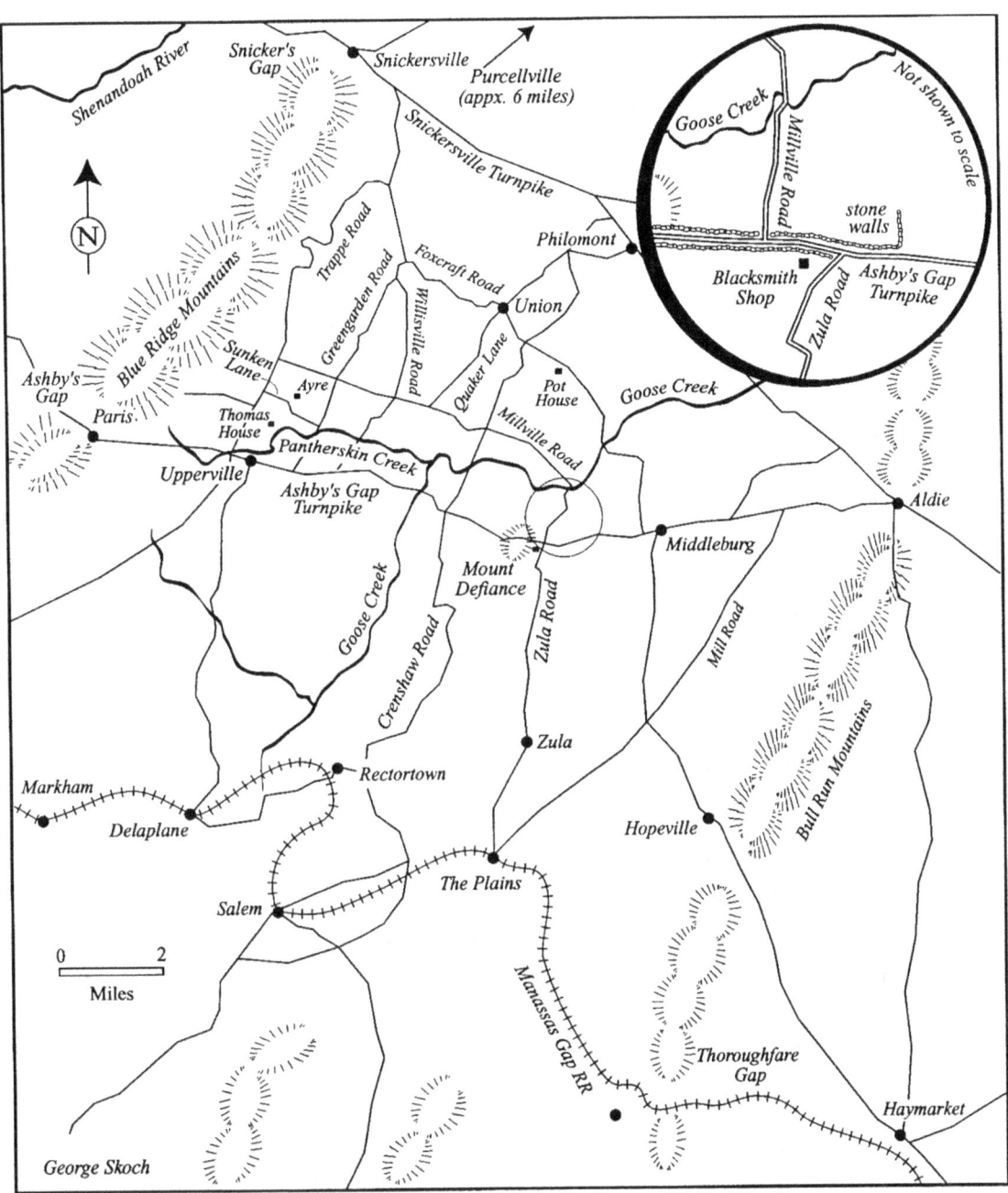

3.2: Loudoun Valley, Middleburg and Upperville

Carolina Cavalry was temporarily commanded by Lieutenant Colonel W. H. F. Payne (on loan from the 4th Virginia). Stuart was at the head of the column with Robertson's brigade, followed by Chambliss and his command.

Their first day on the road was uneventful, and one member of the 2nd North Carolina remembered that "There was but little grain for horse feed in this section but there were magnificent fields of clover and orchard grass. The men were dismounted twice a day and each would hold his horse by the bridle until he fed himself."[65]

The next morning Chambliss moved his cavalrymen up to the Manassas Gap Railroad and along the road from White Plains to Thoroughfare Gap. His job was to detect and assess the presence of the enemy if in the area.[66]

On the morning of June 17, B. H. Robertson's brigade (including the 4th and 5th North Carolina) moved to Rectortown and held so he could move in support of either Chambliss at Thoroughfare Gap or Munford at Aldie. Stuart moved over to Middleburg to set up his headquarters for the day — he took his staff and two squadrons from the 4th Virginia Cavalry as an escort.[67]

While Stuart had his orders to establish a shield for R. E. Lee's army on the march, Pleasonton's orders from Hooker were equally clear on June 17, 1863. His instructions were:

...put the main body of your command in the vicinity of Aldie, and push out reconnaissance toward Winchester, Berryville, and Harper's Ferry.

The commanding general [Hooker] relies upon you with your cavalry force to give him information of where the enemy is, his force, and his movements. You have a sufficient cavalry force to do this. Drive in pickets, if necessary, and get us information. It is better that we should lose men than to be without knowledge of the enemy, as we now seem to be..., and [Hooker] directs that you leave nothing undone to give him the fullest information.[68]

Pleasonton's instructions must have arrived early on June 17, because he acted on them and sent the following instructions to David McM. Gregg, commanding the Second Division, at 3:00 A.M. on the same day:

The general commanding directs that you have your command ready to move at 5 o'clock this A.M., to march and encamp at Aldie to-night. One regiment of your command will be sent through Thoroughfare Gap as far as Middleburg to-night, scouting the country well in that vicinity. These headquarters will be at Aldie to-night.[69]

D. McM. Gregg had his command on the march for Aldie early and selected Alfred N. Duffié's command, the 1st Rhode Island Cavalry, to pass through Thoroughfare Gap and then turn north for Middleburg. Munford with Fitz Lee's brigade had pickets east of Aldie by the time D. McM. Gregg's advance brigade, commanded by Judson Kilpatrick, arrived. Further south, Chambliss with W. H. F. Lee's brigade had pickets waiting for Duffié as he came through Thoroughfare Gap — both Union moves were anticipated and detected immediately by Stuart's cavalry.

Aldie

Thomas Munford approached Aldie with the 1st, 4th, and 5th Virginia — he had sent most of the 2nd and 3rd Virginia north from Middleburg when he passed through. He sent a company ahead to scout the town and set pickets, but they were met just east of Aldie by Kilpatrick's advance. Munford's scouting party was driven back to his 5th Virginia. Munford's 5th Virginia under Rosser, and Kilpatrick's 2nd New York deployed and engaged in a brief fight through the streets of Aldie. As more troops arrived on both sides, the fighting escalated throughout the day. The fighting was severe, and both sides were pushed back at different times. Munford was finally ordered to withdraw to Middleburg around 4:00 P.M., and Pleasonton did get to spend the night in Aldie as originally planned.[70]

After Munford was withdrawn from the Aldie area, Pleasonton was quick to acknowledge that he had driven off Fitz Lee's brigade with only one division of his own. Pleasonton seemed content to hold at Aldie and not push for Middleburg until the next morning. He was apparently still confident Duffié and the 1st Rhode Island Cavalry were through Thoroughfare Gap and settled for the night at Middleburg. It should have occurred to him that he had just seen Munford take Fitz Lee's brigade back in the direction of Middleburg.[71] But Duffié had more than that to contend with on June 17, and he would have to handle it on his own — there would be no support from Gregg or Pleasonton.

Thoroughfare Gap

Also on the morning of June 17, John R. Chambliss moved his command along the Manassas Gap Railroad toward Thoroughfare Gap. His job was to detect the enemy's presence in the gap as well as keep a line of communication open to Wade Hampton who was still below the Rappahannock — they were instructed to avoid any serious fighting along the way.

The 9th Virginia was in front of the column on June 17, and they were the first to see Alfred N. Duffié and the 1st Rhode Island Cavalry emerge from the pass. A few shots were exchanged and the 9th Virginia fell back on its support and formed a line of battle. Their line was sufficiently west of the pass to allow

Duffié's advance through the pass at around 9:30 that morning. The presence of Chambliss's skirmishers slowed Duffié, so his column of only 275 cavalrymen did not clear the pass until around 11 A.M. The Federal cavalrymen followed their orders and turned north along the Bull Run Mountains, then headed for the town of Hopewell on the road to Middleburg.[72]

As Duffié moved his column north toward Middleburg, he knew he was being followed at a distance but was otherwise not bothered by Chambliss's cavalrymen. Chambliss was a good distance behind Duffié because he expected more Union troops to arrive through Thoroughfare Gap that morning — it apparently did not seem reasonable that Pleasonton would send just one small regiment. He was justly concerned that any Union troops following Duffié would be in a position to execute a flank or rear attack on his command, so Chambliss waited a reasonable period of time before following Duffié north.

Chambliss sent one dispatch to Stuart at Middleburg early, indicating there were no enemy in Thoroughfare Gap, then, shortly thereafter, he sent another describing his encounter with Duffié — apparently neither message got through. In any case, Chambliss had collected his brigade on the road Duffié took to Middleburg by late afternoon and marched well into the night at a very cautious pace. One member of Chambliss's column described the pursuit in these words:

As this Rhode Island regiment moved on towards Middleburg, we followed them, quite ignorant of their numbers, and how soon they might turn to attack us. We were ordered to be in readiness to fight at any moment. Very soon the twilight dusk settled over us, and then came the darkness. An order passed down the line giving us a watchword and reply for distinguishing friend from foe in a night battle. With sabres drawn and in silence, we marched by fours in a darkness that hid us from our comrades at our side, and halted about nine or ten o'clock, and went into camp on the edge of a large field, where we ate our supper, fed our horses, and lay down for sleep.[73]

Duffié arrived near Middleburg at 4:00 P.M., but his afternoon and evening were far more eventful than was that of Chambliss, because he had orders to spend the night in Middleburg — which resulted in overbooking because J. E. B. Stuart and his escort were already there and settling in for the evening.

MIDDLEBURG

J. E. B. Stuart and his staff had their escort of two squadrons from the 4th Virginia with them at Middleburg on June 17. They had pickets set on the roads coming from Aldie and up from the Thoroughfare Gap area. Duffié's advance met and drove Stuart's pickets into town around 4:00 P.M. A member of Stuart's staff observed that the advance troopers from the 1st Rhode Island Cavalry arrived so quickly and unexpectedly that "…Stuart and his staff were compelled to make a retreat more rapid than was consistent with dignity and comfort." While the cavalrymen from the 4th Virginia engaged Duffié's advance for around a half hour, Stuart withdrew along Ashby's Gap Turnpike back to Rector's Cross Roads. Stuart then sent instructions to Munford for a withdrawal from Aldie, and to Chambliss to immediately move their brigades to Middleburg (Stuart's courier did not find Chambliss who was still near Thoroughfare Gap and just getting his pursuit of Duffié underway). Stuart immediately sent B. H. Robertson's command (the 4th and 5th North Carolina) to Middleburg from Rectortown where they had been held in reserve. Stuart was a bit miffed that his comfortable and promising afternoon in Middleburg had been so unceremoniously brought to an end.[74]

Even though Duffié had driven Stuart and his guard from Middleburg, he knew Confederate cavalry were west, east, and south of him. He set about barricading and posting pickets at the entrances to town. Duffié instructed his officers "…to hold the town at all hazards…." He sent word to Kilpatrick at Aldie and hoped re-enforcements would be sent in time. It was about 7:00 P.M. when Duffié knew that enemy troops were approaching from Aldie, Union, and Rectortown (and that Chambliss's command was still somewhere south of him). He and his 275 cavalrymen had no way out and were determined to hold their position — after all, their orders were to spend the night in Middleburg.[75]

Duffié's most immediate problem came from the west in the form of Robertson's 4th and 5th North Carolina Cavalry, numbering about 900. Robertson arrived about half a mile west of town just before nightfall where skirmishers from the 4th Virginia were still in line. Duffié described what followed:

The enemy surrounded the town and stormed the barricades, but were gallantly repulsed by my men with great slaughter. They did not, however, desist, but, confident of success, again attacked, and made three successive charges. I was compelled to retire on the road by which I came, that being the only one open to retreat. With all that was left of my command, I crossed Little River northeast [southeast] of Middleburg, and bivouacked for the night, establishing strong pickets on the river.[76]

The Federals did have a compelling case for withdrawal because the cavalrymen from the 4th and 5th North Carolina were in the process of dismounting for a final charge upon Duffié's men. Unfortunately for Duffié and his troopers, by the time they were out of town and reached a point where it felt safe to bivouac for the night, they chose a clearing that Chambliss and W. H. F. Lee's brigade had also selected on that dark night. The two commands were within sight of one another once the dawn arrived.

The next morning, June 18, was full of surprises for the men of both blue and gray. According to Lieutenant G. W. Beale, of the 9th Virginia Cavalry,

In the gray mist of the early dawn, a detail of men were sent by us to a barn located in the field of our bivouac. As they approached it, the Federals were discovered and their presence reported. There followed among us bridling and saddling in hot haste... [and we left at a gallop]. The Rhode Island men began a rapid attempt to escape as soon as they perceived the situation they were in, taking in their flight a road leading towards the Bull Run mountain. Captain Haynes was too close on them to admit of their rallying and giving battle. Twice, or oftener, they attempted to turn and face him, and at each point several of their dead marked the points where such attempts were made. The pursuit was continued till the mountain crest was reached....[77]

Most of the Union cavalrymen were surrounded and captured; some were killed in hand-to-hand fighting that lasted more than an hour. Only with great effort did Duffié and 27 of his men manage to escape the melee and head for the road leading to Hopewell Gap and over the Bull Run Mountains. Duffié and the handful of his troopers made it back to Centreville on the afternoon of June 19. Duffié reported the loss of about 260 officers and men, but some stragglers continued to return through Union lines during the afternoon and next day.[78]

Chambliss and his command spent the rest of the morning collecting and paroling the prisoners. The brigade was then ordered to continue the march for Middleburg. According to Captain Graham of the 2nd North Carolina Cavalry, it was their day to rotate to the front of the column but Chambliss thought there might be a small force of enemy encamped near the road, so he passed a Virginia regiment to the front. To Graham, this was a case of allowing the Virginia regiment to collect the spoils of war as they passed through the area in which the fighting had taken place earlier. Then, in Graham's words, "On nearing Middleburg and ascertaining that the enemy were in force in the vicinity, the 2nd was passed to the front."[79]

As the men of the 2nd North Carolina and their brigade filed into town, they passed a corner store and on the porch they saw some fellow North Carolinians "...laid side by side the dead bodies of five or six of our men who had been killed the previous evening in the charge by Robinson against Duffié's regiment."[80] Chambliss settled his command near Robertson's 4th and 5th North Carolina.

June 18 was an unusually hot day, around 100 in the shade and 110 under the direct sun. It was a good day to rest, but first Chambliss's and Robertson's brigades were ordered to withdraw just west of town and take positions on Mount Defiance that ran across Ashby's Gap Turnpike. By dropping the line back, west of Middleburg, the town did not become part of the target for the artillery dual that took place during the day. Munford's command (Fitz Lee's brigade) was moved up to the road leading to Snicker's Gap. Stuart knew Pleasonton's job was to move on one or both of the turnpikes leading to the passes over the Blue Ridge Mountains—Stuart put troopers on both roads. He also knew Pleasonton was bringing a very large cavalry force and several brigades of infantry. Stuart was prepared to meet the enemy with Chambliss's four regiments and Robertson's two regiments on the Ashby's Gap Turnpike, and Munford's command with five regiments on the Snickersville Turnpike. Hampton was waiting at Warrenton and Jones was on his way up to join Stuart but would not arrive until the following day.[81]

Early on the morning of June 18, Pleasonton sent Colonel J. I. Gregg's brigade west on Ashby's Gap turnpike to Middleburg; and Colonel William Gamble's brigade, from Buford's division, northwest along the road to Snickersville and on to Snicker's Gap for a view of the Valley beyond.

As Gamble's brigade moved northwest toward Snicker's Gap, Munford's pickets in front of him caused him to pull up and delay along the way. By afternoon Gamble had pushed up near Snickersville, but at that point Munford brought his brigade up from near Union and formed a line across Gamble's path. Gamble was about two miles from Snicker's Gap but about ten miles from any support back at Aldie—caution prevailed and he turned his column back toward Aldie. Munford was joined by W. E. Jones's brigade later that day so Gamble probably made a good choice—even though their mission was not accomplished.

Over on Ashby's Gap Turnpike by late morning June 18, D. McM. Gregg arrived in front of Middleburg and drove Stuart's pickets back through town and thus regained what Duffié had briefly held the previous afternoon.

D. McM. Gregg's pickets moved through town and engaged Chambliss's and Robertson's pickets most of the day—they skirmished but made no attack. Chambliss had his men on Mount Defiance, on both sides of the road leading to Ashby's Gap and ready for battle, but no assault was made on their position.[82] Gregg did not send more than a picket force into Middleburg and did not demonstrate much enthusiasm for challenging Stuart's cavalrymen stretched across the road west of town. Perhaps the Union commander's desire to complete his mission and view the Shenandoah Valley from Ashby's Gap was also dampened by the thunderstorm. Perhaps Stuart's unusual tactic of falling back rather than attacking caused his enemy to suspect a trap. No matter what combination of reasons prevailed, around nightfall Gregg was ordered to withdraw and spend the night about a mile and a half east of Middleburg.

Pleasonton had also sent two regiments under Colonel O. DeForest, of Stahel's command, southwest toward Warrenton the day before, and they were approaching that town on June 18. Stuart was aware of the third Union probe and had ordered Hampton to stop at Warrenton with his command and wait for DeForest and his two regiments.

De Forest did not make a serious move on Warrenton, and beyond to the Blue Ridge. The Union move on Warrenton was met and stopped by Hampton on June 18. Apparently Hampton's resistance, a sudden heavy thunderstorm, and nightfall combined to convince the Union commander that the best course of action was to withdraw all the way back to Centreville. Late that night, in the heavy rain, Hampton started his men north to join Stuart and their comrades in front of Pleasonton's main force.

Pleasonton's three pronged push through the Confederate cavalry to the Blue Ridge Mountains was without results on June 18. Hooker knew no more about the condition and location of the Army of Northern Virginia at the end of the day than he had at its beginning. R. E. Lee had marched undetected for another day toward Pennsylvania.

When Alfred Pleasonton again moved his men west to Middleburg early on June 19, D. McM. Gregg's command remained on the Ashby's Gap Turnpike while John Buford took two brigades (Gamble's and the Reserve Brigade) north from town hoping to turn west and then drop down and hit Stuart in the flank back on Ashby's Gap Turnpike. Their flank march encountered enemy resistance sooner than expected, however—Confederate pickets were waiting about a mile and a half up from Middleburg on the north side of Goose Creek. The brief encounter alerted Munford who had Fitz Lee's brigade at Union and W. E. Jones who had his brigade camped near Bloomfield.[83]

Munford and Jones were under orders to delay any force they met but to avoid a major fight, so they sent only two regiments to greet and slow Buford's column. They found them near Leithtown (or Pot House). Buford got there first and formed a line of battle just minutes before the Confederates arrived. Buford had artillery and easily drove the Virginians back.

In the midst of a lull in the fighting near Pot House, Buford was instructed to send the two regiments from the Reserve Brigade south to Ashby's Gap Turnpike and hit Stuart's flank. Buford sent the 2nd and 6th United States Cavalry under Major Whiting south along Millville Road toward the sounds of fighting. Serious fighting had been taking place on the pike from morning into the afternoon.

Over on Ashby's Gap Turnpike, Stuart had his troops in a strong position to resist D. McM.

Gregg's move west of Middleburg on the morning of June 19. Confederate cavalrymen were positioned on and near high ground, with Chambliss's 13th Virginia on the north side of the pike behind a wall that paralleled the pike and then turned for a bit along the hill. The cavalrymen from the 13th Virginia were dismounted and had a commanding view facing east and south down upon the pike. Just behind the hill was a small ridge called Mount Defiance that ran across the pike. The 9th Virginia was also north of the pike, mounted and waiting just behind the ridge. South of the pike, Stuart's line stepped back from the 13th Virginia's position across the pike and was manned by the 2nd North Carolina and Robertson's 4th and 5th North Carolina Cavalry. The North Carolinians were along Zula Road which ran south from the pike. Stuart had placed McGregor's and Moorman's batteries on the ridge (Mount Defiance) running from the pike south to a wooded area that sheltered Robertson's brigade. The 2nd North Carolina was just behind the artillery facing east and north behind the wall along the pike — like the 13th Virginia, they too had a commanding view of the pike.

Stuart spent the very early morning inspecting his line, and then returned to his staff just behind the 2nd North Carolina's position. Around daybreak, Stuart stretched himself out under a large tree on the top of Mount Defiance for a short rest — an artillery exchange got under way at about the same time. Union forces moved through Middleburg, but hesitated before they launched their attack.[84]

General David McM. Gregg had sent Colonel J. I. Gregg's brigade through town first, then Kilpatrick's brigade followed. J. I. Gregg, D. McM. Gregg's cousin, had sent the 4th Pennsylvania forward to clear the town of Stuart's small picket force — which was done in short order. With that complete, General Gregg formed his line just west of town and in sight of Mount Defiance. From that position they drew Stuart's artillery fire and responded in kind.

The 6th Ohio and 2nd New York from Kilpatrick's brigade were placed north of the Ashby's Gap Turnpike and would march at the 13th Virginia. General Gregg placed some of the 1st Maine on the pike with the 10th New York just behind them and on the south side of the road. He extended his line south from the 10th New York with the balance of the 1st Maine, the 16th and 4th Pennsylvania. The regiments on and south of the pike were from Colonel J. I. Gregg's brigade and faced the North Carolinians near Zula Road and Mount Defiance. Stuart had started the artillery fire while General Gregg was forming his line west of town to establish the range and generally heighten anticipation — at this time Stuart decided to take a short rest under the tree.

Stuart had more time to rest than he expected because once the Union commanders saw the strength of the Confederate position, they had to rethink their plan of attack. Except for artillery exchanges and minor fire from skirmishers periodically, a lull covered the field while Union commanders collected their thoughts. Colonel J. I. Gregg was particularly concerned about sending a force down the pike between the 13th Virginia on the north and the 2nd North Carolina on the south side of the pike, both regiments behind stone walls and on high ground. This approach would also be into the face of Stuart's artillery. In addition, because of the staggered Confederate line which broke as it crossed the pike, by the time J. I. Gregg's men got to the artillery and the 2nd North Carolina near the blacksmith's shop on Mount Defiance, the 13th Virginia from across the road and behind a wall would be on their right flank. Add to this unappealing approach to battle along the pike, J. I. Gregg's men south of the pike had to cross a large open field while charging the artillery and B. H. Robertson's regiments in the woods.

D. McM. Gregg finally agreed to send Kilpatrick's two regiments north of the pike at the 13th Virginia simultaneously with the attack south of the road and followed by the move up the pike. General Gregg was under pressure to move things along and he knew Pleasonton had been told "It is better that we should lose men than to be without knowledge of the enemy, as we now seem to be...." The only advantage Colonel Gregg carried into the fight was superior and apparently expendable numbers.[85]

The serious fighting got under way around 10:00 A.M. North of the pike the 2nd New York and 6th Ohio moved on Chambliss's 13th Virginia, and hoped to occupy them and turn their flank from the north if possible. South of the pike, Colonel Gregg sent the Pennsylvania regiments on foot across the open field at Robinson's two regiments concealed in the woods. They were assisted by mounted companies from the 1st Maine who charged under the artillery fire and helped push the dismounted 4th and 5th North Carolina troops deep into the woods. In fierce fighting from tree to tree the two Pennsylvania regiments and some of the 1st Maine and 10th New York were able to push Robinson's men from the woods and send them scrambling for their horses in the rear. Many of the North Carolinians were captured — mainly from the 4th North Carolina which took the brunt of the attack.

The fighting south of the pike ended Stuart's rest. He and his staff first heard sharp firing from Robertson's position. Then they saw some of their dismounted cavalrymen emerge from the woods for the rear.[86]

At about the same time, Stuart should have been able to see the mounted men of the 1st Maine charging directly up the pike. The men from Maine charged in column of fours between the walls lined with the enemy and directly at a gun or two in the road itself near the blacksmith's shop. They first passed the sharpshooters from the 13th Virginia, north of the road and then approached the Confederate artillery piece in the road about the same time they came under heavy fire from the 2nd North Carolina Cavalry sharpshooters from behind the wall south of the pike.

Just after Stuart saw the enemy advancing on his right and at his front, he saw most of the Union troopers, who had pushed Robertson's men through the woods, turn to their right along Zula Road and make for the blacksmith's shop near the pike — they were heading for the Confederate guns and the dismounted 2nd North Carolina. This prompted Stuart to call up Colonel Beale's 9th Virginia from across the pike and behind the ridge.[87]

Just as the Confederate gun in the road was about to be lost, the 9th Virginia charged the 1st Maine from the north side of the pike, across from the blacksmith's shop. After severe fighting, Beale's 9th Virginian pushed the Maine cavalrymen back down the road past the 13th Virginia sharpshooters again and into the 10th New York's skirmish line where the Confederates were forced to turn back. It was about this same time the men of the 9th Virginia (and the 2nd North Carolina) began to receive fire from south of the pike, from rapidly approaching Pennsylvanians who had just pushed Robinson's brigade from the woods and beyond. Soon the dismounted men from the 2nd North Carolina, and the 16th and 4th Pennsylvania were in a heated exchange, while the mounted men, both blue and gray, continued their charges and countercharges. The fight between the 9th Virginia and mounted men of the Union degenerated into severe hand-to-hand fighting.[88]

At one point, the 9th Virginian, with the help of the sharpshooters both north and south of the walls lining the pike, pushed the mounted Federals back and took a number of prisoners. In the middle of this fighting, Lieutenant Beale of the 9th Virginia made some insightful observations which he later put in writing. His observations illustrate the thin line between surviving or not in the heat of battle — it can turn on one's ability to control his anger and the mood of his opponent in a heated moment of battle. Lieutenant Beale noted, in one case, how a Union cavalryman had been "...unhorsed, and had backed up against an oak in the grove, and having fired his last cartridge, was defending himself with rocks, which he furiously hurled at his assailants until he fell from their pistol shots dead at the roots of the tree." In another case, one in which young Beale himself was directly involved, he recorded that a "...soldier in blue, young, handsome and student-like, had his horse shot under him near me, and I called to him to hand me his arms. Looking momentarily for another charge by a friendly regiment, and so hoping to be liberated, he was slow in unfastening his sabre belt, and when I struck him on the shoulder with the side of my sword to make him hasten the operation, he undertook to remonstrate against my striking a prisoner." The young Yankee was finally captured but lived to fight another day.[89] Soon the Union forces mounted another charge and in turn pushed the 9th Virginia back to and then over Mount Defiance.

By noon or shortly thereafter on the north side of the pike, the dismounted men from the 10th and 2nd New York, and 6th Ohio had pushed the 13th Virginia from the east-facing portion of the wall behind which the Virginians had been firing. These Union troops were then in a position to sweep along the Confederate line facing south behind the east-west leg of the wall. Also by that time, the 9th Virginia had been pushed over the ridge, and Colonel

Gregg's Pennsylvanians had scattered Robertson's brigade and were fighting in front of the blacksmith's shop with the dismounted 2nd North Carolina.

The 2nd North Carolina was busy on two fronts during most of the melee. They had to contend with the mounted 10th New York on the pike and the dismounted Pennsylvanians on Zula Road in front of the blacksmith's shop. Also, as Robertson's brigade was pushed back, the 2nd North Carolina's right flank and rear were increasingly exposed.

As the mounted portion of the 10th New York first reached the crest of Mount Defiance, they received so much heat from the dismounted 2nd North Carolina and the mounted 9th Virginia, they pulled back to their skirmish line just about the time another squadron from the 10th New York was ready to try its hand at pushing Chambliss's men from Mount Defiance. As the fresh squadron of the 10th New York charged up the pike and fought their way to the crest of the ridge, pushing the 9th Virginia and fighting with the 2nd North Carolina on their left, they could see Chambliss reforming the 9th Virginia and the mounted men of the 13th Virginia, so the Federals decided to stand their ground for the moment. Colonel Beale of the 9th Virginia had just been wounded, and Chambliss took charge of the 9th and 13th Virginia regiments as he formed them for a countercharge at the 10th New York atop the ridge. The charge was hardly underway when Stuart ordered a pullback to the next high ground along the Ashby's Gap Turnpike.

As Stuart's cavalrymen were being pressed from the east, north, and south, Major von Borcke of Stuart's staff went to the front, near the 2nd North Carolina's position and observed the overwhelming enemy force closing in on two and perhaps soon three sides. He returned to Stuart, reported the odds and recommended a pull back. Stuart, however, was convinced he could still carry the day and that he would spend the evening in Middleburg, so he sent von Borcke forward to take another look. The Major reported that the situation was even worse than minutes before — it was time to pull back to a stronger position. Stuart was still reluctant to concede that his position was untenable, but the sight of his troops being pushed back on the north side of the pike and the second wave of Union cavalrymen thundering westward on the pike made a believer out of him, and he ordered his artillery to begin their withdrawal, accompanied by mounted men from Chambliss's and Robertson's commands.[90] Stuart and his staff stayed near the front, just behind the still dismounted men of the 2nd North Carolina who were left to slow the enemy advance on and south of the pike — the dismounted men of the 13th Virginia were already falling back on the north side of the pike also in an orderly fashion.

Chambliss and his 9th and 13th Virginia regiments had their hands full on the north side of the pike, so any instructions that reached the 2nd North Carolina came directly from Stuart. The dismounted men of the 2nd North Carolina were ordered to alternately hold and fall back while slowing the enemy advance and allowing the artillery to be relocated and the rest of the regiments to form a new line on the ridge just west of Mount Defiance. One member of Stuart's staff, just behind the 2nd North Carolina's position, described the scene in these words:

As soon as the men of the 2nd NC left the fence the enemy's skirmishers, who were only a short distance in the woods in front, ran forward and occupied it, when they commenced pouring a galling fire into our ranks. Lt. Roberts, of the 2nd NC, who was then in charge of the line here attracted the attention and won the admiration of Stuart.... his part of the line fell back across the open field with a steadiness.... halting and returning the fire with all the promptness and regularity of an every day drill.[91]

Lieutenant William P. Roberts, of Company C, was just 21 years of age at the time (he would, by the end of the war be Robert E. Lee's youngest brigadier general). Lieutenant Roberts, of course, was able to shine that day because the other men of the 2nd North Carolina also did a magnificent job of slowing the Union advance and minimizing the losses taken by their comrades.

As the withdrawal was under way, Stuart and his staff stayed close enough to come under heavy fire and Major von Borcke was seriously wounded — he lived, but his fighting days were over.[92]

When Stuart moved his line back, Pleasonton's forces did not push for further gains, and the fighting along the Ashby's Gap Turnpike was over soon after mid-day. However, there was an encounter just north of the Confederate's new position during the afternoon and into the evening along Millville Road near Goose Creek. Buford had sent Whiting and the Reserve Brigade south along Millville Road earlier, but by the time they crossed the creek they ran into some of Chambliss's pickets from the 13th Virginia. The Confederate pickets immediately notified their commanders and were reinforced by more of Chambliss's command.

Fighting between Chambliss's troops and Whiting's 2nd and 6th United States Cavalry of the Reserve Brigade ended around 6:00 P.M. Whiting dropped down and joined D. McM. Gregg's men along the Ashby's Gap Turnpike, and Confederate pickets remained west and north of the Reserve Brigade for the night. Buford took Gamble's brigade back to Aldie for the night.

Pleasonton again occupied Middleburg, and he found it necessary to inform his superiors that he also held the town of Union.[93] It was commonplace for Pleasonton's claims to exceed his achievements—and that was the case here. In fact, Buford had returned to near Aldie for the night and Munford's brigade was still camped near Union on the night of June 19.

Chambliss's 13th Virginia spent a wet night on the north side of Ashby's Gap Turnpike watching Stuart's immediate left flank. The 9th Virginia and the 2nd North Carolina spent the night on the new Confederate line near the pike.

It was the end of the third day of fighting between the two cavalries and Pleasonton was but little closer to peering into the Shenandoah Valley from Ashby's or Snicker's gaps, which was after all his assignment. R. E. Lee had gained another day for his march north into Pennsylvania.

Though Pleasonton had not gained the information requested by his superiors earlier in the day, Union commanders had information from other sources indicating that R. E. Lee's army was moving northward through the Shenandoah Valley. By evening on the 19th, Hooker was checking with his commander at Harper's Ferry to confirm that Ewell's corps had crossed the Potomac and was already in Maryland. Fortunately for Hooker, he had "eyes and ears" that were in a better position than Pleasonton's. In fact on that same evening, Pleasonton notified Hooker he thought "...they [Longstreet and other Confederates] may attempt to mass their force there [Upperville], and throw it through Thoroughfare Gap by night." Such misinformation was not much to show for three days of fighting in order to penetrate Stuart's lines and gain information.[94]

On the other hand, Stuart knew he could not defeat Pleasonton's larger cavalry, which was supported with infantry, so he sought to delay them—which he did again on that day, and made Hooker wait another day before he could confirm what he suspected about R. E. Lee's movements. Hooker still did not know enough about R. E. Lee's movements to formulate a counter plan.[95]

The next day, June 20, the cavalrymen did not fight each other, just the elements, and otherwise rested or relocated—there had been another thunderstorm the night before and more was on the horizon. Stuart maneuvered to strengthen his positions.

Wade Hampton and his brigade arrived from Warrenton during the day allowing Stuart to strengthen his left as far as Snicker's Gap. Stuart kept Robertson's and Hampton's brigades along with most of his artillery on his line just west of Mount Defiance on the Ashby's Gap Turnpike. He sent Munford with Fitz Lee's brigade to protect Snicker's Gap. In addition, Stuart moved W. H. F. Lee's brigade under Chambliss, including the 2nd North Carolina Cavalry, across Goose Creek to join forces with W. E. Jones's brigade near the town of Union. Otherwise, it was a restful day. The night was less than restful, however, for the men of the 2nd North Carolina according to Captain Graham. At a later date, he wrote:

This was one of the most unpleasant experiences of my army life. I commanded the advance skirmish line which we maintained all night; the line dismounted and placed along a "stake and ridered" rail fence. It rained nearly all night and a stream of water several inches deep ran down the fence row. The only way to avoid the water was to run a rail across the lock and roost upon it.[96]

By June 21, Pleasonton was determined to complete the mission—to pierce R. E. Lee's shield and penetrate the passes through the Blue Ridge Mountains. In spite of his lack of success to date, Pleasonton asked to have his mission expanded from just information gathering to include doing serious damage to Stuart's whole cavalry force. This was clearly an offer his commanding general could not refuse. Pleasonton got infantry support and approval to cripple Stuart's cavalry.[97]

Pleasonton placed three regiments from Kilpatrick's cavalry brigade (the 2nd and 4th New York and 6th Ohio) on the north side of Ashby's Gap Turnpike with three more regiments just behind them from Colonel J. I. Gregg's cavalry brigade (the 4th Pennsylvania, 1st Maine and 10th New York). He then placed four regiments from Colonel S. Vincent's Infantry brigade (the 83rd Pennsylvania, 20th Maine, 44th New York and 16th Michigan) south of the pike. His plan was to have the infantry sweep to the south and hit Stuart's right flank while the latter was fully engaged in front. Leaving nothing to chance, Pleasonton again planned to send Buford around Stuart's left flank — Buford's flanking operation included Gamble's and Devin's brigades as well as the Reserve Brigade under Starr.

By morning, Stuart's line on the pike was where it had been drawn on the afternoon of June 19, about two miles west of Middleburg. He had Hampton's brigade on both sides of Ashby's Gap Turnpike with Robertson's two North Carolina regiments on his left up the Millville Road — protecting Hampton's left. Chambliss had been moved from the Millville Road, south of Goose Creek, up near the town of Willisville, not too far from Jones's camp near Union. Chambliss's and Jones's brigades were then both camped north of the creek, with pickets extended from Robertson's left, up to Millville Road which basically paralleled Ashby's Gap Turnpike to Trappe Road, and east to Foxcroft Road and Goose Creek. Munford was further northwest, on Snickersville Turnpike and would remain above the fighting on June 21.

The Fights on Ashby's Gap Turnpike and Near Upperville, June 21

The troopers' adrenalin was set in motion by an hour-or-so long artillery duel to sense the enemy's positions and resolve for the opening act on June 21. Pleasonton's first move was to send an infantry regiment around Hampton's right flank — Colonel Vincent sent the 83rd Pennsylvania wide left. After giving the flanking move time to get well underway, Pleasonton ordered Vincent to send another infantry regiment at Hart's battery near the pike and at Hampton's sharpshooters — Vincent sent the 16th Michigan.[98]

Pleasonton hoped to sweep Hampton's dismounted cavalry and Hart's artillery aside in short order, but as usual Hampton's men were in a strong position and would not easily be pushed aside. The initial Union advance was slow, then stalled, so Pleasonton ordered Vincent to send more infantry at the Confederate line. Vincent called up the 44th New York and the 20th Maine to assist the 16th Michigan. The 83rd Pennsylvania was still searching for Hampton's flank — they swung a little too far south to arrive in a timely manner. After the infantry's opening push, Kilpatrick's and J. I. Gregg's cavalry brigades entered the fighting, but Vincent's infantry did most of the fighting during the early part of the day.

Finally, the pressure on Hampton's cavalrymen and Hart's guns grew too intense, and Hart was ordered to begin the first pullback of the day. While Hart was reestablishing his battery on the next high ground to the west, along the pike, Hampton's command was hit on its right flank by the 83rd Pennsylvania. The 1st North Carolina was Hampton's right hand that day and took the brunt of the assault, but held long enough for Hart to begin pounding the Union advance again from a new position to the rear. Under cover provided by Hart's battery, Hampton pulled his cavalry back to a new position just below Hart.

Hampton, Hart, and Robertson (on the north side of the pike) continued to fall back ridge by ridge in a similar fashion — fighting, then covering each other's orderly pull back for most of the day. This process achieved delay at a minimal cost while R. E. Lee continued his march for another day.[99]

While Stuart was conducting his series of withdrawals, he became concerned for Chambliss and Jones, who were north of Ashby's Gap Turnpike and Goose Creek. Stuart did not want Buford, who was paralleling his line of march and periodically attempting to drop down to Ashby's Gap Turnpike, to get between himself and Chambliss and Jones. Consequently, Stuart requested Chambliss and Jones to begin an orderly pullback as well, and then drop south and join him at Upperville before Buford got between them or joined General Gregg at that place.

The final fight for the day on Ashby's Gap Turnpike took place first in front of and then about two miles west of Upperville. On the Union side, Vincent's infantry had done most of the fighting and had marched well over ten miles between fights—they were spent. D. McM. Gregg's relatively fresh cavalry would have to carry the load in the last fights that afternoon near Upperville.

Stuart formed his line just east of Upperville and wanted to hold the intersection of the pike and Trappe Road open long enough for Chambliss and Jones to drop south on Trappe Road and join their comrades for the march to Ashby's Gap. He still had Hampton south of the pike and Robertson north of it stretched to Pantherskin Creek. (Pantherskin Creek basically ran east-west at that point and directly into Goose Creek which came from the south and crossed the pike to form a confluence of the creeks.)

Just as D. McM. Gregg started his attack, with Kilpatrick's brigade heading for B. H. Robertson's brigade, the dismounted men of the 5th North Carolina, on Robertson's left, looked across Pantherskin Creek and saw Buford's command coming in their direction. They did not realize Buford had already tried to cross the creek, and it would be no easy matter for him to hit their flank as first feared. More importantly, just after the 5th North Carolina Cavalry sharpshooters saw Buford, the latter saw Chambliss's train and the 2nd North Carolina heading for the pike along Trappe Road. Buford made for the 2nd North Carolina rather than the 5th Cavalry. However, Buford's change of course was too late to keep the men of the 5th North Carolina from breaking and causing serious confusion on the left of Stuart's line in front of Upperville.

B. H. Robertson tried to bring some order to his line and to conduct an orderly retreat and reformation, but with little initial success. Encouraged by Robertson's confusion, Kilpatrick saw a great opportunity and charged down the pike toward town, but Hampton was able to head for the pike and hit Kilpatrick at their front and left flank.

There was a bloody clash and fighting until Kilpatrick's force pulled back. Fighting became mixed and spread along the entire line—Hampton was everywhere conducting a masterful symphony of bloodshed. At one point, Kilpatrick tried to rally his men by leading a charge personally, but his men broke again, and he became Hampton's prisoner. Then Pleasonton threw Starr's Reserve Brigade from Buford's division at Hampton. In time, Hampton's three regiments had both Union brigades plus the Reserve Brigade in disorder, and hand-to-hand fighting was severe—J. E. B. Stuart himself was in the middle of the melee, fighting along with his men.[100]

Hampton's stand against the Yankees gave Robertson time to drop back west of Upperville, collect his troops and form a new line west of Trappe Road. That meant only Hampton's stand was keeping the intersection of Trappe Road open for Chambliss and Jones to join Stuart.

When Pleasonton sent more troops up and north of the pike at Robertson's new position, Hampton's left flank became too exposed and his position untenable. Hampton had to organize an orderly retreat under very difficult circumstances. Finally, Robertson's men were able to help cover Hampton's pullback. By this time, Chambliss and Jones had been pushed west of Trappe Road and were heading for Paris and Ashby's Gap across country. Not only was the intersection on the pike not open to them, but they had been forced from Trappe Road in a separate action.

THE 2ND NORTH CAROLINA AND THE FIGHT ON TRAPPE ROAD, JUNE 21

John Buford left the Aldie area early on the morning of June 21 with the brigades commanded by William Gamble and Thomas Devin—The Reserve Brigade that had been sent to D. McM. Gregg on June 19 rejoined them at Middleburg. Buford's goal was to strike a major blow at Stuart's left as J. I. Gregg's and Kilpatrick's brigades, along with Vincent's infantry brigade, occupied them on the pike.

Buford led his three brigades north from Middleburg on the Foxcroft Road, then turned left just before reaching Goose Creek. They marched along the south bank of the creek until they could see Robertson's North Carolinians on Stuart's left. Buford could not overcome the difficulties of the terrain, however, and was unable to get into a position to hit Robertson's left flank. Consequently, he turned his cavalrymen back along the creek toward

Foxcroft Road and forded Goose Creek near that point.

On the opposite side of the creek Buford's men encountered enemy pickets—the Confederates had again been instructed to slow, not engage, any approaching enemy, so they withdrew after a brief exchange. At that point, both Chambliss and Jones were alerted to the approaching enemy—Chambliss's command was strong along the north side of the creek and centered around Willisville; Jones was camped near the town of Union and extended his pickets from Chambliss's left across to the junction of Foxcroft Road and Goose Creek.

Buford continued along Goose Creek, mostly south, toward Millville where he again hoped to cross the creek and fall upon Robertson's left. Jones had sharpshooters from the 11th and 12th Virginia in front of Buford's column most of the morning and caused him considerable grief. Their effectiveness can be measured by Buford's impression that he had three enemy regiments in front of him early in the day. There were, however, only several squadrons from the 11th and 12th Virginia, and by midday they were supported by a squadron from Chambliss's 9th Virginia Cavalry. The main body of the 9th Virginia and the 2nd North Carolina Cavalry were just in front of the Confederate rearguard. In any case, it was sufficient to delay Buford's arrival at Millville until around noon.

When Buford formulated his plan to move along Goose Creek, overtake Stuart's line, drop south to the pike, and turn the Confederate left, he clearly did not expect the sort of resistance he received from Chambliss's and Jones's cavalrymen north of Goose Creek. Buford was frustrated throughout the morning, largely because of the need to stop, unlimber, deploy, fire a few rounds, then reform the column and get underway every mile or so.[101]

His frustration reached a peak when he finally got to Millville and sent the Reserve Brigade under Major Starr across Goose Creek only to find that he was too late—the fighting on Ashby's Gap Turnpike had already moved further west, and he had missed his chance to hit the Confederate left at that point. The delays mattered.[102] The Reserve Brigade under Starr was instructed to continue on and join D. McM. Gregg on the pike. Buford took Gamble and Devin toward Upperville staying north of the creek and made another sprint for Stuart's line on Ashby's Gap Turnpike. This time as far west as Upperville.

It was around this time Stuart sent a message to Chambliss instructing him and Jones to begin a pull back toward Upperville. Upon receiving Stuart's instructions to head for Upperville, Chambliss collected his troops and train and began moving west along Millville Road. Jones started his column southwest for Millville Road where he would connect with Chambliss's column. Jones left Lomax with sharpshooters from the 11th and 12th Virginia cavalries as the rearguard in front of Buford. Throughout the early afternoon, Chambliss and Jones made good time executing their pullback largely because Buford still did not consider them a worthy target. He still had his eyes fixed on the Confederate force on Ashby's Gap Turnpike.

By the time Jones got to Millville Road, he fell in behind Chambliss's command already heading toward the Blue Ridge Mountains. Chambliss had left a squadron to hold the intersection open until Jones arrived and to inform the latter that Buford was at the time between them and Pantherskin Creek. The Confederate column with its wagons and artillery had to stay on the roads and did not have the "luxury" afforded Buford to cut across country north of Pantherskin Creek for Upperville. Consequently, Chambliss and Jones had to travel west, actually slightly northwest, then make a sharp left turn and head south on Trappe Road along the base of the mountains.

The Confederate wagons and artillery occupied the narrow roads with the mounted cavalry on either side of the road. In this part of Virginia the roads were usually lined on both sides with stone fences around three or four feet high, and the train on the road filled the space between the walls. This meant the cavalry had to travel on the other side of the walls, through the fields on each side. The fields were, of course, marked off with walls of their own; each of which had to be torn down to allow the horsemen to travel parallel to the road.

Lomax's rear guard continued to slow Buford while the latter continued his focus on getting to the pike as soon as possible to help D. McM. Gregg. Both were important because Chambliss and Jones needed all the help they could get in the race for Upperville. The race lasted about three hours.

Once the Confederate column reached Trappe Road and turned south for Upperville, Chambliss's brigade was still in front, and the 2nd North Carolina was at the front of its brigade, traveling through the fields on the east side of the walled road — the wagons and artillery still on the road itself. Some of the 10th Virginia followed the 2nd North Carolina on the east side of the road; others were in the road itself, escorting artillery. The 9th and probably the 13th Virginia were on the west or mountain side of the road.

Just after 3:00 P.M., around the time the Confederates were turning south on Trappe Road, Buford left Millville Road in another attempt to reach and cross Pantherskin Creek and help General Gregg on the pike, who appeared to Buford, in need of assistance. As Buford approached the creek Gregg was beginning his attack on Stuart's line just east of Upperville. (That was probably about the time Robertson's 5th North Carolina saw Buford coming at their flank and broke.) As Buford neared the creek, he realized again he could not easily get at Robertson on the left of Stuart's line, and as this realization settled in, Buford saw the head of Chambliss's column to the west, on Trappe Road heading south for Upperville. In his words, he noticed "…a train of wagons and a few troopers to my right marching at a trot, apparently making for Ashby's Gag." Buford decided to go for the Confederates on Trappe Road.[103]

The "few troopers" in Buford's line of sight were the cavalrymen of the 2nd North Carolina, and they were moving into a very vulnerable position. The men of the 2nd North Carolina were making their way through the fields just east of the wall bordering the east side of the road — to keep pace with the train, they had pulled down stone walls as they crossed from one field to another or crossed side roads. They had just pushed their way through the two stone walls bordering a sunken lane and passed through into a small field only to be confronted with another stone wall on the south side of the small field. After taking down the next wall and passing through the small field and into an old field, and before reaching the orchard by the Thomas House, they were in an open space (the old field) which ran from their left flank east to a bottom near Greengarden Road. The sunken lane also came up from the bottom.

Buford had Gamble move forward and dismount sharpshooters on the sunken lane where it nearly faced west, facing the 2nd North Carolina's left flank. Gamble poised his mounted troopers to charge up from the bottom through the old field and into the 2nd North Carolina. Devin's brigade was a short distance behind Gamble.

Once the 2nd North Carolina was in the old field, fully exposed and nearly enclosed by stone walls, Gamble's sharpshooters opened fire with a heavy volley which startled the horsemen who were moving at a trot.[104]

Immediately, the men of the 2nd North Carolina wheeled to the left and in column of four charged across the old field for the Union troopers behind the stone wall on the sunken lane. Their instincts were to attack, their job was to slow the enemy while their train moved west of Trappe Road on Mountain Road and through fields. The 2nd North Carolina charged nearly to the wall where the firing from the Union sharpshooters was too great, and they had to pull back.[105]

George P. Bryan of Company G, 2nd North Carolina in a letter to his father explained the scene from his vantage point: "I was shot at a rock fence … while the reg't. was charging some sharpshooters behind it. We had to charge in a line across an old field some ½ mile exposed to the fire of the sharpshooters all the way. I was wounded just as we had driven the enemy from the fence by a pistol ball across the top of my head."[106] If the Union sharpshooters were driven from the wall, it was probably just to a new position behind the wall bordering the other side of the sunken lane — a position from which they could unleash a second round directly into the 2nd North Carolina cavalrymen who were stopped across the lane by the first wall. It was at that point the 2nd North Carolina pulled back across the old field to near where they had first been fired upon.

When the 2nd North Carolina first came under fire from the sharpshooter and began their charge, Preston R. Chew and his artillery crew threw themselves into action. They were the 2nd North Carolina's only comrades to instinctively go for the enemy and help the cavalrymen. They took out a wall on the east side of the road and unlimbered their guns in the small field while most of Chew's escort headed across the wall on the west side of the road and up the hill to safety and to get a better view. Apparently for most of the Confederates marching behind the 2nd North Carolina, the Union sharpshooters' fire got their attention, but their first sight of the enemy was after the 2nd North Carolina had made their charge, and Gamble's mounted men were in their first charge. John Z. H. Scott with the 10th Virginia later wrote:

I rode on a while in front of it [a section of their artillery] ... [when] a squadron of Yankees [Gamble's mounted men] intending to cut off retreat along the road we were on came dashing across the fields and got within some three hundred yards of myself and of this piece of artillery before they were observed — I felt no uneasiness for myself — but simply leaped the stone fence on the opposite side of the road and rode up on the hill to see, as I fully expected — the easy capture of the gun — The gunners however never thought of such a thing — In less time than it takes to tell it they dismounted, rushed at the stone fence and partly pulling and partly pushing the stone down they reduced the fence at one point speedily to a heap of rocks, over which and up the hill the horses dragged the gun, the connoneers followed in a run actually loaded the piece with cannister and dropping the trail, and aiming in an instant the charge was sent square into the Yankee squadron at a distance of about a hundred yards — They were staggered and confounded by the shot and before they could recover from their astonishment, another charge followed and set them in motion the other way.[107]

Scott probably got to the safety of the knoll on the west side of Trappe Road soon after Colonel Beale of the 9th Virginia — Beale had observed the 2nd North Carolina's charge and Gamble's mounted men at the bottom before they started their charge. In any case, a number of the cavalrymen from the 9th and 10th Virginia had good seats from which to observe the life and death struggle that engulfed the 2nd North Carolina.

Things happened quickly as Chew was readying his gun for the first shot, and the 2nd North Carolina was pulling back to the area near where they were first hit, Gamble was coming up from the bottom at full charge and heading for the 2nd North Carolina. All the while the Union sharpshooters on the sunken lane were still peppering the mounted men from the 2nd North Carolina. As Gamble's mounted force approached, "The North Carolinians met the charge with a shout...." At about the same time, Chew's guns got off their first rounds into Gamble's charging cavalrymen. This caused part of Gamble's charging force to veer off to the right before the cavalries collided and head for Chew's guns. Soon after the cavalry clash, some men from the 10th Virginia who were behind the 2nd North Carolina made their way into the old field and joined in the cavalry melee. It was also around this time Chew's artillerymen may have been joined by guns from another unit making a total of perhaps four or five guns in the small field.[108]

Shortly after the cavalry fight was underway and Chew's artillerymen got off their second shot into Gamble's men, the two guns assigned to Chambliss's brigade were settled on the knoll west of Trappe Road and began firing. The 9th Virginia Cavalry was beside the guns and was finally ordered to assist the 2nd North Carolina. Colonel R. L. T. Beale of the 9th Virginia described his position and entry into the fighting in these words:

Deeming it useless to make fight against such odds, we were directing our march to the foot of the mountain in rear of our guns, and out of range of the musketry, when orders came for the regiment to relieve the Second North Carolina, as the position must be held for a time. Turning to the left and making openings in the stone walls to pass through, we were joined by Lieutenant-Colonel Lewis with another squadron. As we passed into the field a fresh body of mounted men emerged from the bottom to our right. These Lewis was ordered to charge with his squadron, while the other squadrons were directed against the troops who were engaging the North Carolinians. A mixed hand-to-hand fight was kept up for moments, when, finding fresh squadrons of Yankees pressing up from the bottom, we got back through the stone walls and into the field beyond as best we could.[109]

Clearly, the 2nd North Carolina was engaged for some time before the 9th Virginia arrived. Consequently, the severe fighting lasted for several minutes or an eternity depending on when one entered the old field. The length of time it took the 9th Virginia and ultimately Jones's 12th and 11th Virginia cavalries to join the fight certainly seemed to some of the men in the 2nd North Carolina like an eternity — later Graham of the 2nd North Carolina offered the following comment on the situation: "I do not believe there was an engagement during the war in which a body of troops was more forsaken by comrades than the 'Second Horse' was on that occasion."[110]

While the 2nd North Carolina and other troopers from Chambliss's brigade were still engaged with Gamble's 8th Illinois, the 3rd Indiana, and 12th Illinois, Jones had also gotten into position to enter the fight. From just up the road, Jones had noticed the guns in trouble so he sent the 12th and behind them the 11th Virginia cavalries into the small field. The 12th headed for the endangered artillery and then the 11th Virginia came to their assistance. The fighting was heated and then Jones's 7th Virginia came up and joined the fray. Then more Union artillery arrived supported by the 8th New York. The fighting continued with charge after charge using both saber and pistol, and lasted for around one hour by some accounts—and certainly it seemed longer to some than to others.[111]

The cavalrymen on both sides had reached the point of exhaustion at about the same time and withdrawal was inevitable. By that time, the cavalries had also become mixed and Jones's men were further into the old field and some men from the 2nd North Carolina were closer to Chew's guns, which set the stage for the final scenes of the fight.

It came as more Union cavalrymen charged Chambliss's troops and Chew's guns, causing the Confederates to begin a pull back, and in the process Chew was in danger of losing his guns in the small field. Responding to the danger, Lieutenant William P. Roberts of Company C, 2nd North Carolina rallied a squad of men as his regiment was withdrawing and charged the enemy with enough determination to allow the guns to limber up and retire.[112] It was also around this time Devin's brigade charged up from the bottom and Gamble's men began pulling back. There were no replacement regiments for Chambliss and Jones, and Devin's cavalrymen pushed the last of the confederates from the field—the 2nd North Carolina among them.

The men from Chambliss's and Jones's brigades who were engaged east of Trappe Road followed their comrades and trains west into the foothills, then south to the community of Paris where Stuart was collecting his cavalrymen. They were pursued but not vigorously. Chew's guns were primarily responsible for the distance maintained between the Confederates and Gamble's and Devin's advanced troopers. When Chambliss's and Jones's column reached the Ashby's Gap pike and the bulk of Stuart's cavalry could be seen gathered near Paris, the Union pursuit pulled back and rested for the night.

Longstreet had sent troops back to occupy Ashby's Gap for the night, and Stuart moved his cavalry through the pass "for rest and refreshments." Chambliss's brigade bivouacked for the night near the bank of the Shenandoah River.[113]

Pleasonton had hurt but certainly not destroyed Stuart's cavalry, nor had he reached the Blue Ridge Mountains in a timely manner. By the time he could report Longstreet's presence to Hooker, it was no longer news. Stuart could rest for the night; his shielding mission was accomplished—R. E. Lee's army was well on its way north.[114]

The cost of shielding The Army of Northern Virginia's march north was high for Stuart's cavalry. They suffered numerous losses between June 17 and 21, 1863. A partial tally includes the following: 305 men lost around Aldie on June 17; 99 lost near Middleburg on June 19; and 209 men lost around Upperville on June 21.[115]

The records indicate 12 men killed and mortally wounded near Upperville on June 21, but clearly does not include those lost in that category on Trappe Road. Colonel Gamble alone reported burying 18 Confederates in the old field off Trappe Road that day and others were mortally wounded. That suggests while the fighting on Trappe Road was shorter in duration than the fighting on the pike that day, it was more violent. Jones reported 14 men killed on that day but not all in the fight on Trappe Road. From Chambliss's brigade, Colonel Beale reported that "Though we were in this fight only a few minutes, twenty-seven of the small number engaged were missing. We suffered most from the deadly aim of the muskets or rifles fired from the breastwork of the stone fence...."[116]

In the several days of fighting, clearly the 2nd North Carolina was most seriously involved on June 21 on Trappe Road where they suffered 21 recorded losses—seven men killed or mortally wounded, which constitutes over half the men killed in Stuart's cavalry on that day. If Gamble's burial count (18) was close to accurate, the 2nd North Carolina appeared to take the heaviest losses from among the seven Confederate regiments fighting in the old field off Trappe Road that day. This is understandable because the 2nd North Carolina absorbed the first assault and was engaged longer than any other unit fighting in the old field.

While the 2nd North Carolina was engaged on the 19th near Middleburg, they lost 4 men: 3 killed or mortally wounded, 1 wounded and captured. Two days later on Trappe Road, near Upperville, they had 7 men killed or mortally wounded, 11 wounded, 3 wounded and captured, and 1 captured. The impact of the losses on the 2nd North Carolina Cavalry regiment was suggested by Captain Graham of Company K when he estimated the regiment lost "...over half of the men it took into action, either killed or wounded."[117] Captain Graham's comment might well have been a slight exaggeration influenced by the perception he derived from the fighting in his immediate vicinity, but it also does reflect the small number of effective men in the regiment after the Battle of Brandy Station. His comment suggests the 2nd North Carolina carried only about 50 mounted and armed men into battle on Trappe Road on June 21—the number was probably closer to seventy-five. Some of the men who carried the burden of the numbers are listed in the table below.

The 2nd North Carolina lost four men in the fighting along Zula Road and Ashby's Gap Turnpike on June 19, 1863. They were probably lost while the regiment slowed the approaching enemy, allowing their cavalry and artillery comrades to fall back from Mount Defiance to the next ridge. However, most of the losses taken by the men in the 2nd Cavalry in the series of battles between Middleburg and Upperville were on Trappe Road on June 21, 1863.

Every cavalryman had a story and was more than a name on a casualty list, but one in particular emerged from the fighting in Loudoun Valley between June 17 and 21, 1863. He was George Pettigrew Bryan, Company G, 2nd North Carolina Cavalry; he was the only officer wounded and captured from the regiment on Trappe Road; and his story is both amazing and tragic. It illustrates both the horrors of war and the optimism of ambitious youth that was lost in the war. George wrote a letter to his father, to which I referred several pages above, from the West's Building Hospital in Baltimore on September 25, 1863 while recovering from his wound received on June 21, just off Trappe Road. It is lengthy but worth reading—it is, in part, as follows:

Losses in the 2nd North Carolina Cavalry, June 19–21, 1863

Trooper	Age	Co.	Fate
James Blythe	26	C	mortally wounded
Simeon T. Benn	23	H	mortally wounded
Joseph Brady	29	H	killed
James H. Cox	27	H	wounded & captured
Nicholas McGuire	33	A	killed
James M. Waugh	19	B	killed
Kenneth R. C. Britt	20	C	wounded
William J. Holt	24	C	wounded
Alexander Bedsole	21	D	wounded
Thomas Carter	25	D	wounded
Neill J. Shaw	30	D	wounded
Caleb G. Stephens	26	D	wounded
Robert D. Allman	24	E	wounded & captured
John W. Holden		F	wounded
George P. Bryan	23	G	wounded & captured
George Osborne	40	G	killed
Henry J. Barham		H	captured
Abner L. Hoggard	28	H	wounded & captured
Hiram Lassiter	23	H	killed
William S. Moore	22	H	killed
Charles W. Smith	21	H	killed
James A. Cole	35	I	killed
Ninian W. Gray		K	wounded
Charles Harris	26	K	wounded
Edward G. Wyese		K	wounded

The source used here is *North Carolina Troops 1861–1865, A Roster*, compiled by Louis H. Manarin (Raleigh, N.C., State Division of Archives and History), vol. II, Cavalry, pp, 104–177. (See Appendix for more information on the men listed above, page 395.)

Dear Father. ...I am in as good health as ever in my life and tho' the fare is what a prisoner must expect, I make out very well. I would not know from any inconvenience or pain I suffer that I was wounded. I was shot at a rock fence near Ashby's Gap while the reg't. was charging some sharpshooters behind it. We had to charge in a line across an old field some ¾ mile exposed to the fire of the sharpshooters all the way. I was wounded just as we had driven the enemy from the fence by a pistol ball across the top of my head. The ball entered my skull a little to the left of the middle of the front part of my head & ranging a little to the right across the top of my head to the back. I was so close that there was no fracture. The shot grooving out a track thro' the outer, middle & lower divisions of the skull, leaving a thin crating over the brain. It knocked me senseless from my horse. The Reg't was in column of fours behind me at the time but the horse immediately behind me stepped so sharply on the inside of my left thigh that I was roused sufficiently to see my danger & make a spring for the fence which put me out the way of the remainder of the horses. I could easily have escaped in the confusion but for my left side being paralyzed. I recovered from my stun in about half hour & was soon visited by one of the enemy who examined me & went off saying that it was not worth while to take me to the hospital as I would die in a few minutes anyhow.

I was of a different opinion as I had felt my wound and discovered there was still a covering to my brain however I did not contradict him as I felt my side regaining life every minute & determined to make my way to some woods near by & gain some house during the night. While lying against the fence a reg't of the enemy's cavalry charged in column of fours past me. The horses tread on my cloths but carefully kept off of me, fearing an unsteady foothold. I was in much greater danger after I was wounded than before as the enemy took cover under the fence again & our men from our side of it shelled them & used their carbines against them. My only chance was to lie as close to the ground as possible & await the termination of the fight.... With the help of my sabre-scabbard I now climbed over the fence into the lane which separated me from another fence & the woods beyond it & to my great disappointment, found a couple of officers talking very earnestly in the middle of the road. One seemed to be a staff officer giving orders to the other (to judge by their motions) for every time one would start towards me the others would call him back & continue the conversation. I had lost my sabre out of scabbard as soon as I fell from horse and my pistol I had hidden under a rock as soon as I came to myself, I found my arm extended & my finger on trigger which was a rather bold position for one who was unable to fight, so the first thing I did was to come to a more peaceable attitude & hide my pistol. Without arms & without means of moving faster than a child can crawl I thought my chance of escape from a prison very slight. Fortunately however I got over the fence before the colloqly [colloquy] was over & took my course directly up the fence toward the two officers who probably supposed I would have taken any other direction in preference & thus lost me. I lay down in the thickest place I could find & began to think myself safe when a company of cavalry going on picket probably came directly to me choosing the thickest part of the woods to escape the shell. They halted near me & officer in command sent a Sergeant with a wounded horse to take me to the hospital. He came up to me, commenced unbuckling my sabre belt & holster & offered to let me ride his wounded horse which I declined as my leg was paining me so that I could not ride. While this was going on one of our shells exploded over middle of company wounding & killing men & horses in every direction. I finally reached the field hospital where 2 surgeons were very busy cutting off legs & feet almost every one seeming to be wounded in one or the other place. As they were too busy here to attend to my wound I was sent further to the rear still to another hospital where I found the Surgeons very kind & attentive. They dressed my head very nicely & sent me to a barn with six or eight of our men & officers.... I reached the Stanton Hospital Washington Tuesday night late & remained there for nearly six weeks when we were sent to the Lincoln Hospital in the same city. Remaining here about 3 weeks we were sent to West's Building Hospital where the men were paroled & sent South, & I the only officer along was detained.

Since I have been here my health has been very good & my wound improving. The Drs. seem to think the bone will replace and in six weeks I will be as sound as ever.... We the officers are expected to start for Johnson's Island every hour where we will probably remain for a long while. It is a dreary prospect but can not be avoided so we have to make the best of our ill fortune & patiently wait to be exchanged. We get the papers and discuss about exchanging. The first thing in the morning is "what is the news about exchanging" & the last thing at night is probability of good news in the morning. Every disappointment only seems to make us more hopeful for the morrow. I pass my time reading the papers, playing drafts & reading some few books which I get hold of. I expect a work on Engineering which I will devote myself to as long as it lasts & I will get another on the first opportunity. At Johnston's Island I expect to pass my time very profitably in study of all different kinds as long as I am a prisoner so that my misfortune will be of some use to me after all....[118]

REGROUP AND CONTINUE NORTH

After some rest and nourishment, J. E. B. Stuart had his cavalrymen on the road again the morning after. In his words, "When the mist had sufficiently cleared away..., it was evident the enemy was retiring, and the cavalry was ordered up immediately to the front, to follow."[119] Both cavalries were still tired, bruised, and depleted — it would not be a rapid withdrawal or pursuit. Most of the further abuse inflicted on Pleasonton's men came from the barrels of Chew's guns which were casually followed by Chambliss's and Jones's brigades east along Ashby's Gap Turnpike — the latter engaging in skirmishes only here and there mostly when unavoidable.

Pleasonton was giving up the ground won at such a high price in the previous days, but there was not much point in doing otherwise. He and his cavalry were not capable of pushing Longstreet's and Stuart's men through Ashby's Gap so they could peer into the Shenandoah Valley, and there was no point in holding Upperville.

As the cavalrymen with Chambliss and Jones followed the Union troops along the pike, Colonel Beale from Chambliss's brigade made the following observation, "We saw some of the graves of our fallen comrades, and numerous others of Federal soldiers, reminding us of the deadly strife in which we had been engaged on the two preceding days...." Those words do not reflect the thoughts of men looking for a fight that day. Indeed they were more inclined to follow at a respectable distance until reaching Middleburg where they then broke off all skirmishing and pulled back along the pike. Chambliss's brigade camped near the pike for the night and next day pulling only picket duty.[120]

By June 23, Stuart had Jones's brigade near Snickersville, Fitz Lee's brigade, still under Munford, between Union and Middleburg. Stuart with Hampton's, Robertson's, and W. H. F. Lee's brigades were on the Ashby's Gap Turnpike between Rector's Cross Roads and Ashby's Gap. They then moved to Salem where Stuart was once again gathering his partially rested, partially effective cavalry brigades. They were assembled for the next phase of R. E. Lee's invasion of Pennsylvania, which had not stopped while the cavalry was engaged at Aldie, Middleburg, and Upperville.

The Ride-around to Gettysburg

J. E. B. Stuart sent a message through James Longstreet to Robert E. Lee early on June 22, in which he expressed his desire to move north as soon as possible. Stuart's message did not provide R. E. Lee with any useful information about the enemy, which prompted R. E. Lee to ask "Do you know where he [the enemy] is and what he is doing? I fear he will steal a march on us, and get across the Potomac before we are aware." It was clear, Stuart's first order of business was to locate and determine Joseph Hooker's movements, if any. Apparently Stuart assumed he would soon know the whereabouts and intensions of Hooker and was more concerned with what he could do after locating the enemy. R. E. Lee's reply to Stuart that day did address the latter's concern by adding instructions to leave two brigades to guard the Blue Ridge Mountain passes and the army's rear, and move his other three brigades into Maryland if he found that Hooker was moving northward. Stuart was further instructed to take a position on Richard S. Ewell's right once he was north of the Potomac — part of his assignment was to keep Ewell informed of the enemy's movements and to collect all the supplies he could for the army. At 3:30 P.M., R. E. Lee notified Ewell of his instructions to Stuart. By 4:00 P.M., Lee sent a message to Longstreet for Stuart. Longstreet responded with the following: "I have forwarded your letter to General Stuart, with the suggestion that he pass by the enemy's rear if he thinks that he may get through." Stuart had suggested the ride-around to R. E. Lee as early as the 22nd and continued to do so the following day — finally the mission developed into something more to Stuart's liking.[121]

Of course, passing between the Union army and its Capital rather than between the two opposing armies would increase the likelihood of capturing wagon trains sent to supply Hooker's troops — which became part of the assignment. However, the cost of such a route could deprive R. E. Lee of his "eyes and ears."[122]

Stuart spent June 24 gathering his three favorite brigades — Fitz Lee's, W. H. F. Lee's, and Wade Hampton's — near the town of Salem. Hampton's brigade was tired and battered but only had to drop down from the Ashby's Gap Turnpike to Salem. Fitz Lee had to bring his troops down from near Snicker's Gap, but their spirits had to be high — they had not been in any serous fighting since June 17 at Aldie, and, most importantly, Fitz Lee was back at the head of his brigade. He had missed the fighting at Brandy Station and Aldie due to a serious flareup of his inflammatory rheumatism. W. H. F. Lee's brigade was still under the temporary command of Chambliss. This apparently was not a problem for Stuart because he liked Chambliss, who was after all a Virginian, a West Pointer, young, and the son of a Confederate Congressman — he was Stuart's sort of man. Stuart decided to leave Robertson's and Jones's brigades behind to guard the upper passes in the Blue Ridge. He sent instructions for them to watch the passes and then follow R. E. Lee's infantry north.[123]

Once gathered, Stuart had his column prepare three days' rations and prepare to move toward the Bull Run Mountains after nightfall. Stuart was certain the enemy would be watching the valley from atop the mountains, so he waited for the cover of darkness, hoping to reach the pass undetected. Around 1:00 A.M. on June 25, Stuart started his troopers eastward. Chambliss's command with the 2nd North Carolina was in the saddle and heading for Thoroughfare Gap about an hour later. When Stuart's column reached Thoroughfare Gap, they found it occupied by Hancock's Corps, so they moved down and passed through Glasscock's Gap without incident.[124]

Once through the pass, Stuart planned to get in Hooker's rear and then decide if the enemy was active or not, and if it were practicable to pass around Hooker, or if he should return to the Shenandoah Valley and follow R. E. Lee north. It is not too likely Stuart ever gave the latter possibility much consideration.

After passing through the Bull Run Mountains, Stuart headed for Hay Market, but in the process he again encountered Hancock's II Corps which was heading north. As it turned out, the Union infantry was on the shortest route to a town called Gettysburg in Pennsylvania — very close to the route Stuart had planned to take north. Stuart's choice at the time was to follow Hooker's army, or to swing around to the east of his enemy's column. Stuart took the latter course, so the Confederate cavalry had to back track just a bit and follow a wider arch, south and east, to get around his enemy's rear. Stuart decided it was practicable; he could get around Hooker without "hindrance," do damage to the enemy, and still join Ewell in a timely manner.[125]

Stuart's lead brigade encountered a Union column heading north through Haymarket and fought briefly, but did not stay around for a time-consuming battle. Rather, he withdrew to Buckland and sent Fitz Lee on to Gainesville with his brigade while the others spent the rest of the day grazing their horses. They stayed between Buckland and Gainesville for the night.[126]

On June 26, the Confederate cavalry headed slightly southeast through Brentsville, then turned north for Fairfax Court House. Their horses had grown steadily weaker from the hard fighting and marching since Brandy Station and lack of nourishment.[127]

When Chambliss's command reached the Occoquan Creek, they stopped to graze and rest their horses. At that time the decision was made to furlough a number of troopers with horses unfit for the march ahead. This process was also followed in the other brigades. The decision was prompted by the slow pace they had been making — they were moving slower than usual for infantry — but also because it was obvious that some of the horses had simply "succumbed" from the ordeal. They hoped to pick up the pace by sending their prisoners to the rear, but this had the effect of thinning the already depleted ranks of many regiments. Among those lost to this task was Milas Cavin of Company B, 2nd North Carolina who was still mounted on the horse of fallen comrade, James Waugh, since June 21. Milas and several others from the regiment escorted a "squad" of prisoners back to Culpeper and were then instructed to ride to Winchester. Milas wrote his sister of his detached duty and added, "…but I do not know whether we will meet up with our regiment there or not." The uncertainty Milas was experiencing was in the end far easier to live with than what the others in his regiment would experience before they met again. In any case, the Confederate cavalry was already east of Hooker's army and it was no longer practicable to head west for the Shenandoah Valley and to cross the Potomac in R. E. Lee's path.[128]

Hoping to be more fleet of hoof, Stuart's cavalrymen moved on. When they reached Fairfax Station, Hampton's brigade was in front and skirmished with the Union cavalry stationed there. They drove the Federals from the station and took some prisoners, arms, and equipment. They then took Fairfax Court House on their route north.

Stuart's cavalrymen were in need of nutritional and spiritual uplifting by the time they arrived at Fairfax, and they found it among the Union stores. When one member of his staff arrived on the scene he observed that "Every trooper carried before him upon the pommel of his saddle a bale of smoking tobacco, or a drum of figs; every hand grasped a pile of gingercakes, which were rapidly disappearing." He also noted that at the time, "It was impossible

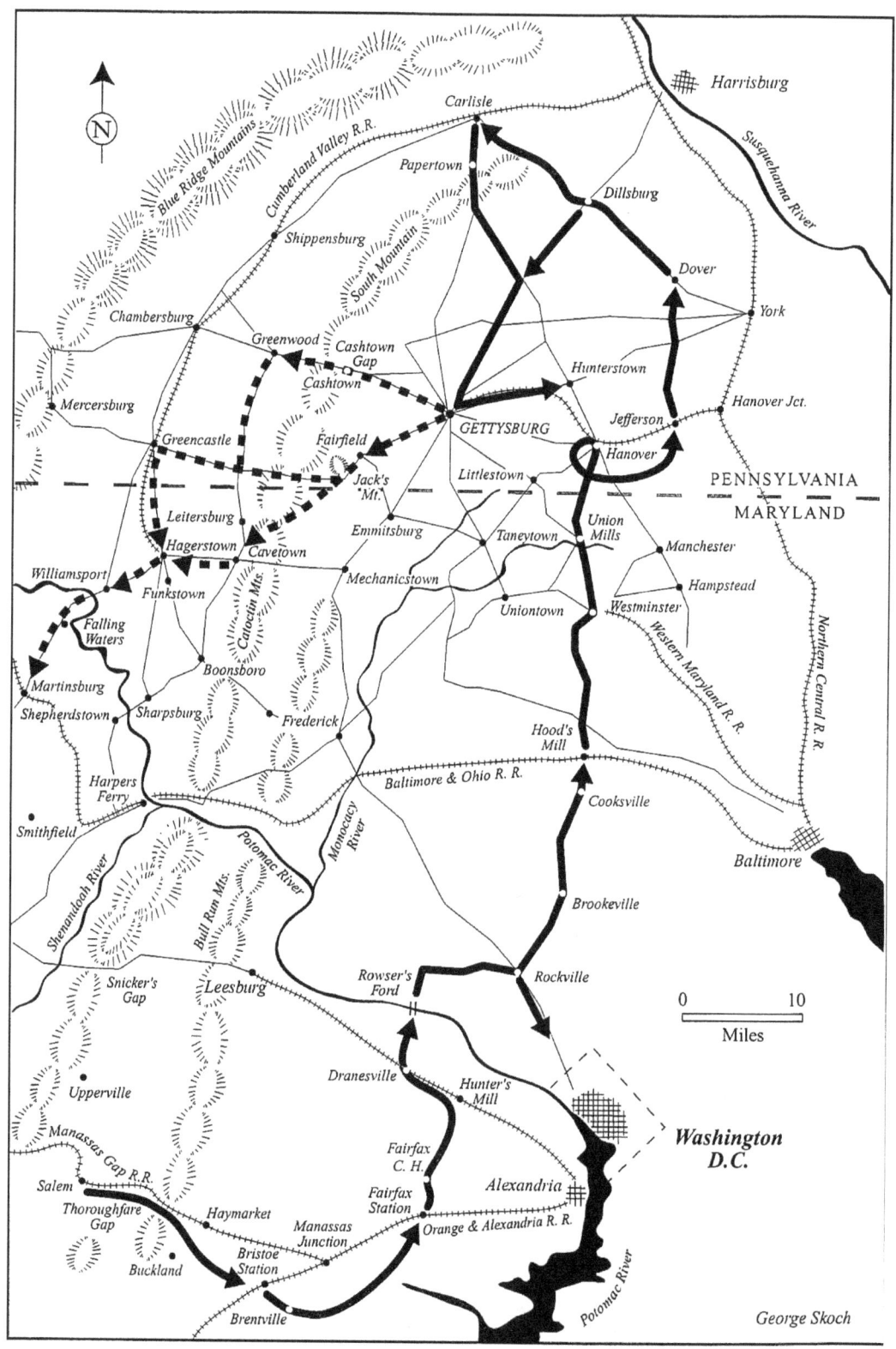

3.3: Stuart's Route to Gettysburg and Back

to forbare from laughing at the spectacle which the cavalry column presented. Every man had on a white straw hat, and a pair of snowy cotton gloves."[129]

By the time Chambliss's command arrived at Fairfax, some spoils were still to be had and were welcome as the cavalrymen had had little to eat for several days and by June 27, most had nothing. By the time the 9th Virginia arrived, one member of the regiment remembered "There were many nice things taken here, and consumed by us ravenous rebs." However, many of the troopers were denied supplies due to their nervousness about enemy cavalry in the vicinity.[130]

Apparently the resourceful North Carolinians were among those who did not leave empty-handed. Captain Graham of the 2nd North Carolina later described the scene in these words:

> The only rations we had for more than two days was a piece of our bread 2x4x½ inch. On Saturday about noon we reached Fairfax Station here we captured a lot of commissary supplies principally butter and crackers (hard-tack). My men got them some cheap straw hats from a store, filled haversacks with crackers and the hats with butter. It was midday and a hot June Day. The butter melted and most of it escaped: the men dipped the crackers in the hats and had the first satisfactory meal in four days.[131]

A truly satisfactory meal was in order as was some rest for both man and horse. By the time Stuart had his cavalrymen back on the march, they had spent several more hours. The 2nd North Carolina, like other regiments, had lost more than that; some of the cavalrymen who were not sent back at Occoquan Creek because their horses were finished were sent to the rear while resting at Fairfax. No count was taken of how many cavalrymen were sent to the rear for lack of fit mounts on the roads to the Potomac, but in Captain Graham's words, "...a considerable squad turned to the rear at Fairfax."[132]

Once Stuart's column reached Hunter's Mill on the turnpike running from Alexandria to Leesburg, Stuart took the pike northwest for about five miles to Dranesville, then due north for Rowser's Ford on the Potomac River. When they arrived near Dranesville, they learned Sedgwick's VI Corps had left the area that morning. They were still close on the enemy's rear. Stuart moved Hampton's cavalrymen cautiously north from Dranesville for the nearly five mile march to the Potomac. Stuart left Chambliss's command west of Dranesville until Fitz Lee could close up and get positioned to cross the river.[133]

Before reaching the river themselves but after several hours of cautious marching from Dranesville, the men in Chambliss's command noticed a marked slowing of the column and knew the front brigade had reached some obstacle up front—Stuart and Hampton had reached the Potomac and had to test the waters before making a slow crossing. At the ford, Stuart had to make some important decisions on the spot. He knew the artillery would be completely submerged so he quickly decided to have cavalrymen carry the artillery shells and powder bags in their arms as they rode across the river. The water was deep and swift, but the river had to be forded, then and there.[134]

Once Fitz Lee's brigade was up, Chambliss began his move to the river. Colonel Beale of the 9th Virginia recounted their approach in these terms: "About sunset we began bearing to the right, taking by-paths and the cover of the woods, and winding through valleys, seemingly as though our wary General was approaching some unsuspecting foe."[135] There was reason to be cautious; just west of Dranesville they came across still smoldering camp fires the Union infantry had left earlier in the day.

The 2nd North Carolina was on Chambliss's left and in sight of enemy infantry near Leesburg while waiting for Fitz Lee's command to close up. Captain Graham of the 2nd North Carolina Cavalry remembered the approach and crossing.

> We ... came in sight of Hancock's rear near Leesburg; placing pickets we halted until after sunset, and then coming back several miles turned through a pine thicket without a road and having to use our hands to keep from losing our hats went into the road that leads to the Potomac river at Rowser's ford. The river I should judge was over half a mile wide and half way up the saddle skirt. We forded in single file.[136]

By the time Hampton's brigade and most of the artillery were across, night fell. When Chambliss's command arrived at the ford, the air was dark and calm, and the water was still deep and swift. Darkness meant the cavalrymen could not see the opposite shore; the swift current meant it was next to impossible to traverse in a line perpendicular to the shoreline. In Captain Graham's words, "…a man on each bank would watch the line and call when any person would get too far down, and be in danger of getting into too deep water. When we crossed it was nine or ten o'clock and no moon; each one had to follow his file leader. It was midnight before all were over."[137]

Once across the river, the cavalrymen collected on the strip of land that served as the tow-path and separated the Potomac River from the Chesapeake & Ohio Canal — they ran parallel for over 180 miles. The canal was too deep to ford, but fortunately for Stuart's cavalrymen, a nearby lock that Hampton's advance had located was used to make the crossing — it was not as dangerous as the ford had been, but it was also slow.

While waiting for the troops to pass over the canal, some forty-two vessels had arrived at the crossing and each was looted of goods that could be used — for instance, an ample supply of grain was found and taken along with other supplies. Two of the vessels were carrying Union troops on their way to Washington — they became prisoners and were marched off to Rockville. Stuart spared boats that were privately owned, but stranded them by turning them sidewise and cutting a sluice gate to the river. He hoped to leave them high and dry for sixty to ninety days, thus crippling a major supply line to the Union army for the same period of time.[138]

Like their comrades, Chambliss's cavalrymen had had another sleepless night and their horses had not had nourishment for 24 hours — but they had crossed the Potomac. On June 28, the column rested for several hours after the crossing. It had been very taxing on the men and horses, and they were allowed to rest and the horses to feast on some of the fine grass in fields not ravaged by war as were those in Virginia.[139]

Stuart had his column back on the march by late morning, heading northeast for Rockville. The 2nd North Carolina was on the road by 10 o'clock that Sunday morning. The time spent allowing the horses to rest and feed was costly in the end, but vitally important at the time. A member of Stuart's staff, W. W. Blackford, noted "Poor Magic [his new mare] looked as thin as a snake but cocked her ear as gayly as ever. Manassas [his other thoroughbred horse] had been wounded during our attack on Hancock's coups at Haymarket, but could still do duty, though much in want of food.... I rode Manassas on the march and had Magic led, saving her for the big battle that we knew was brewing."[140] Horses carrying privates had no such replacements, no relief, and consequently they were in worse condition — and, of course, the private would not be as swift in the next battle or chase.

THE COSTLY PRIZE

As the column moved toward Rockville, Hampton was in front and Chambliss's command next. While on the road, Hampton's men encountered small parties of enemy and took captive a number of wagons with teams. At one point, Chambliss's cavalrymen were called forward and had a running fight with the Second New York Cavalry but when it came to the chase, the speed of the Union horses left the Confederates behind.[141]

Within a mile or so of Rockville, Chambliss pulled his command off the road to feed the horses. While feeding, they were passed by Hampton's brigade. However, when Hampton reached Rockville, he saw evidence of the enemy in town, and Chambliss's command was ordered forward at a trot. Just outside of town, Stuart formed the cavalrymen in line, but the enemy had left town and Stuart, with Chambliss's men, took possession of the town without a contest.[142]

Rockville was on the turnpike running from Washington to Frederick, and Stuart realized it was a main line of communication and supply to Hooker's army, so he set his men to destroying the telegraph line for miles in both directions. While they were disrupting the line of communication from Washington to the Army of the Potomac, an opportunity to disrupt the supply line appeared on the horizon. A large supply train of more than 150 fully loaded wagons destined for Hooker's army was seen coming from Washington — when the front wagons were spotted the rear of the train was only about three or four miles outside Washington. The train was about 8 miles long.[143]

Chambliss's command was ordered onto the pike. Once outside of town, a rear guard was placed on their right flank. Then the 9th Virginia and the 2nd North Carolina moved out at a trot down the pike toward the oncoming train. Soon the Union wagon train was within sight. Colonel Beale remembered, "As we passed a house near the pike a lady ran out clapping her hands in eager excitement, and exclaiming: 'Push on; you have nearly caught them!' After riding a mile or so, we saw the guard of the train, a small party of cavalry, drawn up in line directly across the road, as if to bar our passage. The troopers having the fastest horses were now ordered forward to reinforce the men in advance; but before they got within two hundred yards of them, the enemy wheeled and fled...." As the train's guard saw Chambliss's regiments move from a trot to a charge, they turned, along with the front wagons, in an attempt to retreat along the same road the eight-mile-long train was advancing. Needless to say, there was considerable confusion, but most wagons managed to turn and make a chase out it. The slowness of mules pulling loaded wagons and the confusion among them was welcomed by the charging Confederates who were fueled primarily by adrenalin. Captain Graham of the 2nd North Carolina, charging with his regiment thought briefly of his exhausted mounts, as they pushed their horses down the road. One of Graham's responsibilities was to keep as many of his men mounted as possible, so the issue was often on his mind.[144]

As the drivers of the Union wagons along the train saw the charging cavalrymen many of them leaped from their seats and ran for cover in the woods. This left many of the unattended wagons under the control of frightened mules running wildly and crashing wagons into one another. Chambliss's men made order from the confusion, and as wagons were overtaken, they were turned and sent toward Rockville under guard.[145]

By the time Chambliss's cavalrymen had gathered the last of the wagons, they were within five miles of the Union capital, and Stuart briefly thought of the grand prize but settled for the wagon train. Colonel Beale left us a pretty good description of the captured loot.

The others [wagons] were loaded principally with oats and corn. Bakers' bread, crackers, whiskey in bottles of great variety, sugar, hams, with some tin and woodenware, knives and forks, were also found. The bacon and crackers, as well as the whiskey, proved to our jaded and hungry troopers most acceptable. The train consisted of three new ambulances, two of which were captured by Hampton, and one hundred and seventy-five wagons, drawn by nine hundred mules. The wagons were brand new, the mules fat and sleek, and the harness in use for the first time. Such a train we had never seen before and did not see again.[146]

Stuart knew the Army of Northern Virginia needed the supply train, but he also knew he had to move rapidly from this point on to get around Hooker's column. The latter need would be compromised because he decided to keep the supply train. By evening, Stuart had to move his tired troopers and about 175 additional wagons pulled by mules that were difficult to move rapidly as they too became hungry. When we consider what transpired on what remained of June 28, the picture of Stuart's dilemma becomes more complete.

Stuart learned that Hooker's troops were nearing Frederick, and he would have a very difficult time circling north of him to join Ewell or any part of the Army of Northern Virginia. Once Stuart knew the enemy was at Frederick, his only reasonable route from Rockville was to Westminster and then perhaps he could turn his column northwest to Gettysburg and cross above Hooker's army. Going north toward Westminster at that time was not a bad idea, but Stuart did not know on June 28 that it was a good idea. He did not know the location of R. E. Lee's infantry. He did not know Ewell had troops near Carlisle and York, Pennsylvania more than seventy miles north of his position. Nor did he know Early was camped near Gettysburg, Pennsylvania; and Longstreet and A. P. Hill were near Chambersburg, Pennsylvania. Only Stuart's column had not yet arrived in Pennsylvania—he needed to catch up. All in all, taking the route from Rockville to Westminster would get Stuart closer to Ewell and on a direct route to Gettysburg through Littletown. Stuart needed to get to Littletown and Gettysburg before Hooker's troops got that far north. To accomplish this, Stuart would have to make better time than he had during the several previous days.

Moving more or less parallel, Joseph Hooker's army was only a short distance north of Stuart's column because he had hesitated to start north after R. E. Lee's infantry. When Hooker first learned of the Confederate move north earlier in the month, he wanted to attack and take Richmond in General Lee's absence. Some time was lost while President Lincoln persuaded Hooker to attack the Army of Northern Virginia, defeat it, and win the war. Some felt Hooker was unwilling, perhaps afraid, to meet R. E. Lee in battle — Lincoln was among them. Only after R. E. Lee had his whole army across the Potomac did Hooker finally move north to confront the invader. Once under way, Hooker moved his army rapidly, paralleling the Army of Northern Virginia and in the process staying between R. E. Lee's infantry and Stuart's cavalry.

June 28 was a pivotal day for Hooker just as it was for Stuart. On that day, Lincoln removed Hooker from his command and replaced him with General George G. Meade. When Meade took command, his army was camped around Frederick and had around 90,000 men ready for battle. The Union army was concentrated, and aimed at Gettysburg. Meade had good information on the location of his enemy, and he moved quickly toward him.[147]

R. E. Lee's infantry was spread in an arch above Gettysburg, running from Chambersburg to Carlisle to York. Lee needed to know where the enemy was; he needed his "eyes and ears"; he needed J. E. B. Stuart. Stuart sent messages to R. E. Lee on June 28 when he learned of the enemy presence near Frederick, but he sent them in all the wrong directions — none arrived. On the same day, however, one of Longstreet's scouts brought word of the approaching Union army.

Learning of his enemy's concentrated strength and location, R. E. Lee instructed Ewell to pull his troops from Carlisle and York and move toward him at Chambersburg. In a follow-up message, Lee instructed Ewell to be ready to drop down on Gettysburg if conditions require it.[148] R. E. Lee did not know Stuart was heading directly north and planned to meet Ewell's forces in that area, but R. E. Lee could not have waited even if he had known — Stuart was simply too far behind schedule. Stuart knew nothing of his infantry comrades' positions or proposed movements on that day. Both armies were converging on Gettysburg; only Stuart did not know that.

Stuart spent most of the late afternoon and evening of June 28 at Rockville trying to collect his men and wares — both old and newly acquired. Among his recently acquired encumbrances, accumulated over a period of several days, were around 400 prisoners — to be fed, to be controlled and marched. Stuart knew he had to lighten his load if he were to pass the Union army on his left. So, while Chambliss's and Hampton's commands were collecting themselves and their captured wagons for yet another march, Stuart decided to begin the process of paroling the prisoners. Stuart sent Fitz Lee and his command out of Rockville first, and Chambliss's command was put on the road around sunset.[149]

The parole process took hours at Rockville, was continued on the road, and it consumed several more hours that night at Brookeville. The remainder of the prisoners were paroled the next day at Cooksville. Fitz Lee's brigade crossed the B & O Railroad early on June 29 and most of Stuart's column was across by the end of the day. As they crossed the road, men were detailed to spend most of the day tearing up tracks in both directions. Without the appropriate tools, it was exhausting work for men who had not slept in over 24 hours. Fitz Lee reached Westminster by early evening and had a serious hand-to-hand engagement with a squadron of the 1st Delaware Cavalry. While driving them off, he lost several men and gathered more prisoners. The Union cavalrymen withdrew to their support — Kilpatrick's cavalry was just up the road to Gettysburg at Littlestown. The Confederate cavalrymen spent the night just beyond Westminster. They did not get much rest, however, because in Stuart's words, "Here, for the first time since leaving Rector's Cross-Roads, we obtained a full supply of forage, but the delay and difficulty of procuring it kept many of the men up all night." Fitz Lee's command remained in front throughout June 29 and spent the night near Union Mills.[150]

Like most of Stuart's cavalrymen, the men in Chambliss's command were in the saddle for most of 24 hours by the time they passed through Westminster. Colonel Beale of the 9th Virginia remembered June 29 in these terms: "This weary day passed without halting, and as night approached we learned that the head of the column was fighting. We now reached Westminster, and our 24 hours' march was rewarded with an ample supply of rations for man and horse, much of it appropriated without orders from the large railroad depot at this place. A quiet night's rest here after 48 hours spent in the saddle greatly refreshed us."[151]

Indeed, that night Stuart's entire column was on the pike that ran from Baltimore to Gettysburg, and they had a pretty straight route to Gettysburg. However, the pike to Gettysburg ran through Littlestown, just 6 or 7 miles northwest of Union Mills, and during the night Stuart learned that Kilpatrick's cavalry division was already camped at Littlestown. With the pike blocked, and with it his ability to begin his swing west and over the Army of the Potomac, Stuart sent his column along a slower back road to Hanover — north rather than northwest. It was at this time, according to one member of Stuart's staff, they realized that capturing rather than burning the wagon train outside of Rockville was a mistake. Their slow column was losing ground in their near parallel march with Kilpatrick's command, and Stuart's need to separate his brigades by the length of the wagon train made them vulnerable to attack by the large Union cavalry force a few miles to their left — it was reasonable to expect an encounter soon.[152]

Stuart took his column on the secondary road to Hanover early on the morning of June 30. Chambliss's command was again in front and Hampton's brigade was in the rear, behind the very long wagon train. Fitz Lee's command was put out on the left flank between the road to Hanover and Kilpatrick at Littlestown.

Horses for the Taking

After marching for several miles, the men in Chambliss's command were fully aware of having crossed into Pennsylvania — they were now the invaders, and not all of them were comfortable in that role. Their awareness of the situation was heightened when each regiment was ordered to form a detail with one officer and send them off into the countryside to collect horses for their dismounted comrades. Satisfied they were in enemy territory, some cavalrymen took it upon themselves to break ranks when an opportunity presented itself and help themselves to "enemy property." Colonel Beale later gave an example of such behavior when they passed the first county store in Pennsylvania. He said of his cavalrymen, "...trooper after trooper escaping from the ranks quickly filled it with Confederates, who, without asking the price, were proceeding to help themselves to any and every article they needed or fancied. However, the first field officer who discovered what was going on, rode quietly up and cleared the store, compelling the men to put back what they had taken, and posted a guard to remain until the command had passed."[153]

Robert E. Lee had made it clear back on June 21, in General Orders, No. 72, that no individual connected with his army was at liberty to injure, destroy, or take any private property while in enemy territory. What some men did at the country store was subject to "prompt and rigorous punishment." The field officer's action was typical and sufficient in most cases. Sending details of men under the command of an officer to collect horses for the army's use was expressly permitted — in addition, R. E. Lee's order spelled out the "regulations for procuring supplies."[154]

It was clear Colonel R. L. T. Beale of the 9th Virginia felt no obligation to stop his men when they were looting the country store. But there is no indication he encouraged it — he simply understood it. He was apparently more than happy to let the field officer enforce General Lee's order. On the other hand, Beale had no obvious problem enforcing the order to send a detail from his regiment into the countryside to collect horses. However, he did feel the need to justify the action years later when he wrote of it. He spoke of Pennsylvania "...whose armed sons we had so often seen upon the soil of our native Virginia. The time had come to pay back in some measure the misdeeds of the men who, with sword and fire, had made our homesteads heaps of ruin, and, in many instances, left our wives and children not a horse, nor cow, nor sheep, nor hog, nor living fowl of any kind."[155] There is nonetheless often an air of awkwardness when trying to justify actions that the writer despised most in the behavior of his enemy.

Captain Graham of the 2nd North Carolina did not have mixed feelings about "impressing" horses for the use of his dismounted men — in fact he went a step beyond and encouraged the activity while still in Maryland. Graham later argued that during the war, back in Hillsboro, North Carolina, his mother had had her carriage horses impressed for service in the artillery, and she needed them as President of the Ladies Soldiers Aid Society. So why then should the people of Maryland be exempt from such inconveniences? When he later wrote of his experiences in the Gettysburg campaign, he said, "If the Maryland people through whose section we were passing were our friends beyond 'chin music' they had one of the few opportunities afforded to make substantial contributions; if Confederates took their property the Federals could not punish them for aiding us." Graham's feelings were expressed in his actions as well as his words while traveling through Maryland — he clearly felt R. E. Lee's orders could be "bent" when confronted by immediate needs. He explained,

I confess to disobedience of this order. When a man's horse gave out it was simply a question of whether he should be abandoned in the enemy country or afforded means of escape. I chose the latter, and would mention one or two men to "ride and tie" with him during the day and when night came, tell him to get the first horse he could lay his hands on. I recollect giving these directions to Sergeant Strayhorn and J. K. Umstead and there may have been others. The owner would follow next morning, find his horse, report to Gen. Stuart who would give orders to give up the horse and prefer charges against the rider. I simply repeated the program of the previous day.[156]

Once Captain Graham entered Pennsylvania, he obviously had no difficulty collecting horses for service in the Confederacy. He was an obvious choice to head the squad from the 2nd North Carolina — moreover, in this action he could satisfy his men's needs for mounts while obeying Robert E. Lee's orders. Being a practical man, Graham saw no need to justify the policy of taking horses from Pennsylvanian farmers, rather he saw it as a competition among Confederate squads from every regiment all vying for the horses in the area. In his immediate area, the competition was from the Virginia regiments in his own brigade — and their brigade commander was on loan from one of his competitors, the 13th Virginia Cavalry. Perhaps Graham was too eager; perhaps Chambliss was too covetous of his own. Whatever the case, once again Captain Graham's own words cannot be surpassed in explaining his actions and observations:

Having been placed in command of the impressing squad for the 2nd Horse I knew it might require fast moving perhaps faster to the rear than the front. I concluded I would ride one of Uncle Sam's mules, and got one of the men (Henry Tilley) to try several for me; some of them landed him on the earth pretty soon after mounting, but he found one I thought would answer, upon which I placed one of the wagon saddles, turned my horse over to Bob Walker, whose horse had given out. Mounted the mule and getting the men started out to get ahead of the command, as the first-out would have nearest field to glean. The Colonel commanding the brigade [Chambliss] stopped me and I reported to Lt. Col. Paine [temporary commander of the 2nd North Carolina Cavalry] and told him the only reason he [Chambliss] could have was to allow the other regiments to get ahead of the 2nd. Col. Paine sent him a message by a courier that he would be glad for his regiment to have equal show with the others; shortly word came for the squad to proceed. I had gotten some three miles from the command, had about 20 horses, was standing with one man in the road waiting for the others.... I however got in with my horses and prisoner and sent the latter on to the provost guard.[157]

While waiting in the road for the others in his squad, Graham saw a Union officer emerge from the woods and took him prisoner — he was from the 18th Pennsylvania Cavalry. When Graham asked him why he was out there alone, he replied: "We attacked Stuart on the pike and were routed." Graham then asked where his regiment was and he replied, "Scattered in those woods." That was the first knowledge Graham had that a clash was taking place at Hanover, and he knew his brigade was in front that day. He described his reaction to the news in these words: "I signaled my men in and we struck out for the pike. There were only six of us. It was one of the most unpleasant rides I ever took. The probability was that at any time a squad of the 18th Pennsylvania too numerous for us would overhaul us and captors would become prisoners." He and his five comrades along with their new horses and prisoner did make it through the day safely, which is more than could be said for most of the men in the 2nd North Carolina Cavalry.[158]

While on the road to Hanover, Stuart still considered the possibility of turning left at Hanover and heading west toward Gettysburg if Union forces did not get there before him. Judson Kilpatrick's route to Hanover was shorter than Stuart's, but more importantly, the Union column was not encumbered with the wagon train the Confederates were escorting. Stuart was aware of this but still reluctant to abandon his prize.[159] Kilpatrick, on the other hand, was in a hurry to pass through Hanover and cut off Early's command traveling from York west to join R. E. Lee. The Union command knew where their enemy's infantry was, but Kilpatrick was either unaware of Stuart's presence on his immediate right or simply not concerned with it.[160]

Greetings at Hanover, Pennsylvania, June 30

Judson Kilpatrick's Union cavalry division left Littlestown for Hanover early on June 30. His rear brigade reached Hanover around 8:00 A.M. on the Littlestown road with the 1st Vermont in the lead; followed by the 1st West Virginia, Elder's battery, the 5th New York, and the 18th Pennsylvania in the rear. The Union column was relatively close, and as each regiment passed through the town, it paused long enough for refreshments and warm greetings from the citizens who lined the main street and Central Square — some of the troopers even dismounted and moved among the friendly faces. Kilpatrick was taking his column north toward Abbottstown and Harrisburg, still hoping to intercept Early's force. The last of the 5th New York was leaving town on Abbottstown Street when it heard small arms fire from south of town. Almost immediately a portion of the 18th Pennsylvania was driven in among them on the streets of Hanover.[161]

The Confederate column approached Hanover on a back road coming from just outside of Union Mills (leading into Westminster road). Stuart's cavalrymen were strung out with Chambliss's small command in front, then the captured wagon train, followed by Hampton's brigade. Once they discovered Kilpatrick's column was already passing through Hanover, the Confederates had to admit they were at a great disadvantage because their column was divided front to rear by the wagon train, and Fitz Lee's brigade was west of Stuart's line of march. If Chambliss's command was sent at Kilpatrick's column, it would not have support in the immediate area.[162]

Chambliss's column was halted long enough to draw the brigade close. Then it approached the suburb of Pennville near where the route (Westminster road) intersected the main pike entering Hanover from Littlestown — the pike occupied by Kilpatrick's column. Naturally, Stuart decided to attack Kilpatrick's rear with only Chambliss's small brigade on hand. The 13th Virginia was in front that day followed by the 9th Virginia. Stuart rode with Chambliss, a little further down the road near the 2nd North Carolina.[163]

The first notable encounter of the day involved a detachment of 25 men under Lieutenant Shields of the 18th Pennsylvania which had been moving on the Union right flank of their column when they came into contact with the 13th Virginia east of the suburb of Pennville. Shields's detachment was scattered and many captured — Shields himself managed to get away but, as indicated earlier, he was captured by Captain Graham of the 2nd North Carolina who was still on a horse-sequestering detail.

According to R. L. T. Beale of the 9th Virginia, the 13th was in front, followed by two squadrons of the 9th Virginia, as they approached the intersection. Also, apparently while the brigade was halted on Westminster road, the 2nd North Carolina was moved to the road on Chambliss's left. Probably the pike coming from Littlestown on which Kilpatrick's column was traveling. The end of the Union column was passing through Pennville and across the intersection of the Littlestown and Westminster roads as the 13th Virginia approached on Westminster road. It seemed to Colonel Beale that the 13th Virginia hesitated approaching the intersection, and a squadron from the 9th Virginia was sent forward to hit the 18th Pennsylvania in the flank as it passed through the intersection. The hesitation by the 13th was also noted by members of the 2nd North Carolina on the other road, who later reported to Captain Graham — and Graham wrote "Here the Regt. [2nd North Carolina] behaved in a most gallant manner, charging a heavy force of Yankees where two Regts. though double the 2nd in numbers refused to charge." Lieutenant G. W. Beale of the 9th Virginia remembered "...the 13th, 9th and 2nd N.C. regiments were ordered to charge." Beale added, the heaviest losses were "...principally from the N.C. regiment." In any case, by the time the 9th and 13th Virginia were moving, the 2nd North Carolina was in full charge up the pike and into the rear of the enemy column. It appears the 10th Virginia was held in reserve, back near Chambliss—most of their observations were made from south of the Forney farm on the Littletown and Westminster road.[164]

The 2nd North Carolina hit the 18th Pennsylvania and drove them through town.

The charge pushed up Frederick Street and into the Center Square where fierce fighting took place. Most of the citizens who had been mingling with the Union troops fled into shops or their homes when the 2nd North Carolina cavalrymen arrived with yells, sabers high in the

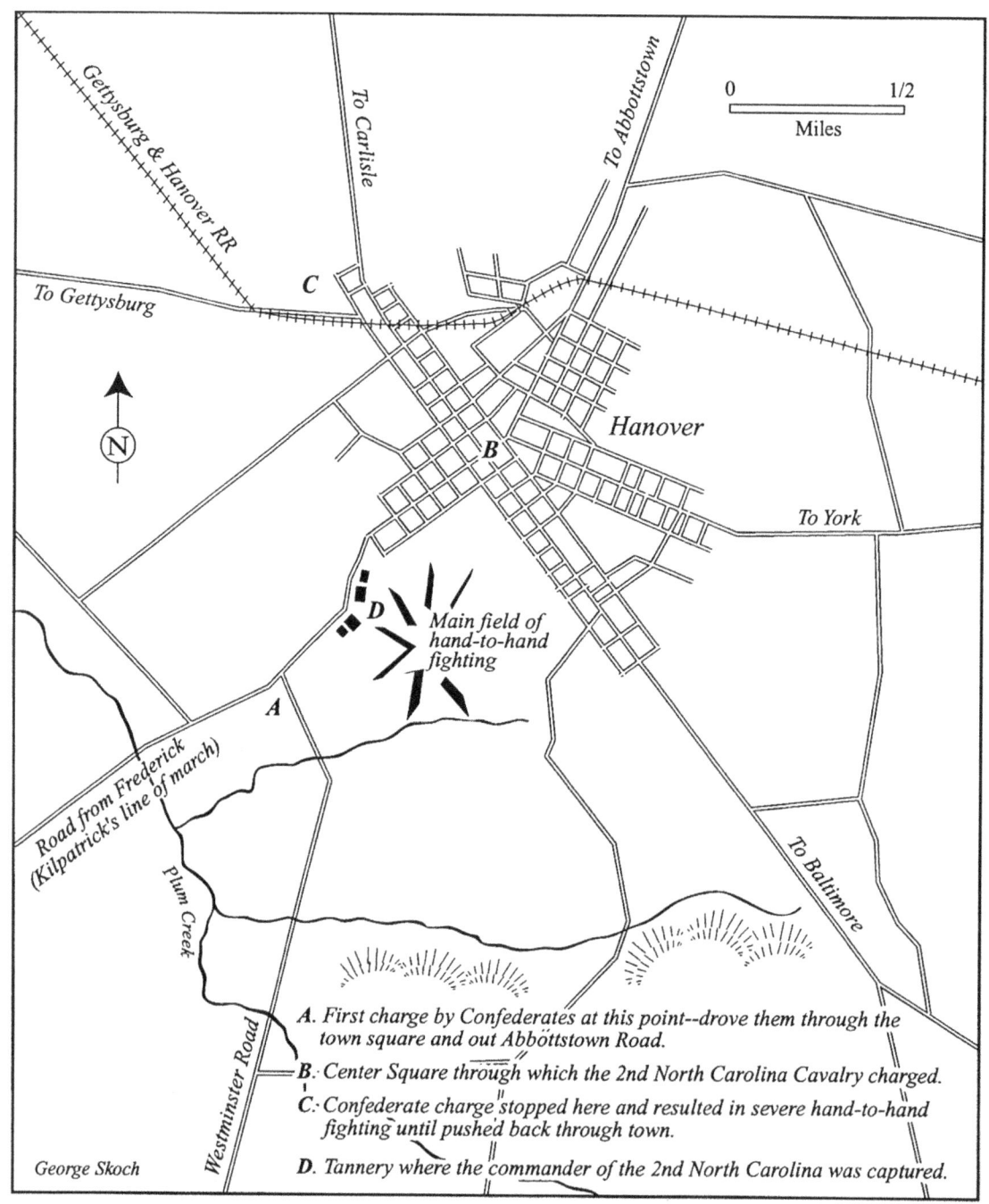

3.4: Cavalry Encounter at Hanover

air, and revolvers discharging. Within minutes, dead and wounded men and horses seemed everywhere in Center Square.[165]

For instance, Sergeant Isaac Peale, Company H, 2nd North Carolina had his horse shot out from under him and as he fell his head hit the pavement. Some years later, a Hanover resident recalled and described the incident in these words:

> During the fighting in the Square, Sergeant Peale, of North Carolina, was seriously wounded at the northeast angle of the Square. In falling from his horse, his head struck a stone which fractured his skull. This was chiefly the cause of his death. He too, with other Confederates wounded, was taken to the improvised hospital at Marion Hall and in the Flickinger foundry on York Street. After the Federal soldiers were taken care of, the surgeons and Hanover citizens looked after the wounded Confederates.... Surgeon Gardner and Dr. Smith presently stood by the cot upon which Sergeant Peale ... was lying.... He was in a dazed condition. The doctors tried to treat the fractured skull, when he arose from his stupor and asked for a clergyman. It was discovered that he belonged to the Catholic Church. Father Kittanning ... was sent for. When the parish priest arrived, he administered the last rites of the church to the dying soldier, who breathed his last in the hospital on the following day. Sergeant Peale was a man of large stature and possibly 40 years old. When asked if he had any relatives living, he answered that he had a sister in North Carolina.[166]

To his caregivers Isaac Peale may have appeared to be 40 years old but at the time was only 28 years of age.

As the fighting worked its way through town, the 2nd North Carolina remained in front of the Confederate force. They pushed the 18th Pennsylvania out Carlisle street and out the northern end of the square, then out the left fork on Abbottstown road, jamming them into the rest of Kilpatrick's column. The 2nd North Carolina pressed its enemy to the railroad tracks in both directions.

On Abbottstown road the 2nd North Carolina's charge was checked by remnants of the 18th Pennsylvania, and the 5th New York. A large body of men from the 18th Pennsylvania were driven into the rear of the 5th New York stopping the chase and resulting in hand-to-hand fighting which caused considerable confusion in the Union column. The main body of the New York regiment, however, faced about and charged into the 2nd North Carolina's flank without waiting for orders. They fought mostly with saber and pistol close in, along the railroad tracks until they meshed with the fighting on Carlisle street. The Confederate drive along Carlisle street also slowed after they had pushed Union troops just past the railroad crossing. Meanwhile, fighting on many of the town's side streets included some of Chambliss's men from the 9th and 13th Virginia. Many of the men from the 18th Pennsylvania were forced to flee town on foot through backyards and gardens.[167]

For about 20 minutes the town of Hanover was occupied by the 2nd North Carolina Cavalry and some of their comrades while hand-to-hand fighting took place just beyond the railroad tracks, on and between both roads leading from the square. The men of the 2nd North Carolina fighting along the railroad tracks soon found that they had no organized Confederate force coming up on their rear or flanks and that the 5th New York was in a position to overwhelm them from the front and on their flanks while some troopers from the 18th Pennsylvania had been rallied and closed in behind them. The possibility of losing what remained of the regiment was great and considering the 2nd North Carolina entered Hanover with no more than 50 cavalrymen it was not likely they could fight their way out in an organized manner.

While confused hand-to-hand fighting took place, Union commanders quickly organized the better part of three regiments to fight the 2nd North Carolina in the northwest section of town — the 1st West Virginia had also turned and followed the 5th New York into the melee along the railroad tracks. By the time the fighting had escalated, the 2nd North Carolina's commander had already left for the rear, escorting a prisoner south along Frederick street.

When 2nd North Carolina cavalrymen were surrounded and overwhelmed by superior numbers, they broke to the rear. The North Carolinians had to get back through and out of town before they reached support — they individually executed their retreat in a variety of ways. For many, this meant running a gauntlet southward back through the square and out Frederick road. For others the only hope for getting back through enemy troops that had closed around them was to dismount and run through backyards and gardens. As the retreating Confederates made their way through town and out Frederick Street, residents fired at them from their homes with what arms they had at hand. This was a new experience for most of the men in the 2nd North Carolina; they knew they were fighting in enemy territory.

The 2nd North Carolina obviously had to leave their dead and wounded in the streets of Hanover as they scampered for their lives. They were joined in their retreat by cavalrymen from the Virginia regiments who had made it into town and were also fighting in the streets of Hanover.

While fighting was taking place along the railroad tracks northwest of town, the 2nd North Carolina's temporary commander, W. H. F. Payne, and one of his staff decided to escort a prisoner to the rear, back along Frederick Street. About the same time, R. L. T. Beale was ambling along the same road toward town behind two squadrons of his 9th Virginia cavalry. Stuart and his staff were also on Frederick Street heading into town but a little ahead of Colonel Beale. It apparently did not greatly concern Payne, Beale, and Stuart that the main fighting along the railroad front was being carried out by the handful of cavalrymen the 2nd North Carolina was able to throw into the rear of the Union column. Most of the 9th and 13th Virginia Cavalry, who were available, were engaged in fighting the enemy that had been passed by the 2nd North Carolina's charge through town. Those Virginians were engaged in hand-to-hand fighting throughout town. Stuart and Beale soon learned that the small force they had sent into Kilpatrick's column could not hold their gains— W. H. F. Payne, commanding the 2nd North Carolina, had problems of his own.

W. H. F. Payne was no longer free to rally what was left of his command when they raced down Frederick Street in retreat because he was in the process of being tanned and captured. As indicated earlier, once the 2nd North Carolina had captured the town and just before the full Union counterattack dropped down from Abbottstown road, Payne started for the rear with an aide and a prisoner in tow. Payne's prisoner described how the tables were turned.

Just outside of town was situated a tannery, the vats of which were not covered and very close to the street. I was walking along beside the colonel's orderly, and as we came near these tannery vats, I saw a carbine lying on the ground. When I came up to it, I quickly took it, and seeing it was loaded I fired and killed Payne's horse, which in its death struggles fell over towards the vats, throwing Payne head first into one of them completely under the tanning liquid. Seeing the colonel was safe enough for the moment I turned my attention to the orderly, who finding his pistol had fouled and was useless, was about to jump his horse over the fence to the right and escape that way if he could, but not being able to do so, concluded he had better surrender. The reason I did not fire upon him was that the last shot in the captured carbine was fired at the colonel's horse. As the orderly did not know this it was my play to make him think that instant death awaited him if he attempted to escape.

So I took him in and disarmed him, and made him help to get the colonel out of the tanning liquid. [Colonel Payne] ... presented a most laughable sight.[168]

The Union soldier who captured Payne and his orderly was living proof that it is better to be lucky than just about anything else in war.

Stuart's experience on Frederick Street that morning was more exciting than Beale's and less unfortunate than Payne's.[169] Like Beale, Stuart and his staff had their casual gait into Hanover interrupted by the retreating cavalrymen from Chambliss's command. As the Union cavalrymen pushed the 2nd North Carolina from the railroad tracks and through town, men from the 9th and 13th Virginia added momentum to the disorderly retreat. Stuart rode forward trying to rally the horsemen passing him along the road, but Union troops were right on their heels. The tired and battered Confederate cavalrymen were in no mood to slow down, let alone stop, turn, regroup, and countercharge. They had been under fire from an overwhelming enemy in their rear and citizens on their flanks firing from their homes along the road from town. However, some of Chambliss's cavalrymen had stopped and turned to fight near the Forney farm just south of the tannery and Stuart along with some of his staff joined in the fighting.[170]

As more Union troops poured south along the road, however, the Confederates began to withdraw and Stuart like many others suddenly realized, they were about to be overwhelmed by the charging Federals. Just south of the Forney farm, the road they occupied was lined with hedges, and some thought Stuart was about to be captured, but the thought clearly never entered his mind. In the words of a staff member on the road with Stuart, his reactions were quick and unequivocal—he was out of there in grand fashion.

Stuart pulled up and, waving his sabre with a merry laugh, shouted to me, "Rally them, Blackford!" and then lifted his mare, Virginia, over the hedge into the field.... I had only that morning, fortunately, mounted Magic, having had her led previously, and Stuart had done the same with Virginia, so they were fresh. As we alighted in the field, we found ourselves within ten paces of the front of a flanking party of twenty-five or thirty men which was accompanying the charging regiment, and they called to us to halt; but as we let our two thorough-breds out, they followed in hot pursuit, firing as fast as they could cock their pistols. The field was in tall timothy grass and we did not see, nor did our horses until close to it, a huge gully fifteen feet wide and as many deep stretched across our path. There were only a couple of strides of distance for our horses to regulate their step, and Magic had to rise at least six feet from the brink. Stuart and myself were riding side by side and as soon as Magic rose I turned my head to see how Virginia had done it, and I shall never forget the glimpse I then saw of this beautiful animal away up in mid-air over the chasm and Stuart's fine figure sitting erect and firm in the saddle. Magic, seeing the size of the place and having received a very unusual sharp application of my spurs, had put out her strength to its full in this leap and she landed six or seven feet beyond the further bank, making a stride of certainly twenty-seven feet. The moment our horses rose, our pursuers saw that their was something there, and it was with difficulty they could pull up in time to avoid plunging headlong into it....[171]

Privates and others with horses not so carefully bred nor from time-to-time led rather than rode did not make the further bank and landed in heaps at the bottom of the gully—Stuart and some of his staff stopped and took the time to laugh at the unfortunates' situation.[172] They were another sort of breed.

While Stuart and some of his staff were having their laugh, the men of the 2nd North Carolina were, in the words of their captured commander being "...almost cut to pieces." Captain Graham of the 2nd North Carolina, who returned from his horse detail just after his comrades had been forced from town, also recalled that day with some bitterness, "General Stuart ... left the regiment [2nd North Carolina Cavalry] to its own defense. Hardly thirty men escaped being killed or captured. Most of these came out on foot through gardens or enclosures which offered protection." Of course Captain Graham was upset because his regiment had been sent into Kilpatrick's column, knowing there was not adequate support for them should they be successful and break through the enemy column.[173]

In any case, part of the Union force charging south through the field was stopped by the gully Stuart so successfully cleared in one mighty leap, but others were stopped by a Confederate countercharge. R. L. T. Beale and some of his men were still south of the fighting taking place around Forney's farm and could see Stuart's difficulty in the field. Beale and the cavalrymen near him were able to tear down a section of the fence between Westminster road and the field in which Stuart and others were being pursued and send in a small party of mounted men to stop the Union advance to the east of Frederick Street. This was the second attempt made by Chambliss's men to stop the Union advance; one near the farm and next in the open field. Both involved a small number of Confederates and were hastily organized, but resulted in severe hand-to-hand fighting with saber and pistol. At that time the Federal forces on the road and in the field pulled back a short way and began to regroup. Stuart and his staff made it back to safety along with most of Chambliss's cavalrymen.[174]

Just after the short-lived Confederate stand near the Forney farm, and around the time Colonel Beale made his countercharge into the field, John F. Fransworth arrived at the Union front and reformed his men for another charge against the hastily drawn line formed by remnants of the 2nd North Carolina and the 9th, 10th, and 13th Virginia Cavalry. They were able to push Chambliss's line back along Westminster road until the Confederates held once again. It was apparently during this fight (or during the fight near Forney's farm), a private from the 5th New York captured the 13th Virginia's regimental flag. Once the Union advance was stopped, they formed a line across the road and held the intersection of the Littlestown (Frederick Street) and Westminster roads—their line extended eastward across the field below Hanover. By that time, Kilpatrick had placed most of his artillery on the hills just northwest of town.

While Federal forces were settling in, Colonel Beale with a handful of men rode to the rear to collect his scattered 9th Virginia. Once sufficiently to the rear, Beale came upon the brigade commander, Chambliss, who had seen Stuart and party nearly surrounded and feared he had been captured. The two Confederate commanders collected their thoughts and Chambliss sent Beale to the hills south of their position and east of Westminster Road to gather all the able men he could find among the regimental wagons parked there and bring them forward.[175]

As Beale approached the hills, he was pleased to find Stuart and many of his staff there and in the process of forming a skirmish line of cavalrymen from Chambliss's command and directing artillery fire. Beale moved most of the cavalrymen in the area forward to Chambliss's line which held while Stuart continued to establish their artillery on the hills behind. The Confederate skirmish line gave and took heavy fire, pulling back slowly as the pressure on their flanks grew. Stuart himself stayed on the hill tops directing artillery fire at the slowly advancing enemy skirmish line and the Union artillery on the other side of town. Once the Confederates were established on and at the base of the hills, the Union advance was less vigorous, but continued to probe their enemy's line — Chambliss's small command, on both sides of the Westminster Road, was able to hold. The artillery duel continued overhead for some time.[176]

By early afternoon, Wade Hampton had arrived with most of his brigade and took a position on the Confederate right, extending the arched line from the hills behind Chambliss's command northward to the road leading to the town of York. Hampton had left the huge captured wagon train a couple of miles back and moved to the sounds of fighting. Fitz Lee arrived soon after the fighting in town was over, and just in time to save the captured wagon train Hampton had left south of town. (Captain Graham of the 2nd North Carolina and his handful of horse-fetchers arrived at the wagon train just after Hampton left for the front and remained there.) Fitz Lee's command then moved up on the left of Chambliss's line, between the Littlestown and Westminster roads.[177] Later in the day, he moved most of his command around behind the hills on which Stuart and his artillery were perched.

By the time Stuart's scattered brigades arrived, Kilpatrick had returned to Hanover with most of his division and set up his headquarters in town. Farnsworth's command was in front of Hampton, and George A. Custer's brigade in front of Chambliss's and for a while Fitz Lee's commands. The dismounted Michigan line, in front of the 2nd North Carolina and their comrades in Chambliss's command, kept up a steady fire with seven-shot repeating Spencer rifles, but the Confederates held.[178] All three Confederate brigades took losses throughout the afternoon, but the heavy losses were sustained before noon by Chambliss's command. By evening the violence at Hanover was mostly over.

According to Stuart's official report, from the time they left Rector's Cross Roads on June 23 through the battle at Hanover on June 30, the following losses were taken by the brigade: 9th

Combat Losses in the 2nd North Carolina Cavalry, June 30, 1863

Trooper	Age	Co.	Fate
Jacob E. Williams	33	A	captured
George W. Sanderson	26	A	captured
John B. Jordon	23	C	killed
Isaac Walters		C	captured
John H. Hubbard	28	D	captured
Prentice E. Tucke	38	E	captured
William Cane	35	G	captured
Mills L. Eure	28	G	captured
Artemas C. Harrell	20	G	captured
Henry A. Kerman	25	G	captured
Ferney L. Roy	22	G	captured
Isham P. Bennett	29	H	captured
Samuel N. Buxton	22	H	captured
John D. Edwards	21	H	captured
James B. W. Foster	61	H	captured
Joseph A. Garris	24	H	captured
William R. Grant	25	H	captured
Isaac Peele	28	H	mortally wounded
William H. Sumner	23	H	captured
Samuel P. Terry		K	wounded/captured
Stephen O. Terry		K	captured
Robert S. Walker		K	wounded/captured
Robert Y. Walker		K	wounded/captured

The source used here is *North Carolina Troops 1861–1865, A Roster,* compiled by Louis H. Manarin (Raleigh, N.C., State Division of Archives and History), vol. II, Cavalry, pp. 104–177. (See Appendix for more information on the men listed above, page 396.)

Virginia Cavalry lost 19 men; 10th Virginia Cavalry lost 2 men; 13th Virginia Cavalry lost 17 men.[179]

Once again, Stuart's report had no numbers for the 2nd North Carolina Cavalry — this was probably because no regimental report was filed, and concern for their numbers was apparently lacking at the brigade level.

While the numbers are similar for two of the Virginia regiments and the 2nd North Carolina, the impact was much more devastating for the latter because the other regiments in the brigade carried more than twice the number of effective men into battle on that day.

Captain Graham wrote, "In this affair we lost 22 men, 2 officers out of 50 carried into action."[180]

A quick survey of the 2nd North Carolina's recorded losses at Hanover on June 30, 1863 indicates of the 23 lost, only 7 returned to fight again with the regiment (there is a possibility two additional men made it back for the last few days of the war in Virginia). This low rate of return partially explains why it was so difficult for the 2nd North Carolina to rebuild after the Gettysburg Campaign.

Stuart Continues the Search for His Infantry

The Confederate and Federal lines held their positions below Hanover until nightfall. Stuart knew there was little to be gained at Hanover, and he had been instructed to join and assist Richard S. Ewell's command — but first, he had to find them. Furthermore, he still did not know the location of R. E. Lee and the rest of his army.

Stuart knew R. E. Lee was to the west of his position, and ultimately he needed to turn in that direction, over the top of Kilpatrick's cavalry. But the roads out of Hanover heading west to Gettysburg and north toward Carlisle were held by Kilpatrick. He took his remaining option and started his troops on another all-night march east toward York, where he hoped to get word of Ewell's command, and from there he could turn northwest and head for Carlisle. From Carlisle he could pass north of Kilpatrick's cavalry and then join the Army of Northern Virginia to the southwest — assuming Kilpatrick did not beat him to Carlisle.

Stuart's men were exhausted, hungry, and back in the saddle. For most of the march to Carlisle, Fitz Lee's brigade led, Chambliss escorted the captured wagon train in the middle, and Hampton was the rear guard. Before reaching York, Stuart learned that General Early had left the area, so upon reaching the small village of Jefferson around nightfall, he turned his column north for Dover. At Jefferson, Stuart left a member of his staff to wait for Hampton's command and instruct the latter to also turn north and head for Dover, then Carlisle. Stuart then moved to the front of Fitz Lee's command — they reached Dover early on the morning of July 1, 1863.[181]

Early in the day, Stuart sent a member of his staff along General Early's trail to locate them and get any orders for the cavalry sent by R. E. Lee; later in the day, Fitz Lee sent a member of his staff on a similar mission. One should be successful.

Neither man nor beast could bear the march. The horses had not been properly fed for days, and many of them were still worn from the previous day's marching and fighting at Hanover. The men were not in much better shape. Most of them had not slept since they left the Union Mills area 24 hours earlier, and some had been in life and death struggles during the first half of the day before. That was the general condition of Stuart's column as Fitz Lee's brigade led them toward Carlisle on the 1st of July.

The head of the column reached Dillsburg and paused for about an hour to rest and consider their position — Stuart was still riding with Fitz Lee's command, and they had not heard from the men sent to locate their infantry. They moved on and reached Carlisle by late afternoon. There was probably some relief to find that Kilpatrick had not moved his Union cavalry north from Hanover to block Stuart's move west at Carlisle, but there was certainly some depression to find that Ewell's infantry was no longer in the area. The only greeting Stuart and Fitz Lee received at Carlisle was from a considerable force of enemy militia with artillery. Stuart had hoped to briefly occupy the town and requisition rations for his troopers. He demanded unconditional surrender or bombardment — but the Union militia and civic leaders were not about to capitulate, so Fitz Lee placed his men around the town and engaged in an artillery duel throughout the evening.[182]

Around midnight, Stuart received word by way of the messenger he had sent early in day to find Early's command and hopefully instructions from R. E. Lee. The word was that R. E. Lee had been engaged with the enemy at Gettysburg during the day, and the cavalry was needed at that place. Stuart immediately sent word to Hampton at the rear of the Confederate column to turn south from Dillsburg toward Gettysburg. Instructions were also sent to Chambliss, whose command had already passed Dillsburg, to follow closely and head for Gettysburg. Stuart pulled Fitz Lee's brigade back from Carlisle and started them south at about 1 A.M. on the morning of July 2 with the intention of joining Hampton en route to Gettysburg. It is not clear Stuart knew at what point Chambliss and the captured wagon train would be able to turn south. Nonetheless, Stuart hoped to reach Gettysburg with all three of his brigades by the morning of July 2.[183]

Hampton received Stuart's instruction in a timely manner and was able to turn his command at Dillsburg, well before dawn and head south for Gettysburg. He had a shorter route and would become the head of Stuart's column as they approached Gettysburg.[184]

Chambliss received word of the turn southward somewhere between Dillsburg and Carlisle and turned his command west just short of Carlisle, eventually following Fitz Lee's route to Gettysburg. The brigade was in some disarray since the fighting at Hanover and was strung out along the wagon train for approximately 10 miles, which meant the head of Chambliss's column was near Carlisle when the rear was hardly clear of Dillsburg.

We should recall, Captain Graham and five other cavalrymen from the 2nd North Carolina, had been on horse detail when their regiment charged into Hanover, and they rejoined their brigade on the battle line during the afternoon of June 30; but apparently they were not able to find their regiment by the time Stuart's column left Hanover toward Carlisle. In Graham's words: "Learning of the capture of my regiment [2nd North Carolina Cavalry] I joined the wagon guard and so continued until we reached Gettysburg. We passed Carlisle on Wednesday night [actually very early morning on the 2nd]."[185]

There were some members of the 2nd North Carolina who had been assigned to accompany the regimental wagon because they or their horses were not serviceable. Those few, perhaps 20 to 25 men, who rode away from Hanover and were more or less ready for battle, accompanied the 10th Virginia which had a North Carolinian company of its own.

After the loss of their commander, W. H. F. Payne, at Hanover, the remnant of the 2nd North Carolina should have been under the command of Captain Strange, but there is no record of this. Strange may not have been available, because at a later date, Captain W. A. Graham of Company K wrote that he was the commander of the 2nd North Carolina at that time because he, Graham, was the regiment's senior officer in the field. Major Clinton M. Andrews was on leave and did not participate in the Gettysburg Campaign. With Graham separated from the regiment, however, we can not be certain who was in command of the mounted remnant of the 2nd North Carolina between Hanover and Gettysburg.[186]

In any case, at least half of the 2nd North Carolina was dispersed along the length of Chambliss's long column — W. A. Graham and his five comrades with the wagon train, the ill and dismounted with the regimental wagons. The effective members were in yet another place riding with the 10th Virginia Cavalry.

As noted, Captain Graham of the 2nd North Carolina remembered passing just under Carlisle in the very early morning on July 2; Colonel Beale of the 9th Virginia remembered passing very near, perhaps in sight of, Carlisle before cutting across country to the pike leading to the small village of Papertown and then Gettysburg. They were just behind Fitz Lee's column.

Stuart's column was already stretched thin and full of gaps by the night of July 1, and the condition got worse that night and on the last leg of their journey to Gettysburg. They managed to cover a great deal of territory by marching day and night (all night June 30 and July 1), and stopping for only one hour twice each day — in the case of Chambliss's command at around 9:00 in the morning and the evening. Fatigue became overwhelming as the hours passed. Stuart described the condition of his cavalrymen in these words, "After a series of exciting combats and night marches, it was a severe tax to their endurance. Whole regiments slept in the saddle, their faithful animals keeping to road unguided. In some instances they fell from their horses, overcome with physical fatigue and sleepiness."[187]

In addition to the fatigue among the men and horses, the column continued to be slowed by the burden of the wagons and prisoners. A member of Stuart's staff remembered the captured wagons and men as "...a source of unmitigated annoyance." When they left Hanover on the evening of June 30, Stuart's brigades escorted around 400 prisoners that were taken since they had paroled approximately that same number at Cooksville a couple of days before. These captured Yankees were also hungry and tired and were probably not inclined to hurry along. Once the column turned north in the direction of Dover, Stuart started to parole the hungry and tired captives during their brief rest stops — but they could not "parole" the hungry and tired mules that were pulling the captured wagons.[188]

It was the job of Chambliss's small command to keep the mules safe and moving because Stuart was less willing to give up his captured wagon train than he was his prisoners. He later acknowledged that the wagon train had become an embarrassment by the time they left Hanover, but he felt that by heading east from that place, then heading north, he would find his infantry near York or Carlisle and thus save his captured wagon train and its much needed supplies for the Army of Northern Virginia. In large part, the difficulty stemmed from the fact that hungry and tired mules were not like the cavalrymen's "...faithful animals keeping to road unguided," when the horsemen fell asleep in the saddle. When a wagon driver fell asleep at the reins, the mule stopped and followed suit or stepped off the road to feed on what was growing in the area. Often the wagons in the rear were unaware of the reason for the column's stopping and would wait a reasonable time before sending someone forward to investigate the blockage. Even without prisoners, Chambliss's command and the wagons did not move at a good pace.[189]

At a later date, when writing of the ordeal Colonel R. L. T. Beale of Chambliss's command, recalled the "...now thoroughly-hated wagon-train." Nonetheless, with the 2nd North Carolina scattered along the train, Chambliss had to keep his command moving. He acquired a local guide and took the train across fields, and headed for the small village of Papertown near where they "captured" a load of scarce writing paper from a mill as they took their one hour morning rest. Colonel Beale described the scene early on July 2:

On reaching Papertown a halt was made for the command to close up. Here some of our men were busy in a search for ration, but most of them, suffering an agony for sleep, lay on the road with bridles in hand, some on rocks, and others on the wet earth, slumbering soundly.

Our slumbers lasted only for an hour. Resuming the saddle, we moved over the mountain spurs along a broad macadamized road leading towards Gettysburg. The sound of cannonading reached our ears during the march, and once or twice we were put into position in order of battle. We saw no enemy, however. The gardens along the line of our march suffered heavily from frequent charges by our hungry men. The author's individual share of these captures was two onions, fresh and juicy, washed down with a bottle of good domestic wine, kindly supplied to him by our accomplished brigade commander [Chambliss].[190]

The Cavalry Joins the Battle of Gettysburg, July 2

Wade Hampton and his command were the first of Stuart's cavalrymen to arrive in the Gettysburg area. He was ordered to move to the Confederate left, but before he could get into position, he was told to return to the village of Hunterstown about five miles above Gettysburg because Judson Kilpatrick's cavalry was moving to that place in an effort to flank the Confederate infantry.[191]

Hampton arrived from the south and took a position about a mile outside of Hunterstown. He then sent about 80 men into the village to detect Kilpatrick's arrival, and around 4:00 P.M., his pickets were driven in. The 18th Pennsylvania arrived and pushed the Confederates back to Hampton's position on a ridge. The Union commander moved into the village and sent John F. Fransworth's brigade out the road heading west, and George A. Custer's brigade out the road to Gettysburg. Hampton was drawn up across Custer's route. With his brigade positioned along the road and artillery support in place, Custer led a company in a charge down the road, lined on both sides by fences, directly at Hampton's position. They were greeted by more than 500 Confederate cavalrymen. Severe fighting with pistol and saber took place for several minutes, then Custer and fewer than half the men he led into battle were driven back into their support. The men from Cobb's Legion followed but were rapidly driven back by fire from seven-shot Spencer rifles and Union artillery. Hampton lost more than 20 men, and Custer more than that — it was a short but bloody encounter. Both sides held their positions until well into the night when Alfred Pleasonton instructed Kilpatrick to withdraw. Hampton's men held the village until morning.[192]

Upon arriving in the area, Stuart had sent a member of his staff ahead to Robert E. Lee's headquarters for orders, and he was instructed to place his cavalry on the Confederate left, which arched above Gettysburg. As the cavalrymen continued to arrive on the afternoon of July 2, they were positioned as instructed: Fitz Lee with his brigade first and finally Chambliss's command — Hampton brought most of his brigade over from Hunterstown during the night. To strengthen his depleted and worn-out troops on the left, Stuart had Jenkins's small brigade added to his command the next morning.[193]

At some point before joining Stuart on the Confederate left, Chambliss got rid of the captured wagon train — he probably sent it to the Army of Northern Virginia's quartermaster. Captain Graham of the 2nd North Carolina, who traveled to Gettysburg with the captured wagon train, later noted, "Thursday [July 2] P.M. about six o' clock we carried the wagon train into Lee's lines not having lost a single vehicle." Chambliss himself may have accompanied the wagons into R. E. Lee's line, because he sent his mounted men on to the Confederate left during the afternoon under the temporary command of Colonel J. Lucius Davis of the 10th Virginia Cavalry — the approximately two dozen mounted men of the 2nd North Carolina Cavalry were with the 10th Virginia, while those not fit for fighting stayed with the wagons.[194]

Many of the Confederate cavalrymen spent part of the evening locating their regiments before they settled in for the first night's rest they had had in eight days. Stuart's chief of staff, H. B. McClellan, attempted to express his relief in these words: "On the ninth night they rested within the shelter of the army, and with a grateful sense of relief which words cannot express."[195]

While some members of Stuart's staff were grateful for a good night's rest, Stuart did not often see the need for such trivial luxuries on a battle's eve for himself or his cavalrymen. For instance, after R. L. T. Beale had the 9th Virginia in place on the left and was in conversation with Colonel J. L. Davis, temporarily in command of the brigade, orders arrived from Stuart for the brigade to stay in the saddle all night and remain alert. According to Beale, Davis replied "...that the request would be cheerfully complied with; but that the utmost verge of endurance by men and horses had been reached, and that whatever the morrow might bring, we feared that neither horses nor men could be used either to march or fight." Once reminded that his cavalrymen were no more than human, Stuart was reasonable — he simply seldom factored in the fatigue variable on his own. The cavalrymen of W. H. F. Lee's brigade (now temporally commanded by J. L. Davis) were soon ordered to dismount and rest for the night. They moved into the fields where their horses could feed, and the troopers fed on captured livestock before resting for the night.[196]

With his cavalrymen settled in, Stuart rode to R. E. Lee's camp the evening of July 2, he understood why he had missed his planned connection with Ewell on his trip north and what had taken place during the first two days at Gettysburg.

Stuart learned that on June 28, R. E. Lee was informed of Hooker's, then George G. Meade's, pursuit of his army north, and Lee began to pull his infantry to him, near Chambersburg. R. E. Lee pulled Ewell's command in from York and Carlisle. Longstreet and A. P. Hill were already near. He also learned that R. E. Lee had little information about Meade and the Army of the Potomac until July 1 — only that they were drawing near. Meade, on the other hand, knew the Army of Northern Virginia was being concentrated near Gettysburg, and he pointed his army in that direction. Gettysburg was a hub for many roads in that section of Pennsylvania, and Meade knew he could head for R. E. Lee in any direction from that location.[197]

Stuart was also told the first Confederates

to approach Gettysburg were from Heth's division in A. P. Hill's corps. The activities of the previous few days were described as follows: late on June 30, when Stuart was leaving Hanover, J. Pettigrew of Heth's division approached Gettysburg. Pettigrew came upon Union cavalry outposts just west of town and reported the potential resistance. Soon after Pettigrew made his report, A. P. Hill returned from a meeting with R. E. Lee and informed his commanders that their best intelligence indicated only a small force of Union cavalry was in Gettysburg. So, early on July 1, 1863, Heth marched southeast to Gettysburg. They soon found the enemy in heavy force and were stopped after some savage fighting. R. E. Lee arrived and made it clear he did not want a major battle until Ewell and Longstreet arrived.[198]

By July 1, the Union line was stronger and building. Part of Ewell's command had also arrived just north of Gettysburg by then, and he received the same instructions given to A. P. Hill: avoid a major engagement if possible until all Confederate forces arrive. Nonetheless, Confederate forces were soon engaged north of Gettysburg in severe fighting. R. E. Lee reiterated to Heth that he did not want a general engagement until Longstreet arrived, and all three corps could be thrown at the enemy. By then matters were out of his control and fighting escalated. Just as the Confederate force north of town was about to be thrown back in defeat, Early's division arrived and immediately plunged itself into the battle on the left. At about the same time, R. E. Lee had A. P. Hill send Henry Heth's command forward. Finally, R. E. Lee told A. P. Hill and Ewell to send everything they could get up at their enemy. The Confederates pushed Meade's XI Corps from Seminary Ridge to Cemetery Hill. Some 5,000 Union prisoners were taken that afternoon.[199]

Longstreet joined R. E. Lee on Seminary Ridge around 5:00 P.M. He urged Lee to take defensive action and spoke against any effort to storm the strong Union position along Cemetery Ridge. Later, R. E. Lee rode over to Ewell's camp—Ewell was also in a defensive frame of mind as they discussed possibilities for the next day.[200]

It was around this same time, Stuart's messengers arrived in the Confederate line and were able to return to Stuart outside of Carlisle with instructions to bring his cavalry to Gettysburg quickly. The returning messengers carried the news of the great successes A. P. Hill and Ewell had had that day.

Robert E. Lee had determined to attack on the morning of July 2. It was close to midday, however, before R. E. Lee had his intelligence reports and managed to instruct Longstreet to position his men for attack. Then R. E. Lee rode off for another meeting with Ewell on the left of his line. When Lee returned, he was not pleased to find that Longstreet had not hurried his men into position for the attack. Longstreet was against the attack and reluctant to initiate the move before his entire command was up—Pickett was not yet in the field. Longstreet reportedly told John B. Hood, "I never like to go into battle with one boot off." Longstreet's enthusiasm for that fight was dangerously low, and he moved toward the ridge not knowing exactly where the Union left rested.[201]

Once Longstreet was underway, he learned that R. E. Lee's information was faulty. Longstreet discovered the Union left extended south to Round Top, but Longstreet would not adjust the plan. Longstreet's command executed a disorganized offensive against a very difficult objective. It was as if each division fought a separate battle. Nonetheless, the men fought hard for several hours.[202]

On the Confederate left, Ewell's men finally launched an assault near the end of the day, but it was also disjointed and gained little. By the end of July 2, the Union forces were stronger, the Confederate forces tired and battered. In addition, both armies were depleted—each army lost about 9,000 men on July 2 which brought the combined losses for both days to approximately 35,000 men.[203] Of course, such losses suggest that generals on both sides were doing something wrong.

Stuart rode back to his command late on July 2 much better informed, but probably not feeling terribly good about how useful he and his cavalry had been up to that point.

Gettysburg's East Cavalry Field, July 3

During his visit to Robert E. Lee's headquarters on Seminary Ridge, J. E. B. Stuart was given instructions for the next day. He was told to guard Ewell's left flank, but Stuart also hoped conditions would favor an attack on the Union infantry's right flank and rear. Actually Stuart had little idea what Pleasonton and Kilpatrick had placed before him and what the possibilities would be on the following day.

Stuart moved his cavalrymen into place cautiously on the morning of July 3, 1863. First he took Jenkins's and Chambliss's brigades from Stallsmith Lane "…secretly through the woods to a position, and hoped to effect a surprise upon the enemy's rear." The position he took was on Cress Ridge which "…completely controlled a wide plain of cultivated fields stretching toward Hanover on the left, and reaching … the enemy held position." He placed two brigades just behind Cress Ridge.[204]

Stuart rode with Jenkins's brigade, which was temporally under the command of Lieutenant Colonel Vincent A. Witcher — they were in the lead and moved beyond the woods, westward, to become the far right of the cavalry line, near Hoffman Ridge. Witcher's command included Jackson's Battery. Moving at the same time, but just behind Witcher, Chambliss's command followed and pulled up with their right on Witcher's left and their left still near the woods just behind Cress Ridge. Even though Stuart wanted to hit the Union infantry in the rear if conditions were right, he faced his cavalry line southeast — toward his enemy's cavalry.

Hampton's and Fitz Lee's commands were on the left of Chambliss's regiments and formed the end of Stuart's cavalry line. Stuart had instructed Hampton to move his command into the woods, on Cress Ridge, northeast of Chambliss's men and stretching to Stallsmith Lane; he had instructed Fitz Lee to place his men on the other side of the lane, on Hampton's left but a little southeast. He also instructed Hampton and Fitz Lee to remain concealed in woods while he secretly moved Witcher and Chambliss into place.

The Rummel farm buildings were front and center of Stuart's line, with a small party of skirmishers in and to the front of the farm buildings. The Confederate front line was behind a small tributary called Little's Run, which was about three-fourths of a mile northwest of Lott's house.[205]

Chambliss probably rejoined his command on the morning of July 3 as they prepared to take their positions for the anticipated fight. Early that morning, the brigade had moved a mile or two to the left along the York turnpike and then bore to the right, following Stuart's and Witcher's command into the woods. Chambliss's cavalrymen numbered little more than 300 that day, but most had rested and eaten. Once in position just southwest of the woods, sharpshooters from each regiment were dismounted and sent forward about 300 yards into Rummel's barnyard — the sharpshooters were behind walls, just to the left of the barn. Most of Jenkins's brigade moved forward and took positions to the right of the barn, and later moved southwest of the Rummel farm, along Little's Run.[206]

When Chambliss's command was moving along York Turnpike early that morning, the 2nd North Carolina had not yet gathered around their regimental commander. Captain Graham of Company K was the regiment's senior officer in the field on the morning of July 3, 1863, and he spent the morning gathering the remnants of the 2nd North Carolina. He had a handful, perhaps 5 or 6 cavalrymen, with him from escort duty with the wagon train; and he gathered a few more who had been on teamster duty with the regiment's wagon train and were able to borrow mounts of some sort. Graham then found the remainder of his regiment, the mounted troopers from the 2nd North Carolina who rode away from Hanover, with Captain Clements and his North Carolina company in the 10th Virginia Cavalry. Graham found about 25 of his men with Clements, and they determined with certainty he was the senior officer present, so he assumed command of some 30 to 40 effective cavalrymen who would represent the 2nd North Carolina Cavalry on East Cavalry Field on the third and final day of the Battle of Gettysburg.[207]

On the morning of July 3, Alfred Pleasonton, after some discussion, sent David McM. Gregg east on Hanover Road to the intersection of Low Dutch Road. D. McM. Gregg took J. Irvin Gregg's and John B. McIntosh's brigades from his command and George A. Custer's brigade from Judson Kilpatrick's command. Custer's command (about 1,900 strong) led the column and arrived at the intersection around 10:00 A.M. He established a skirmish line along Little's Run and sent out patrols looking for Stuart's cavalry thought to be in the area. Custer

Three • Cavalry Shield for the Gettysburg Campaign

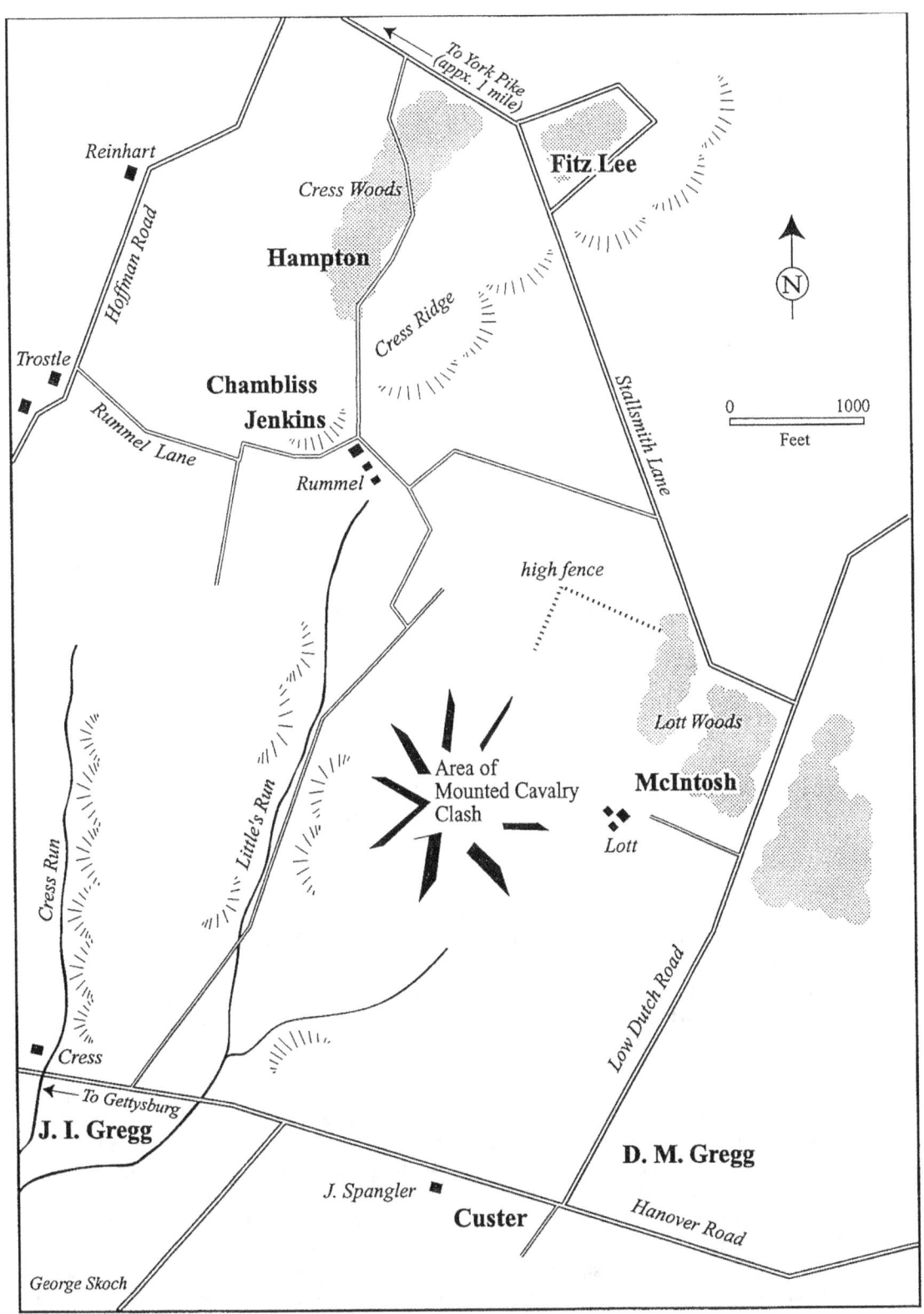

3.5: Gettysburg, East Cavalry Field

then spread the rest of his command along Hanover Road and up Low Dutch Road. When D. McM. Gregg arrived, he placed J. Irvin Gregg's brigade (about 1,000 strong) from Custer's left, west to the right of George G. Meade's infantry, and McIntosh's brigade (with about 900 men) in reserve. Once the fighting began, D. McM. Gregg moved McIntosh up Low Dutch Road to the Lott Woods, on Custer's right.[208]

David McM. Gregg's job was to keep the Confederate cavalry off his infantry's rear. On the other side, Stuart later said, once he had felt D. McM. Gregg's presence, his plan was simply "...to employ in front with sharpshooters, and move a command of cavalry upon their [Gregg's] left flank from a position lately held by me...."[209] Once both cavalries were in position, neither general had overly ambitious goals for the day.

Around midday, Stuart was still with Witcher's troops and ordered Jackson's Battery of that brigade to fire four shots in different directions. Some historians have speculated these shots may have been to alert his comrades that he was in position, but that explanation was brought into question because Stuart later said once Hampton and Fitz Lee were in position, he sent for them to join him in an elevated view of the field spread before them. Because Stuart had sent a messenger to the two commanders requesting their presence, it is not likely he fired the guns for their benefit. It is more probable the shots were intended to elicit a response from any Union forces that might be out there. If the latter were Stuart's purpose, it worked. Custer's guns from along the Hanover Road responded almost immediately.[210]

When the artillery duel began, most of the men from the 2nd North Carolina were dismounted in a field just southwest of the woods behind Cress Ridge. By the time they were in position, the field seemed to radiate as much heat as the bright sun above. Their commander, W. A. Graham, described their position as "...in the hottest sunshine I ever felt, some four of us put our heads under a little bush not two feet high nor so broad across."[211]

Around 1:00 P.M., McIntosh moved up to replace Custer's brigade. McIntosh moved the 1st New Jersey up Low Dutch Road past the Lott farm and into the woods just to the north. The 3rd Pennsylvania and 1st Maryland also moved up the road and into the fields just west of the Lott farm. The Union commanders were still not certain what Stuart had in front of them, so around 2:00 P.M. McIntosh sent forward a skirmish line made up of men from the 1st New Jersey. They advanced to about Little's Run where they drew up to meet Witcher's skirmishers who had been sent forward to a fence on the southeastern edge of Rummel's place to meet the Union probe. Brisk fighting took place between the two skirmish lines. Then Stuart moved a battery to the edge of the woods on the ridge and began firing on the Union skirmishers. Pennington's guns from just north of Hanover Road and Chester's guns near Lott's house responded.[212]

Then McIntosh sent 2 squadrons from the 3rd Pennsylvania forward to Little's Run on the left of the 1st New Jersey, and the Purnell Legion forward and to the right of the 1st New Jersey. Stuart responded by sending more dismounted men from Witcher's and Chambliss's commands into the Rummel farm. Colonel R. L. T. Beale of the 9th Virginia remembered there was a lull in the "grandest and most terrific" artillery exchange he had ever heard, when "...several hundred enemy skirmishers were thrown forward to reinforce and extend the right of their skirmish-line."[213]

When Stuart sent the dismounted men from Chambliss's command forward, he had also brought up a section of horse artillery and placed it in the woods just to the left of Captain Graham and his sweltering men from the 2nd North Carolina. Graham and some of his men were moved to the edge of the woods to protect the artillery — the others were moved forward with their brigade to support the line near Rummel's place. Those left behind were soon subjected to artillery fire as well as fire from the Union skirmish line.[214]

The commander of the 2nd North Carolina who was, along with his men, in the midst of the duel, later said, "I do not suppose it ever has been equaled by land forces in steadiness of discharge and roar of guns." Certainly artillery duels not only equaled but surpassed the exchanges in East Cavalry Field that day, but for the men lying under it, it must have been near overwhelming. Shortly after Graham and some of his men were moved closer to the artillery at the edge of the woods, Graham took a minnie ball in his thigh while lying on the ground and holding the reins of his horse. With Captain Graham down, the command of the 2nd North Carolina in East Cavalry Field devolved to Lieutenant Joseph Baker of Company D.[215]

Union artillery increased its fire and the fighting escalated. Union guns were deadly accurate that afternoon and Stuart's battery on the ridge was soon forced to pull back. Then the Union guns took aim on Rummel's barn which housed sharpshooters from Witcher's and Chambliss's commands.[216]

By early afternoon, the intense firing from the skirmish lines and the artillery had everybody's attention. It was perhaps more of a diversion than Stuart needed. He still had not contemplated throwing Hampton's and Fitz Lee's commands against McIntosh on the skirmish line. He still saw the skirmish action as a diversion to mask a planned mounted attack around the D. McM. Gregg's flank. In order for his surprise flank attack to work, however, Hampton's and Fitz Lee's presence had to remain undetected, and his skirmish line had to hold until all the Confederate forces were in place. Unfortunately for Stuart, McIntosh was aware of Hampton on the ridge and Fitz Lee on Stallsmith Lane. In fact, their presence prompted the Union commander to ask D. McM. Gregg for reinforcements.

Their presence became known shortly after Hampton received his notice to meet with Stuart. Hampton did not think it wise for him and Fitz Lee to both leave the field, so he went first — leaving Fitz Lee in command on the left. He was not able to find Stuart, so returned to his command just in time to stop a charge by his brigade ordered by Fitz Lee. The ill-advised charge was stopped but not before both brigades on the left had moved forward and were seen by the Union commanders around the Lott house and woods.[217] Nonetheless, Stuart apparently thought he could still pull-off his mounted flank attack. He continued to send support to the skirmish line — that line had to hold until he communicated with Hampton and Fitz Lee about the planned flank-attack.

Meanwhile, the presence of the additional two Confederate brigades and the escalating fighting along the skirmish line convinced D. McM. Gregg that Stuart was contemplating something bigger, namely a move against the Union infantry's flank or rear. So D. McM. Gregg was fully ready to engage not only the skirmish line, but whatever Stuart had brought. D. McM. Gregg's other brigade was a few miles away along Hanover Road and had to be brought up, but G. A. Custer's command was still at hand, and D. McM. Gregg ordered him into the skirmish immediately in response to McIntosh's request for reinforcements.[218]

Custer sent the 5th Michigan to support the left of McIntosh's skirmish line. They dismounted and opened fire with their Spencer repeating rifles just as a dismounted charge was made by troopers from Chambliss's command. The Confederate charge overran part of the Union line, but the firepower brought by the 5th Michigan slowed the advance. Men from the 2nd North Carolina were among the charging Confederates Stuart sent at McIntosh's line, and they had their moments of success.[219]

In W. A. Graham's words, they "...took part in the charge which occurred soon after and assisted in cutting off and capturing a squad of the enemy." When Chambliss's dismounted men had stopped and were hotly engaged with the 5th Michigan and the regrouped members of J. B. McIntosh's brigade, Stuart sent a mounted charge from Chambliss's cavalries. They rode past the Rummel barn and hit the right flank of the 5th Michigan.[220] R. L. T. Beale described the charge from his point of view:

The mounted men of our brigade were now ordered to charge. They passed through the yard of the barn, under a raking fire from the guns to our right, and, doubling the head of the bottom, dashed up the slope to meet the foe. The little band led by Chambliss did not apparently exceed two hundred men. Reaching a fence which separated them from the enemy, they halted in line, and used their carbines until the fence was thrown down. It seemed to one who stood in a place of comparative safety that the enemy slackened their fire, curious to see if so few would dare to cross sabres with them. When the fence had been thrown down the brigade, with headlong impetuosity, hurled its column upon the enemy's line, and for a few moments sabres flashed and pistols cracked.[221]

The mounted charge by Chambliss's command drove the Federal skirmish line so far that Stuart became concerned for their return trip. In Stuart's words, "Their impetuosity carried them too far, and the charge being very much prolonged, their horses, already jaded by hard marching, failed under it. Their movement was too rapid to be stopped by couriers, and the enemy perceiving it, were turning upon them with fresh horses." The fresh Union horses aimed at the tired Confederates were mounted by the men of the 7th Michigan Cavalry and led in the countercharge by Custer. Some of the 5th Michigan turned and joined the 7th in driving Chambliss's troopers back into their line.[222]

Chambliss's mounted charge had been effective and they managed to take a number of prisoners, but hardly had they moved their captives to the rear when the countercharge by the 7th Michigan pushed them back across Little's Run and into Rummel's barnyard. At that point, Chambliss's men turned and more hand-to-hand fighting took place. Chambliss's small command had again lost heavily and a number of them became prisoners. In the clash of saber and exchange of pistol fire, Colonel R. L. T. Beale's son, Lieutenant George W. Beale of the 9th Virginia, lost his horse to three minnie balls, but managed to scramble to safety.

The Michigan men on horseback who pushed as far as Rummel's barnyard also came under fire from Chambliss's skirmishers who had been driven back from the area a short while before. The men from the 7th Michigan who had charged to Rummel's barnyard also had to consider the 1st Virginia Cavalry on their right flank behind a high fence. They pulled back across Little's Run and joined their fellow Michiganders who were fighting at the high fence.[223]

The Michigan cavalrymen who had not pursued Chambliss's men to Rummel's barnyard charged directly to a high fence between Little's Run and Lott Woods, up to the skirmish line Fitz Lee had moved across Stallsmith Lane and established facing McIntosh's right flank.[224]

By the time Chambliss had made his mounted charge at the 5th Michigan, some of McIntosh's men were running low on ammunition and his line was thinned. Around the same time, Fitz Lee saw the opportunity to hit McIntosh's line in its right flank and relieve some of the pressure on Chambliss's dismounted troops. He moved skirmishers from the 1st Virginia Cavalry across Stallsmith Lane and the first field, and set a strong line behind a high fence — this line helped stop the charge by Custer and part of the 7th Michigan.

Fighting at the high fence was close and intense. The Michigan men stopped and exchanging fire with the 1st Virginia skirmishers just across the fence. By the time the Michigan cavalrymen reached the fence, mounted men of the 1st Virginia Cavalry had charged forward and reinforced their comrades. As the 1st Virginia exchanged fire with the Michigan men, that portion of the 3rd Pennsylvania which had been held in reserve opened fire on the Virginian's flank from near Lott Woods. The 1st Virginia took fire from across the fence, from their left flank, and finally from Union artillery before they began to scatter. In the meantime, some of Witcher's and Chambliss's dismounted skirmishers (the remnants of the 2nd North Carolina were among them) had moved forward again and were firing into the Michigan cavalrymen at the fence. After emptying their carbines and pistols, the Michigan men began to lose cohesion also.[225]

The final straw for the rookies of the 7th Michigan Cavalry was the sight of Confederate cavalry storming in their direction from Cress Ridge. When Chambliss's mounted troops were hotly engaged in Rummel's barnyard, Chambliss had sent for reinforcement, but it was slow in coming. Chambliss had sent his request to Fitz Lee on Stuart's far left. While Chambliss's men were fighting for their lives, Fitz Lee informed Chambliss's messenger that Wade Hampton was closer to his command, and the request for assistance should be taken to Hampton. From his position, Hampton could see the melee that engulfed Chambliss's cavalrymen, so he ordered Colonel Laurence Baker to send two regiments in support of Chambliss's mounted men. Baker sent the 1st North Carolina and the Jefferson Davis Legion sweeping down from Cress Ridge, through Rummel's barnyard, and directly into the 7th Michigan. Custer and his men were driven back toward Chester's guns and the Lott house — they were eventually driven past Chester's guns and Lott's house to the Low Dutch Road. Custer had led the 7th Michigan into their very first fight; he took them to the high fence, stopped and exchanged fire with the enemy until their guns were emptied, and more than 100 of them were lost in battle.[226]

The mounted men from the 1st Virginia joined the 1st North Carolina and Jefferson Davis Legion in clearing the field. The 1st Virginia threatened the Union guns near the Lott house and Hampton's men considered heading south for Pennington's guns near Hanover Road — but the men from all three Confederate regiments were being raked by heavy fire from both artillery positions and under constant fire from skirmishers on both flanks, so they pulled up and back.[227]

After Custer and the 7th Michigan broke and were pushed back to Low Dutch Road, Custer rode down to Hanover Road and took command of the 1st Michigan as D. McM. Gregg was about to send them into action. Custer quickly moved them for a charge toward the high fence from which he had just been driven. At about the same time, Hampton began his descent from Cress Ridge.[228]

Hampton had watched his 1st North Carolina and Jefferson Davis Legion drive the 7th Michigan from the field and continue their charge too far in the direction of Hanover Road, so he decided to ride into the field of battle to take charge of his two regiments personally. Much to his surprise as he raced down the ridge and into the fields, he turned to see most of his 1st and 2nd South Carolina and Phillips Legion, as well as most of Fitz Lee's brigade (except for the 4th Virginia) charging in good order right behind him. Hampton's assistant adjutant general had misunderstood Hampton's move down the ridge and assumed he intended the whole brigade to follow. Apparently, when Hampton's command was in motion, Fitz Lee saw no need for his brigade to remain on Stallsmith Lane as spectators, and immediately joined the charge.[229] Stuart probably watched the spectacular charge with no less surprise than Hampton.

The training and drill Hampton had put his men through paid dividends that day, as the "mistaken" charge seemed to instinctively flow in behind Hampton. It was a formidable sight. Captain William E. Miller of the 3rd Pennsylvania was in a position to see Hampton's column form and flow down the ridge into the open fields. In his words,

A grander spectacle than their advance has rarely been beheld. They marched with well-aligned fronts and steady reins. Their polished saber-blades dazzled in the sun. All eyes turned upon them. Chester on the right, Kinney in the center, and Pennington on the left opened fire with well-directed aim. Shell and shrapnel met the advancing Confederates and tore through their ranks. Closing the gaps as though nothing had happened, on they came. As they drew nearer, canister was substituted by our artillerymen for shell, and horse after horse staggered and fell. Still they came on.[230]

As Hampton's command swept through Rummel's farm, what remained of Chambliss's command mounted and joined in the charge as Fitz Lee's regiments joined them from the Confederate left. While Hampton and Fitz Lee led the Confederates through the storm of Union shell then canister, Custer was leading the 1st Michigan in a full charge directly at them.

The 1st Michigan left from near Pennington's battery north of Hanover Road and rode under the shell and canister until it was stopped on their behalf. Custer led the Michigan men drawn up in close column of squadrons on a collision course with the oncoming Confederate column — he quickly stepped the gait to a gallop which matched that of Hampton's column. Miller of the 3rd Pennsylvania described the scene in these words, "As the two columns approached each other the pace of each increased, when suddenly a crash, like the falling of timber, betokened the crisis. So sudden and violent was the collision that many of the horses were turned end over end and crushed their riders beneath them. The clashing of sabers, the firing of pistol, the demands for surrender and cries of the combatants now filled the air."[231] The point of contact was in an area where the Confederates' left flank was exposed to McIntosh's men near Lott's place, but not near enough for Custer's men to be exposed to fire from Witcher's and Chambliss's sharpshooters.

Just before the collision, Union commanders on their left and right flanks began to rally parts of various regiments and hit the Confederate column from both sides. McIntosh mobilized officers on his left and right to mount remnants of his command and those from Custer's 5th and 7th Michigan in the area for a series of charges into the flank and front of the Confederate column.

The 3rd Pennsylvania hit Hampton's column in the flank about two-thirds the way down — they first sent in a volley from their carbines and then charged with drawn sabers. Then troopers from the 1st New Jersey charged from Lott Woods and hit just behind the head of the Confederate column. Another charge from the Union left (including Newhall, Treichel and Rogers), hit the Confederate column in the right flank.[232]

The devastating artillery fire during the initial charge, the head-on collision with the 1st Michigan, and, about the same time, the flank attacks from several directions finally caused the head of the Confederate column to waver and then become disorganized as those in the rear had to avoid smashing into their own men who had been stopped or dropped in front of them. Then the force from the 3rd Pennsylvania emerged from the Lott Woods and cut through the Confederate column and drove back a portion of the column as far as Rummel's barnyard. There the Pennsylvanians met stubborn resistance from Witcher's and Chambliss's men.

Hampton was wounded twice and carried from the field as hand-to-hand fighting became general at the front, rear, and both sides of the Confederate force. Stuart's cavalrymen slowly began to pull back near Rummel's farm, and McIntosh pursued them to Little's Run where he again established a skirmish line.[233]

Both cavalries had had enough fighting for the day. D. McM. Gregg was content that the threat to Meade's rear and flank was over. It was equally clear to Stuart that he could not break through Gregg's cavalry and do damage to Meade's infantry. Gregg still had a relatively fresh brigade in reserve and Stuart's troops were spent. Stuart could also claim limited success—he had kept Ewell's flank and rear safe.[234]

Stuart rode to the front to satisfy himself the Union cavalrymen were finished for the day. As he and some of his staff rode past Rummel's barn, they observed the artillery exchange that resumed when the cavalry battle ended. Stuart's attention was drawn to the premature bursting of Confederate shells overhead, and he withdrew his line to the woods on top of Cress Ridge. "The inferiority of their ammunition was painfully evident.... Breathed and McGregor, however, held their position until nightfall."[235]

After dark, Stuart moved his cavalry from Cress Ridge to the York Road and camped for the night. From there he went to R. E. Lee's camp to see how his day had gone. He learned the Army of Northern Virginia had withdrawn to the ridges west of Gettysburg, consequently, "His command was now in an isolated and exposed position...."[236]

Colonel Beale reported that the losses sustained by the 9th Virginia as a percentage of the number of men in the field on that day were greater than on any other day.[237] The same could certainly be said for the 2nd North Carolina which sent fewer than 40 men into battle on July 3, and suffered 7 recorded losses.

Combat Losses in the 2nd North Carolina Cavalry, East Cavalry Field, Gettysburg July 3, 1863

Trooper	Age	Co.	Fate
G. Manning		D	captured
William Lane		E	captured
Asa Rodgers		G	captured
Uriah R. Parrish	25	I	wounded
William A. Graham Jr.	24	K	wounded
J. M. Larner		K	captured
L. H. Wyese		K	captured

The source used here is *North Carolina Troops 1861–1865, A Roster*, compiled by Louis H. Manarin (Raleigh, N.C., State Division of Archives and History), vol. II, Cavalry, pp. 104–177. (See Appendix for more information on the men listed above, page 397.)

Given the overall level of violence in the Battle of Gettysburg, the losses of the 2nd North Carolina Cavalry were not overwhelming, but they did represent a loss of more than 18 percent of its effective force, and when added to the previous losses during the Gettysburg Campaign, it can easily be said the regiment was near extinction.

The 2nd North Carolina once again lost its commanding officer, William A. Graham Jr., in the field that day, but he left us with a few of his impressions. After Graham was wounded in the early afternoon, he described his unforgettable experience in these words: "I was carried to a barn, the 'field hospital' where the ball was extracted about sunset." He went on to say, in the field hospital,

The groans and moans of those being operated upon and of the dying made this an unpleasant place. I secured a staff and hobbled to a house about one hundred yards off and spent the night with a Dutchman who was not at home, but his beds were all prepared as if for company and I was not at all lonesome as several others came in. Next morning we did not know what would be the next move, while it did not seem that we had been victorious there was no panic but a willingness to renew the conflict if ordered. The ambulances came to carry the wounded. None were from my regiment. I secured the horse of a man of the 9th Va. Cavalry who was so badly wounded that he could not sit up. I found I could not ride horseback; the only chance then was to sit by the driver of the ambulance; this I did to Williamsport where I found ambulances of the regiment.[238]

THE CONFEDERATE INFANTRY AT GETTYSBURG

The Confederate infantry had an even worse time of it on July 3. Apparently R. E. Lee felt the fighting on July 2 had forced Meade to strengthen his flanks at the expense of his middle. He then reasoned that on the morning of July 3, his Confederates should hit the middle of Meade's line on Cemetery Ridge. Longstreet once again argued against such an attack, but R. E. Lee paid little attention. Instead, he ordered Longstreet to send Pickett's division, their only fresh troopers, along with two from A. P. Hill's command across an open field, up a difficult ridge, into heavy Union artillery and dug-in infantry.[239]

The plan was for Pickett's men to pierce the Union middle and be joined by Ewell's men pressing down across Culp's Hill. Ewell launched his attack on the Union right around dawn, but by mid-morning his up-hill attack had been pushed back by a superior force.[240]

On the Confederate right, Longstreet was so opposed to the attack, he would not give George Pickett a direct order to attack — in response to a direct request for an order to march, Longstreet only dropped his head implying Pickett could go ahead. Finally, just after 1:00 P.M., Longstreet's artillery began bombarding the center of the Union line.[241]

Around 3:00 P.M. on July 3, 1863, Pickett's troopers moved forward. The Confederate artillery went silent, the Union artillery intensified, and the Confederate infantrymen marched into it. The horrible story of the slaughter that followed has been told many times, and this is not the place to repeat it. Those Confederate infantrymen who could still walk or crawl were forced to retire back to Seminary Ridge. Longstreet collected his disorganized men as best he could for the expected Union pursuit which did not come. Gloom settled over Seminary Ridge for the night and did not lift the next day. The combined losses for both armies over the three days of fighting rose to over 50,000 men.[242]

Retreat from Gettysburg: Cavalry All Around, July 4–14

Just about the time R. E. Lee's infantry was slowly withdrawing across Emmitsburg Road and up Seminary Ridge to the west, J. E. B. Stuart was withdrawing his cavalry from Cress Ridge above East Cavalry Field to the York Road where they encamped for the night. Once his men were settling in camps, Stuart rode over to R. E. Lee on Seminary Ridge for the news of the day and the plan for July 4. He learned of the losses sustained and the need to retreat. Stuart then returned to his men on York Road, knowing they were isolated and exposed to both Union infantry and cavalry that night — they withdrew early the next morning.[243]

By early afternoon, on July 4, just about the time it began to rain, R. E. Lee started the wagons and ambulances filled with an estimated 10,000 wounded men for the Potomac River. They gathered near Cashtown before heading south for Williamsport on the river. R. E. Lee selected Brigadier General John D. Imboden to escort his precious cargo of supplies and wounded men back to Virginia because he was eager to provide maximum protection by using the freshest available troops and a competent commander, knowing they would be a target of Union cavalry along the way. Imboden's train was about 17 miles long and had approximately 50 difficult miles to travel. Some of R. E. Lee's supply wagons and wounded could not make it to Cashtown to join Imboden and had to move ahead of the infantry column through Fairfield, then through the Catochin Mountains and on to Hagerstown — but most of the wagons and ambulances did manage to join Imboden at Cashtown.

Once R. E. Lee had his supplies and wounded on their way, he continued to wait for Meade's army to storm across Emmitsburg Road toward Seminary Ridge — they had been waiting for the attack all morning, but it did not come. The Confederate infantry started to retreat after dark. A. P. Hill's corps led the column, followed by Longstreet; Ewell's corps brought up the rear. They would not be difficult to find and harass; R. E. Lee's main column was over 15 miles long and the Potomac River was some 40 miles away.[244] (See map 3.3.)

J. E. B. Stuart and his cavalry did not play a

major role in the Battle of Gettysburg, but they did have a major and critical role to play shielding the retreat to Virginia. Stuart moved his cavalry near Seminary Ridge early in the morning on July 4. He then sent Beverly H. Robertson's and William E. Jones's small brigades to Fairfield to protect the small wagon train headed in that direction and on to protect the Jack Mountain passes (Monterey Pass). The army in retreat was to take the route to the north of Jack Mountain, and they would expect the Union army to use the pass south of the mountain to cut off the Confederate column.

John Buford's cavalry command had been sent to Westminster on July 3 to guard Union supplies. H. Judson Kilpatrick's cavalry was moved toward Emmitsburg on the afternoon of the 4th. The latter's responsibility was to attack and generally harass the flanks and rear of the retreating Confederates. Cavalrymen from Kilpatrick's division moved to meet R. E. Lee's train heading for Fairfield, and eventually Jones's and Robertson's cavalrymen who had been assigned to protect the train and column heading for Fairfield.

Robertson's 4th and 5th North Carolina cavalries, and Jones's 6th, 7th, and 11th Virginia cavalries had arrived in the Cashtown area on the morning of July 3. Early the next morning, they received instructions to move down to Fairfield and protect the wagon and ambulance train passing through the mountains near that place. Jones moved out first, and his 7th Virginia was the first to encounter Kilpatrick's Union cavalry as they were stalking the Confederate train near Fairfield. Jones moved his 6th Virginia up to support the 7th — his 11th regiment was held in reserve. Robertson's 4th North Carolina under D. D. Ferebee, and 5th North Carolina under James B. Gordon were at the rear of the Confederate cavalry column headed for Fairfield. Jones was able to beat off the enemy cavalry, and the Confederate train continued on. Robertson and Jones then headed for the southern road around Jack Mountain on the road already crowded with wagons, ambulances, and wounded men able to walk — it was slow going, and with no guarantee the Confederate cavalry would get to the pass before Kilpatrick's cavalry.[245]

While plodding along the muddy road with the train, Robertson and Jones received word that Kilpatrick's cavalry was heading for Ewell's wagon train. The two cavalry brigades picked up their pace and set out to intercept the enemy cavalry, but they had to travel roads jammed with slow-moving wagons to arrive at the expected point of attack. The Union cavalrymen, on the other hand, headed for Jack Mountain on a muddy but uncluttered road, and moved as rapidly as possible, hoping to catch the Confederate wagons in the pass. Jones tried to move ahead with his 6th Virginia and Robertson's 4th North Carolina, but had little luck. His column became strung-out and arrived with too little, too late.

Kilpatrick got to the pass before Jones and Robertson and after several hours of severe fighting, his troops were able to push aside the small cavalry command riding at the head of the wagons. Kilpatrick then took the hill and positioned his guns hoping to do serious damage to the train. Once he had his guns in place, the Federals began to shell the wagons and ambulances. The train and its small escort finally received help when Robertson's 5th North Carolina managed to move up.

As the 5th North Carolina Cavalry approached the mountain pass, it learned the enemy was already there, and it would have to fight for position. The 5th North Carolina, led by James B. Gordon, fought through the night until they gained and defended the pass, and thus held it open for R. E. Lee's infantry which took the road late that night.[246] Nevertheless, when Kilpatrick withdrew early on the morning of July 5, he took with him numerous prisoners and captured wagons.

Stuart had been instructed to send W. E. Jones and B. H. Robertson to protect the mountain passes between Fairfield and Hagerstown and to designate a small cavalry command, not to exceed two squadrons, to ride at the head of the wagon train. In addition, he was instructed to place an escort at the head of the infantry column, and a similar command to ride at the rear of the retreating army — the lead command was to report to A. P. Hill, and the rear guard to Richard S. Ewell. Stuart was also instructed to send one or two brigades to Cashtown Road and on to Chambersburg and hold that flank until the rear of the army (Ewell's command) was past Fairfield — Stuart sent Fitz Lee who was with his own brigade and in command of Wade Hampton's (the latter was under the temporary command of Colonel Laurence Baker since Hampton had been wounded the day before). After holding at Chambersburg, Fitz Lee was instructed to take his command toward Greencastle and to continue guarding the right and rear of the army on its way to Hagerstown and Williamsport. Fitz Lee was well behind Imboden on his designated route. Stuart was told to take the rest of his cavalry down to Emmitsburg and then across the Catochin Mountains and South Mountain to Cavetown and Boonsboro, guarding the left and rear of the Army of Northern Virginia. Soon Stuart was underway toward Emmitsburg with John R. Chambliss (W. H. F. Lee's brigade) and Milton J. Ferguson (Albert G. Jenkins's brigade). The remnant of the 2nd North Carolina Cavalry, perhaps 25 mounted men, along with a reduced 9th, 10th, and 13th Virginia Cavalries made up Chambliss's command.[247]

Imboden's Wagon Train

By the time the Confederates had firm control of the pass around Jack Mountain, John D. Imboden's wagons and ambulances had passed from Cashtown and were heading for Marion, between Chambersburg and Greencastle, where they turned south.

After Robert E. Lee had placed Imboden in command of the main wagon train gathering near Cashtown, most of the wagons and ambulances from the Gettysburg area were instructed to head for Cashtown and wait for instructions from Imboden. In addition, a battalion from the Washington Artillery of Louisiana was assigned to Imboden's train, and moved from Gettysburg at 9:00 A.M. on the morning of July 4. When the artillery reached Imboden at Cashtown, its guns were placed along the train at about one mile intervals in a pouring rain. As indicated, Imboden's train was around 17 miles long with Fitz Lee's and Wade Hampton's brigades following at some distance. The march to Williamsport began soon after they were in place. It was a hard march. According to the commander of the artillery, they did not stop once to feed and only once for water before they reached Williamsport — around 50 miles away on slow, muddy and crowded roads.[248]

The 2nd North Carolina Cavalry wagons and ambulances were among those assembled at Cashtown — Captain Graham of the 2nd North Carolina was wounded in East Cavalry Field on the 3rd and rode an ambulance belonging to another regiment to Cashtown on July 4. Graham, along with the other wounded from the regiment, the regiment's teamsters, and cavalrymen without mounts, all traveled with Imboden's train to Williamsport.[249]

Considering the heavy rains, muddy roads, and the generally poor condition of the men and beasts in the train, they made good time. In addition to the impediments provided by nature, the train was hit by detachments of Union cavalry at several points along the route. For instance, Imboden's train came under attack near Greencastle. The enemy was soon driven off, but the train lost about 130 wagons and 200 men. Among the losses were wagons belonging to Fitz Lee's cavalry brigade. (The latter brigade lost some 60 wagons in the attack.)[250] The 2nd North Carolina suffered only two recorded losses at Greencastle on July 5, 1863.

From Greencastle, Imboden led his train south on the Williamsport Road which ran about five miles west of Hagerstown, through Cunningham's Crossroads located about half way between Greencastle and Williamsport. As the train reached Cunningham's Crossroads, still on July 5, they were hit again by a larger force of Union cavalry than earlier in the day. About 200 Union cavalrymen arrived near the crossroads and waited for a vulnerable, unguarded, segment to pass in front of them before they launched their attack. Again, Imboden's train lost heavily before the attackers were driven off. They lost more than 100 wagons, 600 animals, and 600 men (about half of whom were wounded men from the Battle of Gettysburg).

Late in the day, J. Irvin Gregg's cavalry was drawing closer to the rear of Imboden's train, when they had an encounter with Fitz Lee's cavalry command near the rear of the train.

In spite of the bad road conditions and the attacks along the way, the head of Imboden's train of supplies and wounded men pulled into Williamsport late on July 5 and began to semi-circle the wagons with their backs to the raging Potomac River.

Cavalry on the Infantry's Left Flank

After W. E. Jones and B. H. Robertson had been sent to Fairfield and Jack Mountain pass, and Fitz Lee had been sent to Cashtown and on to Chambersburg to ride at J. D. Imboden's rear, J. E. B. Stuart led the rest of his cavalry to cover the left flank of R. E. Lee's retreat.

After sunset on July 4, Stuart led his column past the front of R. E. Lee's infantry as it still faced Cemetery Ridge. Stuart rode with J. R. Chambliss's (W. H. F. Lee's) and M. J. Ferguson's (Jenkins's) brigades. It was in that passing the men of Chambliss's command including the 2nd North Carolina cavalrymen learned the extent to which their infantry comrades had fallen the day before. Their route kept them east of the Catochin Mountains as they headed for Emmitsburg, before turning westward through the mountains.

After passing Cemetery Ridge, Stuart and his cavalrymen moved into some very dense woods. The rain and darkness on the road caused them to hold up and wait several hours for daylight. While waiting, they were able to get a guide, and when the road could be seen, they were back on it. They arrived at Emmitsburg at dawn and learned that a large body of Union cavalry had passed through on the previous afternoon, July 4, heading for one of the passes in the Catochin Mountains—the passes Robertson and Jones had been instructed to hold open. Stuart reasoned the Union cavalry would be handled there, so he spent some time in Emmitsburg gathering supplies, and 60 or 70 prisoners in and around town.[251]

From Emmitsburg, Stuart led his two brigades south to a small village called Mechanicstown (Cooperstown). They stopped there to feed and rest their horses. From there he took his men westward through the mountains. After passing through the Catochin Mountains, the road forked. Stuart thought his best chance of passing through South Mountain would be to divide his force and pass through at two different places. He sent Ferguson down the left fork, and he accompanied Chambliss's command on the other. As Chambliss's cavalrymen came through the west end of the pass, heading for Smithtown, they encountered Kilpatrick's pickets.[252]

After Kilpatrick had left Jack Mountain (Monterey) early on July 5, he moved down to Smithtown. There he and his men were resting and preparing for a Sunday dinner provided by the townspeople, when Stuart and Chambliss's command arrived. Kilpatrick's dinner had to wait. He placed his troops on hills around town and formed a skirmish line at the base of South Mountain to stop Chambliss's command which included the remaining mounted men of the 2nd North Carolina Cavalry and J. E. B. Stuart.

Stuart and his cavalrymen had to fight their way out of the pass. In Stuart's words, "Before reaching the western entrance to this pass, I found it held by the enemy, and had to dismount a large portion of the command, and fight from crag to crag of the mountain to dislodge the enemy already posted." Once through the pass, Stuart positioned his artillery, formed his skirmish line and engaged Kilpatrick's troops for a short while, before Kilpatrick withdrew and moved his men south to Boonsboro. Kilpatrick did not want to go head-to-head with Stuart's cavalry that day—even when it was only Chambliss's small brigade in front of them.[253]

Around sunset, Stuart and Chambliss's command cleared the mountain pass, and received word that Ferguson's command on the other road had also hit some resistance. Stuart sent a message to Ferguson instructing him to back off and follow the route Stuart had taken through the mountains if he had not yet passed through. Ferguson was making good headway on his passage through South Mountain, but when he got Stuart's message, he pulled back and took the route that had been used by Chambliss's command—Ferguson caught up with Stuart west of the mountains during the night. Then Stuart sent a company from the 9th Virginia in the direction of Leitersburg, telling them to be watchful because the enemy cavalry might be there. Stuart sent a dispatch with them for R. E. Lee who was expected to be several miles west of that place. From Leitersburg the dispatch was sent west with a detachment of ten men to find R. E. Lee. The dispatch carriers returned about 3:00 A.M. on July 6, not having found R. E. Lee, but they could report having seen many broken wagons from the Confederate train along the road side. They could also report having seen a large body of about 300 Yankee cavalry marching toward Leitersburg—but they did not present a problem. When Stuart arrived at Leitersburg with the rest of Chambliss's command, they all enjoyed a good breakfast.[254]

While at Leitersburg, Stuart heard from R. E. Lee and was assured that most of Kilpatrick's cavalry was already down near Boonsboro. By this time, Robertson, with his and Jones's command, caught up with Stuart — Jones and a few of his staff had been separated from his brigade during heavy fighting in the pass near Jack Mountain so arrived from the west rather than the north along with the rest of his brigade. Jones was able to inform Stuart of Imboden's arrival at Williamsport with the wagons and ambulances that survived the trip.[255]

Stuart knew at that time he must hold Hagerstown open for R. E. Lee's army. When he left Leitersburg, Stuart sent Chambliss's and Robertson's brigades directly to Hagerstown — he noted in his report that they were "...together a very small command." Stuart headed for Cavetown with the rest of his cavalry. Once at Cavetown, Stuart sent Jones with his men southwest along the Boonsboro Road for a few miles then instructed them to turn west for Funkstown and hold that position which covered the eastern front of Hagerstown. Stuart and Ferguson's command accompanied Jones as far as Cavetown, then turned off for Chewsville and on to Hagerstown. When Stuart arrived at Cavetown, he learned that a large force of enemy cavalry had left Boonsboro and was nearing Hagerstown. He knew Chambliss's small command was going to need assistance at Hagerstown so Stuart hurried along with Ferguson and his men.[256]

Kilpatrick left Boonsboro early on July 6 for Hagerstown because he had heard that Stuart was entrenched there to protect the passage of his army and his wagon trains at Williamsport. At about the same time, John Buford left for Williamsport to attack and destroy Imboden's wagons and ambulances held up there.[257]

HAGERSTOWN

It is difficult to know if the mounted remnant of the 2nd North Carolina Cavalry was traveling as a separate unit of around 25 men who rode away from Gettysburg, or if they were attached to another unit, perhaps Captain William B. Clement's North Carolina company (Company B) in the 10th Virginia Cavalry of Chambliss's brigade. Recall, when the 2nd North Carolina left Hanover, on June 30 for the round-about trip to Gettysburg they were a few men stronger and were also without their commander, Payne, so they traveled with Captain Clement's North Carolina men in the 10th Virginia. On July 3, east of Gettysburg, Captain Graham of the 2nd North Carolina took command of the regiment until later in the day when he was wounded. Leaving Gettysburg in retreat, the regiment was smaller and was under the command of Lieutenant Joseph Baker of Company D. Very likely Chambliss once again attached the remnants of the 2nd North Carolina to Captain Clement. In any case, they were with or alongside the 10th Virginia and the 9th and 13th Virginia Cavalries in Chambliss's command during the retreat and in the melee that occurred at Hagerstown on July 6.

Chambliss arrived at Hagerstown just before Kilpatrick's cavalrymen, but the enemy was fast approaching from the southeast. The 9th Virginia was sent into town first and began to post pickets on the roads coming from the south and east. About the same time, the Union cavalry was seen approaching on the road from Boonsboro. J. Lucius Davis drew his 10th Virginia in a line across the main street of town as the Confederate pickets were driven back into their line. Davis in turn charged the fast-approaching enemy. The clash was violent, and Davis's horse was shot, and he was wounded and captured. The fighting was hand-to-hand, as small groups of men slashed and fired at one another at close range in various locations throughout town. As more Union troops entered town, the 10th Virginia and their comrades slowly pulled back along the main street, then regrouped and turned to fight again. By that time, Chambliss's entire command, including the 2nd North Carolina, was fighting in the streets of Hagerstown. Before becoming overwhelmed, Chambliss withdrew his cavalrymen to a hill above town where they regrouped before heading back into town.[258]

From the north side of town, Chambliss dismounted some of his men and began reentry in order to dislodge the Union troops from Hagerstown. The cavalrymen were soon joined by Alfred Iverson's small infantry command. Iverson arrived while Chambliss and Robertson were engaged with the Union troops in town. He sent the wagons he was escorting to the rear, deployed skirmishers and joined in the fight — helping to push the enemy from Hagerstown. Stuart and Ferguson came up during the fight.[259]

Soon after they regained a foothold in town and were almost out of ammunition, the dismounted Confederate men were attacked by a squadron of Federal cavalrymen from the First West Virginia, who came charging up the main street. Once the charging Federals came within the range of Chambliss's dismounted men, they were also within the range of Iverson's skirmishers and they received a heavy fire at close range from both. After the dismounted Confederates emptied their guns into the charging enemy, Chambliss's mounted troopers then charged the disorganized West Virginians, driving them from town and capturing most of them. The 4th and 5th North Carolina cavalries of Robertson's brigade came up on the enemy's flank to help rout Kilpatrick's brigade.[260]

When Stuart and Ferguson arrived at Hagerstown, it was occupied by troopers from Kilpatrick's cavalry, and found Iverson's small body of infantry and Chambliss's and Robertson's small cavalries brigades at the north end of Hagerstown trying to retake the town. W. E. Jones then arrived on Stuart's left from the Funkstown area.[261] Stuart was eager to join in the fight but according to him, their "…operations were here much embarrassed by our great difficulty in preventing this latter force [Chambliss's] from mistaking us for the enemy, several shots striking very near our column." Of course, "friendly fire" is never welcome, but Chambliss's men were engaged in a hard fight and had been pushed from town, and were in the process of driving the enemy back out of town when Stuart arrived on the scene near the enemy's rear at a rapid pace.[262]

By afternoon, Ferguson's and Jones's commands had joined Chambliss's and Robertson's troopers as well as Kilpatrick's cavalrymen in the conflict, and hand-to-hand fighting was general throughout the town for several hours. When the Confederates finally pushed Kilpatrick's cavalry from Hagerstown, they retreated along the only route left to them, southwest on the road to Williamsport — Jones had brought his command up on the road from Boonsboro, which was the route Kilpatrick's men had arrived on. As Chambliss's men pursued the enemy along the turnpike toward Williamsport, with the 13th Virginia in front, followed by the 9th. Robertson's 4th and 5th North Carolina cavalries (with fewer than 900 troopers left in the saddle) rode with Ferguson's command to the left of the pike, both led by Stuart. The Confederate cavalrymen moved at a trot. Iverson, along with his wagons and infantry, slowly dropped behind on the march to Williamsport — the latter arrived that night.[263]

It is difficult to estimate the losses for Stuart's command at Hagerstown that day, but the loss of 263 men in Kilpatrick's brigades suggest the Confederate losses were also high — perhaps more than 100 but probably fewer than 200.[264] There were three men lost from the 2nd North Carolina, which carried fewer than 25 horsemen into the town that day.

As they pushed Kilpatrick's men toward Williamsport, Chambliss and his troopers were subjected to artillery and skirmishers' fire from time-to-time from guns placed on high ground along the route and small bodies of dismounted Union cavalry in front of the artillery — though they consistently pulled back as the Confederates approached. However, at one point the Federals made a more serious stand on some high ground between Hagerstown and Williamsport — they again placed their artillery on a small hill, with skirmishers just in front and on both sides of the road. The 13th Virginia was at the front of Chambliss's column, until they chased some enemy cavalry, who had been firing at them from the side of the road, into a woods. The departure of the 13th Virginia left the 9th at the front of Chambliss's column — they then faced the enemy volleys of canister that raked furrows in the occupants of the pike. The 9th quickened its pace as it moved up the hill toward the enemy guns, with Lieutenant George Beale and Sergeant Richard Washington leading the charge. Within twenty paces of the guns, the last canister was fired and some of the men at the head of the 9th Virginia dropped and others scattered — George Beale survived, Richard Washington did not. By the time the Confederate cavalrymen passed through the line; the guns were deserted, but enemy riflemen fired upon them from both sides of the road. At that point, Colonel Beale recalled hearing Stuart arrive to call the men of the 9th back, off the pike and into the field on the left, exclaiming, "That place will be too hot for you." Stuart lost the opportunity to capture the enemy guns with his move, but he saved many of his men.[265]

Stuart then brought up Ferguson's command at the charge, and the 9th Virginia rallied without regard to companies and charged the center of the Union line that had by then been reinforced by troops Kilpatrick had not sent into Hagerstown. When Kilpatrick sent a brigade into Hagerstown, he kept two brigades back and they moved between Stuart and Williamsport during the march. The remainder of Chambliss's command followed close in the charge up the pike until "...the whole body of the enemy were wheeling and running." Kilpatrick did not again rally his troops, and Stuart's cavalrymen moved to Williamsport without further difficulty.[266]

WILLIAMSPORT

About the time Stuart's cavalrymen were leaving Hagerstown, he heard artillery fire from Williamsport which concerned him — he had to hold Williamsport where R. E. Lee's wagons had collected, and the Army of Northern Virginia hoped to cross the Potomac. The sounds of war told him Buford was at Williamsport. When Stuart finally had Kilpatrick's cavalry on the run toward Williamsport, he pushed them rapidly past Buford's right flank and rear — Buford was still pounding the door of Williamsport with artillery and skirmish lines. Buford had hoped to receive reinforcements from Kilpatrick, but when the latter arrived he knew that was not in the cards — in Buford's words, "Just before dark, Kilpatrick's troops gave way, passing to my rear by the right, and were closely followed by the enemy." Buford would have seen a couple of dozen cavalrymen from the 2nd North Carolina and the rest of Chambliss's command close on Kilpatrick's retreating men.[267]

As indicated, about the same time Kilpatrick had led his men to Hagerstown, early on July 6, Buford's division had marched from Boonsboro directly to Williamsport. Thus, while Stuart was making his march to Williamsport, the Confederates already in Williamsport were threatened by Buford. Imboden had arrived at Williamsport with his train the day before, and his train was Buford's target. Imboden spent most of the day defending the wagons he escorted there as best he could — and his best was good enough until reinforced by Stuart's cavalry.

When Imboden reached Williamsport on July 5, he saw the river was too high for his wagons and ambulances to cross safely. However, he was able to begin the slow process of sending thousands of wounded across on two ferries that were still functioning. When Imboden pulled his wagons up, he mobilized his handful of infantry, cavalry, wounded, and teamsters for defense of the train and the seriously wounded in ambulances. Fortunately for Imboden and his command, his small battalion from the Washington Artillery under Eshleman arrived at Williamsport at 3:00 A.M. on July 6. Imboden immediately placed his artillery across the roads coming from Boonsboro and Hagerstown. This offered the exhausted artillerymen a chance for several hours of rest on the line. They had fought at Gettysburg and then marched hard along with Imboden's train for "...forty-two hours, without sleep, rest, or subsistence."[268]

Around 5:00 P.M. July 6, Buford arrived with cavalry and artillery on the road from Boonsboro and soon after on the road from Hagerstown — Imboden had both roads covered with his artillery and rag-tag collection of troopers. The artillery duel was as severe as the hand-to-hand fighting on the periphery of Williamsport that day. Certainly Imboden's ill-equipped force was happy to see Chambliss's cavalry drive Kilpatrick's men behind Buford's line, causing the latter to reconsider his ongoing siege of Williamsport. Just about the time Chambliss's command arrived at Williamsport, Fitz Lee's cavalry command was approaching town on the direct road from Greencastle.[269]

Upon arriving at Williamsport, Chambliss's command began to collect the men by regiments — many of whom had become scattered along the column in the difficult march and fighting from Hagerstown. Also, by the time the brigade arrived at Williamsport, Major Clinton M. Andrews, of the 2nd North Carolina, had returned to duty and found himself the senior officer in the regiment. He once again took command of the regiment — Andrews had missed the entire Gettysburg Campaign and was certainly shocked to see what was left of his regiment. The regiment numbered fewer than 25 men at the time, but Andrews apparently had with him several of his cavalrymen who had also returned to duty while the campaign was underway. The 2nd North Carolina Cavalry lost two more men in the fight to keep Buford's command out of Williamsport and away from the Confederate wagons.[270]

Most of Chambliss's men camped on the hills above Williamsport, while others were immediately placed on picket duty. Pickets were pushed along the roads leading to Williamsport until contact was made with enemy skirmishers. On the night of July 7, the rest of Stuart's cavalry settled along the road from Hagerstown to Boonsboro. Pickett's battered infantry command arrived and relieved Chambliss's cavalry around Williamsport on July 8, and the cavalry brigade moved to Stuart's front. By late in the day, Stuart's cavalry shield was placed as follows: Ferguson's command on the southern end, in front of their infantry; then Jones's brigade to their north, just east of Hagerstown and to the Cavetown road; Chambliss's command was northeast of Hagerstown; and Robertson's brigade was just north of Chambliss.[271]

By July 8 and 9, Stuart was shielding the wagons and troops at Williamsport with a line that extended from above Hagerstown to Funkstown and to Williamsport. Stuart's cavalry was instructed to establish a shield around R. E. Lee's trains and infantry, as the latter continued to arrive and entrench. R. E. Lee wanted his infantry dug in as firmly as possible in case Meade's army was up before the Potomac was down. The concern was real. Meade's army was closing in by July 8, but they spent the next four days consolidating their force for the final attack on the Army of Northern Virginia. Finally, R. E. Lee extended his line from Williamsport, southeast past Falling Waters, the other place he hoped to cross the Potomac. For Lee's army, waiting meant digging works along his nearly ten-mile front. Also while waiting for the river to drop or Meade to attack, the Confederates continued to send artillery, ammunition, and the wounded across the river by rafts.

BOONSBORO ROAD

John Buford and his division spent the night of the 7th in Boonsboro, with an advance brigade pushed up the Hagerstown Road. That got Stuart's attention and reinforced his notion that any cavalry attack would come from the Boonsboro area. Consequently, on July 8, Stuart decided to make a strong demonstration with a good portion of his cavalry toward Boonsboro to discourage an enemy attack from that direction. Stuart brought up most of Fitz Lee's, Hampton's (under Baker), Jones's, and W. H. F. Lee's (under Chambliss) brigades, as well as artillery. Stuart's command moved on the road to Boonsboro through Funkstown around 5:00 A.M., and Jones's men made first contact with Buford's line, with Chambliss's and Fitz Lee's commands alongside. The Confederates moved out on both sides of the Hagerstown-Boonsboro Road pushing Buford's advance units back to their division near Boonsboro. Stuart got within a couple of miles of town by mid-morning and stood in front of Buford's division.[272]

Stuart's Horse Artillery started firing at Buford's skirmish line early in the day — the line was spread into muddy fields on both sides of the road. Union artillery soon joined the chorus. The artilleries dueled, as did the skirmish lines until ammunition began to run low by mid-afternoon.

Kilpatrick had moved to the left of Buford's line, and as the fighting neared Boonsboro, Ferguson's Confederates came up on the road from Williamsport and pressed Kilpatrick. The latter gave way first, Buford's line followed as Stuart pushed them back to Boonsboro. Stuart's ammunition was by then also running low, and he had an additional cause for concern — the Union infantry had begun to arrive the day before and much of it was camped in the area of Boonsboro. In addition, Stuart knew he had made his presence felt, and the enemy would hesitate before moving on Williamsport and Hagerstown. Stuart pulled back and settled for the night near Funkstown. Ferguson and his men moved back to Williamsport. By the end of the day, Stuart was satisfied that his demonstration had given the enemy reason to pause, so he pulled back. Chambliss's command was among those pulled back near Funkstown where they were still under artillery fire until they passed back through their own infantry lines near the Hagerstown Road — where they spent the night.[273]

According to Stuart, his men drove the Union troopers back into their infantry. According to Buford, his men drove the Confederates back four miles — both statements were correct and in that order.[274]

The Union cavalry lost 80 men around Boonsboro in the fighting that day, and Stuart may also have lost close to that number of men. The 2nd North Carolina Cavalry recorded one man wounded in the fighting that day.

Stuart's cavalrymen spent most of the next day

forming their line and digging in — their left flank was near Hagerstown, their right extended just south of Funkstown, and their backs were on the Antietam Creek. Stuart's line held throughout July 9 and experienced only one minor attack from Buford's men in the late afternoon.

By July 10, most of Meade's infantry was in front of R. E. Lee's line. The Union First, Sixth, and Eleventh Corps were in position behind Buford's cavalry. With such support, Meade was ready to have Buford probe R. E. Lee's line.

Buford's cavalry division came up the Hagerstown-Boonsboro road again on the morning of July 10 and pushed Stuart's cavalry back through Funkstown into their infantry line. Jones's, Chambliss's, and Robertson's commands were north of the main fighting on that day. Stuart placed cavalry units on both flanks of the infantry line and held. A regiment from Ferguson's and Fitz Lee's commands were most heavily engaged, but the major part of the defense was conducted by the entrenched infantry under the direct eye of R. E. Lee. The Confederate infantry and cavalry held fast, and around 3:00 P.M., Buford pulled back when his ammunition was exhausted. Buford apparently felt he could not easily penetrate the enemy's line, and he made no further serious attempts to get at the Confederate wagon trains near Williamsport. Buford pulled back through Boonsboro to near Bakersville on July 11 and remained there until the morning of July 14.[275]

While Buford was probing the Confederate line on July 10, most of Chambliss's command moved about a mile northeast of Hagerstown, until they found their enemy. By that time, their enemy was most of Meade's army. R. E. Lee's army was just southeast of Hagerstown, waiting for Meade to attack. Chambliss's command stretched from Hagerstown for about a mile to the northeast. Robertson's two small regiments were still on Chambliss's left — both brigades watched Meade's right.[276]

On July 11, Kilpatrick's cavalry division was moved from the Boonsboro area to the right wing of the Union line, around Hagerstown. R. E. Lee and J. E. B. Stuart were not quite ready to pull their cavalry from in front of their infantry, but R. E. Lee did ask Stuart to move more cavalry to the left, just northwest of Hagerstown. Stuart was further instructed to pull his entire cavalry to their left when pressed by the enemy infantry.[277]

On the 12th, Meade's infantry moved in the direction of Hagerstown and Stuart had his line pull back in an orderly manner and collect on the left of R. E. Lee's then well-entrenched infantry line. Kilpatrick was sent forward with his cavalry division and a brigade of infantry to take Hagerstown. Around dawn, Chambliss's men were aware of the Union cavalry massing in front of them, and they were moved up to reinforce Robertson on the left. Orders were given to all company officers to have their men saddle up and mount as rapidly as possible. The Confederate cavalry line was about two and a half miles in front of Ewell's infantry at that point. The enemy came, Chambliss and Robertson fell back, hill by hill, slowing the enemy as much as possible. This move put Meade's forces in position to easily cross Antietam Creek and move on Hagerstown, but he hesitated.[278]

Just before backing into Hagerstown, a strong Union column charged Chambliss's line and drove them through town.[279] Both Chambliss and Robertson lost a number of men as they were driven back.

Kilpatrick claimed to take 100 prisoners from Chambliss's and Robertson's small commands that day. In spite of his tendency to exaggerate his successes, Kilpatrick did capture several men from Chambliss's command, two of whom were from the 2nd North Carolina.[280]

On the evening of July 12, R. E. Lee instructed Stuart to expect an attack in front of Longstreet and A. P. Hill, and when it came, the cavalry should hit the enemy's right flank — but Stuart was also instructed to keep an eye on the road to Chambersburg. Accordingly, after the fighting on July 12, the Confederate line was shortened, and their left rested on the road to Greencastle, just west of Hagerstown. Chambliss's command regrouped and was moved to block the Greencastle Road coming in from the north. By late evening, R. E. Lee told Stuart that Longstreet was sufficiently entrenched and no longer needed Fitz Lee's cavalry shield. Fitz Lee's command was then moved up to support Chambliss on the left, while Jones's command covered the line from the Cavetown Road to the Funkstown Road. On July 13, Stuart extended his cavalry pickets from just west of Hagerstown and to the north as far as Chambersburg—covering over three miles into dangerous territory. It was raining heavily again that day as the Confederate cavalrymen held their positions, waiting for Meade's attack which still did not come.[281]

Getting Back Across the Potomac

Conditions had changed by July 13: Meade had collected a force he considered sufficient to destroy the Army of Northern Virginia, the Potomac River had receded enough to make fording a possibility at Williamsport, and the Confederates had repaired the pontoon bridge at Falling Waters. It was time for R. E. Lee to take his army home.

In addition, much to R. E. Lee's surprise, Meade did not attack, so by afternoon, R. E. Lee instructed Ewell's corps to retreat across the Potomac at Williamsport; and Longstreet's and A. P. Hill's corps were ordered to use the pontoon bridge at Falling Waters for the same purpose. The withdrawal of artillery, wagons, and infantry was to begin around midnight. Also on the afternoon of July 13, Stuart received the following instructions.

I wish you to place your cavalry in position before night, so as to relieve the infantry along the whole extent of their lines when they retire, and take the place of their sharpshooters when withdrawn. They will be withdrawn about 12 o'clock to-night. Direct your men to be very vigilant and bold, and not let the enemy discover that our lines have been vacated. At daylight withdraw your skirmishers, and retire with all your force to cross the river.[282]

Covering R. E. Lee's retreat had reached its final and potentially most difficult stage—the cavalry had to hold and slow any enemy attempts to attack the retreating columns while crossing the Potomac. After nightfall, Fitz Lee's cavalrymen replaced Longstreet's men in the trenches; Hampton's men (under Laurence Baker) took the place of A. P. Hill's men; and Jones's brigade along with the much reduced commands of Chambliss and Robertson relieved Ewell's men on the far left of the Confederate line as they pulled out for the river at Williamsport.

It was a dark and rainy night so the crossing was slow. Ewell had the best road and was across by 8:00 A.M. the next day. The routes to Falling Waters were slower, and the crossing itself was slower because all the artillery, ammunition wagons, and ambulances that could not ford the river, had to be sent down to the pontoon bridge. Consequently, it was daylight on July 14 before Longstreet and A. P. Hill started their troops across, which also explains why Fitz Lee's command was not able to cross at the bridge that morning.[283]

Not long after Longstreet and A. P. Hill were lining up at the pontoon bridge, both Kilpatrick and Buford were on their way to Falling Waters. Around 11:00 A.M., Union cavalry appeared at the rear of Longstreet's column still about a mile and a half from the bridge. With Ewell and Stuart nearly across the Potomac, Kilpatrick moved down to join Buford at Falling Waters, and he was free to join Buford in an attack on the slower moving columns of Longstreet and A. P. Hill heading for the crossing at Falling Waters. Buford came up from Bakersville to hit the column in the flank, and got between his enemy and the pontoon bridge at one point.[284]

Longstreet's and A. P. Hill's cavalry support was initially assigned to Fitz Lee's brigade. Fitz Lee was instructed to follow A. P. Hill across the pontoon bridge around daylight, but Fitz Lee apparently thought his task was primarily to cross the river at daylight and covering A. P. Hill's rear was less important. Whatever his reasoning at the time, when Fitz Lee saw that the pontoon bridge still full of Longstreet's men, he took most of his cavalrymen up to Williamsport and forded the river at that point. He left two squadrons to protect the infantry crossing at Falling Waters. Apparently Stuart and Fitz Lee did not realize how far behind schedule A. P. Hill's column was and that both Buford and Kilpatrick were converging on Falling Waters. If they had, they would certainly have increased the cavalry protection, not reduced it.[285]

The problem for A. P. Hill was compounded when Fitz Lee's two squadrons crossed the pontoon bridge after Longstreet's column, thinking it was the end of A. P. Hill's column. When A. P. Hill's column finally approached Falling Waters, there was no Confederate cavalry on their flanks, and the troopers near the end of his column had to fight their way to the river. Among the wagons and men in A. P. Hill's rear were some of the 2nd North Carolina Cavalry's wagons, teamsters, and men in Company Q unable to ford the river up at Williamsport. The fighting was severe, and Buford caused

Confederate Cavalry Losses from Gettysburg to the Potomac

Retreat Totals by Brigade		Retreat Totals by Regiments	
Robertson	144	13th Virginia	37
W. H. F. Lee*	100	9th Virginia	30
Fitz Lee	96	10th Virginia	22
Hampton	76	2nd North Carolina*	11
Jones	39		

The numbers in this table are from J. E. B. Stuart's report no. 565, O. R., vol. XXVII, part 2, pp. 716–717.

*No report was submitted for the 2nd North Carolina, but a count of the regiment's losses was made from the Roster. The number was also added to the totals for W. H. F. Lee.

---

considerable confusion in A. P. Hill's column while taking around 500 prisoners.[286]

There was naturally some bitterness among infantrymen stemming from the absence of cavalry support for the rear guard of A. P. Hill's column. Longstreet had been left at the bridge by R. E. Lee to oversee the passage of A. P. Hill's men, and he was particularly incensed by the absence of Fitz Lee's cavalry. Indeed, Longstreet strongly suggested the loss of the North Carolinian Brigadier General Johnston Pettigrew was attributable to Fitz Lee's failure to perform. In Longstreet's words:

The division of the Third Corps under General Pettigrew formed the rear of the infantry line, which was to be covered by Fitzhugh Lee's cavalry. But the cavalry brigadier rode off and crossed the river, leaving, it is said, a squadron for the duty, and the squadron followed the example of the brigadier. The consequence was that when Kilpatrick's cavalry rode up it was taken to be the Confederates ordered for their rear-guard. Instead of friends, however, General Pettigrew found a foe. He was surprised by a dashing cavalry charge, was wounded, and died after a few days.[287]

When left to make judgments on his own, Fitz Lee often made bad ones. His comrades often paid the price, but his career seldom did. Fitz Lee's conduct in the fighting at Gettysburg on July 3 was also brought under some question by Wade Hampton when Fitz Lee impetuously ordered a charge that exposed their position. Hampton made it clear in his battle report that he was not responsible for the ill-advised charge into East Cavalry Field.[288] In spite of these problems, and as is often the case, high command only knows what is transmitted in reports, and when Stuart wrote his report on the campaign he had the following to say about Robert E. Lee's nephew, Fitzhugh Lee:

I desire to mention among the brigadier-generals one whose enlarged comprehensions of the functions of cavalry, whose diligent attention to the preservation of its efficiency, and intelligent appreciation and faithful performance of the duties confided to him, point to as one of the first cavalry leaders on the continent, and richly entitle to promotion. I allude to Brig. Gen. Fitz. Lee.[289]

Of course, such selective praise is how careers are often made, and Fitz Lee's promotions did follow as did Hampton's—however, Pettigrew's career ended, but his reputation did not.

By morning on July 14, Chambliss's command crossed by fording the Potomac at Williamsport along with most of Stuart's cavalry. W. W.

Combat Losses in the 2nd North Carolina Cavalry During the Retreat, July 4–13, 1863

Trooper	Age	Co.	Fate
Drury W. Reardon	26	D	captured near Williamsport
Reuben Winbourn	30	E	captured near Hagerstown
George H. Edwards	26	G	captured near Hagerstown
Lambert P. Garrard	24	K	killed at Hagerstown
James Potter	32	G	captured at Greencastle
Uriah R. Parrish	25	I	captured at Greencastle
Andrew P. York		A	wounded & captured at Williamsport
David C. Harvell	25	A	wounded near Falling Waters
Henry G. Thornell	29	E	captured near Falling Waters
Spencer R. Chaplin		G	captured at Falling Waters
William Burns	30	I	captured at Falling Waters

The source used here is *North Carolina Troops 1861–1865, A Roster*, compiled by Louis H. Manarin (Raleigh, N.C., State Division of Archives and History), vol. II, Cavalry, pp. 104–177. (See Appendix for more information on the men listed above, page 398.)

Blackford of Stuart's staff, noted that the cavalry followed Ewell's column across, and they too had a hard time of it. According to the cavalryman, even though on horseback they got almost as wet as the infantry, and then they had to sit in a wet saddle for hours while the infantrymen could walk and thereby stay warmer. Probably not many infantrymen looked upon their mounted comrades as carrying a greater burden then they, however. Certainly none of the troopers had an easy time of it. Blackford, and no doubt many others, felt ill from exposure and mostly remembered being wet, cold, hungry, and exhausted on that dark rainy morning.[290] In any case, the men in Robert E. Lee's army who were fortunate enough to return from Gettysburg were back in Virginia by 1:00 P.M.

There are no recorded cavalry losses for the crossing at Williamsport, but among the losses sustained by Longstreet's and A. P. Hill's men at Falling Waters that day, were four men from the 2nd North Carolina Cavalry. These men were among those in Company Q, men without serviceable mounts or who were ill or who fought alongside teamsters and General Pettigrew's rear guard to save the last of the wagons trying to cross at Falling Waters. This train included the regiment's wagons that had to cross at the pontoon bridge because they could not ford the river at Williamsport.[291]

As expected, Cavalry losses were relatively heavy during the retreat. The record of Stuart's losses is not complete but it shows the following.

The numbers suggest Stuart's two smallest brigades suffered the heaviest losses. Robertson's North Carolina brigade of only two regiments and W. H. F. Lee's brigade under the command of Chambliss both took enormous losses relative to their initial sizes.

While the entire brigade certainly shared the pain of the heavy losses during the retreat, the 2nd North Carolina Cavalry's losses are amplified by their relative impact. The 2nd North Carolina left Gettysburg with about 25 men in the saddle — and lost at least 11 during the retreat. Their losses are listed in the table.

The small force of effective horsemen in the 2nd North Carolina probably numbered fewer than 20 men when they crossed the Potomac at Williamsport on July 14, 1863. The regiment's wagons along with its wounded and horseless troopers were more numerous and were among the last of Robert E. Lee's army to cross the river at Falling Waters that day.

Four

Reorganizations and Winter Campaigns

Robert E. Lee took his army across the Potomac and headed south through Martinsburg. He had planned to take his army across the Shenandoah River and continue south through Loudoun County, east of the Blue Ridge Mountains, but the river was too high. He halted his army near Bunker Hill on the road to Winchester — the men rested while they waited for the water to subside. The Army of Northern Virginia stretched back through Martinsburg on July 15, 1863. George G. Meade's infantry was not following, but his cavalry was threatening.[1]

After crossing the Potomac, Stuart took his staff to a wonderful farm called the Bower, where they had stayed on a previous occasion. They always enjoyed making the best of any situation, and some of his staff were able to momentarily set aside the tragedy of Gettysburg and the ordeal of getting back to Virginia. For instance, W. W. Blackford after describing the horrible sights of their wagon trains crossing the Potomac immediately appreciated their new comforts on July 15. In his words: "Our camp was pitched at the old place in his park and our pleasant, gay life was resumed, with the lovely daughters and nieces of our host." Perhaps a little apologetic for his elation, Blackford added, "A shade of sadness hung over our meeting, however, when we thought how many who were with us during our former visit were dead or absent from wounds."[2]

Stuart had a little trouble settling into the good life at the Bower after the defeat at Gettysburg because he had become a target for mounting criticism of the cavalry's absence from the front of the Army of Northern Virginia from late June to July 2. He went to unusual lengths to justify his activities in the days prior to the Battle of Gettysburg in his after-battle report of August 20, 1863.[3]

Another reason Stuart had little time for enjoying the gaiety at the Bower was the presence of enemy cavalry south of the Potomac. The second half of July was still an active time for cavalrymen. Once back in Virginia, Hampton's brigade (still under the command of Laurence Baker) was assigned picket duty on the Potomac, from Falling Waters to Hedgesville. Beverly H. Robertson was sent to the fords on the Shenandoah River, and the other brigades were moved back toward Leetown. Almost as soon as Stuart arrived at the Bower on the 15th, he learned that a large force of enemy cavalry had crossed the river at Harper's Ferry and was spotted between Shepherdstown and Leetown — Harper's Ferry was again in Union hands. (Leetown was about 4 miles northeast of Smithfield and about 10 miles west of Harper's Ferry.) Stuart was concerned the enemy cavalry might turn north and head for Martinsburg, so he decided to attack them as a preventative measure.[4]

Meade collected and re-supplied John Buford's and H. Judson Kilpatrick's cavalry divisions at Berlin, Maryland on July 15. He also sent four corps of his army to Berlin and three corps to Harper's Ferry. While the Union troops were gathering that morning, D. McM. Gregg, commanding the Second Cavalry Division, was sent to Shepherdstown across the Potomac to find and harass the retreating Confederates near Charlestown. He was able to inform Meade that R. E. Lee's army was spread along the road from Martinsburg to Winchester and headed for Winchester.[5]

The Fight Near Shepherdstown

D. McM. Gregg's probe alerted Stuart to the presence of enemy cavalry between Shepherdstown and Leetown which threatened R. E. Lee's column. Early on the 16th, Stuart sent Fitz Lee's brigade to meet the pursuers with J. R. Chambliss's very small brigade (including the remnants of the 2nd North Carolina which may have numbered nearly fifty effective men) in support. Albert G. Jenkins's brigade was instructed to move from Martinsburg toward Shepherdstown. William E. Jones and his brigade were already near Charlestown.[6]

Just as he was formulating his plan of attack, Stuart was summoned to R. E. Lee at Bunker Hill, so he placed the operation in Fitz Lee's hands. Fitz Lee moved his command along the pike toward Shepherdstown until he encountered D. McM. Gregg's cavalry. He then dismounted his and Chambliss's men on the turnpike and steadily drove Gregg's cavalrymen back. The fighting was sharp and Gregg lost about 70 men, but his troopers finally fell back to a strong position behind stone walls and barricades where they were able to hold. Fitz Lee's and Chambliss's men remained in front of their enemy, fighting until nightfall. Jenkins's brigade came up during the fight but stayed in support. Jones was not instructed to move toward Shepherdstown. During the night, D. McM. Gregg withdrew his command to Harper's Ferry. Stuart joined his troops during the fight and then moved toward Leetown.[7] (See map 2.3.)

With the enemy cavalry present, Robert E. Lee wanted Stuart to move the main body of his cavalry across the Shenandoah and establish a shield down in Loudoun County, but the river was still too high for the cavalry to cross with its supply wagons—the scouts sent across had to swim their horses over. Stuart was forced to hold most of his cavalry near Leetown until July 22. Meade used this time to move his cavalry south into Loudoun County; and Stuart became concerned the enemy cavalry might get between his cavalry and Richmond. Meanwhile, R. E. Lee had Longstreet's corps steadily moving south through the Shenandoah Valley, headed for Front Royal and then Chester Gap. R. E. Lee wanted Longstreet to stay south of Meade's cavalry, and Stuart wanted to be between Longstreet and the enemy's cavalry. It was going to be a close race. Stuart had sent Robertson's cavalry brigade to Longstreet as an advance guard. L. Baker's command (Hampton's brigade) covered the rear of Ewell's column; and Jones's brigade was assigned picket duty on the lower Shenandoah. Jones was then instructed to follow the last of Robert E. Lee's column south. Fitz Lee's, Chambliss's, and Jenkins's brigades set out on a forced march along the Shenandoah for Front Royal where they hoped to cross the river and head east for Manassas Gap in order to protect the flank of R. E. Lee's retreating infantry column.[8] (See map 2.2.)

It would be difficult because Meade had already moved a cavalry division into Loudoun County and occupied Snicker's Gap by July 17. Indeed, Meade had four infantry corps and two cavalry divisions across the Potomac by the end of the day. The next day, he sent a cavalry division along the eastern side of the Blue Ridge Mountains to take and hold the mountain passes as far as Chester Gap. Meade's intention was to push his infantry to Warrenton in Fauquier County and on to Culpeper Court House. Meade also sent a cavalry force toward Aldie to protect the Orange & Alexandria Railroad as far as Warrenton Junction—thus keeping his supply line open to Warrenton, his destination.[9]

By July 19, Meade had his three columns marching south, with two divisions of cavalry in front and on his right flank along the mountains. He had learned that the Army of Northern Virginia was moving south in the Valley, had already passed Front Royal and was heading for Culpeper.[10]

Longstreet was ordered to cross the Shenandoah and occupy Ashby's Gap on July 19. However, he still could not ford the swollen river, and his scouts told him that Union cavalry already occupied the eastern end of Ashby's Gap. Longstreet then continued his march south, hoping to cross the mountains at Manassas or Chester Gaps. At Front Royal, the river was still too high for fording, but the remains of a pontoon bridge were still in place, and Longstreet was able to get a brigade across to hold the western end of Manassas and Chester Gaps. On July 20, Union cavalry tried to push through both gaps, but Longstreet's men held the passes, and Buford's men had to back off, but maintained control of the eastern entrances to both gaps. Longstreet's column continued south and reached Culpeper Court House on July 24.[11]

By July 22, Buford moved his wagon train to Warrenton, and on the next day, he had his whole division concentrated near Barbee's Cross Roads. Buford's division held Warrenton, Fayetteville, and had pickets on the Rappahannock

River from Sulphur Springs to Kelly's Ford, across from Brandy Station.[12]

On the 23rd, back at Manassas Gap, Meade made another attempt to get into the Shenandoah Valley. He pushed his Third Corps through the mountains and by the end of the day had fought his way to within a few miles of Front Royal. The next morning, he learned that Ewell's corps had passed during the night and all that could be seen was Jones's cavalry near the rear of the column. Meade had the unpleasant task of once again reporting to his superiors that "Finding the enemy entirely beyond my reach, I have withdrawn the army...." Meade withdrew from Manassas Gap and concentrated his forces near Warrenton and Warrenton Junction.[13]

A little further south, still on July 23, Stuart (with Fitz Lee's, Chambliss's, and Jenkins's commands) was finally able to pass Longstreet on the column's left and march through Chester Gap and move near Amissville, below the Rappahannock River, where he encountered Union cavalry. The next day Stuart and his cavalrymen endeavored to cover the left flank of A. P. Hill's column as it moved into Culpeper County — Hill and his command had started its march south through the Shenandoah Valley on July 21, accompanied by R. E. Lee. On July 24, R. E. Lee joined Longstreet's column as it entered Culpeper Court House.[14]

On the 24th, R. E. Lee was aware that Meade had pushed through Manassas Gap the day before and threatened Ewell's rear. In a message to Stuart, Lee pointed out that Stuart had obviously misgauged the threat to Ewell's column. R. E. Lee went on to say, "I want you to do all in your power to cover the passage of the troops through the mountains, and also gain what information you can as regards the advance of the enemy." It is surprising at that late date in the retreat, R. E. Lee felt compelled to remind Stuart what his job entailed — it was probably meant to be only a minor scolding. Normally Lee had unbounded confidence in Stuart's judgment and efficiency. R. E. Lee went on to instruct Stuart in these words: "A scout yesterday informed me that the enemy was running the trains as far as White Plains, and citizens informed him that they were advancing toward Rappahannock Station. You had better extend Chambliss, Jr., farther down the river [the Rappahannock], if you find that the enemy is extending that way."[15]

Chambliss's command, including the 2nd North Carolina Cavalry, was placed on picket duty from around Hazel Run, southeast along the Rappahannock. It had not been an easy trip for them and even though they had time to rest, it would take a while to recover — they were still tired, hungry, partially armed and disorganized. Their condition was described by one member of Chambliss's command just a few days after arriving, on July 27. Private Collins of the 10th Virginia Cavalry wrote his wife the following account:

...I am not all together well I have been suffering very much on this trip with head ache I think as much from hunger as any thing else we have been bringing up the rear all the way and there was no chance to get a mouthful on the way as such a large army was ahead of us ... evry house eat out along the road and we could not leave the road for fear of being caught by the Yankees So it was the third day before I got a meal and that was diner we traveled night and day and head ache nearly *killed* me I am suffering with it now but not so bad thogh I get something to eat now by paying high for it I have not drawn a mouthful from the government for a fortnight I can graze Barney though he dont look as nice as if he had plenty of grain we drew some grain yesterday I hope it will be better We have stoped here [twelve miles from Culpeper C. H. on Hazel Run] on picket the rest of the army is at Culpeper where I think they are going to make a stand I have not found any of my things yet cloths or nothing else *obine* gave me a navy pistol and best Sharps Carbine I ever saw The man that had my Carbine lost it in Pennsylvania Ben Rodgers has my saddle ____ at the wagon all rite we are all exchanging....[16]

Many of the cavalrymen in Chambliss's command spent the first couple of days south of the Rappahannock finding their regiments and wagons. During their first few weeks back from the Gettysburg Campaign, many of the 2nd North Carolina cavalrymen who were absent and had missed the campaign began to return — the regiment remained one of Stuart's smallest units, but it avoided extinction. They did not have much time to collect themselves, however, because picket duty was immediate; their enemy was just across the river in an unknown strength, but certainly in greater numbers and better equipped than they.

Once Stuart had his Rappahannock line in place, he passed some of the criticism that was being leveled at him because of his late arrival at Gettysburg onto to his cavalrymen. He vented his displeasure in two General Orders.[17] The first, No. 25 dated July 29 opened with these words: "The nondescript, irregular body of men, known as Company Q, which has so long disgraced the cavalry service, and degraded the individuals resorting to it, is hereby abolished." Stuart went on to say the sick and disabled men would be sent to hospitals. Unserviceable horses would be sent to the camp for disabled horses in each division. Efficient provost guards would be organized immediately to stay with the wagon trains to prevent men from joining the trains when the mood struck them. When they did, from that time forward, they would be arrested. If any officer under the rank of a brigade commander, granted permission for such absences, the officer would be arrested and tried. A provost guard was also organized for each brigade with the duty to prevent straggling and disorders of every kind, and in battle to arrest any man going to the rear and compel them to return to the front. Also, no brigade, regiment, or company officer will have the authority to issue permits for leaves to travel 5 miles from brigade headquarters in any direction. Stuart ended his General Order with these words: "Let the straggler be disgraced in the eyes of all honest and patriotic men; let the artful dodger on the battlefield receive the retributive bullet of his gallant comrade; let every man recognize his duty to his oppressed country as his sole motive, and vengeance on a ruthless invader his constant aim."

The next day, July 30, Stuart issued General Orders No. 26 on how a cavalrymen should fight. He said the need for this General Order was to "correct the defects in the mode of fighting pursued by this division." The defects were clearly on the increase and he felt his "oral injunctions" had been in vain. Stuart provided instructions for how to move into battle; how to sit a horse; how to hold a saber; and among other things, when to use a pistol. Then he went into detail instructing, one after the other, brigade, regiment, and squadron commanders where to place themselves relative to their columns. The orders provided supplemental guidelines for drill while in camp.

The message was clear, Union cavalrymen were in all respects better than before the Gettysburg Campaign, and Stuart's men would have to improve to meet the new reality.

The cavalrymen had ample opportunity to put Stuart's orders into practice from the day they were issued because there was continual skirmishing along the front, and scouting parties were sent forward from time to time. For instance, on July 30 some men from the 2nd North Carolina engaged the enemy and three men were wounded, captured, and sent back to a Federal hospital in Winchester.

The regiment's recorded combat losses from the time they re-crossed the Potomac on July 14 through August of 1863 are summarized in the table below.

Combat Losses in the 2nd North Carolina Cavalry from the Potomac to the Rappahannock, July 1863

Trooper	Age	Co.	Fate
William H. Wellington	34	D	wounded July 17
George C. Dunn	22	K	wounded mid–July
Robert H. Morrison	43	B	captured July 30
Richard H. Barnes	26	E	captured July 30
William O'Quinn	28	D	captured July 30

Information contained in this table came from Compiled Service Records as summarized by Louis H. Manarin, *North Carolina Troops: 1861–1865, A Roster*, vol. II, pp. 98–177. (See Appendix for more information on the men listed above, page 398.)

The opposing armies settled into uncomfortable lines on each side of the Rappahannock River. R. E. Lee and Stuart expected Meade to attack at any time, but the Union resolve to attack was mired in politics. When Meade had failed to destroy the Army of Northern Virginia before it was able to retreat across the Potomac on July 14, President Lincoln let it be known he felt the war could have been won, then and there. He verbalized his suspicions of "bad faith" or worse on the part of Meade — the President made it clear he was very dissatisfied with the outcome. Meade heard of Lincoln's dissatisfaction and offered his resignation. Of course, Lincoln, could not fire the general who had delivered the victory at Gettysburg, so he did not accept the resignation. This situation festered and began to manifest itself in the decision about when to attack R. E. Lee's army. Lincoln and Meade tap-danced around image and responsibility for the next attack on Lee for several days.[18]

Finally on August 1, Meade notified Lincoln through Halleck that Buford's cavalry had crossed the Rappahannock River at 10:00 A.M. and had engaged Stuart's cavalry. Meade claimed to have driven Jones's and Hampton's cavalry brigades back toward Culpeper Court House into A. P. Hill's line. At which time Buford backed off and settled in between the Rappahannock and Brandy Station. On August 3, R. E. Lee moved Longstreet and A. P. Hill from Culpeper Court House across the Rapidan. He had previously moved Ewell's corps from Madison to south of the Rapidan. The Army of Northern Virginia's line was south of the Rapidan by August 4. Meade was correct in his earlier assumption, R. E. Lee did avoid a general engagement with the Union army between the rivers; instead, he dropped below the Rapidan to a more defensible position.[19]

Once R. E. Lee had his infantry settled below the Rapidan, he wrote Stuart at Culpeper Court House requesting that the cavalry remain there. In his words, "If we leave Culpeper, the enemy will enter it. If you can hold it without sacrificing your men, it will be well. So long as you remain, your supplies can be forwarded by rail to the Court-House.... If you are forced back, it will be best to come back to the rivers, where you can get good grazing." It was clear, R. E. Lee simply wanted to keep the enemy between Brandy Station and the Rappahannock as long as the cost was not too great. That was the cavalry's job — uncomfortable most of the time and dangerous from time to time.[20]

Chambliss's command was part of the front line from Brandy Station to Mountain Run on August 4, when Colonel R. L. T. Beale of the 9th Virginia recorded that an advance on their position was made by some cavalrymen from John Buford's division. Buford, on the other hand, reported that "This afternoon the enemy made an advance, with a strong force of cavalry (say 2,000) and six guns, for the purpose of seeing what we were about." Buford went on to describe the action as follows, "He drove my picket line back about 1,500 yards, when the division came up, and in turn drove him nearly 2 miles. My picket line to-night is 800 yards in advance of where it was yesterday. The enemy's reconnaissance was an utter failure. My casualties are trifling, say 5 to 10." There was a small fight, involving thousands of men, resulting in few casualties, and accomplishing nothing for either side.[21]

Aside from such infrequent clashes, the men on both picket lines maintained an uneasy peace. For instance, a young man in Jones's brigade characterized the atmosphere in these words: "This state of things remained for several weeks. Not a shot was fired during all that time, and so well-acquainted did the pickets of each army become, that it was not an uncommon thing to see them marching across the fields to meet each other and exchange greetings, and often the Confederates traded tobacco for coffee and sugar.... This got to be so common that Gen. Stuart had to issue an order forbidding it."[22]

Routine picket duty south of the Rappahannock continued until September 13, when Meade made another push south to confront R. E. Lee's army. By midday, Alfred Pleasonton notified Meade that his cavalry had "...advanced as far as General Buford did on the 4th August last."[23]

Though the Confederate cavalry in front of Pleasonton had officially been reorganized by September 13, regiments had not yet been fully shuffled into their new brigades — the 2nd North Carolina was still physically with Chambliss, in W. H. F. Lee's brigade. Chambliss's command had rotated to a position between Brandy Station and Culpeper Court House by the morning of the 13th, and Colonel R. L. T. Beale of the 9th Virginia was in temporary command of the brigade in Chambliss's absence. Jones's brigade, under the temporary command of Lunsford L. Lomax, was on the front line, facing Kelley's Ford.[24]

Stuart had received advanced warning; he knew the enemy was coming across the river early that morning, yet he did not take to the field. Instead he left L. L. Lomax in charge of the engagement. However, Stuart prepare for his uninvited guests. He ordered all regiments to have their camps packed up and to move their wagons, ambulances, and camp equipment to the rear, toward the Rapidan. One of the messages sent by Stuart reached R. L. T. Beale at Chambliss's headquarters at 3:30 A.M., and instructed him to have his pickets communicate with Lomax.[25]

Lomax's brigade stood in front of Buford's cavalrymen when the latter crossed the river early that morning. We can assume Stuart passed along R. E. Lee's instructions of September 4, not to sacrifice his men. One member of Lomax's 6th Virginia regiment recalled the morning in these words:

As they advanced we gradually fell back, and when we had retreated about a mile, they began firing on us.... We returned the fire, and began to dispute their passage. But as they had a much larger force we gradually released the territory, fighting as we retreated.

My part of the line carried me directly through the streets of Culpeper, and the fighting in and around the town was the heaviest that we encountered.[26]

At the break of dawn, R. L. T. Beale moved the 2nd North Carolina and the rest of Chambliss's command forward and set skirmishers to the right of Lomax's men and in front of Kilpatrick's advancing cavalrymen. A member of R. L. T. Beale's command also noted the swift and superior force coming at them from the river, so they too began an orderly pullback to Culpeper Court House. One Confederate described the scene in these words: "In this movement, a heavy fusillade was kept up by the skirmish lines and artillery on each side." It was during this retreat that R. L. T. Beale was hit in the leg — the shot splintered the bone and he had to be removed from the field. Momentarily, W. H. F. Lee's brigade was again without a commander, but after some brief confusion they fought on.[27]

The Confederate cavalrymen were able to slow the advancing Federal force just long enough for the last train to leave the station in Culpeper carrying their wounded and supplies south. As the train pulled out, fighting continued through town. Then dropping south of town, the 2nd North Carolina and its brigade, alongside Lomax's, continued to make charges into the advancing enemy cavalry when possible, but each time Union infantry soon appeared, and the Confederates fell back again.[28] The intensity of the Confederate resistance during their withdrawal to the Rapidan is well expressed by a Union brigade commander in Kilpatrick's cavalry division.

After gaining this position and the town of Culpeper, I was fired on by a battery posted in thick woods on the left of the railroad, and ordered the Fifth New York Cavalry to charge and take it. They charged most bravely, but the ground being bad, were much broken, and on gaining the crest of the hill were attacked by a much larger body of cavalry and driven back. They were gallantly rallied by General Kilpatrick in person, under heavy fire, and advanced again to the front. At that moment I was on the right of the railroad, and ordering the Second New York to come in on the right of the Fifth.

I rode over and led the Fifth again into the woods. Here we met with General Custer [commanding the Second Brigade], who was heavily engaged, and did all that men could do to advance. We were, however, overpowered by numbers and the Second New York were flanked and their extreme right driven in. At this juncture the affair looked badly and I feared the command would be driven back, but I brought up the First [West] Virginia Cavalry, the last regiment at my command, which had only the day before been supplied with Spencer's rifles....

This timely re-enforcement changed the event and the rebels were driven back in confusion, followed by my brigade through the woods and across the fields.[29]

In one of his messages to Meade on September 13, Pleasonton acknowledged the Confederate cavalrymen's resistance when he reported "The enemy are falling back slowly. We are pushing them as fast as possible." As decimated as Chambliss's command was, it clearly did not give way easily.[30]

It was near nightfall when Lomax's and Chambliss's commands crossed the Rapidan and moved into their own infantry line. Pleasonton's cavalry arrived at the Rapidan River early on the morning of September 14. They took strong positions at the Somerville and Raccoon Fords, but they could not effect a crossing because the Confederate cavalry, supported by infantry and artillery, was too strong on the opposite shore. By September 15, Pleasonton informed Meade that the enemy force across the Rapidan was even stronger, and that under heavy fire Buford had withdrawn into some woods. Even after infantry support for Pleasonton's cavalry arrived on September 17, the Federals found the riverside too hot and pulled back a safe distance.[31]

Gouverneur K. Warren with his Second Corps of infantry remained near Buford's line only briefly, then pulled back and occupied Culpeper Court House. Meade continued to send his army across the Rappahannock and settled them around Culpeper on September 16. He sent two corps forward to the Rapidan but did not attempt a crossing. In Meade's words, "An examination of the enemy's position proved it entirely out of the question to attempt to force the passage of the river in his immediate front." Meade then began the process of planning a flank movement against the Army of Northern Virginia.[32]

While picketing the Rappahannock River and holding Culpeper Court House in August and for the first couple of weeks in September, the 2nd North Carolina Cavalry suffered several losses. The recorded losses are summarized in the following table.

Combat Losses in the 2nd North Carolina Cavalry from August to September 16, 1863

Trooper	Age	Co.	Fate
George R. Britton	27	E	captured, Aug. 21
John Lomis		C	captured, Sept. 13
James M. Gordon	26	I	captured, Sept. 16
Comodore G. Muse	20	I	captured, Sept. 16

Information contained in this table came from Compiled Service Records as summarized by Louis H. Manarin, *North Carolina Troops: 1861–1865, A Roster*, vol. II, pp. 98–177. (See Appendix for more information on the men listed above, page 398.)

Cavalry Reorganization and Leadership Change

Before taking his army north Robert E. Lee wrote President Davis largely at the urging of J. E. B. Stuart of the need to reorganize the cavalry. Stuart felt he had an overabundance of commanders deserving of the rank of brigadier general but too few positions for them. He wanted more brigades. R. E. Lee and Stuart were also aware that with so many brigades, they could argue for a level of command between the brigades and Stuart himself. R. E. Lee proposed to Davis that two cavalry divisions be created, each led by newly-appointed major generals. They naturally had two men in mind for these jobs: Wade Hampton, who was a wealthy planter from South Carolina before the war and had demonstrated an exceptional instinct for warfare and leadership, and Fitzhugh Lee, who was above all else, politically correct in the eyes of Stuart. Fitz Lee was a Virginian, a West Pointer, and R. E. Lee's nephew. When recommending his nephew to Davis, R. E. Lee pointed out that no other cavalry officer had done "better service."[33] Once R. E. Lee's recommendations were accepted, Stuart technically had two divisions under his command and as such he was a corps commander, but he did not get promoted to Lieutenant General, a rank commensurate with his position.

R. E. Lee also recommended to Davis the creation of at least one new brigade. He argued the existing brigades were too large—not in number of men, of course, but in the number of regiments, legions, and battalions in each brigade. The new brigade would create a spot for one of the would-be brigadier generals Stuart had his eye on. Other commands would be available at the brigade level with the promotion of Wade Hampton and Fitz Lee from brigadier generals to major generals. In addition, Beverly H. Robertson had requested to be relieved of his command of the North Carolina Brigade soon after the Gettysburg Campaign. Reorganization of the cavalry offered R. E. Lee and Stuart the opportunity to relieve him of his command.[34]

Robert E. Lee requested that Hampton's former brigade be given to Colonel Matthew C. Butler of the 2nd South Carolina Cavalry, and Fitz Lee's former brigade be given to Colonel William C. Wickham of the 4th Virginia Cavalry. He also requested that Colonel Lawrence S. Baker of the 1st North Carolina Cavalry receive Robertson's North Carolina Brigade. Colonel Lunsford L. Lomax was recommended for the new brigade.

The reorganization of the Cavalry Corps of the Army of Northern Virginia was now completed. (See table on following page for the regiments and brigades.)[35]

THE NORTH CAROLINA CAVALRY BRIGADE

Even though a North Carolina brigade under the command of Beverly H. Robertson had existed before the Gettysburg Campaign, it was not very inclusive. Most notably, it did not include the 1st and 2nd North Carolina cavalries. There had been discontent among North Carolinians, who for various reasons felt they would be better treated and appreciated in their own unit, and these feelings were made known publicly. For instance as early as February of 1863, while stationed on the Rappahannock,

---

Stuart's Cavalry Corps, September 9, 1863

Wade Hampton's First Cavalry Division

W. E. Jones's Brigade (replaced by Thomas Rosser on October 10, 1863)
    6th Virginia — J. S. Green
    7th Virginia — R. H. Dulany
    12th Virginia — A. W. Harman
    35th Virginia Battalion — E. V. White

L. S. Baker's Brigade (replaced by James B. Gordon on October 5, 1863)
    1st North Carolina — J. B. Gordon
    2nd North Carolina — W. G. Robinson*
    4th North Carolina — D. D. Ferebee
    5th North Carolina — S. B. Evens

M. C. Butler's Brigade (commanded by Pierce M. B. Young)
    Cobb's Georgia Legion — P. M. B. Young
    Jeff. Davis Miss. Legion — J. F. Waring
    Phillips Georgia Legion — W. W. Rich
    2nd South Carolina — T. J. Lipscomb

Fitzhugh Lee's Second Cavalry Division

W. H. F. Lee's Brigade (commanded by J. R. Chambliss)
    1st South Carolina — J. L. Black
    9th Virginia — R. L. T. Beale
    10th Virginia — J. L. Davis
    13th Virginia — J. R. Chambliss

L. L. Lomax's Brigade
    1st Maryland Battalion — R. Brown
    5th Virginia — T. L. Rosser
    11th Virginia — O. R. Funsten
    15th Virginia — W. B. Ball

W. C. Wickham's Brigade
    1st Virginia — R. W. Carter
    2nd Virginia — T. T. Munford
    3rd Virginia — T. H. Owen
    4th Virginia — W. H. Payne

*William G. Robinson was officially commander of the 2nd North Carolina Cavalry, but he was seldom present, and Clinton M. Andrews was in command once again at the time of reorganization.

---

members of the 1st North Carolina Cavalry sent an open letter, to the State Journal that was reprinted for wider circulation. It was titled "Our Cavalry—Honor To Whom It Is Due," and included the following comments:

It is the desire, Mr. Editor, of nearly every officer of this regiment that North Carolina should have a brigade of cavalry, commanded by a North Carolinian General. We have enough cavalry to make a splendid brigade and a number of competent men to command it. Its regiments are now scattered over Virginia and North Carolina, with scarcely more than a regiment to a brigade, and they are commanded by officers not of our State. We feel that we could do better service, be better cared for, and more justice done us by being brigaded together.[36]

R. E. Lee was responding to such well-known and longstanding discontent when he pressed for the expanded North Carolina brigade and the need to have it commanded by a North Carolinian. Its first commander was the newly appointed Brigadier General Lawrence Baker. Baker was the senior North Carolina cavalryman and the choice of R. E. Lee and J. E. B. Stuart, but he was seriously wounded before he had a chance to take command of the brigade. Colonel Dennis D. Ferebee was the next senior North Carolinian in the brigade, and he assumed temporary command of the brigade upon its formation. According to a communication passed along by Major W. H. Cheek, of the 1st North Carolina, the 1st, 2nd, 4th, and 5th North Carolina Cavalries were already operating as a brigade for the action at Jack's Shop on September 22, 1863—Ferebee was in command of the North Carolina Brigade for that fight. (The 1st North Carolina was under the temporary command of Lieutenant Colonel Ruffin while James B. Gordon was temporarily commanding Butler's brigade.)[37]

James B. Gordon of the 1st North Carolina Cavalry was assigned temporary command of Hampton's former brigade during August and most of September, pending M. C. Butler's return to service—later P. M. B. Young was selected for the temporary commander of Butler's brigade and Gordon was returned to the North Carolina brigade. By late September, R. E. Lee had grown concerned about Lawrence Baker's fitness for active duty, so he gave him the command of the North Carolina cavalry regiments still in North Carolina, and sought a permanent commander for the North Carolina Cavalry Brigade in Stuart's cavalry. D. D. Ferebee of the 4th North Carolina was then still in temporary command of the brigade, but R. E. Lee passed over him and gave the command to the more ambitious and aggressive James B.

Gordon. Gordon accepted his commission on October 5, 1863 along with the North Carolina Cavalry Brigade.[38] Thus, in the month of September 1863, the 2nd North Carolina Cavalry found itself in a new all North Carolina brigade, with a new brigadier general who was also a North Carolinian. It must have felt a little more like home.

THE 2ND NORTH CAROLINA CAVALRY REGIMENT

Command of the 2nd North Carolina Cavalry was apparently a difficult position to hold. After Colonel Solomon Williams was killed on June 9, 1863, the regiment was temporarily led by Lieutenant Colonel W. F. Payne of the 4th Virginia until he was captured on June 30. Captain Graham of Company K, 2nd North Carolina was more or less in command from Hanover to Gettysburg until he was wounded on July 3. Lieutenant Joseph Baker of Company D was apparently in command of the handful of survivors during the retreat to Williamsport. At Williamsport, Captain James W. Strange of Company D rejoined the regiment and was identified as the senior officer in the field, so he was in command until Major Clinton M. Andrews rejoined the regiment and resumed temporary command — Andrews was the regiment's temporary commander before W. F. Payne was assigned to the task for a short while late in 1862 and again in June of 1863.

The position of permanent commander of the 2nd North Carolina Cavalry was offered to James B. Gordon of the 1st North Carolina on July 13, 1863, but he declined the offer on July 23, hoping for a more important command — which he got. He became Colonel of the 1st North Carolina, and soon afterward brigadier general of the North Carolina brigade.[39]

William G. Robinson, who was captured in the fiasco at Gillett's Farm back in North Carolina on April 13, 1862, had returned from prison and was promoted to colonel on September 9, 1863 to rank from July 23 — the day Gordon declined the command. W. G. Robinson was colonel of the 2nd North Carolina for several months until he requested a transfer to the Navy Department before May of 1864. Robinson was not physically in command of the regiment long enough to make a difference — according to William P. Roberts of Company C, "In August, 1863 ... after the transfer of Colonel Gordon, Major C. M. Andrews, late Captain Company B, became Colonel and commanded the regiment till June, 1864."[40] (Gordon was technically commander of the 2nd North Carolina Cavalry for ten days.) Clinton M. Andrews was promoted to colonel February 18, 1864 and finally took command of the regiment on more than a temporary basis.

Shortly after being pushed back behind the Rapidan River on September 13, Stuart's cavalry regiments moved into their new brigades where called for by the reorganization. The North Carolina Cavalry Brigade was pulled together under the temporary command of Colonel Dennis Ferebee, and the 2nd North Carolina under the temporary command of Clinton M. Andrews when called into action September 22, 1863.

The Fight at Jack's Shop, September 22

On September 16, General Meade had acknowledged the only way to proceed against R. E. Lee's army behind the Rapidan River was with a flank attack. Orders went out on the afternoon of the 20th to have the cavalry explore the Robertson and Rapidan Rivers above Rapidan Station. An additional message read, "The object of the reconnaissance is to ascertain the position and force of the enemy between those rivers and along the Rapidan, the number and character of the roads leading to the Rapidan..., and of the character of the fords.... It is particularly desirable to learn the character of the south bank of the Rapidan along the road leading to Orange Court House from Burronsville, since it is along that road that the army may march, should Orange Court-House be approached from above." Early on September 21, Meade had Pleasonton put Kilpatrick's and Buford's cavalry divisions in motion. The next morning, Buford reported to Pleasonton that he and Kilpatrick had reached Madison Court House (about 15 miles southwest of Culpeper Court House) before sundown the day before. Kilpatrick arrived first and had to drive off a handful of Confederate cavalrymen posted in the town. Kilpatrick then moved toward Baronsville and on to Liberty Mills on the Rapidan to examine the roads and fords in that direction. Buford took a different route from Madison and planned to connect with Kilpatrick at Liberty Mills.[41]

The routes taken by the Union cavalry divisions led directly into the area held by Hampton's division of Stuart's cavalry. As part of that division the newly formed North Carolina brigade, including the 2nd North Carolina, was resting directly on Buford's and Kilpatrick's paths. On September 20, the day Pleasonton ordered his cavalry divisions into action, the Federal signal corps intercepted a short message from Colonel D. D. Ferebee (temporary commander of the North Carolina brigade) containing these words: "Send wagons of Second North Carolina Cavalry to them to-day near Robertson's River."[42] Buford planned to concentrate his and Kilpatrick's cavalry divisions in precisely that area on the night of September 22, after having made their examination of the roads and rivers in the surrounding area. Buford knew Stuart had cavalry between Robertson's River and the Rapidan, with a small force of Confederate infantry at Liberty Mills. Yet early on the morning of the 22nd, Buford and Kilpatrick led their divisions into the hornet's nest.[43]

By the time Buford and Kilpatrick approached Madison Court House on the afternoon of September 21, Stuart knew he was about to confront a strong Union probe on the left wing of the Army of Northern Virginia. Stuart also knew his job was to keep the enemy cavalry out of the area or drive them out before they learned too much. By the time he collected his troops, it was too late to keep them out, so he had to engage them and drive them out as soon as possible. Stuart had to confront the Union's First and Third Divisions with Hampton's new, not yet cohesive, and very depleted division. Fitz Lee and his division were on the right wing of R. E. Lee's army, while Hampton was still recovering from severe wounds he received at Gettysburg. Consequently, Stuart rode with Hampton's division and its temporary leadership. During the night, Stuart sent orders to the three brigades of Hampton's division instructing them to be in the saddle at the break of day on September 22. As indicated, at that time Hampton's division consisted of: W. E. Jones's brigade, under the temporary command of Colonel Funsten;[44] Butler's brigade, under the temporary command of James B. Gordon ; and Laurence S. Baker's North Carolina brigade, under the temporary command of Dennis D. Ferebee.

D. D. Ferebee's North Carolina command consisted of the 1st North Carolina Cavalry under the temporary command of Lieutenant Colonel Thomas Ruffin; the 4th North Carolina, Ferebee's regiment, was under a temporary commander because Ferebee was commanding the brigade; the 5th North Carolina was commanded by Lieutenant Colonel S. B. Evens; and the 2nd North Carolina Cavalry was under the temporary command of Clinton M. Andrews.

Ferebee led the small North Carolina brigade into battle that day with approximately 500 mounted men. Even the 1st North Carolina could only mount around 130 men on September 22. The other regiments in the brigade, on average, had about the same number — the 2nd North Carolina Cavalry being by far the smallest. The North Carolina cavalry regiments had not yet recovered from the devastation they experienced during the Gettysburg Campaign. When they took to the road, Ferebee's command was followed by about 1,500 men from Jones's and Butler's brigades. Stuart and his band of about 2,000 horsemen were all alerted and on the road at sunup.[45]

Stuart collected the cavalrymen of Hampton's division just outside Madison Court House and headed for Liberty Mills, following Buford's trail. He rode at the head of the column with Ferebee and the North Carolina brigade. The 1st North Carolina Cavalry led the column, followed by the 2nd North Carolina, then the 5th and 4th North Carolina cavalries.[46]

At about 1:00 A.M., the North Carolina regiments received orders to be in the saddle by daybreak. Lieutenant Colonel Ruffin rode at the head of the 1st North Carolina at Stuart's side, about 100 yards behind the advance guard. When they passed a small community called Jack's Shop, Ruffin had to stop and have his horse attended to — Major W. H. Cheek temporarily took his place at the head of the 1st North Carolina. The company in advance was proceeding cautiously with sabers drawn, expecting to encounter Buford's cavalry at any moment. Stuart had instructed the advance to charge the enemy at first sight. Cheek was instructed to follow and support their charge with the remainder of the regiment. Just beyond Jack's Shop, Cheek saw his advance guard take up the gallop. He had the rest of the 1st North Carolina draw sabers and strike the same gait. Just before they broke into a full charge, Stuart yelled to Major Cheek, "Be careful, and do not run into an ambush."[47] Stuart probably was concerned about sending a small regiment under the command of a Major not well known to him directly at Buford's cavalry division, but he nonetheless sent the Major off with a word of caution. Stuart then turned off the road to wait for the other regiments in the North Carolina brigade to pull up.

Major Cheek and the 1st North Carolina Cavalry drove Buford's rear guard for a short distance before they pulled up. They had come to "a skirt of pines, extending on either side of the road." Across the road and in the pines Buford had a strong line of dismounted cavalrymen. The power of suggestion from Stuart's parting words or reality caused Cheek to fear he was approaching an ambush, so he wisely halted his men and remembered his only instructions; "…do not run into an ambush." He ordered his men to "Return sabres!" "Unsling carbines!" "Fire on the enemy!"[48]

With his men engaged, Cheek, rode back to Stuart and was instructed to dismount his regiment, form a line in the field to the right of the pike, and then charge the Union skirmish line.[49] Then the 5th North Carolina was moved up and was also dismounted and joined the front skirmish line. Both the 1st and 5th North Carolina made several attempts to drive Buford's line back, but it was too strong.

In face of such a formidable line of mounted and dismounted brigades and heavy artillery fire, the 1st and 5th North Carolina were called back to where Stuart had established his main line with the 2nd and 4th North Carolina as well as portions of Butler's and Jones's brigades. The fight raged for several hours, and even though Buford could not be moved, he did not seem eager to press his numerical advantage with a charge.[50]

Stuart's command fought under heavy skirmish and artillery fire, before Stuart met with Ferebee, Gordon, and others and decided the enemy was too strong to take. So as the artillery fire became more threatening, they pulled their main line back 200 yards to reduce the heat and wait until Buford made his intentions clearer (Buford was probably waiting for Kilpatrick to arrive). The opposing lines continued their engagement in what Private Paul B. Means of the 5th North Carolina termed "one of the very fiercest fights of the war." The artillery fire continued throughout.[51]

As the North Carolina regiments were being overwhelmed in their front, they felt Buford's troopers coming at their flank as well, so they dropped back. By the time they had pulled back about a mile, the men of the 1st and 5th North Carolina heard firing coming from behind them. At about the same time, the Confederates came into a field and saw their artillery posted on a small hill.[52]

In the words of Stuart's adjutant-general, H. B. McClellan:

While Stuart was thus engaged in a severe fight he received information that a large body of the enemy's cavalry had turned his left and had gained possession of the road in his rear, thus cutting him off from the ford at Liberty Mills. It was necessary to withdraw from Buford to meet this attack; but the moment that the withdrawal commenced Buford pressed on Stuart's lines with vigor. It seemed for a time that Stuart had at last been caught where he could not escape serious damage. Kilpatrick had already thrown a body of dismounted men across the road between Stuart and the ford, and he was thus enclosed in front and rear. Buford pressed so heavily that several mounted charges were necessary to hold him in check. The battle was soon brought within the compass of an open field, near the center of which a little hill gave position for the Confederate artillery. The scene was now extremely animated. Stuart's artillery was firing in both directions from the hill, and within sight of each other his regiments were charging in opposite directions.[53]

As mentioned, when Buford was sure of Kilpatrick's presence, he moved on the North Carolina brigade with full force. Ferebee's command began to move into a small open field in which they initially felt exposed, but from which they almost immediately could see upon a small hill, Stuart and his Horse Artillery. Stuart was on horseback orchestrating McGregor's Battery in two, sometimes three directions simultaneously—two guns on Buford's line and two on Kilpatrick's. With the men of the 1st and 5th under the shelter of the artillery, Stuart felt they could hold. So he and his staff rode back to the rest of his division— where, the 2nd and 4th North Carolina with part of Butler's and Jones's brigades had been holding Kilpatrick's advance on their rear and flanks.[54]

The 2nd and 4th North Carolina cavalries had fallen back and were turned to meet Kilpatrick at their rear and on their flanks. Captain James W. Strange of the 2nd North Carolina described the situation in these words, "We fought them at great disadvantage for several hours until our ammunition gave out, and that, together with the enemy's making a flank movement, compelled us to fall back; in doing so we encountered a party in our rear." Stuart knew he was surrounded as did the eager Union commanders. Stuart sent a member of his staff along the line to make sure every man understood the seriousness of their situation. Stuart's message to his men was reportedly simple, "Boys it's a fight to captivity, death or victory." To which at least one North Carolinian replied, "We'll go out of here if there isn't but one of us left." And the others cheered the sentiment.[55]

At that point, Stuart was looking for an escape route through the rear, through Kilpatrick's lines. If Kilpatrick's command could simply have held, with Buford pressing the 1st and 5th North Carolina back, Stuart would have lost his guns and perhaps a good portion of Hampton's division. The Confederate cavalrymen, however, kept pressing, and exchanged charges and counter-charges until Kilpatrick's line began to waver. Finally, Stuart ordered two regiments (very likely the 2nd and 4th North Carolina) to make a determined charge and break Kilpatrick's line. H. B. McClellan of Stuart's staff remembered: "One of these regiments charged, mounted, up to the fence behind which Kilpatrick's men were dismounted, threw down the fence in their faces, and cleared the road for Stuart's retreat." From that point on, Kilpatrick's line began to crumble, cavalrymen from all three of Hampton's brigades participated in the next charge. Captain Strange of the 2nd North Carolina described it as a "...spirited charge, made by portions of the whole division, soon put them [Kilpatrick's cavalrymen] to flight." Having broken the Union line, Stuart withdrew rapidly from the engagement with Buford, and retired across the Rapidan at Liberty Mills, where he was soon reinforced by Wilcox's division of infantry."[56]

While the 1st and 5th North Carolina cavalries still struggled to hold Buford's troops, a member of the 1st North Carolina gratefully noted, that the 2nd and 4th North Carolina had punched their way through Kilpatrick's line, "...we see a crowd of blue jackets coming in divested of arms, canteens and spurs. Colonel Ferebee, with a part of his command [the 2nd and 4th regiments] and a miscellaneous crowd from every command, had charged and cut the Yankee line." The trooper from the 1st North Carolina went on to recall, the Yankees drew back, "...and we made our way quietly to the river."[57]

Once pushed across, Kilpatrick became engaged with Confederate infantry.[58] By the time the 1st and 5th North Carolina regiments got to the river, they were able to see Kilpatrick's command on the other side of the Rapidan. Kilpatrick's command was unable to countercharge in the face of the Confederate infantry, so they apparently simply attempted to regroup and hold their ground. Stuart, however, not content to have escaped encirclement, regrouped his cavalrymen for another go at Kilpatrick. George S. Dewey of the 1st North Carolina described the final fight of the day in these words:

When we arrived there we beheld another large column of the enemy [Kilpatrick's Division] across the river and about two miles above. We crossed at Liberty Mills and took a road leading to them. The evening was far advanced ... yet they must be driven back before night. We found a body of our infantry deploying along a fence and through a field, holding them in check. We went to their left, under a ridge of hills, into a wood.... We came out of the woods to the left and in front of the infantry.

The Yankees were prepared for us, and opened a heavy fire of artillery with their usual accuracy. General Stuart now orders the charge. The last rays of the sun are glistening on our sabers as we raise the warcry and ply the rowels of our weary steeds. They participate in the excitement and, forgetting their weariness, dash forward. It is a long charge, over hills and gullies.

The enemy has limbered up and taken his artillery back to a safer position; further on we see a large body of cavalry, who open on us with their rifles. We make for them through a shower of grape and rifle balls.

Just before we reach them they break and run, leaving an impassable branch between us. At the same time a body of their sharpshooters open on us from the right. We turn on them and close the day by capturing all who made a stand — twenty-four in number."[59]

The charge Stuart ordered probably included most, if not all, of the mounted men under his command that day — including the 2nd North Carolina Cavalry.

Apparently Buford had pushed as far as the river but had been unable to see the trouble Kilpatrick was having because he did not pursue the 1st and 5th North Carolina across the Rapidan.[60]

As darkness came, though Stuart had had a close call earlier, he could end the day with a small sense of success. Kilpatrick had had a hard day and ended it with his troops scattered and in retreat. Buford obviously felt better about the day; he reported that he had met Stuart's cavalry and had "whipped" and "dispersed" them, and that his reconnaissance mission was a success.[61]

John Buford did not mention in his report that he and Kilpatrick had encircled J. E. B. Stuart and Hampton's division, but were unable to capture the big prize — perhaps Stuart himself. He did not report that Stuart's troopers were able to fight their way out of near annihilation and regroup to scatter Kilpatrick's command at the end of the day.

Buford was able to report that he took about 100 prisoners, perhaps 15 wagons, and a small herd of beef-cattle. In addition, he was once again able to report that "The casualties in the First Division are trifling." Buford also noted that Kilpatrick's losses were more severe.[62]

Stuart did not file a report on the North Carolina brigade's activity, so it is difficult to determine the Confederate losses. Nonetheless, the brigade sustained heavy losses in the fighting around Jack's Shop. One estimate put the brigade's losses at ninety-two men — out of only about 500 men carried into the battle. The 1st North Carolina was estimated to have had about 130 mounted men on the field that day and to have lost 33 of them.[63]

The 2nd North Carolina, which was still the smallest regiment in the brigade, also took heavy losses that day. The recorded losses are listed on the following table.

For a couple of weeks after the fight at Jack's Shop, the men of the 2nd North Carolina Cavalry, along with the other regiments in the North Carolina brigade, settled into more or less routine picket and scouting duties. On oc-

Combat Losses in the 2nd North Carolina Cavalry, Jack's Shop on September 22, 1863

Trooper	Age	Co.	Fate
William B. McCabe		C	killed in action
Jonathan Carter	18	D	captured
Neill A. Wilks	22	D	mortally wounded
Lawson Campbell	38	E	captured
Robert H. Haybarger	33	E	mortally wounded
Pinkney A. Tatum		F	captured
Joseph G. Liscomb	26	H	captured
Jacob A. Matthews	25	H	wounded & captured
H. E. Taylor	24	H	captured
Benjamin Joshua Vincent		H	captured
Joseph H. Wheeler	35	H	captured
Joseph H. Dixon	24	I	killed in action
Henry T. Bowling		K	wounded in action

Information contained in this table came from Compiled Service Records as summarized by Louis H. Manarin, *North Carolina Troops: 1861–1865, A Roster*, vol. II, pp. 98–177. (See Appendix for more information on the men listed above, page 399.)

casion this duty took them some distance from their camp. For instance, on September 27, 1863 the Union commander of the Third Army Corps, W. H. French, reported that "The enemy have a force of cavalry not far in rear of the Sixth Corps, and send daily scouting parties behind us, between our line and Hazel River." General French also reported that a Federal officer who had been seriously wounded was shot by a Lieutenant in the 2nd North Carolina Cavalry — William B. Tidwell of Company A.[64] One of the 2nd North Carolina's squadrons may have been among those cavalrymen operating behind Union lines up near the Hazel River, because scouting parties were routinely sent in several directions from the regiment's camp.

Most scouting parties received assignments that kept them closer to camp however. One such instance was reported by Captain James W. Strange of Company D in an open letter to his hometown newspaper when he wrote, "I was sent off with 20 men on a country expedition yesterday [the latter part of September]; went as far as Madison C. H. and captured 2 Yankees, all that we saw.... We had 2 days hard marching and are today resting ourselves and horses." Private Lockhart wrote his sister on October 2 and gave us the general location of their camp and description of their duty in these words: "Our regiment goes on picket every fourth day: we go on picket a Monday morning and will stay on until Tuesday morning." Captain Strange ended his report with this assessment: "Our troops here are in good spirits and confident of success whenever Meade sees fit to make his advance across the Rapidan."[65]

While the cavalrymen of the 2nd North Carolina and the rest of Stuart's cavalry kept an eye on Meade's army south of the Rappahannock River, R. E. Lee was growing increasingly aware of Meade's concentration of forces for a move on the Army of Northern Virginia's left wing. The Union cavalry probe on September 22 was confirmation of R. E. Lee's expectations. He wrote President Davis the following day, pointing out the extent to which Meade was building his force just north of Culpeper Court House. R. E. Lee wrote him again on the 27th and opened his letter with these words: "The enemy has made no serious advance yet. All his preparations indicate that intention." By September 30, however, R. E. Lee was less certain Meade was about to attack—the Union concentration still had cavalry massed on the Confederate left, but by this time, R. E. Lee speculated that might also suggest Meade was preparing a defense.[66]

Robert E. Lee was a master of defense, and he was prepared—but he had little patience for postponing action. If Meade would not attack, he would.

The Bristoe Campaign, October 9–20

In September, Robert E. Lee had lost most of Longstreet's command to the fighting in Tennessee, and Meade had lost the 11th and 12th corps to that theater. By early October, Meade was camped north of Culpeper Court House waiting for some of the troops to return, and waiting for new draftees to fill his ranks. While waiting, he had two Corps placed as far south as the Rapidan River, and he was still considering attacking R. E. Lee by turning his left flank, but Lee decided to attack Meade and moved first.[67]

R. E. Lee collected Ewell's and A. P. Hill's corps near Madison Court House on the morning of October 9 and started them for Culpeper Court House. They were heading for Meade's right flank, which, R. E. Lee hoped, would cause Meade to withdraw allowing Lee to hit his enemy while on the move and do serious damage. With so many infantrymen in motion, one might expect another epic battle, but both infantries spent most of this campaign getting into position—consequently, this campaign was largely a series of cavalry battles.[68]

Stuart left Fitz Lee's cavalry division to hold the Rapidan line and to cover the army's rear as they pulled out while he took Hampton's division (Wade Hampton was still recovering from his wounds) to the right of R. E. Lee's column shielding it from Meade's army as the Confederates moved north and east. The division led by Stuart included Gordon's North Carolina brigade, Butler's brigade (temporarily commanded by Colonel P. M. B. Young), and Jones's brigade (temporarily commanded by Colonel O. R. Funsten). Stuart collected his cavalrymen near Madison Court House and Robertson's River on the evening of October 9.[69]

The North Carolina brigade went into the campaign under the command of James B. Gordon. (Gordon replaced Baker as commander of the North Carolina Cavalry Brigade on October 5, 1863.)[70] Colonel Thomas Ruffin replaced Gordon as the commander of the 1st North Carolina Cavalry Regiment; the 2nd North Carolina's commander, Lieutenant Colonel William G. Robinson, still had not returned from his capture some 18 months before, so the regiment was once again under the able, temporary leadership of Major Clinton M. Andrews; Colonel D. D. Ferebee returned to command the 4th North Carolina once Gordon assumed command of the brigade; and Lieutenant Colonel Stephen Evans commanded the 5th North Carolina Cavalry.

Stuart led Hampton's division directly toward Culpeper Court House near where the enemy was camped in considerable force. Meade was surprised to hear the Army of Northern Virginia was mobilized early on October 9, but he was quick to respond. By 6:30 A.M., Alfred Pleasonton was directed to move his cavalry and find out what R. E. Lee was up to. Pleasonton was instructed to mobilize D. McM. Gregg's division "as rapidly as possible and march day and night until he reaches Culpeper Court House." Judson Kilpatrick was ordered to have his division watch Madison Court House and the roads leading to Woodville and Culpeper Court House — he was instructed to attack and impede the progress of the enemy if they move up from Madison Court House. John Buford was ordered to head for Germanna Ford, further east on the Rapidan River, and to force a crossing, join forces with General Newton's infantry command, and then turn westward and follow the enemy.[71]

Kilpatrick was in position to observe R. E. Lee's infantry collect around Madison Court House on the 9th and camp there for the night. However, he was not certain of the whereabouts of Stuart's cavalry. The positions of the two cavalries and their orders determined that when Stuart moved Hampton's division from Madison Court House toward Culpeper Court House, he would clash with Kilpatrick's division; and when Buford moved his division down to the Rapidan, he would encounter Fitz Lee's division.[72]

At sunup October 10, Stuart's cavalry left the Madison Court House area and moved directly for James City — he was leading his brigades directly at the enemies' strength in order to hold their attention while R. E. Lee put his infantry in motion. Gordon's North Carolina brigade moved out first on the road for Russell's Ford on the Robertson River.[73]

The 4th North Carolina Cavalry was in the front with the other three North Carolina regiments close behind. As they approached Russell's Ford, they encountered Union pickets, and the 4th North Carolina pushed them back into their support which consisted of an infantry regiment (the 120th New York Infantry) and a small force of Kilpatrick's cavalry. Stuart had Gordon dismount a portion of his men and attack the enemy in their front — he was instructed to follow closely with the remainder of the North Carolina brigade. At the same time, Stuart led P. M. B. Young and his command through woods to hit the Union force in its right flank. The Union troops had drawn up in line of battle, but when hit from two directions, they broke and pulled back. Stuart reported that between 75 and 100 excellent arms were taken and as many prisoners. Once across the Robertson River, Oliver R. Funsten's command was detached as the advance guard and moved with the infantry. Ewell instructed Funsten to move up and hold Griffensburg on the Sperryville and Culpeper Court House road. He moved out ahead of A. P. Hill and Ewell. James B. Gordon's and Young's cavalrymen pursued the scattered Federals along the road to James City, where they encountered Kilpatrick's main line of defense.[74]

Kilpatrick had Brigadier General George A. Custer at James City; Colonel J. Irvin Gregg (of the Second Cavalry Division) on Custer's left; and General Henry E. Davies's brigade on his right extending as far as the Sperryville pike. As Stuart approached James City with Young's and Gordon's brigades, Kilpatrick pulled his brigades out of town, back to a strong position among the hills overlooking the town. The Union line included artillery and infantrymen from French's division as well as Kilpatrick's cavalrymen. This time, Stuart placed Young's command in front of the Union line, and the North Carolina Brigade on their right. He brought up two pieces of artillery from Young's command to answer the steady artillery fire from around six Federal guns. Sharpshooter as well as artillery fire was steady until nightfall. Stuart did not attack; his instructions at that point were to keep the enemy off the infantry's flanks. The Confederates felt that could best be accomplished with demonstrations rather than all-out attacks. After dark, Stuart ordered his men into bivouac on their line of battle.[75]

While Kilpatrick's men were engaged at James City on the 10th, H. E. Davies was positioned far enough to the Union right to observe the Confederate infantry column moving west of him toward Woodville which would threaten Meade's right flank — Meade learned of this on October 10, when Pleasonton sent the following message: "It would appear the enemy's infantry are much nearer than we had supposed, and looks more like a fight here in the morning."[76]

Once Meade knew R. E. Lee's army was attempting to turn his flank, he began to withdraw his infantry along the Orange & Alexandria Railroad, in order to keep R. E. Lee's forces from taking his rear. By the time R. E. Lee got to Culpeper Court House, Meade was gone.

Meanwhile Buford and his cavalry division left Stevensburg, just south of Brandy Station, on the morning of the 10th, with orders to move south to the Rapidan. Buford moved faster that day than instructions from Pleasonton, which led to considerable confusion about what Buford was to accomplish and where he was to meet his infantry support. Nonetheless, Buford's troops reached the river around midday, and his troops fought their way across Germanna Ford, pushing Fitz Lee's skirmishers back. The next morning, Buford sent Pleasonton the following message from Morton's Ford: "My supports are not to be found. Rumor says they have marched back to Culpeper. I shall remain for further instruction. We found a small regiment of infantry and the dismounted men of Fitz. Lee's brigade."[77]

Stuart, Gordon and Young spent the night at James City in front of Kilpatrick's division. Funsten spent the night near Griffinsburg holding the road to Woodville and Sperryville open for the infantry. Fitz Lee spent the night on the Rapidan River near Raccoon Ford watching Buford and his command.

On October 11, R. E. Lee received word from Stuart that his plan was working; his move toward Meade's right flank caused the latter to withdraw his infantry. With Meade on the move, R. E. Lee took his infantry just west of and past Culpeper Court House hoping to find Mead near Warrenton in Fauquier County. R. E. Lee divided his infantry for the trip to Warrenton. He sent Ewell toward Griffinsburg, Sperryville, Amissville and to Warrenton, and A. P. Hill to Sulphur Springs (Warrenton Springs) and on to Warrenton. Meade left his cavalry in Culpeper County to cover his withdrawal, and Stuart's cavalrymen would continue to shield Lee's column and press Meade's rear.[78] (See map 2.2.)

Early on October 11, Buford learned that Kilpatrick had pulled back from James City during the night and that his commanding general "had changed the programme." Also that morning in his camp south of the Rapidan, Buford received orders from the previous day instructing him not to cross the Rapidan but to pull back and cross the Rappahannock at Kelly's Ford. Buford proceeded to re-cross the Rapidan, while Fitz Lee sent Lomax's and W. H. F. Lee's (still under Chambliss's command) brigades at him. Fitz Lee took Wickham's brigade across the river up at Raccoon Ford. According to Buford, Fitz Lee's men followed him all the way back to Stevensburg. According to Fitz Lee, he drove Buford's cavalrymen all the way to Stevensburg and on to Brandy Station.[79]

Back at James City, Stuart had the troops directly under his command mobilized early on the 11th, and soon realized that Kilpatrick had withdrawn during the night toward Culpeper Court House. Young's command (Butler's brigade) was left to hold James City, while Stuart took Gordon's North Carolina brigade northwest toward Griffinsburg rather than follow Kilpatrick directly to Culpeper Court House. Stuart was taking no chances. He stayed close on his infantry's flank, between Kilpatrick and R. E. Lee's column.

Stuart met Funsten's command (Jones's brigade) at Griffinsburg around 11:00 A.M. that morning, and sent the 11th Virginia up to the Sperryville and Warrenton road while the rest of Funsten's command was sent up to intersect the Sperryville and Culpeper Court House pike. Gordon and his North Carolinians were sent to the same pike, to Funsten's right, toward Stone-House Mountain. They were then pushing Kilpatrick's force back on Culpeper Court House. The 12th Virginia of Funsten's command was sent after an isolated Union infantry regiment, but otherwise the move to Culpeper Court House was not seriously challenged.[80]

The Union forces continued to fall back leaving their deserted camps for the Confederate cavalrymen to explore. As Stuart approached Culpeper Court House, he knew Meade had withdrawn his infantry so R. E. Lee's infantry had the opportunity to hit the enemy while in retreat.

Stuart easily pushed back the small cavalry force left in Culpeper Court House, took the town and moved out a short distance to meet Kilpatrick's cavalry just east of town where they had set their artillery and were prepared to make a stand. Stuart moved forward with the two remaining regiments under Funsten (the 7th and 12th Virginia), and the main bodies of the four North Carolina regiments still with Gordon that day (the 1st, 2nd, 4th, and 5th North Carolina).[81] (The other regiments of

Funsten's command had been detached to move along with the infantry column.) In all, Stuart had about 1,500 cavalrymen with him, and Kilpatrick had around 4,000. Soon after Stuart arrived, he decided to test Kilpatrick's forward position and his resolve to hold it by sending the North Carolinians forward in a strong "demonstration."[82]

Gordon sent the 4th North Carolina in first with the 5th and 2nd regiments right behind them. They all advanced under heavy artillery and sharpshooter fire. As the 4th North Carolina moved forward, they "encountered a detachment of Kilpatrick's cavalry which after a stubborn resistance was driven back with considerable loss." The North Carolina brigade drove Kilpatrick's front line back across Mountain Run and into his main body — which by then had been pushed back to just below Brandy Station. In this fight Colonel Ferebee and others were wounded. The 5th North Carolina followed the 4th in the charge and lost two lieutenants, both severely wounded about the head, and other men as well. The 2nd North Carolina Cavalry lost Lieutenant John C. Baker and Private Charles J. Saunders in this fight — both were wounded. Baker died of his wounds a month later.[83]

The size of the enemy force and the strong position taken by Kilpatrick helped Stuart decide not to make a frontal attack across open ground. Rather, he left some artillery in front of Kilpatrick and took Funsten's and Gordon's commands directly toward Brandy Station on the Rixeyville road.[84]

Stuart's plan was to move around Kilpatrick's right and on to Fleetwood Hill (ridge) just above Brandy Station; thereby "intercepting the enemy on their line of retreat along the railroad toward the Rappahannock." Kilpatrick also saw the advantage of occupying the heights and headed in the same direction; this put Stuart on his left when the two cavalry commands came together. Stuart had Funsten's command in front on a nearly parallel but collision course with Kilpatrick's column. Gordon's North Carolina regiments were behind Funsten's and thus on Kilpatrick's flank. At about this same time, Stuart and others in his command became aware of Fitz Lee's pursuit of Buford's division from the Rapidan. The sound and smoke from Fitz Lee's guns made their presence known to all those in the race for Fleetwood Hill — Fitz Lee and Buford were fighting around Stevensburg. Buford stood his ground because when he reached Stevensburg, he saw the rear guard of the Union Fifth Corps still moving toward the Rappahannock to cross at Kelly's Ford. Kilpatrick also knew he had to keep Stuart from passing around his right and reaching the still-retreating Union column. Stuart on the other hand, with the presence of Fitz Lee's division, saw the opportunity to do some damage to the enemy cavalry as well as keep them away from R. E. Lee's column. Indeed, the opportunity to do serious damage to Kilpatrick's command racing along the east side of the railroad tracks toward Brandy Station was enormous with Gordon on their left flank and Fitz Lee's cavalrymen on their right. According to one member of the 6th Virginia under Fitz Lee's command, however, as they watched Kilpatrick race by in order to avoid being cut off, "we had the finest opportunity to assail these troops in flank, we sat quietly upon our horses, waiting for orders. After they [Kilpatrick] passed, we were ordered forward, but even then only went in a trot." Kilpatrick escaped the forces on his right flank, but the stage was set for an escalation of the fighting. The two brigades of Hampton's division under Stuart's command would have to take on Kilpatrick's division — help from Fitz Lee would be too little and too late.[85] (See map 3.1.)

As indicated, Gordon's command was moving along Kilpatrick's left flank, so when Fitz Lee's presence was known, Gordon sent the 1st North Carolina to attack what appeared to be a detached Union regiment traveling on their right. The North Carolinians did their job, capturing or killing at least 60 Union cavalrymen. The 1st North Carolina regiment, however, then found itself in front of Custer's brigade. At about the same time, Funsten's 12th Virginia, at the head of the column, saw Kilpatrick's advance moving closer to the heights and made a charge. After some severe fighting the men of the 12th Virginia managed to push the enemy back. Funsten's other regiment, the 7th Virginia, had been separated during the race for Fleetwood Hill and came up in the rear of Gordon's command — which proved fortunate for the North Carolinians who soon found themselves in some difficulty.[86]

About the time the 1st North Carolina made its attack on Kilpatrick's apparent rear, the 4th and 5th North Carolina were moved rapidly forward in support of the 12th Virginia's attack on the enemy's front. The 4th and 5th were placed on a partly sunken road, below a rise, where they watched the 12th Virginia make its attack and waited for orders to join the fight—both Stuart and Gordon were there to give the much anticipated orders when the appropriate moment arrived. Before that moment, however, the 18th Pennsylvania Cavalry came over a rise and hit the 4th and 5th North Carolina on their unprotected flank. What followed was described by a member of the 5th North Carolina Cavalry in these words: "when suddenly the Eighteenth Pennsylvania, in regiment front, led by General Davies, fell like a tornado on the sixty-third [5th] and Fifty-ninth [4th], over the open elevation which had concealed them, and both the Fifty-ninth and Sixty-third broke in confusion to their left until the Seventh Virginia, most opportunely coming up, charged the Eighteen Pennsylvania on their left flank, and they fled." The location of the 2nd North Carolina during this fight is not clear, but if they had been with the 4th and 5th cavalry regiments, it would likely have been noted because the encounter has been described often—in addition, none of the after-battle reports mentioned their presence, but that was usually the case, even when they were on site, primarily because of their small numbers.[87]

When Gordon reported on the day's events, he simply stated, "Near Mr. Bott's house the Fourth and Fifth were charged in flank by the Eighteenth Pennsylvania and broke in considerable confusion. The brigade took no further active operations during the day." Members of the North Carolina regiments, however, had more difficulty rationalizing what they had done. For instance, Daniel B. Coltrane of the 5th North Carolina Cavalry wrote "That was the only time I can remember that the 63rd broke and ran. We were beaten in some engagement. But we came out of them still in formation and under control of our officers.... We reformed in the next few minutes and were ready to charge which shows we were good veteran troopers."[88]

Meanwhile, Kilpatrick had enough troopers to occupy Stuart's men, and still move toward Fleetwood Hill along with his artillery—which he did. Stuart's artillery had been left some distance behind due to the rapid movement of Funsten's and Gordon's commands along the railroad tracks heading for Brandy Station. Fitz Lee did not come up and join Stuart as the latter had hoped because he mistakenly assumed Funsten's and Gordon's cavalrymen moving toward Brandy Station were enemy, and he paused to shell them for an uncomfortable length of time before he realized they were his comrades. At some point, Fitz Lee did get up and join Stuart, but not until the Union cavalry had Fleetwood Hill and covered their infantry's escape route to the Rappahannock. Kilpatrick and Buford also united and made an orderly withdrawal over the river by 8:00 P.M. October 11. Stuart's disappointment at not being able to close on Kilpatrick's command and deliver them a serious blow is evident in his summary comment on the activities: "The time gained to the enemy by the breaking of the two North Carolina regiments, and General Lee's belief that I was the enemy, enabled the enemy to gain Fleetwood Heights and place his artillery in position."[89]

Fighting continued until evening, but Stuart's force was unable to break through the combined force of Kilpatrick's and Buford's divisions under the command of Pleasonton.[90]

However, Stuart's cavalrymen did push their enemy beyond Fleetwood Hill and bivouac for the night on the plush farm of Mr. John Minor Botts. In his official report, Buford noted that much of the fighting took place near Mr. Botts's farm—Buford knew him well, because he was a Union supporter. For that reason, his farm was not ravaged by Meade's army while they were camped in the area during the weeks preceding this fight. On October 11 however, Mr. Botts's good fortune came to an end—for awhile. Not only did one of the Confederate Cavalry charges take place directly through his front yard, but that night nearly 3,000 Confederate cavalrymen made themselves "guests" on his farm. It was one of the few places in the area that still had undisturbed corn fields and fence rails. After the fighting, Stuart's cavalrymen fed their horses in his corn field, and made wonderful camp fires of his rails. One Confederate noted that "The next morning there were very few fence rails and very little corn left. The men could be heard to say while building high their fires, 'pile on boys, they are nothing but d—d old Union rails.'

Botts came down Monday morning and said he would like to get a certificate of the quantity of corn used and rails burnt. He was dismissed very cavalierly."[91]

Early on October 12, Stuart sent word to P. M. B. Young, commanding Butler's brigade, to move up from James City to Culpeper Court House and protect the supplies being unloaded for transport to the upper Hazel River and on to the army.[92] Then Stuart instructed Colonel T. L. Rosser and his 5th Virginia Cavalry to stand watch on the Rappahannock.[93]

Stuart thought Rosser's command at the river, and Young's at Culpeper Court House would be more than enough to discourage any Union cavalry probes into the area while he moved north with R. E. Lee. However, Stuart had not realized how effectively he had shielded his army from Meade's view, nor did he realize how willing Meade was to do battle. Indeed, Meade had been led to believe that R. E. Lee's army was still at Culpeper Court House on the morning of the 12th, so he sent the Second, Fifth, and Sixth Corps along with Buford's cavalry division back across the Rappahannock toward Brandy Station to do battle at Culpeper Court House. Rosser managed to slow Buford's advance and consequently Meade's infantry, which gave Young time to get into position near Culpeper Court House. By afternoon Young and his brigade had arrived, and soon afterward, they received a message that a large enemy force was on the way. Young moved out of town to an area known as Slaughter's Hill and put his artillery in place and dismounted most of his men in line of battle — Rosser's men dropped back and joined Young's line. By the time the Federal column arrived, the Confederates were able to confront them with considerable fire power. It was near nightfall and the Union commanders were still unaware of the size of the force in front of them, so they settled in for the night after receiving heavy fire from Young's guns and sharpshooters.[94]

Young's cavalrymen did all they could to disguise the smallness of their force, but during the night, Meade received word from D. McM. Gregg informing him that he had been pushed from the Hazel Run in the morning and the Rappahannock in the afternoon, and that the enemy column was crossing up at Sulphur Springs in heavy force. Gregg's cavalry was first pushed by Ewell's column — Funsten's 11th Virginia had been sent to that position the day before, and by the afternoon of the 12th the rest of Funsten's brigade was at the head of Ewell's command pushing Gregg. Once D. McM. Gregg's situation was known, Meade immediately withdrew his force from Culpeper — his infantry was back across the Rappahannock by midnight, and Buford's cavalry division was over the river by daylight on October 13. The Confederate commanders, Young and Rosser, had a better morning than they had expected. Meade knew R. E. Lee would be at Warrenton before he could reach the area, so he sent his men to Auburn and Catlett's Station where he hoped to be in position to confront his enemy.[95]

Meanwhile, also on the morning of October 12, Stuart with Fitz Lee's cavalry division and Funsten's and Gordon's brigades moved up to intercept Ewell's column on the road to Jeffersonton as it crossed the Hazel River. Funsten's command moved to the head of Ewell's men, and Fitz Lee's division and Gordon's North Carolina brigade moved on Ewell's flank.[96]

Upon reaching the head of Ewell's column, Funsten was instructed by R. E. Lee to move forward and to cut off some enemy cavalry that was in and around Jeffersonton. When Funsten moved up, he found his previously detached 11th Virginia already at the head of Ewell's men and discovered they had driven the enemy cavalry (the 13th Pennsylvania and 10th New York Cavalries) back into town. The Federal cavalry had fallen back and was in a strong position by the time Funsten arrived, but once he threw the 7th Virginia to the left and the 12th Virginia to the right, the fighting became very heavy, and Funsten finally drove and scattered the enemy. The Army of Northern Virginia continued its march to Warrenton Springs on the upper Rappahannock (called Carter's Run or Hedgeman's River above the springs).[97] (See map 2.2.)

Stuart sent two regiments to cross the Rappahannock higher up, and he moved in advance of Ewell's column to force a crossing at Warrenton Springs. Stuart was met at the river by well manned rifle-pits and mounted cavalrymen as well as artillery posted along the hills just behind — all from D. McM. Gregg's cavalry division. Funsten sent the 7th and 11th Virginia to cross at nearby fords, and the 12th Virginia was sent directly at the bridge. The 12th Virginia was also forced to ford the river because the bridge had been taken out of service by Gregg's men.[98]

There is a high probability regiments other than Funsten's Virginia units participated in the forced crossing that day. Funsten wrote a very detailed account of the part his men played in storming across the river and occupying the far bank. Unfortunately, when James B. Gordon wrote his report, he provided us with one of his masterful understatements of the role played by his North Carolinians at the river that day—unlike most commanders on both sides, he frequently understated the contribution made by himself and his men. In this instance, he simply reported, "I crossed Hazel [Hedgeman's] River about sunset and moved to Warrenton that night and occupied the town." As is often the case, the contrast in reporting styles at the brigade level leads to some units not being mentioned in summary reports written further up the chain of command. Consequently, when Stuart wrote his battle report, the Virginia regiments appear to have been acting alone that day. This naturally bothered some of the North Carolinians who were there, because like many others, they knew that not being mentioned in your commander's battle report implied that you had not preformed well that day. Many also felt that Stuart had difficulty seeing non–Virginian units in any battle. In any case, Stuart's failure to mention Gordon's regiments in this fight prompted Private Means of the 5th North Carolina to write, "At this crossing of the river the Sixty-third [5th Cavalry] was in a glorious charge of which General Stuart, innocently and inadvertently, of course, gives all the praise to the Twelfth Virginia. But the Sixty-third was certainly in that charge as men now still living well know." There is a good probability that the other North Carolina cavalry regiments—including the 2nd North Carolina—were also in the action that evening.[99]

The certainty of the day was that Stuart's cavalrymen carried the position, and after the bridge was restored, a sufficient number of Ewell's infantrymen crossed before nightfall to secure the position. Though the crossing was made and the day had ended, there was no rest for the cavalry yet. Stuart sent Funsten and Gordon with their commands to Warrenton, another 7 or 8 mile march, where they finally bivouacked for the night. Fitz Lee's command had moved up earlier, and it spent the night at Fox's Mill on the upper Rappahannock.[100]

Fighting Between Auburn and Catlett's Station

By October 13, R. E. Lee wrote the Secretary of War informing him that he had hit Meade on his right flank, and Meade retired north of the Rappahannock—and that most of their contact with the enemy to date had been by Stuart's cavalry. For the most part, the latter being successful.[101]

The report was written as R. E. Lee was concentrating his army around Warrenton, and Stuart's cavalry shield was set east of town facing the suspected location of Meade's column. R. E. Lee was not certain how far Meade's column had managed to get along the Orange & Alexandria Railroad. Around 10:00 A.M., Lee asked Stuart to take his cavalry east as far as the railroad, to Catlett's Station and locate the enemy, and if successful to determine their direction and strength. Stuart sent Lomax's brigade from Fitz Lee's division first—Fitz Lee and the rest of his command were not yet at Warrenton but would soon arrive and follow Lomax in the direction of Catlett's Station. Stuart marched with Funsten's three regiments and Gordon's four regiments toward Auburn and then Catlett's Station. Funsten's and Gordon's commands had been so heavily engaged over the previous four days that their ammunition was exhausted. Consequently, they had to wait a short while for their ordnance wagons to catch up. When Stuart finally left for Catlett's Station, he had his two cavalry brigades, seven pieces of artillery, and five ordnance wagons.[102] (See map 2.2.)

When Lomax arrived at Auburn, he learned that Meade's army was at Warrenton Junction in large numbers. He waited at Auburn for Stuart to arrive with Funsten and Gordon to get new instructions in light of the development. On hearing the news, Stuart instructed Lomax to stay at Auburn and keep the route back to Warrenton open for him while he moved on to Catlett's Station with Funsten's and Gordon's commands. As Stuart headed east for the railroad, he sent a small party of men under W. W. Blackford south to Three Mile Station on the railroad branch that runs from Warrenton Junction to the town of Warrenton.[103]

Stuart then took his command across Cedar Run at Auburn and past St. Stephen's Church to within a mile or two of Catlett's Station from where he was able to see what R. E. Lee had hoped for — Meade's army on the move. R. E. Lee's original plan was to get Meade on the road, and then strike his army while it was in motion. In Stuart's eyes, Meade was vulnerable. Meade's infantry, artillery, and wagons were marching in a steady stream northward. In addition, there was an immense park of wagons in the fields between Warrenton Junction and Catlett's Station — what a prize. Stuart immediately sent word to R. E. Lee back at Warrenton to bring his army east and hit Meade's retreating column in the flank.[104]

When Stuart's messenger rode west to find R. E. Lee, he was surprised to find that Union forces occupied Auburn. The courier sent word back to Stuart, informing him that the enemy was in force at his cavalry's rear — then the messenger found a way through the enemy column and went on to Warrenton. As it turned out, Meade had two columns heading north: one along the railroad, the other several miles northwest of the rail line and going directly through Three Mile Station, Auburn, and on to Greenwich. (Meade's army divided around Warrenton Junction and planned to reunite at Bristoe Station or above.) Meade's plan was obviously to move his troops north more quickly by using two roads, but in the process, he had unwittingly trapped J. E. B. Stuart and two of his brigades between the columns. Union cavalry in advance of Meade's column arrived at Auburn and were held by Lomax's men until Union infantry began to arrive. Just before Lomax was overwhelmed, his division commander, Fitz Lee, arrived and had him pull back. They camped on the road back to Warrenton. A Union infantry column was then between Stuart's two cavalry brigades and Fitz Lee's division. In addition, by afternoon October 13, Meade had both D. McM. Gregg's and Kilpatrick's cavalry divisions milling around the front of his two columns. For all practical purposes, they had Stuart and the two small brigades with him in a deadly triangle.[105]

The messenger carrying word of Union troops in Auburn reached the North Carolina brigade at the end of Stuart's cavalry column in late afternoon. James B. Gordon immediately sent word up their line of march to Stuart. While Stuart was watching the massive enemy column march by his front, he received word of the large column passing the rear of his command. He had the option of trying to punch his way through the Federal column passing near Auburn but considered the possible loss of his wagons, artillery, and ambulances too great. Stuart decided to lie low until the enemy passed or R. E. Lee arrived with his army. He moved back toward Auburn, almost in sight of it, where he found a small heavily wooded valley just off the road — ideal for concealing his wagons, artillery, and cavalrymen with all their horses. He quietly moved his command into the small valley. His advance and rear-guards were drawn in and given orders not to return enemy fire — they wanted to disappear. The little valley had ridges of small hills between the Confederate cavalrymen and the Federal columns on either side. Stuart managed to move his artillery to the top of the hills facing Auburn. They were close enough to hear the muffled sounds of hoofs, wagon wheels, and men talking along the road just west of their hiding place — the Union column was passing them at a distance of approximately 150 yards. H. B. McClellan of Stuart's staff remembered, "How thankful we were for those hills! How thankful for that darkness! An hour of daylight would have wrought our destruction."[106]

As night fell, some of Stuart's men lined the hills and looked down across a small open field to the threatening column of marching men. W. W. Blackford, also of Stuart's staff and an incurable romantic, noted while watching the column pass that "Almost every man, it seemed, carried a lantern which gave the scene a very picturesque effect in the dark, still night." H. B. McClellan recalled, "This was the only occasion on which I remember to have seen Stuart give outward manifestation of his deep concern. So close were we to the marching columns of the enemy that we could distinctly hear the orders of the officers as they closed up the column." An observer for the *Richmond Examiner* wrote, "Our situation was extremely critical; any accident — the accidental discharge of a pistol would have disclosed out position, and then, in view of the overwhelming force of the enemy, nothing awaited us but destruction or surrender. Stuart gave his officers and men to understand that surrender was not to be thought of, but that the enemy was to be fought to the last."[107]

Once again, Stuart made certain that the word was spread throughout Funsten's command and Gordon's North Carolina regiments conveying the full seriousness of their situation. Stuart dismounted most of Funsten's command and some of Gordon's, placing them in a close line of battle as sharpshooters; some of Gordon's cavalrymen remained in their saddles for the night — few slept. There was nothing left to do but wait and keep quiet — neither was an easy task to accomplish. Stuart's concern for their situation was manifested in a stringent order he issued that no noise of any description should be made during the night. John E. Cooke of Stuart's staff remembered the tense atmosphere in these words: "The men sat motionless and silent in the saddle, listening, throughout the long hours of the night. No man spoke; no sound was heard from human lips as the little force remained *perdu* [lost] in the darkness." Silence was difficult to maintain because of the large number of animals confined with the cavalrymen, especially the mules attached to the artillery and supply wagons. W. W. Blackford recalled that "...it was necessary to place a man at the head of every mule in the ambulances to keep them from betraying our presence, for the poor beasts needed food and water, and often we would hear an incipient bray brought to a premature close by a whack over the head from a sabre scabbard."[108]

Stuart managed a short nap for himself but mostly he waited to hear from R. E. Lee. He sent several messengers through the lines to inform Lee of his situation and the possible enemy target. Stuart felt he was in a good position to assist R. E. Lee's infantry should it arrive in time. In the meantime, his staff kept an eye open for a break in the Union column to the west, which might offer the possibility for Stuart to race his little command through to a more favorable position to wait for R. E. Lee — but no gap in the enemy line was apparent during the long night. The other hope that filled many a Confederate mind that night was that the end of the Union column would have passed by Auburn by dawn, or even that the columns would have passed Warrenton Junction by that time, leaving a more difficult but possible avenue of escape to the south. Neither possibility materialized before dawn.[109]

Soon it was apparent daylight would be with them before R. E. Lee could arrive. Stuart and his men knew their waiting was near an end, and they would soon have to dash for the ford and get back across Cedar Run as best they could. When there was just enough light, they gazed out over the small clearing near the road toward the only passable ford in the area and saw a sight that made their hearts skip a beat and then rapidly make up for it. H. B. McClellan described the scene: "As day began to dawn it was manifest that a collision of some kind was unavoidable. Upon the adjacent hill-tops and on the same side of Cedar Run with ourselves, but between us and the ford, a large force of infantry had halted, stacked arms, and were building camp-fires and preparing for breakfast. And now hearts beat quick with suspense, and saddle-girths were tightened, and arms were made ready; for the moment of our discovery could not be far distant, and at that moment we must attack." Stuart moved his guns nearer the crest of the hill overlooking the enemy bivouac and waited some more.[110]

Shortly, there was the distant sound of musket fire coming from the other side of Auburn, near the road to Warrenton. Stuart may have suspected Fitz Lee's cavalry command was in that area, but he had not heard from them since he left Lomax and his brigade at Auburn the day before; what Stuart hoped for was the arrival of R. E. Lee and the infantry. Dense fog at first light gave Stuart's men a few more moments to contemplate their situation. It also carried surrounding sounds more readily to their ears — the sounds of the enemy enjoying their breakfast, and the guns to the far west. Stuart waited until the gunfire in the distance "appeared more general, when, believing that it was our attack in earnest, I opened seven guns upon the enemy and rained a storm of canister and shell upon the masses of men, muskets, and coffee-pots." Private Coltrane of the 5th North Carolina remembered when Stuart opened fire on the quiet breakfast scene, "Their surprise and confusion was wonderful to behold. Coffee pots fell into the fires; men jumped for their weapons; some ran; others fell in their tracks."[111]

Apparently Stuart's first thoughts when he opened fire on the Union bivouac were that he would be pounding the enemy from the east as R. E. Lee's infantry hit them from the west. If that was his thinking, it was soon corrected — no effective Confederate attack was coming from the west out of Warrenton. The next line in Stuart's battle report reads: "Strange to say, the fire of our infantry ceased as soon as I opened, and I soon found myself maintaining an unequal contest with an army corps...." In other words, oops! Whatever Stuart's initial reasons may have been, once he opened fire on the enemy below, he had only to think about getting his small command out of the little valley and across the run — including his artillery and wagons.[112]

The Union troopers rallied within minutes and returned fire from a nearby hill into Stuart's guns, and infantrymen moved up the hill at both of the Confederate flanks. Stuart started his wagons and pulled his artillery down into the little valley to follow the wagons. Gordon and the North Carolina regiments were on the left and noticed the rapid advance of the enemy in the direction of the road the Confederates needed to exit the little valley and head for the ford. Understanding the need to slow the Union infantry's charge long enough to allow Stuart's command to exit the valley and head for the run, Gordon sent Colonel Ruffin and his 1st North Carolina up and over the hill directly into the enemy artillery fire and their oncoming infantry. Lieutenant Colonel W. H. H. Cowles, of the 1st North Carolina, who led his squadron in the charge, described the experience in these words: "Through the open field, facing the enemy's fire, the gallant regiment, with sabres drawn, followed its gallant leader, when suddenly there was a stop, a recoil — the brave and gallant Ruffin, with several others, had been shot down at the head of the column, which caused some disorder." Cowles rallied his squadron for another charge; shortly thereafter Major R. Barringer rallied a portion of the regiment for a charge that scattered some and slowed others in the Union lines. From his position, Cowles could see more lines of enemy infantry forming and moving in their direction, so he pulled his squadron back and up a small hill to where Gordon was positioned for further orders. Gordon instructed him to continue his pull back because the charge by the 1st North Carolina had achieved its purpose — Stuart's train had just about cleared the valley and was on its way to the ford.[113]

The 1st North Carolina took heavy losses but most of the regiment joined Stuart's column and made for the run — between one third and one half of the mounted men in the regiment were lost that morning. The other North Carolina regiments assisted in mobilizing the wagons and artillery and escorting them out of the valley and through the ford. Funsten's command mounted up and fell in behind the Confederate column.[114]

Once across Cedar Run, Stuart collected his men and moved across the road heading up to Greenwich. At that point, Stuart stopped his men so they could eat, while he rode off to find R. E. Lee.[115]

Stuart found R. E. Lee's camp just beyond Auburn, and received instructions for the next attempt to engage Meade's main column. The Army of Northern Virginia was going to continue its pursuit of Meade's army east to Bristoe Station. Fitz Lee was instructed to move toward New Baltimore, Gainesville, and then to the vicinity of Bristoe Station, staying on the left flank of the army. Stuart led Funsten's and Gordon's brigades along the right flank of R. E. Lee's army. Stuart sent word back to Young to move his brigade up and meet the rest of Hampton's division at Bristoe Station.[116]

Bristoe Station

While Stuart and his men were contained for the night, he lost track of their enemy's Second and Third Corps and had nothing to report on their whereabouts — Robert E. Lee, nonetheless, moved his army forward toward Bristoe Station where he thought he might encounter Meade's army in some force — large or small. A. P. Hill was in front of R. E. Lee's column on October 14 and was the first to pick up the scent of Meade's column after they passed through Greenwich around 10:00 A.M. From there, A. P. Hill's command followed the road to Bristoe which was strewn with knapsacks, blankets, and an occasional gun — the true sign of a rapidly retreating army, and a sight that perhaps caused A. P. Hill and his officers to become overly enthusiastic. A. P. Hill and his command were the first Confederates to arrive at Bristoe Station that afternoon, and he was eager to engage the enemy. Upon arrival, Hill saw what he thought to be the Union's Third Corps and moved in to punish it, but as he was mid-attack, he was hit in the flank by the Second Corps that had been parked behind a long railroad embankment. A. P. Hill's troops were seriously hurt—the 27th North Carolina was devastated, losing just under 70 percent of its 416 men. In all, A. P. Hill lost more than 1,300 men by evening. A. P. Hill was widely blamed for being too eager and hasty, and he shouldered the blame for the entire disaster at Bristoe Station. Part of Hill's miscalculation was engaging the enemy without knowing the size of the force in front of him — it was his responsibility to know. His serious lack of information, however, might have been averted if his "eyes and ears" had been at his flank. But there was no official blame leveled at J. E. B. Stuart, because after all, he was not there.[117]

Stuart went to the wrong place. He had lost sight of the main column without realizing there was a problem. In his words: "while with Funsten's and Gordon's brigade I moved on the right flank of the army toward Bristoe, aiming to keep on the right of our infantry skirmishers. It so happened that a battalion of skirmishers of Rodes's division left the line of march pursued by the column and branched off toward Catlett's Station. Keeping on the right of these skirmishers, I found myself very much put out of my course, and, in consequence, my column did not reach Bristoe until after dark."[118]

After the fight, R. E. Lee's main column arrived at Bristoe — he was deeply depressed when he surveyed the carnage with A. P. Hill. Then he and his army tried to sleep in line of battle. Stuart arrived after sundown with Funsten's and Gordon's brigades. Fitz Lee also arrived during the night from the left flank of the army. As the Confederates continued to arrive, Meade's army continued to pull out.[119]

COVERING YET ANOTHER PULLBACK

On the morning of October 15, the Federal force in front of R. E. Lee's army was once again gone, so Lee began his preparations to withdraw from Meade's column. As they approached the Union capital, Meade's supply lines got shorter and R. E. Lee's got longer — consequently, Meade got stronger but Lee did not. On the same day, R. E. Lee notified the Secretary of War from Bristoe Station that "It is impossible for us to remain where we are, as the country is destitute of provisions for men and animals.... The counties of Culpeper, Fauquier, and Prince William have been relieved for the time being, but when we retire may be reoccupied. Though the enemy has suffered less than I wished." In his report, General Lee was trying to convey, without having to say it, that nothing lasting had been achieved and no significant damage had been done to Meade's army. R. E. Lee again gave Stuart the job of shielding the Confederate withdrawal. Stuart's job was to pursue the enemy to Manassas Junction and Bull Run and keep them there — Stuart was instructed to be as bold as necessary to give the impression the whole Confederate army was still behind him.[120] (See maps 2.2 and 2.4.)

Stuart's cavalry harassed the retiring Federals for the next couple of days. He had Fitz Lee's division with him as well as most of Hampton's (Young's command had not yet caught up). As they took the road for Manassas Junction, Gordon's North Carolina brigade was in front, and they encountered enemy pickets near the junction. Gordon dismounted most of the men in his regiments, and, according to Private Paul Means of the 5th North Carolina, they launched "a fierce attack on them, which lasted till late in the afternoon, and drove them across Bull Run." It was about that time, Stuart learned of a Federal wagon train traveling on his side of Bull Run — he wanted it before it could get across. He called it a "promised prize." The North Carolina brigade was gathered and sent directly for the train. About two miles below the junction they encountered a large force of Union cavalry which they boldly attacked. Gordon led the attack into the front of the well-posted enemy, while Stuart took Funsten's command on a circuitous route in the direction of Yates's Ford on Bull Run where he hoped to flank the enemy. Gordon started with an artillery duel and soon had his dismounted cavalrymen engaged. Shortly after the fighting began, Buford arrived with support for the Union rear guard. The North Carolinians challenged but could not break through Buford's line — fighting continued until nightfall. It was just dark when Stuart arrived near where the North Carolinians had been battling and sent the 12th Virginia at the enemy. At about the same time, Lomax arrived with his brigade, after having driven a force back across the run up at McLean's Ford. By the time Gordon's support arrived, however, the day was gone, and soon afterwards so was Buford and his wagons. The Federals withdrew across Bull Run.[121]

On October 16, Lomax and his brigade were sent to Bristoe Station where they were threatened by enemy cavalry throughout the day, though not seriously. Fitz Lee and most of his division remained at Manassas and then joined Lomax at Bristoe on the 17th and 18th of the month. Young's command arrived near Manassas Junction on the night of the 15th to fill out Hampton's division which was still under the direct command of J. E. B. Stuart. Funsten was ordered to move his brigade toward Gainesville, and on the night of the 16th, he was relieved by Brigadier General T. Rosser, the new commander of Jones's former brigade.[122]

On the same day, Stuart moved Hampton's division toward Groveton, intending to cross Bull Run above Sudley Ford and get behind the enemy. They made slow progress. As they approached Groveton, they skirmished with the enemy, and battled poor road conditions, all of which slowed the operation. Nonetheless, they crossed Bull Run and headed for the Bull Run Mountains. Gordon and his North Carolina brigade did locate the Union right flank, and, according to Gordon, they made "a demonstration upon the enemy's flank and rear." The North Carolinians bivouacked near Stone Castle that night. On the 17th, Stuart took Hampton's division to within three miles of Aldie, and by late afternoon the lead command, Young's brigade, came upon the enemy near Frying Pan. Troopers from his and Gordon's brigade dismounted and engaged their enemy for more than two hours. Stuart was satisfied that after a couple of hours skirmishing, he had determined the strength and position of the enemy in the area, and thus accomplished the purpose of his expedition. Claiming satisfaction, Stuart "secretly" and at their "leisure" withdrew Hampton's men and they spent the night near Little River turnpike—the next morning they pulled back toward Gainesville.[123]

Judson Kilpatrick had monitored Stuart's movements, and on October 17 he reported, "My scouts have been all day inside the cavalry pickets, but have failed to gain any information of the main army of the rebels." At that time, R. E. Lee and his main army was still in and around Bristoe Station—but their bags were packed. General Lee put his army on the march for the Rappahannock River early the next morning. Stuart had managed to keep the Federal cavalry away while preparations were under way and allowed the army to withdraw without being harassed.[124]

THE BUCKLAND RACES

On October 18, Stuart pulled Hampton's command back to Gainesville, and by nightfall, he learned that Kilpatrick's cavalry division was coming his way.[125]

Meade became interested in pursuing the retreating Confederates but not close enough to bring on a major engagement. Kilpatrick's division was sent out to stay on Stuart's rear—but Kilpatrick and his men had not fared well at the hands of Stuart's cavalrymen on previous meetings, so he was perhaps too eager to climb up Stuart's rear guard and regain some pride for himself and his men.

During the night of October 18, Kilpatrick's advance met and drove in Stuart's pickets. Stuart knew the numbers were not in his favor when Hampton's depleted division stood in front of Kilpatrick's, so he had Young's brigade saddle up and move back to Hay Market in a heavy rainstorm. When pulling back, Stuart found that his pickets still held Gainesville so he was able to pass through that place and move toward Buckland without difficulty. Stuart remained concerned about his rear guard, so he sent a message to Fitz Lee, who had his division camped near Auburn, requesting that he move up and cover Stuart's flank. Stuart felt if Fitz Lee had his division alongside Hampton's, they could easily handle Kilpatrick, so he waited for Fitz Lee to arrive from Auburn.[126] (See map 2.2.)

Stuart selected advantageous positions along Broad Run near Buckland Mills early on the 19th and placed his artillery and sharpshooters—if Kilpatrick arrived before Fitz Lee, he was ready. That day, Stuart's rear guard was Young's brigade, and they felt Kilpatrick's presence as early as 8:00 A.M. Young's rear regiment fought continuously until they joined Stuart's line at Buckland a couple of hours later. Young's brigade rested, while Rosser's (who had just relieved Funsten) and Gordon's North Carolinians held the line, waiting for Kilpatrick.[127]

Kilpatrick had sent one regiment to Hay Market and another to Greenwich in order to discover Stuart's position. Both parties determined that the Confederate cavalry had pulled back toward Buckland Mills. Shortly thereafter, Kilpatrick had his command in front of Stuart on Broad Run. After more than two hours of heavy fighting, Kilpatrick was unable to push across the run held by Rosser's and Gordon's men, so he began to look toward Stuart's flanks.[128]

As Kilpatrick readied his men for a flank move, Stuart heard from Fitz Lee. He had an interesting proposal for Stuart: if Hampton's division withdrew in the direction of Warrenton, they would draw Kilpatrick with them, and then as Fitz Lee came up from Auburn, he could hit the Federals in the flank and rear. Stuart liked the idea and agreed. Stuart sent word back to Fitz Lee that Hampton's command would retreat until they heard his signal gun, then they would turn and attack Kilpatrick. The timing of Stuart's pullback was perfect for him, but very imperfect for Kilpatrick.[129]

Just about the time Stuart began his withdrawal, Kilpatrick ordered George A. Custer to charge the bridge across the run and establish his sharpshooters in the buildings on the other side — which he did. Kilpatrick was convinced that Stuart's withdrawal resulted from Custer's successful storming of the bridge. Thus, in the pursuit that followed, though Kilpatrick did not seem to suspect he was being drawn into a trap, he was nonetheless cautious.[130]

Stuart slowly withdrew Hampton's command through New Baltimore and toward Warrenton. Kilpatrick delayed a short while before following; he waited for his scouts to return with any word of enemy on his flanks before he pushed after Stuart. Most of Stuart's cavalrymen did not know the plan and were puzzled by their commander's willingness to repeatedly withdraw with almost no fighting. As the process continued, Kilpatrick's cautious approach grew bolder, and his troops arrived at Stuart's rear around 3:30 P.M. Stuart set a line of skirmishers and kept the column slowly moving toward Warrenton. Soon after Stuart had his line posted at Chestnut Hill (about two and a half miles before Warrenton), he heard the sound of artillery back in the direction of Buckland, and he knew Fitz Lee had begun his attack on Kilpatrick's flank and rear. The order passed among the dismounted Confederate cavalrymen to mount up. In the words of one North Carolina private, "Immediately we wheeled, under Stuart's own orders, and astonished the enemy with a ferocious attack."[131]

When Stuart turned Hampton's brigades, he placed Gordon's North Carolina brigade in the center and Young's and Rosser's on each flank. With sabers drawn, the North Carolinians were ordered up the pike where they met the enemy posted near New Baltimore. It was the 1st North Carolina Cavalry's day to be in front — the 2nd North Carolina was next. Gordon led his cavalrymen up the road. Captain Cowles of the 1st North Carolina was at the rear of his regiment's column but soon decided to move up where he suspected the action would be. As he moved forward along the column, he arrived at the crest of a hill that allowed him to see the action in front — he described the scene for us:

The fire of the enemy was taking effect on our column, which had halted, the head of the column resting upon the crest of a hill...: Our own column resting in the road with sabres drawn and ready for action, with mounted skirmishers on either flank [Young and Rosser] responding to the enemy's fire; General Stuart and Gordon on the right of the road viewing intently the situation; the enemy's column (the pick and flower of the Federal cavalry) confronting us and stretching in column of fours, completely covering the highway in our front as far as we could see, with mounted skirmishers on either flank and evidently in readiness to charge. Not a moment was to be lost; ... Stuart called quickly: "Now Gordon, is your time! " and Gordon as promptly: "Charge with the First North Carolina!" ...Down from the crest of that ridge the regiment poured like an avalanche. With flashing sabres and the impetuous speed of a war-horse, nothing could withstand it...; break they must, and break they did.[132]

The North Carolinians' target was straight up the pike, Henry E. Davies's brigade. Major Rufus Barringer was at the head of the regiment along with Captain Cowles. Once under way, the charge up the pike included all the North Carolina regiments. In the words of Paul Means of the 5th North Carolina, Kilpatrick's cavalrymen, "fought stubbornly at first but nothing could resist the impetuous charges of the Sixty-third [5th Cavalry] and other North Carolinians and those boasting [Union] columns broke in confusion." In his report, Gordon noted that Captain Cowles "captured (with a portion of the First and Second Regiments) 5 wagons and 2 ambulances." Many of the 2nd North Carolina Cavalry's men with the fastest horses, as well as some riders from the other regiments in Gordon's brigade, became mixed with the charging men of the lead regiment. As the Union cavalrymen broke, Young and his brigade were charging through the woods on the right of the pike in an effort to hit the enemy in the flank, but the Federal cavalrymen soon fled so rapidly, they never got into the battle. Once the Union cavalrymen broke, the race for Buckland was on. Davies's Union cavalrymen were pushed back into Fitz Lee's stalemate with Custer. The rapid pace of Davies's retreat put Custer and his men in a dangerous position and caused them to execute a rapid retreat from their fight with Fitz Lee's command near Broad Run.[133]

Kilpatrick had left G. A. Custer near Broad Run to cover his flank and rear. That put him in Fitz Lee's path as the latter came up from Auburn. Fitz Lee had expected to hit Kilpatrick without serious opposition, but Custer and his command were between the two. Custer withstood Fitz Lee's attack, and a severe fight continued until Kilpatrick's front gave way under the charge by the North Carolina regiments. Custer was forced to leave his fight with Fitz Lee quickly when Davies's men raced into his position. Custer managed to keep order among his command, however, and he got most of his men along with his artillery back across Broad Run at Buckland. Some of Davies's men crossed with Custer. In the surrounding panic, Custer was unable to save his headquarters wagons, baggage, and papers— most of which were captured by a force led by Cowles which included cavalrymen from the 1st and 2nd North Carolina cavalries.[134]

What came to be known in Confederate ranks as the "Buckland Races," saw Union cavalrymen fleeing as rapidly as possible through New Baltimore, Buckland (at which point Custer's men joined the rapid retreat), across Broad Run, and on to Hay Market. According to Private Means of the 5th North Carolina, Gordon's brigade "pursued them relentlessly and almost resistlessly, the horses at full speed the whole distance." At one point, the 18th Pennsylvania Cavalry was "ridden down by its own cavalry," and found it necessary to offer some resistance, as the North Carolinians crawled up their backs. Still fresh in the minds of the men in the 4th and 5th North Carolina was how the Pennsylvanians had humiliated them — recall, just days before near Brandy Station, the 18th Pennsylvania had surprised the two Confederate regiments as they swept down upon them and caused them to panic and break in full view of their comrades in Hampton's division. Private Means proudly described the regiments' second meeting in October in these words: "The Eighteenth Pennsylvania too, was in the panic and rout. The Sixty-third [5th North Carolina Cavalry] rode and cut and slashed into their ranks furiously, and they sadly learned as the Sixty-third joyously found that 'there is retribution in history.'"[135]

Fitz Lee and his division pursued the fleeing enemy down the pike toward Gainesville. With Hampton's division, Stuart continued the chase to the left toward Hay Market. Both Confederate commands drove the fleeing Union horsemen into their infantry lines.

When he heard of the cavalry chase, R. E. Lee had a little something to be pleased about. He wrote Stuart on the 19th, telling him "The plan was well conceived and skillfully executed." For Stuart, the "Buckland Races" marked the end of the Bristoe Campaign.[136]

The Confederate line was once again on the Rappahannock by October 19, 1863, and on that day R. E. Lee conveyed the following instructions for Stuart and his cavalrymen:

It is not my design for you to advance or to cross the Potomac, but to withdraw on the line formerly designated, when you think it advantageous to do so. I have ordered the iron from the railroad for some miles north of the Rappahannock to be hauled across the river. I desire you, while this operation continues, to have a brigade near the railroad, with pickets at Catlett's, in order to give the working parties and wagons notice of any advance of the enemy's cavalry, and to cover their movements as much as possible.[137]

After guarding the work crews, Stuart's command leisurely returned south of the Rappahannock on October 20. Gordon's North Carolinians, along with most of Stuart's cavalrymen, took up picket posts along the Rappahannock and Hazel Rivers.

The 2nd North Carolina Cavalry was engaged in the fights involving Gordon's North Carolina brigade, and many of the recorded losses for the regiment could have been from any one of those battles. The uncertainty results from a lack of specificity in reporting. For instance, for three of the men listed below, the records simply indicate they were lost in the Bristoe Campaign in the month of October, and in two other cases, the records only list the date of admission to the hospital in Richmond with wounds. However, the absence of details does not alter the magnitude of the recorded losses taken by the 2nd North Carolina Cavalry during the campaign.

Combat Losses in the 2nd North Carolina Cavalry Bristoe Campaign October 8–20, 1863

Trooper	Age	Co.	Fate
William A. Luckey	35	B	wounded October 10
Charles J. Saunders	30	E	wounded October 11
John C. Baker	22	I	mortally October 11
James S. Ozment		F	captured October 12–13
Edwin D. Parker		F/S	captured October 14
James H. White	20	B	captured October 14
John M. Saunders	35	A	wounded October 19
John Tilly		K	mortally October 19
Jesse M. Walker	25	A	wounded October
Charles W. Small		C	wounded October
James M. Winburn	31	G	wounded severely October

Information contained in this table came from Compiled Service Records as summarized by Louis H. Manarin, *North Carolina Troops: 1861–1865, A Roster*, vol. II, pp. 98–177. (See Appendix for more information on the men listed above, page 399.)

MEADE CROSSES THE RAPPAHANNOCK

On November 7, the Army of the Potomac once again moved to the Rappahannock — George Meade meant to force his way across the river. John Sedgwick, commanding the Fifth and Sixth Corps moved on Rappahannock Station; and William H. French marched on Kelly's Ford with the First, Second, and Third Corps. On the north side of the river at Rappahannock Station, Robert E. Lee had two brigades which Sedgwick's command pushed back and across the river with little difficulty, capturing Confederate artillery and some 1,600 men. French had even less difficulty at Kelly's Ford. By the next morning Meade's army was across the Rappahannock.[138]

The Federals moved their army through Brandy Station and on toward Culpeper Court House with cavalry out front. As they approached Culpeper, Meade learned that the Army of Northern Virginia had pulled back to establish a new line on the south side of the Rapidan River. At that point, Meade was content to consolidate his force in a line from below Kelly's Ford, through Brandy Station, and up to Welford's Ford on the Hazel River. He wanted to rebuild the bridges and the railroad line and establish Brandy Station as his supply depot before he stretched his supply line any further.[139]

By November 16, Meade reported "...the road was put in order and the bridge built over the Rappahannock, and by the 19th the sidings for a depot at Brandy Station were constructed, and supplies for the use of the army brought up and delivered." Now Meade was ready to push across the Rapidan and confront Robert E. Lee.[140]

Though Robert E. Lee had A. P. Hill's command was on the left, Ewell's command was on the right, and Stuart's cavalry on both sides of the railroad, he did not offer any serious resistance to Meade's approach.[141]

After Meade's troops had crossed the river, R. E. Lee's army spent the night on a line between Culpeper Court House and Brandy Station, but that line was considered even less defensible than their previous one, so they dropped back and re-crossed the Rapidan to a much more defensible position.[142]

James B. Gordon's North Carolina Cavalry Brigade along with the rest of Wade Hampton's division and Fitz Lee's division covered the retreat to the Rapidan River. Hampton returned to active duty on November 8, just in time to spend the day skirmishing with the enemy's advance.

Once south of the Rapidan, Stuart's cavalry built winter quarters and patrolled the river. They occasionally crossed it to probe the Union Cavalry shield that Meade had between his army and the Rapidan. Men from the 2nd North Carolina had one such encounter with the enemy up the Robertson River on November 11, in which Benjamin O. Wade was captured. Another instance a few days later on November 18, Hampton took a small detachment from Gordon's North Carolina brigade "on a little prospecting tour of his own." The first Union force they met was once again the 18th Pennsylvania Cavalry. They surprised the Federals at breakfast and captured "83 horses, 10 mules, 1 ambulance, 1 hospital wagon, 1 forge, and a host of prisoners." More importantly however, for the men of the 5th North Carolina, was the opportunity to capture the 18th Pennsylvania's payroll and funds. You will recall, the 5th North Carolina felt history had given them some retribution during the "Buckland Race" in late October for the humiliation the 5th had received at the hands of the 18th Pennsylvania earlier in October. The men of the 5th North Carolina took the 18th Pennsylvania's payday and divided the greenbacks among themselves—the score was finally settled between the regiments. According to Private Means of the 5th regiment, "the Sixty-third [5th Cavalry] North Carolina and the Eighteenth Pennsylvania then and there agreed never again to refer to the affair between us at John Minor Botts's [near Fleetwood Hill]. It was a final settlement between gentlemen, and both sides prefer to hear no more talk about our matters by outsiders." On that note, this writer will change the subject.[143]

The Mine Run Campaign, November 26–December 2

George Meade had his supply lines in place and appeared ready to advance on the Rapidan by November 19, but he spent another week getting there. He crossed the Rapidan "in three columns at Jacob's and Germanna Mills and Culpeper [Ely's] Ford; no opposition." The following day Meade moved the Third and Sixth Corps from Jacob's Mill toward Robertson's Tavern on the Orange Turnpike; the Second Corps also onto the turnpike; and the Third and First Corps on the Orange Plank Road.[144] (See map 2.5.)

Stuart's cavalrymen were patrolling the river and posted at the fords when Meade's men arrived. They were in small numbers at the principle fords with no orders to slow the enemy in any significant way, but rather to detect any advance and report it to their commanders. That was not always an easy assignment. For instance, John W. Rogers of Company C, 2nd North Carolina Cavalry was taken prisoner along with others on the Rapidan when Meade's cavalry stormed across the fords in force.

R. E. Lee's cavalrymen did their job; they warned him on November 26 that the enemy was crossing at Germanna and Ely's Fords. He was not sure, however, if Meade planned a move on Fredericksburg or a move on the Confederate left flank in order to draw them from their entrenchments. That uncertainty made defense difficult, so R. E. Lee decided the best course of action was to attack the invaders. During the night of the 26th, he moved his infantry from the upper Rapidan, eastward toward the enemy: Richard S. Ewell's corps, under the command of Jubal A. Early, was sent to the Orange Turnpike toward Locust Grove; and A. P. Hill's command was sent, on a nearly parallel route, across the Orange Plank Road. The next day, General Early's command met the Union Third Corps on the plank road about 4 miles from Robertson's Tavern, near Locast Grove. Both sides called it a "spirited engagement." Then the Union Second Corps moved up, joined the fight and occupied the tavern on Orange Plank Road. A. P. Hill's column was led by Hampton's cavalry division when it encountered the Federals near New Hope Church. The Union Fifth Corps was heading westward on the plank road with D. McM. Gregg's cavalry division out in front.[145]

At the opening of the Mine Run Campaign, the three brigades in Hampton's cavalry division were commanded by James B. Gordon, P. M. B. Young, and Thomas L. Rosser. These brigades were placed between the two approaching armies. Rosser's brigade was off guarding the roads coming from the Germanna and Ely's Fords to Fredericksburg, and they made a large haul of Union material when they successfully attacked a wagon train near Wilderness Tavern on the Orange Turnpike (they captured 18 wagons, 280 mules, and 150 prisoners). Due to miscommunications, Young's brigade and Hampton himself were late in leaving camp on November 27. Stuart made what appears to have been a token effort to find Hampton, and then took command of Gordon's brigade and moved impatiently to the front of A. P. Hill's column.[146]

Gordon's regiments were commanded by the following men: the 1st North Carolina Cavalry by Major R. Barringer; the 2nd, 4th, and 5th regiments by Colonel W. G. Robinson, Colonel D. D. Ferebee, and Lieutenant Colonel S. B. Evens, respectively. Colonel William G. Robinson had just returned to duty and taken command of the 2nd North Carolina Cavalry. (This was the first time Robinson led cavalrymen from his regiment into battle since the fiasco at Gillett's farm in North Carolina on April 13, 1862 — at which time he was wounded and captured.)

Stuart, with the North Carolinians, was eager to stop the continued progress of Meade's army, so he moved his cavalrymen toward the Union cavalry near New Hope Church at about 11:00 A.M. on November 27.

In the clash near New Hope Church, the North Carolina cavalrymen, in Stuart's words, "had to maintain a very unequal contest, which was greatly aggravated by a deficiency in ammunition for carbines and rifles, fighting on foot, owing to the peculiar undergrowth, being the only practicable mode of warfare." In spite of the odds and the hurried pace, which resulted in a lack of preparedness, Gordon's North Carolinians drove the enemy cavalry back to their infantry support and then held — they stopped the Federal advance. In the late afternoon, Henry Heth's infantry division arrived and relieved the North Carolinians. With Confederate infantry on the Orange Plank Road in front of D. McM. Gregg's cavalry and the Fifth Corps, Stuart held Gordon's troopers to the right of the road covering the Confederate flank — Stuart had received word of enemy troops moving around the right. Further to the left of the Confederate line, Ewell's command was under pressure and needed cavalry support up front between his men and the enemy. Gordon answered the request by sending a detachment of North Carolina cavalrymen under the command of W. H. Cowles of the 1st North Carolina, and in a brief action, Cowles was seriously wounded. In spite of the present danger, most of the North Carolina cavalrymen settled in for the night just off the plank road and kept a "good line of videttes along the whole front, Gen. Stuart retired for the night, to a place near Verdiersville." Before Stuart had left for the night, Hampton arrived with Young's brigade, and the latter was dismounted and placed on the infantry's flank. Skirmishing between the lines and on the flanks continued throughout the afternoon and evening.[147]

Of course, there were other cavalry clashes November 27. For instance, Fitz Lee's cavalry division met Kilpatrick's cavalry as they were attempting to cross the Rapidan at Morton's and Raccoon Fords — Kilpatrick was pushed back. In addition, Major John S. Mosby and his cavalrymen made nuisances of themselves by hitting Meade from the rear at Brandy Station — they destroyed a number of wagons and made off with 112 mules.[148]

Robert E. Lee pulled his line back to the west side of Mine Run in the late evening of November 27, and the Union First and Sixth Corps were brought up during the night. The next day, the armies of both Meade and R. E. Lee faced one another across Mine Run. The Confederates built an impressive line of earthworks, and Meade hesitated at the sight of them. Then R. E. Lee saw Meade's troops throwing up earthworks and showing their artillery. He was puzzled and still uncertain of Meade's intentions. He again called on his cavalry. R. E. Lee instructed Stuart to take Hampton's division around the Federal left and determine their "position and situation." While the infantries continued to jockey for better positions on the flanks well into the night of November 28, Stuart instructed Hampton to have his cavalry ready to march at an early hour the next morning. Hampton saw that all three of his brigades were supplied with ammunition, and then he waited at his headquarters for further instructions. Stuart was on the road early Sunday morning the 29th, and heading southeast toward Shady Grove Church near the camps of Hampton's cavalry brigades. He sent a courier ahead, instructing Hampton to bring his division up and meet him on Catharpin Road, but the message Hampton received lacked clarity or did not arrive in time. In any case, Stuart grew impatient waiting for Hampton, and moved to Rosser's brigade headquarters. Once there, Stuart ordered Rosser's brigade into their saddles and onto Catharpin Road heading up to the Orange Plank Road — the roads intersected just east of Parker's Store. Stuart then sent a courier to Gordon's headquarters, instructing the North Carolina brigade to also mount up and head for the plank road. At some point, Stuart sent a message to Hampton at his headquarters to move up and meet him at Gordon's or Rosser's headquarters. Hampton immediately rode to Gordon's headquarters and found them in the process of moving out. He then moved to Young's camp and had him also prepare to move out for the Orange Plank Road. Young had his command on the Catharpin Road about one hour behind Gordon's North Carolinians. Once Hampton had set Young in motion, he rode to Rosser's camp and found that he and his men were already gone. (That a division commander as capable as Hampton was the last to know that most of his brigades were mobilized and heading for the enemy can best be explained by Stuart's eagerness to find the enemy and complete his assignment.) Hampton then rode with Young's brigade, about one mile behind the North Carolina brigade on Catharpin Road, heading for the plank road. Even further up the Catharpin Road, Stuart rode with Rosser and his command — they turned off the road, however, just before getting to the Orange Plank Road in order to arrive near Parker's Store.[149]

Stuart and his staff were the first to arrive at the Orange Plank Road near a railroad cut — at that point, his cavalry was around the Union flank and behind their line across Orange Plank Road. As they arrived, Stuart and his party exchanged "greetings" with Federal pickets before a squadron from Rosser's brigade came up. The pickets they encountered were from D. McM. Gregg's cavalry division, and Rosser's cavalrymen drove them back into their camp near Parker's Store. Union skirmishers then opened a heavy fire on the advancing Confederates causing them to pull back and regroup. Rosser and his cavalrymen were under great pressure but continued to push forward. The first attempt to storm the Union camp was not successful, but the next was, and Rosser's men were able to capture some arms and equipment. The scene in the occupied camp was, in the words of Lieutenant Garnett of Stuart's staff, "a scene of disgraceful confusion. The men, attracted by the rich plunder of the camp, were scattered about picking up what ever they could find, and it was an utter impossibility to make them return to their ranks." It took awhile to restore order among Rosser's men, which gave the Union commanders time to respond, and they did. Gregg sent three regiments and a battery of artillery toward Parker's Store more rapidly than expected and threatened Rosser flank by moving some troops on the railroad cut. To avoid being flanked, Stuart ordered Rosser to pull back and take a position on the south side of the railroad cut. From that position, Rosser regrouped and continued skirmishing with Gregg's cavalry — they held the line with great difficulty until Gordon's North Carolina brigade arrived.[150]

When Hampton and Young were about one mile from Parker's Store, they heard the fighting that had engulfed Rosser's command. Hampton had already sent word to Gordon, who was very near the fighting by then, to move up on Rosser's right. Just before Gordon arrived at the plank road, he received orders from one of Stuart's couriers "to move up rapidly; that the enemy were pressing back General Rosser." At around the same time, Hampton, still about one mile from Parker's Store, also received instructions to hurry up in support of Rosser — Stuart's courier led Hampton and Young as they moved to a trot for the plank road.[151]

As soon as Gordon arrived at the Orange Plank Road, he reported to Stuart and was immediately ordered to move to Rosser's right and attack the enemy in front of him. When Gordon moved his North Carolinians into position, he "found General Rosser's command on the east [south] of the railroad cut ... about 800 yards from Parker's Store, save one regiment on the Orange Plank Road about a mile east of the store. He was falling back skirmishing with the enemy to the east [south] of the road. The regiment down the road was not near the enemy." Gordon dismounted the 2nd North Carolina Cavalry and a portion of the 5th — placed them under the command of Captain Reese of the 2nd North Carolina, who immediately led a charge into the enemy's line. Gordon described the action as seen by the North Carolinians[152]:

My dismounted men were ordered to charge the Yankee skirmishers, which was done in handsome style, driving them from the railroad cut across the plank road out of their camps, and scattering them through the woods, capturing a number of prisoners, some horses, overcoats, blankets, guns, and their camp equipage. A large number of prisoners would have been captured (as my right had swung around to the right and rear of the enemy's left) had it not been for a false rumor brought in by courier that a column of Yankee infantry were moving up the plank road in my rear. I received orders from General Rosser (stating they were from General Stuart) to withdraw my command east [south] of the plank road, which stopped the pursuit on the right.

The charge and follow-through by the 2nd North Carolina Cavalry and a portion of the 5th Cavalry as well as the support of the remainder of the North Carolina brigade allowed Rosser to regroup and join Young's command, which had come up on their left. They continued the pursuit of Gregg's cavalrymen. The North Carolina brigade's successful charge was rewarded with a rest as it was ordered to hold the road at Parker's Store while Hampton's other two brigades continued to push the enemy further along the road. Gordon then sent the 5th North Carolina back with the prisoners. The rest of the North Carolina brigade was relieved and ordered into camp after about one hour. It was by then a dark and very cold night — again.[153]

There is little doubt that the aggressive approach and well entrenched line made by R. E. Lee's army, and the aggressive move by Stuart's cavalrymen around the Union left made an impression on Meade by the day's end. Meade reported to his superior: "The army was in position by the morning of the 29th, and on that afternoon General Warren, with the Second Corps, was sent to the plank road, where the enemy was also found strongly entrenched. Every effort has been made, as yet without avail."[154]

The two armies continued to face each other across Mine Run for the next couple of days. Hampton's cavalry brigades were placed on the Confederate right — some dismounted, others remained in their saddles. The cavalrymen from time-to-time scouted the enemy's positions which led to light skirmishing, but no serious action. The men tried to stay warm and waited to be attacked; Meade was waiting for just the right opportunity. There was a break from the lull on the 30th when Union skirmishers from the First and Third Corps advanced across Mine Run during the day, but overly cautious Union commanders continued to assess the probability of success until the day was gone, and the skirmishers were pulled back. That day, like each day on Mine Run, Stuart rode his lines and then slowly rode back to his camp near Verdiersville for the night.[155]

Nothing much happened on December 1, but when daylight arrived the following day, R. E. Lee and his commanders were immediately aware of the absence of enemy pickets. Confederate skirmishers moved forward to make contact — they were gone. R. E. Lee set his army in pursuit. A. P. Hill's command was moved along the Orange Plank Road; and Early's command was sent up the Orange Turnpike. Stuart instructed Hampton to have his cavalry division sweep around the Confederate right as far as Chancellorsville, and if the enemy were not found on the roads leading to Spotsylvania, they were instructed to press up to the Rapidan.[156]

Before long, it was discovered that Meade was withdrawing across the Rapidan at Germanna and Ely's Fords. A. P. Hill's command was halted on the Orange Plank Road after advancing about 8 miles; and Early's and Stuart's commands pushed as far as Germanna Ford only to find the enemy had crossed. Meade recrossed the Rapidan on December 2 because he was unable to penetrate or turn R. E. Lee's line.[157]

The recorded losses taken by the 2nd North Carolina Cavalry in action just prior to and during the Mine Run Campaign were as follows:

Combat Losses in the 2nd North Carolina Cavalry Mine Run Campaign, November 1863

Trooper	Age	Co.	Fate
Benjamin O. Wade	35	I	captured, Nov. 11
John W. Rogers		C	captured, Nov. 26
John A. Parker		C	captured, Nov. 28
Nicholas J. Harrell	26	C	wounded, Nov. 29
Randall H. Reese*	26	H	killed, Nov. 29
Virginius Copeland*		H	mortally wounded, Nov. 29
Michael McGuire	25	A	mortally wounded, late Nov.
Felix E. Woodward	23	E	captured, Mine Run, Nov. 30

Information contained in this table came from Compiled Service Records as summarized by Louis H. Manarin, *North Carolina Troops: 1861–1865, A Roster*, vol. II, pp. 98–177, unless otherwise indicated. (See Appendix for more information on the men listed above, page 400.)
*Reese and Copeland were mentioned in Gordon's after-battle report, *O. R.*, vol. XXIX, part 1, p. 903.

The locations and dates of losses indicate the men of the 2nd North Carolina Cavalry were patrolling and picketing along the Rapidan and up the Robertson River during the month of November and into the Mine Run Campaign.

As usual, there were many wounded in the dismounted charge on the Union line near Mine Run who did not require hospitalization, and thus their pain was not recorded. In addition, the 2nd Cavalry's brigade commander, James B. Gordon, once again had a close call when his horse was shot out from under him and he crashed to the ground.[158]

Captain William P. Roberts of Company C had only the following to say about the campaign: "Mine Run and other places, and until its close, the gallant little regiment was always in readiness and took its place in front whenever called upon to do so." The 2nd Cavalry's dismounted charge into the enemy's line on November 29, 1863 was a harbinger of things to come, and Confederate commanders from that day forward knew they could call on the 2nd North Carolina cavalrymen when such a charge was called for.[159]

Winter Camp: "Rain, Sleet and Snow make camp-life almost unbearable"

Just days after the Mine Run Campaign, the cavalry moved into winter quarters. A member of Stuart's staff, Lieutenant Theodore S. Garnett, wrote of the conditions and activities that occupied their time:

Winter had set in with more than usual severity when the troops returned to their old camps around Orange Court House, and along the Rapidan. A great part of the Cavalry had been disbanded and been sent home to procure fresh horses even before the Mine Run Campaign began, — and now this absolutely necessary process to fill up our ranks was continued by Gen. Stuart. The system of "Horse Details" was greatly enlarged, and every effort was made to organize more efficiently and equip more thoroughly our still badly provided Cavalry Corps....

Immediately on our return to the old camp, the waste places were rebuilt, the wooden chimneys were daubed afresh with the red mud of old Orange, the wall-tents were again pitched in front of them, and we settled down for the winter.... Dull days would come; it was impossible to escape them; Rain, Sleet and Snow make camp-life almost unbearable.[160]

Stuart's camp was near Orange Court House, but most of the brigades under his command, except for those along the Rapidan River, were scattered throughout Virginia. It was a relatively simple matter to temporally disband many of the Virginia cavalry regiments and let them go home where they might better resuscitate themselves and their horses. In fact, most of the cavalrymen in Fitz Lee's division wintered at or very near their homes. Getting the Carolinians and other Southerners in Hampton's division home so that they could better deal with their weakened horses or lack of them was not as easily achieved. In the case of North Carolinians, much of Hampton's and Gordon's energy and time was spent trying to locate the men in a place where they might better prepare for the coming spring campaign. When the commanders were not able to send the regiments home, they had to find a way to keep them warm enough and fed enough to be around for the next campaign. Rebuilding the number of serviceable horses and recruiting new men for the North Carolina brigade was a particularly difficult task while they remained in Virginia during the long and cold months of winter camp. In spite of their needs most of the North Carolinians spent most of the winter in Virginia because it was not universally acknowledged that all their needs could best be met if they were in North Carolina, and not incidentally, somebody had to be on picket, scout the enemy lines, and be ready to confront any one of the many enemy invasions, rumored or real.

LOCATIONS AND DUTIES

Camp locations were generally influenced by duty assignments — if the regiment is assigned to picket duty, it makes sense to camp nearby. On the other hand, if the troopers are also considered to be part of the defense of Richmond when needed, then they should be near enough to be effective there. Of course, another consideration is the availability of sustenance for both men and horses. If winter camp is to be a time and place for rebuilding a regiment, forage should be nearby.

The troopers in Hampton's division who remained on duty in Virginia had to be placed in locations that met the variety of needs listed above. This spread them rather thin because their main picket line was along the Rapidan River and later the Orange Plank Road as well;

and most of the rumored invasions were about Richmond coming under attack from the Peninsula.

The regiments in Hampton's division were also among those most in need of rebuilding, especially those regiments decimated during 1863 — such as the 2nd North Carolina. In addition to meeting the daily needs of his men, one of Gordon's major responsibilities was to field a strong brigade for the next spring campaign which was only a few months away. One of Hampton's major responsibilities was to help his brigade commanders meet these needs and at the same time have a cavalry force capable of responding to the current needs of the army.

Once in winter camp on December 7, Hampton wrote directly to Robert E. Lee suggesting how his cavalrymen might best survive the winter and rebuild for the next spring campaign. Hampton pointed out how most of his men were a great distance from their homes and thus were having difficulty keeping themselves mounted due to the high and increasing prices for horses in Virginia. He communicated his concern that many of his best men might have to move into the infantry for that very reason. Hampton recommended that Gordon's and Young's (Butler's) brigades be sent to the Roanoke River, near Weldon, less than 10 miles below the North Carolina border — where he felt they could better obtain forage and affordable horses. He added that in his view the North Carolina regiments would greatly increase their numbers if they were allowed to winter in their home state. Hampton went on to say, "...if the horses are kept here this winter on short forage, these brigades will not be in condition for active service, nor will they ever be able to fill up their ranks."[161]

Robert E. Lee put into effect what he considered a more workable plan. He answered Hampton's letter on January 23 explaining what he preferred to do. He sent Rosser's brigade of Virginia regiments to the lower Shenandoah Valley which was near home for many of them, as Hampton had suggested. Beyond that, he basically rejected Hampton's suggestions saying that he hoped there was sufficient forage down near Milford Station along the Richmond to Fredericksburg railroad because Gordon's and Young's brigades had been sent to that area. R. E. Lee went on to say it was impossible to send any of the regiments back to South Carolina; and his official reports indicated a shortage of forage down around the Roanoke in northern North Carolina. The only relief Lee could offer was to suggest that Hampton have two regiments from each brigade (Gordon's and Young's) fall back to greener pastures, leaving one on duty at all times from each brigade, and alternate the regiments. R. E. Lee hoped by rotating the regiments, each North Carolina company would have enough time in their home counties to recruit horses and men.[162]

Meanwhile, the 2nd North Carolina Cavalry, camped some distance from Stuart's cavalry headquarters, received little assistance from the Confederate army for feeding men and beasts. A couple of weeks after the Mine Run Campaign, the men of the 2nd North Carolina were already hard pressed to sustain themselves and their horses. The men often had to fend for themselves; having some money did help. Private Levi Lockhart wrote his sister and explained the condition around their camp, near Milford, in these words: "We can get anything here to eat that we want by paying a high price for it; Irish potatoes, six dollars per bushel; sweet potatoes, eight dollars; chickens, from three to five dollars a piece." One way or another, the cavalrymen managed to feed themselves and care for their horses. A couple of weeks later, Private Lockhart again wrote his sister and explained how he was handling his horse's well-being: "I gave William Monk $80.00, when he started home with my horse; I told him to take pay out of it for taking my horse and to leave the rest of it at home." (A trooper's pay in the 2nd North Carolina was erratic, but pay for the service of their horses was more regular — the latter typically amounted to $12 per month.)[163]

Robert E. Lee was not insensitive to the special needs of southern cavalrymen far from their homes. He simply had other concerns to juggle. In fact the day after Lee wrote Hampton, he wrote the Secretary of War in Richmond and outlined the difficulties:

The cavalry of this army, by its hard service, summer and winter, and through the deficiency of forage in the latter season, had become very much reduced. This is especially true of the two southern brigades, which have not the same opportunities of remounting themselves with those from Virginia. The enemy have always had on this line a cavalry force greatly superior in numbers, and will doubtless recruit their cavalry divisions largely before the next campaign. I hear of no recruits coming to this army, and see but little prospect of any, as they all choose the regiments and companies (already filled to overflowing) which are not called upon for very active duty. I think it is of the highest importance that steps should be taken to strengthen our cavalry.[164]

R. E. Lee's recommendations for strengthening the cavalry centered on getting more units from South Carolina. A few days after Lee's letter, Stuart entered the discussion when he suggested the War Department put pressure on South Carolina and Georgia to send some of their well-manned cavalry regiments to him. He pointed out that Brigadier General Butler was still in South Carolina recovering from wounds, and he could select some men from the large units there and bring them to Virginia for inclusion in the depleted South Carolina regiments under his command. Neither R. E. Lee nor Stuart had recommendations for enhancing the North Carolina regiments under their command.[165] That was Gordon's job, who in turn, for the most part, left it to the regiments.

As indicated, Gordon's North Carolina brigade was located near Milford Station on the Richmond, Fredericksburg & Potomac Railroad. R. E. Lee had placed them there hoping the forage was better than on the Rapidan River where the major part of their picketing duties were performed, and where they could move to Richmond if needed.[166] (See map 2.5.)

Their picket duties along the Rapidan took them as far as Jacob's Ford, which meant they often had to travel up to thirty miles in freezing weather to picket the river for several days at a time on a rotation basis. In addition, the North Carolinian cavalrymen went on scouts that ranged even farther. For instance, according to the Union Provost Marshal General in Alexandria, a squad of six North Carolina cavalrymen from Gordon's brigade conducted a small raid near Accotink (5 or 10 miles below Alexandria) — they arrived at that place on January 12. That scout took the Confederate cavalrymen about 45 miles above their camp.[167]

In addition, Hampton was under constant pressure to send cavalry to Richmond in response to the many false alarms of Union troops moving up the Peninsula. On January 30, he acknowledged that he had his men ready to move to any point that became threatened, even to shield Richmond from an attack coming up the Peninsula. He also pointed out that his force was so depleted that he would be unable to withstand even an assault that came down the railroad from Alexandria — which he felt was just as likely as an attack up the Peninsula. Hampton pointed out that if he left men on his picket lines, at best he would be able to mount a force of around 700 to 800 men (the 2nd North Carolina Cavalry could mount closer to 50 than 100 men at that time). He also mentioned that he was prepared to send his dismounted cavalrymen down to Colonel Bradley Johnson at Hanover Junction if that place became threatened. Hampton and Gordon had already sent the dismounted North Carolinians to Orange Court House, and by the end of January he was suggesting that Stuart send them over to Hanover Junction if he thought the threat was greater. Hampton estimated 75 to 100 dismounted men from Gordon's North Carolina brigade were in Orange County. The use of all dismounted cavalrymen was a result of Stuart's earlier orders that disbanded Company Q and required that they must be usefully employed or move to the infantry.[168]

In addition to using all his available men for picket duty and keeping them ready at all times to march toward suspected enemy advances from the Peninsula and elsewhere, throughout the winter he continued to send men from his cavalry division as far as Stafford and Fauquier County on scouting missions.[169]

Private Means of the 5th North Carolina described their stay in winter quarters as "Long, weary, winter work well done." In addition to doing their work well, they apparently also stayed militarily fit. In late December, Stuart inspected the North Carolina brigade's camp near Milford Station and wrote the following to Hampton: "I desire to express my high gratification at the good order and military discipline in Gordon's and Young's Brigades during my recent visit to them."[170]

RESUSCITATE AND RECRUIT, BOTH MEN AND HORSES

In addition to performing their duties at the places described above, the cavalry units had to rebuild. Stuart's Aide-de-Camp, Garnett, wrote that cavalrymen had been sent on Horse Details since early October, and that program was still under way during the early months of

1864.[171] By February 1864, the program was expanded to include entire squadrons or regiments as R. E. Lee had recommended to Hampton. This allowed two of the North Carolina regiments to be relieved of duty and travel home for about a month at a time to get remounted.

Private Means pointed out that the men of the 5th North Carolina Cavalry were sent home for fresh horses necessary for the inevitable spring campaign. He went on to write, "The regiment [5th North Carolina Cavalry] temporarily disbanded at Henderson, N.C., in March, 1864, that each man might go to his home for a new horse, or the recuperation of the one he had and himself." At the end of the regimental leave, the captain of each company reassembled his men with their horses at a designated place, and marched to Richmond where they once again became a regiment. Once reassembled, the 5th North Carolina numbered around 500 mounted men. The 4th North Carolina went on Horse Detail in a similar manner during that cold and hard winter. (The 4th was officially detached from Gordon's brigade on April 22, 1864.) The 1st and 2nd North Carolina Cavalry were not so fortunate. Some were allowed to go on Horse Detail, but never the entire regiment in such a systematic manner. Most men in the 2nd North Carolina were kept on duty during the winter. However, the Company Muster Roll for a number of the cavalrymen in the 2nd North Carolina, show they were "Absent on horse detail of thirty days since April 26, 1864," but the regiment stayed on duty.[172]

Individual North Carolinians in the 1st and 2nd Cavalries were at best absent on Horse Details for a month, while winter camp lasted nearly five months that year, thus they had to be maintained in Virginia for the balance of the winter. It was Hampton's job to get his share of the clothing, food, and forage available to the Army of Northern Virginia for his cavalrymen; and it was Gordon's job to supply his North Carolinians as best he could while they were on duty in Virginia.

Hampton remained close to his troops and could see them deteriorating. He knew more was needed if they were to be ready for the spring campaign, and he was enough of a politician to know the wheel that squeaked the loudest got the "grease." So he entered into an exchange of ideas with Stuart and R. E. Lee about where his men should be stationed. He achieved little, and R. E. Lee ended the debate several days later by saying, "General H. [Hampton] had better [remain] within reach of Hanover Court-House, and his depot had better not be so exposed as it would be at Lloyd's; but he must establish himself where he can get supplies." In other words, Hampton should not move any of his men too far south, but should find another way to feed them and their horses.[173]

By February 6, R. E. Lee and his commanders kept their eyes on the left of their line—Ewell was reporting the enemy in force at Morton's Ford, on the Rapidan. R. E. Lee instructed Stuart to "Endeavor to find out enemy's intentions and direction." And he added, "If his army is in motion we must concentrate and fight him. You had better prepare Wickham to move to the front." Later the same day, Stuart was notified that Ewell reported two enemy infantry regiments had indeed crossed at Morton's Ford. Stuart immediately instructed Hampton to "Have one brigade ready to move at short notice. Indications at Morton's Ford may make it necessary for you to move to the support of your picket-line. Get up some hard bread."[174] Some of Gordon's North Carolina cavalrymen were on the picket line.

Wesley Merritt, commanding Buford's former First Cavalry Division, crossed the Robertson River on February 6 at two different fords and drove the Confederate pickets back at both places (John Buford had died of an illness on December 16, 1863). The next day, Merritt moved his artillery and cavalry toward Barnett's Ford and engaged Lomax's men with skirmish and artillery fire until around 1:00 P.M. when he received orders to withdraw.[175]

As Merritt moved his division to the Robertson River, Kilpatrick moved directly to the Rapidan with his. Kilpatrick crossed at Germanna and Ely's Fords at about 11:00 A.M. on February 6. He then sent columns in several direction to probe the Confederate line. One column which he described as a "considerable force" met a small body of enemy cavalry and drove them back across the Orange Plank Road. He also sent a regiment to Jacob's Ford where they captured the picket. Kilpatrick went into camp that night on the plank road coming from Germanna Ford. By 9 o'clock on the next morning, he was back across the Rapidan.[176]

Kilpatrick was able to report that R. E.

Lee's army was in basically the same place as last November when Meade retired across the Rapidan, and that Hampton's cavalry was over near Hamilton's Crossing. Kilpatrick also learned that "A large number of his [Hampton's] men are without horses or arms; 240 of his men picket the river from Germanna to the United States Ford; only a few of the last detail sent had horses." Kilpatrick's information was pretty accurate. A good number of Hampton's cavalry were without mounts, and many without adequate arms. Actually many of the men on the picket lines, with and without horses, were Gordon's North Carolinians, and a small number of them were taken prisoner.[177]

Gordon had men from the 2nd North Carolina Cavalry posted along the river from Jacob's down to Ely's Ford, and along the Orange Plank Road. When Kilpatrick's men came across, some men from the 2nd North Carolina were on picket at the fords, and some of the cavalrymen were without horses—the latter were easily captured. Others were driven back. Kilpatrick stated his men captured the picket force at Jacob's Ford on February 6, and North Carolinians were certainly among them. Kilpatrick's cavalrymen also encountered men from Gordon's command down on the Orange Plank Road, and that was near where they took three more prisoners from the 2nd North Carolina. In his brief report of this incident on the Rapidan, R. E. Lee simply said, "The guard at the ford (a lieutenant and 25 men), while bravely resisting the passage of the enemy, were captured."[178]

By the time the regiment's commander told Hampton how depleted the 2nd North Carolina was, it was back under the command of Major Clinton M. Andrews. He was promoted to Lieutenant Colonel on February 12, 1863, and just six days later, Andrews was rewarded for his superior leadership of the 2nd North Carolina Cavalry whenever summoned, and promoted to Colonel of the regiment.[179]

After the flurry of excitement and some losses on February 6 and 7, the cavalrymen of Hampton's division went back on picket, and stood at the ready to march for any action that was not another false alarm. The next call for Hampton to move his cavalry came from General Elzey. Elzey again requested cavalry because Richmond was about to be attacked from the Peninsula. This most recent alarm came on February 11, and Hampton naturally received it with some skepticism—there had already been too many false alarms, and his men and horses were too weary to be put on the march each time. Hampton now waited for confirmation of any attack before he put his cavalrymen on the road. It was another false alarm; the Union force returned to Williamsburg. A couple of days later, R. E. Lee commended Hampton for being careful not to waste what little resources he had left. The message said that General Lee himself "...has been very much annoyed by the false alarms from Richmond, and the distress which it had caused among the men and horses in moving during winter season."[180]

At that point, Hampton had very few troops available at any given time. In Hampton's words, "The last fruitless expedition did my horses much harm. In the North Carolina brigade only the Second Regiment is here, the First being on picket duty, and the major commanding it reports this morning [February 12] but 65 horses for duty, and in Young's brigade I do not think that more than 350 men can be mounted."[181]

In any case, trying to remain in a state of readiness for every perceived threat coming at Richmond and continually performing picket duties in harsh conditions was taking its toll on the horses, the men, and their commanders. Lee and Hampton were obviously impatient with the continual false alarms that further taxed the already exhausted cavalry.

Kilpatrick's Expedition to Richmond, February 28–March 4, 1864

The next alarm was not false, nor was it the beginning of the 1864 campaign; it was H. Judson Kilpatrick's expedition against Richmond. The politician in Kilpatrick drove him to action. He knew his career would not be advanced by sitting in his camp near Stevensburg, and he knew Richmond was not strongly defended. He also knew Hampton's cavalry, which rested between him and Richmond, was few in number and poorly equipped—that much he had learned from the last probe across the Rapidan on February 6 and 7. With all that in mind, he devised a plan to attack Richmond with a strong force of cavalry.

Kilpatrick's plan was to cross the Rapidan with around 4,000 cavalrymen and six guns at Ely's Ford; then move to Spotsylvania Court House; and from there send a sufficient force of cavalry to destroy the Virginia Central Railroad which would prevent R. E. Lee from sending re-enforcements in a timely manner. Kilpatrick proposed to move ahead with the main force to Hanover Junction, and from there along Brook Road to Richmond. Small detachments were to go in several directions, cutting communications between Kilpatrick's planned route and the Army of Northern Virginia. Kilpatrick's explicit purposes for the expedition were both political and military—more emphasis was given to one over the other depending on to whom he was currently selling the idea.[182]

At best, Kilpatrick received a tepid response to his plan from his immediate commanders, Generals Pleasonton and Meade. They weighed the possible costs of such an expedition against what they considered questionable gains. Kilpatrick was determined, however, and on February 12, he took his plan directly to President Lincoln. Kilpatrick sold the plan as a bold effort to liberate all the Union prisoners of war held in Richmond. That would obviously be a morale booster for the troops as well as the war weary people of the Union. Kilpatrick spread icing on the cake by agreeing to distribute copies of "the President's amnesty proclamation to the rebel command in our front, and to the inhabitants of Virginia in the various counties about Richmond." Always eager for something to happen, Lincoln supported Kilpatrick's plan—as did his Secretary of War. On the other hand, Pleasonton voiced his disapproval by officially stating that he thought the plan was "not feasible at this time." He went on to say, " In reference to the president's proclamation, I will most willingly undertake to have it freely circulated in any section of Virginia that may be desired. I do not think I am promising too much in naming even Richmond." Sufficient pressure on Meade and Pleasonton got them to go along with, if not enthusiastically support, Kilpatrick's expedition to the enemy's capital—the symbolism of taking Richmond was also a political prize too great to ignore.[183]

By February 27, Kilpatrick had everyone aboard and had accepted some additions to his basic plan. Further up the Rapidan, a diversionary force of infantry and cavalry would be sent across at the left flank of the Confederate line. It would then feint a move on Charlottesville. George Custer was designated to lead the cavalry force of 1,500 toward the enemy's left, and John Sedgwick with two divisions of infantry was ordered to make for Madison Court House. The latter was scheduled to arrive there Sunday afternoon, February 28.[184]

Perhaps the most notable addition to Kilpatrick's plan was the young and ambitious Colonel Ulric Dahlgren. Kilpatrick was apparently reluctant at first to give the young man a prominent role in the expedition, but ultimately enough controversy surrounded the issue to make it an attractive feature. Kilpatrick let Dahlgren take the advance force of 460 men. With that settled the parting message from Meade's headquarters to Kilpatrick on the 27th made it clear that the plan was his "...with the sanction of the President and the Secretary of War." and thus no detailed instructions came from Meade's headquarters. Kilpatrick was on his own and ordered to move out the next morning.[185]

George A. Custer was ordered to move on the Confederate left and arrive at Madison Court House on the evening of February 28. He was able to maintain his schedule and left Madison for Charlottesville around midnight. Stuart's camp was at Orange Court House, just east of Custer's route, but Custer managed to pass around the left of the Confederate line long before Stuart knew what was going on. The Federal cavalrymen arrived in the vicinity of Charlottesville in early afternoon on February 29. Once Stuart got word of Custer's presence and was able to determine his direction, he and Wickham's brigade from Fitz Lee's cavalry division started for Charlottesville. William C. Wickham's brigade had just replaced Lomax's brigade which had been doing the picket duty on the upper fords of the Rapidan. Wickham's men were relatively fresh, so they were able to monitor Custer's progress soon after they left Madison Court House. After some hours on the march, Stuart received word that Custer was pulling back. Stuart then turned his pursuit northward, hoping to catch the enemy around Stannardsville. The Confederate cavalrymen got between Custer and his destination, Madison Court House, but Custer's men managed to charge through the Confederate cavalrymen and get back to Madison where Sedgwick's infantry was holding.[186]

While Custer was at Madison Court House fully occupying Stuart's attention, Kilpatrick's expedition left camp at Stevensburg with 3,582 men and a battery of U.S. Horse Artillery. His cavalrymen were picked from both the First and Second Cavalry Divisions. They left camp at 7:00 P.M. February 28, and headed for Ely's Ford on the Rapidan.[187]

Kilpatrick's advance under the command of Ulric Dahlgren reached Ely's Ford around 11:00 P.M. and managed to get a small party across undetected. That well-executed maneuver allowed them to get behind the small picket of 15 Confederate cavalrymen and capture the lot of them. Unfortunately for the Confederates not one picket managed to escape and take word of the Union crossing back to P. M. B. Young (still commanding Butler's brigade). Kilpatrick managed to get his entire column across the river without disturbing the Confederate pickets further up and down the line. Dahlgren then moved the advance rapidly to Spotsylvania Court House and on to the Virginia Central Railroad to disrupt R. E. Lee's communications with Richmond. Dahlgren was then instructed to cross the James River, move down river, and attack Richmond from the south in coordination with Kilpatrick's planned attack from the north.[188] (See map 2.4.)

Kilpatrick moved his main column rapidly past Spotsylvania Court House on the morning of February 29 and then south to Beaver Dam Station on the Virginia Central Railroad. Around 1:00 P.M., they paused at the station, just long enough to destroy the station and considerable track. From there, they moved rapidly toward Richmond. Kilpatrick and his men went into camp early that evening just about 9 miles from Ground Squirrel Bridge on the South Anna River. The Union column was back on the road early the next morning planning to cross Ground Squirrel Bridge and move on Richmond, but the column was misdirected. On their unintended route, the Federal cavalrymen came upon an enemy picket line in front of a small force of infantry. This slowed Kilpatrick's column a bit.[189]

Meanwhile, Wade Hampton was paying the price for having his few available cavalrymen spread thinly over the picket line. Judson Kilpatrick had been able to punch through the line at Ely's Ford undetected. With its cavalry spread so thin, the eyes and ears of the Army of Northern Virginia were not able to sense the enemy presence with any degree of certainty.

Pierce M. B. Young, commanding the picket line around Ely's Ford, got his first indication that Kilpatrick had crossed the Rapidan at about 11:00 A.M. on March 1, by then Kilpatrick was already approaching Ashland and the South Anna River. During the night, Young had received an uncertain report from a citizen suggesting a column had passed the previous night, and at about the same time he received word from a scout near Culpeper Court House that the enemy was on the move in that area. None of the information was adequate to justify the movement of his brigade in any direction. Young immediately telegraphed Stuart and Hampton as well as the provost marshal at Hanover Junction informing them of what little he knew. He then ordered his brigade to cook some rations and stay ready to move out. While waiting to hear from Stuart or Hampton, Young received another report from a citizen that a column of enemy cavalry had passed him during the early part of the day. Young telegraphed Hampton again at his headquarters near Milford on the Richmond Fredericksburg & Potomac Railroad to confirm the report and get orders. Hampton replied with instructions to have his men ready to march on short notice.[190]

Hampton had also begun to receive word that the enemy was heading for the Rapidan by late morning on the 29th; and he also sent word to Stuart that there was apparently movement on their front, and his information indicated Kilpatrick was "Supposed to be coming to Ely's Ford." (By the time Hampton sent this message, Kilpatrick had already passed through Ely's Ford.) By 12:30 P.M., Hampton sent another communication to Stuart passing along Young's second report from a citizen about an enemy column across the Rapidan heading for the Virginia Central Railroad. By 10:30 on the night of the 29th Hampton still had not heard from Stuart (who was busy tracking Custer to the west) so he sent another message in Stuart's direction telling him that Kilpatrick had passed him and reached Beaver Dam Station several hours earlier that evening. He also informed

Stuart that he had sent part of the North Carolina brigade to Beaver Dam on the North Anna River, on Kilpatrick's trail.[191]

As soon as Hampton learned what direction Kilpatrick was taking he put the 1st North Carolina Cavalry and the available men from the 2nd North Carolina under Clinton M. Andrews on the road. Hampton's mounted force at Milford that day was 253 men from the 1st North Carolina and 53 men from the 2nd North Carolina. He sent them all after Kilpatrick. Hampton also sent word to the Maryland Cavalry under Colonel Bradley T. Johnson, stationed at Hanover Junction, to be ready to join him where the Virginia Central meets the R. F. & P. Railroad. However, the Marylanders were already aware of Kilpatrick's presence and had moved to stay between their enemy and Richmond. After leaving men at various rivers and bridges, Johnson took his remaining 60 cavalrymen and four guns and made for Ashland, and then on to Yellow Tavern just north of Richmond. By then Kilpatrick's advance was already at the outer defenses of Richmond and had their guns pounding the Confederate city about that time. Johnson intercepted a courier from Dahlgren to Kilpatrick with a message that described their intention to attack the city from both sides. Johnson knew he did not have time to wait for reinforcement, so he threw his entire force of 60 men at Kilpatrick, driving his rear guard in on the main body of the Union column. Kilpatrick put his plan to attack the city on hold until the next day and went into camp. Johnson moved his men into camp between Kilpatrick and Richmond. During the night, the 1st and 2nd North Carolina cavalries arrived in the area.[192]

Once again, Kilpatrick's luck at the outset was incredible. Only one regiment and part of another near Hampton could be immediately put on his trail—they were the 1st and 2nd North Carolina Cavalries. Hampton took command of these North Carolinians because their brigade commander, James B. Gordon, was on leave back in his home state. The 1st North Carolina was under the command of Colonel Cheek, and the 2nd Cavalry was under the command of newly appointed Colonel Andrews. Hampton placed Cheek, the senior colonel in the camp, in charge of the 306 cavalrymen. They prepared several days rations and were on the road by 8:00 P.M. February 29. Their job was clear enough, track down and stop Kilpatrick's expedition against Richmond when the opportunity presents itself. Hampton remained at Milford waiting for some word from Stuart.[193]

The men with the 1st and 2nd North Carolina cavalries marched after Kilpatrick's column under less than ideal circumstances. In the words of Colonel Cheek, "We left camp about midnight [other accounts put the time at about 8 o'clock] on the last day of February and marched continuously through a terrible storm of rain, hail, sleet and snow, until about midnight of the first of March we came in sight of camp-fires between Atlee's Station and Richmond." Hampton caught up with his North Carolinians early on the morning of March 1, and they headed toward Hanover Court House where they hoped to come upon the enemy. They were late; Kilpatrick was already at the outer-defenses of Richmond. According to Captain Ford of the 1st North Carolina Cavalry, Hampton knew well "his force was too small to seriously embarrass the movements of the enemy by direct attack, kept his men in hand, waiting to strike the enemy a blow under the fifth rib when it was possible to be accomplished. All of Monday night and Tuesday we were in the saddle and on the alert, though not all the time in motion. Keeping at a respectful and safe distance from Kilpatrick, and avoiding an encounter." From Hanover Court House, Hampton moved down, paralleling the Virginia Central Railroad. By then, the cavalry was having difficulty maintaining even a slow pace because almost constant rain all day and night caused the roads to be deep in mud, making each step more difficult for the exhausted horses. It was also slow going for the two pieces of artillery from Hart's Battery Hampton had brought along. Nonetheless, they plodded on and as they approached Atlee's Station, about nine miles north of Richmond, they could see camp fires off to their right in the direction of Brook Road and in front between the station and Richmond. Hampton's advance troopers took some small arms fire as they approached the station but were under orders not to return fire. Hampton did not want to fire until he was sure the campfires were kept by their enemy.[194]

THE FIGHT AT ATLEE'S STATION

Once fired upon, Hampton dismounted about 100 men and approached the station. The enemy pickets had fallen back so Hampton occupied the station house with no difficulty. From there he approached the camp in front of his column, toward Richmond. The North Carolinians moved down the road and again came upon enemy pickets who, after firing a few shots, retired. Hampton's men were still under instructions not to return fire until they knew who they were firing at. Apparently in their haste to fall back, the pickets failed to sound the alarm in the Union camps behind them. W. H. Cheek sent scouts forward immediately, and they came across a horse left by one of the pickets. The horse was tied to a fence and bore a new saddle, blanket, and bridle — it clearly belonged to a Union cavalrymen. The Confederate advance sent word back that the camps in front were occupied by the enemy. Surprisingly, they were all asleep around their campfires in the midst of some woods. It was now the turn of Kilpatrick's men to be surprised.[195] (See map 2.1 or 2.4.)

Colonel Cheek and the cavalrymen from the 1st and 2nd North Carolina moved slowly through the snowstorm toward the silent enemy camp — this was the rear camp in Kilpatrick's cluster of three, each containing about one brigade of hand-picked Union cavalrymen. Cheek dismounted about 120 of his 306 men, and moved them cautiously to within 50 yards of the camp and then had them lie down in the snow to wait for the sound of their artillery whistling overhead. If it had not been so cold, they probably would have enjoyed the prone position for their wait. They had been in their saddles for over 24 hours before arriving in this position. Their ride through a night, a day, and most of another night had been through heavy rain, sleet, and hail, and then snow, and now they had lie down in the snow with only their frozen clothes between them and it — they had to endure, motionless and in silence. The other 186 or so men under Cheek's command sat quietly, frozen in their saddles, which may have been a little more tolerable, while Hampton brought up the two guns from Hart's Battery and placed them carefully on a rise.[196]

The dismounted men were instructed to wait until 14 shots had passed over their heads, then charge the enemy camp. The guns were placed at very close range and the shots were executed in rapid succession. Everything was designed to heighten the surprise and thus the impact of his charging mass of 306 cavalrymen. Captain N. P. Ford and his squadron of forty men were among those lying in the snow, and he remembered the "dismounted men counted the shells with great precision as they went over their heads into the enemy camp, which were fired with that rapidity which would indicate to a startled foe the presence of as many batteries as there were pieces." Then, again in Ford's words, "those dismounted men rose and charged the enemy's camp with all the noise that could emanate from forty mouths with the dreaded rebel yell; and from forty well-handled repeating carbines; all of this conducted by old 'vets' who so well knew that what we lacked in numbers must be compensated for in noise and rattle." In a similar account, Colonel Cheek recalled, "When the first shell flew over him, Captain Blair was ordered to rise, raise the yell and charge the camp. The scheme proved a perfect success. The enemy was surprised, demoralized and stampeded." The mounted North Carolinians followed closely on their comrade's heels and quickly formed a shield between the camp and the fleeing enemy in case they were able to regroup and countercharge. The charge was so effective and the pursuit by the mounted Confederates so quick, there was no countercharge. Hampton said his North Carolinians that night "were fully equal to the most difficult duty of soldiers — a night attack." Of course, at least one thing is more difficult than making a night attack, and that is being surprised by one.[197]

The Confederate cavalrymen drove the sleepy, disoriented, and panicked enemy from their camp, and some of them pursued the fleeing Federals for a short distance — a distance sufficient to push them into the next of Kilpatrick's camps further down the road. A good number of the men in the second camp apparently also scampered to the front camp where Kilpatrick had already heard the sounds of the guns. After having his rear guard hit by the Marylanders earlier in the night, Kilpatrick had backed off from his attack on Richmond and put his front brigade into camp at around 1:00 A.M. March 2. The North Carolinians had launched their attack on Kilpatrick's rear brigade shortly before that hour.[198]

Kilpatrick continued to hear guns from up the road after Hampton's attack on his rear camp, due to the manner in which the pursuit took place. A short while after Cheek's command had stormed the Union camp, Hampton restored order to the joyful North Carolinians, who were appreciating the warm fires and equipment left by the Union cavalrymen and set them on the road in pursuit of the fleeing enemy. During the pursuit the Confederate cavalrymen moved slowly after their prey. It was dark and the snow was heavy, and by then they knew thousands of enemy cavalrymen were in front of them. With that in mind, the Confederates shelled the road in front as they moved along. However, after a short while wisdom prevailed and Hampton stopped the pursuit until daylight. The Confederate cavalrymen moved back to the captured Union camp and enjoyed the warm fires, blankets and other abandoned Federal accoutrements.[199]

Hampton's pursuit continued long enough for the sounds of his guns to be heard in Kilpatrick's front camp, and if the sounds were not heard as far away as his camp at Mechanicsville, he heard from some of his retreating cavalrymen. The discomfort Kilpatrick felt that early morning as a result of both attacks at his rear can be sensed in these comments from his after-battle report: "The night was intensely dark, cold, and stormy.... Not knowing the strength of the enemy, I abandoned all further ideas of releasing our prisoners, and at 1:00 A.M. moved to the intersection of.... Here we went into camp."[200]

When Hampton had his cavalrymen back in pursuit after daybreak, Kilpatrick had already moved his brigades away from Richmond. Kilpatrick pulled back to Old Church and waited for Dahlgren to arrive from south of the city. While waiting, his troops were harassed by Confederate cavalrymen who were driven back each time, with prisoners being taken. Kilpatrick learned "From the prisoners ... that they belonged to Hampton's Division, and that it was he who attacked me the night before; that he had with him a large force of mounted infantry and cavalry and four pieces of artillery." Kilpatrick's first moves of the day gave Hampton the impression he was going to force his way through the Confederate cavalry line and march north to rejoin his army. Hampton knew his horses could not endure a rapid and sustained march, and thinking Kilpatrick was going to head north, he moved his North Carolinian cavalrymen back north along the railroad and concentrated his force back near their former camps. Further confrontation was avoided because Kilpatrick actually marched southeast for Williamsburg.[201]

By the time Hampton's cavalrymen had charged into the enemy camp early in the morning of March 2, they were far fewer in number than the 306 who had left camp on February 29 — they had been reduced by the need to post pickets, send out scouts, and by broken-down horses. Nonetheless, the representatives from the North Carolina brigade took: 87 prisoners (including a brigadier general), 133 horses, 55 guns, 35 pistols, 46 sabers, 45 saddles, 43 bridles, 39 halters, and numerous blankets and other items of great value at the time. The men from the 1st and 2nd North Carolina had considerable time in the former Union camp to collect and exchange the many treasures of the night. When Colonel Cheek was asked to explain the discrepancy between the number of horses captured and the number of saddles, bridles, and halters listed on his report of property captured he simply replied, "When we know that the horses when captured were tied up and unsaddled, I can account for the difference only by the system of exchanges that we know is always practiced on such occasions. If the number of saddles, bridles, and halters should be made to correspond with the number of horses, I have no doubt the report would much nearer approximate the truth." I have no record of how the inquiring Assistant Adjutant General responded to Colonel Cheek's "explanation," but there was no denying many more North Carolinians rode the next day on good Union saddles and with much more.[202]

Ulric Dahlgren's planned simultaneous attack on Richmond never materialized for a number of reasons including his inability to get across the James River and his inability to find and communicate with Kilpatrick. Dahlgren had sent detachments in several directions, looking for any part of Kilpatrick's large command.[203]

One of Dahlgren's detachments ran into one of Hampton's detachments carrying wounded to Richmond early on the morning of March 3. Hampton had sent his wounded by a roundabout route in order to avoid running into Kilpatrick's column. The Confederate ambulance train was under the care of the 2nd

North Carolina Cavalry's Assistant Surgeon, Thomas E. Williams, and they were little more than an mile out of the captured camp when the front ambulance encountered Dahlgren's detachment. Reportedly, the driver of the front ambulance was still so elated over their just completed victory that, in the darkness and still blinding snow, he enthusiastically described the amazing details of the rout, without realizing he was talking to a Union officer. According to Captain Ford of the 1st North Carolina Cavalry, "Dr. Williams coming up at this juncture, realizing from some cause, perhaps from pronunciation ... that he was in the presence of the enemy, remarked to the officer in command that he supposed that he and his train were captured. The officer asked him what command had done all this mischief. Dr. Williams discreetly replied that it was Hampton's Division. After a few remarks the officer dismissed Dr. Williams, telling him he did not wish to be encumbered with wounded, thinking that he was doubtless in a very critical situation, marched no further in the direction of the camp-fires he had been seeking, but filed off by a left-hand road, making all possible haste to the Peninsula." The Union officer also probably appreciated the fact that all but two of the wounded men in the train of ambulances were Federal cavalrymen on their way to hospitals—albeit prison hospitals. This encounter probably played a part in Dahlgren's decision to swing wide around Hampton's force of unknown size in order to get to Gloucester Point.[204]

Dahlgren himself was with one of his detachments when they unexpectedly encountered some cavalrymen from the 9th Virginia who were in his path, recruiting along with some Home Guard from the area. They had gotten as far as King and Queen Court House when Dahlgren and some of his men rode into an ambush in which he was mortally wounded by a shotgun blast. The remnant of Dahlgren's command reached Kilpatrick on the evening of March 3 at their camp near Tunstall's Station.[205]

Kilpatrick's expedition ended with his retreat to Williamsburg, and Hampton taking his cavalrymen from the 1st and 2nd North Carolina cavalries back to their camps near Milford.

THE MOOD OF WINTER CAMP CONTINUED

By mid–March James B. Gordon returned from his furlough in time to visit with Governor Vance who was on a tour of his North Carolina units in Virginia. The governor felt he should visit the front line troops and bolster their spirits because there had been meetings of citizens back in North Carolina discussing the sanity and morality of negotiating a peace to end the war. Reports of these meetings and debates over the issue of peace were carried in most of the newspapers available to the troops. Naturally, many troopers were given cause to wonder why they were there, while others were angered or depressed. Governor Vance personally visited troops to assure them that their state was behind them, and their service was necessary and noble—and above all, their sacrifices were appreciated. Governor Vance was a very impressive speaker and apparently even J. E. B. Stuart was captivated to such a degree he attended many of the governor's speeches. As one attendee noted, "It was an interesting sight to witness these old heroes wipe away tears, and a few moments later be convulsed with laughter." By most accounts, the speaking tour was a great success—the governor left in his wake many troopers who were once again proud to be North Carolinians and to be fighting in Virginia. The harsh weather made the speaking tour difficult at times, but Governor Vance was able to pay a short visit to the North Carolina Cavalry Brigade's camp near Milford before he headed back to Raleigh on April 4. Of course he was probably only greeted by about 200 men from the 1st and 2nd North Carolina—many men from those regiments were on picket and scout activities, and the 4th and 5th North Carolina Cavalry regiments were still on detached duty.[206]

Less than a week after Hampton's North Carolinians had chased the enemy from the doorsteps of Richmond, he was again fighting for sustenance for his cavalry. On March 9, Hampton felt compelled to write Stuart about the continued hard duty performed by his regiments and the lack of hay forage for his horses. He mentioned that the situation was aggravated because it was known that the cavalry had received such forage, but none of it had reached his command. Rather it was shipped to the left of the Confederate line where the Virginia regiments perform much lighter duty. He reminded Stuart that Fitz Lee's Virginia regiments, disbanded for the winter and gone to their homes were now returning very full, and they could easily replace his worn-out troops.[207]

The friction between Hampton and Stuart grew during March of 1864. By mid-month, Stuart wrote Hampton that when Butler returned from South Carolina, Young's command should be divided, giving the two South Carolina regiments to Butler and an all South Carolina brigade would be filled out when new regiments arrived from that state. Stuart went on to say that Young could keep the legions and he would eventually get a Georgia regiment. Such manipulation of the regiments under his command did not sit well with Hampton, so he went over Stuart's head but sent the message through Stuart, when he wrote these words to R. E. Lee's headquarters: "I have received no orders from competent authority to break up one of my brigades, and until such orders come I shall not divide Butler's brigade. I respectfully request the commanding general not to authorize any change in my command without at least consulting my wishes on the subject." Apparently someone in the chain-of-command was listening, because by March 29, Hampton was in South Carolina helping Butler organize and bring the 4th, 5th, and 6th South Carolina regiments to Virginia, where they would operate in an all South Carolina brigade under Butler. This also allowed the 1st and 2nd South Carolina Cavalries to return home for rest and recruiting. However, there was little relief for the 1st and 2nd North Carolina regiments still rotating into picket duty out of their camp near Milford — some 40 miles from their picket lines.[208]

Milas A. Cavin of Company B, 2nd North Carolina Cavalry described the regiment's duty for most of the month of April 1864 in a letter to his aunt. In his words,

Our regiment is now on picket on the Rapidan river some 40 miles from camp. We have been out some 22 or 23 days. but we are expecting to be relieved and hope to return to camp in a few days. But excuse me this evening as I must fit for going on post as a vidette. We will be relieved from post in the morning, April 30th So upon returning from the lines to our reserve camp this morning we received our mail from our regular camp.... We expect to be relieved from picket Tuesday.[209]

Just before his description of picket duty, Private Cavin told his aunt, "We have had a right pleasant winter and were a considerable part of the time in camp, and had what we have learned to consider pretty comfortable quarters, we have been pretty well fed and clothed and upon the whole had a much better time than we had the winter before." Later in the letter, he expressed his appreciation for the mail he received that day — some of which had been hand carried by a neighbor and comrade. Apparently his courier-neighbor had tried to make the folks back home feel better by telling them Milas was fine and well satisfied with his lot as a soldier. His family wrote back expressing how pleased they were with Milas's condition. Milas was quick to correct their impressions by writing, "It seems that John Elim would have you all believe that I am satisfied. Well you must know that I cannot be satisfied in spending the prime of my life in the midst of danger, privations and exposures which we have to under go in the army. Besides aggravations and temptations of the most grievous character." Milas went on to point out that he has learned there is simply no point in complaining about things over which one has no control, and that he was being patient and hoping to "live to see better days."

The cavalrymen of the 2nd North Carolina were still spread far and wide performing their duties and fending for themselves. For instance, while Private Cavin and his company were spread along the Rapidan for nearly a month, Private George W. Walker of Company K wrote his cousin on May 1, 1864 from camp on the Rappahannock of his activity and condition. He wrote, "I am on a fishing detail on the Rappahannock River, and I get plenty of fish to eat."[210]

No matter how they filled their time and their stomachs, most of the cavalrymen surely would rather have spent the winter at home. One trooper in the 2nd North Carolina Cavalry who very much wanted a furlough that winter but was unwilling to risk going on a horse detail and failing to return with horses was Private Milas Cavin. The thirty-two year old private discussed his possibility of getting a furlough with his aunt in these terms and with his tongue firmly planted in his cheek.

I have not succeeded yet in getting a furlough. I could have gone on the last detail that was sent for horses. but I did not think it best to do so. I may get a furlough yet and if I do not I have several plans thought upon hoping that I may succeed in some one of them. Aunt Jenni can't you select a wife for me that I may get a furlough to go home and get married it seems that furloughs of that kind are being granted, and I expect that a choice that you would make would please me exactly.[211]

By mid–April, Stuart was getting serious about collecting his cavalry units for the coming spring campaign, especially those that had had some opportunity to revitalize themselves. For instance, in Hampton's absence, Stuart wrote directly to Gordon asking him to immediately recall the 4th and 5th North Carolina cavalries from North Carolina. Stuart went on to say that the recall orders should include the phrase, "Pursuant to instructions from the Comdg. General." Perhaps such an appeal to a higher authority was made to avoid any controversy about giving instructions to brigades in Hampton's division during the latter's absence. In any case, Stuart's concern for the 1st and 2nd North Carolina cavalries was once again limited to a promise of sustenance to come, and a hope that they would be fit when called upon to fight again. In Stuart's words: "It will be impossible to afford any respite to the rest of your Brigade [the 1st and 2nd Cavalries], as active operations will soon commence, but it is hoped that the supply of corn, which will be ample, and the coming grass, will be sufficient for your command's maintenance in a state of efficiency." The men and horses of the 1st and 2nd North Carolina cavalries must have felt fulfilled by the often repeated promise of sustenance to come—their horses would be fed when the spring grass appeared.

Even though, in Stuart's words, there was to be no respite for the 1st and 2nd North Carolina, James B. Gordon was encouraged by the possibility of having all four of his North Carolina regiments together again, and with at least two of them stronger than when winter began.[212]

Gordon was pleased because the 4th North Carolina had started winter camp with 82 effective men and a seriously wounded commander; and by early Spring, Colonel Ferebee was back and the regiment had an effective force of over 400 men.[213]

In addition, Gordon was receiving a revitalized 5th North Carolina Cavalry. Early in 1864, the 5th North Carolina Cavalry was also sent home to rest and recruit. They disbanded at Henderson, North Carolina and reassembled around mid–April by companies and rode to Richmond. At that time, they reportedly were "in splendid condition and numbering over 500 effective men and officers."[214]

The recorded losses taken by the 2nd North Carolina Cavalry from the end of the Mine Run Campaign on November 30, 1863 until the beginning of the spring campaign on May 3, 1864 are listed in the table below.

Combat Losses in the 2nd North Carolina Cavalry December 1863–April 1864

Trooper	Age	Co.	Fate
Alberter B. Dale	22	A	wounded January 30
James Newell		F	captured February 6
Alexander L. Maness	20	I	captured February 7
Asa Williams	25	I	captured February 7
Elias Williams	22	I	captured February 7
Thomas R. Manchester	20	A	captured February 18
Kenneth R. C. Britt	20	C	wounded April 28

Information contained in this table came from Compiled Service Records as summarized by Louis H. Manarin, *North Carolina Troops: 1861–1865, A Roster*, vol. II, pp. 98–177. (See Appendix for more information on the men listed above, page 400.)

With the exception of the losses taken on February 6 and 7, the men killed, wounded, or captured were on picket or scouts and lost in minor encounters with the enemy. The four men captured on February 6 and 7 were on picket at the fords along the Rapidan when Merritt and Kilpatrick led their divisions across the river to probe R. E. Lee's defenses. In addition to the 7 combat losses listed above, the regiment lost 24 men from December 1, 1863 through April of 1864—losses for reasons such as transfers, death from illness, discharges for health reasons, and desertions (there were 7 of the latter during winter camp). The total loss of 32 men during winter camp does not include those who became ineffective as cavalrymen due to their horses becoming unserviceable during that time.

Even though the 2nd North Carolina did not have the opportunity to disband and return to their homes to recruit as did the 4th and 5th North Carolina cavalries, they nonetheless did manage to add 73 recruits to the regiment during the five months in winter camp. The regiment received one new recruit during the harsh months of December and January. Most recruitment efforts were made at the company level in their home counties. One such effort was made by John P. Lockhart, First Lieutenant, commanding Company K and appeared on January 20, 1864. In an open letter to his hometown newspaper, he thanked the citizens for sending his company 15 pairs of socks and 7 pairs of gloves, and then wrote the following: "Permit me further to say to the young men of old Orange, that if any one wishes to join the cavalry service, they will always find my company open and ready to receive them, provided they furnish themselves with good serviceable horses. We number seventy men, as good as ever slung a carbine or drew a sabre, and would like to increase the number to eighty." The result of such efforts must have been disappointing. Company K received no new recruits in January, only one in February, and four in March. The entire regiment, in fact, only received one new recruit in January, 22 in February, and 43 in March — perhaps the increased number of volunteers in March resulted from their high profile actions in pushing Kilpatrick's expedition against Richmond out of the area early that month.[215]

Based on the available information, the net gain in manpower for the 2nd North Carolina Cavalry was around 41 men, plus the number of men who regained serviceable horses over those who lost them during this period. The regiment probably had as many as 200 healthy and mounted men by the end of winter camp, during the first part of May 1864. Major William P. Roberts's assessment of the 2nd North Carolina was "during the winter the regiment was greatly augmented in strength and discipline, so that when the campaign of 1864 opened, it was in fair condition, although numerically much smaller than any other regiment of the brigade...." In his words, the regiment was "greatly augmented" yet only in "fair" condition. As indicated above, the 2nd North Carolina was probably a bit stronger by the end of winter camp than when it went in. Roberts went on to point out that the 2nd never fully recovered from the fighting during the Gettysburg Campaign, especially the fights at Upperville and Hanover.[216]

Shuffling the Regiment and the Brigade, Mid-April to May 3

As indicated, by late March Wade Hampton was in South Carolina helping Matthew C. Butler prepare new regiments for service in Virginia. He did not return to duty in Virginia until May 2. (James B. Gordon had returned from his leave and was back in Richmond by March 14 on his way to Milford.) While Hampton was away, the War Department in Richmond, Robert E. Lee and J. E. B. Stuart made a number of changes that affected his command as well as others.

CHANGES IN THE 2ND NORTH CAROLINA CAVALRY

Regimental leadership underwent several important changes during winter camp. Colonel William G. Robinson had apparently had enough of the hardship and neglect so asked for and received a transfer to the Navy Department. Some of the men in the 2nd North Carolina Cavalry had been very vocal about their feelings and were not unhappy to see Robinson leave. For instance, one member of the regiment wrote the following from headquarters on January 18: "This Regiment is at present under command of Major C. M. Andrews of Statesville, N.C., who has had command more than half the time since the Reg't entered the service — owing to the absence of Lt. Col. Robinson, who has been in Europe for nearly a year. Maj. Andrews is an efficient officer and an accomplished gentleman, respected and confided in by his junior officers, and will we trust, soon be promoted by Gov. Vance to the Colonelcy of the Reg't."[217]

On February 12, 1864, Clinton M. Andrews was promoted from Major to Lieutenant

Colonel. The 2nd North Carolina Cavalry had not had a Lieutenant Colonel since Robinson was promoted to Colonel (even though Robinson was absent during most of his tenure as Lieutenant Colonel). Andrews held the position of Lieutenant Colonel for only six days when he was promoted to Colonel of the regiment. As is often the case, the wheels of bureaucracy turned slowly and in mid–April Stuart, while trying to pull his cavalry together for the coming campaign, had to raise the issue of Andrews's commission with Gordon. In a letter to Gordon, Stuart included the following urging: "It is important that Col. Andrews should be brought before an Examining Board at once, to have his commission determined. Is it advisable to order a new Board."[218]

In any case, when Andrews moved up rapidly in mid–February, he left vacancies in his wake. The position of Lieutenant Colonel would not be filled until James L. Gaines was brought in from the brigade's staff in March of 1865 — there was apparently no obvious candidate to promote from within the regiment. However, Andrews's recently vacated position of Major was filled immediately. Captain William P. Roberts of Company C was appointed major of the regiment on February 18. Roberts was only 23 and had been a Captain only since August of 1863.

Gordon, Hampton, and Stuart in some combination must have had great confidence in W. P. Roberts because they passed over other captains in the regiment who had more experience and wanted the position. Most specifically, James W. Strange, who had been captain of Company D since the regiment was formed back in mid–1861— and he had commanded the regiment for short periods of time, when called upon to do so. His anger was so great that on March 17, he resigned in protest, and took a position in another department, as captain in the 2nd Battalion North Carolina Local Defense Troops.

Changes in the North Carolina Brigade

Within Gordon's North Carolina brigade the most notable changes during winter camp were that the 4th and 5th regiments were permitted to return to their home state and replenish themselves. The 4th Cavalry was able to mount 490 men by the first of May. The 5th regiment numbered over 500 men in the saddle upon their return.[219]

Unfortunately for Gordon, the 4th North Carolina Cavalry was detached from his brigade and assigned to Beauregard's command. According to the same Special Orders No. 94, the 3rd North Carolina Cavalry under Colonel John A. Baker was ordered to report immediately for assignment to Gordon's North Carolina brigade. An exchange of the experienced 4th regiment and its commander, Colonel Ferebee, for the 3rd North Carolina Cavalry was certainly not on Gordon's wish list, yet that would have been preferable to what happened. In fact, Beauregard had been given the latitude to accept the 4th regiment and retain the 3rd until the expedition against New Bern was complete. The 3rd Cavalry did not actually join the North Carolina brigade until the end of May 1864.[220]

The 5th North Carolina Cavalry was detained in Richmond on its way back to Gordon's brigade in mid–April, but when Hampton returned from South Carolina and reported for duty on May 2, he immediately started sending the necessary messages, and on that same day Special Orders No. 102 was issued in Richmond containing the following: "The Fifth Regiment North Carolina Cavalry, now on temporary service near this city, will immediately proceed to the headquarters Army of Northern Virginia ... for assignment to duty with Brigadier-General Gordon's brigade."[221]

The 1st and 2nd North Carolina cavalries were at hand for Hampton and Gordon as they had been throughout the hard winter. As they gathered their forces around May 1, these two regiments were not the strongest of the North Carolina regiments, but they were the veteran units. They were the old war horses who brought a level of confidence based on experience to the brigade. They had suffered and toughened during the battles of 1863 and the winter that followed. The high esteem in which both the 1st and 2nd North Carolina cavalries were held by their follow cavalrymen is evident in the comment by Private Paul Means of the 5th North Carolina when he took pride in the fact that General Hampton had placed his regiment "side by side with the Ninth [1st] and Nineteenth [2nd] in his attachment and estimate of merit, without the slightest difference as to either. A great tribute of love and confidence to our regiment from a *very great source.*²²²

General Hampton was moved to express his attachment to and confidence in the North Carolina brigade when he was notifying Gordon that they had been removed from his division.

CHANGES IN THE DIVISIONS

There was pressure for a third cavalry division — the impetus came from the return of Robert E. Lee's second son, W. H. F. Lee, who was wounded during the battle at Brandy Station on June 9, 1863, and then captured while recuperating. W. H. F. Lee was exchanged along with several members of the 2nd North Carolina Cavalry in mid–March. In addition, the young Lee was saddened by the recent loss of his wife — his father, among others, was eager to move him back into active service. After all, W. H. F. Lee was a good commander. His former brigade, in which the 2nd North Carolina Cavalry had served before moving to the North Carolina brigade, was given to Colonel John R. Chambliss in his absence. Consequently when W. H. F. Lee was promoted to the rank of Major General on April 23, 1864, he needed a division. After some thought and second thoughts Chambliss's brigade was taken from Fitz Lee's division, and James B. Gordon's North Carolina brigade was taken from Wade Hampton, and both were given to W. H. F. Lee's new division of cavalry. By the beginning of the 1864 campaign, Stuart's cavalry corps contained: Fitz Lee's division with L. L. Lomax's and W. C. Wickham's brigades; Hampton's division with P. M. B. Young's, M. C. Butler's and T. L. Rosser's brigades; and William H. F. Lee's division with J. R. Chambliss's and J. B. Gordon's brigades.²²³

Stuart and his superiors apparently thought it created a better balance among the divisions if Gordon's North Carolinians served under a Virginian, and Rosser's Virginians served under a Carolinian. The logic of the decision to organize the brigades in that manner was not shared by Hampton and most of the North Carolinians. In fact on May 5, the day Ulysses S. Grant's army was crossing the Rapidan, Hampton was ordered by Stuart to give Gordon the following instructions: "proceed without delay with your command to the vicinity of Shady Grove, where you will concentrate your brigade and report for further orders to Major-General Stuart." In relaying the instructions to Gordon, Hampton's Assistant Adjutant General Barker also wrote,

I am directed by Major-General Hampton, in communicating the above orders, to express to you, and through you to your whole brigade, the surprise with which he had received the orders, and the pain it causes him to execute them. He indulges the hope that his wishes may be consulted, and that a new assignment may be made as soon as the present emergency shall have passed, which will return your brigade to his division and give him back the troops to whom he has become so attached and whom he has learned to trust in times of danger and trial.

Indulging this hope, he refrains from saying farewell, but will watch the performance of officers and men in the approaching contest with the same interest as if they were under his own command, confident that your regiments should be eventually returned to him they will bring back unsullied banners and a record of glory increased and illustrated by new achievements in the coming campaign.²²⁴

The feelings of confidence and respect flowed in both directions, and the North Carolina cavalrymen were not pleased about being removed from Hampton's division. Private Means of the 5th North Carolina acknowledged that over time the cavalrymen came to see their new division commander, W. H. F. Lee, as a fine commander, and they became very attached to him, "but [he was] not such a man or commander as Hampton, whom we loved personally and officially. There was sad regret on our part as there was with General Hampton at this transfer."²²⁵

Unavoidably occupied with these thoughts, Hampton and Gordon along with the cavalrymen of the North Carolina brigade had to place themselves in front of the advancing Union army. General Grant was crossing the Rapidan River to launch his spring campaign. Hampton, Gordon and their North Carolinians managed to put their priorities in order and put up a good fight in the days that followed, but they continued to make it clear they preferred to have the North Carolina Cavalry Brigade remain in Hampton's division.

Five

Grant's Overland Campaign, May 4 to Mid-June 1864

With his re-election on the horizon, President Lincoln governed a war-weary nation by the spring of 1864. He needed the war to end. He brought Ulysses S. Grant in from his successes in the west and promoted him to lieutenant general. Grant took charge of the Union armies in the east, and his primary objective became the destruction of Robert E. Lee's Army of Northern Virginia. He planned to use all the armies at his disposal and coordinate his attack across the land. The Army of the Potomac, still commanded by George G. Meade, would be his hammer, pounding the rebel army on the anvil of R. E. Lee's determination and skill as a general. The other armies at Grant's disposal would be used to guide the enemy into position. Lincoln was desperate for victory, and Grant was determined to provide it, no matter the cost.[1]

President Davis had also endured political opposition to a war that had become too costly, too bloody and too long for many of his constituents. By the Confederate elections in the fall of 1863, political opposition had become increasingly vocal within the Confederacy and was fueled by the devastating defeat at Gettysburg. There was a strong movement for peace in North Carolina, but Governor Zebulon B. Vance fought off attackers and managed to keep his pro–Confederate administration in office as did others of like mind across the Confederacy—yet the issue was now raised and would never completely go away. Then came the deprivations of the hard winter.[2]

As deprivation and discontent brought about by the long war spread throughout the south during the winter, it became increasingly difficult for the Army of Northern Virginia to keep and recruit willing and able men to fight on the front lines. In an effort to maintain the strength of its army, the southerners had extended the draft age to fifty on the high end and seventeen on the other and required troopers whose enlistments were expiring to remain in the service.

It had been a hard year; nonetheless, the men in the Army of Northern Virginia managed to survive in surprisingly high spirits as the spring of 1864 arrived. Consequently, R. E. Lee was able to field an army lacking in manpower and equipment relative to the enemy, but ready for the coming fights. One historian may have overstated the case when he characterized the men of Robert E. Lee's army in these words: "They had become a band of brothers fighting from motives of pride in themselves, comradeship with each other, and devotion to Marse Robert." However, this characterization does explain how the Confederate fighting men were able to do what they soon accomplished in the spring of 1864. In addition, by spring R. E. Lee and many other southerners believed their best chance of leaving the conflict as an independent nation was to maintain a costly war until the northern election and hope for the defeat of Lincoln and his supporters.[3]

With all the political considerations in mind, Grant launched his Overland Campaign on May 4, 1864, beginning a seven week effort to flank Robert E. Lee's right and pull him out into open fields of battle. The gentlemanly facade often painted on the ugly face of war was gone—the goal was relentless pursuit and destruction of the Army of Northern Virginia. The armies started maneuvering one another on May 4 at the Wilderness of Spotsylvania, and continued jousting southward toward Richmond and finally Petersburg where they dug in by late June.

The Battle of the Wilderness, May 4–6

Since early April, Robert E. Lee had been expecting George G. Meade to bring his Army of the Potomac across the Rapidan. His expectations were met on May 4, 1864 when Grant launched his three-front attack in Virginia—the plan was to perform the tragedy on three stages simultaneously. The script called for Meade's army to take center stage by crossing the Rapidan, marching rapidly south through the Wilderness of Spotsylvania, then turn west around R. E. Lee's right wing and behind his strong fortifications along the river. Benjamin F. Butler's Army of the James was instructed to head up the peninsula along the north side of the James River at Richmond. And finally, Franz Sigel and his army were to start south through the Shenandoah Valley, then head east and threaten R. E. Lee's left wing. U. S. Grant's objective was not to conquer and occupy more southern territory but to draw the Army of Northern Virginia out of its strong defensive position and into an open field where the Union's dominant numbers in infantry, cavalry, and artillery could make a difference.[4]

Just prior to launching his spring campaign, Grant set up his headquarters near Meade's in Culpeper County rather than Washington City, this emphasized the central role assigned to the Army of the Potomac in the pending drama. Meade had his Second, Fifth, and Sixth infantry corps as well as the army's cavalry positioned to move across the Rapidan early on May 4 — Ambrose E. Burnside's Ninth Corps, operating semi-independently, was on its way from Annapolis and would support Meade's army where needed.

Grant had brought Philip H. Sheridan from the west and placed him in charge of the Army of the Potomac's cavalry. They reorganized the cavalry into three divisions, under brigadier generals David McM. Gregg, James H. Wilson, and Alfred A. Torbert. As commanders, D. McM. Gregg had more cavalry experience than the others — Wilson had the least. The Army of the Potomac's cavalry was stronger and more experienced than it had ever been. It was almost able to hold its own against the Confederate cavaliers under J. E. B. Stuart during the Gettysburg Campaign, and by the spring of 1864 might still be defeated from time-to-time but would not be dominated as before. Indeed, as the Federal cavalry grew stronger the Confederate cavalry had an increasingly difficult time resuscitating itself.[5]

R. E. Lee had brought James Longstreet and his First Corps back from Tennessee, and by late April they were settled around Gordonsville. Lieutenant Generals R. S. Ewell and A. P. Hill were also at hand with their Second and Third Corps. R. E. Lee's cavalry was still commanded by J. E. B. Stuart and was composed of three divisions. The divisions were led by Wade Hampton, Fitz Lee, and W. H. F. Lee. The infantry commands along with some of Stuart's cavalry and artillery combined to give R. E. Lee an army of approximately 65,000 men facing Meade's Army of the Potomac supported by Burnside's Ninth Corps which together constituted a much larger force (most estimates put the Union force at about 115,000). Stuart's cavalry numbered about 8,000 effective cavalrymen in face of Sheridan's approximately 12,000.[6]

As indicated, for several days R. E. Lee knew Meade was mobilizing his army to attack across the Rapidan but he did not know the direction the main push would take. One thing Lee was certain of, if Meade and his army crossed into the Wilderness that is where he wanted to meet them. The Confederate commanding general knew if they fought in the dense wilderness, the enemy's superiority in numbers would be neutralized — especially in the cavalry and artillery. In order to cover all possibilities, however, R. E. Lee held his Second and Third Corps back near Orange Court House until Meade made his move, when he was across the river. Longstreet and his First Corps were held back near Gordonsville ready to move in any one of several directions. No significant force was placed along the river at the major fords because R. E. Lee wanted to keep his army concentrated until Meade committed to a direction — either toward Fredericksburg, Richmond, or Gordonsville (the junction of the Orange & Alexandria and the Virginia Central Railroads).[7] (See map 2.5.)

When Sheridan's cavalrymen led Meade's troops across the Rapidan, Stuart's cavalry was still scattered across central and southern Virginia. Stuart had Fitz Lee's division nearby with Lunsford L. Lomax's and William C. Wickham's brigades; they were concentrated near Hamilton's Crossing, below Fredericksburg. Wade Hampton and some of his division were also at hand. When Hampton returned to duty on the Rapidan line May 2, he found at his disposal James B. Gordon's North Carolina brigade with the 1st and 2nd regiments, and Pierce M. B. Young's command with not more than three full companies—Thomas L. Rosser's small brigade was patrolling over near Orange Court House but was moved by Stuart over to Catharpin Road for the fighting on May 5. The 1st North Carolina Cavalry was patrolling the area near Morton's Ford and as far down as Germanna Ford. The 2nd North Carolina had just been relieved of that duty a day or two earlier and was back in its camp between Bowling Green and Guinea Station on the Richmond, Fredericksburg & Potomac Railroad. Gordon's camp was near Guinea Station, and Hampton's was near Milford. (Gordon's 5th North Carolina arrived from Richmond in time to join the fighting late on May 6.) When Hampton left camp and marched forward to meet Sheridan's cavalry advance on May 5, he had with him the 2nd North Carolina Cavalry under Gordon's command.[8]

Grant Crosses the Rapidan

The Union plan was to cross the Rapidan at Germanna and Ely's Fords and dash through the Wilderness. The troops crossing at Germanna were to sweep west on Orange Plank Road; those crossing at Ely's Ford were to head for Catharpin Road, then turn west through Todd's Tavern. Both columns hoped to met R. E. Lee's army near Orange Court House. Grant and his commanders had no desire to fight in the thick, dark area known as the Wilderness. They planned to move their main force quickly to clear the Wilderness and met Lee south of the dense forest, in open fields.[9]

Sheridan's cavalry crossed the Rapidan first. James H. Wilson's cavalry division took Germanna Ford with little difficulty and started down Germanna Plank Road toward Wilderness Tavern on the Orange Turnpike. D. McM. Gregg's cavalrymen crossed the river at Ely's Ford and headed through Chancellorsville toward Catharpin Road—there were no opposing forces to greet them only thinly spread cavalrymen on picket duty. Commanded by Winfield S. Hancock, the Union's Second Corps followed D. McM. Gregg over Ely's Ford. The Fifth Corps, then the Sixth, commanded by Gouverneur K. Warren and Sedgwick respectively, followed James H. Wilson's cavalrymen across at Germanna Ford.[10]

As indicated, the 1st North Carolina Cavalry was patrolling Germanna Ford so were the first to detect Wilson's Union cavalrymen coming across the river. At 9:00 A.M., Major William H. H. Cowles of the 1st North Carolina notified Richard S. Ewell, who was poised to advance from Orange Court House, of what appeared to be a heavy cavalry force with wagon trains moving south along the Germanna Plank Road. A couple of hours later, Cowles notified Stuart that Wilson's strong cavalry force had advanced to a half mile below Locust Grove. Cowles mentioned that he would slow them as much as possible with his small cavalry detachment. The remainder of the regiment was watching the fords further up river. Wilson and his cavalrymen spent most of their day on Orange Plank Road roaming up to the Orange Turnpike and down to Catharpin Road. As planned, around 3:00 P.M. May 4 G. K. Warren notified Meade's headquarters that his whole infantry command had reached the Old Wilderness Tavern—John Sedgwick's corps was just behind him. Just before 8:00 P.M., Wilson notified Warren that he had pulled his cavalry division in and they were concentrated at Parker's Store on the Orange Plank Road.[11]

Shortly after Wilson had crossed D. McM. Gregg's cavalry was across at Ely's Ford. Soon after, Gregg sent a regiment east toward Fredericksburg and their movement was detected. Fitz Lee's cavalry was near Hamilton's Crossing but he had patrols up as far as Fredericksburg. The cavalry commander reported the following to Stuart, "Enemy advancing in heavy cavalry force on plank road toward Fredericksburg." When this movement was communicated up to R. E. Lee's headquarters it added to the uncertainty R. E. Lee felt about Meade's main point of attack. This meant the available Confederate cavalry would have to close in and meet the Union cavalry columns. Hampton sent a message to Stuart indicating he planned to pull detachments from the 1st North Carolina back to the Catharpin Road and connect to Fitz Lee's command near the road heading down to Spotsylvania Court House. Stuart brought Rosser's brigade of Hampton's command over from Orange Court House to stand in front of Wilson's Union cavalry and moved Fitz Lee's two brigades up below Fredericksburg to stand before D. McM. Gregg's advancing column. Hampton was still in his camp waiting for orders to bring up the 2nd North Carolina Cavalry late on May 4.[12]

Meade himself crossed the river at Germanna Ford early May 4 and by afternoon he put his infantry into camp between Germanna Ford and the Wilderness Tavern, still in the Wilderness. Grant crossed the Rapidan late morning and set up camp near Meade's. For reasons not entirely clear, the Union army stopped for the evening and night in a place where they did not want to fight the Army of Northern Virginia the next morning — in the Wilderness. Clearly Grant did not expect R. E. Lee to advance on his position. When the Union army went into camp however, they gave R. E. Lee time to sort out his intelligence reports of the day and to settle in his mind what Meade's most likely direction would be the following day. All the while, R. E. Lee began moving his infantry into the Wilderness toward Meade's army.[13]

ROBERT E. LEE'S RESPONSE

By late morning on May 4, Robert E. Lee had determined to meet Grant's army in the Wilderness — not wait for him to attack. He started Ewell east on the Orange Turnpike with his Second Corps; at about the same time he started A. P. Hill's Third Corps along the Orange Plank Road. Also, near mid-day, Longstreet had the First Corps on the road from Gordonsville toward Richard's Shop on the Catharpin Road. By nightfall Ewell had his command at Robertson's Tavern (near Locust Grove), and later A. P. Hill camped near Verdiersville on the Orange Turnpike. Longstreet stopped his command for the night near Brock's Bridge on the North Anna River. He was confident, though not realistic when he notified R. E. Lee that he could have his men on the Orange Turnpike by noon on May 5. R. E. Lee's plan was for Longstreet to arrive at just the right moment and hit Meade's army in the flank as Ewell and A. P. Hill had the Army of the Potomac engaged in their front on the Orange Turnpike and the Orange Plank Road. R. E. Lee needed Ewell and A. P. Hill with five thin divisions to hold Meade's ten strong divisions until Longstreet arrived with his two divisions. R. E. Lee hoped Longstreet understood the critical nature of the timing — but apparently he did not.[14]

By afternoon on May 4, Stuart and his staff were also moving toward the front line along Orange Plank Road to the Confederate right. They rode through the dense, dark Wilderness — it was after sundown when they reached their line that stretched across the road near Mine Run. Rosser's brigade from Hampton's division was just behind them. Stuart stopped in the middle of the road, faced about and watched Rosser's regiments approach and turn into the Confederate line. Except for a few cavalrymen in the advance of the brigade, the horsemen did not know they were being lead to the front by Stuart himself. They were inspired as they saw him standing in the road where they were turning into the line. A member of Stuart's staff described the nighttime scene for us:

Stuart was recognized by his men who greeted him with enthusiastic shouts as regiment after regiment followed each other, filed off before him along the rear of the infantry. It was an impromptu ovation to the Chief of the Cavalry Corps.... Stuart himself a little in advance of us with his plumped hat in his hand, looked like an equestrian Statue — both man and horse being as motionless as marble — his fine soldierly figure fully revealed in the light of the camp fires that were blazing brightly on both sides of the road, as far as the eye could reach and lighting up the foreground splendidly.

The cavalry came up in columns of four at full trot, saluting the General with a shout as they wheeled off, at a gallop, toward their designated positions while the infantry, catching inspiration from their cheers, mingled their loud hurras with their's, In one grand chorus of twice ten thousand voices. It was really a grand spectacle to see these gallant horsemen coming toward us out of the gloom of night into the glare of the fires, making the welkin ring with their wild war cries and the earth to tremble beneath their horses hoofs.[15]

Stuart and his staff set up camp near Verdiersville on the plank road. He notified R. E. Lee of Wilson's cavalry in the area and then they spread their blankets under trees to rest.[16] Most of the cavalrymen were anxious for the pending fight after too many months in winter camp and picket duty. It is doubtful, however, that any of them could have anticipated the intense and sustained violence they were about to experience over the next six weeks —

so they settled into their last good sleep for a while.

During the evening of May 4, Meade became increasingly concerned about his wagon train with Fitz Lee's cavalry coming up from Hamilton's Crossing so he pulled Alfred T. A. Torbert's cavalry division back to help protect the wagons. Sheridan was not altogether pleased because that left only Wilson's cavalry division to shield Warren and Sedgwick, and D. McM. Gregg's cavalry to hold the way open for Hancock's infantrymen.[17]

Early the next morning, Meade moved Hancock from Chancellorsville down to Catharpin Road and toward Todd's Tavern; Warren was sent along a wagon road from Wilderness Tavern toward Parker's Store which was down on the Orange Plank Road; and Sedgwick was scheduled to follow Warren. With tens of thousands of men and wagons all moving toward just two destinations, the roads and byways were severely congested and by early morning already hot and dusty. Hancock's infantry was additionally impeded by having to move forward without cavalry eyes before them. D. McM. Gregg was scheduled to be in advance of their column but he was bogged down northeast of Todd's Tavern. Warren also had to move toward the enemy without a cavalry shield because apparently no one knew for certain where Wilson was on the morning of May 5. This seems strange because at 5:00 that morning, Wilson sent the following message to Meade's headquarters: "In accordance with orders received yesterday my command is in motion toward the Catharpin road." Of course, Wilson knew where he was—right in the path of the oncoming Army of Northern Virginia, while Torbert and D. McM. Gregg had their cavalry commands assigned to Meade's left where the only real threat was from Fitz Lee's small cavalry division.[18]

A Bad Day in the Wilderness — May 5, 1864

R. E. Lee's two corps marched east to meet Meade's army. The Confederate command was not eager to encounter the enemy's main force before Longstreet arrived with his First Corps, but it happened. Warren's Corps was heading for Wilderness Tavern with Sedgwick's just behind. Once under way, Warren learned of Confederate troops coming east on the Orange Turnpike, and he concentrated his force to met them. He paid little attention to the Orange Plank Road — he apparently assumed his left was covered by Wilson's cavalry at Parker's Store. Later in the morning Meade learned that R. E. Lee also had infantry advancing east along Orange Plank Road and would be in a position to hit Warren's flank. Meade had his army out of position because he had expected R. E. Lee to be digging in around Mine Run for a defensive stand. Lee had once again surprised his adversaries by coming at them instead of waiting for them. Meade had started the day on the offense, moving westward slowly with no cavalry escort, planning to attack the enemy entrenchments. By midmorning Meade was preparing to defend against R. E. Lee's approach along both roads.[19]

Tens of thousands of infantrymen fought fiercely through the day and into the evening in the dense and dark wilderness soon filled with smoke and fires ignited mostly by artillery. They were often firing at unseen enemies and occasionally at their comrades. Hancock's strong division joined Warren's and hit the Confederate right by early evening — it was not clear that R. E. Lee's army would be able to hold until the next day when Longstreet was expected. A. P. Hill's thin line was almost broken more than once, but held. On balance, R. E. Lee's commanders made better decisions than did Grant's, and by the end of the day the two infantries fought to a stand-off. R. E. Lee had managed to hold Grant's army and to survive until Longstreet's expected time of arrival. Grant felt he was still in a position to turn the Confederate right the next morning.[20]

Cavalry Encounter Between Wilson and Rosser

Before dawn on May 5, Wilson started his cavalry division from Parker's Store south to Catharpin Road and then right (west) on the road where he came face-to-face with Rosser's cavalry brigade which had been sent to shield both Longstreet's approach and A. P. Hill's right. Though Rosser was part of Hampton's cavalry division, he was moved to Catharpin Road from near Orange Court House under Stuart's instructions — Hampton had no idea where Rosser was on May 2, and Rosser had not yet rejoined his division commander by the 5th of the month.[21]

When the cavalrymen from Wilson's division and Rosser's brigade met the fighting was severe. Wilson had dismounted many of his troops and thrown out a strong picket line. Rosser accepted the challenge and charged. The Union front line was driven back into its support and then into Wilson's main body of dismounted cavalry and artillery, which held. More charges were made; sometimes mounted, sometimes not. Wilson's artillery made the Confederate cavalrymen pay a very high price as they charged into shrapnel and canister each time they tried to dislodge the enemy line. Finally, Rosser was compelled to pull back and spare some of his men in the face of overwhelming numbers and firepower. Soon after Rosser fell back to where he had originally encountered Wilson's picket line, he sent word to Stuart of his difficult fight.[22]

Around midmorning, Rosser received support from the Horse Artillery. The artillery had been mobilized early on the morning of May 5 when Major R. P. Chew sent McGregor's battery to W. H. F. Lee at Orange Court House, and Thomson's, Johnston's, and Shoemaker's batteries toward Richard's Shop on Catharpin Road—the latter was a fortunate choice for Rosser's men later that morning. Chew estimated his artillery would arrived at the front around 9:00 A.M., and with hard marching, held his schedule. Stuart and some of his staff also arrived and became involved in Rosser's fight.[23]

While Wilson was totally occupied with Rosser's cavalrymen, he failed to detect the movement of A. P. Hill's infantry marching east along the Orange Plank Road, just north of him. Around noon Wilson realized that he was some distance from his army with Confederate infantry to the north and cavalry to the west and south. He began to withdraw eastward. When Wilson began to move, Rosser not content to hold Catharpin Road open became even more aggressive and pursued the Federals with a vengeance — driving them back to Todd's Tavern on Brock Road.[24]

Before Wilson's men started backing into Todd's Tavern, Generals Meade and Sheridan had become concerned about Wilson's absence. By early afternoon Sheridan was asked to locate Wilson's command — he in turn asked D. McM. Gregg, who was nearing Todd's Tavern from the north to find the wayward cavalry commander. Gregg did not have to look far. As he entered Todd's Tavern around 2:00 P.M., Wilson's battered troops were being pushed into town from the west.[25]

D. McM. Gregg sent two fresh regiments through Wilson's exhausted column to stop Rosser's advance. When the fresh Union cavalrymen and artillery made their way to Wilson's rear, they halted Rosser's advance and formed a line about two miles west of Todd's Tavern. Naturally Wilson claimed victory as did Rosser — and of course they both had their moments to claim. Of particular importance was the fact that Rosser had managed to hold Catharpin Road open for Longstreet's arrival early on May 6. Notwithstanding the fact that due to the heavy pressure A. P. Hill had been under during the day, R. E. Lee had decided to redirect Longstreet to the Orange Plank Road to come in behind Hill rather than on Catharpin Road.[26]

HAMPTON AND HIS 2ND NORTH CAROLINA CAVALRY MOVE UP

On the morning of May 5, while Rosser's command engaged Wilson's cavalrymen on Catharpin Road, the 1st North Carolina Cavalry was still on duty shielding Ewell's left to the Rapidan — including Locust Grove and the river fords from Germanna to Jacob's. Ewell did not want his left flank surprised from across the river as he moved east along Orange Turnpike. As we have seen, Rosser's brigade aggressively shielded the Confederate right throughout the day. The rest of Hampton's cavalry division was moving toward the battlefield or waiting for assignments. The 5th North Carolina Cavalry was on its way from Richmond, and the cavalrymen of the 2nd North Carolina were held in camp with their commander, James B. Gordon.[27]

Wade Hampton was in an awkward position because earlier he had been ordered to send Gordon's North Carolina brigade to W. H. F. Lee at Orange Court House. They had been assigned to the latter's new division, but Hampton needed them to help protect the Confederate right. Before he was able to establish communications with Stuart, Hampton had sent a message to R. E. Lee informing him that if he sent Gordon's North Carolina brigade off, he would be left with only 200 men from his division to cover the area between Germanna Ford and Fitz Lee's left below Fredericksburg. Determined not to be left empty-handed in the confusion of the day Hampton kept Gordon and the 2nd North Carolina Cavalry with him.[28]

As indicated, Hampton was having difficulty corresponding with Stuart early on May 5 and at one point he sent a message to Robert E. Lee which began with the words, "Receiving no orders from General Stuart, I fear he is absent." By that afternoon, however, Hampton had received instructions from Stuart to mobilize Gordon and the North Carolina cavalrymen still in camp. Hampton's entire response to Stuart around 2:30 P.M. was "Dispatch received. Will order pickets out and will advise General Lee." Hampton then instructed Gordon to take the 2nd North Carolina Cavalry and concentrate his command in the vicinity of Shady Grove. It took the 2nd North Carolina most of what remained of the day to get into place around Shady Grove. This assignment included placing pickets along Catharpin Road. With the 1st North Carolina already stretched too thin, and the 5th cavalry not yet in the area, that meant Gordon had only the 2nd North Carolina to concentrate at Shady Grove as ordered. He was accompanied by Hampton and a small number of men from Young's command. Initially Gordon's assignment placed him just behind Rosser as the latter pushed Wilson's cavalry command to Todd's Tavern. The 2nd North Carolina cavalrymen along with some of Young's men were then on Catharpin Road covering A. P. Hill's right flank, while still holding the road open for Longstreet's anticipated arrival the following day.[29]

The North Carolina brigade's new division commander, W. H. F. Lee, was near Orange Court House covering the Confederate rear and was also having trouble corresponding with the very mobile J. E. B. Stuart. On May 6, W. H. F. Lee acknowledged receipt of Stuart's message that had been sent on the 4th. In his message to a member of Stuart's staff, W. H. F. Lee added: "Please impress upon the general the necessity of sending me my other brigade [Gordon's North Carolina brigade] as soon as it can be spared." It should be recalled that at that time with Gordon's unit absent, W. H. F. Lee's entire division consisted of Chambliss's brigade. On the other hand, it also appeared from the message that the division commander understood that Gordon's command was needed over on Catharpin Road at the moment.

Soon after W. H. F. Lee sent his message to Stuart's camp, he was directed to take Chambliss's brigade around the enemy lines toward Stevensburg in Culpeper County to do what damage he could to the Union supply line.[30]

Over on Brock Road early on May 5, D. McM. Gregg had moved his cavalry in advance of Hancock's infantry down to Todd's Tavern. As indicated, he had to seal off Rosser's advance along Catharpin Road, but he also had orders to push south out of Todd's Tavern. Orders aside, D. McM. Gregg was stalled at the tavern because Fitz Lee's cavalry division had moved up through Spotsylvania Court House during the day and blocked the road in front of his column. Fitz Lee's and D. McM. Gregg's cavalrymen clashed about two miles south of Todd's Tavern on Brock's Road. D. McM. Gregg's cavalry division was blocked for the night from the west and south of Todd's Tavern. Sheridan pulled Wilson's division back to the wagon train near Chancellorsville; and Torbert's command was camped for the night several miles southwest of Chancellorsville.[31]

An Even Worse Day in the Wilderness — May 6, 1864

At dawn on May 6, Grant put in motion his plan to concentrate his attack on R. E. Lee's right wing. It was a good plan because A. P. Hill's corps had been seriously weakened in the previous day's fighting. The problem for the Union was that R. E. Lee planned to bring Longstreet's corps in on his right to join Hill as soon as he arrived in the Wilderness. Meade had to defeat Hill before Longstreet arrived for Grant's plan to work.[32]

The Federal infantrymen moved first and with force against A. P. Hill's thin line. The assault worked its way up the Confederate line all the way to Ewell's left. Hill's position was not fortified as well as Ewell's, and they had to contend with Hancock's relatively fresh men. Consequently, A. P. Hill's line could not hold and they were pushed back into R. E. Lee's field headquarters. Lee personally commanded the troops at that point inspiring them to make a stand and hold until Longstreet arrived.[33]

Longstreet himself was on the line when the Federal assault began, but he had ridden ahead of his infantry column to confirm his approach. As a result, his presence was of little immediate help to the men on A. P. Hill's line, but Longstreet was impressed with a sense of urgency and rode rapidly back toward his column in order to move them as quickly as possible to the fight. It was midmorning, however, before Longstreet's advanced units doubled-timed through A. P. Hill's line across Orange Plank Road and soon were driving the enemy back to near the line on which the day's battle began.[34]

Once Longstreet had his command fully up and the enemy pushed back, he had time to consider his plan of attack. As he collected information and his thoughts, he learned of an unfinished railroad cut through the dense woods of the Wilderness. Longstreet sent three brigades east along the unfinished railroad bed, and around mid-day they hit the unsuspecting enemy in their left flank, triggering an all-out assault by the Confederate line. Both Confederate lines moved forward rapidly at a right angle to one another through smoke, fire, and the dense wilderness. Through this veil, Longstreet fell wounded from Confederate fire. That stalled the drive, and it was afternoon before R. E. Lee was able to restore order to his right wing. The pause was just what Hancock needed to collect his scattered forces, and Burnside's command had time to arrive and support Hancock's troopers.

On the Confederate left, Ewell's command was successful in holding and finally turning the Union right flank. The 1st North Carolina Cavalry was still patrolling along Ewell's left and was able to provide information to the Confederate commanders on that end of the line about a weak spot in the Union right. That information made a second Confederate flank attack possible. When the right side of Grant's line broke, near panic spread along the entire Union line, but Ewell's pursuit soon bogged down in confusion as they tried to race through the dense smoke-filled Wilderness. Not fully realizing the Wilderness had suddenly become an ally, many Union commanders wanted to execute an orderly general pullback, but Grant insisted that there was no turning back. He had told President Lincoln as much, and he was not about to agree to a retreat back over the Rapidan.[35]

However, the day was by no means a victory for anyone. It was another standoff, and by the end of the day they all had gained nothing at a very high price. Losses for the armies engaged in the Battle of the Wilderness (May 4–6) have been estimated at over 15,000 for the Union, and just over 11,000 for the Confederacy.[36]

More Cavalry Action

Once again, the cavalries fought on the periphery of the deadly battle. Nonetheless, cavalrymen were fighting and risks were being taken and a price was being paid. Late on May 5, Sheridan pulled Wilson's beleaguered cavalrymen back to rest and moved George A. Custer's and Thomas C. Devin's brigades from Torbert's cavalry division forward to help D. McM. Gregg along Brock Road.[37]

At 2:00 A.M. on May 6, Custer's command moved to Brock Road, a few miles north of Todd's Tavern. Custer was sent to confront Rosser's cavalry while Gregg pushed his division south along the road to Spotsylvania into Fitz Lee's cavalry. Then Custer was to push west along the Catharpin Road into Gordon's 2nd North Carolina. That evening the 5th North Carolina caught up with its brigade and fought beside the 2nd North Carolina.[38]

By the time Custer had his command in place early on May 6, Rosser had begun to move toward Brock Road, so the two cavalries clashed just east of where the unfinished railroad cut crossed Brock Road. D. McM. Gregg had sent Custer two guns, and the latter initially had little trouble holding his position but then Stuart moved artillery support up to Rosser's front also and a fiercely contested stand-off was established. By 1:30 in the afternoon, Stuart who was with Rosser and his troopers reported that he was moving Rosser's command forward again and planned to occupy the position they had held earlier in the day near the intersection of the railroad cut and Brock Road. Though Rosser's command was seriously depleted from the previous day's fighting against Wilson's division, it moved on Custer's fresher and stronger brigade. The pressure on Custer grew when Rosser received support from two companies sent by Young and the Union cavalrymen began to give ground. Rosser and his support were then stopped when, in Custer's words, "Colonel Devin, with his command, arrived in the nick of time and rendered good service." In the end, Stuart also reported that Rosser's brigade was "very much reduced by hard fighting" that day and the one before. Custer and Devin were held and unable to move west to hit Longstreet who was by then overwhelming Hancock's left. When Devin moved up to Brock Road, he was under orders from his division commander, Torbert, to join Custer and then under Custer's command to attack Longstreet. This assignment was not fulfilled. Nonetheless, Custer felt he had protected his army's left flank; and Rosser felt he had protected, first A. P. Hill's right flank and then Longstreet's rear and right flank over the course of the day.[39]

More importantly, perhaps, Rosser's determined fighting had caused Hancock to divert some of his infantry from A. P. Hill's front on Orange Plank Road to the sound of fighting on Brock Road. The dismounted cavalrymen under Stuart's and Rosser's command along with their guns made such a racket throughout the morning that Hancock became increasingly convinced that Longstreet's anticipated arrival was taking place on his left flank before it actually occurred. In other words, by noon Rosser's and Fitz Lee's commands (along with most of the 2nd North Carolina and two companies from Cobb's Legion) had fully occupied Custer's and Devin's brigades, Gregg's division, and some of Hancock's infantry. The most important result of the cavalry action by Confederates west and south of Todd's Tavern was to slow Hancock's assault on A. P. Hill's line, and in so doing influence the outcome of the day's fighting, because Longstreet's men got to the front in time.[40]

During the day when Custer could not push southwest past Rosser's cavalrymen, and D. McM. Gregg could not push his command through Fitz Lee's line just south of Todd's Tavern or through Gordon's to the west, Sheridan's cavalry lost its offensive posture and confidence. In addition, events on the infantry's front combined to shake the cavalry commander's confidence in a Union victory that day. For instance, shortly after 1:00 P.M. Sheridan received a message from Andrew A. Humphreys (Meade's Chief of Staff) indicating that Longstreet had turned Hancock's left, and that Sheridan should pull his cavalry back to protect the Union's wagons. Not long afterward, he received word of the successful flank attack on their right by Ewell's command — and the Union cavalry commanders certainly knew there was near panic along their infantry's line and that there was a real possibility Longstreet's or Hampton's commands could come between the Union cavalrymen near Todd's Tavern and their main army. Consequently, with his instructions from Meade (transmitted by Humphreys) and the accumulating worrisome events along the infantry line, Sheridan, without the consent of Grant, pulled D. McM. Gregg's command back northeast of Todd's Tavern. Sheridan also began to scout a retreat to the Rapidan; and in fact started some wagons in that direction. As Sheridan's cavalrymen pulled back, Stuart's horsemen were nipping at their heels well into the night.[41]

It is difficult to track the exact location of the 2nd North Carolina Cavalry throughout May 6 but it is certain they were the unit under James B. Gordon's direct command that day. They apparently rode most of the night and were in position, picketing along Catharpin Road and forming a skirmish line at Corbin's Bridge by early morning. In addition, they were scouting north from Shady Grove as far as the detachments from the 1st North Carolina which were still spread along Ewell's left as far as the Germanna Plank Road. Early in the day, the 2nd North Carolina Cavalry was primarily engaged in the push from Corbin's Bridge to Todd's Tavern. Keep in mind Stuart and Rosser's command were near the intersection of the railroad cut and Brock Road, and Fitz Lee's force was concentrated at the southern entrance to Todd's Tavern on the road from Spotsylvania. Gregg's main force at Todd's Tavern was at Fitz Lee's front but they also had to probe and defend against any Confederate force coming from the west along Catharpin Road, from Shady Grove — that force was primarily the 2nd North Carolina Cavalry.

By late in the day, two North Carolinian regiments were dismounted and fighting under the watchful eye of Gordon, who was sometimes mounted and occasionally on foot as he continually paced back and forth along his line. Gregg's assignment was to move around Longstreet's right wing, but by evening, the 2nd Cavalry had been joined by the 5th North Carolina and both regiments held their ground.[42]

Early on May 6, Stuart sent a message to Gordon on Catharpin Road asking if he thought the enemy he was fighting might be infantry. Stuart had good reason to make the inquiry because earlier in the morning a detachment from Gordon's 1st North Carolina reported an enemy infantry column heading for Gordon's flank. The enemy infantry changed course, however, and Gordon later responded, "I have no good reason for thinking I was fighting infantry, save from the number and manner of firing and reports of officers." By dusk, D. McM. Gregg was pulling his cavalrymen back along Catharpin Road from Todd's Tavern toward Chancellorsville. The Cavalrymen from the 2nd North Carolina had helped contain Gregg at Todd's Tavern that day by holding the road west of the tavern and preventing the flank attack Gregg was instructed to carry out early in the day. To flank Longstreet's right as per Sheridan's early instructions Gregg would first have had to move between Rosser's right and Fitz Lee's left, along Catharpin Road and across Corbin's Bridge — that route was blocked most of the day by the 2nd North Carolina Cavalry and also late in the day by the 5th North Carolina.[43]

The 2nd North Carolina Cavalry was engaged throughout the day and had three recorded losses.

Combat Losses in the 2nd North Carolina Cavalry, The Battle of the Wilderness

Trooper	Age	Co.	Fate
Jesse R. E. Pittman	26	E	wounded, May 6, 1864
Charles J. Saunders	30	E	wounded, May 6, 1864
Romulus W. Saunders		F	wounded, May 6, 1864

Information contained in this table came from Compiled Service Records as summarized by Louis H. Manarin, *North Carolina Troops: 1861–1865, A Roster*, vol. II, pages 98–177. (See Appendix for more information on the men listed above, page 400.)

Stalemate: Grant Moves to Spotsylvania Court House, May 7–12

On the morning of May 7, Robert E. Lee and his troops were somewhat satisfied because after two days of hard fighting they had held Grant's Army of the Potomac and Burnside's Ninth Army to a standstill. Lee spent most of the day collecting his thoughts, men, and equipment continuing to have his men fortify their line. After two hard days in the Wilderness, Lee fully understood the necessity of entrenching and defending when confronted by the Union's larger and better equipped armies. He also had time to ponder what Grant might do next. R. E. Lee was a little surprised the Union army had not withdrawn across the Rapidan after two days of hard fighting. After all that was the pattern. But Grant was more concerned with finishing his mission than repeating the pattern of his predecessors.[44]

Early in the day, Grant determined to continue his march around R. E. Lee's right and head toward Richmond, drawing the enemy army out in the open. Grant was still convinced that with the new rifled muskets his men carried, if the two opposing armies marched at one another in an open field as in past battles his men could annihilate the Confederates. (The new rifles were more accurate at three times the distance than the smoothbore muskets most of the Confederates still carried.) Grant also knew where he wanted to be and spent the better part of the day preparing for a surprise night march southeast. He meant to draw R. E. Lee's army out of its barricades and fight it before the Confederates could again fortify against the more numerous and deadly Union rifles. The next stop was Spotsylvania Court House. If he could get there before Lee, he would position his army between the Army of Northern Virginia and the Confederate capital.[45]

Clearing the Road to Spotsylvania Court House

Before the Union army could begin its move Brock Road had to be cleared of enemy cavalry. Confederate cavalry had moved into Todd's Tavern as D. McM. Gregg pulled out the night before. Of course, clearing the road was a job for Sheridan.

The Union cavalry commander sent Wesley Merritt with Custer's brigade and Devin's command along Furnace Road to Brock Road. Once there, they turned south toward Todd's Tavern. Merritt held Alfred Gibbs's command in the rear, still watching the wagons but in a position to support the units moved forward. Sheridan had J. Irvin Gregg's and Davies's commands move west on Catharpin Road toward the tavern. (See map 2.5.)

Stuart had Fitz Lee's command, consisting of Wickham's and Lomax's brigades, at Todd's Tavern and along Brock Road; Hampton's command was on Catharpin Road where it crossed the Po River at Corbin's Bridge ready to move toward Brock Road if called upon. He still had fewer than three full companies from Young's brigade, and Gordon's North Carolinians. Recall that Gordon's North Carolina brigade had just been assigned to W. H. F. Lee's new division, but Hampton had been allowed to keep them with him during the fighting on May 5 and 6. With only Chambliss's brigade from his division, W. H. F. Lee had been moved from just west of the confluence of the Robertson and Rapidan Rivers to Morton's Ford on the Rapidan to watch for an attack coming from the Shenandoah Valley. By May 7, W. H. F. Lee was still making requests to have Gordon's North Carolinians moved up to his command on the Rapidan. W. H. F. Lee sent a message on the 7th to Lieutenant Colonel W. H. Taylor of his father's staff containing the following: "All quiet in my front. Would like to have Gordon as soon as possible. If you see Stuart jog his memory." Later that day in a message to Stuart, Hampton naturally consented to orders received and said he would send Gordon's brigade to its new division the following day. But he also argued strongly for letting W. H. F. Lee continue his river-watch with one brigade and let Gordon stay where he was—where the action was. Hampton went on to say, "Gordon's men will fight none the worse for being with their old comrades and in their old command, and we certainly need cavalry here." Whatever the next day might bring, on May 7 Gordon once again was fighting alongside Hampton and had the 2nd and 5th North Carolina cavalries with him — the 1st North Carolina was still on duty along the lower Rapidan fords. Rosser's brigade of Hampton's division had taken heavy losses in the fighting of the previous two days and was moved to the rear for a short rest.[46]

On May 7, as Merritt's men advanced along Brock Road, they encountered Fitz Lee's cavalrymen, and fighting escalated between the cavalries. Fitz Lee defended Todd's Tavern by dismounting his men and placing them behind log barricades. Merritt sent dismounted men into the woods to snipe at the enemy while the main body of Union cavalry tried mounted charges against the protected Confederates.

Merritt took heavy losses early in the fighting and made little headway.

Merritt needed help dislodging the Confederate cavalry, and by mid-morning it was possible. Meade assigned guard duty on the wagon train to the infantry, and gave Sheridan permission to throw his entire cavalry at Stuart's cavalry around Todd's Tavern. Gibbs's command was immediately sent up to Merritt's line on the north side of the tavern.

Sheridan sent David McM. Gregg with his division west along Catharpin Road until it branched, sending a fork southward but still toward Brock Road. D. McM. Gregg's command was split at that point — one brigade sent directly at Todd's Tavern to the west under Colonel J. Irvin Gregg's command, while the other brigade under Henry E. Davies's command went southwest to intersect Brock road below Fitz Lee's position. This would put enemy cavalry in front of Fitz Lee, on his right flank, as well as to his rear. Sheridan's plan was to first entrap and dispose of Fitz Lee's two brigades at the tavern, then have Colonel J. I. Gregg's brigade continue west on Catharpin Road through Gordon's North Carolina regiments, and then contain R. E. Lee's right flank—thus opening the way for Grant's infantry column.

The first hitch in Sheridan's plan came quickly as Fitz Lee, sensing difficulty, pulled his Confederate cavalrymen back along Brock Road, and had them erect new barricades across the road just below where the road taken by Davies's command intersected Brock Road. The Confederate pullback was slow and offered as much resistance as necessary. Consequently, it was mid-afternoon before Merritt's command coming from the north and Colonel J. I. Gregg's brigade from the east finally met at Todd's Tavern. Merritt left Custer's brigade above the tavern near the intersection of Brock and Furnace Roads to cover their rear while he had Devin's and Gibbs's commands move south of the tavern along Brock Road to confront Fitz Lee at his new line of barricades. As Merritt took his cavalrymen through Todd's Tavern toward the waiting Fitz Lee, J. I. Gregg was given the task of protecting their right flank, out Catharpin Road toward Corbin's Bridge.[47]

Moving west along Catharpin Road, J. I. Gregg had little trouble until he reached the bridge across the Po. Hampton's command was spread along the far side of the river on both sides of Corbin's Bridge. Some of Hampton's division and Gordon's 2nd and 5th North Carolina Cavalries were on the line across Catharpin Road, behind the Po River. Hampton's position was formidable and J. I. Gregg decided to back off and engage Hampton closer to Todd's Tavern where support was near if needed. Just west of the tavern, J. I. Gregg erected earthworks, put artillery in place, and waited for Hampton's men.[48]

He did not wait long. Gordon's 2nd North Carolina and a small portion of Young's brigade were pounding at the tavern's newly erected gates just about the time they were closed. A member of Stuart's staff rode over to see how Hampton was doing and decided to move up to his advance line which had by then pushed to the entrenched enemy in front of Todd's Tavern. The staff member described the scene as he approached the line:

We then rode up to the barricade and were peeping thro' it when all at once two loud reports startled us, and at the same instant two shells passed overhead a few feet above the barricade, and went hurtling up the road, passing over an entire regiment which was marching at a walk towards the barricade, and dropping harmlessly at the rear of the column. The regiment was immediately withdrawn to one side of the road, and dismounting, prepared to fight on foot. Gen. Gordon soon arrived on the ground, and sending forward his line, soon became hotly engaged.[49]

The Confederates left their barricades and charged the Union entrenchments only to be repulsed by heavy enemy artillery and rifle fire. It was a standoff. Around sunset, Stuart took some of Rosser's men to support Gordon's left on Catharpin Road. Then under the eyes of both Wade Hampton and J. E. B. Stuart, Gordon again sent his men against the enemy's barricades. The fire was too severe, so Stuart ordered the North Carolinians to pull back. J. I. Gregg had positioned himself well. His line was just east of a clearing that had to be crossed by the advancing Confederates. After several attempts to cross the open space, the long range rifles and guns of the enemy convinced the Confederate commanders to have their men throw up earthworks and settle in just west of the clearing. Stuart had not yet received orders to start a general engagement.[50]

After darkness settled in, Stuart instructed Gordon to move back quietly and camp near Shady Grove Church. To insure a low profile during the pullback, a member of Stuart's staff rode along the North Carolinian's line urging quiet prior to and during the withdrawal — he described his success in these words:

...speaking in a low voice and cautioning the men to come off quietly as the lines were so close together that any conversation in the ordinary tone could have been distinctly heard. But in spite of my instructions, one old "Tar-heel," in the exuberance of his spirits, perched himself on a pine stump and clapping his arms to his sides in imitation of the lord of the barnyard, uttered a loud, clear crow, which however came near terminating fatally, for at the very same instant a Yankee fired in the direction of the noise, the bullet passing just in front of my horse and striking the stump on which our "chicken" was sitting. That shut him up effectively, and he "rolled off his log" amid the laughter of his comrades. As we came out, the men exchanged alternate "cheers" and "groans" with the Yankees, and the two lines chaffed each other considerably, calling one another names neither euphonious nor endearing.[51]

Meanwhile over on Brock Road, Merritt was still trying to clear the path for Grant's march to Spotsylvania Court House, but he hit Fitz Lee's new line of dismounted cavalrymen again about a mile south of Todd's Tavern. At that point, a line of Confederate barricades shielded Wickham's brigade, while about half a mile back, Lomax's brigade was dismounted behind its barricade of logs and fence rails. Gibbs's brigade was the first to hit Wickham's line. The Federals hit their enemy with heavy artillery first, then charged the barricades. Wickham's line extended well into the woods on either side of the road, and his men held. Continually underestimating his enemy's position and determination, Gibbs soon found himself in trouble as gaping holes were blown through his line. He finally had to ask for support, and Devin's command was sent forward to plug the holes in Gibbs's line and stabilize the Union front. With Davies's command also on the line, the battle grew even hotter. The fighting continued so intensely that Wickham's barricades caught fire, adding to the heat from enemy rifles and artillery, and finally causing the first Confederate line to drop back to Lomax's position. Fitz Lee fought well and formed a strong line with Wickham's command on one side of the road and Lomax's on the other.[52]

The fighting continued into the late afternoon, and as more Federal troopers moved to the front, their superior firepower became overwhelming and Fitz Lee's left began to break. At that point, the Confederate commander sent a request over to Stuart near Catharpin Road for support from Hampton's command. Hampton had no troops to spare: he still had his hands full with J. I. Gregg's stand, and he continued to resist W. H. F. Lee's effort, through Stuart, to have Gordon's North Carolinians sent to Morton's Ford on the Rapidan. With barricades ablaze, and troops exhausted, wounded, or dead, Fitz Lee finally got the relief he sought when darkness fell — along with many of his men.[53]

Rather than continue the fight into the darkness, Sheridan withdrew his men about a mile or so toward Todd's Tavern. This move allowed Davies to fall back and spend the evening with Colonel J. I. Gregg at Todd's Tavern while Gibbs formed a line on Brock Road in front of Fitz Lee. J. I. Gregg's line continued to hold Hampton to the west of the tavern, and Custer spent the night on Brock Road north of the tavern. Sheridan was elated over having captured Todd's Tavern again. From the tavern that evening, he informed Meade that his cavalry had "made a very handsome fight," and had sealed off Catharpin Road and pushed Stuart's cavalry miles down Brock Road. He also pointed out that he had taken prisoners from Lomax's, Wickham's, Rosser's, Young's, Gordon's, and Chambliss's brigades.[54]

A major problem with that night's scene at the tavern was that Sheridan's assignment had not been to hold Todd's Tavern for the night, but rather to clear Confederate troops from Brock Road so Grant could start his night march to Spotsylvania Court House. Grant planned to have marching infantry on Brock Road heading for Spotsylvania Court House no later than early the next morning. This problem was compounded by the fact that Sheridan's pull-back to the tavern allowed Fitz Lee time to regroup his command and rebuild barricades for the next day, which made Grant's passage even more difficult. There were two main roads leading to Grant's destination — one off of Catharpin Road and the other, Brock Road. Hampton was held back from Brock Road, but was still on Catharpin Road; Fitz Lee remained on Brock Road. Neither path was clear for Grant's infantry; a cavalry fight would be required the next morning, and Grant had to revise his timetable.[55]

During the calm but nervous night, after surveying the area for roads toward Spotsylvania Court House, a member of Stuart's staff wrote these words in his diary:

Saturday, May 7th. This day spent like the last marching and fighting. What a curse war is. The dreadful sights I have seen this week in this Wilderness will never be banished from my memory. The woods are on fire in various places and horrible to think of hundreds of wounded men are in danger of being roasted alive. I am more than ever convinced that those who were instrumental in bringing the curse of this cruel war upon the country have committed an unpardonable crime against humanity which deserved not only the maledictions of mankind, but likewise the anathemas of an offended God.[56]

Robert E. Lee Races for Spotsylvania Court House

By late afternoon on the 7th, R. E. Lee sent instructions to Stuart over on Catharpin Road to examine and become familiar with all the roads south of their position. He wanted to know what roads were available to the Army of Northern Virginia should Grant have his infantry follow Sheridan south on Brock Road toward Spotsylvania Court House. By evening, R. E. Lee had instructed Richard H. Anderson to quietly pull Longstreet's First Corps out of the line after dark and start for Catharpin Road and then Corbin's Bridge. From there R. E. Lee knew he could send them up to Todd's Tavern if he had anticipated Grant's move incorrectly, but if, as Lee then suspected, Grant was heading for Spotsylvania Court House Anderson could readily turn southeast on the road to the court house and the race would be on.[57]

Sheridan ordered his cavalrymen southeast on Brock Road at 5:00 A.M. on May 8 — his task was still to clear the road for the Union infantry march to Spotsylvania Court House. It was a more difficult task by morning than the one he left the night before because Fitz Lee had regrouped and dug in. In addition, the delay had allowed Robert E. Lee to get his First Corps, commanded by Anderson, on the road for the court house, thus adding a dimension of urgency to Sheridan's job.

Grant had his infantry on the road and heading for Brock Road and the court house around midnight. He had his troops muffle the sounds of an army on the march so as not to prematurely alert the enemy of his movement. He wanted to get the head of his column around the Confederate right before they noticed. He did not know that R. E. Lee had already set the First Corps in motion toward Spotsylvania Court House. Grant may have had the idea first, but R. E. Lee had his advance troops mobilized almost as early, and Anderson did not have enemy cavalry in front of him.

Though he had Anderson in motion toward Spotsylvania Court House, when dawn came on May 8, R. E. Lee was not absolutely certain of Grant's intentions. He sent skirmishers out along his line to try to get a sense of what Grant had in mind for the day. He soon learned Grant was not going to withdraw. R. E. Lee then had to decide if his enemy was getting ready to attack Fredericksburg or Spotsylvania Court House. In either case, Lee's reaction would have to take into account that Longstreet was seriously wounded and out of the picture for awhile; A. P. Hill was too ill to command his corps; and Ewell was also not well and was in a depressed mood. R. E. Lee's most fit and able commander was J. E. B. Stuart. His cavalry, though only partially there, had performed its scouting and shielding tasks well during the Battle of the Wilderness and the following day. R. E. Lee certainly took some comfort knowing Stuart's cavalry was there and positioned to lead the Confederates southeast if need be. If the direction was Spotsylvania Court House, Stuart and his cavalrymen were in front of the enemy. Lee knew he had to count heavily on Stuart to perform again and felt he could.[58]

As Grant's infantry started for Brock Road from the Orange Turnpike area, the roads became very congested and movement was difficult at best. Finally, Warren took his command south on Brock Road and Sedgwick took his east to Chancellorsville. Grant was enthusiastically cheered by his men when he turned them south on Brock Road rather than North for the Rapidan. Meade took the same route as Warren and arrived at Todd's Tavern around 1:00 A.M. on May 8. Meade was not happy to find D. McM. Gregg and Merritt bedded down for the night, when they had not yet finished clearing Brock Road for the approaching Union infantry. Meade apparently had put his army in motion thinking the road was free of enemy cavalry. He made it clear that he felt Sheridan had failed to do his job. Meade immediately ordered Sheridan's cavalrymen into action. He sent D. McM. Gregg's division west on Catharpin Road to clear it as far as Corbin's Bridge and hold Hampton's cavalry behind that point. Meade gave Merritt orders to move his command down Brock Road to Spotsylvania Court House as rapidly as possible and then shield the western approaches to the village.[59]

The advance troops of Warren's Fifth Corps reached Merritt's line across Brock Road around 3:30 on the morning of May 8 to the sound of dismounted cavalrymen skirmishing with the enemy. Warren's infantry column continued to arrive with no place to go. They came to a halt and began to form an unplanned bivouac along Brock Road.[60]

As pressure grew behind him, Merritt had to move Fitz Lee's cavalrymen out of the way quickly, but that was not going to be easy. Fitz Lee had his men dismounted behind newly constructed barricades and Breathed's artillery was well placed to greet the Union cavalry as it approached. The fighting was again deadly. Sheridan arrived at the front to encourage his troops, but Merritt could not push through the Confederate cavalry. As the Union infantry continued to accumulate behind him, Merritt finally had to ask Warren to bring some of his infantry forward and storm over Fitz Lee's cavalrymen. The infantrymen were ordered to take the barricade using only bayonets. They formed a line and marched on the Confederates. The Confederate cavalrymen fell back, contesting every step of the Union advance. Though considerable numbers of men had been lost on both sides, the Union advance could not be stopped. An entire army was moving on their heels. Finally Fitz Lee found a hill, Laurel Hill, just off Brock Road near the intersection with Old Courthouse Road, still about a mile above Spotsylvania Court House. He decided to make a stand with the Old Courthouse Road at his back if he needed to withdraw in that direction. As he was collecting his men for a final stand before reaching the village, Fitz Lee learned that Wilson's Union cavalry division had just reached Spotsylvania Court House at his rear. There was little he could do but hope they did not come at his rear immediately. Fitz Lee could not turn his front from Warren's infantry line which was still coming in force.[61]

Fitz Lee's concerns were not unfounded.

James Wilson's cavalry division had been resting near Chancellorsville after their hard fighting against Rosser's brigade on May 6, when Sheridan ordered them toward Spotsylvania Court House early on the morning of the 8th. Wilson's command had a wide arch to march, but it was unobstructed by the enemy. It swung southeast out of Chancellorsville and arched down on Spotsylvania Court House from the northeast, and arrived about the time Fitz Lee was making a stand at Laurel Hill on Brock Road. Wilson wasted no time; he sent a brigade up Brock Road from the court house to hit Fitz Lee in the rear and open the route for Meade's marching column.[62] (See map 2.5.)

By then Stuart and some of his staff had joined Fitz Lee and his cavalrymen. Their only hope was for the timely arrival of Anderson with Longstreet's First Corps. Anderson had dropped south from the Confederate line, crossed the Po at Corbin's Bridge, and taken a road eastward paralleling the Po until the river turned south across his path at Block House Bridge. From there he continued east with his command to the Block House where his route crossed the Old Courthouse Road. At that point, the village of Spotsylvania Court House was about a mile ahead of him, and Fitz Lee on Laurel Hill was just about a mile north of him.

Anderson's advance arrived at the Block House Bridge around 7:30 A.M., and they had artillery with them. Shortly after they settled in at the bridge, Anderson's advance units received word from Stuart that he needed artillery up the Old Courthouse Road, at Laurel Hill immediately because the enemy's infantry was massing for an attack and Grant's army was about to overrun his position. Just as Anderson was sending support to Stuart, he learned that Wilson's cavalry was entering Spotsylvania Court House, and he would also have to move in that direction quickly.[63]

Anderson sent artillery and two brigades of infantry to support the cavalrymen on Laurel Hill. Stuart personally went down the south side of the hill to guide Anderson's men and guns into position. He placed the guns and sent one infantry brigade across Brock Road. Stuart's line was in place just minutes before Warren's Union infantry marched into sight. The Confederate First Corps commanded by Anderson had won the race between infantries. Grant's infantry had an earlier start, the shorter route, better roads, and the element of surprise on its side—yet Grant lost the race, albeit only by minutes. R. E. Lee's infantry had conditions opposite to all that, yet he had two brigades of cavalry in front of Grant's column. Among other things, Fitz Lee's cavalry had slowed Grant's advancing army allowing Anderson to arrive just in time. All that was left was more fighting.[64]

The Infantries Clash Near Spotsylvania Court House

Warren arrived at the front of his column, he decided to attack immediately—to drive the Confederates from the hill and push through to the village. Warren launched his attack on Stuart's line at about 8:30 on the morning of May 8. The Union Fifth Corps came forward in waves, allowing Stuart's guns and muskets ample time to reload and make the charging Federals drop, either dead or for cover in any available ditch. Unit after unit charged Stuart's well chosen and barricaded position only to be battered and pushed back.[65]

Warren regrouped and launched a second attack a couple of hours later. By then more of his troops had arrived at the front, but Anderson had also increasingly moved more of the Confederate First Corps into the barricades. This attack met with no more success than the first, and the Federal infantrymen built their own barricades and dug trenches as protection from the continuous hail of gunfire coming in their direction. In most cases, they did not wait for instructions from their commanders before protecting themselves. By noon, Warren himself felt defeated and conceded that he did not have the resources to occupy Spotsylvania Court House.[66]

Meanwhile, as Stuart and Anderson fought Warren's command coming from the north, Wilson was still coming through Spotsylvania Court House so he sent a brigade north on Brock Road at the Confederate rear. Stuart sent a regiment, the 3rd Virginia Cavalry toward the village to protect their rear from just such an attack. About the same time, Anderson sent two infantry brigades around the village to encircle Wilson's command. Wilson sent a courier to Sheridan communicating his desperate situation and recalled the cavalrymen he had sent up to Laurel Hill in an effort to hold on to the prize he was first to take—Spotsylvania Court

House. Sheridan sent word back to Wilson that he had no support to send and that he was about to be cut off from the main body of the army. Wilson was fully aware of the latter, and wasted no time withdrawing from the village. He was out just as the Confederates stormed in.[67]

Midday saw a major artillery duel between the lines until both sides tired of it. Warren's infantry and artillery were at a standstill, he could not break through the Confederate First Corps. Warren had made it clear to Meade that he needed reinforcements to break through — the rest of Grant's army would just have to line up along Brock Road behind him. Meade responded by sending Hancock's Second Corps to Todd's Tavern to hold the enemy back on Catharpin Road — he did not want to give R. E. Lee the opportunity of coming down Brock Road at the Union rear. The Union column on Brock Road was threatened because the Confederate Second and Third Corps were still northwest of them, and during the day R. E. Lee started Ewell's corps toward Spotsylvania Court House. Hampton's cavalry command was still holding Corbin's Bridge on Catharpin Road as Ewell's Second Corps began to move behind them toward the action around the court house. By late afternoon, the entire Confederate Second Corps had passed south behind Hampton's cavalry screen (General Early started A. P. Hill's Third Corps in the same direction later in the day.), and Grant's army continued to pass through Todd's Tavern with their flank and eventually their rear shielded by Hancock's infantry corps. About the same time, Meade hurried Sedgwick's Sixth Corps from below Chancellorsville to help Warren in front of Spotsylvania Court House. It took Sedgwick around five hours to get into position for a joint attack by both Union corps. By the time they were ready, however, three Confederate divisions from Ewell's corps had joined Anderson's two divisions on the line just above Spotsylvania Court House. The two opposing armies formed an immense and immediate standoff — there was skirmishing all along the line but not much else during the afternoon. In the evening, Warren and Sedgwick tried to coordinate an attack, but by the time it was underway, the Confederate line was too strong and the Union assault failed once again. Late on May 8, R. E. Lee, Ewell, and Anderson bivouacked for the night near the Block House — General Early with A. P. Hill's corps would join them by evening of the next day.[68]

Meanwhile, back in the Wilderness, General Early had his Third Corps in motion for Spotsylvania Court House. R. E. Lee had instructed Early to take his column through Todd's Tavern, and then turn south along Brock Road as soon as the enemy was no longer in front of his line. That was a good idea in that it would have put him at the enemy's rear, except for the fact that Hancock's infantry corps had replaced Colonel J. I. Gregg's cavalry brigade at the tavern. Early wisely sent Mahone's division ahead before he set his entire corps in that direction. Hampton's cavalry sensors knew a Federal force was still at Todd's Tavern, and the cavalry commander offered his assistance to General Early; but they were apparently unaware of the size of the enemy's force by early evening. Hancock had a brigade forward on Catharpin Road, about halfway between Corbin's Bridge and Todd's Tavern. The Confederates struck the enemy from the north with some of Mahone's infantry and from the west with Young's and Rosser's cavalry from Hampton's division. (Gordon's 2nd and 5th North Carolina regiments remained in support near Corbin's Bridge.)[69]

The Confederates drove Hancock's advance back along Catharpin Road into their entrenchments in front of Todd's Tavern. General Early realized the Union infantry was in force at the tavern and on Brock Road, and if he followed his prescribed route, in his words, his "...march would have led through his [the enemy's] entire army." Early pulled back a bit and put his command down for the night between Todd's Tavern and Corbin's Bridge. Very early on the morning of May 9, Hampton passed along a message from R. E. Lee instructing Early to take the alternate route to Spotsylvania — the one taken earlier by Anderson and Ewell.[70]

General Early had his command on the Confederate line about a mile northwest of Spotsylvania Court House later in the day, and his men had some time to rest. Grant's army did not attack on May 9. The Union soldiers were also allowed to rest that day, when they were not entrenching and positioning their artillery.[71]

The Cavalries Move Toward Richmond, May 9

While the Union army was being battered at Laurel Hill, some of its commanders were already trying to salvage the day and rationalize their failure to clear Brock Road. By early afternoon on May 8, the brewing storm between Meade and Sheridan came to a head and the thunder could be heard by many of the men around Meade's headquarters as Sheridan exchanged blame with Meade over the disastrous events of the previous night and that morning. In addition, Meade was still interested in using cavalry to guard the wagons, and Sheridan did not want to waste his resources on such duty. Sheridan reportedly "replied with spirit, 'If I am permitted to cut loose from this army I'll draw Stuart after me, and whip him, too.' This was the principal object of the Richmond raid." In the end, Grant, with Meade agreeing, gave Sheridan what he wanted. He was allowed to immediately collect his cavalry, his ammunition and supply wagons and go after Stuart's cavalry. The infantry took over guarding the wagon trains, clearing its own path, and searching for the enemy's flanks. Sheridan was happy, but Meade's army would have to spend the next several bloody days without their eyes and ears.[72]

Sheridan immediately concentrated his cavalrymen just southeast of Chancellorsville. As the Union cavalrymen poured into their camps, they re-supplied and readied for a campaign—additional units were supplied with the new seven-shot Spencer carbines. The supply and ammunition wagons were packed and readied. While these routine preparations were underway, Sheridan worked out his plan. He knew he had to draw Stuart's cavalry from the battle lines currently in place, so he took his cavalry toward the Confederate capital. If his direction appeared to threaten Richmond and its supply lines, he knew Stuart would collect his cavalrymen and follow. He set a course east for Telegraph Road below Fredericksburg, then south. His route took the Union cavalry column east of the ominous infantry battle brewing near Spotsylvania Court House. Once he reached Telegraph Road his initial plan called for him to proceed directly to Yellow Tavern just north of Richmond. When he got to Jerrell's Mill, however, he detoured and headed for Chilesburg on Mountain Road. Sheridan wanted to be at least a day away from the confrontation between R. E. Lee and Grant before he tangled with Stuart in a major way. He calculated there would be fewer enemy posts and patrols on Mountain Road as he approached Richmond, and in any event, Mountain Road more or less paralleled Telegraph Road and rejoined it just above Yellow Tavern, about 7 or 8 miles north of Richmond. In addition, along the way near Beaver Dam Station, Sheridan knew his route would cross the Virginia Central Railroad, and he could disrupt that important Confederate supply line as he moved south. He knew such a course would get Stuart's full attention.[73]

Stuart's cavalry would not otherwise be an easy target because it was spread far and wide. On the afternoon of May 8, W. H. F. Lee, with only Chambliss's brigade from his division, was at Verdiersville mobilizing for a trip north of the Rapidan to scout the camp sites and depots formerly occupied by the enemy army as far as Stevensburg near Brandy Station. W. H. F. Lee's other brigade, James B. Gordon's North Carolinians, was still near Hampton's division (from his own brigade, Hampton had a portion of Young's brigade and Rosser's brigade on hand). In addition, Gordon's brigade itself was further divided during the day. The 1st North Carolina was pulled from its picket duties near the Germanna and Ely's Fords and sent to its new division commander, W. H. F. Lee. They collected near Verdiersville early on May 8, but remained for only a couple of hours before being detached from W. H. F. Lee and sent to join Gordon and their North Carolina brigade as they readied themselves for a move toward Spotsylvania Court House to meet Stuart. The 2nd and 5th North Carolina cavalries were still with Gordon and close to Hampton on Catharpin Road shielding their infantry's march to Spotsylvania Court House. Fitz Lee's division (consisting of Wickham's and Lomax's brigades) was on the line at Laurel Hill, just above Spotsylvania Court House. On May 8, Stuart was not yet aware of Sheridan's instructions to concentrate his cavalry for a fight with him, so no Confederate move to consolidate cavalry in response to Sheridan's plan was made on that day.[74]

Before dawn on May 9, Sheridan had more than 10,000 men in their saddles and heading south amid a palatable air of excitement—the cavalrymen felt they were launching a major campaign against Richmond. They marched in three divisions commanded by Wesley Merritt, David McM. Gregg, and James H. Wilson — and were accompanied by six batteries of horse artillery in a column nearly thirteen miles long. As planned, Sheridan took his column in a wide swing around the poised infantries. He wanted his column to be noticed and it was. Once he was underway, Confederate cavalry scouts began to probe the column to sense its size, composition, and direction, but were expected and of no concern to the Federals.[75]

Stuart and his staff pulled out of the line and back to Spotsylvania Court House shortly after 4:00 A.M. on May 9. After arriving, he was told by his scouts of Sheridan's column — but the only cavalry Stuart had in the area were Fitz Lee's two brigades on the Confederate far right. Cavalry patrols were undertaken by Wickham's brigade. They kept an eye on the marching Union cavalry during the morning, then just after midday General Early began to arrive near Spotsylvania Court House with the Third Corps and was placed on the right of their line. Once Early was in place the remainder of Wickham's cavalry brigade was released to harass Sheridan's rear.

Wickham moved his command at a hurried pace and after nearly three hours of hard riding, the Confederates caught Sheridan's rear guard just as it finished crossing the Ta River where it intersected Telegraph Road at Jerrell's Mill. The Union rear guard formed a line across Mountain Road (which branched from Telegraph Road at Jerrell's Mill), but no serious charge was made by Wickham's men. The Confederates made one charge into the column's rear regiment which scattered and hurried up the road. At that point, the Union rear guard and pursuing Confederates just exchanged shots and threatened additional attacks. After about half an hour, Sheridan's rear guard packed up and moved along. Wickham's job was not to engage the enemy column in any serious manner, but to harass them, slow them if possible, and most importantly to keep Stuart informed. This he did by following on their flank, probing for weak spots and making a general nuisance of himself.[76]

Fighting at the rear of the Union column in no way hindered the rather pleasant and more or less uninterrupted ride near the front of Sheridan's marching column. Sheridan advanced through Chilesburg by early evening, nearly 15 miles ahead of his rear guard. Wilson's and D. McM. Gregg's divisions camped for the night near Anderson's Ford on the North Anna River.

While the Union camps were being set up Sheridan sent a party across the river toward Beaver Dam Station on the Virginia Central Railroad. In a heavy rainstorm the Federals reached the station just as two trains were waiting to unload Confederate supplies and take away nearly 300 Union prisoners. The Union cavalrymen led by George A. Custer freed their comrades and captured the supplies that included food and medical stores sorely needed by R. E. Lee's army. Custer's men took what they could carry and burned the remainder along with the station. In addition, during the night Custer's men were augmented with others from Merritt's division and were able to destroy nearly ten miles of railroad track. Sheridan had already accomplished one of his secondary objectives before dawn on May 10.[77]

STUART GATHERS HIS CAVALRY WHILE IN PURSUIT

Early in the afternoon of May 9, Stuart and his staff left their temporary headquarters near Spotsylvania Court House and rode to catch up with Fitz Lee's command. Stuart was in high spirits as he rode off ahead of his men — he sensed a major cavalry battle brewing. Stuart overtook Fitz Lee just after nightfall, not long after Fitz Lee and Lomax's brigade had joined Wickham's command which was still on Sheridan's rear guard. Some skirmishing was still going on when Stuart arrived but soon diminished in the darkness.[78]

Before Stuart set out to catch up with Fitz Lee's command, he sent instructions for Gordon's North Carolina brigade to move forward and join him near Spotsylvania Court House. He left Hampton with nearly two brigades to defend the line west of Todd's Tavern. W. H. F. Lee returned the following day from Culpeper County with Chambliss's brigade to reinforce Hampton's small command. The North Carolina brigade was no longer detached to Hampton, but still detached from W. H. F. Lee's new division. They were attached to Stuart.[79]

Soon after receiving orders to head south, Gordon moved his brigade below the Confed-

Five • Grant's Overland Campaign, May 4 to Mid-June 1864

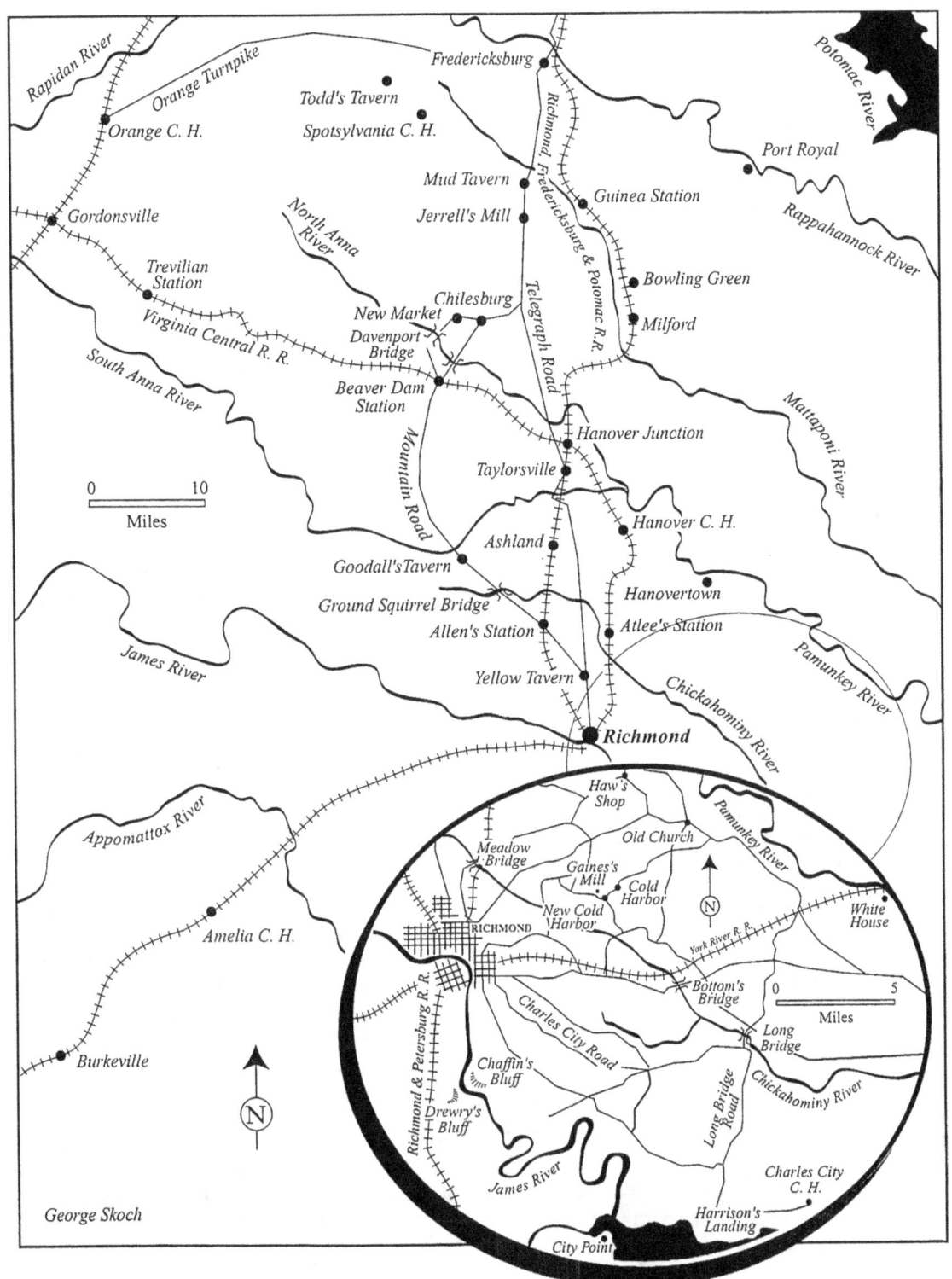

5.1: From the Wilderness to Petersburg

erate line at Spotsylvania Court House and on to Telegraph Road. The North Carolinians had farther to march and left later than Fitz Lee's command, so they were several hours behind their fellow Confederates on Sheridan's trail. Gordon marched his command as far as Mud Tavern below the Po River and camped for the night. Gordon's command was near full strength with the 1st, 2nd and the replenished 5th North Carolina cavalries in his column (the 3rd North Carolina, though assigned to him, was still detained in North Carolina). Stuart wanted the North Carolina brigade with him and Fitz Lee's two brigades before he entered a major battle with Sheridan's three divisions (all three Confederate brigades totaled between 4,000 and 4,500 men).[80]

Shortly after Stuart caught up with Fitz Lee, he sent a member of his staff, T. S. Garnett, to locate Gordon's column and hurry them forward. Garnett had to ride back about 5 or 6 miles to Mud Tavern where he found Gordon's North Carolina regiments making camp for the night. Gordon's Quartermaster had managed to obtain corn and forage, and the men with their horses were settling in to partake of it and rest. Garnett described his arrival in these words:

Dismounting I approached the house and inquiring for Gen. Gordon I was answered by that officer himself from the porch of a small house near the roadside. Making my way to him in the dark, he eagerly inquired after Stuart and I delivered my orders. "Gen. Stuart wants you to come right ahead, General," said I; to which Gordon replied, "By G__d, my men shall not move one foot till they fed up." He then said that it was out of the question to move his brigade until they had taken some rest. They had marched from Locust Grove since day break, over 40 miles, without stopping to feed or water, and then changing his tone, he kindly invited me to come and lie down by him on the porch. I did so, and in a few minutes we were both fast asleep. I was waked by Gen. Gordon, who had just ordered the brigade to move, and remounting we rode along together on our way to join Genl. Stuart.[81]

Gordon and his three North Carolina regiments reached Stuart's camp near the small village of Chilesburg very early on May 10. They had marched about 50 miles in less than 24 hours and had slept for only a few of those. Nonetheless, by the time they arrived Stuart had devised a plan of attack on Sheridan's column, and the cavalrymen were back in their saddles shortly after dawn. Stuart knew his three brigades were no match for Sheridan's three division, so he wanted to hit the enemy when they were about halfway across the North Anna River, and thus deal with them in two parts. Fitz Lee sent Lomax's brigade back to Stuart just before or about the same time Gordon arrived at Stuart's camp with the North Carolina brigade. Apparently Fitz Lee did not know Stuart also had Gordon's command with him near Chilesburg. In any case, Stuart divided his troops leaving Fitz Lee with his command on Mountain Road to press Sheridan's rear to the river while taking Gordon's brigade from Chilesburg westward to New Market, then south to the North Anna. From there Stuart planned to cross the river at Davenport Bridge, then turn to hit the front half of the Union column near Beaver Dam Station.[82]

Sheridan had camped Merritt's command below the North Anna River so they could spend a good deal of the night destroying the railroad on both sides of Beaver Dam Station. Wilson's and D. McM. Gregg's divisions were camped north of the river. About midway through the night, Sheridan knew that Stuart was collecting his cavalry behind him near Chilesburg and began to suspect that Stuart might try exactly what he planned to do—cross the North Anna upstream, probably at Davenport Bridge, and head for the Union flank around Beaver Dam Station. To protect his western flank, Sheridan had Merritt send the 5th United States Cavalry and the 1st New York Dragoons, under the command of Captain A. K. Arnold, upriver toward Davenport Bridge in case Stuart did come at the Union flank by that route. They were instructed to hold the bridge at all costs.[83]

When he started out early on the morning of May 10, Stuart apparently had little or no doubt that with shrewd maneuvering and hard fighting his cavalry force of just over 4,000 could hit Sheridan's column of nearly 12,000 in the rear and flank and do them significant harm. With such confidence Stuart and Gordon took their cavalrymen up river to cross at Davenport Bridge.

The head of Stuart's column left camp before dawn — Stuart left around 9:00 A.M. About the time Gordon had his troopers mounted Fitz Lee's guns began to pound the rear of the

Union column. The artillery fire was partly meant to divert attention from Gordon's departure, but it primarily created an unpleasant setting for Sheridan's men as they prepared and consumed breakfast.

Just after daybreak Sheridan started D. McM. Gregg's division over the river — Wilson's followed. Confederate horse artillery pulled up close enough to lob shells at the ford as the Federals crossed. Nonetheless, Sheridan's rear divisions crossed the river and fell in with Merritt's division already near Beaver Dam Station.[84]

Before daybreak, Arnold's detachment from Merritt's division started up river from Beaver Dam Station toward Davenport Bridge to block Stuart's anticipated crossing. They got to the bridge just after sunup and found Confederate engineers already there repairing the previously damaged bridge for Stuart's arrival. Arnold's men drove off the work crew and did additional damage to the bridge. It would be a wet crossing for Gordon's cavalrymen. Arnold waited for Stuart's column at a small ford just below the bridge and shortly spotted Confederate troopers when they approached the bridge, then turned away and headed up river in search of another ford. Arnold sent a small detachment up their side of the river to monitor the enemy's search for a usable ford. The Confederates, led by the 5th North Carolina, soon found a crossing point and when they approached the river they could see "On the opposite hills, skirted with heavy timbers, mounted videttes of the enemy," which indicated to them the main Union column was just ahead.[85]

The arrival of the North Carolina brigade across the river was quickly communicated to Arnold. He responded immediately by sending his two regiments up to the ford. Gordon sent sharpshooters from the 5th North Carolina forward and drove Arnold's dismounted men back from the south shore. As the Union sharpshooters were being pushed back Gordon sent a mounted squadron from the 5th North Carolina charging across with sabers high and voices shrill directly toward Arnold's advancing troopers. Even though the ford was almost impassable — according to one North Carolinian, "Horses and riders went down in the stream, yet up they grappled and soon reached the bank, which was readily cleared of the party holding it, and which gave the regiment an exciting chase for several miles."[86]

Just as it appeared the fighting would escalate and Gordon's other regiments moved forward, Sheridan summoned Arnold back to the Union column. Sheridan had already moved through Beaver Dam Station — indeed Wilson's division had passed with Wickham's brigade at its heels. By the time Arnold regrouped and neared the station, he found he had Wickham in front of him and Gordon on his rear. The cavalrymen from either Wickham's or Arnold's commands charged, and fierce fighting with pistols and sabers took place. Before he was badly beaten, however, Arnold managed to throw out a line of skirmishers along Wickham's flank and take most of his men around the Confederates and race for the rear of Sheridan's column with Wickham's men hot on their trail. Arnold lost nearly 70 men that morning.[87]

Stuart collected Wickham's, Lomax's, and Gordon's brigades just below the remains of Beaver Dam Station. Some of Wickham's men followed Arnold to Sheridan's column and continued on with great difficulty. The Federals had learned well how to keep their enemy off their rear. They felled trees and placed whatever obstacles they could find across the road to impede the progress of their pursuers.[88]

STUART'S RIDE-AROUND TO YELLOW TAVERN

Stuart was still fully aware that the relative size of the two cavalry forces meant he could not confront Sheridan in an open battlefield; and hanging on Sheridan's rear doing little was not in Stuart's nature. He needed a better plan, a way to ambush Sheridan near enough to Richmond to gain support from the City's defenses. He needed to get in front of the Union column, so the road full of obstacles before him was not a reasonable course. Stuart decided his best chance was to leave Gordon's North Carolina brigade to press Sheridan's rear guard — which included clearing the road of barricades when necessary as they went along and attacking when an opportunity presented itself, causing the Union rear guard to lag behind its column and not be immediately available at the front when the main engagement takes place. Stuart would take Fitz Lee and his two brigades east toward Hanover Junction, then south along Telegraph Road to Taylorsville, and on to Yellow Tavern just above Richmond where he hoped to be waiting for Sheridan. Stuart's men and horses were tired, but they would have to ride nearly all day and night to reach the intersection above Yellow Tavern before the head of Sheridan's column.[89]

Stuart pushed his column hard, taking byroads that generally paralleled the Virginia Central Railroad—he knew he had to cover as much ground as possible on May 10. They made good time and around 9:00 P.M. Fitz Lee's two brigades were pulling into Hanover Junction just east of Telegraph Road. From there Stuart sent a progress report to General Braxton Bragg at Richmond (he had been sending reports to Bragg throughout the day). With a tired cavalry at the end of a long day's march Stuart seemed eager to make sure the general at Richmond knew what was approaching his doorstep and that Stuart's cavalry was not sufficient to stop it.[90] Stuart wrote:

While pursuing the enemy from Beaver Dam on the Richmond road the barricading was so serious an obstruction that a road parallel to their line of march was taken by my command, and the head of the column will rest near Taylorsville to-night.... Should he attack Richmond I will certainly move [in] his rear and do what I can; at the same time, I hope to be able to strike him if he endeavors to escape. His force is large, and if attack is made on Richmond it will be principally as dismounted cavalry, which fight better than enemy's infantry.[91]

When Stuart penned that message to Bragg he sounded less than optimistic about the possibility he could get around Sheridan's front before reaching Yellow Tavern. Perhaps he simply did not want Richmond defenses to count on his timely arrival. On the other hand, while at Hanover Junction Stuart learned that the head of Sheridan's column was already at Ground Squirrel Bridge over on the other road—that put him a lot closer to Yellow Tavern than the Confederates. In any case, in his message Stuart made it clear if Sheridan wanted to attack Richmond, it would happen. There was no Confederate cavalry between the enemy and Richmond.[92]

Speculation about Stuart's level of confidence at that moment aside, we can be certain he was not about to give up the race for Yellow Tavern, and only when pressed by Fitz Lee did he acquiesce and allow his cavalrymen to take some much needed food and rest. However Stuart moved on to Taylorsville to get the head of his column a couple of miles further down the road before he rested a few hours. As he left Hanover Junction, Stuart made clear to his staff that he expected Fitz Lee's men to be on the road by 1:00 A.M. May 11. To ensure that occurred he instructed H. B. McClellan of his staff to remain in Fitz Lee's camp and ordered him not to close his eyes until he saw the cavalrymen in their saddles and on the road. They kept their schedule and joined Stuart at Taylorsville.[93]

At 2:00 A.M. Stuart notified General Bragg at Richmond that he and his men were about to leave Taylorsville along the Richmond, Fredericksburg and Potomac Railroad toward the rail stop at Ashland. He informed Richmond that if he got to Ashland before the enemy, he would move over to Telegraph Road and hurry for the intersection of Mountain and Telegraph Roads just above Yellow Tavern.[94]

THE NORTH CAROLINA CAVALRY PRESSES SHERIDAN'S COLUMN

On the morning of May 10 when Sheridan marched south out of Beaver Dam Station, he wanted to get his column across the South Anna River by the end of the day. Once he was that far south, he looked forward to doing battle with Stuart's cavalry. The Union column reached Ground Squirrel Bridge on the South Anna River a little after 4:00 P.M.; they had marched about 18 miles since breakfast. Sheridan led his column across the bridge, and after his rear guard caught up, instructed them to burn the bridge. Union pickets were set along the southern shore to watch for and discourage the crossing of those pesky North Carolinians who had been harassing them throughout the long, hot march that day. While Sheridan's men were settling in that evening, Stuart was pushing Fitz Lee's two brigades for another five hours to reach Hanover Junction. Sheridan felt less pressured by time and allowed his cavalrymen to cook supper, care for their horses, and get a good night's sleep.[95] (See map 5.1.)

The next morning, Sheridan divided his command for the last leg of his march toward Richmond. D. McM. Gregg's division had been at the head of the column the day before, so on May 11, they got to remain on the south side of the river and protect Sheridan's rear. Just after sunup, Sheridan had Merritt's and Wilson's divisions on the road. Their course was through

Goodall's Tavern and along a road paralleling Mountain Road to the Richmond, Fredericksburg and Potomac Railroad at Allen's Station. From there that road continued for a couple of miles before it rejoined Mountain Road for a short distance before the latter road intersected Telegraph Road just above Yellow Tavern. From around Ground Squirrel Bridge to the intersection on Telegraph Road the Federal cavalrymen had to march little more than ten miles that day. (Stuart's column had to march a little farther from Hanover Junction to meet their enemy just above Yellow Tavern later in the day.)[96]

As Sheridan marched toward Goodall's Tavern, Davies's brigade was sent due east to Ashland Station. His mission was to tear up the station and tracks, then head south along the rail bed to rejoin the column as it passed through Allen's Station. Before Sheridan's main column met Stuart and Fitz Lee's brigades just above Yellow Tavern, both Gregg, back at Ground Squirrel Bridge, and Davies, over at Ashland Station, would have some fighting to do.[97]

Fighting at Ground Squirrel Bridge and Goodall's Tavern, May 11

Gordon's North Carolina brigade had marched over 40 miles with little food, water, or rest on May 9; then with very little rest, they were back in their saddles the next morning marching toward Chilesburg, and from there they took a circuitous route across the North Anna and down to Beaver Dam Station, fighting a good deal of the way. Once they were assigned the task of pursuing Sheridan's column on May 10, they had already marched and fought over 10 miles, and had another 15 miles to cover in the same manner before they could rest and eat just north of the South Anna River that night. One cavalryman from North Carolina remembered that trying time as one in which "Our horses like ourselves were worn and ill-fed. We hardly remembered what remounts were."[98]

As indicated above, the head of the Union column crossed the South Anna River around 4:00 P.M. and rested more than fifteen miles from the column's rear. Their rear guard would take the remainder of the day to catch up because they periodically stopped to defend themselves and drop trees across the path of the oncoming North Carolinians. In spite of the obstacles throughout the day the Confederates stayed close and were constantly on the rear guard's flanks. Squads would move forward through wooded areas, suddenly appearing on their enemy's flanks, sending a few volleys into the marching column, scattering it momentarily, then disappearing into the woods.[99]

Gordon's North Carolina brigade stopped for a brief rest that night in sight of the enemy's campfires across the South Anna River. The next morning, May 11, they were back in the saddle around 3 o'clock, ready to pursue Sheridan's cavalry once again. Sheridan's rear guard had burned the bridge over the river but Gordon wasted no time searching for an alternative crossing point.[100]

When Sheridan left D. McM. Gregg's division to cover his rear at the South Anna River, he was confident there would be little or no pressure from that direction — with the bridge burned, the river was considered unfordable. Gordon and his North Carolinians had a different view, however. Soon after Sheridan had his column on the road heading south, Gregg's pickets along the south shore of the river called for support. A small squad of men was sent to the river in support of the picket line, while the rest of Gregg's command continued to prepare for their trip south to catch up with the main column. Suddenly there were increased sounds of musket fire, and dismounted Union soldiers were pushed back into their picket camp, some head-over-heels, and the cavalrymen raced for their mounts.[101]

Gordon was determined to stay on the rear of the enemy's column, thereby being near the action when Stuart arrived at Sheridan's front. He looked fast and hard for a way to cross the river and found a ford thought to be impassable by D. McM. Gregg's men, even some of his own because of the fifteen-foot-high banks. No matter, Gordon was going to take his brigade across. He rapidly moved to the front of his column, and in the words of one of his cavalrymen, "He galloped to this ford with the Sixty-third [5th cavalry] in front ... and with a mighty plunge he led the way, and over that old ford every man of his brigade followed him. Some were seriously hurt, but we were out there expecting to get hurt." Federal pickets along the south shore fired at them as they hit the water, but in a matter of minutes the North Carolina regiments crossed the river and charged up the steep embankment into the enemy pickets driving them back. Then a detachment from the 2nd North Carolina was sent forward and drove the skirmishers back through their picket camp along Mountain Road. The chaos soon spread back to Gregg's main camp around Goodall's place as the picket force raced back for support. After passing through the enemy's picket camp, most of the North Carolina cavalrymen quickly dismounted and filed into a small lane leading to Gregg's main camp. A squadron of Confederate horsemen remained in their saddles and took the lead. The brigade marched down the road in column of fours in the face of heavy fire from Union skirmishers. According to Private Paul B. Means of the 5th North Carolina Cavalry, "In splendid style we swung out into line on the right of that road and went at their dismounted men with a steady step and fire, and drove them back in disorder and confusion." The dismounted 2nd North Carolina and some of the 5th marched into the skirmishers' steady but retreating fire and drove the enemy back to their main camp near Goodall's Tavern. They suddenly saw the 1st Maine and 10th New York Cavalries mounted and ready to charge up the road. Gordon quickly brought the mounted 1st North Carolina and a mounted squadron from the 5th past their dismounted comrades in a full charge into the oncoming enemy. Pistols were emptied at close range and saber-to-saber fighting took place among the mounted cavalrymen. As the dismounted North Carolinians approached the melee, the mounted Federals withdrew in a rapid and disorganized manner. When the Confederates reached Gregg's camp, Union sharpshooters continued firing from the woods and from the tavern and outbuildings as well as the barns and stables. Behind such barricades, the Union cavalrymen were able to stop the rapid Confederate advance. Hard fighting continued for several hours, but the North Carolinians could not dislodge the enemy sharpshooters. Gordon did not have artillery with him, which meant a frontal attack on the buildings would have been exceedingly wasteful.[102]

Finally, Gordon took command of the 1st North Carolina Cavalry and sent Colonel Cheek on a flanking move around the buildings with a squadron from the 5th North Carolina. Cheek hit the left flank of the Union line and drove them back in confusion. At about the same time, Gordon charged with the remainder of his brigade, encouraging D. McM. Gregg's men to back out of the tavern complex onto the open road. Gordon then dismounted the 1st and the squadron of the 5th North Carolina cavalries and pushed his dismounted troopers down the road at the retreating Union line. Gordon sent the 2nd North Carolina into the woods to again flank Gregg's line. This resulted in fighting on two sides in fierce hand-to-hand combat with sabers slashing, pistols firing, and men falling. Cheek remembered that "...we had the most desperate hand-to-hand conflict I ever witnessed." Even the 1st Maine Cavalry, considered to be one of the Union's best, was overwhelmed and broke in confusion as the cavalrymen individually took the road in disorganized retreat.[103]

Gordon regrouped his North Carolinians, with the 2nd Cavalry in front, and pursued the Federals down the road. Then D. McM. Gregg's cavalry regrouped and formed a line across the road, as the 2nd North Carolina approached, Colonel C. M. Andrews at the head of his regiment ordered a charge directly into the Union line. The 1st and 5th North Carolina followed. The Union line quickly broke and fell back on a second line protected by barricades and well placed artillery. As the 2nd North Carolina continued its charge, Gregg's artillery raked the road with grape and canister. The Union guns continued to pour canister into Gordon's men, while Gregg regrouped his men, forming a two-hundred-yard-long line centered on the main road near Ground Squirrel Church. As Union artillery pounded the North Carolinians, the reorganized Union line of dismounted cavalry repeatedly emptied their muskets and revolvers into Gordon's men.[104]

Gordon was unable to charge and disable the Union artillery, so he organized another move around the enemy's flank. He sent Cheek with a squadron from the 1st North Carolina into the woods for more than 100 yards, around the right of D. McM. Gregg's line. Cheek's squadron got into position and charged, while the remainder of the Confederate cavalrymen did the same in front of the enemy. From there, hand-to-hand fighting ensued once again and reverberated along the Union line.[105]

Finally, the pressure was too great in front and on his flank so D. McM. Gregg pulled his men back. Some of the North Carolinians followed in close pursuit while others remained in the hastily abandoned Union camp for a short rest and to collect the spoils left behind. The Federal cavalrymen from Ground Squirrel Church to the rear of Sheridan's column executed an efficient and by then typical rear guard action. Under constant and heavy assaults from Gordon's North Carolina regiments, Gregg had his men repeatedly fall back, dismount, form a skirmish line and repel threatened and real attacks alike — this continued for several hours and over many miles. However, the battered Union cavalrymen continued to stand between Sheridan's main column and their pursuers.[106]

As D. McM. Gregg's men were enduring the assaults of Gordon's command, Davies's command was also having a time of it several miles to the east at Ashland.

Stuart Meets Sheridan Near Yellow Tavern, May 11

The head of Stuart's and Fitz Lee's column had passed through Ashland by the time Davies and his Union cavalrymen arrived. The Confederate column was strung out and as Davies approached the station, Lomax's brigade had passed through and Wickham's was arriving. The 2nd Virginia Cavalry was in a position to confront Davies's brigade, but were driven back and unable to keep the Federals from setting fire to the depot and looting several buildings. As more Confederate cavalry arrived, the scene was set for a major battle. However, Davies did not want to get that involved while so far from Sheridan's main column, so he turned south for Sheridan. Fitz Lee and Stuart had already turned toward Telegraph Road and on to the intersection with Mountain Road.[107] (See map 5.1.)

As Davies rejoined Sheridan, the head of the main column had set a comfortable pace along Mountain Road while Stuart was hurrying his cavalry south on Telegraph Road. Most of the distance covered by Stuart and his cavalrymen from Taylorsville was made at a gallop. Consequently, at around 8 A.M. on the morning of May 11, Lomax and his cavalrymen arrived at the intersection of the two roads toward which the opposing cavalries marched. They were the first to arrive but were relatively few in number, exhausted and in questionable condition for the inevitable battle with Sheridan and his divisions.[108]

Beyond where the roads intersected, they became one which was called Brook Turnpike. This went to Yellow Tavern and on to Richmond. Lomax stayed just above the intersection, and formed his brigade in a line of battle along Telegraph Road. While he was in the process Fitz Lee arrived and joined in the preparations. They placed the 6th Virginia near the intersection, with the 5th and 15th Virginia along Telegraph Road facing west. They had sharpshooters out on the left and in front of the line to detect early arrivals from Sheridan's column. Apparently, their plan was to charge into Sheridan's left flank as he approached the intersection. Then they waited.[109]

Stuart arrived at Lomax's line before Sheridan and had time to approve the reception organized for their enemy's arrival. Wickham's brigade was still back some distance on Telegraph Road due to the time they lost fighting Davies at Ashland. When Wickham arrived, Stuart placed his brigade west of and perpendicular to the road connecting to Lomax's right. If Sheridan came at Lomax's front, then Wickham could come down on Sheridan's left flank. In case Sheridan continued on to Brook Turnpike toward Yellow Tavern, Stuart planned to hit the enemy in the flank and rear from Telegraph Road. Hoping to deliver a devastating blow to the Union column, Stuart sent an aide on to Richmond to inquire about the possibility of sending a force from Richmond's defenses up Brook Turnpike to catch Sheridan in a Confederate vise.[110]

Sheridan's column began to arrive around 9:00 A.M. and turned to face Lomax's left. Devin's command was at the base of Telegraph Road, Gibbs to his left, and Custer further to the Union left near the mouth of Mountain Road. Merritt's entire division formed in front of Lomax's worn-out brigade. Then as Custer moved forward, Wickham's brigade arrived and filed onto the ridge west of the road. Merritt sent skirmishers forward to probe Stuart's line, but Sheridan did not like the odds and decided to avoid a full-scale battle until Wilson arrived with his division. Nonetheless, Custer on the left was particularly aggressive in probing his enemy's line because he was concerned about Confederate artillery on the ridge with Wickham's line, facing south, at his left. Custer tried to gain a comfort zone by pushing Lomax's skirmish line in but was driven back. He regrouped and pushed forward again and in hand-to-hand fighting was able to push Lomax's skirmishers back east of Telegraph Road. Confederate artillery brought Custer's advance to a halt but in the meantime most of Merritt's command had also pushed forward and made gains against Lomax's line. Gibbs's and Devin's men hit Lomax's left at about the same time with their seven-shot carbines and pushed them along the Confederate line in deadly confusion. Those of Lomax's men who were not killed or did not scatter were captured. When Lomax regrouped his men along the ridge occupied by Wickham, but on the east side of the road, he had several hundred fewer men.[111] Young Private Hopkins, who was among Lomax's men, later remembered the scene in these words:

There we halted for the purpose of stopping the enemy's advance, for the sunken road furnished us some protection, but they did not stop. They marched on, firing as they came.

Their line was longer and thicker than ours, and it was evident that we were about to be surrounded. Some of our men mounted the fence in the rear and fled across the fields. Others stood their ground and were captured, I among them.[112]

Gibbs pulled up his advance because Custer had withdrawn under heavy fire from Wickham's sharpshooters and artillery along the ridge west of Telegraph Road. That gave Lomax time to reform on the ridge at Wickham's left. Once Stuart's entire command was positioned on the ridge and his outnumbered force had held Sheridan, he apparently felt they could continue to be successful if reinforced.[113]

As Sheridan had suspected, Merritt's division alone could not easily defeat Stuart's two brigades, so he enforced his earlier decision to wait for Wilson's division. While waiting, Sheridan sent Devin south toward Richmond to determine the likelihood Stuart might be reinforced from that place. Devin approached the city's defenses and returned to tell Sheridan that Stuart was not likely to receive support from Richmond.[114]

Stuart took command of Lomax's men east of the road, while Fitz Lee stood with Wickham's command west of the road. They waited to hear from Bragg in Richmond or Gordon from behind the enemy, or from Sheridan in front of them. While waiting, Stuart received a message from Gordon who was still harassing the rear of Sheridan's column over on Mountain Road. Gordon told of his North Carolina brigade's victory at Ground Squirrel Bridge and Goodall's Tavern. On hearing the news Stuart slapped his thigh and said in loud voice, "Bully for Gordon!" Then in a lowered voice he said, "I wish he was here!"[115]

Around 2:00 P.M. Stuart's aide returned from Richmond with word that General Bragg had agreed to send reinforcements from the city. By 3 o'clock, Stuart regained his optimism and sent a message back to Bragg indicating he hoped his cavalry and the force sent from Richmond could catch Sheridan between coordinated attacks. He felt sure Sheridan could not get away from such an attack. Stuart also predicted Gordon and his North Carolinians would join him, and added, "As soon as Gordon joins my right I will try them again, and expect to get so as to command the intersection."[116]

By late afternoon Stuart was still waiting. To arrive in a timely manner, Gordon would have had to circle around Gregg's and Wilson's divisions and come up on Stuart's right flank. That would take some time; even if he were in a position to move his command immediately. Of course, Sheridan was waiting for Wilson's division to catch up. They were in the second position of his column—not far behind Merritt's division. Sheridan was luckier than Stuart that day. His reinforcements arrived first which added measurably to his already superior numbers. As Wilson's division arrived, Sheridan moved them into position on the west side of Telegraph Road facing Wickham's line and moved Merritt's command on the road and east of it. Custer's brigade was placed on the road prepared to pierce the center of the Confederate line. Sheridan had a division in front of Wickham's brigade and a division in front of Lomax's brigade, and if Gordon's brigade got near Sheridan, he still had another division in his rear, Gregg's, to occupy the late arrival. Sheridan liked these odds and decided to hesitate no longer. By 4:00 P.M. on May 11, Sheridan's men assaulted on the Confederate line. Stuart would have to fight without his reinforcements.[117]

With Sheridan's thousands of mounted and dismounted cavalrymen formed for the attack, the artillery sounded off first from both lines. Then from the sky, thunder and lightening joined the chorus, or sounded a warning. A thunderstorm quickly covered the battlefield

Sheridan sent a mounted charge into the battery anchoring the center of the Confederate line — directly up Telegraph Road. On either side of the road he had dismounted cavalrymen. Custer was given the opportunity to lead the mounted charge up the road. He led the 1st and 7th Michigan and the 1st Vermont Cavalry up the road and into the Baltimore Light Artillery, which had joined Stuart the day before.[118]

Confederate artillery raked the ominous blue line as it moved forward. Stuart remained mounted so he could move along the line to the hottest spots, as was his custom. He did not have far to ride that afternoon; he was perched, binoculars in hand, on Telegraph Road. He spotted Custer's mounted command gathering near a woods and knew they were about to make a mounted charge, that they would come first. He warned Sergeant William Poindexter, who was nearby, that the mounted charge would take the Baltimore Light Artillery if Custer was not met by a mounted countercharge. Stuart ordered up a portion of the 1st Virginia of Wickham's brigade being held in reserve.[119]

When Custer charged, Wilson's and Gibbs's dismounted lines moved forward. Added to the thunder of both artillery and the sky, came the sound of hundreds of thundering hoofs. As the Union horsemen gained momentum, a squad from Lomax's 6th Virginia sprang out front with a countercharge down Telegraph Road. They crashed into the enemy, bringing the 1st Michigan to a stop for a hand-to-hand fight that brought first the sounds of carbines, then of pistols, and finally the thud of sabers striking skulls.[120]

Some of Wilson's dismounted men made it through the artillery and small arms fire to overrun a portion of Wickham's line. Union lines continued to move up the ridge. Stuart quickly rode over to the Baltimore Light Artillery. It clearly had become the focal point of the blue tide as it rolled up the ridge. The men were reassured by his presence — Stuart had been the Colonel of the 1st Virginia in 1861 when the Marylanders joined the cavalry regiment. The gunners from Maryland with Stuart at their side held their ground as enemy cavalry rushed through them and on both sides and continued to come at their front in an endless mass. Then, after the enemy had passed them on both sides, the 1st Virginia came charging from the rear, causing the Union cavalry to rapidly reverse course. The Virginian's inadvertently drove the enemy back into Stuart's position. Almost immediately, Stuart and the troops near him were surrounded by chaos and the enemy. Men and horses were running and spinning as pistols fired and sabers cut in all directions. Stuart was still shouting orders as he slashed with his saber after emptying his pistols. He was excited, in his element, almost enjoying the rush until he was mortally wounded by a pistol shot from a retreating Union cavalryman.[121]

The 1st Virginia managed to push the enemy from the ridge near the threatened artillery, but the Confederate line could not withstand the onslaught much longer. Michigan and Vermont cavalrymen were still storming up Telegraph Road directly at the center of the Confederate line. Shortly, some of the Confederate units broke and others were pulled back. As they scattered, most made it north across the Chickahominy River. Some of Wickham's command moved west toward Ashland, while some of Lomax's command circled and headed south for Richmond. Most of Stuart's staff joined the death vigil in Richmond, and after James E. B. Stuart's death on May 12, they rode up and reported to R. E. Lee near Spotsylvania Court House. Several of them were immediately assigned to Wade Hampton who was still in the area. Wickham had lost around 100 men, and Lomax nearly 200 that day.[122]

Many Union cavalrymen considered their victory near Yellow Tavern as the turning point in the relationship between the cavalries operating in Virginia, and the loss of Stuart was a major factor in the new dynamics.[123]

THE NORTH CAROLINA BRIGADE AT ALLEN'S STATION, MAY 11

As Stuart was making what turned out to be his last stand against the Union cavalry, James B. Gordon was still very occupied with General D. McM. Gregg's division over near Allen's Station, some four miles to the west. Gordon and his North Carolinians had been close on the enemy's rear harassing them since the fighting around Goodall's Tavern earlier in the day. Then as D. McM. Gregg passed through Allen's Station, he left a detachment behind to perform the ritual tearing up of tracks. As they were performing their duty, Gordon's command caught up and quickly organized themselves for a charge. Colonel J. I. Gregg was in command of the Union troops at Allen's Station, and he quickly moved his men to a nearby ridge and positioned his artillery well. The North Carolinian regiments charged toward the Union line through the same thunder and lightening storm that was covering the carnage over near Yellow Tavern.[124]

J. I. Gregg's artillery raked through Gordon's charging cavalrymen and brought them to an abrupt halt before they neared the Union line. Both sides exchanged musket and rifle fire while the Union artillery continued tearing into the North Carolinians well after darkness promised to shield them — the Union artillery would wait for lightning to illuminate the Confederate positions and then shell them in the darkness. Gordon was still without guns to retaliate.[125]

Gordon and his North Carolina brigade had pressed D. McM. Gregg's division so tightly against Wilson's column that Gregg considered his fighting at Allen's Station as part of the general battle between Sheridan and Stuart — they were, after all, only a few miles apart that evening. In his report D. McM. Gregg said, "On the 11th, near Ground Squirrel Church, this division, marching in rear, was attacked by Gordon's brigade of rebel cavalry. The attacks of the enemy were repeated during the entire day, thus forming a part of the general engagement with the enemy at Yellow Tavern." The North Carolinians did their job, did their best, but it did not matter.[126]

At the time some Union commanders, Wilson for one, felt Sheridan's victory near Yellow Tavern was a turning point in the history of the two cavalries— marking the ascendancy of the Union cavalry. In the larger picture, however, Sheridan's campaign against Stuart was costly for the Union also. In the end, Sheridan's victory was not as important as what his campaign cost Grant and his men back at Spotsylvania Court House.[127]

U. S. Grant and R. E. Lee at Spotsylvania Court House, May 10–13

For days Grant assaulted R. E. Lee's fortified line arched above Spotsylvania Court House with blind charge after charge. R. E. Lee had kept some cavalrymen on his flanks; Grant had kept very few. Fighting was heavy on May 10 but a major attack planned by Grant for the late afternoon was postponed due to indecisiveness and a lack of coordination. When finally executed, it was repulsed at great cost to both sides. It was Grant's bloodiest day yet in his new campaign. Grant spent the following day assessing his position and planning the next assault against the Confederate line, providing the men on both sides a welcome rest and time to think about their possible futures. R. E. Lee and his generals spent most of the day wondering when Grant would attack next. Finally, early on May 12 Grant made an all-out assault on the Confederate line (at the "Mule Shoe"), which rose to a crescendo at a place in the line known as the Bloody Angle. The worst fighting was over by afternoon with another impasse achieved, and Bloody Angle had earned its name. Very early on the morning of May 13 the Confederates pulled back to a stronger position.[128]

President Lincoln was pleased with both Grant's victories and his willingness to pursue the enemy even after no victory was in hand. R. E. Lee would build sound earthworks, but Grant would still charge. Lincoln liked that. Grant's aggressiveness would eventually prevail but in the meantime the price was high. From the day Grant had his army cross the Rapidan on May 4 through the fighting on May 12, the Union's combat losses totaled over 33,000 men. Grant knew the price was high but he also knew the Confederates could not sustain such losses for long. In the same period of time, Robert E. Lee had lost approximately 23,000 men. Considering the relative size of the two armies and their abilities to replace lost men, the Confederate loss was more devastating.[129]

While R. E. Lee's and Grant's infantrymen bled and died on May 12, their cavalrymen were not having a very good day either.

The Cavalries After Yellow Tavern

On May 11, J. E. B. Stuart had been carried from the battlefield near Yellow Tavern, and the job of collecting his two defeated and scattered cavalry brigades fell to Fitz Lee. His uncle and commanding general, R. E. Lee, had his hands full up near Spotsylvania Court House and was not able to respond immediately to the cavalry's needs. Most of Stuart's staff were in Richmond stunned by the pending death of their beloved leader. Fitz Lee spent the night north of the Chickahominy River — probably more than a little disoriented and uncertain about what to do next. He knew his command was in no condition to attack, so all he could do was try to anticipate Sheridan's next move, because that would dictate his response. During the night Fitz Lee received word that Richmond's defenses on the north side of the city were being reinforced and he concluded that if he moved down to Meadow Bridge he could contain Sheridan while the forces in Richmond could pound the trapped enemy. Accordingly, Fitz Lee put his command back into the saddle and moved down the north side of the Chickahominy to block Meadow Bridge.[130]

Sheridan's cavalrymen spent the night of May 11 camped around Yellow Tavern in considerably higher spirits than their Confederate counterparts. Sheridan had originally planned to circle east of Richmond and meet B. F. Butler on the James River for a joint action against the city. But he was only 6 or 7 miles above the city and more full of confidence than usual. He had his command on Brook Turnpike which ran south to Richmond. The city's outer defenses were not strong. They were manned by only a token force and were about a mile and a half in front of Richmond's second or intermediate line of defense. Even the main line of defense just outside the city was not particularly strong at that time. Sheridan knew that a major part of the force stationed at Richmond was on the other side of town facing B. F. Butler's Union army. For those reasons the city made a tempting target. Nonetheless, he decided to swing around Richmond as planned and join Butler on the James — but he would not make a wide swing around the city. He was feeling confident and did not want to give the appearance of pulling back. Sheridan rode forward that evening, down Brook Turnpike past Richmond's outer defense to Brook Church. There he saw a military road that led due east, between the city's outer and intermediate defensive lines, then turn northeast to cross the Chickahominy River at Meadow Bridge. Sheridan planned to take his command on that route and cross the bridge; then turn south for the James River at Fair Oaks Station — that would be the quickest route around the city. That route would also give him a bold and daring exit.[131] (See map 2.1.)

Around 11:00 P.M. May 11, Sheridan's column headed south on Brook Turnpike. Wilson's division was in the lead, then Torbert's division still under the command of Merritt. D. McM. Gregg's division was in the rear. Slowed by rain, mud, and the need to clear the road of wires connected to land mines, Sheridan's column took four hours to travel about three miles from Yellow Tavern to Brook Church. Around 3:00 A.M. on May 12 Wilson turned his command east on the military road from the church. Merritt's and Gregg's divisions stopped near Brook Church and waited for daylight. The pace of Sheridan's march gave Richmond time to strengthen its main line of defense ensuring that the invaders could not continue directly south. No adequate roads led west from Sheridan's new position at Brook Church. Fitz Lee with his two brigades were still somewhere north of Sheridan, and Gordon's North Carolina regiments were still pressing Sheridan's rear guard. The Union cavalry commander now had no choice — he had to continue east before going south.[132]

As indicated, while Fitz Lee was gathering his cavalrymen and groping for a plan, he realized he and the Richmond defenses had Sheridan in a box; if he could move his cavalrymen south quickly enough, they could close the lid on Sheridan's only escape route. Fitz Lee knew the heavy rains had limited Sheridan's options. The Union cavalry would have to head for the Meadows Bridge and cross to the north side of the Chickahominy. Fitz Lee decided to take his cavalry down and block the crossing.[133]

Wilson's command was first down the military road and consequently the first to come under heavy fire from Richmond's defenses. Wilson turned his men off the military road along Meadow Bridge Road and formed a line of dismounted men facing Richmond's intermediate line of defense. He placed his artillery on a rise called Strawberry Hill. From there the sides had a brisk artillery exchange. The heavy artillery in the city's fortified inner line of defense dominated Wilson's guns. That combined with brisk musket fire kept Wilson's command under great pressure. After his situation stabilized, he was instructed to hold while Sheridan moved his column along the military road behind Wilson's line for Meadow Bridge. The city's line was to a large extent manned by non-military Confederate personnel, and while they kept Wilson pinned down, they were not about to assault his line. It would be up to Fitz Lee and his cavalrymen to hit Sheridan at the bridge.[134]

By the time Wilson had his line formed facing south, Merritt and D. McM. Gregg had moved well along the military road. Merritt moved his command to Meadow Bridge and found it damaged and Fitz Lee's cavalrymen on the other side — he had to stop and fight and repair. That meant D. McM. Gregg also had to pull up his column and turn his attention to the North Carolinians on his rear. He was about a half mile along the road when he turned his command to face Gordon's brigade. D. McM. Gregg placed J. I. Gregg's brigade in a line north of the road, Davies's brigade south of the military road, and he moved his artillery onto a small rise behind his line of dismounted cavalrymen. D. McM. Gregg had gained respect for the North Carolina regiments that had charged into and driven back some of his best men over the previous several days, so he was not about to take his rear guard obligations lightly. He had his entire division, all ten regiments, in front of Gordon's three tired and battle worn regiments.[135]

Gordon turned his cavalrymen east onto the military road not hesitating but moving with caution to test D. McM. Gregg's line. He dismounted the 1st and 2nd North Carolina cavalrymen and pushed them forward slowly. Gordon's initial plan was to let the dismounted troopers push and weaken the enemy line enough to allow the still mounted 5th North Carolina to charge the enemy line and punch through to the Union battery on the rise just behind. As they approached, however, it became clear that the enemy line extended well beyond Gordon's on both sides of the road and was much deeper and had reserves and was covered by artillery. Gordon understood that even if the North Carolinians could break through the enemy line at one point, they would easily be surrounded. He wisely pulled up and sent a courier to Richmond requesting reinforcements and if possible artillery.[136]

Sheridan's exit was going well, Wilson's and Gregg's commands were holding the Confederates off while Merritt's men moved to clear the route across Meadow Bridge. Fitz Lee had managed to get cavalrymen to the bridge and tear off its planking, making it temporarily impassable. The Virginia cavalrymen were well-entrenched on the north side of the bridge. Merritt sent Custer's brigade to the bridge with a repair crew and instructions to push back the enemy skirmishers and repair it. There was a railway bridge near Meadow Bridge which allowed the Virginia Central Railroad to cross the Chickahominy. Custer used the rail approach, its embankment shielded sharpshooters while other dismounted men waded neck deep through the flooded lowlands and up near the river's edge. They got close enough to fire with accuracy at the Virginians on the other side — keeping the Virginian's heads low while Custer started others across the railroad bridge. The Federal cavalrymen were able to drive Fitz Lee's cavalrymen back and secure a foothold on the north shore. This allowed Custer to send the repair crew to Meadow Bridge. Fitz Lee's defense was not sufficient to hold the Union advance which had a very difficult approach to the bridges over the Chickahominy. Sheridan's men were fighting on three fronts with their wagons and field hospitals in the center.[137]

Rain began coming down in torrents making it easier to sit and hold a position, but Sheridan was in a hurry — the longer he remained where he was, the more likely it was the enemy in front of Wilson and D. McM. Gregg would be reinforced from Butler's front on the other side of town. Custer had a good foothold on the north side of Meadow Bridge, but if Fitz Lee were able to mount a strong attack, the Federal advance could easily be pushed back across the river. As Sheridan grew concerned over the delays in repairing the bridge, the Richmond command was moving to reinforce Gordon, the line in front of Wilson, and to send an Alabama brigade north on Meadow Bridge Road into Wilson's line. The Confederate hope was to crush Sheridan between these relatively fresh troops and Fitz Lee's line at the bridge. The weak link in the Confederate chain that could have bound the Union cavalry turned out to be the battered men on Fitz Lee's line at Meadow Bridge.[138]

THE NORTH CAROLINA BRIGADE AND THE BATTLE OF BROOK CHURCH, MAY 12

As stated earlier, James B. Gordon and his North Carolinians came upon their enemy over on the west end of the military road early on May 12, but did not have the force to dislodge the Union line. According to one member of the 5th North Carolina, "Gordon dismounted the Ninth [1st] and Nineteenth [2nd] North Carolina and attacked him [the enemy] fiercely...." After the first assault, Gordon sent to Richmond for support, and around 9:00 A.M., support began to arrive. He received two new guns, manned by new recruits. Gordon placed them over near the mounted 5th North Carolina on his right, and they were in position quickly. Private Means of the 5th North Carolina later remembered the gun crew sent from Richmond and recorded this impression: "And oh! such artillery! It was the most beautiful in all its appearances that we ever beheld. The smoke of battle had never been about it." Beauty aside; what Gordon needed at the moment was experienced men, and the new gunners were not that. They had fired their guns before, but never at an enemy that fired back. As soon as the Confederate guns fired a round, a Union battery responded. The reply came from guns that redirected their fire away from the North Carolina line and sent canister at Gordon's new artillerymen, inflicting upon them considerable dirt and noise, and soon panic. The Private from the 5th North Carolina described the scene as follows[139]:

—canister for the first time in its history rattled around those beautiful guns and among its wheels and every man about the battery flew into the ditches of those old entrenchments. Gordon was furious. He raved and begged. He called it "Band Box Artillery," which would have occurred only to him, possibly, under such a fire. But those artillerists "held the trenches faithfully" against Richmond's invaders. Some few of them could not even stand that and came through the woods by us. We laughed at them, ridiculed them and asked them to go back and man their guns. But they looked at us as if they thought we were surely crazy.

In the meantime, Gordon had started the dismounted men from the 1st and 2nd North Carolina cavalries toward their enemy's line for a second time, and they were also being swept with canister from Union batteries and musket fire from D. McM. Gregg's dismounted men. Gordon could not afford to have his only two guns idle for even a moment once the enemy artillery was opened upon his advancing line, but all his efforts to get his gunners back on the job failed. After expressing his anger and disgust in various ways, he wheeled his horse and raced off to assist the men of his 1st and 2nd cavalries who were charging into the face of enemy fire.[140]

Gordon's North Carolinians received some support from a more experienced battery shortly after the first gun-crew scattered, and the new arrivals drew some of the fire from D. McM. Gregg's guns. That alone was helpful to the dismounted chargers. Then later around 10:00 A.M., reinforcements arrived from Hunton's command. Gordon placed an infantry regiment on each flank of his dismounted cavalrymen. This extended his line almost as far as D. McM. Gregg's front in each direction, and they all moved forward. The dismounted cavalrymen got ahead of their infantry and could not sustain their gains. Gordon finally got his cavalrymen and his infantry reinforcements to advance in line, but the Union line was too deep and strongly entrenched. They could not be dislodged. Gordon's line settled in for an exchange of musket fire under a hail of artillery shells coming from both sides.[141]

Meanwhile, more of Hunton's troops arrived from Richmond and were sent toward Gordon's right on the south side of the road. The new arrivals were the City Battalion and they moved in facing northward at Gregg's left flank. These troopers from the city were not seasoned veterans and made inviting targets for their enemy. Davies's cavalrymen were well entrenched on the Union flank and D. McM. Gregg moved the 1st Maine over to support Davies. After the Federals tired of using the city's militia for target practice, the 1st New Jersey launched a dismounted charge and scattered what remained of the men from Richmond's home guard.[142]

While the Richmond militia was being decimated, Gordon was riding along his line on both sides of the road instilling confidence in his men by his personal display of courage. His men encouraged him to dismount. He was an obvious target, and they were concerned for his safety. Before he finished his explanation of why he needed to set an example under the circumstance, he was mortally wounded and fell from his horse. When Gordon fell, he passed command of the North Carolina brigade to Colonel Clinton M. Andrews of the 2nd North Carolina Cavalry—the latter being the senior officer still standing in the field. Andrews immediately saw the futility of a mounted charge to silence the enemy's guns, so he dismounted the 5th North Carolina and had them join the line on the north side of the road, near the 1st North Carolina — that left the 2nd North Carolina on the cavalry line, south of the military road.[143]

The 5th Cavalry was moved as the 19th Virginia infantry arrived from Richmond and filed in on his right. The recent arrivals from Richmond came along the same course previously taken by the city's militia, and as the 19th Virginia was moved in to hit D. McM. Gregg's left, they were abruptly aware that Wilson's right wing, that had been facing Richmond, had become joined to D. McM. Gregg's left. The Virginians marched into battle and were hit hard in their front and flank — they ground to a halt.[144]

Just before 2:00 P.M., Andrews assumed he had gained strength on his right so he again sent his line forward under heavy fire. After struggling forward, the dismounted North Carolina cavalrymen noticed the infantry support on their right flank was not keeping pace with them. Hunton had sent his Richmond units in one at a time and did not coordinate his attacks with Andrews's North Carolina line. The men from Richmond were sacrificed for no gain whatsoever — indeed, their presence was costly to the North Carolinians because first Gordon and then Andrews expected support which did not materialize as they moved forward in anticipation. In the end, their enemy were not pressed. Most of Sheridan's command was across the Chickahominy before nightfall, but scattered skirmishing continued on Andrews's and Hunton's front across the military road well into the evening.[145]

In the pouring rainstorm, while James B. Gordon and then Clinton M. Andrews were desperately trying to break D. McM. Gregg's line on the west, Archibald Gracie had moved his Confederate brigade out to Richmond's middle line of defense hoping to drive James H. Wilson's line back into Sheridan's flank, but they were unable to get beyond their fortifications. Wilson had his artillery continually pounding the Confederate line — and at times, Sheridan himself was riding among Wilson's batteries encouraging them and having Merritt send them more ammunition as they spent theirs. Wilson's line was secure by 3 o'clock that afternoon.[146]

D. McM. Gregg's and Wilson's dismounted cavalrymen had fought hard and provided Merritt's men the time they needed to take, hold, and repair the Meadow Bridge over the Chickahominy. By around 4:00 P.M., the bridge was covered with mismatched planks taken from nearby farms, and just sound enough to move some of Merritt's men across the river and push Fitz Lee's remaining skirmish line further from the river and back into their reserve entrenchments. Then in short order, Merritt's cavalrymen stormed over the bridge and drove Fitz Lee's command from their entrenchments — the Confederates were overwhelmed by numbers and force. According to Merritt, it took only a very few minutes to relocate the enemy. The remnants of Wickham's and Lomax's brigades pulled back above Mechanicsville and formed lines on Old Church Road. Fitz Lee collected his staff and most of his men near Polegreen Church, about 4 miles from Mechanicsville. He thought Sheridan would head north to rejoin Grant, and he intended to stand in Sheridan's path. Instead, Merritt's command alone pushed to Mechanicsville and skirmished with Fitz Lee's troopers; allowing the rest of Sheridan's column to pass below them. Then Merritt moved his men down to Gaines's Mill for the night.[147]

The bulk of Sheridan's command moved along the north side of the Chickahominy River and spent the night of May 12 below Gaines's Mill. The next day they continued along the river and spent the night near Bottom's Bridge; then they went back over the river the next morning. Sheridan then took his cavalry south to Haxall's Landing on the James River. Sheridan's march to Richmond and attempt to destroy Stuart's cavalry was not a total success, but his troops had damaged the Confederate cavalry leadership immeasurably.[148]

Fitz Lee's men spent the night of the 12th wet, exhausted, hungry, and beaten — conditions that had existed for two days and nights running. The North Carolina brigade followed Sheridan's column across the Chickahominy River and then moved north to join Fitz Lee's command. Fitz Lee's men and their North Carolinian comrades had completely exhausted their ammunition and rations during the marching and fighting over the previous week, so they settled in Mechanicsville on May 13 to rest and re-stock their supply wagons from the stores in the Richmond command. The North Carolina cavalrymen spent the next couple of days recuperating and picketing along the Chickahominy and down toward the James.[149]

The reported losses taken by the 2nd North Carolina Cavalry were few considering the amount of fighting they had done on Catharpin Road and around Todd's Tavern as well as during their pursuit of Sheridan on the latter's campaign toward Richmond. Among their greatest losses was the mortal wounding of their brigade commander, James B. Gordon. With Gordon down and Andrew called to command the North Carolina brigade, there was no report of the battle and losses taken by the 2nd Cavalry on May 12. The recorded losses for the 2nd Cavalry are listed in the table below.

Combat Losses in the 2nd North Carolina Cavalry May 7–11, 1864

Trooper	Age	Co.	Fate
A. H. Martin	27	A	killed, May 8
Samuel Bryson	39	A	captured, May 9
William H. Ivey		H	captured, May 10
Shubal G. Worth		F&S	killed, May 11
Gideon Newell		F	wounded, May 11
Jesse V. Roberts*		K	wounded, May
Willie P. Tilly*	29	K	wounded, May

Information contained in this table came from Compiled Service Records as summarized by Louis H. Manarin, *North Carolina Troops: 1861–1865, A Roster*, vol. II, pages 98–177. (See Appendix for more information on the men listed above, page 400.)

*As was often the case, the recorded losses during this march did not reflect the severity of the 2nd North Carolina Cavalry's engagement. Captain Lockhart of Company K, in a series of articles to his company's hometown newspaper, from time-to-time drew attention to the injuries and near losses in his company alone that did not get recorded in the muster rolls. For instance on the march described above, Private Jesse V. Roberts and Private Willie P. Tilley were slightly wounded, and Corporal James D. Lewis "had his gun shot all to pieces in his hands." Such minor occurrences were numerous and were recorded in the experiences of the cavalrymen, if not in the muster rolls. See John P. Lockhart, *Hillsborough Recorder*, June 1, 1864, page 3, col. 2.

Replacing James Ewell Brown Stuart as commander of his cavalry corps would not have been an easy task for Robert E. Lee even under ideal circumstances — having Grant's army in front of him and not going away was not a good time to consider the possibilities. There were two candidates for the job. The first was Fitzhugh Lee, R. E. Lee's nephew, fellow West Pointer, and fellow Virginian; the second possibility was Wade Hampton, a planter from South Carolina with no formal military training, but from a family that understood the military. Hampton's father and grandfather had both been generals (Wade Hampton I and II). In addition, Wade Hampton III was one of the wealthiest men in the Confederacy. He was not someone who could easily be moved aside. In terms of rank, Hampton was the senior. He had been promoted to brigadier general a couple of weeks before Fitz Lee. Yet, on paper, it was not an obvious choice — Fitz Lee had the formal training, plus he had always been among J. E. B. Stuart's inner circle of associates. Wade Hampton had never been close to Stuart, and often he was a thorn in Stuart's side when he felt his Carolina cavalrymen were treated poorly relative to their Virginia counterparts. There was also friction between Hampton and Fitz Lee and some of the latter's commanders. It was not an easy choice for R. E. Lee for a variety of reasons. Among the factors making R. E. Lee's decision difficult was Wade Hampton's natural abilities as a military leader. R. E. Lee's non-choice at the time was to let his three cavalry divisions under Fitz Lee, Wade Hampton, and W. H. F. Lee operate as separate commands and report to him.[150]

Stalemate: Grant Moves to the North Anna River, May 20

On May 12, R. E. Lee had personally managed the fighting within the Mule Shoe so early the next morning he pulled his men back and into a more defensible line just below the bloodied site — from near Block House Bridge on the left, to just above Spotsylvania Court House on the right. The Confederate line was nearly where it had been before all the blood-letting of the previous two days. The Confederates sprawled out on the muddy ground too tired to eat and too soiled to care — many were already aware that they would never forget what horror they had just been through. Nor were Grant and many of his men feeling particularly victorious — they had killed thousands and lost thousands of men. If their goal had been to pull R. E. Lee's army out into an open battle field and annihilate them, then they had achieved little. Grant had to feel his position in front of the Army of Northern Virginia on June 13 was not terribly different from what it had been six days earlier. Grant spent the day determining what his enemy had done and collecting his own command. Still, Grant could not react quickly to the Confederate early morning move because he did not have his cavalry with him. He had to probe for R. E. Lee's line with infantry.[151]

On June 14, Grant again attempted to dislodge R. E. Lee's army by shifting his troops to the left during the night, and then to surprise and overpower the Confederate right near Spotsylvania Court House early in the morning. Once again, however, the Confederate infantry benefited greatly for having cavalry on both flanks. In this instance, Chambliss's cavalrymen spotted the Union buildup around 8:00 A.M. on the 14th, so General Early positioned and used his artillery to disrupt the enemy while he organized an offensive. In addition, Chambliss dismounted some of his cavalrymen and harassed Grant's left for several hours under very hot fire before they were forced to drop back. By then, R. E. Lee had Early organize some of his command to attack the Union build-up. General Early used dismounted cavalrymen from Chambliss's brigade to charge one Union flank while he sent infantry at their front and other flank. The Confederates surprised their enemy with a well-organized and forceful attack at the point of the concentration—causing them to flee to the rear. Among those bolting from their positions when the Confederates came storming out of the woods from several directions was General Meade himself. Indeed, Meade was nearly captured by a member of W. H. F. Lee's 13th Virginia Cavalry. Shortly after Early's success, R. E. Lee sent word to Hampton's cavalry on the Confederate left, still near Shady Grove Church, to organize a mission to slip around and behind Grant's right wing. Hampton sent Rosser's brigade on its mission about 5:00 P.M. on May 14. Rosser found what his commander needed to know and made his presence felt. R. E. Lee knew much more about his enemy's strength, positions, and movements than Grant did about his. Confederate cavalry on Grant's left and right flanks alerted him to his need to strengthen those areas as he continued to organize a major move on R. E. Lee's main line.[152]

It had been raining heavily for several days so any move through the deep mud was impractical; consequently, on May 15 Grant did not move. Hampton and his horse artillery was particularly active on Grant's right, with his cavalrymen aggressively scouting around the north end of the Union line while W. H. F. Lee had Chambliss's brigade engaged in similar activity on the southern end of the line. The few cavalrymen Grant had pulled together were no match for the Confederate horsemen. These activities by the cavalries and the inactivity of the infantries continued through the next day.[153]

On May 17, R. E. Lee received some good news. Beauregard had finally attacked B. F. Butler below the James River and pushed him back into an area known as the Bermuda Hundred—an area largely confined by the confluence of the James and Appomattox Rivers. However, R. E. Lee could only wait for Grant to move because he did not have the strength to go on the offensive.

Grant planned a major move against the Army of Northern Virginia early in the morning of May 18. During the night he began moving troops from his left to the north end of his line, where he expected to launch an overwhelming attack on the unsuspecting Confederate left. The divisions Grant moved to the north end of his line turned south, facing R. E. Lee's left wing. His troops were in place by 4:00 A.M., and the artillery started another bloody day. Poorly coordinated attacks resulted in a frustrated Grant putting an end to his assault on the Confederate entrenchments about five hours later.[154]

Grant gave up trying to assault his entrenched enemy. He planned another attempt to lure R. E. Lee out into an open battlefield. Grant raced for the North Anna River, hoping to engage R. E. Lee before he could entrench. Lee had foreseen such a possible move, so sent Ewell's command southeast to Mud Tavern on Telegraph Road, just in case Grant moved south. Ewell's assignment was to entrench at the tavern and block Grant's route south. R. E. Lee was not yet certain the race for the North Anna River was on, but he was in it nonetheless and prepared once again to make Grant take a longer route if a move southward was in the offing. (See map 5.1.)

Grant's plan was once again to swing around the Confederate right, and get between the enemy army and Richmond. Grant lost a day before starting south because Ewell's command launched an attack late on the afternoon of May 19. Nonetheless, late on the 20th Grant sent W. S. Hancock's command southeast toward Guinea Station, then along the Richmond, Fredericksburg & Potomac Railroad to Milford Station and on to Hanover Junction where they would join the rest of Grant's army. G. K. Warren was scheduled to leave shortly after Hancock and take a shorter route directly down Telegraph Road. The Union moves were detected early largely because they did not have cavalry to screen their movements, and R. E. Lee had cavalry on both flanks. (By this time, Chambliss's brigade from W. H. F. Lee's division was stretched across all routes heading south.)

For the most part, Grant avoided Ewell's command at Mud Tavern because he did not want another major engagement near that place — he stayed with his plan to move around the Confederate right by changing Warren's course and sending him southeast to follow Hancock. By the time Warren left the Spotsylvania line, Hancock's men were already marching through Bowling Green. Once Grant had Warren fully in motion, he and his staff left the line for the North Anna River. Shortly thereafter, R. E. Lee had seen enough movement to be convinced his enemy was moving toward Richmond and not preparing for another fight near Spotsylvania. R. E. Lee then started Ewell's command directly south along the Telegraph Road with Anderson's (Longstreet's) command to follow. R. E. Lee would concentrate his army around Hanover Junction just across the North Anna River. He sent A. P. Hill and his command on a more westerly route which crossed the North Anna up river and then along the Virginia Central Railroad to Hanover Junction. Lee hoped to beat Grant to the North Anna River and entrench his army in Grant's path. The Confederates had an advantage, partly because they had a shorter route, but also because Hancock's advance encountered more enemy cavalry than did R. E. Lee's column. R. E. Lee was concerned along the way that Sheridan's cavalry might come from the south and get to Hanover Junction first.[155]

GRANT CALLS SHERIDAN BACK TO HIM

On May 21, as Robert E. Lee put his army in motion for Hanover Junction, he sent the following message to General John C. Breckinridge: "Remain at Junction. Defend the position. Get up your transportation and be prepared to move. Fitz Lee is following cavalry." R. E. Lee concern was warranted because Grant had called Sheridan forward on May 17. Sheridan moved northward immediately, and was noticed.

After escaping across Meadow Bridge on May 12, Sheridan had taken his cavalry down around Haxall's Landing on the James River where he set up camp and rested his cavalry May 14 through 17. After the fight on May 12, the North Carolina brigade under Clinton M. Andrews moved along with Fitz Lee's command to the line east of Richmond between the Chickahominy and James Rivers. According to Major Galloway of the 5th North Carolina Cavalry, after a few days rest following the fight with Sheridan's column at Brook Church until mid–June, "Not a day passed without some hostile firing, no two nights did we sleep on the same ground."[156]

When Sheridan received his orders to start north and join Grant, Fitz Lee spread his command in an arch shielding Richmond on the southeast. The Confederate cavalrymen had scouting parties roaming the area between White House on the Pamunkey River and Bottom's Bridge on the Chickahominy and a picket line that extended down from Bottom's Bridge across Charles City and Darbytown Roads as far as New Market Road where they connected with other Confederate defenses. Fitz Lee's cavalrymen were spread over approximately 12 miles, and his line consisted of his two depleted brigades, commanded by Wickham and Lomax, and the battered North Carolina brigade commanded by Clinton M. Andrews of the 2nd North Carolina Cavalry. In addition to being part of Richmond's shield, the cavalrymen with Fitz Lee were keeping their eyes on Sheridan's cavalry. Fitz Lee's concern was that he might start the Union cavalry south across the James River to join Butler or attack Richmond on his own from the south side of the river. Fitz Lee had a party of 30 cavalrymen forward monitoring Sheridan's movements at all times. When the Confederate cavalrymen detected movement in Sheridan's cavalry late on May 17, it was in a northerly direction, however, so Fitz Lee notified his superiors immediately.[157] (See map 2.1.)

On that same day President Davis wired R. E. Lee with these desperate sounding words: "Hanover Junction is threatened by Sheridan and is unsafe. The supplies there will be brought here [Richmond] if it can be done by morning. If this cannot be done, shall they be sent to Guiney's, or to what point?" When Grant called Sheridan back to him, he got a lot of people's attention.[158]

On the 18th, R. E. Lee responded to his nephew's warning of Sheridan's mobilization with these instructions: "Collect all the cavalry and watch his [Sheridan's] course. Notify those on his route and keep me advised. Protect railroad and depots, if possible." Fitz Lee quickly gathered and readied the three small brigades under his command. The cavalrymen in Fitz Lee's command numbered around 3,000, many of whom were still recovering from two defeats, the loss of cavalry commanders, as well as the usual shortage of forage for their horses. Fitz Lee moved his cavalrymen through Mechanicsville and up the Virginia Central Railroad to Atlee's Station, all the while keeping Confederate commanders informed of Sheridan's progress. His command was strong enough to march along the west side of Sheridan's column, staying between the enemy column and the railroad, but he could not bring on a general engagement with Sheridan's column.[159]

Once on the road, Sheridan had some difficulty locating Grant because the latter was on the road toward the North Anna River. Nonetheless, initially Sheridan knew he needed to head north, then at some point turn west. Sheridan first headed for the Chickahominy River; crossed over and spent the night of the 18th camped around Baltimore Crossroads. The going was slow because rivers were high, bridges were out, and the roads were muddy. These conditions were an advantage for Fitz Lee, who spent most of the 18th collecting and putting his cavalrymen on the road. The Confederate cavalrymen camped near Atlee's Station on the night of May 19.[160]

While camped near Baltimore Crossroads, Sheridan realized he would have to cross the swollen Pamunkey River to find Grant and his army. He sent for a pontoon bridge, and while waiting, sent Custer and his brigade to Hanover Court House on a bridge destroying mission to draw enemy eyes away from his stalled column. At the same time and for the same purpose, he sent D. McM. Gregg and Wilson with their divisions on a demonstration toward Cold Harbor and Mechanicsville — Sheridan kept most of Merritt's command (Torbert's First Division) with him.[161]

Near Gaines's Mill on May 20, D. McM. Gregg and Wilson came in contact with Fitz Lee's skirmishers. The Confederate cavalrymen dropped back slowly until Fitz Lee arrived with reinforcements, then the opposing lines held and exchanged fire — neither side apparently interested in pursuing a major attack on the other's position. Meanwhile, Custer had moved along the south side of the Pamunkey, through Hanovertown and on to Hanover Court House where he burned some small bridges, tore up some rail-track, and raided the station. When Fitz Lee heard of Custer's mischief at the court house, he left Colonel C. M. Andrews and his North Carolina brigade (still the 1st, 2nd, and 5th cavalries) in front of McM. Gregg's and Wilson's divisions. Fitz Lee headed for Custer with Wickham's and Lomax's brigades. While the Confederate cavalryman knew his possibilities were limited in front of two enemy divisions, he felt he could handle Custer and his brigade. Fitz Lee arrived at the court house around night-fall, only to find that Custer was not interested in a major fight and was pulling back in front of his advance.[162]

Meanwhile, late on May 20 Sheridan and Merritt arrived at White House and pushed the Confederate pickets there back to Tunstall's Station on the Richmond & York River Railroad. D. McM. Gregg returned from his demonstration and joined Sheridan there on May 22. Once across the Pamunkey, they camped for the night on the Mattapony River (at Aylett's). Custer returned from his mission around Hanover Court House on the same day — his brigade also crossed the river and made camp.[163]

The small North Carolina brigade in front of D. McM. Gregg's and Wilson's demonstration near Gaines's Mill were able to hold because the Federal cavalrymen were not interested in a major engagement at the time. Fitz Lee had his pickets in the right place, and moved his command quickly on the 20th and early on May 21, so he was able to report Sheridan's every move.[164]

By May 22, Sheridan was on the road again and on the 24th he rejoined the Army of the Potomac near Chesterfield Station, a couple of miles above the North Anna River. His return marked the end of his campaign to destroy R. E. Lee's cavalry and disrupt Confederate supply lines. On the 25th, Wilson's division was moved to the right of Grant's army, and Sheridan's other two divisions rested until Grant was ready to move again — with his cavalry next time.

Robert E. Lee must have taken some comfort knowing that Hampton and others had held Hancock's division just below Milford Station on May 21, thus allowing his Confederate column to move toward Hanover Station without difficulties on its flank; and Fitz Lee had established his headquarters at Atlee's Station on the Virginia Central Railroad, protecting the southern approach to Hanover Station. These challenging tasks required the cavalry to be at full strength; consequently while Sheridan was enjoying his return to Grant, both Fitz Lee and Hampton were trying to strengthen their commands.[165]

Wade Hampton and some of his cavalry had been moved from the Confederate left at the Spotsylvania battlefield to Milford Station where they stood in the path of Hancock's advancing column, and he needed his full command. From that place he continued his request that Richmond send forward his South Carolina brigades that were delayed near the city. His message on May 19, was short and simple: "Can my cavalry now be sent up? I need them greatly." Unfortunately for the Confederates, the need for cavalry far outstripped the supply, and commanders around and below Richmond were hesitant to lose any troops in their defenses.

Fitz Lee's command was closer to the cavalry action around Richmond, so he received what reinforcements were in the area. For instance, late on May 20, the 5th South Carolina Cavalry of M. C. Butler's brigade, under the command of Colonel John Dunovant, arrived near Hanover Station on its way up to Hampton, but was held there and incorporated into Fitz Lee's line. In addition, because W. H. F. Lee was not making serious attempts to have his North Carolina brigade join him and Chambliss's brigade — it continued to be detached to Fitz Lee, who simply needed the North Carolinians more at the time. In fact both Robert E. and Fitz Lee were trying to bring the North Carolina brigade up to strength by moving the 3rd North Carolina up to the front along the North Anna River.

Earlier in the month, the 3rd North Carolina started in the direction of its new brigade but encountered a number of delays below and at Richmond — where cavalry was also very much in demand. In his effort to accumulate cavalry, Fitz Lee finally, on May 16, passed on a message to Bragg at Richmond from R. E. Lee in which the latter declared, "If more cavalry be detached from this army it will be impossible to ascertain the enemy's movements. The cavalry from North Carolina and South Carolina must be called upon, and any other that can be had and put in one body." Bragg had stopped the 3rd North Carolina on its journey north to help protect Richmond and was reluctant to send it on.[166]

Finally on May 19, Special Orders No. 116 were issued which included the following: "Colonel Baker, commanding Third Regiment North Carolina Cavalry, now on duty with General G. T. Beauregard, will report immediately with his command to Maj. Gen. Fitz. Lee, north of Richmond." This order was issued just after R. E. Lee had ordered Fitz Lee to march along with the enemy cavalry northward toward Hanover Junction. The 3rd North Carolina reached Richmond on May 22, and from there was sent up to Hanover Junction along with other cavalrymen under the command of Brigadier General Pierce M. B. Young of Hampton's division. They finally arrived at Hanover Court House on May 26.[167]

Additional cavalry forces were also sent up to Fitz Lee's command from the Richmond area along with Pierce M. B. Young, who had been on a special assignment. Young had been pulled from Hampton around the time fighting started on the Spotsylvania battlefield. He was moved down to the Virginia/North Carolina border — near Danville, over 100 miles southwest of Petersburg. His assignment was to gather dismounted and no longer fully equipped cavalrymen, as well as wait for the new arrivals from North and South Carolina. Many of the new arrivals would also be in need of mounts and equipment before they would be fit for active service. Young's assignment was to outfit them and send them on to R. E. Lee's Army of Northern Virginia, but, as indicated in the case of the 3rd North Carolina Cavalry, Bragg and Beauregard were continually trying to attach cavalrymen to their commands as soon as Young could get them ready. Among Young's resuscitated cavalrymen were many from the battered North Carolina brigade.[168]

Fully outfitted or not, by May 20 Young had been moved to Richmond with his collection of cavalrymen. At that point, his command included the 3rd North Carolina Cavalry and some of M. C. Butler's South Carolina brigade who were destined for Hampton's division. Butler was not yet with them — he had had his foot blown off in the Battle of Brandy Station the previous June and had been in his home state recuperating and recruiting. He would join his new brigade in Virginia shortly. Special Orders No. 118 was issued the next day, and it instructed Young to take his collection of cavalrymen to Fitz Lee.[169]

Politics and the Attack at Wilson's Wharf, May 24

As indicated earlier, by May 24 Sheridan was resting his cavalry above the North Anna/Pamunkey River and enjoying a visit with Grant. At the same time, Fitz Lee was trying to gather reinforcements for his command while he watched the Pamunkey for any attempt by Grant to head south for Richmond. With Sheridan quiet, though Grant was in the middle of stormy battles with R. E. Lee, forces were at work to pull the major part of Fitz Lee's cavalry from the line below the Pamunkey for an expedition some though irrational from a military and other perspectives.

One would expect R. E. Lee to have objected to such an expedition, but he had been operating at half strength for days due to a bout with dysentery — and while ill was also very occupied on the 23rd and 24th with Grant's advances. On May 23, Grant had troops across the North Anna River, and the Battle of Jericho Mills was taking place. R. E. Lee spent the night reforming his line and entrenching. As expected, on the morning of May 24, Grant sent his army from several directions across the North Anna at the Confederate "V"-shaped entrenchments and once again fought to a stalemate. R. E. Lee had little time for politics oozing from Richmond those days.[170]

While R. E. Lee was busy around the river, one of the matters occupying President Davis was the racial dimension of the war. Earlier in May, when B. F. Butler moved his Union army up the James River, he established fortifications along the way to protect his supply line. One of these outposts was at Wilson's Wharf under the command of Brigadier General Edward A. Wild, who commanded a brigade of black troops. Wild had already lost an arm as a result of earlier fighting but not his enthusiasm for the war — he was a strong abolitionist and was instrumental in forming what was known as "Wild's African Brigade." By the time Wild reached his new post at Wilson's Wharf, he was well known around Richmond as particularly sympathetic to slaves, and he enhanced that image once he settled in on the James. He had his troops make forays into the countryside freeing slaves and, when possible, recruiting them for his brigade. He apparently also did not discourage his troopers' eagerness to "get even." For instance, in one case his troopers took a planter, W. H. Clopon, who was known in the area for his cruelty, tied him to a tree and whipped him for the amusement of the black troops — some of Clopon's former slaves were allowed to add strokes during the demonstration. Wild termed the incident "the administration of Poetical justice." No matter what the justification, such beatings instilled fear in the population in and around Richmond, and fueled the rumor that certainly exaggerated the reports of Wild's men marching through the countryside committing atrocities. In any case, there was enough truth in the reports reaching Richmond to stir the population, and eventually Davis, to action. By May 23, most of the infantry around Richmond had been sent to the fighting on the North Anna River, so Davis had General Bragg of the Richmond command call on Fitz Lee's cavalrymen to give the appearance of doing something about the problem emanating from Wilson's Wharf on the James River.[171]

The 1st, 2nd, and 5th North Carolina cavalries were directly involved in the less than memorable fight at Wilson's Wharf (Kennon's Landing). Fitz Lee organized and led an expedition into enemy lines to attack the fortification at Wilson's Wharf. He called for a "detail of picked men for specially dangerous work." Some sources estimated that Fitz Lee collected as many as 800 men from Wickham's brigade, and 750 from Lomax's. In addition, he collected perhaps 400 men from the North Carolina brigade commanded by C. M. Andrews. He left Lomax in charge of the camp at Atlee's Station and the cavalrymen who remained on picket duty. He also took a number of men from the fresh and full 5th South Carolina Cavalry as well as their commander, Colonel Dunovant.[172]

On May 23, Fitz Lee received "verbal instructions" from General Bragg to form the expeditionary force and take what was described as a relatively weak Union stronghold at Wilson's Wharf. By 4:00 P.M., Fitz Lee had selected his force and was on the road. They marched all night, over 50 miles, and late the next morning were in front of the enemy fortification at Wilson's Wharf. The Confederates easily drove in the enemy pickets and advanced posts to the main Union fortification on the river. When the attackers arrived, it was immediately apparent that their intelligence was less than inadequate; indeed, it was wrong. Their knowledge of the fortifications and size of the enemy force they were sent to capture was based on reports from private citizens in the area and passed along through Davis and Bragg to Fitz Lee — apparently no military personnel had scouted the installations at the wharf. Afterwards, Fitz Lee had this to say about the nature of his target: "It is proper to say that their numbers were represented to be about 1500 encamped only behind rifle pits, and upon that data the expedition was planned." Once they reached their destination, however, the reality was immediately evident. Private Means of the 5th North Carolina Cavalry described what lay before the tired men in Fitz Lee's command in these words: "It consisted of a fort built in semi-circle form on a bluff of the river with each end resting on the James, with heavy parapets and a canal of water the entire front of the half circle. There was open ground for several hundred yards all around the fort covered with abattis and large fallen pine trees to impede assailants." Fitz Lee's description of the enemy fortifications is similar but also pointed out "the nature and thickness of the intertwined abattis and width of ditch being in themselves insurmountable."[173]

Even though the enemy fortifications before him were much more formidable than he had prepared for, Fitz Lee decided to give it a try. In his words, "I nevertheless resolved to make an attempt for the capture of the place, now that the march had been made." One hopes there was a better reason for spending the lives of his men in pursuit of an unattainable goal ("insurmountable" fortifications), than simply, we have come all this way, so why not give it a go.[174]

Fitz Lee divided his force into two detachments: Wickham commanded the troopers from his brigade; while the men from Lomax's brigade, the North Carolina brigade, and the 5th South Carolina regiment were placed under the newly arrived Colonel Dunovant from South Carolina. He then sent his men forward, and skirmishing took place for about an hour and a half. Then Fitz Lee sent Brigadier General Wild a note, under a flag of truce, "containing a summons to surrender in the name of Maj. Gen. Fitz Lee." It contained an unconventional warning from Fitz Lee — he demanded surrender and added that if they complied, "...the garrison should be turned over to the authorities at Richmond as prisoners of war, but if this proposition was rejected he would not be answerable for the consequences when he took the place." One can suppose Fitz Lee put forth his warning because the fort was primarily manned by Wild's brigade, the First U.S. Colored Troops. Wild certainly understood the racial undertones of Fitz Lee's comment when he replied, "We will try that." The fighting resumed.[175]

Wickham's command was sent around through some woods to attack the lower or eastern end of the fort. While they were moving into position, Dunovant was to make a demonstration at the other end of the fortifications. Once Dunovant's command had drawn the attention and fire of the Union troopers, artillery, and gunboats, then Wickham was instructed to assault the fort. Dunovant moved his men forward and began harassing the Union fortifications and gunboats, but did not order his men to charge the fort. The North Carolinians were with Dunovant on the Confederate right. The 5th cavalry was in the middle with the 1st and 2nd North Carolina on either side of their comrades. The Union guns along and on the river responded to Dunovant's presence. While the Confederates on the right were waiting for the order to charge, Private

Means of the 5th North Carolina recalled the situation years later in these terms: "The shells were chiefly 100-pounders. We could see them plainly coming at and over us; great black masses, as big as nail kegs, hurtling in the air and making the earth tremble under us and the atmosphere jar and quake around us when they burst. They certainly were terrifying." During the shelling, some of Fitz Lee's dismounted men managed to maintained a steady fire all along the line, but most waited for instructions to charge. Once in place on the right, they lay on the ground eating strawberries for more than an hour waiting for the signal to attack. From that position the cavalrymen could see "…platoon after platoon of reinforcements coming over the bluff into the fort on the decline next to [them]…."[176]

Over on the left of the Confederate line, Wickham took his men out of the woods and charged the fort. He took them across the open space under heavy fire as far as the "insurmountable" ditch and abattis, and was forced to stop and quickly retire — his command took heavy losses during the pullback. In all, Wickham's command had at least 10 men killed and more than 40 wounded.[177]

Once Wickham's charge on the left began, Dunovant's line received the signal to charge, and the North Carolinians rose "with a mighty yell for that terrible charge." They climbed a high rail-fence and ran straight and fast across the open space, toward the fort. As the charge was made, Private Means later recalled, "The shells from the 100-pounders, 20-pounders and 12-pounders were still bursting over us and other parts of the line." The charge was met by increased firing from the Union batteries in the fort and from the gun boats on each flank, as well as musket fire from all along the fortification. Fitz Lee had brought only one gun with him, and it could not be positioned to adequately support either his left of right. The North Carolinian experience was described as follows[178]:

Yelling and firing as we went and receiving fierce front and cross fires into our ranks from rifles and artillery in the fort and the gunboats; we were within thirty feet of the fort when we saw the utter hopelessness of the attack. The line halted a moment; the order to retreat was given and we retired under that awful fire from the most useless and unwise attack and the most single failure we were ever engaged in.[179]

Fitz Lee was not eager to have marched 50 miles for such a failure, so he instructed his men to regroup and prepared for an all-out assault along his entire line. Before he ordered the charge, however, he reported that "…a subsequent close personal reconnaissance, showed the work to be too elaborate and the orders were countermanded. Accordingly I withdrew my command, encamping for the night at Charles City C. H." Fitz Lee marched his column back toward Atlee's Station on May 25, and arrived there the next day.[180]

Near the fort, as the withdrawal began, Private Means of the 5th North Carolina Cavalry was wounded and carried out on the back of a Virginian cavalryman from Lomax's brigade. After a brief hospital stay he received a three month furlough. He remembered a friend near to him "was wounded by one of those 100-pounders. It passed at least ten feet from him and paralyzed his right arm by concussion of the air. There was no visible flesh injury to the arm, but it fell useless to his side, and quickly turned black its entire length, and he never recovered the use of it during his life time." James T. Armstrong of the 2nd North Carolina was captured, and James R. Harris of the same regiment was among those wounded seriously enough to have it reported. In all, about 20 Confederates were left dead in the field and as many more were captured; there is no good measure of the number of men wounded in what Private Means called this most "useless & unwise attack."[181]

As Fitz Lee and his column were approaching Wilson's Wharf early on May 24, he sent a message to General Bragg in Richmond telling him of reports received about Sheridan's cavalry probes across the Pamunkey River into R. E. Lee's line. He recommended that the small cavalry force he had left in the Richmond area be mobilized and sent to R. E. Lee because of the movement in the enemy's cavalry. Lomax had been left at Atlee's Station and from there he was to command the cavalry line in Fitz Lee's absence. Because of the Union aggressiveness that morning, R. E. Lee had also called for Lomax and most of the cavalrymen under his command to move in the direction of Hanover Court House. Fitz Lee had left behind only a small contingent of the North Carolina Cavalry brigade, and Lomax moved them to one of the suspected targets of Sheridan's cavalry — the road near Hanover Court House. The small number of men left under Lomax's command probably seemed easy prey for Union cavalry as they crossed the river and moved toward the court house to determine their enemy's strength and position.[182]

Among the North Carolinians moved up by Lomax was a small force of men from the 2nd North Carolina Cavalry; they found themselves in front of a major Union probe into R. E. Lee's line. They were attacked near the court house and were soon overwhelmed and broke in an "unfortunate stampede," to use Major William P. Roberts's description of the event. Roberts of Company C later recalled,

by accident I was in command of the regiment when the stampede occurred and in the midst of it, when the best officers and men seemed to be demoralized, the Color Sergeant of the regiment, Private Ramsey, of Company B, brought his flag to me, as I had ordered him to do when he could not rally his men around it, and, offering it to me, said: "Major, will you stand by the flag?" Everything was then in a perfect rout, myself with the rest, and I replied: "Ramsey, d__n the flag; I don't want it;" but he insisted upon giving me the flag, and said he was only obeying orders from me, often repeated.

His brave words inspired a few, and the rally was sounded and what a moment before seemed ignominious flight and the capture of our entire force, turned out to be victory for us in the end. Around the flag a few of us turned and met our pursuers, and most of them were captured before they reached the Pamunkey river. God bless the brave boy![183]

Major W. P. Roberts was all of 22 years old at the time.

Within a couple of days, Fitz Lee returned with his expeditionary force, and the North Carolina brigade was again united and patrolling the line near Hanover Court House. On May 26 they were joined by Colonel John A. Baker and the 3rd North Carolina Cavalry. The exhausted and depleted 1st, 2nd, and 5th North Carolina cavalrymen welcomed the fresh and near complete 3rd Cavalry. The North Carolina brigade had been marching and fighting nearly every day and night since leaving their camp near Bowling Green on May 5. The day before the 3rd Cavalry arrived, Captain Lockhart of the 2nd North Carolina wrote the folks back home and described their condition in these words,

"Our soldiers, although nearly worn out with fatigue, are in fine spirits and seem eager to meet the enemy. I have not had my shoes off in fifteen days. Excuse this letter, as it was written on my haversack while my horse was grazing."[184]

When Colonel J. A. Baker arrived with his 3rd Cavalry, he was the ranking Colonel in the brigade and immediately replaced Clinton M. Andrews as acting commander — Andrews went back to commanding the 2nd North Carolina Cavalry. James B. Gordon had died of his wounds on May 18, and no permanent replacement had yet been made. As the cavalrymen received another temporary commander, some of their thoughts continued to include Colonel Gordon. For instance, on May 22 John P. Lockhart of the 2nd North Carolina Cavalry wrote of their loss in these words: "our beloved and gallant Brigadier Gen. J. B. Gordon" was lost, and "It is enough to make every cavalryman weep to know that Gens. Stuart and Gordon are no more."[185]

In little more than a week, the 2nd North Carolina Cavalry had been engaged in a variety of actions and the following were among the losses.

Combat Losses in the 2nd North Carolina Cavalry May 16–24, 1864

Trooper	Age	Co.	Fate
John Batts		E	wounded, May 16
H. H. Ashbrook		E	mortally wounded, May 17
George D. Weatherly		F	wounded, May 17
Justin E. Best	37	C	wounded, May 18
George McClintock		F	wounded, May 18
Owen A. G. Wood		F	captured, May 20
Robert S. Walker		K	wounded, May 22
James T. Armstrong	21	G	captured, May 24
James R. Harris	23	K	wounded, May 24

Information contained in this table came from Compiled Service Records as summarized by Louis H. Manarin, *North Carolina Troops: 1861–1865, A Roster*, vol. II, pages 98–177. (See Appendix for more information on the men listed above, page 401.)

Stalemate: Grant Moves to Cold Harbor, May 27

By May 26, Grant realized the Confederate line at the North Anna River was stronger than any of their previous positions, so he bypassed it.

He once again set his army in motion, swinging around R. E. Lee's right wing. That night Alfred T. A. Torbert, who had rejoined his cavalry division, started down the north side of the Pamunkey River — Sheridan rode with him. The cavalry led Meade's VI (commanded by Wright), II (Hancock), V (Warren), and IX (Burnside) Corps. Torbert and his men marched all night to cross near Hanovertown early on the morning of May 27, where they encountered the North Carolina Cavalry brigade — this meeting marked the beginning of the Cold Harbor Campaign for the cavalry.[186] (See map 5.1.)

FIGHTING FROM HANOVERTOWN THROUGH HANOVER COURT HOUSE, MAY 27

Torbert sent cavalrymen from Custer's brigade forward to drive the North Carolinian pickets from the river bank and allow the engineers to put down a pontoon bridge. About an hour passed before the Union cavalry division was able to cross the river, and by that time the North Carolina brigade had collected itself and prepared to engage the advancing column. Custer's brigade went over first, followed by Merritt's and Devin's brigades. After passing through Hanovertown, Custer led the Union cavalrymen westward on Hanover River Road. He soon came to a fork in the road — one road led to Hanover Court House and the other to Haw's Shop. Torbert had Custer divide his command, sending two regiments along the river road toward Hanover Court House and the other two on the road toward Haw's Shop. Merritt's brigade followed Custer and his two regiments, while Devin and his brigade moved behind Custer's regiments heading for Hanover Court House.[187]

Custer's regiments on the river road were slowed by having to push nearly one hundred North Carolinians from the 3rd cavalry back along the road toward the court house. After a short distance, the Federals had pushed the enemy advance into its support — into the main body of the North Carolina brigade, which was by then composed of the 1st, 2nd, 3rd, and 5th cavalry regiments. Colonel John A. Baker, who had taken command of the brigade the night before, moved his men forward rapidly and drew a line in front of the advancing enemy. In the meantime, Colonel Bradley T. Johnson's Maryland cavalry, temporarily attached to Fitz Lee and in the area, was ordered to assist Baker. They devised a plan whereby the North Carolinians would hold the oncoming Union force, while Johnson took his command and a squadron from the 5th North Carolina around the right to hit the enemy in the flank.[188]

Unfortunately for the Marylanders, Torbert had also decided to hit his enemy in the flank. He instructed Custer to change course with his two regiments and head northwest toward the right flank of the North Carolina line. This put them on a collision course with Johnson's flanking move.

Up on the Hanover River Road, the Union advance had been stopped by the Confederate line across the road. The line was formed by the 1st, 2nd, and 5th North Carolina cavalries — they absorbed the 3rd cavalry as it fell back from the Union advance. As Custer's two regiments approached, the fighting intensified but Baker's line held. Then Devin's brigade arrived with more artillery and moved forward to hit the left of the North Carolina line.

The advancing Union force was too large with too much fire power — Baker's men had to fall back in stages. At about the same time, the Union flanking move coming up from near Haw's Shop hit the North Carolina line on its right flank causing them to drop back more quickly. While the North Carolinians were hotly engaged on the river road, the Union flanking force pushed along the same road occupied by Johnson's Maryland command and caught the latter by surprise, hardly allowing them time to form a line of battle. Johnson had the 5th North Carolina squadron up front, and they were quickly driven back into the Marylanders' column. Then Johnson's cavalrymen made several charges into the advancing enemy line but each time were driven back. Custer pushed Johnson's men back several miles before he stopped to regroup. He then turned his Michigan regiments toward the North Carolina brigade's right flank. Baker sent detachments from the 1st and 3rd Regiments at the oncoming Union flank attack, leaving the 2nd North Carolina and parts of the other three North Carolina regiments to slow the enemy advancing at their front along the river road. Devin's cavalrymen were concentrating on the Confederate left which was primarily held by the 2nd North Carolina Cavalry. At that point, Devin's regiments overwhelmed the Confederates and took a number of prisoners, at least four of whom were from the 2nd North Carolina Cavalry. Under enormous pressure, the entire North Carolina line fell back beyond the Union flanking move and formed a new line. Once they had stabilized their line, the North Carolinians were reinforced by Wickham's brigade and waited for another enemy advance. Both Johnson and Baker took heavy losses but were able to slow the attackers.[189]

The North Carolinians felt Johnson's command did not perform well, causing them to fall back rapidly to protect their right wing. The Marylanders felt Baker's command should have been able to hold Devin's advance on Hanover River Road more effectively. Each Confederate command was trying to salvage some pride when, in fact, Torbert's cavalry division was capable of overwhelming both Baker's and Johnson's commands under just about any circumstances.

According to one member of the North Carolina brigade, throughout the day's fighting, Baker was "directing and supervising every movement." Many in the brigade were pleased with their new commander's presence at the front. Of course, some cavalrymen were still unsure of his judgment. After all, it was Baker's first day on the job, and he was being assessed by those who had most at stake. The following illustrates the concerns of one member of the brigade as reported by another.

Passing a member of the brigade the evening of the fight, he said: "Col. Baker seems to be very brave." "Yes," I replied, "he will carry you as far into the ranks of the enemy as any other living man." "But," said he, "I'm afraid he will *lead* us so far in that he cannot get us out again." "You have only to judge his future by his past," I said, and left him seemingly much pleased and relieved.[190]

The North Carolinians and Marylanders had made Grant's cavalry advance fight for their position south of the Pamunkey River, but the Union cavalry had crossed and their infantry followed. Grant had his Sixth Corps in motion to follow Torbert's cavalry across near Hanovertown. By early morning, May 27, J. A. Baker was in a position to report to R. E. Lee, through Lomax who was near Hanover Court House, that the enemy cavalry and infantry were crossing the Pamunkey in force. R. E. Lee was quick to react to the news from the North Carolina brigade, and by 8:30 A.M., Ewell had his orders to withdraw quietly from the North Anna line, so as not to be seen, and move down to the south side of the South Anna River. R. E. Lee was again moving quickly to block Grant's flanking move.[191]

By late afternoon on May 27, Fitz Lee reported that the enemy cavalry had collected near Haw's Shop and Enon Church, so he was heading for Atlee's Station where he planned to join Hampton and his command. In fact, as this campaign opened, all three of Robert E. Lee's cavalry divisions along with their commanders, Wade Hampton, Fitz Lee and W. H. F. Lee, were gathering at Atlee's Station. From there, the cavalrymen planned to move to Haw's Shop or Hanovertown the next morning and confront Grant's cavalry. Lomax's was the only brigade remaining at Hanover Court House.[192] (See map 2.1.)

Earlier, when Wade Hampton was moved from in front of Hancock's column at Milford Station, he and his command were placed on R. E. Lee's left while the latter was engaged with Grant's army on May 23 and 25. Hampton's cavalry had several heated skirmishes in that position, and when Grant began to move his army on the 27th, Hampton was sent down to Atlee's Station to join forces with Fitz Lee's command. In addition, by May 27, Special Orders No. 123 instructed Colonel Pierce M. B. Young to move toward Hanover Court House from Richmond with the cavalry under his command and report to R. E. Lee, who was still near Hanover Junction.[193]

By May 24 and 25, Chambliss's brigade of W. H. F. Lee's division was also picketing and skirmishing along the North Anna River and New Found Creek. On the 27th, W. H. F. Lee and Chambliss's brigade started south and east to join the rest of R. E. Lee's cavalry. Most of Chambliss's brigade marched through Ashland toward Atlee's Station. As indicated above, the other half of W. H. F. Lee's command, the North Carolina brigade, was already in the area between Hanover Court House and Hanovertown. J. A. Baker, with his North Carolinians reported to W. H. F. Lee near Atlee's Station late on May 27.[194]

Lomax's brigade of Fitz Lee's command

was sent to picket the crossing at the South Anna River. Young's brigade under the command of Colonel Wright of Hampton's cavalry was also sent in that direction to cover R. E. Lee's infantry as it moved across the South Anna.[195]

Cavalry Fight at Haw's Shop (the Fight at Buckeye), May 28

By early morning May 28, both Torbert's and D. McM. Gregg's cavalry divisions as well as a division of Grant's infantry were across the Pamunkey River. Grant needed to know where the Army of Northern Virginia was as he moved his infantry corps across the river. Sheridan sent D. McM. Gregg's division from Hanovertown to Haw's Shop, leaving Torbert's cavalry to hold the Hanover River Road and protect the infantry's right flank as it continued across the river at Hanovertown. Later in the day, Grant's Sixth Corps crossed the Pamunkey and relieved Torbert's cavalry division. Torbert then moved down to Haw's Shop to join D. McM. Gregg's cavalry division which was in need of assistance by the afternoon because R. E. Lee had most of his cavalry headed for Haw's Shop early that morning—Lee wanted his cavalry to discover how much of Grant's infantry had crossed the river and where they were headed. Both Grant and R. E. Lee needed reliable information about the other's infantry, so each sent his cavalry to find it.[196]

Robert E. Lee's cavalry marched under Wade Hampton's command—he was the senior major general among the Confederate cavalry commanders. Hampton was instructed to move his three small divisions from Atlee's Station toward Haw's Shop and confirm the presence and direction of Grant's infantry. Fitz Lee moved out first with Wickham's brigade from his division; they were followed by M. C. Butler's South Carolina cavalrymen who had recently arrived, and Rosser's brigade from Hampton's division; the rear of the column was brought up by most of W. H. F. Lee's division (Some of Chambliss's and most of the North Carolina brigade). The North Carolina brigade brought up W. H. F. Lee's rear on May 28—they had been more heavily engaged the previous day than the other units in their division so were positioned for a relatively easy day.[197]

It is hard to determine precisely how much of W. H. F. Lee's two brigades were with him as he moved out with Hampton on the morning of May 28, but it is clear Chambliss's brigade was not complete. George W. Beale of the 9th Virginia Cavalry wrote that on May 27 his regiment was moving, at least initially, with Chambliss and his brigade from R. E. Lee's left on the North Anna line through Ashland. The 9th Virginia Cavalry and perhaps others from Chambliss's brigade had instructions to move east and get behind Warren's Fifth Corps of Union infantry after they crossed the Pamunkey and began to move south. The 9th Virginia Cavalry's assignment was to annoy Warren's rear and pick up any stragglers. Beale described the horrible residual effects of war left in Warren's wake as he moved south after crossing at Hanovertown. What is clear from his descriptions is that at least one of Chambliss's regiments was southeast of Haw's Shop on the road to Old Church while Hampton's command was engaged with D. McM. Gregg's cavalry division just west of Haw's Shop. According to R. L. T. Beale, Colonel of the 9th Virginia Cavalry, they spent the night of May 27 on the road to Old Church and while marching the next morning could hear the rattle of small arms coming from Haw's Shop. Colonel Beale then moved his regiment toward the sound of fighting. Beale remembered, "On reaching there we were posted to protect the flank of the men engaged." The 9th Virginia was moved forward and engaged in some skirmishing before being pulled back.[198]

Apparently, the approach and involvement of the 9th Virginia was separate from the action seen by the troops brought by Hampton from Atlee's Station—which included the North Carolina brigade of W. H. F. Lee's division.

As Hampton's column neared Haw's Shop, Fitz Lee's troopers came upon the enemy first and drove them back. Davies was moving his Union cavalry brigade west along the road to Atlee's Station when their advance was driven back by Wickham's brigade. As the two opposing columns met, troopers on both sides accumulated at their fronts and exchanged mounted charges. Then each dismounted to form battle lines. As Wickham's command was forming, Rosser's brigade from Hampton's division moved up on their left. When W. H. F. Lee's command began arriving, they were sent to Rosser's left—the Confederate far left. In an after-the-war report, Hampton wrote, "Genl. Wm. Lee had been sent on a road leading to our left, with directions to turn the right flank of the enemy if he could do so." The North Carolina brigade, under the command of Baker, was with W. H. F. Lee as he marched toward the Union right. (Apparently some of the North Carolinians remained on picket duty between Hanover Court House and Ashland — along with Johnson's Maryland cavalrymen.)[199]

The dismounted cavalry lines tried to advance on their opponents, but were driven back each time. Severe fighting took place on both sides of the road leading to Atlee's Station from Haw's Shop. As the cavalrymen exchanged fire, artillery from both sides entered the contest and dramatically raised the stakes. D. McM. Gregg and Hampton both sent their reserve units into the line hoping to cause the other to break. The standoff was finally broken after Torbert's division on the Hanover River Road was relieved by the Union's VI Infantry Corps and sent to assist D. McM. Gregg just west of Haw's Shop. When Torbert arrived, he sent Custer's brigade at the center and Merritt's at the Confederate left. Fighting intensified — mostly hand-to-hand and bloody.[200]

Meanwhile over on the Confederate left, W. H. F. Lee's flanking move approached D. McM. Gregg's right and encountered Merritt's newly arrived command. The encounter was described by a member of the North Carolina brigade in these terms:

Gen. W. H. F. Lee, with our brigade, swung round by means of by ways on the enemy's right flank, and opened a heavy artillery fire upon them, at the same time throwing out his dismounted skirmishers, who engaged the enemy hotly, driving them back some distance. The fight raged for several hours along the entire line ... our men firmly holding their ground with their carbines.[201]

Of course, W. H. F. Lee's mission was to turn the Union right rather than simply hold his ground, but he and his men were not able to get into a position to flank the Union line once it was reinforced by Merritt's brigade. Merritt's and W. H. F. Lee's cavalrymen exchanged fire but were not seriously engaged. However, W. H. F. Lee did manage to get his artillery close enough to do some damage to the Union right.[202]

The fight straddling the road to Atlee's Station continued for several hours, and both sides were pushed to near breaking. By evening, Hampton received reports indicating the Union Sixth Infantry Corps had arrived from the river road. That day his mission was to gain information about the presence of Grant's infantry south of the Pamunkey. Late in the day Hampton could report Grant did have infantry south of the river as far as Haw's Shop. In addition, by that time Hampton knew he could not move the reinforced enemy line in front of him, so he withdrew his command. Unfortunately for the Confederates, Wickham withdrew too quickly which left a hole in the center of their line exposing the inner flanks of both T. L. Rosser's and M. C. Butler's commands. D. McM. Gregg had a different view. He claimed his rapid advance on the Confederate center drove Wickham's command back in confusion — his advance probably did account for the rapidity with which the center of the Confederate line fell back. In any case, Rosser withdrew his command without loss, but Union forces were able to storm through the hole in the center of the line and turn Butler's left flank before they could fall back. Butler himself had not yet joined his brigade, and the temporary commander of his troops was overwhelmed in Hampton's eyes, so the latter rode over and brought the South Carolinians out without a heavy loss.[203]

The Confederate troops dropped back about 300 yards and reformed their line, but made no further attack. During the day, while the fight between the cavalries raged, Hampton contacted General Early, whose infantry was close enough to get to the rear of the Union line in front of Hampton, but Early declined the opportunity; and D. McM. Gregg's cavalrymen were spared the pounding that might have been.[204]

By the end of the day, based on information from captured infantrymen from the enemy's Fifth and Sixth Corps, Hampton could report to R. E. Lee that Grant's infantry was across the Pamunkey River; but Sheridan could not inform Grant of the location of R. E. Lee's infantry. Yet, as is often the case, both sides claimed some success, and both commands had several hundred fewer cavalrymen.

By the time the cavalry fighting was at an end near Haw's Shop, R. E. Lee was at Atlee's Station and his army was on the move. Once he knew Grant's infantry was south of the river and Hampton's cavalry was being pushed back along the road to Atlee's Station, he called upon General Breckinridge to move his infantrymen in line between Atlee's Station and Totopotomoy Creek to protect his army on its move south. Breckinridge's infantry was in place by late afternoon and relieved Hampton's cavalrymen on the new line between the marching armies.[205]

All three of R. E. Lee's cavalry divisions camped near Atlee's Station again that night. It was the first night W. H. F. Lee's division went into camp with all its regiments—Chambliss's 9th, 10th, and 13th Virginia cavalries; and the 1st, 2nd, 3rd, and 5th North Carolina cavalries under the temporary command of John A. Baker.

Sheridan's cavalry did not advance toward the Totopotomoy and Breckinridge's line during the night of May 28. In fact, after nightfall Sheridan's cavalry was also relieved on the line near Haw's Shop and returned to the Pamunkey, a short distance below Hanovertown and then moved down the road to Old Church where they went into camp early on May 29.[206]

As Grant and R. E. Lee continued to shift their armies south on May 29, their cavalries also moved in that direction staying between the opposing forces. Sheridan sent Wilson's division to picket Grant's right. Gregg's and Torbert's divisions were sent to picket the road from Old Church to Cold Harbor.[207]

The Confederates made similar moves. R. E. Lee sent Fitz Lee's division to their right, near Mechanicsville; W. H. F. Lee's division to their left, once again picketing the Hanover River Road to the Union line west of Hanovertown; and Hampton held two of his brigades near Atlee's Station. Hampton sent M. C. Butler, who had just returned to service after recuperating from the loss of his foot, with his brigade down to Meadow Bridge near Richmond to assess his newly organized brigade.[208]

The road from Old Church to Cold Harbor was important to Grant and Sheridan because on it the enemy could harass the Union wagons traveling to and from White House, which was becoming their main supply base on the Pamunkey. Torbert's cavalry division was picketing the road.[209]

At about 4:00 P.M. on May 30, Devin's brigade of Torbert's division was attacked on the road from Old Church to Cold Harbor by M. C. Butler's South Carolina brigade, which had stopped at Cold Harbor on the way to the Meadow Bridge area. The fight soon became severe and lasted about three hours. Finally, Torbert had to bring up Merritt's brigade and two regiments from Custer's brigade. With this force Torbert was able to push the Confederates back in stages for a distance of about 3 miles and finally back to Cold Harbor. The fighting was again all done by dismounted cavalrymen. Torbert's exhausted men stopped the pursuit about a mile and a half before Cold Harbor and bivouacked. That evening, Butler notified Fitz Lee of his encounter with Sheridan's cavalry and the next day Fitz Lee moved his cavalrymen to Cold Harbor and relieved Butler's South Carolina Cavalry Brigade.[210]

As indicated, several miles north of M. C. Butler's stand at Cold Harbor, the North Carolina Cavalry Brigade was picketing the river road when Wilson sent Chapman's brigade of Union cavalry across the Pamunkey near Hanovertown. (Wilson's cavalry had stayed north of the river while Grant's infantry crossed.) After Chapman's brigade moved a couple of miles along the road to Hanover Court House, they came upon North Carolinian pickets. The two opposing cavalries skirmished until nightfall when both sides posted strong picket lines, and Chapman camped his brigade on Crump's Swamp.[211]

Pierce M. B. Young had finally arrived at Hanover Court House from Richmond on May 30, along with many of the cavalrymen he had been refitting near Danville on the North Carolina border. However, Young was not returned to his own brigade in Hampton's division, rather he was temporarily assigned to command the North Carolina brigade in W. H. F. Lee's division. Young's new command remained concentrated near Hanover Court House and spread along the river road toward Hanovertown with enemy cavalry a couple of miles down the road. J. A. Baker was moved back to his 3rd North Carolina Cavalry.

The Cavalry at Cold Harbor and Hanover Court House, May 31

The stage was set for two cavalry conflicts below the Pamunkey River on May 31: one on the road between Old Church and Old Cold Harbor; the other involving the 2nd North Carolina Cavalry around Hanover Court House.

On the morning of the 31st, Sheridan joined Torbert and discussed a plan to take Old Cold Harbor. Sheridan was still concerned about keeping his supply lines open to their base at White House, so he felt controlling the area between the base and Old Church and Old Cold Harbor was essential.[212]

In response to M. C. Butler's encounter on May 30, Fitz Lee had collected his command near Old Cold Harbor — his job was still to shield R. E. Lee's troop movements. On the other side, Sheridan did not want Confederate cavalry so close to his supply line and his concerns were heightened by Butler's presence and determined fight around Old Cold Harbor. Consequently, on May 31 Torbert's command was moved into position and he attacked in the afternoon. D. McM. Gregg's division was moved up for support but was not needed. Torbert sent Merritt's brigade up the main road to Old Cold Harbor with Custer's brigade just behind. Devin's command was sent by another road just to the left but with the same destination. Merritt's command was the first to engage Fitz Lee's dismounted cavalrymen, and they drove the Confederates back about one and a half miles to a breastworks made of earth and fence rails from behind which they made a strong stand. Torbert sent Custer's command up on Merritt's left, connecting with Devin on the far left. The Union plan was for Devin to approach Old Cold Harbor from a lower road and turn the Confederate right, but they were unable to do so. In addition, Custer and Merritt were unable to break the line across the road to Old Cold Harbor. Finally, Merritt moved to turn the left of the Confederate line and was successful, causing them to pull back and leave the breastworks. Fitz Lee's cavalrymen were driven through and just beyond Old Cold Harbor. When Fitz Lee was pushed from Cold Harbor, R. E. Lee felt certain his enemy was moving in that direction, so he extended his line on the right to cover the place. R. E. Lee started R. F. Hoke's infantry division in that direction, and late on May 31 Hoke's advance began to relieve Fitz Lee's cavalrymen. Before the Confederate infantry began to arrive, however, Torbert was feeling exposed at Cold Harbor, about 3 miles in front of D. McM. Gregg's division, so he pulled back for the night. By morning, however, Grant had notified Sheridan that "Cold Harbor be held at all hazards."

Sheridan moved back into Cold Harbor before daybreak on June 1, just as the Confederates were preparing to retake the place. Now both Grant and R. E. Lee wanted control of the area around Cold Harbor.[213]

Once entrenched, Sheridan's cavalrymen were able to use their batteries and repeating carbines with deadly effect, and Hoke's infantrymen could not retake Cold Harbor. They fought from daylight to around 10:00 A.M. when Grant's Sixth Infantry Corps arrived and replaced Sheridan's cavalrymen. Throughout the day, infantry and artillery from both sides continued to enter the lines near Cold Harbor, and fighting escalated accordingly — but neither side won a clear dominance over the other on May 31. Fitz Lee kept his Confederate cavalrymen on the line for another day. Sheridan moved his men toward the Chickahominy and covered the infantry's left until the afternoon when Hancock's command came up and relieved them. The two Union cavalry divisions then moved down the Chickahominy near Prospect Church and camped for the night.[214]

Early on May 31, while Sheridan had Torbert's and D. McM. Gregg's divisions fighting around Cold Harbor, Wilson's cavalry division was covering Grant's right, which put them in front of W. H. F. Lee's two cavalry brigades. W. H. F. Lee had his command around Hanover Court House and out the river road to Hanovertown. The North Carolina regiments were easternmost along the road to Hanovertown. This was P. M. B. Young's first day in command of the North Carolina brigade, and it was to be a busy one from its outset.[215]

Wilson and his division of Union cavalry were instructed to swing around the Confederate left and send a force to the South Anna River and the two railroads in the area to destroy bridges and rail track. Then Sheridan apparently relieved Wilson of the destruction business around the South Anna and told him to concentrate on protecting the army's right wing — which is what he was doing on the Hanover River Road on May 30 when he skirmished with cavalrymen from the North Carolina brigade. Wilson established a line southwest of the Pamunkey near Crump's Swamp that night. By early the next morning, Wilson had both John B. McIntosh's and George H. Chapman's brigades with him on the river road.[216]

Early on May 31, Wilson took his division up the river road to take Hanover Court House and the railroads there and beyond. His advance soon ran into pickets from the North Carolina brigade and pushed them toward the court house. The North Carolina regiments had formed a line with their left at the court house and their right stretching beyond the Virginia Central Railroad. A member of the North Carolina brigade described the scene:

The 1st, 2nd, 3rd, and 5th regiments were dismounted and double quicked in with as much *élan* as old veteran infantry. The scene was grand…, as our boys jaded and worn rushed over a hill and saw the long black lines of the enemy sweeping over a wide plain, rushing to gain the position that lay before them. At the same time the white clouds of smoke from our cannon gave assurances that we had help from behind; our boys dashed impetuously forward hardly waiting to fire.[217]

The North Carolinians attacked the advancing Union column and drove them back a short distance into their main force. From that point, according to Rufus Barringer (then of the 1st North Carolina), "pretty much the entire Brigade was dismounted, and withstood, with undaunted spirit, a fierce and overwhelming attack of the enemy." The 2nd North Carolina was on the left extending to the court house, then the 3rd Cavalry; the Confederate right was held by the 5th North Carolina as far as the station on the Virginia Central Railroad. The 1st North Carolina stood ready just behind the line. W. H. F. Lee held Chambliss's Virginian regiments in reserve. Late in the day, Union forces came at their front and initiated flanking moves around both sides. McIntosh's brigade overwhelmed the dismounted Confederates and pushed the North Carolina cavalrymen from Hanover Court House. Chambliss sent some of his Virginia cavalrymen in but it was too little, too late. The fighting was over by 9:00 P.M., when the North Carolina regiments pulled back and reformed their line just south of the court house and held for the remainder of that night. The 1st North Carolina spent the night drawn up in a line across the road between their comrades and the enemy in Hanover Court House.[218]

Wilson was in Hanover Court House by 11:00 P.M. when he reported "…after a very sharp fight drove the enemy from a very strong position on the north side of Mechump's Creek, and through Hanover Court-House, taking some prisoners and killing quite a number. The rebels were commanded in person by General Young, and were probably his brigade, and two pieces of artillery." It was reasonable for Wilson to assume Young was commanding his own brigade from Hampton's division, but in fact he had been fighting with the North Carolina brigade of W. H. F. Lee's division. Wilson went on to report that his "…men were fatigued from their fighting to-day, and ammunition exhausted. I have therefore concluded to halt for the night, recruit men and horses, get ammunition and provisions, so as to push out at the first dawn of day." Certainly, the North Carolina cavalrymen were just as exhausted and low on ammunition when Young withdrew them to a position south of Hanover Court House. His command and their division commander, W. H. F. Lee, along with most of Chambliss's brigade, camped for the night near Wickham's large plantation on the road to Ashland.[219]

By the end of the day, Wilson had one brigade covering the roads heading south from Hanover Court House and another covering the roads to Hanovertown. He had Grant's right wing covered.[220]

Cavalry Fight at Ashland, June 1

At 4:00 A.M. June 1, James H. Wilson had his Federal cavalrymen on the road heading for the railroad bridges over the South Anna River and Ashland Station on the Richmond, Fredericksburg & Potomac Railroad. He sent John B. McIntosh, commanding the First Brigade, westward toward Ashland and George H. Chapman's brigade to the bridge where the Virginia Central crossed the South Anna River, then west along the river to the bridge carrying the Richmond, Fredericksburg & Potomac Railroad.[221] (See map 5.1.)

As Chapman moved his command toward the Virginia Central Railroad, he came upon a fight near Hanover Court House between McIntosh's 2nd New York Cavalry and a cavalry battalion from Maryland. Chapman helped push the Confederates back. From there he moved his division along the railroad toward the South Anna River and destroyed the railroad bridge. He then moved over to destroy structures on the Richmond, Fredericksburg & Potomac Railroad. They only encountered minor resistance from a handful of guards at each bridge and accomplished their destruction in good time. While in the final stages of destroying water tanks, rail track, and the like, Chapman received word from Wilson to retire to Hanover Court House quickly. McIntosh was under great pressure at Ashland.[222]

McIntosh had taken his command from Hanover Court House early on June 1, heading toward Ashland — but his path was obstructed. Early that morning, the 2nd North Carolina Cavalry relieved the 1st regiment across the road leading to Ashland. They were the first to greet McIntosh's advancing column.[223] W. H. F. Lee and the rest of his command were in the position they had fallen back to the night before, and they were ready for McIntosh's cavalrymen. A member of W. H. F. Lee's staff (Theodore S. Garnett, formerly of J. E. B. Stuart's staff) described the scene created by McIntosh's approach as viewed first by the 2nd North Carolina Cavalry and then their brigade.

The morning of the 1st June found us drawn up, mounted and in line, on the high ground just south of Wickham's, an excellent position to meet the advancing enemy. Their long blue lines, both mounted and dismounted stretched entirely across the level meadows and wheat fields of Wickham's fine plantation. Anticipating their attack on our front with every advantage in our favor I was hopeful of an easy repulse. They seemed to be in no hurry to begin the fight and we waited patiently for them to open the ball. I was sitting my horse near Gen. Lee, watching the splendid pageant of ever-increasing numbers of blue horseman, fully displayed to our view in the plains below, when one of our scouts rode up and told the General that the enemy were moving a heavy column around our right-flank, then very much exposed and easily turned.[224]

Wilson was advancing his command on parallel roads, and the southernmost route was taking his men toward W. H. F. Lee's right flank. Once he was aware of his enemy on his flank and considered the large force in front of his command, W. H. F. Lee pulled his North Carolina brigade back along the road toward Ashland and brought them into position out of sight of McIntosh's column, just east of the village.

W. H. F. Lee left Bradley T. Johnson and his Maryland command with two pieces of artillery in front of McIntosh. They were instructed to hold if possible or retire slowly along the road to Ashland, impeding the enemy's progress. As W. H. F. Lee was resting his men just east of Ashland, he had some thoughts about the Marylanders he had left in front of the advancing enemy, so he ordered Garnett of his staff to take a squadron from the 3rd North Carolina to assist Johnson. Garnett rode over to the commander of the 3rd Cavalry at the time, Major Roger Moore, and told him of his assignment. Moore was reluctant to send a squadron of his men into a fight under Garnett, whom he did not know well, and insisted that he go with them. Garnett welcomed his company and assistance, and they started up the road to join the Marylanders.[225]

Johnson had been fighting the enemy from hilltop to hilltop as he and his Maryland cavalrymen slowly dropped back — hoping that reinforcements would arrive from some quarter. Then in an effort to slow McIntosh's column even more, Johnson ordered a charge into the enemy column. They could not penetrate the advance, and their well-liked Lieutenant Colonel, Ridgely Brown, who led the charge was shot through the head and died instantly. Garnett and Moore arrived with the squadron of North Carolinians just as the charge had been repulsed. Garnett approached Johnson and explained that W. H. F. Lee had sent a squadron to assist, with his compliments. Johnson rather brusquely replied, "I don't want your Squadron — take it back — Col. Brown has just been killed — I cannot stop the enemy here — I am now falling back across the Railroad." Garnett was at first a little surprised by the reaction, then quickly realized W. H. F. Lee had to be advised that the enemy advance could not be stopped by the force left behind, so he took the squadron back at a gallop toward Ashland just as the Marylanders were stepping aside.[226]

As they neared Ashland, Garnett and his cavalrymen could hear gunfire in front of them so they picked up their pace, "...and pushing ahead at a run, we crossed that road just as the head of the enemy's column appeared on our left coming at a charge, and the rear of our Squadron swept across their front within pistol shot. But neither party fired a shot, doubtless their surprise was as great as ours...." Immediately after passing in front of the enemy's charge, the squadron rode into Young's North Carolina line which had been moved just south of Ashland and was drawn up across Telegraph Road.[227]

McIntosh's cavalrymen pushed their way into Ashland, driving the North Carolina skirmishers south and began to damage railroad property. The Federals covered this operation by sending forward a line to hold W. H. F. Lee's North Carolina brigade south of the village. Skirmishing was heated along the line, but neither side deemed it necessary to mount a serious charge. W. H. F. Lee sent a large portion of Chambliss's brigade into the woods around Ashland where they spent most of the day skirmishing with enemy cavalrymen on similar assignments. Meanwhile, McIntosh's force continued to file into the village. By the time W. H. F. Lee was bringing pressure on the Union troops in the village, he received a message from Hampton informing him that he had sent three regiments from Rosser's brigade at the rear of the enemy column. The Union cavalrymen who were not yet at Ashland were driven into it at a rapid pace. Hampton requested that Lee mount a charge from the south of Ashland. At that point, W. H. F. Lee dismounted the remainder of the North Carolina Cavalry and sent them forward — the men of the 5th North Carolina Cavalry, led at that point by Garnett, pushed the enemy in front of them into the path of Rosser's charging cavalrymen coming from the east. At the same time, other North Carolinian cavalrymen, also dismounted, were pushing into the enemy line at various points — they were led by P. M. B. Young. The North Carolinians charged for over a mile under heavy fire and drove the enemy from their strong position near the center of the village. At one point in the line, according to an observer in the 1st North Carolina regiment, when some members of the 3rd North Carolina ran out of ammunition, they "actually fought the enemy with stone and brick-bats." Severe hand-to-hand combat ran the distance of the North Carolina brigade's line. Obviously by that time McIntosh had put all his men to fighting the Confederates which limited what they could achieve in destroying the railroad. His Union cavalry division was under attack from three directions and was at great risk of being seriously hurt. However, the Union commander did manage to send a message to Chapman requesting assistance.[228]

While much of Chambliss's brigade was fighting in the woods around the village, the main body of the North Carolina brigade continued to push in from Telegraph Road, south of the village and on the western flank.[229] As the North Carolinian charge was well under way, Garnett, with the 5th Cavalry, swung around the station and passed by Rosser's command, coming in from the east, witnessing a sight that burned into his memory and he vividly recalled years later:

> Just at this moment the sound and smoke of battle was heavy, deafening and blinding, but I saw coming out of the line on the Telegraph Road an officer, supported by two others, on his horse, shot through the breast and bleeding profusely, whom I recognized as my very gallant old friend, Genl. P. M. B. Young, of Georgia.[230]

The North Carolina brigade had lost another commander at a critical moment. Rosser was in the immediate area and had some success orchestrating the fight in his sector by sending his and some of the North Carolina regiments into the line at appropriate points. However, Wade Hampton felt the North Carolina brigade failed to dislodge the enemy in their first assault because Young had been wounded and the command temporarily lost direction. In any case, within minutes, W. H. F. Lee was able to reform the North Carolina brigade and launch another attack. The close range fighting raged for around three hours with artillery from both sides also firing from close in. In the meantime, Hampton took the 10th Virginia, one squadron from Rosser's 7th Virginia, and one from W. H. F. Lee's 3rd North Carolina around to attack McIntosh's right flank. Hampton felt the Union line was falling back at several points when the reinforcements sent by Chapman approached Ashland from the north on Telegraph Road. The 1st Vermont cavalrymen approached slowly as the road was lined with dense forest. Chapman's troopers dismounted and marched in line across the road for a short distance, then Confederate cavalrymen attacked them in the front and flank. The Vermont regiment was kept busy from the moment they came into contact with the enemy and were only able to connect with McIntosh's forces late in the day. Nonetheless, Wilson felt they drew enough attention to allow McIntosh to withdraw most of his command from Ashland and move toward Hanover

Court House. However, Hampton felt McIntosh was able to withdraw because nightfall brought the fighting to a halt. There was probably some truth to both interpretations.[231]

After dark the Federals left. The men from the 1st Vermont mounted and followed McIntosh's column. Both Chapman's and McIntosh's divisions along with Wilson camped for the night between Hanover Court House and Hanovertown on the Pamunkey. Wilson summed up the day in these words: "It was by that time almost night, and having been engaged in almost constant fighting for two days, ammunition was getting scarce. I withdrew with the division, carrying off all the wounded whom the ambulances would accommodate, and leaving the others in the hands of the enemy. Our loss in the two days was about 200 in killed, wounded, and prisoners." Wilson was not trying to paint his two days of conflict with the North Carolina brigade and the troops of Chambliss's and Rosser's commands as victorious — it was a high price to pay for the temporary decommissioning of a couple of bridges over the South Anna River and a water tank or two.[232]

Neither could the Confederates have felt overwhelmed by successes during those two days. For instance, Garnett of W. H. F. Lee's staff wrote: "The whole affair was badly managed on our part, and what should have been a great victory for us must be numbered among the lost opportunities." He felt they should have destroyed McIntosh's division. In addition to Garnett's perceived loss, the North Carolina brigade had a more tangible loss to deal with — they had lost another temporary commander when Pierce M. B. Young was severely wounded.[233]

Even though Brigadier General Young had commanded the North Carolinians for only two days, they were seriously engaged a good deal of the time, and many of the cavalrymen liked their temporary commander's style. Major Galloway of the 5th North Carolina Cavalry was sufficiently impressed to remember Pierce M. B. Young from Georgia in these terms: "He was the beau ideal of a cavalry leader and he took our hearts by storm." The phrase, "Here goes for hell or promotion" was often Young's cry as he led the North Carolinians into action. Young's style was similar to that of the late J. E. B. Stuart, and many cavalrymen missed it.[234]

As indicated in other places, the records are not always accurate when reflecting where and when cavalrymen were killed, wounded, or captured, but the following is a partial list of men from the 2nd North Carolina Cavalry were lost during the fighting near Hanovertown, Hanover Court House, and Ashland.

Combat Losses in the 2nd North Carolina Cavalry May 27–June 1, 1864

Trooper	Age	Co.	Fate
F. D. Abernathy		B	captured, May 27
Ephraim D, Robbins	24	E	captured, May 27
Henderson B. Thomas	28	I	captured, May 27
William C. Hall	27	K	captured, May 27
Robert W. Atkinson	24	E	captured, May 29
George W. Johnson	27	H	wounded, May
F. W. Sapp		A	captured, June 1

Information contained in this table came from Compiled Service Records as summarized by Louis H. Manarin, *North Carolina Troops: 1861–1865, A Roster*, vol. II, pages 98–177. (See Appendix for more information on the men listed above, page 401.)

THE SECOND CAVALRY FIGHT AT HAW'S SHOP, JUNE 3

By early morning June 3, most of the troopers from both armies were in place. The opposing lines of infantrymen were across the road running between Old and New Cold Harbor. R. E. Lee had his men well entrenched and Grant sent his men at them. It was a bloody morning as the Confederates withstood one uncoordinated assault after another.[235] By the time Grant was calling it a day around Cold Harbor, unplanned fighting again erupted up at Haw's Shop between the cavalries.

After fighting in and around Ashland on June 1, Wade Hampton took his division back to Atlee's Station, while W. H. F. Lee made camp with most of his division just south of Ashland to watch Wilson's cavalry division. Many North Carolina cavalrymen were sent to picket the roads north and east of Ashland. Colonel John A. Baker of the 3rd North Carolina was again given temporary command of the North Carolina brigade. On June 2, W. H. F. Lee took his division to Atlee's Station, then rested for the day and night near Hampton's command.[236]

After the fight at Ashland, Wilson's Union cavalrymen remained on the Union right until the morning of June 3, when they were ordered to move back above the Totopotomoy and drive their enemy's pickets from Haw's Shop and hopefully hit R. E. Lee's line in the left flank. Wilson's assignment was compromised by Hampton's move that same morning, however. Hampton and W. H. F. Lee were marching with the North Carolina brigade to Haw's Shop from Atlee's Station.[237]

Wilson arrived at Haw's Shop around midday and settled into some of the breastworks left from the previous battle. He sent pickets out on the road from Atlee's Station and others but was not expecting visitors. A short while later, Baker and the North Carolina Cavalry Brigade came down the road and at the first sight of enemy pickets, charged. The North Carolina cavalrymen drove the pickets back rapidly into Chapman's line. W. H. F. Lee immediately had Baker dismount the 2nd and 5th North Carolina cavalries—commanded by Colonel C. M. Andrews and Major McNeill, respectively. The men from the 2nd North Carolina Cavalry were led into this battle by Lieutenant Colonel William P. Roberts, and those from the 5th Regiment were led by Captain Shaw. The 2nd North Carolina went in first with a dismounted charge against their enemy's breastworks. They moved forward rapidly as artillery shells flew overhead into the opposing lines. The Union position was strong and difficult to dislodge—several attempts were needed before any movement was detectable. During one of the charges, W. P. Roberts received a slight wound to his head but remained in the field. Rufus Barringer of the 1st North Carolina observed the dismounted action and remembered that the cavalrymen of the 2nd and 5th regiments "...charged at once the enemy's line, which was driven rapidly through a thick wood, back into a line of works, which was charged, and carried in a most impetuous style, driving the enemy back upon another line of entrenchments, with heavy support." The same observer noted that "this spirited and dashing affair was executed under the eye of Gen. Hampton, and elicited his special commendation." In addition, their own division commander, W. H. F. Lee saw the cavalrymen in action and was equally impressed. The 2nd North Carolina Cavalry had fought with W. H. F. Lee a year earlier at Brandy Station as well as on other occasions, so he was probably not altogether surprised to witness their well-executed charges against an entrenched enemy—nonetheless, he was sufficiently impressed to issue a congratulatory order noting the gallant manner in which the 2nd and 5th North Carolina cavalries had conducted themselves that day.[238]

After the 2nd and 5th North Carolina pushed Wilson's line back, the Union cavalrymen, supported by infantry, rallied and drove the Confederates back nearly to their starting point. William P. Roberts had his command quickly throw up breastworks and wait for the Union attack. They came but the entrenched 2nd and 5th North Carolina held. Finally the Union line extended well beyond Roberts's breastworks on both flanks, and they were ordered to withdraw toward Enon Church. Once there, the 2nd and 5th managed to stop the Federal countercharge. They were relieved by the 3rd North Carolina which continued fighting on the line for about another hour before withdrawing, leaving only a few pickets on the road. Union commander, Wilson, described the encounter—in his words, "Parts of both brigades ... dismounted and pushed forward, driving the rebel cavalry, also dismounted, over three lines of breastworks in succession. With a small mounted force they were pursued to Mount Carmel Church. The rebels fought stubbornly." To Hampton, the clash appeared in these terms: "...found the enemy posted in earth works near, the Brigade [the 2nd and 5th Regiments] under command of Col. Baker of the 3rd N.C. Regt. & attacked promptly. After a sharp affair, he carried the works in handsome style, with his gallant North Carolinians, driving the enemy to our interior line, Col. Baker commanded on this occasion, to the entire satisfaction of his Division commander [W. H. F. Lee] & myself, whilst the conduct of the Officers and men, was admirable." As is often the case, no matter how many men are in a brawl, they each see and report a different part of it. In the end, however, there was some small victory possible for each because they did not have the same goals. Hampton probed and found the enemy, which was his mission for the day, while Wilson left McIntosh's brigade in control of Haw's Shop, which was part of his assignment, as the rest of his command marched back to the Totopotomoy.[239]

The cavalrymen listed below were among those

lost to the 2nd North Carolina Cavalry in the second fight around Haw's Shop, on June 3.

Combat Losses in the 2nd North Carolina Cavalry Haw's Shop, June 3, 1864

Trooper	Age	Co.	Fate
Radford Dishman		B	killed
Samuel A. Knox	20	B	wounded
William P. Roberts*	22	F&S	wounded
Liberty Chapman	22	D	captured
William H. Vaughn	22	D	captured
Joseph Baker*	34	D	killed
John B. Person	30	D	wounded
Richard M. Allison	42	B	wounded
Hembree C. Ledford	24	A	wounded
Andrew Jackson		I	captured

Information contained in this table came from Compiled Service Records as summarized by Louis H. Manarin, *North Carolina Troops: 1861–1865, A Roster*, vol. II, pages 98–177. (See Appendix for more information on the men listed above, page 402.)
*William P. Roberts remembered that Lieutenant Joseph Baker of Company D was lost during the fight at Haw's Shop on June 3, 1864. See William P. Roberts, "Additional Sketch Nineteenth Regiment (Second Cavalry)," p. 101.

Sheridan had moved D. McM. Gregg's and Torbert's cavalry divisions down to the Chickahominy River as far as Bottom's Bridge by nightfall on June 2. Fitz Lee's cavalry command was relieved on the Cold Harbor line on the afternoon of June 2 by Breckinridge's infantry and was ordered to move with C. M. Butler's brigade (from Hampton's division) to form a line along the south shore of the Chickahominy, standing between Sheridan and R. E. Lee's extreme right wing. Butler's brigade consisted of the 4th, 5th, and 6th South Carolina regiments and numbered over 1,200 men. It was perhaps the strongest Confederate cavalry brigade in the area (but certainly not the most experienced). Butler's South Carolina brigade arrived at the bridge first and notified Fitz Lee of Sheridan's arrival—Butler told Lee he was prepared to hold the bridge. Nonetheless, Fitz Lee moved his command down near Bottom's Bridge immediately. The situation was stable along the Chickahominy for several days, and Fitz Lee's command remained there until June 7.[240]

After the cavalry fight at Haw's Shop, W. H. F. Lee's command also moved southwest nearly ten miles to Meadow's Bridge on the Chickahominy River, where they rested several days. Then Chambliss's brigade was sent to roam the area around Grant's right as far as Old Church and to send scouts as far as White House on the Pamunkey. W. H. F. Lee kept the North Carolina brigade near his new headquarters at Malvern Hill. From there the North Carolinians pulled picket duty on the Chickahominy from above Bottom's Bridge to Long Bridge and the vicinity.[241]

On the evening of June 6 while camped near Meadow Bridge Rufus Barringer of the 1st North Carolina Cavalry learned he had been promoted and was the new commander of the North Carolina brigade to replace the late James B. Gordon.[242]

During this time of constant fighting and movement the North Carolina brigade underwent important changes in leadership. The loss of Stuart and Gordon was difficult for the cavalrymen to deal with, but there were also important changes in how the cavalry fought its daily battles. Stuart's special instructions issued to the cavalrymen in his corps after the Gettysburg Campaign were no longer as applicable as they were in the early years of the war. There were fewer mounted charges and more firing of rifles from entrenchments. In the first half of 1864, the cavalrymen learned to fight like infantrymen and move from fight to fight like cavalrymen. Rufus Barringer remembered later that when he took permanent command of the North Carolina brigade, the war was advancing through a period he described as follows: "…the sabre grew into less and less favor, and the policy of the great Tennessee cavalrymen, General N. B. Forest, was adopted, of using the revolver on horse and the rifle on foot."¹ The bravado of the charge with saber out front was used less frequently.[243]

The day after Barringer took command of the North Carolina brigade, he and his brigade were detached and moved down river to picket the lower bridges and fords—including Bottom's and Long Bridges on the Chickahominy River. The North Carolinians were R. E. Lee's shield on the Confederate right, and in a matter of days their position became even more important as both Hampton and Fitz Lee prepared their divisions to pursue Sheridan on his expedition to the Virginia Central Railroad toward Trevilian Station. Once Hampton and Fitz Lee had their commands marching westward,

Chambliss's Virginians of W. H. F. Lee's division had to cover the Confederate left — leaving the North Carolina brigade to shield the right along the Chickahominy down to the James River. Barringer's North Carolina brigade had support from the Richmond defenses from time to time, but had primary responsibility on that end of the line. W. H. F. Lee's two small cavalry brigades had to be the eyes and ears for the Army of Northern Virginia. On the Union side, with Sheridan and most of his cavalry on their expedition, only Wilson's division remained to shield Grant's army while it prepared its next move.[244]

In early June, while the fighting was taking place, R. E. Lee continued to extend and entrench his new line from Totopotomoy Creek, through Cold Harbor and down to the Chickahominy River — a line about twelve miles long. Grant's infantry also continued to file into a line facing the enemy, facing southwest, mostly west — almost to the Totopotomoy. By dawn on June 2, it was apparent to most this was going to be the site of the next bloodbath. The day was spent getting ready and on the 3rd, Grant once again gave the order to attack. The Confederate complex of entrenchments was remarkable, ultimately impenetrable yet Union infantrymen were sent at them all along the line. It took hardly an hour to lose another 7,000 men from the north, as nearly 1,500 from the south met similar fates. This final futile attempt to dislodge R. E. Lee's command caused Grant to pause and reconsider his position. When he reflected on his June 3 attacks, he concluded, "In this attempt our loss was heavy, while that of the enemy, I have reason to believe, was comparatively light. It was the only general attack made from the Rapidan to the James which did not inflict upon the enemy losses to compensate for our own." These losses also made a deep impression on his men.[245]

It had been nearly a month since Grant launched his Overland Campaign, and fighting had been almost constant with the armies in front of one another almost every day. At every stop, R. E. Lee would entrench; Grant would not back off but rather attack in costly and largely unsuccessful attempts to dislodge the Confederates. In less than a month, R. E. Lee had lost around 25,000 men, while Grant lost nearly 45,000. Nonetheless, the scene was set for the tragedy to continue.[246]

GRANT'S NEW PLAN

As fighting at Cold Harbor resulted in yet another costly stalemate, Grant developed a new plan to draw R. E. Lee out of his entrenchments by moving in three direction. First he planned to send the cavalry off, in his words, "...to Charlottesville and Gordonsville to effectively break up the railroad connection between Richmond and the Shenandoah Valley and Lynchburg; and when the cavalry got well off to move the army to the south of the James River, by the enemy's right flank, where I felt I could cut off all his resources of supply except by the canal." Grant planned to move David Hunter out of the Shenandoah Valley and have him destroy the Confederate supply depot at Lynchburg and then move eastward destroying the Virginia Central Railroad. The plan also called for Hunter to Join Sheridan's cavalry near Charlottesville along the proposed path of destruction. Sheridan was scheduled to take two cavalry divisions on June 7 and begin destroying the same railroad hit by Hunter, but coming from the eastern end of the rails and heading west until the two Union forces meet. Once Sheridan and Hunter joined forces, they were to move south of Richmond and join the Army of the Potomac. While Hunter and Sheridan had everyone's attention, Grant planned to pull out of Cold Harbor and quickly move across the James River, drawing with him R. E. Lee and the Army of Northern Virginia. Conquering Petersburg and thereby cutting the remaining rail network that supplied Richmond was also part of Grant's plan. On June 9, General Benjamin F. Butler and August Kautz's cavalry were to move on Petersburg, capture the city if possible but at least cut the rail connections across the Appomattox River. To secure the move on Petersburg, Grant planned to send General William F. Smith and his command to Petersburg by the waterways — down the Pamunkey to City Point and then to Petersburg in advance of the rest of the Army of the Potomac. He was certain such a move would draw R. E. Lee out into the open for a final fight. This plan was a little more complicated than Grant's previous ones — all of which had been designed to draw the Confederates out of their entrenchments — but it still required

Grant's infantry to get where they were going before R. E. Lee, and most importantly before Lee's infantry could again entrench. If all went well, B. F. Butler and Kautz could take and hold Petersburg before R. E. Lee's infantry got there. If not, certainly W. F. Smith could beat R. E. Lee to Petersburg and reinforce B. F. Butler. However, Grant's problems were familiar. R. E. Lee had a shorter route, and more importantly the Confederates had Beauregard's small command already in the area. Nonetheless, Grant was confident his plan would work this time.[247]

Grant's moves got off to a good start but soon faltered. For one thing, Grant had not anticipated the lively and determined response R. E. Lee was able to get from his men. At the same time, Grant and his top commanders expected more from their men than they were able to get.[248]

By this time in the campaign, Grant assumed R. E. Lee's men must be beaten, must be ready to walk back to their homes. Grant wrote that morale was high among Confederate soldiers even after Antietam and Gettysburg, but "The battles of the Wilderness, Spotsylvania, North Anna, and Cold Harbor, bloody and terrible as they were on our side, were even more damaging to the enemy, and so crippled him as to make him wary ever after of taking the offensive." Grant concluded the morale among the Confederate troopers must be low, while his army must be full of confidence, sensing the victory he felt was near.[249]

While Grant assumed his troops had higher morale than the enemy, he was himself a bit discouraged. Once again he had been unable to defeat the well entrenched Army of Northern Virginia. He had spent his men; thousands of them had been lost in seemingly hopeless charges into R. E. Lee's defenses — perhaps some had been lost as a response to his frustration. His report on the events seem to reflect the somewhat rambling reflections and justifications for what he was trying to accomplish during the campaign — perhaps it was less a justification than an effort to remind himself that it was all worth it.[250]

Once Hunter had moved out of the Shenandoah Valley, R. E. Lee sent Jubal Early toward Lynchburg to meet him. General Early's command and been beaten down in numbers but not in spirit — he carried about 10,000 men to meet Hunter's approximately 15,000. When Hunter arrived at Early's entrenchments at Lynchburg, he decided conditions were not right and he pulled back — well into West Virginia. This left the Valley open to the Confederates, and R. E. Lee left General Early there to worry Grant and hopefully draw from the latter's strength around Richmond.[251]

Sheridan's move on the railroad coming to Richmond from the west was just a bit more successful than Hunter's had been, but it too was not what Grant had hoped for. Sheridan moved with around 7,000 horsemen, and R. E. Lee sent Hampton with his and Fitz Lee's divisions, about 5,000 cavalrymen, after Sheridan. (W. H. F. Lee and his North Carolina brigade spread themselves even more thinly on the Chickahominy as they relieved Fitz Lee's command.) Hampton's command caught Sheridan's cavalry near Trevilian Station, northwest of Richmond on June 11. For two days the cavalries fought, suffering the bloodiest cavalry battle of the war.[252]

Two days prior to the cavalry fight at Trevilian Station the North Carolina brigade in its new position along the lower Chickahominy settled into the Confederate line, though somewhat unsettled by the ominous blue army massed in front of them. Just as the cavalrymen with Hampton and Sheridan expected a major battle, so did the men of the 2nd North Carolina Cavalry — perhaps from Grant's infantry.[253]

During this tense time on June 9, John P. Lockhart of the 2nd North Carolina Cavalry wrote to his mother and sister from near Gaines's Mill about midway in the North Carolina line along the Chickahominy. He described the atmosphere in these words.

We are in the frontline of fortifications, about one mile from Gaines' Farm. The Yankees' breastworks are about three hundred yards from ours. At one point they are not more than seventy-five or a hundred yards. Evening before last the Yanks sent in a flag of truce to bury their dead, and the pickets have quit firing at each other in our brigade since then; before, we could not raise our heads above the works but what they would fire at us, but now we can walk about, out of our works and look at each other as much as we please. The hills are blue with them about here.

We have three lines of troops at this point. Clingman's Brigade is in the rear of ours. The front runs around the bow of a hill and we have got a ditch cut about four feet deep, through the hill in our rear to get out to get water in time of an engagement.

...I think the Yankees are going to make a desperate struggle to break our lines at this place, but if they don't mind they will have the dust to bite if they charge our ranks at this point.... I believe the sharp-shooters are going to commence firing again, and if they do, we will not see any more peace while we stay on this front line.[254]

After describing the scene at the front Lockhart ended his letter with words more suited for a parent's ears: "Well, Mother, we are getting first rate rations now. We get a half pound of meat per day, plenty of bread, coffee and sugar, and sometimes rice and peas and onions, etc.... Our Company [K] is getting along very well; no casualties since May 10th; I am tolerable well...." Actually, Robert S. Walker, was wounded on May 22, James R. Harris was wounded on May 24, and William C. Hall was captured on May 27 — all from Company K, 2nd North Carolina Cavalry. Nonetheless, Lockhart's description of their rations was likely accurate considering their proximity to Richmond and its supplies.

The attack John P. Lockhart and his fellow cavalrymen expected came while they were on duty near Long Bridge — the 2nd North Carolina had rotated into picket duty along that section of the Chickahominy on June 12. The next day, young John W. Gordon of Company C noted in his diary, "The enemy crossed the Chickahominy in large force, but not held in check by our brigade until evening when part of Heth's division relieved us and we about sunset marched toward Malvern Hill, where we arrived about ten o'clock."[255] It was difficult for the cavalrymen to gauge the magnitude and intent of the Union move across Bottom's Bridge that day, but they remained alert — it might be another probe or a major move by Grant's army. (See map 2.1.)

Stalemate: Grant Moves Toward Petersburg, June 12

While Generals Early and Hampton were occupied west of Richmond and R. E. Lee had one eye cast in their direction, Grant made his move out of Cold Harbor after nightfall on June 12. He had already sent Smith's command to Petersburg by the rivers — now he moved the Fifth Corps across the Chickahominy at Long Bridge and on to White Oak Swamp to cover the crossing of the other corps. The Fifth Corps was shielded by Wilson's cavalry division. Grant's pullout and move across the James toward Petersburg was well executed, so it was days before R. E. Lee was certain that Grant was moving on Petersburg and not Richmond.[256]

Early in the day on June 13, R. E. Lee's pickets found that Grant had left the Cold Harbor line, so they crossed to the south side of the Chickahominy and moved eastward from Richmond to establish a shield for the capital. R. E. Lee sent the cavalry out to find Grant's new position. By the 14th, Lee knew that Grant had troops crossing to the James, and Lee was ready to send Hoke back to Beauregard. Grant had two corps approaching Petersburg on the 15th of the month. The Union Eighteenth Corps reached Petersburg first, but did not realize that Beauregard had only a small force, about 2,500 men, so they hesitated. Even though Petersburg's defenses were thinly manned, the invaders could see heavy breastworks, trenches, and ditches that ran for more than ten miles — with cannon carefully placed and visible here and there. The sight would give any reasonable man cause to pause and ponder the wisdom of a frontal attack. Union troops finally advanced late in the day and overran about a mile of the line, capturing a number of guns. After dark, however, Beauregard's men dug a new line, and were finally reinforced with two infantry divisions. On the 16th R. E. Lee sent George E. Pickett's still decimated division and Charles W. Field's command, both in Richard H. Anderson's corps, to Beauregard's line. Under great pressure Beauregard had pulled his line from the Bermuda Hundreds back to Petersburg. R. E. Lee was at Drewry's Bluff when the last Union infantry crossed the James late on June 16 — they were followed by their cavalry around midnight. By June 17, R. E. Lee realized that Grant was sending his main army at Petersburg. By nightfall Beauregard's line was on the outskirts of Petersburg where the Confederates held.[257]

Grant's command continued to move south and by June 18 Beauregard was facing approximately 70,000 Union infantrymen. However, by the time the Union forces were able to mount a serious attack, R. E. Lee had most of his command in the line. More importantly, the nearly exhausted Confederate troops were ready to defend Petersburg and fight for Robert E. Lee. On the other side, Meade and other Union commanders were desperately trying to get their troops to assault the formidable enemy line.[258]

CAVALRY ACTION WHILE GRANT MOVED TO THE JAMES RIVER

When Grant moved out of Cold Harbor on June 12, the North Carolina Cavalry was on the line in the trenches on the Confederate right picketing the lower Chickahominy River. Chambliss and his brigade were still on the Confederate left. On the 11th, Chambliss reported that one of his scouts found very little activity around the Union supply depot at White House on the river, and that there was talk of Grant going to the James in a few days. On the morning of the 13th, Chambliss described his line from Cold Harbor to Old Church, and noted that he had dropped down near Gaines's house that evening and all indications were still suggesting Grant was about to move his army rather than attack. In fact, later in the day, W. H. F. Lee learned from Chambliss that the enemy had left their front and appeared to be heading down river toward White House, and Burnside's command was also on the move.[259]

While Chambliss was detecting Grant's early moves, the Union commander not only had his infantry in motion, but had Wilson's cavalry division covering the front and rear of his move toward Long Bridge. Wilson and several of his brigades arrived at Long Bridge on June 12. Warren was also there with Grant's Fifth Corps. By midnight, Wilson had Chapman's brigade across the Chickahominy and, as the head of Warren's infantry column appeared, Chapman was ordered to advance. He found in front of him pickets from the North Carolina Cavalry Brigade who immediately did their job—they slowly withdrew toward White Oak Swamp and notified their commander.[260]

Very early on the morning of June 13, W. H. F. Lee in his headquarters near Malvern Hill received an urgent message from Barringer, who was still headquartered near Bottom's Bridge, stating that the enemy had driven in his pickets at Long Bridge and was constructing a pontoon bridge at that point. The 2nd North Carolina Cavalry had rotated into the picket line the day before. W. H. F. Lee immediately notified R. E. Lee, and put the two North Carolina cavalry regiments still in camp, along with one piece of artillery, on the road toward the bridge.[261]

By 7:00 A.M., W. H. F. Lee, his staff and the North Carolina brigade collected on the north side of White Oak Swamp and posted artillery in some old breastworks. Wilson also moved his Union cavalry and some artillery up and exchanged fire for a while, but made no attempt to cross White Oak at that point because of the strong position taken by the North Carolinians. Crawford's division of Warren's infantry came up and held the line in front of the North Carolina brigade, while Wilson moved his cavalrymen toward Riddle's Shop, near Richmond. The point of the move toward Richmond was to keep R. E. Lee uncertain about Grant's direction as long as possible. A detachment from the North Carolina Cavalry Brigade caught up with Chapman's cavalry, around 4:00 P.M. and had a brief skirmish. By 11:00 P.M., Wilson withdrew Chapman's brigade and sent them on the Charles City Court House road toward Samaria Church (Saint Mary's Church). His cavalry had done their job that day—they kept the only Confederate cavalry in the area busy while Grant's infantry moved east of them, heading south. Barringer's North Carolina brigade had pulled back from White Oak Swamp about an hour earlier leaving infantry from Heth's division to hold the Confederate position.[262]

Wilson camped Chapman's brigade at Nance's Shop around 2:00 A.M. on June 14. Just to their cavalry's rear early that morning, Grant's infantry started crossing the James River and heading for Petersburg. By afternoon, the last of Grant's infantry crossed the Chickahominy at Long Bridge with Wilson's other cavalry brigade, commanded by McIntosh, following them over.[263]

While Wilson was reuniting his cavalry near Samaria Church on June 14, W. H. F. Lee had Barringer's North Carolina brigade near Harrison's Landing and Wilcox's house, where they had followed some of Grant's trains. When the North Carolinians arrived at the James, they watched the last of Grant's column cross for the day just down river. They were in awe at the sight of the vast Union wagon trains stretching along the opposite shore, and "a forest of masts crowded the southern shore and armed vessels lay in the river." A member of W. H. F. Lee's staff went on to mention that "I could read the names of several large steamers and one or two ugly looking customers had up steam and were moving slowly up and down stream." These gun boats were worrisome because, as the North Carolina column of cavalrymen approached the river, well within range. Any action by Barringer's small cavalry was altogether pointless—but, as if demanding to at least be noticed, W. H. F. Lee had two guns from McGregor's Battery brought across the wide open plain and onto a high bluff where they could survey the awesome panorama on the river and its opposite shore. McGregor's guns sent several rounds into the shipping and then into the camps, causing momentary panic among the soldiers and mules—and the Federal gun boats noticed. Garnett of W. H. F. Lee's staff, summed up the nonsense of the day and price paid with the following comments:

Only a few rounds had been fired when a long, low-lying, dun-colored gun-boat came slowly up stream, and before she arrived fairly opposite to the position of our battery, Capt. McGregor gave his order to "limber up" and we retired—just in time to escape destruction. As we were driving back across the open plain, a heavy shell passed over the battery, in exact line, and burst with tremendous force, only a short distance ahead of us in front of the leading gun. Before we got out of the field another shell passed over us and struck in our column as it stood in the main road, with its exposed flank, killing two men and horses. The column was speedily moved, and night coming on we marched back to our old position near Malvern Hill.[264]

The 2nd North Carolina Cavalry's recorder losses during the several days before Grant moved to Petersburg were as follows.

Combat Losses in the 2nd North Carolina Cavalry June 10–16, 1864

Trooper	Age	Co.	Fate
Edward W. Porter	22	D	wounded, June 13, 1864
Daniel R. McDonald	31	I	captured, June 14, 1864

Information contained in this table came from Compiled Service Records as summarized by Louis H. Manarin, *North Carolina Troops: 1861–1865, A Roster*, vol. II, pages 98–177. (See Appendix for more information on the men listed above, page 402.)

On June 15, James H. Wilson's Union cavalrymen and the North Carolina regiments spent the day demonstrating and probing into one another's positions from White Oak Swamp to Malvern Hill. Early that morning, Barringer's North Carolinians were skirmishing with enemy cavalry on the road from Samaria Church to Rock's. Barringer's command was pushed out of Rock's and had a hard fight to push their way back. Meanwhile, other cavalrymen from Wilson's division pushed W. H. F. Lee's staff and pickets from Malvern Hill until Colonel M. W. Gary's Confederate cavalrymen (of the Department of Richmond) arrived and drove the enemy back. By evening, Gary was pushing Wilson's cavalrymen back along the road from Riddell's to Nance's Shop, while Barringer and his North Carolinians were pushing enemy cavalry back on all roads south of Gary's route. By evening of the 15th, A. P. Hill had moved his infantry command down, with his left on White Oak Swamp, and M. W. Gary's cavalry between him and the enemy horsemen.[265]

Chambliss's brigade stayed northwest of the action between the Chickahominy and Pamunkey Rivers, and he continued to report that increasingly there was no enemy in the area. He continued to be concerned, however, that Sheridan might return from his raids on the Virginia Central at any time and hit the Confederate rear, so he remained in the area.[266]

On June 16, Barringer's North Carolina brigade continued to skirmish and probe Wilson's cavalry screen covering the rear of Grant's column as it crossed the James. They fought again at Rocks, Malvern Hill, Nance's Shop, Phillip's Farm, Crenshaw's, and Herring Creek. While probing the Union screen, the North Carolina regiments also formed a picket line between Malvern Hill and Grant's column to keep Wilson's cavalry probes back. On June 16, the 2nd North Carolina was placed on the picket line in front of W. H. F. Lee's headquarters at Malvern Hill. While Confederate generals tried to understand the magnitude and significance of Grant's movements, Private John W. Gordon of the 2nd North Carolina Cavalry spent a second day on the picket line without rations and wondered when he might next find something to eat.[267]

Other North Carolinians followed W. H. F. Lee on a probe into the enemy column which once again took them to the James, near

Wilcox's Landing, on June 17. From there he looked across the river at Grant's massive army and reported by late afternoon, "Can see no opportunity of doing anything, as the Peninsula is flanked by large number of gun boats. There are ten in sight from this place." About an hour later R. E. Lee sent his son a short message that read, "Push after enemy and endeavor to ascertain what has become of Grant's army. Inform General Hill." If Grant had known that as of late afternoon on June 17, R. E. Lee still had to ask such a question, he certainly would have been proud of the cavalry screen Wilson's horsemen had provided. Though R. E. Lee still felt some uncertainty about the location of the main body of Grant's army, on the basis of reports coming from Beauregard around Petersburg, he had started troops in that direction. During the night of June 17, W. H. F. Lee, concerned that perhaps his first message had not been received, sent another containing these words, "Grant's entire army is across the river. His cavalry [Wilson's division] crossed about 3 P.M. to-day." The confirmation received, R. E. Lee could move his main force south of Richmond.[268]

On June 18, W. H. F. Lee had Barringer and his North Carolina brigade in camp near Malvern Hill while his other brigade, under Chambliss, was still up patrolling the south side of the Pamunkey. Chambliss was not yet aware of Sheridan's return from Trevilian's Station but he anticipated it. He was also expecting Hampton to return that day and wanted to stay in the area should the two cavalries once again clash at the Pamunkey.[269]

The cavalry that had been on Robert E. Lee's line was still widely dispersed by the time he decided to send his army across the James River. Colonel Gary's cavalry remained with the Richmond defenses, and Chambliss remained north of the James to cooperate with Hampton in delaying Sheridan as he approached White House. Hampton was ordered to stay with and attack Sheridan when possible—if Sheridan escaped, Hampton had instructions to move quickly to Petersburg. On June 18, Robert E. Lee ordered W. H. F. Lee to proceed to Petersburg with Barringer and his North Carolina brigade as rapidly as possible because Wilson's cavalry division was already there. Around noon, W. H. F. Lee and his North Carolina regiments left Malvern Hill and crossed the James on a pontoon bridge at Chaffin's Bluff—a short distance down river from Drewry's Bluff. They halted for the night at Swift Creek. On that occasion, seventeen-year-old John W. Gordon noted in his diary: "My horse being unfit for duty, I marched on foot. I am still without rations. I halted 4 miles from Suip [Swift] Creek." The next day the North Carolinians continued south and marched through Petersburg then southwest out Boydton Plank Road.[270]

While Private Gordon contemplated his tired feet and empty stomach, late on June 18, R. E. Lee sent the above information to President Davis and closed with the P.S.: "I go to Petersburg."[271]

Six

The Siege of Petersburg, Mid-June 1864 to April 1865

By June 18, 1864 both Robert E. Lee and Ulysses S. Grant had amassed their main forces around Petersburg. Lee knew well what his new position meant. Some days earlier he had told General Jabul Early that if Grant gets across the James River and to the gates of Petersburg, the Army of Northern Virginia will have but one option — to defend against a siege. In Lee's words, "...and then it will be a mere question of time."[1]

However, Grant did not have siege on his mind. He had not totally abandoned the goal of his Overland Campaign. He still sought to destroy the Army of Northern Virginia, but his repeated moves toward Richmond and then Petersburg could no longer be used to draw R. E. Lee out of his entrenchments — Grant's army was already in front of those cities. He needed another lure. As Grant stood before Petersburg, he knew the city was a railroad hub through which much of the supplies heading for Richmond had to pass. He would try but if he could not take Petersburg, he at least wanted to destroy or capture its supply lines coming from the south and west. The first targets in this revised agenda were the Weldon Railroad coming up from North Carolina, the Richmond & Danville Railroad coming from the south and west, feeding both Richmond and Petersburg, and the South Side Railroad coming from the Richmond & Danville. Grant decided to envelop Petersburg, cut off Richmond, and, of course, draw R. E. Lee's army out of its trenches in search of supplies. Though by this time he was beginning to speak less of destroying the Army of Northern Virginia immediately.

Initial Efforts to Envelop Petersburg

Grant's first effort was to send infantry around the Confederate right, take the Weldon Railroad and circle around Petersburg northward to dismantle and hold the South Side Railroad. By June 21, 1864 Meade had the Second Corps moving into position on the Union left — extending the line from the Fifth Corps. The new line was along the Jerusalem Plank Road, facing west toward the Weldon. The men of the Second Corps began arriving around midday and immediately began entrenching and sent out skirmishing parties toward the railroad.[2]

Also by that time, W. H. F. Lee had his North Carolina Cavalry brigade, commanded by Rufus Barringer, spread along the Weldon Railroad — their job was to detect and impede any Union movement at or around the Confederate right, and specifically, any assault on the railroad. Hampton's and Fitz Lee's cavalry divisions were still on Sheridan's trail leading from Trevilian Station to the Union supply depot at White House on the Pamunkey River. Consequently, once again the North Carolina cavalry regiments were posted directly in the path of Grant's next planned move. To add momentum to the Union move, the Sixth Corps moved up behind the Second as the push westward across the Weldon Railroad began.

The Union skirmishers sent out from the Second Corps were the first to encounter the North Carolina cavalrymen who had set their screen just east of the railroad. Skirmishing took place along an approximately two mile stretch of the area between Jerusalem Plank Road and the railroad and lasted for several hours. Then the Federals made a more serious probe toward the Weldon. Francis C. Barlow, commanding the 1st Division of the Union Second Corps, was sent to probe the Confederate strength on and just west of the railroad — he had some cavalry with him, but they proved to be of little use against the Confederate cavalry that met him a mile or two in front of the railroad. Barlow met the North Carolina cavalrymen near the Davis farm.[3]

Fight Around Davis's Farm, June 21

Around 1:00 P.M. June 21, Barlow reported that he and his Union infantrymen were about two and a half miles from the railroad, and his "cavalry report the enemy in force and have had a little firing. It is nothing. I am pushing on my skirmishers." The North Carolina cavalrymen sent word of the enemy advance and Rufus Barringer concentrated his force in front of the oncoming Union infantry.[4] Barringer described the scene:

We were wholly without support, but the thick undergrowth and other surroundings favored a vigorous resistance in a dismounted fight. I selected high point for my horse artillery under McGregor, and as far as possible screened it from the enemy's view. I also kept the Fifth Cavalry (Sixty-third North Carolina Regiment) mounted, in reserve to support McGregor and otherwise act as emergency might require. I then dismounted the First, Second and Third Cavalry, and formed two heavy skirmish lines, well concealed in thick undergrowth in front of the railroad, with instructions for the first line not to fire until the Federals were in less than one hundred yards of them, and then after a single volley to slowly retire on the second line, where the real fight was to be made. At this juncture also the full battery of four guns was to open.[5]

About an hour after his first report that afternoon, Barlow reported they had advanced not more than another half mile toward the railroad, and he acknowledged his encounter with Barringer's first line of defense — "We have had quite a skirmish with what I think are the enemy's cavalry, dismounted. We drove them back and are advancing. Our cavalry is of no use to us." Barlow's encounter with the first line of North Carolina cavalrymen gave him an unwarranted sense of confidence, and he pushed his men forward.[6] According to Private Means of the 5th North Carolina, Barlow sent his men into a very deadly situation.

The enemy mistook the movement of our [first] line for a flight. They poured into the woods by thousands. Suddenly McGregor's guns opened; for a moment the heavy lines of the enemy faltered and then fell back under the shock of this splendid battery, but rallying quickly they again rushed forward when all at once a furious, deadly fire from the dismounted men [of the 1st, 2nd, and 3rd North Carolina], at short range, cut them down by scores. The Federal officers dashed bravely forward and called upon their men to follow. But volley after volley thinned their ranks and they broke and fled.[7]

The difficulty some of Barlow's officers had motivating their men to charge into the face of fierce enemy fire can probably be explained as the same hesitation exhibited by many reasonable men in the month after May 1864. Meade and his commanders had been having difficulty getting their troopers to attack enemy entrenchments around Petersburg for days as a result of the bloody fighting they had been a part of in the Wilderness, near Spotsylvania Court House, and Cold Harbor. Many of the Union fighting men had developed what came to be known as the "Cold Harbor Syndrome." While Confederate troops, at least as tired and probably even hungrier, were ready to defend Petersburg and fight for Robert E. Lee.[8]

Nonetheless, the Union forces did move toward the North Carolina line slowly and unevenly. At the farthest advance of Barlow's troopers, the opposing lines were very near one another and both sides took prisoners in the close fighting. After a while, Union infantrymen began to break and in the confusion that followed, John Baker commanding the 3rd North Carolina and several other men charged forward rather imprudently and were captured — among those captured with Baker was Barringer's aide, Lieutenant F. C. Foard. Baker was never exchanged and did not return to service in his regiment; On the other hand, Foard "made a daring and miraculous escape by jumping from a car window of a fast running train between Washington and Baltimore," and returned to Barringer's staff.[9]

Just after 10:00 P.M. on June 21, David B. Birney, commanding the 3rd Division of the Union Second Army Corps, reported that his division was in place on the left of their line near Jerusalem Plank Road and that the following had taken place: "The withdrawal of Barlow's [1st] division from the reconnaissance toward the Weldon railroad brought on an attack of the enemy on my left flank toward dark.

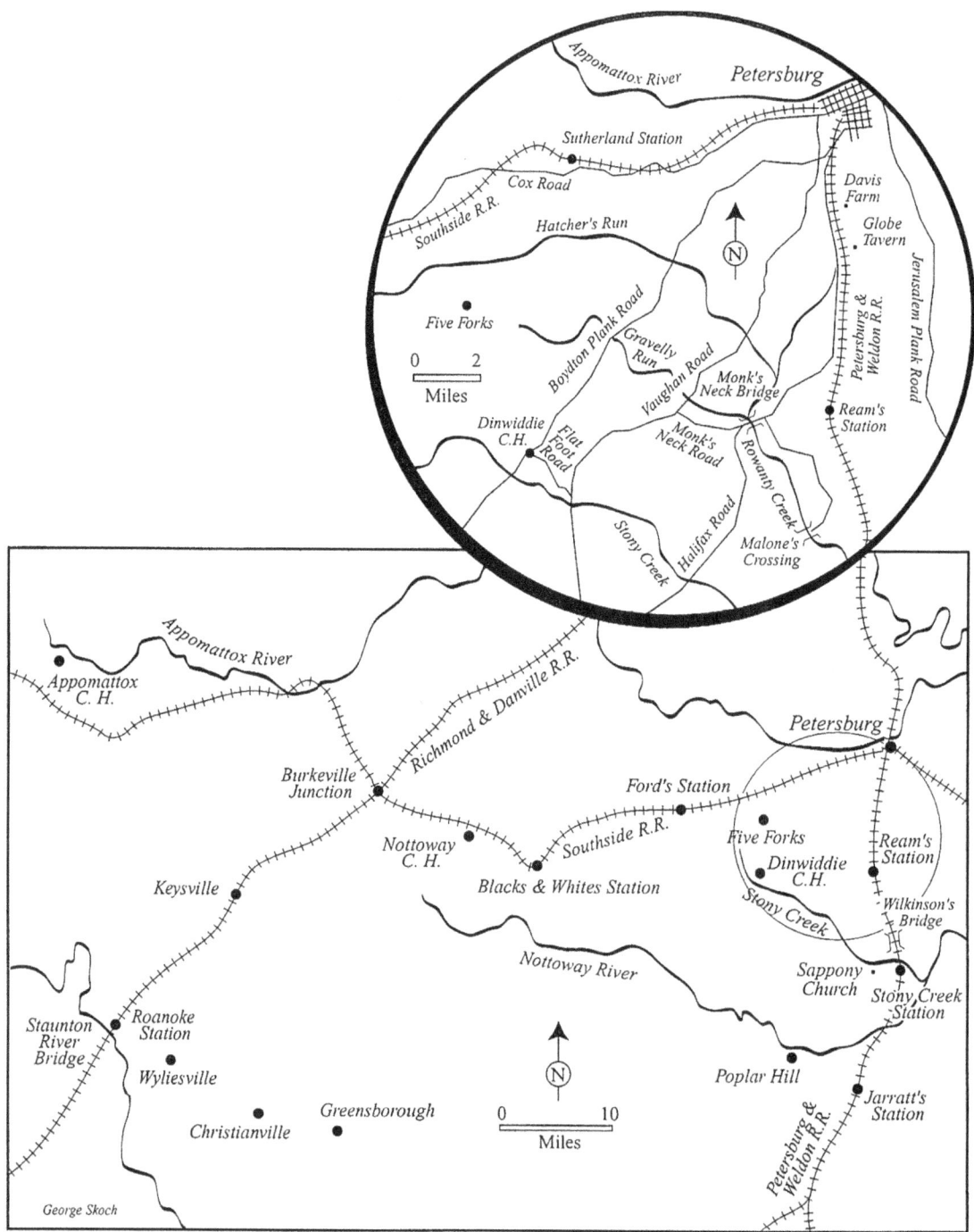

6.1: Siege of Petersburg and Wilson-Kautz Raid

The [Birney's] cavalry was driven back, but my infantry soon checked the [enemy] advance. It was reported to me as consisting of cavalry and infantry."[10]

Birney was correct; by the time his 3rd Di-vision came up to support the wavering 1st division under Barlow, Barringer's North Carolina cavalrymen had been supported by Wilcox's infantry division from A. P. Hill's Third Army Corps. Wilcox's infantrymen and the North Carolina cavalrymen pursued Barlow's retreating command into the line held by Birney's division—to within a few hundred yards of Jerusalem Plank Road where they fought until darkness fell.[11]

When Wade Hampton later wrote of the North Carolina Brigade's fighting on June 21, he may have overlooked the infantry support they received late in the day, but he made clear his appreciation for a job well done.

On the 21st the N.C. Brigade was attacked in its new position by a strong force of Infantry & after a brisk fight, not only repulsed the assaulting column, but drove them from the field, forcing them to leave their dead & wounded & capturing prisoners from nine Regiments.[12]

According to Barringer, the resistance offered by the North Carolinians resulted in 40 dead and 20 prisoners left behind by the Union force and in 27 recorded losses in his command. Among the Confederates lost that day, at least six were from the 2nd North Carolina Cavalry.[13]

Combat Losses in the 2nd North Carolina Cavalry Near Davis's Farm, June 21

Trooper	Age	Co.	Fate
Robert J. Barkley	30	B	killed
John Jones	36	E	mortally wounded
Franklin F. Gurganus	25	G	wounded
Albert F. Faucett	27	K	wounded
Levi Y. Lockhart	24	K	captured
Jesse V. Roberts		K	captured

Information contained in this table came from Compiled Service Records as summarized by Louis H. Manarin, *North Carolina Troops: 1861–1865, A Roster*, vol. II, pages 98–177. (See Appendix for more information on the men listed above, page 402.)

With the Union's Second Corps stopped before the Weldon Railroad, R. E. Lee had time to move more troops down and expand his right as Grant moved more divisions south extending his left. Wilcox's and Mahone's divisions from A. P. Hill's command were moved down to ultimately stop Grant's flanking move. On June 22, Grant's Second and Sixth Corps tried to coordinate another attack on the Confederate right and encircle Petersburg but failed, and the Union line along Jerusalem Plank Road dug in deeper. Whether it was widely acknowledged by Union commanders at the time or not, the Siege of Petersburg had begun. The beginning of the siege marked the end of the major battles that had characterized Grant's Overland Campaign during the previous six weeks. Grant now had his enemy pinned down, but he had not yet destroyed the Army of Northern Virginia. However, this siege was the longest operation of the war and it ultimately wore the Army of Northern Virginia down to a shadow of its former self—it did not end for nine and one half months. Once the infantry lines along the Weldon Railroad were in place, Grant again tried to cut R. E. Lee's and Petersburg's supply lines by sending cavalry under the command of James H. Wilson and August Kautz on a railroad raid just as Sheridan was returning from his unsuccessful raid as far as Trevilian Station on the Virginia Central Railroad.[14]

NORTH OF THE JAMES, THE BATTLE OF SAMARIA CHURCH, JUNE 24

Sheridan's return trip from Trevilian Station was not an easy one. Wade Hampton's cavalry command harassed the rear of his column most of the way. Robert E. Lee was kept informed of Sheridan's return to the Richmond area, and on June 16 he sent a message to Hampton, who was still in pursuit of Sheridan, informing him that Martin Gary's cavalry command and John Chambliss's brigade were still north of the James River and were instructed to join him to "crush" Sheridan. By June 18, Hampton was instructed to bring his cavalry to the right of the Confederate line as soon as possible, if Sheridan made it to the Union supply depot at the White House on the Pamunkey River.[15] (See map 2.1.)

The Union column reached the Pamunkey River on June 17, and the next day Sheridan's cavalrymen were arriving at the White House. Hampton did not immediately head south according to his earlier instructions once Sheridan arrived at the Union depot; rather he stayed to fight a while. When Hampton's men arrived, they began skirmishing and shelling the Union depot. Fitz Lee's cavalrymen crossed the Pamunkey on June 20 and were joined by Chambliss's brigade. When Wilson and Kautz began their railroad raid south of Petersburg on June 21, Sheridan's troops were skirmishing with Confederate cavalrymen near the White

House supply depot. A couple of days later, Sheridan was assigned the task of escorting the supply train carrying goods from the White House to south of the James—it consisted of about 900 wagons and stretched over four miles. At the same time, Chambliss's men were already engaging the Union cavalrymen as far south as Charles City Court House, and the cavalries had minor engagements as Sheridan's cavalry screened the train's move toward Deep Bottom. Hampton was taking his main force toward Bottom's Bridge. On June 24, Gary's cavalry command joined Hampton. Hampton collected and stretched his command in a line with their left reaching north to near Nance's Shop—he was positioned for a major confrontation with Sheridan. The battle centered on Samaria (Saint Mary's) Church. Sheridan's force was driven back toward Charles City Court House but survived. The Union cavalrymen crossed the James River the next day and were ordered to move down to the Jerusalem Plank Road to assist Wilson's reentry. Most of the Union supplies made it across intact, but Sheridan had not kept Hampton engaged north of the James until Wilson's railroad raid was complete.[16]

Hampton's command did not have the strength to follow their enemy to the river and he was instructed to head for Petersburg while Fitz Lee was to follow with his division. Chambliss's brigade was moved quickly south of Petersburg to reinforce the 3rd North Carolina Cavalry between Wilson's returning column and the Weldon Railroad.[17]

Wilson and Kautz Raid on the Railroads, June 22–July 1

While Sheridan and Hampton were making their way back from Trevilian Station, and Barringer's North Carolina brigade was fighting around Davis's farm on June 21, James H. Wilson received orders from Meade to mobilize his cavalry division and four regiments of August Kautz's cavalry command from the Army of The James. If Grant's infantry could not get around the Confederate right, maybe his cavalry could. They were instructed to head for Burkesville where the Petersburg & Lynchburg, and Richmond & Danville Railroads intersect. Their task was to do as much damage as possible to the Richmond & Danville, the South Side (running from Burkesville to Petersburg), and the Petersburg & Weldon Railroads. They were to continue their destruction until the enemy stopped them. Wilson was told that as he began his raid, Meade's infantry would push across and hold the Weldon Railroad around Reams's Station, thus protecting the cavalrymen's return if necessary. Wilson was also assured that Sheridan, who was then near the Union White House depot on the Pamunkey River, would keep Hampton's and Fitz Lee's cavalries busy north of the James. If Sheridan could keep that promise, only W. H. F. Lee's North Carolina Cavalry brigade and Dearing's small cavalry command were left to limit the destructive mission assigned to the Union raiding party. In addition to the assurances, Wilson was told that the cavalry operation was all a part of Grant's larger plan for isolating Petersburg and ultimately Richmond. It was an important mission, and he set out with a force of about 5,500 cavalrymen.[18] (See map 6.1.)

As indicated, when the Union raid began, W. H. F. Lee's Virginia brigade under Chambliss was still north of the James and by then fighting Sheridan's men in conjunction with Hampton's command. To strengthen the Army of Northern Virginia's critical right wing, Special Orders No. 26 on June 19 ordered Brigadier General James Dearing with his 4th North Carolina, 7th Confederate, and 62nd Georgia cavalries to join Barringer's North Carolina brigade near Jerusalem Plank Road and attach to W. H. F. Lee's division. However, Dearing's brigade was not yet an effective replacement for Chambliss's Virginia regiments—they had just been brigaded on May 5 under the temporary command of Dearing. Nonetheless, the cavalrymen under W. H. F. Lee would have to get to know one another on the road because Wilson had his command under way at 2:00 A.M. on June 22.[19]

Wilson's planned route took him around the Confederate right—down the Jerusalem Plank Road, then over to the Weldon and on to Reams's Station; then west to Dinwiddie Court House; then north through Five Forks to the South Side Railroad. From there they planned to follow the railroad to Burkesville and out the Richmond & Danville Railroad as far as possible. Kautz's command was in advance of the Union column heading for Reams's Station. They encountered pickets from Barringer's

North Carolina brigade soon after they turned south along Jerusalem Plank Road. They had no difficulty driving the enemy pickets from their path; consequently, the Confederate commanders were made aware of the Union column. Kautz learned from captured pickets that W. H. F. Lee's command was guarding the railroad. So, he took evasive action by moving westward to the Boydton Plank Road and then on to Dinwiddie Court House. Wilson's division continued directly toward Reams's Station along the Jerusalem Plank Road without delay.[20]

While W. H. F. Lee was determining the direction and size of Wilson's column, he received orders to mobilize Barringer's 1st, 2nd, and 5th North Carolina cavalries along with Dearing small brigade and McGregor's battery. They were quickly in pursuit of the enemy cavalry (he left the 3rd North Carolina Cavalry to picket the Weldon on the Confederate right).

Wilson's column cut over to the Weldon from Jerusalem Plank Road just before Reams's Station, and cavalrymen were detached to destroy railroad property. However, destruction around the station was brought to a premature end that afternoon as the rear of Wilson's column, brought up by Chapman's brigade, was still passing over the tracks, the advance of W. H. F. Lee's column came up on their right. The Confederates sent out skirmishers and directed their artillery at the Union column which hurried them along. By the time W. H. F. Lee pushed the rear of Wilson's column out of Reams's Station, he was fully aware of the enemy's direction and he too set a course toward Dinwiddie Court House.[21]

The columns of combatants, led by Kautz's command, followed by Wilson's division and finally W. H. F. Lee's small command went west to and through Dinwiddie Court House. The two opposing cavalries turned north through Five Forks and struck the South Side Railroad and each other at about the same time.

There was also some contact along the route. From Reams's Station, W. H. F. Lee's cavalry pressed the rear of Wilson's column until well after dark. Chapman's brigade, still positioned at the rear of the Union column, was compelled to acknowledge the Confederate presence — he wrote: "From this point [Reams's Station] the enemy (W. H. F. Lee's cavalrymen) followed the rear on the column closely, keeping up a continual skirmish until a couple of hours after night-fall." The North Carolina cavalrymen had to stay close because the Union cavalrymen had a well defined mission, but the Confederates were not sure what the agenda was or how long it would take. Barringer's men remained close when they reached Dinwiddie Court House, and more serious fighting took place with the Union rear guard around 4:00 P.M. — some prisoners were taken and the enemy was once again hurried along. Finally Chapman's rear guard pulled up for the night when it reached Ford's Station on the South Side Railroad around 11:00 P.M. on June 22. The head of Kautz's column had reached the South Side around 4:00 P.M. and Ford's Station a couple of hours later where they captured and destroyed 2 locomotives, 16 cars, and burned the depot buildings. Before bedding down around midnight, Kautz's men also tore up several miles of track and burned the ties, using the heat to bend the rails on the first day of their mission.[22]

In addition to engaging in the dangerous sport of skirmishing with the enemy, the North Carolinians had to battle the elements — one of Barringer's North Carolina cavalrymen remembered "The weather was exceedingly hot and it was terribly dusty. In close column it was almost impossible to breathe or see for the dust, so we were forced to march in column of twos and with long intervals between regiments...."[23]

BLACKS AND WHITES, JUNE 23, 1864

August Kautz's cavalrymen remained at the head of the Union column as it started westward along the South Side Railroad around 1:00 A.M. on June 23. They continued to tear up track as they passed through Blacks & Whites Station and by Nottoway Court House. Kautz was unopposed and arrived at Burkesville around 3:00 P.M. Farther back in the column, Wilson had a more difficult day.[24]

Wilson's cavalrymen followed Kautz along the railroad destroying what the advance regiments had missed — they did a thorough job as far as Blacks & Whites Station. Near that small station, Wilson and his lead brigade, commanded by McIntosh, mistakenly took a road that led them three or four miles out of their way, southwest of the railroad. Chapman's brigade remained at work on the railroad between Blacks & Whites Station and Nottoway

Court House. Meanwhile, W. H. F. Lee had taken a shorter route from Ford's Station early in the morning. He realized that he could not stop Wilson's handiwork from the rear, so he left the railroad, took a somewhat shorter road and marched rapidly to be in a position to hit the enemy column farther up the line. The combination of factors allowed the Confederates to get between the Union divisions and catch Wilson's division divided near Blacks & Whites—only Chapman's brigade was on the railroad to receive the head of W. H. F. Lee's Confederate column. It was near noon when Chapman's men saw Dearing's Confederates coming from the northeast — it was the beginning of the first major battle during the Wilson-Kautz Raid on the railroads. It is known to some as the Battle of Nottoway and to others as the Battle at Blacks and Whites (because the fighting was near a place called Oak Grove where the main road crosses the railroad, it is also sometimes referred to as the Battle of the Grove). The North Carolinian cavalrymen refer to it as the Battle at Blacks & Whites, so this book does the same.[25]

When Dearing's cavalrymen approached the railroad they were dismounted and rapidly formed for attack—McGregor's artillery was also quickly moved forward and put into position. The 2nd North Carolina was a short distance behind Dearing's command and W. H. F. Lee rapidly moved them up on Dearing's right. (Colonel Clinton M. Andrews commanding the 2nd Cavalry was too ill to take the field that morning, and the command was led into battle by twenty-two-year-old Major William P. Roberts.) The Confederate line formed rapidly and charged Chapman's formidable command. Chapman had also quickly put his men in a line of battle along and just south of the railroad to receive the oncoming Confederates. The Federals immediately counterattacked, and the dismounted cavalrymen from Dearing's small brigade and the 2nd North Carolina were no match for Chapman's numbers and firepower. In short order, Dearing's men were overwhelmed and began to break. Union cavalrymen were quick to pursue and push them back across the railroad tracks. At about the same time, the 2nd North Carolina's advance was stopped near the railroad. This put Chapman's men in a position to hit the 2nd North Carolina's left flank and to momentarily captured McGregor's guns. At the sight of Dearing's men retreating in some confusion and his guns falling rapidly into enemy hands, W. H. F. Lee quickly sent for his other two North Carolina regiments which were still strung-out in column of twos. In Barringer's column, the 2nd North Carolina was followed by the 1st, then the brigade's short wagon train, and finally the 5th North Carolina. The 2nd North Carolina had been well in advance of the rest of Barringer's command, so their exposure up front almost lasted too long.[26]

At the sound of gunfire coming from the front of their column, the North Carolina cavalrymen in the 1st and 5th regiments closed up and quickened their pace. Within minutes, W. H. F. Lee's message arrived instructing them to move up as rapidly as possible. The North Carolinians immediately moved to a gallop as they formed into column of fours and raced for the front. When they arrived, they saw W. H. F. Lee on horseback by the side of the road shouting, "Save the guns! Save the guns!" That command was followed by "Prepare to fight on foot; dismount; front into line; double-quick, march!" The cavalrymen from the 1st North Carolina charged forward and went in on the left of the rapidly retreating men from Dearing's command. The firing became even more intense as Barringer's and Chapman's dismounted cavalrymen clashed in close combat around McGregor's guns. The 5th North Carolina also moved up rapidly and went in on the right of the 1st Cavalry, partially through Dearing's men who were still falling back. From their position, the troopers in the 5th Cavalry could see the cavalrymen from the 2nd North Carolina on the far right. The men of the 2nd Cavalry were still under intense fire and were slowly falling back in good order. In the initial charge when Dearing's men broke, the 2nd Cavalry's left flank became exposed and came under heavy fire from two directions. Their situation was desperate as they saw the men from Dearing's brigade disappear to the rear. Major W. P. Roberts and the men of the 2nd Cavalry retained their composure, however, and were able to execute a slow, orderly retreat until the welcome sight of the men from the 5th North Carolina appeared on their left. Men from the 1st and 5th North Carolina pushed the Federals back far enough to insure the recapture of McGregor's guns and stop their enemy's advance. At the sight of their reinforcements, the

2nd North Carolina reversed its direction and joined their comrades in the advance. With the taste of victory still fresh on their palates, Chapman's Union cavalrymen were turned and pushed back south of the railroad — but it was not a reversal easily achieved.[27]

As the 5th North Carolina passed Dearing's command, Private Means, on the right of his 5th Cavalry, looked to his right and noticed that the 2nd North Carolina had not fled its line. They were still furiously engaged with Chapman's oncoming force and were in danger of having their flank turned when Dearing's line broke. Private Means later described the action on his right:

Roberts' courage never failed. He saw everything in battle just as lightning reads a landscape, absolutely unperturbed. He took in the situation at a glance. His orders rang out clear and strong. His regiment faced and wheeled to the left, the personification of his orders. And in a moment the fire of the Nineteenth [2nd North Carolina Cavalry] and the fire of the extreme right of the Sixty-third [5th Cavalry] was pouring into Chapman's left flank and rear. The tide of battle was turned and McGregor's guns and the day were saved.[28]

As indicated above, young Major W. P. Roberts led the 2nd North Carolina Cavalry into battle near Blacks and Whites and was understandably proud of his men. After giving the cavalrymen of the 1st North Carolina, on the left of the line, credit for saving McGregor's guns and for pushing Chapman's right back across the railroad, Roberts wrote: "This was one of the most satisfactory engagements that I witnessed during the war, and the old Second sustained its reputation quite manfully." Roberts briefly mentioned the bravery of his men to make a point, and he typically made no mention of his role in the fighting — he had no tolerance for after-battle boasting from his men or himself. (Unlike many commanders, when Roberts mentioned his participation in specific actions, it was typically to illustrate his own shortcomings or near failures.) Nonetheless, about this fight he wrote: "There was stubborn fighting and much individual gallantry shown by some of my men during the day, and I remember that Sergeant Nicholas Harrell, of Company C, a perfectly reliable man, informed me at the close of the engagement, that during the day he had placed *hors de combate* on no less than six of the enemy." Roberts made this uncharacteristic comment on how hard his men fought that day because he felt they had been overlooked by their brigade commander when praise was dispensed at the end of the fighting.[29]

Barringer had spent most of the day on the center-left and left, near his former regiment the 1st North Carolina as was his habit, and consequently he reported and praised the action and men he observed directly. Barringer issued General Orders, No, 11 on July 4, 1864 in which he described the fighting at Blacks & Whites in these words: "On the 23rd ult., at Blacks and Whites, the 1st regiment, with a dash and spirit worthy of themselves, turned the tide of the battle, saved the day, and drove back the triumphant advance of a whole brigade of the enemy cavalry."[30] That Barringer overlooked the contribution made by the men of the 2nd Cavalry that day, probably explains why Private Means of the 5th Cavalry went to great lengths to give Roberts and his men their due. In any case, young Roberts's bravery extended beyond the battlefield when it came time to defend his men — which is why he soon became one of the more popular commanders of the 2nd North Carolina Cavalry. Roberts later described the situation in these words,

The brigade commander did not witness the action of this regiment [2nd North Carolina Cavalry], nor did I receive an order from him during the day, but he got possessed with an idea somehow, or other, that the Ninth [1st North Carolina] alone was entitled to all praise, and published an order to that effect as soon as the brigade returned to camp. I declined to have the order read to my men on dress parade, and there was friction between the brigade commander and myself, but I carried my point in the end. I did not object to his congratulating the Ninth upon its splendid behavior, but I did object to his partiality.[31]

Apparently Barringer thought about the situation later and spoke with others near the right of the Confederate line, because when he wrote a summary of his brigade's actions for the press in January 1865, after praising the 1st North Carolina commanded by Major Cowles for saving the artillery, he said: "The Second under Major Roberts, (...) promptly facing to the left, hitching his line to Major Cowles', joined in the charge, both being gallantly supported by the Fifth...." Then in a letter to his brother just after the war, Barringer wrote,

"On the 23rd Gen'l Dearing attacked them [Chapman's command] in the flank near Blacks & Whites; but he was forced to yield to overwhelming numbers, when the tide of battle was suddenly turned by the heroic conduct of the 1st & 2nd Regiments." In addition, at an even later date, when he wrote a brief history of the 1st North Carolina Cavalry, he told of the guns being saved by the 1st Cavalry and mentioned that, "Just at this juncture, however, a detachment of the Second Cavalry, under Major W. P. Roberts, managed to get in the Federal rear and right across the railroad track."[32]

After being pushed south of the railroad, Chapman's Union line regrouped and held as fighting continued through the afternoon. In his words: "The enemy bringing up strong re-enforcements my line again retired to its original position along the railroad, from which repeated attempts of the enemy failed to dislodge them." Wilson also wrote in his report that, "This was one of the most determined cavalry engagements in which this division had participated, and resulted in serious injury to the enemy.... Our loss was about 75 killed, wounded, and missing...." From the field on June 24, W. H. F. Lee estimated his losses to be from 60 to 100 men since leaving camp.[33]

As Chapman indicated, after the initial charges and countercharges were made and the lines stabilized, Barringer's men continued their efforts to dislodge their enemy under a heavy and constant fire but with no success. Barringer described the afternoon in these words, "And now for several hours the battle raged. Whole trees and saplings were cut down with shells and minie-balls, until night ended the conflict." (At some point during that violent afternoon and evening, Colonel Clinton M. Andrews struggled to the front to join his 2nd North Carolina Cavalry and received a serious wound to his thigh—he later died of complications resulting from the amputation of his leg.)[34]

Near daylight on June 24, Chapman quietly withdrew his men from the line and followed Wilson's and McIntosh's brigades along the South Side toward Berkeville and onto the Richmond & Danville Railroad. They spent most of the day marching along the rail bed—Kautz's command still a considerable distance in front of Wilson's column continued to destroy as much of the railroad as possible. The commander of Kautz's lead brigade reported that they marched "...along the Richmond and Danville Railroad, halting every few hours and sending out parties to destroy the track, stations, water tanks, &c. marching in this manner we reached Keysville. We halted for the night and again sent out heavy working parties to destroy the road." Wilson's command with Chapman's battered brigade followed along doing much the same. As indicated, Kautz's cavalrymen began arriving at Keysville early in the afternoon and later in the day, while Kautz was still working on the railroad, Wilson arrived with his column—the entire Union command spent the night in the recently created ruins. Just before sundown, W. H. F. Lee's advance arrived on Chapman's rear and skirmished until after night fall.[35]

W. H. F. Lee got a late start on the 24th. He spent time consolidating his men who were fit to march and took the time to locate rations for them and to rest and graze their horses. While there, his scouts brought news of Kautz's arrival at Burkeville and his movement down the Danville Railroad. By afternoon, the Confederate cavalrymen were again in pursuit of Wilson's men. W. H. F. Lee left Dearing's command near Blacks and Whites to rest and regroup. He also sent some of his artillery back because he was out of ammunition. With both Union divisions at Keysville and W. H. F. Lee with only three depleted and tired regiments from the North Carolina brigade, the Confederate commander decided not to become seriously engaged that night.[36]

Early the next morning, the Federal troops were on the march again with Chapman's brigade at the rear of Wilson's column. Kautz's lead brigade was on the road by 4:00 A.M. and continued its periodic stops to destroy the railroad. It also located three lumber mills within a few miles of the railroad and decided to destroy them—the reasoning was to deprive the Confederates of material with which to rebuild the road. Kautz's advance continued on through Roanoke Station and pulled up just short of the railroad bridge, the Staunton River Bridge.[37]

Kautz's advance drove the enemy pickets across the bridge, but the Confederates had a strong position and were determined to hold the bridge. The bridge was guarded by Junior and Senior Reserves and disabled soldiers. A colonel from the 12th North Carolina, who lived nearby and was home convalescing from wounds received earlier, assisted the raw troops and was wounded again in the process. The young and old Confederates had some artillery and used it well. They repulsed Kautz's attempts to take or burn the bridge. The Union troops were never able to get closer than seventy or eighty yards of the bridge. In his official report, Kautz wrote that "…the burning of the bridge was, therefore, reluctantly abandoned."[38]

Wilson rode with his two brigades at the rear of the Union column. After he crossed the Little Roanoke with McIntosh's brigade and their wagons, Wilson pulled up for the night behind Kautz north of the Staunton River Bridge. He sent instructions forward for Kautz to burn the bridge if he could not take it. About the time Kautz was attempting to fulfill his instructions, Chapman at the rear of Wilson's column again came under attack from Barringer's North Carolina regiments. At that point, the Union column was hotly engaged in front and rear. Again, however, the three North Carolina regiments did not try to overrun Wilson's rear, just harass it, make them use up their ammunition, and hopefully hurry them along.[39]

Wilson's original orders were to push along the Danville Railroad as far as possible and when the enemy stopped his progress, return to the Army of the Potomac, east of Petersburg. With the Confederate reserves and disabled in front and W. H. F. Lee's North Carolina brigade at his rear, Wilson decided it was time to end his raid on the railroads. In his words, "Finding that the bridge could not be carried without severe loss, if at all, the enemy being again close upon my rear … I determined to push no farther south, but to endeavor to reach the army by returning toward Petersburg."[40]

Barringer had his regiments so close to Chapman's rear guard that Wilson found it necessary to "extricate" his command at midnight. He sent McIntosh out first, then the wagons followed by Chapman's command. Kautz covered the escape, then followed. The North Carolina cavalrymen were held back by long range shelling and exhaustion. By daylight, Wilson's advance reached Wyliesville on its eastward march for Petersburg. His men rested there for two hours, had coffee and were back on the road for Christianville and Greensboro—they marched a short distance farther and camped for the night.[41]

W. H. F. Lee gave his exhausted cavalrymen time to rest and regroup on the morning of June 26. Dearing's command caught up with the North Carolinians, and they accompanied a select detachment from Barringer's brigade on the trail of the Union column. By that time, the North Carolina brigade had been reduced to fewer than 300 effective men. The primary cause of the reduction was the breakdown of their horses—the Confederates had not been able to replace their horses after the six weeks of hard campaigning before they started in pursuit of Wilson and Kautz. When forming the detachment of North Carolinians to follow Wilson's column, Barringer used a very practical method of selection. A member to the 5th North Carolina remembered, "It was more a selection of horses than men. Horses able to make rapid and continuous pursuit. Company H, and I suppose all other companies of the regiment, passed single file before these officers and they selected the horses." The cavalrymen from the North Carolina regiments and Dearing command had to ride hard and stay close to the enemy's rear. They harassed them from time to time making Wilson's men drop lines of skirmishers across the road to slow the Confederates. W. H. F. Lee's main column, the North Carolinians not detached, moved at a more leisurely pace on Wilson's left flank.[42]

During the pursuit, W. H. F. Lee had kept his father well aware of Wilson's movements which encouraged R. E. Lee to have Hampton move quickly south of Petersburg. Hampton with his two brigades and Chambliss's brigade crossed the James River on June 26. Hampton sent Chambliss's command on toward Reams's Station—they had not been on the long march to Trevilian Station and back earlier in the month so were less worn. Hampton hoped his two brigades might have the opportunity for some rest once across the James River, but they were disappointed. The day after crossing, Hampton was ordered to move his command down to Stony Creek Depot and intercept Wilson's Union column before it could reach the safety of Meade's line. Hampton moved quickly. Fitz Lee was not far behind with his division, but he was ordered to hold at Chaffin's Bluff. Hampton's advance arrived at Stony Creek Depot around midday on June 28—Chambliss's brigade of W. H. F. Lee's division was already in the area. Once Hampton had the opportunity to assess the situation, he requested that some infantry and artillery be moved to Reams's Station — two brigades of infantry from Mahone's division and artillery were quickly moved. Hampton informed R. E. Lee that he intended to attack Wilson at Sappony Church and requested that Fitz Lee and his cavalrymen be brought down to Reams's Station to help Mahone's infantry brigades. The Confederates were ready to greet Wilson and Kautz upon their return, and the latter did not expect the welcome.[43]

Meanwhile, early on the morning of June 27, Wilson had his column marching eastward again with little opportunity for rest or foraging. They crossed the Nottoway River just after mid-day on June 28 — at that point, they stopped for some water and rest. While there, Wilson learned to his dismay that the Confederates had a small infantry force and two small detachments of cavalry at Stony Creek Depot on the Weldon Railroad — the place he planned to cross the road before turning northeast for Meade's army.[44]

However, Wilson was confident the small enemy force at Stony Creek would not alter his planned route, so he sent his advance unit forward at a rapid pace with instructions to clear the road for his main column. The Confederate picket was driven back with little difficulty; then suddenly Wilson's advance regiment was attacked by a strong force of dismounted cavalry and pushed back into their main column. McIntosh moved a brigade up and stopped the Confederate advance. In the process Wilson learned from prisoners taken that the dismounted troopers were part of Hampton's cavalry. The small enemy cavalry force Wilson had been warned about turned out to be the advance of Hampton's command which had just arrived from near Richmond. Wilson's worst nightmare was at hand — recall that before Wilson left on his railroad raid, he asked for and received assurances from Meade and Sheridan that Hampton would be occupied north of the James until his mission was over. He was also assured Meade's infantry would have possession of the Weldon Railroad. The reality awaiting Wilson was that Sheridan had not controlled Hampton, and Meade had not penetrated A. P. Hill's line on the Weldon.[45]

The advance units from both cavalries were quickly and fiercely engaged just west of Stony Creek Depot near Sappony Church. Hampton's advance greeted the Federal cavalry column, but was pressed slowly back as more of Wilson's command arrived. While Hampton's men were being pressed, Chambliss arrived from Stony Creek Depot with his 9th, 10, and 13th Virginia regiments. Chambliss was able to stop Wilson's advance. As the cavalrymen began to settle into opposing lines, Union artillery arrived and poured shot and shell at the Confederates. Around 4:00 P.M., Confederate artillery arrived and replied. Meanwhile, the balance of Hampton's brigades continued to arrive and was moved to the front with Chambliss. Shortly afterwards, about 200 men arrived from Holcombe's Infantry Legion and were put in the middle of the Confederate line. Wilson was soon aware that he would not be able to cross the Weldon at that point, so late in the day when Kautz came up with his column, Wilson sent him and the wagons on a night march in an arch, northwest and then back to the Weldon Railroad at Reams's Station, about ten miles north of Stony Creek Depot. Wilson hoped that though Sheridan had not been able to hold Hampton north of the James, at least Meade could have taken and held the railroad around Reams's Station.[46]

While Kautz was on the road, Hampton strengthened his line and prepared to attack Wilson at daybreak. Wilson understood that his best chance was also to head for Reams's Station and the protection of Meade's infantry, but first he had to withdraw his two brigades carefully, minimizing his losses. On the other side, Hampton felt his force was seriously outnumbered, and he was reluctant to start with a frontal attack, so around sunup he dismounted and sent portions of Butler's and Rosser's brigades, under the command of Butler, at Wilson's left flank. At the same time, he sent Chambliss's command forward along with his whole line. The Union line was overwhelmed and broke. Chapman and many of his Union cavalrymen were cut off from their horses, but he and about 300 men from his brigade escaped on their own and rejoined Wilson around midday. Others were scattered and with or without mounts tried to make off on their own. However, Wilson escaped with the main body of his command and fought his way toward Reams's Station — more or less following Kautz's earlier route. After a short delay, Butler's brigade was on Wilson's path, followed by Chambliss's three regiments and artillery. Hampton moved with Chambliss's command most of the day and they encountered and pursued a portion of the Union column that had scattered. Wilson arrived on Kautz's line near Reams's Station around noon on June 29.[47]

The First Battle at Reams's Station, June 29

Early on June 29, 1864, about the same time Hampton attacked Wilson down around Sappony Church, Kautz and his column approached Reams's Station. Kautz's advance was stopped and driven back in confusion by Mahone's infantry. Kautz regrouped his men and tried again to break through the enemy line in front of the station, but with no success. He then entrenched his line and waited for Meade to arrive with reinforcements, but of course, Meade was not in the area. His only support was Wilson who reached Kautz in the afternoon and learned of their enemy's presence and Meade's absence from the station. Wilson immediately sent McIntosh's brigade forward to break through to the station. They had no success. Then Wilson massed his entire force, by then even Chapman had arrived with his small band of escapees from Sappony Church, with the ambulances and wagons in his rear to "make a vigorous attempt to break through." Wilson intended to head north to Petersburg, still hoping to find Meade's infantry on the rail line, but as he readied his command, he found his enemy's infantry in line of battle with a large skirmish line out front advancing down his intended route of escape. At about the same time, Wilson got word of Fitz Lee's two cavalry brigades advancing on his left flank.[48]

Fitz Lee had been ordered to move his cavalrymen across the James on June 28 and proceed to Petersburg. From there he was sent to Reams's Station. When Fitz Lee arrived at the station, he found Mahone's two infantry brigades drawn up in line of battle across the country road coming into the station. He was told Mahone was reluctant to attack because his two small brigades were no match for the two divisions in front of him. Fitz Lee immediately dismounted two regiments from Lomax's brigade and one from Wickham's, under the command of Lomax, and sent them on a small road through some woods to attack the enemy's left flank. Once the dismounted cavalrymen were well on their way, Mahone readied his men for a frontal attack.[49]

Wilson saw Mahone and knew of the dismounted cavalrymen moving on his left, so he wanted reinforcements. By that time, the effective cavalrymen in the two divisions under Wilson's command probably did not outnumber the enemy in front of him. He sent word to Meade at City Point on the James requesting immediate assistance and then reconsidered his plan to head north.[50]

Wilson's request for help at Reams's Station made it to Grant and Meade at City Point, and the generals moved immediately to send infantry support — which they knew could not make it in time. Considering the importance of time, the Union generals then sent a message to Sheridan asking him to move his cavalry in support of Wilson's division. Sheridan apparently felt little urgency in the matter and even less responsibility for letting Hampton get south of the James in the first place. Sheridan's slowness in responding to Wilson's call for assistance added fuel to the fiery debate that continued for years between Wilson and Sheridan over why Wilson nearly lost his entire command upon returning from his railroad raid. In any case, Sheridan's cavalrymen arrived at Reams's Station about 7:00 P.M. on June 30, long after Meade's infantrymen had arrived and driven off the few Confederates remaining at the station.[51]

In the early afternoon on June 29, just after Wilson sent his request for assistance, he decided to pull his command back south along the railroad toward Jarratt's Station. Before his planned retreat could be executed, however, Mahone's infantry came forward, and Fitz Lee sent three mounted regiments in a charge under the command of Wickham. About that same time the dismounted Confederate cavalrymen hit Wilson's left. Wilson's tired and discouraged line broke and fell back. Kautz's and McIntosh's lines were quickly overwhelmed and divided. Kautz's and Wilson's commands became separated and split into numerous smaller groups, all attempting to get away as best they could. By different routes, some of Kautz's men dropped back and joined Wilson and the bulk of his command near Stony Creek where they tried to make a stand against Fitz Lee's cavalrymen, but could not rally effectively. Here Fitz Lee's men captured the enemy's guns and turned them on their former masters—Lee's own guns trailed far behind his fast moving horsemen. Wilson's men had to fight continually, but they still retreated south along the Weldon Railroad. Wilson did manage to get the remnants of his command through Jarratt's Station around dawn on June 30, and then turn east and head for the safety of Meade's army. From Reams's Station to Jarratt's, the Union cavalrymen scrambled and fought along the Weldon for about 20 miles. About 1,000 of Wilson's men escaped with Kautz, and about 500 of Kautz's men returned with Wilson's column. Hampton arrived back at Stony Creek Depot after Wilson had been chased through. Hampton then moved to Jarrett's Station on the morning of June 30 but was too late to intercept Wilson—Hampton had no word from Fitz Lee until 9:00 A.M. when a message from Fitz Lee to R. E. Lee passed through Hampton's hands. Only then did the latter know where Fitz Lee and the enemy's main body was located. At that point, Hampton sent Chambliss's Virginia brigade and others after Wilson's column, relieving some of Fitz Lee's exhausted troops. Hampton later lamented the lack of coordination between the two Confederate cavalry divisions and the lost opportunity to destroy Wilson's and Kautz's commands because of the lack of communication.[52]

The detachment of cavalry from W. H. F. Lee's command, though exhausted, was spread around the rear of Wilson and Kautz throughout June 28—making any retreat westward impossible. Nonetheless, as various Union units became trapped, many of them found it necessary to break and make off as best they could. Some found heading west the only opening, until they encountered detached North Carolina cavalrymen from Barringer's brigade. For instance, a sergeant from the 5th North Carolina Cavalry captured a Federal Colonel and his "magnificent gray horse superbly caparisoned." Unfortunately for the sergeant, General Barringer came along and desired the horse for himself—the general made sure the sergeant got "a serviceable black chunk of a horse" in the "exchange."[53]

While the detachment of men from the North Carolina Brigade and Dearing's' command followed closely on the trail of Wilson's and Kautz's column, the main body of Barringer's brigade, with its broken down body of horses, marched toward Petersburg—they covered about 15 miles on June 27, and about 25 miles on June 28 after which they spent the night still in Lunenburg County.[54]

The accomplishments of Wilson's railroad raid were of short duration—the supply lines to Petersburg were reportedly running again by July 5. A. A. Humphreys of Meade's staff wrote, "Notwithstanding our attempts to destroy the Confederate lines of supply, they still remained sufficient for the wants of the Confederacy.... The repair of the two roads injured by Wilson was begun at once." The cost to the Union forces of the temporary interruption of supplies was considerable, however. They lost around 1,500 men, 12 guns, and all their wagons. Also important were the small arms and equipment captured by Confederate cavalrymen. For example, Colonel R. L. T. Beale of Chambliss's brigade noted that "Some Henry rifles (sixteen-shooters) were taken on the day previous.... All of our men not previously supplied were now furnished with good McClellan saddles and colt revolvers."[55]

Barringer estimated when he began chasing Wilson and Kautz on their railroad raid, he had 1,200 effective North Carolina cavalrymen in his column; after the fight at Blacks and Whites he had 1,000; and after fighting on Wilson's rear in front of the Roanoke River, he had fewer than 300 effective cavalrymen to pursue Wilson and Kautz eastward to the Weldon Railroad. Most of the reduction in Barringer's command resulted from the marching, the heat, and the lack of rest and nourishment for both men and horses. The 2nd North Carolina Cavalry had six recorded combat losses from the fight at Blacks and Whites.[56]

Duty Along the Weldon Railroad, July

Rufus Barringer and the main body of his North Carolina cavalrymen marched 12 miles on June 29 and spent the night in Nottoway County. They continued on the 30th another 15 miles and spent the night in Amelia County, above the South Side Railroad. After marching

Combat Losses in the 2nd North Carolina Cavalry Wilson-Kautz Railroad Raid

Trooper	Age	Co.	Fate
Clinton M. Andrews		F&S	mortally wounded, June 23
Charles H. Elder	33	D	wounded, Jun 23
John Scoggins Jr.	26	I	killed, June 23
William J. Hare	30	I	mortally wounded, June 23
Edward G. Wyese		K	killed, June 23
Willie P. Tilley	29	K	killed, June 24

Information contained in this table came from Compiled Service Records as summarized by Louis H. Manarin, *North Carolina Troops: 1861–1865, A Roster*, vol. II, pages 98–177. (See Appendix for more information on the men listed above, page 402.)

about 18 miles on July 1, the 2nd North Carolina Cavalry camped for the night on the Appomattox River — the rest of their brigade was nearby. July 2 was spent resting their animals — they had no forage for them and could not push too hard. On July 3, the 2nd Cavalry, still under the command of young Major William P. Roberts, marched 25 miles and joined the rest of the brigade on Gravelly Run, about six miles from the Weldon Railroad. They were united with their sister brigade, Chambliss's Virginians, who were camped along Hatcher's and Gravely runs in Dinwiddie County.[57]

Despite no general engagement along their section of the Petersburg line during this time, Captain Lockhart of the 2nd North Carolina Cavalry described the underlying tension along the line in this manner: "In some places the lines are not more than three hundred yards apart, and the skirmishers are constantly engaged in picking at each other day and night, but without any material result." The cavalrymen received rations on a fairly regular basis, but their horses were still on half rations of corn because of the disruption of supplies coming up on the Weldon line — supplies were being moved north by wagon from Stony Creek Depot. Conditions were not good, and after several days of fighting and marching, it was more than some could endure. These conditions were described to the enemy when a member of the 2nd North Carolina Cavalry out on scouting duty, deserted into enemy lines late on July 5. Three deserters from the 5th North Carolina went into enemy lines on July 21, but most of the cavalrymen continued to endure the ordeal.[58]

From their camps on Hatcher's and Gravely Runs, the Virginia and North Carolina brigades once again pulled picket duty along the Weldon from just below Reams's Station northward. For instance, cavalrymen from Company C, 2nd North Carolina relieved the 5th Cavalry near Reams's Station on July 8, and in turn were relieved by the 3rd regiment on July 16. Others from Company K of the 2nd North Carolina were relieved on picket duty July 18 about four miles south of Petersburg. The regiments rotated into picket duty along the Weldon until July 28. One member of the 2nd North Carolina described the camp's setting in these words: "Nothing romantic or picturesque in scenery, however, but on the contrary somewhat repulsive to the eyes of these 'tar heels.'" Without the excitement of fighting and interesting scenery while on a march, the North Carolinians had time to think about things of questionable importance, such as politics. For instance, the same cavalryman from the 2nd North Carolina who did not think much of the Virginia landscape along the Weldon wrote an open letter to the *Daily Confederate* in which he vented his strong opinions on the governor's race in North Carolina. He presumed to speak for his comrades in arms when he wrote that they are not fearful about their ability to win the war, but "...there is something that gives us great uneasiness — and that is, the *harrowing* idea of having such a man as Holden at the *helm of State*. Great God! What are our fathers, brothers and friends at home thinking of?" After many more such lines, the writer ends his thoughts with "*Holden must be crushed. Vance shall be our Governor.*"[59]

During their rest between marching and fighting, the North Carolinian cavalrymen also had a special assignment at the request of R. E. Lee (in addition to picketing and scouting). On July 26, 1864, R. E. Lee issued an order authorizing Barringer's regiments "...to take possession of all cavalry arms, equipments and accoutrements in the hands of civilians or other unauthorized persons in the State of North Carolina, when he is satisfied that such arms, &c., are legitimately the property of the Confederate States. All arms, &c., dropped by our troops or the enemy on their lines of march or on the battle fields, or left or sold by officers or privates to persons not in the military service, are the property of the Confederate States."⁶⁰ Soon after this assignment was given, Barringer issued a notice for all, that reads in part as follows:

Under this authority, I desire especially to gather up McClellan saddles. These saddles were captured from the enemy. There can be no private property in them. Partisan Rangers and others have no right to sell them, except to the government, which pays fixed prices for the captures....

This brigade is much in need of good saddles. Many of those we have are ruining the horses' backs.... Those now at home, and especially all on "horse detail," are required to gather up these saddles, also Sharp's rifles, Colt's repeaters, and other cavalry arms and equipment....

I claim no right at present either to seize or impress these arms and equipments, but I confidently expect every honest man not in the field, to give them up. They ought to be ashamed, in a time like this to be seen with them.⁶¹

This new assignment had to have been received with mixed feelings and hesitation as the cavalrymen returned to their home counties on leave or while out on horse duty. Nonetheless, the time spent in camp and on picket was a needed break from the marching and fighting during the months of May and June.

While camped near Gravelly Run, they recruited some horses, a few men, and collected their stragglers. In addition, many of their exhausted and broken-down mounts were made whole again. Within a couple of weeks, Barringer's brigade approached its normal level of effectiveness. In fact, many cavalrymen in the North Carolina brigade were better equipped than ever before — Barringer remembered, "More than half of this regiment [1st North Carolina Cavalry] were armed and equipped from the enemy."⁶²

The 2nd North Carolina Cavalry's losses during this period of rebuilding resulted from sporadic firing along the line and scouting duty. Those lost to the regiment included the following.

Grant's Demonstrations Against Richmond

As indicated, Robert E. Lee's cavalry settled into guarding the right of the Confederate line for about a month after the Wilson-Kautz Raid

Combat Losses in the 2nd North Carolina Cavalry Picketing and Scouting the Weldon Railroad

Trooper	Age	Co.	Fate
Alexander T. Allen		F	captured, July 5
M. M. Kibbler		G	wounded, died July 10
David H. Idol		D	captured, July 13
Elijah Sheffield	28	I	wounded, July 26
W. Eatmon		E	wounded, July
Nathaniel C. Tucker		F	wounded, July
William D. Dale*	26	A	wounded, May 4–July 26
John E. McEwen*	24	B	wounded, May 4–July 26
Milas C. Jordon*		B	wounded, May 4–July 26
John J. Hardin*	29	B	wounded, May 4–July 26
S. R. Moore*	42	B	wounded, May 4–July 26
Nicholas J. Battle*	34	C	wounded, May 4–July 26
John T. Cross*	26	C	wounded, May 4–July 26
Henry Hofler*	25	C	wounded, May 4–July 26
Jesse C. Stone*	22	D	wounded, May 4–July 26
David Stafford*		F	wounded, May 4–July 26
William S. Spruill*		G	wounded, May 4–July 26
William Fuller*	28	G	wounded, May 4–July 26
John W. Snell*	22	G	wounded, May 4–July 26
William Garner*	30	I	wounded, May 4–July 26
George W. Walker*		K	wounded, May 4–July 26

Information contained in this table came from Compiled Service Records as summarized by Louis H. Manarin, *North Carolina Troops: 1861–1865, A Roster*, vol. II, pages 98–177. (See Appendix for more information on the men listed above, page 403.)

*The names marked with an asterisk are from a list compiled by Lieutenant Edward M. Jordan, Adjutant with the 2nd North Carolina Cavalry, which can be found in: Lieutenant Edward M. Jordan, "Casualties in 2nd Regiment, N.C. Cavalry, Since May 1, 1864," *Daily Confederate*, July 27, 1864, page 2, col. 5.

before any significant movement took place. W. H. F. Lee's division (Dearing's brigade attached) was placed on the line just below Petersburg; Fitz Lee's division in the center, near Reams's Station; and Hampton's division on the far right, around Stony Creek Depot.[63] Grant was continually trying to make something happen to break what was beginning to look like another stalemate. He kept one eye on Petersburg and the Confederate right for weakness and tried to create some by threatening Richmond from time to time. While the cat-and-mouse game went on around Petersburg and Richmond, Grant kept his other eye on General Early's activities from the Shenandoah Valley to Washington, D. C..

Grant Threatens Richmond

As usual, Grant had more than one iron in the fire and more than one was always near hot enough to cause his enemy a problem. By late July, one of his moves was just about ready to burst under the Confederate defenses. A regiment from Burnside's Corps, largely made up of Pennsylvania coal miners, had been secretly digging a tunnel under a portion of the Confederate line in front of Petersburg, and it was nearly complete — it was about 500 feet long. The plan was to place several hundred kegs of blasting powder under the Confederate line and blow it out of existence. Union infantry would then storm through the crater and carry the day; perhaps even the city. Grant knew this plan had a greater chance of success if the Confederate line at Petersburg was thin. Consequently, he decided to make a demonstration in front of Richmond, causing R. E. Lee to send troops from Petersburg to north of the James River. Grant had settled Meade with most of the Army of the Potomac on the Petersburg line and south along the Weldon Railroad. Burnside's command was east of Petersburg. On July 26, Grant put Union feet and hooves in motion when he moved Hancock's Second Corps, and Sheridan with Torbert's and D. McM. Gregg's cavalry divisions from their positions on the Petersburg line to an area north of the James— he wanted a credible demonstration in front of Richmond. Of course, there were a couple of side shows to the main event that Grant hoped would materialize. For instance, in addition to enticing R. E. Lee to weaken the Petersburg line to strengthen the Richmond defenses, Grant hoped the explosive action around Petersburg would allow Sheridan to continue on around Richmond and do a proper job of cutting the supply line to the Confederate capital along the Virginia Central Railroad.[64]

W. H. F. Lee's division was the first to be moved in response to Union troop movements. On July 28, young John W. Gordon of Company C, 2nd North Carolina Cavalry, wrote in his diary, "Held elections in the brigade for Gov. of N. Ca. I cast my first vote at the age of seventeen." Just hours after casting their votes, the North Carolina brigade broke camp and marched through Petersburg — they covered around 20 miles that day and spent the night on the turnpike between Petersburg and Richmond. They were on the road again early the next morning and crossed the James River as they had the month before at Chaffin's Bluff. This move was a direct response to Grant's movement of troops to the area. Apparently Robert E. Lee was not overly concerned though because he moved Fitz Lee's division to the area but not to the front. Fitz Lee moved his division to the north side of the James River late on July 28. He reached Chaffin's Bluff by morning on the 29th, but in his report simply said: "Marched back to camp near Reams's on night of 31st." R. E. Lee left Hampton and his division on the Weldon Railroad.[65]

Kautz's cavalry division joined Sheridan at Deep Bottom, while Wilson's battered division remained south of the James River. Hancock and Sheridan moved across the James early August 27 — the cavalry first. The Second Corps was moved to support the cavalry if it succeeded in penetrating the Richmond defenses. Hancock's command was positioned to keep Confederate troops from crossing and hitting the cavalry in the flank or rear. Hancock and Sheridan moved up and then turned toward the city with cavalry on the right. The Confederate front line of pickets was pushed back with little difficulty, and both Hancock's and Sheridan's men moved to their enemy's entrenchments across the roads leading to Richmond. There were three main roads that led to Richmond: the one nearest the river was the New Market Road; the middle road was Darbytown Road; and the next was the Charles City Road. The Confederate line was on the west bank of Bailey's Creek, running from the James to Fussell's Mill on the left.[66] (See map 2.1.)

Grant did not intend to make a frontal assault on the strong Confederate entrenchments. Rather he wanted the Second Corps to make a strong demonstration in front of the line, while the cavalry turned the enemy's left flank near the Charles City Road. However, Sheridan had difficulty turning the left because R. E. Lee had already sent Wilcox's and Kershaw's infantry divisions to the Richmond front and Heth's division joined the line on the 27th. The Richmond line was stronger than the Union commanders had anticipated.[67]

Early in the day Sheridan's advance troops drove the Confederate pickets back and moved toward the enemy line at a charge. Kershaw immediately threw infantrymen into a counter charge and drove the Union cavalrymen back into Sheridan's main body which was more than the Confederates were equipped to handle. Kershaw's troops came upon dismounted Union cavalrymen formed in a line and with their repeating carbines firing at close range. The Confederates fell back.[68]

As indicated, R. E. Lee anticipated Grant's move in time and sent infantry to reinforce the Richmond line — just as Grant had hoped he would. R. E. Lee had moved Field's and Kershaw's divisions from Longstreet's corps, and Heth's and Wilcox's from A. P. Hill's corps north of the James. Grant, Sheridan, and Hancock were all surprised, however, that R. E. Lee had detected their "secret" move north of the James and was able to in turn secretly reinforce the Richmond line in a timely manner. R. E. Lee also had W. H. F. Lee's cavalry division at the front.

From Chaffin's Bluff on the morning of July 29, the 2nd North Carolina Cavalry and the rest of their brigade moved toward Malvern Hill where they found the enemy in line of battle — by afternoon they fought as part of the Confederate line. The North Carolina brigade was principally engaged in the fighting around Fussell's Mill and skirmished well into the night as far as Riddle's Shop. After sundown they withdrew about four miles and camped for the night.[69]

Hancock's inability to penetrate the Confederate line encouraged Grant to forget sending Sheridan around Richmond on another railroad-raid. But it also encouraged him to quickly move back across the James and let Burnside attack the Confederate line a day ahead of schedule. Grant felt the Petersburg line had been sufficiently weakened by the movement of Confederate troops to defend Richmond, so he moved on Petersburg. On the night of July 29, Hancock and Sheridan re-crossed the James to join Burnside's explosive assault on the Petersburg line. Hancock moved into the Union line around Petersburg and Sheridan moved his cavalry down to Lee's Mill on the Union left. The attack was scheduled for pre-dawn on August 30.[70]

Even though Beauregard had detected Burnside's tunneling project shortly after it had begun, he and R. E. Lee, after considering alternatives, decided to let it run its course and station guns where they could provide a crossfire when necessary. Nonetheless, when the explosion occurred it was greater than the generals on either side anticipated and thus contained an element of surprise for all. It was imperative that Burnside's troops move quickly through the crater blown in the ground and carry the Confederate line. Unfortunately for Burnside's men, their own parapets and abatis had not been prepared to allow them through. It took too long for Burnside to get his men to the crater. Once they got there, it was nearly impossible see the crater through the smoke, dust, and debris — it was 170 feet across and about 40 feet deep. In addition, the first Union troops to arrive at the crater had been sent without their general and with little direction — they filed into the debris-filled hole and added to the confusion. The Confederates were also initially stunned. Their first reaction was to move away from the explosion a couple of hundred yards on either side — creating an inviting gap in their line. It came down to a question of which generals could rally their men first and fill the gap. Union troops got to and beyond the crater first, but were disoriented and without much guidance. Just as they were about to move behind and along the Confederate line, their enemy came at full charge, driving them back into the crater and to their original entrenchments. Meade soon realized that this offensive effort had failed and with Grant's approval withdrew all his troops to their original positions. Meade alone reported a loss of men numbering over 4,400. Meade asked President Lincoln for a Court of Inquiry on the cause of the botched attack, and it was granted.[71]

South of Petersburg near the Weldon Railroad, M. C. Butler's cavalry command (Hampton's division) had a brisk fight with Sheridan's cavalrymen near Lee's Mill on July 30. The 2nd North Carolina Cavalry and its division spent July 30 camped four miles behind the Confederate line north of the James River, preparing to go back to the Weldon Railroad, south of Petersburg.[72]

A private in the 2nd North Carolina Cavalry summed up the move to save Richmond as a rather routine experience. W. H. F. Lee had been ordered to take cavalrymen to the defense of Richmond, so they rode day and night to arrive on the line July 29; on the 30th they were up early and saddled and cooked rations for a long march, but did not move. The next day at 1:00 A.M. they were in their saddles and once again heading for Chaffin's Bluff and across the James.[73]

The 2nd North Carolina Back South of Petersburg

Once all three of R. E. Lee's cavalry divisions were again south of Petersburg, he spread them along the Weldon Railroad where they were charged with keeping that supply line to the city open. The 2nd North Carolina Cavalry was once again picketing from near Reams's Station to within a few miles of Petersburg — one private wrote home on August 7, and said, "We have come back to our old camp, about five miles south of Petersburg. We left Malvern Hill last Sunday night and arrived here yesterday."[74]

The cavalrymen were hardly settled along the Weldon when R. E. Lee perceived the need for his troops elsewhere. He began to thin his line in order to send reinforcements to General Early in northern Virginia. He sent Kershaw's infantry division and then some cavalry from his frequently targeted right.

Fitz Lee and his cavalrymen from Lomax's and Wickham's brigades had been back in their camp near Reams's Station for only a few days when on August 5, R. E. Lee sent them to Richmond and then on to R. H. Anderson at Culpeper Court House. Fitz Lee arrived there on the 11th, then his orders were changed instructing him to move to Front Royal in front of Kershaw's infantry division which had moved into the area under R. H. Anderson. They marched north and reached Williamsport on the Potomac on August 26. On the 27th, Fitz Lee marched to Leetown. He fought enemy cavalry on August 28 and 29. On September 1, they were fighting near Winchester along with Anderson and Early. Fitz Lee and his command continued fighting in the area until September 19 — it was around that time he was wounded and sent to Richmond to recuperate.[75] (See map 2.3.)

After Fitz Lee was moved to northern Virginia, the other two cavalry divisions closed up and stayed on the Weldon line for another five days before their ranks were again thinned. On August 10, R. E. Lee instructed Hampton to move his division north of the James. He was aware that Grant had put Sheridan in command of a small army and sent them after General Early. Hampton was also told to leave Dearing's brigade with W. H. F. Lee's command which would spread itself to cover the picket line Hampton's men were leaving. Once Hampton was underway, he was given orders to proceed to R. H. Anderson in Culpeper County. The purpose was to threaten the Union flank if they move into the Shenandoah Valley in an effort to stop Early.[76]

Both Grant and R. E. Lee reduced their cavalry strength on the Petersburg line. As indicated, Grant could not ignore General Early's presence in the Shenandoah Valley and the additional units R. E. Lee sent his way — Early's command was increasingly seen as a threat to the Federal Capital. Lee had left General Early near the Shenandoah Valley since mid-June; and by July 6, Early had crossed the Potomac. On July 11 he had his Confederate force at the Washington defenses, just five miles from President Lincoln's residence. Early had been making a general nuisance of himself, and concern grew as he received additional reinforcements. When R. E. Lee sent Fitz Lee's cavalry division up to assist Anderson on August 5, Grant had already, four days earlier, made arrangements to have Sheridan deal with the problem. The day after the embarrassment in front of Petersburg, called the Battle of the Crater, Sheridan was made commander of the newly formed Army of the Shenandoah. In addition to infantry, Sheridan initially took Albert T. A. Torbert's cavalry division, and a few days later he was given James H. Wilson's command — he took two of his three cavalry divisions. Grant's initial instructions were specific; in a message to Meade, he wrote, "The enemy's cavalry is now in Pennsylvania, and it is important that we should get a mounted force after them. If Sheridan is able for duty I wish you would send him to report to me in person. I shall send him to command all the forces against Early." Grant wrote Halleck of Sheridan's mission that same day; adding these words to emphasize his concern: "…I want Sheridan put in command of all the troops in the field, with instructions to put himself south of the enemy and follow him to the death."[77]

W. H. F. Lee's two brigades along with Dearing's small brigade were left to picket the Weldon. Their line was thin, and they were busy. A private in the 2nd Cavalry summarized their duty during the first two weeks of August in his diary:

August
   4th About six o'clock in evening we left S. Creek, passed through Petersburg and relieved the 4th Reg't. [4th North Carolina Cavalry, Dearing's brigade] on picket near Reams Station.
   5th After standing picket all day, we are relieved by the 62nd Geor. [of Dearing's brigade] about eleven o'clock at night. Then go five miles up the line and halt on the railroad until day.
   6th As soon as it is day we mount, and go three miles and relieve the 9th Virginia [of Chambliss's brigade] on picket, and at 12 o'clock we are relieved by the 1st Reg't. [1st North Carolina Cavalry] and return to camp.
   12th We go on picket again and relieve the 5th Reg't. [5th North Carolina Cavalry].
   14th Were relieved by infantry. Returned to camp and fed our horses. At four o'clock we start on a march [to fight north of the James once again].[78]

Hampton and his cavalry division were still on the road to Culpeper when on August 14, R. E. Lee sent a short message to General Ewell in Richmond, instructing Hampton "…to return to Richmond as soon as practicable with his whole command." By the time the message reached Hampton it was late in the day and his men were already camped for the night. Hampton moved early the next morning. Grant had launched another attack on Richmond, and W. H. F. Lee's cavalry command had been quickly moved up to meet the enemy, leaving only Dearing small cavalry brigade to guard the Weldon Railroad.[79]

By mid–August, according to Barringer, his North Carolina regiments had spent nearly six weeks after the Wilson-Kautz Raid in "…rest and quiet, which were devoted, with unremitting energy, to the work of recruiting, organizing, drill and discipline." This allowed Barringer to put around 1,500 men and horses on the road north to defend Richmond once again.[80]

Not incidentally, while Wade Hampton had his division on the road to Culpeper County on August 11, Special Orders No. 189 was issued which stated, "Maj. Genl. Wade Hampton is assigned to the command of the Cavalry of this Army." R. E. Lee was apparently also convinced it was necessary to have better coordination among the cavalry divisions, and Wade Hampton of South Carolina was the man to replace J. E. B. Stuart. Hampton would be too busy for the next couple of weeks to savor the promotion, however.[81]

GRANT THREATENS RICHMOND AGAIN, AUGUST 14–18

R. E. Lee's continual strengthening of his force between the Shenandoah Valley and Washington D.C. was a concern for Grant because he had for weeks wanted to reduce the size of his force defending the Federal Capital. Specifically, he wanted to bring the Sixth and Nineteenth Corps down to oppose Richmond. If he did that, however, it would leave only Hunter's command to defend the Capital, a force not sufficient given the growing number of Confederates in the area. In response, Grant felt pressed to force R. E. Lee to bring some of his troops in northern Virginia back to the Richmond-Petersburg line. Another Union move against Richmond was called for.[82]

Grant's plan to demonstrate against Richmond had two possible outcomes. Either R. E. Lee would bring troops back from northern Virginia or thin his line at Petersburg even more — either or both would please Grant. Early in the day on August 13, Grant instructed Winfield S. Hancock and his Second Army Corps, along with about 9,000 men from D. B. Birney's Tenth Army Corps, and D. McM. Gregg's cavalry division, to move north of the James. His instructions were basically the same as they had been two weeks earlier, except for the route he was to take across the James. Hancock was in command of the party, but Grant was very "hands-on" during the operation. The main body of B. F. Butler's Army of the James remained just across the river in the Bermuda

Hundred, but could be called upon if necessary. Kautz's cavalry was left on the Petersburg line.[83]

Hancock's infantry was first moved to City Point, then up river to give a false sense of its destination to the Confederates. Once across the James, Birney's column stayed close to the river. He was the first to drive in the Confederate pickets and take prisoners, but Birney was instructed to hold off his attack until Hancock had his divisions in place. Hancock notified Grant of their movements at 8:15 A.M. on August 14. Mott moved up the New Market Road, and Barlow with nearly 10,000 men under his command marched further to the right near Fussell's Mill. D. McM. Gregg's cavalry moved to the far right of the Union advance. Once the infantry had control of the Darbytown and Charles City Roads, the plan was for the cavalry to make a dash for Richmond. The plan seemed workable, except that the Confederate line was once again stronger than Grant and his commanders had anticipated, and Hancock's troops did not respond ideally. After three attempts to break through the Confederate line, they called it a day.[84]

Grant continued to watch for a weakening of the Petersburg line, but by late evening on the 14th when he reported the day's events to Washington, he could only report that Hancock's force had fought the enemy and taken some prisoners who revealed that the Confederate infantry was primarily from Field's division supported by remnants of Pickett's division. Grant had evidence at that time indicating the Confederate line around Petersburg was being weakened.[85]

Late on the evening of August 14, Hancock reported that D. McM. Gregg's cavalry was pressing the enemy on the Charles City Road and had pushed the Confederate troopers from their first line of rifle-pits. The Union cavalrymen were poised to strike Richmond if not seriously opposed and if their infantry moved as planned.[86]

FIGHTS AROUND WHITE'S TAVERN AND WHITE OAK SWAMP, AUGUST 15, 16

The Confederate line under attack was commanded by Charles W. Field. The right of his line rested at Chaffin's Bluff and the left at Fussell's Mill. Fussell's Mill was just southeast of Richmond where the three main roads coming from the river to the city nearly came together (the three roads primarily used by the Union forces to approach Richmond were the New Market, Darbytown, and Charles City Roads).[87] (See map 2.1.)

As expected, Grant's attack did prompt an immediate response from R. E. Lee. A few minutes into August 15, C. W. Field was sent word that two infantry brigades and W. H. F. Lee's cavalry division were on their way. He was also informed that Hampton and his cavalry division had been recalled and were on their way to the Richmond line. Field used the cavalry to extend his far left. He thought that necessary because his far left did not have time to entrench as thoroughly as the rest of the Confederate line, and the enemy's cavalry had been placed there.[88]

The North Carolina brigade was ordered to the front in a forced march on the night of the 14th. They crossed the James at Chaffin's Bluff and moved directly behind Field's line, past Fussell's Mill, which had been the Confederate left, to Charles City Road. The North Carolinians were accompanied by Chambliss's brigade. The two brigades marched night and day and engaged the enemy on Charles City Road early August 15.[89]

On August 14, Hancock's men made several minor attempts to assault the Confederate line, but were easily turned back. No serious attack was made on the 14th, but during the night Hancock positioned his troops for an early morning assault on the Confederate line. He moved most of Birney's command and some of Mott's further to the Union right, facing Fussell's Mill. Barlow's command was still on Darbytown Road, back near the intersection with Long Bridge Road. D. McM. Gregg's cavalry was to cover the movement on the Union right along Charles City Road.[90]

THE CAVALRY ON CHARLES CITY ROAD, AUGUST 15

Early on the 15th, D. McM. Gregg moved his cavalry up Charles City Road toward White's Tavern. At 8:00 A.M., he reported to Hancock that his advance was within a mile of the tavern, and that he was pressing the enemy. As D. McM. Gregg's command was pushing the Confederate pickets, W. H. F. Lee and his command were approaching down the Charles City Road with Barringer's North Carolina brigade in front. Just after passing White's Tavern, the North Carolinians came upon Union cavalrymen (near Fisher's Farm). W. H. F. Lee ordered Barringer to move his regiments forward and attack. Barringer dismounted the 5th North Carolina and sent them at the enemy in a charge with the 2nd and 3rd cavalries right behind. The Union advance was quickly turned yet repeatedly tried to face the oncoming Confederates and make a stand. They were overwhelmed each time. Finally D. McM. Gregg's men broke and were driven over three miles with the North Carolina regiments hot on their heels. The dismounted Confederates rapidly pursued their enemy until exhausted. At that time, Barringer sent a mounted squadron after the retreating Federals and pushed to D. McM. Gregg's strong, well entrenched line of infantry and dismounted cavalry at Wilson's farm. The mounted North Carolina troopers continued their charge, and according to a writer for the *Richmond Enquirer*, "Cutting and slashing, they unquailingly dashed upon the heels of the flying herd—leaping their works through the opposing ranks—sabreing and taking out several prisoners, and, in the midst of the excitement that ensued, dashed back without losing a single man." Barringer's cavalrymen did drive D. McM. Gregg's troops off the road and across White Oak Swamp (after crossing Deep Creek), causing their main line to fall back.[91]

Around midday, D. McM. Gregg reported to Hancock that "The enemy are making a spirited advance, but are held by one of my brigades dismounted." As just indicated, however, his advance brigade did not hold, and was driven into their main Union line which then was also slowly pushed back as more of Barringer's dismounted cavalrymen arrived. By 1:30 P.M., Hancock reported to Grant that W. H. F. Lee's cavalry had driven D. McM. Gregg out of the entrenchments he had taken from the Confederates the previous day.[92]

Shortly after Barringer's cavalrymen drove the Union troopers out of and past their entrenchments, Hancock sent an infantry force to hit the Confederate horsemen in the flank. He also sent more infantry support directly to D. McM. Gregg who by then had been pushed back to the intersection of Long Bridge Road and the Charles City Road.[93]

With his infantry support, D. McM. Gregg regrouped after the initial attack by the North Carolina regiments and mounted a strong and rapid advance along the north side of White Oak Swamp with both infantry and dismounted cavalry. The 2nd North Carolina Cavalry, under the command of Major William P. Roberts, had been moved north of White Oak Swamp and was directly in the path of the advancing Union force.[94] A writer for the *Richmond Enquirer* described the scene:

He [Roberts] gallantly faced his command and withstood the shock of the pressing assailants, who swept around on the flanks of his limited line, seeming to engulph his heroic little band in the swooping wings of their heavy lines; but the sagacity and cool determined valor of this young officer, at no time allowed them an undue advantage. Stubbornly contesting every inch of ground, falling back in good order before this overwhelming odds, the 1st North Carolina reached his support, rushing up with a yell, which event caused the enemy to believe that large reinforcements were arriving.[95]

Roberts and his 2nd North Carolina Cavalry had been swamped by infantry and cavalry and come under attack on their right flank by Birney's approaching infantry. Apparently W. H. F. Lee did not send Chambliss's Virginia regiments forward and ordered Barringer to retreat in an orderly fashion to more defensible ground south of the swamp. Somehow the 2nd North Carolina, north of the swamp, did not get the message—they were the Confederate's front line when their comrades were ordered to fall back. Their desperate situation was finally recognized, however, and Barringer sent the 1st Cavalry forward to assist their withdrawal.[96] Major Roberts described the view:

The entire division was soon withdrawn by some miscarriage of orders, as I afterwards learned, and it was not very long before the enemy advanced in great numbers upon my little command, but it stood up against this onslaught as only brave men can. At one time the regiment was practically surrounded, and its annihilation seemed complete, but in the nick of time up dashed the Ninth North Carolina [1st Cavalry], led by the gallant Colonel W. H. Cheek, who finally responded to my wishes and put his regiment where I suggested it should be put, and by his action I was enabled to extricate my men.[97]

In his summary of that day's action, Barringer praised the stubborn resistance made by W. P. Roberts and the 2nd Cavalry as they inflicted unusual punishment on the enemy for every inch of ground given up. Barringer went on to say, "...when he [Roberts] was ordered to retire across White Oak Swamp, which he did in excellent order, the enemy showing no disposition to follow him. This Regiment [2nd North Carolina] suffered pretty severely in this engagement." Indeed, commanders of both the 1st and 2nd North Carolina cavalries noted the severity of their fighting and their considerable losses that day. After nightfall, the 2nd North Carolina and the rest of Barringer's brigade were relieved by Chambliss's brigade and fell back about two miles from the line for the night.[98]

According to the Union view of the fighting, when confronted by both the 1st and 2nd North Carolina cavalries and the possibility of a much larger force in front of them on the next day, D. McM. Gregg halted his advance and did not press across the swamp. By late afternoon, Hancock reported to Grant that they had succeeded in pushing W. H. F. Lee's cavalry back as far as the entrenchments held by D. McM. Gregg's men early that morning.[99]

During the day, Hancock sent a message to Grant stating that he had captured a member of Barringer's staff and others from W. H. F. Lee's division. But his captures were not enough to lift his mood. Later that night, Hancock heard of D. McM. Gregg's shortage of water and forage for his horses, so instructed him to send for some because they "...may be here for several days." Even later on August 15, Hancock wrote these words to B. F. Butler, "I am well out on the Charles City and Central [Darbytown] Roads. The day has been consumed in affairs with cavalry and in reconnaissance. To-morrow morning at daylight I hope to commence more serious work." In his after-battle report, Hancock later wrote, "Another day thus passed without accomplishing anything commensurate with my wishes."[100]

Cavalry Fighting Near White Oak Swamp, August 16

Hancock and his commanders spent much of the night preparing for a major attack on the Confederate line early on August 16. His infantry on New Market and Darbytown Roads were facing C. W. Field's division of R. H. Anderson's First Army Corps, and on the Union right Birney's command was to launch the main assault on a section of the line that included troopers from Wilcox's and Mahone's divisions of A. P. Hill's Third Corps. On the Union's far right, on Charles City Road, D. McM. Gregg's cavalry supported by Nelson A. Miles's infantry brigade of Barlow's division was to move as far up the road as possible and make a strong diversion against W. H. F. Lee's cavalry before Birney launched the main attack.[101]

During the late morning, Hancock's force assaulted Field's line just to the left of Fussell's Mill—according to Field, the most vulnerable part of his line. In addition, the three roads leading to Richmond were all near Fussel's Mill and were all occupied by Union forces. The Confederate line was assaulted more than once, and at one point Field's left was cut off. Union forces poured through the gap, but Field rallied and drove the Federals back. He later recalled, "At this time not only the day but Richmond seemed to be gone."[102]

Over near Charles City Road, D. McM. Gregg started the activity early by attacking W. H. F. Lee's advance regiment on picket near Deep Creek. Colonel J. I. Gregg's cavalry and Mile's infantry made the initial attack, with the rest of the Union cavalry ready if needed. Because the North Carolina brigade did the major part of the fighting on August 15, Chambliss's brigade was on the picket line during the night and in the Union's direct line of attack the next morning. Chambliss had the 13th Virginia on the front line, and he camped a short distance behind with his 9th and 10th Virginia. Early on the 16th, Chambliss and his staff moved out to join his 13th Virginia—he left the 9th and 10th cavalries to follow. Many of the cavalrymen in the 9th and 10th Virginia were some distance from camp in search of water. Not realizing they were needed at the front, they returned and formed at a leisurely pace. Consequently, the 13th Virginia was on its own at the front for longer than it could stand. About the time Chambliss joined his advance regiment, D. McM. Gregg's force came up and hit their picket line. The fighting was hard, and Chambliss dashed back and forth along his line encouraging his men to stand and fight until support arrived. He was a conspicuous target that was not missed that morning—Chambliss fell mortally wounded and was dead by the time his enemy came upon his body. The Union cavalry also fought hard and pushed Chambliss's front line back in confusion. The 9th and 10th Virginia arrived soon after the fighting started but were not sufficient to stop the enemy's rising tide. As the 9th Virginia moved forward at a trot, they were fired upon and immediately dismounted forming a line across the road. After a brief but rapid exchange of fire with a dismounted enemy, they discovered firing was also coming from their flank and rear. The Confederates began to fall back before they reached the 13th Cavalry or knew of Chambliss's fate.[103]

Once W. H. F. Lee received word of the assault on Chambliss's command at the front, he rushed forward with Barringer's North Carolina brigade to confront the Federal assault on the Virginia regiments which had fallen back around White's Tavern. Barringer hurried the 1st, 2nd, and 3rd North Carolina regiments to the retreating line tenuously held by Chambliss's troops—it was the 1st North Carolina's turn to be in front, and the 2nd Cavalry followed. William P. Roberts, commanding the 2nd North Carolina Cavalry, described the scene from his position in these words:

...hurried to the front in columns of fours, the Nineteenth [2nd Cavalry] being the last of the division. Suddenly I saw the regiments to my front bear to the right, and immediately thereafter came an order from General Lee [W. H. F. Lee] ... for the Nineteenth to hurry to the front. The command "trot," "gallop," was given, and in a short while I reported to the Major-General [W. H. F. Lee]. My orders were to relieve the regiment to my front, the Ninth Virginia, I think it was, and he further said to me: "Roberts, you know what to do, but the line must be held."[104]

As the 2nd North Carolina and the rest of their brigade reached Chambliss's beleaguered men, they immediately dismounted and formed a line to the left of the road—their sister brigade being on the right. This stopped the Union advance.[105] An observer noted that once the North Carolinians were on the line and the Virginians regrouped, "With this disposition our lines were advanced, under a heavy fire, at a double quick, driving the enemy from his first position."[106]

Once Barringer arrived on the left of Chambliss's brigade and helped stop the Union advance, W. H. F. Lee's line prepared to advance against D. McM. Gregg's cavalry and Miles's infantry. Both sides spent some time jockeying to flank their enemy's line but not much happened until the Confederate cavalry was reinforced by the arrival of Hampton's division.

Hampton took his command around the left. Then W. H. F. Lee ordered his cavalrymen on both sides of the road to charge the center. At the sound of the signal gun, the Confederate cavalrymen advanced at a double quick under heavy fire and through thick woods that made it difficult to see men thirty yards away. Finally the Union line broke and was driven back into its support—the Confederate cavalrymen were not able to dislodge the main force. The fighting continued fiercely, but W. H. F. Lee's line made no headway until a burst of fire came from their right. John Gregg's Texas infantry brigade (from Field's division) and Gary's South Carolina cavalry (also sent by Field) came from the direction of Fussell's Mill and hit the Union flank (the flank attack occurred just before 11:00 A.M. according to Miles). The combined Confederate force was overwhelming, and D. McM. Gregg's Union cavalrymen and Miles's infantry were soon driven back even harder and faster than they had advanced earlier in the day. A member of the 2nd North Carolina described the scene on the left side of the road: "The Yankees held their ground pretty well for a while, pouring volley after volley of minie balls into our ranks, mixed with torrents of grape and canister. Our lines never wavered for a moment, but rushed forward determined to conquer or die in the attempt." According to Barringer, the 2nd North Carolina Cavalry was among the first to storm the enemy works and took heavy losses at that point (including the mortal wounding of Captain George P. Bryan of Company G). The Union troops were pushed across Deep Creek (one of two small creeks crossing Charles City Road between White's Tavern and the intersection with Long Bridge Road). Many of the Federal troops made it back across the swamp in a disorganized fashion, losing horses and equipment in the process. In fact, D. McM. Gregg lost hundreds of men and horses that afternoon—though the Confederate cavalrymen were most grateful for the latter. Captain Lockhart of the 2nd North Carolina described the scene in these words: "The enemy were routed, throwing away knapsacks, haversacks, canteens, and their guns, fled in confusion. The ground was strewn with dead Yankees and their plunder for about one mile." Just after 3:00 P.M., D. McM. Gregg could take the time to notify Hancock that he was "...holding to north side of Deep Creek. Our last advance was met by a superior force of infantry, which moved up from the direction of Fussell's Mill; the force is now retiring to my left and in the direction of the mill. The firing in my front has ceased." W. H. F. Lee's cavalry remained in front of the Union cavalry line.[107]

D. McM. Gregg's problems on Charles City Road were compounded on the 16th by Hampton's arrival on the road just after Barringer's North Carolinians had stopped the Union pursuit of Chambliss's command. As indicated, while on the road to Culpeper, Hampton was promoted to commander of the cavalry corps in R. E. Lee's army, while Matthew C. Butler took over the management of Hampton's division which still included Butler's, Rosser's and Young's brigades. When Hampton arrived on the scene, he met with W. H. F. Lee, who was more familiar with the situation at hand, and they decided Hampton should take some of Butler's, Rosser's and Young's commands around to the enemy's right and attempt to gain their rear, while W. H. F. Lee would take his division at their front. Gary's cavalry brigade from the Richmond defenses was also near the Confederate left. The men with Hampton were mostly held in reserve and only slightly engaged. W. H. F. Lee's cavalrymen carried the day. Hampton had arrived in time to witness the Confederate line form and push the Union infantry and cavalry past where they started the day. According to Hampton, "...Lee [W. H. F. Lee] moved his line forward, & in a gallant charge not only regained the ground he had lost, but drove the enemy in confusion across Deep Creek."[108]

To earn this praise from the cavalry commander, the 2nd North Carolina Cavalry, along with the other regiments in its division, had to pay a high price. The 2nd Cavalry had seven men killed or wounded that day.[109]

While D. McM. Gregg created his diversion over on Charles City Road and paid dearly for it, some of Birney's command advanced against the Confederate line near Fussell's Mill and after a severe fight, managed to capture hundreds of prisoners from Wilcox's and Mahone's commands of A. P. Hill's corps—Birney's attack finally got underway shortly after noon. The Confederates soon rallied, however, and retook their line. Hancock's infantry and cavalry had little to show for some serious fighting at the end of the day.[110]

A Slow but Dangerous Day, August 17

At 9:30 on the evening of August 16, Grant sent a message to Hancock informing the latter of a trick he had up his sleeve. Grant wrote, "I have ordered to Strawberry Plains steamers ostensibly to bring down the Second Corps. It is intended as a ruse to make the enemy believe you are withdrawing, and to bring them out to attack you."[111]

The next day, the Union steamers pulled out of Deep Bottom heading back to City Point, hoping the Confederates would think they carried Hancock's command from the battlefield. The ruse did not work, and the Confederate line remained in place. Chambliss's cavalry brigade, under the command of Colonel J. Lucius Davis, was on picket duty that day and most of the following. That left W. H. F. Lee with the North Carolina Brigade for other activities, the most obvious of which was to investigate the suspicious movements at Deep Bottom. Among the cavalrymen sent to observe the commotion at Deep Bottom were men from the 2nd North Carolina Cavalry, and they had a hard day. One member of the 2nd North Carolina was mortally wounded, and two of his comrades were captured at that place.[112]

Aside from such skirmishes and brief encounters, very few were killed that day. Rather, attention was paid to retrieving and burying the dead from the previous day's fighting. A truce was agreed upon for a couple of hours in the early evening, and some bodies were exchanged—the remains of General Chambliss was among them.

The lull in the fighting on August 17 gave young Private Gaston B. Lockhart of the 2nd North Carolina Cavalry a chance to write his mother—he had only been in the service for about four and a half months. Gaston started by telling her that he and his older brother, John also of the 2nd Cavalry, were by the "blessing of God" both alive and well. Then he went on to tell her more than she probably wanted to know.

Our regiment was in some hard fighting yesterday and the day before. We gave the Yankees a bad whipping, and ran them back for a mile and a half; we are now on the battlefield that we ran the Yankees off, about five miles from Malvern Hill. John Umstead was wounded in the finger, and James A. Homes was mortally wounded and since died; no one else hurt belonging to our Company. We lost about thirty-five men from the Regiment, Killed, wounded and missing.[113]

Grant Prepares His Next Move

While Hancock was waiting to see if Grant's ruse would draw the enemy from its works, Grant was in the process of finalizing another alternative approach to easing the pressure on Sheridan in northern Virginia and cutting the supply routes to Petersburg. He sent a report to Halleck in Washington, D. C. on August 16, in which he stated, "I have relieved the Fifth Corps [Warren's] from the trenches, and have it ready to march around Petersburg if the enemy can be induced to throw troops enough north of the James to justify it." Once Birney's men had taken prisoners from A. P. Hill's corps north of the James, Grant knew R. E. Lee's right, just south of Petersburg, was weakened. In addition, he believed most of R. E. Lee's cavalry had been sent from their far right, on the Weldon Railroad, up to the Charles City Road (Hancock had also reported that Dearing's small brigade was with W. H. F. Lee, but it remained on the Weldon). Nonetheless, R. E. Lee apparently had not moved as much of his force to Richmond as Grant had hoped, because Grant still did not feel an attack on Petersburg was reasonable, but a lesser target was thought practical. Pursuant to these thoughts and his desires, on August 17 Grant sent a message to Meade on the Petersburg line in which he set out his scaled down version of what he wanted. He described his flexible plan as follows:

Under these circumstance no decisive result could be expected from moving a single corps by our left; but they might get to the Weldon road and, with the aid of a little cavalry, cut and destroy a few miles of it. You may, therefore, start Warren in the morning. I do not want him to fight any unequal battles nor to assault fortifications.... If he cannot strike the road near the enemy's line enclosing Petersburg he can strike or feel farther south. If he finds the enemy extending along the railroad, showing front whenever he does, let him remain, holding them there.... I want, if possible, to make such demonstrations as will force Lee to withdraw a portion of his troops from the Valley, so that Sheridan can strike a blow against the balance.[114]

By 2:00 P.M. on the 17th, Meade notified Grant that Warren was ready to move early the next morning, and two regiments of cavalry from Kautz's command would be sent with him. Throughout the day, however, Meade continued to express his concern about the strength of A. P. Hill's and Beauregard's commands on the Petersburg line. He was reluctant to send Warren and some of Kautz's cavalry down until the Confederate line in front of him was weakened further. Meade and Grant continued to exchange messages well into the night juggling the one's concerns and the other's desires. By day's end, Warren was sent to the Weldon.[115]

Finally after 10:00 P.M. on August 17, Hancock received a message from Grant informing him that Warren was instructed to move south of the city and strike the Weldon Railroad early the next morning. Grant reminded Hancock to be alert for the movement of Confederate troops from in front of his line to below Petersburg, and to attack any weakness on his front. Hancock remained north of the James River until August 20, and held the North Carolina Cavalry there just about as long. The fighting north of the James continued, making it more difficult for R. E. Lee to meet Warren's advance on the Weldon Railroad in a timely manner.[116]

Another Day of Fighting on the Charles City Road, August 18

On August 18, R. E. Lee instructed his infantry and cavalry to attack Hancock's line — but it was early evening before Field's Confederate infantry came out of their works above Fussell's Mill and attacked Birney's line. The fighting was hard for about half an hour, when troops from Barlow's command hit the Confederate line in the left flank. The Confederates pulled back, and it was too late in the day for any further action.[117]

Meanwhile, the cavalries clashed over near Charles City and Long Bridge Roads. D. McM. Gregg's cavalry line was across Charles City Road just below Deep Creek. Hampton sent W. H. F. Lee and Barringer's North Carolina brigade straight ahead to attack on the Charles City Road (most of Chambliss's brigade, under the command of Davis, was on picket duty on the 17th and 18th); and Hampton's division, commanded by M. C. Butler, was sent to the left, across the White Oak Swamp and instructed to move on the enemy's right flank and rear. Hampton rode with W. H. F. Lee, Barringer, and the North Carolina regiments.[118] (See map 2.1.)

M. C. Butler took his command over White Oak Swamp and moved to Long Bridge Road. He arrived about 11:00 A.M., and waited for the appointed signal to attack the enemy at the road's intersection with Charles City Road. It was around 5:00 P.M. when M. C. Butler finally heard the signal to attack, which he did immediately and drove the Union cavalrymen from the intersection to Riddell's Shop. Butler had been instructed to take the intersection and wait for W. H. F. Lee's command to arrive along the Charles City Road. Butler took about 30 prisoners, from D. McM. Gregg's cavalry division and waited.[119]

While M. C. Butler was taking his command around the enemy's flank, W. H. F. Lee and his North Carolinians went directly at the Union position on Charles City Road. Hampton described the action for Robert E. Lee the following day, "General William H. F. Lee made a very handsome and successful fight yesterday. He drove the enemy two miles and a half, killing many and capturing 110 prisoners, representing two brigades of infantry, in addition to D. McM. Gregg's division of cavalry. I have not witnessed a more gallant affair with our cavalry this campaign than the one of yesterday." The cavalry Hampton was praising that day was the North Carolina Brigade.[120]

Private Gordon of the 2nd North Carolina Cavalry, described the evening in his characteristic, matter-of-fact style: "August 18th, In the evening we advanced and had a little skirmish with the enemy, and shelled the woods around us. At night we fell back two miles and bivouacked."[121]

Union commanders, Hancock and D. McM. Gregg, knew that by sundown their cavalry on Charles City Road and Deep Creek was being driven and had W. H. F. Lee's cavalry in front of them and M. C. Butler's command in their rear at the intersection of Charles City and Long Bridge Roads. Early in the day, Hampton's plan was to unite W. H. F. Lee's and Butler's commands at the intersection, but that was overly ambitious—while the North Carolina regiments were able to push the enemy cavalry more then two miles down the road, they were not close to their rendezvous with Butler. According to Hampton, the main problem was his guide, who did not get him from W. H. F. Lee's position on Charles City Road to White Oak Bridge to signal Butler until nearly sunset. Butler was at the intersection until 9:00 P.M. when he was ordered to move back to his camp near W. H. F. Lee's cavalrymen.[122]

By the end of the day, it did not matter—the fighting in front of Richmond had ceased to be useful and Grant was moving on.

Combat Losses in the 2nd North Carolina Cavalry North of the James River in Mid-August, 1864

Trooper	Age	Co.	Fate
Bartlett Y. Tyson	30	I	wounded, Aug. 15
Rufus J. Byrum	23	I	killed, Aug. 15
George W. Rowan	20	A	killed, Aug. 15
John J. Bryan	26	E	wounded, Aug.
Thomas Felton	24	E	wounded, Aug.
Thomas E. Reese	19	H	captured, Aug. 15
James G. Lowery		A	killed, Aug. 16
Joseph Paschal	24	I	wounded, Aug. 16
John H. Steele	27	B	wounded, Aug. 16
Lewis R. Cowper	36	C	mortally wounded, Aug. 16
George P. Bryan	24	G	killed, Aug. 16
Romulus S. Barham	22	H	wounded, Aug. 16
John Umstead*		K	wounded, Aug. 16
James A. Holmes**	24	K	mortally wounded, Aug. 16
John T. Meloney	32	B	mortally wounded, Aug. 17
Charles Hofler	21	C	captured, Aug. 17
Edward A. Sheaffer	40	D	captured, Aug. 17
Junius H. Barham	26	H	wounded, Aug. 18

Information contained in this table came from Compiled Service Records as summarized by Louis H. Manarin, *North Carolina Troops: 1861–1865, A Roster*, vol. II, pages 98–177. (See Appendix for more information on the men listed above, page 403.)

*Gaston B. Lockhart to mother, August 17, 1864 from camp near Malvern Hill, in Lockhart Family Letters, Rare Book, Manuscript, and Special Collections Library, Duke University; also J. P. Lockhart, *Hillsborough Recorder*, August 24, 1864, page 2, cols. 2, 3.

**The Roster of North Carolina Troops, lists James A Holmes as killed in action on June 10th; however, his captain, John P. Lockhart, was very specific when he provided the following in the source cited above, "James A. Holmes of my company fell mortally wounded in the charge [of August 16, 1864].... He died the next morning, and was buried near White Tavern on the Charles City Road."

W. H. F. Lee's cavalry had been an important part of limiting Grant's move on Richmond to a demonstration, but it had been costly for both sides. The 2nd North Carolina took heavy losses in the fighting on August 15 and 16, and lost three men when sent to investigate Grant's ruse on the river. They were again involved in the fighting on the 18th, but did not carry the heaviest burden that day.

It is not surprising that by the time Muster Roles were compiled many men who received wounds, some serious, did not have them recorded for the records that survived. For instance, Gaston B. Lockhart was under the impression the 2nd North Carolina Cavalry had about 35 men killed, wounded, or missing from the fighting on August 15 and 16. In addition, their commander, William P. Roberts, who fought alongside the cavalrymen of the 2nd North Carolina remembered that on August 16, "more then thirty officers and men [were] killed in a few minutes." Of course, we are dealing with perceptions and estimates, but it is probably safe to assume the number of men killed, wounded, and captured from that small regiment, on those two days, was somewhere between 16 and 30.[123]

Grant Makes His Move for the Weldon Railroad

George G. Meade reluctantly relieved the Fifth Corps on the Petersburg line during the night of August 14, replacing them by extending the Ninth Corps into its entrenchments. By the 16th, Meade was satisfied that only three enemy infantry divisions were left on the Petersburg line, so he ordered G. K. Warren to move his Fifth Corps to the Weldon Railroad. Warren's instructions were clear: he was to move at 4:00 A.M. the next morning; establish a base on the Weldon as near to the enemy entrenchments as possible; destroy the railroad as far south as possible, until strong resistance was reached, then hold; and probe the enemy's line for weaknesses that could be exploited, but not to "fight under serious disadvantages or assault fortifications." To assist Warren, August V. Kautz was instructed to place two brigades of cavalry at his service.[124]

By 11:00 A.M. August 18, Warren reported that the last of his divisions were on the Weldon about two miles south of the intersection with Vaughan Road (near Globe Tavern). Warren left a small force near Globe Tavern to begin tearing up the railroad — they only had to contend with pickets from Dearing's small cavalry brigade. The main body of Warren's command moved up the railroad toward the intersection with Vaughan Road — R. B. Ayres's division in advance. Just after 2:00 P.M., Warren reported that they encountered considerable resistance. They had met two of Henry Heth's infantry brigades from A. P. Hill's command. A couple of hours later, Warren reported Ayres had lost some ground, but he had ordered Ayres and S. W. Crawford to regroup and advance again. Warren managed to get a foothold on the Weldon but not much else — he had Confederate infantry between him and Petersburg and to the west, as well as enemy cavalry south of him along the railroad. At 5:00 P.M., Meade sent Grant this assessment: "I fancy he [Warren] will not be able to do more than effect a lodgment on the road and that the enemy will vigorously dispute this." An hour later, Meade sent another message to Grant, "Warren is directed to maintain his hold and entrench himself. When may we look for Hancock?" Grant responded with assurances Hancock would send Mott's division from north of the James to support the Petersburg line and thus free additional infantry support for the Fifth Corps. Warren spent the evening and most of the night entrenching his position on the railroad with his right nearly two miles south of the main Confederate entrenchments of Petersburg. He fully expected the enemy to make every effort to push him off the road the next morning. Warren received assurances that Motts' infantry was on the way — but it would take more than a day; and that Kautz was sending another cavalry regiment as soon as possible.[125]

Late on the 18th, Grant notified Washington D. C. that they held a section of the Weldon Railroad. The next day President Lincoln sent a message to Grant expressing his gratification at the success in pushing across and seizing the Weldon, and that it would be a heavy blow to the enemy if it could be held.[126]

However, Meade was not yet assessing his success. He was still unsure Warren could hold his position on the Weldon until Hancock returned from north of the James, but Grant reassured him there would be less pressure on him around Petersburg as long as Hancock detained a large Confederate force around Richmond. More importantly, early August 19, Grant explained to Meade that, he was "...anxious to force the enemy to withdraw from the Valley the re-enforcements he has sent to J. Early, and I think the best way to do it is to threaten as long a line as possible. If, therefore, there is no necessity for it, I shall not withdraw Hancock for the present."[127]

Grant's concerns about Sheridan's ability to control Early in northern Virginia had been heightened when it was confirmed that Fitz Lee's cavalry division and Kershaw's infantry division were on the way to the Shenandoah Valley to support J. Early.[128]

The loss of the Weldon Railroad would make it more difficult for the Confederacy to supply the Army of Northern Virginia and Petersburg. Its loss may have been inevitable, but it was not yet acceptable to the Confederates; so on August 19 they made their first attempt to remove Grant's foothold from the Weldon — it was not an easy day for Warren's troopers. That evening he reported to Meade's headquarters, "The enemy broke through the line I had just established between my position and that on the plank road, and moving rapidly on my right flank, compelled the whole of Crawford's and Ayres's division to fall back. A heavy fight took place, and the whole line has been regained, taking many prisoners." It has been estimated that Warren lost more than 2,500 men that day. He nonetheless assured headquarters that he would collect his command and be ready to fight come the next dawn.[129]

Beauregard had sent three Confederate brigades from the Petersburg defenses to support Heth during the day, but no serious Confederate troop movements had yet taken place. Even though D. McM. Gregg sent another cavalry brigade to Warren on August 19, the latter could not yet be sure of his enemy's strength, so he moved back a mile or two into an open space he considered more defensible than the woods surrounding his position at nightfall on August 19. He and his troops were more comfortable on the 20th.[130]

As indicated earlier, Mott's division was moved south of the James River to support Warren's move on the Weldon Railroad August 18. The remaining divisions under Hancock's command were withdrawn from north of the James after night fall on August 20.[131]

R. E. Lee's Response to Grant's Move on the Weldon

When Warren had moved his troops to the Weldon, they first encountered Dearing's cavalry brigade left by W. H. F. Lee to guard the road. At 10:15 A.M. August 18, Dearing notified Beauregard on the Petersburg line: "Enemy has driven in my pickets and reserves in front of Yellow House. I am just going up with another regiment." By noon, Dearing sent the following: "Enemy is advancing in force both upon railroad and Vaughan road." Beauregard notified R. E. Lee, who had moved up to Chaffin's Bluff leaving Beauregard in command of the Petersburg line, that he was sending two brigades to help confront Warren, but he had to have them back on his line by nightfall. Later in the afternoon, A. P. Hill notified Beauregard that he had two divisions of the enemy in front of him. By 7:00 P.M., Beauregard notified R. E. Lee that Heth desired and needed reinforcements and that the three brigades he had sent during the day were all that he could send to Heth. He reiterated that the brigades must return to his Petersburg line during the night.[132]

Early on the 19th, Beauregard reaffirmed to R. E. Lee that the enemy had fortified its position on the Weldon, and he "...will endeavor to-day to dislodge Warren with four brigades of our infantry and the division of cavalry you have promised." Throughout the day Beauregard kept R. E. Lee informed of Union troop and supply movements to the railroad south of Petersburg from City Point. The task was became more difficult by the hour.[133]

Robert E. Lee had promised Beauregard a cavalry division, but it could not arrive from north of the James in time for the August 19 attack. Back north of the James, on Charles City Road, early warnings from R. E. Lee to Hampton about the pending need to move the cavalry back south of the James elicited a less than enthusiastic response from the commander of the cavalry. On the afternoon of August 19 Hampton reported to R. E. Lee that his cavalry's horses were in need of rest and grazing. As a result, W. H. F. Lee's division received orders to march for the James River and prepare to cross at Chaffin's Bluff. They did and were near Swift

Creek when they stopped for the night. The next day they marched south of Petersburg.[134]

Hampton with his division, then under the command of M. C. Butler, rested at Chaffin's Bluff. R. E. Lee returned to Petersburg and on the morning of August 21 sent a message to C. W. Field at Chaffin's Bluff requesting that if Hancock had left his front, he should send as many of his brigades as possible south of Petersburg. Lee added, "If Gregg has left request Hampton to report to me." Later that afternoon, R. E. Lee sent the same instructions directly to Hampton, and Hampton moved.[135]

The 2nd North Carolina Cavalry had marched to the James on August 19 with their division. They crossed again at Chaffin's Bluff and ended the day at Swift Creek. While on the march, William P. Roberts was promoted to colonel and given command of the 2nd North Carolina Cavalry. Major W. P. Roberts had been given temporary command of the 2nd North Carolina Cavalry during and since the fighting at Blacks and Whites on June 23—on that day, the regiment's colonel, Clinton M. Andrews, was mortally wounded. W. P. Roberts continued in temporary command of the regiment until August 19, when he was promoted to rank as colonel from June 23, 1864.[136]

The Focus on the Destruction of the Weldon Railroad

The Union hold on the Weldon Railroad around Globe Tavern meant the Confederates could still bring supplies for Petersburg to within one day of the city by loading wagons and swinging around the Union foothold at the tavern. That was not good enough. The Union command decided it wanted to destroy the railroad for at least another 13 miles south of the tavern, to Rowanty Creek. If successful, the Confederates would have to load their supplies from the train at Stony Creek Depot onto wagons and take them to Dinwiddie Court House, then along the Boydton Plank Road to Petersburg—a trip of about thirty miles. Grant's goal was clear. On August 22, he wrote Meade, "It is my desire to hold the Weldon road, if it can be held, and to thoroughly destroy it as far south as possible. I do not expect to attack the enemy behind his intrenchments, unless he sends off a large part of his force." Hancock's command would be brought back south of the James and onto the Weldon for the purpose of destroying the railroad south of Globe Tavern. His job north of the James was at an end in any case.[137]

Hancock noted in his report that "Nothing of great interest occurred during the 20th." That was about to change. Grant ordered him back with his command, and instructed Meade to send him forward to support Warren. Thus Hancock and his troops moved back below the James and marched under exhausting conditions to the rear of Warren's operation where they arrived on August 21. The next day, they began destroying the Weldon Railroad. D. McM. Gregg and his cavalry were also pulled back from the Charles City Road on August 20, and moved down to the Weldon to shield Hancock's work. W. H. F. Lee's cavalry was already on the road, and his North Carolina brigade arrived there late on August 20.[138]

Early on the 20th, in a hard rain, W. P. Roberts led the 2nd North Carolina Cavalry from Swift Creek through Petersburg and out the railroad tracks for a couple of miles where they stopped for a short rest. Around sunset, they were in the saddle again and took a roundabout route toward Reams's Station on the Weldon where they stopped for the night. The North Carolina brigade missed A. P. Hill's first attempt to regain the Weldon on the 19th, but they were just in time for the second attempt. About 3:00 A.M., the cavalrymen of the 2nd North Carolina were on the road marching for about four miles to just west of Reams's Station, then halted until daylight. Union troops had moved west of the railroad, and were dug in near the Poplar Spring Church. It was the 2nd North Carolina Cavalry's job to dislodge and drive the enemy back from Poplar Spring Church across the railroad if possible.[139]

The Fight at Poplar Spring Church, August 21, 1864

The Confederate's second attempt to push Warren from his foothold on the Weldon had two dimensions to it: the infantry fight for Globe Tavern and the cavalry fight near Poplar Spring Church. Both fights took place August 21.

A. P. Hill's attack on Warren's entrenched infantrymen was unsuccessful and costly for a variety of reasons—not enough manpower being but one of the most important.[140]

W. H. F. Lee sent Chambliss's former

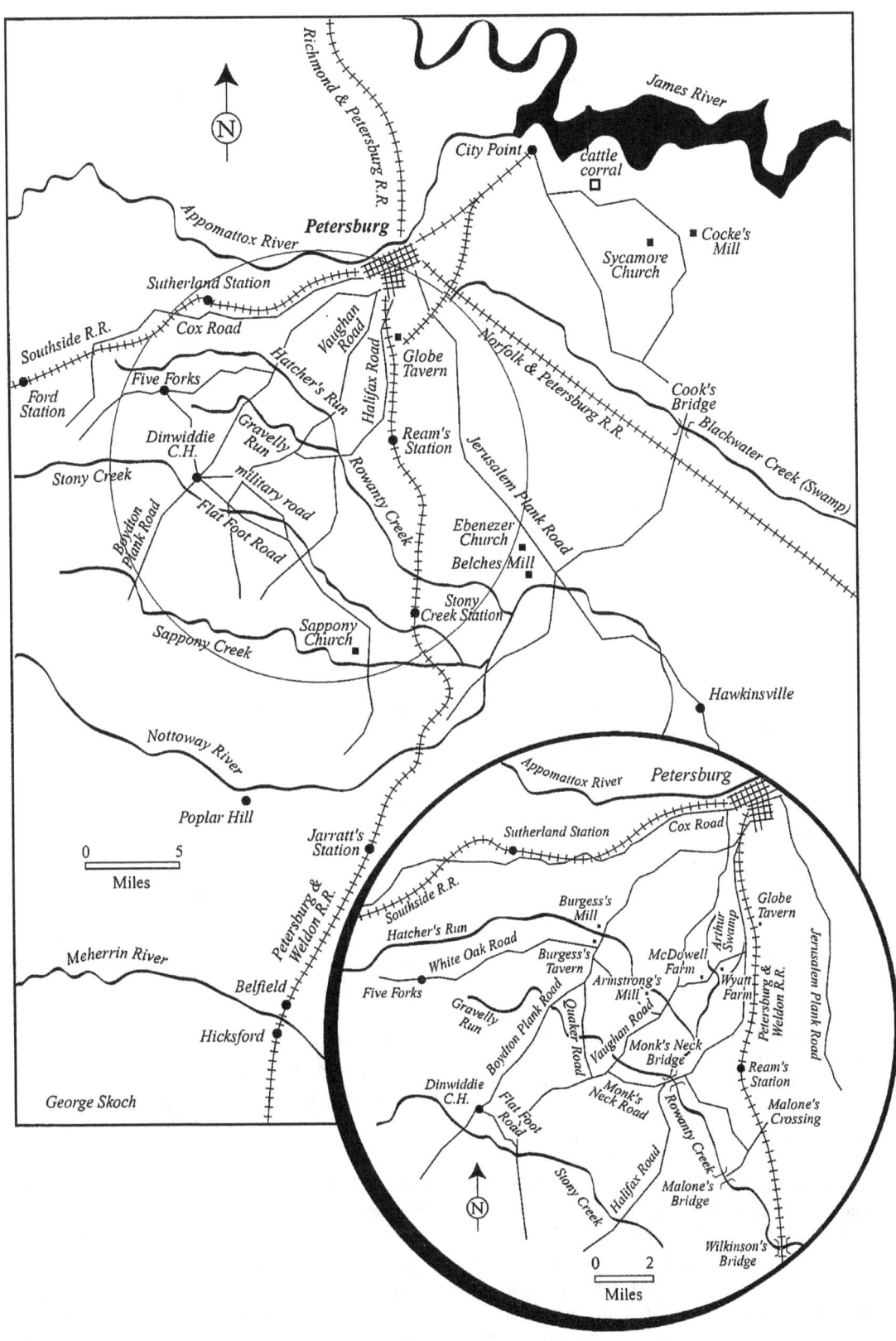

6.2: Grant's Moves South and West of Peterburg

brigade to cover the left of A. P. Hill's infantry line. He placed his other brigade, Barringer's North Carolina, again on the Confederate right advancing on the Weldon Railroad. On the night of August 20, the 2nd North Carolina Cavalry was camped near the Boydton Plank Road near the Vaughan Road which ran into a small road on which the Poplar Spring Church was located. The North Carolinians were still tired from the hard march from above the James, but nonetheless they were awakened by the sound of "Boots and Saddles" long before the sun greeted them. As they took to the road, they could still hear the skirmishing that had been sounding all night—it came from the nearby front line. They were soon on the Vaughan Road about a mile or so from the Weldon (near the Seven Mile or Yellow House).[141]

The head of the Confederate cavalry column soon encountered the Union pickets and pushed. They continued on and shortly came upon the enemy's reserves, at which time a platoon from the North Carolina Brigade was dismounted and rapidly sent forward to test the strength of the enemy. The 2nd Cavalry was posted on the left of Vaughan Road, and two squadrons were sent forward. The Confederate cavalrymen spread out until their left connected with their infantry already on the line. By that time, the fighting on the right of the 2nd Cavalry had intensified and was nearing a general conflict. Two Union batteries, one in front and one to the right of the cavalrymen, opened fire on their position, which disrupted the still mounted men from the 2nd North Carolina, who were in an open field near a woods, as well as the skirmishers who were caught in a devastating crossfire from the enemy's artillery. Once the enemy artillery had the Confederates' attention, Union infantry started through the woods, advancing on the North Carolina cavalrymen's line. The woods provided some protection for the Union troops as they fired volley after volley into the still mounted men of the 2nd Cavalry in the open field. The dismounted Confederate cavalrymen stood their ground, fired back and slowed the Union advance. This allowed the remainder of the 2nd Cavalry to dismount, send their horses to the rear, and step back to a more defensible line. From there, they skirmished until darkness came. By the end of the day, the North Carolina cavalrymen had a well-entrenched Union infantry far superior in number in front of them, yet were able to halt its advance.[142]

While the 2nd Cavalry had its hands full with Union infantry and artillery, the rest of the North Carolina Cavalry Brigade was also busy helping to push enemy back east of the Weldon. When the 3rd Cavalry encountered the enemy, with the 5th North Carolina in support, they "...drove the enemy into their advanced works, after taking his works forced him rapidly through the woods into heavy entrenchments along the Weldon Railroad." Once the Confederate advance was underway, the 5th North Carolina was moved up on the right of the 3rd Cavalry and together fought to within a few yards of the railroad. At that point, they realized they were far in advance of the rest of their line and were coming under great pressure on their right while their left was exposed. The 3rd and 5th regiments fell back to where the 2nd Cavalry had held. The 1st Cavalry was moved to their right where pressure was increasing. The new North Carolina Cavalry line held until dark when they were ordered to fall back. Warren's Fifth Corps had not been able to advance on the Confederate supply routes, but they had retained their position on the railroad. W. H. F. Lee's cavalry failed to push Union troops from the Weldon, while A. P. Hill's infantry had not regained the mile long stretch of track around Globe Tavern.[143]

According to Barringer, his North Carolina brigade lost 68 men that day—38 were from the 5th Cavalry. The 2nd North Carolina also took several casualties—including those listed in the table below.[144]

Combat Losses in the 2nd North Carolina Cavalry Around Poplar Spring Church, August 21, 1864

Trooper	Age	Co.	Fate
Aurelius Scott	22	C	wounded
William G. Warren	36	C	wounded
J. B. Eatmon		E	wounded
John W. Snell	21	G	wounded
Thomas J. Harris		K	wounded

Information contained in this table came from Compiled Service Records as summarized by Louis H. Manarin, *North Carolina Troops: 1861–1865, A Roster*, vol. II, pages 98–177. (See Appendix for more information on the men listed above, page 404.)

After sundown on August 21, the 2nd North Carolina returned to camp, about three miles behind the line. They remained near camp on August 22 and then marched 17 miles the next day to once again become the right of the Confederate line. By the end of the day, the regiment was on picket duty on the extreme right, three miles from Stony Creek along with W. H. F. Lee's entire division. The men of the 2nd Cavalry were relieved on the picket line by the 9th Virginia on August 24.[145]

After the fighting on August 21, a major part of W. H. F. Lee's assignment was to protect the supply route from Stone Creek Depot to Dinwiddie Court House and on to Petersburg. R. E. Lee already had wagon trains rolling on this alternate supply route. The picket line in front of Reams's Station was vacated when W. H. F. Lee moved his command to Stony Creek. The gap was filled when Hampton arrived with his cavalry division under the command of M. C. Butler. All the while, Union troops continued to destroy railroad track around Reams's Station, with their protective skirmish line a mile or so west of the station. Consequently, soon after Hampton and Butler arrived, another minor attempt was made to disrupt Union destruction work on the Weldon. On August 23, it was M. C. Butler's turn to push the enemy back from Monk's Neck Bridge where the old Stage Road crossed Rowanty Creek about two miles west of Reams's Station. The Confederates managed to push the Union line back to the station after some severe fighting, but not off the railroad. The Union forces at Reams's Station were behind strong works—the force included two of Hancock's infantry divisions. There was not much more Hampton and the cavalry division with him could do beyond pushing the first line. Nonetheless, after assessing the situation late on the 23rd and early the next day, Hampton decided Hancock's corps at the station was paying more attention to tearing up the road than guarding themselves—they appeared vulnerable. Hampton knew regaining Reams's Station was important even if the railroad was lost at Globe Tavern. On the 24th, he recommended to R. E. Lee that an attack be made on the place with help from some of A. P. Hill's infantry. Just minutes after receiving Hampton's recommendations, R. E. Lee responded, telling Hampton that A. P. Hill was on his way down with Heth's division, and that Hill was in charge of the operation. Hampton received R. E. Lee's message and later rode out to personally guide A. P. Hill's column to Monk's Neck Bridge where they camped for the night and formulated their plan of attack for the next morning.[146]

By nightfall of the 24th, Hancock's command had destroyed the railroad for about three miles south of Reams's Station and planned to do another five miles in the coming days. Hancock's two divisions again spent the night around Reams's Station.[147]

It was significant that Hampton convinced R. E. Lee to make another go at the Union presence on the Weldon because R. E. Lee had pretty much given up the idea of regaining the use of the Weldon as far as Petersburg to supply his troops and the city. He wrote President Davis and the Secretary of War on August 22 reminding them that he had for some time felt the Weldon was indefensible because of the proximity of the enemy's line to the railroad south of Petersburg. Nonetheless, as he pointed out, his troops had made two serious efforts to push Warren's command back east of the railroad and regain its use, the first on August 19 and the next two days later. R. E. Lee felt both efforts were all that could be expected given the small size of the force he had been able to move into the fights relative to the strength of the enemy. He further acknowledged that even if he could push Warren's force back from the railroad, he did not have the number of troops needed to defend the road from future attacks—he was certain Union forces could retake and destroy sections of the Weldon at any point. Thus, on the 22nd R. E. Lee informed his superiors that he was certain the best course was to abandon further efforts to dislodge the enemy from the Weldon. R. E. Lee went on to say that he was sure Grant's efforts had turned from trying to overpower his defenses around Petersburg and Richmond and were now directed at compelling the Confederates to evacuate their lines by cutting off their supplies. R. E. Lee also suggested[148]:

Under these circumstances, we should use every effort to maintain ourselves by our remaining line of communications. The most intelligent and energetic officers should be charged with the duty of superintending the transportation of supplies over all the roads upon which the army depends.... I shall do all in my power to get supplies by the Weldon road, bring them as far as Stony Creek by rail, and thence by wagons. One train [wagons] has already been sent out for this purpose, and another is preparing to start. If we can get through the next month or six weeks the corn crop will begin to be available in Virginia.... Our supply of corn is exhausted to-day.[149]

On the same day R. E. Lee and the Secretary of War were exchanging their ideas on the implications of losing the Weldon, W. H. F. Lee's cavalry division was moved down near Stony Creek and in position to safeguard the wagon trains moving supplies from Stony Creek Depot toward Dinwiddie Court house and on to Petersburg. The North Carolina cavalrymen were on the far right, nearest to Stony Creek Depot. They had been given the all-important job of protecting the wagon trains. Naturally that meant they were once again the most likely targets of Union cavalry on the new, alternate Confederate supply line.

The Confederate Secretary of War responded to R. E. Lee the next day, acknowledging the importance of supply problems and saying "...with regret, that the enemy have effected a permanent lodgment on the Weldon railroad." He added, "I do not disguise from you or myself that there may be very serious strain within the next two months in providing adequate supplies." Later on August 23, R. E. Lee again replied to the Secretary of War, adding a final depressing note on the Confederates' state of affairs: "Without some increase of strength [more troops], I cannot see how we are to escape the natural military consequences of the enemy's numerical superiority." As indicated, the consequence uppermost on R. E. Lee's mind that day and the one before was the permanent loss of his supply line on the Weldon Railroad — with a sufficient number of dispensable men he would be able to push the Union forces off the Weldon and regain its use. However, the reality of his numbers meant he had to hold the other railroads, the Danville and South Side, and retain use of the Weldon as far north as possible — at least as far as Stony Creek Depot. That was why he unhesitatingly approved Hampton's proposal to attack Hancock at Reams's Station.[150]

As indicated earlier, after M. C. Butler's cavalry pushed the Union front line back from Monk's Neck Bridge to Reams's Station on August 23, Hampton decided that the Union force around Reams's Station could be attacked to "advantage." On the afternoon of the 24th, R. E. Lee approved Hampton's plan, and told him "...do all in your power to punish the enemy. You ought to have your scouts to ascertain their position and the best point to attack them." R. E. Lee still did not believe they could take and hold the entire railroad, but there was not much else to do except attack in an effort to stop further destruction south of Reams's Station.[151]

Hampton already had his cavalrymen scouting the lines early on August 24. Barringer, then temporarily commanding W. H. F. Lee's division, notified M. C. Butler that "The enemy did not seem inclined to advance beyond Malone's Crossing. They have a skirmish line in front of Malone's Crossing (toward Reams' Station), and Barlow's division (a deserter says) is there tearing up the railroad. A large body of their cavalry, supposed to be a brigade, moved on their left yesterday at 3 P.M. I have heard nothing of them, but have sent out scouts toward Stony Creek to see if they have possibly crossed below me." Confederate scouts were getting snapshots of Hancock moving the Second Division up early on August 24 relieving the First Division in the entrenchments — and the First Division moving to destroy more of the railroad toward the crossing of Rowanty Creek. Regardless of enemy strength, Hampton knew doing nothing was not a viable option. He met with A. P. Hill late on the 24th and determined their plan of attack. It was agreed Hampton would move his cavalry first; then Hill would move his infantry up near Monk's Neck Bridge, about three miles west of the station early on the 25th, and wait for word from Hampton.[152]

THE BATTLE AT REAMS'S STATION, AUGUST 25, 1864

A. P. Hill moved his command onto the road heading east which crossed the railroad just south of Reams's Station. He spread his force in line on both sides of the road to facing their enemy's line — Hill had Henry Heth and Cadmus M. Wilcox with their commands up front. On the other side, Hancock's men were expecting the Confederate infantry and were strongly entrenched just west of the railroad, straddling the same road. Hancock had suspended all destruction of the railroad early on August 25 until he knew what his enemy was up to—he waited several hours and was just about to send a detail of his men back to work when Hampton made his first strike against the Union cavalry shield on the southern end of their line. Hancock sent John Gibbon's division (the would-be destruction crew that day) to support S. P. Spear's cavalry on the Union left.[153]

Cavalry shielded the Union line south of Reams's Station. The cavalrymen were clustered about Malone's Crossing on the morning of August 25. Hampton took his cavalry in that direction. He sent Barringer with his North Carolina brigade over to and up the Halifax Road, which crosses over to the east side of the Weldon, and up to Malone's Crossing. Hampton sent W. H. F. Lee's other brigade, the late Chambliss's brigade under the command of Colonel J. Lucius Davis, up Malone's Road, over Malone's Bridge and on toward the crossing to join with Barringer and his command. J. L. Davis's command was supported by T. L. Rosser's and P. M. B. Young's (commanded by Wright) brigades under Butler's command. (Hampton had left J. Dunovant's brigade to cover the left flank and rear of A. P. Hill's line.) Hampton rode with J. L Davis and M. C. Butler across Malone's Bridge and around 9:00 A.M. encountered enemy cavalry belonging to Colonel S. P. Spear's command and drove them back to a line of support. At that point, J. L. Davis dismounted a portion of his command and sent them at the Union line. Colonel R. L. T. Beale's 9th Virginia went up first and found that the Union line extended well beyond their line, so the 10th Virginia was sent to the Confederate right, to extend just beyond their flank. With reinforcements arriving, the men of the 9th Virginia rose up with a yell and charged the enemy line, carrying it with little difficulty. McGregor's battery joined the rout at that point, and the Union cavalry was pushed through Malone's Crossing and up the railroad to Reams's Station.[154]

Just as S. P. Spear's cavalry was in confused and rapid retreat, Hancock sent J. Gibbon's infantry division to stop the Confederate cavalry onslaught. The Union infantry made attempts to turn both of Hampton's flanks but failed, and the cavalrymen held. In fact, Hampton's cavalrymen pushed Gibbon's infantry back until the line stabilized with the Union troops behind fortifications thrown up earlier. Hampton's cavalrymen attacked again and drove Gibbon's command even further. In Hancock's view, "The enemy's dismounted cavalry now made an attack on the left, driving General Gibbon's division from its breastworks ... and the enemy, elated at their easy success at this point, were pressing on with loud cheers when they were met by a heavy flank fire from the dismounted cavalry, occupying the extreme left, and their advance was summarily checked." The dismounted Union cavalry that hit Hampton's advancing troopers in the flank and brought the drive to an end were from D. McM. Gregg's command. Once Hampton had driven Gibbon's division from its fortification, he knew he had the enemy infantry's attention on their southern flank, so it was time for A. P. Hill to strike from the west. Hampton sent word to Hill indicating it was a good time for the Confederate infantry to enter the battle. Hill replied asking Hampton to withdraw a bit down the railroad allowing the enemy to follow so that Hill's infantry might hit them in the rear. Hampton complied and pulled his cavalry back about 400 yards, but the Union infantry was reluctant to follow and advanced slowly. A. P. Hill's first assault on the Union line occurred around 2:00 that afternoon. Hampton did not drop back too far, because he knew he was close to having cut Gregg's cavalry off from their infantry support, and he wanted to pounce on them. Before he hit D. McM. Gregg's cavalry, however, he wanted Barringer to bring up the North Carolina regiments from over on Halifax Road—he sent for them immediately.[155]

Barringer and his North Carolina regiments left camp near Stony Creek early August 25 and headed north along Halifax Road toward Malone's Crossing where they planned to meet Hampton and the rest of the cavalry. Barringer was then commanding W. H. F. Lee's division during the latter's illness, but Chambliss's former brigade (commanded by J. L. Davis) was over with Hampton's column, so Barringer was basically with his North Carolina Brigade. Along the way, they encountered the enemy.

Barringer and his fellow North Carolinians came upon the enemy's first line of works not far along the Halifax Road, near Tucker's Farm. Barringer moved the 3rd Cavalry to protect the rear and dismounted the 1st Cavalry for the charge, with the 2nd and 5th Cavalries in close support. Without hesitation, the Confederates made a vigorous attack upon the Union first line of defense just east of the Weldon Railroad.[156]

Soon after Barringer's men had driven their enemy back to their second line of defense, a message arrived from Hampton informing Barringer that he had a portion of the Union cavalry cut off, and he wanted the North Carolinians to come up quickly and hit their flank in a joint attack. Barringer remounted his troopers and made off for the enemy cavalry retreating from Hampton's push, near Malone's Crossing. As the North Carolina regiments rushed northward to intercept the fleeing enemy cavalry in their flank, they came upon a strongly fortified Union line fully manned by infantry. They were too late, the targeted Union cavalry had already crossed Barringer's path into the safety of their line. About that time, Barringer received another message from Hampton indicating the vulnerable enemy cavalry had indeed moved back and avoided the trap. Once Hancock realized Gibbon's infantry had rapidly fallen back and exposed D. McM. Gregg's flank, the Union cavalry was pulled back from their exposed position apparently just in time.[157]

A disappointed Barringer then moved his brigade up behind Hampton just as the latter's line was dropping back about 400 yards at A. P. Hill's suggestion. Hampton then instructed Barringer to leave a strong picket on the Halifax Road and join the right of Hampton's line which was facing north, near Malone's Crossing. Later, Hampton remembered that in the midst of the maneuvering for position before the coming fight, he moved to secure his right flank and hit the enemy's flank if possible — in his words, "I dismounted the Second North Carolina Regiment, under Colonel Roberts, ordering him to take position on the right of the line and to turn the flank of the enemy if an opportunity offered."[158]

Events had been taking place rapidly up to that point as the commanders prepared their lines for a major assault, and the succession of changed orders filtered back among the still advancing Confederate cavalrymen. Through the eyes of a private in the 2nd North Carolina the events unfolded as follows:

As soon as the Brigade could about wheel we moved off at gallop, expecting at every moment to meet up with (as we termed it,) the doomed party [D. McM. Gregg's cavalry]. But from some cause or other the bird had flown, and instead of meeting up with the party that were reported cut off, we encountered a heavy line of infantry, with which we skirmished a while, but hearing that the enemy were in our rear, (and as all troops are rather sensitive about their rear and flank,) considerable uneasiness was expressed at the time, and in a short while our skirmishers were withdrawn, the column moved back to the railroad, where we joined the balance of our command.... We were not permitted to remain inactive long the old 2d was called upon to dismount, and was immediately pushed forward under the command of our gallant Col. W. P. Roberts, who merits still higher promotion for his bravery and the skillful manner in which he has handled his command during the recent campaign.[159]

The North Carolina regiments were then on the far right of the Confederate line facing a well-fortified enemy behind an advance line of earth works and rifle pits. The Union line resembled a horse shoe across the Weldon with the open end facing east. The lower end of the line was bent slightly to the north in order to protect the only road exiting the Union enclosure — it was an escape route to Jerusalem Plank Road if needed. The bulk of D. McM. Gregg's cavalry was placed near the Union escape route to help protect it. The Confederate cavalry prepared to coordinate its attack on the Union line facing southeast with A. P. Hill's assault on the Union line facing west.

In his second charge of the day, A. P. Hill went forward with three North Carolina brigades. According to one Confederate observer, however, the advance was soon "checked by the terrible fire of grape, canister and musketry poured into their ranks." The charging troopers did not break but dropped to the ground and waited for support, which arrived soon. Then they resumed the charge, under what seemed to be even heavier fire, to and over the enemy's defenses. Many of the Union infantrymen who were not captured fled in disorder, dropping their guns and equipment to facilitate their flight. Union artillery was captured and quickly turned on their former owners by Pegram's gunners, adding to the bloody retreat of Hancock's line.[160]

Over on the Confederate right, the cavalry line waited to coordinate its assault with the infantry's advance. Hampton heard A. P. Hill's artillery open fire at about 5:00 P.M. and sent orders to his cavalrymen to advance along the entire line. Hampton watched from a position overlooking the field as his dismounted cavalrymen stormed and leaped over the enemy breast works. Colonel W. P. Roberts and the 2nd North Carolina were ordered in first and remained out in front all the way to the enemy's barricades. Hampton's position allowed him to observe the charge, and in his relatively short after-battle report, he wrote, "Colonel Roberts, with his regiment, charged here one line of rifle-pits, carrying it handsomely, and capturing from 60 to 70 prisoners."[161]

Barringer concurred when he wrote, "The Second Regiment, led by Col. Roberts, in advance, closely supported by the other Regiments, charged, and were among the first troops to reach the works, sweeping the enemy before them in the wildest confusion." A private in the 2nd North Carolina sent a report to a newspaper at the time, which reads[162]:

We advanced near a mile [dismounted] before we came upon the enemy, where we found them strongly posted behind breastworks. Knowing that but little could be accomplished by fighting them at a distance entrenched as they were, we made at them in double quick time, driving them like chaff before the wind, capturing quite a number of prisoners. Everyone thought we had won enough glory for the day. But not so with the officials.[163]

After Hampton watched the 2nd North Carolina and other regiments storm and push back the Union line, he was made aware that A. P. Hill's infantrymen were pushing the enemy eastward across the Weldon, so he ordered his men to back off, and form a line east of the railroad, still facing north. Hampton dismounted most of his cavalrymen and placed Chambliss's brigade, under J. L. Davis, on the left, anchored on the railroad; the North Carolina Brigade in the middle; and P. M. B. Young's brigade on the right. T. L. Rosser's brigade formed a second line in their rear. He then instructed the commanders to keep their left on the railroad and advance slowly, while the right should advance more rapidly—J. L. Davis's regiments on the left were to act as a slowly advancing hinge and the rest of the line as a gate with P. M. B. Young's brigade on the right, moving rapidly and swinging the gate closed on the rear of the enemy line.[164]

The Confederate cavalrymen, both walking on the left and running on the right, had very rough terrain to cover. Their enemy had cut down timber and created obstacles to slow just such attacks upon them. Heavy fire from artillery and musketry made the charge even more difficult. In his after-battle report, Hampton had this to say about the last charge of the day: "Here he [the enemy] made a stubborn stand, and for a few moments checked our advance, but the spirit of the men was so fine that they charged the breast-works with the utmost gallantry, carried them, and captured the force holding them."[165] Again from the 2nd North Carolina Cavalry we have a private's view, confirming Hampton's observation about his men's spirit:

In an hour or so after the first charge we were again ordered forward, not having lost a man killed in the first charge from the 2d, and being already elated with our achievements, our men moved off to the second charge in fine spirits, fully confident of success, and well did they perform their duty. As soon as the enemy were encountered in their second line of entrenchments, which were very formidable indeed, our boys raised a yell (which always strikes terror in the cowardly,) and pushed at them in double quick, faltering not in the least until they arrived at the breastworks, routing the enemy completely, and capturing a large number of prisoners. The ground was completely covered with arms and knapsacks. Night having closed in upon us, we had to stop the pursuit....[166]

While the 2nd North Carolina Cavalry was at the front of the fighting all day, other regiments were naturally by their side, though it was not equally clear to all observers who was there and who was not in the midst of that confused afternoon. For instance, a newspaper report indicated that the 2nd North Carolina was closely and most actively supported by the 9th Virginia, while those closest to the action gave that honor to the 10th Virginia Cavalry. Major Clement of the 10th Virginia in a letter to his wife on August 29, 1864 revealed his displeasure over the misplaced public credit with these words: "Gen'l comdg the Division came to my camp day before yesterday to compliment me upon the gallant maneuver in which my men conducted them selves during the fight, I see some news paper had coupled the 9th Va. Reg't with the 2d N.C. in taking those works, which is a mistake it was the 'Bloody 10th.'" Roberts of the 2nd North Carolina supported Clement's view years later when he wrote, "The fact is, the great brunt of the battle, so far as the cavalry participated, was borne by the Nineteenth North Carolina [2nd Cavalry] and the Tenth Virginia, and these two regiments, unsupported, carried the last of the entrenchments held by the enemy. It was just at dark, I remember, and I never witnessed a more splendid charge."[167]

At the end of the day, Barringer took special satisfaction in the infantry's response to his cavalrymen's conduct while fighting dismounted as infantrymen. He expressed his pleasure in these words: "And here, be it said in due credit, that our once jeered cavaliers elicited the special commendation of the infantry, and for once, shook hands over one common victory."[168]

According to one of those North Carolina infantryman, "The cavalry vied with the infantry in their headlong assault upon the enemy's lines. The Second North Carolina, under General W. P. Roberts, of Gates County, carried the first line of rifle-pits on the right, and the cavalry all swept over the main line."[169]

On August 28, R. E. Lee found time to write his wife, and mention that "On the 25th Fitzhugh's [as W. H. F. Lee was called within his immediate family] division behaved splendidly, charging on foot the enemy's works on the right, & capturing the men at their posts with their arms, &c. The North Carolina brigades signalized themselves, & behaved most handsomely." The following day, R. E. Lee sent a letter to Governor Z. B. Vance of North Carolina in which he expressed his admiration for the gallantry and good conduct of the North Carolinians. After praising the infantry, he said, "…the brigade of Gen. Barringer bore a conspicuous part in the operations of the cavalry, which were no less distinguished for boldness and efficiency than those of the infantry."[170]

In the end, Hancock's command was able to retain control of the road heading east to Jerusalem Plank Road until nightfall, and use it to escape during the night. A good portion of D. McM. Gregg's cavalry helped hold the road during the latter part of the day and remained to cover the retreat. Then he moved his cavalrymen to Jerusalem Plank Road early August 26 and held that position. Meade reported to Grant that by 8:00 P.M. Hancock had lost the railroad around Reams's Station, and in addition to better than 2,000 men, they also lost eight pieces of artillery.[171]

A. P. Hill's and Hampton's troopers had retaken Reams's Station and the Weldon Railroad south of there, but Union forces still held the railroad for about a mile around Globe Tavern and would continue to deny the Confederacy that direct rail route from the south to Petersburg for the remainder of the war.

When Hampton listed his losses, he had: 6 men killed, 25 wounded, and 2 missing in M. C. Butler's division; and 10 killed, 50 wounded, and 1 missing in W. H. F. Lee's division (commanded by Barringer). More than one observer who witnessed the 2nd North Carolina Cavalry at the front that day was surprised that they had no cavalrymen from the regiment killed in the first charge. Later in the day, however, they did have men seriously wounded. W. P. Roberts remembered: "Our losses were small, but our captures were great, and the old Second Cavalry did splendid work."[172]

After the fighting, the 2nd North Carolina Cavalry marched slowly back to camp on the military road 3 or 4 miles east of Dinwiddie Court House in a heavy rain and thunderstorm, nursing numerous wounds—apparently only four of which warranted reporting.

Combat Losses in the 2nd North Carolina Cavalry Battle at Reams's Station, August 25, 1864

Trooper	Age	Co.	Fate
James W. Johnson	33	H	wounded
Henry I. Kimball	30	B	wounded
James A. Shuford	31	B	wounded
Joseph E. Harrell		C	wounded

Information contained in this table came from Compiled Service Records as summarized by Louis H. Manarin, *North Carolina Troops: 1861–1865, A Roster*, vol. II, pages 98–177. (See Appendix for more information on the men listed above, page 404.)

Barringer recalled the difficult days in August 1864 for his cavalrymen: "Thus in ten days our division had crossed and recrossed the James River; had marched to Stony Creek and then back to Reams's Station, makes nearly one hundred miles night and day marching, and in the meantime fighting eight severe actions."

However, the hard month of August ended on a relatively quiet note for the North Carolina cavalrymen, and September started in the same way.[173]

On August 26, R. E. Lee sent a message of thanks to Hampton for a job well done by the cavalry. He also instructed him to have Dearing's brigade do all the picketing for a while and let W. H. F. Lee's and Butler's commands rest while they refreshed their horses, if possible. However, apparently it was not possible to rest all the cavalrymen, because the North Carolina regiments were on picket duty the morning following the Battle at Reams's Station. Hampton notified R. E. Lee's headquarters that his pickets were moved to a line two miles east of Reams's Station by morning on August 26. The 3rd North Carolina had remained on picket duty during the fighting and was relieved the next morning. John W. Gordon, of the 2nd North Carolina Cavalry, wrote the following entry in his diary: "August 26, go on picket duty, relieve the 3rd Cavalry." And he followed that entry with "August 27, relieved by the 1st Cavalry."[174]

Both sides could claim a little success from the battles for control of the Weldon Railroad: R. E. Lee regained use of the road as far north as Reams's Station and had a buffer zone for the Stony Creek Depot; but more importantly, Grant still interfered with supplies coming up by holding on to the salient which extended across the railroad and encompassed Globe Tavern. However of more immediate importance to the weary troopers at the time was that quiet reigned along the lines for a couple of weeks because Grant and R. E. Lee both remained on guard, each expecting the other to take the initiative.[175]

In addition to watching for attacks, both sides were engaged in some clean-up. For instance, on August 27, D. McM. Gregg sent a message requesting that burial parties from his command be allowed beyond the Confederate picket line to bury their dead comrades. The same day, Hampton replied it would not be possible, but he had ordered all their dead to be buried and all their wounded had been collected and were under the charge of Union surgeons. One Union report on the losses at Reams's Station shows: 140 killed, 529 wounded, and just over 2,000 captured or missing.[176]

Picket Duty, an Adventure, and More Picketing

While the infantry settled into entrenchments, the North Carolina cavalrymen rested and tried to settle into the monotony of picket duty but were typically restless after a few days. Indeed by September 5, their commander, Wade Hampton, was once again looking for opportunities to make something happen; R. E. Lee was equally eager.

As early as September 3, R. E. Lee had suggested to Hampton that the enemy's huge supply depot around City Point (south of the confluence of the Appomattox and James Rivers) was vulnerable. Hampton sent his favorite scout in that direction, and on September 5 when the scout returned from his journey far behind Grant's lines, he spelled out in detail the size and disposition of the Union force around the depot and the prize. The prize was large, nearly 3,000 heads of cattle, guarded by only 120 men and 30 unarmed citizens. Of course, the surrounding area had more enemy troopers. One regiment of cavalry at Sycamore Church, about four miles south of the cattle, would have to be dealt with; and a large body of Union cavalry several miles northwest of Prince George Court House, was camped near City Point. They could be expected to join the adventure. The only truly dangerous place, according to the scout, would be on the return when the enemy would probably come south from their main line and attack the Confederates as they crossed the Jerusalem Plank Road heading west.[177]

Hampton formulated a plan for his expedition and sent it to R. E. Lee, who approved it on September 9. His concern was also for the return trip when they would be encumbered with cattle, and their presence known, and their route passing directly south of the Union cavalry. He suggested Hampton take a wide swing around the enemy left "…to give ample space for your flank pickets to notify you of danger." With approval, Hampton moved forward with his raid on the Union cattle.[178]

His troopers were ready for their adventure on the evening of August 13, when a young private in the 2nd North Carolina wrote the following diary entry: "Our camp is now on the Military road, four miles from Dinwiddie Court House and eight from Petersburg. This evening we are ordered to cook up five days rations and be ready to move by day in the morning." Of course, the troopers did not know where they were going because secrecy was important.[179]

HAMPTON'S BEEF STEAK RAID, SEPTEMBER 14–17

Hampton moved his cavalrymen early on September 14. He left very few men on the flank of the Petersburg line and took Barringer's North Carolina brigade and Chambliss's former brigade (together constituting W. H. F. Lee's division), as well as Rosser's and Dearing's brigades, and a detachment of 100 men from Young's and Dunovant's brigades. Hampton, and those cavalrymen camped near him, moved down Boydton Plank Road, past Gravelly Run. Along the way they picked up W. H. F. Lee's division and moved southeast toward Stony Creek Depot—well below the enemy line. They reached Rowanty Creek at Wilkinson's Bridge and camped for the remainder of the day—the cavalrymen were able to unsaddle their horses and rest until night. It was essential that this large body of cavalrymen remain undetected until they arrived at their target, so they were back in their saddles after dark and quietly on their way.[180]

Hampton took his men across Wilkinson's bridge early September 15 and with a rapid march headed toward Ebenezer Church near the Jerusalem Plank Road and on to Cook's Bridge on the Blackwater. Hampton had selected Cook's Bridge for his crossing because it had been destroyed, and the enemy would not think it a reasonable place to launch a raid. While his engineers threw up a bridge, the Confederate men and their horses rested and had a feed. Hampton used the time to discuss the plan of attack with his officers and give them their assignments.[181] (See map 6.2.)

The plan called for W. H. F. Lee's two brigades to leave the column first and move to the left. They should be the first to encounter enemy pickets, and they were told to drive them in, which would hopefully be the first notice to their enemy's cavalry that the Confederates were behind their lines. Once the Union pickets were driven in, Barringer and J. L. Davis were to move their brigades up and block the roads between the main enemy cavalry camp and Sycamore Church to the east. Hampton was to take T. L. Rosser's brigade and the detachment of 100 men under Miller as well as Dearing's small brigade to Sycamore Church. Just before arriving at the church, Dearing's command was to move off to the right and guard against a flank attack coming from the east. The plan called for Rosser's command to attack the cavalry regiment stationed at Sycamore Church, neutralize them and move on to the cattle about three miles to the north.[182]

It was important that all three Confederate columns get into position without prematurely alerting the Union cavalry—and they did. Rosser launched his attack on their enemy at Sycamore Church at 5:00 A.M. September 16. The roads leading into town were well-barricaded, and the Union cavalrymen had time to rally and put up a stubborn but brief fight before they were overwhelmed by Rosser's men. The scattered Union cavalry left their dead around the town and their wounded to be captured along with others, as well as much of their camp supplies which went to Confederate hands. At the sound of Rosser's first firing, W. H. F. Lee and Dearing both moved forward to their assigned tasks.[183]

Dearing attacked the small force they expected to find around Cocke's Mill, then spread his command to shield Rosser's raid on the cattle from any enemy approaching from the east.[184]

M. C. Rosser's shield on the west was established and held by Barringer's and J. L. Davis's commands. The Confederate presence to the west was recorded by Henry E. Davies, commanding the Union's Second Cavalry Division, as follows:

Early that morning the enemy's cavalry, moving down the Powhatan road, made a strong demonstration on General Kautz's picket-line, driving in a number of his posts and capturing a large portion of the First District of Columbia Cavalry, in camp on that road. This force, as I subsequently learned, was the cavalry division of General W. H. F. Lee, and his demonstration was made to cover the movement of Hampton, who with three brigades marched to Coggins' Point and drove off the herd of cattle at that place in charge of a detachment of the thirteenth Pennsylvania Cavalry, many of whom were made prisoners.[185]

W. H. F. Lee had split his command, sending one brigade to the left to take the 3rd New York Cavalry's camps, and the other brigade to the right, toward a force made of cavalrymen from the 11th Pennsylvania and the 1st District of Columbia commands. A member of the 9th Virginia in J. L. Davis's command noted that when the sounds of Rosser's fighting reached them "...our brigade charged down the main road which we were to hold, guarded by only a squadron or so of the enemy. These unsuspecting creatures, though warned of our approach by the firing below, had barely time to escape, and that without waiting to put on their clothing. Their tents, many horses, clothing and camp equipage, fell into the hands of us eager adventurers." Davis's brigade also took about 25 prisoners at that point. Barringer's North Carolina brigade was on the other road standing between Rosser's push toward the cattle and Kautz's cavalry. Their initial encounter with the enemy was recorded by a member of the 2nd North Carolina in his diary as follows: "Just at the dawn of day, we charged a squadron of Yankee Cavalry, capturing 24 prisoners. We kept on two miles to a cross road...."[186]

Union commanders received notice of W. H. F. Lee's minor assaults on A. V. Kautz's pickets as early as 6:00 A.M. but dismissed them as isolated and unimportant incidents. About an hour and one half later, Kautz suspected the action was indeed an attack on the 1st District of Columbia Cavalry, and it had succeeded. He realized by 8:30 A.M. that Hampton had something else in mind—the cattle. Kautz then headed for Sycamore Church to find the remnants of the Union camp Hampton had already passed through with the stolen cattle. By noon, Kautz and about 600 men were hot on Hampton's trail, but about four hours behind the head of the cattle drive. Kautz's column could at best hope to harass the Confederate rear, not retrieve the stolen cattle. For that purpose, they would need a larger force; one that had a chance of hitting the Confederate column in the middle or nearer the front. The main Union pursuit was made by H. E. Davies commanding just over 2,000 cavalrymen from the Second Division—they were pulled from the Petersburg line and got started around 12:30 P.M. They were under way about two hours after the head of Hampton's column began crossing Cook's Bridge on the Blackwater. H. E. Davies needed to move rapidly and did, heading down Jerusalem Plank Road hoping to cut off Hampton's column before it got west of the road.[187]

Hampton had his three columns pulling back with their loot in hand and on the hoof by 8:00 A.M. that same morning—he made off with just under 3,000 head of beef. The three Confederate commands withdrew along the routes they came on and reunited before they reached the Blackwater. Barringer's North Carolina brigade was instructed to cover the withdrawal at Sycamore Church and bring up the rear of the column. The 2nd North Carolina was the last to pull out. Their commander, W. P. Roberts, remembered and wrote the following of that morning[188]:

I received orders from him [Hampton] in person to bring up the rear. The regiment remained in the vicinity of where the cattle were captured for nearly an hour after the entire command had been withdrawn, and I at once, busied myself in making the necessary disposition of the regiment to protect our rear. Very soon the Federal cavalry began to press me and there were a number of mounted charges given and received during the day, but I was hardly pressed and was glad when night came to end the pursuit. The day's work was a hard one; ... but I managed to keep my command so well in hand that I lost only one or two men, I think, before reaching Belcher's mill [Belches's].[189]

Kautz's advance began arriving at Sycamore Church just before noon on August 16, and Hampton's column was well on the road with the exception of the 2nd North Carolina, the Confederate rear guard. Roberts's job was to keep Kautz far enough behind that Hampton did not have to be concerned with him, and he accomplished that.

Once Hampton had his command reunited and on a course for their lines, he sent Rosser forward to hold Jerusalem Plank Road. Then Dearing's and Miller's commands moved in the middle of the long column near the huge cattle herd and the wagons. As indicated, W. H. F. Lee's command brought up the rear to defend against their expected enemy pursuers.[190]

When Hampton had the cattle across the Blackwater (and counted as they crossed the small bridge), heading for the plank road, he rode forward to find Rosser. He had not gone far before he received word from Rosser that a heavy force of enemy cavalry was coming south on Jerusalem Plank Road—it was, of course, H. E. Davies with his column of 2,000 mounted men. Hampton ordered Rosser to set a line of battle at Ebenezer Church, and then Hampton ordered the column with the cattle to swing south and cross Jerusalem Plank Road about two miles below the church at which the line of battle had been drawn.[191]

Rosser came under attack from H. E. Davies's column around 2:00 P.M., while the cattle were moved safely and then westward. The large Union force pushed Rosser's pickets in with little difficulty, but Rosser's line near Ebenezer Church firmed up and held. As the rest of the Confederate column arrived, they were moved to support Rosser's line. Miller's command of 100 cavalrymen came along not long after Rosser's line had stabilized, and then Dearing's small brigade arrived. Word was sent back to the rear brigades of W. H. F. Lee's command, but they had been the column's rear guard and consequently were still behind a considerable distance due to minor skirmishing along the way.[192]

With the increased size of the Confederate force in front of him, H. E. Davies was hesitant to charge with great zeal but was content to hold his position and make only minor charges to test the Confederate line — they remained engaged until around 8:00 P.M. H. E. Davies reported that he was waiting for Kautz to come up on the enemy column's rear.[193]

J. L. Davis's command (Chambliss's brigade) had been hurried to the front from near the end of the Confederate column to assist Rosser. Later, one view from the rear provided this description: "We made haste to reach him, sometimes at a trot, sometimes at a gallop, for fifteen miles, and at full speed came into line of battle just as the sun went down. The enemy was lavishing profuse attentions upon us in the way of solid shot and shells; but we faced him resolutely and sent back searing and glittering like meteors at night shot, for shot." Shortly after Davies's command arrived, troopers from Barringer's North Carolina brigade made their appearance on the line — Barringer's men settled into the line near Belcher's Mill [Belches's Mill]. As they arrived, Hampton knew the threat to Rosser's position had diminished, and he was losing daylight. His thoughts turned from just holding the Union cavalry back, away from the cattle, to doing some damage to the hesitant enemy line in front of him. He took W. H. F. Lee's command out of the line they had just joined and around the flank to attack their enemy from the rear. By the time they were in position, however, daylight was gone, and Hampton did not attack. He had W. H. F. Lee's brigades rejoin Rosser's line and help fend off the last easily repulsed charges of the day.[194]

Well into his stalemate, H. E. Davies received word that the cattle had passed through Sycamore Church at sunrise that day, and he concluded they must be well southwest of his position. He had still heard nothing of Kautz's command, so he withdrew his command. Around that same time, Kautz had again come upon the Confederate rear guard, but he did not attack because he was not sure H. E. Davies was in position to attack at the head of the enemy column. Once Hampton received word that the cattle were safely across the Nottoway, he left four squadrons at the church and moved the rest of his command back, fearing his enemy might send a large force along the railroad to get between him and the cattle column. Actually, H. E. Davies did send a brigade in that direction but much too late. Hampton took his column to Wilkinson's Bridge to cover any attempted flanking move and spent the night near Rowanty Creek. J. L. Davis's brigade pulled into camp around midnight, and Barringer's North Carolinians later.[195]

As Hampton pulled his command back from Ebenezer Church, Barringer's brigade was left to cover the pullback, and the 2nd North Carolina Cavalry was again instructed to cover their rear. According to Barringer, the rear guard had "some pretty hard fighting at Belcher's Mill [Belches's] and other well-guarded points near Ebenezer Church...." While covering Hampton's exit, the 2nd North Carolina came under attack by the cavalry force H. E. Davies left on the line and possibly Kautz's advance troops that had been on their trail most of the day. In any case, one private in the 2nd Cavalry noted that while on rear guard duty, "...we were attacked both in front and rear. About 11 o'clock, we dismounted and drove back the rear party while some other brigade kept off the front." Otherwise, the 2nd Cavalry had frequent but minor skirmishing during the trip home.[196]

The 2nd North Carolina Cavalry moved back to its camp near the military road east of Dinwiddie Court House, and the rest of their brigade moved to their old camps between Malone's Bridge on the Rowanty Creek and Stony Creek to resume picket and scouting duties. W. P. Roberts reported no serious losses in his 2nd Cavalry during Hampton's expedition. In fact, Hampton counted his total losses as 10 men killed, 47 wounded, and 4 missing. He listed among his gains 2,468 heads of beef, 304 prisoners, and 11 captured wagons.[197]

Grant Moves on Richmond and Across the Weldon Again

Aside from minor skirmishing, it was pretty quiet along the Weldon Railroad and the wagon train route on the Boydton Plank Road for ten days or so after the "beef steak raid." By the latter part of September, however, Grant was ready to make another move on Richmond. It was similar in purpose to the earlier moves on the city — to stimulate activity and perhaps a breakthrough on one of the lines. As always, Grant would like to have had Richmond fall into his hands, but he would also have been satisfied for awhile if he managed to control additional Confederate supply lines to the city. Similarly, he would like to take Petersburg but would have been satisfied if this move resulted in taking the South Side Railroad coming into the city from the west and/or taking Boydton Plank Road used by the wagon trains. Grant planned to make his moves and be prepared to force the issue at any point depending on from where R. E. Lee pulled troops to defend the capital. This time he used Benjamin F. Butler's troops located in Bermuda Hundreds. Edward O. C. Ord, commanding the Eighteenth Corps and David B. Birney with the Tenth crossed the James River during the night of September 28 and headed for Richmond. Ord took the river road, while Birney advanced to the New Market and Darbytown Roads. Kautz and his cavalry command moved to the Darbytown Road. Grant had a major portion of the Army of the James mobilized for this effort, and they were soon seriously engaged north of the James. Union troopers made a forceful assault on the fortifications at Fort Harrison near Chaffin's Bluff early the next morning. Additional attacks made that day and on the 30th were without much success. On those two days, Union losses were estimated at 394 killed, 1,554 wounded, and 324 missing.[198] (See map 2.1.)

As B. F. Butler's troops moved north of the James, Meade was instructed to move his troops on the Petersburg line just enough to give the Confederates the impression that Union troops were collecting below Petersburg. Grant also instructed Meade that if he saw a significant reduction in his enemy's line around Petersburg, he should be prepared to move against the city or below it and then up to the South Side Railroad. In addition, if he got control of the South Side, he was instructed to hold it at all costs. If movement in that direction became possible, he was advised to pay attention to the possibility of capturing the Boydton Plank Road (the main Confederate wagon train route for supplies coming from Stony Creek Depot).[199]

In addition to Meade's movement of troops, Grant also planned a strong demonstration below Petersburg. D. McM. Gregg's cavalry had been concentrated on the Union left, and their assignment called for deep probes into the Confederate right, perhaps as far as Boydton Plank Road. Ultimately, D. McM. Gregg led about 4,300 cavalrymen south on the Halifax Road early on September 29 (which was close to the number of mounted cavalrymen Hampton was able to field that day). Gregg split his command when they reached lower Church Road. Colonel C. Smith was sent toward Boydton Plank road, while H. E. Davies stayed near the Weldon Railroad heading for Reams's Station.[200]

The Confederates had A. P. Hill's corps and Johnson's division as well as Hampton's two cavalry divisions in front of Meade and D. McM. Gregg (A. P. Hill was in command, because Beauregard moved to help their cause further south).[201]

When Meade began to shuffle his troops on September 29, A. P. Hill sent H. Heth's and C. M. Wilcox's divisions forward to their first line of defense. The Confederate main line south of Petersburg had been extended southwest, shielding Boydton Plank Road to within a mile or so of Hatcher's Run. Hampton's cavalry was still on the Confederate right — J. Dunovant's brigade was camped up on Boydton Plank Road near Hatcher's Run; Major H. Farley's foot brigade, cavalrymen without mounts, was camped a few miles southeast of Dunovant on Vaughan Road; P. M. B. Young's brigade was camped a couple of miles southwest of that position but still on Vaughan Road; and J. L. Davis's command (Chambliss's former brigade) was camped still farther down the Vaughan Road, past its intersection with

Quaker Road and the military road. R. Barringer's North Carolina brigade was camped several miles southeast of Davis's position on the military road. (Hampton lost the services of Rosser's brigade just a couple of days before when they were sent to the Shenandoah Valley.) Hampton also had R. P. Chew's three batteries of horse artillery nearby[202]

The locations of the cavalry camps were well considered. After the Confederates lost use of the Weldon above Reams's Station, they loaded supplies from rail cars to wagons at Stony Creek Depot and moved them along Flat Foot Road through Dinwiddie Court House and then up Boydton Plank Road. To shorten the route, they built the military road that connected Flat Foot Road to Vaughan Road where it intersected with Quaker Road — thus bypassing Dinwiddie Court House and saving miles. Hampton had his cavalry camps close to the very important supply route that constituted the Confederate line from Dunovant's position just above Hatcher's Run to Barringer's camp between Rowanty and Stony Creeks — the 2nd North Carolina Cavalry camp was on the new military road.[203]

The area between the Confederate cavalry line and Jerusalem Plank Road east of the Weldon was patrolled and probed by both Hampton's cavalrymen and Union forces. That meant any serious effort by Union cavalry to target the supply route along Boydton Plank Road would start from Globe Tavern and drop south along the Weldon or the Jerusalem Plank Road; then turn west, and push Hampton's pickets back with serious resistance, likely around Vaughan Road. Of course, that is what Grant, Meade, and D. McM. Gregg had in mind for the morning of September 29.

D. McM. Gregg's cavalry column was on the road early, and moved from the Jerusalem Plank Road over to the Halifax Road staying behind Warren's picket line. They moved south until they came to the Church Road, at which point D. McM. Gregg put Charles H. Smith and his 2nd Brigade in the advance position and sent them westward toward the Vaughan Road. H. E. Davies's 1st Brigade was sent further down the railroad toward Reams's Station to drive back any force and capture supplies there.[204]

While D. McM. Gregg moved his cavalry into position, Hampton was planning a more leisurely morning on September 29. He had scheduled a review of W. H. F. Lee's North Carolina brigade and J. L. Davis's Virginia brigade — there had been less time and fewer inclination for reviews in 1864 than in 1863, so many faced the event with mixed emotions. (The event received such advanced billing that while advancing west of the Weldon, D. McM. Gregg was told of the planned event by a citizen along his march.) However, before the review took place, the division was called northward because the serious fighting north of the James River near Chaffin's Bluff was already underway. W. H. F. Lee took his command up to and along Boydton Plank Road toward Petersburg. Before they reached Petersburg, however, D. McM. Gregg's cavalry encountered and was pushing M. C. Butler's cavalry pickets back toward Hatcher's Run. The Confederate command feared this might be an all-out assault on the South Side Railroad, so Hampton halted W. H. F. Lee's command and held them up on Boydton Plank Road for most of the day — they were near Petersburg and ready to head north or south once their commander had a better idea of what Grant was up to.[205] (See map 6.2.)

Meanwhile, C. H. Smith's Union troopers had moved along the Lower Church Road to the intersection with Wyatt's Road which they took toward Vaughan Road. Around 7:00 A.M. on the 29th his troopers were probing for a route to Vaughan Road west of Wyatt's place. C. H. Smith set up a rear guard position at Wyatt's farm and sent four regiments toward Vaughan Road. When Smith's advance regiment reached Arthur's Swamp, less than a mile west of Wyatt's place, they met some Confederate pickets from Dunovant's command. The pickets were pushed back to their support near Hatcher's Run. Smith's cavalrymen then moved slowly westward, passed McDowell's farm and west of Vaughan Road. They met with more resistance there, but were able to push it aside and head for Hatcher's Run. At that point, Farley's horseless cavalrymen stopped the Union advance giving Hampton time to form Young's brigade into a defensible line. By afternoon, as Hampton was forming his line to stop D. McM. Gregg's advance, he ordered W. H. F. Lee to leave J. L. Davis's Virginia brigade and artillery on Boydton Plank Road and bring Barringer's North Carolina regiments to join the fight. Hampton's line was already formidable, with most of P. M. B. Young's and J. Dunovant's brigades in place. They were ready to meet their enemy, but Hampton was still not certain what force was poised behind his enemy's cavalry. That was why he sent for the North Carolina regiments. D. McM. Gregg, on the other hand, did not see his mission that day as one that included a serious fight, so he tried to get closer to Boydton Plank Road by going around Hampton's flank. However, M. C. Butler moved to block the attempt. By early afternoon, D. McM. Gregg decided he was not strong enough to fight the cavalry in front of him and worried that enemy infantry might be too close, so he had C. H. Smith's command pull back. They moved east near McDowell's Farm.[206]

Fighting at McDowell's and Wyatt's Farms, September 29, 1864

By the time D. McM. Gregg's cavalry had refused to get seriously engaged and was settled into their new line around McDowell's place, Hampton realized there was no major infantry force behind his enemy's cavalry — he had been considering the possibility this action was the beginning of a major assault on the South Side Railroad. With that in mind, Hampton was not eager to call off the fight. So the Confederates moved up, and around 4:00 P.M., Hampton had M. C. Butler test the Union line in front of them; it turned out to be just a forward picket line easily pushed back to C. H. Smith's main line around McDowell's farm. At the farm, serious fighting resulted in no significant movement by either line. Then, according to Hampton, W. H. F. Lee arrived with three regiments from Barringer's North Carolina brigade.[207]

Barringer had left the 1st North Carolina on picket duty, and held his 3rd Cavalry in reserve. When the 2nd and 5th North Carolina arrived, they were immediately dismounted and rapidly moved to the line. Major McNeil moved up with his 5th Cavalry, and W. P. Roberts took the 2nd Cavalry forward. Roberts was put in command of both North Carolina regiments. Arriving on the line, they saw the enemy in a wood, and W. H. F. Lee ordered a charge. Without hesitating, W. P. Roberts took his command forward and in the process drew upon themselves "a very heavy fire, both from their front and right." Nonetheless, fresh and eager, the North Carolinians continued their charge into the Union left. At about the same time, M. C. Butler sent his regiments at C. H. Smith's center and right, but met with stubborn resistance. However, the 2nd North Carolina and its support ran over the 4th and 13th Pennsylvania Cavalry and captured a number of them, including Major James Peale of the 4th Pennsylvania. In a summary account of the day, the following was reported for the 13th Pennsylvania, "...when the brigade was attacked and fought until dark, the regiment losing 500 yards of ground, after two dismounted charges, losing 2 officers and 30 men killed, wounded, and missing." Barringer's strong move nearly flanked the Union line while their center and right was holding. Sensing a problem, the center of the Union line pulled back before being flanked. C. H. Smith then managed to gather his men into works that had been erected on the high ground near the Wyatt's house.[208]

The new Union line was east of Arthur's Swamp and just west of Wyatt's place. Hampton's dismounted cavalrymen continued to press hard against C. H. Smith's well-positioned line, but the latter did not give way.[209]

By the time C. H. Smith had his men settled into their new line, his infantry support arrived from Globe Tavern and joined the cavalrymen in the works — but did not become engaged. (Meade, back at Globe Tavern, had heard sounds of fighting on Gregg's front and gave instructions to send an infantry brigade down Halifax Road to support the cavalry.) Around the same time, Hampton's cavalry stormed across Wyatt's farm and formed a line close to their enemy's works, but by the time they were set for an assault on the Union stronghold, night had fallen and it was deemed impractical. At that point, the battle de-escalated into light skirmishing around the farmhouse. About 9:00 P.M., Hampton established a picket line, and M. C. Butler took Dunovant's and Young's brigades back to their camps. W. H. F. Lee rode with Barringer and his North Carolina Brigade back to spend the night near J. L. Davis's Virginia brigade. They were camped from the Boydton Plank Road to the Confederate entrenchments built to shield the upper stretch of the supply route. The 2nd North Carolina marched to the outer fortifications southeast of the plank road.[210]

Though most of the Confederate cavalrymen had returned to their camps for the night,

D. McM. Gregg could not pull back beyond the Weldon because the Union plan called for continued demonstrations and some fighting the next day — they knew this battle was not over. D. McM. Gregg spent the night with his forces concentrated at Wyatt's farm and Reams's Station. His infantry support was ordered back to Globe Tavern and since C. H. Smith's cavalry brigade was spent, Gregg moved his 1st Brigade into the front line. H. E. Davies and his men arrived on the line around 10:00 P.M. and relieved Smith's troopers. D. McM. Gregg and C. H. Smith then rode back to Halifax Road for the night.[211]

JONES'S FARM, SEPTEMBER 30

R. E. Lee could not do much on September 30 but wait for Grant to attack north of the James and below Petersburg. It was expected, but there were not enough Confederate troops to cover even the most probable points of attack. Union success north of the James the day before made the fall of Richmond a real possibility, so R. E. Lee had to be ready to strengthen his line around the capital if a major push developed there. Given his shortage of manpower, the best R. E. Lee could do was hold great numbers of troops in reserve, ready to move in any direction. As indicated, many of the Confederate troops had been pulled out of the Petersburg line and sent north of the James. Many were held in reserve and were ready to move on the morning of September 30. This worried R. E. Lee. He knew the roads to the all important supply routes on the Boydton Plank Road and the South Side Railroad were very vulnerable.[212]

Grant instructed Meade late on September 29 to be ready to move the next morning around 8:00 A.M., but to wait for an opportunity or instructions to attack.[213]

Grant was sure the Petersburg line was weakened by the increased Confederate strength north of the James. The Union plan for September 30 called for Warren to move his infantry out first on the Poplar Spring Church road, and shortly have the Fifth and Ninth Corps join forces. D. McM. Gregg was to move his cavalry as far as the Peebles's farm — just west of the Weldon, near the Union stronghold at Globe Tavern. If they were successful in breaking through the Confederate lines, they were to head for the supply lines.[214]

Around 9:00 A.M., Meade had the Fifth and Ninth Corps on the road. Warren's Fifth Corps was in advance and moved to the Halifax Road, then exited the Union fortifications that enclosed Globe Tavern and protruded across the Weldon Railroad. The column headed west on Poplar Spring Road toward Peebles's farm which was near the Confederate outer defenses. The outer defenses were lightly manned by Confederate horse artillery and cavalry — the 2nd North Carolina Cavalry was among those near the right of these recently constructed works. Most of the infantry had been pulled from these outer works and were behind Petersburg ready to move north or south. One Confederate fortification was in G. K. Warren's path, however; it was called Fort Archer and was located near Peebles's farm. The fort gave Warren's command pause and time to let the Ninth Corps catch up before launching an attack. While they waited, the Confederates moved some troops back to the Boydton Plank Road — the 2nd North Carolina Cavalry was moved back to the plank road from the outer defenses around noon. About an hour later a division of infantry from Warren's corps attacked the fort.[215]

After a brief fight, the Confederate troops fell back to their main line of earthworks that extended from the Petersburg defenses, southwest in front of the Boydton Plank Road to protect that supply route and roads leading up to the South Side Railroad. There was a pause in the fighting as the Union forces occupied their enemy's outer defensive line. By mid-afternoon A. P. Hill ordered his infantrymen to the line below Petersburg and prepared to attack Warren's line. In consultation with A. P. Hill, Hampton moved W. H. F. Lee's cavalry into position to strike the enemy on their left flank. As four Confederate infantry brigades moved into position, the Union Ninth Corps began to move through the line held by Warren's Fifth Corps. The Ninth Corps moved forward and formed for a charge on the Confederate line, only to be met by a countercharge. The Union troopers were pushed back in confusion. Part of the rout was due to the flank attack around the Union left by W. H. F. Lee's cavalry, causing the whole line to drop back. Some of the Fifth Corps came forward and stabilized the Union line, but not before W. H. F. Lee's cavalrymen had captured hundreds of prisoners.[216]

W. H. F. Lee also moved the 2nd North Carolina Cavalry from up on Boydton Plank Road into the flank attack on the Union left. Private Gordon of the 2nd Cavalry wrote the following in his diary that night: "Just before night we go around and come in behind the Yankee works. Our forces captured part of the Yankee line of works and two regiments of Yankees with their colours. At 10 o'clock we go back to the Plank road and bivouack for the night."[217]

The next day, October 1, Meade wanted to push the Confederate works along Boydton Plank Road with more force. During the night he moved a division of the Second Corps up on the left of Ninth and Fifth Corps in order to advance on the Boydton Plank Road. Hampton expected Meade to attempt to regain the ground he had lost on the 30th, so he placed W. H. F. Lee's two brigades and Dearing's near Fort MacRae on the right of the first line of works. The move was prompted when M. C. Butler's cavalry came under attack over on the Vaughan Road by some of D. McM. Gregg's cavalrymen. Hampton took two of W. H. F. Lee's Virginian regiments and hit the Union cavalrymen in the rear, driving them back to their entrenchments near McDowell's place. Furthermore, Hampton wanted to mount a formidable attack on the Union line, so he sent word to W. H. F. Lee requesting that two more regiments be sent to him — the 2nd North Carolina Cavalry, on the line at Fort MacRae, was relieved by the 3rd North Carolina and moved toward Vaughan Road and Gravelly Run, presumably along with one other regiment. Meanwhile, the Union infantry line advanced to the Confederate works along the plank road, but thought the enemy line there too formidable to attack. From these positions skirmishing took place along the line during October 1 and 2, but the serious fighting was over. The troopers held their positions until Grant and his commanders called off the assault both north of the James and south of Petersburg.[218]

By the time the 2nd North Carolina Cavalry reached Gravelly Run prepared to join Hampton's attack, the operation was called off. The success of the Confederate infantry had contributed to Hampton's decision not to attack D. McM. Gregg's cavalry near McDowell's house. Thus, the 2nd North Carolina was left standing in the rain near Gravelly Run around midday and did not fight that day. Private Gordon of the 2nd North Carolina described the two days of waiting in these words:

October 1st. As soon as it is day we go to the left of the enemy and are posted behind the outer line of works, where we are relieved by the 3rd Reg't.

We go out to and down the plank road to Perkins'-mills on Gravel run, when we halt about 12 o'clock. It has rained hard all day and night.

October 2nd. This morning we go back and through up a line of works a little in advance of those we left last night. They having been captured from the 3rd Reg't. We lie behind our works all day and night expecting the Yankees to advance.

October 3rd. Remain behind our breast-works until evening, when we go back to Perkins'-mill.

October 4th. We leave the mill in the evening and return to our camp on Stony Creek.[219]

Actually, when the 2nd North Carolina Cavalry returned to the front line on October 2, it was involved in skirmishing below Harmon Road as it moved to establish a line of works near Fort MacRae in front of the position the 3rd North Carolina had been pushed from the night before. The men of the 2nd Cavalry were among the last cavalrymen in the trenches protecting their infantry's right flank. In general, however, by October 2 the fighting stopped and the clean-up began.

The Union losses north of the James totaled about 3,300, and the Confederate estimates totaled around half that number. The fighting below Petersburg resulted in about 2,900 men lost to the Union, and the Confederates lost slightly fewer than half that number.[220]

The 2nd North Carolina Cavalry took several losses during the first two weeks of September, resulting from encounters while on scouting missions, picket duty, or pursuing Union cavalry probes across the Weldon Railroad. Later in the month, they took losses while defending the supply route along Boydton Plank Road. Some of the men lost to the 2nd North Carolina Cavalry are in the following list.

Grant's Last Attempts to Encircle Petersburg Before Winter Camp

By mid–October, Grant could not understand how the Army of Northern Virginia continued to resist his advances, one after another. Several

Combat Losses in the 2nd North Carolina Cavalry During September 1864

Trooper	Age	Co.	Fate
James M. Shields	26	A	captured, September 3
Wilson L. Spruill	26	G	wounded, September 7
John J. Hardin	29	B	captured, September 10
Vincent Barns	39	E	wounded, September 12
J. R. Hood		B	captured, September 17
James N. Turner		D	killed, September 29
Jacob Isley		G	killed, September 29
Willie G. Sharp	22	E	wounded, September
Nathaniel C. Tucker		F	wounded, September
Joel B. Reid	19	B	killed, September

Information contained in this table came from Compiled Service Records as summarized by Louis H. Manarin, *North Carolina Troops: 1861–1865, A Roster*, vol. II, pages 98–177. (See Appendix for more information on the men listed above, page 404.)

attempts directly at Richmond had failed, and many attempts to get around the Confederate right and cut Petersburg's supply lines on the Boydton Plank Road and, more importantly, the South Side Railroad had also failed. However, he was still convinced his enemy's army was about to collapse, but he was not sure another major attack should be attempted in the Fall of 1864.[221]

On the other hand, Meade was eager for another attempt to get around the enemy's right flank. He had been getting a lot of bad press and wanted another chance to show what he was capable of doing before they pulled in for the winter. Meade knew that after the Union probe on the Confederate right during the last days of September, R. E. Lee had hastily extended his line in front of Boydton Plank Road as far as Hatcher's Run; and he knew that part of the line was vulnerable. In the end, Meade was able to convince Grant to try one more sweep around their enemy before winter. On October 24, Grant wrote Meade the following: "Make your preparations to march out at an early hour on the 27th to gain possession of the South Side Railroad, and to hold it, and fortify back to your present left." Those were ambitious instructions in that if Meade could fortify back to his present position, he would also have taken control of the wagon train route along Boydton Plank Road. Grant went on to make clear it was Meade's plan when he added: "In commencing your advance, move in three columns, exactly as proposed by yourself in our conversation of last evening, and with the same force you proposed to take." That was exactly what Meade wanted—a chance to demonstrate he could plan and initiate action, not just follow instructions.[222]

Meade's plan was to hit the weakened enemy in the hastily thrown up works with a large, overwhelming force. He would take 30,000 to 35,000 infantrymen, considerable artillery, and a cavalry force of about 3,000 men. Basically, Meade took the Second Corps (Hancock's), two divisions from the Fifth Corps (Warren's), a major part of the Ninth Corps (under Parke), and D. McM. Gregg's cavalry.[223]

W. S. Hancock was to drop south and then move westward to the intersection of Hatcher's Run and Vaughan Road; then on to Boydton Plank Road; then west on White Oak Road, paralleling the South Side Railroad. Once on White Oak, west of the Confederate entrenchments, they planned to head north to the South Side Railroad. Hancock and the cavalry planned to go around the newly extended Confederate works. J. G. Parke was to head directly at the front of the new enemy works while Hancock and D. McM. Gregg were making their sweep. Warren and his Fifth Corps were to head for Armstrong's Mill and be prepared to support Parke and the Ninth Corps. If Parke was unable to break through his enemy's line, then Warren would drop down and move on Hancock's right for the sweep to the targeted railroad. Meade's force moved out around 3:00 A.M. on October 27. (Of course, Grant also had B. F. Butler's command ready to move simultaneously on Richmond.)[224]

Fighting Along the Boydton Plank Road, October 27–28, 1864

Hancock and his command crossed Hatcher's Run near Armstrong's Mill, and to his left D. McM. Gregg's cavalry crossed the Rowanty Creek at Monk's Neck Bridge. Hampton's pickets were driven in along both lines of march. M. C. Butler was ordered forward to block the

Union forces moving from Vaughan Road toward Boydton Plank Road, while Hampton moved down the plank road to block the enemy cavalry coming up on Quaker Road. Dunovant's brigade was stretched as far down as Monk's Neck Bridge and offered the first resistance to Gregg's cavalry column as it came west. The Union cavalry column continued west to Quaker Road which they took heading north for the Boydton Plank Road. A mile or so up the road, they came to the blockage created by Hampton and some of his cavalrymen at Quaker Bridge over Gravelly Run. Hampton had sent word to W. H. F. Lee to move rapidly up and hit their enemy's cavalry in the rear when the fighting started at the bridge — Hampton was confident the Union cavalry caught between their forces would be destroyed. D. McM. Gregg knew that W. H. F. Lee's division was in camp behind him near Stony Creek, or they were on their way toward his rear. Consequently, he understood he could not stand for long, fighting his way across Quaker Bridge.[225]

Fortunately for D. McM. Gregg, getting his column over the bridge took very little time because Hampton offered little resistance and slowly pulled back. Just before W. H. F. Lee was in position, Hampton received word that a Union force was advancing rapidly from Armstrong's Mill to Boydton Plank Road which would take them to Hampton's rear, so he quickly pulled back from his confrontation with D. McM. Gregg's cavalrymen. Gregg crossed Gravelly Run and burned the bridge behind him. Hampton had hoped Dearing's cavalry brigade would come down from A. P. Hill's line to cover his rear, but that did not occur. As Hampton pulled back to the plank road, he soon discovered his enemy crossing that road and heading west on White Oak Road. Hancock's advance had actually moved around the left of the Confederate works and was entering White Oak Road which nearly paralleled the South Side Railroad — Hampton knew he had to get a force in front of them rapidly, so he sent for the nearest, M. C. Butler's command. Hampton left some cavalrymen and artillery on Boydton Plank Road near Wilson's House to stop Gregg's advance from the Quaker Road and ordered M. C. Butler to White Oak Road immediately. Hancock's advance was just where they wanted to be.[226]

D. McM. Gregg's Union cavalrymen then had an easy time of it on Quaker Road and continued up to Boydton Plank Road — they were on the plank road before one o'clock in the afternoon. Their only immediate problem was still on their rear, but that did not slow their advance. This progress, along with the troops on the White Oak Road, must have delighted Meade and Grant, both of whom had been on the front just behind Parke's line since around 9:30 that morning. By 1:00 P.M., Hancock received orders to slow his infantry advance on the plank road and not press west on the White Oak Road. About the same time, Hampton's presence on the plank road was detected between D. McM. Gregg's cavalry on the same road and Hancock's advance on White Oak Road. That situation should have worried Hampton more than the Union commanders, but the pause in the Union advance westward gave Hampton time to collect M. C. Butler and his command and move west, then up to White Oak Road and form a line in front of Hancock's advance just before they started their move west on the road. Even if concentrated, Hampton's cavalry was not expected to stop Meade's combined infantry and cavalry force, but to detect and then slow the enemy advance until infantry could be moved in front of them. By early afternoon, Hampton had his cavalry in position to meet his responsibilities. Once he stopped Hancock's advance, he strengthened his line across the road with his left on Burgess's Mill Pond and managed to repulse more than one enemy infantry attack. About this time, Meade and Grant both visited the line on Boydton Plank Road and were a little disconcerted to see how strongly their enemy was posted in their planned path to the South Side Railroad.[227]

Meanwhile, H. Heth, commanding the Confederate works along Boydton Plank Road, had heard the fighting between Hampton and their enemy's cavalry and infantry and sent some help from the right of his line. H. Heth sent Dearing's brigade and J. L. Davis's command just west of Hatcher's Run overlooking Burgess's Mill. In addition, A. P. Hill had ordered W. Mahone to take three of his brigades down to the right of their line.[228]

While the Confederates were closing around Hancock's and D. McM. Gregg's commands, Grant and Meade were meeting by the side of Boydton Plank Road. Just before 4:00 P.M. Grant had seen enough. His enemy was too well entrenched to move, so he would have to abandon another attempt to move on the South Side Railroad. A very disappointed Grant and Meade moved back from the front, but before they left Grant told Hancock to keep his men on the line until noon the next day in an effort to bring on an attack from the enemy. Grant wanted to have some sort of small victory for the press—the Federal election being so close and all.[229]

By the time the Union commanders had decided to abandon their mission, and at most hoped to incite an attack on their own positions, Hampton and Heth had already decided to accommodate them. Hampton, firmly planted on White Oak Road, heard of Heth's infantry advance on Hancock's position from the north and knew W. H. F. Lee was sitting on D. McM. Gregg's rear and ready to advance from the south—so Hampton readied for a coordinated attack on Hancock and Gregg. As arranged, at the sound of Heth's musketry, Hampton ordered M. C. Butler to attack, while W. H. F. Lee had been instructed to do the same.[230]

The Confederates rushed to close the box around their enemy, but not all with equal success. It was after 4:00 P.M. when the fighting got started on Boydton Plank Road (near Wilson's Farm), Hatcher's Run, and Burgess's Mill. Darkness ended the violence.[231]

W. H. F. Lee's Cavalry, Gravelly Run and Boydton Plank Road (Wilson's Farm)

As indicated, early in the day when D. McM. Gregg and his cavalry column were halted at the bridge over Gravelly Run on the Quaker Road, they were forced to stop and deploy their advance because Hampton, with M. C. Butler, had formed a line of battle at the run. Hampton pulled most of his men back before a major fight took place, but while the Union column fought its way through the small force Hampton left behind, the head of W. H. F. Lee's column came up from Stony Creek and arrived at the intersection of Vaughan and Quaker (and the military) Roads.

According to H. E. Davies, his brigade was bringing up the rear of the Union column when they were hit near the intersection of Vaughan and Quaker Roads while waiting for D. McM. Gregg's advance to fight its way across Gravelly Run. In his words, "Here W. H. F. Lee's division, coming up from Stony Creek, made a spirited attack upon the rear of my command...." W. H. F. Lee had taken J. L. Davis's (Chambliss's) Virginia brigade west to Boydton Plank Road and left Barringer and his North Carolina regiments to attack the Union cavalry's rear guard. Barringer described the action that followed in these terms: "On receiving orders from Gen. Lee to attack, Gen. Barringer dismounted parts of the First and Second Regiments, and proceeded to advance, but found the enemy already retiring; only a few shots were fired by each party."[232]

Barringer's North Carolinians stayed on their enemy's rear and were engaged in light skirmishing as they slowly approached the bridge over Gravelly Run. Once H. E. Davies had the last of the Union column over the bridge, under the eyes and fire of Barringer's cavalrymen, he burned it. H. E. Davies and his Union cavalrymen continued up the road and on to Boydton Plank Road while Barringer and his men moved westward to join W. H. F. Lee and the rest of their division over on the plank road—from there they marched rapidly northward and across Gravelly Run.[233]

W. H. F. Lee's command caught up with D. McM. Gregg's cavalry on Boydton Plank Road around Wilson's farm and formed for an attack. According to Barringer,

...we were ordered by Gen Lee to dismount the First and Second regiments [North Carolina Cavalry] and put them in on the left of the road, forming a line of battle with the Ninth and Thirteenth Virginia Regiments then actively engaged on our right. Gen. Barringer being ordered to advance his lines, the troops went forward with great alacrity; but Major McNeil, who accompanied the Regiment, soon found himself in advance of the Virginia Regiments, on his right, who, for some reason, had not moved at the same time. Our line now overlapped the enemy's right, Col. Cheek and Maj. McNeil, were now ordered to oblique to the right, which flanked the enemy, and brought our fire upon his main force concealed in the woods.[234]

As the battle heated up, the whole line was ordered to advance and did. By then Hampton had dropped down and sent word to W. H. F. Lee that D. McM. Gregg and Hancock were pretty well boxed in and he should prepare to launch a major attack at the sounds of musketry coming from Heth's front on the north or from Hampton's front to the northwest of their enemy. In the meantime, the 3rd and 5th North Carolina, which had been left mounted and in support of McGregor's batteries, came up and joined the line. W. H. F. Lee then moved the 1st and 5th North Carolina to the front on both sides of the Boydton Plank Road and left the Virginia troopers from J. L. Davis's brigade on their right. McGregor's Battery was also moved forward and placed on the Boydton Plank Road among the cavalrymen of the 5th North Carolina. About the time this new Confederate line was formed, the fighting on all fronts heated up considerably. Early in the day, the 2nd North Carolina was engaged in the continual skirmishing with their enemy, but in the final disposition of troops they were held in a support position to protect their artillery. Judging by the battering the artillerymen took, the 2nd Cavalry must also have been in the midst of considerable firing. The intensity of feelings and fighting on the Boydton Plank Road near Wilson's house that day was recorded by one member of the 5th North Carolina as "one of the most important actions and greatest victories that the Sixty-third [5th Cavalry] North Carolina Regiment was ever engaged in." Barringer himself listed the fighting that day among the North Carolina brigade's finest moments when he wrote, "...but the most important of all was the battle at Wilson's farm on the 27th of October, when Grant seized the Boydton plank-road, and we repeated the operation at Reams' Station and with like success."[235]

Once the battle was raging, Hampton took his cavalry down and spread them between Butler's force up on White Oak Road and W. H. F. Lee's near Wilson's farm on Boydton Plank Road, effectively sealing off the western front. From that view point, Hampton was later able to report that W. H. F. Lee "...attacked with great spirit driving the enemy rapidly and handsomely to Bevel's House." According to Hampton, his cavalry "...had driven him [the enemy] in on all the roads, and he was massed in the field around the houses of Bond and Burgess. The night having grown very dark and a heavy rain coming on I was forced to pause in my attack, but I ordered the line held all night, so that we might attack at daylight the next morning."[236]

Late in the day, H. E. Davies took his Union cavalry brigade from Boydton Plank Road back down to Gravely Run for the night. After dark, Colonel W. P. Roberts of the 2nd North Carolina Cavalry sent a party back down Quaker Road where it encountered Davies's pickets and drove them into their reserves. The cavalrymen of the 2nd North Carolina managed to come away with three captured horses and a number of arms.[237]

Young Private Gordon of the 2nd North Carolina Cavalry recorded the day in his diary in these words, "We marched to the Petersburg and Boydton plank road and we held as a support to one of our batteries. Part of our brigade is dismounted and engaging the enemy. At night after the fighting has ceased our regiment is put on picket on the battle field. We remain on post until 12 o'clock next morning."[238]

As a result of the October attack, Barringer reported losses in his North Carolina brigade as 3 killed, 65 wounded, and 2 missing. The 2nd North Carolina Cavalry recorded the following losses.[239]

Combat Losses in the 2nd North Carolina Cavalry During October 1864

Trooper	Age	Co.	Fate
Virgil A. Burns	24	I	captured, October 11
Hardy Burns	25	I	captured, October 24
Amaziah M. Price	24	A	captured, October 27
Jared T. Childs		F&S	captured, October 27

Information contained in this table came from Compiled Service Records as summarized by Louis H. Manarin, *North Carolina Troops: 1861–1865, A Roster*, vol. II, pages 98–177. (See Appendix for more information on the men listed above, page 404.)

On October 28, as the armies returned to their previous positions. Hampton moved Butler's and Barringer's commands back to their camps. The 2nd North Carolina, along with others, was first in the order of rotation for picket duty. On picket, the 2nd North Carolina helped canvass the abandoned Union lines and found the usual remains of a force that had pulled back rapidly from battle and had time to reflect on the accomplishments of the previous days. For instance, a diary entry October 28, 1864 from a private in the 2nd North Carolina Cavalry reads, "October 28th. Part of our men charge a hospital full of Yankee wounded which they left last night and captured a hundred prisoners. This is the 3rd time they have attempted to extend their line to the South Side Railroad and been defeated. In the evening we returned to our camp on Stony Creek."[240]

By October 29, the 2nd North Carolina, along with the other cavalrymen in its division, settled into the picket line Hampton established from the end of their infantry's entrenchments near Hatcher's Run down to Stony Creek. Occasionally Union scouting parties would probe the "everyman's land" between the Weldon Railroad and Vaughan Road which routinely required a Confederate cavalry party to saddle up and ride to put a stop to the intrusion. Such assignments were not welcome in what had already become a cold and hungry season. The 2nd North Carolina was called upon to counter several such probes between the end of October and the end of the first week in December 1864—they had minor but notable skirmishes near Boisseau's Farm, Gravelly Run, Hargrove's House, and a few other places without names.[241]

The Confederate cavalrymen were by and large ready to set up winter quarters and rebuild their units. However, Grant was not quite ready. He had shut down activities up around Richmond for the winter, but not below Petersburg. A reminder that Grant did not give up a campaign easily occurred late on the morning of December 1. The cavalrymen of the 2nd North Carolina were ordered into their saddles and headed for Stony Creek Depot which had come under attack. As they approached the station, they could see the smoke billowing above the scene. They were too late to save most of the station, but managed to drive the raiding party off. Their advance got just close enough to lose one man who was captured and taken off. Most of the regiment went on to pursue the raiding party for about eight miles toward the Union line before turning back. They arrived back at the depot around 11:00 P.M. and returned to their camp the next morning. It was a most unwelcome diversion, but somebody had to respond. The 2nd Cavalry relieved the 5th North Carolina on the picket line "…along the Stage road and on Saponi Creek on the 5th of December." As the cavalrymen took up their picket posts, Grant and Meade were already positioning troops for another move on the Confederate right.[242]

Warren's Raid to Belfield, December 8

On December 5, 1864, Grant sent the following instructions to Meade: "You may make immediate preparations to move down the Weldon railroad for the purpose of effectually destroying it as far south as Hicksford, or farther if practicable." It still bothered Grant that he had not been able to destroy the Weldon at and below Stony Creek Depot. R. E. Lee had adjusted to the loss of the Weldon line around Globe Tavern, and his army and Petersburg were still getting supplies from that line by wagon trains from Stony Creek Depot. Grant decided that he should destroy the Weldon all the way down to Hicksford, making it even more difficult for R. E. Lee to supply his army and the city under his protection. The attack on Stony Creek Depot on December 1 was followed by plans to move again in that direction with an irresistible force. This was not another move to flank the Army of Northern Virginia or to create weak spots elsewhere on the Confederate line; its energy was focused on destroying more of the Weldon Railroad and lengthening the wagon supply line for the winter. Grant instructed Meade to mobilize for the tour of destruction on December 5 and be ready to move down the Weldon by the 7th of the month.[243]

G. K. Warren was in command of the action, and he took the three divisions in his Fifth Corps, Mott's division from the Second Corps, and D. McM. Gregg's cavalry division—about 22,000 infantry and 4,200 cavalrymen. R. E. Lee had said on earlier occasions that when and wherever Grant wanted to attack and destroy sections of the Weldon Railroad he had the force to do so, and the Confederates did not have the force to stop him. Nonetheless, the Confederates had to throw what they had in the area in front of the Union raiding party—and what they had was largely Hampton's battered, tired, and cold cavalrymen.[244]

D. McM. Gregg's cavalry moved along the Jerusalem Plank Road on the cold and rainy/snowy morning of December 7—at 4:00 A.M., of course. Their infantry followed the same course. Meade had little information about Hampton's cavalry movements into the area below Stony Creek Depot—Warren's destination. Soon after Warren was underway, however,

Meade was informed that deserters from the 1st North Carolina Cavalry had entered their lines the night before and told them that Barringer's North Carolina brigade had returned to camps above Stony Creek December 2, after the brief encounter around the depot the day before. This had to be reassuring and suggest that their only initial resistance would come from enemy pickets. Meade and Warren could assume Hampton did not suspect another move on the Weldon at Stony Creek Depot or below. When the Union cavalry crossed Warwick Swamp at Protor's and Lee's Mills, they encountered the first Confederate cavalrymen Hampton was notified of the strong force advancing down Jerusalem Plank Road.[245]

The Union column continued south on Jerusalem Plank Road as far as Hawkinsville then went southwest toward the Weldon. The cavalry crossed the Nottoway River in the afternoon of December 7, but Warren's infantry column had to wait for a bridge to be put in place. Late in the day, about half of the Union infantry was across, and they camped on both sides of the river. Their cavalry and some infantry moved on to Sussex Court House for the night. The next morning they moved for the railroad just below Stony Creek Station.[246]

H. E. Davies's cavalry brigade reached the Halifax Road around 9:00 A.M. December 8, where they met a small party of enemy cavalry. C. H. Smith's brigade arrived next and was sent north on the railroad to destroy the railroad bridge over the Nottoway. As Union cavalry continued to arrive on the Halifax Road, D. McM. Gregg put his men to work destroying track.[247]

The Confederates were also moving on the morning of December 7. Hampton had his cavalrymen once again heading for Stony Creek Depot. The 2nd North Carolina was relieved from picket duty by troopers from Dearing's brigade and joined the rest of its brigade on the march to the depot. After marching most of the day, Hampton sent Butler's and W. H. F. Lee's divisions east and southeast to probe the raiding column. The 2nd North Carolina Cavalry was delayed a bit while being withdrawn from the picket line and reached the depot after most of their division had moved through. They immediately moved east a few miles until they forded the Nottoway and found their division — at that point, they joined in a light skirmish on Halifax Road. From this and other minor encounters, Hampton determined the size and likely destination of the Union column — most importantly, he discovered he was at the rear of the Union cavalry column. He wanted to be in front of them, so he moved his cavalrymen back west of the railroad and then rapidly around the Union advance and headed for Belfield on the Meherrin River — he wanted to get there before his enemy. Hampton had small parties of cavalrymen over near the railroad, near the Union cavalry's advance to monitor and, if possible, slow the column as it moved south along the Weldon. Meanwhile, to the rear of D. McM. Gregg's cavalry, most of Warren's infantrymen spent the latter part of December 8 destroying the rails from the Nottoway River Bridge to Jarratt's Station.[248]

By early afternoon on December 8, Hampton received word that A. P. Hill was on his way with an infantry force to help stop the Union mission of destruction on the Weldon. Hampton urged A. P. Hill to hurry on their long march, and he had his cavalrymen back on the road at 2:00 the next morning. The head of Hampton's column approached Belfield around daylight on December 9 — by hard marching they arrived before their enemy. Hampton immediately placed his cavalrymen to help defend Hicksford and the railroad bridge over the Meherrin River.[249]

The town and railroad bridge was defended by Junior and Senior Reserves from both North Carolina and Virginia when Hampton's cavalrymen arrived, and Hampton moved most of his men into the existing line of defense. Barringer moved the 5th North Carolina north of the river, in front of the existing line of defense to help protect the railroad bridge. The 2nd North Carolina Cavalry was sent about a mile up the Meherrin to hold the nearest passable ford (Cook's Ford) — Hampton was concerned the enemy cavalry might try to hit his left flank by crossing up river. Another regiment was sent about four miles down river to protect the Confederate right.[250]

The Union cavalry arrived in front of Belfield around 3:00 P.M. on December 9. They approached slowly and went into a line of battle in a similar manner. When it came, the assault on the Confederate line was, in Hampton's words, "...a feeble one, and it was not renewed, though a sharp fire was kept up until after night." In the words of one private from the

5th North Carolina, "When they finally came, we were ready for them, but they showed even less inclination to fight than we did. At least we had to move to keep warm while they had warm overcoats. It was a terrible night of cold and rain and sleet, and when dawn came it was no better." Another private from that North Carolina regiment agreed with the previous assessment, especially the harsh weather, and added: "And all that night Colonel W. P. Roberts, with the Nineteenth North Carolina Regiment [2nd Cavalry], picketed and guarded the Meherrin above Hicksford while others slept as well as they could."[251]

When the 2nd North Carolina moved up river early in the day, they fortified themselves at Cook's Ford. Pickets were also sent out along the river in both directions. Then they waited and watched the dampness on and around them turn to ice.[252]

Hampton met with A. P. Hill during the night and planned a coordinated attack for the morning of December 10. However, by the time Hampton and his men arose and made preparations for their attack, their enemy had pulled back. D. McM. Gregg was instructed to withdraw his cavalrymen from in front of Hampton's early on December 10 — he was instructed to have one brigade fall back early to be Warren's advance on the roads back to their lines.[253]

As soon as Hampton discovered his enemy was gone, he sent word to A. P. Hill, and sent W. H. F. Lee's division after the enemy column. Understandably the men in Hampton's command were not eager to go on the offensive early that freezing morning. Most had not had anything to eat in two or three days, and all were cold and wet. Going on the offensive meant first they had to go out and tear down the barricades that had been erected to keep their enemy back — though a small problem, a great annoyance to many under the circumstances. Nonetheless, the 2nd Cavalry did cross the Meherrin at Belfield and joined the pursuit of the retreating Union column, skirmishing with them until nightfall. The pursuit was so close that at one point the Union rear guard set a trap and men from the 3rd North Carolina Cavalry rode into it losing around 15 men, killed or wounded. At another point, the 2nd North Carolina came on the rear of their enemy column and according to their commander, a squadron lead by "Captain A. F. Harrell, made a splendid charge and captured some prisoners." Darkness brought the pursuit to an end for the 2nd North Carolina as they were ordered back to their camp near Stony Creek along with most of Hampton's cavalrymen — one regiment continued the pursuit for another day.[254]

On December 8, Grant had heard that R. E. Lee was pulling some infantry from his right and sending them to Hampton at Belfield. This news once again excited the possibility that Meade might after all be able to get around the Confederate line and hit the South Side Railroad while the action continued on the Weldon. However, the news of troop movements lacked certainty, and word of troops coming down from General Early's battered command in the Valley to join the right of the Confederate line kept filtering into Union headquarters. This resulted in hesitation, and the possibility was debated throughout the next day. However, the possibility was sufficiently tantalizing to both Grant and Meade, to warrant sending a force of three brigades of infantry, three regiments of cavalry, and artillery all under the command of General N. Miles to probe the Confederate line around Hatcher's Run while the debate was ongoing. Hampton had left Young's cavalry brigade on the run, and they with the help of others were able to offer enough resistance to slow, halt, and eventually cause the withdrawal of Miles's probe. On the afternoon of December 10, Meade also pulled his force up on Hatcher's Run back into their lines.[255]

Even though Grant's revived hope to interrupt the Confederate supply line on the South Side Railroad did not materialize, Warren's expedition was a success. They did destroy the Weldon down as far as the Meherrin River, and that was their objective. It did make the job of hauling supplies from the Weldon to Petersburg more difficult and increase the Confederate's hardship during the winter. It took until early March 1865 before the Weldon was again usable as far north as Stony Creek Depot.

Hampton reported his losses in Warren's Raid on the Weldon as "slight." According to Barringer, his North Carolina regiments suffered the following losses: the 1st Cavalry, 33 killed, 83 wounded, 22 missing for a total of 138; the

2nd Cavalry took 16 killed, 71 wounded, 22 missing for a total of 109; the 3rd regiment had 19 killed, 86 wounded, and 46 missing for a total of 158; and the 5th Cavalry had 30 killed, 137 wounded, and 41 missing for a total of 208. The roster only reflects the following for the 2nd North Carolina—and they were all on December 10—during the pursuit.

Combat Losses in the 2nd North Carolina Cavalry During December 1864

Trooper	Age	Co.	Fate
Jonathan McClain	20	D	captured, December 1
George McClintock		F	captured, December 10
Charles F. Regan	24	I	captured, December 10
Ira J. Waters		K	captured, December 10
Barzelia B. Wendley		K	captured, December 10
J. M. Shaw		G	captured, December 12
Leonard Shughart		G	captured, December 12

Information contained in this table came from Compiled Service Records as summarized by Louis H. Manarin, *North Carolina Troops: 1861–1865, A Roster*, vol. II, pages 98–177. (See Appendix for more information on the men listed above, page 405.)

After Warren's raid to Belfield, the 2nd Cavalry moved camp farther south by about 20 miles, from near Stony Creek to Cook's Ford on the Meherrin River, about a mile from Belfield, December 18. This became their winter camp, and it lasted until February 23, 1865. While in winter camp, the cavalrymen of the 2nd North Carolina, indeed the whole brigade, had the usual picketing and scouting duties as well as an occasional special assignment.

Equipping the Regiment— A Special Assignment

During this winter camp, a special assignment grew out of the need for cavalry equipment. The process of arming and equipping Confederate cavalrymen by picking up Union material left in battlefields started early in the war and was an individual effort as much as it was directed in a systematic way by commanders from R. E. Lee on down. W. P. Roberts remembered when his 2nd North Carolina Cavalry came to the Army of Northern Virginia in late 1862, "It went to meet the enemy, too, poorly armed and equipped. But I am glad to bear testimony to the fact that in the campaigns from 1863 to 1865, it was equipped almost entirely by captures from the enemy, including bridles and saddles, carbines, pistols, swords, canteens, blankets, and every article necessary to a thorough equipment of a trooper." The system worked well whether individual troopers picked up what they needed, or their commanders sent out details to gather the arms and equipment left by their enemy to be later distributed by quartermasters. As long as the army was being equipped it was not a major problem. Increasingly, however, some troopers did a little business on the side by picking up more than they needed and selling it to civilians for cash or food. As time went on, local citizens themselves entered the business of picking up their own souvenirs from near by battlefields. As it became harder for R. E. Lee to supply his cavalrymen, especially the North Carolina regiments, he moved to regain control of the situation. As early as July 26, 1864, R. E. Lee officially authorized General Barringer "…to take possession of all cavalry arms, equipments and accoutrements in the hands of civilians or other unauthorized persons in the State of North Carolina." He went on to say, "No persons in the military service had a right to sell or otherwise dispose of arms, &c,… General Barringer will not delegate this authority to any one except commissioned officers of his own command.…" This must have been a difficult assignment for Barringer and his staff, but within a month he asked for and received some help from the *Daily Confederate* published in Raleigh when they ran an editorial asking citizens to cooperate in the effort to collect materials. The piece included the following: "The brigade of Gen. Barringer is among the best in the service, but it had suffered much in the almost constant battles and skirmishes in which it has been engaged since May last. Its efficiency is much impaired for the want of carbines, saddles and other cavalry accoutrements of the best kind; and there is no doubt of the fact that these are now to be found in private hands.… They have been taken from the battle-field as trophies of war, or when captured from prisoners, have been sent [home] and often sold...." The editorial ends with the "...call on the private citizens of the State to see that these arms and equipments are returned.... If they are not returned by this means, other and more stringent measures will be adopted by those having the power."[256]

More stringent measures were needed to help supply the North Carolina cavalry regiments and they were still being implemented in December of 1864 when young John W. Gordon of the 2nd North Carolina was assigned to one of the details sent out among the people of Virginia to gather materials. He was a Virginian, which probably softened the edge on this special assignment. The assignment, in his view, was apparently a nice change of pace. He wrote in his diary of this experience:

December 22nd. Today I am detailed and sent off to hunt up saddles and other equipments belonging to the government and in the hands of citizens. I go about fifteen miles today. Cross the Nottoway at Wyatts Mill and stop at a Mrs. Johnson's'.

23rd. I start off early this morning go nearly to Dinwiddie Court House and turn to the left. About night I strike the Petersburg and Boydton plank road and travel up it two miles, stop at Williamsons' a short turn, cross the Nottoway by bridge and at the junction of the Boydton and Lawrenceville roads, I take the latter which is the left hand. I stop tonight at Col. Edmunds' two miles from Williamsons'.

24th. After a good nights rest on a feather bed and a hearty breakfast I ride again. My intention is to go the same way the Wilson raiders went last Summer. So I keep up the Lawrenceville road. I stopped near Smokey Ordinary and got dinner then went a few miles further and stopped for the night at Col. Blickks.

25th. To day is Christmas though with us there is no difference between this and Sunday and any other day. About twelve o'clock, I start again and go to Pwellborn about 12 miles and stop at Mr. Wm. Phipps'. I left the plank road this evening to my right.

26th. Today I feel but little like riding and Mr. Phipps' is such a nice place to stop, I shall stay with him until morning again.

27th. About 9 o'clock I bid Mr. Phipps a reluctant farewell and put out for camp abut 18 miles off. I stopped at a house and got dinner. Leave by Hick's ford, crossed the river and reached camp about night. I have been gone five days and have lived upon the best of the land.[257]

John made no mention of arms and equipment he may have gathered nor of making a stop at the quartermaster's camp to deliver them — probably just an oversight. However, he did seem to enjoy the assignment.

SCOUTS AND PICKETS

While in winter quarters, young John W. Gordon also had his turn at scouting a distance from camp. In January of 1865, he was sent down to eastern North Carolina to scout with five other men and stayed for eight days.[258]

On February 26, 1865, Private Gordon's diary entry reads, "I have neglected to note anything that has occurred since the 27th of December 1864, since that time we have been on picket, once stood eight days. Have been up to Dinwiddie Court House and on the Boydton plank road after the Yankees, with whom we had a skirmish. Have heard various reports about moving to different places and have been under marching orders several times."[259]

A private in the 5th North Carolina Cavalry had similar assignments and noted the additional hardship on the men and horses due to being so far south of their picket posts. He remembered that "It was especially hard on the cavalry. We had to march thirty miles to picket from our quarters near Belfield, and frequent movements of the enemy forced us to long hard marches.... The raids of the enemy kept our communications cut for most of the winter." The cavalry's presence was required there because Belfield had become the main depot for supplies coming up the Weldon Railroad after Warren's raiders destroyed the tracks down to that point. By late February, however, the Confederates had repaired the Weldon as far as Stony Creek Station, which allowed them to reestablish their depot at that point. On February 23 the 2nd North Carolina broke winter camp near Belfield and moved to Stony Creek Station. This made their ride to picket posts a little easier for about a month.[260]

While in winter camp at Belfield, the many skirmishes in which the 2nd Cavalry was involved, resulted in only two recorded losses.

Grant made one last major effort to capture supplies moving along the Boydton Plank Road on February 5, 1865. He had a reluctant Meade mobilize the Second and Fifth Infantry Corps and much of D. McM. Gregg's cavalry for a drive through the Confederate right near Hatcher's Run.

Combat Losses in the 2nd North Carolina Cavalry January–February 1865

Trooper	Age	Co.	Fate
Bradford L. Honeycut	29	A	wounded, c. February 1
Henry G. Thornell	31	E	wounded, c. February 23

Information contained in this table came from Compiled Service Records as summarized by Louis H. Manarin, *North Carolina Troops: 1861–1865, A Roster*, vol. II, pages 98–177. (See Appendix for more information on the men listed above, page 405.)

Robert E. Lee's troopers held the line as best they could, but the Union cavalry finally broke through to the supply line along the Boydton Plank Road. They went as far as Dinwiddie Court House only to find there was no massive wagon-train to be captured — D. McM. Gregg took a total of eighteen wagons during his mission. As Meade had feared, their losses far outweighed the gains from the operation. The Union lost about 1,500 men; the Confederacy about 1,000.[261]

Grant's move on the wagon train route was not met with a great deal of enthusiasm by Confederate troopers either — especially not by the worn-out and discouraged cavalrymen. For instance, when the alert reached the 2nd North Carolina Cavalry's camp, early on February 5, all the men with serviceable horses were ordered out of camp to defend their supply line. It is difficult to say just how widespread Private Milas Cavin's feelings were, but he made his clear. He was one of those who remained in camp because he claimed his horse had distemper. Private Cavin wrote his mother on February 11 and made it clear he did not mind missing the action of the previous days. In fact he told her that he had "...a very nice time since the command went out. I have just heard the command is coming in this evening."[262]

On February 8, Robert E. Lee described what Private Cavin missed by staying in camp when he wrote the following to the Secretary of War:

All the disposable force of the right wing of the army has been operating against the enemy beyond Hatcher's Run since Sunday [February 5]. Yesterday, the most inclement day of the winter, they had to be retained in line of battle, having been in the same condition to two previous days and nights. I regret to be obliged to state that under these circumstances, heightened by assaults and fire of the enemy, some of the men had been without meat for three days, and all were suffering from reduced rations and scant clothing, exposed to battle, cold, hail, and sleet.... The physical strength of the men, if their courage survives, must fail under this treatment.... I had to bring William H. F. Lee's Division forty miles Sunday night to get him in position.[263]

Other cavalrymen in Barringer's North Carolina brigade were also worn nearly to the breaking point after the fighting and marching of the previous summer and fall and the deprivation of the cold winter. Private Coltrane of the 5th North Carolina Cavalry described his mood and the conditions that prevailed in terms that would probably have elicited considerable agreement from his comrades.[264]

I don't remember a time when I was not hungry, nor a day when my horse was well-fed. The country was almost exhausted of forage, and our rations from the army commissary were scant, unpalatable foods which we would have scorned four years earlier. The raids of the enemy kept our communications cut for most of the winter.

My horse became so exhausted that I asked for a permit to go home for another one. I received a fifteen-day furlough in March and started back to North Carolina sometimes riding and sometimes leading my poor, exhausted horse. We Confederate privates felt that we were beaten, so by that time we were just doggedly hanging on. I realized this and it was a great temptation to stay at home, yet I reported back on March 25, 1865.[265]

Private Coltrane returned to his regiment in time for the journey to Appomattox Court House.

Like privates Milas Gavin of the 2nd North Carolina Cavalry and Daniel B. Coltrane of the 5th Cavalry, Robert E. Lee did not anticipate the coming Spring with much hope. A peace settlement did not materialize. He knew his line was too long to be sustained, and because of that, it would be difficult to collect his command if necessary without falling back so far that both Richmond and Petersburg would fall into Union hands. He hoped to be able to fall back as far as Burkeville if necessary, but not as far as Appomattox Court House.

Seven

The Appomattox Campaign

The Spring campaign of 1865 found Robert E. Lee in a desperate situation. Ulysses S. Grant's cavalry was stronger than ever and Philip H. Sheridan had just devastated Jubal Early's corps at Waynesboro on March 2. By mid–March Sheridan was heading for the Richmond-Petersburg area. Then on March 23, Joseph E. Johnston telegraphed that William T. Sherman had just combined with Scholfield at Goldsboro, North Carolina, to form an unstoppable force. R. E. Lee knew he could no longer sit in front of Grant, guarding Richmond and Petersburg. If Grant did not encircle R. E. Lee with P. H. Sheridan's cavalry and thereby cut his supply routes as well as his escape routes soon, then W. T. Sherman would certainly arrive from North Carolina and take the Army of Northern Virginia from the flank or rear. R. E. Lee's concern began to shift from keeping his supply routes open to keeping the escape routes from Richmond and Petersburg open long enough to use them. This meant keeping Sheridan's cavalry back until the retreat could be executed. R. E. Lee knew the remnants of his cavalry were no match for Sheridan — especially after he had sent Wade Hampton and Matthew C. Butler's cavalry division to South Carolina in January. Robert E. Lee was understandably nervous, but so was General Grant.[1]

The Union was tired of the prolonged war and Grant knew it. He felt the war must come to an end decisively before political forces reached a settlement. With that in mind, Grant was worried that R. E. Lee might take his army from the Richmond-Petersburg line during the night and join Johnston in North Carolina, thereby prolonging the war. Grant hoped to engage Lee's army and not let go until it was destroyed.[2]

By March 14, Grant had good reason to suspect R. E. Lee was preparing for a withdrawal from his entrenchments — he knew Lee had been sending supplies back toward Lynchburg. Also by that date, Grant received the following correspondence from George G. Meade: "I have examined the cavalry deserters, and they say positively that two brigades of W. H. F. Lee's division, hitherto at Stony Creek, moved yesterday morning with all their transportation toward Dinwiddie Court-House, leaving no one at Stony Creek." The Confederate brigades he referred to were Rufus Barringer's North Carolina brigade and R. L. T. Beale's Virginia brigade (formerly J. L. Davis's). W. H. F. Lee's third brigade (formerly James Dearing's) was commanded by William P. Roberts and was still on picket duty near the right flank of the Petersburg line. Meade's report aside, W. H. F. Lee's command did not move to Dinwiddie Court House until Sheridan had already made his move toward that place on March 29. In any case, Meade knew they were moving and was only speculating about where W. H. F. Lee's cavalry was heading.[3]

Robert E. Lee felt sure Grant would try to cut his escape routes by sweeping south of the Confederate line, then north to the South Side Railroad. To meet the challenge, Lee had his strongest cavalry unit on his right wing, on the Weldon Railroad to Stony Creek, and along the wagon train route. He had W. H. F. Lee's cavalry division spread thinly along those routes.

Grant was in a hurry. So was R. E. Lee. Once Lee's retreat got underway, the North Carolina Cavalry Brigade was protecting the rear and flank of the Army of Northern Virginia most of the way to Appomattox Court House. Today the events that took place there and along the way are collectively referred to as the Appomattox Campaign. At crucial points during the campaign, the 2nd North Carolina Cavalry was devastated to the point of losing its identity as a fighting unit.

Grant's Spring Offensive Against the Army of Northern Virginia

U. S. Grant issued orders for George G. Meade, Edward O. C. Ord, and Philip H. Sheridan to be underway on March 29, 1865. Grant's most urgent task was to get Sheridan around the right wing of R. E. Lee's entrenchments which only extended southwest of Petersburg as far as the intersection of White Oak and Claiborne's Roads. His goal was to block Lee's retreat routes on Boydton Plank Road and the South Side Railroad. This would not be an easy task. Grant had known for months that if he could have cut these supply routes to Petersburg, the Confederate army would not have survived many days. Raid after raid during the previous months sought to cut those routes—the failure of each raid required the next. Nonetheless, Grant believed the numerical superiority of Sheridan's cavalry, with infantry close behind, could now be successful.[4]

Sheridan moved early on March 29. He marched down the Jerusalem Plank Road through Reams's Station and headed for Malone's Bridge on Rowanty Creek. From there his plan was to cross Hatcher's Run near Monk's Neck Bridge, head for Dinwiddie Court House; then turn north, traveling west of R. E. Lee's line and head for the South Side Railroad.

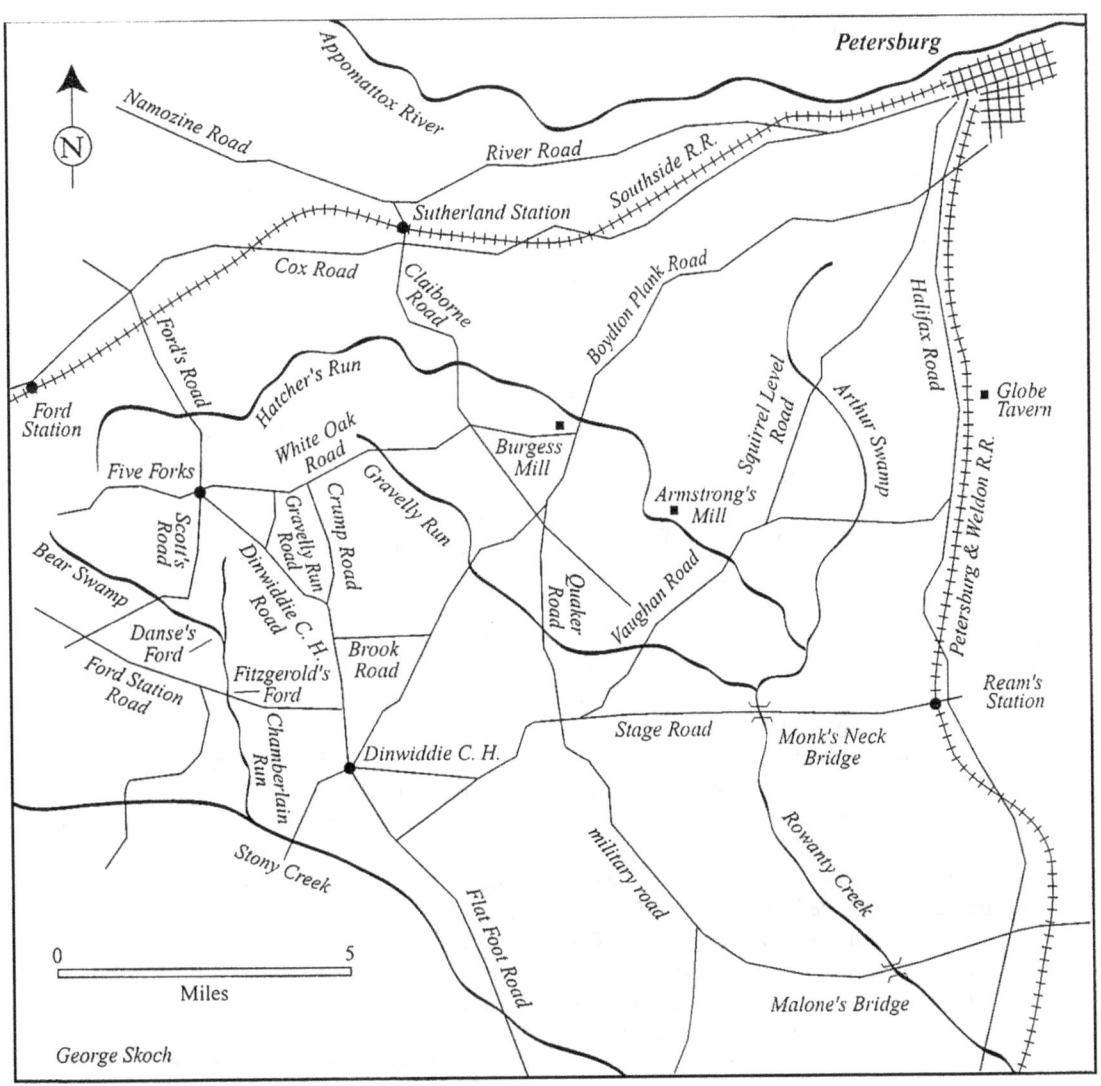

7.1: To Chamberlain's Run and Five Forks

Sheridan was aware that the Union Second and Fifth Corps (infantry) would soon be in position on Vaughan Road south of Hatcher's Run and extending to the Dinwiddie Court House area. A. A. Humphreys was ordered to cross Hatcher's Run on Vaughan Road; while G. K. Warren was directed to cross the same run at Monk's Neck Bridge. Grant hoped these moves would draw R. E. Lee's forces out of their entrenchments. If Lee did not come out to meet Sheridan, then Sheridan was to head for and destroy sections of the Danville and South Side Railroads. However, encounters between the two armies on the 29th led Grant to alter his immediate goals — by the end of the day he was more optimistic. Sheridan's role was to be more aggressive. He was ordered to attack, turn R. E. Lee's right wing and engage their enemy behind the Confederate line. While Sheridan was executing this revised plan, the infantry would simultaneously attack the entrenchments where they were most vulnerable.[5]

It apparently did occur to Grant and others that R. E. Lee's line was already extended west beyond what was prudent — necessary, perhaps, but not tenable. On March 30, Grant directed E. O. C. Ord, Horatio G. Wright, and John G. Parke to find the points at which Lee's Petersburg line was thin and thus vulnerable to frontal attack. Both Wright and Parke reported that the Confederate entrenchments in front of them could be successfully attacked.[6]

ROBERT E. LEE'S REACTION

As indicated earlier, Robert E. Lee knew he could not sit and defend the Richmond-Petersburg area through another campaign. His right flank was exposed and thin, and beyond Sutherland Station on the South Side Railroad his supply and escape routes were vulnerable. His line east of Petersburg had been pushed in to the point where the Union line facing it included Fort Stedman. Desperate for ideas and hope, he approved a plan offered by John B. Gordon to storm and retake Fort Stedman early on March 25, 1865. Lee hoped to turn Grant's attention away from the Confederate right. The attack failed for a number of reasons — all of which emphasized the obvious: R. E. Lee's line could not hold. And Lee knew Grant had his cavalry on the move under Sheridan.[7]

On March 27, 1865, James Longstreet sent the following correspondence from the Richmond area to W. H. Taylor, Assistant Adjutant-General:

Gary's scouts report Sheridan's force passing Malvern Hill yesterday at 8 a.m., going up river. The last of the column passed at 3 p.m. Kautz's men told citizens they were under orders and expected to go to North Carolina. Sheridan left White House hurriedly, leaving a quantity of saddles, bridles, ammunition, and a great many sacks of oats. He received 2,000 fresh horses at White House.[8]

The next day, Longstreet continued to keep his superiors informed of Union cavalry movements around Richmond and heading south.

There was no hesitation. R. E. Lee's cavalry would be sent to slow Sheridan — but Sheridan had approximately 13,000 sabers, while Lee could at most assemble around 5,000. In addition, Sheridan's cavalrymen were well fed, well equipped, well mounted, and well led. The same could not be said for R. E. Lee's cavalry. In addition, Sheridan had substantial infantry support on the roads to Dinwiddie Court House and Five Forks in G. K. Warren's Fifth and A. A. Humphreys's Second Corps.[9] The Confederate cavalry force would have to be supplemented with infantry if Grant's cavalry was to be blocked, but from where?

On the issue of infantry support for the cavalry, R. E. Lee and Longstreet were concerned about how to pull troops from their already thin line of entrenchments without Grant noticing the increased vulnerability along the line. They settled for using George E. Pickett's command. It was not exactly a reserve command, but it had already been divided and sent here and there as a perceived need arose. R. E. Lee decided Pickett's three uncommitted brigades could probably be sent to the Confederate right without being noticed, and Longstreet concurred. Pickett's command had had relatively uneventful posts since Gettysburg, and for numerous and obvious reasons they had an unusually high rate of desertions and low morale. Nonetheless, it was their time again.[10]

Robert E. Lee created a special mobile force under Pickett that would move to the Confederate right and extend the line westward about another four miles, but remain mobile enough to keep Sheridan away from the South Side Railroad. The mobile force would include George H. Steuart's, Montgomery D. Corse's, and William R. Terry's infantry brigades under the command of Colonel Joseph Mayo—Pickett's other brigade, under Eppa Hunton was to stay with Longstreet up on the James River. Pickett's three brigades boarded trains in Petersburg and were moved to Sutherland Station on the South Side Railroad. The last of them arrived there late on March 29. In addition, by the time Pickett's men were in place on the right the following day, Pickett received William H. Wallace's and Matthew W. Ransom's small brigades from Bushrod R. Johnson's division (Anderson's corps). The cavalry in Pickett's mobile force included the divisions of William H. F. Lee and Fitzhugh Lee, as well as "...a small sprinkling of Rosser's Division."[11]

Fitz Lee's cavalry division had been on the Confederate left, so it was necessary to bring them down to Petersburg and then send them west to the Five Forks area. Fitz Lee brought the remnants of Thomas T. Munford's and William H. F. Payne's brigades, leaving Martin W. Gary's brigade on the left of the line. All of Fitz Lee's men without mounts were also left behind—his division provided about 900 cavalrymen to Pickett's mobile force. A good portion of Thomas L. Rosser's division was also made part of the mobile force—but it was also weak and small in number, perhaps 1,000 to 1,200 men. The strength of the Confederate cavalry would have to come from W. H. F. Lee's division, which numbered fewer than 3,000 cavalrymen. The latter number seems about right, and is difficult to dispute. For instance, years later, Rufus Barringer remembered that at the outset of the Appomattox Campaign, his four North Carolina regiments "averaged about 400 effective men each." If correct, that would put his effective force at about 1,600 (the 2nd North Carolina was typically smaller than the other regiments, however). W. H. F. Lee's Virginia brigade, commanded by R. L. T. Beale, was probably smaller, while his third brigade, W. P. Roberts's, had fewer than half that number. Though relatively adequate in numbers, W. H. F. Lee's cavalry division had been performing the task of shielding the Confederate right during the winter of 1864–1865. Most of W. H. F. Lee's pickets regularly made the exhausting march from their camps, north to the Confederate's Petersburg line. The 2nd North Carolina was among Barringer's regiments taking part in that grueling ordeal right up to their move toward Dinwiddie Court House on March 29 when everything intensified.[12]

Thus, when the spring campaign began, W. H. F. Lee's division was made up of Richard L. T. Beale's, William P. Roberts's, and Rufus Barringer's brigades. (John R. Chambliss's former brigade was commanded by J. L. Davis until October 17 when command was given to R. L. T. Beale of the 9th Virginia Cavalry.)[13]

When Rosser was given command of a division, James Dearing took his former brigade. Newly appointed brigadier general William P. Roberts of the 2nd North Carolina was given command of Dearing's former brigade—Roberts was commissioned on February 21, 1865. Roberts's command included the 4th North Carolina Cavalry, the 16th North Carolina battalion of cavalry (the 7th North Carolina Cavalry), and part of the 8th Regiment of Georgia Cavalry.[14]

R. Barringer's North Carolina brigade still consisted of the 1st, 2nd, 3rd, and 5th cavalries. As his regiments were mobilized, the 1st North Carolina Cavalry was commanded by Colonel William H. Cheek; the 2nd Cavalry was commanded by James L. Gaines (Gaines was promoted to colonel when W. P. Roberts left to command his own brigade in February of 1865); the 3rd Cavalry was commanded by Lieutenant Colonel Roger Moore (he had been in command since John A. Baker was captured on June 21, 1864), and the 5th North Carolina Cavalry was led by its Colonel James H. McNeill.

All three Confederate cavalry divisions were placed under Fitz Lee for this operation as they collected in the Five Forks area. Once gathered, the Confederates had a cavalry force numbering about 4,600 men under Fitz Lee, and they were organized in the following units (see table following page).

On March 27, Fitz Lee received orders to have his command ready and to "...move at daylight to-morrow to the south side [railroad], reporting to General R. E. Lee, with as much forage as you can collect and carry. You will leave your dismounts on the Nine-Mile road in the works." About 390 men were left behind.[16]

Fitz Lee moved with his cavalrymen to Pe-

Cavalry in R. E. Lee's Mobile Force
Beginning Order of Battle for Their Last Campaign*:

Fitzhugh Lee's Division (Thomas L. Munford)

Munford's Brigade
    1st Virginia — William A. Morgan
    2nd Virginia — Cary Breckinridge
    3rd Virginia — Thomas H. Owen
    4th Virginia — Charles Old
Payne's Brigade (William H. Payne)
    5th Virginia — James H. Allen
    6th Virginia — Daniel T. Richards
    8th Virginia — Thomas P. Bowen?
    15th Virginia
    36th Virginia Btn. — James W. Sweeney
Gary's Brigade (Martin W. Gary)
    7th Georgia — William H. Burroughs
    7th South Carolina — Alexander C. Haskell
    Hampton Legion South Carolina — Thomas M. Logan
    24th Virginia — William T. Robins

W. H. F. Lee's Division (W. H. F. Lee)

Barringer's Brigade (Rufus Barringer)
    1st North Carolina — William H. Cheek
    2nd North Carolina — James L. Gaines (Major John P. Lockhart)**
    3rd North Carolina — Roger Moore
    5th North Carolina — James H. McNeill (Captain John R. Erwin)**
Beale's Brigade (Samuel H. Burt)
    9th Virginia — Thomas Waller
    10th Virginia — Robert A. Caskie
    13th Virginia — Jefferson C. Phillips
    14th Virginia
Roberts's Brigade (William P. Roberts)
    4th North Carolina — Dennis D. Ferebee
    7th North Carolina (16th N.C. Btn.) — Thomas B. Edelin

Rosser's Division (Thomas L. Rosser)

Dearing's Brigade (James Dearing)
    7th Virginia
    11th Virginia
    12th Virginia
    35th Virginia Btn.
McCausland's Brigade
    16th Virginia
    17th Virginia
    21st Virginia
    22nd Virginia

*Not all the regiments listed here were with Fitz Lee at the opening of the campaign, but they arrived soon afterward with the withdrawal from the Richmond-Petersburg line. As indicated, the best estimates put Fitz Lee at Five Forks with about 4,000 cavalrymen, and the total force for all the regiments listed above near 5,500 (not all being effective). **Lockhart and Erwin replaced their colonels on March 31. According to Major John M. Galloway, who was in Petersburg recuperating from a wound, he returned after McNeill fell and took command of the 5th Cavalry just before heading for Farmville. On the other hand, Paul B. Means, also of the 5th North Carolina, had a letter from Captain John R. Erwin stating that he commanded the regiment from Chamberlain's Run through the march from Appomattox Station.[15]

tersburg and reported to R. E. Lee. He was instructed to meet Pickett's infantry and W. H. F. Lee's and Rosser's cavalries at Sutherland Station. Apparently, it was at this time Fitz Lee was given command of all three cavalry divisions in order to better coordinate the confrontation with Sheridan. Ultimately, he was instructed to attack Sheridan and drive him from Dinwiddie Court House — not just block his path north to the South Side Railroad. R. E. Lee hoped such aggressiveness on his part would give Grant pause and the Army of Northern Virginia a little more time.

As indicated, W. H. F. Lee's and Rosser's divisions were camped around and south of Petersburg, reaching south to Stony Creek Station on the Weldon Railroad. The two divisions would have to swing west before turning north for Sutherland Station and the Five Forks area because Grant's forces were already between most of them and the Petersburg line.[17]

W. H. F. Lee's command was camped near Stony Creek Station — more than forty miles from the Five Forks area. W. H. F. Lee had patrols in the area as far north as the Confederates' Petersburg line and west to Dinwiddie Court House. Roberts's small brigade was on White Oak Road covering the right flank of the Petersburg entrenchments. Consequently, his cavalrymen were clashing with Union patrols early in March. For instance, one Union correspondence dated March 18 included this comment: "William H. Lee's cavalry has been moved from Stony Creek to Dinwiddie Court-House, and his division pickets the whole line from Stony Creek to the Boydton plank road. The line is very thin."[18] The report was correct in stating that W. H. F. Lee's cavalry was picketing the area through which Grant intended to make his initial thrust.

On March 29, W. P. Roberts's brigade was the first to experience the increased activity in a series of clashes with Union patrols sent out to feel for the right flank of the Confederate line. Roberts's brigade held their position on Richard H. Anderson's right until April 1 — Roberts's pickets would be the link between Pickett's mobile force at Five Forks and the Petersburg entrenchments. W. P. Shaw of the 4th North Carolina Cavalry wrote that "On 30 and 31 March, our regiment was continually in the immediate front of Sheridan's cavalry and had a number of sharp encounters with the enemy at Boisseau's and other points along the line of the White Oak road."[19]

Grant's increased activity in the area started early. For instance, in Union Special Order No. 74 on March 21, Simon G. Griffin was ordered to post a picket reserve of at least 300 men at a bridgehead across Hatcher's Run; Romeyn B. Ayres was ordered to double his picket reserves; and Samuel W. Crawford was ordered to post a picket reserve of 150 men at the Goshen house and the same number at the junction of the Church and Halifax roads. Such pickets and patrols determined the strength and location of Confederate resistance. Another Union report dated March 29 contained the following: "Barringer's brigade, and perhaps a division of cavalry, passed down Quaker road to Stony Creek yesterday. No enemy met; a few scouts seen."[20] Such reports contained much inaccurate information and speculation, but nonetheless indicated Union awareness of Barringer's North Carolina brigade in the area, and that he had some of his cavalry patrolling Stony Creek to the Dinwiddie Court House area by March 28.

Sheridan was not only aware of Barringer's cavalrymen in the area, but apparently also understood that W. H. F. Lee had orders to move his division closer in on the right of the Confederate line. In fact, Sheridan has given us a good description of the route and its condition taken by W. H. F. Lee's division and the North Carolina Cavalry:

> Gregg's brigade ... was held on the Boydton plank road, and guarded the crossing of Stony Creek, forcing the enemy's cavalry, that was moving from Stony Creek Depot to form a connection with the right of their army, to make a wide detour, as I had anticipated, on the roads south of Stony Creek and west of Chamberlain's Bed — a very fatiguing march in the bad conditions of the roads. A very heavy rain fell this day, aggravating the swampy nature of the ground, and rendering the movements of troops almost impossible.[21]

W. H. F. Lee's swing around J. Irvin Gregg's brigade (of George Crook's division) and the swollen creeks took them about two miles southwest of Dinwiddie Court House before they turned north — certainly not the direct route from their previous camp to the Five Forks area. Barringer recalled the ordeal in these terms: "Rain had fallen in torrents, and our column was forced to make a long detour South and West of Dinwiddie, in order to head

Stony Creek. Marching night and day, and leaving our trains behind, we effected a crossing late on the 30th, and camped that night on the White Oak Road near the famous Five Forks." They joined Fitz Lee in camp near Five Forks later that night.[22] Of course, the march to Five Forks was more eventful than suggested in the above statement by the brigade commander.

First Encounters

As Grant's cavalry and infantry entered the area patrolled by W. H. F. Lee's cavalry division on March 29, they met little or no resistance. Confederate cavalrymen's orders were to move toward Five Forks and Sutherland Station on the South Side Railroad. W. H. F. Lee started the main body of his cavalry division toward Dinwiddie Court House on that morning except for the pickets and patrols who were engaged in delaying tactics such as burning bridges and dropping trees across roads. They were not under orders to confront Sheridan's move toward Dinwiddie Court House with force.[23]

When Sheridan and his troops reached Malone's Bridge on Rowanty Creek, they found it had been burned by Confederate troops—again, probably W. H. L. Lee's cavalrymen. J. I. Gregg's brigade was in the advance, and while they were waiting for a pontoon bridge to be constructed had a brief exchange of fire across the Creek with a small number of Confederate cavalry pickets—probably those who had burned the bridge. Out-manned and out-gunned, the Confederate cavalrymen were driven back and across Stony Creek.[24] (See map 6.2.)

After crossing Rowanty Creek, Sheridan's column continued to find only minor resistance, but he learned of a strong cavalry force south of his route consisting of W. H. F. Lee's and Rosser's divisions, so he left his wagon trains at the burned bridge in the protection of George A. Custer's division and moved as fast as possible toward Dinwiddie Court House. He wanted to keep the Confederate cavalry to his south and make them swing wide around the court house before turning north to support the Confederate right.[25]

The Union infantry also met with little opposition initially. A. A. Humphreys with his Second Corps crossed Hatcher's Run at the Vaughan Road with relative ease. G. K. Warren and the Fifth Corps crossed at Monk's Neck Bridge. Warren reported: "At 4.45 A.M. the head of the column reached the crossing of Rowanty Creek. A few shots were fired by the enemy's lookouts there, probably as an alarm signal, but no opposition was made to our crossing." After they were across, for the first mile or so, they also had to continually clear the road of debris such as fallen trees placed there by W. H. F. Lee's cavalrymen.[26]

Throughout the first day of the campaign G. K. Warren continued to note the presence of W. H. F. Lee's cavalry, and by nightfall he positioned Ayres's command to protect the Union flank and rear. It was "…a measure rendered necessary for the security of our position and trains, which later might be attacked by the enemy's cavalry (Barringer's) that had been reported to have passed south of us." Ayres was straddling Quaker Road just above Gravelly Run. W. H. F. Lee's North Carolina cavalrymen were making their presence felt.[27]

Fitz Lee's cavalry division spent most of the second day getting into position. On the morning of March 30 his cavalrymen marched from the Sutherland Station area through Five Forks and headed for Dinwiddie Court House. After passing Five Forks, however, they ran into Union cavalry. The encounter amounted to more than just the two sides locating each other because Grant was so pleased with his infantry's successes the previous day, he ordered Sheridan to forget about the railroads and attack the Confederate right. Thus Merritt moved Devin's division through Dinwiddie Court House and quickly toward Five Forks.

Both cavalries were alternately driven back and both sides took prisoners, but neither Fitz Lee nor Sheridan achieved his objective. However, by the end of the day Sheridan and Fitz Lee knew exactly where the enemy cavalry was—at their front.[28] Sheridan had to be a little concerned about the arrival of W. H. F. Lee's and Rosser's divisions which were taking the long way around, below Dinwiddie Court House. In addition to the fact that W. H. F. Lee's and Rosser's cavalries had not yet arrived, it was important that Fitz Lee's men held off Sheridan's first move because Pickett was also not quite in place.

From Sutherland Station, Pickett had moved his troops down Claiborne Road to the intersection with White Oak Road, and on the morning of March 30, Robert E. Lee rode from Petersburg to meet with Pickett and others and set the plan of attack.[29] They were apparently unaware that the night before Sheridan had ordered an attack on Five Forks, and that Fitz Lee was meeting it with his own thrust toward Dinwiddie Court House that very morning.

On this same morning, on White Oak Road, G. Pickett was joined by W. H. Wallace's and M. W. Ransom's small brigades sent by Richard H. Anderson the day before. In fact, while moving west along the line on March 29, these two brigades met and repulsed the serious assault on the Confederate line made by Joshua L. Chamberlain and others. Pickett's mobile force also received W. J. Pegram and six of his guns at this time.[30]

After the meeting with R. E. Lee, Pickett marched his force west along White Oak Road to Five Forks, about four miles away. He was there by 4:30 P.M. and met Fitz Lee who had finished his fight and pulled back to Five Forks. By 10:00 P.M. they were all settled-in along White Oak Road—it was about this time, W. H. F. Lee and Rosser arrived with their cavalrymen.

George E. Pickett apparently had plenty of time and counsel while preparing his attack for the morning of March 31, 1865. He had met with Robert E. Lee and others, had most of the day to consider and reconsider the details, and then in the evening he held another council which included Fitz Lee, the commander of the cavalry in the special mobile force. Of course, the mobile force would attack Sheridan. That was R. E. Lee's plan from the outset.

Early on March 31, Munford's command (formerly Fitz Lee's division) moved out from Five Forks along the Dinwiddie Court House Road which took them southeast as far as Gravelly Run Road. The road then turned south directly toward Dinwiddie Court House. Munford posted a strong force at the intersections of Dinwiddie Court House with Gravelly Run and Crump Roads. As Munford moved out, he made first contact with the advance troops of Devin's cavalry near the Gravelly Run Road. Once firm contact was made, Munford had been instructed to hold until he "...heard the rattle of Fitz Lee's guns in sufficient volume to indicate a serious engagement...." Then Munford was to attack the enemy in front of him.[31]

Most of Pickett's infantry and Fitz Lee's other two cavalry divisions left Five Forks shortly after Munford. Around daybreak, they moved on to Scott's Road which leaves the forks going directly south then turns a bit westerly and crosses Bear Swamp. Their plan was to have Pickett's and Fitz Lee's troops drop down along the west side of Chamberlain's Run and prepare to turn east and cross the run at two pre-selected fords, and thus hit Sheridan's force in the flank as it faced Munford. W. H. F. Lee's and Rosser's cavalry divisions were in advance of Pickett's infantry, and they continued south to Fitzgerald's Ford. They planned to cross there and make their eastward thrust into Sheridan's flank along Ford Station Road. Pickett planned to cross Chamberlain's Run at Danse's Ford with his infantry.[32]

Their plan probably would have worked well in the early years of the war, but now the plan had two important impediments to its success—the leadership of the Confederate cavalry was not what it had once been, and the Union cavalry's leadership was considerably improved from what it had been. Sheridan had anticipated Pickett's flank attack across Chamberlain's Run.

Wesley Merritt assigned George Crook's division to guard their left flank and particularly to hold Fitzgerald's Ford on Chamberlain's Run. Crook placed Charles H. Smith's brigade to cover Fitzgerald's Ford and Davies's brigade about a mile up the run at Danse's Ford. Crook held J. I. Gregg's brigade in reserve.[33] Merritt kept Thomas C. Devin's division in front of Munford and Custer's back behind Dinwiddie Court House in reserve still guarding the wagon trains.

In addition, the Confederate attack was not well coordinated. W. H. F. Lee's cavalry encountered Smith's forces before Pickett was in place and badly executed a charge across Fitzgerald's Ford that triggered Munford's advance, again before Pickett was ready to cross the run at Danse's Ford.

"Dreadful conflict at Chamberlain's Run on the 31st of March"

When Fitz Lee's cavalry moved west of Chamberlain's Run, then south, W. H. F. Lee's division was in front, and Barringer's North

Carolina brigade was at the head of the column. Barringer had the 1st Cavalry under Colonel Cheek; the 2nd Cavalry under Lieutenant Colonel Gaines; and the 5th Cavalry under Colonel McNeill. He had a total of about 900 men in the field that day. (The 3rd Cavalry was in the rear guarding the wagon trains.) As Barringer approached Chamberlain's Run at Fitzgerald's Ford, he sent a squadron from the 5th Cavalry forward. This alerted the Union forces and caused C. H. Smith to immediately place the 2nd New York and 6th Ohio in line, dismounted to hold the east side of Chamberlain's Run — he also sent a battalion of the 1st Maine across the run to locate the enemy.[34]

First Encounter

The 1st Maine Battalion crossed the run with no difficulty and deployed. When Barringer's brigade encountered the 1st Maine west of Chamberlain's Run, it stopped and organized for an attack. W. H. F. Lee ordered Barringer to dismount his front regiment, the 5th North Carolina Cavalry, and push the advancing 1st Maine back across the run. McNeill and the 5th Cavalry had difficulty dislodging their enemy from the heavy forest and undergrowth, so Barringer was ordered to dismount the 1st and 2nd North Carolina cavalries and attack in force. The 2nd North Carolina was sent at their enemy's center, the 5th on the right, and the 1st on the left. R. L. T. Beale's Virginia brigade remained mounted in reserve. The North Carolina brigade advanced under the command of W. H. F. Lee. As planned, the 2nd Cavalry hit the center and the 1st and 5th swept the flanks.

W. H. Cheek was instructed to take the 1st North Carolina just north of Fitzgerald's Ford, dismount and prepare to cross the run. The 2nd and 5th North Carolina cavalries were ordered to dismount and push the 1st Maine back through the ford. The 1st Maine's squadron was driven back across the run into their support troops.[35] Once the North Carolinians reached Fitzgerald's Ford they formed in column of fours. The 5th North Carolina was to the right of the entrance to the ford, and the 2nd North Carolina to the left of it. The initial plan called for the 1st and 5th North Carolina to cross at about the same time and then wait while the 2nd followed the 5th at the ford. After all three regiments successfully forded Chamberlain's Run, the 2nd North Carolina Cavalry planned to connect its left to the 1st North Carolina.[36]

This was more easily planned than executed. There was a narrow corridor to Fitzgerald's Ford, and it was lined with briars and a deep swamp. In addition, there was "...a bluff to the immediate right of the ford, and on our side of it, and other obstructions of fallen timber on both sides of the stream, that it could not be crossed, for battle, except at the ford." Across the run, the ground rose rapidly up to the Union line containing the 2nd New York and the 6th Ohio.[37]

As planned, once the North Carolinians gained access to the ford, the 5th Cavalry began to cross in column of fours, each man holding his rifle in one hand and cartridge box in the other, high above his head. It was not a pleasant experience; they "crossed that ford under a galling, withering fire from Henry rifles, that shot sixteen times each without loading, fired by an entrenched enemy." Then, according to instructions, as each company reached the far bank of Chamberlain's Run, it moved to the right of Ford Station Road and waited for the 2nd North Carolina Cavalry to cross. And here, "...somebody blundered. Blundered awfully, but with the best intention."[38]

Before the 2nd North Carolina could begin its crossing, apparently W. H. F. Lee ordered Colonel Savage and the mounted 13th Virginia from Beale's brigade to charge across the ford in an effort to divert the heavy Union fire from the 5th North Carolina which had already crossed the run and from the 2nd Cavalry as it crossed. Unfortunately for the Confederates, only a squadron of the mounted Virginians understood their orders, and they charged across the ford and up the incline on the others side in a force too weak to be effective.[39] The men of the 2nd North Carolina were then ordered into the ford on foot in column of fours and began to make their way to the eastern shore with rifles and cartridge boxes held overhead.

Under McNeill, the 5th North Carolina advanced slowly waiting for the 2nd Cavalry to form on its left — then the mounted Virginia squadron charged past them and toward the Union line. As the Virginians were driving the 2nd New York Rifles and 6th Ohio from their first line, C. H. Smith sent the 1st Maine and the 13th Ohio forward in good order. Confronted by Smith's four advancing regiments, the Virginia horsemen wheeled in all directions, broke and dashed back to the ford with a brigade of repeating rifles at their backs inciting panic. As the retreating Virginian horsemen flew past the dismounted 5th North Carolina Cavalry, several efforts were made to stop them but to no avail — the problem was by the time the mounted Virginians hit the ford, only about two squadrons of the 2nd North Carolina had made it across. The horsemen plowed into the ford and its occupants, driving many of the dismounted cavalrymen into deeper water below the ford. The above account of the blunder at Chamberlain's Run is based on the writing of Paul B. Means, a private in the 5th North Carolina, who watched the men of the 2nd North Carolina get ridden down and out of the narrow ford. Another private in the same unit, Daniel B. Coltrane, recalled the initial fording by the 2nd North Carolina in these terms, "...they were immobilized by a Virginia squadron which broke in front of them. Somebody had made a grave mistake. Men were shot down in the ford or swept off by the current and drowned." The impact this event had on the men of the 2nd North Carolina Cavalry was clearly remembered by those who watched as well as those who were run down. Most of the men from the 2nd North Carolina made it back to the west side of Chamberlain's Run but with nothing accomplished for their losses and risks except frayed nerves, exhaustion, and lost equipment.[40]

With a full Union cavalry brigade now charging down upon them, the 5th North Carolina and those men of the 2nd North Carolina who had made it across the run were forced to follow the mounted horsemen back across the ford. When the Confederates hit the water, they were slowed and the Union brigade, unimpeded, drew closer and the fire grew even more accurate at the closer range — the 2nd and 5th North Carolina suffered greatly. Commanders of both regiments were lost early in the fighting. Nevertheless, Barringer managed to organize his North Carolina troops on the west side of the run and stop the Union advance.[41]

When the morning's activities got underway, the 1st North Carolina was dismounted and placed about 150 yards north of Fitzgerald's Ford. The 1st Cavalry was scheduled to cross the run and wait for the 2nd North Carolina to connect with their right, but, as recounted above, the 2nd North Carolina was denied the opportunity to complete its crossing, leaving a gap between the 1st and 5th North Carolina of more than one hundred yards. The 1st North Carolina made its crossing and drove the enemy back. Then they experienced firing on their right flank as well as at their front — they were isolated and could not advance farther without exposing their rear and potentially being completely cut off from their brigade. Holding on the east shore of Chamberlain's Run was untenable due to increasing Union fire. Their situation was much like that of the 5th North Carolina — except they could not see what was going wrong with the plan of attack as a result of the unscheduled mounted charge by one of Beale's Virginia regiments.[42]

At a later date, Barringer wrote of "the dreadful conflict at Chamberlain's Run on the 31st of March," and noted that in the morning alone his North Carolina brigade lost over 20 officers killed and over 100 men killed and wounded. Among them were Major McLeod of the 1st North Carolina Cavalry; Colonel Gaines of the 2nd North Carolina Cavalry who was seriously wounded and lost his arm; and Colonel McNeill of the 5th North Carolina Cavalry who was killed.[43]

Meanwhile, east of Chamberlain's Run, Munford had started his push against Devin's division when he heard sustained gun fire from the direction of Fitzgerald's Ford. He drove the Union force back slowly but steadily until Crook's flank was in jeopardy of being exposed to Pickett's thrust across Chamberlain's Run at Danse's Ford once it got underway — but first there was a lull in the fighting.[44]

West of Chamberlain's Run, the North Carolina brigade had several hours to regroup, collect their thoughts, and fill their cartridge boxes before they were ordered to charge again. The men of the 5th North Carolina were certainly shaken by their exposure to severe fire and their rapid retreat, as well as the loss of their Colonel McNeill and others that morning. The 1st North Carolina had to recover from similar experiences, and in addition had to overcome some intense and mixed feelings about being sent across the run and not supported on their right as the plan called for. The cavalrymen of the 2nd North Carolina also had a difficult time getting themselves together in a couple of hours for the next charge. The men of the 2nd Cavalry who reached the east side of the run were subject to heavy Union fire and the need to retreat along with the 5th North Carolina. The men who were held by the water when the Virginia cavalrymen dashed back wildly across the narrow ford certainly had additional physical and mental problems to contend with. The dismounted men of the 2nd Cavalry were ridden through and over, and finally pushed from the ford into deeper waters. If they were not injured, they lost or sustained damage to their weapons. If they were not drowned, they were certainly shaken; one can easily imagine they were angry with their commander or the mounted Virginia horsemen who rode them down. Whatever the intensity and scope of the problems the men of the North Carolina brigade had to deal with, they needed to establish new leadership and be ready to fight again — soon.

Around 2:00 P.M., W. H. F. Lee and Barringer learned that Pickett and Fitz Lee were driving across Chamberlain's Run up at Danse's Ford. Barringer's brigade was ordered to attack the enemy and drive them from Chamberlain's Run. Barringer protested to W. H. F. Lee because of the extent to which his troops had been damaged that morning — but to no avail. Barringer's effort to convince W. H. F. Lee to send R. L. T. Beale's Virginia regiments across first and his in support took so much time that finally Fitz Lee rode over from Danse's Ford. His horse covered with foam, Fitz Lee peremptorily ordered the attack by Barringer's North Carolina Brigade.[45]

With the enemy well entrenched across the run, Barringer knew the only chance his men had of fording the run on foot was to have an element of surprise. He hoped to achieve that by feigning an attack along the line and then suddenly assault in column. Barringer again placed the 1st North Carolina about 150 yards above Fitzgerald's Ford and instructed them to cross the run as rapidly as possible, and in close formation. Their job was to attract the attention and first fire of the Union line.[46]

Then Barringer gathered the 2nd and 5th North Carolina cavalries in front of the ford, but back just enough to be concealed by brush and timber. There he told them of the afternoon's objective, and ordered them "...to charge across the ford at all hazards, just as soon as the enemy's fire was fairly concentrated on the 1st Reg't. & to carry the works opposite the ford at any & every sacrifice."[47]

Colonel Cheek gave the command — "Forward!" And the 1st North Carolina stepped into Chamberlain's Run for the second time that day in an unbroken line. Immediately, they began to receive the enemy's fire from all the works along the eastern shore. The run at that point was about one hundred yards wide, and still full of brush, brambles, rocks, and rails — and more than waist-deep at that point. The 1st North Carolina was about halfway across, "...when, with a terrific yell, the dismounted 2nd & 5th Regiments charged across the ford, ran the Federals out of their works...." The 1st North Carolina Cavalry crossed and was joined by R. L. T. Beale's Virginia brigade on its left.[48]

In essence, it was the same plan used earlier that day except this time the 2nd North Carolina stepped into Fitzgerald's Ford first, followed by the 5th North Carolina. Major John P. Lockhart led the 2nd Cavalry over the run in face of heavy fire from the Union line. Once across, he deployed to the left of the road and eventually connected to the right wing of the 1st North Carolina. The 5th, led by Captain John R. Erwin, followed on the 2nd North Carolina's heels and formed on the right of Ford Station Road. Once across, John R. Erwin and John P. Lockhart "...gave their orders to charge at the same moment and grandly, gloriously, with a wild rush and yell they went forward over those works and drove Sheridan's splendid soldiers miles back...." With the Union forces in retreat, W. H. F. Lee's Virginia brigade moved to the front and pushed the enemy toward Dinwiddie Court House.[49]

On the Union side, after his morning success, C. H. Smith put his entire brigade in front of Fitzgerald's Ford — they were dismounted and spent two or three hours around midday building breastworks. These works were quickly overrun by the North Carolinians, and C. H. Smith's brigade was steadily pushed southeast toward Dinwiddie Court House Road. At some point during his retreat, Smith learned that Pickett had forced his way across Chamberlain's Run up at Danse's Ford, and the Union forces there and on Dinwiddie Court House Road were retreating.[50]

Indeed, Pickett had finally forced his way across Danse's Ford and pushed H. E. Davies back. When Davies was supported by Stagg's and Fitzhugh's brigades, they were pushed south along Dinwiddie Court House Road where Pickett was joined by Munford's cavalry. Word of the developments along Dinwiddie Court House Road encouraged C. H. Smith to fall back and in line with other Union brigades near the Court House. By evening, G. A. Custer's division had been moved up north of Dinwiddie Court House and was straddling the road coming south with the retreating Federal forces on it. Smith's brigade fell in on the left of Custer's brigades. Once Pickett and W. H. F. Lee approached the line in front of Dinwiddie Court House, "A spirited, obstinate contest ensued, which lasted until night, Smith's brigade, General Sheridan says, bearing the brunt of the cavalry attack."[51] Into the evening, Barringer's North Carolinian cavalrymen pressed Smith's line.

As darkness absorbed the fighting, Pickett's infantry faced south, with Munford's cavalry on his left, and W. H. F. Lee's and Rosser's divisions on his right—W. H. F. Lee's cavalrymen spent the night resting and picketing as far back as Fitzgerald's Ford.

By the time W. H. F. Lee's cavalrymen had crossed Chamberlain's Run and moved along Ford Station Road to join Pickett, their losses were staggering. Private Paul Means of the 5th North Carolina remembered the fight at Chamberlain's Run in these terms: "This was the most fearful and fiercest battle we were ever in."[52] The contribution made by W. H. F. Lee's cavalrymen did not go unnoticed by the infantry. Walter Harrison of Pickett's staff later described the activities of W. H. F. Lee's division on that day with these words:

This was in effect one of the most severe cavalry fights of the wars. General W. H. F. Lee was directed to force a crossing at this point, immediately in face of a superior force of the enemy having all the advantages of position, with a deep stream of water in front. His loss was terrible. Out of fifteen hundred mounted men, he had about five hundred put *hors du combat* on the field.[53]

Keep in mind most of the fighting at and near Fitzgerald's Ford was by Barringer's North Carolina brigade, and he later indicated that after the second crossing his brigade took additional losses amounting to ten more officers and over fifty more men. At the end of the day, Barringer lamented that his brigade only had two remaining field officers—Colonel Cheek of the 1st North Carolina, and Major Lockhart of the 2nd North Carolina. (Lockhart would be wounded the next day.) Soon after the events of March 31, while in prison, Barringer wrote in his pocket diary, "My loss this day was 170 killed, wounded and captured, of which 30 were officers."[54]

William P. Roberts and his brigade spent March 31 on White Oak Road covering the right flank of the Petersburg entrenchments. Nonetheless, he had the opportunity to move toward Five Forks and see his old regiment, the 2nd North Carolina Cavalry, after the fight that day. He described the occasion as follows:

I distinctly remember that after the battle of Chamberlain's Run, I passed the regiment on the road, and its great loss in splendid officers and gallant men made such an impression upon me that I wept like a child. Its losses had been so many that I scarcely recognized it.[55]

The 2nd North Carolina's men were severely hurt on March 31, but with their leadership in disarray and the injuries so numerous, most losses were not recorded, or the records did not survive the retreat. The only recorded losses for the regiment are listed below.

Combat Losses in the 2nd North Carolina Cavalry on March 31, 1865

Trooper	Age	Co.	Fate
James L. Gaines		F&S	severely wounded
George W. Hathaway	20	C	killed
Nicholas J. Harrell	27	C	wounded
William S. Caveness	23	I	mortally wounded
Edward M. Jordan*		F&S	severely wounded
Turner*		F&S	severely wounded

The source used here is *North Carolina Troops 1861–1865, A Roster*, compiled by Louis H. Manarin (Raleigh, N.C., State Division of Archives and History), vol. II, Cavalry, pp. 104–177. (See Appendix for more on the men listed above, page 405.)

*Barringer said he lost Lieutenants Jordan and Turner of the 2nd Cavalry at Chamberlain's Run, though the official records do not reflect their losses. R. Barringer, "Ninth Regiment (First Cavalry)," p. 441.

According to William P. Roberts, after James L. Gaines was wounded, the 2nd North Carolina Cavalry was commanded by "Captain

J. P. Lockhart, a gallant officer, formerly of my old squadron, Company K. Lockhart, I am told, led it through all the engagements following Chamberlain Run, and under his command the regiment lost none of its prestige for gallantry and devotion to duty."⁵⁶

The Battle of Five Forks, April 1, 1865

George E. Pickett was poised to attack with his mobile force on the morning of April 1, but during the night he was made aware of Union troops on his left flank and near his rear. He gave up the ground his men had won and pulled back to Five Forks. W. H. F. Lee's cavalry division returned over Fitzgerald's Ford around daylight and marched for White Oak Road where they took a position on Pickett's right, about a mile west of Five Forks. Munford followed the infantry back to White Oak Road.⁵⁷

Pickett notified R. E. Lee of his need to fall back to Five Forks soon after he learned about the large Union force positioned to envelop his command. R. E. Lee replied with the now infamous request to "Hold Five Forks at all hazards. Protect road to Ford's Depot and prevent Union forces from striking the South Side Railroad."⁵⁸

It was understood with the fall back to Five Forks, Pickett's opportunity to attack passed. April 1, 1865 would be Sheridan's and Warren's time to take the offensive. During the early morning hours, Confederate troops spread themselves along White Oak Road. Once at Five Forks, Pickett centered his infantry on that intersection with Matthew W. Ransom's North Carolina brigade on the east end. Then coming westward was W. H. Wallace's brigade, while G. H. Steuart's brigade touched Ford's Road at the intersection called Five Forks. Pickett placed J. Mayo's (Terry's brigade) then M. D. Corse's brigades west of the forks. Ransom's brigade on the left was "refused" (bent back, nearly perpendicular to the road). This suggests Pickett considered Ransom the end of his line, yet Munford's cavalrymen were east of Ransom. W. P. Roberts's small cavalry brigade was even further east along White Oak Road as an early warning system, or perhaps it was there to create an illusion, suggesting to Sheridan that Pickett's line was actually connected to the main Confederate entrenchments near Claiborne's Road.

The Confederate cavalry was placed at both ends of the infantry line. W. H. F. Lee's division was posted on the right, the west end of the line. Barringer had the 5th North Carolina (then under the command of Captain John R. Erwin of Company F) dismount and spread along the White Oak Road in a little field, fronting on a great open expanse — they were the westernmost troops on Pickett's line of light entrenchments, just west of and connecting to Corse's infantry brigade. The 2nd and 3rd North Carolina cavalries were in the same little field with the 5th North Carolina, but remained mounted (the 2nd Cavalry was commanded by Captain John P. Lockhart). According to the brigade's custom, the 1st North Carolina rotated off on April 1— the 3rd North Carolina had been off the day before. The 1st Cavalry was sent to the extreme right of the battlefield, some two miles from the line, with no expectation of taking part in any battle that day.⁵⁹ Apparently some or all of R. L. T. Beale's Virginia brigade of W. H. F. Lee's division had been detached to Corse's command and dismounted nearby, but east of the 5th North Carolina Cavalry.⁶⁰

At least one regiment of Munford's cavalrymen (the 8th Virginia) was posted at the other end of the infantry line on the Confederate left. Later, Munford said, while in retreat he joined the 3rd and 11th Virginia cavalries near Ford's Road and Hatcher's Run. Apparently his other Virginia regiments were spread along Ford's Road toward Five Forks.⁶¹ This opened a considerable gap between Pickett's main line, ending with Munford's 8th Virginia Cavalry, and R. H. Anderson's forces on the west end of the Confederate Petersburg entrenchments. The gap was nominally covered by pickets from W. P. Roberts's small cavalry brigade — which primarily consisted of the 4th and 7th North Carolina cavalries. Roberts had been on the right flank of the Petersburg line most of the winter, and now he had to spread his meager ranks to connect with Munford's pickets.

George E. Pickett's entire line was thin, but it was positioned to address Robert E. Lee's concern for protecting Ford's Road leading to the South Side Railroad and not Pickett's concern about being cut off from the main Confederate line running from Petersburg to Claiborne's Road. In reality, the thinness of the entire Confederate line made it vulnerable at many points, but none more so than the area covered by Roberts's brigade. This was also evident to Sheridan and he probed this weakness in the Confederate line even before his troops were completely deployed and ready to attack Pickett's line. Pickett placed his artillery on the left between Ransom and Munford, and at Five Forks. His mobile force immediately set about entrenching itself. Rosser's cavalry division was sent to the rear along Ford's Road, just north of Hatcher's Run with the wagon trains.[62]

The mood on the Confederate line is difficult to determine, but since Gettysburg not much had happened to bolster confidence among Pickett's infantrymen. Even the previous day's small victory was diminished when the ground gained was given back during the early morning hours. Now most of his men were behind hastily erected, light entrenchments waiting for the Federals to attack. Add to this mood the certainty that they were hungry and tired. Confidence in leadership would be essential in such a situation.

The cavalry was not in much better condition. In terms of leadership nearly every North Carolina regiment had been decimated, and the commander of cavalry certainly inspired confidence among some of his troopers. The cavalry did not have J. E. B. Stuart or Wade Hampton with them, so they, like the infantry, could only look to the commanding general, Robert E. Lee. The cavalrymen had to feel he would come up with something to save the day.

The condition of Pickett's troops and the defenses hastily erected were later characterized by one historian in these words: "The descent of those Virginia soldiers from their furious charge up Cemetery Ridge to their pathetic defense of a wooded crossroads [Five Forks] was the epitome of their army's decline." Such statements may have also applied to the North Carolinians on Pickett's line — infantrymen as well as cavalrymen. In any case, their resolve and leadership would soon be tested when they see what Grant pits against them in a matter of hours.[63]

Sheridan had W. Merritt's 1st (T. C. Devin) and 3rd (G. A. Custer) cavalry divisions in line south of White Oak Road and straddling Scott's Road. Custer's division faced White Oak Road west of Five Forks, and Devin's division faced the road east of Five Forks as far as Ransom's front. Custer's men were not heavily engaged the previous day and were relatively fresh. His column followed W. H. F. Lee's division during the early morning hours, with his left following along the east bank of Chamberlain's Run. Custer placed Capehart's brigade on the west end of the Federal line, followed by Wells's and Pennington's brigades. Pennington's right was on Scott's Road connecting to Fitzhugh's cavalry brigade of Devin's division. Devin placed Stagg's and Gibbs's cavalry brigades on the east end of Sheridan's cavalry line. Sheridan then waited for Warren to get his Fifth Infantry Corps in place.[64]

G. K. Warren could confidently move his infantry to face Pickett's left without much concern for his flank facing Anderson's remaining, entrenched Confederate troops. At 1:00 P.M. on April 1, Warren received the order to move his troops into position straddling Gravelly Run Road facing northwest — their target would be Munford's cavalry regiment and Ransom's refused leg of Pickett's infantry line. When in place, the length of Warren's line would be about 1,000 yards. The placement of Warren's troops was determined by Sheridan, along with the instructions that all the troops should be in place before the attack began. Sheridan wanted one quick, heavy blow at Pickett's left. Ayres division was to be placed west of Gravelly Run Road, and Crawford's division to the right of it. Griffin's division was just behind and to the right of Crawford. Ayres's division was the last of Warren's troops to get in line of battle. They were in place around 4:00 P.M. Sheridan's cavalry was ready to attack by 1:00 o'clock, about the time he ordered Warren to move his infantry up for an attack. Sheridan waited impatiently while Warren efficiently moved his troops into line of battle.[65]

A Bad Day for Roberts's North Carolina Cavalrymen on Pickett's Left

Before Warren's forces were in place, Sheridan learned of troop movements on his right that might put his force at risk from Confederates coming west along White Oak Road. R. H. Anderson had already sent Wallace's and Ransom's regiments to Pickett, but Sheridan was concerned that Anderson might send additional support after the fight for Five Forks got underway. Sheridan was aware of Anderson's weakened condition, but he saw no reason to leave his right flank vulnerable, so he moved to block White Oak Road at the most vulnerable point in the Confederate line—the section held by W. P. Roberts's thin line of cavalrymen.

Sheridan sent Mackenzie's cavalry force, two brigades, up the Crump Road "...with directions to gain the White Oak road if possible, but to attack at all hazards any enemy found, and if successful then march down that road and join me [Sheridan]." Mackenzie's force met Roberts's picket line, drove through them with relative ease, sending part of Roberts's men to the east and into Anderson's entrenchments; the others were forced to the west and sought cover with Munford's 8th Virginia Cavalry.[66] W. P. Shaw of Roberts's brigade recalled the encounter:

Our regiment [the 4th North Carolina] now reduced to a handful of effective men, was dismounted and placed in the road near Five Forks, behind a barricade of rails and brush, with an open field in front, where soon appeared a large force of the enemy's cavalry, which in a broad column charged down upon our position which was gallantly held until the mounted troops in large numbers had leaped their horses over the rail piles and gotten in the rear of us. Fortunately for us on the opposite side of the road was a well timbered wood which offered protection to our men who had been run over and ordered to surrender, and most of them made their way back to their horses with comparatively small loss....[67]

Roberts's men were veteran fighters as was he, but he had commanded this small brigade for only about one month (he was the youngest brigadier general in the Army of Northern Virginia at the age of 24) and he lacked field officers—a crucial point when forces are spread thin along a picket line and out of view of their commander.[68]

Mackenzie's encounter with Roberts was the first important fight of the day. When it was over, Mackenzie left a small force across White Oak Road to block any Confederate advance from the east and then turned his troops westward along the road. On his way to join Sheridan near Five Forks, Mackenzie met Warren's infantry as it crossed White Oak Road and began the main battle of the day.[69]

OUT TO LUNCH

Roberts's picket line absorbed the first thrust of the Union attack and sounded the alarm. When Roberts's men were pushed into the front line of the 8th Virginia, the event was communicated Munford, who felt the news from that front was important enough to personally ride to Fitz Lee's headquarters. (Munford got the news about 1:00 P.M.)

Munford carried the news that Pickett's mobile force was cut off from the Army of Northern Virginia. That was something Pickett wanted to avoid. When Munford arrived with the news, he found Fitz Lee mounted and ready to ride off. Munford handed Fitz Lee the dispatch he had received describing the assault and rout of Roberts's position. Fitz Lee read it and said, "Well, Munford, I wish you would go over in person at once and see what this means and, if necessary, order up your division and let me hear from you." Fitz Lee then rode off without telling Munford he could be reached someplace other than his or Pickett's headquarters—the latter place being a reasonable possibility because Munford saw Fitz Lee join Pickett and the two of them ride off. Apparently Fitz Lee did not tell Pickett what had happened to Roberts on the east end of the line—hard to imagine, but Pickett later said he did not know, and Fitz Lee never claimed to have told Pickett this news. In any case, they rode off together within minutes of Fitz Lee learning of the attack on their left.[70]

Years later, Fitz Lee said he was not concerned about serious entrenchments for the troops nor about Roberts's rout because he did not feel Sheridan would attack that afternoon. One must assume those were indeed his feelings at the time, or he certainly would not have taken an extended lunch. (Pickett apparently felt the same way about Sheridan's intentions that afternoon.) Then again, maybe reason had little to do with Fitz Lee's and Pickett's lack of concern about the situation. Maybe they were simply in the mood for a good old-fashioned shad-bake, and General Rosser had invited them both to his camp north of Hatcher's Run for such a lunch. By all accounts, it was a wonderful feast and a leisurely time.[71]

While Pickett and Fitz Lee were enjoying the baked shad and general merriment, Sheridan was tugging at the tether of the time it took to get Warren's infantry in line of battle. One observer described Sheridan's mood in these terms: "He made every possible appeal for promptness, he dismounted from his horse, paced up and down, struck the clinched fist of one hand into the palm of the other, and fretted like a caged tiger." There is no question about which of the opposing generals had the greater "fire in his belly" that day. Certainly Sheridan could have learned something about being mellow and enjoying the afternoon from Pickett and Fitz Lee; but they could probably have learned something about being ready in the face of the enemy from Sheridan. On April 1, 1865, Sheridan's posture would pay the greater dividend by far.[72]

Throughout the afternoon, Munford sent couriers to the headquarters of Fitz Lee and Pickett to inform them of the Union infantry buildup along his front. Couriers rode the length of the line, but no one knew where the two generals were — no one had been informed they were leaving the field. Munford and his men watched the Union force accumulate for about three hours before they saw Warren's infantry march toward the 8th Virginia.[73]

The sounds of battle did not reach the shadbake until Warren was well engaged, a little after 4:00 P.M. When Pickett did leave for his troops at the front, he had a two-mile ride — and was late. Fitz Lee did not make it to the front.

Assault on the Confederate Left

Sheridan planned to attack the Confederate left with Warren's Fifth Corps, while Merritt's cavalry executed a feint at the west end of the line. Devin's and Custer's cavalry commands were to advance once they heard the firing from Warren's end of the Union line.[74]

As indicated, shortly after 4:00 P.M., Sheridan sent Warren's troopers forward. After crossing White Oak Road, Ayres turned his men left and headed toward Ransom's refused line. Crawford's division went in just to the right of Ayres, and in the process pushed Munford's skirmishers back. Crawford's momentum carried him too far north before he turned west, so he ended up far behind the Confederate line — which, as it turned out, did not matter much because he had an easier push westward to Ford's Road. Munford's retreating 8th Virginia was in front of Crawford the entire way. Munford described the scene:[75]

Suddenly two full Divisions of Warren's Corps, Crawford's and Ayres's, debauched upon the White Oak road. They were in magnificent array, exposing a full front of probably 1000 yards long....

But what could we do? A handful to a houseful! We could do nothing but shoot and run. At their first fire the smoke enveloped them completely and as soon as it drifted so that we could see them advancing again we poured into them our salute of death — then turned and scooted through the woods like a flock of wild turkeys.

...on all sides the battle raged now. My men scattered like wild turkeys came together again like wild turkeys at the bugle's call; the sharp cracking of their carbines was answered as they fell into skirmish line, now firing now retreating as it became necessary....

Munford estimated he retreated in the above fashion for a full two miles, dropping back to Ford's Road north of the Confederate line.

When Crawford began pushing Munford, Sheridan led Ayres's division across White Oak Road and westward over Ransom's line. One Union observer noted that Ayres's men "...with fixed bayonets and a rousing cheer dashed over the earth-works, sweeping everything before them, killing or capturing every man in their immediate front whose legs had not saved him...." This same observer noted that "Sheridan now rushed into the midst of the broken lines, and cried out: 'Where is my battle-flag?' ... Bullets were humming like a swarm of bees.... All the time Sheridan was dashing from one point of the line to another, waving his flag, shaking his fist, encouraging, threatening, praying, swearing, the very incarnation of battle...."[76]

The sounds of Sheridan's battle eventually alerted Pickett to the fact his lunch was over.[77] It was probably soon after the fall of Ransom's breast-works that Pickett's thoughts wandered from his afternoon festivities, and he asked Rosser for a courier so he could communicate with his troops at Five Forks — the couriers with Pickett's message were not out of sight before one of them was captured and the other raced back to inform Rosser and the other generals that Union forces were approaching Ford's Road. Pickett was immediately in the saddle and at great risk to himself and some of Munford's men, managed to get down Ford's Road and join his troops just west of Five Forks. Fitz Lee hesitated, probably just a moment, and was unable to get past Crawford's troops on Ford's

Road south of Hatcher's Run.[78] Fitz Lee took command of Rosser's troops and guarded Ford's Road above Hatcher's Run for the remainder of the day.

On the Confederate left, Ransom's men who tried to hold the line were soon pushed west into Wallace's men. Then both Ransom's and Wallace's troops were killed, captured, or fell back. It was over quickly, and thousands of Confederates were captured. As Ayres's division was collecting prisoners and regrouping, Griffin and his division joined him in the battle line. Sheridan had broken the Confederate line, and he and his men were eager for total victory as they continued to charge along the line.[79]

Ransom's and Wallace's men who managed to retreat moved into Steuart's line — which now had to front on the east as well as the south. Steuart's new line was just east of Ford's Road and still north of White Oak Road — this was the last stand before Five Forks, which Pickett was instructed to hold at all hazards.

Steuart made a courageous stand just east of the forks. Griffin's division was sent at Steuart's line first, and the fighting was intense; but, at this point, Steuart and the remnants of Ransom's and Wallace's brigades faced Devin's cavalry on the south, Griffin's and Ayres's divisions on the east, while Crawford's and Mackenzie's troops were north of them extending to Ford's Road.

While Sheridan's and Warren's troopers were pressing Steuart's position, Pickett made it past Crawford's men on Ford's Road and went to Mayo west of Ford's Road at Five Forks. There he ordered some of Mayo's men up Ford's Road to stop Crawford's advance and some to support Steuart's line. It was too little, too late. Crawford pushed across Ford's Road and pressed the remnants of Munford's cavalry westward as well as Mayo's men back to White Oak Road. Mayo's men were dead, captured, or scattered. Munford's cavalry rode into the woods west of Ford's Road, while Munford, himself, dropped down to White Oak Road hoping to find one of his generals — he found Pickett fighting to hold the last line of the day.

After reaching Ford's Road, Warren, at the head of Crawford's men, made it to White Oak Road and headed west into Corse's brigade. Corse also had turned his line to face east into the dark blue tidal-wave — all the while he was still under attack by one of Wells's regiments from Custer's cavalry to his south.[80] Corse held firm, then was ordered to fall back, north, because Custer's other cavalrymen were by then west of his position on the Confederate far right.

Assault on the Confederate Right

Most of Corse's infantry, with a few survivors from Ransom's, Wallace's, Steuart's, and Mayo's brigades who were driven back into them, held the last infantry position on Pickett's line, enabling many Confederates, both infantry and cavalry, to escape the Federal force coming from the east along what had earlier been Pickett's line.[81] Barringer's North Carolina Brigade shielded Corse's right flank and rear from Custer's cavalry division.

At the first sound of Warren's attack on Munford and Ransom, just after 4:00 P.M., Devin started his dismounted cavalry toward White Oak Road — toward Wallace's and Steuart's line. West of Scott's Road, Custer moved Pennington's brigade forward at about the same time in the direction of Mayo's and Corse's positions. Contrary to Merritt's original plan which called for a cavalry feint against the Confederate right, Custer wanted Pennington's brigade to draw fire so he could launch a mounted attack on Barringer's North Carolina cavalry on the far right. Custer's plan would take almost one and a half hours to execute because the Confederate line in front of Pennington held and drove him back. In addition, Pennington's lack of success exposed Devin's left flank and resulted in his pullback. Pennington and Devin regrouped and attacked a second time. Again Pennington was slowed, but Devin pushed on into Steuart and Wallace. By this time, Ayres's division was pushing Ransom into Wallace, and Devin was pressuring Wallace's position from the east as well as the south. Only when Pickett pulled some of Mayo's men to oppose Crawford north of the Confederate line was Pennington able to have some success against Mayo's position on White Oak Road. Finally, with Mayo's position weakened, and the tattered remnants of Ransom's and Wallace's brigades pushed into Steuart's men, Devin's division and Pennington's brigade carried the Confederate line in front of them — they managed this just before Ayres's and

Griffin's divisions arrived, but not before the impact of the latter's successes had arrived.[82]

While Devin's division and Pennington's brigade were making their early attempts to push back the Confederates, Custer was trying to press Corse's and Barringer's positions on the far right of the Confederate line. Custer kept Wells's and Capehart's brigades mounted and moved them in front of Corse and Barringer. He sent Wells's 15th New York at Corse's front and his 8th New York at the Confederate artillery located between Corse's and Barringer's brigades. The New Yorkers were to draw fire so Custer could make his move on the North Carolina brigade. According to Custer, as soon as Warren created the first sounds of battle a little after 4:00 P.M., Wells and Capehart galloped against their enemy's right. The New Yorkers paid a high price, but Custer did take his other cavalrymen around the Confederate line and into a position facing east. Most of Barringer's brigade turned west to face him.[83]

Throughout the afternoon, Custer heard the Union infantry coming west along Pickett's line and knew Corse's position would be the next and perhaps last target—certainly he wanted some of that day's glory. With his men at the west end of the Confederate line, Custer felt he was in a position to push Barringer's North Carolina regiments into Corse's command and then take Corse before Warren and Sheridan got there with their final push.

On the other hand, Corse's task was to hold on long enough for some of the Confederate troops from the other infantry brigades to escape north through the woods. Corse was mostly facing east to hold Warren's divisions and counting on Barringer's North Carolina cavalrymen to watch his rear and flank.

CAVALRY CLASH ON THE WESTERN FRONT

Paul B. Means, a private in the 5th North Carolina Cavalry, described the threatening circumstances experienced by his comrades:

Just about sundown ... I saw the mightiest mass of men I ever looked at in battle, in the most perfect lines I ever witnessed, come forward with loud cheers, waving the beautiful Stars and Stripes, and sweep like a storm over Pickett's works about two hundred yards to our left. [Means was referring to Warren's infantry rolling up Pickett's line from east to west.] All Pickett's veterans between us and these storming lines fled in utter rout and confusion down the White Oak road right back of that little field and in full sight of us all.... Those great federal lines in order to envelop our forces to their right and front wheeled grandly to the right as they victoriously stormed Pickett's works and did not come down on us at once.[84]

After Mayo had been overrun, and as Warren moved with Crawford's men toward Corse's position, Custer was running out of time so he made his final move. Barringer was with the 2nd, 3rd, and 5th North Carolina cavalries in the little field just north of White Oak Road that Private Means referred to. They faced a large open expanse to their south. The mounted men of the 2nd North Carolina Cavalry faced Custer to the west and south, while Warren's Union infantrymen stormed Corse's line at their rear. They held firm and waited for Custer's charge. The 5th North Carolina was dismounted behind a small improvised breastworks with Corse's men on their left. Paul B. Means also described the drama experienced by the North Carolina cavalrymen in the last fight before Robert E. Lee's final retreat:

In front of that little field, all over that great open expanse came Custer's great division ... converging down on the Sixty-third [the 5th Cavalry], the Nineteenth [the 2nd Cavalry] and the Forty-first [the 3rd Cavalry] North Carolina. The voices of Custer and his officers rang out in clear, clarion tones, orders that every old cavalryman in that little field distinctly heard and knew to mean our utter destruction if executed. Every man in that little field knew Pickett was routed and that it could be but a short time till that "army with banners" to our left would also come down upon us. But not a man moved in those little, low works. To all appearances they were kneeling dead.... He [Captain Erwin] rose and repeated it so that his entire little line heard it: "Hold your fire till that coming cavalry reaches the edge of the field and till I order it." Those kneeling men were not dead; they were just obeying orders.... The Nineteenth [2nd Cavalry] and Forty-first [3rd Cavalry] had their orders. They sat still in their saddles, every man with his sword or his pistol in his hand. That splendid cavalry under the Stars and Stripes came on grandly; they reached the edge of the field, a great, loud, bass voice ... said "Fire!" An awful volley answered from the rifles of the Sixty-third and then they rattled with one continuous fire. The magnificent riders "in blue" in front to that fire fell from their saddles and recoiled just to come again. As that "order to fire" was given the Nineteenth and Forty-first rode forward into Custer's "serried ranks" as if they really expected to "annihilate" them.

The shock of the collision was terrible. Orders rang out on both sides clear-cut and loud. Sabers rang on each other with a cold steel ring that only the bravest veterans can stand. Pistol shots here and there and everywhere emptied saddles and burnt, with powder flashes, faces with death's pallor on them. Each side knew what was at stake, and this saber slashing lasted longer than I ever saw one.[85]

The Union cavalrymen regrouped and charged several times. But Custer's men were unable to advance beyond the first point of contact with the North Carolinians. The contest ended when W. H. F. Lee rode onto the field and ordered Barringer to withdraw his force, the dismounted men first. This order was precipitated by Warren's success on Corse's line, and the mass of Federal troops on Barringer's left and rear — all moving toward the North Carolina cavalrymen. On Barringer's orders, "The Nineteenth [2nd Cavalry] and Forty-first [3rd Cavalry] began to retire slowly. The dismounted Sixty-third [5th Cavalry] withdrew with their faces to the foe, firing as they fell back."[86]

In his report on these events, Pickett later described the scene in these words,

One of the most brilliant cavalry engagements of the war took place on this part of the field.... The enemy made a most determined attack in heavy force (cavalry), but were in turn charged by Gen. W. H. F. Lee, completely driving them off the field. This, with the firm stand made by Corse's men, and those that could be rallied at this point, enabled many to escape capture.[87]

Pickett's reference to W. H. F. Lee's command in that field meant Barringer's 2nd, and 3rd North Carolina Cavalry — the 5th North Carolina was dismounted at the end of Corse's line; the 1st N.C. was off the field that day; and Beale's Virginia brigade was also dismounted and on the line near Corse's brigade. Pickett's claim that the North Carolinians completely drove Custer off the field was an overstatement. However, Custer's cavalry was held and that was a great achievement by the men of the 3rd North Carolina and the battered men of the 2nd North Carolina who had survived Chamberlain's Run the day before.

Barringer summed up their contribution with his usual tendency to simplify: "Meanwhile his cavalry passed our front in overwhelming numbers and sought to turn my right flank — thereby enveloping the entire force engaged. Again and again the 2nd, 3rd & 5th Regiments charged this cavalry — impeding their progress and enabling our fleeing army to escape."[88] There is no evidence that the men of the 5th North Carolina remounted and joined the 2nd and 3rd cavalry regiments in the last charges at Custer's troops, but some of them may well have.

In the end, Warren overwhelmed and pushed Corse's brigade from the last breastworks in Pickett's line. Custer, with Capehart's and Wells's brigades, was denied glory that day by Barringer's 2nd and 3rd North Carolina cavalry regiments. Every Federal division in the Battle of Five Forks that day overran the Confederates at their front, except Custer's — he did not advance from his point of contact with the North Carolina cavalrymen. But he would have another opportunity.

Among the last Confederates to leave the fight that day were the mounted men of the 2nd and 3rd North Carolina cavalries — many of them were among the captured. Among the 2nd North Carolina Cavalry's losses that afternoon were:

Combat Losses in the 2nd North Carolina Cavalry at Five Forks on April 1, 1865

Trooper	Age	Co.	Fate
John Lockhart*	30	F/S	wounded
Nicholas J. Harrell	27	C	captured
Josephus H. Smith	21	C	killed
Charles T. Davis	26	D	wounded
Evans Jacobs		F	captured
George A. Johns		F	captured
Jennings W. Lambeth		F	captured
J. R. Ponton	17	F	wounded
Jerome A. Sapp		F	captured
George D. Weatherly		F	captured
William M. Jarvis	26	G	captured
Solomon F. Dean		H	captured
Albert G. Voss		H	captured

The source used here is *North Carolina Troops 1861–1865, A Roster*, compiled by Louis H. Manarin (Raleigh, N.C., State Division of Archives and History), vol. II, Cavalry, pp. 104–177. (See Appendix for more information on the men listed above, page 405.)

*Barringer reported that Lockhart was wounded on April 1. Roberts reported that Lockhart continued to command the regiment until April 9, 1865. R. Barringer, "Ninth Regiment (First Cavalry)," pp. 441–442; W. P. Roberts, "Additional Sketch Nineteenth Regiment (Second Cavalry)," p. 107.

The veteran cavalrymen knew they could win a charge, even win a battle, and yet lose a war — that day they only won a couple of charges. The outlook was bleak for the men of the 2nd North Carolina Cavalry and their comrades.

What remained of W. H. F. Lee's and Munford's cavalry divisions headed north and after crossing Hatcher's Run, turned east for Ford's Road. There they joined Fitz Lee and Rosser's division. The 2nd North Carolina and the rest of Fitz Lee's cavalry went into camp that night, near the South Side Railroad. They were between Ford Depot and Sutherland Station.[89] During the night, Anderson joined Fitz Lee with what remained of his infantry command and the remnants of Pickett's mobile force.

Earlier in the day Anderson had been sent from the Petersburg entrenchments to support Pickett's force at Five Forks. At 5:45 P.M., Anderson received orders to move to Church Crossing (Ford's Road) on the South Side; by 6:30 he was on his way. It was already too late to help Pickett. Early the next morning, around 2:00, B. Johnson joined his comrades at Church Crossing. The Confederates would get only a few hours rest before the retreat. Early on April 2, the last of R. E. Lee's men in the western end of the Petersburg entrenchments fell back to Sutherland Station. From there, they joined the remnants of Pickett's and Anderson's infantries for the retreat.[90]

On April 2, Sheridan took control of the South Side Railroad — he already had the Boydton Plank Road. The Army of Northern Virginia left the Richmond-Petersburg lines by nightfall.

The Retreat Begins

Fitz Lee's cavalrymen started April 2 with an extraordinary sense of gloom. Among their concerns were events taking place at Richmond and Petersburg — they had listened to the sounds and seen the flashes of fighting throughout the night. They knew the situation there was desperate because of their loss at Five Forks. They stood "to horse" waiting for orders. They also knew Merritt's Union cavalrymen were all along the White Oak Road and would soon be heading for the South Side Railroad on the several roads coming up to it. Their orders from the day before were to protect the South Side Railroad. Pickett, Anderson, and Fitz Lee also waited for orders and knew the situation had changed considerably in the past twenty-four hours.[91]

While three of his commanders were waiting on the South Side Railroad, Robert E. Lee decided to leave the Richmond-Petersburg area as soon as possible — but he would have to hold Petersburg until nightfall if possible. General Lee and his army began to evacuate Petersburg around 8:00 P.M. They moved north of the Appomattox River, and headed west for their only possible escape route to North Carolina.[92]

Anderson and Pickett received their new orders by late morning — they were instructed to move to Amelia Court House. Their commanding general planned to meet them there. Pickett had lost nearly his entire command — only a few hundred men were left in his division. His losses included most of the two brigades he had on loan from Anderson. On April 2, Pickett was ordered to report to Anderson; not much was heard from him for the remainder of the war.[93]

Fitz Lee's cavalry was directed to cover the rear of Anderson's column as it moved out. Munford's command set pickets on the Cox Road and approaches from the south. W. H. F. Lee's cavalry was also along Cox Road and had a force at the intersection with Ford's Road coming up from Five Forks — at that point Cox Road is on the north side of the railroad. Captain Charles W. Pearson of the 5th North Carolina Cavalry described the scene on the morning of April 2 in these terms: "The brigade had been dismounted and was throwing up defenses. The road and fields soon became filled with retreating men, wagons, ambulances and every description of army hangers-on. We were ordered to remount." Barringer's North Carolina brigade was ordered to saddle and to cover the infantry column's rear as it left the area — at that time, the brigade numbered about 900 men.[94]

Devin's Union cavalry division approached the railroad from Ford's Road. They unlimbered their guns and quickly pushed back Barringer's pickets. According to Devin, "The railroad was then torn up, ties burnt, and rails heated and bent." Devin continued to push W. H. F. Lee's cavalry north a short distance to Cox Road, then by way of Brown's Road, up to Scott's Cross Roads on Namozine

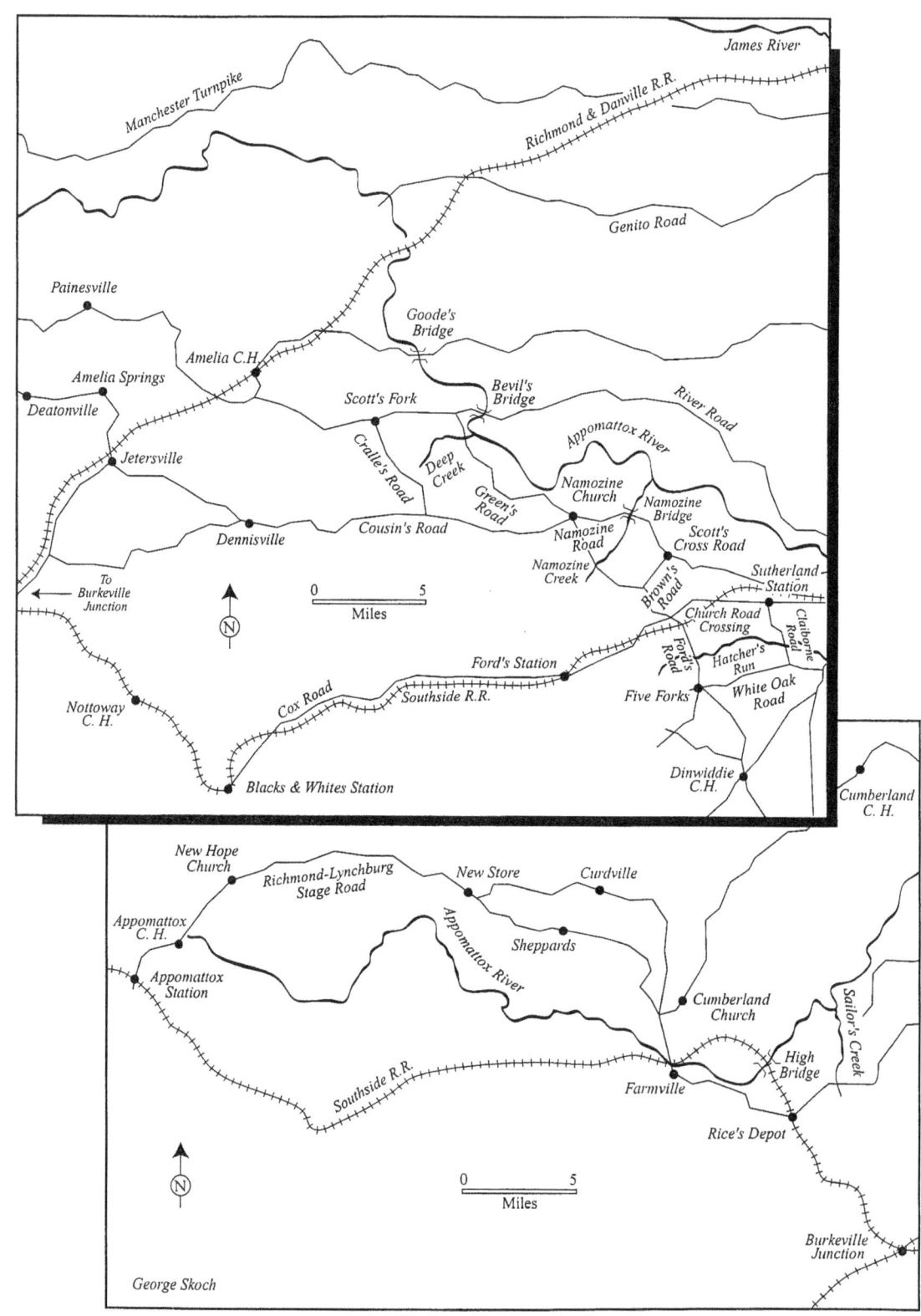

7.2: The Route to Appomattox Court House

Road. Along the way, Devin's cavalry made charges which were met with counter-charges. Barringer's cavalrymen were instructed to delay the pursuing enemy, but avoid serious engagements. Merritt described their activity in these words: "The cavalry in our front opposed the column from time to time at points favorable for resistance, building barricades of rails and logs, but he was easily dislodged and driven by the advance back...." The men of the 2nd North Carolina Cavalry had hard work to do while in harms way, and they did it well. By the time Merritt's cavalry, with Devin's division still in front, pushed Barringer to Scott's Cross Roads, R. H. Anderson's infantry was already on Namozine Road heading for Amelia Court House.[95]

Bushrod R. Johnson's division of R. H. Anderson's corps reached the Namozine Road at Scott's Cross Roads by 3:00 P.M. Between 5:00 and 6:00 P.M., Fitz Lee informed Johnson that the federal cavalry was hot on his heels and gaining ground. Johnson knew Confederate cavalry had been skirmishing with enemy cavalry at his rear all day, and as pressure increased Johnson complied with Fitz Lee's request to stop and form a line to meet the enemy. Johnson halted the remnants of his division and quickly began to put barricades across Namozine Road. Soon, Devin's division came in sight of Johnson's and Fitz Lee's troopers. From about 6:30 until 8:00 P.M. Union cavalry attempted to overcome the Confederate barricades, but were held back. Darkness fell and the action stopped. Merritt summarized the delay at the crossroads: "Here a spirited fight took place, in which the First Division was engaged with the enemy's infantry. The enemy used his artillery freely."[96]

Around the time fighting stopped near Scott's Cross Roads, Robert E. Lee had his evacuation of Petersburg and its defenses underway. During the night of April 2, Robert E. Lee and his army marched out of Petersburg and along the north side of the Appomattox River. Longstreet's command, under Ewell, left Richmond traveling southwest on a course that would have them join R. E. Lee before they crossed the Appomattox River — their plan was to take the army across at Genito's, Goode's, and Bevil's bridges. They planned to meet Anderson and Fitz Lee at Amelia Court House. R. E. Lee and Longstreet did not fall under serious attack the first day of their retreat because on April 3, Grant's forces were busy occupying the Confederate entrenchments on the Richmond-Petersburg line, and the cities themselves. The same cannot be said for Anderson over on Namozine Road with Fitz Lee's cavalry covering his retreat. The Confederates retreating westward on the south side of the Appomattox River were constantly pressed by Sheridan's cavalry.[97]

The Battle at Namozine Church, April 3

After the fight at Scott's Cross Roads, B. R. Johnson's and W. H. F. Lee's divisions took a short rest and were on the road again by 11:00 P.M. By then they had fallen behind the rest of Anderson's command and there would be even more delays. By 2:00 A.M. on April 3, Johnson's command and the cavalry at their rear were across Namozine Creek. W. P. Roberts's cavalry brigade and a Virginia regiment were left to hold the ford at Namozine Creek — they were to delay Sheridan's cavalry and then fall back and bring up the rear of the Confederate column. Roberts's men got rear guard that day because they had arrived too late to participate in the fight at Scott's Cross Roads— they had been on an alternate route.[98]

William P. Roberts's men took time to destroy the bridge at Namozine Creek and obstruct the ford with fallen trees and other debris to slow the Union advance. Soon after Roberts's men were in place at the ford, Custer's division appeared and began firing canister. While that was underway, the dismounted 1st Vermont of Wells's brigade moved along the creek, then crossed and hit Roberts's men in the flank. Roberts made a hasty retreat and most got away. When Roberts's command caught the Confederate column, they were told to move up, and Barringer's North Carolina brigade was placed in the rear again. As Roberts was moving forward, past their fellow North Carolinians, some of Custer's cavalrymen came from a byroad and hit Barringer's men on their flank — it was a complete surprise. Surprises usually create panic and a stampede and this was no exception. The immediate reaction of the exhausted and hungry cavalrymen of Barringer's brigade was to get out of there. Cavalry regiments, one after the other, crashed into the one in front of them. Finally the momentum was halted, and men from both cavalry brigades made a stand and drove the Union cavalrymen back. When order was restored in Barringer's command, they continued their march — though a little more tattered than before. Their march from Namozine Creek to their next fight at Namozine Church was about 5 miles.[99]

By 6 A.M., Johnson's infantrymen moved past Namozine Church, then marched west on Green's Road. Anderson's column had taken Cousin's Road (the extension of Namozine Road). After traveling a bit, Johnson dropped down to Cousin's Road and joined the rest of the infantry column and Fitz Lee with some of his cavalry. Fitz Lee sent Munford's and Rosser's cavalry divisions with Anderson, while he waited at the church for his cousin, W. H. F. Lee. (Fitz Lee would join Anderson's column shortly.) After meeting with Fitz Lee, W. H. F. Lee sent Beale's and Roberts's brigades after Johnson on Green's Road, and left Barringer's North Carolina brigade to slow Custer's division near Namozine Church.[100]

By the time Barringer and his cavalrymen got to Namozine Church, the infantry and the rest of the cavalry had already passed. Fitz Lee and W. H. F. Lee, along with members of their staffs, had waited — they had instructions for Barringer's North Carolinians. As the three commanders met, Private Paul B. Means and others overheard the following:

"General Lee[W. H. F.], you must leave our *best* brigade here and hold this position to the last. The safety of our army depends upon it, and I [Fitz Lee] will move on in rear of the retreat with the rest of the cavalry." I [Means] heard those words. All there heard them and we all knew what they signified — the destruction of the brigade chosen. General W. H. F. Lee instantly turned to General Barringer and said: "General Barringer, you have heard the orders; you must do that duty here." All the other generals and staffs moved off at once. The head of the enemy's column was then in full view.[101]

Barringer mentioned to W. H. F. Lee that his command had been at the point of fighting or at the rear-guard skirmishing for several days and was utterly exhausted and had suffered a great loss of officers. He was told there was no alternative.[102]

Private Means of the 5th North Carolina Cavalry left us a description of the fight at Namozine Church — he was close to the 2nd North Carolina and his view of the action is largely what follows. Barringer moved quickly to place the 1st, 2nd, and 5th North Carolina cavalries. The 2nd North Carolina was "mounted by fours" in the center of Barringer's line, just northwest of the intersection of Cousin's and Green's Roads. The 1st North Carolina was mounted "in close single line," in some woods, and on the 2nd Cavalry's left. The 5th North Carolina was "dismounted in line," on the right of Barringer's line — they straddled Cousin's Road and stretched from Green's Road to near the Namozine Church grounds. As usual, every fourth man in the 5th North Carolina remained mounted and held the horses of three of his comrades. They were sent up the road behind the 2nd North Carolina and near one of McGregor's guns — the dismounted men would never see their horses again.[103]

Wells's brigade of Custer's division was the first to appear in Barringer's front. Approaching the intersection near Namozine Church, Wells placed the 8th New York to the right of Namozine Road; the 1st Vermont left of the road; and the 15th New York in close support. The 2nd and 5th North Carolina saw the Vermont regiment emerging from a woods across an open field, about 400 yards away. By the time the North Carolinians formed their line of battle, the Federal cavalry was also in position and charged "magnificently." There was heavy fire from both sides, and the Union cavalrymen were driven back several times.

Barringer was with the dismounted 5th Cavalry when he saw a "great flanking column" sweeping around the left of his 1st North Carolina Cavalry. He sent Private Means over to see how Colonel Cheek of the 1st Cavalry was doing and to encourage him to hold. Private Means found the 1st North Carolina "...firing furiously into the flankers and they getting nearer, as they moved and under the excitement of the battle, were firing right into the faces of the Ninth [1st North Carolina Cavalry]." When Means asker Colonel Cheek how he was doing, and reminded him of the need to hold the position, Cheek reportedly said, "Present my compliments to General Barringer and tell him that we will hold to the last. But this can not last much longer. Look yonder!"[104]

Several minutes earlier, when Fitz Lee had given his instructions and left the field, he said hold "to the last." To the North Carolinians left at the rear and facing the overwhelming Federal cavalry, Fitz Lee's instruction came to mean: hold to the last possible minute. Private Coltrane, also of the 5th North Carolina, was convinced when Fitz and then W. H. F. Lee gave their instructions to Barringer, they more than likely meant hold to the last man, because the generals did not bother to tell Barringer's men where to meet the Confederate column after the fight. Years later, Coltrane made the comment, "I don't suppose the officers thought that any of us would live long enough to need the information."[105]

When Private Means returned to Barringer and the 5th North Carolina, the firing had become even more intense and one of the dismounted men on the line rose up "...and said: 'Please get me some ammunition. I have fired my last cartridge.' He was told: 'No ammunition can be brought in here now; borrow some, John.' He smiled, kneeled down and 'borrowed' two cartridges." About this time Wells's 15th New York came in on the heels of the 8th New York and the 1st Vermont.[106]

The 15th New York joined the party as the 1st Vermont bore down on the positions of the 5th and 2nd North Carolina cavalries and the 1st North Carolina was flanked by the 8th New York and was breaking. In the heat of this battle, Barringer ordered the 2nd North Carolina Cavalry to countercharge the 1st Vermont. This charge by the remnants of the exhausted 2nd North Carolina was meant to slow the Union cavalry and perhaps give the 5th North Carolina time to remount and follow the 1st North Carolina Cavalry into the woods. Whatever Barringer's intent, it was hopeless. The 2nd North Carolina collided with the 1st Vermont about midway across the field, and was turned without much damage to the Vermonters.

The 2nd North Carolina Cavalry's charge into the oncoming 1st Vermont and their support troops indicated to all that the last minute had arrived. With the 1st North Carolina fleeing across the road and into the woods and the 2nd North Carolina on its futile charge, Barringer ordered the 5th Cavalry to fall back. According to Private Means, the 5th Cavalry, with Captain John R. Erwin at their head, was majestically marched "by twos" off their last battlefield. They had an additional problem, however; they could not get up and cross Green's Road to their horses. The 8th New York in their sweep around Barringer's left was approaching the road with the 1st North Carolina in full retreat at their front; and the 1st Vermont, and probably the 15th New York, were heading toward the intersection of Green's and Cousin's Roads with the 2nd North Carolina in full retreat at their front. With no alternative, the dismounted 5th followed Barringer on a lane going into the woods.[107]

After traveling through lanes and woods for some miles, Barringer moved out to see if the cavalry patrol in front of them was Confederate or enemy — it was the enemy and he was captured. Captain Erwin then led the battered 5th North Carolina through the woods, on foot, for days. They avoided capture, but never rejoined the Army of Northern Virginia. After learning of Robert E. Lee's surrender, each captain took command of his company and they found their way to their home counties in North Carolina. By the time they reached their homes, most learned of Joseph E. Johnston's surrender near Raleigh.[108]

The 1st North Carolina Cavalry had also been in a very precarious situation soon after the fight around Namozine Church commenced. The 8th New York passed them on the left, and the 1st Vermont charged up the road on their right. Many cavalrymen from the 1st North Carolina managed to escape when Colonel Cheek led his command across the road and into some woods.[109]

Many of the men in the 2nd North Carolina Cavalry were lost in the initial collision with the 1st Vermont, and others were lost after their charge had been turned. After being driven back across Cousin's Road, and up Green's Road, the 2nd North Carolina was hit in its flank by the 8th New York where more losses were sustained. Those who survived the fighting near Namozine Church on April 3 managed to catch up with W. H. F. Lee, and then Anderson's and Fitz Lee's column and move toward Amelia Court House.

Colonel Cheek of the 1st North Carolina left us with this observation of the fight that day: "This engagement at Namozine Church was the crushing blow to General W. H. F. Lee's cavalry division. No regiment of his command that was present at this battle ever made an organized fight afterwards." His qualification on this statement reflects the fact that only Barringer's 1st, 2nd, and 5th regiments were on that field, that day. Barringer's 3rd North Carolina was still out on picket duty and not on the battlefield. W. H. F. Lee's brigades under Beale and Roberts were with the infantry in advance.[110]

The sacrifices made that day by the North Carolinians were noticed by the cavalry commander in his final report: "At another of the temporary halts upon this march to check the enemy in the vicinity of Namozine Church, that very excellent North Carolina brigade, of W. H. F. Lee's division, suffered severely."[111]

The losses taken by the 2nd North Carolina Cavalry on April 3 were associated with the fighting near Namozine Church, but probably at different stages of the fight. For instance, the 2nd North Carolina first charged and collided with the 1st Vermont; then they were hit by the 8th New York (and perhaps the 15th New York) in their flank.[112] This is further suggested by the locations given by Union officers when they captured cavalrymen from the 2nd North Carolina. Some were listed as taken at Aberdeen Church (when the Yankee officer taking the prisoners asked where he was and was told Namozine Church, he must have heard "Aberdeen Church"), and some prisoners were probably taken by another Union officer who recorded the location of the capture as near Amelia Court House (or perhaps on the road to Amelia Court House). A short distance from the battlefield, another Union officer reported capturing Mingrella Credle and John Moore on the Appomattox River; yet another even reported taking James Johnson at Jetersville. The two larger groups of prisoners were taken at, or very near, the battle site; the others were probably taken after they had been scattered and made it some distance before being captured. Most were captured, when their horses were lost or exhausted during the charge or flank attack.

The following is certainly a partial list of the wounded and killed. As the regiment moved quickly from the battle field, few observations and surely no records were made of the fallen men. As always, many men no doubt rode off with survivable wounds that no one bothered to note. In addition, some stragglers would not drift back into the ranks for days if at all, and finally, the Union troopers could not always identify the dead on the battlefields before they were quickly buried.

Combat Losses in the 2nd North Carolina Cavalry on April 3, 1865

Trooper	Age	Co.	Fate
Parnell T. Kearns		A	captured
William F. Linvill		A	captured
Henry N. Miller		A	captured
James J. McLean	38	B	captured
John T. Cross	26	C	captured
William T. Goodman		C	captured
Joseph E. Harrell		C	captured
John R. Haskins		C	captured
Aurelius Scott		C	captured
Alexander Autry	27	D	captured
Charles H. Elder	35	D	captured
John J. Rogers	35	D	captured
James E. R. Winstead	27	E	captured
Ellington Frazier		F	captured
Pinkney Gordon		F	captured
William J. Tadlock	24	H	captured
Daniel M. Baker	31	I	captured
Thomas J. Sherman		I	captured
John W. Rhew		K	captured
Isaac Taylor		K	captured
Henry F. Tritt		A	captured
James A. Ramsey	25	B	captured
Augustus D. Troutman	20	B	captured
William M. Waugh	27	B	captured
Robert P. Lawrence	25	C	captured
Daniel A. Patterson	24	D	captured
Yancy S. Corem		F	captured
John T. Edwards		F	captured
Jordan Parrish	23	I	captured
William R. Webb		K	captured
Mingrella Credle	24	G	captured
John Moore		H	captured
James B. Johnson	37	H	captured
Benjamin T. Boyed	27	C	wounded
Robert P. Hofter	29	C	wounded
George W. Jones		C	wounded
Neill G. Biggs	23	D	wounded
William C. Faucette	28	D	wounded
John J. Bryan	28	E	wounded
James H. Harris	24	G	wounded
James H. Johnson	24	H	wounded
John Bowling		K	wounded
Ninian W. Gray		K	wounded
Isaiah S. Harris	27	G	mortally wounded

The source used here is *North Carolina Troops 1861–1865, A Roster*, compiled by Louis H. Manarin (Raleigh, N.C., State Division of Archives and History), vol. II, Cavalry, pp. 104–177. (See Appendix for more information on the men listed above, page 406.)

A puzzling aspect of the day's activities is the capture of the 2nd North Carolina Cavalry's battle flag, now identified and located at The Museum of The Confederacy in Richmond, Virginia (identified as WD304). The Museum also has a letter written by Lieutenant Thomas W. Custer (the General's brother), dated 1866, in which he states that he captured the 2nd North Carolina's flag April 2, 1865 at Namozine Church. The 2nd North Carolina had again been decimated at that place and probably lost its flag there, but not on that date — the place was apparently more memorable than the date, so perhaps it is a simple and unimportant mistake. Then again, though Thomas Custer was awarded a Medal of Honor for capturing the 2nd North Carolina Cavalry's battle flag, we need to keep in mind that Thomas Custer was in the 6th Michigan Cavalry of Devin's cavalry division which was not in the fight with Barringer's North Carolinians at Namozine Church. If Thomas Custer was in possession of the 2nd Cavalry's flag, he did not capture it in the battle at Namozine Church. According to General Devin, his division was marching behind George A. Custer's Third Division on April 3 and camped for the night at Deep Creek which means Thomas Custer and the 6th Michigan probably passed through the battlefield long after the fight was over.[113] It is not known at this time if Thomas Custer picked up the battle flag while passing through the area, or if the troops in his command took it from scattered stragglers left behind after the combatants had moved on, or if he came by it in some other manner.

General George A. Custer collected his forces near Namozine Church after the battle and dispatched Wells's brigade to follow Fitz Lee with Munford's and Rosser's divisions down Cousin's Road. He also directed Capehart's brigade to follow W. H. F. Lee's command and the remnants of the 1st and 2nd North Carolina cavalries on Green's Road. He sent a regiment from Pennington's brigade with Wells and Capehart on their respective routes — Pennington and the rest of his command stayed at the crossroads and followed later.[114]

Throughout the day, the remains of Barringer's brigade, some of the 1st, 2nd, and 3rd North Carolina cavalries, caught up with Roberts's brigade and W. H. F. Lee, and moved with them — all hoping to join their commanding general, Robert E. Lee, at Amelia Court House. The 2nd North Carolina Cavalry had maintained its organization and effectiveness until the Battle at Namozine Church, but with the capture of Barringer and most of his staff, and the great losses by the 2nd Cavalry, its survival as an organized fighting force was questionable. Nevertheless, according to General Roberts, after Namozine Church the 2nd North Carolina Cavalry, "…what was left of it, with some scattering remnants of the other regiments of the [North Carolina] brigade, reported to me by orders from General Lee, and became a part of my brigade until the surrender at Appomattox."[115]

It would be easy to declare the 2nd North Carolina Cavalry spent after the fight at Namozine Church, and this story at an end — but as long as one man from the 2nd North Carolina Cavalry rode to fight at Appomattox, the story must go with him.

Five More Days to Appomattox Court House

After the Namozine Church battle, W. H. F. Lee's command continued the retreat on Green's Road with Johnson's men, all of whom dropped down to join Anderson's column on Cousin's Road. The disorganized men of Barringer's former brigade joined W. H. F. Lee throughout the day. The North Carolinian cavalrymen who stayed together were skirmishing with Capehart's brigade at their heels most of the way.[116] Once they reached Anderson's column, they had to work their way to the front of his troops — by early morning of April 4, they were at the head of Anderson's column.

Anderson's orders were to proceed to Bevil's Bridge on the Appomattox River and hold it until R. E. Lee got there with the rest of the Army of Northern Virginia. Anderson arrived at Bevil's Bridge before nightfall and waited. While he was waiting, Pickett arrived with the remnants of his mobile force which by then numbered only a few hundred men. Apparently Anderson was saddened to learn that almost every man in the two brigades he had detached to Pickett before the battle of Five Forks had been lost there on April 1.[117]

The bulk of Sheridan's cavalry had been following Anderson along the Namozine Road. Behind the Union cavalry came Griffin's Fifth

Infantry Corps, then Humphreys's Second Corps, then Wright's Sixth Corps—the Union forces all hoping to get south of R. E. Lee's army before they consolidated at Amelia Court House and moved down into North Carolina.[118]

By this time the Federals recognized that Anderson was heading for Amelia Court House hoping to join Robert E. Lee and his army. According to Merritt they had seen large bodies of Confederate infantry and wagon trains on the north side of the Appomattox River heading for Bevil's and Goode's bridges. They were correct. By April 3, R. E. Lee's army was approaching the Genito, Goode's, and Bevil's Bridges. In fact, that evening most of Longstreet's men were across the Appomattox at Goode's Bridge. High waters eventually forced all of the troops with Robert E. Lee, and later Richard S. Ewell's command, to cross at Goode's Bridge.[119] Longstreet's troops finished crossing the Appomattox very early on the morning of April 4. John B. Gordon's command was not far behind. Ewell had not yet arrived at Goode's Bridge.

Longstreet headed for Amelia Court House after he had crossed the river and collected his command. He was on the road by sunup on April 4. Other Confederate commanders were not far behind. During the journey, Federal cavalry constantly harassed Longstreet's left flank, and he had no cavalry protection at the time which made Sheridan's job easier. Fitz Lee and his cavalry were at Bevil's Bridge with Anderson. However, Sheridan only intended to slow the Confederate column, which he did, and that made a difference.[120]

Of course, Robert E. Lee had more than one problem during his journey. First his army lost time because it had to cross the Appomattox by one bridge. Then it was slowed by Federal cavalry on the march to Amelia Court House. Each delay gave Grant's infantry time to catch up with Sheridan's cavalry and form an impenetrable line south of the Army of Northern Virginia, blocking its way to North Carolina. R. E. Lee had a one day lead on Grant's infantry at the outset of the retreat. Now, nature and Sheridan were combining to dissipate Lee's chances of getting around Grant and dropping into North Carolina.

Fight at Amelia Court House, April 4

Soon after Longstreet left Goode's Bridge toward Amelia Court House, Johnson of Anderson's corps led his division from its camp near Bevil's Bridge for the same destination. Johnson marched in the rear of Pickett's small and partially armed command. Anderson's troops were also harassed by Union cavalry along the way. They marched about four miles on April 4 when the Union cavalry and artillery forced Johnson's command to form a defensive line until nightfall. Fitz Lee's cavalry came up during the night and formed on Johnson's right flank where they rested until 3:00 A.M.[121] During the remainder of the march to Amelia Court House, most of Fitz Lee's cavalrymen were busy keeping Sheridan's cavalrymen away from Anderson's left flank and rear. W. H. F. Lee's cavalrymen were sent far in advance of Anderson's column. His division then consisted of R. L. T. Beale's Virginia brigade and W. P. Robert's North Carolinians—which included remnants of Barringer's 1st, 2nd, and 3rd North Carolina regiments.

As W. H. F. Lee's men approached the town, they received word that a force of Federal cavalry was approaching the court house from the south. This was around the time R. E. Lee and Longstreet were arriving at the head of their column. The infantry could not be brought up in time to handle the enemy cavalry south of town, so a squadron from the 14th Virginia Cavalry was hurried forward with W. P. Roberts's North Carolinians close behind.[122]

The Virginia squadron entered town, turned south and rode for about three miles when they met enemy cavalry. The Virginians dismounted and had a vigorous exchange with the Union troops. While this was going on, W. P. Roberts galloped up and ordered the squadron to mount and move into an open field. Roberts and his mixed command of North Carolinians started to advance when the Federal troops charged. The Confederates met them with a counter charge, using mostly pistols and finally engaging in hand-to-hand fighting. During the fighting, R. E. Lee and some of his staff rode out to observe the encounter and just behind the clashing troops an interesting incident took place, one that some Confederates liked to tell. Samuel M. Gaines of the 14th Virginia wrote the following:

...a Federal officer, riding in advance of his men, dashed into our ranks. Instantly three or four pistols were turned upon him and a command rang out, "Don't shoot!"

I thought I recognized in the command the voice of General [Robert E.] Lee, and, turning, saw him at my horse's heels, with his hand raised, his countenance and posture indicating intense anxiety for the safety of the Federal officer.

One of our men seized his bridal, and thus stopping his horse, and it was then discovered that he was wounded and unable to control the animal. In another instant, but for general Lee's quick outcry, he would have been riddled with bullets. The general had taken in the situation, when it had occurred to no one else on our side, and thus saved the life of the gallant Federal officer.[123]

Years later, W. P. Roberts remembered the encounter as one in which his "little band of heroic men" on that day, "…met and successfully resisted the charging columns of General Custer near Amelia Courthouse, saving, in all probability, the great Lee from capture…."[124] Regardless of how remembered, all the men there that day took something from the encounter. Among them were the battered men of the 2nd North Carolina who still rode with W. P. Roberts.

Earlier on April 4, when Robert E. Lee and James Longstreet arrived at Amelia Court House, they went directly to the railroad station to get and distribute the rations Lee had ordered sent before he left Petersburg — however, the 350,000 rations were not there. It was another devastating delay for R. E. Lee's army. R. E. Lee's army continued to arrive throughout the day and waited for rations — details were sent into the surrounding area to gather food. R. E. Lee could not move his exhausted and hungry men further without nourishment. On the other hand, he knew that he had lost his one day lead on Grant's infantry. When Lee's wagons returned to camp with very little food to show for their effort, moods were depressed and the situation seemed even more hopeless. R. E. Lee also knew his troops, hungry or not, had to reach Burkeville before Grant's infantry. It would now be a very close race. The Confederates left some artillery and wagons at Amelia Court House and had the infantry and the remaining wagons travel separately to move the infantry more rapidly to Jetersville and then Burkeville. The troops, shrouded in gloom, started slowly for Jetersville at about 1:00 P.M. on April 5 — they knew Sheridan's cavalry and perhaps some infantry was in their path. W. H. F. Lee's cavalry was in front again that day with Longstreet's column just behind. The cavalrymen were an early warning system.[125]

THE ROAD BLOCK AND FIGHTING AROUND JETERSVILLE, APRIL 5

Robert E. Lee planned to march to Jetersville and Burkeville, pushing his way through Sheridan's cavalry if necessary — that would only be possible if Grant's infantry was not yet there. After passing through Jetersville, R. E. Lee and Longstreet rode ahead and were up front when they heard firing. It was W. H. F. Lee's skirmishers engaging Sheridan's dismounted cavalry on the army's route south. W. H. F. Lee rode to his rear and came upon the generals. The cavalryman told his superiors that Sheridan's command was in force at their front, and enemy infantry was probably also there or very near. Actually by that time, Griffin and the Fifth Corps had already joined Sheridan. R. E. Lee's instincts were correct when he decided not to attempt a break-through of Sheridan's line in order to continue on to Burkeville. The Army of Northern Virginia's delays, especially at Amelia Court House, had allowed Sheridan's cavalry and the Union's infantry to block their march south to North Carolina. Robert E. Lee had imagined his situation was bad, but his reality was even worse. Grant's Fifth Corps was entrenched; his Second Corps was arriving, with his Sixth Corps right behind them.[126]

Robert E. Lee turned Longstreet's command and headed back toward Jetersville before coming upon Sheridan's line. R. E. Lee planned to head northwest, then west and try again to pass west of Grant and head south for the North Carolina line. W. H. F. Lee's cavalry (Roberts's and Beale's commands) stayed engaged with the enemy for the remainder of the day withdrawing slowly as it became necessary. A colonel and lieutenant in Roberts's command described their hopes and actions with these words: "…and again at Jetersville the Seventy-fifth [7th North Carolina Cavalry] did good work, not failing to charge time and again until W. P. Roberts saw that it was useless to continue to throw his weak line against Sheridan's vast army in the vain endeavor to break through so as to enable R. E. Lee to retreat by Burkeville…."[127]

Meade did not start moving his infantry toward Jetersville until around 8:00 P.M. In part he was delayed because he met with resistance from Confederate cavalry, but more importantly, he was waiting for the Sixth Corps to catch up. Meade's plan was to push R. E. Lee's army back and attack them at Amelia Court House early on the morning of April 6 with the Second, Fifth, and Sixth Corps. However, R. E. Lee and his army would not be there.[128]

Earlier on the 5th, while R. E. Lee accompanied Longstreet's command south through Jetersville, Gary's cavalry escorted the wagon trains on a different route from Amelia Court House. Meanwhile, Sheridan sent Henry E. Davies and his brigade to locate the Confederate wagon trains. That took Davies to Amelia Springs and on to Painesville where he learned that Confederate trains were passing about four miles outside of town. When Davies found the wagon trains which were under the command of Custis Lee (R. E. Lee's oldest son), he attacked them and drove off Gary's cavalry—taking hundreds of prisoners and horses, 5 guns, and 11 flags—and burned nearly 200 wagons. The Union brigade then started back to Jetersville with its prizes. Shortly after leaving Painesville, the victorious Davies and his command were attacked at their rear by Gary's regrouped Confederate cavalry and delayed by a running fight as far as Amelia Springs. When R. E. Lee got the news of Davies's attack on his trains, he sent Fitz Lee with Rosser's and Munford's cavalry divisions after Davies. Around nightfall, Fitz Lee and his command caught Davies and drove him back to Sheridan's position near Jetersville.[129] Fitz Lee then took his command into camp for the night near Amelia Springs—leaving some troops within shouting distance of the enemy lines. W. P. Roberts's and R. L. T. Beale's cavalry commands were still occupied to the south at the rear of the Confederate column that had pulled out of Jetersville and was heading for Deatonsville.

Most Confederate cavalrymen were on alert along the line that night including the 2nd North Carolina cavalrymen and their comrades in Roberts's and Beale's commands. A member of Gary's brigade remembered that first night in sight of the enemy's outpost during the retreat and wrote:

All around us through the stillness floated the music of the Yankee bands, mocking with their beautiful music our desperate condition; yet our men around their fires were enjoying it as much, and, seemingly, with as light hearts as the owners of it. Occasionally, as a bugle call would ring out, which always sounds to a trooper as a challenge to arms, a different expression would show itself, and a harder look take the place of the softer one induced by "Home, Sweet Home," or "Annie Lawrie."[130]

Robert E. Lee's new plan for retreat was well underway by the afternoon of April 5. The plan had Longstreet backtrack a short distance along the railroad, then head northwest to Amelia Springs. From that point the army would head southwest to Deatonsville and then drop down to Rice's Station and move on to Farmville. The move was well over twenty miles and most of the way the roads were crowded with wagons slogging through mud—the wagons were heavy and slowed a process that needed to be rapid. The retreating army and the wagon trains merged near Deatonsville, and from that point on the troopers spent most of their time marching alongside the wagons in the darkness of night. They would have to march all night—then maybe they could arrive at Farmville before Grant's infantry.[131]

On their new course, R. E. Lee again rode with Longstreet's command, and when they passed through Amelia Springs during the night, R. E. Lee met with Fitz Lee who had settled most of his cavalrymen for the night. Fitz Lee was instructed to move his men at daylight and catch up to Longstreet—Fitz Lee had the commands of Rosser, Munford, and Gary near him. W. H. F. Lee, with Roberts's and Beale's commands, was still detached and held his position in front of the enemy north of Jetersville. Their task was to hold the Union forces while Longstreet turned the army and then fall back and guard the rear of the retreating column.[132]

Apparently, Gordon was not aware of what Roberts's and Beale's commands had encountered just south of Jetersville and was probably wondering why his tired and hungry troops had to turn and march through Amelia Springs. In response to his concerns, at 4:00 A.M. R. E. Lee sent a message to Gordon explaining that he had expected to be attacked at Jetersville and for that reason had ordered troops to Deatonsville as rapidly as possible even though the men and animals were exhausted. R. E. Lee further explained that by leaving the cavalry (Fitz Lee and the cavalrymen with him) at Amelia Springs for the night, he hoped the Confederate rear would be secure to Deatonsville.[133] However, Fitz Lee was instructed to pull out early on April 6 and move rapidly to catch Longstreet at Rice's Station. Roberts's and Beale's cavalrymen were at Gordon's rear through the next morning—facing the main body of the enemy coming from south of Jetersville.

James Longstreet's command began arriving at Rice's Station about sunup on April 6. They were fortunate to have passed through Deatonsville before the wagon trains arrived so did not have to share the road with them to Rice's Station—they made pretty good time. Longstreet had been instructed to wait there as the rest of the army drew up. Their action that day was not severe, but it was more-or-less constant. Union general Ord's command approached the station but was held back throughout the day. Fitz Lee's cavalry arrived during the late morning, but Longstreet did not use them in his fight to hold Rice's Station because during the morning he received information indicating that Ord had sent a detachment to burn High Bridge on the Appomattox River. Longstreet felt the bridge was essential because the remaining wagon trains would have to cross the Appomattox at that point and then turn down to Farmville. Consequently, when Fitz Lee's cavalry command arrived, Longstreet immediately sent Rosser's men to High Bridge. Soon after, Munford and then Gary arrived with their commands and Longstreet sent them to help Rosser at High Bridge.[134]

The Battles at High Bridge and Sailor's Creek, April 6

Around midday just below High Bridge, Rosser's and Munford's troops confronted Union forces. The fierce battle degenerated into hand-to-hand fighting before it was over. The Confederate cavalry was victorious, reminiscent of years past. Rosser rode back to Longstreet at Rice's Station sporting the spoils of his much needed victory.[135]

The rest of R. E. Lee's infantry was stretched far behind Longstreet's command. Anderson, Ewell, and Gordon were encumbered by numerous heavy wagons—all sharing the same muddy roads since Deatonsville. As indicated, Gordon brought up the rear, with Roberts's North Carolinians and Beale's Virginia cavalrymen at his rear the first part of the day. The Union cavalry and infantry were close behind during most of the retreat from Jetersville. They were hitting Gordon in the flanks and W. H. F. Lee in the rear. Roberts's and Beale's commands would skirmish with the pursuing Union forces and then drop back to keep up with Gordon's column. At several points during the retreat, Gordon and his cavalry escort took stands to slow the Federal column at their heels. One such stand was at Deatonsville where Gordon, supported by Roberts's and Beale's commands, threw up breastworks to slow the advancing Second Corps. Gordon's command was overwhelmed at that place, and lost several hundred men and several battle flags—they were pushed beyond Deatonsville.[136]

The Confederate column was continually stretched because of Sheridan's cavalrymen and the slow pace of the wagons. This resulted in large gaps between Longstreet's, Anderson's, and Ewell's commands. Due to the gaps between commands, Gordon took the wrong road. About three miles out of Deatonsville the road forked. Longstreet and those who followed him took the left fork toward Rice's Station. At the rearguard position, Gordon mistakenly took the more northern route toward High Bridge. Gordon had lost sight of Ewell's command and followed the wagon train heading for High Bridge. This was particularly hazardous because by midday Union forces were marching through fields on a parallel course in sight of the Confederate column.[137]

Further up the column, the Union cavalry was positioned to exploit the growing weaknesses, and they attacked until the Confederates were forced to stop and form battle lines. Crook, Devin, and Custer all brought their commands up from their more southern, but parallel route to hit the Confederates at various points.[138] All three Confederate commanders, Anderson, Ewell, and Gordon found themselves in serious trouble at about the same time. The attacks escalated throughout the afternoon, and once the Union infantry pulled up along their left flank, it became hopeless.

Meade knew early in the day that R. E. Lee was trying to pass north of him and head for Deatonsville, so he had put his infantry on the road. Humphreys's Second Corps left their position just south of Jetersville headed north and turned west near Amelia Springs to fall in behind Gordon's Confederate column. Griffin's Fifth Corps was on Humphreys's right, heading toward Amelia Court House. Wright and his Sixth Corps followed Sheridan on a more westerly route and stayed south of the Army of Northern Virginia blocking all routes south.[139] They converged in an area called Sailor's Creeks.

Three major fights took place in the Sailor's Creek area April 6. By late afternoon, Sheridan's cavalry had turned north to block Anderson's route to Rice's Station. Wright's Sixth Corps came in on Ewell's rear — between Ewell and Gordon. Finally, Humphreys brought Gordon to a halt.[140]

Years later, John B. Gordon remembered that by the afternoon the gap between his command and Richard S. Ewell broadened and was soon filled by a large Union force which surrounded Ewell and a large part of his command, forcing their surrender.[141] Ewell's command of about 3,000 was not more than 300 at the close of the day — Ewell and several other generals were also taken prisoner. Anderson was hit from more than one direction and lost nearly 3,000 men and two generals. The Confederate losses in the two commands totaled around 6,000 men on April 6, 1865 near Sailor's Creek. Nether Ewell nor Anderson had artillery or cavalry support.

Gordon also had a bad day. Toward the end of the day, Gordon had the enemy massed at his front and on both flanks. By evening his position had become even more untenable because W. H. F. Lee's cavalry had been taken from him earlier in the day and moved to another part of the line. Finally, Gordon's command was driven from the field in confusion, but not totally captured.[142] When Gordon collected his command and most of the wagons near High Bridge, he had lost thirteen flags, four guns, and more than 1,700 men.[143]

As indicated earlier, Humphreys's Second Corps was on Gordon's and W. H. F. Lee's heels from the start of the day. Some years later, Gordon described the retreat — early in the day, perhaps most of the day on April 6. It was an experience shared by the men in the 2nd North Carolina Cavalry and their comrades in W. H. F. Lee's division:

To bring up the rear and adequately protect the retreating army was an impossible task. With characteristic vigor General Grant pressed the pursuit. Soon began the continuous and final battle. Fighting all day, marching all night, with exhaustion and hunger claiming their victims at every mile of the march, with charges of their infantry in rear and of cavalry on the flanks, it seemed the war god had turned loose all his furies to revel in havoc. On and on, hour after hour, from hilltop to hilltop, the lines were alternatively forming, fighting, and retreating, making one almost continuous shifting battle.

Here, in one direction, a battery of artillery became involved; there, in another, a blocked ammunition train required rescue: and thus came short but sharp little battles which made up the side shows of the main performance, while the different divisions of Lee's lion-hearted army were being broken and scattered or captured.[144]

Gordon's words described the day well. He also noted that by the end of the day the different divisions of the army were broken and scattered or captured — his reference was to the commands of Anderson, Ewell, and his own. The best information available at this time suggests that Roberts's and Beale's cavalrymen were mostly involved in what Gordon called the almost continuous "side shows," and not one of the three "main performances."

Little information indicates where W. H. F. Lee's cavalrymen were placed after being removed from Gordon's rear. Company Rosters give places and dates for individuals who were lost, but they were primarily stragglers or men on scouting duty. For instance, in Beale's brigade, the 9th Virginia Cavalry had four men captured in different locations at the South Side Railroad, Jetersville, and Amelia Court House, but they may have been stragglers. The record further shows that one cavalryman was captured at Sailor's Creek on April 6, but he may well have been without a mount and working the wagon trains when captured. The 10th Virginia Cavalry had men captured at two locations on this day: two at New Store and three at Blacks and Whites. The losses in Beale's 13th Virginia Cavalry make a little more sense: two men captured at Sailor's Creek and two at Farmville. A fifth man was captured at Amelia Court House, but again they may well have been stragglers. On the other hand, the two captured at Farmville may have been among the many cavalrymen Longstreet sent ahead of his column to Farmville late at night on April 6. Again, it is possible that the two captured at Sailor's Creek were with the wagon trains.

W. P. Roberts's 4th North Carolina Cavalry

had three losses that day. One man was captured at Amelia Court House and may have been a straggler. The other two were captured near the battlefields of that day: one at High Bridge and the other at Harper's farm which is in the area of Union cavalry attacks on Anderson during the afternoon. The 7th North Carolina Cavalry had no recorded losses for April 6.

The recorded losses for the cavalrymen in Barringer's former North Carolina brigade also show little evidence of organized fighting on that afternoon. The 1st North Carolina Cavalry had three losses: one at Amelia Court House, perhaps a straggler; one wounded at Burkeville Junction (this is not in R. E. Lee's line of retreat, but it was the place Colonel Cheek of the 1st North Carolina was captured while on a special mission the day before); and one man was captured at Sailor's Creek, probably with the wagons. The records for the 3rd North Carolina Cavalry show no losses for this day. The 2nd North Carolina Cavalry had four men captured on April 6. Two men were listed as taken on the South Side Railroad, which could be near High Bridge or Farmville — the latter makes more sense because the other two cavalrymen were captured at Farmville. Again recall, Longstreet sent the cavalry ahead of his column into Farmville just after nightfall on April 6.[145]

Recorded losses for April 4, 5, and 6 indicate the 2nd North Carolina Cavalry was engaged at various points along the journey.

Combat Losses in the 2nd North Carolina Cavalry on April 4, 5 & 6, 1865

Trooper	Age	Co.	Fate
Perry Lucas	39	E	captured
Pleasant C. Kelly		F	captured
William S. Lee		F	captured
Balum Hornada		G	captured
Samuel G. J. Dalton		F	captured
Henry N. Price	26	D	wounded
Stephen O. Terry		K	captured
Daniel J. Gooch	18	C	wounded
P.A. Kroover		G	captured
David L. Tate		H	captured
William L. Stilly	27	G	captured
Dallas Wahab	20	G	captured

The source used here is *North Carolina Troops 1861–1865, A Roster*, compiled by Louis H. Manarin (Raleigh, N.C., State Division of Archives and History), vol. II, Cavalry, pp. 104–177. (See Appendix for more information on the men listed above, page 407.)

From Rice's Station to Farmville

The cavalry units in W. H. F. Lee's command were moved separately from Gordon's rear on April 6, but by the end of the day joined the rest of the cavalry under Fitz Lee at Rice's Station in preparation for Longstreet's move to Farmville. It is clear Roberts's and Beale's cavalrymen were moved up to Longstreet before the three main fights late that afternoon because as Longstreet noted, he did not know of the disasters at Sailor's Creeks until the next morning.[146]

The men of the 2nd North Carolina Cavalry and their comrades in Fitz Lee's command left Rice's Station behind Longstreet late April 6 thinking the day had gone pretty well, considering the circumstances. Around nightfall, Longstreet gave up his wait at Rice's Station and marched for Farmville. It was another night march and another attempt to get around Grant's army and head south. Most, if not all, of Fitz Lee's cavalry command covered Longstreet's rear on the night march. After crossing Bush River, Longstreet relieved the cavalry and sent them forward to Farmville. This may have been when the 2nd North Carolina took its losses on April 6. In Farmville, Longstreet and Fitz Lee found a supply train waiting for them and most of the troops were given two days' rations — the first distribution of food for many since leaving the Petersburg-Richmond area.[147]

Longstreet crossed the Appomattox River at Farmville early in the morning of April 7, and his troops prepared their breakfast. Time was taken for this much needed meal, though Sheridan's cavalry and some Union infantry were on their heels and the option of retreating south or even west from Farmville was not open. As some of the Confederates prepared their much anticipated meal, they felt some urgency. Union forces were crossing the Appomattox with little difficulty and threatening their escape route north of Farmville. R. E. Lee and Longstreet learned that after survivors of Gordon's and Mahone's commands had crossed the Appomattox at High Bridge and the wagon bridge just below, they had not successfully destroyed the two bridges. Humphreys's Second Corps followed Gordon across the river and threatened to cut R. E. Lee's escape route north of Farmville. R. E. Lee wanted Longstreet up with Gordon and Mahone to keep their route open. Consequently, Longstreet's men were soon "ordered under arms and put in quick march, but Gen. Lee urged double-quick."[148]

Federal cavalry was harassing Fitz Lee's troops around and through the town until they crossed the river. Most of the Confederate cavalry crossed the Appomattox after Longstreet at a ford just above Farmville. A. A. Humphreys indicated Fitz Lee had all his cavalry with him when he marched for Farmville, but that is not likely. In any case, W. H. F. Lee's cavalry division was either with Fitz Lee or somewhere along Longstreet's column going through Farmville.[149]

Gary's cavalry brigade was among the last to leave Farmville and as they passed through the main part of town on the morning of April 7, they joined the rest of Fitz Lee's cavalry gathering in a large field. Fitz Lee and Rosser were there with other "distinguished cavalry officers," one of whom may have been W. H. F. Lee with Beale's and Roberts's commands. When Edward M. Boykin of Gary's brigade described the scene, he did not mention W. H. F. Lee. However he did say that at one point "…all the cavalry of the army of Northern Virginia, looking on…."[150]

Union forces were pushing into town and the Confederate cavalry stayed long enough to slow their advance. The Federal column paused to bring up artillery, unlimber and fire at the Confederate cavalry on the edge of town. Fitz Lee had dismounted most of his cavalry and formed a line. Boykin and the 7th South Carolina Cavalry were among those mounted in front of the line and observed: "The shells went over our heads, but struck a few feet in front of General Lee's dismounted line, making gaps in it as they did so." As more Federal troops collected, the bridge at Farmville was burned and Fitz Lee led his cavalry along the Appomattox for about two miles and crossed them at a ford. Gary's brigade was the last to cross the river.[151]

After crossing the river, Fitz Lee gave his men a short rest and then headed north following Longstreet. At this point in the retreat many Confederate cavalrymen were forced to walk beside their exhausted and broken horses a good deal of the time. So when they had opportunities to get fresh and healthy mounts, they did. Needless to say, they made few friends among the local inhabitants as they pressed into service every horse they could locate.[152]

Though the bridges at Farmville had been burned, some of the Union cavalry forded the Appomattox River. J. Irvin Gregg's command of George Crook's division was soon pressing the rear of the Confederate column. Gregg led his cavalrymen in an attack on the wagons near the end of the column. In turn, Munford led a frontal attack on Gregg's force, and Rosser's men hit them on their flank. The Federal cavalrymen were driven back, and many prisoners were taken including J. I. Gregg himself. Bryan Grimes's North Carolina infantry division (of Gordon's corps) and William Owen's artillery were also involved in the encounter with J. I. Gregg. Gary's cavalry brigade came up just about the time the fighting ended. John E. Cooke, formerly of J. E. B. Stuart's staff and then on William N. Pendleton's staff, estimated that at this time Fitz Lee had a force of about 1,500 cavalry on broken down horses. Just after the encounter with J. I. Gregg's cavalry, Fitz Lee sent W. H. F. Lee's command on ahead to support the front of the Confederate column. Fitz Lee and the rest of his cavalry did not move forward, but stayed in place for the remainder of the day.[153]

Robert E. Lee was within a 100 yards of J. I. Gregg's attack and after it was over a conversation took place in the road between R. E. Lee and W. H. F. Lee. Some years later, John E. Cooke recalled the exchange between the Lees just after their cavalrymen had beaten J. I. Gregg's troops, "to the great satisfaction of General Lee, who said to his son, General W. H. F. Lee: 'Keep your command together and in good spirits, general — don't let them think of surrender — I will get you out of this'."[154] We can reasonably assume W. H. F. Lee communicated his father's message to his commanders, Roberts and Beale, in spirit if not in his words. In any case, with that optimistic note, the 2nd North Carolina Cavalry moved toward the front and the next fight. W. H. F. Lee's command was moving to support William Mahone's left flank.

After J. I. Gregg's failed attack on the wagons, the Union forces on the rear of the Confederate column stayed in place and skirmishers and artillery fired at each other throughout the day. With at least one charge by some of Gary's cavalrymen, the stand-off lasted until nightfall. Fitz Lee indicated his position near Crook's troops was held until about midnight. When the retreat resumed, the cavalry followed

Longstreet's command, and that position was maintained throughout April 8.[155]

THE FIGHT AT CUMBERLAND CHURCH

Early on April 7, Robert E. Lee started Longstreet on his march from Farmville heading north. After marching a few miles, his command was placed on Gordon's right, facing east. Gordon was on Mahone's right, also facing east. Mahone was facing north across their route of retreat because Federal troops, most of Humphreys's command, had followed Gordon across the Appomattox on the wagon bridge near High Bridge. They did not turn southwest to Farmville, but headed northwest to get around and block the Confederate column before it could turn. Humphreys's Second Corps faced west in front of Longstreet and Gordon and arched its line to face south at Mahone's front. R. E. Lee's entrenchments formed an arc over and east of Cumberland Church.

As indicated, Mahone was facing north into Scott's brigade of Humphreys's corps. Mahone's left flank was the most vulnerable place on the Confederate line. Of course, that was where Humphreys struck first — Scott's troopers were sent in behind their bayonets at about 4:15 P.M. As Mahone's left flank was threatened, Longstreet sent G. T. Anderson's brigade to help hold the flank, which they did.[156]

Some Confederate cavalrymen were on G. T. Anderson's left as they counter-attacked. At the time Munford's, Rosser's, and Gary's commands were all fully engaged to the rear with Crook's division. Consequently, only Roberts's and Beale's commands of W. H. F. Lee's division were supporting Anderson and Mahone at the northern end of the Confederate column.

Humphreys's command was not strong enough to hold the Confederate column because the latter was not sufficiently weakened by J. I. Gregg's attack on the southern end of the column. Humphreys did not know the bridge at Farmville had been burned and that the bulk of the Union force had not yet crossed the Appomattox River to attack R. E. Lee from the rear. When he heard the sounds of battle coming from the attack by J. I. Gregg, Humphreys thought that Sheridan's cavalry and the infantry's Fifth Corps were attacking the rear of the Confederate column. But he was wrong; it was only J. I. Gregg's cavalry and the Confederates did not have to pull troopers from the front of their column to protect the rear. Thus Humphreys could not hold and R. E. Lee was able to continue his desperate retreat. The 2nd North Carolina Cavalry and their comrades covered the line as the Army of Northern Virginia marched through. By evening Grant was headquartered in Farmville and thinking about R. E. Lee's imminent surrender, perhaps at Appomattox.[157]

Robert E. Lee's plan for the next day was to head for Appomattox Station on the South Side Railroad where he might find more rations before turning south for North Carolina. Of course, the challenge was to get there before Grant's infantry.

At this time, the remnants of Robert E. Lee's army were collected into two corps — one under Longstreet, the other under Gordon. The cavalry remained under Fitz Lee. When the decision was made for yet another night march, Longstreet led his command north for another 5 miles, then turned west and went through Curdsville. R. E. Lee again rode with Longstreet. Gordon led his command out of Cumberland Church along the Lynchburg Wagon Road parallel to Longstreet's route for about 2.5 miles, then on to the Richmond-Lynchburg Stage Road where Gordon turned west toward New Store. Some of Fitz Lee's cavalry followed Gordon. Fitz Lee said he and his cavalry were at the rear of Longstreet's Corps and stayed in that position throughout April 8. However, as usual, the cavalry command was divided among several positions along the column. Also, according to Humphreys, we know Gordon had cavalry protecting his rear and finally we know that Gary's cavalry was with Walker's artillery which left toward Appomattox long before the rest of the army — Gary's cavalry and Walker's artillery were the first to arrive at Appomattox. W. H. F. Lee's cavalrymen were with Gordon's column.[158]

Early in the morning on April 8, Grant again sent his troops in pursuit of R. E. Lee's men. Wright's Sixth Corps was following Longstreet; Humphreys's Second Corps was on Gordon's trail; the Fifth Corps with most of Sheridan's cavalry were sent westward along the South Side Railroad. The cavalry and the Fifth Corps had a shorter route to Appomattox Station than did the Army of Northern Virginia, and they made every effort to capitalize on their advantage.

Though Sheridan's cavalry was not at the rear of the Confederate column on April 8, the Federal infantry keep pressure on the Confederate cavalry following Longstreet and Gordon. For instance, Munford recalled the day in these terms: "But while the Cavalry of the enemy were gone we who were in the rear of Longstreet's Corps were being closely followed and persistently pressed by the enemy's Infantry. My men were dismounted constantly and deployed as rear guard."[159] The cavalry covering Gordon's column more than likely included men from the 2nd North Carolina Cavalry and they certainly had a similar time of it that day.

Early April 8, another message from Grant was passed to R. E. Lee—it took several hours to reach Lee who was riding with Longstreet more than likely near the head of the column.[160] Part of the delay in receiving the message was because Grant sent it through Humphreys's column to the Confederate cavalry in front of them (W. H. F. Lee's command). Humphreys was following Gordon's column and R. E. Lee was traveling with Longstreet on a near parallel road. The message had to work its way up one column and then be taken to the road on which Longstreet and the commanding general were making their retreat. Rosser's command was at the rear of Longstreet's column when the message for Robert E. Lee arrived and the message was passed to one of his men. Then Rosser had to send it up through Longstreet's column to R. E. Lee—cavalrymen probably rode at a reasonable speed, but it took awhile. The message contained a response to an earlier message from R. E. Lee on possible conditions of surrender. Lee in turn responded to Grant that day—no surrender yet.

By late afternoon, the two Confederate corps converged on New Store, still about a nine hour march to Appomattox Court House. Gordon arrived first and passed through town. Longstreet had to halt while Gordon's men passed by, then Longstreet's troops fell in behind. Humphreys's Second Corps arrived near New Store early that evening not far behind Gordon and rested his men for a few hours just outside of town. Humphreys was followed by Wright's Sixth Corps on the road to Appomattox.

Walker's Confederate artillery and Gary's cavalry brigade (numbering about 500 men) had left New Store much earlier in the morning and passed Appomattox Court House by midday. They marched past the court house for a couple of miles and got within half mile of Appomattox Station when they encountered pickets from Custer's cavalry force. Custer had his men spread along a half mile front on the north side of the South Side Railroad and centered on the station. All the supplies and rations R. E. Lee had hoped to find at Appomattox Station were there, but in the hands of Sheridan's cavalrymen. Walker sent part of his artillery on and took the rest back to the Appomattox Court House area along with Gary's cavalrymen.

Gordon arrived in the vicinity of the court house around 3:00 P.M. April 8. At that time, R. E. Lee's army was stretched from the court house along Stage Road for about ten miles. Most of W. H. F. Lee's cavalrymen arrived during the morning and were camped along the road. The 1st, 2nd, and 4th North Carolina cavalries initially camped about six miles from Appomattox Court House.[161] That position in the ten-mile string of encampments suggests W. H. F. Lee's division with Roberts's and Beale's commands dropped behind Gordon's troopers though they had arrived at the court house ahead of the infantrymen. During the late afternoon and evening, the men of the 2nd North Carolina Cavalry were certainly not encouraged by the sounds of fighting coming from their front—Walker's artillery and Gary's dismounted cavalry were engaged with the enemy near Appomattox Station through the evening.[162]

The men of the Army of Northern Virginia received some rations and rest for the remainder of their last full day as an army. Of course, the army was smaller this day, just as it had become smaller each day of the retreat. It diminished partly because of fighting, but also due to large number of desertions. Every day of the retreat saw a thinning of the Confederate ranks from desertions. April 8 was no different. Often as troopers passed familiar roads that led to their homes, they just hung their equipment on a tree or fence and walked home.[163]

That afternoon, it occurred to Fitz Lee that Sheridan's cavalry had not been on his rear throughout the day and that it was very likely Sheridan took a more direct route along the South Side Railroad to Appomattox Station—

which was exactly what he had done. Fitz Lee rode along the column to find R. E. Lee and express his concerns. He asked to have his cavalry moved to the front in the event Sheridan was arriving soon. R. E. Lee instructed him to do so. Fitz Lee's thinking was correct, but his timing was a little off. Union cavalry was already at Appomattox Station and Walker's artillery as well as Gary's cavalry had already had several skirmishes with them by the time Fitz Lee got approval to move his cavalry forward.

By early evening, Fitz Lee arrived back where Rosser's and Munford's commands had settled in — still about 10 miles from the court house. W. H. F. Lee's command was settled in farther up the column, about six miles from the court house — still at the rear of Gordon's encampment. Fitz Lee left a small rear guard for Longstreet and moved Rosser and Munford forward during the evening. Fitz Lee arrived at W. H. F. Lee's position in the column around 10:00 or 11:00 P.M. and the bugle sounded for Roberts's and Beale's commands to "Mount your horses." The cavalrymen had gotten a few hours rest and some got a few hours more after they arrived near the court house while waiting for morning action. According to Private W. L. Moffett of Beale's brigade, they passed to the front of the army "...and formed into line of battle, were dismounted and ordered to stand and hold horses and keep awake." Others may have been more fortunate. According to Lieutenant E. J. Holt of Roberts's command, by 4:00 A.M. on April 9, they were awakened on the Lynchburg Road about three-quarters of a mile from the court house.[164]

During the evening of April 8, Custer's probes to find the Confederate column helped R. E. Lee determine Custer's location, but R. E. Lee remained unsure of the location of Grant's Fifth Infantry Corps. Based on his awareness of Custer's presence, the loss of all supplies and rations at Appomattox Station and the weakness of his own army, R. E. Lee summoned his last council of war.

Robert E. Lee's field headquarters was set up about a mile behind the court house in the woods. He held council with generals Longstreet, Gordon, and Fitz Lee — the commanders of his three remaining corps. They met "...by a low-burning bivouac-fire. There was no tent there, no table, no chairs, and no camp-stools. On blankets spread upon the ground or on saddles at the roots of the trees, we sat around the great commander." The four generals decided that, in R. E. Lee's words, "Fitz Lee, with the cavalry, supported by Gordon, was ordered to drive the enemy from his front, wheel to the left, and cover the passage of the trains; while Longstreet, who from Rice's Station had formed the rear guard, should close up and hold the position." Robert E. Lee also made it clear if the Union infantry was on the line in the morning, all would be considered lost and he would surrender the Army of Northern Virginia. Fitz Lee requested that if the army was surrendered, he wanted to take his cavalry out, perhaps down to North Carolina, to continue the fight.[165]

Fitz Lee probably made his feelings known to his three division commanders as well. He called Munford up from the rear to R. E. Lee's headquarters and told him of the army's dire straits. Munford then requested that he be given a place on the far right of the line because most of his men were from the Appomattox area and knew the woods and byroads well — thus giving them a great opportunity to escape to Lynchburg should the army be surrendered. Fitz Lee reportedly replied, "Bully for you, Munford. You shall have the right of the line." Around 1:00 A.M., Rosser expressed his ideas concerning surrender to Gordon. His position was that if the army was to be surrendered, he and his men would ride from the field and continue the war in North Carolina. Soon after his meeting with Gordon, Rosser released all the prisoners held by his command.[166]

Once again, the situation was even worse than Robert E. Lee had imagined. The jaws of the vise closing around him included Humphreys's Second Corps and Wright's Sixth Crops camped within three miles of Longstreet's rear on the night of April 8. Grant's lower jaw was his cavalry already in place and blocking R. E. Lee's access to Appomattox Station. Sheridan was also prepared to attack the next morning. He had moved Charles H. Smith's cavalry brigade from Crook's division to his front line for the morning attack. The attack would at least delay the Army of Northern Virginia until the power of the lower jaw arrived — the Fifth Corps to combine with Sheridan and close the vise. Griffin and Ord were also making every effort to reach Sheridan in time for the morning attack.

They pushed their infantrymen over a thirty mile march on April 8 and through most of the night. They knew if Sheridan could hold R. E. Lee until they got to Appomattox, it would end there.

The Last Battle: Appomattox Court House, April 9

The Army of Northern Virginia's attack formation was decided the night before and put into place before dawn on April 9. The line ran from the right, the northwest end, to the Confederate left, and centered on the Richmond-Lynchburg Stage Road. R. E. Lee wanted to continue his retreat to the west along the Stage Road. That meant his front line had to advance and wheel left until the line was across and nearly parallel to the Stage Road and south of it. The right would have to advance over the greatest distance while the left of the Confederate line could simply hold its position. If successful, the Stage Road would be open and the wagon trains could escape along with the army. Once Fitz Lee's cavalry and John B. Gordon's infantry corps cleared the road, Longstreet would move in and help hold the line.

Fitz Lee's cavalry was placed on the right. They were on the latch side of the "swinging gate," not the hinge side, so when the line wheeled left, they had more ground to cover. But they were mounted and able to cover the ground rapidly — indeed get out ahead of the infantry, if necessary. W. H. F. Lee's two brigades, W. P. Roberts's and R. L. T. Beale's, were on J. B. Gordon's immediate right and numbered around 400 cavalrymen. T. L. Rosser's command was next and T. T. Munford's troopers were on the end of the Confederate line. Combined, Fitz Lee's three divisions brought about 2,400 cavalrymen to the line that morning. C. H. Smith's Union command was north of the stage road and would need to be pushed back some distance to clear the escape route — that would primarily fall to the cavalry. Gordon had his skirmish line out in front of and along his entire battle line running for about three-quarters of a mile.[167]

The remnant of the 2nd North Carolina Cavalry, still commanded by John P. Lockhart, was with W. P. Roberts when ordered to horse at about 4:00 A.M. April 9. They marched through the village to about one-third of a mile west of the court house and formed a line facing southwest. They remained in that position, mounted, until sunrise — the sun felt good to the cold, hungry, sleepy, and tattered North Carolinians. With the sun came a chaplain from an unidentified regiment who rode out in front of Roberts's command and "made an earnest and fervent prayer." After all, it was Palm Sunday. Soon after he finished, the North Carolinians were subjected to artillery fire, but remained mounted and in line. The Union skirmish line was supported by two pieces of artillery in front of Gordon's right and W. H. F. Lee's cavalrymen.[168]

Bryan Grimes had his North Carolina infantry on the line early and waited for orders from Gordon. Fitz Lee and Gordon rode up a little later and began to discuss the order of attack. Gordon thought the enemy in front was cavalry, thus Fitz Lee's cavalry should lead the Confederate attack. Fitz Lee argued there was mostly infantry at their front, consequently Gordon's infantry should lead off. Grimes got impatient with the discussion, probably because it was apparent neither Gordon nor Fitz Lee wanted to order their men into what the two generals believed would be the last battle for the Army of Northern Virginia. Who would send out the last trooper to die in Virginia? Apparently neither Gordon nor Lee wanted that honor. And it seems Grimes was much less convinced that surrender was imminent. He finally intervened and pointed out it was somebody's responsibility to advance. Grimes offered to take his division out first but indicated that he had to have support — his division could not open the Stage Road alone. Gordon's reply was for Grimes to drive the enemy back and take the other two divisions if he wanted. Grimes then formed Gordon's corps for the attack.[169]

Skirmishers on both sides had been firing at one another for some time before the main Confederate line began to move. Around dawn, a shell came shrieking over the heads of W. H. F. Lee's cavalrymen and the buglers sounded: "To mount." Instantly, Poague's artillery, just to the left of Roberts's and Beale's commands, responded — there was then a constant flow of shells passing over the heads of the cavalrymen. With the outbreak of artillery fire, the men of the 2nd North Carolina Cavalry and their comrades gave for the last time in battle the "Rebel

Yell" as the cavalry rode out a step ahead of Grimes's infantry. They advanced "...slow at first, then at a trot and as Poague's guns ceased firing we charged...."[170] As Grimes and his infantry stepped out, the enemy artillery focused primarily on them. At that point, cavalrymen from Roberts's and Beale's commands wheeled left in front of Gordon's skirmishers and rode directly into the left flank of the Union artillery and dismounted support troops. The remainder of W. H. F. Lee's cavalrymen headed for C. H. Smith's brigade which straddled the Stage Road—from north to south, they were the 13th Ohio, 2nd New York Mounted Rifles, 1st Maine, 6th Ohio, and 13th Ohio. Davies's brigade, also of Crook's division, was behind Smith.

Roberts's and Beale's men, who rode into Smith's skirmishers and pushed them back into their main line, were greeted with fire from seven-shot Spencer repeating carbines and sixteen shot Henry repeaters probably making them think they had a full division in front of them. Nonetheless Roberts's North Carolinians pressed forward until Smith's line began to give way. G. Crook then sent support for Smith from Mackenzie's and Young's (D. McM. Gregg's former division) commands. The Union cavalry continued to give way before W. H. F. Lee's cavalry and Grimes's infantry. Then Merritt sent Custer's division to the line for support. When both Custer's and Devin's commands reached the battlefield, they joined on Smith's right facing Grimes's North Carolina infantry—the Confederates continued to advance. W. H. F. Lee's cavalrymen clashed with Mackenzie's and Young's men as well as Smith's as they drove forward. The Confederate advance stopped when Grant's infantry joined the Union line. The Twenty-fourth Corps replaced Crook's line of cavalry, the Fifth Corps fell in behind Devin and the Confederate attack was over.[171]

The Last Cavalry Charge

Roberts's and Beale's cavalrymen made the initial charge with sabers and pistols drawn as they swooped into the flank of the Union artillery and the dismounted cavalrymen from the 1st Maine who had been placed in support of the guns. The charge had to penetrate a wall of shells, grape, canister, and carbine fire. The Confederate cavalrymen who went for the artillery rode rapidly across an undulating field which at times had them shielded from the fire of the Union guns which were about 700 or 800 yards from the Confederate line. When the Confederate cavalrymen got within about 200 yards, the gunners and supporting troops began to break—those who did not get away into the woods were captured along with the guns. About fifty prisoners were taken at that point by Roberts and his North Carolina cavalrymen.[172]

W. H. F. Lee's cavalrymen continued to push the 1st Maine back into Smith's line—for about one-quarter of a mile. Then W. P. Roberts returned to the position where they had first encountered the artillery and regrouped his men. He then had his men join the other members of W. H. F. Lee's command pushing Smith's entire line back into their support troops.[173]

The remaining men of the 2nd North Carolina Cavalry were among the cavalrymen making the charge at their enemy's artillery position. General W. P. Roberts acknowledged their presence with this comment:

In fact, the little brigade did more than its share from the White Oak road to Appomattox, and on the morning of the surrender it was ordered to the front on the right of our lines. It faithfully and bravely responded to the last call, and with the remnant of the Nineteenth North Carolina [2nd Cavalry], took the last guns captured by the Army of Northern Virginia, and I am sure they fired the last shots as well.[174]

J. P. Leach of Bryan Grimes's 53rd North Carolina Infantry also remembered the early minutes of the fight. He wrote:

We were ordered to charge the battery and went forward at double-quick, but before going two hundred yards the guns were silenced and in a few moments were brought galloping toward my command, each gun having six horses....

The battery of four guns had been flanked by cavalry of Gen. Wm. P. Roberts and surrendered to him before the infantry could reach them, a fortunate circumstance which I recall with lasting gratitude for the "butter-milk" brigade.[175]

After taking the Union artillery out and pushing their support troops, Roberts's men joined with Beale's brigade and Grimes's infantry to push Smith's brigade southwest and off the Richmond-Lynchburg Stage Road until they had opened the retreat route for the little Army of Northern Virginia.

Once the men were fighting along the line and the Union infantry was visible in great numbers, as well as their cavalry, Robert E. Lee sent a member of his staff to Gordon, asking if he thought he could push the enemy sufficiently to open the road. Gordon replied, "Tell General Lee that my command has been fought to a frazzle, and unless Longstreet can unite in the movement, or prevent these forces from coming upon my rear, I cannot long go forward." Unfortunately for the Confederates, Longstreet already had his hands full and was being pushed by Humphreys's Second Corps, and Wright's Sixth Corps coming up. R. E. Lee knew by this time that Ord's Army of the James was in front of Gordon. Sheridan's cavalry and Griffin's Fifth Corps were also at his front.[176]

As indicated, before the Union infantry was on the line, Grimes's infantry and W. H. F. Lee's cavalry were able to push back Sheridan's cavalry. Grimes halted his line about one-quarter of a mile south of the Stage Road and turned Cox's brigade facing west as he became increasingly concerned about Ord's build-up to the southwest near Smith's cavalry—his concern was if he advanced any farther, they could get to his rear. Shortly thereafter, the men of Roberts's and Beale's cavalries halted their advance also—they could see battle flags of the 62nd Ohio, 199th Pennsylvania, 39th Illinois, 67th Ohio, 10th Connecticut, 11th Maine, and others. Nonetheless, Grimes felt he could hold the escape road open for the army, so he sent a message back to Gordon to that effect. Gordon's reply was for Grimes to withdraw his command immediately.[177]

Confederate Cavalry, Wide-Right

Earlier in the morning, just after W. H. F. Lee had moved his cavalry into action, Rosser moved his cavalrymen to the southwest, apparently in an attempt to get around the left of the Union line around Smith's brigade. Rosser's command may have made contact with the enemy soon after the North Carolinians did, though they went wide to the west in search of the Union left. As he took his command around Smith, they briefly encountered troops from Mackenzie's and Young's commands and perhaps Osborn's infantry.[178]

Munford left shortly after Rosser and took his men westward. He went out to the west and into woods where he came upon Union troopers. He turned a little more to his right and moved forward again. He continued on until he ran into pickets from Henry E. Davies brigade, also from Crook's division. Munford's command continued around the Union left until reaching the Lynchburg Road. From this point, Munford apparently decided the Union forces were too overwhelming. He not only saw Davies's and Mackinzie's cavalrymen, but also Union infantry in great force. Around the same time, a large column of enemy cavalry moved to his front. There was a charge by Federal cavalrymen, and a countercharge. The latter was apparently not Munford's call. Neither did a great deal of damage. The encounter ended when an officer appeared on the field with a flag of truce. Munford decided that because he had already started his men west on the Lynchburg Road, the conditions of surrender did not apply to his command. After traveling several miles down the road, various units began to take roads home as they appeared. However, Munford with a small fraction of his command did get as far as Lynchburg.[179]

Munford's and Rosser's commands were far to the west of the fighting that occupied Roberts's command and the remainder of W. H. F. Lee's cavalrymen. Munford and Rosser apparently intended to test the ease with which they might be able to get around the enemy. Whatever the original intent, Fitz Lee positioned them well to leave the field and avoid surrender. He had informed Munford and Rosser of R. E. Lee's determination to surrender if the enemy's infantry appeared on the battlefield, and their infantry was very evident. Fitz Lee certainly also told his two division commanders that it was his intention to leave the field and not surrender the cavalry with the Army of Northern Virginia. Whether Munford's and Rosser's exit was premature or ill-advised is hard to say, but their positions out on the far right facilitated the move once Fitz Lee halted W. H. F. Lee's cavalrymen.

Fitz Lee may not have told his cousin, W. H. F. Lee, of his plan to leave the field if surrender appeared imminent, but it is more likely W. H. F. Lee decided for himself to keep his command on the field to the end. His North Carolinian cavalrymen were accustomed to being the last to leave a battlefield.

Certainly the early battlefield scene had changed dramatically and rapidly as two infantry corps appeared on the Union line. The Confederate advance had halted and Union officers were riding in several directions carrying flags of truce. Fitz Lee felt justified in acting on his previously announced plan for his cavalry. He apparently also instructed Roberts's and Beale's commands to leave the battlefield. In his final battle report to R. E. Lee, Fitz Lee wrote:

Upon hearing that the Army of Northern Virginia had surrendered, the men were generally dispersed and rode off to their homes, subject to reassembling for a continuation of the struggle. I rode out in person with a portion of W. H. F. Lee's division, the nearest to me at the time, and previous to the negotiations between the commanders of the two armies. It will be recalled that my action was in accordance with the views I had expressed in the council the night before — that if a surrender was compelled the next day, I would try to extricate the cavalry, provided it could be done without compromising the action of the commanding general, but that I would not avail myself of a cessation of hostilities pending the existence of a flag of truce.[180]

Fitz Lee rode off the field with members of R. L. T. Beale's Virginia regiments. W. H. F. Lee rode back alone and passed Private Moffett who was still guarding the guns and prisoners his unit had captured earlier. The Private asked his commander where Beale's brigade was and W. H. F. Lee responded, "It was gone; you turn them fellows aloose and come with me." W. H. F. Lee continued to the rear and met with Generals R. E. Lee, Gordon, Pendleton, Pickett, and Longstreet.[181]

W. P. Roberts had been told to withdraw and leave the battlefield, but not much else. As he pulled back with his cavalrymen and was nearing the court house, he met Garnett of his staff and asked him if he had heard anything about a surrender. Garnett was surprised by the question and replied in the negative. Roberts informed Garnett that R. E. Lee was indeed going to surrender the army and he had "…just received orders to leave here and march to Buckingham Court House, where General Fitz Lee says the cavalry will rendezvous." However, Buckingham Court House was in the opposite direction of where the other Confederate cavalry units had gone — it was northeast of Appomattox.

William P. Roberts and Garnett took what was left of their small command (including cavalrymen from the 2nd North Carolina) and moved past the Appomattox Court House, a few hundred yard west of it. Then they went into a trot and reached a good road on which they headed for Buckingham. After going a short distance, they slowed to "a walk, a silent and solemn procession of about 100 men…." The 100 men Garnett referred to probably included some cavalrymen from each of the 1st, 2nd, 3rd, 4th, and 7th North Carolina cavalries.

They had traveled a couple of miles when a member of Fitz Lee's staff overtook them and indicated Fitz Lee wanted them to stop and wait for him to arrive. The cavalrymen were placed in line along the side of the road to wait. When Fitz Lee came into sight, Roberts rode out to meet him. In a matter of minutes, Roberts returned and told Garnett to disband the command. Garnett turned to the troopers and said: "Men, General Roberts says you can break ranks and disband. We bid you goodbye, and you may go back to North Carolina in any way you choose." After delivering his farewell, Garnett later wrote: "Unclasping my sabre from my belt, I threw it far from me, so as to let the men know that I, at least, considered the war at an end." Garnett went on to say, "In two minutes there was not a man to be seen, and General Roberts, his Adjutant-General [Garnett] and Courier Forbes were left there, the sole representatives of Roberts's cavalry brigade."[182] There were apparently no longer any pretenses of continuing the war contained in Fitz Lee's final instructions to the North Carolina cavalrymen.

Sending cavalrymen home rather than surrendering them at Appomattox was of mixed value. Those who rode away were able to take their broken down horses with them, and that was a certainty at the time and important to a cavalryman. On the negative side of such an exit is the fact that the North Carolinian cavalrymen who did not surrender at Appomattox Court House were considered prisoners of war if taken while heading home. However, most of the men made it to their homes and went in for their paroles at a later date with varying degrees of success.

There were 219 men from the 2nd North Carolina Cavalry who went in for paroles at other places and at later dates. Some men were already home when the truce was called at Appomattox Court House on April 9, 1865, but most were in route or scattered. Probably only a few from the 2nd Cavalry were among the 100 or so cavalrymen with Roberts and Garnett just after they left the battlefield.

Among those who did not wait for a parole at Appomattox Court House was Captain John P. Lockhart, the last commander of the 2nd North Carolina from March 31 until his departure which was sometime in the afternoon of April 9, 1865. He may have been one of the men with Roberts until the command was dispersed, or he may have left with others earlier. Whatever the case, he was paroled at Greensboro, North Carolina May 23, 1865.

Some of the men dispersed and sent home under instructions from Fitz Lee were not as lucky as those who stayed to surrender at Appomattox. Some men were captured after April 9 and placed in prison camps for weeks or months before being released. Several unfortunates were sent to places as distant as Ohio for imprisonment. For example: Claudius P. Erwin of company B, 2nd North Carolina Cavalry, was captured in Taylorsville, N.C. April 14, and then confined at Camp Chase, Ohio; Calvin M. Sharpe, also of company B was captured in Iredell Co., N.C. April 14 and also confined at Camp Chase, Ohio. Both Erwin and Sharpe were released June 13, 1865. J. R. Ponton of company F was captured in a Petersburg Hospital April 13 and sent to Camp Hamilton Prison (he was released on May 31); William H. Grant of company C was captured at Blacks & Whites, Virginia, April 17, 1865 and paroled. Most of the men in the 2nd North Carolina probably had experiences similar to the other cavalrymen from Barringer's former brigade. Of course, the men were near total exhaustion, but so were their means of escape — their horses. Joshua B. Hill was an Orderly Sergeant in the 3rd North Carolina Cavalry, and he observed, "A few had escaped; most of them had been taken, man by man, dismounted from horses which hunger, disease and wounds rendered incapable of supporting their starving but dauntless riders."[183]

At least two men of the 2nd North Carolina Cavalry were shot during the last day of their fighting. They were William H. Strayhorn of company K, wounded and sent to a Petersburg hospital April 9, 1865, and R. M. Brady of company B, wounded and sent to a Petersburg hospital April 11, 1865 — Brady was transferred to Point of Rocks, Virginia, where he died May 16, 1865. Perhaps he was the last cavalryman of the 2nd North Carolina to die as a direct result of the war.

It is probably not uncommon for men who for years had endured daily danger and deprivation in the pursuit of lofty principles associated with their right to secede, to suddenly begin thinking of down-to-earth, almost trivial issues — but it is always a little surprising when they manage to do so. For instance, leaving the battlefield for home with their horse was very important to most cavalrymen — even though most horses were well worn and barely able to make the journey, it was important. They could probably retain a little dignity in defeat if they arrived home as they left, a mounted cavalryman.

Indeed, this issue was not so trivial that it went unmentioned by their commanding generals. The positive element in Fitz Lee's decision to disperse his men rather than have them surrendered at Appomattox was to insure that the men did not lose their horses as part of the surrender package. A few days after the last battle, Fitz Lee acknowledged that one of the reason for dispersing his cavalrymen was based on the ownership of horses in any surrender. Because cavalrymen in the Army of Northern Virginia owned their own horses, and in most cases they would be essential for getting a crop in the ground once the men arrived home, Fitz Lee felt his men had a right to keep their own mounts and it was unlikely any terms of surrender would allow that. He certainly meant well, but he was wrong. Even though this was the positive element in Fitz Lee's decision to disperse his troopers, it was, as it turned out, not necessary. It was unnecessary because Robert E. Lee also felt that the ownership of horses was an important issue and mentioned it to Grant near the end of the surrender negotiations — Grant agreed to allow those men in the former Army of Northern Virginia to take their horses home with them.[184] Consequently, not much was actually gained by riding off the battlefield before the surrender, and some cavalrymen paid a high price — as hindsight makes clear.

William H. F. Lee's cavalry division surrendered only 298 men and officers at Appomattox Court House April 9. The distribution of these men among the brigades was as follows:[185]

Cavalrymen Surrendered at Appomattox from W. H. F. Lee's Division

	Officers	Men	Totals
W. H. F. Lee and staff	7	1	8
Barringer's brigade	2	21	23
Beale's brigade	22	152	174
Roberts's brigade	5	88	93
TOTALS	36	262	298

Most of the 23 men in Barringer's North Carolina brigade were probably cavalrymen without horses on wagon duty or among the wounded. There were eight men from the 1st North Carolina; seven men and two officers from the 2nd North Carolina Cavalry; one man from the 3rd North Carolina; and five men from the 5th North Carolina Cavalry among those paroled at Appomattox.[186]

Among the men surrendered and paroled at Appomattox Court House were nine cavalrymen from the 2nd North Carolina[187] (See following table).

Colonel James L. Gaines was in an ambulance without his newly amputated arm when he surrendered and was paroled (he had been wounded March 31 at Chamberlain's Run). The other cavalrymen paroled at Appomattox Court House were either taken within the 20 mile radius allowed by the Union commissioners or were troopers without serviceable horses at the time. Three generals from each army were appointed commissioners with the task of arranging the conditions of surrender. They decided that the surrender at Appomattox Court House applied to all Confederate troops within a 20 mile radius, except for cavalrymen who escaped before the surrender. The conditions for the capture or walk-ins of cavalrymen was to be decided on a case-by-case basis—which meant in many instances, arbitrarily. This approach explains why some 2nd North Carolina cavalrymen when captured were paroled, and others sent to prison.[188]

The war ended for those paroled at Appomattox April 9, 1865. For the men who were captured before April 9 and were on their way to or already in prison, the war would last longer. At least 76 men from the 2nd North Carolina Cavalry were in Federal prisons on April 9 in the following locations: 52 men at Point Lookout; 5 men at Fort Delaware; 6 at Elmira, N.Y.; and 13 men in other places.[189]

As this history is read, the battles fought and experiences endured by the men of the 2nd North Carolina Cavalry and cavalrymen like them are not forgotten.

2nd North Carolina Cavalry Men Surrendered at Appomattox Court House

Trooper	Co.	Fate
James L. Gaines	F&S	paroled April 9, 1865
Edward M. Jordon	F&S	paroled April 9, 1865
H. Reed	A	paroled April 9, 1865
W. P. White	A	paroled April 9, 1865
Joshua Melvin	D	paroled April 9, 1865
Ephraim Barnes	E	paroled April 9, 1865
I. B. Phatan	E	paroled April 9, 1865
John Dalrymple	I	paroled April 9, 1865
G. W. Stone	I	paroled April 9, 1865

The source used here is *North Carolina Troops 1861–1865, A Roster*, compiled by Louis H. Manarin (Raleigh, N.C., State Division of Archives and History), vol. II, Cavalry, pp. 104–177.

Appendix: Combat Losses in the 2nd North Carolina Cavalry[1]

• **Battle of New Bern.** Tully M. Forbes was mustered in as sergeant in Company C. He was captured near New Bern on March 14, and exchanged on August 5, 1862. In February 1863, Sergeant Forbes transferred to the 12th Battalion North Carolina Cavalry. Private Joseph J. Ellis was also captured in or near New Bern and exchanged on August 5, 1862. Private Ellis died of illness on April 12, 1864 at Bowling Green, Virginia. Private Nicholas J. Battle joined Company C when he was 31 years of age. He was captured at or near New Bern, and paroled by December 1862. He returned to fight with the regiment. Private Hiram Barber of Company I was also captured at or near New Bern and paroled soon afterwards. He also returned to fight with his regiment after his parole.

• **Mid-March to Mid-April.** Private Andrew N. Reid enlisted at the age of 18. Less than one year later, on March 30, 1862 he was killed in action while on picket near Deep Gully, North Carolina (about 8 miles west of New Bern, just north of the Trent River). The two cavalrymen mentioned in Lieutenant Lockhart's scouting report from Company C, were Private James H. Kelly who enlisted at the age of 21; his muster roll information states, "missing in skirmish, now on parole, being taken prisoner;" Private Kelly returned to service with the regiment; and Private Hugh Wilbur Collins who enlisted at the age of 22 and was captured along with Kelly; his muster information includes, "missing in skirmish, now on parole, being taken prisoner, absent on parole through December 1862." Private Collins returned to service with the regiment until September of 1863, when he transferred to the 13th Regiment Virginia Cavalry. Willie H. Perry was mustered in as a corporal at the age of 20. Corporal Perry was captured following the Battle of New Bern and his muster roll includes the following: "Prisoner of war. Died at Moorehead City April 16, 1862." Corporal Perry may have been on Lieutenant Lockhart's scout to Moorehead City around April 8, 1862, but there is no record of any cavalrymen from his Company E being on the scout. He was probably on a different mission that took him around 40 miles south of New Bern.

• **Gillett's Farm, April 13, 1862.** Lieutenant Colonel William G. Robinson was wounded and captured in a desperate attempt to salvage his operation with a charge into the rear of the farm house. He was imprisoned and later exchanged. On September 9, 1863, Robinson was promoted to colonel, to rank from July 23, 1863. He was officially dropped from the 2nd Cavalry on May 25, 1864, when the Secretary of War transferred him to the Navy Department. Private John A. Braddy enlisted at the age of 35. The notation in his record simply reads, "Killed in action at Gillett's Farm, Onslow County, April 13, 1862." Private Alexander C. McDougald was a carpenter before he enlisted at the age of 32. He was seriously wounded at Gillett's farm. He was finally discharged from the regiment on March 24, 1863 because of his wound. Private Love Melvin enlisted at the age 19. He was seriously wounded in the fight at Gillett's Farm and died eleven days later on April 24, 1862. Private Jesse R. E. Pittman enlisted at the age of 24. He was also seriously wounded at Gillett's Farm on April 13, 1862. On the muster roll for March–April 1863, he was still listed as "at home on sick furlough. Disabled by wounds." Private Pittman was finally admitted to a hospital in Richmond on May 6, 1864 with a gunshot wound in the arm and retired to the Invalid Corps on August 18, 1864 — the latter may not have been the same wound received at Gillett's Farm. Corporal John M. Gaster enlisted at the age of 31. He received a severe wound in his "shoulder joint at the Gillett fight." It was serious enough to have him discharged at Camp Johnson near Kinston on May 19, 1862. Josiah Turner, Jr. was captain of Company K, a rank he held through training camp. His record shows that he was wounded in the heart on April 13, 1862 at Gillett's Farm. His brigade commander, Robert Ransom, however, went on record stating that after the fight he personally examined the captain and found that all his injuries occurred from a fall from his horse. Perhaps the wound to his heart came from Ransom's public accusations. In any case, Captain Turner resigned on November 8, 1862. Private John H. Vanstory enlisted on February 22, 1862. The record states he was wounded while on picket duty on April 13, 1862 — if that is accurate, then he was not a part of the event at Gillett's Farm.

• **April 14–July 27, 1862.** Private H. Zimmerman enlisted at the age of 22. The records simply show he was "Killed in action at Tuscarora, N.C., April 14, 1862." Private Lambert P. Garrard enlisted at 22 years of age. He was "Injured by his horse falling in skirmish on April 15, 1862." Private Garrard returned to service with the regiment and fought with them until the retreat from Gettysburg nearly a year later. Private William B. Whitworth enlisted on June 17, 1861, and less than a year later, on April 17, 1862, was killed while on picket duty. Private John Taylor Cross enlisted at the age of 23 and was shot in the chest while fighting near Sawyer's

Mill. He and a handful of men from his Company C were surrounded and, along with his neighbor from Gates County, Lieutenant W. P. Roberts, had to fight their way through the Union encirclement. Private Cross was still listed as "Absent wounded" through February 1863. He returned to fight with the regiment for more than another two years. There is little available information on Private W. T. Brown except that he was "Captured at Williamsburg, Va., May 5, 1862" and exchanged on August 5, 1862. He was a member of Company A, one of the units unaccounted for during the May–June 1862 period. This suggests that his company may have been detached to the Williamsburg area for awhile in May of 1862. Sergeant Jesse A. Cahoon enlisted at the age of 23. After nearly three months of service he was captured on May 9 and was paroled and exchanged that same month. He returned to service with the 2nd Cavalry and was appointed corporal during September–October 1862, and then quickly promoted to sergeant during November–December of 1862. Sergeant Cahoon apparently showed great promise until he had had enough of the war and "deserted this company June 3, 1864." Private Joseph W. Tarkenton enlisted at the age of 18. He was also in Company G and captured in the same action as Sergeant Cahoon on May 9, 1862 — probably while on picket duty. Private Tarkenton was paroled the same day as was the sergeant from his company. He also returned to fight with his regiment. George Lee D. McLelland, Jr., enlisted at the age of 18. He was a private when he was captured on May 13, 1862 near Kinston while on picket duty. He was paroled and exchanged by the end of the month, and returned to duty — G. L. D. McLelland, Jr. was appointed Bugler during May–June 1863 and remained in that position. Private Beauford Rhea enlisted at the age of 24. Almost one year later, on May 15, 1862, he was killed in the desperate fight near Foscoe's Farm, when fewer than 50 men from the 2nd Cavalry handled four times that number of their enemy. Private William Henry Neal was already a farmer when at the age of 18 he enlisted on September 10, 1861. He was also lost in the fight at Foscoe's Farm — wounded and captured. Private Neal was exchanged in August of 1862 and finally discharged on December 11, 1862 because of "wounds received at Foscoe's, N.C., May 15, 1862." Private James J. McLean enlisted at the age of 36. He was captured in the fighting around Pollocksville on May 16, 1862, and paroled six days later. Private McLean returned to fight with his regiment. Private John F. Miller, also from Company B, enlisted at the age of 32. He was captured near Pollocksville during the fight of May 16, 1862 — he was also paroled six days later, and returned to fight with his unit another day. Private Jones S. Henderson enlisted at the age of 20. He was wounded in action at Pollocksville in May of 1862, and returned to his company to fight and get wounded again at a later date. Private John A. Battle enlisted at the age of 26, and was captured during a skirmish in May 1862 and paroled soon after. J. A. Battle returned to his regiment, only to die in a Richmond hospital from "Typhoid Pneumonia" on December 17, 1863. Three cavalrymen from Company K were captured while on picket duty May 26 and 27. Private Thomas Bunch was captured on July 26, 1862, and exchanged on October 6, 1862. The rest of Private Bunch's record reads as follows: "Sentenced to prison upon conviction of charge of desertion on January 27, 1864, and released under presidential pardon for volunteering in the Winter Legion for the defense of Richmond against the Sheridan Raid." Private Robert Samuel Walker enlisted on September 19, 1861, and was captured on July 26 and exchanged on October 6, 1862 along with Private Bunch. Private Walker returned to fight with his regiment. Private N. B. Dudley enlisted at the age of 23. His military career was short but not deadly. He was captured on July 27, 1862 and exchanged on October 6 of that year along with others from the company. Private Dudley, however, was discharged while he was a prisoner of war on July 31, 1862 for "Physical disability."

• **Bachelor's Creek, July 28, 1862.** Corporal Grier R. Black enlisted at the age of 21 — he was mustered in as a corporal. Corporal Black's record reads as follows: "Killed in action at Frenche's on Batchelor Creek, 13 miles from New Bern, N.C., July 28, 1862." Private John J. Harden enlisted at the age of 26. After his capture on July 28, 1862, he was confined until exchanged on October 6, 1862, after which he returned to fight with his regiment. Corporal Samuel A. Knox enlisted at the age of 18. After his capture, he was also exchanged on October 6, 1862. He had mustered in as a private, but was appointed corporal in March–April 1863. Privates Cornelius Medlock and James H. Puckett were captured together; they were also both exchanged on October 6, 1862. Private William F. Reid enlisted at the age of 19. He was captured and confined along with the others in Company B, and exchanged with them on October 6, 1862. Private W. F. Reid returned to fight with the regiment until he died in winter camp in Occupation, Essex County, Va. on January 27, 1863 of "pneumonia." Private William J. Reid was a farmer before he enlisted on June 18, 1861 at the age of 19. He was "Wounded in left arm above the elbow in the skirmish at Jerry French Place," near Bachelor Creek, N.C., July 28, 1862 and captured same day. Admitted to Federal hospital at New Bern, N.C., the same day and had his arm amputated. He was paroled October 8, 1862, and discharged on February 26, 1863 "by reason of disability." Edwin P. Rogers Sr. enlisted on June 18, 1861 when he gave his age as 24 (Edwin P. Rogers, Jr. enlisted on the same day, at the same place, for the same Company B, and gave his age as 18 — he was probably a nephew). Edwin Rogers Sr. mustered in as a private, and was captured along with the others in his company on July 28, 1862 and confined until exchanged on October 6, 1862. He was appointed blacksmith during March–April 1863, and remained with the regiment. Sergeant Marcus J. Shook enlisted at the age of 25 — he mustered in as sergeant. He was captured along with many of his men near Bachelor Creek and confined until released on October 6, 1862. He was promoted to 1st sergeant January–February 1863, and stayed with the regiment until the end. Private George C. White enlisted on February 20, 1862 at the age of 23. He was captured along with the others and exchanged with most of them on October 6, 1862 — Private White also returned to the regiment.

• **August 1862.** Privates Alexander Autry and John H. Hubbard both enlisted in June 1861 at the ages of 24 and 26 respectively and were captured on August 6, 1862. They were both exchanged two months later and returned to fight with their regiment to the end. Private George R. Britton enlisted at the age of 25. He was captured on August 6, 1862 and exchanged on October 6, 1862. He also returned to his regiment.

• **October 1862.** Private David Panther enlisted on

June 18, 1861 at the age of 18. He was one of the 13 men rejected by Colonel Laurence S. Baker of the 1st North Carolina on August 3, 1861, but he waited two months, then went to another county and reenlisted in Company A. Private Panther was wounded in early October 1862, and died in a Culpeper Court House hospital on October 13, 1862 from "gunshot wound and fever." Private Henry G. Thornell enlisted on June 4, 1861 at the age of 27. He was captured while on picket or patrol around Warrenton and was exchanged after a couple of weeks in confinement, on October 31, 1862. After his parole, he returned to fight with the regiment. Private Rufus Rentfrow enlisted on June 3, 1861 at the age of 23. He was captured on October 19, 1861, and exchanged on November 2, 1862. He also returned to fight with his regiment. Private Joseph C. Melton enlisted on June 22, 1861 at the age of 30. He was captured on October 21, 1862, and exchanged on November 2, 1862. Private Melton returned to his regiment for the remainder of the war.

• *November, 1862–April 27, 1863.* Private Henry Moore enlisted on November 10, 1861 at the age of 45. He was admitted to a hospital in Richmond on December 24, 1862 with a gunshot wound through his right foot. Private Moore returned to service and was transferred to the C. S. Navy on April 25, 1864. Three cavalrymen from the regiment were captured near Dumfries while on Stuart's Christmas raid along the Union supply line. Private Hiram L. Leister was captured at Dumfries and confined at Old Capitol Prison until exchanged on March 29, 1863—he died at Jordon's Springs Hospital, near Winchester, Va. on July 8, 1863. Sergeant Joseph T. Summers enlisted on June 18, 1861 at the age of 27. He entered as a private, was appointed corporal early in 1862, and promoted to sergeant on December 1, 1862. Summers was also captured while on the Christmas raid to Dumfries. He was confined until exchanged on March 29, 1863, and soon returned to fight with his regiment. Private Robert F. Moore enlisted on February 21, 1862 at the age of 28. He was captured at Fairfax Court House, probably the furthest point reached by Stuart's raid, and confined until exchanged on March 29, 1863. Private Moore returned to fight with his regiment. Sergeant Robert C. Ozment was a brick mason when he enlisted on June 27, 1861 at 24. He was promoted to sergeant during March–April 1862. Sergeant Ozment was reported "wounded and at home on furlough" during May–June 1863; he may well have been wounded in April of that year. He was discharged on March 5, 1865 due to "a gunshot wound of the right femur fracturing the bone." Private M. S. Coffey was a farmer when he enlisted on August 10, 1861 at the age of 19. He was admitted to a hospital in Richmond on April 6, 1863 with a gunshot wound to the abdomen. He was later transferred to London, Tenn. on April 23, 1863, and was discharged on June 5, 1863 with an "abscess of the liver." Four cavalrymen were captured near Hazel River on April 15, 1863, as Hooker's Union cavalrymen made a last effort to salvage their raid across the Rappahannock River. Most if not all of the men from the 2nd North Carolina Cavalry who were captured that morning were among the dismounted men in rifle pits, left unsupported in front of the charging enemy cavalry. Private John Kelly enlisted on June 18, 1861 at 24. He was captured at Hazel Run, and exchanged before May 13, 1863—after which he returned to his regiment. Private John H. Rhea enlisted on June 18, 1861 at the age of 21. Private Rhea was captured at Willford's Ford on Hazel Run, confined and exchanged on May 13, 1863. He was on parole for six months. Robert H. Sumrow enlisted on June 18, 1861, and was mustered in as a corporal at the age of 27. He was reduced to private late in 1862. Private Sumrow was captured on the Hazel River, and exchanged on May 13, 1863 after which he returned to fight with his regiment. Private Archibald T. Clark enlisted on June 12, 1861 at 22. He was captured near Culpeper Court House on April 15 — probably after being pushed from the rifle pits on the Hazel River. Private Clark was exchanged on May 13, 1863, and returned to his regiment.

• *April 29–May 7, 1863.* Private James Easom enlisted on July 22, 1861 at the age of 22. He was in his enemy's path early on April 29 and was overrun and captured at that point. Private Easom was then exchanged on May 13, 1863, later to return to his regiment. Jacob Dale enlisted on June 1861 at the age of 37. He was captured, and exchanged on May 13, 1863—he returned to service with the regiment. Private William H. Wellington enlisted on June 8, 1861 at the age of 32. He was captured, confined, and exchanged May 13, 1863—he also returned to fight with his regiment. Private Jesse Simpson enlisted on June 6, 1861 at the age of 22. He too was captured and confined—he was exchanged on May 23, 1863. Private Simpson returned to his regiment, and was transferred to the 52nd Regiment N.C., Troops on December 7, 1864. Private James L. Drake enlisted on March 11, 1863 at the age of 22. He was only in the service about six weeks when he was captured, imprisoned, and then exchanged on May 13, 1861. He returned to the regiment, only to be admitted to a Petersburg hospital on July 8, 1864 with "dysenteria, acute." Private Drake was transferred to Weldon, N.C. on July 22, 1864, and died four days later of "diarrhea, chronic." Private James H. Cox enlisted on July 6, 1861 at the age of 25. He was captured, confined, and exchanged on May 13, 1863. He was back with his regiment in less than a month and joined them for the Gettysburg Campaign. Private Augustus Cullifer was 19 years of age when he enlisted on July 6, 1861. He went on to be captured, confined, and exchanged on May 13, 1863 — he also returned to the regiment. John A. P. Conoly enlisted on July 20,1861 at the age of 27. He mustered in as a private, but moved up in rank rapidly: he was appointed corporal in May 1862; promoted to sergeant in June 1862; elected 2nd lieutenant March 10, 1863. He was captured on April 30, 1863, confined at Old Capitol Prison, Washington, D.C. on May 18, and exchanged in June of 1863. Conoly returned to his company and was appointed 1st lieutenant on October 5, 1864, and then captain on March 21, 1865 to rank from September 27, 1864. Private Alexander Bedsole enlisted on June 21,1861 at the age of 19. He was captured on April 30, confined, and exchanged on May 23, 1863. Private Bedsole returned to his regiment in time to fight in the bloody battle at Upperville on June 21, 1863. Private Richard McGlogan enlisted on December 1, 1862 at the age of 46 as a substitute. The Federal Provost Marshal records indicate he was captured near Fredericksburg on April 30, and sent to Washington, D.C. on May 1, 1863. Thereafter he was listed as a deserter. Private Warren C. Moore enlisted on June 21, 1861 at the age of 41. He was captured near Fredericksburg, and exchanged on May 23, 1863. He returned to the regiment and was discharged on September 15, 1864. Private John W.

Simms enlisted on June 21, 1861 at the age of 18. He was captured on April 30, 1863, confined, and exchanged on May 23, 1863 — he returned to his regiment. William H. Warren enlisted on July 15, 1861 at the age of 20. He mustered in as a sergeant and was appointed 1st sergeant July–August 1862; he was an "O. Sergeant" during September–October 1862, and a private from November 1862 through October 1863; he was captured on April 30, 1863, and exchanged on May 23, 1863. He returned to his regiment and was appointed quartermaster sergeant July–August 1864. Private John W. Pritchard enlisted on July 6, 1861 at 30 years of age. He was captured near Fredericksburg, and exchanged on May 13, 1863. Private Pritchard returned to the regiment, but transferred to the 44th Regiment N.C. Troops on November 3, 1864. Private Ellas Williams enlisted on August 9, 1861 at 20 years of age. He was captured near Fredericksburg, confined, and exchanged on May 23, 1863. Private Williams returned to fight with his regiment another day. Private Yancy S. Corem enlisted on June 20, 1861. He was wounded and admitted to a hospital in Charlottesville on May 2 with a gunshot wound — he returned to duty with his regiment on June 25, 1863, and fought to the end. Thomas J. Mims enlisted on June 12, 1861 at the age of 46 as a farrier (responsible for shoeing horses), but was in the thick of the action on May 2 when he was captured by his enemy. He was confined and exchanged on May 23, 1863, then admitted to a Richmond hospital on June 8 with "rheumatism chronic," then furloughed for 30 days on September 28, 1863. By February 2, 1865 Thomas Mims' wife made a claim for the balance of his pay, which was due a deceased soldier. Private James Carter enlisted on August 14, 1861 at the age of 21. He was captured on May 3, 1863 near Fredericksburg, and exchanged on May 23 of that year. Private Carter returned to his regiment. Private William J. Davis enlisted on June 12, 1861 at the age of 24. He was captured near Fredericksburg, confined, and exchanged on May 23, 1863. He returned to fight with his regiment until he transferred to the 51st Regiment N.C. Troops on January 13, 1865. Private Neill A. Johnson enlisted on June 22, 1861 at the age of 22. He was also captured on May 3 near Fredericksburg, confined, and exchanged on May 23, 1863. He returned to the regiment. Private James F. Price enlisted on June 20, 1861 at the age of 22. He was captured near Fredericksburg, confined, and exchanged on May 23, 1863, after which he returned to his regiment. Private Hardy Burns enlisted on July 17, 1861 at the age of 23. He was captured on May 3, confined, and exchanged on May 23, 1863. He returned to fight with his regiment. Private Rufus J. Byrum enlisted on August 27, 1861 at the age of 21. He was captured along with the others near Fredericksburg, confined, and exchanged on May 23, 1863. Private Byrum returned to the 2nd North Carolina Cavalry, only to be killed in action a little more than a year later.

• *Second Squadron, August–September, 1862.* Private Henry T. Bowling enlisted on September 10, 1861. He was captured during the raid on Plymouth, N.C. on August 31, 1862. He was exchanged on October 6, 1862, and returned to service with the regiment. William Henry Brothers enlisted on June 17, 1861. He was wounded in the fight at Washington, N.C. on September 6, 1862. He returned to duty and was appointed corporal in May–June 1863. John G. Boothe at the age of 38 was appointed captain of Company C when the unit was formed. Captain Boothe resigned on May 1, 1863 because of "aneurism of the sub-clavian artery resulting from a wound received in the service." Private John Gray enlisted on September 11, 1861 at the age of 20. Five days short of one year later, he was killed in the fighting at Washington, North Carolina. Private Levi S. Walker enlisted on September 16, 1861. He was captured during the fight at Washington, and exchanged on October 6, 1862 after which he returned to service.

• *Second Squadron, October 1862–Mid-May 1863.* Private James F. M. Terry enlisted on September 10, 1861. He was captured near Suffolk sometime around April 9 and exchanged during May–June 1863. Private Terry returned to fight with his regiment. Private Barzelia B. Wendley enlisted on January 1, 1862 and was also captured near Suffolk, Virginia, on the same day. He was exchanged at some unknown date and returned to fight with the regiment.

• *Brandy Station, June 9, 1863.* Colonel Solomon Williams was a West Point graduate and became a captain in the U.S. Army before resigning his commission to return to North Carolina at the outbreak of war in 1861. He commanded infantry until he took command of the 2nd Cavalry. While Williams and his command was in northern Virginia, he was married to the daughter of a captain in the Confederate Navy. About two weeks later he was killed in the Battle of Brandy Station. Corporal John O. Brown enlisted on June 18, 1861 at the age of 23. He was mustered in as a private and appointed corporal just five months later. Corporal Brown was killed in action near Brandy Station on June 9, 1863. Private William E. Foster enlisted in Company I on September 4, 1861 at the age of 24 and transferred to Company A on January 1, 1863. He was captured near Beverly Ford on June 9, 1863, and confined at Old Capitol Prison in Washington, D.C. until paroled and exchanged on June 30, 1863. Private Foster was received by the Provost Marshal General in Washington, D.C. on March 1, 1864 as a "deserter." He took the Oath of Allegiance and was provided transportation to Philadelphia. Private Joseph Tucker enlisted on June 18, 1861 at the age of 27. He was captured near Beverly Ford on June 9 and confined at Point Lookout until exchanged on June 30, 1863 — he returned to fight with the regiment. Captain S. Jay Andrews was appointed 1st lieutenant at the age of 19 on June 21, 1861. He was promoted to captain from September 6, 1862. Captain Andrews was wounded near Brandy Station on June 9. His leg was amputated, and he retired to the Invalid Corps on September 14, 1864. Sergeant Joseph T. Summers enlisted on June 18, 1861 at the age of 27. He mustered in as private and was appointed corporal in January–February 1862, and promoted to Sergeant on December 1, 1862. Sergeant Summers was captured during a raid near Dumphries, Virginia, on November 28, 1862, and confined until paroled and exchanged on March 29, 1863. On June 9 in the Battle of Brandy Station, he was seriously wounded, and in April 1864 he was detailed as a nurse, then retired to the Invalid Corps on January 9, 1865 — at that time, he was assigned to the post surgeon in Raleigh. Edward M. Jordon transferred from the infantry to the 2nd Cavalry on August 12, 1861 as a private. He was detailed as regimental quartermaster sergeant in September–October 1862, and as sergeant-major in March–April 1863. Jordon was wounded in action at Brandy Station and admitted to a hospital in Richmond on June 21 and furloughed for 35 days on June 25, 1863. He was elected 2nd lieutenant on December 15, 1863 and was transferred to the regiment's Field and Staff as adjutant with the rank of 1st lieutenant on August 3, 1864. Lieutenant Jordon remained with the 2nd Cavalry and was one of a handful who was paroled at Appomattox Court House on April 9, 1865. Private John F. Haslett transferred to the 2nd Cavalry from the infantry on September 16, 1862. He was wounded in action at Brandy Station, and in July 1863 he was furloughed from a Charlottesville, Virginia, hospital for 40 days. He was last mentioned in the September–October 1863 muster roll as "absent without leave" (keep in mind there are few muster roll records after September 1864). David Elbert Riddick transferred to the 2nd Cavalry from the infantry on September 1, 1862. He was appointed Corporal in May–June 1863. Riddick was captured near Beverly Ford on June 9, 1863 and exchanged on June 30. He was promoted to sergeant in September 1864, and to 2nd lieutenant on January 8, 1865 to rank from June 3, 1864. Riddick remained with the regiment and was on leave during most of February 1865. Private Orange Roundtree was born in Gates County and enlisted there on June 17, 1861 at the age of 19. He was seriously wounded near Brandy Station on June 9, 1863 and died of his wounds in a Richmond hospital on August 3, 1863. Sergeant John G. Overby enlisted on June 29, 1861 as a private. He was appointed sergeant in January–February 1862. He was wounded and transported along with Joseph T. Summers to a hospital in Gordonsville (see the note for the table above). There was no record of his wound or being taken to the hospital in the company muster roll which simply listed Sergeant Overby as "absent without leave since February 15, 1864. Dropped since August 30, 1864." Private John W. Gordon enlisted on March 20, 1863 in Virginia at the age of 17. Young Gordon was in the service less than three months when he was wounded and captured near Brandy Station. He was confined in a hospital in Washington, D.C. until transferred to Point Lookout.[2] Private Gordon was paroled and exchanged on March 6, 1864. When his parole was over, he left his home again on May 31, 1864 to join his comrades in the 2nd Cavalry. He left a short diary in which he recorded many of his observations from May 1864 through February 1865 — we will have the opportunity to visit his work on several occasions. Private Lucian Baggott enlisted on August 16, 1861 at the age of 23. He was wounded in the "upper part left thigh (flesh)" in action near Brandy Station on June 9, 1863, and was furloughed from a Richmond Hospital on June 18 for 30 days. He returned to fight with the regiment. Private William Gills enlisted on August 6, 1861 at the age of 26. He was captured near Beverly Ford on June 9, 1863 and exchanged at City Point on June 30. He was reported "absent sick" in October 1863. Private John W. King enlisted on July 16, 1861 when he was 28 years of age. He was captured near Beverly Ford on June 9, 1863. He was also paroled at City Point on June 30, 1863 — he returned to service with his regiment. Private Daniel W. Jones enlisted on June 18, 1861. He was wounded near Brandy Station. He was accounted for until he retired to the Invalid Corps on January 6, 1865. Captain Pinkney A. Tatum enlisted on June 17, 1861 and was mustered in as 1st sergeant. He was appointed 3rd lieutenant as of October 12, 1861, promoted to 1st lieutenant on December 1, 1862, and promoted to captain on May 11, 1863. Tatum was wounded on June 9, 1863, but remained with his company. James Jarvis enlisted on July 18, 1861 at the age of 21, and was mustered in as corporal — he was reduced to ranks in September–October 1862. He was wounded in action near Brandy Station on June 9, 1863 with a "gunshot wound of abdomen." Jarvis returned to fight with his regiment and was elected 3rd lieutenant on December 30, 1863 and promoted to 2nd lieutenant on September 13, 1863. Private Jones S. Henderson enlisted on July 15, 1861 at the age of 20. He had been wounded at Pollocksville, N.C. in May 1862 and was wounded again near Brandy Station on June 9, 1863. He transferred to the infantry on January 16, 1864 (the fate of many cavalrymen who could not replace their horses). Private Thomas Raleigh enlisted on April 30, 1863 at the age of 25. His comrades reported him "captured at Brandy Station, Va., 9 June," but no Federal records indicate his capture or imprisonment. For whatever reason, his military service lasted only about five weeks. Private James H. Bunch enlisted on July 6, 1861 at the age of 22. His record only indicates "Killed in action at Brandy Station, Va., June 9, 1863." Private James A. Buxton enlisted on January 1, 1863 at the age of 18. Six months later he was wounded in action near Brandy Station. He returned to fight with the regiment for the remainder of the war. John G. Blassingame was originally a 2nd lieutenant in the 1st North Carolina Cavalry, but resigned on October 1, 1861, and was elected 2nd lieutenant in Company I of the 2nd North Carolina Cavalry on April 4, 1862. He was detached to command Company F during the Battle of Brandy Station when he was mortally wounded — he died of his wounds June 11, 1863. Private William M. Dalrymple enlisted on June 12, 1861 at 24 years of age. He served as blacksmith from July through October 1862. He was captured near Beverly Ford on June 9, 1863, and paroled and exchanged at City Point on June 30, 1863. He returned to fight with the regiment. Private Alexander Lane Maness enlisted on August 27, 1861 at the age of 18. He was captured near Beverly Ford on June 9, 1863, and paroled and exchanged on June 30 of that year. Private Maness returned to fight with his regiment for the remainder of the war. Private Henderson Asbell enlisted on November 11, 1861. He was captured near Beverly Ford on June 9 and exchanged on June 30, 1863 — after which he returned to the regiment. Private James Asbell also enlisted on November 11, 1861. He was wounded in action near Brandy Station on June 9, 1863. He was still listed as "absent wounded" through October 1863. Corporal Henry J. Blalock enlisted on September 10, 1861 at the age of 18 and mustered in as private — he was appointed corporal in March–April 1863. Henry Blalock was killed in action near Brandy Station on June 9, 1863. Private John W. Carden enlisted on September 11, 1861 at the age of 22. He was wounded near Brandy Station on June 9, 1863 and later returned to service with the regiment. Private Charles R. Wilson enlisted on February 9, 1863. He was wounded near Brandy Station on June 9, 1863 — his record thereafter reads, "discharged 1863 as mail contractor."

• *June 19–21, 1863.* Private James Blythe enlisted on July 16, 1861 at the age of 24. He was wounded in the head near Middleburg on June 19, and died of his wounds two days later. Private Simeon T. Benn enlisted on July 6, 1861 at the age of 21. He was wounded in action near Middleburg, and died of his wounds in Petersburg on June 30, 1863. Private Joseph Brady enlisted on July 6, 1861 when he was 27 years of age. He was killed in action near Middleburg. Private James H. Cox enlisted on July 6, 1861 at the age of 25. He had been captured near Fredericksburg on April 29, 1863 in the prelude to the Battle of Chancellorsville, and he was back with his regiment in less than a month after being paroled and exchanged. Private Cox was then wounded and captured near Middleburg on June 19, 1863. There is no date given for his exchange, but he was admitted to a Richmond hospital on October 24, 1863. His wound was described as "gunshot wound of left leg. Amputated." Private Cox received a 60 day furlough on November 3, 1863. Nicholas McGuire enlisted on June 18, 1861 at the age of 30 — he mustered in as private and was appointed farrier from June to October 1862. He was killed in action near Upperville on June 21, 1863. Private James M. Waugh turned 18 years of age and enlisted in the 2nd Cavalry on February 1, 1862. Private Waugh was killed in action near Upperville on June 21, 1863. Private Kenneth R. C. Britt enlisted on June 28, 1861 at the age of 18. He was wounded in action near Upperville on June 21, and returned to action with the regiment. Private William J. Holt enlisted on June 18, 1861 at the age of 22. He was detailed to the Ordinance Department, Kinston, North Carolina on March 20, 1862 through October 1862. Private Holt was wounded in action near Upperville, and stayed with the regiment — he was absent on detail with an unserviceable horse from August 1, 1863 through September 1864. Private Alexander Bedsole enlisted on June 21, 1861 when he was 19 years old. He had been captured near Fredericksburg on April 30; paroled and exchanged on May 23, 1863. He was back in action and wounded near Upperville on June 21 — he stayed with the regiment, and was employed on "extra duty as a shoemaker February 1–28, 1865." Private Thomas Carter enlisted on July 8, 1861 at the age of 23. He was wounded in action near Upperville and admitted to a hospital in Richmond. Private Carter was furloughed from the hospital on September 29, 1863 for 60 days. By April 1864, he was "detailed to light duty at Fayetteville, N.C." Private Neill J. Shaw enlisted on July 29, 1861 at the age of 28. He was wounded in action near Upperville on June 21, 1863, and remained with the regiment. Private Caleb G. Stephens enlisted on August 14, 1861 at the age of 24. He also was wounded near Upperville and remained with the 2nd Cavalry. Private Robert D. Allman enlisted on June 4, 1861 at the age of 22. He was wounded and captured near Upperville on June 21, 1863 — there are no records showing his parole or exchange. Lieutenant John W. Holden enlisted on June 22, 1861, and was mustered in as private. In December 1862 he was elected 3rd lieutenant, then promoted to 2nd lieutenant by February 10, 1863, and to 1st lieutenant on May 11, 1863. He was wounded on June 21, 1863 and admitted to a Richmond hospital with a gunshot wound, "fractured ulna of right arm." On July 21, 1863, he was furloughed for 60 days, and on December 12 of that year he submitted his resignation because "having been wounded ... so disabled as to render myself unable for military service." George Pettigrew Bryan was appointed 3rd lieutenant at the age of 22, to rank from September 30, 1861. He was promoted to 2nd lieutenant on August 30, 1862, and to 1st lieutenant on September 1, 1862. He was seriously wounded and captured in the fighting on Trappe Road on June 21, 1863. He was confined in the hospital at the Old Capitol Prison, and while being cared for there, he was visited by several prominent individuals who were friends of his father (see his letter from that place, transcribed on pages 144–145). Lieutenant Bryan was among the first prisoners to then be transferred to Point Lookout for confinement, and while there he was promoted to captain of Company G. He was paroled and exchanged on March 10, 1864. Private George Osborne enlisted on July 18, 1861 at the age of 38. He was killed in action near Upperville on June 21, 1863. Private Henry Junius Barham transferred to the 2nd Cavalry from the infantry in March–April 1863. He was captured near Upperville on June 21, and paroled and exchanged at City Point on June 30, 1863. Private Abner L. Hoggard enlisted on July 6, 1861 at the age of 26. He was wounded and captured in the fighting on Trappe Road on June 21, 1863, and confined in hospitals in Washington, D.C., and Baltimore until paroled and exchanged on August 24, 1863. He was back with his unit until July 26, 1864 when he was listed as "deserted to enemy," but Federal records do not show receiving a prisoner by that name in 1864. Private Hiram Lassiter enlisted on July 6, 1861 at the age of 21. He was killed in action near Upperville on June 21, 1863. Private William S. Moore enlisted at the 4th of July celebration in Bertie County in 1861 at the age of 20. He was killed in action near Upperville on June 21, 1863. Private Charles W. Smith enlisted on July 6, 1861 at the age of 19. He also was killed in action near Upperville on June 21, 1863. James A. Cole enlisted on July 15, 1861 at the age of 33. He was mustered in as sergeant and was appointed 2nd lieutenant on June 12, 1863. He was killed in action near Upperville just over one week later. Private Ninian W. Gray enlisted on December 20, 1862, and was wounded near Middleburg on June 17–18, 1863, or near Upperville on June 21 — probably the latter. In any case, he stayed with the regiment for the duration of the war. Private Charles Harris enlisted on September 10, 1861 at the age of 24. He was wounded in action near Upperville on June 21, 1863, but remained on duty. Private Edward G. Wyese enlisted on February 1, 1862. He was wounded in action near Upperville on June 21, 1863 and stayed with the regiment to fight one more year.

• **June 30, 1863.** Lieutenant Jacob E. Williams enlisted on June 18, 1861 at the age of 31. He was mustered in as 1st sergeant and elected 3rd lieutenant in November 1862. Williams was captured at Hanover and confined at Johnson's Island, Ohio, until he was transferred to City Point, Virginia, for exchange on February 24, 1865 (there is no record of the actual exchange). Sergeant George W. Sanderson enlisted on June 18, 1861 when he was 24 years old. He entered as a private and was appointed 1st sergeant in November 1862. He was captured at Hanover, and confined at Fort Delaware until transferred to Point Lookout on October 15, 1863. Sergeant Sanderson was exchanged February 18, 1865, and was still on parole when the war ended with his regiment. Private John B. Gordon enlisted on June 17, 1861 at the age of 21. He was mustered in as 1st sergeant, but took a reduced to ranks in May–June 1863. A few weeks later, he was killed in action at Hanover. Private Isaac Walters transferred to the 2nd North Carolina Cavalry from the infantry on September 16, 1862. He was captured at Hanover and confined at Point Lookout where he died on December 28, 1863 of "chronic diarrhea." Corporal John H. Hubbard enlisted on June 18, 1861 at the age of 26, with the rank of private. He was captured on August 6, 1862 and confined for two months before exchanged. A few months later, Hubbard was appointed corporal. Corporal Hubbard was captured again at Hanover and confined at Elmira, New York and exchanged on March 15, 1865 — too late to rejoin his regiment before the war's end. Prentice E. Tucke enlisted on June 10, 1861 at the age of 36. He mustered in as private and was elected 2nd lieutenant April 26, 1863. Tucke was captured at Hanover and confined at Johnson's Island, Ohio where he resigned on August 25, 1863. Because of his recent promotion, he simply had to state that he had no "intention to return to the service." He took the Oath of Allegiance on October 7, 1863. Private William Cane enlisted on January 1, 1863 in Essex County Virginia at the age of 35. Company muster rolls show Private Cane captured at Westminster, some 20 miles south of Hanover on June 30 — if that was the case, his horse may have given out and he became a straggler. On the other hand, Federal prisoner of war records show him captured at Hanover on June 29, 1863. (The dates and places are mixed, but close enough to list him here.) In any case, he was confined at Fort Delaware for the remainder of the war. Captain Miles L. Eure was appointed 2nd lieutenant, Company C at the age of 26. He transferred to Company G upon his appointment to captain July 1, 1862. Captain Eure submitted his resignation on June 23, 1863 due to his desire to "attend the session of the Legislature of N.C." While waiting for his resignation to be accepted, he remained with his unit and was captured at Hanover, and confined at Johnson's Island Ohio, until transferred to Point Lookout on February 20, 1865 for exchange (there is no record of the actual exchange). Artemas C. Harrell enlisted on September 8, 1861 at the age of 18. He was captured at Hanover on June 30, 1863, and exchanged August 1 of that same year. He returned to his regiment and was appointed sergeant a year later — then ordinance sergeant in September 1864. (Sergeant Harrell apparently harbored no ill feeling about his experience in Hanover, Pennsylvania, because after the war he settled in the state and raised his family there.) Private Henry A. Kerman enlisted on July 28, 1861 at the age of 23. He was among the captured at Hanover and confined at Point Lookout until exchanged on March 16, 1865 — it is unlikely he was able to rejoin the regiment after his parole and before they left for Appomattox. Private Ferney L. Roy enlisted on February 16, 1862 at the age of 20, and as a substitute for Archbell Bedford. Private Roy was captured at Hanover and confined at Fort Delaware until exchanged on March 16, 1865 — again, too late to join up with the regiment before the end of the war. Corporal Isham P. Bennett enlisted on July 6, 1861 at the age of 27 and was mustered in as Private. He was captured at Hanover and confined until exchanged about one month later. Bennett was appointed corporal in July–August 1864 and remained with the regiment. Samuel N. Buxton enlisted on July 6, 1861 at the age of 20, and was mustered in as sergeant. He was elected 3rd lieutenant on July 10, 1862, and appointed 2nd lieutenant on June 11, 1863. A couple of weeks later, he was captured at Hanover, and confined at Fort Delaware until exchanged on March 20, 1864. While Buxton was in prison, he was promoted to captain as of November 29, 1863. Captain Buxton was reported as "absent on leave" in the December 31, 1864 inspection report, due to an illness he contracted while on prison — there is no record indicating he was able to return to service. Private John D. Edwards enlisted on July 6, 1861 at 19 years of age. He was captured on June 30, 1863, and confined at Fort Delaware until transferred to Point Lookout on October 18, 1863. He was paroled and exchanged on February 10, 1865. He was shown on the rolls of a detachment of paroled prisoners at Camp Lee, near Richmond on February 17, 1865 — he may have had the opportunity to rejoin the regiment for the last weeks of the war. Private James B. W. Foster enlisted on July 6, 1861 at the age of 59. He was captured at Hanover and confined at Fort Delaware where he died of "general debility" on August 26, 1863 (at 61 years of age) — he was buried in the National Cemetery in Salem, New Jersey. Private Joseph A. Garris enlisted on September 1, 1861 at the age of 23. He was captured in the Battle of Hanover and confined at Fort Delaware until transferred to Point Lookout prison on October 18, 1863. He was exchanged on September 22, 1864, and released from a Richmond hospital six days later. Private William R. Grant enlisted on July 6, 1861 when he was 23 years old. He was captured at Hanover the day after the battle, and confined at Fort Delaware until transferred to Point Lookout on October 18, 1863 where he died of "chronic diarrhea" on November 6, 1863. Private Isaac Peele enlisted on July 6, 1861 at the age of 26. He was captured while fighting in the streets of Hanover after being wounded and falling from his horse — he fractured his skull when he hit the pavement which was reported as his cause of death (see the discussion of his situation presented earlier in this section). Private William H. Sumner enlisted on July 6, 1861 at the age of 21. He was captured at Hanover and confined at Fort Delaware where he died on October 14, 1863 for unstated reasons — he was buried in Salem, New Jersey. Private Samuel P. Terry enlisted on February 24, 1862, and was wounded and captured at Hanover. Private Terry was confined in hospitals until paroled and exchanged on August 20, 1863 — he returned to service with the regiment. Sergeant Stephen O. Terry enlisted on September 10, 1861, was mustered in as private, and was appointed corporal on May 27, 1863. About one month later, he was captured at Hanover, and confined at Fort Delaware until transferred to Point Lookout on October 18, 1863. While in prison, he was promoted to sergeant — he was back with the regiment by late 1863. Private Robert Samuel Walker enlisted on September 19, 1861. He was captured while on picket duty just days before his company was transferred from Kinston to Hamilton, North Carolina on August 1, 1862. He was exchanged on October 6, 1862 and returned to his unit. He was wounded and captured at Hanover on June 30, 1863, and he was back with his company by August 1863 when he was listed "absent detailed to buy a horse." Private Robert Walker acquired his horse and returned to service with the regiment. Private Robert Young Walker enlisted on September 10, 1861. He was wounded and captured at Hanover and confined until paroled on August 23, 1863 at Baltimore, Maryland — after which, he returned to the regiment.

• *East Cavalry Field, Gettysburg, July 3, 1863.* Little is recorded for Private G. Manning except that he was captured near Gettysburg on July 3, 1863 and confined at Fort Delaware until transferred to Point Lookout on October 18, 1863. He was paroled and exchanged on May 8, 1864. Private William Lane was also captured near Gettysburg on July 3, 1863, and was confined at

Fort Delaware where he died for unstated reasons on February 3, 1864. Asa Rodgers enlisted on November 1, 1862 in Hertford County, North Carolina, while the regiment was up north defending the town of Warrenton, Virginia — he mustered in as a Bugler. He was captured at Gettysburg on July 3, 1863, and confined at Fort Delaware until paroled and exchanged on December 28, 1863, after which he returned to fight with the regiment as a private. Private Uriah R. Parrish enlisted on July 13, 1861 at the age of 23. He was wounded in action at Gettysburg on July 3 and placed in one of the regiment's ambulances among Imboden's wagon train the next day for the trip back to Virginia. (However, he was captured on July 5 when Imboden's train was attacked at Greencastle by Union cavalry.) Captain William Alexander Graham, Jr., was appointed 1st lieutenant in September 1861, to rank from August 30, 1861 at the age of 22. He was appointed captain on November 8, 1862, and was in command of the regiment's Second Squadron while on detached duty — including service under Longstreet during the Suffolk Campaign. He was wounded in action in East Cavalry Field on July 3, 1863. He submitted his resignation on November 20, 1863, and was appointed Assistant Adjutant General of North Carolina with the rank of major. Private J. M. Larner was captured at Gettysburg on July 3, 1863, and confined at Fort Delaware until paroled and exchanged on February 18, 1865 — he was probably unable to rejoin the regiment before the war in Virginia was over. Private L. H. Wyese enlisted on November 1, 1862, and was captured at Gettysburg on the 4th of July. No date for his exchange is given, but he was back with the regiment by August of 1864.

• *During the Retreat, July 4–13, 1863.* On July 7, Stuart had his cavalrymen pushing Buford's cavalry along Boonsboro road, and in the process, Private Drury W. Reardon was captured. He was confined at Point Lookout where he died of "chronic Diarrhea" on February 15, 1864. When Chambliss's command was holding the Confederate left, Meade made his move toward Hagerstown on July 12, 1863. The North Carolinians were in the front and were pushed through town by an overwhelming Union force — they lost the following two men during that action. Reuben Winbourn enlisted on June 15, 1861 at the age of 28. He was captured near Hagerstown when pushed through town on July 12. He was confined at Point Lookout until exchanged on March 20, 1864, after which he returned to the regiment. Private George H. Edwards enlisted on July 4, 1861 at the age of 24. He was captured near Hagerstown on July 12, 1863 and confined at Point Lookout for the remainder of the war — he was released on June 12, 1865. Private Lambert P. Garrand enlisted on September 10, 1861 at the age of 22. He was injured during a skirmish on April 15, 1862 and returned to service with the regiment. Then in one of the skirmishes on the Confederate left, he was killed at Hagerstown on July 8, 1863. The other seven men of the 2nd North Carolina who were lost during the retreat from Gettysburg were among the wounded or men without mounts traveling with Imboden's wagon train to Williamsport, or with the wagons forced to cross the Potomac at Falling Waters without cavalry support. When Imboden's train was hit on July 5 at Greencastle, two men from the regiment were taken by the enemy. Private James Potter had enlisted on July 6, 1861 at the age of 30. After his capture, he was confined at Fort Delaware until transferred to Point Lookout on October 18, 1863, where he died in the hospital on February 12, 1864 of "chronic diarrhea." Private Uriah R. Parrish was seriously wounded at East Cavalry Field on July 3, and captured on July 5 while being transported to the Potomac. Private Parrish died in a hospital in Gettysburg on August 30, 1863. The 2nd North Carolina lost one man at Williamsport while helping to defend Imboden's wagon train waiting for the opportunity to cross the river. He was Private Andrew P. York — he enlisted on August 13, 1862. He was wounded and then captured at Williamsport, from there he was admitted to a Federal hospital in Hagerstown in August of 1863. Four men from the regiment crossed the Potomac at Falling Waters with the wagon train. One was Private David C. Harvell who enlisted on June 18, 1861 at the age of 23. He was wounded during the Gettysburg Campaign and admitted to a Richmond hospital on July 16, 1863 with a gunshot wound to his left arm. He returned to duty on August 4, until he was captured in South Carolina on May 24, 1865. Private Henry G. Thornell enlisted early at the age of 27. He was captured back on October 17, 1862 while on duty in Warrenton, and exchanged a couple of weeks later. He was captured again near Falling Waters on July 14, 1863 and confined at Point Lookout until exchanged on May 3, 1864 — after which he returned to the regiment. Private Spencer R. Chaplin enlisted on July 27, 1861. He was also captured at Falling Waters on July 14. He was released after taking the Oath of Allegiance to the U.S. in Washington on December 15, 1863. Private William Burns enlisted on July 17, 1861 at the age of 28. He was captured at Falling Waters on July 14, 1863 and confined at Point Lookout until released for exchange on March 17, 1864.

• *From the Potomac to the Rappahannock, July 1863.* Private William H. Wellington enlisted on June 8, 1861 at the age of 32. He was captured near Fredericksburg on April 29, 1863 and exchanged on May 13. Private Wellington was then wounded near Shepherdstown on July 17 — he returned to action, but his wounds combined with new ones resulted in his retirement to the Invalid Corps in January of 1865. Private George C. Dunn enlisted on September 10, 1861 at the age of 20. He was wounded around Leetown soon after the regiment was back across the Potomac. He returned to service before September 1864. In a skirmish with Union forces on July 30, three men from the regiment were wounded and captured. Private Robert H. Morrison enlisted on June 18, 1861 at 41 years of age. He was captured on the 30th and sent to a Federal hospital in Winchester. There is no date for his parole or exchange, but he appeared in a Confederate hospital in Richmond by the end of August, and returned to duty later. Private Richard H. Barnes enlisted on June 15, 1861 at the age of 24. He was also captured and sent back to a Federal hospital in Winchester — there is no record of his parole or exchange, but his company muster roll indicates he had died by September of 1863. The third cavalryman captured on July 30 and sent back to a hospital in Winchester was William O'Quinn. He enlisted on July 22, 1861 at the age of 26. He was exchanged by September 7, and retired to the Invalid Corps on September 28, 1864.

• *August–September 16, 1863.* Private George R. Britton enlisted on June 10, 1861 at the age of 25. He was captured on August 6, 1862, and exchanged two months later. Private Britton was captured for a second time on

August 21, 1863 while on picket along the Rappahannock River — he was sent to Old Capital Prison in Washington, D.C. where he took the Oath of Allegiance to the U.S. on September 26, 1863, and was sent to Philadelphia. Private John Lomis was captured along with many others in his brigade during the fighting near Culpeper on September 13. He was confined at Old Capital Prison in Washington, D.C. on October 19, 1863, and then transferred to Point Lookout, Maryland prison on October 27 of that year. Nothing more was heard of him. James M. Gordon enlisted on September 19, 1861 at the age of 24. He mustered in as private and was appointed corporal on June 14, 1863. Corporal Gordon was captured during the Union army's occupation of Culpeper Court House on September 16, confined at Point Lookout until transferred to Elmira, N.Y., on August 16, 1864. He died there October 25, 1864 of "chronic diarrhea." Young Corporal Commodore G. Muse enlisted on September 9, 1861 at the age of 18. He also mustered in as a private and was appointed corporal on June 4, 1863. He was also captured near Culpeper Court House on September 16, and confined at Elmira, N.Y. where he died of "variola" on May 11, 1865 — about one month after his army surrendered.

• *Jack's Shop, September 22, 1863.* Private William B. McCabe enlisted on January 8, 1862 as a substitute for Cullen Askew. He served well and was killed in action at Jack's Shop on September 22, 1863. Private Jonathan Carter enlisted on August 12, 1861 at the age of 16. Nearly two years later, he was captured while fighting at Jack's Shop, and confined at Elmira, New York until released for exchange on March 10, 1865 — it is not likely he had time to rejoin the regiment before the war ended. Corporal Neill A. Wilks enlisted on August 1, 1861 at 20 years of age. He mustered in as private and was appointed corporal on April 1, 1863. Corporal Wilks was wounded in the fight at Jack's Shop and died of his wounds two days later. Private Lawson Campbell enlisted on June 4, 1861 at 38 years of age. He was captured on September 22, 1863 and confined at Point Lookout until exchanged on April 27, 1864 — after which he returned to service with the regiment. Private Robert H. Haybarger enlisted on June 10, 1861 at the age of 31. He was seriously wounded at Jack's Shop, and died of his wounds on October 1, 1863. Pinkney A. Tatum enlisted on June 17, 1861 and was mustered in as 1st sergeant. He was then appointed 3rd lieutenant as of October 12, 1861 and promoted to 1st lieutenant two months later. He was promoted to captain on May 11, 1863. Captain Tatum was captured near Madison Court House on September 22, 1963 and confined at Fort Delaware and Johnson's Island, Ohio until June 7, 1865. Private Joseph G. Liscomb enlisted on July 6, 1861 at the age of 26. He was captured near Madison Court House on September 22, 1863 and confined at Point Lookout until exchanged on February 24, 1865. Private Jacob A. Matthews enlisted on March 1, 1862 at the age of 24. He was wounded and captured at Jack's Shop and then confined in a hospital in Washington, D.C. where he lost a foot, before being transferred to Point Lookout on February 4, 1864 and exchanged on April 30, 1864. He then received a 30 day leave from a hospital in Richmond on May 6, 1864. Private H. E. Taylor traveled from Northampton County, North Carolina to enlist in Culpeper County, Virginia, on November 1, 1862 — at the age of 22. He was captured at Madison Court House on September 22, 1863 and confined at Point Lookout where he died on June 22, 1864. Private Benjamin Joshua Vincent transferred from the Virginia infantry on August 18, 1863. About one month later, he was captured near Madison Court House and confined at Elmira, N.Y., until released on June 15, 1865. Private Joseph H. Wheeler enlisted on July 6, 1861 at the age of 33. He was captured near Madison Court House while fighting on September 22, 1863. Private Wheeler was first confined at Point Lookout and then transferred to Elmira, N.Y., on August 16, 1864 where he remained until exchanged on March 15, 1865 — he was then admitted to a hospital in Richmond until March 21 when he received a 30 day furlough which turned out to be for the duration of the war. Private Joseph H. Dixon enlisted on August 17, 1861 at the age of 22. He was killed in action at Jack's Shop on September 22, 1863. Private Henry T. Bowling enlisted on September 10, 1861. He was captured in the raid on Plymouth, North Carolina on August 31, 1862 and confined for just over one month. A little more than a year later, he was wounded in the fighting at Jack's Shop and furloughed for 60 days on December 9, 1863 — then because of his wounds, he was retired to the Invalid Corps on January 6, 1865 — he served in Confederate hospitals until the end of the war.

• *Cavalry Bristoe Campaign, October 8–20, 1863.* Private William A. Luckey Sr. enlisted on June 18, 1861. He was listed among those discharged during training camp on August 18, 1861, but he must have returned — because he was again listed among the wounded taken to the hospital on October 10, 1863. Private Charles J. Saunders enlisted on June 14, 1861 at the age of 28. He was wounded at Culpeper Court House on October 11, 1863 but was back fighting with the regiment at the beginning of the Spring 1864 campaign. John C. Baker enlisted on July 12, 1861 at the age of 20. He mustered in as sergeant, and was reduced to corporal in November–December of that year. By the end of the following year, he was promoted to sergeant, and to 2nd lieutenant June 21, 1863. Lieutenant Baker was mortally wounded at Culpeper Court House and died from those wounds on November 11, 1863. Private James S. Ozment enlisted on June 17, 1861. He was captured near Winchester, Virginia, on October 12–13, 1863 and confined at Point Lookout until exchanged on February 13, 1865. Edwin D. Parker was a musician who enlisted on June 10, 1861 at the age of 36. He transferred to the Field and Staff of the regiment as chief bugler in March–April 1862. He was captured at Warrenton, Virginia, on October 14, 1863 and confined at Point Lookout — there is no record of his release. Private James H. White enlisted on May 15, 1863 at the age of 18. Five months later, on October 14, he was captured near Catlett's Station and confined at Point Lookout until exchanged on March 5, 1865. Private John M. Saunders enlisted on June 18, 1861 at the age of 33. He was admitted to a hospital in Richmond with a gunshot wound to his left side on October 19, 1863. On November 6, 1863 he was given a 30-day furlough, after which he returned to the regiment. Private John Tilley enlisted on February 4, 1862 along with Henry Tilley, his brother or cousin — there were already four other Tilley men in Company K from Orange County when they enlisted. John Tilley was wounded in action at Buckland on October 19, 1863, died from his wounds five days later (four of the six Tilley men in Company K survived the war). Private Jesse M. Walker enlisted on June 18, 1861 at the age of 23. He mustered in as private and was appointed sergeant on October 27, 1861 (just as they concluded training camp). He was reduced in rank to private a couple of months later. Private Walker was slightly wounded in the Bristoe Campaign in October, 1863 but stayed with the regiment. Sergeant Charles W. Small started the war in the 17th Regiment North Carolina Troops and re-enlisted in the 2nd Cavalry on October 23, 1862. He mustered in as a private and was appointed sergeant in May–June 1863. He was wounded in the Bristoe Campaign in October 1–22, 1863 which resulted in the loss of his right arm — Sergeant Small retired to the Invalid Corps on November 4, 1864. Private James M. Winburn enlisted on July 10, 1861 at the age of 29. He was severely wounded in the Bristoe Campaign in October 1863, but made it back to North Carolina where he entered Federal lines at Washington and surrendered. He was returned to Fort Monroe, Virginia, on March 13, 1864 with the comment "Rebel deserter;" he took the Oath of Amnesty there on April 4, 1865 — just five days before the surrender at Appomattox Court House.

• *Mine Run Campaign, November 1863.* Benjamin O. Wade enlisted on August 20, 1863 at the age of 33. He was captured while on picket duty on the Robinson River, November 11, 1863 and confined at Point Lookout until exchanged on September 18, 1864 — he was then given a "sick furlough." John W. Rogers enlisted on April 26, 1862 and was captured on the Rapidan River on November 26, 1863. He was confined at Point Lookout where he died on June 2, 1864 — no cause of death was given. Private John A. Parker enlisted on September 6, 1861. He was captured while scouting the enemy line at Mine Run on November 28, 1863 and confined at Point Lookout until exchanged on February 24, 1865 — Private Parker was admitted to a Richmond hospital with "bronchitis" on March 5, and given a 60 day furlough on March 16, 1865 (thus he missed the Appomattox Campaign in late March and early April of that year). Nicholas J. Harrell enlisted on August 5, 1861 at the age of 24. He mustered in as private, was appointed corporal in January–February, 1862, and promoted to sergeant in March–April 1863. Sergeant Harrell was wounded in the dismounted charge made by the regiment near Parker's Store on November 29, and was sent to a hospital at Camp Winder, near Richmond, until released in late December 1863 — after which he returned to the regiment. Randall H. Reese enlisted on July 6, 1861 at the age of 24. He mustered in as sergeant, was elected 3rd lieutenant on January 1, 1862, was promoted to 2nd lieutenant on July 10, 1862, then to 1st lieutenant on October 1, 1862, and then promoted to captain on June 11, 1863. A little more than five months later, he was killed in the dismounted charge at Mine Run.[3] Virginius Copeland started the war in the 15th Regiment North Carolina Troops, and transferred to the 2nd Cavalry on February 2, 1863 as a private. He was appointed 2nd lieutenant on April 1, 1863, and promoted to 1st lieutenant on November 29, 1863. On the day of his last promotion he was wounded and sent to a hospital in Charlottesville where he died of his wounds on December 6, 1863. Private Michael McGuire enlisted on August 10, 1861 at the age of 23. He was wounded at Mine Run and admitted to a Charlottesville hospital on December 2, 1863 with a gunshot wound — he died there on January 7, 1864. Felix E. Woodward enlisted on June 3, 1861 at the age of 21. He mustered in as corporal and was promoted to sergeant in May–June 1862. Sergeant Woodward was captured on November 30 at Mine Run and confined at Point Lookout until exchanged on March 10, 1864 — after which he returned to the regiment.

• *December 1863–April 1864.* Private Alberter B. Dale enlisted on June 18, 1861 at the age of 20. He took a gunshot wound in the shoulder and was admitted to a Richmond hospital on January 30, 1864 — he later returned to active duty. Private James Newell enlisted on June 26, 1861. He was captured on the Rapidan River on February 26, 1864 and confined at Fort Delaware until June 19, 1865. Private Alexander Lane Maness enlisted on August 27, 1861 at 18 years of age. He was captured at Beverly Ford on June 9, 1863 and exchanged on June 30 of that year. Then he was captured on the Rapidan on February 7, 1864 and confined until May 3, 1865. Asa Williams enlisted on July 17, 1861 at the age of 23. He mustered in as corporal and was reduced in ranks November–December 1861. He was captured on the Rapidan on February 7, 1864 and confined at Old Capitol Prison in Washington, D.C. until he died of "Typhoid fever" on March 20, 1864. Private Elias Williams enlisted on August 9, 1961 at the age of 20. He was captured near Fredericksburg on April 30, 1863 and exchanged on May 23, 1863. He was captured a second time on the Rapidan February 7, 1864, and confined at Fort Delaware until exchanged on September 30, 1864. Private Thomas R. Manchester enlisted on June 18, 1861 when he was only 18 years of age. He was captured in Cherokee County, North Carolina (probably on a horse detail) on February 18, 1864 and confined at Louisville, Kentucky until transferred to Fort Delaware on February 29. Private Manchester died of a "punctured wound" in Fort Delaware on January 22, 1865. Private Kenneth R. C. Britt enlisted on June 28, 1861 at the age of 18. He was apparently a scrappy young man who managed to be where the action was twice too often. He was wounded in the action on Trappe Road near Upperville on June 21, 1863 and then again on April 28, 1864 when he was wounded in the left hip — he nonetheless returned to service with the regiment before September of 1864.

• *Battle of the Wilderness.* Private Jesse R. E. Pittman enlisted on June 10, 1861 at the age of 24. He was wounded in action on April 13, 1862 and returned to the regiment. Private Pittman was wounded for a second time and entered a hospital in Richmond with a severe gunshot wound to his arm — he was retired to the Invalid Corps on August 18, 1864. Private Charles J. Saunders enlisted on June 14, 1861 at the age of 28. He was wounded on October 11, 1863, and then again when he took a shell fragment in his arm and was admitted to a Richmond hospital on May 6, 1864 — he was retired to the Invalid Corps on November 14, 1864 and thereafter pulled light guard duty. First Lieutenant Romulus W. Saunders worked his way up from private. He was wounded in the thigh and sent to a hospital in Danville on May 6, 1864. Saunders was furloughed on May 24, and resigned from the 2nd North Carolina Cavalry on September 22 of that year. At that time he was conscripted into the infantry — by December of 1864 he was assigned to the 52nd Regiment N.C. Troops.

• *May 7–11, 1864.* Private A. H. Martin enlisted on October 23, 1862 at the age of 25. He was killed in action near White Hall on Catharpin Road May 8, 1864 — the day before the regiment moved with the North Carolina Brigade to help Stuart track Sheridan's move toward Richmond. Sergeant Samuel Bryson enlisted on June 18, 1861 at the age of 37. He mustered in as a private and was appointed sergeant on June 1, 1862. He was captured near Spotsylvania Court House on May 9, as the regiment moved south from Catharpin Road to join Stuart's pursuit of Sheridan. He was confined at Elmira, New York until June 20, 1865 — he was released after taking the Oath of Allegiance. Second Lieutenant William H. Ivey enlisted on July 3, 1861. He mustered in as a private and was appointed corporal in March–April 1862, and was promoted to quartermaster sergeant in May–June 1862, and then elected 2nd lieutenant on December 1, 1863. He was captured near the Wilderness, probably near Catharpin Road, just after the main body of the regiment had moved to join Stuart's column. He was confined at Fort Delaware until transferred to Hilton Head, S.C. on August 20, 1864; he remained there until March 12, 1865 when he was returned to Fort Delaware — he was confined there until he took the Oath of Allegiance on June 16, 1865. The regiment's adjutant, Lieutenant Shubal G. Worth was appointed 1st lieutenant on November 27, 1863 and was killed while leading men of the 2nd North Carolina in one of the charges made into Sheridan's rear guard while pursuing them to the South Anna River — he was asked to take some men and charge a Union battery, which he attempted unsuccessfully. Private Jesse V. Roberts transferred into the 2nd Cavalry from the infantry on September 29, 1863. He was "slightly wounded in the left side, the ball passing through his cartridge box, thus saving his life." Private Roberts remained with the regiment. Private Willie P. Tilley enlisted on July 8, 1862 at the age of 27. He "was very slightly wounded in the hand" while the regiment was in pursuit of Sheridan's cavalry. Private Tilley remained with his unit.

• *May 16–24, 1864.* Private John Batts enlisted on February 16, 1864 and three months later was admitted to a hospital in Richmond with a gunshot wound in his ankle — on June 3, 1864 he received a 60 day furlough and later returned to service. Private H. H. Ashbrook was hospitalized for illness in August 1862 and furloughed for 40 days in October of that year. He returned to service and was wounded by a shotgun blast and taken to a hospital in Richmond on May 17 where he died on June 13, 1864. Private George D. Weatherly enlisted on June 26, 1863. He was admitted to a Richmond hospital with a gunshot wound on May 18 and was furloughed for 60 days on June 7, 1864. Private Weatherly was still "absent at home wounded" in September, but returned and fought again with the regiment. Private Justin E. Best enlisted on February 14, 1863 at the age of 36. He was also hit by a shotgun blast and admitted to a hospital in Richmond on May 18, 1864. He received a 60 day furlough on June 10, then returned to service with the regiment. Private George McClintock enlisted on March 5, 1864 and was admitted to a hospital in Danville with a gunshot wound to the shoulder a little more than two months later. He healed and returned to the regiment. Private Owen A. G. Wood enlisted on June 10, 1861. He was captured and imprisoned at Point Lookout, Maryland until he was exchanged at Venus Point, Savannah River, Georgia on November 15, 1864. He returned to service until the end of the war. Private Robert Samuel Walker had been captured on July 26, 1862 and exchanged in October of that year; he was wounded and captured at Hanover, Pennsylvania on June 30, 1863. He returned to the regiment by July 1863 and then went on a horse detail to find another horse. After he was remounted, he saw action until admitted to a Richmond hospital on May 22 with a gunshot from which he recovered and returned to service. Private James Thomas Armstrong enlisted on August 16, 1861 at the age of 19. He was captured at Wilson's Wharf on the James River and confined at Point Lookout, Maryland until paroled and exchanged on March 16, 1865 — he probably did not get back to the regiment in time to fight in the Appomattox Campaign. James R. Harris enlisted on September 10, 1861 at the age of 21. He mustered in as corporal and was promoted to sergeant in March 1862, and to 2nd lieutenant on September 1, 1863. He was wounded in action on May 24 and admitted to a hospital in Raleigh, N.C. on September 27, 1864 with a fractured hand from a gunshot wound.

• *May 27–June 1, 1864.* Private F. D. Abernathy enlisted on February 16, 1864 and was captured in the fighting around Hanover Junction on May 27. He was confined at Elmira, New York, where he died in prison from "chronic diarrhea" on August 6, 1864. Ephraim D. Robbins enlisted on June 22, 1861 at the age of 22. He mustered in as private, and was elected 3rd lieutenant in June of 1862, promoted to 2nd lieutenant in July of 1862, and to 1st lieutenant on September 19, 1863. He was captured near the Pamunkey River and confined at Fort Delaware until he took the Oath of Allegiance on June 16, 1865. Henderson B. Thomas enlisted on July 17, 1861 when he was 26 years old. He was mustered in as private and appointed corporal in May of 1862, promoted to sergeant in June of 1863 and elected 2nd lieutenant in October of 1863. He was captured near Hanover Court House and taken to Fort Delaware where he remained for the balance of the war — he took the oath on the same date as Robbins. Private William C. Hall enlisted on September 10, 1861 at 24 years of age. His horse was shot out from under him and he was captured near Hanover Court House and was confined at Elmira, New York until he died of "chronic diarrhea" on October 27, 1864. Robert W. Atkinson enlisted on June 10, 1861 at the age of 22. He entered as 3rd lieutenant, was promoted to 2nd lieutenant in June of 1862, and to 1st lieutenant in July of that year. Atkinson was captured near Fredericksburg on April 30, 1863 and paroled at Old Capitol Prison on May 18, 1863. He was captured for a second time at Hanover Court House — he is listed in the Roster of Troops as a captain but no date is given for his promotion to that rank. In any case, he was of some interest to his captors judging by the trouble they went to in finding the proper location for him. He was first sent to Point Lookout, Maryland; then to Washington, D.C. on July 16, 1864; from there he was sent to Fort Delaware on July 22, 1864; and on August 20, 1864 to Hilton Head, South Carolina. While at Hilton Head, Atkinson's name was included in a list of prisoners asking to take the Oath of Allegiance dated March 6, 1865. The entry includes the endorsement that "the above named prisoners to be turned over to the Provost Marshal General in New York City." Clearly, by that time many good men who had endured much, had had enough. Private George W. Johnson enlisted on July 6, 1861 at the age of 25. He was wounded in action near Ashland — it was serious enough to be recorded but apparently did not warrant sending him to Richmond for treatment. He stayed with the regiment to fight again. Private F. W. Sapp enlisted on March 18, 1864 and was captured near Hanover Court House about ten weeks later. Private Sapp was confined at Point Lookout, Maryland; from there he was taken to Elmira, New York on July 12, 1864. From there, he was being transported by train through Pennsylvania when the train crashed on July 15, 1864 — he was listed as "killed or missing" as a result of the accident.

• *Haw's Shop, June 3, 1864.* Private Radford Dishman had been fighting with the 2nd North Carolina Cavalry for just over two years when he was killed in action on June 3, 1864. Samuel A. Knox was with the regiment from its first days when he enlisted at the age of 18 — he was captured in July 1862 and exchanged in October 1862. Samuel was promoted to corporal in March of 1863, but his career ended when he was wounded on June 3, 1864 and admitted to a hospital at Danville the following day. He was furloughed June 7 and died of his wounds June 19, 1864. William P. Roberts began his military experience at the age of 19 when he helped form Company C. He was appointed 2nd lieutenant in training camp and had moved through the ranks to major by February of 1864. On June 3, he was leading one of several charges when he was "disabled by a wound in the head, but did not leave the field," and remained with the regiment. Private Liberty Chapman enlisted on July 15, 1862 at the age of 20. He was listed as captured near Gaines's Mill on June 3, 1864, and confined at Elmira, New York where he remained until he took the Oath of Allegiance on June 19, 1865. Private William H. Vaughn enlisted on June 8, 1861 at the age of 20. He was also taken at Gaines's Mill and sent on to Elmira where he was held until the end of the war. First lieutenant Joseph Baker started the war as a 2nd lieutenant at the age of 32 and ended it when he was killed in action during the fight near Haw's Shop — but the younger William P. Roberts later only recalled that he was "...either killed or captured, and his fate was never afterwards ascertained." John B. Person enlisted on July 6, 1861 at the age of 28. He mustered in as sergeant and was elected 2nd lieutenant in November of 1861. He was admitted to a hospital in Richmond on June 2, 1864 with "a gunshot wound to the pelvis." He was furloughed for 30 days on September 8, 1864 but was never able to return to the regiment. First Lieutenant Richard M. Allison began his military career as a 2nd lieutenant at the age of 40 and was promoted by September 1862. He was wounded and then admitted to a hospital in Richmond on June 4, 1864 with a gunshot wound to the left thigh. Allison was furloughed for 60 days on July 12, 1864 but was unable to return to service with the regiment. Hembree C. Ledford mustered in as private and was appointed sergeant around October 1863. He was admitted to a hospital in Richmond on June 4, 1864 with a gunshot wound in the arm — he was furloughed on July 18, 1864 and returned to service with the regiment. Andrew Jackson enlisted on September 11, 1862 at the age of 46 as a substitute for William J. Judd. He was captured near Gaines's Mill on June 3, 1864 and confined at Elmira, New York until exchanged in March 1865. On March 22, he was admitted to a hospital in Richmond with "debilitas" and furloughed for 30 days on March 28, 1865 — which lasted him through the end of the war.

• *June 10–16, 1864.* Private Edward W. Porter enlisted on July 2, 1861 at the age of 20. He was admitted to a Richmond hospital on June 13, 1864 with a gunshot wound, and furloughed on June 30 for 30 days. While on furlough, he was attached to the 2nd Battalion N.C. Local Defense Troops where he remained through 1864 — by January 1865 he was back with the 2nd North Carolina Cavalry. Sergeant Daniel R. McDonald entered service at age 29 with the rank of sergeant which he retained throughout the war. He was captured on June 14, 1864 in Bedford County, Virginia, about 20 miles west of Lynchburg (probably on a scouting mission along the Lynchburg & Petersburg Railroad). He was confined at Point Lookout, Maryland until exchanged around March 11, 1865.

• *Near Davis's Farm, June 21.* Private Robert J. Barkley of Iredell County enlisted in June 1861 at the age of 27. He was "killed in action, June 21, 1864." Private John Jones enlisted in June of 1861 at the age of 33 and was mortally wounded on June 21, 1864. He died three days later from the wounds he received during the fighting at Davis's Farm. Private Franklin F. Gurganus enlisted in July 1861 at the age of 22. He was wounded on June 21, and listed as "absent suffering from wound," in September 1864 — he was finally retired to the Invalid Corps on November 23, 1864. Captain John P. Lockhart wrote his mother about the capture of his brother, Corporal Levi Y. Lockhart and his comrade Private Jesse V. Roberts. John wrote, "He and Jesse Roberts were sent out to ascertain where the enemy was, near where the left of the 3rd N.C. Cav. was — and it had fallen back, and went up among the Yankees before they knew where they were." Levi Lockhart was paroled and exchanged on September 22, 1864; Jesse Roberts was confined at Point Lookout, Maryland until paroled and exchanged on March 14, 1865. Lieutenant Albert F. Faucett enlisted in September 1861 at the age of 24 and mustered in with the rank of sergeant. He was elected 3rd lieutenant March 10, 1862; appointed 2nd lieutenant on June 2, 1862; and promoted to 1st lieutenant on September 30, 1863. Lieutenant Faucett received a severe wound under his left arm from a minnie ball and was admitted to a Hospital in Petersburg; then he was finally retired to the Invalid Corps on February 14, 1865. Before Faucett left the field, however, he presented John and Levi Lockhart's younger brother, Gaston Lockhart, with his pistol for his gallantry on the field of battle that day. (Nineteen-year-old Gaston had enlisted less than three months before the fight at Davis's Farm.)[4]

• *Wilson-Kautz Railroad Raid.* Clinton M. Andrews, colonel of the regiment, was "wounded in the thigh and died from the effects of amputation."[5] Sergeant Charles H. Elder enlisted on June 8, 1861 at age 30. He was wounded in the thigh but remained in active service. Corporal John Scoggins, Jr. enlisted in July 1861 at the age of 23, and was appointed corporal on April 1, 1864. He was killed in action less than three months later. Sergeant William J. Hare enlisted in September of 1861 at the age of 27. He was appointed corporal in November–December 1862, and promoted to sergeant on April 1, 1864. Sergeant Hare was mortally wounded on June 23, and died from his wounds on June 27, 1864. Private Edward G. Wyese enlisted in February of 1862. He was wounded in the severe fighting around Upperville on June 21, 1863, but lived to fight again, until he was "shot through the head and instantly killed" in the action at Blacks and Whites. Private Willie P. Tilley enlisted in July 1862 at the age of 27. He was then killed in the skirmishing around Keysville late on June 24, when his North Carolina brigade caught up with Wilson's division.

• **Picketing and Scouting the Weldon Railroad.** Private Alexander T. Allen enlisted in June of 1861 and was captured near Petersburg on July 5, 1864. He was confined at Elmira, N.Y., where he died of "variola" February 1, 1865. Private M. M. Kibbler enlisted March 3, 1864 and died from gunshot wounds while in a Richmond Hospital on July 10, 1864. Private David H. Idol was captured near Washington, D.C. on July 13, 1864 and confined at Old Capitol Prison in Washington until transferred to Elmira, N.Y. July 23, 1864—he took the Oath and was released May 15, 1865. Sergeant Elijah Sheffield enlisted in August 1861 as a private at the age of 25. He was appointed sergeant on April 1, 1864. Sergeant Sheffield was admitted to a hospital at Danville with a gunshot wound in the right side, and was furloughed July 26, 1864—he retired to the Invalid Corps October 6, 1864. Private W. Eatmon had enlisted only five months prior to receiving a wound to the hand in July of 1864; he was retired to the Invalid Corps September 22, 1864. Second Lieutenant Nathaniel C. Tucker was severely wounded, and remained "absent at home wounded" through September 1864. Private William D. Dale was wounded in action but was listed as present for muster through September 1864 (the last record available). Corporal John E. McEwen was wounded in the leg but remained in the service. Private Milas Chauncey Jordon was wounded in the arm and was present for muster through September 1864. Private John J. Hardin had been captured during the battle at Bachelor's Creek in N.C. July 28, 1862 (the regiment lost nine other men there) and exchanged on October 6, 1862; and he was wounded in the foot between May and mid–July of 1864, but returned to active service. Private S. R. Moore had enlisted around three months before he was wounded in the leg and returned to active service until discharged in March 1865 for "disease of the kidneys" at 43 years of age. Private Nicholas J. Battle had been captured along with three other men from the regiment during their first battle at New Bern March 14, 1862 and later paroled; he was wounded in the leg between May and mid–July of 1864 and returned to active service. John Taylor Cross had been wounded at Sawyer's, N.C. in May of 1862 and returned to service; he was again severely wounded in the leg between May and mid–July of 1864, yet returned to active service. Private Henry Hofler was wounded in the foot, but returned to service through September 1864. Private Jesse C. Stone was wounded in the hand and remained with the regiment through September 1864. Private David Stafford was only in the military for around five months when he was severely wounded; he was transferred to the Invalid Corps on November 26, 1864. Private William S. Spruill transferred into the 2nd Cavalry in July 1864 from the 52nd North Carolina infantry and was wounded shortly thereafter; he was transferred back to his former regiment December of 1864. Private William Fuller was wounded and was present through September 1864. John W. Snell was wounded, yet remained with the regiment. Private William Garner received a "painful" wound, and remained with the regiment through September 1864. Private George W. Walker was wounded but was still with the regiment through September 1864.

• **North of the James in Mid-August, 1864.** Third Lieutenant Bartlett Y. Tyson was wounded near Deep Bottom on August 15 and admitted to a hospital in Richmond with a gunshot wound "through right leg injuring tibia;" he was retired to the Invalid Corps on March 13, 1865. Private Rufus J. Byrum was captured near Fredericksburg on May 3, 1863 and imprisoned until exchanged 20 days later; he was then killed near Deep Bottom on August 15, 1864. Private George W. Rowan was also killed in action during the fighting around Richmond on the 15th. Sergeant John J. Bryan was wounded in the right heel on August 15 and furloughed for 60 days from a Richmond hospital later in the month. Corporal Thomas Felton was wounded in the right hand—his middle finger was amputated and he returned to service. Private Thomas E. Reese was captured on August 15; there is no further military record of him. Private James G. Lowery was killed in the fighting around Richmond on August 16, 1864. Private Joseph Paschal was wounded in the right thigh and admitted to a Richmond hospital the next day—he was furloughed from the hospital for 60 days in early November 1864, and returned to the Invalid Corps February 22, 1865. Private John H. Steele was also wounded in the right thigh on the 16th, and admitted to a hospital in Richmond where he died from his wound on September 10, 1864. Captain Lewis R. Cowper was a personal friend of his colonel, W. P. Roberts; they shared a hometown, came up through the ranks together and respected one another to the end. Cowper was fifteen years older than his colonel, and indeed older than most of the men in Company C, yet he was admired by the youngest, John W. Gordon. Captain Cowper was wounded in action near White Oak Swamp on August 16 and admitted to a hospital in Richmond where he died from his wounds on September 6, 1864. Captain George Pettigrew Bryan was shot through the head, trampled by a horse, and captured on June 21, 1863 near Upperville; he survived, and then was imprisoned and exchanged on March 10, 1864 and returned to duty; he lived to be killed in action on August 16, 1864 near White Oak Swamp. Corporal Romulus S. Barham was wounded on the 16th near White's Tavern and admitted to a hospital in Richmond the following day with a gunshot wound to the "face, lower side, right jaw, passing out below left eye;" he was furloughed for 30 days on September 8, 1864. Private John Wesley Umstead enlisted for service in March 1864 and was admitted to a hospital in Richmond August 16 with a gunshot wound to his left hand; he returned to duty on the 27th of the month. Private James A. Holmes entered service as a corporal and was promoted to captain in February 1862—apparently rank did not interest him because he resigned his rank in January 1863; he was again a private when killed in action. Private John T. Meloney was wounded in the fighting around Richmond, and died from his wounds August 17, 1864. Private Charles Hofler was captured near Deep Bottom August 17, and confined at Point Lookout where he died October 15, 1864. Private Edward A. Sheaffer was also captured near Deep Bottom on August 17 and confined at Point Lookout until exchanged on March 17, 1865; he was admitted to a Richmond hospital on April 14, 1865 with "chronic rheumatism"—he was by then 40 years of age. Private Junius Henry Barham was wounded in the right thigh on the 18th near White's Tavern; he was admitted to a hospital in Richmond where his leg was amputated; he was furloughed from the hospital December 17, 1864. As indicated above, Junius' younger brother, Romulus, also of Company H, lost a portion of his face two days earlier fighting near the same tavern.

• *Near Poplar Spring Church, August 21, 1864.* Private Aurelius Scott enlisted on February 20, 1862 at the age of 19. He was admitted to a Petersburg hospital on August 21, 1864 with a gunshot wound to his right thigh and received a 40 day furlough on September 1 of that year, then returned to the regiment. Corporal William G. Warren enlisted in May of 1862 at the age of 34. He was appointed corporal in May–June 1863. Corporal Warren was admitted to a hospital in Petersburg on August 21, 1864 with a gunshot wound in his right hand. Three days later he was released and given a 30 day furlough. Private J. B. Eatmon enlisted on April 12, 1864 and was admitted to a Petersburg hospital on August 21 of that year with a gunshot wound to his right hand. Private Eatmon also received a 30 day furlough on August 24. Private John W. Snell enlisted in July 1861 at the age of 19. He was admitted to a Petersburg hospital on August 21 with a gunshot wound to his left thigh and was released with a 60 day furlough December 1, 1864. Private Thomas J. Harris received a gunshot wound to the hand and was sent to a hospital in Petersburg; he was furloughed for 30 days on August 24, 1864.

• *Battle at Reams's Station, August 25, 1864.* Private James W. Johnson enlisted in July 1861 at the age of 30. He was wounded in action at Reams's Station and admitted to a hospital in Raleigh August 28. He was released the following day and given a 60 day furlough. Private Henry I. Kimball enlisted in March 1862. His record only shows "absent in hospital. Wounded August 25, 1864." Private James A. Shuford enlisted in June 1861 at the age of 28. His muster records also simply state "absent in hospital. Wounded August 25, 1864." Private Joseph E. Harrell transferred into the 2nd Cavalry from the infantry on January 1, 1864. His record also simply shows "absent wounded in hospital since August 25, 1864."

• *September 1864.* Private James M. Shields enlisted in June 1861 at the age of 23. He was captured September 3 near Lee's Mill about 3 miles east of Reams's Station, east of the Jerusalem Plank Road on Warwick Swamp. Private Shields was confined at Point Lookout until he was paroled and exchanged on March 15, 1865 — it is doubtful he made it back to the regiment in time for the march to Appomattox Court House. Sergeant James L. Spruill enlisted in August 1861 as a private; he was a blacksmith by July–August 1862, appointed corporal by September–October 1862 and promoted to sergeant by March–April 1863. Sergeant Spruill died from wounds in a Richmond hospital September 7, 1864 — he was probably wounded in early September or late August. Private John J. Hardin enlisted in June of 1861 at the age of 26. He was captured on July 28, 1862 — nine other men from Company B were lost on that day. They were surprised by the enemy while out on picket duty near Bachelor's Creek, North Carolina. Private Hardin was confined until exchanged in Virginia on October 6, 1862. He returned to service with the regiment and was captured near Petersburg September 10, 1864. He was imprisoned at Point Lookout where he died of "pneumonia" on February 19, 1865. Private Vincent Barnes enlisted in July 1861 at the age of 36. He mustered in as a 1st Sergeant and was appointed sergeant major August 19, 1861. Soon after leaving training camp Barns was reduced to ranks. Private Barns was admitted to a hospital at Wilmington, North Carolina with gunshot wounds on September 12, 1864 — he was probably wounded a day or two earlier. He was back on duty with the regiment on November 9, 1864. Private J. R. Hood is a bit of a mystery; there are no records of his enlistment date or place; and after he was captured near Petersburg on September 17, 1864 and sent to City Point two days later, there is no record of his confinement or release. Captain James Neill Turner started the war with the Engineer Corps, in Company B of the 2nd North Carolina Cavalry as a 2nd lieutenant and became captain in Company D. Captain Turner led his men in the charge to the enemy line near Gravely Run on September 29, 1864 and drove them nearly two miles to the Wyatt farm where he was killed in action. Private Jacob Isley enlisted on March 3, 1864 and he was killed in action September 15 while the regiment was holding the line near Ebenezer Church allowing Hampton to escape with his cattle; or he was killed during the charge at Wyatt's farm on September 29, 1864 — unfortunately the records are not complete enough to be more precise. Private Willie G. Sharp enlisted in June of 1861 at the age of 19. He was listed as "absent wounded" in September of 1864 and was released from a hospital in Goldsboro, North Carolina October 13, 1864 and returned to duty. Lieutenant Nathaniel C. Tucker enlisted in June 1861 as a private. He was appointed corporal in March–April 1862, promoted to sergeant January–February 1863, and promoted to 2nd lieutenant to rank as of August 18, 1863. In September of 1864, Lieutenant Tucker was listed as "absent at home wounded." Private Joel B. Reid enlisted in Culpeper County, Virginia, on April 14, 1863 at the age of 17. He fought with the regiment through September of 1864 — at that time his muster card states "Killed his Yankee in their camp and fell himself."

• *October 1864.* Virgil and Hardy Burns both resided in Moore County when they enlisted on July 17, 1861 at the ages of 22 and 23, respectively. Private Hardy Burns was captured along with five other cavalrymen from the 2nd North Carolina at the Battle of Chancellorsville on May 3, 1863. He was exchanged May 23 and returned to the regiment. Private Virgil A. Burns was appointed blacksmith in November 1862. Virgil was reportedly captured October 11, 1864 near Bermuda Hundred. At that time the regiment was engaged in routine scouts and picketing; given the distance Private Burns was from his camp, he was probably on a scouting mission when captured. Hardy was also captured near the same place, but reportedly six days later, and presumably he was there on the same sort of business as Virgil. In any case, the records do not show a place of confinement, but they do show that both Hardy and Virgil took the Oath of Allegiance; and Hardy was provided transportation to Baltimore, Maryland, while Virgil was provided transportation to Grant County, Indiana. Amaziah M. Price was mustered in as a private and appointed bugler for Company A between July and October of 1862. Bugler Price was captured near Petersburg October 27, 1864 — the only other cavalryman from the regiment captured that day was an assistant surgeon. Amaziah was confined at Point Lookout until released June 16, 1865. Jared T. Childs transferred to the Field and Staff of the 2nd North Carolina Cavalry October 16, 1864 as an assistant surgeon. Less than two weeks later he was captured near Petersburg and confined at Fort

Delaware. He was transferred to Fort Monroe December 5, and released January 6, 1865.

• *December 1864.* Private Jonathan McClain (McClam) was captured December 1 while the regiment was sent to stop the raid on Stony Creek Depot and was confined at Point Lookout until released on June 29, 1865. Private George McClintock enlisted on the 5th of March 1864 as the Battle of the Wilderness got underway. He was with the regiment monitoring Sheridan's cavalry until the Union commander started his move north to rejoin Grant's army on May 18, 1864 — on that day, while monitoring the enemy cavalry too closely, George was wounded in the shoulder and sent to the hospital in Danville. He returned to service and was captured December 10, 1865 while pursuing the enemy cavalry as they pulled back from their raid on the Weldon Railroad. Private McClintock was confined at Point Lookout until June 29, 1865. Private Charles F. Regan enlisted in July of 1861 at the age of 21 and managed to stay well until December 10, 1864 when he too was captured. He was confined at Point Lookout until June 19, 1865. Private Ira J. Waters enlisted in January 1862 and was with his regiment until captured while pursuing the enemy cavalry from the Weldon Raid December 10, 1964; he was confined at Point Lookout until June 21, 1865. Private Barzella B. Wendley enlisted in January 1862. He was captured while covering Longstreet's flank during the Suffolk Campaign April 9, 1863. Ira returned to the regiment, and was captured again December 10, 1864 while pursuing the enemy cavalry. Private Wendley was confined at Point Lookout until June 21, 1865. J. M. Shaw and Leonard Shughart were apparently among the last to be withdrawn from the pursuit of Warren's column on December 11— they may have been injured or weakened stragglers who could not keep up with the pullback, or they may have been part of the force Hampton left on the Union rear for an extra day. Private J. M. Shaw was confined at Point Lookout until May 14, 1865. Private Leonard Shughart enlisted in February 1864, and after his capture on December 12 of that year, he was exchanged on January 21, 1865. Leonard was admitted to a Hospital in Richmond on the same day, and furloughed from there on January 24, 1865 — he probably was not back in time for the march to Appomattox Court House.

• *January–February 1865.* Private Bradford L. Honeycut enlisted in Company B of the 2nd Cavalry in June 1861 at 25 years of age. He was listed as a deserter on September 24, 1861, but returned to service five weeks later — considering the lack of discipline, equipment, and training in the early weeks of training camp, it might be fair to say Bradford simply went home for a spell. He was probably not happy in Company B because he was transferred to Company A, April 1, 1864. There was no date or place given for the fight in which Private Honeycut was wounded in the arm, but by the time he arrived in the hospital at Raleigh February 3, 1865, his arm had already been amputated. He received a 60-day furlough February 20, so probably did not get back to his unit in time for the march to Appomattox. Private Thornell enlisted in June of 1861 at the age of 27. He was captured during one of the skirmishes outside Warrenton, Virginia, October 17, 1862; he was exchanged October 31 of that year. Henry was captured again near Falling Waters, Maryland July 14, 1863 while returning from the difficult journey to and from Gettysburg. He was confined at Point Lookout until exchanged May 3, 1864. He was admitted to a hospital in Raleigh February 23, 1865 with a gunshot wound to the right hand, and listed as a "deserter" from the hospital March 7, 1865 — considering that many privates felt the war was lost by that time, and taking into account Henry's service and condition, he probably deserves to be remembered in a more favorable light than the official roll indicates.

• *March 31, 1865.* James L. Gaines had been assistant adjutant general for Barringer's brigade before being appointed lieutenant colonel on March 1, 1865. He took command of the 2nd North Carolina Cavalry when William P. Roberts left to command Dearing's former brigade. Gaines was seriously wounded early in the fighting at Chamberlain's Run and had his arm amputated in a field hospital. He continued to travel with the regiment's wagons and was paroled at Appomattox Court House on April 9, 1865. George W. Hathaway enlisted September 15, 1862 at the age of 18. He mustered in as private and was appointed 2nd lieutenant before November 21, 1864, and then promoted to 1st lieutenant January 6, 1865. His career ended when he was killed in action at Chamberlain's Run. Nicholas J. Harrell enlisted August 5, 1861 at the age of 24. He had moved from private to sergeant when he was seriously wounded at the Battle of Mine Run in late 1863. He had moved to 2nd lieutenant when he was wounded at Chamberlain's Run — he, like many others wounded that day, stayed with the regiment to fight the next day. William S. Caveness enlisted on August 6, 1861 at the age of 20. He mustered in as private and was appointed corporal June 14, 1863. He was mortally wounded near Chamberlain's Run on March 31, 1865. Edward M. Jordan transferred from the infantry into Company C of the 2nd North Carolina Cavalry August 12, 1861 as a private. He was seriously wounded at the Battle of Brandy Station in mid–1863, but returned to fight with his company until appointed adjutant for the regiment with the rank of 1st lieutenant. He was wounded at Chamberlain's Run, but stayed with the regiment until paroled at Appomattox Court House. A Lieutenant Turner was reported wounded at Chamberlain's Run, and the only Lieutenant Turner still with the regiment in March of 1865 was Julian S. Turner of Company K. He enlisted on September 10, 1861 at the age of 28. Turner mustered in as a 1st sergeant but was reduced to the ranks by June of 1862; then promoted to 3rd lieutenant on September 13, 1864. Lieutenant Turner stayed with the regiment and was later paroled at Goldsboro, North Carolina on May 4, 1865.

• *Five Forks, April 1, 1865.* John P. Lockhart enlisted September 10, 1861 at the age of 26 and mustered in as 2nd lieutenant. He was promoted to 1st lieutenant November 8, 1862, and to captain, September 30, 1863. When the regiment's temporary command, James L. Gaines, was wounded early in the fighting at Chamberlain Run, John P. Lockhart was put in command of the 2nd Cavalry and rode at their front during the day — in the process he was wounded and his hat took a ball. In addition, his horse was shot from under him in the fighting around Five Forks. According to Rufus Barringer, Lockhart survived Chamberlain Run only "..., to get a ball the next day, which he still bears." Nonetheless, he managed to lead the men of the 2nd Cavalry through the last fight at Appomattox Court House. Second Lieutenant Nicholas J. Harrell had been seriously wounded at Mine Run in 1863 and wounded again at Chamberlain Run, March 31, 1865. The next day, he along with many of his comrades in the 2nd Cavalry stayed on the field and covered the retreat of others at Five Forks, only to be surrounded and captured along with around 5,000 other Confederate soldiers on April 1, 1865. He was confined at Point Lookout until released June 27, 1865. Private Josephus H. Smith, Jr. of Company C enlisted in 1864 at the age of 20. He fought until he was killed in action at Five Forks. Private Charles T. Davis enlisted October 10, 1864 at the age of 25. Less than six months later he was wounded in action at Five Forks and admitted to a Danville hospital on April 3 with a gunshot wound "in thorax, right side." He returned to duty just in time for the finale on April 9, 1865. Private Evans Jacobs enlisted March 5, 1864, and was captured at Five Forks. He was confined at Hart's Island, N.Y. until released on June 15, 1865. Sergeant George A. Johns enlisted June 27, 1861. He mustered in as corporal and was promoted to sergeant by June 1862. He was appointed regimental suttler April 15, 1863, but retained his rank and position in Company F. He was captured at Five Forks and confined at Point Lookout until released June 6, 1865. Jennings W. Lambeth enlisted February 22, 1862, and was mustered in as private. He was reported to be "absent at home wounded" in May–June 1863, but returned to fight with the regiment until captured at Five Forks. He was confined at Point Lookout until released on June 28, 1865. Private J. R. Ponton was wounded in action at Five Forks and captured. He was reported in a Petersburg hospital on April 13 and transferred to Fort Monroe on May 4. He was then confined in the military prison at Camp Hamilton, Va. May 25 until released on May 31, 1865. Private Ponton's hospital records show his age as 17. Private Jerome A. Sapp enlisted July 14, 1862. He was captured at Five Forks and confined at Point Lookout until released June 30, 1865. Private George D. Weatherly enlisted June 26, 1863. He was in a Richmond hospital in May 1864 with a gunshot wound, and furloughed in June—he was "absent at home wounded" through September 1864. He was then captured at Five Forks and confined at Point Lookout until released on June 21, 1865. Sergeant William M. Jarvis enlisted July 18, 1861 at the age of 22. He mustered in as a private; was appointed corporal by October 1862, and promoted to sergeant by August 1864. Jarvis was captured at Five Forks and confined at Point Lookout until released June 19, 1865. Private Solomon F. Dean was from Forsyth County. He was also captured at Five Forks and confined at Point Lookout until released June 12, 1865. Private Albert G. Voss was conscripted on November 26, 1864. He was captured on April 1, 1865 at Hatcher's Run, about a mile above Five Forks—probably during the retreat to the South Side Railroad. Voss was confined Elmira, N.Y. until released July 7, 1865.

• *April 3, 1865.* Private Parnell T. Kearns was conscripted in March 1864 and remained in State service at Raleigh until assigned to the 2nd North Carolina Cavalry on September 27, 1864. Private Kearns was fighting with the regiment when captured around Namozine Church. He was confined at Point Lookout until released on June 6, 1865. Private William F. Linvill enlisted on March 1, 1864 and fought with the regiment until captured around Namozine Church on April 3. He was confined at Point Lookout until June 28, 1865. Private Henry N. Miller enlisted in September 1864, and was captured around Namozine Church. He was confined at Point Lookout until released on June 29, 1865. Private James J. McLean enlisted on June 29, 1861 at the age of 36. He was captured near Pollocksville, N.C. in May 1862 and released about a week later. He was again captured around Namozine Church on April 3, 1865 and confined at Point Lookout until June 29, 1865. Private John Taylor Cross of Gates County enlisted on June 17, 1861 at the age of 23. He was wounded near Sawyer's Mill, N.C. while on picket with Lieutenant William P. Roberts, also of Gates County, in May 1862. He recovered and fought until captured around Namozine Church. Private Cross was confined at Point Lookout until June 26, 1865. Private William Thomas Goodman transferred to the 2nd Cavalry from the infantry on September 16, 1862. He was discharged August 20, 1863 after furnishing a substitute (just after returning from the Gettysburg Campaign). However, Private Goodman did return to fight with the regiment because the Federal Provost Marshal records list him as captured around Namozine Church April 3, 1865. He was confined at Point Lookout until released June 17, 1865. Private Joseph E. Harrell transferred to the 2nd North Carolina Cavalry from the infantry January 1, 1864. He was wounded in the Battle of Reams's Station on August 25, 1864. Private Harrell was later captured around Namozine Church and confined at Point Lookout until June 13, 1865. Private John R. Haskins enlisted February 29, 1864 and was assigned to Company C at Raleigh on March 3, 1864. A year and a month later he was captured around Namozine Church and confined at Point Lookout until June 14, 1865. Private Aurelius Scott enlisted February 20, 1862. He was wounded in August 1864, and returned to the regiment. Private Scott was then captured around Namozine Church April 3, 1865 and confined at Point Lookout until June 19, 1865. Private Alexander Autry enlisted June 16, 1861 at the age of 24. He was captured first August 6, 1862 and released two months later. He was captured again around Namozine Church and confined at Point Lookout until June 22, 1865. Charles H. Elder enlisted June 8, 1861 when he was 30 years of age. He mustered in as sergeant and held that rank. Sergeant Elder was wounded in action June 23, 1864 and returned to fight again. He was then captured around Namozine Church and confined until June 26, 1865. Private John J. Rogers enlisted July 18, 1861 at the age of 29. He fought with the regiment until captured around Namozine Church and was confined at Point Lookout where he died of "disease of heart" May 8, 1865. James E. R. Winstead enlisted June 10, 1861 at the age of 23. He mustered in as private and was appointed corporal August 19, 1861. He was captured and then paroled at Hanover Court House May 3, 1863. He was promoted to sergeant during May–June 1863. Sergeant Winstead was captured around Namozine Church and confined at Point Lookout until June 21, 1865. Private Ellington Frazier enlisted February 28, 1864, and was captured around Namozine Church April 3, 1865. He was confined at Point Lookout until June 26, 1865. Private Pinkney Gordon enlisted on February 22. 1862 and was captured around Namozine Church. He was confined at Point Lookout until released June 8, 1865. William J. Tadlock enlisted July 5, 1861 at the age of 19. He mustered in as private and was appointed corporal during July–August, 1864. Corporal Tadlock was captured around Namozine Church and confined at Point

Lookout until June 21, 1865. Private Daniel M. Baker enlisted on July 12, 1861 at the age of 28. He was captured around Namozine Church on April 3, 1865 and confined at Point Lookout until June 23 of that year. Private Thomas J. Sherman was captured around Namozine Church April 3 and confined at Point Lookout until June 5, 1865. Private John Wilson Rhew enlisted February 24, 1862. He was captured around Namozine Church on April 3, 1865 and confined at Point Lookout where he died of "diarrhea chronic" June 8, 1865. Private Isaac Taylor enlisted January 28, 1862. He was captured around Namozine Church and confined at Point Lookout until June 21, 1865.

The following men from the 2nd Cavalry were also taken near Namozine Church but probably by a different Union unit — they were all listed as captured near Amelia Court House. Private Henry F. Tritt was captured April 3 and confined at Point Lookout until taking the Oath of Allegiance June 21, 1865. Private James A. Ramsey enlisted September 29, 1861 at the age of 21. After he was captured, he was also confined at Point Lookout until June 17, 1865. Like most men in Company B, Private Augustus Davidson Troutman was from Iredell County, N.C., but he traveled to Culpeper County, Va. to enlist in May 1863 at the age of 18. After he was captured, he was confined at Point Lookout until June 20, 1865. William Moses Waugh enlisted August 22, 1861 at the age of 24. He was appointed corporal December 1, 1862. After his capture he was confined at Point Lookout until June 30, 1865. Private Robert P. Lawrence enlisted June 29, 1861 at the age of 21. He was appointed bugler during November–December 1862, then reduced in rank in mid-1864. After his capture, he was confined at Point Lookout until June 28, 1865. Daniel A. Patterson enlisted June 21, 1861 at the age of 21. He mustered in as a sergeant and was appointed 1st sergeant on December 1, 1862. After his capture, he was sent to Point Lookout until June 17, 1865. Private Yancy S. Corem enlisted June 20, 1861. He spent time in a Charlottesville hospital for a gunshot wound in May of 1863 and returned to duty a month later. After his capture April 3, 1865, he was confined at Point Lookout until June 24, 1865. John T. Edwards enlisted June 10, 1861. He mustered in as a private and made corporal late in the war. After his capture he was confined at Point Lookout until June 26, 1865. Private Jordan Parrish enlisted July 18, 1861 at 19 years of age. After his capture he was confined at Point Lookout until June 16, 1865. Private William R. Webb enlisted March 5, 1864. He was captured less than one year later and confined at Hart's Island, N.Y. until June 19, 1865.

The following three cavalrymen were probably captured in the skirmishing around Jetersville, or after the major fighting at Namozine Church when men had scattered in various directions. Mingrella Credle enlisted July 15, 1861 at the age of 21. He mustered in as a private, and was appointed corporal during July–August, 1864. After he was captured near the Appomattox River, he was confined at Point Lookout until June 24, 1865. Private John Moore was also captured on the river and confined at Point Lookout until he took the Oath of Allegiance June 29, 1865. Private James B. Johnson enlisted July 6, 1861 at the age of 33. He was taken at Jetersville Station and confined at Point Lookout until June 14, 1865.

The following men were wounded in the fighting April 3, 1865, and all but one were taken to a hospital in Danville, Virginia, that same day. Private Benjamin T. Boyed enlisted July 2, 1861 at the age of 21. He received a gunshot wound to the "right forearm flesh," and was admitted to the hospital April 3 and furloughed for 30 days on April 9, 1865. Robert P. Hoffer enlisted June 22, 1861 at the age of 25. He was one of seven Hoffers from Gates County, N.C. to enlist in Company C. Hoffer was wounded in the right arm and was also released from the hospital on April 9 with a 30-day furlough. Private George W. Jones transferred to the 2nd Cavalry from the 17th Regiment N.C. Troops in October 1862. He was wounded in the right side of his chest and admitted to the hospital on April 3. He was released and furloughed for 60 days on April 8, 1865. Private Neill G. Biggs enlisted on June 17, 1861 at the age of 19. He was admitted to the hospital April 3 with a gunshot wound to his abdomen, and was furloughed for 60 days on April 8, 1865. William C. Faucette enlisted on July 26, 1861 at the age of 23. He mustered in as sergeant and was promoted to 1st sergeant during July–August 1864. Sergeant Faucette was admitted to a hospital in Danville on April 3, 1865 with a gunshot wound "on scalp, left side, flesh." He returned home and was paroled at Greensboro, North Carolina May 19, 1865. First Sergeant John J. Bryan enlisted June 10, 1861 at the age of 24. He mustered in as a corporal and was promoted to orderly sergeant during May–June 1862, and to 1st sergeant during July–August 1864. Sergeant Bryan was wounded August 15, 1864 and spent some time in a Richmond hospital; he was again wounded and sent to the hospital on April 3, 1865. He was released with a 60-day furlough April 9, 1865. Private James Henry Harris enlisted July 16, 1861 at the age of 20. He was admitted to the hospital at Danville April 3 with a gunshot wound to his right elbow. He made it to a hospital in Greensboro and was paroled from there April 28, 1865. James H. Johnson enlisted on July 6, 1861 at 20 years of age. He mustered in as a private and was appointed corporal during July–August 1864. He took a gunshot wound in his right cheek and was admitted to the hospital on April 3. He was given a 60-day furlough April 8, 1865. John Bowling enlisted September 10, 1861. He was mustered in as a private and was appointed bugler during January–February 1863. He was wounded in the hand and admitted to a hospital in Danville April 3, 1865. Private Ninian W. Gray enlisted December 20, 1862, and was wounded at Middleburg June 18 or Upperville June 21, 1863. He was again wounded and admitted to a hospital with a gunshot wound to his face April 3, 1865. On April 8, he was given a 60-day furlough. All the men listed above were in a Danville hospital, a couple of miles above the North Carolina border, and released on the day their army reached Appomattox Court House or the following day when Robert E. Lee surrendered. Private Isaiah S. Harris was not so lucky. He enlisted July 12, 1861 at the age of 23. He was in a Petersburg hospital when he was captured April 3 with a gunshot wound to his right lung. Private Harris died there April 14, 1865.

• *April 4, 5, 6, 1865.* Private Perry Lucas enlisted July 15, 1862 at the age of 34. He was captured April 4 and confined at Point Lookout until June 28, 1865. Private Pleasant C. Kelly enlisted March 5, 1864. He was captured at Amelia Court House April 4 and confined at Point Lookout until released June 22, 1865. William S. Lee enlisted June 17, 1861. He mustered in as a private, and transferred to the regiment's Field and Staff as color bearer September 15, 1861. He returned to Company F during January–February 1862, and was appointed corporal during May–June 1862. Corporal Lee was captured near Amelia Court House April 4 and confined at Point Lookout until June 28, 1865. Private Balum Hornada enlisted March 3, 1864. He was captured April 4 near Amelia Court House and confined at Point Lookout until June 24, 1865. Private Samuel G. J. Dalton resided in Stokes County, N.C. when he enlisted. He was captured at Jetersville Station April 4. He was confined at Point Lookout until June 26, 1865. Private Henry N. Price enlisted June 20, 1861 at the age of 22. He was admitted to a hospital in Danville with a gunshot wound to his left leg April 4. He was furloughed for 40 days April 8, 1865. Stephen O. Terry enlisted September 10, 1861. He mustered in as a private and was appointed corporal May 27, 1863. Corporal Terry was captured at Hanover, Penn. in June of 1863 and exchanged May 30, 1864. While in prison, he was promoted to sergeant. Sergeant Terry was again captured April 5, 1865 and confined at Hart's Island, N.Y. until June 19, 1865. Private Daniel Joseph Gooch enlisted October 1, 1864 at the age of 17. He was admitted to the hospital at Danville with a gunshot wound in his left side April 5, 1865. There is no record of his death, release, or parole. Private P. A. Kroover came to the regiment from New Orleans, Louisiana. He was captured at Farmville April 6, 1865 and confined at Newport News, Va. until June 30, 1865. Private David L. Tate resided in Guilford County when he joined the 2nd Cavalry. He was captured near Farmville April 6 and confined until June 16, 1865. He died in a hospital at Fort Monroe, Va. of typhoid fever July 6, 1865. Private William L. Stilly enlisted April 28, 1863 at the age of 23. He remained in service with the state until assigned to the 2nd Cavalry January 1, 1864. He was captured April 6 near the South Side Railroad and confined at Point Lookout until June 30, 1865. Dallas Wahab joined the regiment in Fauquier County, Va. November 1, 1862 at the age of 18. He mustered in as a private and was appointed corporal during July–August 1864. Corporal Wahab was captured April 6 near the South Side Railroad and confined at Newport News until June 30, 1865.

Chapter Notes

ABBREVIATIONS: **MC**—Museum of the Confederacy, Richmond, Virginia; **NARS**—National Archives and Records Service, General Services Administration, Washington, D.C.; **NCDA**—North Carolina Division of Archives and History, Raleigh, N.C.; **SCL-DU**—Rare Book, Manuscript, and Special Collections Library, Duke University, Durham, N.C.; **SHC-UNC**—Southern Historical Collection, University of North Carolina, Chapel Hill, N.C.; **VHS**—Virginia Historical Society, Richmond, Virginia; **SCL-USC**—South Caroliniana Library, University of South Carolina, Columbia, S.C.; **O.R.**—*The War of the Rebellion: A Compilation of the Official Records of the Union and Confederate Armies.* 70 vols., 128 parts. Washington, D.C.: Government Printing Office, 1880-1901. All references are to Series I, unless otherwise indicated; **SHSP**—*Southern Historical Society Papers*, 52 vols., Jones, J. William, *et al.*, editors, Richmond: Southern Historical Society, 1876-1959; ***Our Living & Our Dead***—*Our Living and Our Dead: Devoted to North Carolina—Her Present, and Her Future*, 4 vols., S. D. Pool, editor, Raleigh, N.C.: North Carolina Branch of the Southern Historical Society, September 1874-August 1876; ***Battles & Leaders***—*Battles and Leaders of the Civil War*, 4 vols., Robert U. Johnson and Clarence C. Buel, editors, New York: 1887-1888. Reprint, New York: Castle Books, 1956; **CMH**—*Confederate Military History*, vol. 4 (North Carolina), 12 vols. Clement A. Evans, editor, Atlanta, 1899.

Preface

1. The facts leading to North Carolina's decision to secede are discussed in greater detail in John G. Barrett, *The Civil War in North Carolina* (Chapel Hill, 1963), p3–16; also see James M. McPherson, *Battle Cry of Freedom* (New York, 1989), p276–282.

One

1. In addition to Ransom, Captain Solomon Williams, of Nash County, North Carolina, also resigned his commission in the U.S. Army, and returned to serve his state—he too was a graduate of West Point. Colonel Williams took command of the 12th North Carolina Infantry. It would be a year before Solomon Williams became the second commander of the 2nd North Carolina Cavalry. *Weekly Raleigh Register* (Ransom), July 3, 1861, p1; and (Williams), May 22, 1861, p1.
2. *Weekly Raleigh Register*, May 29, 1861, p3.
3. *Fayetteville Observer Weekly*, Aug 19, 1861, p1, col 2; *Weekly Raleigh Register*, July 24, 1861, p2 (originally published in the Washington, N.C. *Dispatch*, July 10, 1861).
4. *Fayetteville Observer Weekly*, Aug 26, 1861, p3, col 3; *Fayetteville Observer Weekly*, Sept 16, 1861, p1, col 3.
5. In an effort to attract guests the hotel was still advertising its availability and rates in the *Raleigh Register* in mid–1862. It became a Confederate hospital by late 1862 and remained so throughout the war. Across the railroad (the old Raleigh & Gaston) from the old hotel site is a Confederate cemetery containing 52 soldiers who died at the hotel/hospital—most of them were cavalrymen. The 2nd North Carolina Cavalry's training camp was just east of the cemetery. Camp Beauregard (at Ridgeway), where the 1st North Carolina Cavalry trained, was only about 30 miles from the cemetery. Samuel Thomas Peace, Sr., *Vance County, North Carolina: A Short History* (Henderson, N.C.: 1955), p352–357.
6. As quoted in T. Harrell Allen, *Lee's Last Major General: Bryan Grimes* (Mason City, Ia., 1999), p27. Later as a Major General, Grimes stood at the front of John B. Gordon's command and led them in the last organized charge into battle by the Army of Northern Virginia at Appomattox Court House on April 9, 1865—the remnants of the 2nd North Carolina Cavalry were at his right hand on that day and charged in advance of his infantry.
7. The source for these numbers is L. H. Manarin, *North Carolina Troops*, vII, Cavalry, p104–177. The Roster of Troops took most of its information from the Compiled Service Record which are primarily based on Company Muster Roll cards. The greatest error in these numbers result from not fully representing losses.
8. Even though the ranks of the Cherokee Rangers had been screened, the company did not remain in the 1st North Carolina Cavalry. Shortly after the screening process, the 1st Cavalry moved out to Camp Beauregard in Warren County, but the Cherokee Rangers remained in Asheville. The company had been selected by and assigned to the 1st Cavalry while their Captain Hayes was in Raleigh attending the State Legislature. Apparently while in Raleigh, Hayes was persuaded to join Colonel Spruill's Cavalry Legion (Spruill was also in Raleigh attending the State Convention). When Hayes returned to

Ashville, he made it clear he preferred to be a part of Spruill's legion. The Cherokee Rangers became Company A of Spruill's 2nd North Carolina Cavalry. Politics played an important role in many of the early decisions affecting the 2nd Cavalry. R. Barringer, "Ninth Regiment (First Cavalry)," p417; W. A. Curtis, "Sketches of Company A, 2nd Regiment of North Carolina Cavalry," in S. D. Pool, editor, *Our Living and Our Dead*, v2, p42–43.

9. Thomas Branson to sister, Emily, Camp Clark, Aug 19, 1861, the "Branson Family Papers," 1848–1925, P.C. 1507.1, in NCDA.

10. *Weekly Raleigh Register*, Sept 11, 1861, p1.

11. Reprinted in the *Fayetteville Observer Weekly*, Sept 30, 1861, p1, col 3.

12. Thomas Branson to sister, Emily, on Aug 19, 1861, from Camp Clark, "Branson Family Papers," P.C. 1507.1, p1–4, in NCDA.

13. C. J. Hartley, *Stuart's Tarheels* (Baltimore, 1996), p58–59.

14. Branson to sister, Sept 21, 1861, "Branson Family Papers," P.C. 1507.1, p2, in NCDA.

15. A. Gordon, "Organization of Troops," p3–4; also C. J. Hartley, *Stuart's Tarheels* (Baltimore, 1996), p58.

16. Branson to Sister Emily, in "Branson Family Papers," P. C. 1507.1, p4, in NCDA.

17. Special Order No. 5, dated Oct 4, 1861, in NCDA.

18. W. A. Curtis, "Sketched of Company A," in *Our Living and Our Dead*, v2, p41 and 44.

19. Letter from Captain of Ordnance in Raleigh to Lieutenant Colonel Robinson, Kittrell's dated Oct 12, 1861 in "Emma Henderson Dunn Papers," 1852–1903, no. 1867, folder no. 1, in SHC-UNC.

20. Battalion Order No. 1, Battalion Headquarters, Camp Clark, Oct 13, 1861; Special Orders No. 3, Headquarters 2nd Cavalry, Oct 18 1861, Camp Clark, NCDA.

21. Daniel H. Hill, *Bethel to Sharpsburg* (Wilmington, N.C., 1992), v1, p183–187.

22. *Hillsborough Recorder Weekly*, Oct 30, 1861, p3, col 1–2.

23. *Hillsborough Recorder Weekly*, Nov 20, 1861, p3, col 1.

24. *Hillsborough Recorder Weekly*, Dec 11, 1861, p3, col 2.

25. We are all indebted to Ellen Lockhart of Orange County for corresponding on a regular basis with her brothers, cousins, and friends in the 2nd Cavalry (and other regiments), and for saving their letters to her. Levi Lockhart to Ellen Lockhart in Dec 1861 from Camp Washington, "Lockhart Family Letters," in SCL-DU.

26. W. A. Graham Jr., "Nineteenth Regiment (Second Cavalry)," p80–81.

27. *Fayetteville Observer Weekly*, Nov 18, 1861, p2, col 2.

28. *Hillsborough Recorder Weekly*, Dec 11, 1861, p3, col 2.

29. Special Orders No. 5, Nov 5th 1861, Camp Clark, in NCDA.

30. W. A. Curtis, "Sketched of Company A," in *Our Living and Our Dead*, v2, p42.

31. W. A. Curtis, "Sketched of Company A," in *Our Living and Our Dead*, v2, p43.

32. J. G. Barrett, *The Civil War in North Carolina* (Chapel Hill, 1963), p62.

33. *O.R.*, vIV, p576.

34. D. H. Hill, *O.R.*, vIV, p694.

35. Gatlin to Hill on Oct 28, 1861 from Goldsboro, N.C.; in National Archive, Washington, D. C., R. G. 109, War Department Collection of Confederate Records, "Special Orders" by R. C. Gatlin (bound volume of originals).

36. Gatlin, *O.R.*, vLI, part 2, p365.

37. Special Orders, No. 224, *O.R.*, vIV, p700; Special Orders No. 240, *O.R.*, vIV, p705.

38. Gatlin, *O.R.*, vIV, p705.

39. Gatlin, *O.R.*, vLI, part 2, p401; Huger, *O.R.*, vIV, p718; Clark, *O.R.*, vIV, p711–712; Special Orders No. 272, *O.R.*, vIV, p715.

40. Clark, *O.R.*, vIV, p717; Benjamin, *O.R.*, vIV, p717–718.

41. Gatlin, *O.R.*, vLI, part 2, p442.

42. "The Burnside Fleet," *Weekly Raleigh Register*, Jan 15, 1862, p2.

43. Letter from Thomas Branson dated Jan 8, 1862; Thomas Branson to sister, Emily, on Jan 21, 1862. Both letters from "Branson Family Papers," 1848–1925, P. C. 1507.1, in NCDA.

44. James W. Bacon to Ellen Lockhart on Jan 25, 1862 from Camp Fisher, "Lockhart Family Letters," in SCL-DU.

45. In a correspondence from Brigadier General Gatlin to the Governor of North Carolina, Henry T. Clark, on Feb 21, 1862, Gatlin said Winton was defended by "Col. Solomon Williams' regiment." That was an error. The officer in command at Winton was William T. Williams. *O.R.*, vLI, part 2, p476. (Colonel Solomon Williams took command of the 2nd North Carolina Cavalry on June 6, 1862.)

46. Thomas C. Parramore, "The Burning of Winton in 1862," *North Carolina Historical Review*, 1962, v39, p18–31. Also see, J. G. Barrett, *The Civil War in North Carolina* (Chapel Hill, 1963), pp., 91–95. This act clearly established Colonel Hawkins as a leader with no sense of history and certainly no vision of the future — to this date, historians and the stories they tell are suffering for such losses while no known military importance can be attached to the records intentionally destroyed in the court house that day.

47. Gatlin to Clark, on Feb 22, 1862 from Goldsboro; Gatlin to Branch, on Feb 21, 1862 from Goldsboro; Gatlin to Martin, on Feb 24, 1862, in , R. G. 109, War Department Collection of Confederate Records, "Special Orders" by R. C. Gatlin (bound volume of originals), NARS; *O.R.*, vLI, part 2, p476; *O.R.*, vIX, p434.

48. *O.R.*, v9, p449.

49. Henry T. Clark, *O.R.*, Series IV, vI, p987.

50. J. G. Barrett, *The Civil War in North Carolina* (Chapel Hill, 1963), p95–107.

51. Rush C. Hawkins, "Early Coast Operations in North Carolina," *Battles and Leader*, v1, p647–648. Brevet Brigadier-General Hawkins was the commander of the 9th New York (Zouaves) — he was the same commander who lead the invasion and burning of Winton, North Carolina on Feb 20, 1862.

52. Branch, *O.R.*, vIX, p246; Campbell, *O.R.*, vIX, p250; Spruill, *O.R.*, vIX, p252; Vance, *O.R.*, vIX, p255.

53. Vance, *O.R.*, vIX, p255; Haughton, *O.R.*, vIX, p268.

54. Vance, *O.R.*, vIX, p255; E. J. Hess, *Lee's Tar Heels* (Chapel Hill, 2002), p 12.

55. Branch, *O.R.*, vIX, p244.

56. Branch, *O.R.*, vIX, p244–245; Hoke, *O.R.*, vIX, p259–260.

57. Reno, *O.R.*, vIX, p221; William S. Clark, *O.R.*, vIX, p225.

58. H. J. B. Clark, *O.R.*, vIX, p267–268.

59. Sinclair, *O.R.*, vIX, p262–263.

60. Branch, *O.R.*, vIX, p245.

61. H. J. B. Clark, *O.R.*, vIX, p267; William S. Clark, *O.R.*, vIX, p225–226.

62. William S. Clark, *O.R.*, vIX, p226.

63. E. J. Hess, *Lee's Tar Heels* (Chapel Hill, 2002), p12–15.

64. Hoke, *O.R.*, vIX, p260–261.

65. Spruill, *O.R.*, vIX, p253.

66. "The Fight at Newbern," *Weekly Raleigh Register*, March 26, 1862, p1.

67. From the *Raleigh Standard*, reprinted in the *Fayetteville Observer*, March 24, 1862, p4, col 3; From the *Raleigh Standard*, reprinted in the *Fayetteville Observer*, March 31, 1862, p1, col 1.

68. *Hillsboro Recorder* Weekly, April 16, 1862, p3, col 2.

69. Spruill, *O.R.*, vIX, p253.

70. Branch, *O.R.*, vIX, p245; Barbour, *O.R.*, vIX, p266; Sinclair, *O.R.*, vIX, p263.

71. Branch, *O.R.*, vIX, p245; Hoke, *O.R.*, vIX, p260–261.

72. Branch, *O.R.*, vIX, p245; From the *Raleigh Standard*, reprinted in the *Fayetteville Observer*, March 24, 1862, p4, col 2.

73. Hoke, *O.R.*, vIX, p260–261.

74. Graham, *Hillsboro Recorder Weekly*, April 9, 1862, p3,

col 1; *Fayetteville Observer*, April 7, 1862, p3, col 2; Spruill, *O.R.*, vIX, p252.
75. Spruill, *O.R.*, vIX, p252.
76. Spruill, *O.R.*, vIX, p252.
77. *Fayetteville Observer*, April 7, 1862, p3, col 2.
78. Spruill, *O.R.*, vIX, p254; *Fayetteville Observer*, April 7, 1862, p3, col 2.
79. Spruill, *O.R.*, vIX, p254.
80. *Hillsboro Recorder*, reprinted in the *Fayetteville Observer*, April 7, 1862, p1, col 3.
81. *Fayetteville Observer*, April 14, 1862, p2, col 5.
82. Vance, *O.R.*, vIX, p255–256.
83. E. J. Hess, *Lee's Tar Hells* (Chapel Hill, 2002), p16.
84. *Fayetteville Observer*, April 14, 1862, p2, col 5; Vance, *O.R.*, vIX, p257; Hoke, *O.R.*, vIX, p261.
85. As quoted in J. G. Barrett, *The Civil War in North Carolina* (Chapel Hill, 1963), p106.
86. *O.R.*, vIX, p445; Branch, *O.R.*, vIX, p248.
87. Gatlin, *O.R.*, vIV, p578; Special Orders Nos. 53, *O.R.*, vIX, p447.
88. *O.R.*, vIX, p459–460.
89. W. A. Graham Jr., "Nineteenth Regiment (Second Cavalry)," vII, p81. Lieutenant, later Captain, Graham of Company K was with the regiment until wounded at Gettysburg on July 3, 1863; Lockhart, *Hillsborough Recorder Weekly*, April 16, 1862, p3, col 2; Captain Strange of Company D sent his thanks to the people of Cumberland County in the *Fayetteville Observer*, April 14, 1862, p4, col 1; Lieutenant Graham of Company K thanked the people in Orange County for their help. *Hillsborough Recorder Weekly*, April 9, 1862, p3, col 1–2.
90. W. A. Graham Jr., "Nineteenth Regiment (Second Cavalry)," vII, p82.
91. The Company Muster Roll information indicates the Regiment was dispersed as follows in the March–April period: Company A, Kinston; Company B, Kinston; Company E, Camp Johnston near Kinston; Company G, Camp Johnston near Kinston; Company H, Camp below Kinston; Company K, Camp near Kinston; Company C, Trenton; Company D, Trenton; Companies F & I, not stated. Company Muster Roll, "C. S. R. of Confederate Soldiers who served in Organizations from the State of N.C.; 2nd Cavalry (19th State Troops)," Microcopy 270, roll 11, NARS.
92. Boothe, *O.R.*, vIX, p295–296.
93. Ransom, *O.R.*, vIX, p300; "The Cavalry Skirmish," *Fayetteville Observer*, April 28, 1862, p1, col 4; "Nineteenth Reg., Second Cavalry. The Skirmish at Gillett's, below Trenton," *Hillsborough Recorder Weekly*, April 23, p3, cols. 1 and 2.
94. Ransom, *O.R.*, vIX, p300–303. See the response by Robert E. Lee which follows Ransom's report in the Official Record. Also, apparently most of Captain Turner's injuries were about the head, even though the entry for Turner in the Roster of North Carolina Troops reads "Wounded in heart April 13, 1862 at Gillett's...." The wound to Turner's heart might have been a reference to the blow dealt him by Ransom — the latter blow was one from which he apparently never fully recovered.
95. D. S. Freeman, *Lee's Lieutenants* (N.Y., 1995), v2, p327–328.
96. R. E. Lee in Ransom, *O.R.*, vIX, p303.
97. This was apparent throughout his leadership — for instance, in a letter to J. E. B. Stuart on May 31, 1863, there was a question of doing justice to a young Lieutenant accused on inconclusive evidence, and General Lee restated the tone of the process by saying "This is a case, in my opinion, where possible error is better than probable wrong." R. E. Lee, *O.R.*, vXXV, part 2, p844.
98. Ransom, *O.R.*, vIX, p302.
99. "The Affair Below Trenton," *Weekly Raleigh Register*, April 23, 1862, p1.
100. "Nineteenth Reg., Second Cavalry. The Skirmish at Gillett's, below Trenton," *Hillsborough Recorder Weekly*, April 23, p3, cols. 1 and 2.

101. Holmes, *O.R.*, vIX, p465; Lee, *O.R.*, vIX, p467; R. E. Lee, *O.R.*, vIX, p467–468; Holmes, *O.R.*, vIX, p468.
102. I believe companies H and I are the two companies in Virginia with Ransom because the company muster records show Company H near Fredericksburg June through Oct 1862, and Company I in camp near Richmond May–June 1862. The May–June reports were typically written in July and the fact that the company was in North Carolina in May probably did not seem worth noting. Also, the inventory of regiments for the Army of Northern Virginia, dated July 23, 1862, lists "North Carolina Cavalry (2 companies)" in Brigadier General Ransom's Brigade. The 1st North Carolina was listed separately in the report as part of J. E. B. Stuart's Cavalry Brigade. *O.R.*, vXIV, p651, 652.
103. R. E. Lee, *O.R.*, vIX, p472.
104. *O.R.*, Series I, vIX, p473–475.
105. Martin, *O.R.*, vIX, p473.
106. "From Capt. Strange's Company," *Fayetteville Observer*, June 23, 1862, p3, col 3.
107. According to one report, all the companies of the 2nd Cavalry except Companies A and F were in their new camp on June 17. "From Capt. Strange's Company," *Fayetteville Observer*, June 23, 1862, p3, col 3; also see, The Company Muster Rolls for May–June contained the following information about the location of each company at the time: A, not stated; B, Camp Johnston; C, Hamilton (they were near Trenton / Pollocksville); D, Trenton; E and F, not stated; G, Trenton; H, Fredericksburg (as there June–Oct); I, camp near Richmond; K, Camp Johnston.
108. P. T. Bennett, "General Junius Daniel," *SHSP*, v18, p344; *CMH*, v4, p307.
109. "Successful Skirmish," *Raleigh Standard* reprinted in the *Fayetteville Observer*, May 5, 1862, p2, col 4.
110. "Outposts of the Army, May 17, 1862," *Raleigh Standard*, reprinted with commentary in the *Fayetteville Observer*, May 26, 1862, p2, col 4.
111. "Cavalry Skirmishes," *Hillsborough Recorder* Weekly, May 28, 1862, p3, col 1.
112. *Raleigh Register Weekly*, May 21, p2.
113. Sanford, *O.R.*, vIX, p349.
114. Foster, *O.R.*, vIX, p413.
115. R. E. Lee, *O.R.*, vIX, p475.
116. Holmes, *O.R.*, vIX, p476.
117. R. E. Lee, *O.R.*, vIX, p478–479.
118. "Important From Kinston,'" *Raleigh Daily Telegraph*, Aug 3, reprinted in the *Hillsborough Recorder Weekly*, Aug 7, 1862, p3, col 3.
119. *O.R.*, vIX, p479.
120. Hill, *O.R.*, vIX, p480; Special Orders No. 179, dated Aug 11, noted that Pettigrew had "... reported for duty, is assigned to command of the brigade now commanded by Col. Junius Danial of Maj. Gen. D. H. Hill's command...." *O.R.*, vXIV, p672; At the time, there was the possibility General Lee and others were a little out of touch with the many reorganization efforts at the brigade level. For instance, several weeks after the first exchange regarding Pettigrew, General Lee requested that Pettigrew be given command of a brigade. Major General G. W. Smith responded to him, pointing out that Pettigrew already had a brigade. To which General Lee could simple respond on Oct 3, 1862, "I have received your letter of the 26th ultimo. When I applied for Brigadier-General Pettigrew, I did not know that he was assigned to the command of a brigade. I do not desire that he should be disturbed." R. E. Lee, *O.R.*, vXIX, part 2, p689.
121. R. E. Lee, *O.R.*, vXII, part 3, p944.
122. Smith, *O.R.*, vXVIII, p743–744.
123. R. E. Lee, v14, p651.
124. Clingman, *O.R.*, vIX, p477.
125. "Important From Kinston," *Raleigh Daily Telegraph*, Aug 3, reprinted in the *Hillsborough Recorder Weekly*, Aug 7, 1862, p3, col 3.

Two

1. W. A. Graham, "Nineteenth Regiment (Second Cavalry)," p87.
2. The events described in this section for the months May through Sept 1862 are based on the following sources unless otherwise noted: D. S. Freeman, *Lee's Lieutenants* (New York, 1995), v1, p201–224, 225–243, 275–302, 503–537, 557–580, 588–604, v2, p1–62, 63–80, 81–95, 103–119, 144–152; J. M. McPherson, *Battle Cry of Freedom* (1988, New York, 1989), p454–472, 534–545, 557–562, 568–571.
3. As quoted in D. S. Freeman, *Lee's Lieutenants* (New York, 1995), v1, p265.
4. R. E. Lee, *O.R.*, vXI, part 3, p590; D. S. Freeman, *Lee's Lieutenants* (New York, 1995), v1, p278.
5. See: F. J. Porter, "Hanover Court House and Gaines's Mill," p326–343; D. H. Hill, "Lee's Attacks North of the Chickahominy," p347–362; W. B. Franklin, "Rear-guard Fighting During the Change of Base," p366–382; D. H. Hill, "McClellan's Change of Base and Malvern Hill," p383–395; J. Longstreet, "The Seven Days, Including Frayser's Farm," p396–405; F. J. Porter, "The Battle of Malvern Hill," p406–427.
6. E. P. Alexander, *Military Memoirs of a Confederate* (New York, 1993), p157, 174.
7. This property was handed down to W. H. F. Lee from his great grandmother, Martha Custis Washington. The widow Martha Custis lived on this property when courted by George Washington.
8. Stuart, *O.R.*, vXI, part 2, p516–517.
9. Stuart, *O.R.*, vXI, part 2, p517.
10. D. H. Hill, "McClellan's Change of Base and Malvern Hill," p394; W. W. Blackford, *War Years with Jeb Stuart* (Baton Rouge, 1993), p86–87.
11. Jackson's command included his former division under Winder, as well as Ewell's and A. P. Hill's divisions; Longstreet's command included his division and the divisions of D. R. Jones's, McLaws's, D. H. Hill's and R. H. Anderson's. See, D. S. Freeman, *Lee's Lieutenants* (New York, 1995), v1, p671–673.
12. D. H. Hill had performed as well as any of Lee's generals during the Seven Days' Battles, but he was moved out of the Army of Virginia to replace Holmes as the commander of troops south of the James River and in North Carolina when the latter was transferred out west. D. H. Hill left on July 21.
13. Smith, *O.R.*, vXII, part 3, p948.
14. Smith, *O.R.*, vXVIII, p743.
15. R. E. Lee, *O.R.*, vXIX, part 1, p145.
16. Stuart, *O.R.*, vXIX, part 1, p817.
17. R. E. Lee, *O.R.*, vXIX, part 2, p605–606.
18. Stuart *O.R.*, vXIX, part 1, p818.
19. R. E. Lee, *O.R.*, vXIX, part 2, p609.
20. R. E. Lee *O.R.*, vXIX, part 1, p151; Stuart, *O.R.*, vXIX, part 1, p820–821.
21. Stuart, *O.R.*, vXIX, part 1, p821; R. E. Lee, *O.R.*, vXIX, part 1, p152–153.
22. Lincoln was privately frustrated with G. B. McClellan for not having destroyed Lee's army at Antietam Creek or before they got back to Virginia, but he publicly touted their victory. On Sept 22, 1862, Lincoln announced to his cabinet that he had made a covenant with God that if Lee was driven from Maryland then he would issue his Emancipation Proclamation. Under the powers available to him, Lincoln's move was to free the slaves in the seceded states — he could only seize enemy "property," he could not free slaves in states not in rebellion. Much controversy swirled around this Proclamation in the North. Did it mean, for instance, if Lee had decisively carried the day at Sharpsburg, Lincoln would not have issued the Proclamation? Another curiosity stemmed from the notion that unless the states in rebellion returned to the Union by Jan 1, their slaves "…shall be then, henceforward, and forever free." Did this mean if the southern states had returned by that date, the slaves would not have been free? In any case, the meaning of the Proclamation and level of commitment to emancipation was questioned, even in the military, and McClellan, with his political allies in Washington, was near the center of it. Indeed, the opposition to Lincoln in McClellan's army almost got out of hand and on Oct 7, McClellan had to issue a general order reminding his men that the military must remain subordinate to civil authority. For a more complete survey of the controversies surrounding Lincoln's Proclamation see, J. M. McPherson, *Battle Cry of Freedom* (New York, 1989), p557–560.
23. Davis, *O.R.*, vXIX, part 2, p634. When the 2nd North Carolina Cavalry arrived in Warrenton a couple of weeks later, they were in Chambliss's command. Even though Chambliss was reporting to R. E. Lee, his command was still under G. W. Smith and not yet part of Robert E. Lee's Army of Northern Virginia — that would take more formal reorganization.
24. R. E. Lee, *O.R.*, vXIX, part 2, p641–642.
25. R. E. Lee, *O.R.*, vXIX, part 2, p640.
26. *O.R.*, vXVIII, p751.
27. The Company Muster Rolls contain only this one reference to their activity during the week and a half stay at Culpeper. Company Muster Roll, "Compiled Service Records of Confederate Soldiers Who Served in Organizations from The State of North Carolina," Second Cavalry (19th State Troops), National Archives Microfilm Publication, Microcopy No. 270, Roll 11, NARS.
28. W. H. F. Payne's account of his activities and the results are in an autobiographical letter he wrote for Joseph R. Anderson on Dec 13, 1903. this letter and other papers of Colonel Payne are in the Museum of the Confederacy in Richmond. Some of Payne's papers have been printed in cooperation with the Museum in the Sept 1999 issue of *North & South*, v2, number 7, p76–89.
29. W. H. F. "Rooney" Lee was promoted to brigadier general on Oct 3, 1862 to rank from Sept 19. *O.R.*, vXIX, part 2, p705.
30. As quoted in Henry B. McClellan, *I Rode with Jeb Stuart* (Bloomington, 1958), p146.
31. H. B. McClellan, *I Rode with Jeb Stuart* (Bloomington, 1958), p157–158.
32. W. W. Blackford, *War Years with Jeb Stuart* (Baton Rouge, 1993), p177; H. B. McClellan, *I Rode with Jeb Stuart* (Bloomington, 1958), p158–160.
33. Andrews, Addendum Series I, *O.R. Supplement*, v3, p601–603; Andrews also sent a report to Governor Vance of North Carolina which was reprinted as follows: Major Clinton M. Andrews, "Second N.C. Cavalry — Another Haul of Live Yankees and Other Brutes," *Weekly Raleigh Register*, Nov 5, 1862, p3, column 1. Samuel N. Mason, Dec 9, 1862, letter to his father from below Fredericksburg, Special Collections item P. C. 755, NCDA.
34. Stahel, *O.R.*, vXIX, part 2, p97–98.
35. Stahel, *O.R.*, vXIX, part 2, p453.
36. R. E. Lee, *O.R.*, vXIX, part 2, p669.
37. R. E. Lee, *O.R.*, vXIX, part 2, p676.
38. R. E. Lee, *O.R.*, vXIX, part 2, p678.
39. R. E. Lee, *O.R.*, vXIX, part 2, p680.
40. Sigle, *O.R.*, vXIX, part 2, p100.
41. Asmussen, *O.R.*, vXIX, part 2, p502; Bayard, *O.R.*, vXIX, part 2, p518.
42. Autobiographical letter from William H. F. Payne to Joseph R. Anderson on Dec 13, 1903, p80, MC.
43. G. B. McClellan, *O.R.*, vXIX, part 1, p87.
44. Stuart outlined their activities during the early days of Nov in his official report of operations from Oct 30–Nov 6. *O.R.*, vXIX, part 2, p140–145.
45. H. B. McClellan, *I Rode with Jeb Stuart*, (Bloomington, 1958), p186.
46. Bayard, *O.R.*, vXIX, part 2, p518.
47. Pleasonton, *O.R.*, vXIX, part 2, p519.
48. H. B. McClellan, *I Rode with Jeb Stuart*, (Bloomington, 1958), p170, 171.
49. H. B. McClellan, *I Rode with Jeb Stuart*, (Bloomington, 1958), p171.

50. Company Muster Roll, "Compiled Service Records of Confederate Soldiers Who Served in Organizations from The State of North Carolina," Second Cavalry (19th State Troops), National Archives Microfilm Publication, Microcopy No. 270, Roll 11, NARS.
51. H. B. McClellan, *I Rode with Jeb Stuart*, (Bloomington, 1958), p171.
52. H. B. McClellan, *I Rode with Jeb Stuart*, (Bloomington, 1958), p88, 177.
53. Colburn for McClellan, *O.R.*, vXIX, part 2, p547.
54. H. B. McClellan, *I Rode with Stuart*, (Bloomington, 1958), p181.
55. Stuart, *O.R.*, vXIX, part 2, p144. The manner and extent to which the 1st North Carolina Cavalry suffered is discussed in greater detail in C. J. Hartley, *Stuart's Tarheels, James B. Gordon and His North Carolina Cavalry*, (Baltimore, 1996), p163–169.
56. Stuart, *O.R.*, vXIX, part 2, p144.
57. Sigel, *O.R.*, vXIX, part 2, p547.
58. Pleasonton, *O.R.*, vXIX, part 2, p117.
59. H. B. McClellan, *I Rode with Jeb Stuart*, (Bloomington, 1958), p88.
60. Stuart, *O.R.*, vXIX, part 2, p144.
61. Stuart, *O.R.*, vXIX, part 2, p144; Lee, *O.R.*, vXIX, part 2, p703.
62. Autobiographical letter from William H. F. Payne to Joseph R. Anderson on Dec 13, 1903, p80, MC.
63. G. B. McClellan, *O.R.*, vXIX, part 1, p88.
64. R. E. Lee, *O.R.*, vXIX, part 2, p695; also see Lee to Davis, *O.R.*, vXIX, part 2, p698.
65. R. E. Lee, *O.R.*, vXIX, part 2, p701–702.
66. Lincoln, Nov 5, 1862, *O.R.*, vXIX, part 2, p545. G. B. McClellan bid his troops farewell from the gallery of the Warren Green Hotel in Warrenton—the new headquarters for the Army of the Potomac. McClellan left town early on the morning of Nov 9.
67. R. E. Lee, *O.R.*, vXIX, part 2, p704; Sigel, *O.R.*, vXIX, part 2, p550.
68. Long, *O.R.*, vXIX, part 2, p704; Stuart, *O.R.*, vXIX, part 2, p144–145; R. E. Lee, *O.R.*, vXIX, part 2, p707. Autobiographical letter from William H. F. Payne to Joseph R. Anderson on Dec 13, 1903, p81, MC; W. A. Graham, "Nineteenth Regiment (Second Cavalry)," p87.
69. Taylor for Lee, *O.R.*, vXIX, part 2, p705.
70. In late Oct, Lee had reorganized the Army of Northern Virginia into two Corps. The First Corps was under Longstreet, and the Second under Jackson—formal announcement of this organization came on Nov 6, 1862. Reorganization of the cavalry was also needed because Lee was convinced it should play a larger role in the war—what it had shown to date impressed him. D. S. Freeman, *Lee's Lieutenants*, (New York, 1995), v2, p269–280.
71. Special Orders No. 238, *O.R.*, vXIX, part 2, p712–713; H. B. McClellan, *I Rode with Jeb Stuart* (Bloomington, 1958), note on p186–187.
72. R. L. T. Beale, *History of the Ninth Virginia Cavalry in the War Between the States* (Amissville, Va., 1981), p54.
73. R. E. Lee to Randolph, *O.R.*, vXIX, part 2, p709; R. E. Lee to Smith, *O.R.*, vXIX, part 2, p709–710.
74. R. E. Lee, *O.R.*, vXIX, part 2, p716; R. E. Lee, *O.R.*, vXXI, p1013–1014; also see R. E. Lee, *O.R.*, vXXI, p1020–1021.
75. R. E. Lee, *O.R.*, vXXI, p1013. One gets the feeling R. E. Lee is engaged in just a bit of micro-management in this assignment. Even thought his son had by that time proven himself to be a very capable commander of the 9th Regiment Virginia Cavalry, it was his first assignment as commander of his own brigade. Another point of interest stemming from the relationship has to do with R. E. Lee's custom of ending his official correspondences with a version of "I am, most respectfully, your obedient servant," or "I have the honor to be, with great respect, your obedient servant." One can infer a moment of awkwardness in General Lee's sign-off when he uncharacteristically ended with "&c." rather than "your obedient servant."
76. R. E. Lee, *O.R.*, vXXI, p1019; R. E. Lee, "The Battle of Fredericksburg," *O.R.*, vXXI, p550–551. On Nov 18, R. E. Lee again sent Stuart across the Rappahannock to confirm the suspected movements of the Army of the Potomac. According to R. E. Lee, Stuart's findings "... confirmed the previous reports, and it was clear that the whole Federal Army, under Burnside, was moving toward Fredericksburg."
77. J. M. McPherson, *Battle Cry of Freedom* (New York, 1998), p570.
78. R. E. Lee, *O.R.*, vXXI, p1020.
79. R. E. Lee, *O.R.*, vXXI, p551.
80. R. E. Lee, *O.R.*, vXXI, p551.
81. G. W. Beale, *A Lieutenant of Cavalry in Lee's Army* (Baltimore, 1994), p56.
82. G. W. Beale, *A Lieutenant of Cavalry in Lee's Army* (Baltimore, 1994), p56–57.
83. R. L. T. Beale, *History of the Ninth Virginia Cavalry* (Amissville, 1981), p54–55, 59–61.
84. J. A. Early, *The Memoirs of General Jubal A. Early* (New York, 1994), p166.
85. G. W. Beale, *A Lieutenant of Cavalry in Lee's Army* (Baltimore, 1994), p57.
86. Samuel N. Mason, Dec 9, 1862, letter to his father from below Fredericksburg, Special Collections item P. C. 755, NCDA.
87. W. Allen, *The Army of Northern Virginia in 1862* (Dayton, Ohio, 1984), p469; R. E. Lee, "The Confederate Army," p147.
88. J. H. Moore, "With Jackson at Hamilton's Crossing," p141; J. Early, *The Memoirs of General Jubal A. Early* (New York, 1994), p171.
89. G. W. Beale, *A Lieutenant of Cavalry in Lee's Army* (Baltimore, 1994), p63; R. L. T. Beale, *History of the Ninth Virginia Cavalry* (Amissville, 1981), p56; H. B. McClellan, *I Rode with Jeb Stuart* (Bloomington, 1958), p192.
90. J. M. McPherson, *Battle Cry of Freedom* (New York, 1989), p571–572; D. S. Freeman, *Lee's Lieutenants* (New York, 1995), v2, p332–358 (on the Confederate right) and 359–368 (on the Confederate left); G. McWhiney and P. D. Jamieson, *Attack and Die: Civil War Military Tactics and the Southern Heritage* (Tuscaloosa, 1982); D. S. Freeman, *Lee's Lieutenants* (New York, 1995), v2, p341; H. von Borcke, *Memoirs of the Confederate War for Independence* (Nashville, 1999), p306.
91. The Company Muster Rolls for the 2nd North Carolina Cavalry show the following for Company B, "during Saturday and Saturday night of the Fredericksburg fight we were employed as sharpshooters on the right of ... battle," and for Company I, "Saturday night we were sharpshooters at Fredericksburg on right of our line." "Compiled Service Records of Confederate Soldiers Who Served in Organizations from The State of North Carolina," Second Cavalry (19th State Troops), National Archives Microfilm Publication, Microcopy No. 270, Roll 11, NARS.
92. G. W. Beale, *A Lieutenant of Cavalry in Lee's Army* (Baltimore, 1994), p64–66.
93. R. L. T. Beale, *History of the Ninth Virginia Cavalry* (Amissville, 1981), p57; J. Early, *The Memoirs of General Jubal A. Early* (New York, 1994), p184.
94. D. S. Freeman, *Lee's Lieutenants* (New York, 1995), v2, p397–399; H. B. McClellan, *I Rode with Jeb Stuart* (Bloomington, 1958), p197.
95. Stuart, *O.R.*, vXXI, p731; also see D. S. Freeman, *Lee's Lieutenants* (New York, 1995), v2, p400.
96. W. H. F. Lee, *O.R.*, vXXI, p742; Stuart, *O.R.*, vXXI, p731; D. S. Freeman, *Lee's Lieutenants* (New York, 1995), v2, p400.
97. Stuart, *O.R.*, vXXI, p732.
98. Stuart, *O.R.*, vXXI, p732–733.
99. Stuart, *O.R.*, vXXI, p733.
100. Stuart, *O.R.*, vXXI, p734.
101. Stuart, *O.R.*, vXXI, p734–735; also see, D. S. Freeman, *Lee's Lieutenants* (New York, 1995), v2, p400–406.
102. D. S. Freeman, *Lee's Lieutenants* (New York, 1995), v2, p428.

103. H. von Borcke, *Memoirs of the Confederate War for Independence* (Nashville, 1999), p350.
104. D. S. Freeman, *Lee's Lieutenants* (New York, 1995), p428.
105. Note to Stuart with letter to Hampton enclosed: R. E. Lee, *O.R.*, vXXI, p1101.
106. J. M. McPherson, *Battle Cry of Freedom* (New York, 1989), p584–585; D. S. Freeman, *Lee's Lieutenants* (New York, 1995), v2, p429; Stoneman, *O.R.*, vXXV, part 2, p60.
107. H. von Borcke, *Memoirs* (Nashville, 1999), p353; H. B. McClellan, *I Rode with Jeb Stuart* (Bloomington, 1958), p204; C. J. Hartley, *Stuart's Tarheels* (Baltimore, 1996), p183–185.
108. R. E. Lee, *O.R.*, vXXV, part 2, p642.
109. A. B. Nicholson, Chm'n., "Camp of 2nd N.C. Cavalry, Essex Co., Va.," *Fayetteville Observer*, March 23, 1863, p1, col 5.
110. W. H. F. Lee, *O.R.*, vXXV, part 1, p20.
111. D. S. Freeman, *Lee's Lieutenants* (New York, 1995), v2, p457–464.
112. R. E. Lee, *O.R.*, vXXV, part 2, p664.
113. Muster Roll reports for the 2nd North Carolina Cavalry, Company D, show they "left camp in Essex County on April 4 under orders for Orange County C. H., which we reached on April 8. We stayed there until the 12th and then on to Culpeper C. H., where we arrived that afternoon. the next day all our dismounted men numbering about 130 were ordered to rifle pits to guard the different fords along the Rappahannock." The same information is shown in Company E's report. (Companies A, F, G, H, and I show near Culpeper C. H. for March–April. Co. B has no entry.) These records indicate that they arrived at Culpeper on the 12th, and were on picket duty at Upper Rappahannock fords by April 13. "Compiled Service Records of Confederate Soldiers Who Served in Organizations from The State of North Carolina," Second Cavalry (19th State Troops), National Archives Microfilm Publication, Microcopy No. 270, Roll 11, NARS. Also see, R. L. T. Beale, *History of the Ninth Virginia Cavalry* (Amissville, 1981), p60.
114. R. E. Lee, *O.R.*, vXXV, part 2, p703.
115. Milas Cavin letter to his mother, April 13, 1863 in "Milas A. Cavin Papers," Private Collections # 399, NCDA.
116. Stoneman, *O.R.*, vXXV, part 2, p60.
117. Hooker, *O.R.*, vXXV, part 2, p199–200.
118. R. E. Lee, *O.R.*, vXXV, part 2, p792; W. W. Blackford, *War Years with Jeb Stuart* (Baton Rouge, 1993), p203.
119. Taylor for Stoneman, *O.R.*, vXXV, part 2, p204–205.
120. W. W. Blackford, *War Years with Jeb Stuart* (Baton Rouge, 1993), p203; also see, H. B. McClellan, *I Rode with Jeb Stuart* (Bloomington, 1958), p220.
121. Milas A. Cavin letter to his father from Culpeper Court House on May 29, 1863, in "Milas A. Cavin Papers," Special Collections # 399, NCDA.
122. H. B. McClellan, *I Rode with Jeb Stuart* (Bloomington, 1958), p218–220; Strange, *O.R.*, vXXV, part 1, p87.
123. Buford, *O.R.*, vXXV, part 1, p1088; G. W. Beale, *A Lieutenant of Cavalry in Lee's Army* (Baltimore, 1994), p75–76; Strange, *O.R.*, vXXV, part 1, p87.
124. *O.R.*, vXXV, part 2, p213–214.
125. W. H. F. Lee, *O.R.*, vXXV, part 1, p85; G. W. Beale, *A Lieutenant of Cavalry in Lee's Army* (Baltimore, 1994), p76–78.
126. Hooker and Lincoln, *O.R.*, vXXV, part 2, p214; Hooker, *O.R.*, vXXV, part 2, p238.
127. J. M. McPherson, *Battle Cry of Freedom* (New York, 1989), p639.
128. R. E. Lee, *O.R.*, vXXV, part 2, p724–725.
129. H. B. McClellan, *I Rode with Jeb Stuart* (Bloomington, 1958), p224–225.
130. *O.R.*, vXXV, part 1, p794.
131. Fitzhugh Lee, *General Lee, A Biography of Robert E. Lee* (New York, 1994), p240–243.
132. Devin, *O.R.*, vXXV, part 1, p777–780.
133. Devin, *O.R.*, vXXV, part 1, p777; H. B. McClellan, *I Rode with Jeb Stuart* (Bloomington, 1958), p225–226.
134. "Compiled Service Records of Confederate Soldiers Who Served in Organizations from The State of North Carolina," Second Cavalry (19th State Troops), National Archives Microfilm Publication, Microcopy No. 270, Roll 11, NARS.
135. Devin, *O.R.*, vXXV, part 1, p777.
136. Beardsly in Devin's report: *O.R.*, vXXV, part 1, p778. The First North Carolina Cavalry was not on the Rappahannock that day — they were doing R&R with Wade Hampton's brigade. The brigade was not mobilized for this campaign until May 3, when the Secretary of War called on Hampton to ready his forces and head for the Chancellorsville area. Immediately the 1st North Carolina, which was bivouacked 21 miles away, began to march toward Hampton at Lynchburg. On May 3, Hampton notified the Secretary of War that his brigade was in motion. On May 4, he sent the following: "Two regiments ordered to Farmville, three to Gordonsville. I leave to-day for Gordonsville; have no information; would be glad to hear from Fredericksburg." The only North Carolina Cavalry on the Rappahannock near Kelly's Ford on April 28 and 29 was the 2nd North Carolina Cavalry. The confusion probably resulted from the fact that when the 6th New York crossed the river, it was under the command of Lieutenant Colonel McVicar, but later Captain Beardsly wrote the regiment's report for Colonel Devin. See: Hampton, *O.R.*, vXXV, part 2, p772; and C. J. Hartley, *Stuart's Tarheels* (Baltimore, 1996), p189–190.
137. W. H. F. Lee, *O.R.*, vXXV, part 1, p1098; W. H. F. Lee, "Memoranda of The Operations of Brigadier General W. H. F. Lee's Command During General Stoneman's Raid into Virginia," p181.
138. Kellogg in Devin, *O.R.*, vXXV, part 1, p777; H. B. McClellan, *I Rode with Jeb Stuart* (Bloomington, 1958), p226; R. L. T. Beale, *History of the Ninth Virginia Cavalry* (Amissville, 1981), p62.
139. Most of the 10th was down in the Beaver Dam area and Lousia Court House when called up — they moved toward the Rapidan that day, April 29. Some of the companies of the 10th Virginia Cavalry arrived near Chancellorsville in time to be useful, others met with W. H. F. Lee and the 9th and 13th Virginia Cavalries to engage Stoneman's raid on Lee's lines of communication with Richmond. William Bailey Clement's letter to his wife on May 3, 1863, from camp near Rapidan, in "William Bailey Clement Papers," Private Collection Papers, PC. 409, NCDA.
140. Wickham, *O.R.*, vXXV, part 1, p1045–1046; H. B. McClellan, *I Rode with Jeb Stuart* (Bloomington, 1958) p226; R. L. T. Beale, *History of the Ninth Virginia Cavalry* (Amissville, 1981), p62.
141. Wickham, *O.R.*, vXXV, part 1, p1048.
142. B. F. Fordney, *Stoneman at Chancellorsville, the Coming of age of Union Cavalry* (Shippensburg, Pa., 1998), p19–20.
143. Stuart, *O.R.*, XXV, part 1, p1046; W. H. F. Lee, *O.R.*, XXV, part 1, p1098; H. B. McClellan, *I Rode with Jeb Stuart* (Bloomington, 1958), p227.
144. Beardsley in Devin's *O.R.*, XXV, part 1, p778; Pleasonton, *O.R.*, XXV, part 1, p774; Ruger, *O.R.*, vXXV, p707.
145. Years later, when justifying Stuart's selective actions of that day, H. B. McClellan pointed out that in fact Slocum's column was opposed and slowed during the entire march. It is still unclear whether W. H. F. Lee or Stuart himself ordered the 2nd North Carolina Cavalry to place themselves in front of Slocum's push to the Rapidan, but it was common for the cavalry commanders during that time to "forget" where they had placed the 2nd North Carolina Cavalry. In any case, it is clear that H. B. McClellan learned of the opposition in front of Slocum after the war was over by reading Union reports of the march. Even years later when Stuart's Assistant Adjutant General, H. B. McClellan, was pointing fingers, he inadvertently acknowledged that they did not know at the time who was in front of the advancing enemy. In his words, "What officer was in command of this Confederate picket does not appear; nor can it be stated why he failed to notify the Ely's Ford picket; nor why he failed to communicate his movements to Stuart. It is reasonable, as well as charitable, to suppose that he made the effort to perform

these evident duties, but that his couriers also were captured." (H. B. McClellan, *I Rode with Jeb Stuart* [Bloomington, 1958], footnote on p227–229.) The latter supposition was reasonable because Stuart had sent two couriers to Germanna and Ely's Fords and neither got through. McClellan conferred with his friend, W. H. F. Lee, on more than one occasion after the war while sorting out the facts for his book which suggests that perhaps W. H. F. Lee was not the commander who ordered W. H. Payne to take the 2nd North Carolina Cavalry in front of the advancing enemy column. On the other hand, Stuart did know the location of the 2nd North Carolina Cavalry before the afternoon of April 30, when R. E. Lee noted that Stuart had ordered the cavalrymen to report to him earlier — how much earlier, we do not know, perhaps the day before just after they had crossed the Rapidan. (R. E. Lee, O.R., vXXV, part 2, p761.) Perhaps Stuart knew of the 2nd North Carolina Cavalry's actions that day, but, of course, he did not survive the war and was not available to clarify the matter.

146. Ruger, O.R., vXXV, part 1, p707; Williams, O.R., vXXV, part 1, p677; Hawley, O.R., vXXV, part 1, p719; O.R., vXXV, part 1, p172.
147. Huey, O.R., vXXV, part 1, p783.
148. Recall, Stuart called Colonel J. L. Davis of the 10th Virginia Cavalry up from Beaver Dam (some of them were at Louisa Court House) — W. H. F. Lee had left the 10th Virginia Cavalry there when he moved his brigade to the Rappahannock in early April. Most of the 10th Virginia left for the Rapidan on April 29.
149. R. E. Lee, O.R., vXXV, part 2, p759–760.
150. Anderson, O.R., vXXV, part 1, p849.
151. Anderson, O.R., vXXV, part 1, p850.
152. Stuart, O.R., vXXV, part 1, p1047.
153. R. E. Lee, O.R., vXXV, part 2, p761. More than a month later, on June 6, Anderson wrote in his report on the fighting around Chancellorsville that Colonel Owen and his men from the 3rd Virginia joined him on the afternoon of May 30 and threw out pickets to his front and on both flanks. There was no mention of the 2nd North Carolina Cavalry in this report. Anderson, O.R., vXXV, part 1, p850.
154. R. E. Lee and Special Orders, No. 121, O.R., vXXV, part 2, p758–763; R. E. Lee, O.R., vXXV, part 1, p797.
155. D. S. Freeman, *Lee's Lieutenants* (New York, 1995), v2, p531; McLaws, O.R., vXXV, part 1, p825.
156. McLaws, O.R., vXXV, part 1, p825; D. S. Freeman, *Lee's Lieutenants* (New York, 1995), v2, p532–538.
157. H. B. McClellan, *I Rode with Jeb Stuart* (Bloomington, 1958), p231–232; Wickham, O.R., vXXV, part 1, p1048.
158. Fitzhugh Lee, *General Lee* (New York, 1994), p245–246; D. S. Freeman, *Lee's Lieutenants* (New York, 1995), v2, p538–541.
159. Fitzhugh Lee, *General Lee* (New York, 1994), p247–253; R. E. Lee, O.R., vXXV, part 1, p798.
160. H. B. McClellan, *I Rode with Jeb Stuart* (Bloomington, 1958), p235–237; H. von Borcke, *Memoirs* (Nashville, 1999), p386.
161. Fitzhugh Lee, *General Lee* (New York, 1994), p247–253; R. E. Lee, O.R., vXXV, part 1, p799.
162. H. B. McClellan, *I Rode with Jeb Stuart* (Bloomington, 1958), p235–236.
163. H. B. McClellan, *I Rode with Jeb Stuart* (Bloomington, 1958), p237–249.
164. R. E. Lee, O.R., vXXV, part 2, p769; H. B. McClellan, *I Rode with Jeb Stuart* (Bloomington, 1958), p251–254; Fitzhugh Lee, *General Lee* (New York, 1994), p253.
165. Anderson, O.R., vXXV, part 1, p853; Wilcox, O.R., vXXV, part 1, p857; R. E. Lee, O.R., vXXV, part 1, p801–802; H. B. McClellan, *I Rode with Jeb Stuart* (Bloomington, 1958), p255; D. N. Couch, "The Chancellorsville Campaign," p164, 171; J. M. McPherson, *Battle Cry of Freedom* (New York, 1989), p644–645.
166. On May 5, Pleasonton was ordered with the cavalry under his command to secure the fords from the north side of the Rappahannock. On May 6, he said we had "returned to our old camps." Pleasonton, O.R., vXXV, part 1, p776.
167. Stoneman, O.R., vXXV, part 1, p1063.
168. The activities of Stoneman's columns are described in: Stoneman, O.R., vXXV, part 1, p1057–1064; W. H. F. Lee, O.R., vXXV, part 1, p1097–1098.
169. B. F. Fordney, *Stoneman at Chancellorsville* (Shippensburg, Pa., 1998), p50–52; E. G. Longacre, *Lincoln's Cavalrymen* (Mechanicsburg, 2000), p147.
170. Clingman, O.R., vIX, p477.
171. J. G. Barrett, *The Civil War in North Carolina* (Chapel Hill, 1963), p133.
172. Letter from Levi Y. Lockhart to Sister from Camp Springgreen on Aug 17, 1862, in "Lockhart Family Letters," SCL-DU.
173. "The Late Attack on Washington, N.N.CC.— Distinguished Gallantry of Captain Tucker's Company," *Weekly Raleigh Register*, Sept 24, 1862, p2, col 3.
174. Captain Boothe of Company C was in command of the 2nd squadron at Hamilton. When it was clear his recovery would not leave him fit for further service, he resigned on May 1, 1863. On that date, James M. Wynn became Captain of Company C. William A. Graham of Company K became the commander of the 2nd Squadron following the loss of Captain Boothe on Sept 6, 1862. Graham was not yet Captain of Company K, but he had been in command. Company K had been in a similar situation — their Captain, Josiah Turner, had been seriously wounded in April of 1862, but did not resign until Nov 8, 1862, at which time William A. Graham was appointed Captain of Company K.
175. Mix, O.R., vXVIII, p7–10; letter from Levi Lockhart to his sister on Sept 14, 1862, in "Lockhart Family Letters," SCL-DU.
176. Foster, O.R., vXVIII, p4–6.
177. Member of Tuckers Cavalry Company, "The Late Attack on Washington, N.C...." *Weekly Raleigh Register*, Sept 24, 1862, p2, col 3; Lieutenant, Company K, 2nd Cavalry, *Hillsborough Recorder Weekly*, Sept 17, 1862, seven p from p1, col 1; J. G. Barrett, *The Civil War in North Carolina* (Chapel Hill, 1963), p134.
178. W. A. Graham, "Nineteenth Regiment (Second Cavalry)," p88. Also, Private Levi Lockhart wrote his sister from Hamilton, North Carolina on Sept 14. By Oct 19, Levi's cousin, also in the Second Squadron, wrote from Drewry's Bluff, both in "Lockhart Family Letters," SCL-DU. The regiment's Company Muster Roll information for Sept–Oct show for Company C, that soon after (the fight at Washington) orders came from Brigadier General Martin "to proceed to Va. to rejoin our Regiment but at Petersburg ordered by Major General French to go to Drewry's Bluff and report to Brigadier General Daniels;" and for Company K, "Marched from Spring Green, Martin County to Drewry's Bluff, distance 120 miles." Also see, "Abstract from Field Return of troops commanded by Maj. Gen. G. W. Smith, Oct 1, 1862," O.R., vXVIII, p751.
179. G. W. Smith, O.R., vXVIII, p743–744, 747–748, 749.
180. Spear, O.R., vXVIII, p125; Peck, O.R., vXVIII, p510.
181. O.R. Atlas, Series I, vXI, Plate XVII.
182. W. A. Graham, "Nineteenth Regiment (Second Cavalry)," p88.
183. Letter from William H. Strayhorn to his cousin dated Jan 11, 1863, in "Margaret F. Craig Papers," SCL-DU.
184. G. H. Steuart, O.R., vXIX, part 2, p664–665; report by Lieutenant W. P. Roberts of Company C, 2nd North Carolina Cavalry, in Compiled Service Records-NARA.
185. Vance, O.R., vXVIII, p860–861.
186. Letter from William H. Strayhorn to his cousin dated Jan 11, 1863, , in "Margaret F. Craig Papers," SCL-DU.
187. G. W. Smith, O.R., vXVIII, p794.
188. Melton for G. W. Smith, O.R., vXVIII, p802; D. H. Hill, O.R., vXVIII, p188. On March 15, Colonel Jack Brown at his headquarters near Drewry's Bluff stated he had "Capt. W. A. Graham, commanding Second Squadron, Second North Carolina Cavalry" in his command at that place. There is a

note attached to Graham's name indicating they had been there "since ordered to Petersburg." *O.R.*, vXVIII, p921.
  189. Seddon, *O.R.*, vXVIII, p815.
  190. Seddon, *O.R.*, vXVIII, p883; R. E. Lee, *O.R.*, vXVIII, p882, 883–884.
  191. Cooper, *O.R.*, vXVIII, p884; Seddon, *O.R.*, vXVIII, p890; *O.R.*, vXVIII, p2, and *O.R.*, vXVIII, Special Orders, p895; Brown, *O.R.*, vXVIII, p921.
  192. Pendleton, *O.R.*, vXXV, part 2, p651; J. W. Gordon, "Pleasant Days in War Time," p93.
  193. J. W. Gordon, "Pleasant Days in War Time," p93–94.
  194. Dodge, *O.R.*, vXVIII, p179–180.
  195. D. S. Freeman, *Lee's Lieutenants* (New York, 1995), v2, p477–478; Confederate purchasing agents had been buying supplies for the Army throughout North Carolina and further south for sometime and it usually involved some politics and economics. This is amply illustrated by a communication from Governor Z. B. Vance of North Carolina to President Davis back on Nov 12, 1862; Vance, *O.R.*, vXVIII, p771.
  196. Elzey, *O.R.*, vXVIII, p871; Longstreet, *O.R.*, vXVIII, p918.
  197. Brown, *O.R.*, vXVIII, p921.
  198. Elzey sent Wise's brigade toward Yorktown on April 8, and they were to attack the Union outpost at Williamsburg on the morning of April 11. Elzey notified R. E. Lee of his plan in a correspondence dated April 7, and Lee approved of Elzey's planned diversion toward Yorktown in a message dated April 11. R. E. Lee, *O.R.*, vXVIII, p979.
  199. D. S. Freeman, *Lee's Lieutenants* (New York, 1995), v2, p479.
  200. W. Harrison, *Pickett's Men: A Fragment of War History* (Gaithersburg, Md., 1988), p75–76. Also see D. S. Freeman, *Lee's Lieutenants* (New York, 1995), v2, p481–483.
  201. Private Levi also pointed out that they had left seven men in the 2nd N.C. Hospital in Petersburg and one at Jerusalem. Letter from Levi Y. Lockhart to his sister, Ellen Lockhart, on March 24, 1863 from Wakefield, Virginia, in "Lockhart Family Letters," SCL-DU.
  202. At this time, the total effective cavalrymen in the other eight companies of the 2nd North Carolina Cavalry on the Rappahannock totaled just 110.
  203. Private Walker was one of the men the squadron had left in the hospital at Petersburg. He caught up with his comrades at Wakefield, and in his first letter from there he noted the hard march his squadron had made from Petersburg, "It rained, and hailed, and snowed for two days and nights on them, and I was glad that I was not with them, for if I had been with them, I do not know what I should have done." Letter from George W. Walker to his cousin, Ellen Lockhart, on March 29, 1863 from Wakefield, Virginia, in "Lockhart Family Letters," SCL-DU.
  204. S. A. Cormier, *The Siege of Suffolk* (Lynchburg, 1989), p55–56.
  205. Longstreet, *O.R.*, Series I, vXVIII, p963.
  206. Graham was specific about the places, if not the times, they were engaged—he said: "There were engagements with the enemy at Providence Church and Chuckatuck." The fight at Chuckatuck was more than likely during their withdrawal several weeks later. W. A. Graham, "Nineteenth Regiment (Second Cavalry)," p88; S. A. Cormier, *The Siege of Suffolk* (Lynchburg, 1863), p88–89.
  207. Longstreet, *O.R.*, vXVIII, p997.
  208. H. B. Simpson, *Hood's Texas Brigade: Lee's Grenadier Guard* (Dallas, 1983), p228.
  209. While patrolling the area south of Smithfield, the Second Squadron normally went as far as and beyond Chuckatuck, putting some of them in position to see a frequent curiosity which was a small problem for Longstreet—the curious problem was General George Pickett. In 1852, Pickett lost his wife of less than a year, and by 1863, he was 38 years old, still a widower, and very much in love with a young lady who happened to live near Chuckatuck, north of Western Branch. On numerous occasions, Longstreet gave Pickett permission to ride as fast as he could to visit his lady and return before morning—maybe getting some sleep before he was back on duty. After awhile, Longstreet must have figured Pickett's absence, even when he was physically there, was getting out of hand and needed to be less frequent—Longstreet decided Pickett should be in camp most evenings. Pickett protested to Longstreet's staff and apparently managed to make his visits from time-to-time. D. S. Freeman, *Lee's Lieutenants* (New York, 1995), v2, p491–492. Pickett's willingness to leave his command with the enemy in front of them would have more serious consequences when he did so to attend a clambake at Five Forks on April 1, 1865.
  210. J. W. Gordon, "Pleasant Days in War Time," p95.
  211. S. A. Cromier, *The Siege of Suffolk* (Lynchburg, 1863), p104.
  212. S. A. Cromier, *The Siege of Suffolk* (Lynchburg, 1863), p226.
  213. Longstreet, *O.R.*, vXVIII, p1001; R. E. Lee, *O.R.*, vXVIII, p1024–1025.
  214. D. B. Sanger, *James Longstreet, I. Soldier* (Baton Rouge, 1952), p143, 144; Sorrel for Longstreet, *O.R.*, vLI, p695.
  215. One such event took place on April 22, and has been described in the following: S. A. Cromier, *The Siege of Suffolk* (Lynchburg, 1863), p171, 226; Cushing, *O.R. Navy*, v8, p771–772.
  216. Levi Y. Lockhart's letter to his sister on April 27, 1863 from camp near Suffolk, in "Lockhart Family Letters," SCL-DU. When Captain Josiah Turner resigned on Nov 8, 1862, William A. Graham was promoted to captain, and John P. Lockhart was promoted to 1st lieutenant in Graham's place. When Graham retired on Nov 20, 1863, John P. Lockhart became captain of Company K of the 2nd North Carolina Cavalry.
  217. R. E. Lee, *O.R.*, vXVIII, p1024–1025.
  218. Longstreet, *O.R.*, vXVIII, p1032 and 1037; J. Longstreet, *From Manassas to Appomattox, Memoirs of the Civil War in America* (Bloomington, 1960), p326–327.
  219. Longstreet, *O.R.*, vXVIII, p1038.
  220. Just two days earlier, on May 1, 1863, captain of the 2nd Squadron, John Boothe, found it necessary to resign because of an "aneurysm of the sub-clavian artery resulting from a wound received...." at Washington, N.C. on Sept 6, 1862. James M. Wynn of Hertford County was promoted to captain of Company C on May 1, 1863. Wynn was probably acting captain from Sept 7, 1862 until his appointment in May of 1863. William A. Graham, of Company K, remained in command of the Second Squadron of the 2nd Regiment North Carolina Cavalry.
  221. Union commanders on the Confederate right had word of the pending withdrawal about 11:00 P.M. on May 3 from a couple of deserters. Other deserters confirmed the report, but by the time Union forces got to the enemy earthworks on the Confederate right, they were empty. Dodge, *O.R.*, vXVIII, p300.
  222. *O.R.*, Series I, vXVIII, p275–279 for Major General John J. Peck's report, and p316–320 for Colonel Arthur H. Dutton's report—both with the U.S. Army, commanding at Suffolk. Also see S. A. Cromier, *The Siege of Suffolk* (Lynchburg, 1863), p266.
  223. Crosby, *O.R.*, vXVIII, p321–322.
  224. *O.R.*, vXVIII, p320.
  225. S. A. Cromier, *The Siege of Suffolk* (Lynchburg, 1863), p270–272.
  226. Longstreet, *O.R.*, vXVIII, p1040.
  227. Sorrel for Longstreet, *O.R.*, vXVIII, p1045.
  228. Ferebee via Longstreet, *O.R.*, vXVIII, p740.
  229. French, *O.R.*, vXVIII, p706.
  230. D. S. Freeman, *Lee's Lieutenants* (N.Y., 1995), v2, p684.

Three

  1. W. A. Graham, "Nineteenth Regiment (Second Cavalry)," p88; D. S. Freeman, *Lee's Lieutenants* (New York, 1995), v3, p1.

2. Payne was back with the 2nd North Carolina by March of 1863 and commanded the regiment until Colonel Solomon Williams returned on June 8. Payne resumed command of the 2nd North Carolina by June 10 and stayed with them until he was captured at Hanover, Pennsylvania on June 30 of 1863.
3. Years later, H. B. McClellan estimated the number of cavalrymen present for the review at about 4,000. H. B. McClellan, *I Rode with Jeb Stuart* (Bloomington, 1958), p261. The Official Report submitted by Stuart's staff on May 25 indicated the three brigades present contained 5,071. *O.R.*, vXXV, part 2, p823.
4. Message from Robert Y. Walker to Lieutenant John P. Lockhart, May 1863, in "Lockhart Family Letters," SCL-DU.
5. H. von Borcke, *Memoirs* (Nashville, 1999), p411.
6. W. W. Blackford, *War Years with Jeb Stuart* (Baton Rouge, 1993), p211–212.
7. H. von Borcke, *Memoirs* (Nashville, 1999), p411; H. B. McClellan, *I Rode with Jeb Stuart* (Bloomington, 1958), p261.
8. William A. Graham, "From Brandy Station to The Heights of Gettysburg," *The News and Observer*, Feb 7, 1904, p2.
9. D. S. Freeman, *Lee's Lieutenants* (New York, 1995), v3, p3–4.
10. J. E. Cooke, *Wearing of the Gray, Being Personal Portraits, Scenes and Adventures of the War* (Bloomington, 1959), p305–306; W. W. Blackford, *War Years with Jeb Stuart* (Baton Rouge, 1993), p212–213; J. N. Opie, *A Rebel Cavalryman with Lee, Stuart and Jackson* (Dayton, Ohio, 1997), p145–146.
11. G. W. Beale, *A Lieutenant of Cavalry in Lee's Army* (Baltimore, 1994), p83.
12. R. E. Lee, *O.R.*, Series I, vXXV, part 2, p820–821.
13. *O.R.*, Series I, vXXV, part 2, p823.
14. *O.R.*, Series I, vXXV, part 2, p819–820.
15. *O.R.*, Series I, vXXV, part 2, p823.
16. R. E. Lee, *O.R.*, vXXV, part 2, p836–837.
17. Stuart, *O.R.*, vXXV, part 2, p825.
18. W. A. Graham, "From Brandy Station to The Heights of Gettysburg," *The News and Observer*, Feb 7, 1904, p2.
19. One can readily find recruitment advertisements for the 1st North Carolina Cavalry, but we are hard pressed to find them for the 2nd Cavalry. For instance, see: *Fayetteville Observer*, Feb 24, 1862, p1, col 2; and *The Weekly Raleigh Register*, March 25, 1863, p3, col 4.
20. W. A. Graham, "Nineteenth Regiment (Second Cavalry)," p88–89.
21. My general discussion of the larger battle at Brandy Station on June 9, 1863 is drawn from the histories listed at the end of this note. I have made more specific references to these and other materials where it seemed appropriate. The reader is directed to the following works for a more complete discussion of the larger battle. For accounts by people who were there, see H. B. McClellan, *I Rode with Jeb Stuart* (Bloomington, 1958), p257–295; H. von Borcke and J. Scheibert, *The Great Cavalry Battle of Brandy Station* (Gaithersburg, Maryland, 1976), p43–72; G. W. Beale, *A Lieutenant of Cavalry in Lee's Army* (Baltimore, 1994), p80–99; J. N. Opie, *A Rebel Cavalryman* (Dayton, 1997) p147–157. For historians' views see: D. S. Freeman, *Lee's Lieutenants* (New York, 1995), v3, p1–19; C. J. Hartley, *Stuart's Tarheels* (Baltimore, 1996), p196–214; Clark B. Hall, "The Battle of Brandy Station," *Civil War Times Illustrated*, (May/June 1990) p32–42, 45; E. G. Longacre, *The Cavalry at Gettysburg* (Lincoln, 1993), p65–86; Patrick Brennan, "Thunder On The Plains of Brandy," *North & South*, part I, p14–34, and part II, p32–51.
22. Buford, *O.R.*, vXXVII, part 3, p8.
23. Halleck, *O.R.*, vXXVII, part 1, p31; Pleasonton, *O.R.*, vXXVII, part 3, p32.
24. Butterfield for Hooker, *O.R.*, vXXVII, part 3, p27–28.
25. L. W. Hopkins, *From Bull Run to Appomattox* (Baltimore, 1908), p90.
26. L. W. Hopkins, *From Bull Run to Appomattox* (Baltimore, 1908), p90–91.
27. J. N. Opie, *A Rebel Cavalryman* (Dayton, 1997), p148–150. Private Opie ended his chapter with the following comment: "That night, after the fighting was over, the soldiers of my company crowded around me, confusing me with compliments, calling me Antony and Murat, until, feeling that I did not justly deserve their commendations, I remarked, 'O pshaw! boys, my horse ran away with me.'" With those words, he lost the opportunity to become one of the war's heroes, but did history one better by remaining an honest man.
28. W. A. Graham, "Nineteenth Regiment (Second Cavalry)," p90; Colonel Williams had just returned to duty from his honeymoon leave the day before. The regiment's temporary commander, Lieutenant Colonel W. H. F. Payne of the 4th Virginia, was back with his old regiment near Brandy Station. Payne and the 4th Virginia Cavalry fought along side the 2nd South Carolina near Stevensburg that morning. Payne's duties that day were identified by H. B. McClellan with this comment: "The communication between Butler and Wickham was made through Lieutenant Colonel W. H. Payne, of the 4th Virginia." (See, H. B. McClellan, *I Rode with Jeb Stuart* (Bloomington, 1958), p288.) Payne later stated that he commanded the 2nd North Carolina in the Battle of Brandy Station—but that was a mistake, Colonel Sol. Williams was clearly in command of the regiment on June 9, 1863 (for Payne's comment, see: J. Coski, "Forgotten Warrior," *North & South*, p81, col 1.
29. W. A. Graham, "Nineteenth Regiment (Second Cavalry)," p91; G. W. Beale, *A Lieutenant of Cavalry in Lee's Army* (Baltimore, 1994), p86; Jones, *O.R.*, vXXVII, part 2, p749.
30. H. B. McClellan, *I Rode with Jeb Stuart* (Bloomington, 1958), p266; G. W. Beale, *A Lieutenant of Cavalry in Lee's Army* (Baltimore, 1994), p86; Marshall, *O.R.*, vXXVII, part 2, p757–758; "The Rappahannock Cavalry Fight," *Fayetteville Observer*, June 22, 1863, p2, col 2.
31. Flood, *O.R.*, vXXVII, part 1, p821–822; Mudge, *O.R.*, vXXVII, part 1, p1043–1044.
32. G. W. Beale, *A Lieutenant of Cavalry in Lee's Army* (Baltimore, 1994), p86–87; Pleasonton at 11:00 A.M., *O.R.*, vXXVII, part 1, p903.
33. At one point, George W. Beale put the 2nd North Carolina as well as the 4th Virginia there but that was a misprint—it was Hampton's 2nd South Carolina. G. W. Beale, *A Lieutenant of Cavalry in Lee's Army* (Baltimore, 1994), p90.
34. H. B. McClellan, *I Rode with Jeb Stuart* (Bloomington, 1958), p285–291.
35. H. B. McClellan, *I Rode with Jeb Stuart* (Bloomington, 1958), p288.
36. H. B. McClellan, *I Rode with Jeb Stuart* (Bloomington, 1958), p269–271.
37. According to Stuart's adjutant, Lieutenant W. W. Blackford, he had no reason to have been concerned about enemy troops arriving from Kelly's Ford, but as soon as trouble was perceived, Stuart went into action. Lieutenant Blackford was sent down the line to alert all the commanders. W. W. Blackford, *War Years with Jeb Stuart* (Baton Rouge, 1993), p215; Jones, *O.R.*, vXXVII, part 2, p749.
38. G. M. Neese, *Three Years in the Confederate Horse Artillery* (New York, 1911), p176; W. W. Blackford, *War Years with Jeb Stuart* (Baton Rouge, 1993), p215–216, 217.
39. D. S. Freeman, *Lee's Lieutenants* (New York, 1995), v3, p12.
40. Pleasonton, *O.R.*, vXXVII, part 1, p903.
41. "The Rappahannock Cavalry Fight," *Fayetteville Observer*, June 22, 1863, p2, col 2.
42. Marshall, *O.R.*, vXXVII, part 2, p758.
43. R. L. T. Beale, *History of the Ninth Virginia Cavalry* (Amissville, 1981), p68–69.
44. G. W. Beale, *A Lieutenant of Cavalry in Lee's Army* (Baltimore, 1994), p96.
45. H. B. McClellan, *I Rode with Jeb Stuart* (Bloomington, 1958), p282–283.
46. W. A. Graham, "Nineteenth Regiment (Second Cavalry)," pages 91–92; for a view of the afternoon's fighting

through eyes in the 10th Virginia, see, R. J. Driver, Jr., *10th Virginia Cavalry* (Lynchburg, Virginia, 1992), p36–38.

47. G. W. Beale, *A Lieutenant of Cavalry in Lee's Army* (Baltimore, 1994), p96.

48. Pleasonton, *O.R.*, vXXVII, part 1, p903–904.

49. *O.R.*, vXXVII, part 1, p905.

50. "The Rappahannock Cavalry Fight," *Fayetteville Observer*, June 22, 1863, p2, col 2.

51. As indicated, W. H. F. Lee was wounded during this engagement. Consequently, he missed the events of the late afternoon, and never filed a report on the brigade's activities on June 9, 1863. W. H. F. Lee was probably told about the later stages of the encounter by his good family friend, R. L. T. Beale (who was commanding the 9th Virginia), while he was recuperating from his leg wound at Beale's home. (W. H. F. Lee was captured there and remained a prisoner until March 1864.) The Regimental commander of the 2nd North Carolina, Sol. Williams, was killed a few minutes after W. H. F. Lee was wounded and obviously had no chance to report the activities of his regiment. Several years after the war, R. L. T. Beale was kind enough to write an account of what he remembered for H. B. McClellan when the latter wrote his account of the war. McClellan stated that he had no firsthand knowledge of what W. H. F. Lee's brigade was doing, given his involvement at Fleetwood Hill. So McClellan's account was largely based on the written information from R. L. T. Beale, and a walk and talk with W. H. F. Lee over the battle field several years after the war. Both Lee and McClellan probably relied heavily on R. L. T. Beale's account, which primarily focused on his regiment's immediate contest. See, H. B. McClellan, *I Rode with Jeb Stuart* (Bloomington, 1958), p267, note 1; W. A. Graham, "Nineteenth Regiment (Second Cavalry)," p93–94.

52. Turner, *O.R.*, vXXVII, part 2, p720.

53. William F. Fox, *Regimental Losses in the American Civil War* (Albany, 1889), chapter XIV, p545.

54. G. W. Beale, *A Lieutenant of Cavalry in Lee's Army* (Baltimore, 1994), p97. On the point of Union losses being more severe on Buford's front, see a supporting conclusion in: C. B. Hall, "The Battle of Brandy Station," *Civil War Times Illustrated*, p 45.

55. Adjutant General's Department, Roll of Honor, vols. 3 and 4, "A Sketch of the Nineteenth Regiment N.C. Troops. (Cavalry)," Microfilm no. S.1.80P., third page, NCDA.

56. Chambliss, *O.R.*, vXXVII, part 2, p771–772. It is understandable Colonel Chambliss did not feel he was in a position to write on the brigade's activities for the day or afternoon but it is unfortunate he did not deem it proper to submit a report on the activities of the sharpshooters under his command throughout the day. Unfortunately, by the time W. H. F. Lee was released from captivity and returned to service he was concerned with current matters and did not file a detailed report of the day's activities.

57. W. A. Graham, "Nineteenth Regiment (Second Cavalry)," p94–95.

58. W. A. Graham, "Nineteenth Regiment (Second Cavalry)," p93; Stuart, *O.R.*, vXXVII, part 2, p684.

59. Raleigh, Adjutant General's Department, Roll of Honor, vols. 3 and 4, "A Sketch of the Nineteenth Regiment N.C. Troops. (Cavalry)," Microfilm no. S.1.80P., third page, NCDA; J. E. Moore, "Over the Grave of Colonel Sol. Williams," p138.

60. Pleasonton, *O.R.*, vXXVII, part 3, p84.

61. W. A. Graham, "Nineteenth Regiment (Second Cavalry)," p91–92.

62. W. A. Graham, "Nineteenth Regiment (Second Cavalry)," p95.

63. H. B. McClellan, *I Rode with Jeb Stuart* (Bloomington, 1958), p296.

64. Stuart, *O.R.*, vXXVII, part 2, p688.

65. W. A. Graham, "From Brandy Station to The Heights of Gettysburg," *The News and Observer*, Feb 7, 1904, p2.

66. Stuart, *O.R.*, vXXVII, part 2, p688; R. L. T. Beale, *History of the Ninth Virginia Cavalry* (Amissville, 1981), p70.

67. H. B. McClellan, *I Rode with Jeb Stuart* (Bloomington, 1958), p298, 303; H. von Borcke, *Memoirs* (Nashville, 1999), p425; Stuart, *O.R.*, vXXVII, part 2, p688.

68. S. Williams for Hooker, *O.R.*, vXXVII, part 3, p172.

69. A. J. Alexander for Pleasonton, *O.R.*, vXXVII, part 3, p171.

70. I have relied heavily on the work of Robert F. O'Neill Jr. for the descriptions of the fighting at Aldie, Middleburg, and Upperville unless otherwise noted. For a more comprehensive and in-depth description of these three battles, the reader should see: R. F. O'Neill Jr., *The Cavalry Battles of Aldie, Middleburg and Upperville, June 10–27, 1863* (Lynchburg, 1993). For the battle around Aldie see p31–65.

71. More than one historian, after studying this situation, has had critical if not damning words for Pleasonton's judgment if not his motives for sending Duffié on such a mission. For instance, Edward Longacre, a student of the Army of the Potomac, had this to say: "The same day, Pleasonton committed a more serious mistake — perhaps deliberately — when he sent Colonel Duffié and his 275 Rhode Islanders on what amounted to a suicide mission, then abandoned them to their fate." E. G. Longacre, *Lincoln's Cavalrymen*, (Mechanicsburg, 2000), p167. Also see R. F. O'Neill, Jr., *The Cavalry Battles of Aldie, Middleburg and Upperville* (Lynchburg, 1993), p67.

72. R. L. T. Beale, *History of the Ninth Virginia Cavalry* (Amissville, 1981), p70; G. W. Beale, *A Lieutenant of Cavalry in Lee's Army* (Baltimore, 1994), p100; Duffié, *O.R.*, vXXVII, part 1, p962–963. When writing their respective histories, both Beales clearly and specifically made the point that the 9th Virginia Cavalry was at the head of the column on June 17 and that they were the troops encountered by Duffié as he emerged from Thoroughfare Gap that morning. Nevertheless, Edward Longacre stated in his 1986 book that the Confederates first encountered by Duffié were "members of Lieutenant Colonel William H. F. Payne's 2nd North Carolina of Chambliss's brigade." The same historian in his 2000 book identified the first troops encountered by Duffié as "... a number of North Carolinians from the brigade of Rooney [W. H. F.] Lee, now under Col. John R. Chambliss, Jr...." The latter could only have been a reference to the 2nd North Carolina cavalrymen. Longacre's cited source in his 1986 work that puts the 2nd North Carolina in front of Duffié is Roy P. Stonesifer, "The Union Cavalry Comes of Age," *Civil War History*, 11 (1965), p279. Stonesifer's only reference to this question is "Meanwhile, Duffié and his 1st Rhode Island (275 men) had proceeded on the morning of June 17 to Thoroughfare Gap. Here his skirmishers encountered sentries of Colonel John R. Chambliss's 2nd North Carolina of W. F. H. Lee's brigade. Not all of Chambliss's regiment was in the vicinity of the Gap, and Duffié pushed through their scattered pickets." No source is given by Stonesifer, however, to support this observation. I have searched elsewhere for supporting evidence indicating the 2nd North Carolina was Duffié's greeting party that morning on the western end of the pass but have found nothing to contradict the Beales's claims that their 9th Virginia was in front of Duffié. See E. G. Longacre, *The Cavalry at Gettysburg* (1993), p110; and E. G. Longacre, *Lincoln's Cavalrymen* (Mechanicsburg, 2000), p167.

73. G. W. Beale, *A Lieutenant of Cavalry in Lee's Army* (Baltimore, 1994), p100.

74. H. B. McClellan, *I Rode with Jeb Stuart* (Bloomington, 1958), p298, 303–304; Duffié, *O.R.*, vXXVII, part 1, p963; also see H. von Borcke, *Memoirs* (Nashville, 1999), p425–426; Paul B. Means, "Additional Sketch Sixty-Third Regiment (Fifth Cavalry), p562.

75. Duffié, *O.R.*, vXXVII, part 1, p963.

76. Duffié, *O.R.*, vXXVII, part 1, p963; also see P. B. Means, "Additional Sketch Sixty-Third Regiment (Fifth Cavalry), p562–563.

77. G. W. Beale, *A Lieutenant of Cavalry in Lee's Army* (Baltimore, 1994), p101.

78. Duffié, *O.R.*, vXXVII, part 1, p963–964; H. B. McClellan, *I Rode with Jeb Stuart* (Bloomington, 1958), p305.

79. W. A. Graham, "From Brandy Station to The Heights of Gettysburg," *The News and Observer*, Feb 7, 1904, p2.
80. G. W. Beale, *A Lieutenant of Cavalry in Lee's Army* (Baltimore, 1994), p101.
81. H. B. McClellan, *I Rode with Jeb Stuart* (Bloomington, 1958), p306; P. B. Means, "Additional Sketch Sixty-Third Regiment (Fifth Cavalry), p563.
82. G. W. Beale, *A Lieutenant of Cavalry in Lee's Army* (Baltimore, 1994), p101.
83. For the description of events on June 19, unless noted, I have relied upon: R. F. O'Neill, Jr., *The Cavalry Battles of Aldie, Middleburg and Upperville* (Lynchburg, 1993), p100–113.
84. T. S. Garnett, Jr., "Annals of the War: Cavalry Service with General Stuart," *Philadelphia Weekly Times*, Feb 8, 1879.
85. S. Williams for Hooker, *O.R.*, vXXVII, part 3, p172.
86. T. S. Garnett, Jr., "Annals of the War: Cavalry Service with General Stuart," *Philadelphia Weekly Times*, Feb 8, 1879.
87. T. S. Garnett, Jr., "Annals of the War: Cavalry Service with General Stuart," *Philadelphia Weekly Times*, Feb 8, 1879.
88. R. L. T. Beale, *History of the Ninth Virginia Cavalry* (Amissville, 1981), p73; G. W. Beale, *A Lieutenant of Cavalry in Lee's Army* (Baltimore, 1994), p102; T. S. Garnett, Jr., "Annals of the War: Cavalry Service with General Stuart," *Philadelphia Weekly Times*, Feb 8, 1879.
89. G. W. Beale, *A Lieutenant of Cavalry in Lee's Army* (Baltimore, 1994), p102.
90. H. von Borcke, *Memoirs* (Nashville, 1999), p429–430.
91. T. S. Garnett, Jr., "Annals of the War: Cavalry Service with General Stuart," *Philadelphia Weekly Times*, Feb 8, 1879.
92. W. W. Blackford, *War Years with Jeb Stuart* (Baton Rouge, 1993), p219–220.
93. Pleasonton, *O.R.*, vXXVII, part 3, p223.
94. Platt, *O.R.*, vXXVII, part 3, p215; Butterfield for Hooker, *O.R.*, vXXVII, part 3, p218; Pleasonton, *O.R.*, vXXVII, part 3, p210. By the morning of June 20, even Pleasonton knew Longstreet was guarding Ashby and Snicker's Gaps and that the Confederate army was moving toward the Potomac, *O.R.*, vXXVII, part 3, p224.
95. H. B. McClellan, *I Rode with Jeb Stuart* (Bloomington, 1958), p307.
96. W. A. Graham, "From Brandy Station to The Heights of Gettysburg," *The News and Observer*, Feb 7, 1904, p2.
97. Pleasonton, *O.R.*, vXXVII, part 1, p911.
98. Just as on the previous several pages, the description of action on June 21, 1863 draws heavily from R. F. O'Neill, Jr., *The Cavalry Battles of Aldie, Middleburg and Upperville* (Lynchburg, 1993), p119–158 unless otherwise noted.
99. H. B. McClellan, *I Rode with Jeb Stuart* (Bloomington, 1958), p308.
100. D. S. Freeman, *Lee's Lieutenants* (New York, 1995), v3, p53; H. B. McClellan, *I Rode with Jeb Stuart* (Bloomington, 1958), p311–312, 313; and Stuart, *O.R.*, vXXVII, part 2, p691.
101. Gamble, *O.R.*, vXXVII, part 1, p932–933.
102. Gamble, *O.R.*, vXXVII, part 1, p932–933; Buford, *O.R.*, vXXVII, part 1, p920–921; Jones, *O.R.*, vXXVII, part 2, p751.
103. Buford, *O.R.*, vXXVII, part 1, p921.
104. From where Colonel R. L. T. Beale stood, Gamble's dismounted cavalrymen probably were indistinguishable from infantry, and their position behind a stone fence appeared to mark a field rather than the sunken lane. R. L. T. Beale, *History of the Ninth Virginia Cavalry* (Amissville, 1981), p74.
105. W. A. Graham, "From Brandy Station to The Heights of Gettysburg," *The News and Observer*, Feb 7, 1904, p2.
106. Bryan's very interesting and useful letter is transcribed more fully at the end of this section. George P. Bryan to his father, West's Building Hospital, Baltimore, Sept 25, 1863, "John Herritage Bryan Papers," Private Collection no. 6, NCDA.
107. John Z. H. Scott, "Memoirs of J. Z. H. Scott, Brother of R. Lewis Scott" (Galveston, July 1, 1891), p14–15, VHS.
108. According to Lieutenant Graham of the 2nd North Carolina, the men from the 10th Virginia who gave assistance were under Major William B. Clements. Clements was a North Carolinian, who on more than one occasion requested that his North Carolina company be transferred to a North Carolina regiment—his requests were never granted. W. A. Graham, "Nineteenth Regiment (Second Cavalry)," p96.
109. R. L. T. Beale, *History of the Ninth Virginia Cavalry* (Amissville, 1981), p74–75.
110. W. A. Graham, "Nineteenth Regiment (Second Cavalry)," p96.
111. The order in which the various regiments entered the field after the 2nd North Carolina was first hit is not consistent across all reports and is difficult to determine, but it is certain at the pitch of the battle, all of Gamble's regiments were involved, as well as the 2nd North Carolina, some of the 7th, 9th, 10th, 11th, and 12th Virginia Cavalry. Gamble, *O.R.*, vXXVII, part 1, p933; Jones, *O.R.*, vXXVII, part 2, p751.
112. W. A. Graham, "From Brandy Station to The Heights of Gettysburg," *The News and Observer*, Feb 7, 1904, p2.
113. Stuart, report of Aug 20, 1863, *O.R.*, vXXVII, part 2, p687; R. L. T. Beale, *History of the Ninth Virginia Cavalry* (Amissville, 1981), p76.
114. D. S. Freeman, *Lee's Lieutenants* (New York, 1995), v3, p55.
115. W. F. Fox, *Regimental Losses in the American Civil War* (Albany, 1889), chapter XIV, p545.
116. Jones, *O.R.*, vXXVII, part 2, p751; R. L. T. Beale, *History of the Ninth Virginia Cavalry* (Amissville, 1981), p75.
117. W. A. Graham, "Nineteenth Regiment (Second Cavalry)," p96.
118. Letter from George P. Bryan to his father, West's Building Hospital, Baltimore, Sept 25, 1863, John Herritage Bryan Papers, Private Collection no. 6, NCDA.
119. Stuart, *O.R.*, vXXVII, part 2, p691.
120. R. L. T. Beale, *History of the Ninth Virginia Cavalry* (Amissville, 1981), p77.
121. R. E. Lee to Stuart, *O.R.*, vXXVII, part 3, p913; R. E. Lee to Ewell, *O.R.*, vXXVII, part 3, p914–915; Longstreet to R. E. Lee, *O.R.*, vXXVII, part 3, p915; At a later date, Stuart said the plan to pass around Hooker's army was part of what he proposed to R. E. Lee and that his commanding general authorized the move, if Stuart thought it practicable. Stuart, *O.R.*, vXXVII, part 2, p692.
122. R. E. Lee to Stuart, *O.R.*, vXXVII, part 3, p923.
123. D. S. Freeman, *Lee's Lieutenants* (New York, 1995), v3, p59–60.
124. R. L. T. Beale, *History of the Ninth Virginia Cavalry* (Amissville, 1981), p77; Stuart, *O.R.*, vXXVII, part 2, p692.
125. J. E. Cooke, *Wearing of the Gray* (Bloomington, 1959), p234–235; Stuart, *O.R.*, vXXVII, part 2, p693.
126. Stuart, *O.R.*, vXXVII, part 2, p693.
127. Stuart, *O.R.*, vXXVII, part 2, p693; D. S. Freeman, *Lee's Lieutenants* (New York, 1995), v3, p63.
128. R. L. T. Beale, *History of the Ninth Virginia Cavalry* (Amissville, 1981), p77; W. A. Graham, "From Brandy Station to The Heights of Gettysburg," *The News and Observer*, Feb 7, 1904, p2; Letter from Milas Cavin to his sister, June 27, 1863 from Culpeper, "Milas A. Cavin Papers," Private Collection, P.C. 399, NCDA; D. S. Freeman, *Lee's Lieutenants* (New York, 1995), v3, p63.
129. J. E. Cooke, *Wearing of the Gray* (Bloomington, 1959), p234.
130. G. W. Beale, *A Lieutenant of Cavalry in Lee's Army* (Baltimore, 1994), p112.
131. W. A. Graham, "From Brandy Station to The Heights of Gettysburg," *The News and Observer*, Feb 7, 1904, p2.
132. D. S. Freeman, *Lee's Lieutenants* (New York, 1995), v3, p64; W. A. Graham, "From Brandy Station to The Heights of Gettysburg," *The News and Observer*, Feb 7, 1904, p2.
133. Stuart, *O.R.*, vXXVII, part 2, p693.
134. R. L. T. Beale, *History of the Ninth Virginia Cavalry* (Amissville, 1981), p78; H. B. McClellan, *I Rode with Jeb Stuart* (Bloomington, 1958), p323.

135. R. L. T. Beale, *History of the Ninth Virginia Cavalry* (Amissville, 1981), p78; Stuart, *O.R.*, vXXVII, part 2, p693.
136. W. A. Graham, "From Brandy Station to The Heights of Gettysburg," *The News and Observer*, Feb 7, 1904, p2.
137. W. A. Graham, "From Brandy Station to The Heights of Gettysburg," *The News and Observer*, Feb 7, 1904, p2. Colonel Beale of the 9th Virginia also described the ordeal with additional observations, in R. L. T. Beale, *History of the Ninth Virginia Cavalry* (Amissville, 1981), p78
138. W. S. Nye, *Here Come the Rebels* (Dayton, 1984), p317; H. B. McClellan, *I Rode with Jeb Stuart* (Bloomington, 1958), p324.
139. W. W. Blackford, *War Years with Jeb Stuart* (Baton Rouge, 1993), p224.
140. W. W. Blackford, *War Years with Jeb Stuart* (Baton Rouge, 1993), p224.
141. Stuart, *O.R.*, vXXVII, part 2, p694.
142. R. L. T. Beale, *History of the Ninth Virginia Cavalry* (Amissville, 1981), p79; Stuart, *O.R.*, vXXVII, part 2, p694.
143. Stuart, *O.R.*, vXXVII, part 2, p694.
144. R. L. T. Beale, *History of the Ninth Virginia Cavalry* (Amissville, 1981), p79; W. A. Graham, "From Brandy Station to The Heights of Gettysburg," *The News and Observer*, Feb 7, 1904, p2; Stuart, *O.R.*, vXXVII, part 2, p694.
145. R. L. T. Beale, *History of the Ninth Virginia Cavalry* (Amissville, 1981), p79–80.
146. R. L. T. Beale, *History of the Ninth Virginia Cavalry* (Amissville, 1981), p80; also see, Stuart, *O.R.*, vXXVII, part 2, p694.
147. J. M. McPherson, *Battle Cry of Freedom* (New York, 1989), p651, 653.
148. R. E. Lee from Chambersburg to Ewell, dated June 28, in Clifford Dowdey and Louis H. Manarin, editors, *The Wartime Papers of Robert E. Lee* (New York, 1987), p534. Their source is at the Virginia Historical Society in Richmond, Virginia.
149. Stuart, *O.R.*, vXXVII, part 2, p694; R. L. T. Beale, *History of the Ninth Virginia Cavalry* (Amissville, 1981), p81.
150. Stuart, *O.R.*, vXXVII, part 2, p695; H. B. McClellan, *I Rode with Jeb Stuart* (Bloomington, 1958), p326.
151. R. L. T. Beale, *History of the Ninth Virginia Cavalry* (Amissville, 1981), p81.
152. Stuart, *O.R.*, vXXVII, part 2, p695; H. B. McClellan, *I Rode with Jeb Stuart* (Bloomington, 1958), p327.
153. R. L. T. Beale, *History of the Ninth Virginia Cavalry* (Amissville, 1981), p81.
154. R. E. Lee, *O.R.*, vXXVII, part 3, p912–913.
155. R. L. T. Beale, *History of the Ninth Virginia Cavalry* (Amissville, 1981), p81.
156. W. A. Graham, "From Brandy Station to The Heights of Gettysburg," *The News and Observer*, Feb 7, 1904, p2. Sergeant William H. Strayhorn remained in his company, and fought to the end. He was wounded during Lee's retreat to Appomattox Court House and died in a Petersburg hospital on April 17, 1865; John Wesley Umstead was wounded in action Aug 16, 1864 at Fussell's Mill but returned to his unit and fought to the end.
157. W. A. Graham, "From Brandy Station to The Heights of Gettysburg," *The News and Observer*, Feb 7, 1904, p2.
158. W. A. Graham, "From Brandy Station to The Heights of Gettysburg," *The News and Observer*, Feb 7, 1904, p2.
159. Stuart, *O.R.*, vXXVII, part 2, p695; H. B. McClellan, *I Rode with Jeb Stuart* (Bloomington, 1958), p327.
160. In his report for that day, Kilpatrick noted that just minutes after receiving word that Stuart's men were approaching Littlestown, the rear of his column was attacked at Hanover. This is curious because Fitz Lee's brigade had driven cavalrymen from Kilpatrick's command from Westminster back on their support on the evening of the 28th, and Stuart's troopers moved up to occupy Union Mills on the evening of the 29th of June. Kilpatrick, *O.R.*, vXXVII, part 1, p986.
161. Hammond, *O.R.*, vXXVII, part 1, p1008.
162. H. B. McClellan, *I Rode with Jeb Stuart* (Bloomington, 1958), p327.
163. R. L. T. Beale, *History of the Ninth Virginia Cavalry* (Amissville, 1981), p82.
164. Colonel Beale said the 2nd North Carolina was moving on a road to their left. R. L. T. Beale, *History of the Ninth Virginia Cavalry* (Amissville, 1981), p82; Blackford said "The 2nd North Carolina Regiment made the first charge through the town, driving the enemy out,..." W. W. Blackford, *War Years with Jeb Stuart* (Baton Rouge, 1993), p225; H. B. McClellan, *I Rode with Jeb Stuart* (Bloomington, 1958), p327–328; R. J. Driver, *10th Virginia Cavalry* (Lynchburg, 1992), p39; Graham, Adjutant General's Department, Roll of Honor, vols. 3 and 4, "A Sketch of the Nineteenth Regiment N.C. Troops. (Cavalry)," Microfilm no. S.1.80P., third page, NCDA; G. W. Beale, *A Lieutenant of Cavalry in Lee's Army* (Baltimore, 1994), p113.
165. G. R. Prowell, *Prelude to Gettysburg, Encounter at Hanover* (Shippensburg, Pa., 1994), p58–59.
166. G. R. Prowell, *Prelude to Gettysburg, Encounter at Hanover* (Shippensburg, Pa., 1994), p113.
167. Hammond, *O.R.*, vXXVII, part 1, p1008.
168. G. R. Prowell, *Prelude to Gettysburg, Encounter at Hanover* (Shippensburg, Pa., 1994), p93.
169. R. L. T. Beale, *History of the Ninth Virginia Cavalry* (Amissville, 1981), p82.
170. G. R. Prowell, *Prelude to Gettysburg, Encounter at Hanover* (Shippensburg, Pa., 1994), p100–101. Samuel Abram Reddick is one of many troopers who never left the Forney farm. Prowell, the local historian, who wrote of the fighting at Hanover had the opportunity to speak with many people who remembered the day. Nonetheless, he recorded an error made by the Forney family about Samuel A. Reddick. Samuel was shot through the chest during the fight and managed to crawl up the steps to the Forney home where he lay for several hours. By evening the family took him into the house where he was comforted along with three wounded Union soldiers. The young man died the next day, but "Before he breathed his last he pulled from his inside pocket a copy of the New Testament and opening the lid, help [held] up to the sister of Mr. Forney the open book. On a flyleaf was the name of his only sister, a young woman residing in North Carolina. "Take this book," he said, "and send it to my home. That address will reach my sister. She gave me this book when I left home two years ago, and she asked me to keep it and bring it back again when the cruel war shall have ended. It has ended now for me." The name of this soldier was Samuel Reddick. He was a sergeant in the Second North Carolina Regiment.... Miss Forney opened a correspondence with the soldier's sister, when it was learned that his father was a clergyman. In reply to her letter the father requested that the soldier's grave be marked.... A year later some friends or relatives came to Hanover, took up the body and sent it to North Carolina, where it was buried in the village graveyard." The Forneys knew the young soldier was the son of Abram Reddick of Hertford County, North Carolina, and they understandably assumed he was a member of the 2nd North Carolina Cavalry which was fighting around their home. However, Samuel was a student at the University of Virginia when the war broke out and he chose to join the 13th Virginia Cavalry along with some of his classmates. Samuel wrote a very interesting letter to his father describing the formation of his convictions and his company. Samuel A. Riddick to his father from Camp Ruffin on Nov 23, 1861, "The Cowpers Papers," no. 3150 in SHC-UNC.
171. W. W. Blackford, *War Years with Jeb Stuart* (Baton Rouge, 1993), p226–227.
172. H. B. McClellan, *I Rode with Jeb Stuart* (Bloomington, 1958), p328.
173. William H. Payne to Joseph R. Anderson, Dec 13, 1903 in J. Coski, "Forgotten Warrior," *North & South*, p81; W. A. Graham, "Nineteenth Regiment (Second Cavalry)," p97; also, a member of Stuart's staff, H. B. McClellan, raised the

question at a later date, when he said "...if it [the 2nd North Carolina] could have been properly supported, would have resulted in the rout of Kilpatrick's command." H. B. McClellan, *I Rode with Jeb Stuart* (Bloomington, 1958), p327–328.

174. R. L. T. Beale, *History of the Ninth Virginia Cavalry* (Amissville, 1981), p82–83; for a general description of the melee around Forney's farm also see T. Alexander, "Gettysburg Cavalry Operations, June 27–July 3, 1863," *Blue and Gray*, p25; for a description of Stuart's dramatic exit from Frederick road and the field, see W. W. Blackford, *War Years with Jeb Stuart* (Baton Rouge, 1993), p226–227.

175. R. L. T. Beale, *History of the Ninth Virginia Cavalry* (Amissville, 1981), p83; Hammond, *O.R.*, vXXVII, part 1, p1008–1009.

176. R. L. T. Beale, *History of the Ninth Virginia Cavalry* (Amissville, 1981), p83; W. W. Blackford, *War Years with Jeb Stuart* (Baton Rouge, 1993), p227.

177. W. A. Graham, "From Brandy Station to The Heights of Gettysburg," *The News and Observer*, Feb 7, 1904, p2, 4. When the turmoil around the wagons settled down, Graham, "Learning of the capture of my [his] regiment I [he] joined the wagon guard and so continued until we [they] reached Gettysburg."

178. J. E. Cooke, *Wearing of the Gray* (Bloomington, Indiana, 1959), p241; T. Alexander, "Gettysburg Cavalry Operations, June 27–July 3, 1863," *Blue and Gray*, p27.

179. Most of the losses were taken at Hanover. The 9th Virginia, however, took several if not close to half of their losses at Westminster the day before. Stuart, *O.R.*, vXXVII, part 2, p713. Colonel R. Beale in his regimental history put the number at about 20; Driver in his regimental history uses Stuart's number; and Balfour in his history of the 13th put the number at 13. R. L. T. Beale, *History of the Ninth Virginia Cavalry* (Amissville, 1981), p83; R. J. Driver, *10th Virginia Cavalry* (Lynchburg, 1992), p38; D. T. Balfour, *13th Virginia Cavalry* (Lynchburg, 1986), p21; on the 9th Virginia at Westminster, see, G. W. Beale, *A Lieutenant of Cavalry in Lee's Army* (Baltimore, 1994), p113, and W. A. Graham, "From Brandy Station to The Heights of Gettysburg," *The News and Observer*, Feb 7, 1904, p2.

180. Adjutant General's Department, Roll of Honor, vols. 3 and 4, "A Sketch of the Nineteenth Regiment N.C. Troops. (Cavalry)," Microfilm no. S.1.80P, third page, NCDA. Captain Graham's count differs a little because he undoubtedly knew of individuals receiving minor wounds who were not reported or entered into company records.

181. J. E. Cooke, *Wearing of the Gray* (Bloomington, Indiana, 1959), p243–244; Stuart, *O.R.*, vXXVII, part 2, p696.

182. Stuart, *O.R.*, vXXVII, part 2, p696–697; W. W. Blackford, *War Years with Jeb Stuart* (Baton Rouge, 1993), p228.

183. Stuart, *O.R.*, vXXVII, part 2, p697; W. W. Blackford, *War Years with Jeb Stuart* (Baton Rouge, 1993), p228.

184. H. B. McClellan, *I Rode with Jeb Stuart* (Bloomington, 1958), p330–331.

185. W. A. Graham, "From Brandy Station to The Heights of Gettysburg," *The News and Observer*, Feb 7, 1904, p4.

186. Adjutant General's Roll of Honor on Oct 1, 1863, as quoted in L. H. Manarin, "19th Regiments N.C. Troops (2nd Regiment N.C. Cavalry)," *North Carolina Troops*, vII, Cavalry, page 101; W. A. Graham, "From Brandy Station to The Heights of Gettysburg," *The News and Observer*, Feb 7, 1904, p4.

187. Stuart, *O.R.*, vXXVII, part 2, p696; W. A. Graham, "Nineteenth Regiment (Second Cavalry)," p98.

188. W. W. Blackford, *War Years with Jeb Stuart* (Baton Rouge, 1993), p228; Stuart, *O.R.*, vXXVII, part 2, p696.

189. W. W. Blackford, *War Years with Jeb Stuart* (Baton Rouge, 1993), p228; Stuart, *O.R.*, vXXVII, part 2, p696; H. B. McClellan, *I Rode with Jeb Stuart* (Bloomington, 1958), p330.

190. R. L. T. Beale, *History of the Ninth Virginia Cavalry* (Amissville, 1981), p84–85.

191. J. E. Cooke, *Wearing of the Gray* (Bloomington, Indiana, 1959), p246; Hampton, *O.R.*, vXXVII, part 2, p724.

192. H. B. McClellan, *I Rode with Jeb Stuart* (Bloomington, 1958), p330–331.

193. H. B. McClellan, *I Rode with Jeb Stuart* (Bloomington, 1958), p332; Stuart, *O.R.*, vXXVII, part 2, p697.

194. W. A. Graham, "From Brandy Station to The Heights of Gettysburg," *The News and Observer*, Feb 7, 1904, p4; R. L. T. Beale, *History of the Ninth Virginia Cavalry* (Amissville, 1981), p85.

195. Stuart, *O.R.*, vXXVII, part 2, p697; H. B. McClellan, *I Rode with Jeb Stuart* (Bloomington, 1958), p332.

196. R. L. T. Beale, *History of the Ninth Virginia Cavalry* (Amissville, 1981), p85–86.

197. J. M. McPherson, *Battle Cry of Freedom* (New York, 1989), p652–653.

198. Hess, *Lee's Tar Heels* (Chapel Hill, 2002), p115–117; D. S. Freeman, *Lee's Lieutenants* (New York, 1995), v3, p77–78, 80–81.

199. D. S. Freeman, *Lee's Lieutenants* (New York, 1995), v3, p82–87, 89, 93–100; J. M. McPherson, *Battle Cry of Freedom* (New York, 1989), p654.

200. J. M. McPherson, *Battle Cry of Freedom* (New York, 1989), p655; D. S. Freeman, *Lee's Lieutenants* (New York, 1995), v3, p106–109.

201. D. S. Freeman, *Lee's Lieutenants* (New York, 1995), v3, p103–105, 111–117.

202. D. S. Freeman, *Lee's Lieutenants* (New York, 1995), v3, p119–120; 128.

203. J. M. McPherson, *Battle Cry of Freedom* (New York, 1989), p660.

204. Stuart, *O.R.*, vXXVII, part 2, p697.

205. W. E. Miller, "The Cavalry Battle Near Gettysburg," p402.

206. R. L. T. Beale, *History of the Ninth Virginia Cavalry* (Amissville, 1981), p86.

207. W. A. Graham, "Nineteenth Regiment (Second Cavalry)," p98; W. A. Graham, "From Brandy Station to The Heights of Gettysburg," *The News and Observer*, Feb 7, 1904, p4.

208. W. E. Miller, "The Cavalry Battle Near Gettysburg," p401.

209. Stuart, *O.R.*, vXXVII, part 2, p698.

210. Stuart, *O.R.*, vXXVII, part 2, p697.

211. W. A. Graham, "From Brandy Station to The Heights of Gettysburg," *The News and Observer*, Feb 7, 1904, p4.

212. W. E. Miller, "The Cavalry Battle Near Gettysburg," p402.

213. R. L. T. Beale, *History of the Ninth Virginia Cavalry* (Amissville, 1981), p87.

214. W. A. Graham, "From Brandy Station to The Heights of Gettysburg," *The News and Observer*, Feb 7, 1904, p4.

215. W. A. Graham, "Nineteenth Regiment (Second Cavalry)," p98.

216. W. A. Graham, "From Brandy Station to The Heights of Gettysburg," *The News and Observer*, Feb 7, 1904, p4; W. E. Miller, "The Cavalry Battle Near Gettysburg," p402.

217. Hampton, *O.R.*, vXXVII, part 2, p724.

218. W. E. Miller, "The Cavalry Battle Near Gettysburg," p402–403.

219. W. E. Miller, "The Cavalry Battle Near Gettysburg," p403.

220. W. A. Graham, "Nineteenth Regiment (Second Cavalry)," p98; R. L. T. Beale, *History of the Ninth Virginia Cavalry* (Amissville, 1981), p88; G. W. Beale, *A Lieutenant of Cavalry in Lee's Army* (Baltimore, 1994), p116.

221. R. L. T. Beale, *History of the Ninth Virginia Cavalry* (Amissville, 1981), p87–88.

222. Stuart, *O.R.*, vXXVII, part 2, p698; W. E. Miller, "The Cavalry Battle Near Gettysburg," p403.

223. R. L. T. Beale, *History of the Ninth Virginia Cavalry* (Amissville, 1981), p88.

224. Stuart, *O.R.*, vXXVII, part 2, p698; H. B. McClellan, *I Rode with Jeb Stuart* (Bloomington, 1958), p340; W. E. Miller, "The Cavalry Battle Near Gettysburg," p403.

225. W. E. Miller, "The Cavalry Battle Near Gettysburg," p404.
226. W. E. Miller, "The Cavalry Battle Near Gettysburg," p404.
227. Hampton, *O.R.*, vXXVII, part 2, p724–725; W. E. Miller, "The Cavalry Battle Near Gettysburg," p404.
228. W. E. Miller, "The Cavalry Battle Near Gettysburg," p403.
229. Hampton, *O.R.*, vXXVII, part 2, p724–725.
230. W. E. Miller, "The Cavalry Battle Near Gettysburg," p404.
231. W. E. Miller, "The Cavalry Battle Near Gettysburg," p404.
232. W. E. Miller, "The Cavalry Battle Near Gettysburg," p404–405.
233. W. E. Miller, "The Cavalry Battle Near Gettysburg," p405; H. B. McClellan, *I Rode with Jeb Stuart* (Bloomington, 1958), p337.
234. H. B. McClellan, *I Rode with Jeb Stuart* (Bloomington, 1958), p341.
235. H. B. McClellan, *I Rode with Jeb Stuart* (Bloomington, 1958), p341.
236. H. B. McClellan, *I Rode with Jeb Stuart* (Bloomington, 1958), p349.
237. R. L. T. Beale, *History of the Ninth Virginia Cavalry* (Amissville, 1981), p89.
238. W. A. Graham, "From Brandy Station to The Heights of Gettysburg," *The News and Observer*, Feb 7, 1904, p4.
239. J. M. McPherson, *Battle Cry of Freedom* (New York, 1989), p661; also see, E. J. Hess, *Lee's Tar Heels* (Chapel Hill, 2002), p141–154.
240. D. S. Freeman, *Lee's Lieutenants* (New York, 1995), v3, p143.
241. D. S. Freeman, *Lee's Lieutenants* (New York, 1995), v3, p151–156; J. M. McPherson, *Battle Cry of Freedom* (New York, 1989), p661.
242. D. S. Freeman, *Lee's Lieutenants* (New York, 1995), v3, p157–164; W. Harrison, *Pickett's Men* (Gaithersburg, 1988), p90–109; J. M. McPherson, *Battle Cry of Freedom* (New York, 1989), p664.
243. H. B. McClellan, *I Rode with Jeb Stuart* (Bloomington, 1958), p349.
244. D. S. Freeman, *Lee's Lieutenants* (New York, 1995), v3, p164–165; R. E. Lee, General Orders, No. 74 in C. Dowdey and L. H. Manarin (editors), *The Wartime Papers of Robert E. Lee* (New York, 1987), p539–540; R. E. Lee, *O.R.*, vXXVII, part 2, p309.
245. W. E. Jones, *O.R.*, vXXVII, part 2, p752; Marshall (commanding the 7th Virginia), *O.R.*, vXXVII, part 2, p760.
246. C. J. Hartley, *Stuart's Tarheels* (Baltimore, 1996), p242.
247. Stuart, *O.R.*, vXXVII, part 2, p699; R. E. Lee, General Orders, No. 74 in C. Dowdey and L. H. Manarin (editors), *The Wartime Papers of Robert E. Lee* (New York, 1987), p539–540.
248. Eshleman, *O.R.*, vXXVII, part 2, p436b.
249. Adjutant General's Roll of Honor on Oct 1, 1863, as quoted in Louis H. Manarin, "19th Regiments N.C. Troops (2nd Regiment N.C. Cavalry)," *North Carolina Troops*, vII, Cavalry, p101.
250. Eshleman, *O.R.*, vXXVII, part 2, p437; Stuart, *O.R.*, vXXVII, part 2, p703.
251. Stuart, *O.R.*, vXXVII, part 2, p700; R. L. T. Beale, *History of the Ninth Virginia Cavalry* (Amissville, 1981), p90.
252. R. L. T. Beale, *History of the Ninth Virginia Cavalry* (Amissville, 1981), p90–91.
253. Stuart, *O.R.*, vXXVII, part 2, p700.
254. J. E. B. Stuart, "Report of Operations After Gettysburg," p67; R. L. T. Beale, *History of the Ninth Virginia Cavalry* (Amissville, 1981), p91–92.
255. Stuart, *O.R.*, vXXVII, part 2, p701.
256. Stuart, *O.R.*, vXXVII, part 2, p701.
257. Kilpatrick, *O.R.*, vXXVII, part 1, p995.
258. R. L. T. Beale, *History of the Ninth Virginia Cavalry* (Amissville, 1981), p92.
259. Iverson, *O.R.*, vXXVII, part 2, p581.
260. R. L. T. Beale, *History of the Ninth Virginia Cavalry* (Amissville, 1981), p92–93; P. B. Means, "Additional Sketch Sixty-Third Regiment (Fifth Cavalry), p570.
261. Stuart, *O.R.*, vXXVII, part 2, p701.
262. Stuart, *O.R.*, vXXVII, part 2, p701. In spite of Stuart's perceived welcome, the men on Chambliss's line were apparently happy to see him. In Colonel Beale's words, "Late in the afternoon loud cheers along our line announced the presence of General Stuart, whose horse's feet clashed against the pavement at the side of the street as he dashed forward to the front." R. L. T. Beale, *History of the Ninth Virginia Cavalry* (Amissville, 1981), p92–93.
263. J. E. B. Stuart, "Report of Operations After Gettysburg," p68; R. L. T. Beale, *History of the Ninth Virginia Cavalry* (Amissville, 1981), p93; Iverson, *O.R.*, vXXVII, part 2, p581.
264. W. F. Fox, *Regimental Losses in the American Civil War (1861–65)*, chapter XIV, p545.
265. Colonel Beale had watched his men charge the guns on the pike and was under the impression the last enemy round of canister had taken his son, George, and he refused to leave his son's body lying in the road, so after Stuart had ordered his men into the field, and Colonel Beale had emptied his revolvers into the Union riflemen on the sides of the road, he rode back to retrieve his son's body. The Colonel found his son had escaped death "…but Sergeant Richard Washington lay dead in the arms of his weeping brother." Lieutenant George Beale was assigned the responsibility for getting his fallen comrade's body back across the Potomac. R. L. T. Beale, *History of the Ninth Virginia Cavalry* (Amissville, 1981), p93–95.
266. R. L. T. Beale, *History of the Ninth Virginia Cavalry* (Amissville, 1981), p94–95.
267. Buford, *O.R.*, vXXVII, part 1, p928.
268. Eshleman, *O.R.*, vXXVII, part 2, p437; W. M. Owen, *In Camp and Battle with the Washington Artillery* (Baton Rouge, 1999), p257–258.
269. J. E. B. Stuart, "Report of Operations After Gettysburg," p69.
270. W. A. Graham quoted in G. R. Prowell, *Prelude to Gettysburg, Encounter at Hanover* (Shippensburg, Pa., 1994), p172.
271. Stuart, *O.R.*, vXXVII, part 2, p703; R. L. T. Beale, *History of the Ninth Virginia Cavalry* (Amissville, 1981), p96; Clement (North Carolina Company in 10th Virginia Cavalry) letter to his wife, from Williamsport on July 9, 1863, in Private Collection Papers, PC 409, "William Bailey Clement Papers," NCDA.
272. J. E. B. Stuart, "Report of Operations After Gettysburg," p70.
273. J. E. B. Stuart, "Report of Operations After Gettysburg," p70.
274. Stuart, *O.R.*, vXXVII, part 2, p703–704; Buford, *O.R.*, vXXVII, part 1, p929; R. L. T. Beale, *History of the Ninth Virginia Cavalry* (Amissville, 1981), p95–96.
275. J. E. B. Stuart, "Report of Operations After Gettysburg," p71; Buford, *O.R.*, vXXVII, part 1, p929; Stuart, *O.R.*, vXXVII, part 2, p704; Devin, *O.R.*, vXXVII, part 1, p941–942.
276. R. L. T. Beale, *History of the Ninth Virginia Cavalry* (Amissville, 1981), p95–96.
277. J. E. B. Stuart, "Report of Operations After Gettysburg," p71; R. E. Lee, *O.R.*, vXXVII, part 3, p994–995.
278. J. E. B. Stuart, "Report of Operations After Gettysburg," p71; Kilpatrick, *O.R.*, vXXVII, part 1, p996; R. L. T. Beale, *History of the Ninth Virginia Cavalry* (Amissville, 1981), p96; Paul B. Means, "Additional Sketch Sixty-Third Regiment (Fifth Cavalry), p570.
279. R. L. T. Beale, *History of the Ninth Virginia Cavalry* (Amissville, 1981), p97.
280. Kilpatrick, *O.R.*, vXXVII, part 1, p996.
281. R. E. Lee, *O.R.*, vXXVII, part 3, p998; Stuart, *O.R.*, vXXVII, part 2, p705; R. L. T. Beale, *History of the Ninth Virginia Cavalry* (Amissville, 1981), p97.

282. R. E. Lee, *O.R.*, vXXVII, part 3, p1001. General Lee added that the cavalry force designated to replace Longstreet in the trenches might afterwards follow Longstreet over the pontoon bridge at Falling Waters. Fitz Lee was given that assignment but found crossing the bridge too difficult, so he left two squadrons to cross with Longstreet and moved the rest of his command up to ford at Williamsport with the rest of the cavalry.
283. R. E. Lee, *O.R.*, vXXVII, part 2, p323; Stuart, *O.R.*, vXXVII, part 2, p705.
284. Buford, *O.R.*, vXXVII, part 1, p929.
285. J. E. B. Stuart, "Report of Operations After Gettysburg," p72; also see, E. J. Hess, *Lee's Tar Heels* (Chapel Hill, 2002), p162–165.
286. Buford, *O.R.*, vXXVII, part 1, p929; R. E. Lee, *O.R.*, vXXVII, part 2, p323.
287. J. Longstreet, *From Manassas to Appomattox* (Bloominton, 1960), p430; also see, Stuart, *O.R.*, vXXVII, part 2, p705; and E. J. Hess, *Lee's Tar Heels* (Chapel Hill, 2002), p164.
288. D. S. Freeman, *Lee's Lieutenants* (New York, 1995), v3, p195, 210–211; Hampton, *O.R.*, vXXVII, part 2, p724.
289. Stuart, *O.R.*, vXXVII, part 2, p709.
290. W. W. Blackford, *War Years with Jeb Stuart* (Baton Rouge, 1993), p234–235; R. L. T. Beale, *History of the Ninth Virginia Cavalry* (Amissville, 1981), p97.
291. Rufus Barringer, "Ninth Regiment (First Cavalry)," p425.

Four

1. R. E. Lee, *O.R.*, vXXVII, part 2, p324.
2. W. W. Blackford, *War Years with Jeb Stuart* (Baton Rouge, 1993), p235.
3. D. S. Freeman, *Lee's Lieutenants* (New York, 1995), v3, p206–208; Stuart, *O.R.*, vXXVII, part 2, p692–705, 707–709.
4. Stuart, *O.R.*, vXXVII, part 2, p705–706.
5. D. McM. Gregg, *O.R.*, vXXVII, part 1, p955; Meade, *O.R.*, vXXVII, part 1, p94–95.
6. Stuart, *O.R.*, vXXVII, part 2, p706.
7. Stuart, *O.R.*, vXXVII, part 2, p706; D. McM. Gregg, *O.R.*, vXXVII, part 1, p955–956.
8. Stuart, *O.R.*, vXXVII, part 2, p706–707.
9. Meade, *O.R.*, vXXVII, part 1, p95–96.
10. Meade, *O.R.*, vXXVII, part 1, p97.
11. J. Longstreet, *From Manassas to Appomattox* (Bloomington, 1960), p431.
12. Buford, *O.R.*, vXXVII, part 1, p929–930.
13. Meade, *O.R.*, vXXVII, part 1, p99.
14. Stuart, *O.R.*, vXXVII, part 2, p707; R. E. Lee, *O.R.*, vXXVII, part 2, p1026, 1037.
15. R. E. Lee, *O.R.*, vXXVII, part 2, p1037.
16. John O. Collins, letter to his wife on July 27, 1863. C589c.2, reel 8 of 42, Confederate Military Manuscripts Series A: in VHS.
17. Stuart, General Orders No. 25, *O.R.*, vXXVII, part 3, p1049–1051; General Orders No. 26, *O.R.*, vXXVII, part 3, p1054–1056.
18. J. M. McPherson, *Battle Cry of Freedom* (New York, 1989), p666–667; Meade, *O.R.*, vXXVII, part 1, p103–104; Halleck, *O.R.*, vXXVII, part 1, p104–105, 105–106; Meade, *O.R.*, vXXVII, part 1, p106–107, and 108–109.
19. Meade, *O.R.*, vXXVII, part 1, p111–112; R. E. Lee, *O.R.*, vXXVII, part 2, p324.
20. R. E. Lee, *O.R.*, vXXVII, part 3, p1075.
21. R. L. T. Beale, *History of the Ninth Virginia Cavalry* (Amissville, 1981), p98; Buford, *O.R.*, vXXIX, part 1, p22.
22. L. W. Hopkins, *From Bull Run to Appomattox* (Baltimore, 1908), p116.
23. H. B. McClellan, *I Rode with Jeb Stuart* (Bloomington, 1958), p372; Pleasonton, *O.R.*, vXXIX, part 1, p111.
24. G. W. Beale, *A Lieutenant of Cavalry in Lee's Army* (Baltimore, 1994), p124; H. B. McClellan, *I Rode with Jeb Stuart* (Bloomington, 1958), p373.
25. G. W. Beale, *A Lieutenant of Cavalry in Lee's Army* (Baltimore, 1994), p124; R. L. T. Beale, *History of the Ninth Virginia Cavalry* (Amissville, 1981), p98–99; H. B. McClellan, *I Rode with Jeb Stuart* (Bloomington, 1958), p373.
26. L. W. Hopkins, *From Bull Run to Appomattox* (Baltimore, 1908), p116–117.
27. G. W. Beale, *A Lieutenant of Cavalry in Lee's Army* (Baltimore, 1994), p124–125.
28. H. B. McClellan, *I Rode with Jeb Stuart* (Bloomington, 1958), p372.
29. H. E. Davies, *O.R.*, vXXIX, part 1, p120–121.
30. Pleasonton, *O.R.*, vXXIX, part 1, p111.
31. H. B. McClellan, *I Rode with Jeb Stuart* (Bloomington, 1958), p374; R. L. T. Beale, *History of the Ninth Virginia Cavalry* (Amissville, 1981), p99; G. W. Beale, *A Lieutenant of Cavalry in Lee's Army* (Baltimore, 1994), p125–126; Pleasonton, *O.R.*, vXXIX, part 1, p112–113; Warren, *O.R.*, vXXIX, part 1, p134.
32. Meade, *O.R.*, vXXIX, part 1, p9.
33. R. E. Lee, *O.R.*, vXXVII, part 3, p1068–1069; D. S. Freeman, *Lee's Lieutenants*, (New York, 1995), v3, p209.
34. R. E. Lee, *O.R.*, vXXVII, part 3, p1069; D. S. Freeman, *Lee's Lieutenants*, (New York, 1995), v3, p209–215.
35. *O.R.*, vXXIX, part 2, p707–708.
36. From the Rappahannock, "Our Cavalry—Honor to Whom It Is Due," *Fayetteville Observer*, Feb 23, 1863, p4, col 4.
37. W. H. Cheek, "Additional Sketch Ninth Regiment (First Cavalry)," p448–449.
38. C. J. Hartley, *Stuart's Tarheels* (Baltimore, 1996), p267–270.
39. C. J. Hartley, *Stuart's Tarheels* (Baltimore, 1996), p250–254.
40. W. P. Roberts, "Additional Sketch Nineteenth Regiment (Second Cavalry)," p101.
41. Meade, *O.R.*, vXXIX, part 1, p9; A. A. Humphreys, *O.R.*, vXXIX, part 2, p214–215; Buford, *O.R.*, vXXIX, part 1, p140.
42. Marston, *O.R.*, vXXIX, part 2, p214.
43. Buford, *O.R.*, vXXIX, part 1, p140.
44. W. E. Jones's brigade went into battle with their commander under arrest for once again arguing with J. E. B. Stuart. Jones had submitted his resignation to R. E. Lee before the Gettysburg Campaign over disagreements with Stuart, but Lee held the resignation. However, by this time Stuart had Jones before a court-martial for disrespect. Jones was eventually found guilty of the charge and his command was given to Thomas Rosser on Oct 10, 1863. Lee said in a letter to President Davis, "I consider General Jones a brave and intelligent officer, but his feelings have become so opposed to General Stuart that I have lost all hope of his being useful in the cavalry here." General Lee requested that Jones be transferred to a cavalry command elsewhere. R. E. Lee, *O.R.*, vXXIX, part 2, p771–772.
45. Dewey, "Skirmishes near Liberty Mills and at Robertson's Ford," *O.R., Supplement*, vV, p588; J. N. Opie, *A Rebel Cavalryman* (Dayton, 1997), p195.
46. Dewey, "Skirmishes near Liberty Mills and at Robertson's Ford," *O.R., Supplement*, vV, p585; P. B. Means, "Additional Sketch Sixty-Third Regiment (Fifth Cavalry)," p572–573; Strange, "From the 2nd N.C. Cavalry," *Fayetteville Observer*, Oct 5, 1863, p1, col 4.
47. W. H. Cheek, "Additional Sketch Ninth Regiment (First Cavalry)," p452.
48. W. H. Cheek, "Additional Sketch Ninth Regiment (First Cavalry)," p452; also in his "From The First N.C. Cavalry," *Fayetteville Observer*, Oct 5, 1863, p2, col 1.
49. W. H. Cheek, "Additional Sketch Ninth Regiment (First Cavalry)," p452–453.
50. W. H. Cheek, "Additional Sketch Ninth Regiment (First Cavalry)," p453.
51. Dewey, "Skirmishes near Liberty Mills and at Robertson's Ford," *O.R., Supplement*, vV, p586–587; P. B. Means, "Additional Sketch Sixty-Third Regiment (Fifth Cavalry)," p573.

52. Cheek, "From The First N.C. Cavalry," *Fayetteville Observer*, Oct 5, 1863, p2, col 1.
53. H. B. McClellan, *I Rode with Jeb Stuart* (Bloomington, 1958), p374–375.
54. P. B. Means, "Additional Sketch Sixty-Third Regiment (Fifth Cavalry)," p573–574.
55. Strange, "From the 2nd N.C. Cavalry," *Fayetteville Observer*, Oct 5, 1863, p1, col 4; P. B. Means, "Additional Sketch Sixty-Third Regiment (Fifth Cavalry)," p573; Daniel B. Coltrane, *The Memoirs of Daniel Branson Coltrane* (Raleigh, 1956), p20.
56. P. B. Means, "Additional Sketch Sixty-Third Regiment (Fifth Cavalry)," p574; H. B. McClellan, *I Rode with Jeb Stuart* (Bloomington, 1958), p374–375; Strange, "From the 2nd N.C. Cavalry," *Fayetteville Observer*, Oct 5, 1863, p1, col 4.
57. Dewey, "Skirmishes near Liberty Mills and at Robertson's Ford," *O.R., Supplement*, vV, p587.
58. Buford, vXXIX, part 1, p141.
59. Dewey, "Skirmishes near Liberty Mills and at Robertson's Ford," *O.R., Supplement*, vV, p587–588.
60. P. B. Means, "Additional Sketch Sixty-Third Regiment (Fifth Cavalry)," p574.
61. Buford, *O.R.*, vXXIX, part 1, p141.
62. Buford, *O.R.*, vXXIX, part 1, p141.
63. Dewey, "Skirmishes near Liberty Mills and at Robertson's Ford," *O.R., Supplement*, vV, p588, 587.
64. French, *O.R.*, vXXIX, part 1, p199. Kilpatrick, who was responsible for controlling the enemy cavalry and keeping it from the rear of his army, was asked to investigate the matter and determine if enemy cavalry were indeed operating in the army's rear. A couple of days later, Kilpatrick made a politically correct report in which he stated that from all the information he could gather, the Union officer shot behind their lines was a victim of "... a scouting party connected with a party of guerrillas.... They cross the river at night and return early in the morning." In other words, the perpetrators were an enemy Kilpatrick was not specifically responsible for at the time. Kilpatrick, *O.R.*, vXXIX, part 1, p198–199.
65. Strange, "From the 2nd N.C. Cavalry," *Fayetteville Observer*, Oct 5, 1863, p1, col 4; Letter from Levi Y. Lockhart, Company K, to his sister from camp near Orange Court House, on Oct 2, 1863, item 203: in "Lockhart Family Letters," SCL-DU.
66. R. E. Lee, in C. Dowdey and L. H. Manarin (eds.), *The Wartime Papers of Robert E. Lee*, (New York, 1987), p602–603, 605–607.
67. D. S. Freeman, *Lee's Lieutenants* (New York, 1995), v3, p239.
68. D. S. Freeman, *Lee's Lieutenants* (New York, 1995), v3, p239–240; J. E. Cooke, *Wearing of the Gray* (Bloomington, 1959), p253.
69. Stuart *O.R.*, vXXIX, part 1, p439.
70. Gordon was born in Wilkes County, North Carolina, and studied at Emory and Henry College in Virginia. He returned to Wilkes County and worked in the mercantile business and became involved in local politics and by 1850, the state legislature. In 1861, he organized a company of State troops and became its captain in the First Regiment, State Troopers. He was commissioned major of the First North Carolina Cavalry, and soon afterward, the regiment was assigned to Stuart's Cavalry. In the spring of 1863, Gordon was commissioned colonel. By Sept of 1863, he was promoted to brigadier general and given the North Carolina Cavalry Brigade. See, C. J. Hartley, *Stuart's Tarheels* (Baltimore, 1996), chapter 3 and elsewhere in the volume.
71. A. A. Humphreys, *O.R.*, vXXIX, part 2, p268.
72. Kilpatrick, *O.R.*, vXXIX, part 1, p373.
73. Stuart, *O.R.*, vXXIX, part 1, p439.
74. Stuart, *O.R.*, vXXIX, part 1, p439–440; H. B. McClellan, *I Rode with Jeb Stuart* (Bloomington, 1958), p377; Gordon, *O.R.*, vXXIX, part 1, p460; Young, *O.R.*, vXXIX, part 1, p458.
75. Stuart *O.R.*, vXXIX, part 1, p440; Young, *O.R.*, part 1, p458; J. E. Cooke, *Wearing of the Gray* (Bloomington, 1959), p252–255.
76. Kilpatrick, *O.R.*, vXXIX, part 1, p374–375.
77. Buford, *O.R.*, vXXIX, part 1, p346–348.
78. D. S. Freeman, *Lee's Lieutenants* (New York, 1995), v3, p239–240; J. E. Cooke, *Wearing of the Gray* (Bloomington, 1959), p253.
79. Buford, *O.R.*, vXXIX, part 1, p348; Fitzhugh Lee, *O.R.*, vXXIX, part 1, p463.
80. Stuart, *O.R.*, vXXIX, part 1, p440–441; Funsten, *O.R.*, vXXIX, part 1, p455; Gordon, *O.R.*, vXXIX, part 1, p460.
81. H. B. McClellan mentioned that Stuart only had three regiments of Gordon's brigade with him around Culpeper Court House on Oct 11, but all four regiments took losses at that place on that day. See H. B. McClellan, *I Rode with Jeb Stuart* (Bloomington, 1958), p378–379. Stuart said he moved forward to Brandy Station with Gordon's command and only two regiments of Funsten's command — he did not say with only three regiments from Gordon's command. See Stuart, *O.R.*, vXXIX, part 1, p441. Also, according to the brief histories provided in the Company Rosters, all four North Carolina regiments fought at Russell Ford, James City, Culpeper Court House, and spent the night of Oct 11 near Brandy Station. For instance, see: L. H. Manarin, *North Carolina Troops* (Raleigh, 1968–1993), vII, p101.
82. H. B. McClellan, *I Rode with Jeb Stuart* (Bloomington, 1958), pages 378–379; Stuart, *O.R.*, vXXIX, part 1, p441.
83. W. P. Shaw, "Fifty-Ninth Regiment (Fourth Cavalry)," p465; P. B. Means, "Additional Sketch Sixty-Third Regiment (Fifth Cavalry)," p575; Gordon, *O.R.*, vXXIX, part 1, p460; Stuart, *O.R.*, vXXIX, part 1, p441. In the after-battle reports, Baker was listed as killed but that was probably an assumption based on the severity of his wounds.
84. H. B. McClellan, *I Rode with Jeb Stuart* (Bloomington, 1958), p378–379; Stuart, *O.R.*, vXXIX, part 1, p441.
85. Stuart, *O.R.*, vXXIX, part 1, p442–443; Kilpatrick, *O.R.*, vXXIX, part 1, p375; Gordon, *O.R.*, vXXIX, part 1, p460; J. N. Opie, *A Rebel Cavalryman* (Dayton, 1997), p196–197.
86. P. B. Means, "Additional Sketch Sixty-Third Regiment (Fifth Cavalry)," p576; Stuart, *O.R.*, vXXIX, part 1, p443.
87. Stuart, *O.R.*, vXXIX, part 1, p443; P. B. Means, "Additional Sketch Sixty-Third Regiment (Fifth Cavalry)," p576–577.
88. Gordon, *O.R.*, vXXIX, part 1, p460; D. B. Coltrane, *Memoirs* (Raleigh, 1956), p22.
89. Buford, *O.R.*, vXXIX, part 1, p349; Meade, *O.R.*, vXXIX, part 1, p10; Stuart, *O.R.*, vXXIX, part 1, p443; H. B. McClellan, *I Rode with Jeb Stuart* (Bloomington, 1958), p379–383.
90. H. B. McClellan, *I Rode with Jeb Stuart* (Bloomington, 1958), p382.
91. "The Late Virginia Campaign," *Richmond Examiner*, reprinted in *Fayetteville Observer*, Nov 2, 1863, p2, col 5; Gordon, *O.R.*, vXXIX, part 1, p460.
92. On Oct 15, 1863, Brigadier General P. M. B. Young was officially ordered to report to Stuart "for assignment to the command of Butler's Brigade." See Special Orders, No. 256; *O.R.*, vXXIX, part 2, p788. By Oct 31, 1863, Butler's former brigade was listed as Young's brigade in Hampton's division: *O.R.*, vXXIX, part 1, p820.
93. Stuart, *O.R.*, vXXIX, part 1, p444; Young, *O.R.*, vXXIX, part 1, p458; H. B. McClellan, *I Rode with Jeb Stuart* (Bloomington, 1958), p383.
94. Meade, *O.R.*, vXXIX, part 1, p10; H. B. McClellan, *I Rode with Jeb Stuart* (Bloomington, 1958), p383–384; Young, *O.R.*, vXXIX, part 1, p458–459.
95. Meade, *O.R.*, vXXIX, part 1, p10; Buford, *O.R.*, vXXIX, part 1, p349; H. B. McClellan, *I Rode with Jeb Stuart* (Bloomington, 1958), p383–386.
96. Stuart, *O.R.*, vXXIX, part 1, p444.
97. Funsten, *O.R.*, vXXIX, part 1, p456; H. B. McClellan, *I Rode with Jeb Stuart* (Bloomington, 1958), p384–385.
98. Stuart, *O.R.*, vXXIX, part 1, p446; H. B. McClellan, *I Rode with Jeb Stuart* (Bloomington, 1958), p386.

99. Stuart, *O.R.*, vXXIX, part 1, p446; Funsten, *O.R.*, vXXIX, part 1, p456–457; Gordon, *O.R.*, vXXIX, part 1, p460; P. B. Means, "Additional Sketch Sixty-Third Regiment (Fifth Cavalry)," p578.
100. Stuart, *O.R.*, vXXIX, part 1, p446; H. B. McClellan, *I Rode with Jeb Stuart* (Bloomington, 1958), p386; Fitz Lee, *O.R.*, vXXIX, part 1, p463.
101. R. E. Lee, *O.R.*, vXXIX, part 1, p405–406; R. E. Lee, in C. Dowdey and L. H. Manarin (eds.), *The Wartime Paper of Robert E. Lee* (New York, 1987), p608.
102. Stuart, *O.R.*, vXXIX, part 1, p447; H. B. McClellan, *I Rode with Jeb Stuart* (Bloomington, 1958), p386–387.
103. Stuart, *O.R.*, vXXIX, part 1, p447; H. B. McClellan, *I Rode with Jeb Stuart* (Bloomington, 1958), p387.
104. Stuart, *O.R.*, vXXIX, part 1, p447; H. B. McClellan, *I Rode with Jeb Stuart* (Bloomington, 1958), p388.
105. Stuart, *O.R.*, vXXIX, part 1, p447; Fitz Lee, *O.R.*, vXXIX, part 1, p463; Brown and Green of Lomax's brigade, *O.R.*, vXXIX, part 1, p467 and 468; D. McM. Gregg, *O.R.*, vXXIX, part 1, p355–356.
106. D. S. Freeman, *Lee's Lieutenants* (New York, 1995), v3, p255–256; W. W. Blackford, *War Years with Jeb Stuart* (Baton Rouge, 1993), p238; H. B. McClellan, *I Rode with Jeb Stuart* (Bloomington, 1958), p389.
107. D. S. Freeman, *Lee's Lieutenants* (New York, 1995), v3, p255–256; W. W. Blackford, *War Years with Jeb Stuart* (Baton Rouge, 1993), p239; H. B. McClellan, *I Rode with Jeb Stuart* (Bloomington, 1958), p389, 390; "The Late Virginia Campaign," *Richmond Examiner*, reprinted in *Fayetteville Observer*, Nov 2, 1863, p2, col 5.
108. P. B. Means, "Additional Sketch Sixty-Third Regiment (Fifth Cavalry)," p579; Stuart, *O.R.*, vXXIX, part 1, p448; J. E. Cooke, *Wearing of the Gray* (Bloomington, 1959), p261; W. W. Blackford, *War Years with Jeb Stuart* (Baton Rouge, 1993), p239–240.
109. H. B. McClellan, *I Rode with Jeb Stuart* (Bloomington, 1958), p391.
110. H. B. McClellan, *I Rode with Jeb Stuart* (Bloomington, 1958), p391–392.
111. Stuart, *O.R.*, vXXIX, part 1, p448; "The Late Virginia Campaign," *Richmond Examiner*, reprinted in *Fayetteville Observer*, Nov 2, 1863, p2, col 5; D. B. Coltrane, *Memoirs* (Raleigh, 1956), p24.
112. Stuart, *O.R.*, vXXIX, part 1, p448; J. E. Cooke of Stuart's staff wrote that the end of the Union columns were both past or near passing their point and in a matter of minutes Stuart could have taken his command out with little resistance, but "Now was his opportunity, not only to extricate himself, but to take vengeance for the long hours of anxiety and peril." Lieutenant Colonel Cowles of the 1st North Carolina concurred when he later wrote, "when it was ascertained that the rear of the enemy's two columns had separated, leaving an open space through which we could pass. My own impression is that General Stuart could not resist the temptation to give the enemy a taste of our mettle in payment for the long hours of suspense in which he had held us completely surrounded." H. B. McClellan, also of Stuart's staff, tells the story as told by Stuart — that Stuart opened fire fully convinced their infantry was attacking the enemy from the west. J. E. Cooke, *Wearing of the Gray* (Bloomington, 1959), p261; Cowles in W. H. Cheek, "Additional Sketch Ninth Regiment (First Cavalry)," p455; H. B. McClellan, *I Rode with Jeb Stuart* (Bloomington, 1958), p391–392.
113. Stuart, *O.R.*, vXXIX, part 1, p448; Cowles in W. H. Cheek, "Additional Sketch Ninth Regiment (First Cavalry)," p456; R. Barringer, "Ninth Regiment (First Cavalry)," p427.
114. P. B. Means, "Additional Sketch Sixty-Third Regiment (Fifth Cavalry)," p581; Stuart, *O.R.*, vXXIX, part 1, p448.
115. Stuart, *O.R.*, vXXIX, part 1, p448; P. B. Means, "Additional Sketch Sixty-Third Regiment (Fifth Cavalry)," p581.
116. Fitz Lee, *O.R.*, vXXIX, part 1, p463; Stuart, *O.R.*, vXXIX, part 1, p448–449.
117. D. S. Freeman, *Lee's Lieutenants* (New York, 1995), v3, p241–247; E. J. Hess, *Lee's Tarheels* (Chapel Hill, 2002), p187–194; "The Late Virginia Campaign," *Richmond Examiner*, reprinted in *Fayetteville Observer*, Nov 2, 1863, p2, col 5.
118. "The Late Virginia Campaign," *Richmond Examiner*, reprinted in *Fayetteville Observer*, Nov 2, 1863, p2, col 5; Stuart, *O.R.*, vXXIX, part 1, p449; Fitz Lee, *O.R.*, vXXIX, part 1, p463.
119. "The Late Virginia Campaign," *Richmond Examiner*, reprinted in *Fayetteville Observer*, Nov 2, 1863, p2, col 5; Stuart, *O.R.*, vXXIX, part 1, p449; Fitz Lee, *O.R.*, vXXIX, part 1, p463.
120. R. E. Lee, *O.R.*, vXXIX, part 1, p406; Stuart, *O.R.*, vXXIX, part 1, p449.
121. P. B. Means, "Additional Sketch Sixty-Third Regiment (Fifth Cavalry)," p581; Stuart, *O.R.*, vXXIX, part 1, p449–450; Gordon, *O.R.*, vXXIX, part 1, p461; Funsten, *O.R.*, vXXIX, part 1, p457; Lomax, *O.R.*, vXXIX, part 1, p466; C. J. Hartley, *Stuart's Tarheels* (Baltimore, 1996), p290–292.
122. By Special Order, No. 256, dated Oct 15, 1863, Brigadier Generals Thomas L. Rosser was assigned to command Jones's former brigade, and P. M. B. Young was assigned to command Butler's brigade: *O.R.*, vXXIX, part 2, p788.
123. Lomax, *O.R.*, vXXIX, part 1, p466; Fitz Lee, *O.R.*, vXXIX, part 1, p463; P. B. Means, "Additional Sketch Sixty-Third Regiment (Fifth Cavalry)," p582; Funsten, *O.R.*, vXXIX, part 1, p457; Stuart, *O.R.*, vXXIX, part 1, p450; Gordon, *O.R.*, vXXIX, part 1, p461; Young, *O.R.*, vXXIX, part 1, p459.
124. Kilpatrick, *O.R.*, vXXIX, part 1, p379–380; R. E. Lee, *O.R.*, vXXIX, part 1, p407–409; Stuart, *O.R.*, vXXIX, part 1, p451.
125. Stuart, *O.R.*, vXXIX, part 1, p451.
126. Stuart, *O.R.*, vXXIX, part 1, p451.
127. Stuart, *O.R.*, vXXIX, part 1, p451; Young, *O.R.*, vXXIX, part 1, p459.
128. Kilpatrick, *O.R.*, vXXIX, part 1, p382; Stuart, *O.R.*, vXXIX, part 1, p451.
129. Stuart, *O.R.*, vXXIX, part 1, p451.
130. Kilpatrick, *O.R.*, vXXIX, part 1, p382.
131. Stuart, *O.R.*, vXXIX, part 1, p451; P. B. Means, "Additional Sketch Sixty-Third Regiment (Fifth Cavalry)," p583; Kilpatrick, *O.R.*, vXXIX, part 1, p383; Young, *O.R.*, vXXIX, part 1, p459.
132. Cowles in W. H. Cheek, "Additional Sketch Ninth Regiment (First Cavalry)," p457–458.
133. Stuart, *O.R.*, vXXIX, part 1, p451; Gordon, *O.R.*, vXXIX, part 1, p461; P. B. Means, "Additional Sketch Sixty-Third Regiment (Fifth Cavalry)," p583; Cowles in W. H. Cheek, "Additional Sketch Ninth Regiment (First Cavalry)," p458–459; Young, *O.R.*, vXXIX, part 1, p459; H. B. McClellan, *I Rode with Jeb Stuart* (Bloomington, 1958), p395.
134. H. B. McClellan, *I Rode with Jeb Stuart* (Bloomington, 1958), p394–395; Gordon, *O.R.*, vXXIX, part 1, p461.
135. P. B. Means, "Additional Sketch Sixty-Third Regiment (Fifth Cavalry)," p583; D. B. Coltrane, *Memoirs* (Raleigh, 1956), p25.
136. R. E. Lee, *O.R.*, vXXIX, part 1, p794; Stuart, *O.R.*, vXXIX, part 1, p452.
137. R. E. Lee, *O.R.*, vXXIX, part 2, p794–795.
138. Meade, *O.R.*, vXXIX, part 1, p11.
139. Meade, *O.R.*, vXXIX, part 1, p11.
140. Meade, *O.R.*, vXXIX, part 1, p11.
141. H. B. McClellan, *I Rode with Jeb Stuart* (Bloomington, 1958), p397; D. S. Freeman, *Lee's Lieutenants* (New York, 1995), v3, p264–267.
142. D. S. Freeman, *Lee's Lieutenants* (New York, 1995), v3, p267.
143. T. S. Garnett, *Riding with Stuart* (Shippensburg, Pa., 1994), p15–16; P. B. Means, "Additional Sketch Sixty-Third Regiment (Fifth Cavalry)," p584–585.
144. Meade, *O.R.*, vXXIX, part 1, p11.
145. R. E. Lee, *O.R.*, vXXIX, part 1, p825; Meade. *O.R.*, vXXIX, part 1, p11–12.

146. Rosser, *O.R.*, vXXIX, part 1, p825; Stuart, *O.R.*, vXXIX, part 1, p898–899.
147. Stuart, *O.R.*, vXXIX, part 1, p898–899; T. S. Garnett, *Riding with Stuart* (Shippensburg, Pa., 1994), p16; R. E. Lee, *O.R.*, vXXIX, part 1, p826.
148. R. E. Lee, *O.R.*, vXXIX, part 1, p826.
149. R. E. Lee, *O.R.*, vXXIX, part 1, p826; Stuart, *O.R.*, vXXIX, part 1, p899; T. S. Garnett, *Riding with Stuart* (Shippensburg, Pa., 1994), p19; Rosser, *O.R.*, vXXIX, part 1, p905; Gordon, *O.R.*, vXXIX, part 1, p902; Young, *O.R.*, vXXIX, part 1, p906; Hampton, *O.R.*, vXXIX, part 1, p902; E. J. Hess, *Lee's Tarheels* (Chapel Hill, 2002), p197–198.
150. T. S. Garnett, *Riding with Stuart* (Shippensburg, Pa., 1994), p20; Rosser, *O.R.*, vXXIX, part 1, p905; Gregg, *O.R.*, vXXIX, part 1, p807; Stuart, *O.R.*, vXXIX, part 1, p900–901.
151. Hampton, *O.R.*, vXXIX, part 1, p902; Gordon, *O.R.*, vXXIX, part 1, p902; Young, *O.R.*, vXXIX, part 1, p907.
152. Gordon, *O.R.*, vXXIX, part 1, p903.
153. Gordon, *O.R.*, vXXIX, part 1, p903; T. S. Garnett, *Riding with Stuart* (Shippensburg, Pa., 1994), p23.
154. Meade, *O.R.*, vXXIX, part 1, p12.
155. Stuart, *O.R.*, vXXIX, part 1, p900; Meade, *O.R.*, vXXIX, part 1, p17; T. S. Garnett, *Riding with Stuart* (Shippensburg, Pa., 1994), p23.
156. R. E. Lee, *O.R.*, vXXIX, part 1, p826.
157. Meade, *O.R.*, vXXIX, part 1, p12.
158. Stuart, *O.R.*, vXXIX, part 1, p901.
159. W. P. Roberts, "Additional Sketch Nineteenth Regiment (Second Cavalry)," p101.
160. T. S. Garnett, *Riding with Stuart* (Shippensburg, Pa., 1994), p25–26.
161. Hampton, *O.R.*, vXXIX, part 2, p862–863.
162. R. E. Lee, *O.R.*, vXXXIII, p1117.
163. Letter from Levi Lockhart to his sister, from camp headquarters, Dec 17, 1863; and Lockhart to his sister, from camp near Guinea Station, Jan 5, 1864, in "Lockhart Family Letters," SCL-DU.
164. R. E. Lee, *O.R.*, vXXXIII, p1118.
165. Stuart, *O.R.*, vXXXIII, p1125.
166. T. S. Garnett, *Riding with Stuart* (Shippensburg, Pa., 1994), p38; *O.R.*, vXXXIII, p19.
167. T. S. Garnett, *Riding with Stuart* (Shippensburg, Pa., 1994), p38; *O.R.*, vXXXIII, p19.
168. Hampton, *O.R.*, vXXXIII, p1132.
169. Hampton, *O.R.*, vXXXIII, p19.
170. Hampton, *O.R.*, vXXXIII, p1132; Stuart as quoted in P. B. Means, "Additional Sketch Sixty-Third Regiment (Fifth Cavalry)," p586.
171. T. S. Garnett, *Riding with Stuart* (Shippensburg, Pa., 1994), p38; *O.R.*, vXXXIII, p25–26.
172. P. B. Means, "Additional Sketch Sixty-Third Regiment (Fifth Cavalry)," p586, 591.
173. Hampton, *O.R.*, vXXXIII, p1140, 1143; Stuart, *O.R.*, vXXXIII, p1143; R. E. Lee, *O.R.*, vXXXIII, p1143.
174. R. E. Lee and Stuart, *O.R.*, vXXXIII, p1148.
175. Merritt, *O.R.*, vXXXIII, p139–140.
176. Kilpatrick, *O.R.*, vXXXIII, p140–141.
177. Kilpatrick, *O.R.*, vXXXIII, p140–141.
178. Kilpatrick, *O.R.*, vXXXIII, p141; Compiled Service Records as summarized by L. H. Manarin, *North Carolina Troops*, vII, p146, 168, 170; R. E. Lee, *O.R.*, vXXXIII, p141.
179. Andrews lived in Iredell County, North Carolina and he enlisted at the age of 31. He was Company B's first captain. He was promoted to major and transferred to the regiment's Field and Staff from Sept 6, 1862. Andrews led the main body of the 2nd North Carolina into Virginia in late Sept of 1862 and served as their commander while Colonel Sol Williams was detached, and on more than one occasion between "permanent" commanders. He made lieutenant colonel on Feb 12, 1864, and Colonel on Feb 18.
180. Hampton, *O.R.*, vXXXIII, p1162; Venable for R. E. Lee, *O.R.*, vXXXIII, p1186.
181. Gordon's 4th and 5th North Carolina regiments were resting and recruiting in their home state. Hampton, *O.R.*, vXXXIII, p1162; J. M. Galloway, "Sixty-Third Regiment (Fifth Cavalry)," p536.
182. Kilpatrick, *O.R.*, vXXXIII, p172.
183. Kilpatrick, *O.R.*, vXXXIII, p172–173; Pleasonton, *O.R.*, vXXXIII, p171–172.
184. Humphreys, *O.R.*, vXXXIII, p598; Pleasonton, *O.R.*, vXXXIII, p599–600.
185. Pleasonton, *O.R.*, vXXXIII, p183; Humphreys, *O.R.*, vXXXIII, p173–174.
186. Pleasonton, *O.R.*, vXXXIII, p599; H. B. McClellan, *I Rode with Jeb Stuart* (Bloomington, 1958), p399–402; T. S. Garnett, *Riding with Stuart* (Shippensburg, Pa., 1994), p40.
187. Pleasonton, *O.R.*, vXXXIII, p182; Kilpatrick, *O.R.*, vXXXIII, p183–184.
188. Kilpatrick, *O.R.*, vXXXIII, p183; Young, *O.R.*, vXXXIII, p203.
189. Kilpatrick, *O.R.*, vXXXIII, p184.
190. Young, *O.R.*, vXXXIII, p203.
191. Hampton, *O.R.*, vXXXIII, p201.
192. Hampton, *O.R.*, vXXXIII, p201; C. A. Evens, "The Maryland Line," p115–118.
193. Hampton, *O.R.*, vXXXIII, p201.
194. Hampton, *O.R.*, vXXXIII, p201; W. H. Cheek, "Additional Sketch Ninth Regiment (First Cavalry)," p460; N. P. Ford, "An Attack on Richmond Foiled," p281.
195. According to Colonel Cheek, Hampton and his staff stayed in the station and sent the cavalrymen under Cheek forward to find out if the camp belonged to friends or foe — his only instructions to Cheek were if he found the fires belonged to the enemy he should harass them all he could. Hampton's and Captain Ford's accounts suggest Hampton stayed with his cavalrymen. Hampton, *O.R.*, vXXXIII, p201; W. H. Cheek, "Additional Sketch Ninth Regiment (First Cavalry)," p460; N. P. Ford, "An Attack on Richmond Foiled," p281.
196. W. H. Cheek, "Additional Sketch Ninth Regiment (First Cavalry)," p460; N. P. Ford, "An Attack on Richmond Foiled," p281.
197. W. H. Cheek, "Additional Sketch Ninth Regiment (First Cavalry)," p460; N. P. Ford, "An Attack on Richmond Foiled," p281–282; Hampton, *O.R.*, vXXXIII, p., 201.
198. W. H. Cheek, "Additional Sketch Ninth Regiment (First Cavalry)," p461; Kilpatrick, *O.R.*, vXXXIII, p185.
199. W. H. Cheek, "Additional Sketch Ninth Regiment (First Cavalry)," p461.
200. Kilpatrick, *O.R.*, vXXXIII, p185.
201. Hampton, *O.R.*, vXXXIII, p201–202; Kilpatrick, *O.R.*, vXXXIII, p185–186; Hampton's journal as quoted in W. J. Green, "Night Attack of the 1st and 2nd North Carolina Cavalry Upon Kilpatrick's Division," p169.
202. Hampton, *O.R.*, vXXXIII, p202; Cheek, *O.R.*, vXXXIII, p204–205; W. H. Cheek, "Additional Sketch Ninth Regiment (First Cavalry)," p461.
203. Meade, *O.R.*, vXXXIII, p171; Kilpatrick, *O.R.*, vXXXIII, p186.
204. N. P. Ford, "An Attack on Richmond Foiled," p282–283.
205. Meade, *O.R.*, vXXXIII, p171; Kilpatrick, *O.R.*, vXXXIII, p186. There were controversies surrounding the death of Dahlgren. The Union commanders were outraged by the manner in which Dahlgren's remains had been treated — stripped, abused, and initially left on a roadside. The Confederate commanders were outraged by a copy of a speech Dahlgren apparently delivered to his command, in which he said, "The bridges once secured, and the prisoners loose and over the river, the bridges will be secured and the city destroyed and Jeff. Davis and cabinet killed." This address was published in newspapers and caused questions to be asked all along the Union chain of command. Finally, on April 1, Robert E. Lee wrote directly to George G. Meade, enclosing photographic copies of the address, asking if Dahlgren's comments and intentions had originated higher up in the Federal chain of command. Lee went on to ask for a more detailed explanation of the purpose of the expeditions against

Richmond. On April 17, Meade's response to R. E. Lee contained the following: "In reply I have to state that neither the United States Government, myself, nor General Kilpatrick authorized, sanctioned, or approved the burning of the city of Richmond and the killing of Mr. Davis and cabinet, nor any other act not required by military necessity and in accordance with the usages of war." According to some scholars, Meade privately suspected Kilpatrick had authored the controversial addresses: see E. G. Longacre, *Lincoln's Cavalrymen* (Mechanicsburg, 2000), p245, note 43. For the broader controversy see, *O.R.*, vXXXIII: Humphreys, Parsons, p175; Kilpatrick, p176; Meade, p177, 180; R. E. Lee, p178; Dahlgren, two items, p178–179.

206. "Gov. Vance Before The Army," *Fayetteville Observer*, April 18, 1864, p1, col 4; J. H. Lane, "Glimpses of Army Life in 1864," p407–408; C. J. Hartley, *Stuart's Tarheels* (Baltimore, 1996), p325–326.

207. Hampton, *O.R.*, vXXXIII, p201.

208. Hampton, *O.R.*, vXXXIII, p200–201, 201–202; Edward L. Wells, *Hampton & His Cavalry '64* (1997), p124–125.

209. Letter from Milas A. Cavin to his aunt from "the woods" on April 29, 1864, P. C. 399, NCDA.

210. George W. Walker to Ellen Lockhart, May 1, 1864, in "Lockhart Family Letters," SCL-DU.

211. Letter from Milas A. Cavin to his aunt from "the woods" on April 29, 1864, P. C. 399, NCDA.

212. Stuart to Gordon, April 13, 1864, Greensboro Historical Museum Archives, Civil War Collection, MSS. Coll. # 16, Series 31.

213. R. Barringer, letter to his brother, V. C. Barringer, dated Jan 27, 1866, from Concord, p5–6, "Rufus Barringer Paper," no. 1028, SHC-UNC; Special Orders No. 94, *O.R.*, vXXXIII, p1306; W. P. Shaw, "Fifty-Ninth Regiment (Fourth Cavalry)," p465.

214. P. B. Means, "Additional Sketch Sixty-Third Regiment (Fifth Cavalry)," p591.

215. John P. Lockhart, *Hillsborough Recorder*, Jan 20, 1864, p2, col 3; the numbers are from the Compiled Service Records as summarized by L. H. Manarin, *North Carolina Troops*, vII, p98–177.

216. W. P. Roberts, "Additional Sketch Nineteenth Regiment (Second Cavalry)," p100.

217. From the "Headquarters 2D N.C. Cavalry," *Fayetteville Observer*, Feb 1, 1864, p4, col 1.

218. Stuart to Gordon, April 13, 1864, Greensboro Historical Museum Archives, Civil War Collection, MSS. Coll. # 16, Series 31.

219. R. Barringer, letter to his brother, V. C. Barringer, dated Jan 27, 1866, from Concord, p6 SHC-UNC; P. B. Means, "Additional Sketch Sixty-Third Regiment (Fifth Cavalry)," p591.

220. Special Orders No. 94, *O.R.*, vXXXIII, p1306; Baker, *O.R.*, vXL, part 3, p804; J. S. Carr, "The Gordon-Barringer Brigade," p581–582.

221. P. B. Means, "Additional Sketch Sixty-Third Regiment (Fifth Cavalry)," p591; Hampton, *O.R.*, vXXXVI, part 2, p941; Special Orders No. 102, *O.R.*, vXXXVI, part 2, p940; Whiting, *O.R.*, vXXXVI, part 2, p942.

222. P. B. Means, "Additional Sketch Sixty-Third Regiment (Fifth Cavalry)," p593.

223. The first draft of the reorganization had Hampton retaining Butler, Young and Gordon; Fitz Lee retaining Lomax and Wickham; and W. H. F. Lee with Rosser and Chambliss—but on reflection, Stuart decided it would be better if Gordon went to W. H. F. Lee. *O.R.*, vXXXVI, part 1, p1027; "North Carolina Officers Exchanged," *Hillsborough Recorder*, March 23, 1864, p2, col 3.

224. Barker for Hampton, *O.R.*, vXXXVI, part 2, p954.

225. P. B. Means, "Additional Sketch Sixty-Third Regiment (Fifth Cavalry)," p592.

Five

1. J. M. McPherson, *Battle Cry of Freedom* (New York, 1989), p713–717.

2. J. M. McPherson, *Battle Cry of Freedom* (New York, 1989), p689–698.

3. J. M. McPherson, *Battle Cry of Freedom* (New York, 1989), p719, 721.

4. A. A. Humphreys, *The Virginia Campaign of 1864 and 1865* (New York, 1995), p6, 9–12; J. M. McPherson, *Battle Cry of Freedom* (New York, 1989), p722.

5. G. C. Rhea, *The Battle of the Wilderness* (Baton Rouge, 1994), p40.

6. The Confederate numbers are generally drawn from field returns for April 20 & 30, 1864 as abstracted in *O.R.*, vXXXIII, p1297-1298. The report has numbers for the Second, Third, and Cavalry Corps. Estimates for the First Corps at that time are around 10,000 men (for the latter estimate, see: D. S. Freeman, *Lee's Lieutenants* (New York, 1995), v3, p342). Similar Federal returns can be found in *O.R.*, vXXXIII, p1036; These numbers are generally used though acknowledged to be estimates. See: G. C. Rhea, *The Battle of the Wilderness* (Baton Rouge, 1994), p21 and 34; J. M. McPherson, *Battle Cry of Freedom* (New York, 1989), p724; Union General Andrew A. Humphreys calculated the Federal strength to be 99,438 "present for duty equipped" on April 30. He calculated Confederate strength at 61,953. See: A. A. Humphreys, *The Virginia Campaign of 1864 and 1865* (New York, 1995), p14. However, some writers have recently disputed these numbers, looking more closely at the Compiled Service Records for individuals in the various units: see A. C. Young, III, "Numbers and Losses in the Army of Northern Virginia," p15–29. Alfred Young would add more than 30,000 men to the size of the Army of Northern Virginia, but most of the size comes from adding units that were in the general area and were, for the most part, added to R. E. Lee's command in late May. Consequently, most of the late arrivals for the Overland Campaign were not available to R. E. Lee during the fights at the Wilderness, Spotsylvania, and Yellow Tavern. In other words, Young states that a "combined figure of 96,000 represents the maximum number of men available to Lee," but he is careful to point out that most of Lee's losses of some 24,000 men were taken during the first half of May, when his Army of Northern Virginia was operating with closer to 66,000 men. That is to say, at no time did R. E. Lee have anywhere near 96,000 effective men in the field. Another interesting conclusion Young comes to is that during the Overland Campaign, R. E. Lee's army lost 24,000 and gained 30,000 men — meaning his command was larger after the campaign than at the outset. However, Lee more than Grant was certainly "robbing Peter to pay Paul." Lee could not significantly increase the size of the Army of Northern Virginia. In any case, even though Young concludes that Lee's army was larger than we thought at the beginning of the campaign and even larger at the end, no one has yet suggested that generals Lee and Grant were able to field armies that were close to equal in size and equipment at any given time during the campaign.

7. D. S. Freeman, *Lee's Lieutenants* (New York, 1995), v3, p343–346; G. C. Rhea, *The Battle of the Wilderness* (Baton Rouge, 1994), p27–28.

8. Hampton, XXXVI, *O.R.*, part 2, p941, 970; R. Barringer, "Ninth Regiment (First Cavalry)," p429; P. B. Means, "Additional Sketch Sixty-Third Regiment (Fifth Cavalry)," p594.

9. A. A. Humphreys, *The Virginia Campaign of 1864 and 1865* (New York, 1995), p10–12; G. C. Rhea, *The Battle of the Wilderness* (Baton Rouge, 1994), p52–55.

10. Meade, *O.R.*, vXXXVI, part 1, p188–189; G. C. Rhea, *The Battle of the Wilderness* (Baton Rouge, 1994), p72–76.

11. Cowles, *O.R.*, vLI, part 2, p888; Warren, *O.R.*, vXXXVI, part 2, p378; Wilson, *O.R.*, vXXXVI, part 2, p378.

12. Fitz Lee, *O.R.*, vLI, part 2, p888; Hampton, *O.R.*, vLI, part 2, p949.

13. G. C. Rhea, *The Battle of the Wilderness* (Baton Rouge, 1994), p55–56.
14. R. E. Lee, *O.R.*, vXXXVI, part 2, p952; G. C. Rhea, *The Battle of the Wilderness* (Baton Rouge, 1994), p80–86, 90; D. S. Freeman, *Lee's Lieutenants* (New York, 1995), v3, p349.
15. Alexander R. Boteler, Diary, "On J. E. B. Stuart's Staff," William E. Brooks Collection, Manuscript Division, Library of Congress, Washington, D. C., p2–3.
16. Stuart, *O.R.*, vLI, part 2, p887–888.
17. G. C. Rhea, *The Battle of the Wilderness* (Baton Rouge, 1994), p91–92.
18. G. C. Rhea, *The Battle of the Wilderness* (Baton Rouge, 1994), p94–95, 108; Wilson, *O.R.*, vXXXVI, part 2, p429.
19. G. C. Rhea, *The Battle of the Wilderness* (Baton Rouge, 1994), p97–108; D. S. Freeman, *Lee's Lieutenants* (New York, 1995), v3, p350–356.
20. G. C. Rhea, *The Battle of the Wilderness* (Baton Rouge, 1994), chapters 3–5; J. M. McPherson, *Battle Cry of Freedom* (New York, 1989), p725.
21. Wilson *O.R.*, vXXXVI, part 1, p877; Garnett of Stuart's staff knew where Rosser had been, and that he had been sent to Catharpin Road: T. S. Garnett, *Riding with Stuart* (Shippensburg, Pa., 1994), p51.
22. A. A. Humphreys, *The Virginia Campaign of 1864 and 1865* (New York, 1995), p35; Kennon, Assistant Inspector General, *O.R.*, vXXXVI, part 1, p1098–1099; G. C. Rhea, *The Battle of the Wilderness* (Baton Rouge, 1994), p113.
23. Chew, *O.R.*, vXXXVI, part 1, p955; G. C. Rhea, *The Battle of the Wilderness* (Baton Rouge, 1994), p113.
24. D. McM. Gregg, *O.R.*, vXXXVI, part 2, p429; G. C. Rhea, *The Battle of the Wilderness* (Baton Rouge, 1994), p256.
25. G. C. Rhea, *The Battle of the Wilderness* (Baton Rouge, 1994), p255; A. A. Humphreys, *The Virginia Campaign of 1864 and 1865* (New York, 1995), p36; Gregg, *O.R.*, vXXXVI, part 2, p429.
26. G. C. Rhea, *The Battle of the Wilderness* (Baton Rouge, 1994), p259–260, 272.
27. Cowles, *O.R.*, vXXXVI, part 2, p952 and 954; Hampton, *O.R.*, vXXXVI, part 2, p953.
28. Hampton, *O.R.*, vXXXVI, part 2, p954 and 593. Stuart spent the early morning in his camp near Verdiersville, and by midmorning he was off to participate in Rosser's fighting.
29. Hampton, *O.R.*, vXXXVI, part 2, p954.
30. W. H. F. Lee, *O.R.*, vXXXVI, part 2, p963–964.
31. Fitzhugh Lee, "Report of Major General Fitzhugh Lee of the Operations of His Cavalry Division, A. N. V. from May 4th 1864 to Sept 19th, 1864," p4, in Eleanor S. Brockenbrough Library, MC; G. C. Rhea, *The Battle of the Wilderness* (Baton Rouge, 1994), p259, 344.
32. Hancock's command was on the Union left, and he was finally alerted to the possible appearance of Longstreet after Confederate prisoners taken on May 5 were questioned and revealed that Longstreet was expected. A. A. Humphreys, *The Virginia Campaign of 1864 and 1865* (New York, 1995), p37.
33. G. C. Rhea, *The Battle of the Wilderness* (Baton Rouge, 1994), Chapters 6–8; J. M. McPherson, *Battle Cry of Freedom* (New York, 1989), p725.
34. J. M. McPherson, *Battle Cry of Freedom* (New York, 1989), p725.
35. G. C. Rhea, *The Battle of the Wilderness* (Baton Rouge, 1994), p404; J. M. McPherson, *Battle Cry of Freedom* (New York, 1989), p726.
36. A. A. Humphreys, *The Virginia Campaign of 1864 and 1865* (New York, 1995), p53; A. C. Young, III, "Numbers and Losses in the Army of Northern Virginia," p26.
37. Forsyth for Sheridan, *O.R.*, vXXXVI, part 2, p429.
38. A. A. Humphreys, *The Virginia Campaign of 1864 and 1865* (New York, 1995), p51.
39. Custer, *O.R.*, vXXXVI, part 2, p466; Stuart, *O.R.*, vLI, part 2, p893–894; Torbert, *O.R.*, vXXXVI, part 2, p467–468.
40. A. A. Humphreys, *The Virginia Campaign of 1864 and 1865* (New York, 1995), p42; Fitzhugh Lee, "Report of the Operations of His Cavalry Division, from May 4th to Sept 19th, 1864," p4–6, in MC; G. C. Rhea, *The Battle of the Wilderness* (Baton Rouge, 1994), p345–350.
41. Early on May 6, Sheridan was instructed to send a division of cavalry (D. McM. Gregg's) along Brock Road, around Longstreet's right and to the enemy's rear. His instructions were to be on the offensive so by merely holding Brock Road and Todd's Tavern he could not have considered the day a success. In spite of Custer's stated satisfaction with fighting Rosser's to a stand off, Sheridan was certainly less satisfied with their achievements that day. By noon, Sheridan knew he could not fulfill his assignment. By 2:35 P.M., he had started wagons toward Ely's Ford on the Rapidan. See, A. A. Humphreys, *The Virginia Campaign of 1864 and 1865* (New York, 1995), p39; Humphreys (at 1 P.M.) and Sheridan (at 2:35 P. M.), *O.R.*, vXXXVI, part 2, p467; G. C. Rhea, *The Battle of the Wilderness* (Baton Rouge, 1994), p379.
42. Exactly when Hampton and Gordon arrived on the battlefield is difficult to determine because Hampton sent Stuart a message indicating he was moving Gordon's 2nd North Carolina and some of Young Cobb's Legion toward Shady Grove. That is not a problem if the message was sent from a position along Catharpin Road, or if it had been sent on May 5 from his camp back near Milford. The problem is, the message is dated May 6 from Milford. Perhaps Hampton sent his cavalrymen ahead while he stayed in camp until morning, or the date on or the location from which the message was sent is in error. All other information indicate that Gordon's and Young's men marched most of the night after leaving their camps near Milford late on May 5. Both Gordon and the 2nd North Carolina were fighting on Catharpin Road on the 6th, and later in the day the 5th North Carolina joined Gordon and the 2nd North Carolina. Wright, with a detachment from Young's brigade, was on Rosser's right on Brock Road. At 8:00 A.M. Cowles of the 1st North Carolina Cavalry warned Brigadier General Gordon that enemy infantry was coming down the Germanna road and might move to threaten his left. Later in the morning, Stuart and Gordon exchanged messages about the nature of the enemy force in front of Gordon's command in the morning's fighting. No men from the 2nd North Carolina Cavalry were taken prisoner that day, but three were wounded in the fighting. The 5th North Carolina also lost several men that day while fighting side by side with the 2nd North Carolina. This suggests Gordon and the 2nd North Carolina Cavalry were fighting on the right flank of the Confederate line early on May 6. Cowles, Gordon, *O.R.*, vXXXVI, part 2, p962, 961; P. B. Means, "Additional Sketch Sixty-Third Regiment (Fifth Cavalry)," p594; Custer, *O.R.*, vXXXVI, part 2, p466.
43. Three separate messages from: Cowles, Gordon and Hampton, *O.R.*, vXXXVI, part 2, p961–962; also see, Fitz Lee, *O.R.*, vLI, part 2, p894.
44. G. C. Rhea, *The Battles for Spotsylvania Court House and the Road to Yellow Tavern* (Baton Rouge, 1997), p5.
45. G. C. Rhea, *The Battles for Spotsylvania Court House and the Road to Yellow Tavern* (Baton Rouge, 1997), p6.
46. Hampton, *O.R.*, vXXXVI, part 2, p970–971; W. H. F. Lee, *O.R.*, vXXXVI, part 2, p962–963, and *O.R.*, vLI, part 2, p898; R. L. T. Beale, *History of the Ninth Virginia Cavalry* (Amissville, 1981), p116–117; Cheek of the 1st North Carolina from near Germanna Ford at 2:00 P.M., *O.R.*, vXXXVI, part 2, p968; Galloway of the 5th North Carolina Cavalry said the 5th cavalry arrived on May 7 in Galloway, "Sixty-third Regiment. (Fifth Cavalry), p536; Means, also of the 5th North Carolina Cavalry, said the regiment fought at White Hall, close to Catharpin Road on the 6th. P. B. Means, "Additional Sketch Sixty-Third Regiment (Fifth Cavalry)," p594.
47. Fitzhugh Lee, "Report of the Operations of His Cavalry Division, from May 4th to Sept 19th, 1864," p607, MC; G. C. Rhea, *The Battles for Spotsylvania Court House and the Road to Yellow Tavern* (Baton Rouge, 1997), p30–32.
48. G. C. Rhea, *The Battles for Spotsylvania Court House and the Road to Yellow Tavern* (Baton Rouge, 1997), p32–33.

49. T. S. Garnett, *Riding with Stuart* (Shippensburg, Pa., 1994), p56–57.
50. "Barringer's N.C. Brigade of Cavalry," *Daily Confederate*, Feb 22, 1865, p2, cols, 3, 4, 5; T. S. Garnett, *Riding with Stuart* (Shippensburg, Pa., 1994), p56–57; G. C. Rhea, *The Battles for Spotsylvania Court House and the Road to Yellow Tavern* (Baton Rouge, 1997), p33.
51. T. S. Garnett, *Riding with Stuart* (Shippensburg, Pa., 1994), p57.
52. G. C. Rhea, *The Battles for Spotsylvania Court House and the Road to Yellow Tavern* (Baton Rouge, 1997), p33–35.
53. G. C. Rhea, *The Battles for Spotsylvania Court House and the Road to Yellow Tavern* (Baton Rouge, 1997), p33–35.
54. G. C. Rhea, *The Battles for Spotsylvania Court House and the Road to Yellow Tavern* (Baton Rouge, 1997), p36; Sheridan, *O.R.*, vXXXVI, part 2, p515–516.
55. G. C. Rhea, *The Battles for Spotsylvania Court House and the Road to Yellow Tavern* (Baton Rouge, 1997), p36–37.
56. Alexander R. Boteler, Diary, William E. Brooks Collection, Manuscript Division, Library of Congress, Washington, D. C., p6.
57. Taylor for R. E. Lee, *O.R.*, vXXXVI, part 2, p969–970, and Taylor again at 7:00 P.M., p969.
58. G. C. Rhea, *The Battles for Spotsylvania Court House and the Road to Yellow Tavern* (Baton Rouge, 1997), p10–11.
59. G. C. Rhea, *The Battles for Spotsylvania Court House and the Road to Yellow Tavern* (Baton Rouge, 1997), p37–44.
60. G. C. Rhea, *The Battles for Spotsylvania Court House and the Road to Yellow Tavern* (Baton Rouge, 1997), p45–46.
61. Fitzhugh Lee, "Report of the Operations of His Cavalry Division, from May 4th to Sept 19th, 1864," p7–9, MC; G. C. Rhea, *The Battles for Spotsylvania Court House and the Road to Yellow Tavern* (Baton Rouge, 1997), p47–50.
62. G. C. Rhea, *The Battles for Spotsylvania Court House and the Road to Yellow Tavern* (Baton Rouge, 1997), p50.
63. G. C. Rhea, *The Battles for Spotsylvania Court House and the Road to Yellow Tavern* (Baton Rouge, 1997), p52.
64. G. C. Rhea, *The Battles for Spotsylvania Court House and the Road to Yellow Tavern* (Baton Rouge, 1997), p52–53.
65. G. C. Rhea, *The Battles for Spotsylvania Court House and the Road to Yellow Tavern* (Baton Rouge, 1997), p53–54.
66. G. C. Rhea, *The Battles for Spotsylvania Court House and the Road to Yellow Tavern* (Baton Rouge, 1997), p62–65.
67. G. C. Rhea, *The Battles for Spotsylvania Court House and the Road to Yellow Tavern* (Baton Rouge, 1997), p65–68.
68. G. C. Rhea, *The Battles for Spotsylvania Court House and the Road to Yellow Tavern* (Baton Rouge, 1997), p71–77, 83–88.
69. J. A. Early, *Memoirs* (New York, 1994), p352; G. C. Rhea, *The Battles for Spotsylvania Court House and the Road to Yellow Tavern* (Baton Rouge, 1997), p78–79.
70. G. C. Rhea, *The Battles for Spotsylvania Court House and the Road to Yellow Tavern* (Baton Rouge, 1997), p80–81; J. A. Early, *Memoir* (New York, 1994), p352.
71. J. A. Early, *Memoir* (New York, 1994), p353; A. A. Humphreys, *The Virginia Campaign of 1864 and 1865* (New York, 1995), p71; G. C. Rhea, *The Battles for Spotsylvania Court House and the Road to Yellow Tavern* (Baton Rouge, 1997), p89–94.
72. T. F. Rodenbough, "Sheridan's Richmond Raid," p189; G. C. Rhea, *The Battles for Spotsylvania Court House and the Road to Yellow Tavern* (Baton Rouge, 1997), p68–69.
73. G. C. Rhea, *The Battles for Spotsylvania Court House and the Road to Yellow Tavern* (Baton Rouge, 1997), p96–99.
74. R. L. T. Beale, *History of the Ninth Virginia Cavalry* (Amissville, 1981), p116–117; "Barringer's N.C. Brigade of Cavalry," *Daily Confederate*, Feb 22, 1865, p2, cols, 3, 4, 5.
75. G. C. Rhea, *The Battles for Spotsylvania Court House and the Road to Yellow Tavern* (Baton Rouge, 1997), p99–100. Another historian placed the number of effective men with Sheridan at closer to 12,000; R. E. L. Krick, "Stuart's Last Ride: A Confederate View of Sheridan's Raid," p128.
76. T. S. Garnett, *Riding with Stuart* (Shippensburg, Pa., 1994), p61; Alexander R. Boteler, Diary, William E. Brooks Collection, Manuscript Division, Library of Congress, Washington, D. C., p6; Fitzhugh Lee, "Report of the Operations of His Cavalry Division, from May 4th to Sept 19th, 1864," p10–11, MC; G. C. Rhea, *The Battles for Spotsylvania Court House and the Road to Yellow Tavern* (Baton Rouge, 1997), p114–117; H. B. McClellan, *I Rode with Jeb Stuart* (Bloomington, 1958), p409–410; "The Raid Around Richmond," *Richmond Enquirer*, May 17, 1864, p1, col 4.
77. G. C. Rhea, *The Battles for Spotsylvania Court House and the Road to Yellow Tavern* (Baton Rouge, 1997), p117–118.
78. T. S. Garnett, *Riding with Stuart* (Shippensburg, Pa., 1994), p61; Fitzhugh Lee, "Report of the Operations of His Cavalry Division, from May 4th to Sept 19th, 1864," p11, MC; G. C. Rhea, *The Battles for Spotsylvania Court House and the Road to Yellow Tavern* (Baton Rouge, 1997), p119.
79. The thinness of Hampton's line in front of Todd's Tavern is illustrated in a message from Rosser on May 10 in which he explains that "The approaches by the Catharpin road are defended by three lines of earth-works.... Stuffed figures were placed on the works to represent sentinels." Rosser, *O.R.*, vLI, part 2, p913–914.
80. *Daily Confederate*, May 23, 1864, p2, col 4; T. S. Garnett, *Riding with Stuart* (Shippensburg, Pa., 1994), p61; H. B. McClellan, *I Rode with Jeb Stuart* (Bloomington, 1958), p410; "Barringer's N.C. Brigade of Cavalry," *Daily Confederate*, Feb 22, 1865, p2, cols, 3, 4, 5; W. H. F. Lee, *O.R.*, vLI, part 2, p913; G. C. Rhea, *The Battles for Spotsylvania Court House and the Road to Yellow Tavern* (Baton Rouge, 1997), p120.
81. T. S. Garnett, *Riding with Stuart* (Shippensburg, Pa., 1994), p62.
82. Writing some years after the war, both T. S. Garnett and H. B. McClellan, of Stuart's staff, remembered that Stuart took only Gordon's brigade up to Davenport Bridge and Fitz Lee kept his command with him — perhaps after Gordon arrived, Stuart sent Lomax back to Fitz Lee. In support of Garnett's and McClellan's recollections, a few days after the event a member of the North Carolina brigade wrote, "A party from Gordon's Brigade were dismounted and engaged the enemy in front across the river, while Wickham and Lomax led around below and Gordon above." I have herein agreed with the above position with less than complete conviction. My uncertainty is founded on and finds expression in the fact that other researchers have determined that Stuart took Lomax's command with the North Carolinians up to Davenport Bridge. This position is supported by Stuart's clear statement of which units he planned to take with him. As Stuart was preparing to leave for the bridge upriver at 8:45 A.M. on the morning of May 10, he dashed off a note to R. E. Lee in which he stated, "The other brigades, Gordon's and Lomax's, will cross above at Davenport's Bridge and will sweep down on south side." This was Stuart's intention at the time, and there is no strong evidence to suggest he changed his plan moments later when he moved out — however, it remains a real possibility. Of course, on this same question, there is Fitz Lee's view from further down the road — he was only aware of having sent Lomax's command to Stuart and did not know Gordon and his North Carolinians had arrived in his rear — perhaps Lomax did not get back to Fitz Lee before the latter was fully engaged with the enemy. T. S. Garnett, *Riding with Stuart* (Shippensburg, Pa., 1994), p63; H. B. McClellan, *I Rode with Jeb Stuart* (Bloomington, 1958), p410; "The Raid Around Richmond," *Richmond Enquirer*, May 17, 1864, p1, col 4; Stuart, *O.R.*, vLI, part 2, p913; Fitzhugh Lee, "Report of the Operations of His Cavalry Division, from May 4th to Sept 19th, 1864," p11, MC. On the same issue see G. C. Rhea, *The Battles for Spotsylvania Court House and the Road to Yellow Tavern* (Baton Rouge, 1997), p120, note number 94.
83. G. C. Rhea, *The Battles for Spotsylvania Court House and the Road to Yellow Tavern* (Baton Rouge, 1997), p189–191.
84. G. C. Rhea, *The Battles for Spotsylvania Court House and the Road to Yellow Tavern* (Baton Rouge, 1997), p191.
85. *Daily Confederate*, May 23, p2, col 4; G. C. Rhea, *The*

Battles for Spotsylvania Court House and the Road to Yellow Tavern (Baton Rouge, 1997), p191.

86. *Daily Confederate*, May 23, p2, col 4; "The Raid Around Richmond," *Richmond Enquirer*, May 17, 1864, p1, col 4; G. C. Rhea, *The Battles for Spotsylvania Court House and the Road to Yellow Tavern* (Baton Rouge, 1997), p191-192.

87. *Daily Confederate*, May 23, p2, col 4; Fitzhugh Lee, "Report of the Operations of His Cavalry Division, from May 4th to Sept 19th, 1864," p11, MC; G. C. Rhea, *The Battles for Spotsylvania Court House and the Road to Yellow Tavern* (Baton Rouge, 1997), p192.

88. *Daily Confederate*, May 23, p2, col 4; G. C. Rhea, *The Battles for Spotsylvania Court House and the Road to Yellow Tavern* (Baton Rouge, 1997), p193.

89. Fitzhugh Lee, "Report of the Operations of His Cavalry Division, from May 4th to Sept 19th, 1864," p12, MC; G. C. Rhea, *The Battles for Spotsylvania Court House and the Road to Yellow Tavern* (Baton Rouge, 1997), p194.

90. Fitzhugh Lee, "Report of the Operations of His Cavalry Division, from May 4th to Sept 19th, 1864," p12, MC.

91. Stuart, *O.R.*, vLI, part 2, p911-912.

92. Stuart, *O.R.*, vLI, part 2, p912; G. C. Rhea, *The Battles for Spotsylvania Court House and the Road to Yellow Tavern* (Baton Rouge, 1997), p196.

93. H. B. McClellan, *I Rode with Jeb Stuart* (Bloomington, 1958), p411.

94. Stuart, *O.R.*, vLI, part 2, p916; Fitzhugh Lee, "Report of the Operations of His Cavalry Division, from May 4th to Sept 19th, 1864," p13, MC; G. C. Rhea, *The Battles for Spotsylvania Court House and the Road to Yellow Tavern* (Baton Rouge, 1997), p197.

95. G. C. Rhea, *The Battles for Spotsylvania Court House and the Road to Yellow Tavern* (Baton Rouge, 1997), p196.

96. G. C. Rhea, *The Battles for Spotsylvania Court House and the Road to Yellow Tavern* (Baton Rouge, 1997), p197.

97. G. C. Rhea, *The Battles for Spotsylvania Court House and the Road to Yellow Tavern* (Baton Rouge, 1997), p197; R. E. L. Krick, "Stuart's Last Ride: A Confederate View of Sheridan's Raid," p134.

98. D. B. Coltrane, *Memoirs* (Raleigh, 1956), p29.

99. R. Barringer, "Ninth Regiment (First Cavalry)," p429; G. C. Rhea, *The Battles for Spotsylvania Court House and the Road to Yellow Tavern* (Baton Rouge, 1997), p194.

100. *Daily Confederate*, May 23, 1864, p2, col 4.

101. *Daily Confederate*, May 23, 1864, p2, col 4; P. B. Means, "Additional Sketch Sixty-Third Regiment (Fifth Cavalry)," p596; G. C. Rhea, *The Battles for Spotsylvania Court House and the Road to Yellow Tavern* (Baton Rouge, 1997), p197.

102. *Daily Confederate*, May 23, 1864, p2, col 4; P. B. Means, "Additional Sketch Sixty-Third Regiment (Fifth Cavalry)," p597-598; W. H. Cheek, "Additional Sketch Ninth Regiment (First Cavalry)," p466; G. C. Rhea, *The Battles for Spotsylvania Court House and the Road to Yellow Tavern* (Baton Rouge, 1997), p198.

103. *Daily Confederate*, May 23, 1864, p2, col 4; "The Raid Around Richmond," *Richmond Enquirer*, May 17, 1864, p1, col 5; W. H. Cheek, "Additional Sketch Ninth Regiment (First Cavalry)," p465-466; G. C. Rhea, *The Battles for Spotsylvania Court House and the Road to Yellow Tavern* (Baton Rouge, 1997), p198-199.

104. "The Raid Around Richmond," *Richmond Enquirer*, May 17, 1864, p1, col 4; G. C. Rhea, *The Battles for Spotsylvania Court House and the Road to Yellow Tavern* (Baton Rouge, 1997), p199.

105. W. H. Cheek, "Additional Sketch Ninth Regiment (First Cavalry)," p465-466; *Daily Confederate*, May 23, p2, col 4; G. C. Rhea, *The Battles for Spotsylvania Court House and the Road to Yellow Tavern* (Baton Rouge, 1997), p199.

106. *Daily Confederate*, May 23, 1864, p2, col 4; G. C. Rhea, *The Battles for Spotsylvania Court House and the Road to Yellow Tavern* (Baton Rouge, 1997), p199.

107. T. S. Garnett, *Riding with Stuart* (Shippensburg, Pa., 1994), p65; Fitzhugh Lee, "Report of the Operations of His Cavalry Division, from May 4th to Sept 19th, 1864," p13, MC; G. C. Rhea, *The Battles for Spotsylvania Court House and the Road to Yellow Tavern* (Baton Rouge, 1997), p199.

108. Sheridan, *O.R.*, vXXVI, part 1, p790; G. C. Rhea, *The Battles for Spotsylvania Court House and the Road to Yellow Tavern* (Baton Rouge, 1997), p201.

109. Fitzhugh Lee, "Report of the Operations of His Cavalry Division, from May 4th to Sept 19th, 1864," p14, MC; G. C. Rhea, *The Battles for Spotsylvania Court House and the Road to Yellow Tavern* (Baton Rouge, 1997), p201.

110. H. B. McClellan, *I Rode with Jeb Stuart* (Bloomington, 1958), p412-413; G. C. Rhea, *The Battles for Spotsylvania Court House and the Road to Yellow Tavern* (Baton Rouge, 1997), p201.

111. G. C. Rhea, *The Battles for Spotsylvania Court House and the Road to Yellow Tavern* (Baton Rouge, 1997), p203-204.

112. L. W. Hopkins, *From Bull Run to Appomattox* (Baltimore, 1908), p158.

113. G. C. Rhea, *The Battles for Spotsylvania Court House and the Road to Yellow Tavern* (Baton Rouge, 1997), p205.

114. G. C. Rhea, *The Battles for Spotsylvania Court House and the Road to Yellow Tavern* (Baton Rouge, 1997), p205.

115. T. S. Garnett, *Riding with Stuart* (Shippensburg, Pa., 1994), p68; Fitzhugh Lee, "Report of the Operations of His Cavalry Division, from May 4th to Sept 19th, 1864," p14, MC; G. C. Rhea, *The Battles for Spotsylvania Court House and the Road to Yellow Tavern* (Baton Rouge, 1997), p205.

116. Stuart to Bragg, May 11, 1864, at 3 o'clock P.M., "Stuart's Last Dispatch," p138-139; G. C. Rhea, *The Battles for Spotsylvania Court House and the Road to Yellow Tavern* (Baton Rouge, 1997), p205-206.

117. G. C. Rhea, *The Battles for Spotsylvania Court House and the Road to Yellow Tavern* (Baton Rouge, 1997), p206.

118. G. C. Rhea, *The Battles for Spotsylvania Court House and the Road to Yellow Tavern* (Baton Rouge, 1997), p207.

119. W. B. Poindexter, "He Proposed to Advance on the Enemy Camp at Yellow Tavern," p119-121; G. C. Rhea, *The Battles for Spotsylvania Court House and the Road to Yellow Tavern* (Baton Rouge, 1997), p207.

120. G. C. Rhea, *The Battles for Spotsylvania Court House and the Road to Yellow Tavern* (Baton Rouge, 1997), p208.

121. W. B. Poindexter, "He Proposed to Advance on the Enemy Camp at Yellow Tavern," p119-121; F. Dorsey, "Fatal Wounding of General J. E. B. Stuart," p236-238; H. B. McClellan, *I Rode with Jeb Stuart* (Bloomington, 1958), p413; G. C. Rhea, *The Battles for Spotsylvania Court House and the Road to Yellow Tavern* (Baton Rouge, 1997), p208.

122. Fitzhugh Lee, "Report of the Operations of His Cavalry Division, from May 4th to Sept 19th, 1864," p15, MC; G. C. Rhea, *The Battles for Spotsylvania Court House and the Road to Yellow Tavern* (Baton Rouge, 1997), p209, 211; T. S. Garnett, *Riding with Stuart* (Shippensburg, Pa., 1994), p73.

123. Wilson, *O.R.*, vXXXVI, part 1, p879; G. C. Rhea, *The Battles for Spotsylvania Court House and the Road to Yellow Tavern* (Baton Rouge, 1997), p211.

124. G. C. Rhea, *The Battles for Spotsylvania Court House and the Road to Yellow Tavern* (Baton Rouge, 1997), p209.

125. "Barringer's N.C. Brigade of Cavalry," *Daily Confederate*, Feb 22, 1865, p2, cols, 3, 4, 5; G. C. Rhea, *The Battles for Spotsylvania Court House and the Road to Yellow Tavern* (Baton Rouge, 1997), p209-210.

126. Gregg, *O.R.*, vXXXVI, part 1, p853.

127. G. C. Rhea, *The Battles for Spotsylvania Court House and the Road to Yellow Tavern* (Baton Rouge, 1997), p212.

128. G. C. Rhea, *The Battles for Spotsylvania Court House and the Road to Yellow Tavern* (Baton Rouge, 1997), p127-188, 212-307.

129. G. C. Rhea, *The Battles for Spotsylvania Court House and the Road to Yellow Tavern* (Baton Rouge, 1997), p319 and 324.

130. Fitzhugh Lee, "Report of the Operations of His Cavalry Division, from May 4th to Sept 19th, 1864," p16, MC.

131. G. C. Rhea, *To the North Anna River* (Baton Rouge, 2000), p38–40.
132. G. C. Rhea, *To the North Anna River* (Baton Rouge, 2000), p40–42.
133. G. C. Rhea, *To the North Anna River* (Baton Rouge, 2000), p43.
134. G. C. Rhea, *To the North Anna River* (Baton Rouge, 2000), p47.
135. T. F. Rodenbough, "Sheridan's Richmond Raid," p191; G. C. Rhea, *To the North Anna River* (Baton Rouge, 2000), p48.
136. P. B. Means, "Additional Sketch Sixty-Third Regiment (Fifth Cavalry)," p602; G. C. Rhea, *To the North Anna River* (Baton Rouge, 2000), p48–49.
137. G. C. Rhea, *To the North Anna River* (Baton Rouge, 2000), p49–50.
138. G. C. Rhea, *To the North Anna River* (Baton Rouge, 2000), p51.
139. P. B. Means, "Additional Sketch Sixty-Third Regiment (Fifth Cavalry)," p602–603.
140. P. B. Means, "Additional Sketch Sixty-Third Regiment (Fifth Cavalry)," p602; "The Raid Around Richmond," *Richmond Enquirer*, May 17, 1864, p1, col 5; G. C. Rhea, *To the North Anna River* (Baton Rouge, 2000), p51–52.
141. "The Raid Around Richmond," *Richmond Enquirer*, May 17, 1864, p1, col 5; G. C. Rhea, *To the North Anna River* (Baton Rouge, 2000), p52.
142. "The Raid Around Richmond," *Richmond Enquirer*, May 17, 1864, p1, col 5; G. C. Rhea, *To the North Anna River* (Baton Rouge, 2000), p52–53.
143. P. B. Means, "Additional Sketch Sixty-Third Regiment (Fifth Cavalry)," p603; "Barringer's N.C. Brigade of Cavalry," *Daily Confederate*, Feb 22, 1865, p2, cols. 3, 4, and 5; G. C. Rhea, *To the North Anna River* (Baton Rouge, 2000), p53.
144. P. B. Means, "Additional Sketch Sixty-Third Regiment (Fifth Cavalry)," p603; G. C. Rhea, *To the North Anna River* (Baton Rouge, 2000), p53.
145. P. B. Means, "Additional Sketch Sixty-Third Regiment (Fifth Cavalry)," p603; "Barringer's N.C. Brigade of Cavalry," *Daily Confederate*, Feb 22, 1865, p2, cols. 3, 4, and 5; Chilton, *O.R.*, vLI, part 2, p925; G. C. Rhea, *To the North Anna River* (Baton Rouge, 2000), p52–53.
146. G. C. Rhea, *To the North Anna River* (Baton Rouge, 2000), p54–55.
147. Merritt, *O.R.*, vXXXVI, part 1, p813–814; Fitzhugh Lee, "Report of the Operations of His Cavalry Division, from May 4th to Sept 19th, 1864," p19, MC; G. C. Rhea, *To the North Anna River* (Baton Rouge, 2000), p55–57.
148. Sheridan, *O.R.*, vXXXVI, part 1, p777–778; D. McM. Gregg, *O.R.*, vXXXVI, part 1, p854. According to Merritt they moved to Malvern Hill on the 14th and stayed there until the night of May 17. Merritt, *O.R.*, vXXXVI, part 1, p814; G. C. Rhea, *To the North Anna River* (Baton Rouge, 2000), p59–60.
149. "Barringer's N.C. Brigade of Cavalry," *Daily Confederate*, Feb 22, 1865, p2, cols. 3, 4, and 5; Fitzhugh Lee, "Report of the Operations of His Cavalry Division, from May 4th to Sept 19th, 1864," p19–20, MC.
150. R. E. Lee formalized his decision in Special Orders no. 126, in which he disbanded Stuart's staff, reassigning several of them to other commands—including Fitz Lee's and W. H. F. Lee's divisions. *O.R.*, vXXXVI, part 2, p1001; G. C. Rhea, *To the North Anna River* (Baton Rouge, 2000), p61–62; E. J. Wittenberg, *Glory Enough for All: Sheridan's Second Raid and the Battle of Trevilian Station* (Dulles, Va., 2001), p18.
151. G. C. Rhea, *To the North Anna River* (Baton Rouge, 2000), p21–28.
152. G. C. Rhea, *To the North Anna River* (Baton Rouge, 2000), p30–33, 75–94.
153. G. C. Rhea, *To the North Anna River* (Baton Rouge, 2000), p95–116.
154. G. C. Rhea, *To the North Anna River* (Baton Rouge, 2000), p133–152.
155. G. C. Rhea, *To the North Anna River* (Baton Rouge, 2000), p212–229.
156. J. M. Galloway, "Sixty-Third Regiment (Fifth Cavalry)," p538.
157. Sheridan, *O.R.*, vXXXVI, part 1, p792; Fitz Lee, *O.R.*, vLI, part 2, p938; Fitz Lee to his cousin, G. W. C. "Custis" Lee, *O.R.*, vLI, part 2, p944–945.
158. R. E. Lee, item 718 in Dowdey and Manarin, *Wartime Papers of Robert E. Lee* (New York, 1987), p745; Davis, *O.R.*, vLI, part 2, p939.
159. R. E. Lee to Fitz Lee, *O.R.*, vLI, part 2, p943; Fitz Lee to his cousin, G. W. C. "Custis" Lee, *O.R.*, vLI, part 2, p944–945; Fitzhugh Lee, "Report of the Operations of His Cavalry Division, from May 4th to Sept 19th, 1864," p20–21, MC; G. C. Rhea, *To the North Anna River* (Baton Rouge, 2000), p195.
160. Sheridan, *O.R.*, vXXXVI, part 1, p792; Fitz Lee, *O.R.*, vLI, part 2, p954.
161. Sheridan, *O.R.*, vXXXVI, part 1, p792; D. McM. Gregg, *O.R.*, vXXXVI, part 1, p854.
162. Fitzhugh Lee, "Report of the Operations of His Cavalry Division, from May 4th to Sept 19th, 1864," p21, MC; G. C. Rhea, *To the North Anna River* (Baton Rouge, 2000), p196–197.
163. Sheridan, *O.R.*, vXXXVI, part 1, p792, 786; D. McM. Gregg, *O.R.*, vXXXVI, part 1, p854.
164. Fitz Lee, *O.R.*, vLI, part 2, p954; Fitz Lee, *O.R.*, vXXXVI, part 3, p815.
165. Wade Hampton, "1864 Narrative," in the Hampton Family Papers, Wade Hampton III report, p37–38, SCL-USC; G. C. Rhea, *To the North Anna River* (Baton Rouge, 2000), p238–239.
166. R. E. Lee in Fitz Lee, *O.R.*, vLI, part 2, p938; Beauregard and Bragg, *O.R.*, vLI, part 3, p801–804.
167. Special Orders No. 116, *O.R.*, vLI, part 2, p950; Sale, *O.R.*, vXXXVI, part 3, p808.
168. Young, *O.R.*, vLI, part 2, p938.
169. Special Orders No. 118, *O.R.*, vXXXVI, part 3, p812–813.
170. G. C. Rhea, *To the North Anna River* (Baton Rouge, 2000), chapters IX and X.
171. G. C. Rhea, *To the North Anna River* (Baton Rouge, 2000), p362–363.
172. G. C. Rhea, *To the North Anna River* (Baton Rouge, 2000), p363. Means said the 5th North Carolina alone supplied 225 men and the brigade a total of over 1,000, but Barringer said the North Carolina brigade detached 225 men under the command of Major McNeil for this expedition. P. B. Means, "Additional Sketch Sixty-Third Regiment (Fifth Cavalry)," p604; "Barringer's N.C. Brigade of Cavalry," *Daily Confederate*, Feb 22, 1865, p2, cols. 3, 4, and 5. Fitz Lee later remembered that his total command on this occasion numbered about 1,600 men, which would be more consistent with Barringer's numbers. Fitzhugh Lee, "Report of the Operations of His Cavalry Division, from May 4th to Sept 19th, 1864," p21 and 24–25, MC.
173. Fitzhugh Lee, "Report of the Operations of His Cavalry Division, from May 4th to Sept 19th, 1864," p23, 25, MC; P. B. Means, "Additional Sketch Sixty-Third Regiment (Fifth Cavalry)," p604.
174. Fitzhugh Lee, "Report of the Operations of His Cavalry Division, from May 4th to Sept 19th, 1864," p22, MC.
175. Wild and Butler, *O.R.*, vXXXVI, part 2, p271–272 and p269. Fitz Lee's attack on the fort at Wilson's Wharf was only one of several assaults on recently established Union installations along the James—another attack had been made on Fort Powhatan May 21, a base just upriver. As a result of the attack on the 21st, racial tensions built among the military commanders in the area. These tensions carried over to several areas of Fitz Lee's attack. For instance, during the attack of the 21st, two men were captured from the Twenty-second U.S. Colored Troops. About a week later and after Fitz Lee had attempted his assault on the fort at Wilson's Wharf, the Union commander at City Point, E. W. Hinks, sent a message to General Butler concerning a report that the two men

captured on the 21st "... were shot to death in Petersburg at a place called the 'Gallows,' designated for the executions of condemned criminals." General Hinks went on to recommend to Butler that if the report were true "... all the prisoners captured from General Fitzhugh Lee, at Wilson's Wharf, on the 18th [24th] instant, be held for execution in retaliation for the murder of the soldiers of the Twenty-second Regiment...." There is no doubt that passions were high during May of 1864 and that they were fueled by the race issue, but apparently Butler did not act on Hinks's recommendation. Of the 20 some men captured from Fitz Lee's command on May 24, only one was from the 2nd North Carolina. He was 21 year-old James T. Armstrong, and he was not executed; he was imprisoned at Point Lookout until March of 1865. Hinks, *O.R.*, vXXXVI, part 3, p287–288.

176. Fitzhugh Lee, "Report of the Operations of His Cavalry Division, from May 4th to Sept 19th, 1864," p23, MC; P. B. Means, "Additional Sketch Sixty-Third Regiment (Fifth Cavalry)," p606–607.

177. Fitzhugh Lee, "Report of the Operations of His Cavalry Division, from May 4th to Sept 19th, 1864," p23, MC.

178. Fitzhugh Lee, "Report of the Operations of His Cavalry Division, from May 4th to Sept 19th, 1864," p23, MC; P. B. Means, "Additional Sketch Sixty-Third Regiment (Fifth Cavalry)," p606–607.

179. P. B. Means, "Additional Sketch Sixty-Third Regiment (Fifth Cavalry)," p606.

180. Fitzhugh Lee, "Report of the Operations of His Cavalry Division, from May 4th to Sept 19th, 1864," p24–25, MC.

181. P. B. Means, "Additional Sketch Sixty-Third Regiment (Fifth Cavalry)," p606.

182. Fitz Lee and Lomax, *O.R.*, vLI, part 2, p957 and 958.

183. W. P. Roberts, "Additional Sketch Nineteenth Regiment (Second Cavalry)," p101.

184. John P. Lockhart, *Hillsborough Recorder,* June 1, 1864, p3, col 2, and June 8, 1864, p2, col 2.

185. John P. Lockhart, *Hillsborough Recorder,* June 1, 1864, p3, col 2.

186. Torbert, *O.R.*, vXXXVI, part 1, p804; One historian who acknowledges this as the opening of the Cold Harbor Campaign unfortunately notes the presence of only a Maryland cavalry unit on the south side of the Pamunkey—failure to mention the North Carolina cavalrymen is a common omission in the literature on other occasions as well. See, E. B. Furguson, *Not War But Murder: Cold Harbor 1864* (New York, 2000), p46–47.

187. Torbert, *O.R.*, vXXXVI, part 1, p804.

188. Sheridan, *O.R.*, vXXXVI, part 1, p793; Torbert, *O.R.*, vXXXVI, part 1, p804.

189. "Barringer's N.C. Brigade of Cavalry," *Daily Confederate*, Feb 22, 1865, p2, cols. 3, 4, and 5; P. B. Means, "Additional Sketch Sixty-Third Regiment (Fifth Cavalry)," p608; C. A. Evens, "The Maryland Line," p120–121; "The Recent Cavalry Operations," *Fayetteville Observer*, June 13, 1864, p2, col 1, reprinted from the *Richmond Enquirer*.

190. "Recent Cavalry Operations," *Richmond Enquirer*, June 17, 1864, p1, col 4.

191. Taylor for R. E. Lee, *O.R.*, vLI, part 2, p962.

192. Fitz Lee, *O.R.*, vLI, part 2, p962 and 963; Fitzhugh Lee, "Report of the Operations of His Cavalry Division, from May 4th to Sept 19th, 1864," p25, MC.

193. Wade Hampton, "1864 Narrative," in the Hampton Family Papers, Wade Hampton III report, p.38, SCL-USC; Special Orders No. 123, *O.R.*, vXXXVI, part 3, p840.

194. R. L. T. Beale, *History of the Ninth Virginia Cavalry* (Amissville, 1981), p121–123 ;"Barringer's N.C. Brigade of Cavalry," *Daily Confederate*, Feb 22, 1865, p2, cols. 3, 4, and 5; John P. Lockhart *Hillsborough Recorder,* June 8, 1864, p2, col 2, written from Atlee's Station on May 28.

195. Fitz Lee, *O.R.* , vLI, part 2, p966.

196. Torbert, *O.R.*, vXXXVI, part 1, p804.

197. Wade Hampton, "1864 Narrative," in the Hampton Family Papers, Wade Hampton III report, p38, SCL-USC;

Fitzhugh Lee, "Report of the Operations of His Cavalry Division, from May 4th to Sept 19th, 1864," p25, MC; T. S. Garnett, *Riding with Stuart* (Shippensburg, Pa., 1994), p74.

198. G. W. Beale, *A Lieutenant of Cavalry in Lee's Army* (Baltimore, 1994), p157; R. L. T. Beale, *History of the Ninth Virginia Cavalry* (Amissville, 1981), p123, 126.

199. Wade Hampton, "1864 Narrative," in the Hampton Family Papers, Wade Hampton III report, p38, SCL-USC; Fitzhugh Lee, "Report of the Operations of His Cavalry Division, from May 4th to Sept 19th, 1864," p25–26, MC; P. B. Means, "Additional Sketch Sixty-Third Regiment (Fifth Cavalry)," p608.

200. Wade Hampton, "1864 Narrative," in the Hampton Family Papers, Wade Hampton III report, p38–39, SCL-USC; Fitzhugh Lee, "Report of the Operations of His Cavalry Division, from May 4th to Sept 19th, 1864," p26, MC. For a more detailed account of the fighting, see: G. C. Rhea, "The Hottest Place I Ever Was In, The Battle of Haw's Shop, May 28, 1864," p42–57.

201. "The Recent Cavalry Operations," *Fayetteville Observer*, June 13, 1864, p2, col 1, reprinted from the *Richmond Enquirer.*

202. Wade Hampton, "1864 Narrative," in the Hampton Family Papers, Wade Hampton III report, p38–39, SCL-USC; "Barringer's N.C. Brigade of Cavalry," *Daily Confederate*, Feb 22, 1865, p2, cols. 3, 4, and 5; "The Recent Cavalry Operations," *Fayetteville Observer*, June 13, 1864, p2, col 1, reprinted from the *Richmond Enquirer*; also see, "Recent Cavalry Operations in Virginia," *Fayetteville Observer*, June 20, 1864, p2, col 3.

203. Hampton was probably very anxious when he saw Wickham's command withdrawn too rapidly and expose the South Carolinian's flank. Hampton's displeasure with Wickham goes back to the Battle of Brandy Station on June 9, 1863 when Wickham's command broke and exposed Butler's South Carolina regiment. In that earlier battle, Butler's foot was blown off, and Wade Hampton's younger brother was killed. Hampton blamed Wickham for the death of his brother and the damage done to the South Carolina cavalry. Butler still had not returned from South Carolina, so Hampton probably felt a special need to watch over his new troops—especially when fighting next to Wickham's command. See, E. S. Wittenburg, *Glory Enough for All* (Dulles, Va., 2001), p18 and note no. 70; W. N. McDonald, *A History of the Laurel Brigade* (Baltimore, 2002), p244.

204. Wade Hampton, "1864 Narrative," in the Hampton Family Papers, Wade Hampton III report, p38–39, SCL-USC; Torbert, *O.R.*, vXXXVI, part 1, p804; McM. Gregg, *O.R.*, vXXXVI, part 1, p854; P. B. Means, "Additional Sketch Sixty-Third Regiment (Fifth Cavalry)," p608.

205. R. E. Lee, *O.R.*, vXXXVI, part 3, p843–844; Fitzhugh Lee, "Report of the Operations of His Cavalry Division, from May 4th to Sept 19th, 1864," p26, MC.

206. Sheridan, *O.R.*, vXXXVI, part 1, p793; Torbert, *O.R.*, vXXXVI, part 1, p804.

207. Sheridan and Torbert, *O.R.*, vXXXVI, part 1, p794 and 805.

208. Wade Hampton, "1864 Narrative," in the Hampton Family Papers, Wade Hampton III report, p39, SCL-USC; Fitzhugh Lee, "Report of the Operations of His Cavalry Division, from May 4th to Sept 19th, 1864," p26, MC.

209. Sheridan, *O.R.*, vXXXVI, part 1, p794; Torbert, *O.R.*, vXXXVI, part 1, p805.

210. Butler, *O.R.*, vLI, part 2, p970; Torbert, *O.R.*, vXXXVI, part 1, p805; Fitzhugh Lee, "Report of the Operations of His Cavalry Division, from May 4th to Sept 19th, 1864," p26, MC.

211. Chapman, *O.R.*, vXXXVI, part 1, p899.

212. Sheridan, *O.R.*, vXXXVI, part 1, p795.

213. Torbert, *O.R.*, vXXXVI, part 1, p805; Fitzhugh Lee, "Report of the Operations of His Cavalry Division, from May 4th to Sept 19th, 1864," p26, MC; R. E. Lee, item 749 in Dowdey and Manarin, *Wartime Papers of Robert E. Lee* (New

York, 1987), p761–762; Sheridan, *O.R.*, vXXXVI, part 1, p794.
214. Sheridan, *O.R.*, vXXXVI, part 1, p794; Fitzhugh Lee, "Report of the Operations of His Cavalry Division, from May 4th to Sept 19th, 1864," p26–27, MC.
215. "Barringer's N.C. Brigade of Cavalry," *Daily Confederate*, Feb 22, 1865, p2, cols. 3, 4, and 5; "The Recent Cavalry Operations," *Fayetteville Observer*, June 13, 1864, p2, col 1, reprinted from the *Richmond Enquirer*.
216. Wilson, May 31, 1864, 1:30 P.M., *O.R.*, vXXXVI, part 1, p871–872.
217. "The Recent Cavalry Operations," *Fayetteville Observer*, June 13, 1864, p2, col 1.
218. "The Recent Cavalry Operations," *Fayetteville Observer*, June 13, 1864, p2, col 1; P. B. Means, "Additional Sketch Sixty-Third Regiment (Fifth Cavalry)," p608; "Barringer's N.C. Brigade of Cavalry," *Daily Confederate*, Feb 22, 1865, p2, cols. 3, 4, and 5; R. L. T. Beale, *History of the Ninth Virginia Cavalry* (Amissville, 1981), p 126.
219. P. B. Means, "Additional Sketch Sixty-Third Regiment (Fifth Cavalry)," p608; "Barringer's N.C. Brigade of Cavalry," *Daily Confederate*, Feb 22, 1865, p2, cols. 3, 4, and 5; Wilson, May 31, 1864, 11:00 P.M., *O.R.*, vXXXVI, part 1, p872–873; T. S. Garnett, *Riding with Stuart* (Shippensburg, Pa., 1994), p76.
220. Wilson, *O.R.*, vXXXVI, part 1, p871–873 and 880–881.
221. Wilson, *O.R.*, vXXXVI, part 1, p873.
222. Chapman, *O.R.*, vXXXVI, part 1, p899–900.
223. "The Recent Cavalry Operations," *Fayetteville Observer*, June 13, 1864, p2, col 1.
224. T. S. Garnett, *Riding with Stuart* (Shippensburg, Pa., 1994), p76.
225. T. S. Garnett, *Riding with Stuart* (Shippensburg, Pa., 1994), p77.
226. C. A. Evens, "The Maryland Line," p122; T. S. Garnett, *Riding with Stuart* (Shippensburg, Pa., 1994), p77.
227. T. S. Garnett, *Riding with Stuart* (Shippensburg, Pa., 1994), p77; "The Recent Cavalry Operations," *Fayetteville Observer*, June 13, 1864, p2, col 1, reprinted from the *Richmond Enquirer*.
228. McIntosh and Chapman, *O.R.*, vXXXVI, part 1, p888 and 900; Wade Hampton, "1864 Narrative," in the Hampton Family Papers, Wade Hampton III report, p40, SCL-USC; T. S. Garnett, *Riding with Stuart* (Shippensburg, Pa., 1994), p77–78; G. W. Beale, *A Lieutenant of Cavalry in Lee's Army* (Baltimore, 1994), p152–154; R. L. T. Beale, *History of the Ninth Virginia Cavalry* (Amissville, 1981), p126–127; "Barringer's N.C. Brigade of Cavalry," *Daily Confederate*, Feb 22, 1865, p2, cols. 3, 4, and 5; G. Baylor, *Bull Run to Bull Run, or Four Years in the Army of Northern Virginia* (Richmond, 1900), p216; "The Recent Cavalry Operations," *Fayetteville Observer*, June 13, 1864, p2, col 1; W. N. McDonald, *A History of the Laurel Brigade* (Baltimore, 2002), p245–248.
229. G. W. Beale, *A Lieutenant of Cavalry in Lee's Army* (Baltimore, 1994), p152–154; T. S. Garnett, *Riding with Stuart* (Shippensburg, Pa., 1994), p78.
230. T. S. Garnett, *Riding with Stuart* (Shippensburg, Pa., 1994), p78.
231. McIntosh and Chapman, *O.R.*, vXXXVI, part 1, p888 and 900; Wilson, *O.R.*, vXXXVI, part 1, p881–882; Wade Hampton, "1864 Narrative," in the Hampton Family Papers, Wade Hampton III report, p40, SCL-USC; T. S. Garnett, *Riding with Stuart* (Shippensburg, Pa., 1994), p78–79.
232. McIntosh and Chapman, *O.R.*, vXXXVI, part 1, p888 and 900; Wilson, *O.R.*, vXXXVI, part 1, p881–882; Wade Hampton, "1864 Narrative," in the Hampton Family Papers, Wade Hampton III report, p40, SCL-USC; T. S. Garnett, *Riding with Stuart* (Shippensburg, Pa., 1994), p78–79.
233. T. S. Garnett, *Riding with Stuart* (Shippensburg, Pa., 1994), p79.
234. "Barringer's N.C. Brigade of Cavalry," *Daily Confederate*, Feb 22, 1865, page 2, cols, 3, 4, 5; John M. Galloway, "Sixty-Third Regiment (Fifth Cavalry)," p537–538.
235. See, E. B. Furguson, *Not War But Murder: Cold Harbor 1864* (New York, 2000), chapters 6–10.
236. T. S. Garnett, *Riding with Stuart* (Shippensburg, Pa., 1994), p79.
237. Wilson, *O.R.*, vXXXVI, part 1, p882; Wade Hampton, "1864 Narrative," in the Hampton Family Papers, Wade Hampton III report, p41–42, SCL-USC.
238. "Barringer's N.C. Brigade of Cavalry," *Daily Confederate*, Feb 22, 1865, p2, cols. 3, 4, and 5; "The Recent Cavalry Operations," *Fayetteville Observer*, June 13, 1864, p2, col 1, reprinted from the *Richmond Enquirer*; W. P. Roberts, "Additional Sketch Nineteenth Regiment (Second Cavalry)," p101; "The Recent Cavalry Operations," *Fayetteville Observer*, June 13, 1864, p2, col 1, reprinted from the *Richmond Enquirer*.
239. "Recent Cavalry Operations," *Richmond Enquirer*, June 17, 1864, p1, col 5; Wilson, *O.R.*, vXXXVI, part 1, p882; Wade Hampton, "1864 Narrative," in the Hampton Family Papers, Wade Hampton III report, p41–42, SCL-USC; "Barringer's N.C. Brigade of Cavalry," *Daily Confederate*, Feb 22, 1865, p2, cols. 3, 4, and 5.
240. Sheridan, *O.R.*, vXXXVI, part 1, p794–795; Fitz Lee, *O.R.*, vLI, part 2, p984; Fitzhugh Lee, "Report of the Operations of His Cavalry Division, from May 4th to Sept 19th, 1864," p27–28, MC; R. E. Lee, *O.R.*, vXXXVI, part 1, p1032; Butler, *O.R.*, vLI, part 2, p978–979.
241. T. S. Garnett, *Riding with Stuart* (Shippensburg, Pa., 1994), p79–80.
242. Special Orders No. 138, *O.R.*, vXXXVI, part 3, p873; "Barringer's N.C. Brigade of Cavalry," *Daily Confederate*, Feb 22, 1865, p2, cols. 3, 4, and 5. Rufus Barringer graduated from UNC at Chapel Hill in 1842, and practiced law and politics. He was devotedly attached to the Union and Constitution and spoke publicly and passionately against secession. Barringer's stand on principles made him very unpopular, but he continued his active opposition to the currents during the months before the war—he warned that secession would lead to the fiercest and bloodiest war in modern times. Once war was inevitable, however, he returned home and raised a company which became Company F of the 1st North Carolina Cavalry, and he became their captain. He was promoted to major in Aug of 1863; to Lieutenant Colonel in Nov 1863; and brigadier general in June of 1864. Barringer led the North Carolina brigade through its battles until captured near Namozine Church on April 3, 1865.
243. R. Barringer, "Ninth Regiment (First Cavalry)," p430.
244. "Barringer's N.C. Brigade of Cavalry," *Daily Confederate*, Feb 22, 1865, p2, cols. 3, 4, and 5; Rufus Barringer letter to his brother, V. C. Barringer, dated Jan 27, 1866 from Concord, North Carolina, p7, SHC-UNC.
245. Grant, *O.R.*, vXXXVI, part 1, p21–22; E. B. Furgurson, *Not War But Murder* (New York, 2000), p99–180; J. M. McPherson, *Battle Cry of Freedom* (New York, 1989), p733, 735.
246. J. M. McPherson, *Battle Cry of Freedom* (New York, 1989), p733.
247. Grant, *O.R.*, vXXXVI, part 1, p22–23; J. M. McPherson, *Battle Cry of Freedom* (New York, 1989), p737.
248. J. M. McPherson, *Battle Cry of Freedom* (New York, 1989), p739.
249. Grant, *O.R.*, vXXXVI, part 1, p23.
250. Grant, *O.R.*, vXXXVI, part 1, p22–23.
251. J. M. McPherson, *Battle Cry of Freedom* (New York, 1989), p739.
252. E. L. Wells, *Hampton & His Cavalry in '64* (Richmond, 1997), p187–223; J. M. McPherson, *Battle Cry of Freedom* (New York, 1989), p739; D. S. Freeman, *Lee's Lieutenants* (New York, 1995), v3, p516–524; Fitzhugh Lee, "Report of the Operations of His Cavalry Division, from May 4th to Sept 19th, 1864," p28, MC; Wade Hampton, "1864 Narrative," in the Hampton Family Papers, Wade Hampton III report, p44–46, 51–54, SCL-USC; E. J. Wittenberh, *Glory Enough for All* (Dulles, Va., 2001), chapters 2–7.
253. Sheridan, *O.R.*, vXXXVI, part 1, p796.

254. John P. Lockhart to mother and sister, June 9, 1864, from Gaines's Farm, in Lockhart Family Letters, SCL-DU.
255. John W. Gordon, Diary, p2–3, North Carolina Collection, MC.
256. Grant, *O.R.*, vXXXVI, part 1, p22–23; E. B. Furguson, *Not War But Murder* (New York, 2000), p241–242; J. M. McPherson, *Battle Cry of Freedom* (New York, 1989), p739–740.
257. G. T. Beauregard, "Four Days of Battle at Petersburg," p540–544; J. M. McPherson, *Battle Cry of Freedom* (New York, 1989), p740.
258. G. T. Beauregard, "Four Days of Battle at Petersburg," p540–544; J. M. McPherson, *Battle Cry of Freedom* (New York, 1989), p741.
259. Chambliss, *O.R.*, vLI, part 2, p998, 1004, and 1010.
260. Wilson, *O.R.*, vXXXVI, part 1, p883.
261. T. S. Garnett, *Riding with Stuart* (Shippensburg, Pa., 1994), p80.
262. Wilson, *O.R.*, vXXXVI, part 1, p883; A. A. Humphreys, *The Virginia Campaign of 1864 and 1865* (New York, 1995), p201–202; John W. Gordon, Diary, p3, North Carolina Collection, MC.
263. Wilson, *O.R.*, vXXXVI, part 1, p884.
264. T. S. Garnett, *Riding with Stuart* (Shippensburg, Pa., 1994), p82.
265. Wilson, *O.R.*, vXXXVI, part 1, p884; W. H. F. Lee, *O.R.*, vLI, part 2, p1018; A. P. Hill, *O.R.*, vLI, part 2, p1017.
266. Chambliss, *O.R.*, vLI, part 2, p1018.
267. Rufus Barringer letter to his brother, V. C. Barringer, dated Jan 27, 1866 from Concord, North Carolina, p7, in SHC-UNC; John W. Gordon, Diary, p3, North Carolina Collection, MC.
268. Rufus Barringer letter to his brother, V. C. Barringer, dated Jan 27, 1866 from Concord, North Carolina, p6–7, in SHC-UNC; P. B. Means, "Additional Sketch Sixty-Third Regiment (Fifth Cavalry)," p609; W. H. F. Lee, *O.R.*, vLI, part 2, p1080; R. E. Lee, *O.R.*, vXL, part 2, p663; W. H. F. Lee, *O.R.*, vLI, part 2, p1020.
269. Chambliss, *O.R.*, vLI, part 2, p1021.
270. John W. Gordon, Diary, p3–4, North Carolina Collection, MC.
271. R. E. Lee, item 801 in Dowdey and Manarin, *Wartime Papers of Robert E. Lee* (New York, 1987), p792; Colonel Gary was active along the north side of the James as well as elsewhere in the area destroying bridges and wharves at places such as Harrison's and Wilcox's Landings. M. W. Gary, *O.R.*, vLI, part 2, p1023.

Six

1. J. William Jones, Personal *Reminiscences of General Robert E. Lee*, p40.
2. A. A. Humphreys, *The Virginia Campaign of 1864 and 1865* (New York, 1995), p227–228; N. A. Trudeau, *The Last Citadel* (Baton Rouge, 1991), p64–65.
3. Lyman to Meade, June 21, 12:55 P.M., *O.R.*, XL, part 2, p275; A. A. Humphreys, *The Virginia Campaign of 1864 and 1865* (New York, 1995), p227.
4. Barringer was able to concentrate most of his North Carolinian cavalrymen in front of Barlow's advance, but many of them stayed at their picket posts along their two mile line and could only hear the noises of battle in the distance. D. B. Coltrane, *Memoirs* (Raleigh, 1956), p31–32.
5. R. Barringer, "Ninth Regiment (First Cavalry)," p431.
6. Barlow's reports at 1:10 and 2:10 on the afternoon of June 21, *O.R.*, vXL, part 2, p276.
7. P. B. Means, "Additional Sketch Sixty-Third Regiment (Fifth Cavalry)," p610.
8. For a discussion of this syndrome, see: J. M. McPherson, *Battle Cry of Freedom* (New York, 1989), p735, 741; *O.R.*, v40, 2, p156–57; N. A. Trudeau, *The Last Citadel* (Baton Rouge, 1991), p64–65.
9. R. Barringer, "Ninth Regiment (First Cavalry)," p431–432; "From the N.C. Cavalry," *Daily Confederate*, July 11, 1864, p2, cols. 4, 5; P. B. Means, "Additional Sketch Sixty-Third Regiment (Fifth Cavalry)," p610.
10. Birney, *O.R.*, vXL, part 2, p275.
11. N. A. Trudeau, *The Last Citadel* (Baton Rouge, 1991), p68.
12. W. Hampton, "1864 Narrative," p42, SCL-USC.
13. R. Barringer, "Ninth Regiment (First Cavalry)," p432; Birney reported that his 3rd division lost 20 men in "Barlow's skirmish." *O.R.*, vXL, part 2, p276.
14. A. A. Humphreys, *The Virginia Campaign of 1864 and 1865* (New York, 1995), p228–229; R. J. Sommers, *Richmond Redeemed* (New York, 1981), pix–x.
15. R. E. Lee, *O.R.*, vXXXVI, part 3, p91; E. J. Wittenburg, *Glory Enough For All* (Washington, D.C., 2001), p215–233.
16. A. A. Humphreys, *The Virginia Campaign of 1864 and 1865* (New York, 1995), p235, 255; *O.R.*, vXXXVI, part 3, p903; E. J. Wittenburg, *Glory Enough For All* (Washington, D.C., 2001), p233–292.
17. *O.R.*, vXXXVI, part 3, p903.
18. Wilson, *O.R.*, vXL, part 1, p625; A. A. Humphreys, *The Virginia Campaign of 1864 and 1865* (New York, 1995), p236–237.
19. Special Orders No. 26, *O.R.*, vXL, part 2, p669; Special Orders No. 105, *O.R.*, vXXXVI, part 2, p958; A. A. Humphreys, *The Virginia Campaign of 1864 and 1865* (New York, 1995), p236–237.
20. Kautz, *O.R.*, vXL, part 1, p730; Wilson, *O.R.*, vXL, part 1, p625; "From the N.C. Cavalry," *Daily Confederate*, July 11, 1864, p2, cols. 4, 5.
21. Chapman, *O.R.*, vXL, part 1, p645; T. S. Garnett, *Riding with Stuart* (Shippensburg, Pa., 1994), p85.
22. Chapman, *O.R.*, vXL, part 1, p645; "From the N.C. Cavalry," *Daily Confederate*, July 11, 1864, p2, cols. 4, 5; "Cavalry Raid Incidents," *Daily Confederate*, Aug 12, 1864, p1, col 1; Cowles in W. H. Cheek, "Additional Sketch Ninth Regiment (First Cavalry)," p468; P. B. Means, "Additional Sketch Sixty-Third Regiment (Fifth Cavalry)," p612; Wilson, *O.R.*, vXL, part 1, p625; Kautz, *O.R.*, vXL, part 1, p731.
23. W. H. H. Cowles in W. H. Cheek, "Additional Sketch Ninth Regiment (First Cavalry)," p468.
24. Kautz, *O.R.*, vXL, part 1, p731.
25. Wilson, *O.R.*, vXL, part 1, p625–626; R. Barringer, "Ninth Regiment (First Cavalry)," p433; A. B. Cummins, *The Wilson-Kautz Raid: More Commonly referred to as the Battle of the Grove, June 21, July 1, 1864* (Blackstone, Va., 1961), p6.
26. Chapman, *O.R.*, vXL, part 1, p645; R. Barringer, "Ninth Regiment (First Cavalry)," p433; P. B. Means, "Additional Sketch Sixty-Third Regiment (Fifth Cavalry)," p613.
27. Chapman, *O.R.*, vXL, part 1, p645; Cowles in W. H. Cheek, "Additional Sketch Ninth Regiment (First Cavalry)," p468–469; P. B. Means, "Additional Sketch Sixty-Third Regiment (Fifth Cavalry)," p613.
28. P. B. Means, "Additional Sketch Sixty-Third Regiment (Fifth Cavalry)," p613–614.
29. W. P. Roberts, "Additional Sketch Nineteenth Regiment (Second Cavalry)," p102.
30. Barringer, General Orders, No. 11, July 4, 1864, reprinted in *Daily Confederate*, July 16, 1865, p2, col 6.
31. W. P. Roberts, "Additional Sketch Nineteenth Regiment (Second Cavalry)," p102–103.
32. Barringer, "Barringer's N.C. Brigade of Cavalry," dated Jan 17, 1865, *Daily Confederate*, Feb 22, 1865, p2, cols. 3, 4, 5; R. Barringer letter to his brother, V. C. Barringer, dated Jan 27, 1866 from Concord, N.C., p7, SHC-UNC; R. Barringer, "Ninth Regiment (First Cavalry)," p433.
33. Chapman, *O.R.*, vXL, part 1, p645; Wilson, *O.R.*, vXL, part 1, p626.
34. R. Barringer, "Ninth Regiment (First Cavalry)," p433; W. P. Roberts, "Additional Sketch Nineteenth Regiment (Second Cavalry)," p102; W. H. F. Lee, *O.R.*, vLI, part 1, p272.
35. Chapman, Kautz, and West, *O.R.*, vXL, part 1, p646, 731, and 734, respectively.

36. R. Barringer letter to his brother, V. C. Barringer, dated Jan 27, 1866 from Concord, N. C, p7, SHC-UNC; P. B. Means, "Additional Sketch Sixty-Third Regiment (Fifth Cavalry)," p614; W. H. F. Lee, *O.R.*, vLI, part 1, p272.

37. Wilson, Chapman, and West, *O.R.*, vXL, part 1, p626, 646, and 734 respectively.

38. C. A. Evens, "Services of the North Carolina Cavalry Along the Rapidan...." p261; Wilson and Kautz, *O.R.*, vXL, part 1, p627 and 731 respectively.

39. Wilson, *O.R.*, vXL, part 1, p627; "Cavalry Raid Incidents (continued)," *Daily Confederate*, Aug 17, 1864, p1, col 1; Barringer, "Barringer's N.C. Brigade of Cavalry," dated Jan 17, 1865, *Daily Confederate*, Feb 22, 1865, p2, cols. 3, 4, 5.

40. Wilson, *O.R.*, vXL, part 1, p627;

41. Wilson, *O.R.*, vXL, part 1, p627; J. M. Galloway, "Sixty-Third Regiment (Fifth Cavalry)," p539.

42. R. Barringer, "Ninth Regiment (First Cavalry)," p434; P. B. Means, "Additional Sketch Sixty-Third Regiment (Fifth Cavalry)," p615, 617–618; J. M. Galloway, "Sixty-Third Regiment (Fifth Cavalry)," p539; A young private in the 2nd North Carolina wrote a diary entry for June 26 that reads, "Here a selection of the best horses is made and the others are sent back towards Petersburg." John W. Gordon, Diary, p6, North Carolina Collection, MC.

43. A. A. Humphreys, *The Virginia Campaign of 1864 and 1865* (New York, 1995), p238; W. Hampton, "1864 Narrative," p55–56, SCL-USC.

44. Wilson, *O.R.*, vXL, part 1, p627.

45. Wilson, *O.R.*, vXL, part 1, p627; E. G. Longacre, *Lincoln's Cavalrymen* (Mechanicsburg, 2000), p290–291.

46. Wilson, *O.R.*, vXL, part 1, p627; R. L. T. Beale, *History of the Ninth Virginia Cavalry* (Amissville, 1981), p133–134; W. Hampton, "1864 Narrative," p57, SCL-USC.

47. Wilson, *O.R.*, vXL, part 1, p627; Chapman, *O.R.*, vXL, part 1, p646; R. L. T. Beale, *History of the Ninth Virginia Cavalry* (Amissville, 1981), p134; W. Hampton, "1864 Narrative," p57–58, SCL-USC.

48. Wilson, Kautz, and Chapman, *O.R.*, vXL, part 1, p628, 732, and 646 respectively; Fitzhugh Lee, "Report of the Operations of His Cavalry Division, from May 4th to Sept 19th, 1864," p34–35, MC; A. A. Humphreys, *The Virginia Campaign of 1864 and 1865* (New York, 1995), p239.

49. Fitzhugh Lee, "Report of the Operations of His Cavalry Division, from May 4th to Sept 19th, 1864," p34–35, MC.

50. Wilson, Kautz, and Chapman, *O.R.*, vXL, part 1, p628, 732, and 646 respectively; A. A. Humphreys, *The Virginia Campaign of 1864 and 1865* (New York, 1995), p239; Fitz Lee estimated that Wilson had over 5,000 men on his line that day but it is very unlikely that number of his cavalrymen made it as far as Reams's Station on that last day of Wilson's railroad raid. Fitzhugh Lee, "Report of the Operations of His Cavalry Division, from May 4th to Sept 19th, 1864," p35, MC.

51. E. G. Longacre, *Lincoln's Cavalrymen* (Mechanicsburg, 2000), p291.

52. Wilson, *O.R.*, vXL, part 1, p629–630; Fitzhugh Lee, "Report of the Operations of His Cavalry Division, from May 4th to Sept 19th, 1864," p35–36, MC; W. Hampton, "1864 Narrative," p58–59, SCL-USC; A. A. Humphreys, *The Virginia Campaign of 1864 and 1865* (New York, 1995), p241.

53. J. M. Galloway, "Sixty-Third Regiment (Fifth Cavalry)," p539. Barringer rode his fine new horse until he was captured on April 3, 1865, at which time the Union colonel from whom the horse was originally taken was at hand and regained his fine mount.

54. John W. Gordon, Diary, p6, North Carolina Collection, MC.

55. A. A. Humphreys, *The Virginia Campaign of 1864 and 1865* (New York, 1995), p241–242; Sharpe to Humphreys, *O.R.*, vXL, part 3, p38; R. L. T. Beale, *History of the Ninth Virginia Cavalry* (Amissville, 1981), p136.

56. R. Barringer letter to his brother, V. C. Barringer, dated Jan 27, 1866 from Concord, N.C., p8, SHC-UNC; R. Barringer, "Ninth Regiment (First Cavalry)," p434.

57. J. W. Gordon, Diary, p7, North Carolina Collection, MC.

58. J. P. Lockhart, *Hillsborough Recorder*, July 13, 1864, page 2, cols. 1, 2; Sharpe and Babcock, *O.R.*, vXL, part 3, p37–38 and 362–363.

59. Gaston B. Lockhart to sister Ellen, July 17, 1864 from camp near Petersburg, in Lockhart Family Letters, SCL-DU; "Camp 2nd N.C. Cavalry, July 24, 1864," *Daily Confederate*, July 27, 1864, p1, col 1.

60. Baldwin for R. E. Lee, *Daily Confederate*, Aug 6, 1864, p1, col 4.

61. Barringer, *Daily Confederate*, Aug 6, 1864, p1, col 4. Six or seven weeks later, the *Daily Confederate* ran a plea to the citizens of the state to turn in the cavalry arms and equipment in their possession because Barringer's brigade had suffered much in recent fighting and, "Its efficiency is much impaired for want of carbines, saddles and other cavalry accoutrements of the best kind; and there is no doubt of the fact that these are now to be found in private hands in almost every portion of the State." "Cavalry Arms and Accoutrements," *Daily Confederate*, Sept 19, 1864, p2, col 2.

62. Gaston B. Lockhart to sister, Ellen, July 17, 1864 from camp near Petersburg, in Lockhart Family Letters, SCL-DU; R. Barringer, "Ninth Regiment (First Cavalry)," p434; R. L. T. Beale, *History of the Ninth Virginia Cavalry* (Amissville, 1981), p136.

63. W. Hampton, "1864 Narrative," p61, SCL-USC.

64. A. A. Humphreys, *The Virginia Campaign of 1864 and 1865* (New York, 1995), p247–248.

65. John W. Gordon, Diary, p7–8, North Carolina Collection, MC; Fitzhugh Lee, "Report of the Operations of His Cavalry Division, from May 4th to Sept 19th, 1864," p37, MC; W. Hampton, "1864 Narrative," p61, SCL-USC.

66. A. A. Humphreys, *The Virginia Campaign of 1864 and 1865* (New York, 1995), p247–249; E. G. Longacre, *Lincoln's Cavalrymen* (Mechanicsburg, 2000), p296.

67. A. A. Humphreys, *The Virginia Campaign of 1864 and 1865* (New York, 1995), p249.

68. A. A. Humphreys, *The Virginia Campaign of 1864 and 1865* (New York, 1995), p249.

69. R. Barringer, "Ninth Regiment (First Cavalry)," p434; P. B. Means, "Additional Sketch Sixty-Third Regiment (Fifth Cavalry)," p618.

70. A. A. Humphreys, *The Virginia Campaign of 1864 and 1865* (New York, 1995), p249, 252, 254.

71. A. A. Humphreys, *The Virginia Campaign of 1864 and 1865* (New York, 1995), p255–264; Fitzhugh Lee, *General Lee* (New York, 1994), p360–361.

72. W. Hampton, "1864 Narrative," p61, SCL-USC; John W. Gordon, Diary, p8, North Carolina Collection, MC.

73. John W. Gordon, Diary, p8, North Carolina Collection, MC.

74. Gaston B. Lockhart to his sister, Aug 7, 1864, in Lockhart Family Letters, SCL-DU.

75. Fitzhugh Lee, "Report of the Operations of His Cavalry Division, from May 4th to Sept 19th, 1864," p37–52, MC.

76. W. Hampton, "1864 Narrative," p63, SCL-USC; R. E. Lee, *O.R.*, vXLII, part 2, p1172.

77. J. M. McPherson, *Battle Cry of Freedom* (New York, 1989), p758; A. A. Humphreys, *The Virginia Campaign of 1864 and 1865* (New York, 1995), p299; Grant, *O.R.*, vXXXVII, part 2, p558 and 559.

78. John W. Gordon, Diary, p9–10, North Carolina Collection, MC.

79. W. Hampton, "1864 Narrative," p66, SCL-USC; R. E. Lee, *O.R.*, vXLII, part 2, p1172; R. E. Lee, *O.R.*, vLI, part 2, p1034 and 1035.

80. R. Barringer letter to his brother, V. C. Barringer, dated Jan 27, 1866 from Concord, N.C., p8, SHC-UNC.

81. W. Hampton, "1864 Narrative," p63, SCL-USC; Special Orders No. 189, *O.R.*, vXLII, part 2, p1171, 1173; R. E. Lee in Dowdey and Manarin, *Wartime Papers of Robert E. Lee* (New York, 1987), item 824, p813.

82. A. A. Humphreys, *The Virginia Campaign of 1864 and 1865* (New York, 1995), p245.
83. Grant, *O.R.*, vXLII, part 2, p167; E. G. Longacre, *Lincoln's Cavalrymen* (Mechanicsburg, 2000), p299.
84. Hancock, *O.R.*, vXLII, part 1, p217–218, and *O.R.*, vXLII, part 2, p172, 173, 174, 180; Grant, *O.R.*, vXLII, p173, 180; A. A. Humphreys, *The Virginia Campaign of 1864 and 1865* (New York, 1995), p268–269.
85. Grant, *O.R.*, vXLII, part 2, p167.
86. *O.R.*, vXLII, part 1, p218.
87. C. W. Field, "Narrative of Major-General C. W. Field," p551–552.
88. Taylor for R. E. Lee, *O.R.*, vXLII, part 2, p1180; C. W. Field, "Narrative of Major-General C. W. Field," p552.
89. D. B. R. (correspondence of the Richmond Enquirer), "Late Cavalry Fighting on the Charles City Road," date line Aug 18, 1864, reprinted in *Daily Confederate*, Sept 2, 1864, p2, col 3; P. B. Means, "Additional Sketch Sixty-Third Regiment (Fifth Cavalry)," p618–619; R. Barringer letter to his brother, V. C. Barringer, dated Jan 27, 1866 from Concord, N.C., p8, SHC-UNC.
90. C. W. Field, "Narrative of Major-General C. W. Field," p551–552. Hancock, *O.R.*, vXLII, part 1, p218; Hancock, *O.R.*, vXLII, part 2, p197, 199; A. A. Humphreys, *The Virginia Campaign of 1864 and 1865* (New York, 1995), p270, 271.
91. D. McM. Gregg, Aug 15, 1864, 8 A.M., *O.R.*, vXLII, part 2, p204; D. B. R. (correspondence of the Richmond Enquirer), "Late Cavalry Fighting on the Charles City Road," date line Aug 18, 1864, reprinted in *Daily Confederate*, Sept 2, 1864, p2, col 3; Barringer, "Barringer's N.C. Brigade of Cavalry," dated Jan 17, 1865, *Daily Confederate*, Feb 22, 1865, p2, cols. 3, 4, 5; P. B. Means, "Additional Sketch Sixty-Third Regiment (Fifth Cavalry)," p619; R. Barringer letter to his brother, V. C. Barringer, dated Jan 27, 1866 from Concord, N.C., p8, SHC-UNC.
92. D. McM. Gregg, Aug 15, 1864, 8 A.M., *O.R.*, vXLII, part 2, p204; P. B. Means, "Additional Sketch Sixty-Third Regiment (Fifth Cavalry)," p619; R. Barringer letter to his brother, V. C. Barringer, dated Jan 27, 1866 from Concord, N.C., p8, SHC-UNC; Hancock, *O.R.*, vXLII, part 2, p198.
93. Hancock, *O.R.*, vXLII, part 2, p198, 199.
94. Barringer, "Barringer's N.C. Brigade of Cavalry," dated Jan 17, 1865, *Daily Confederate*, Feb 22, 1865, p2, cols. 3, 4, 5.
95. D. B. R. (correspondence of the Richmond Enquirer), "Late Cavalry Fighting on the Charles City Road," date line Aug 18, 1864, reprinted in *Daily Confederate*, Sept 2, 1864, p2, col 3.
96. Birney reported to Hancock at 1:50 P.M. that he had also hit the enemy cavalry in their flank that afternoon, *O.R.*, vXLII, part 2, p206; D. B. R. (correspondence of the Richmond Enquirer), "Late Cavalry Fighting on the Charles City Road," date line Aug 18, 1864, reprinted in *Daily Confederate*, Sept 2, 1864, p2, col 3.
97. W. P. Roberts, "Additional Sketch Nineteenth Regiment (Second Cavalry)," p104.
98. R. L. T. Beale, *History of the Ninth Virginia Cavalry* (Amissville, 1981), p139; W. P. Roberts, "Additional Sketch Nineteenth Regiment (Second Cavalry)," p104; W. H. Cheek, "Additional Sketch Ninth Regiment (First Cavalry)," p470; Barringer, "Barringer's N.C. Brigade of Cavalry," dated Jan 17, 1865, *Daily Confederate*, Feb 22, 1865, p2, cols. 3, 4, 5; J. P. Lockhart, *Hillsborough Recorder*, Aug 24, 1864, p2, cols. 2, 3.
99. Hancock, *O.R.*, vXLII, part 2, p198, 199; Birney, *O.R.*, vXLII, part 2, p206.
100. Hancock, *O.R.*, vXLII, part 2, p172, 173, 174, 180, 198, and 199; and *O.R.*, vXLII, part 1, p218.
101. Hancock, *O.R.*, vXLII, part 1, p219.
102. C. W. Field, "Narrative of Major-General C. W. Field," p553.
103. R. L. T. Beale, *History of the Ninth Virginia Cavalry* (Amissville, 1981), p137.
104. W. P. Roberts, "Additional Sketch Nineteenth Regiment (Second Cavalry)," p104.
105. J. P. Lockhart, *Hillsborough Recorder*, Aug 24, 1864, p2, cols. 2, 3.
106. R. Barringer letter to his brother, V. C. Barringer, dated Jan 27, 1866 from Concord, N.C.; p8, SHC-UNC; P. B. Means, "Additional Sketch Sixty-Third Regiment (Fifth Cavalry)," p619; from the *Richmond Enquirer* reprinted in the *Fayetteville Observer*, Aug 29, 1864, p2, col 1.
107. R. Barringer letter to his brother, V. C. Barringer, dated Jan 27, 1866 from Concord, N.C., p8, SHC-UNC; P. B. Means, "Additional Sketch Sixty-Third Regiment (Fifth Cavalry)," p619; from the *Richmond Enquirer* reprinted in the *Fayetteville Observer*, Aug 29, 1864, p2, col 1; J. P. Lockhart, *Hillsborough Recorder*, Aug 24, 1864, p2, cols. 2, 3; Barringer quoted in "Obituary, The Late Captain George Pettigrew Bryan," *Daily Confederate*, Aug 24, 1864, p2, col 5; comment from the 1st Maine Cavalry, *O.R.*, vXLII, part 1, p86; Miles, *O.R.*, vXLII, part 2, p223–224; Barringer, "Barringer's N.C. Brigade of Cavalry," dated Jan 17, 1865, *Daily Confederate*, Feb 22, 1865, p2, col 5; C. W. Field, "Narrative of Major-General C. W. Field," p554.
108. W. Hampton, "1864 Narrative," p67, SCL-USC.
109. All were certainly tragic losses, but one stands out because it was the loss of a young man, George Pettigrew Bryan, who spent the first years of his life full of promise and optimism, and even in war when he was unlucky, he was lucky, until Aug 16, 1864. In most ways he led a privileged life — his father was wealthy and prominent in North Carolina, and he and his brother were educated at the University of North Carolina. Early in the war, George often wrote his younger brother, who was attending the University, and offered him well meaning advice on how to remain a good person and not fall into the ways of the wicked by drinking and engaging in such common practices of students. George regularly expressed a responsibility to his father and to his younger brother — he saw himself as a righteous person. In addition, George seemed to be an ambitious young man set on doing what was right and expected of him. He was 24 years of age when he was severely wounded and captured at Upperville on June 21, 1863 — even then he had few if any doubts about the future. He apparently spent a good deal of his prison-time studying for his future. (His letter to his father illustrates these points and is presented in chapter 3 of this work.) George was promoted to the rank of captain while confined at Point Lookout, Maryland until he was exchanged at City Point on March 10, 1864. Soon after his exchange, he returned to Company G, of the 2nd North Carolina Cavalry, and fought with them until he was killed in action near Charles City Road on Aug 16, 1864 while leading his men in a charge.
110. A. A. Humphreys, *The Virginia Campaign of 1864 and 1865* (New York, 1995), p271; Hancock, *O.R.*, vXLII, part 2, p217–218.
111. Grant, *O.R.*, vXLII, part 2, p222.
112. R. L. T. Beale, *History of the Ninth Virginia Cavalry* (Amissville, 1981), p141; Hancock, *O.R.*, vXLII, part 1, p219–220; Garnett in G. W. Beale, *A Lieutenant of Cavalry in Lee's Army* (Baltimore, 1994), p169.
113. Gaston B. Lockhart to Dear Mother, Aug 17, 1864 from camp near Malvern Hill, in Lockhart Family Letters, SCL-DU.
114. Grant, *O.R.*, vXLII, part 2, p244.
115. Grant to Halleck, *O.R.*, vXLII, part 2, p210; Meade, *O.R.*, vXLII, part 2, p245; Meade and Grant, *O.R.*, vXLII, part 2, p211–212.
116. Grant, *O.R.*, vXLII, part 2, p250; Hancock, *O.R.*, vXLII, part 1, p220.
117. Hancock, *O.R.*, vXLII, part 1, p220; A. A. Humphreys, *The Virginia Campaign of 1864 and 1865* (New York, 1995), p272.
118. W. Hampton, "1864 Narrative," p68, SCL-USC; R. L. T. Beale, *History of the Ninth Virginia Cavalry* (Amissville, 1981), p141.
119. Butler, *O.R.*, vLI, part 2, p1035.

120. Hampton, *O.R.*, vLI, part 2, p1035–1036.
121. John W. Gordon, Diary, p13, North Carolina Collection, MC.
122. Hancock, *O.R.*, vXLII, part 1, p220; D. McM. Gregg, *O.R.*, vXLII, part 2, p321; Butler and Hampton, *O.R.*, vLI, part 2, p1035 and 1036.
123. Gaston B. Lockhart said 2nd N.C. lost 35 men in his Letter to mother, Aug 17, in Lockhart Family Letters, SCL-DU; W. P. Roberts, "Additional Sketch Nineteenth Regiment (Second Cavalry)," p104.
124. A. A. Humphreys, *The Virginia Campaign of 1864 and 1865* (New York, 1995), p272–273; Humphreys, *O.R.*, vXLII, part 2, p251.
125. A. A. Humphreys, *The Virginia Campaign of 1864 and 1865* (New York, 1995), p274–275; Warren, *O.R.*, vXLII, part 2, p273, 274, 275; Meade, *O.R.*, vXLII, part 2, p264, 265; Grant, *O.R.*, vXLII, part 2, p265.
126. Humphreys, *O.R.*, vXLII, part 2, p290; Grant, *O.R.*, vXLII, part 2, p261; Stanton for Lincoln, *O.R.*, vXLII, part 2, p291.
127. Grant, *O.R.*, vXLII, part 2, p293.
128. Grant, *O.R.*, vXLII, part 2, p292.
129. Warren, *O.R.*, vXLII, part 2, p307–308; A. A. Humphreys, *The Virginia Campaign of 1864 and 1865* (New York, 1995), p276.
130. Walker for Hancock, *O.R.*, vXLII, part 2, p321; A. A. Humphreys, *The Virginia Campaign of 1864 and 1865* (New York, 1995), p277.
131. Hancock, *O.R.*, vXLII, part 1, p222.
132. Beauregard with Dearing's dispatch, *O.R.*, vXLII, part 2, p1186, 1187.
133. Beauregard, *O.R.*, vXLII, part 2, p1190.
134. Hampton, *O.R.*, vLI, part 2, p1036; R. L. T. Beale, *History of the Ninth Virginia Cavalry* (Amissville, 1981), p141.
135. R. E. Lee, *O.R.*, vXLII, part 2, p1193.
136. William Paul Roberts was born on July 11, 1841 in Gates County, North Carolina. He was the second of four sons and a daughter born to a farmer and his wife. Roberts enlisted as a sergeant but was immediately made a junior 2nd lieutenant in Company C at the age of 19 when the company entered training camp. He obviously had no military training and no university training. However, he was a good student and experience was one of his teachers. Roberts was 1st lieutenant by May 1, 1863, and captain by Aug of that year. Roberts was appointed Major and transferred to the regiment's Field and Staff on Feb 18, 1864. He took command of the 2nd Cavalry on June 23, 1864. He became R. E. Lee's youngest brigadier general on Feb 23, 1865 — legend has it that Robert E. Lee presented his own gauntlets to the young general for his distinguished gallantry. Roberts's small brigade was formed from the remnants of Dearing's brigade and included the 4th North Carolina Cavalry, the 7th Cavalry (a newly formed regiment also known as the 16th Battalion), and the 8th Georgia Cavalry. When Barringer was captured during the last days of the Appomattox Campaign, W. P. Roberts also commanded the remnants of the North Carolina brigade — including the handful of men left in the 2nd North Carolina Cavalry. Roberts and 94 of his command remained near R. E. Lee for the surrender at Appomattox. After the war, Roberts became a politician; he represented his county at the state's constitutional convention in 1875, served in the state legislature in 1876–1877, was state auditor from 1880 to 1888, and went on to become the United States Counsel at Victoria, British Columbia. He died in 1910 at Norfolk, Virginia.
137. A. A. Humphreys, *The Virginia Campaign of 1864 and 1865* (New York, 1995), p278; Grant, *O.R.*, vXLII, part 2, p391.
138. Hancock, *O.R.*, vXLII, part 1, p220, 222; Grant, *O.R.*, vXLII, part 2, p327; A. A. Humphreys, *The Virginia Campaign of 1864 and 1865* (New York, 1995), p278; for the planned disposition of the troops on Aug 20, see: Humphreys, *O.R.*, vXLII, part 2, p332.
139. John W. Gordon, Diary, p13–14, North Carolina Collection, MC.
140. D. S. Freeman, *Lee's Lieutenants*, 3 vols. (N.Y., 1995), v3, p589.
141. A private in Company K, 2nd North Carolina Cavalry, *Hillsborough Recorder*, Sept 21, 1864, p2, col 4; D. B. R., "Barringer's N.C. Brigade of Cavalry," *Daily Confederate*, Feb 23, 1865, p2, cols. 3, 4.
142. A private in Company K, 2nd North Carolina Cavalry, *Hillsborough Recorder*, Sept 21, 1864, p2, col 4; John W. Gordon, Diary, p13–14, North Carolina Collection, MC.
143. D. B. R., "Barringer's N.C. Brigade of Cavalry," *Daily Confederate*, Feb 23, 1865, p2, cols. 3, 4.
144. D. B. R., "Barringer's N.C. Brigade of Cavalry," *Daily Confederate*, Feb 23, 1865, p2, cols. 3, 4; R. L. T. Beale, *History of the Ninth Virginia Cavalry* (Amissville, 1981), p141.
145. A private in Company K, 2nd North Carolina Cavalry, *Hillsborough Recorder*, Sept 21, 1864, p2, col 4; John W. Gordon, Diary, p14–15, North Carolina Collection, MC.
146. W. Hampton, "1864 Narrative," p70–71, SCL-USC; R. E. Lee, *O.R.*, vXLII, part 2, p1202.
147. A. A. Humphreys, *The Virginia Campaign of 1864 and 1865* (New York, 1995), p279.
148. R. E. Lee, *O.R.*, vXLII, part 2, p1194; and R. E. Lee to Davis in Dowdey and Manarin, *Wartime Papers of Robert E. Lee* (New York, 1987), item 870, p842.
149. R. E. Lee, *O.R.*, vXLII, part 2, p1194–1195.
150. Seddon, *O.R.*, vXLII, part 2, p1199; R. E. Lee, *O.R.*, vXLII, part 2, p1200.
151. W. Hampton, "1864 Narrative," p71, SCL-USC; R. E. Lee, *O.R.*, vXLII, part 2, p1202.
152. Barringer, *O.R.*, vLI, part 2, p1037; Hancock, *O.R.*, vXLII, part 1, p222; C. M. Stedman, "Battle at Reams' Station," p114.
153. C. M. Stedman, "Battle at Reams' Station," p114–116; Hancock, *O.R.*, vXLII, part 1, p223.
154. Hampton, *O.R.*, vXLII, part 1, p942–943; Hancock, *O.R.*, vXLII, part 1, p223; R. L. T. Beale, *History of the Ninth Virginia Cavalry* (Amissville, 1981), p142.
155. Hancock, *O.R.*, vXLII, part 1, p227; "From the Front. Another Battle on the Weldon Road...." *Daily Confederate*, Aug 29, 1864, p2, cols. 3–5; reprinted from the *Petersburg Express*, Spectator, "From Below. The Late Fight — Hampton's Cavalry — their Gallant Conduct...." *Daily Confederate*, Aug 31, 1864, p2, cols. 3,4; Hampton, *O.R.*, vXLII, part 1, p943.
156. P. B. Means, "Additional Sketch Sixty-Third Regiment (Fifth Cavalry)," p620; D. B. R., "Barringer's N.C. Brigade of Cavalry," *Daily Confederate*, Feb 23, 1865, p2, cols. 3–4.
157. D. B. R., "Barringer's N.C. Brigade of Cavalry," *Daily Confederate*, Feb 23, 1865, p2, cols. 3–4; P. B. Means, "Additional Sketch Sixty-Third Regiment (Fifth Cavalry)," p620; Hampton and Hancock, *O.R.*, vXLII, part 1, p943 and 227 respectively.
158. Hampton, *O.R.*, vXLII, part 1, p943.
159. A private in Company K, 2nd North Carolina Cavalry, *Hillsborough Recorder*, Sept 21, 1864, p2, col 4.
160. "From the Front. Another Battle on the Weldon Road...." *Daily Confederate*, Aug 29, 1864, p2, cols. 3–5; reprinted from the *Petersburg Express*, Spectator, "From Below. The Late Fight — Hampton's Cavalry...." *Daily Confederate*, Aug 31, 1864, p2, cols. 3,4; C. M. Stedman, "Battle at Reams' Station," p114–116; Hancock, *O.R.*, vXLII, part 1, p223; Hampton, *O.R.*, vXLII, part 1, p943.
161. Hampton, *O.R.*, vXLII, part 1, p943.
162. D. B. R., "Barringer's N.C. Brigade of Cavalry," *Daily Confederate*, Feb 23, 1865, p2, cols. 3–4.
163. A private in Company K, 2nd North Carolina Cavalry, *Hillsborough Recorder*, Sept 21, 1864, p2, col 4.
164. Hampton, *O.R.*, vXLII, part 1, p943.
165. Hampton, *O.R.*, vXLII, part 1, p943–944.
166. A private in Company K, 2nd North Carolina Cavalry, *Hillsborough Recorder*, Sept 21, 1864, p2, col 4.

167. A correspondent for the *Petersburg Express* had noted that Colonel R. L. T. Beale and his 9th Virginia, and Colonel W. P. Roberts with his 2nd North Carolina Cavalry were signaled out for "special applause" in the cavalry line. Reprinted from the *Petersburg Express*, "From the Front. Another Battle on the Weldon Road...." *Daily Confederate*, Aug 29, 1864, p2, cols. 3–5; Clement letter to his wife on Aug 29, 1864, in William Bailey Clement Papers, Private Collection Papers, PC 409, NCDA; W. P. Roberts, "Additional Sketch Nineteenth Regiment (Second Cavalry)," p103.

168. D. B. R., "Barringer's N.C. Brigade of Cavalry," *Daily Confederate*, Feb 23, 1865, p2, cols. 3–4.

169. C. M. Stedman, "Battle at Reams' Station," p116.

170. R. E. Lee in Dowdey and Manarin, *Wartime Papers of Robert E. Lee* (New York, 1987), item 875, p847; R. E. Lee, *O.R.*, vXLII, part 2, p1206–1207; reprinted in "Tribute to North Carolina—Letter From Gen. Lee," *Daily Confederate*, Sept 5, 1864, p2, col 4.

171. Hancock and D. McM. Gregg, *O.R.*, vXLII, part 1, p227, 607 respectively; Meade, *O.R.*, vXLII, part 2, p470.

172. Hampton, *O.R.*, vXLII, part 1, p943; for an observation of the small number of losses see, reprinted from the *Petersburg Express*, Spectator, "From Below. The Late Fight—Hampton's Cavalry...." *Daily Confederate*, Aug 31, 1864, p2, cols. 3, 4; W. P. Roberts, "Additional Sketch Nineteenth Regiment (Second Cavalry)," p103.

173. R. Barringer, "Ninth Regiment (First Cavalry)," p435.

174. Hampton, *O.R.*, vXLII, part 2, p1231; John W. Gordon, Diary, p16, North Carolina Collection, MC.

175. R. E. Lee, *O.R.*, vXLII, part 2, p1204–1205.

176. D. McM. Gregg and Hampton, *O.R.*, vXLII, part 2, p1231; *O.R.*, vXLII, part 1, p131.

177. Shadburne, *O.R.*, vXLII, part 2, p1236.

178. R. E. Lee, *O.R.*, vXLII, part 2, p1242.

179. John W. Gordon, Diary, p16, North Carolina Collection, MC.

180. Hampton, *O.R.*, vXLII, part 1, p944–94; G. W. Beale, *A Lieutenant of Cavalry in Lee's Army* (Baltimore, 1994), p194–195.

181. Hampton, *O.R.*, vXLII, part 1, p945.

182. Hampton, *O.R.*, vXLII, part 1, p945.

183. Hampton, *O.R.*, vXLII, part 1, p945.

184. Hampton, *O.R.*, vXLII, part 1, p945.

185. H. E. Davies, *O.R.*, vXLII, part 1, p614.

186. G. W. Beale, *A Lieutenant of Cavalry in Lee's Army* (Baltimore, 1994), p195; John W. Gordon, Diary, p17, North Carolina Collection, MC.

187. N. A. Trudeau, *The Last Citadel* (Baton Rouge, 1991), p199; Hampton and H. E. Davies, *O.R.*, vXLII, part 1, p945 and 614.

188. Hampton, *O.R.*, vXLII, part 1, p945.

189. W. P. Roberts, "Additional Sketch Nineteenth Regiment (Second Cavalry)," p105.

190. Hampton, *O.R.*, vXLII, part 1, p945.

191. Hampton, *O.R.*, vXLII, part 1, p945.

192. Hampton, *O.R.*, vXLII, part 1, p946.

193. H. E. Davies Jr., *O.R.*, vXLII, part 1, p614.

194. G. W. Beale, *A Lieutenant of Cavalry in Lee's Army* (Baltimore, 1994), p195–196; R. Barringer letter to his brother, V. C. Barringer, dated Jan 27, 1866 from Concord, N.C., p9, SHC-UNC; H. E. Davies Jr. and Hampton, *O.R.*, vXLII, part 1, p614, 946.

195. H. E. Davies Jr. and Hampton, *O.R.*, vXLII, part 1, p614, 946; N. A. Trudeau, *The Last Citadel* (Baton Rouge, 1991), p201; G. W. Beale, *A Lieutenant of Cavalry in Lee's Army* (Baltimore, 1994), p196.

196. D. B. R., "Barringer's N.C. Brigade of Cavalry," *Daily Confederate*, Feb 23, 1865, p2, cols. 3–4; John W. Gordon, Diary, p18, North Carolina Collection, MC; R. Barringer, "Ninth Regiment (First Cavalry)," p436; P. B. Means, "Additional Sketch Sixty-Third Regiment (Fifth Cavalry)," p626.

197. Hampton, *O.R.*, vXLII, part 1, p946.

198. Grant, *O.R.*, vXXXVI, part 1, p32; A. A. Humphreys, *The Virginia Campaign of 1864 and 1865* (New York, 1995), p284, 289; also see, N. A. Trudeau, *The Last Citadel* (Baton Rouge, 1991), p207.

199. A. A. Humphreys, *The Virginia Campaign of 1864 and 1865* (New York, 1995), p290.

200. Grant, *O.R.*, vXLII, part 2, p1046–1047; A. A. Humphreys, *The Virginia Campaign of 1864 and 1865* (New York, 1995), p290.

201. A. A. Humphreys, *The Virginia Campaign of 1864 and 1865* (New York, 1995), p291–292.

202. R. J. Sommers, *Richmond Redeemed* (New York, 1981), p196–197.

203. R. J. Sommers, *Richmond Redeemed* (New York, 1981), p179.

204. R. J. Sommers, *Richmond Redeemed* (New York, 1981), p192, 197; D. McM. Gregg, *O.R.*, vXLII, part 2, p1106; N. A. Trudeau, *The Last Citadel* (Baton Rouge, 1991), p208.

205. John W. Gordon, Diary, p18, North Carolina Collection, MC; D. McM. Gregg, *O.R.*, vXLII, part 2, p1106–1107; R. J. Sommers, *Richmond Redeemed* (New York, 1981), p196–197.

206. Hampton, *O.R.*, vXLII, part 1, p947; D. McM. Gregg, *O.R.*, vXLII, part 2, p1107; R. J. Sommers, *Richmond Redeemed* (New York, 1981), p197, 199–202; N. A. Trudeau, *The Last Citadel* (Baton Rouge, 1991), p208.

207. Hampton, *O.R.*, vXLII, part 1, p947.

208. D. B. R., "Barringer's N.C. Brigade of Cavalry," *Daily Confederate*, Feb 23, 1865, p2, cols. 3, 4; P. B. Means, "Additional Sketch Sixty-Third Regiment (Fifth Cavalry)," p627; *O.R.*, vXLII, part 1, p94; R. J. Sommers, *Richmond Redeemed* (New York, 1981), p204–205.

209. Hampton, *O.R.*, vXLII, part 1, p947; R. J. Sommers, *Richmond Redeemed* (New York, 1981), p202.

210. R. J. Sommers, *Richmond Redeemed* (New York, 1981), p203–205; Hampton, *O.R.*, vXLII, part 1, p947; John W. Gordon, Diary, p19, North Carolina Collection, MC.

211. D. McM. Gregg at 8 P.M., *O.R.*, vXLII, part 2, p1108; R. J. Sommers, *Richmond Redeemed* (New York, 1981), p205.

212. R. J. Sommers, *Richmond Redeemed* (New York, 1981), p207–208.

213. Grant, 11:30 P.M. Sept 29, *O.R.*, vXLII, part 2, p1094.

214. R. J. Sommers, *Richmond Redeemed* (New York, 1981), p235, 238.

215. N. A. Trudeau, *The Last Citadel* (Baton Rouge, 1991), p212; John W. Gordon, Diary, p19, North Carolina Collection, MC.

216. Hampton, *O.R.*, vXLII, part 1, p947–948; N. A. Trudeau, *The Last Citadel* (Baton Rouge, 1991), p213–214.

217. John W. Gordon, Diary, p19–20, North Carolina Collection, MC.

218. Hampton, *O.R.*, vXLII, part 1, p948; R. J. Sommers, *Richmond Redeemed* (New York, 1981), p375; N. A. Trudeau, *The Last Citadel* (Baton Rouge, 1991), p216.

219. John W. Gordon, Diary, p20–21, North Carolina Collection, MC.

220. R. J. Sommers, *Richmond Redeemed* (New York, 1981), p382–383, 413; N. A. Trudeau, *The Last Citadel* (Baton Rouge, 1991), p217.

221. N. A. Trudeau, *The Last Citadel* (Baton Rouge, 1991), p221.

222. A. A. Humphreys, *The Virginia Campaign of 1864 and 1865* (New York, 1995), p294; Grant, *O.R.*, vXLII, part 3, p317; N. A. Trudeau, *The Last Citadel* (Baton Rouge, 1991), p221–222.

223. A. A. Humphreys, *The Virginia Campaign of 1864 and 1865* (New York, 1995), p294–295; Grant, *O.R.*, vXXXVI, part 1, p32; N. A. Trudeau, *The Last Citadel* (Baton Rouge, 1991), p221–222.

224. A. A. Humphreys, *The Virginia Campaign of 1864 and 1865* (New York, 1995), p295; N. A. Trudeau, *The Last Citadel* (Baton Rouge, 1991), p222–223.

225. W. Hampton, "1864 Narrative," p96, SCL-USC; Hampton, *O.R.*, vXLII, part 1, p949; N. A. Trudeau, *The Last Citadel* (Baton Rouge, 1991), p233.

226. W. Hampton, "1864 Narrative," p96, SCL-USC; Hampton, *O.R.*, vXLII, part 1, p949; N. A. Trudeau, *The Last Citadel* (Baton Rouge, 1991), p234.
227. Hampton, *O.R.*, vXLII, part 1, p949; W. Hampton, "1864 Narrative," p96, SCL-USC; N. A. Trudeau, *The Last Citadel* (Baton Rouge, 1991), p235, 241.
228. Hampton, *O.R.*, vXLII, part 1, p950; N. A. Trudeau, *The Last Citadel* (Baton Rouge, 1991), p237.
229. N. A. Trudeau, *The Last Citadel* (Baton Rouge, 1991), p242–243, 245.
230. Hampton, *O.R.*, vXLII, part 1, p949–950; N. A. Trudeau, *The Last Citadel* (Baton Rouge, 1991), p243.
231. Hampton, *O.R.*, vXLII, part 1, p950; N. A. Trudeau, *The Last Citadel* (Baton Rouge, 1991), p247.
232. H. E. Davies, Jr. and Hampton, *O.R.*, vXLII, part 1, p629, 949; D. B. R., "Barringer's N.C. Brigade of Cavalry," *Daily Confederate*, Feb 23, 1865, p2, cols. 3–4.
233. H. E. Davies, Jr. and Hampton, *O.R.*, vXLII, part 1, p629, 949.
234. D. B. R., "Barringer's N.C. Brigade of Cavalry," *Daily Confederate*, Feb 23, 1865, p2, cols. 3–4.
235. D. B. R., "Barringer's N.C. Brigade of Cavalry," *Daily Confederate*, Feb 23, 1865, p2, cols. 3–4; P. B. Means, "Additional Sketch Sixty-Third Regiment (Fifth Cavalry)," p627, 629; R. Barringer, "Ninth Regiment (First Cavalry)," p436.
236. W. Hampton, "1864 Narrative," p97, SCL-USC; Hampton, *O.R.*, vXLII, part 1, p950.
237. D. B. R., "Barringer's N.C. Brigade of Cavalry," *Daily Confederate*, Feb 23, 1865, p2, cols. 3–4; H. E. Davies, *O.R.*, vXLII, part 1, p629.
238. John W. Gordon, Diary, p21, North Carolina Collection, MC.
239. D. B. R., "Barringer's N.C. Brigade of Cavalry," *Daily Confederate*, Feb 23, 1865, p2, cols. 3–4.
240. John W. Gordon, Diary, p21–22, North Carolina Collection, MC.
241. John W. Gordon, Diary, p22–23, North Carolina Collection, MC; W. Hampton, "1864 Narrative," p105, SCL-USC.
242. John W. Gordon, Diary, p23, North Carolina Collection, MC.
243. Grant, *O.R.*, vXLII, part 3, p804–805; N. A. Trudeau, *The Last Citadel* (Baton Rouge, 1991), p263–264.
244. Williams for Meade, *O.R.*, vXLII, part 3, p828–829; N. A. Trudeau, *The Last Citadel* (Baton Rouge, 1991), p264.
245. Babcock, *O.R.*, vXLII, part 3, p844–845; N. A. Trudeau, *The Last Citadel* (Baton Rouge, 1991), p266.
246. Warren, *O.R.*, vXLII, part 3, p855; N. A. Trudeau, *The Last Citadel* (Baton Rouge, 1991), p268.
247. N. A. Trudeau, *The Last Citadel* (Baton Rouge, 1991), p268.
248. Hampton, *O.R.*, vXLII, part 1, p950–951; John W. Gordon, Diary, p23–24, North Carolina Collection, MC; D. B. R., "Barringer's N.C. Brigade of Cavalry," *Daily Confederate*, Feb 23, 1865, p2, cols. 3–4; P. B. Means, "Additional Sketch Sixty-Third Regiment (Fifth Cavalry)," p633; N. A. Trudeau, *The Last Citadel* (Baton Rouge, 1991), p271.
249. Hampton, *O.R.*, vXLII, part 1, p951.
250. Hampton, *O.R.*, vXLII, part 1, p950–951; R. Barringer, "Ninth Regiment (First Cavalry)," p437; N. A. Trudeau, *The Last Citadel* (Baton Rouge, 1991), p273–274.
251. Hampton, *O.R.*, vXLII, part 1, p951; D. B. Coltrane, *Memoirs* (Raleigh, 1956), p37; P. B. Means, "Additional Sketch Sixty-Third Regiment (Fifth Cavalry)," p634.
252. John W. Gordon, Diary, p24–25, North Carolina Collection, MC.
253. Hampton, *O.R.*, vXLII, part 1, p951; Bibber for D. McM. Gregg, *O.R.*, vXLII, part 3, p919.
254. Hampton, *O.R.*, vXLII, part 1, p951; N. A. Trudeau, *The Last Citadel* (Baton Rouge, 1991), p278–279, 280–281; John W. Gordon, Diary, p25, North Carolina Collection, MC; W. P. Roberts, "Additional Sketch Nineteenth Regiment (Second Cavalry)," p105.
255. Grant and Meade, *O.R.*, vXLII, part 3, p864–892, 921;

Humphreys, *O.R.*, vXLII, part 3, p912–913; N. A. Trudeau, *The Last Citadel* (Baton Rouge, 1991), p270–271, 274–275.
256. W. P. Roberts, "Additional Sketch Nineteenth Regiment (Second Cavalry)," p106; R. E. Lee, reprinted in *Daily Confederate*, Aug 6, 1864, page 1, col 4; and Sept 19, 1864, p2, col 2.
257. John W. Gordon, Diary, p26–28, North Carolina Collection, MC.
258. John W. Gordon, Diary, p29, North Carolina Collection, MC.
259. John W. Gordon, Diary, p29, North Carolina Collection, MC.
260. D. B. Coltrane, *Memoirs* (Raleigh, 1956), p37–38; John W. Gordon, Diary, p29, North Carolina Collection, MC; on Feb 22, Meade notified Grant that he had information indicating the railroad had been restored to Stony Creek and W. H. F. Lee's cavalry had moved from Belfield to Stony Creek, *O.R.*, vXLVI, part 2, p630–631.
261. D. McM. Gregg, *O.R.*, vXLVI, part 2, p409; N. A. Trudeau, *The Last Citadel* (Baton Rouge, 1991), p312–322.
262. Milas Cavin letter to his mother, Feb 11, 1865, in Cavin Papers, P.C. 399, NCDA.
263. R. E. Lee, *O.R.*, vXLVI, part 2, p1209–1210.
264. D. B. Coltrane, *Memoirs* (Raleigh, 1956), p37–38.
265. D. B. Coltrane, *Memoirs* (Raleigh, 1956), p38.

Seven

1. D. S. Freeman, *Lee's Lieutenants* (New York, 1995), v3, p655 and 639.
2. U. S. Grant, *Personal Memoirs* (New York, 1999), p570, 567; D. S. Freeman, *Lee's Lieutenants* (New York, 1995), v3, p645.
3. Grant, *O.R.*, vXLVI, part 2, p963; Meade, *O.R.*, vXVLI, part 2, p963–964; R. Barringer, "Cavalry Sketches," p738.
4. D. S. Freeman, *Lee's Lieutenants* (New York, 1995), v3, p655.
5. A. A. Humphreys, *The Virginia Campaign of 1864 and 1865* (New York, 1995), p324–325, 327; E. Bearss and C. M. Calkins, *The Battle of Five Forks* (Lynchburg, 1985), p14; Sheridan, *O.R.*, vXLVI, part 1, p1101, 1116.
6. A. A. Humphreys, *The Virginia Campaign of 1864 and 1865* (New York, 1995), p329.
7. D. S. Freeman, *Lee's Lieutenants* (New York, 1995), v3, p647–654; and C. M. Calkins, *The Appomattox Campaign* (Conshohocken, Penn., 1997), p11.
8. Longstreet, *O.R.*, vXLVI, part 3, p1357–1360.
9. A. A. Humphreys, *The Virginia Campaign of 1864 and 1865* (New York, 1995), p433; C. M. Calkins, *The Appomattox Campaign* (Conshohocken, 1997), p14.
10. Longstreet, *O.R.*, vXLVI, pt 3, p1360; D. S. Freeman, *R. E. Lee* (New York, 1935), v4, p25; E. Bearss and C. M. Calkins, *The Battle of Five Forks* (Lynchburg, 1985), p10.
11. W. Harrison, *Pickett's Men* (Gaithersburg, 1988), p135, 136.
12. Freeman put W. H. F. Lee's division at about 2,500, D. S. Freeman, *Lee's Lieutenants* (New York, 1995), v3, p657; Bearss and Calkins put his number at 2,400, E. Bearss and C. Calkins, *The Battle of Five Forks* (Lynchburg, 1985), p9–11, note 39; Barringer himself, estimated the number of men in W. H. F. Lee's division at fewer than 3,000, R. Barringer, "Ninth Regiment (First Cavalry),"p. 439; R. K. Krick, *9th Virginia Cavalry* (Lynchburg, 1982), p41–42.
13. R. L. T. Beale, *History of the Ninth Virginia Cavalry* (Amissville, 1981), p146.
14. W. P. Roberts, "Additional Sketch Nineteenth Regiment (Second Cavalry)," p106, 108.
15. W. P. Roberts, "Additional Sketch Nineteenth Regiment (Second Cavalry)," p107, J. M. Galloway, "Sixty-third Regiment (Fifth Cavalry)," p541–542, and P. B. Means, "Additional Sketch Sixty-Third Regiment (Fifth Cavalry)," p646, 653–654.
16. Latrobe for Longstreet, *O.R.*, XLVI, 3, p1358.

17. Fitz Lee, *O.R.*, vXLVI, 1, p1298, 1299; D. S. Freeman, *R. E. Lee* (New York, 1935), v4, p28–29; E. Bearss and C. Calkins, *The Battle of Five Forks* (Lynchburg, 1985), p21.
18. Sharpe, *O.R.*, vXLVI, part 3, p29.
19. W. P. Shaw, "Fifty-Ninth Regiment (Fourth Cavalry)," p469.
20. *O.R.*, vXLVI, part 3, p64; Warren, *O.R.*, vXLVI, part 3, p254.
21. Sheridan, *O.R.*, vXLVI, part 1, p1102.
22. R. Barringer, "Cavalry Sketches," p738; R. Barringer letter to his brother, V. C. Barringer, dated Jan 27, 1866 from Concord, N.C., p10, SHC-UNC. George Crook was given command of David McM. Gregg's division on March 26, 1865 — D. McM. Gregg's resignation was accepted on Feb 8, 1865.
23. W. H. F. Lee, Appomattox Campaign Report, April 11, 1865, VHS.
24. Sheridan, OR, vXLVI, part 1, p1101; E. Bearss and C. Calkins, *The Battle of Five Forks* (Lynchburg, 1985), p14; Merritt, *O.R.*, vXLVI, part 1, p1116; A. A. Humphreys, *The Virginia Campaign of 1864 and 1865* (New York, 1995), p324–325.
25. A. A. Humphreys, *The Virginia Campaign of 1864 and 1865* (New York, 1995), p325; Crook, *O.R.*, vXLVI, part 1, p1141.
26. A. A. Humphreys, *The Virginia Campaign of 1864 and 1865* (New York, 1995), p326; Warren, *O.R.*, vXLVI, part 1, p799.
27. Warren, *O.R.*, vXLVI, part 1, p802, and *O.R.*, vXLVI, part 3, p256.
28. W. Harrison, *Pickett's Men* (Gaithersburg, 1988), p137; Merritt, *O.R.*, vXLVI, part 1, p1116; Fitz Lee, *O.R.*, vXLVI part 1, p1299.
29. W. Harrison, *Pickett's Men* (Gaithersburg, 1988), p136; C. M. Calkins, *The Appomattox Campaign* (Conshohocken, 1997), p20.
30. C. M. Calkins, *The Appomattox Campaign* (Conshohocken, 1997), p20–21.
31. T. T. Munford, "Five Forks—The Waterloo of The Confederacy," VHS, p10; E. Bearss and C. Calkins, *The Battle of Five Forks* (Lynchburg, 1985), p36; A. A. Humphreys, *The Virginia Campaign of 1864 and 1865* (New York, 1995), p334.
32. E. Bearss and C. Calkins, *The Battle of Five Forks* (Lynchburg, 1985), p36.
33. A. A. Humphreys, *The Virginia Campaign of 1864 and 1865* (New York, 1995), p334.
34. R. Barringer, "Cavalry Sketches," p738; W. H. F. Lee, Appomattox Campaign Report, April 11, 1865, VHS.
35. R. Barringer, "Cavalry Sketches," p738–739; Smith, *O.R.*, vXLVI, part 1, p1156–1157.
36. P. B. Means, "Additional Sketch Sixty-Third Regiment (Fifth Cavalry)," p639.
37. P. B. Means, "Additional Sketch Sixty-Third Regiment (Fifth Cavalry)," p639.
38. P. B. Means, "Additional Sketch Sixty-Third Regiment (Fifth Cavalry)," p640.
39. R. Barringer, "Ninth Regiment (First Cavalry)," p. 440.
40. P. B. Means, "Additional Sketch Sixty-Third Regiment (Fifth Cavalry)," p640–641; Smith, *O.R.*, vXLVI, part 1, p1156–1157; D. B. Coltrane, *Memoirs* (Raleigh, 1956), p39.
41. P. B. Means, "Additional Sketch Sixty-Third Regiment (Fifth Cavalry)," p641.
42. W. H. Cheek, "Additional Sketch Ninth Regiment (First Cavalry)," p472.
43. R. Barringer letter to his brother, V. C. Barringer, dated Jan 27, 1866 from Concord, N.C., p10, SHC-UNC.
44. Merritt, *O.R.*, vXLVI, part 1, p1116.
45. R. Barringer, "Cavalry Sketches," p740; P. B. Means, "Additional Sketch Sixty-Third Regiment (Fifth Cavalry)," p642.
46. R. Barringer, "Cavalry Sketches," p740.
47. R. Barringer letter to his brother, V. C. Barringer, dated Jan 27, 1866 from Concord, N.C., p11, SHC-UNC; R. Barringer, "Cavalry Sketches," p740.
48. R. Barringer letter to his brother, V. C. Barringer, dated Jan 27, 1866 from Concord, N.C., p11, SHC-UNC; R. Barringer, "Cavalry Sketches," p741; W. H. Cheek, "Additional Sketch Ninth Regiment (First Cavalry)," p474.
49. P. B. Means, "Additional Sketch Sixty-Third Regiment (Fifth Cavalry)," p642; R. Barringer, "Ninth Regiment (First Cavalry)," pp. 440–441.
50. As the reader is certainly aware, the "reality" of any situation depends on where one is standing to view an event. For instance, Barringer described Smith's retreat in these terms: "In ten minutes the whole Yankee line was in flight and the Confederates in full pursuit. This was kept up for some distance and with great slaughter, until night closed upon us...." Smith's description of events was: "At 5:30 p.m. the enemy opened with four pieces of artillery, and the brigade suddenly discovered that it was confronted by Pickett's division of infantry. The brigade maintained its ground under the hottest fire of which the enemy was capable, losing heavily all the while, till nearly dark, when it ran entirely out of ammunition ... and was forced to fall back to the main road leading from Dinwiddie Court House...." By the time Smith's afternoon adventure reached Sheridan's report, he said the following about Smith's brigade: "His command again held the enemy in check with determined bravery, but the heavy force brought against his right flank [Pickett and Munford] finally compelled him to abandon his position on the creek and fall back to the main line immediately in front of Dinwiddie Court House." Smith and Sheridan would have us believe the North Carolina brigade was not a significant factor in the retreat from Fitzgerald's Ford, but this story is about what the 2nd North Carolina cavalrymen experienced. Consequently, I have emphasized the views of the 2nd North Carolina cavalrymen and not allowed them to be spun out of the battle scene. See: R. Barringer, "Ninth Regiment (First Cavalry)," p441; Smith, *O.R.*, vXLVI, part 1, p1157; Sheridan, *O.R.*, vXLVI, part 1, p1103.
51. A. A. Humphreys, *The Virginia Campaign of 1864 and 1865* (New York, 1995), p335; *O.R.*, vXLVI, part 1, p1103.
52. P. B. Means, "Additional Sketch Sixty-Third Regiment (Fifth Cavalry)," p638.
53. W. Harrison, *Pickett's Men* (Gaithersburg, 1988), p137.
54. R. Barringer letter to his brother, V. C. Barringer, dated Jan 27, 1866 from Concord, N.C., p11–12, SHC-UNC; R. Barringer. "Diary, April-Aug 1865," Rufus Barringer Papers, no page, SHC-UNC.
55. W. P. Roberts, "Additional Sketch Nineteenth Regiment (Second Cavalry)," p107.
56. W. P. Roberts, "Additional Sketch Nineteenth Regiment (Second Cavalry)," p107. Captain John P. Lockhart was from Orange County, North Carolina. He was 26 years old when he enlisted in 1861. Two of his younger brothers were also in the 2nd North Carolina Cavalry — another in the 27th North Carolina (infantry). John P. Lockhart received the rank of 2nd lieutenant in training camp, and was promoted to captain by Sept 30, 1863. Lockhart took command of the 2nd Cavalry on March 31, 1865 at Chamberlain's Run. He left Appomattox Court House with the remnant of the 2nd Cavalry after the battle on April 9, 1865, and was paroled at Greensboro, N.C. on May 23, 1865.
57. A. A. Humphreys, *The Virginia Campaign of 1864 and 1865* (New York, 1995), p342; Fitzhugh Lee, *General Lee* (New York, 1994), p376.
58. D. S. Freeman, *Lee's Lieutenants* (New York, 1995), v3, p661; W. Harrison, *Pickett's Men* (Gaithersburg, 1988), p138; Fitz Lee, *O.R.*, vXLVI, part 1, p1299.
59. P. B. Means, "Additional Sketch Sixty-Third Regiment (Fifth Cavalry)," p645; W. H. Cheek, "Additional Sketch Ninth Regiment (First Cavalry)," p477–478; R. Barringer, "Ninth Regiment (First Cavalry)," p. 442.
60. T. T. Munford, "Five Forks," VHS, p21; A. A. Humphreys, *The Virginia Campaign of 1864 and 1865* (New York, 1995), p351.
61. T. T. Munford, "Five Forks," VHS, p31; E. Bearss and C. Calkins, *The Battle of Five Forks* (Lynchburg, 1985), p78.
62. Sheridan was also aware that Pickett's left wing could

expect little or no help from Anderson on the right of the Petersburg entrenchments around Burgess's Mill. Anderson had attacked the Federals at his front the day before and was too weak to hold his initial gain and incurred heavy losses. Anderson could not again effectively leave his entrenchments—Sheridan knew this; Pickett and Fitz Lee should have known this, but may not have. D. S. Freeman, *Lee's Lieutenants* (New York, 1995), v3, p662 and 664–665; W. Harrison, *Pickett's Men* (Gaithersburg, 1988), p139–140; Fitz, *O.R.*, vXLVI, part 1, p1299; E. Bearss and C. Calkins, *The Battle of Five Forks* (Lynchburg, 1985), p77.

63. This belief among the troopers is expressed well in E. Bearss and C. Calkins, *The Battle of Five Forks* (Lynchburg, 1985), p78; D. S. Freeman, *Lee's Lieutenants* (New York, 1995), v3, p664.

64. A. A. Humphreys, *The Virginia Campaign of 1864 and 1865* (New York, 1995), p343–344; Merritt, *O.R.*, vXLVI, part 1, p1117; Custer, *O.R.*, vXLVI, part 1, p1130.

65. Warren, *O.R.*, vXLVI, part 1, p829–830; A. A. Humphreys, *The Virginia Campaign of 1864 and 1865* (New York, 1995), p346, 347.

66. Sheridan, OR, vXLVI, part 1, p1105; T. T. Munford, "Five Forks," VHS, p23–24.

67. W. P. Shaw, "Fifty-Ninth Regiment (Fourth Cavalry)," p469.

68. D. S. Freeman, *Lee's Lieutenants*, 3 vols. (New York, 1995), v3, p662, and his note no. 44.

69. When Mackenzie met Sheridan, he was sent around the right of Warren's infantry with instructions to move north to Hatcher's Run then turn west to Ford's Road and hold the crossing. Sheridan, *O.R.*, vXLVI, part 1, p1105; A. A. Humphreys, *The Virginia Campaign of 1864 and 1865* (New York, 1995), p347.

70. D. S. Freeman, *Lee's Lieutenants* (New York, 1995), v3, p666; T. T. Munford, "Five Forks," VHS, p24.

71. D. S. Freeman, *Lee's Lieutenants* (New York, 1995), v3, p664, 665.

72. H. Porter, "Five Forks and The Pursuit of Lee," p713. Like some others, I have perhaps been a little hard on Pickett and Fitz Lee for their absentee leadership in the battle at Five Forks, but it is a moral issue as well as a technical one. It is a question of standing by your men when you place them in harms way. The Confederate troops needed and deserved leadership that day, and it was lacking—though Pickett's and Fitz Lee's presence in the battle could not have changed the overwhelming outcome of the day. (The haunting but irrelevant question is, would the presence of Stonewall Jackson, J. E. B. Stuart, or Wade Hampton have made a difference? Probably not.)

73. T. T. Munford, "Five Forks," VHS, p25; D. S. Freeman, *Lee's Lieutenants* (New York, 1995), v3, p670.

74. A. A. Humphreys, *The Virginia Campaign of 1864 and 1865* (New York, 1995), p344; E. Bearss and C. Calkins, *The Battle of Five Forks* (Lynchburg, 1985), p87.

75. A. A. Humphreys, *The Virginia Campaign of 1864 and 1865* (New York, 1995), p350; T. T. Munford, "Five Forks," VHS, p28–29.

76. H. Porter, "Five Forks and The Pursuit of Lee," p713.

77. After the Federal attack was well underway, Pickett and Fitz Lee were still enjoying their extended lunch. Years later, Rosser acknowledged that at one point in the afternoon, two of his pickets rode into camp and reported that the enemy was advancing on all fronts. He added: "These reports were made to Pickett and to Lee and as the position at Five Forks was considered as well chosen and strong but little attention was given to the enemy's advance." As quoted in D. S. Freeman, *Lee's Lieutenants* (New York, 1995), v3, p668.

78. D. S. Freeman, *Lee's Lieutenants* (New York, 1995), v3, p669–670; T. T. Munford, "Five Forks," VHS, p32.

79. J. C. Gorman, *Lee's Last Campaign* (Raleigh, 1866), p32–33.

80. A. A. Humphreys, *The Virginia Campaign of 1864 and 1865* (New York, 1995), p350–351.

81. W. Harrison, *Pickett's Men* (Gaithersburg, 1988), p147.

82. For a more complete account of the fight described here see: E. Bearss and C. Calkins, *The Battle of Five Forks* (Lynchburg, 1985), p103–109.

83. W. H. F. Lee's other brigade, Beale's, was detached to and with Corse's troops. A. A. Humphreys, *The Virginia Campaign of 1864 and 1865* (New York, 1995), p351; T. T. Munford, "Five Forks," VHS, p21; Custer, *O.R.*, vXLVI part 1, p1130.

84. P. B. Means, "Additional Sketch Sixty-Third Regiment (Fifth Cavalry)," p645–646.

85. P. B. Means, "Additional Sketch Sixty-Third Regiment (Fifth Cavalry)," p645–647.

86. P. B. Means, "Additional Sketch Sixty-Third Regiment (Fifth Cavalry)," p647; A. A. Humphreys, *The Virginia Campaign of 1864 and 1865* (New York, 1995), p353.

87. Pickett's report as presented in W. Harrison, *Pickett's Men* (Gaithersburg, 1988), p147; also see T. T. Munford, "Five Forks," VHS, p37.

88. R. Barringer letter to his brother, V. C. Barringer, dated Jan 27, 1866 from Concord, N.C., p12–13, SHC-UNC.

89. P. B. Means, "Additional Sketch Sixty-Third Regiment (Fifth Cavalry)," p648; Fitz Lee, *O.R.*, vXLVI, part 1, p1300; Devin, *O.R.*, vXLVI, part 1, p1124; A. A. Humphreys, *The Virginia Campaign of 1864 and 1865* (New York, 1995), p354.

90. Johnson, *O.R.*, vXLVI, part 1, p1289; C. M. Calkins, *The Appomattox Campaign* (Conshohocken, 1997), p46.

91. T. T. Munford, "Last Days of Fitz Lee's Cavalry Division," VHS, p3.

92. C. M. Calkins, *The Appomattox Campaign* (Conshohocken, 1997), p47–48 and 54–58.

93. D. S. Freeman, *Lee's Lieutenants* (New York, 1995), v3, p688; W. Harrison, *Pickett's Men* (Gaithersburg, 1988), p147–149.

94. T. T. Munford, "Last Days of Fitz Lee's Cavalry Division," VHS, p3; Merritt, *O.R.*, vXLVI, part 1, p1118–1119; Pearson as quoted in Paul B. Means, "Additional Sketch Sixty-Third Regiment (Fifth Cavalry)," p648–649; R. Barringer letter to his brother, V. C. Barringer, dated Jan 27, 1866 from Concord, N.C., p12, SHC-UNC.

95. Devin, *O.R.*, vXLVI, part 1, p1124; Merritt *O.R.*, vXLVI, part 1, p1118–1119.

96. Johnson, *O.R.*, vXLVI, part 1, p1288–1289; Devin, *O.R.*, vXLVI, part 1, p1124; C. M. Calkins, *The Appomattox Campaign* (Conshohocken, 1997), p54; Merritt, *O.R.*, vXLVI, part 1, p1119.

97. Fitz Lee, *O.R.*, vXLVI, part 1, p1300; D. S. Freeman, *Lee's Lieutenants* (New York, 1995), v3, p684–685; C. M. Calkins, *The Appomattox Campaign* (Conshohocken, 1997), p63–69.

98. W. P. Shaw, "Fifty-Ninth Regiment (Fourth Cavalry)," p470.

99. C. M. Calkins, *The Appomattox Campaign* (Conshohocken, 1997), p70; Custer, *O.R.*, vXLVI, part 1, p1131; T. T. Munford, "Last Days of Fitz Lee's Cavalry Division," VHS, p5.

100. Johnson, *O.R.*, vXLVI, part 1, p1289; C. M. Calkins, *The Appomattox Campaign* (Conshohocken, 1997), p72.

101. P. B. Means, "Additional Sketch Sixty-Third Regiment (Fifth Cavalry)," p650. Private Daniel B. Coltrane, also of the 5th N.C. Cavalry, reported overhearing the same conversation. D. B. Coltrane, *Memoirs* (Raleigh, 1956), p41.

102. R. Barringer letter to his brother, V. C. Barringer, dated Jan 27, 1866 from Concord, N.C., p12–13, SHC-UNC.

103. P. B. Means, "Additional Sketch Sixty-Third Regiment (Fifth Cavalry)," p650–653.

104. P. B. Means, "Additional Sketch Sixty-Third Regiment (Fifth Cavalry)," p651.

105. D. B. Coltrane, *Memoirs* (Raleigh, 1956), p42.

106. P. B. Means, "Additional Sketch Sixty-Third Regiment (Fifth Cavalry)," p651; C. M. Calkins, *The Appomattox Campaign* (Conshohocken, 1997), p71.

107. In his battle report, Custer indicated that the 2nd

North Carolina's charge was met by the 8th New York. However, he may not have been in a position to see the details, or the 8th New York also may have turned on the 2nd North Carolina. It is also possible Custer had the first collision of the cavalries confused with the immediate post-charge action where after swinging around the 1st North Carolina, the 8th New York turned toward Green's Road and hit the 2nd North Carolina Cavalry while in retreat from the 1st Vermont. Custer, *O.R.*, vXLVI, part 1, p1131.

108. P. B. Means, "Additional Sketch Sixty-Third Regiment (Fifth Cavalry)," p654; D. B. Coltrane, *Memoirs* (Raleigh, 1956), p44.

109. W. H. Cheek, "Additional Sketch Ninth Regiment (First Cavalry)," p480.

110. W. H. Cheek, "Additional Sketch Ninth Regiment (First Cavalry)," p480; P. B. Means, "Additional Sketch Sixty-Third Regiment (Fifth Cavalry)," p650.

111. Fitz Lee, *O.R.*, vXLVI, part 1, p1301.

112. The 15th New York did take some prisoners at Namozine Church. See Coppinger, *O.R.*, vXLVI, part 1, p1139.

113. Devin, *O.R.*, vXLVI, part 1, p1125.

114. Custer, *O.R.*, vXLVI, part 1, p1131.

115. W. P. Roberts, "Additional Sketch Nineteenth Regiment (Second Cavalry)," p107.

116. Johnson, *O.R.*, vXLVI, part 1, p1289; C. M. Calkins, *The Appomattox Campaign* (Conshohocken, 1997), p72.

117. D. S. Freeman, *Lee's Lieutenants* (New York, 1995), v3, p683, 688.

118. C. M. Calkins, *The Appomattox Campaign* (Conshohocken, 1997), p74.

119. Merritt, *O.R.*, vXLVI, part 1, p1119; C. M. Calkins, *The Appomattox Campaign* (Conshohocken, 1997), p69.

120. J. Longstreet, *From Manassas to Appomattox, Memoirs* (Bloomington, 1960), p609.

121. Johnson, OR, vXLVI, part 1, p1289; Pickett's report as presented in W. Harrison, *Pickett's Men* (Gaithersburg, 1988), p149.

122. J. Longstreet, *From Manassas to Appomattox, Memoirs* (Bloomington, 1960), p609.

123. S. M. Gaines, "How General R. E. Lee Saved The Life Of A Federal Officer," p375-376.

124. W. P. Roberts, "Paroles Of The Army Of Northern Virginia," p387.

125. C. M. Calkins, *The Appomattox Campaign* (Conshohocken, 1997), p75; D. S. Freeman, *Lee's Lieutenants* (New York, 1995), v3, p691.

126. D. S. Freeman, *Lee's Lieutenants* (New York, 1995), v3, p692-693; A. A. Humphreys, *The Virginia Campaign of 1864 and 1865* (New York, 1995), p376.

127. J. T. Kennedy and W. F. Parker, "Seventy-fifth Regiment (Seventh Cavalry)," p90.

128. J. Longstreet, *From Manassas to Appomattox, Memoirs* (Bloomington, 1960), p610; A. A. Humphreys, *The Virginia Campaign of 1864 and 1865* (New York, 1995), p377.

129. Davies, *O.R.*, vXLVI, part 1, p1145; A. A. Humphreys, *The Virginia Campaign of 1864 and 1865* (New York, 1995), p376, 377; C. M. Calkins, *The Appomattox Campaign* (Conshohocken, 1997), p87; Fitz Lee, *O.R.*, vXLVI, part 1, p1301.

130. E. M. Boykin, *The Falling Flag* (Oxford, Miss., 1992), p25.

131. D. S. Freeman, *Lee's Lieutenants* (New York, 1995), v3, p693-694.

132. Fitz Lee, *O.R.*, vXLVI, part 1, p1301.

133. R. E. Lee, *O.R.*, vXLVI, part 3, p1387.

134. J. Longstreet, *From Manassas to Appomattox, Memoirs* (Bloomington, 1960), p612; D. S. Freeman, *Lee's Lieutenants* (New York, 1995), v3, p708.

135. J. Longstreet, *From Manassas to Appomattox, Memoirs* (Bloomington, 1960), p612; T. T. Munford, "Last Days of Fitz Lee's Cavalry Division," VHS, p10-11; D. S. Freeman, *Lee's Lieutenants* (New York, 1995), v3, p708-709; C. M. Calkins, *The Appomattox Campaign* (Conshohocken, 1997), p104; W. M. Owen, *In Camp and Battle with the Washington Artillery* (Baton Rouge, 1999), p376.

136. R. E. Lee, *O.R.*, vXLVI, part 1, p1266; Fitzhugh Lee, *General Lee* (New York, 1994), p384; Wheaton, *O.R.*, vXLVI, part 1, p914.

137. C. M. Calkins, *The Appomattox Campaign* (Conshohocken, 1997), p112-113; J. Longstreet, *From Manassas to Appomattox, Memoirs* (Bloomington, 1960), p611; D. S. Freeman, *Lee's Lieutenants* (New York, 1995), v3, p700; Smith, *O.R.*, vXLVI, part 1, p1158.

138. Crook, *O.R.*, vXLVI, part 1, p1142; Devin, *O.R.*, vXLVI, part 1, p1125; Custer, *O.R.*, vXLVI, part 1, p1132.

139. C. M. Calkins, *The Appomattox Campaign* (Conshohocken, 1997), p99.

140. C. M. Calkins, *The Appomattox Campaign* (Conshohocken, 1997), p114.

141. J. B. Gordon, *Reminiscences of the Civil War* (Baton Rouge, 1993), p429.

142. R. E. Lee, *O.R.*, vXLVI, part 1, p1266; D. S. Freeman, *Lee's Lieutenants* (New York, 1995), v3, p710. In the midst of the constant difficulties made by both man and nature, Gordon managed to notice and remember a micro-incident which yields much understanding of the day. When Gordon's line was breaking and his officers were trying to rally the troops a captain saw a "boy soldier" running as fast as he could to the rear, and called to him, "Why are you running?" Without breaking stride, the boy yelled back, "Golly, captain, I'm running 'cause I can't fly!" See, J. B. Gordon, *Reminiscences of the Civil War* (Baton Rouge, 1993), p424.

143. A. A. Humphreys, *The Virginia Campaign of 1864 and 1865* (New York, 1995), p378-381; Fitzhugh Lee, *General Lee* (New York, 1994), p385; C. M. Calkins, *The Appomattox Campaign* (Conshohocken, 1997), p109-112.

144. J. B. Gordon, *Reminiscences of the Civil War* (Baton Rouge, 1993), p423-424.

145. For the Virginia regiments mentioned above see the rosters in R. K. Krick, *9th Virginia Cavalry* (Lynchburg, 1982), p55-108; R. J. Driver, Jr., *10th Virginia Cavalry* (Lynchburg, 1992), p86-178; D. T. Balfour, *13th Virginia Cavalry* (Lynchburg, 1986), p63-104. For the North Carolina regiments see Louis H. Manarin, *North Carolina Troops 1861-1865, A Roster*, v2, Cavalry: 1st N.C., p7-97; 2nd N.C., p104-177; 3rd N.C., p180-262; 4th N.C., p266-335; and 7th N.C., p655-695.

146. J. Longstreet, *From Manassas to Appomattox, Memoirs* (Bloomington, 1960), p616.

147. C. M. Calkins, *The Appomattox Campaign* (Conshohocken, 1997), p124-125.

148. J. Longstreet, *From Manassas to Appomattox, Memoirs* (Bloomington, 1960), p616.

149. Fitzhugh Lee, *General Lee* (New York, 1994), p385; Fitz Lee, *O.R.*, vXLVI, part 1, p1303; J. Longstreet, *From Manassas to Appomattox, Memoirs* (Bloomington, 1960), p616-617; C. M. Calkins, *The Appomattox Campaign* (Conshohocken, 1997), p116; A. A. Humphreys, *The Virginia Campaign of 1864 and 1865* (New York, 1995), p386. Humphreys did not give a source for this and he had stayed back to cross the river at High Bridge so he would not have seen this himself.

150. E. M. Boykin, *The Falling Flag* (Oxford, Miss., 1992), p33, 35.

151. E. M. Boykin, *The Falling Flag* (Oxford, Miss., 1992), p35.

152. E. M. Boykin, *The Falling Flag* (Oxford, Miss., 1992), p38-39.

153. Fitz Lee, *O.R.*, vXLVI, part 1, p1303; A. A. Humphreys, *The Virginia Campaign of 1864 and 1865* (New York, 1995), p390; C. M. Calkins, *The Appomattox Campaign* (Conshohocken, 1997), p133-134; J. E. Cooke, *Life of R. E. Lee* (Harrisburg, Penn., 1995), p455. Boykin refers to General Lee's division in this fight, and even though the only General Lee commanding a division in that area was W. H. F. Lee, his reference is certainly to Fitz Lee's division then under

the command of Munford. E. M. Boykin, *The Falling Flag* (Oxford, Miss., 1992), p40.

154. J. E. Cooke, *Life of R. E. Lee* (Harrisburg, Penn., 1995), p455.

155. Fitz Lee, *O.R.*, vXLVI, part 1, p1303; E. M. Boykin, *The Falling Flag* (Oxford, Miss., 1992), p42.

156. C. M. Calkins, *The Appomattox Campaign* (Conshohocken, 1997), p131-133.

157. C. M. Calkins, *The Appomattox Campaign* (Conshohocken, 1997), p133-134.

158. C. M. Calkins, *The Battles of Appomattox Station and Appomattox Court House, April 8-9, 1865* (Lynchburg, 1987), p4; C. M. Calkins, *The Appomattox Campaign* (Conshohocken, 1997), p138; Fitz Lee, *O.R.*, vXLVI, part 2, p1303; A. A. Humphreys, *The Virginia Campaign of 1864 and 1865* (New York, 1995), p392.

159. T. T. Munford, "Last Days of Fitz Lee's Cavalry Division," VHS, p15.

160. C. M. Calkins, *The Appomattox Campaign* (Conshohocken, 1997), p148-149.

161. C. M. Calkins, *The Appomattox Campaign* (Conshohocken, 1997), p154; W. P. Shaw, "Fifty-Ninth Regiment (Fourth Cavalry)," p471.

162. W. H. F. Lee, Appomattox Campaign Report, April 11, 1865.

163. C. M. Calkins, *The Battles of Appomattox* (Lynchburg, 1987), p9.

164. T. T. Munford, "Last Days of Fitz Lee's Cavalry Division," VHS, p15; D. S. Freeman, *Lee's Lieutenants* (New York, 1995), v3, p722; W. L. Moffet, "The Last Charge," p14; E. J. Holt, "The last Capture of Guns," p71.

165. J. B. Gordon, *Reminiscences of the Civil War* (Baton Rouge, 1993), p435; R. E. Lee, *O.R.*, vXLVI, part 1, p1266; Fitz Lee, *O.R.*, vXLVI, part 1, p1303, 1304.

166. T. T. Munford, "Last Days of Fitz Lee's Cavalry Division," VHS, p17; C. M. Calkins, *The Battles of Appomattox* (Lynchburg, 1987), p64.

167. T. T. Munford, "Last Days of Fitz Lee's Cavalry Division," VHS, p18; W. H. F. Lee, Appomattox Campaign Report, April 11, 1865, VHS.

168. E. J. Holt, "The last Capture of Guns," p71.

169. D. S. Freeman, *Lee's Lieutenants* (New York, 1995), v3, pages 727-728; T. H. Allen, *Lee's Last Major General, Bryan Grimes* (Mason City, Iowa, 1999), p250-251.

170. W. L. Moffet, response to: E. E. Bouldin, "The Last Charge," p14.

171. C. M. Calkins, *The Appomattox Campaign* (Conshohocken, 1997), page 161, 162; Merritt, *O.R.*, vXLVI, part 1, p1121.

172. The prisoners and guns were quickly sent to the rear under the care of Private Moffett, who watched them until W. H. F. Lee later came by and told him to let them go; it was all over. W. L. Moffet, response to: E. E. Bouldin, "The Last Charge," p14-15.

173. Holt, of the 7th N.C. in E. J. Holt, "The Last Capture of Guns," p71; Garnett, in Henry A. London, "Last at Appomattox," p67-68.

174. W. P. Roberts, "Additional Sketch Nineteenth Regiment (Second Cavalry)," p108. On the issue of who fired the last shot, several other units fighting at that place also feel they fired the last shot of the war in Virginia, and certainly they all deserve to believe they did.

175. H. A. London, "Last at Appomattox," quotes Leach, p68-69.

176. J. B. Gordon, *Reminiscences of the Civil War* (Baton Rouge, 1993), p437-438; C. M. Calkins, *The Appomattox Campaign* (Conshohocken, 1997), p164-165.

177. T. H. Allen, *Lee's Last Major General, Bryan Grimes* (Mason City, Iowa., 1999), p253; C. M. Calkins, *The Appomattox Campaign* (Conshohocken, 1997), p162-163.

178. C. M. Calkins, *The Battles of Appomattox* (Lynchburg, 1987), p64, 123, 124.

179. T. T. Munford, "Last Days of Fitz Lee's Cavalry Division," VHS, p20-23.

180. Fitz Lee, *O.R.*, vXLVI, part 1, p1303-1304.

181. W. L. Moffett, response to: E. E. Bouldin, "The Last Charge," p14-15.

182. W. P. Roberts, "Paroles Of The Army Of Northern Virginia," p387; Garnett, as quoted at length by T. T. Munford, "Last Days of Fitz Lee's Cavalry Division," VHS, p28-29.

183. J. B. Hill, "Forty-first Regiment (Third Cavalry)," p785.

184. Fitz Lee, *O.R.*, vXLVI, part 1, p1304; C. M. Calkins, *The Appomattox Campaign* (Conshohocken, 1997), p173-174.

185. *O.R.*, vXLVI, part 1, p1278.

186. "Supplement to Parole List," *North Carolina Troops, 1861-'65*, v5, p657-658.

187. "Parole List at Appomattox," *North Carolina Troops, 1861-'65*, v5, p567, 657-658.

188. D. S. Freeman, *Lee's Lieutenants* (New York, 1995), v3, p742.

189. *North Carolina Troops 1861-1865, A Roster*, compiled by Louis H. Manarin (Raleigh, N.C., State Division of Archives and History), vII, Cavalry, p104-177.

Appendix

1. *North Carolina Troops 1861-1865, A Roster*, compiled by Louis H. Manarin (Raleigh, N.C., State Division of Archives and History), vII, Cavalry, p104-177. The Roster of Troops took most of its information from the Compiled Service Records which are primarily based on Company Muster Roll cards.

2. John W. Gordon was among the first prisoners of war to be transferred to Point Lookout. On Aug 6, 1863, 500 prisoners were sent there from Old Capitol Prison in Washington, and 800 from Baltimore. By the end of September nearly 4,000 Confederate prisoners were confined at the point (many were transferred from Fort Delaware in Oct 1863), and by Dec 1863 there were more than 9,000. E. W. Beitzell, *Point Lookout Prison Camp for Confederates* (Leonardtown, Maryland), p20.

3. Several captains of other companies joined in drafting a resolution expressing their regret at the death of Captain Reese, "who fell mortally wounded while gallantly leading his men [of Company H] in a charge upon the enemy on Sunday 29th of Nov. 1863." *Fayetteville Observer*, "For the Observer, Camp Gordon's N.C. Cavalry. Dec. 6, 1863," Jan 18, 1864, p1, col 4.

4. John P. Lockhart to mother, Petersburg, June 28, 1864, "Lockhart Family Letters," in SCL-DU; J. P. Lockhart, *Hillsborough Recorder*, July 13, 1864, p2, cols. 1, 2.

5. Colonel Andrews's fate is described in W. P. Roberts, "Additional Sketch Nineteenth Regiment (Second Cavalry)," p102; and by Captain John P. Lockhart who wrote, "Col. C. M. Andrews had his right ankle shivered by a minnie ball, and died soon after it was amputated. It is thought that an overdose of chloroform caused his death." J. P. Lockhart, *Hillsborough Recorder*, July 13, 1864, page 2, cols. 1, 2.

Bibliography

Archival Sources

Duke University, Special Collections Library, Durham, North Carolina:
    Margaret F. Craig Papers.
    Lockhart Family Letters.
Greensboro Historical Museum Archives, Civil War Collection:
    Stuart, J. E. B. Letter to James B. Gordon. MSS. Coll. # 16, Series 31.
Library of Congress, Manuscript Division, Washington, D.C.:
    William E. Brooks Collection.
Museum of the Confederacy, Richmond, Virginia:
    John W. Gordon Diary; North Carolina Collection.
    Lee, Fitzhugh. "Report of Major General Fitzhugh Lee of the Operations of His Cavalry Division, A. N. V. from May 4th 1864 to September 19th, 1864." Eleanor S. Brockenbrough Library.
    Payne, William H. F. Autobiographical letter to Joseph R. Anderson, dated December 13, 1903.
North Carolina Division of Archives and History, Raleigh, North Carolina:
    Adjutant General's Department, Roll of Honor, vols. 3 and 4, "A Sketch of the Nineteenth Regiment N.C. Troops. (Cavalry)," Microfilm no. S.1.80P.
    Branson Family Papers, 1848–1925; P.C. 1507.1.
    John Herritage Bryan Papers, P.C. no. 6.
    Milas A. Cavin Papers, P.C. no. 399.
    William Bailey Clement Papers, P.C. no. 409.
    Mason, Samuel N. Letter to his father, dated December 9, 1862, from below Fredericksburg, P.C. 755.
    Special Order No. 3, Headquarters 2nd Cavalry, dated October 18, 1861.
    Special Order No. 5, dated October 4, 1861.
National Archives and Records Administration, Washington, D.C.:
    War Department Collection of Confederate Records, Special Orders by R. C. Gatlin (bound volume of originals), RG 109.
    Company Muster Roll, Compiled Service Records of Confederate Soldiers Who Served in Organizations from the state of North Carolina; 2nd Cavalry (19th State Troops), RG 109. Microcopy 270, roll 11.
University of North Carolina, Southern Historical Collection, Chapel Hill:
    Rufus Barringer Papers, no. 1028.
    Cowpers Papers, no. 3150.
    Emma Henderson Dunn Papers, 1852–1903; no. 1867, folder no. 1.
University of South Carolina, South Caroliniana Library, Columbia:
    Hampton Family Papers.
Virginia Historical Society, Richmond, Virginia:
    Collins, John O. Letter, Confederate Military Manuscripts Series A, C589c.2, reel 8.
    Lee, William H. F. Appomattox Campaign Report from Appomattox Court House, Va., dated April 11, 1865: MSS3: L515a: 506.
    Munford, Thomas T. "Five Forks—The Waterloo of the Confederacy." MSS5:1 M9237: 1.
    _____. "Last Days of Fitz Lee's Cavalry Division."
    Scott, John Z. H. "Memoirs of J. Z. H. Scott, Brother of R. Lewis Scott." Galveston, July 1, 1891.

Published Works

Alexander, Edward Porter. *Military Memoirs of a Confederate*. Reprint, New York: Da Capo Press, 1993.

Alexander, Ted. "Gettysburg Cavalry Operations, June 27–July 3, 1863." *Blue and Gray* Vol. VI, no. 1 (October 1988), pp. 8–32, 36–41.

Allen, T. Harrell. *Lee's Last Major General, Bryan Grimes of North Carolina*. Mason City, Iowa: Savas Publishing Co., 1999.

Allen, William. *The Army of Northern Virginia in 1862*. Reprint, Dayton, Ohio: Morningside Bookshop, 1984.

Balfour, Daniel T. *13th Virginia Cavalry*. Lynchburg, Va.: H. E. Howard, 1986.

Barrett, John G. *The Civil War in North Carolina*. Chapel Hill: University of North Carolina Press, 1963.

Barringer, R. "Cavalry Sketches." In Pool, Stephen D., ed. *Our Living and Our Dead*. Vol. 3, pp. 738–741.

Barringer, Rufus. "Ninth Regiment (First Cavalry)." In Clark, Walter, ed. *Histories of the Several Regiments and Battalions from North Carolina in the Great War, 1861–1865*. Vol. I, pp. 417–443. Goldsboro, N.C.: Nash Brothers, 1901.

Baylor, George. *Bull Run to Bull Run or Four Years in the Army of Northern Virginia*. Richmond: B. F. Johnson Publishing Co., 1900.

Beale, George W. *A Lieutenant of Cavalry in Lee's Army*. Reprint, Baltimore: Butternut and Blue, 1994.

Beale, Richard L. T. *History of the Ninth Virginia Cavalry in the War Between the States.* Reprint, Amissville, Virginia: American Fundamentalist, 1981.

Bearss, Ed, and Chris Calkins. *The Battle of Five Forks.* Lynchburg: H. E. Howard, 1985.

Beauregard, G. T. "Four Days of Battle at Petersburg." In Johnson, Robert U., and Clarence C. Buel, eds. *Battles and Leaders of the Civil War, 1884–88.* Vol. 42, pp. 540–544.

Beitzell, Edwin W. *Point Lookout Prison Camp for Confederates.* Reprint, Leonardtown, Maryland: St. Mary's County Historical Society, 1972.

Blackford, William W. *War Years with Jeb Stuart.* Reprint, Baton Rouge: Louisiana State University Press, 1993.

Boykin, E. M. *The Falling Flag, Retreat and Surrender at Appomattox.* Reprint, Oxford, Mississippi: The Guild Bindery Press, Inc., 1992.

Brennan, Patrick. "Thunder on the Plains of Brandy." *North & South,* Part I, Vol. 5, no. 3 (April 2002), pp. 14–34, and Part II, Vol. 5, no. 4 (May 2002), pp. 32–51.

Calkins, Chris M. *The Appomattox Campaign: March 29–April 9, 1865.* Conshohocken, Pennsylvania: Combined Books, 1997.

———. *The Battles of Appomattox Station and Appomattox Court House, April 8–9, 1865.* Lynchburg: H. E. Howard, Inc., 1987.

Carr, Julian S. "The Gordon-Barringer Brigade." In Clark, Walter, ed. *Histories of the Several Regiments and Battalions from North Carolina in the Great War, 1861–1865,* Vol. I, pp. 581–582. Goldsboro, N.C.: Nash Brothers, 1901.

Cheek, W. H. "Additional Sketch Ninth Regiment (First Cavalry)." In Clark, Walter, ed. *Histories of the Several Regiments and Battalions from North Carolina in the Great War, 1861–1865.* Vol. I, pp. 445–487. Goldsboro, N.C.: Nash Brothers, 1901.

Coltrane, Daniel B. *The Memoirs of Daniel Branson Coltrane.* Raleigh: Edwards & Broughton Co., 1956.

Cooke, J. E. *Life of Robert E. Lee.* Reprint, Harrisburg, Pa.: The Archive Society, 1995.

Cooke, John Esten. *Wearing of The Gray, Being Personal Portraits and Adventures of The War.* Reprint, Bloomington: Indiana University Press, 1959.

Connelly, Thomas L. *The Marble Man: Robert E. Lee and His Image in American Society.* New York: Alfred A. Knopf, 1977.

Cormier, Steven A. *The Siege of Suffolk: The Forgotten Campaign, April 11–May 4, 1863.* Lynchburg: H. E. Hunt, 1989.

Coski, John. "Forgotten Warrior." *North & South,* Vol. 2, no. 7 (September 1999): pp. 76–89.

Couch, Darius N. "The Chancellorsville Campaign." In Johnson, Robert U., and Clarence C. Buel, eds. *Battles and Leaders of the Civil War, 1884–88.* Vol. 3, pp. 154–171.

Cummins, A. B. *The Wilson-Kautz Raid: More commonly referred to as the Battle of the Grove, June 21, July 1, 1864.* Blackstone, Virginia: Nottoway Publishing Co., July 1961.

Curtis, W. A. "Sketches of Company A, 2nd Regiment of North Carolina Cavalry." In Pool, Stephen D. ed. *Our Living and Our Dead.* Vol. 2, pp. 41–43.

Dorsey, Frank. "Fatal Wounding of General J. E. B. Stuart." *Southern Historical Society Papers,* Vol. 30 (Jan.-Dec. 1902), pp. 236–238.

Dowdey, Clifford, and Louis H. Manarin, eds. *The Wartime Papers of Robert E. Lee.* Reprint, New York: Da Capo Press, 1987.

Driver, Robert J., Jr. *10th Virginia Cavalry.* Lynchburg: H. E. Howard, Inc., 1992.

Early, Jubal A. *The Memoirs of General Jubal A. Early.* Reprint, New York: Konecky & Konecky, 1994.

Evens, Clement A., ed. *Confederate Military History.* 12 vols. Atlanta: 1899.

———. "The Maryland Line." *Confederate Military History.* Vol. 2 (North Carolina), pp. 115–122.

———. "Services of the North Carolina Cavalry Along the Rapidan ... Activity of the Confederate Cavalry." *Confederate Military History.* Vol. 4 (North Carolina), chapter 15, pp. 249–261.

Field, C. W. "Narrative of Major-General C. W. Field." *Southern Historical Society Papers,* vol. 14, pp. 551–554.

Fordney, Ben F. *Stoneman at Chancellorsville: The Coming of Age of Union Cavalry.* Shippensburg, Pa.: White Mane Books, 1998.

Franklin, William B. "Rear-guard Fighting During the Change of Base." In Johnson, Robert U., and Clarence C. Buel, eds. *Battles and Leaders of the Civil War, 1884–88.* Vol. 2, pp. 366–382.

Freeman, Douglas Southall. *Lee's Lieutenants: A Study in Command.* 3 vols. Reprint, New York: Simon & Schuster, 1995.

———. *R. E. Lee, A Biography.* 4 vols. New York: Charles Scribner's Sons, 1935.

Ford, N. P. "An Attack on Richmond Foiled." *Southern Historical Society Papers,* vol. 24, pp. 278–284.

Fox, William F. *Regimental Losses in the American Civil War (1861–65).* Albany: Albany Publishing, 1889.

Furguson, Ernest B. *Not War But Murder: Cold Harbor 1864.* New York: Alfred A. Knopf, 2000.

Gaines, Samuel M. "How General R. E. Lee Saved the Life of a Federal Officer." *Southern Historical Society Papers,* vol. 33, pp. 375–376.

Galloway, John M. "Sixty-Third Regiment (Fifth Cavalry)." In Clark, Walter, ed. *Histories of the Several Regiments and Battalions from North Carolina in the Great War, 1861–1865.* Vol. III, pp. 529–543. Goldsboro, N.C.: Nash Brothers, 1901.

Garnett, T. S. "Cavalry Service with General Stuart." *Annals of the War. Philadelphia Weekly Times.* February 8, 1879.

Garnett, Theodore S. *Riding with Stuart: Reminiscences of an Aide-de-Camp,* Robert J. Trout, ed. Shippensburg, Pa.: White Mane Publishing Co., 1994.

Gordon, A. "Organization of Troops." In Clark, Walter, ed. *Histories of the Several Regiments and Battalions from North Carolina in the Great War, 1861–1865,* Vol. I, pp. 3–49. Goldsboro, N.C.: Nash Brothers, 1901.

Gordon, John B. *Reminiscences of the Civil War.* Reprint, Baton Rouge: Louisiana State University Press, 1993.

Gordon, John W. "Pleasant Days in War Time." *Confederate Veteran,* Vol. 37 (March 1929), pp. 93–95.

Gorman, John C. *Lee's Last Campaign.* Raleigh: William B. Smith & Co., 1866.

Graham, William A. "Nineteenth Regiment (Second Cavalry)." In Clark, Walter, ed. *Histories of the Several Regiments and Battalions from North Carolina in the Great War, 1861–1865*. Vol. II, pp. 79–98. Goldsboro, N. C.: Nash Brothers, 1901.

Grant, Ulysses S. *Personal Memoirs*. Reprint, New York: Penguin Books, 1999.

Green, W. J. "Night Attack of the 1st and 2nd North Carolina Cavalry Upon Kilpatrick's Division." In Pool, Stephen D. ed. *Our Living and Our Dead*. Vol. 2, p. 169.

Hall, Clark B. "The Battle of Brandy Station." *Civil War Times Illustrated*, Vol. 29 (May/June 1990): pp. 32–45.

Harrison, Walter. *Pickett's Men: A Fragment of War History*. Reprint, Gaithersburg, Md.: Olde Soldier Books, Inc., 1988.

Hartley, Chris J. *Stuart's Tarheels: James B. Gordon and His North Carolina Cavalry*. Baltimore: Butternut and Blue, 1996.

Hawkins, Rush C. "Early Coast Operations in North Carolina." In Johnson, Robert U., and Clarence C. Buel, eds. *Battles and Leaders of the Civil War, 1884–88*. Vol. 1, pp. 647–652.

Hess, Earl J. *Lee's Tar Heels: The Pettigrew-Kirkland-MacRae Brigade*. Chapel Hill: The University of North Carolina Press, 2002.

Hill, Daniel H. *Bethel to Sharpsburg*. 2 vols. Wilmington, N.C.: Broadfoot Publishing Co., 1992.

_____. "Lee's Attacks North of the Chickahominy." In Johnson, Robert U., and Clarence C. Buel, eds. *Battles and Leaders of the Civil War, 1884–88*. Vol. 2, pp. 347–362.

_____. "McClellan's Change of Base and Malvern Hill." In Johnson, Robert U., and Clarence C. Buel, eds. *Battles and Leaders of the Civil War, 1884–88*. Vol. 2, pp. 383–395.

Hill, Joshau B. "Forty-First Regiment (Third Cavalry)." In Clark, Walter, ed. *Histories of the Several Regiments and Battalions from North Carolina in the Great War, 1861–1865*. Vol. II, pp. 767–787. Goldsboro, N.C.: Nash Brothers, 1901.

Holt, E. J. "The Last Capture of Guns." In *Five Points in the Record of North Carolina in the Great War of 1861–5*. Pp. 71–72. Raleigh: Report of the Committee, North Carolina Literary and Historical Association, 1904.

Hopkins, Luther W. *From Bull Run to Appomattox, A Boy's View*. Baltimore: Fleet-McGinley Press, 1908.

Humphreys, Andrew A. *The Virginia Campaign of 1864 and 1865: The Army of the Potomac and the Army of the James*. Reprint, New York: Da Capo Press, 1995.

Hunter, Alexander. *Johnny Reb & Billy Yank*. New York: Konecky & Konecky, 1904.

Johnson, Robert U., and Clarence C. Buel, eds. *Battles and Leaders of the Civil war, 1884–1888*. 4 vols. New York: 1887–1888. Reprint, New York: Castle Books, 1956.

Jones, J. William. *Personal Reminiscences of General Robert E. Lee*. Reprint, Baton Rouge: Louisiana State University Press, 1994.

Kennedy, John T., and W. F. Parker. "Seventy-fifth Regiment (Seventh Cavalry)." In Clark, Walter, ed. *Histories of the Several Regiments and Battalions from North Carolina in the Great War, 1861–1865*. Vol. I, pp. 71–96. Goldsboro, N.C.: Nash Brothers, 1901.

Krick, Robert E. L. "Stuart's Last Ride: A Confederate View of Sheridan's Raid." In Gary W. Gallagher, ed. *The Spotsylvania Campaign*. Pp. 127–169. Chapel Hill: University of North Carolina Press, 1998.

Krick, Robert K. *9th Virginia Cavalry*. Lynchburg: H. E. Howard, Inc., 1982.

Lane, J. H. "Glimpses of Army Life in 1864." *Southern Historical Society Papers*, vol. 18, pp. 406–420.

Lee, Fitzhugh. *General Lee, A Biography of Robert E. Lee*. Reprint, New York: Da Capo Press, 1994.

Lee, Robert E. "The Confederate Army." In Johnson, Robert U., and Clarence C. Buel, eds. *Battles and Leaders of the Civil War, 1884–88*. Vol. 3, pp. 146–147.

Lee, William H. F. "Memoranda of the Operations of Brigadier General W. H. F. Lee's Command During General Stoneman's Raid into Virginia." *Southern Historical Society Papers*, vol. 3, pp. 181–182.

London, Henry A. "Last at Appomattox." In *Five Points in the Record of North Carolina in the Great War of 1861–5*. Pp. 59–70. Raleigh: Report of the Committee, North Carolina Literary and Historical Association, 1904.

Longacre, Edward G. *The Cavalry at Gettysburg*. Lincoln: University of Nebraska Press, 1993.

_____. *Lincoln's Cavalrymen: A History of the Mounted Forces of the Army of the Potomac*. Mechanicsburg, Pa.: Stackpole Books, 2000.

Longstreet, James. *From Manassas to Appomattox: Memoirs of the Civil War in America*. Reprint, Bloomington: Indiana University Press, 1960.

_____. "The Seven Days, Including Frayser's Farm." In Johnson, Robert U., and Clarence C. Buel, eds. *Battles and Leaders of the Civil War, 1884–88*. Vol. 2, pp. 396–405.

McClellan, Henry B. *I Rode with Jeb Stuart: The Life and Campaigns of Major General J.E.B. Stuart*. Reprint, Bloomington: Indiana University Press, 1958.

McDonald, William N. *A History of the Laurel Brigade*. Reprint, Baltimore: Johns Hopkins University Press, 2002.

McPherson, James M. *Battle Cry of Freedom: The Civil War Era*. Reprint, New York: Ballantine Books, 1989.

McWhiney, Grady, and Perry D. Jamieson. *Attack and Die: Civil War Military Tactics and the Southern Heritage*. Tuscaloosa: University of Alabama Press, 1982.

Manarin, Louis H. *North Carolina Troops, 1861–1865: A Roster*. 14 vols. Raleigh: North Carolina Division of Archives and History, 1968–1993.

Means, Paul B. "Additional Sketch Sixty-Third Regiment (Fifth Cavalry)." In Clark, Walter, ed. *Histories of the Several Regiments and Battalions from North Carolina in the Great War, 1861–1865*. Vol. III, pp. 545–657. Goldsboro, N.C.: Nash Brothers, 1901.

Miller, William E. "The Cavalry Battle Near Gettysburg." In Johnson, Robert U., and Clarence C. Buel, eds. *Battles and Leaders of the Civil War, 1884–88*. Vol. 3, pp. 397–406.

Moffett, W. L. "The Last Charge." In *Southern Historical Society Papers*, vol. 36, pp. 13–16.

Moore, J. Emory. "Over the Grave of Colonel Sol.

Williams." In Pool, Stephen D. ed. *Our Living and Our Dead*. Vol. 1, p. 138.

Moore, J. H. "With Jackson at Hamilton's Crossing." In Johnson, Robert U., and Clarence C. Buel, eds. *Battles and Leaders of the Civil War, 1884–88*. Vol. 3, pp. 139–141.

Neese, George M. *Three Years in the Confederate Horse Artillery*. New York: Neale Publishing Co., 1911.

Nye, Wilbur S. *Here Come the Rebels*. Dayton: Morningside Bookshop, 1984.

O'Neill, Robert F., Jr. *The Cavalry Battles of Aldie, Middleburg and Upperville, June 10–27, 1863*. Lynchburg: H. E. Howard, Inc., 1993.

Opie, John N. *A Rebel Cavalryman with Lee, Stuart and Jackson*. Reprint, Dayton: Morningside Bookshop, 1997.

Owen, William Miller. *In Camp and Battle with the Washington Artillery of New Orleans*. Reprint, Baton Rouge: Louisiana State University Press, 1999.

Parramore, Thomas C. "The Burning of Winton in 1862." *North Carolina Historical Review*, Vol. 39 (1962): 18–31.

Peace, Samuel T., Jr. *Vance County, North Carolina: A Short History*. Henderson, N.C.: 1955.

Poindexter, William B. "He Proposed to Advance on the Enemy Camp at Yellow Tavern." *Southern Historical Society Papers*, vol. 32 (Jan.-Dec. 1904), pp. 119–121.

Poole, Stephen D., ed. *Our Living and Our Dead: Devoted to North Carolina — Her Present, and Her Future*. 4 cols. Raleigh, N.C.: North Carolina Branch of the Southern Historical Society, September 1874–August 1876.

Porter, Fitz John. "The Battle of Malvern Hill." In Johnson, Robert U., and Clarence C. Buel, eds. *Battles and Leaders of the Civil War, 1884–88*. Vol. 2, pp. 406–427.

_____. "Hanover Court House and Gaines's Mill." In Johnson, Robert U., and Clarence C. Buel, eds. *Battles and Leaders of the Civil War, 1884–88*. Vol. 2, pp. 326–343.

Porter, Horace. "Five Forks and the Pursuit of Lee." In Johnson, Robert U., and Clarence C. Buel, eds. *Battles and Leaders of the Civil War, 1884–88*. Vol. 4, pp. 702–722.

Prowell, George R. *Prelude to Gettysburg, Encounter at Hanover*. Shippensburg, Pa.: Burd Street Press, 1994.

Rhea, Gordon C. *The Battle of the Wilderness, May 5–6, 1864*. Baton Rouge: Louisiana State University Press, 1994.

_____. *The Battles for Spotsylvania Court House and the Road to Yellow Tavern, May 7–12, 1864*. Baton Rouge: Louisiana State University Press, 1997.

_____. "The Hottest Place I Ever Was In." *North & South*, vol. 4, no. 4 (April 2001), 42–57.

_____. *To the North Anna River: Grant and Lee, May 13–25, 1864*. Baton Rouge: Louisiana State University Press, 2000.

Roberts, William P. "Additional Sketch Nineteenth Regiment (Second Cavalry)." In Clark, Walter, ed. *Histories of the Several Regiments and Battalions from North Carolina in the Great War, 1861–1865*. Vol. II, pp. 100–109. Goldsboro, N.C.: Nash Brothers, 1901.

_____. "Paroles of the Army of Northern Virginia." *Southern Historical Society Papers*, vol. 18, p. 387.

Rodenbough, Theo. F. "Sheridan's Richmond Raid." In Johnson, Robert U., and Clarence C. Buel, eds. *Battles and Leaders of the Civil War, 1884–88*. Vol. 4, pp. 188–193.

Sanger, Donald B., and Hay, Thomas R. *James Longstreet: I. Soldier*. Baton Rouge: Louisiana State University Press, 1952.

Shaw, W. P. "Fifty-Ninth Regiment (Fourth Cavalry)." In Clark, Walter, ed. *Histories of the Several Regiments and Battalions from North Carolina in the Great War, 1861–1865*. Vol. III, pp. 455–472. Goldsboro, N. C.: Nash Brothers, 1901.

Simpson, Harold B. *Hood's Texas Brigade: Lee's Grenadier Guard*. Dallas: Alcor Publishing Co., 1983.

Sommers, Richard J. *Richmond Redeemed: The Siege at Petersburg*. New York: Doubleday & Co., 1981.

Southern Historical Society Papers. William Jones et al., eds. 52 vols. Richmond: Southern Historical Society, 1876–1959.

Stedman, Charles M. "Battle at Reams' Station." *Southern Historical Society Papers*, vol. 19, pp. 114–116.

Stuart, James E. B. "Report of Operations After Gettysburg." *Southern Historical Society Papers*, vol. 2, no. 2 (August 1876), pp. 65–78.

_____. "Stuart's Last Dispatch." *Southern Historical Society Papers*, vol. 2 [9], no. 3 (March 1881), pp. 138–139.

Trudeau, Noah A. *The Last Citadel: Petersburg, Virginia, June 1864–April 1865*. Baton Rouge: Louisiana State University Press, 1991.

von Borcke, Heros. *Memoirs of the Confederate War for Independence*. Reprint, Nashville: J. S. Sanders & Co., 1991.

_____, and Justus Schiebert. *The Great Cavalry Battle of Brandy Station, 9 June 1863*. Reprint, Gaithersburg, Md.: Olde Soldier Books, Inc., 1997.

Wells, Edward L. *Hampton & His Cavalry in '64*. Reprint, Camden, S.C.: Culler Printing, 1997.

Wittenberg, Eric J. *Glory Enough for All: Sheridan's Second Raid and the Battle of Trevilian Station*. Washington, D.C.: Brassey's Inc., 2001.

Young, Alfred C. III. "Numbers and Losses in the Army of Northern Virginia." *North & South*, Vol. 3, no. 3 (March 2000), pp. 15–29.

Newspapers

Fayetteville (N.C.) *Observer*
Hillsborough (N.C.) *Recorder*
Raleigh Standard
Raleigh Register
Raleigh Daily Confederate
Raleigh News and Observer
Richmond Enquirer

Index

Allen's Station (May 1864) 259
Amelia Court House 374
Anderson, Richard H.: Chancellorsville Campaign 90–93; Spotsylvania Court House 245, 247; at North Anna River 267; near Richmond 313; April 1, 1865 579; retreat to Appomattox 369, 373; High Bridge & Sailor's Creek, April 1865 377
Andrews, Clinton M. 13, 40; as temporary commander, took the 2nd N.C. Cavalry to Virginia 41; at Warrenton, Va., temporary commander of the 2nd N.C. Cavalry 61, 63–64, 71, 114; retreat from Gettysburg 179; 192; promoted to colonel and took command of the 2nd N.C. Cavalry 193; Jack's Shop 194; Bristoe Campaign 198; promoted to lieutenant colonel, 2nd N.C. Cavalry and colonel just days later in February 1863 221; Kilpatrick's expedition to Richmond 224; 330; Goodall's Tavern 256; Brook Church, May 1864 263; 267–268; Wilson's Wharf, May 1864 271; 273; Haw's Shop, June 1864 284; mortally wounded at Blacks & Whites 300
Appomattox Court House, Battle of (April 9, 1865) 384–389
Army of Northern Virginia 50; Maryland Campaign 54, 56, 59; 2nd N.C. Cavalry 59; Fredericksburg 76; Chancellorsville Campaign 85; 95; retreat from Gettysburg 175, 180–182; Bristoe Campaign 203, 207; 233; at the Weldon R.R. 319; at Appomattox Court House, April 9, 1865 384
Ashland (May 1864) 257; (June 1864) 280
Atlee's Station (March 1864) 224

Bachelor's Creek, N.C. 37–38
Baker, John A. 97, 102–104; 231; took temporary command of the N.C. Cavalry Brigade for the fighting at Hanovertown through Hanover Court House 273–274; 275; Haw's Shop, June 1864 283–284; captured near Davis's farm 293
Baker, Laurence 8, 10; at Gettysburg 170; retreat from Gettysburg 175, 182; 185; took command of the N.C. Cavalry Brigade 191, 194
Barbee's Cross Roads, Va. 68–69
Barringer, Rufus C. 8; Bristoe Campaign 207, 210; Mine Run Campaign 240; 280; took command of the N.C. Cavalry Brigade, south of the Chickahominy 285, 289–290; to Petersburg, June 1864 291; along the Weldon R.R. 292; near Davis's farm 293–294; the Wilson & Kautz Raid 297, 301; Blacks & Whites 298–300; on the Weldon R.R., July 1864 305–306; 310; near Richmond, August 1864 White's Tavern, White Oak Swamp, the Charles City Road 311–317; on the Weldon R.R. 322, 324; temporarily commanding W. H. F. Lee's division 324; Reams's Station, August 1864 325–328; cattle raid, September 1864 330–332; on the Weldon 334; McDowell's and Wyatt's farms, September 1864 335; Boydton Plank Road, October 1864 340–341; south along the Weldon R.R. 343–344; collecting arms and equipment 345; Boydton Plank Road, February 1865 347; spring 1865 351; Chamberlain's Run 355–359; Five Forks, April 1, 1865 360, 364–367; retreat to Appomattox 369; Namozine Church, April 3, 1865 370–371
Battle flag: 2nd N.C. Cavalry 373
Beale, Richard L. T.: Brandy Station 123; 128, 135–136, 142; to Gettysburg 146, 149; Hanover, Pa. 155, 158–160; on to Gettysburg 162–163; at Gettysburg 164, 168–169, 172; retreat from Gettysburg 178; wounded while covering a pullback 189–190; Haw's Shop, May 1864 276; Reams's Station, August 1864 325; took command of Chambliss's former Virginia cavalry brigade 351; spring 1865 348, 351; Chamberlain's Run 356–358; Five Forks, April 1, 1865 360; Amelia Court House 374; Appomattox Court House, April 9, 1865 384, 387
Beauregard, Pierre G. T. 288; defends Petersburg, August 1864 308; around the Weldon R.R. 319
Belfield (December 1864) 342
Blacks & Whites, Battle of (June 23, 1864) 297–303
Boothe, John G. 10, 13, 30, 36; commanding the detached Second Squadron, 2nd N.C. Cavalry 95; wounded 97
Boydton Plank Road (October 1864) 338; Battle of (September 1864) 336
Brandy Station, Battle of (June 1863) 115–128
Bristoe Campaign (October 1863) 198–213
Brook Church (May 1864) 262
Bryan, George Pettigrew: fight on Trappe Road 141, 144; killed near White Oak Swamp, August 1864 314
Bryce's Creek, N.C.: battle around New Bern 31, 34
Buford, John 82; Brandy Station 115, 117–120, 122–124; 133, 137–139; fight on Trappe Road 139–141; retreat from Gettysburg 174, 177, 179–182; 185–186, 189–190; Jack's Shop 193–195; Bristoe Campaign 199–202; died of illness December 1963 220
Burgwyn, Henry K.: New Bern 20, 22, 25, 27–28
Burnside, Ambrose E. 14, 18; on N.C. coast 17; New Bern 21; 39; moved toward Richmond 49–50; commander of the Army of the Potomac 70; 72; Fredericksburg 76; Mud March, January 1863, and lost command of the army 79–80; the Wilderness 234, 240; demonstration against Richmond, August 1864 308
Butler, Benjamin F.: the Wilderness 234; 270; to Richmond, September 1864 333
Butler, Matthew C.: expedition to Maryland and Pennsylvania 61, 63;

Brandy Station 121; took command of Hampton's former brigade 191; 232; Haw's Shop, May 1864 277–278; on the Weldon R.R. 309; took command of Hampton's former division 310, 315; the Charles City Road, August 1864 315–317; on the Weldon 320, 323; Reams's Station, August 1864 325; 333–335; McDowell's and Wyatt's farms, September 1864 335; Boydton Plank Road, September 1864 337; Boydton Plank Road, October 1864 338–340; returned to South Carolina 348

Camp Johnston: near Kinston, N.C. 34–35
Camp Washington: near Edenton, N.C. 11, 13
Chamberlain's Run 355
Chambliss, John R. 54, 57–59; the Rappahannock Line 60, 63–71; 2nd N.C. Cavalry removed from his command 71; Chancellorsville Campaign 87–88; Brandy Station 119–120, 124–126; 128–129; Thoroughfare Gap 130; around Middleburg 131–134, 136–139; 140–143; to Gettysburg 146, 149–154; Hanover, Pa. 155, 159–160; on to Gettysburg 162–163; at Gettysburg 164, 166, 168–172; retreat from Gettysburg 175–183; covering a pullback 185–187, 189–192; Bristoe Campaign 200; 232; Spotsylvania Court House 249; 266, 275; Haw's Shop, May 1864 276, 278; Hanover Court House 280; Ashland 282; 285; above the Chickahominy 289; 290, 295–296; Wilson & Kautz Raid 301–303; Reams's Station, June 1864 304; on the Weldon R.R., July 1864 305; near White's Tavern and White Oak Swamp, mortally wounded, August 1864 311–313
Chancellorsville Campaign (April/May 1863) 85–95
Cheek, W. H. 192; Jack's Shop 194–195; Kilpatrick's expedition to Richmond, near Atlee's Station 225–226; near Goodall's Tavern 256; near White's Tavern, August 1864 312; spring 1865 351; Chamberlain's Run 356, 358; Namozine Church, April 3, 1865 371; captured 379
Chew, R. P.: Brandy Station 122; fight on Trappe Road 141–143; the Wilderness 238; on the Weldon R.R. 334
Clement, William B.: at Gettysburg 166; retreat from Gettysburg 177; Reams's Station, August 1864 327
Cold Harbor, Battle of (May 1864) 273–288
Corse, M. D.: Five Forks, April 1, 1865 360

Crook, George near Dinwiddie Court House 570; Farmville 614; Appomattox Court House, April 9, 1865 622
Culpeper Court House: held by the 2nd N.C. Cavalry 60; 189
Cumberland Church (April 7, 1865) 381
Custer, George A.: Hanover, Pa. 160; Gettysburg 163, 166, 169; Bristoe Campaign 199, 210–211; expedition to Richmond 222; the Wilderness 240; 250; Meadow Bridge, May 1864 262; Hanovertown through Hanover Court House 274; Haw's Shop, May 1864 277; spring 1865 354; Dinwiddie Court House 359; Five Forks, April 1, 1865 364–366; retreat to Appomattox 373, 383; at Appomattox Court House April 9, 1865 385

Dahlgren, Ulric: Kilpatrick's expedition to Richmond 222–223; 226–227
Daniel, Junius 36, 54, 97
Davenport Bridge (May 1864) 252
Davies, Henry E.: Bristoe Campaign 199, 210; Spotsylvania Court House 243; Ashland, May 1864 257; cattle raid, September 1864 330–332; on the Weldon R.R. 333; Boydton Plank Road, October 1864 340–341; south along the Weldon 343; fight at Chamberlain's Run 359; to Appomattox 376; at Appomattox Court House, April 9, 1865 386
Davis, J. Lucius 128; at Gettysburg 164; retreat from Gettysburg 177; temporay command of Chambliss's former brigade 315; Reams's Station, August 1864 325, 327; cattle raid, September 1864 330–332; on the Weldon R.R. 333–334; McDowell's and Wyatt's farms, September 1864 335; Boydton Plank Road, October 1864 339–341
Davis, Jefferson 42, 44, 57, 59, 233, 268; Wilson's Wharf, May 1864 270
Davis's farm (June 1864) 293
Dearing, James A.: Longstreet's Suffolk Campaign 99; Wilson & Kautz Raid 296; Blacks & Whites 298; commanding Rosser's former brigade 351
Devin, Thomas: Chancellorsville Campaign 86–87; 139; the Wilderness 240; near Dinwiddie Court House 355
Dinwiddie Court House (March, 1865) 355
Duffié, Alfred: Brandy Station 116, 120–121; Thouroughfare Gap and Middleburg 130–132

Early, Jubal A.: Maryland Campaign 58; Chancellorsville Campaign 93; Mine Run Campaign 213; Spotsylvania Court House 248; to defend Richmond 250; 266; Haw's Shop, May 1864 277; 287; in the Shenandoah Valley 309
Elzey, Arnold 99; Longstreet's Suffolk Campaign 102; 221
Evans, Stephen: Bristoe Campaign 198; Mine Run Campaign 214
Ewell, Richard S. 53, 95; gathering at Culpeper Court House 109–110; to Gettysburg 128, 152; at Gettysburg 164–165, 173; retreat from Gettysburg 198–200, 204; 212; the Wilderness 234, 236, 240–241; Spotsylvania Court House 248; at North Anna River 266; retreat to Appomattox 369, 374; High Bridge & Sailor's Creek, April 1865 377–378

Ferebee, Dennis: 108; retreat from Gettysburg 174; 192–193; Jack's Shop 194–196; Bristoe Campaign 198, 201; Mine Run Campaign 214; 229, 231
Fisher's Landing: near New Bern 20
Five Forks, Battle of (April 1, 1865) 60
Foscue's farm (May 1862) 36
French, Samuel G.: replaced L. O'B. Branch in N.C. 29, 40, 97–98; Longstreet's Suffolk Campaign 107–108
Funsten, Oliver R.: Bristoe Campaign 198–200, 203, 209

Gaines, James L.: lieutenant colonel of 2nd N.C. Cavalry 231; commanded 2nd N.C. Cavalry, spring 1865 351; wounded in action at Chamberlain's Run 357; the surrender 389
Gamble, William: Middleburg & Upperville 133, 137–138; fight on Trappe Road 139, 141–143
Gary, Martin W.: above the James River, June 1864 290, 295
Gettysburg, Battle of (July 1863) 163–173
Gillett's farm 31–33
Goodall's Tavern 255–256
Gordon, James B.: retreat from Gettysburg 174; temporary command of Hampton's former brigade 192; command of the N.C. Cavalry Brigade 192–193; Jack's Shop 194; Bristoe Campaign 198–199, 204–205; 212; Mine Run Campaign 213, 217; returned from furlough 227; 229–230, 232; the Wilderness 235, 238–239, 241; Spotsylvania Court House 244; to defend Richmond 249, 252;

Ground Squirrel Bridge 255; Goodall's Tavern 256; Yellow Tavern, May 1864 258; Allen's Station, May 1864 259; Brook Church, mortally wounded, May 1864 262–263

Gordon, John B.: retreat to Appomattox 374; High Bridge & Sailor's Creek, April 1865 377; Cumberland Church, April 7, 1865 381; retreat to Appomattox continued 382–383; at Appomattox Court House, April 9, 1865 384, 386

Graham, William A., Jr. 11; New Bern 21, 25; 30; commanding Second Squadron, 2nd N.C. Cavalry 95, 97–98; Longstreet's Suffolk Campaign 102–103, 105–106, 108; Brandy Station 119, 124–128; near Middleburg and Trappe Road 137, 144; to Gettysburg 149–151, 153–154; Hanover, Pa. 155, 159–160; on to Gettysburg 162; at Gettysburg 164, 166, 168–169, 172; retreat from Gettysburg 175, 177; 193

Grant, Ulysses S.: command of armies in Virginia 233; the Wilderness 234, 237, 239; Spotsylvania Court House 242, 245–246, 248; move on Richmond 249; North Anna River 266–267; Cold Harbor 274, 275, 286–287; to Petersburg 288–289; siege of Petersburg 292; 295–296; demonstration against Richmond, July 1864 306–307; demonstration against Richmond, August 1864 308–310; 316; on the Weldon R.R. 318, 320; to Richmond, September 1864 333; Boydton Plank Road, September 1864 336; Boydton Plank Road, October 1864 337–339; 342; Boydton Plank Road, February 1865 346; spring 1865 offensive 348–349; message to Lee, April 8, 1865 382; 383; at Appomattox Court House 388

Gregg, David McM. 82, 84; Brandy Station 116, 119–121; Middleburg & Upperville 130, 133–134, 137, 139; at Gettysburg 166, 168–169, 171–172; 185; Bristoe Campaign 199, 205; Mine Run Campaign 213; the Wilderness 234–235, 237–238, 240–242; Spotsylvania Court House 243, 246; move on Richmond 250, 253–255; Ground Squirrel Bridge 255; Goodall's Tavern 256; Allen's Station, May 1864 259–260; Brook Church, May 1864 262–264; Haw's Shop, May 1864 276–277; Cold Harbor 279; 285; demonstration against Richmond, July 1864 307; moved on Richmond, August 1864 310–311; near White's Tavern, White Oak Swamp, and the Charles City Road, August 1864 311–317; on the Weldon R.R. 319–320; Reams's Station, August 1864 325–326, 328; moved across the Weldon R.R. 333–334; McDowell's and Wyatt's farms, September 1864 335–336; Boydton Plank Road, September 1864 336–337; Boydton Plank Road, October 1864 338–340; south along the Weldon R.R. 342–344; Boydton Plank Road, February 1865 346

Gregg, J. Irvin: Middleburg & Upperville 132, 134, 138–139; at Gettysburg 166, 168; from Gettysburg 175; 199; Spotsylvania Court House 242–245, 248; Allen's Station, May 1864 260; 262; near Richmond 313; spring 1865 353; Dinwiddie Court House 355; captured near Farmville 380.

Grimes, Bryan 8; at Farmville 380; at Appomattox Court House, April 9, 1865 384–385

Ground Squirrel Bridge (May 1864) 255

Hampton, Wade 49; Maryland Cavalry Campaign 56–58; expedition to Maryland & Pennsylvania 61; 66, 68, 71, 76; raids across the Rappahannock 77–78; 79; battling winter 80; 109, 111–113; Brandy Station 116–118, 121–122; 128, 132–133, 137; Upperville 138–139; to Gettysburg 146–147, 149–150, 152–153; Hanover Pa. 155, 160; on to Gettysburg 161–162; at Gettysburg 163–164, 166, 169–172; retreat from Gettysburg 174–175, 183; promoted to major general 191; returned to active duty, November 8, 1863 212; 213; Mine Run Campaign 213–216; 217–221; Kilpatrick's expedition to Richmond 223–224; Atlee's Station 224–226; 227; returned to active duty, May 1864 231; 232; the Wilderness 234–239; Spotsylvania Court House 243, 248; toward Richmond 249; 255–256, 269, 275–276; Haw's Shop, May 1864 276–278; Ashland 282; Haw's Shop, June 1864 284; Trevilian Station 287; north of the James 295–296; Wilson & Kautz Raid 301–303; Reams's Station, June 1864 303–304; moved toward northern Virginia 309; back to Richmond, August 1864 310; took command of the army's cavalry corps, August 1864 310; around White Oak Swamp and the Charles City Road, August 1864 314–317; on the Weldon R.R. 319–320, 323–324; Reams's Station, August 1864 325–329; cattle raid, September 1864 329–332; 333–334; McDowell's and Wyatt's Farms, September 1864 335; Boydton Plank Road, September 1864 336–337; Boydton Plank Road, October 1864 338–342; south along the Weldon R.R. 343–344; returned to South Carolina 348

Hanover, Pa., Battle of (June 1863) 155–163

Hanover Court House (May 1864) 279

Hanovertown through Hanover Court House (May 1864) 274–276

Hawkins, Rush C.: at Winton, N.C. 17

Haw's Shop (May 1864) 276; (June 1864) 283

High Bridge & Sailor's Creek, Battle of (April 1865) 377–379

Hill, Ambrose P. 44–45, 95; gathering at Culpeper Court House 109, 128; at Gettysburg, 164–165; retreat from Gettysburg 173, 182–183; Bristoe Campaign 198–200, 207; 212; Mine Run Campaign 213; the Wilderness 234, 236; Spotsylvania Court House 248; North Anna River 267; along the Weldon R.R. 294–295; around Richmond 313; on the Weldon R.R. 318–319, 322–324; Reams's Station, August 1864 324–328; Boydton Plank Road, September 1864 333, 336; Boydton Plank Road, October 1864 339; south along the Weldon R.R. 343–344

Hill, Daniel H.: in N.C. 14–16, 39–40, 42, 44–45; the Maryland Campaign 56–58; 67, 73; Fredericksburg 102

Hoke, Robert F.: New Bern 21–25, 28; at Cold Harbor 279

Hood, John B. 45; Longstreet's Suffolk Campaign 99, 104–108; 110; at Gettysburg 165

Hooker, Joseph: commander of the Army of the Potomac 80; 82; attack across the Rappahannock 82; 84; the Chancellorsville Campaign 85–86, 92–93; Brandy Station 115, 123; Middleburg & Upperville 128, 130, 143; to Gettysburg & removed from command of the army 151–152

Humphreys, Andrew A.: the Wilderness 241; spring 1865 350, 354; to Appomattox 374; at High Bridge & Sailor's Creek, April 1865 377–378; to Appomattox 379; at Cumberland Church, April 7, 1865 381; 382; at Appomattox Court House, April 9, 1865 386

Imboden, John D.: retreat from Gettysburg 173, 175, 179

Jack's Shop (September 1863) 193

Jackson, Thomas J. 42, 44, 49–50, 54; Maryland Campaign 52–53; Second Battle of Manassas 53; 73, 75; Fredericksburg 76–77; Chancellorsville 85, 91–92; mortally wounded 92

Johnson, Bradley T.: Maryland Cavalry, Hanovertown through Hanover Court House 274; Ashland 281

Johnson, Bushrod R.: retreat to Appomattox 369

Johnston, Joseph E.: commanding the Confederate army in Va. 42–43

Jones, William E. "Grumble": cavalry expedition to Maryland & Pennsylvania 62–63, 71; 111–112; Brandy Station 115, 117–122; 133, 140, 143; retreat from Gettysburg 174–175, 178

Kautz, Augus: Wilson & Kautz Raid 296–297, 300–303; Reams's Station, June 1864 303; demonstration against Richmond, August 1864 307; to the Weldon R.R. 316, 318; cattle raid, September 1864 331–332; 333

Kilpatrick, H. Judson 84; Brandy Station 122; 130; Middleburg & Upperville 131, 134, 138–139; to Gettysburg 152–154; Hanover, Pa. 155, 159–160; at Gettysburg 164, 166; retreat from Gettysburg 174, 176–182; 185; Jack's Shop 193–194, 196–197; Bristoe Campaign 199, 202, 205, 209–211; 220–221; expedition to Richmond 221–224; 226–227

Kinston, N.C. 27, 29, 35, 39–40

Kittrell's Springs, N.C.: 2nd N.C. Cavalry training camp 6–7, 9

Lee, Fitzhugh 46, 49–50; the Maryland Campaign 54, 56–58; expedition to Maryland & Pennsylvania 61–62; 66, 68, 71, 76; Fredericksburg 76; raid across the Rappahannock 78; 79–81; Chancellorsville Campaign 85–87, 89–92; 109–112; Brandy Station 115, 117; to Gettysburg 146–147, 149, 152–153; Hanover, Pa. 155, 160; on to Gettysburg 161–162; at Gettysburg 164, 166, 169–171; retreat from Gettysburg 174–175, 179–183; promoted to major general 183; 185–186; 191; Jack's Shop 194; Bristoe Campaign 199–202, 204–205, 207–211; Mine Run Campaign 214; 217; the Wilderness 234, 236, 238, 240–241; Spotsylvania Court House 243–247; to Richmond 249–250, 252, 254; Yellow Tavern, May 1864 257–258, 260–261; temporary command of Stuart's cavalry 262; Meadow Bridge May 1864 264; 265, 267–269; Wilson's Wharf, May 1864 270–272; 273, 275; Haw's Shop, May 1864 276, 278; at Cold Harbor 279, 285; Trevilian Station 287; 295; Wilson & Kautz Raid 301; Reams's Station, June 1864 303–304; to Richmond July 1864 307; sent to Northern Virginia 309; sent to Pickett, spring 1865 351; command of the cavalry corps in Pickett's mobile force, spring 1865 351; near Five Forks 354; near Dinwiddie Court House 355; fight, at Chamberlain's Run 358; Five Forks, April 1, 1865 362–363, 367; retreat to Appomattox 369; Namozine Church, April 3, 1865 370–371; retreat to Appomattox continued 374, 376–377, 380–383; at Appomattox Court House, April 9, 1865 384, 386–387; the surrender 388

Lee, Robert E.: on fight at Gillett's Farm 32–33; requested N.C. troops 34, 39; 42; commander of the Army of Virginia 43; 43–46, 48–50; Maryland Campaign of 1862 52, 54, 56–59; Second Battle of Manassas 53–54; consolidating forces 59–61; the Rappahannock Line 63–65, 67; 70, 72–73; Fredericksburg 76–77; 79; battling winter 80–82; Chancellorsville Campaign 85, 90–93, 95; 105; gathering at Culpeper Court House 110–112; to Gettysburg 128, 152–153; at Gettysburg 164–165, 173; retreat from Gettysburg 173, 180–181; 186–187, 189, 191–192, 198; Bristoe Campaign 198–200, 209, 211; 212; Mine Run Campaign 213–214, 216; winter camp 218–221, 230; the Wilderness 234, 236, 239–240; Spotsylvania Court House 245–246, 248; 260, 269; at North Anna River 266–268; Union probe across the Pamunkey 272, 275; Cold Harbor 275, 277–279, 283, 286–287; followed Grant to Petersburg 288; 291; Siege of Petersburg 292, 295; Wilson & Kautz Raid 301; along the Weldon R.R., July 1864 305; defends Richmond, August 1864 308; on the Weldon R.R. 319–320, 323–324, 328; cattle raid, September 1864 329; Boydton Plank Road, October 1864 338; 345; Boydton Plank Road, February 1865 347; created a special mobile force, spring 1865 350, 353; met with Pickett 355; on Five Forks, April 1, 1865 360, 367; retreat to Appomattox 373–374; at Amelia Court House 374–375; retreat to Appomattox continued 375–377, 379; at Farmville 380; at Cumberland Church, April 7, 1865 381; 382–383; Appomattox Court House 384, 386; the surrender 388

Lee, William H. F. "Rooney": Seven Days' battles, 46; Stuart's expedition behind enemy lines 50–51; cavalry expedition to Maryland & Pennsylvania 61–63; promotion to brigadier general 65; got a brigade and the 2nd N.C. Cavalry 71–72; to Fredericksburg 73; brigade moved to Port Royal & below 74–76; Fredericksburg 76; returned south of Port Royal 77; raid across the Rappahannock 78–79; 80; battling winter 80–81; 83; fight near Brandy Station 84; Chancellorsville Campaign 85–90, 94–95; preparations to move north 109, 112–114; Brandy Station 115, 117–123; wounded at Brandy Station 124–126; his brigade in the battles at Middleburg & Upperville 128, 130, 132; his brigade to Gettysburg under Chambliss 146; returned to active duty & promoted to major general 232; the Wilderness 234, 238–239; 265; at North Anna River 266; Haw's Shop, May 1864 276–278; Hanover Court House 279–280; Ashland 281–282; Haw's Shop, June 1864 284–285; south of the Chickahominy 289; above the James River, June 1864 290; to Petersburg, June 1864 291; along the Weldon R.R. 292; Wilson & Kautz Raid 297, 300–301; Blacks & Whites 298; defend Richmond, August 1864 307–308, 310; around White's Tavern, White Oak Swamp, and the Charles City Road, August 1864 311–317; on the Weldon R.R. 319–320; Poplar Spring Church, August 1864 320, 322, 324; Reams's Station, August 1864 325; cattle raid, September 1864 330–332; 334; McDowell's and Wyatt's farms, September 1864 335; Boydton Plank Road, September 1864 336–337; Boydton Plank Road, October 1864 339–341; south along the Weldon R.R. 343–344; 347; spring 1865 348, 351, 354–355; fight at Chamberlain's Run 355–356, 358–359; Five Forks, April 1, 1865 360, 366–367; retreat to Appomattox 369; Namozine Church, April 3, 1865 370–373; retreat to Appomattox continued 373; Amelia Court House 374; 375–376; High Bridge & Sailor's Creek, April 1865 377–379; 380; at Cumberland Church, April 7, 1865 381; 382–383; Appomattox Court House, April 9, 1865 384–387; the surrender 388

Lincoln, Abraham 42–43, 45, 49, 54, 59, 70, 80, 82, 85; Hooker & Gettysburg 152; 188–189; expedi-

tion to Richmond 222; 233; about the Weldon Railroad 318
Lockhart, John P. 12–13; New Bern 24; 29, 96; Longstreet's Suffolk Campaign 105; 109; 230; south of the Chickahominy 287; commanding the 2nd N.C. Cavalry at Chamberlain's Run 358; Five Forks, April 1, 1865 360; Appomattox Court House, April 9, 1865 384; some surrendered and were paroled 388
Lomax, Lunsford L. 140, 189–190; gets a new brigade 191–192; Bristoe Campaign 200, 204–205, 208–209; 220, 222, 232; the Wilderness 234; Spotsylvania Court House 244; to Richmond 250; Ashland May 1864 257; Yellow Tavern, May 1864 258–259; Union probe across the Pamunkey 272; Reams's Station, June 1864 303
Longstreet, James 42, 44–45, 49–50; the Maryland Campaign 53, 57–58; Second Battle of Manassas 53; 54, 65, 72–73, 95; Fredericksburg 76–77; Suffolk Campaign 99, 101–108; gathering at Culpeper Court House 109–110; to Gettysburg 128; at Gettysburg 164–165, 173; retreat from Gettysburg 173, 182–183; 186; the Wilderness 234, 236, 239–240; wounded, in the Wilderness 240; retreat to Appomattox 374–377, 379–380; at Cumberland Church, April 7, 1865 381; 382–383; Appomattox Court House, April 9, 1865 384, 386

Martin, James G. 10, 35, 39
Maryland Campaign (1862) 52–61
Mayo, J.: Five Forks, April 1, 1865, 360
McClellan, George B. 42–46, 49–50; Second Battle of Manassas 54; Maryland Campaign 56–59; 66; replaced as commander of the army 70
McDowell's and Wyatt's farms (September 1864) 335
McGregor, William M.: Middleburg & Upperville 134; Jack's Shop 195; 238; on the James River, June 1864 290; around Davis's farm 293; Blacks & Whites 298; Reams's Station, August 1864 325; Boydton Plank Road, October 1864 341; Namozine Church, April 3, 1865 370
McLaws, Lafayette 57–58; 72; Chancellorsville Campaign 91–93
McNeill, James H.: command of the 5th N.C. Cavalry, spring 1865 351; fight at Chamberlain's Run, killed in action 356–357
Meade, George G.: Fredericksburg 77; Chancellorsville Campaign 86–87, 89–90; command of the army

152; retreat from Gettysburg 181–182; 185–190; 193; Bristoe Campaign 198–200, 205, 209; 212; Mine Run Campaign 213–214; expedition to Richmond 222; 233; the Wilderness 234, 236–238, 241; Spotsylvania Court House 243, 246, 248; move on Richmond 249; 266, 289; Siege of Petersburg 292–293; demonstration against Richmond, August 1864 308; moves for the Weldon R.R. 316, 318; Reams's Station, August 1864 328; moves across the Weldon R.R. 333; Boydton Plank Road, September 1864 334, 336–337; Boydton Plank Road, October 1864 338–339; Boydton Plank Road, February 1865 346; spring 1865 offensive, to Appomattox 375; at High Bridge & Sailor's Creek, April 1865 377
Meadow Bridge 262
Merritt, Wesley: took command of Buford's former division 220; Spotsylvania Court House 242–244, 246; move on Richmond 250, 252–254; Yellow Tavern, May 1864 257–258; 262, 264; Hanovertown through Hanover Court House 274; Haw's Shop, May 1864 277–278; Cold Harbor 279; spring 1865 354; near Dinwiddie Court House 355; Five Forks, April 1, 1865 361, 364; retreat to Appomattox 369; at Appomattox Court House, April 9, 1865 385
Middleburg (June 1863) 131
Middleburg & Upperville, Battle of 128–146
Mine Run Campaign (November/December 1863) 213–217
Mosby, John S. 44, 214
Munford, Thomas T. 46; Maryland Campaign 52, 56–59; Brandy Station 117–118, 125; 130; Middleburg & Upperville 128, 131–133, 137–138; brigade commander, spring 1865 351; near Dinwiddie Court House 355; fight, at Chamberlain's Run 359; Five Forks, April 1, 1865 360, 362–364, 367; retreat to Appomattox 376–377; High Bridge & Sailor's Creek, April 1865 377; Farmville 380; 383; Appomattox Court House, April 9, 1865 384, 386

Namozine Church, Battle of (April 3, 1865) 369–373
New Bern, Battle of 19–29
North Anna River, Battle of (May 1864) 265–273
North Carolina Cavalry Brigade 112; a new comander 191–193; Jack's Shop 194–195, 197; Bristoe Campaign 198–203, 205, 207–211; 212–213; Mine Run Campaign 214–216; winter camp 217, 219; Kil-

patrick's expedition to Richmond 224; Atlee's Station 226; visited by Governor Vance 227; 229, 231–232; a new division commander, W. H. F. Lee 232; the Wilderness 235, 238–239; Spotsylvania Court House 243–244; Union move on Richmond 249–250, 252–253; Ground Squirrel Bridge 255; Allen's Station, May 1864 259–260; Brook Church, May 1864 262–264; 267–270; Wilson's Wharf, May 1864 271–272; Union probe across the Pamunkey 272–273; Hanovertown through Hanover Court House 274–275; Haw's Shop, May 1864 276–278; Hanover Court House 279–280; Ashland 282; Haw's Shop, June 1864 283–285; south of the Chickahominy, June 1864 286; Long Bridge on the Chickahominy, June 1864 287; 289; skirmishing above the James River, June 1864 290; to Petersburg, June 1864 291; along the Weldon R.R., June 1864 292; around Davis's farm 293; Wilson & Kautz Raid, June 1864 296–298, 300–301; along the Weldon R.R., July 1864 305–306; around Richmond, August 1864 307–308, 310; near White's Tavern, White Oak Swamp, and the Charles City Road, August 1864 311–318; to the Weldon R.R. 320; Poplar Spring Church, August 1864 322; Reams's Station, August 1864 325–327; beef steak raid, September 1864 330–332; on the Weldon R.R., September 1864 334; McDowell's and Wyatt's farms, September 1864 335; Boydton Plank Road, September 1864 337; Boydton Plank Road, October 1864 340–341; south along the Weldon R.R. (to Belfield) 343–344; Boydton Plank Road, February 1865 347; spring 1865 348, 351; fight, at Chamberlain's Run 356–359; Five Forks, April 1, 1865 364–366; retreat to Appomattox 367, 369; Namozine Church, April 3, 1865 370–373; Amelia Court House 374; High Bridge & Sailor's Creek, April 1865 377, 379; retreat to Appomattox with W. P. Roberts, and Cumberland Church, April 7, 1865 381–382; Appomattox Court House, April 9, 1865 387; the surrender 389
North Carolina, 1st Cavalry 5, 9–10; returned to N.C. 29; Maryland Campaign 56; cavalry expedition to Maryland & Pennsylvania 63; Barbee's Cross Roads 68; at Gettysburg 170; 192; Jack's Shop 194–195; Bristoe Campaign 198, 200–201, 207, 210; Kilpatrick's expedition to Richmond 224; the Wilderness 235, 238, 240–241; Goodall's Tav-

ern 256; Wilson & Kautz Raid 297; Blacks & Whites 298; 310; spring 1865, at Chamberlain's Run 356, 358; Namozine Church, April 3, 1865 370–371; High Bridge & Sailor's Creek, April 1865 379; the surrender 389

North Carolina, 3rd Cavalry 97; Longstreet's Suffolk Campaign 102–106, 108; 231, 269–270; on the Weldon R.R. 322, 329; along the Weldon 341, 344; spring 1865 351; Five Forks, April 1, 1865 360, 365; High Bridge & Sailor's Creek, April 1865 379; the surrender 389

North Carolina, 4th Cavalry 108; Middleburg & Upperville 134; retreat from Gettysburg 174, 178; Jack's Shop 194–196; Bristoe Campaign 198–200, 202; 220, 229, 231; Wilson & Kautz Raid 467; 310; spring 1865 351; High Bridge & Sailor's Creek, April 1865 378

North Carolina, 5th Cavalry: Middleburg & Upperville 134, 139; retreat from Gettysburg 174, 178; Jack's Shop 194–196; Bristoe Campaign 198, 200, 202, 211; 220 229, 231; the Wilderness 232; Goodall's Tavern & Ground Squirrel Bridge 256; Brook Church, May 1864 264; Wilson's Wharf, May 1864 271; Haw's Shop, June 1864 284; Wilson & Kautz Raid 297; Blacks & Whites 298–299; 310; 322; on the Weldon 341; spring 1865 351; fight at Chamberlain's Run 356–358; Five Forks, April 1, 1865 360, 365; Namozine Church, April 3, 1865 371; the surrender 389

North Carolina, 7th Cavalry: spring 1865 351; retreat to Appomattox 375; High Bridge & Sailor's Creek, April 1865 379

Pamunkey River 272–273

Payne, William H. F.: at Warrenton, Va. 60–61, 63, 65–69; returned to his 4th Virginia Cavalry 71; Chancellorsville Campaign 86, 91; 127; Middleburg & Upperville 128–129; Hanover, Pa. 158; brigade commander, spring 1865 351

Pettigrew, James Johnston: retreat from Gettysburg and death 183

Pickett, George E.: Longstreet's Suffolk Campaign 99, 102, 104, 106; at Gettysburg 165, 173; retreat from Gettysburg 180; commands special mobile force, spring 1865 350; to Five Forks 355; near Dinwiddie Court House 355, 358–359; Five Forks, April 1, 1865 360–264, 366–367; retreat to Appomattox 373

Pleasonton, Alfred 62, 67–69; Chancellorsville Campaign 86–87, 89, 95; Brandy Station 115, 120, 122–125; 128, 130; Middleburg & Upperville 132–134, 136–139, 143; at Gettysburg 164, 166; 190, 193; Bristoe Campaign 199–200, 202; expedition to Richmond 222

Plymouth, N.C.: skirmish, 96

Pope, John 49–50; Maryland Campaign 52–53; Second Battle of Manassas 53–54

Poplar Spring Church (August 1864) 320

Port Royal, Va. 80

Ransom, Matthew W.: sent to Pickett 351; Five Forks, April 1, 1865 360

Ransom, Robert 5, 9–10; returned to N.C. 29; critical of 2nd N.C. Cavalry 32–33; back to Virginia 34

Reams's Station, Battle of (June 1864) 303–304; (August 1864) 324–329

Roberts, William P.: near Trenton, N.C. 36; near Pollocksville, N.C. 37; Middleburg & Upperville 136, 143; 230; appointed major of 2nd N.C. Cavalry 231; Union probe across the Pamunkey 273; Haw's Shop, June 1864 284; commanded the 2nd N.C. Cavalry in the battle at Blacks & Whites 298–299; along the Weldon R.R., July 1864 305; near White's Tavern, White Oak Swamp, August 1864 311–312, 314, 318; promoted to colonel of the 2nd N.C. Cavalry on August 19, 1864 320; on the Weldon R.R. 320; Reams's Station, August 1864 326–328; cattle raid, September 1864 331–332; McDowell's and Wyatt's farms, September 1864 335; Boydton Plank Road, October 1864 341; appointed brigadier general and took command of James Dearing's former brigade 348; spring 1865 351; comment on the fight at Chamberlain's Run 359; Five Forks, April 1, 1865 360, 362; Namozine Creek 369; Amelia Court House 374–375; retreat to Appomattox 375; High Bridge & Sailor's Creek, April 1865 377; 380–381; Appomattox Court House, April 9, 1865 384–385, 387

Robertson, Beverley H.: with Jackson's command 49; 51; 112–113; Brandy Station 115, 118; 128, 130; Middleburg & Upperville 131, 134, 136, 139; retreat from Gettysburg 174–175; 185; relieved of command of N.C. Cavalry Brigade 191

Robinson, William G. 6–7, 9, 11, 13, 15; New Bern 24, 26–30; Gillett's farm 31–32, 34; 113, 192–193; Mine Run Campaign 214

Rosser, Thomas 50–51; Maryland Campaign 68–69; 76, 79; 112, 130; appointed commander of W. E. Jones's brigade 192; Bristoe Campaign 203, 209–210; Mine Run Campaign 213–215; 218, 232; the Wilderness 235–241; Spotsylvania Court House 244; 276; Haw's Shop, May 1864 277; Ashland 282; Reams's Station, August 1864 325, 327; cattle raid, September 1864 330–332; commanding a division and sent to Pickett, spring 1865 351, 355; near Dinwiddie Court House 355; Five Forks, April 1, 1865 361–362; retreat to Appomattox 376–377; High Bridge & Sailor's Creek, April 1865 377; Farmville 380; 383; Appomattox Court House, April 9 1865, 384, 386

Ruffin, Thomas: Bristoe Campaign 198

Samaria Church, Battle of (June 1864) 295–296

Shepherdstown 185–186

Sheridan, Philip: the Wilderness 234–235, 237–241; Spotsylvania Court House 242–243, 245–246, 248; move on Richmond 249–250, 252–254; Ground Squirrel Bridge 255; Goodall's Tavern 257; Yellow Tavern, May 1864 257–258, 261, 264; returned to Grant 267–269, 274; Haw's Shop, May 1864 276–278; Cold Harbor 279, 285; Trevilian Station 286–287; Siege of Petersburg 295; 296; demonstration against Richmond, August 1864 307–308; commanding the Army of the Shenandoah 309; spring 1865 349, 354; near Dinwiddie Court House 355, 359; Five Forks, April 1, 1865 360–364, 367; to Appomattox 373, 375; High Bridge & Sailor's Creek, April 1865 377–378; Appomattox Station & Court House 381–383

Smith, Gustavus W. 40–42, 50, 54, 57, 59–60, 67, 98–99

South Carolina Cavalry Brigade 276; at Cold Harbor 278

South Carolina, 2nd Cavalry 56, 121

Spotsylvania Court House, Battle of (May 1864) 242–248

Spruill, Samuel B. 5, 6, 7; New Bern 20, 22–26, 33

Steuart, G. H.: Five Forks, April 1, 1865 360

Stoneman, George 62; command of the Union cavalry 80; 82; attacks across the Rappahannock 82, 84; Chancellorsville Campaign 85–86, 88, 95

Strange, James W. 25, 84, 127, 193; Jack's Shop 196–197; resigned from 2nd N.C. Cavalry 231

Stuart, James E. B. 48; his first expedition 43; Seven Days' battles 46–50; another expedition behind the enemy 52; Maryland Campaign 53–54; 56–58; expedition to Maryland and Pennsylvania, October 1862 61–63; 65–67; Barbee's Cross Roads 68–70; the 2nd N.C. Cavalry into his division 72; Fredericksburg 76; raid across the Rappahannock 78–79; battling winter 80–82; moved cavalry to Culpeper Court House 82; Chancellorsville Campaign 88–90, 92–93; collecting his cavalry for the spring campaign 109, 111; Brandy Station 115, 118; 130; Middleburg & Upperville 131, 134, 137–139; to Gettysburg 145–146, 151–152; Hanover, Pa. 155, 158; on to Gettysburg 160–161; at Gettysburg 164–165, 168, 172; retreat from Gettysburg 173, 176, 178, 180, 182; covering a pullback 185, 187–188; 191; Jack's Shop 194–197; Bristoe Campaign 198–201, 203–211; 212; Mine Run Campaign 214, 216; Kilpatrick's expedition to Richmond 222; 229–23232; the Wilderness 234–236, 241; Spotsylvania Court House 243–244, 246–247; defends Richmond 250, 252–254; Yellow Tavern, mortally wounded, May 1864 257–259

Suffolk Campaign (April 11–May 4, 1863) 99–108

Tatum, Pinkney A. 114; wounded 126–127; clash with Virginia commander, and at Brandy Station 127; captured 197
Torbert, Alfred A.: the Wilderness 234, 237, 239–241; Hanovertown through Hanover Court House 274; Haw's Shop, May 1864 276–278; Cold Harbor 279; 285; demonstration against Richmond, July 1864 307
Trappe Road, Upperville (June 1863) 139

Vance, Zebulon B.: New Bern, 20–28; visiting N.C. troops 227; 233
Virginia, 1st Cavalry 51; Chancellorsville Campaign 92; at Gettysburg 170
Virginia, 2nd Cavalry 46; Maryland Campaign 52, 56; Chancellorsville Campaign 92; Ashland, May 1864 257

Virginia, 3rd Cavalry 67; Chancellorsville Campaign 89, 91–92; Spotsylvania Court House 247; Five Forks, April 1, 1865 360
Virginia, 4th Cavalry 67–68, 121
Virginia, 5th Cavalry 51; Chancellorsville Campaign 92; Bristoe Campaign 203; Yellow Tavern, May 1864 257
Virginia, 6th Cavalry Brandy Station 117; Yellow Tavern, May 1864 257, 259
Virginia, 7th Cavalry 56; Brandy Station 117; 201
Virginia, 8th Cavalry: Five Forks, April 1, 1865 360
Virginia, 9th Cavalry 46, 48; to W. H. F. Lee's new brigade 71–72; 83; Chancellorsville Campaign 87; 128, 135; fight on Trappe Road 140, 142; Hanover, Pa. 155, 158–160; at Gettysburg 170; retreat from Gettysburg 178; 313; High Bridge & Sailor's Creek, April 1865 378
Virginia, 10th Cavalry 81; Chancellorsville Campaign 87, 90; Brandy Station 124; 128; fight on Trappe Road 141; Hanover, Pa. 159–160; on to Gettysburg 162; at Gettysburg 164; retreat from Gettysburg 177; 313; Reams's Station, August 1864 327; High Bridge & Sailor's Creek, April 1865 378
Virginia, 11th Cavalry: Five Forks, April 1, 1865 360
Virginia, 12th Cavalry 51, 56–57; Brandy Station 122; Bristoe Campaign 201
Virginia, 13th Cavalry 54, 57; Rappahannock Line 63, 66; 81; Chancellorsville Campaign 87–88; 128, 134; Hanover, Pa. 155, 158–160; retreat from Gettysburg 178; 313; fight at Chamberlain's Run 356
Virginia, 14th Cavalry: Amelia Court House 374
Virginia, 15th Cavalry 54; the Rappahannock line 63, 66; 81; Chancellorsville Campaign 90, 93; Yellow Tavern, May 1864 257
von Borcke, Heros 80; wounded near Middleburg 136

Wallace, William H.: sent to Pickett 351; Five Forks, April 1, 1865 360
Warren, Gouverneur K.: the Wilderness 235; Spotsylvania Court House 248; to the Weldon R.R. 318; Boydton Plank Road, September 1864 336; south along the Weldon 342; spring 1865 offensive 354; Five Forks, April 1, 1865 361
Warrenton, Va.: protected by 2nd N.C. Cavalry 61
Washington, North Carolina 13, 16, 18, 35, 96, 97
White's Tavern & White Oak Swamp (August 1864) 311
Wickham, William C. 50; takes command of Fitz Lee's former brigade 191; Kilpatrick's expedition to Richmond 222; 232; the Wilderness 234; Spotsylvania Court House 244; to Richmond 250; Yellow Tavern, May 1864 257–258; Wilson's Wharf, May 1864 271; 277
the Wilderness, Battle of (May 1864) 234–242
Williams, Solomon: appointed colonel of 2nd N.C. Cavalry 35; in Kinston, N.C. 39–40; on detached duty 41; returned to regiment 113–114; Brandy Station, killed in action 119, 123–126
Wilson, James H.: the Wilderness 234–235, 238; Spotsylvania Court House 248; move on Richmond 250, 253–254; Yellow Tavern, May 1864 258; 262; Ashland, 280; near the Chickahominy, June 1864 289; Wilson & Kautz Raid 296, 300–302; Reams's Station, June 1864 303
Wilson & Kautz Raid (June 22/July 1) 296–304
Wilson's Wharf (May 1864) 270
Winton, N.C.: burning of 17
Wynn, James M. 11, 26

Yellow Tavern, Battle of (May 1864) 260
Young, Pierce M. B.: Bristoe Campaign 198–199, 203; Mine Run Campaign 213; Kilpatrick's expedition to Richmond 223; 232; the Wilderness 235; 269, 275; in temporary commond of N.C. Cavalry Brigade, May 1864 278; Hanover Court House 279; Ashland, severely wounded 282–283; Reams's Station, August 1864 325, 327; on the Weldon R.R. 333, 335

www.ingramcontent.com/pod-product-compliance
Lightning Source LLC
Chambersburg PA
CBHW080935020526
44116CB00034B/2601